THE LAW OF PRESIDENTIAL POWER
Cases and Materials

THE LAW OF PRESIDENTIAL POWER
Cases and Materials

BY

Peter M. Shane
Professor of Law
University of Iowa

Harold H. Bruff
John S. Redditt Professor of Law
University of Texas at Austin

CAROLINA
ACADEMIC PRESS
POST BOX 51879
DURHAM
N. CAROLINA
27717

For Martha and Beth
P.M.S.

For W.J.B. and M.M.B.
H.H.B.

International Standard Book Number: 0-89089-332-2
Library of Congress Card Catalog Number: 87-72588

Carolina Academic Press
P.O. Box 51879
Durham, North Carolina 27717
(919) 489-7486

Printed in the United States of America

Table of Contents

TABLE OF CASES.. xiii
PREFACE xxi

I. INTRODUCTION.. 3

   A. CONSTITUTIONAL HISTORY: THE CREATION OF THE
      PRESIDENCY.. 4
      1. The Articles of Confederation.................................... 4
      2. Republican Executives in Other Nations 5
      3. State Governors.. 5
      4. The Great Political Theorists 6
      5. Deliberations of the Constitutional Convention 8

   B. COMPETING THEORIES OF THE PRESIDENCY....................... 12
      1. Washington 12
      2. Jefferson 14
      3. Jackson 14
      4. Buchanan 15
      5. Lincoln 16
      6. Wilson on the Post-Civil War Presidency 17
      7. Theodore Roosevelt and Taft 17
      8. Franklin Roosevelt... 19

   C. THE INSTITUTIONAL PRESIDENCY 20

   D. SUPREME COURT ANALYSIS AND SEPARATION OF POWERS
      ISSUES 27

II. FRAMEWORK: THE SEPARATION AND CONFLUENCE OF POWERS...31

   A. ANALYTIC FRAMEWORK.. 31
      1. The Executive and the Judiciary 31
          Marbury v. Madison... 34
          Note: Obtaining Judicial Review of Executive Actions.......... 42
      2. The Executive and Congress (as Mediated by the Courts)......... 47
          Youngstown Sheet & Tube Co. v. Sawyer......................... 47

   B. CONGRESSIONAL DELEGATION AND ITS LIMITS 64
          Amalgamated Meat Cutters & Butcher Workmen v. Connally 75
          Problem: The Limits of Delegated Power......................... 87

   C. PRESIDENTIAL "LEGISLATION," OR, THE OTHER SIDE OF
      DELEGATION: THE ROLE OF THE EXECUTIVE ORDER 88
          AFL-CIO v. Kahn 89
          Problem: Price Controls Under the Credit Control Act of 1969 98
          Note: Private Enforcement of Executive Orders 101

D. VETO POWERS 102
   1. The President's Veto... 102
   2. Pocket Vetoes 106
      Barnes v. Kline 106
   3. Legislative Vetoes.. 112
      Immigration and Naturalization Service v. Chadha 115

III. PROTECTING THE EXERCISE OF PRESIDENTIAL FUNCTIONS 137

A. STATE SECRETS, EXECUTIVE PRIVILEGE, AND PRESIDENTIAL
   PRIVACY 137
   1. Resisting Disclosure to the Public 137
      New York Times v. United States 138
      Snepp v. United States... 149
      Note: Classification of Government Documents....................... 154
      National Security Decision Directive 84: Safeguarding National
         Security Information 156
      Hearing on "National Security Decision Directive 84" 157
   2. Resisting Disclosure in Court.. 162
      United States v. Nixon 163
      Note: State Secrets Privilege 171
   3. Resisting Disclosure to Congress 180
      a. Executive Branch Procedure for Invoking Executive Privilege...... 182
         Memorandum re: Procedures Governing Responses to
            Congressional Requests for Information....................... 182
      b. A Constitutional Requirement of Compromise?.................... 184
         United States v. American Telephone & Telegraph Co............. 184
      c. Case Studies: Executive Response to Congressional Subpoenas ... 187
         Report on "Contempt of Congress" (Anne Gorsuch Burford)..... 189
         United States v. United States House of Representatives 198
         Report on "Contempt of Congress" (James Watt) 200
      d. Note: Political Question Doctrine 208
   4. Congressional Regulation of Aceess to Presidential Documents 210
      Nixon v. Administrator of General Services 210

B. LEGAL ACCOUNTABILITY OF THE PRESIDENT AND HIS
   "INNER CIRCLE" 217
   1. Applicability of Administrative Procedure Statutes 218
      a. Administrative Procedure Act...................................... 218
         Bruff, Judicial Review and the President's Statutory Powers....... 218
      b. Freedom of Information Act 224
         Kissinger v. Reporters Committee for Freedom of the Press 224
      c. Internal Management of the Executive Branch [National
            Environmental Policy Act; Government in the Sunshine Act] . 228
   2. Accessibility of the "Inner Circle" to Congressional Oversight 228
      Report on "Senate Confirmation of Director and Deputy Director
         of the Office of Management and Budget" 229
      Hearing on "The National Security Adviser: Role and
         Accountability" 230
   3. Immunities of Executive Officers from Civil Liability................. 233

Nixon v. Fitzgerald 234
Harlow v. Fitzgerald... 245
Mitchell v. Forsyth 251

IV. THE PRESIDENT AS CHIEF ADMINISTRATOR 259
  A. APPOINTMENTS 259
    1. Executive Officers 259
      Buckley v. Valeo 259
      Note: Presidential Authority and the Civil Service 269
    2. Judges.. 271
      a. Appointments to the Supreme Court 271
        Note: Identifying, Evaluating and Confirming Supreme Court
          Candidates 271
        F.D. Roosevelt, The Coming Crisis and What Can Be Done
          About It 274
        Report on "Reorganization of the Federal Judiciary".............. 277
      b. Appointments to the Court of Appeals........................... 281
        Exec. Order No. 12,059 281
      c. Recess Appointments of Judges 283
        United States v. Woodley.. 283

  B. REMOVALS 290
    1. Separation of Powers Considerations 290
      Myers v. United States.. 291
      Humphrey's Executor v. United States............................... 300
      Bowsher v. Synar 306
    2. First Amendment Limitations...................................... 327
      Branti v. Finkel 328

  C. SUPERVISION OF EXECUTIVE BRANCH POLICYMAKING 332
    1. The Formative Years: Groping for Principles 332
      The President and Accounting Officers 332
      The Jewels of the Princess of Orange 333
    2. The President's Statutory Powers to Manage the Executive Branch... 335
    3. Supervising the Exercise of Discretionary Administrative Authority.. 337
      a. Participation in Administrative Rulemaking 337
        Sierra Club v. Costle 337
      b. Coordinating the Regulatory Process............................ 343
        Report on "Regulatory Organization" 345
        Memorandum re: Proposed Executive Order on Federal
          Regulation.. 355
        Nat'l Academy of Public Administration, Presidential
          Management of Rulemaking in Regulatory Agencies.......... 360

  D. BUDGET AND SPENDING PROCESSES 366
    1. Overview 366
    2. Congressional Control of Spending................................. 368
      Authority for the Continuance of Governmental Functions During a
        Temporary Lapse in Appropriations............................. 369
      Brown v. Califano 375

3.   Executive Control of Spending (Herein, Of Impoundment) 379
     City of New Haven v. United States 384
4.   Constitutional Reform (Herein, of the Item Veto) 390
     Report on "The Line-Item Veto: An Appraisal" 390

V. THE PRESIDENT AND THE FAITHFUL EXECUTION OF THE LAWS .. 395

A. DISCRETIONARY "NON-EXECUTION" OF THE LAWS 396
   1. Unconstitutional Laws 396
      a.   Implementation 396
           Case Study: "Stay" Provisions of the Competition in
             Contracting Act 397
           Hearing on "Constitutionality of GAO's Bid Protest Function" ... 400
      b.   Defending Congress in Court 406
           Hearing on "Representation of Congress and Congressional
             Interests in Court" 407
           Note: Congressional Standing 407
           Barnes v. Kline 409
   2. Laws "Unjustified" in Fact 419
      Note: Commonwealth of Pennsylvania v. Lynn 419
      Case Study: Enforcing the Statutory Exclusion of Alien
        Homosexuals 422
   3. Civil Litigation and the Faithful Execution of the Laws 426
   4. Enforcing the Criminal Law 429
      Smith v. United States 429
      NAACP v. Levi 434
      NAACP v. Bell 437
      Note: Prosecutorial Discretion, Due Process, and the Separation
        of Powers 438
   5. Pardons and Reprieves 439

B. DOES CONGRESS NEED THE PRESIDENT? (HEREIN, OF SPECIAL
   PROSECUTORS AND CONGRESSIONAL AUTHORITY TO REMOVE
   EXECUTION OF THE LAWS FROM PRESIDENTIAL CONTROL) 443
      Nader v. Bork.. 444
      Report on "Independent Special Prosecutor"........................ 448
      Hearings on "Special Prosecutor" 452
      Shane, Special Prosecutor Post Will Survive Legal Test 454
      Notes and Questions on "Independent" Law Enforcement 455

C. DOES THE PRESIDENT NEED CONGRESS? (HEREIN, OF INHERENT
   PRESIDENTIAL AUTHORITY TO EXECUTE THE LAW) 458
   1. General Considerations 459
      In re Neagle 459
      In re Debs 461
   2. Case Studies 466
      a.   Public Lands.. 466
           United States v. Midwest Oil Co................................. 466
      b.   Vindicating Fourteenth Amendment Rights 472
           United States v. City of Philadelphia........................... 472

c. Protecting National Security 483
1. History of Electronic Surveillance............................... 483
Report on "Foreign Intelligence Surveillance Act of 1977" 483
2. Electronic Surveillance and National Security Investigations
Generally 485
United States v. United States District Court 485
Note: Presidential and Congressional Oversight of CIA and
FBI Intelligence Gathering.................................. 492
3. Investigations Under the Foreign Intelligence Surveillance Act
of 1978 497
Report on the "Foreign Intelligence Surveillance Act of 1977" . 497
In the Matter of the Application of the United States for an
Order Authorizing the Physical Search of Nonresidential
Premises and Personal Property 503

VI. THE PRESIDENT AND FOREIGN POLICY 507

A. ANALYTIC FRAMEWORK: THE PRESIDENT'S ROLE IN FOREIGN
AFFAIRS 507
United States v. Curtiss-Wright Corp. 508
Chicago & Southern Airlines, Inc. v. Waterman Steamship Corp..... 513

B. TREATY POWERS.. 520
1. Overview 520
Powers of the President and Senate 520
Permissible Scope of Treaties 523
Legal Impact of Treaties... 523
2. Treaty Termination by the President 525
Goldwater v. Carter (D.C. Cir) 525
Goldwater v. Carter (U.S.) 537

C. EXECUTIVE AGREEMENTS... 541
Note: International Non-Treaty Agreements.......................... 541
United States v. Pink 544
Dames & Moore v. Regan 552

D. OTHER ASPECTS OF CONGRESS' ROLE IN FOREIGN POLICY 568
1. Foreign Policy and Foreign Commerce............................... 568
a. Foreign Trade and the International Emergency Economic
Powers Act... 568
b. Trade Expansion Act 571
Independent Gasoline Marketers Council v. Duncan 571
c. Sales of Military Equipment to Iran 575
2. Foreign Policy and the Independent Regulatory Agencies 579
Westinghouse Electric Corp v. U.S. Nuclear Regulatory
Commission 579
Note: CAB Review of Air Carrier Acquisitions 585
3. Foreign Policy and the Appropriations Power 589
Note: The Iran-Contra Initiative.................................... 589

4. Immigration and Foreign Policy 592

E. INDIVIDUAL RIGHTS AND THE GOVERNMENT'S "MONOPOLY"
   IN FOREIGN AFFAIRS.. 592
   Note: The Logan Act 592
   Haig v. Agee.. 595

VII. THE PRESIDENT AS COMMANDER IN CHIEF 609

A. THE POWER TO COMMIT TROOPS............................... 610
   1. The Scope of the Commander in Chief Clause.................... 610
      The Federalist, No. 69 (Hamilton) 610
      The Prize Cases 610
   2. Case Study: Vietnam... 618
      Meeker, The Legality of United States Participation in the Defense
         of Viet-Nam 618
      Report on "National Commitments".............................. 623
      Mora v. McNamara 637
      Notes and Questions on Vietnam................................ 640
   3. Congress' Efforts to Limit the President's Authority to Commit
         Troops: The War Powers Resolution.......................... 642
      a. The Resolution and its History 642
         War Powers Resolution..................................... 642
         President Nixon's Veto of the War Powers Resolution 645
         Hearings on "War Powers: A Test of Compliance—Relative to the
            Danang Sealift, the Evacuation of Phnom Penh, the
            Evacuation of Saigon, and the Mayaguez Incident" 647
      b. Implementation 650
         1. Iranian Hostage Rescue Attempt......................... 651
            President Carter's Report to Speaker O'Neill Concerning the
               Abortive Rescue Attempt............................. 651
            Legal Opinion by Lloyd Cutler, President's Counsel, on War
               Powers Consultation Relative to the Iran Rescue Mission . 653
         2. Case Study: Lebanon.................................... 653
            Multinational Force in Lebanon Resolution 655
            President Reagan's Signing Statement on Multinational Force
               in Lebanon Resolution 656
            Report on "Multinational Force in Lebanon Resolution"....... 657
         3. Grenada, Libya, and the Persian Gulf 669
         4. Covert Warmaking and the Neutrality Act 671

B. DOMESTIC PRESIDENTIAL POWERS IN WARTIME.................. 672
   1. Civil Liberties 672
      Ex Parte Milligan 674
      Korematsu v. United States.................................... 680
      Notes and Questions on Japanese Internment and its Aftermath 694
   2. Mobilization and Regulation of the Economy.................... 697
      Note: Presidential Economic Controls During World War II 697
      Powers of the President Under the War Labor Disputes Act to Seize
         Properties Affected By Strikes................................ 700

C. PEACETIME AUTHORITY TO USE TROOPS FOR LAW
   ENFORCEMENT (HEREIN, OF THE "POSSE COMITATUS ACT")... 702
      President's Power to Use Federal Troops to Suppress Resistance to
         Enforcement of Federal Court Orders—Little Rock, Arkansas .. 703

VIII. THE TRANSFER OF POWER 711
   A. NOMINATION OF PRESIDENTIAL AND VICE PRESIDENTIAL
      CANDIDATES.. 711
      1. Political Parties and Law Generally 711
         a. Development of Parties and Nominating Systems................... 711
         b. Legal Control of Political Parties 715
            Democratic Party of the United States v. Wisconsin ex. rel.
            La Follette 715
      2. Representation Within Political Parties 725
         Ripon Society v. National Republican Party 725

   B. PRESIDENTIAL ELECTIONS... 734
      1. Campaign Finance... 734
         Buckley v. Valeo 735
         Winpisinger v. Watson 746
      2. Electoral College 750
         Report on "Direct Popular Election of the President and Vice
            President of the United States" 750
         J.A. Best, Prepared Statement on "The Case for the Electoral
            College" 759

   C. IMPEACHMENT 765
      Report on "Constitutional Grounds for Presidential Impeachment" . 766
      Report on "Impeachment of Richard M. Nixon, President of the
         United States" 775

   D. PRESIDENTIAL AND VICE-PRESIDENTIAL SUCCESSION............ 784
      R. Celada, Presidential Continuity and Vice Presidential Vacancy
         Amendment 785
      Note: Reagan-Bush Temporary Power Transfer........................ 789

IX. EPILOGUE: THE FUTURE PRESIDENCY 791
   Cutler, To Form a Government... 791
   Hearing on "One Six-Year Presidential Term" 793

APPENDIX: SELECTED STATUTES AND EXECUTIVE ORDERS........... 813

CONSTITUTION OF THE UNITED STATES 921

INDEX... 937

Table of Cases

Aaron v. Cooper, 703, 709
Abbott Laboratories v. Gardner, 82, 218
Abourezk v. Reagan, 592
Adams v. Richardson, 375
AFGE v. Pierce, 413
AFL-CIO v. Kahn, 88, 89, 97
Agee v. CIA, 161
Agee v. Muskie, 594, 597
Airline Pilots Ass'n Int'l v. Civil Aeronautics Bd., 588
A.L.A. Schechter Poultry Corp. v. United States, 71, 75, 84, 300, 304, 507
Alaska v. Carter, 472
Alaska Airlines, Inc. v. Brock, 134, 387, 389
Alderman v. United States, 491
Alfred A. Knopf v. Colby, 161
Amalgamated Meat Cutters & Butcher Workmen v. Connally, 75, 84, 94, 98, 336
American Int'l Group, Inc. v. Islamic Republic of Iran, 556, 567
American Party of Texas v. White, 738
American Textile Mfrs. Inst., Inc. v. Donovan, 85
Ameron, Inc. v. United States Army Corps of Engineers, 406
Anaconda Copper Company v. Andrus, 472
Anderson v. Celebrezze, 724, 746
Andrus v. Sierra Club, 228
In the matter of the Application of the United States for an Order Authorizing the Physical Search of Nonresident Premises and Personal Property, 503
Aptheker v. Secretary of State, 602
Arizona v. California, 84
Atchison v. Peterson, 470
Atlee v. Laird, 641

Atlee v. Richardson, 641
In re the Attorney General of the United States, 45, 204
Auffmordt v. Hedden, 262

Baker v. Carr, 164, 208, 537
Banco Nacional de Cuba v. Sabbatino, 551
Banzhaf v. Smith, 457
Barenblatt v. United States, 186
Barnes v. Kline, 106, 112, 409, 419
Bas v. Tingy, 641
Berger v. New York, 486
Bernstein v. N.V. Nederlandsche-Amerikaansche Stoomvaart-Maatschappij, 552
Berry v. Reagan, 321
Biddle v. Perovich, 440
Bissonette v. Haig, 710
Bivens v. Six Unknown Named Agents of Federal Bureau of Narcotics, 233, 240, 246, 255, 474
Blaber v. United States, 431
Bloom v. Illinois, 466
Board of Regents of State Colleges v. Roth, 567
Bob Jones University v. United States, 378
Bode v. National Democratic Party, 724, 727
Boutilier v. INS, 423
Bowles v. Willingham, 81
Bowsher v. Synar, 306, 318, 358, 366, 390, 398, 443, 584, 765
Brandon v. Ard, 469
Braniff Airways, Inc. v. CAB, 520
Branti v. Finkel, 328, 331, 721, 747
Brawer v. Horowitz, 479
The Brig Aurora, 65
Brown v. Bd. of Education, 287, 376, 703, 710
Brown v. Califano, 375, 378, 590

Buckley v. Valeo, 117, 124, 197, 215, 259, 267, 305, 316, 319, 324, 355, 402, 406, 735, 745
Buford v. Houtz, 470
Burdick v. United States, 440
Burroughs v. United States, 264
Butte City Water Co. v. Baker, 469
Butz v. Economou, 236, 240, 242, 246, 250

Camfield v. United States, 470
Caminetti v. United States, 503
Carlesi v. New York, 441
Carlson v. Green, 474
Cascade Natural Gas Corp. v. El Paso Natural Gas Co., 426
Champlin Refining Co. v. Corporation Comm'n, 117
Charlton v. Kelly, 531
Chas. T. Main Int'l Inc. v. Khuzestan Water & Power Authority, 556, 565
Cherokee Nation v. Southern Kansas R. Co., 565
Chevron v. Natural Resources Defense Council, Inc., 39
Chicago and Southern Airlines, Inc. v. Waterman Steamship Corp., 513, 519, 585, 588
The Chinese Exclusion Case, 510
CIA v. Sims, 155
Cincinnati Soap Co. v. United States, 380
Citizens for a Better Environment v. Gorsuch, 428
Citizens to Preserve Overton Park, Inc. v. Volpe, 219
City of New Haven v. United States, 384, 389
Clark v. Williard, 548
Cohens v. Virginia, 43, 417
Cole v. Young, 604
Coleman v. Miller, 411, 539
Commodity Futures Trading Commission v. Schor, 315, 321, 323, 326
Common Cause v. Nuclear Regulatory Commission, 228

Contractor's Ass'n of Eastern Pennsylvania v. Secretary of Labor, 92
Conyers v. Reagan, 669
Cooper v. Aaron, 709
Copeland v. Secretary of State, 594
Cousins v. Wigoda, 718, 728
Crockett v. Reagan, 642
Crowell v. Benson, 371
CSC v. Letter Carriers, 330

Dalehite v. United States, 430
Dames & Moore v. Regan, 471, 552, 566
Davis v. Passman, 474
Davis v. Wallace, 130
D.C. Federation of Civic Ass'ns v. Volpe, 135, 341
Deaver v. Seymour, 456
In re Debs, 60, 62, 143, 145, 374, 461, 465, 478, 481, 506, 609, 706
Dellums v. Powell, 205
Dellums v. Smith, 457, 672
Democratic Party of the United States v. Wisconsin ex rel. La Follette, 715, 724, 734
Disconto Gesellschaft v. Umbreit, 549
Dole v. Carter, 543
Dred Scott v. Sandford, 397
Duke Power v. Carolina Env. Study Group, 748
Duncan v. Kahanamoku, 55, 680
Durand v. Hollins, 649, 653

Eastland v. United States Servicemen's Fund, 186, 199, 206
Edwards v. Carter, 523
Edwards v. United States, 106
E.I. du Pont de Nemours & Co. v. Collins, 598
Ellsberg v. Mitchell, 177, 180
Elrod v. Burns, 327
Employers Group v. National War Labor Board, 699
Ex parte Endo, 684, 687
Engel v. Vitale, 737
Environmental Defense Fund v. Thomas, 360

Ernst & Ernst v. Hochfelder, 122
E-Systems Inc. v. United States, 567
Exxon Corp. v. FTC, 194

Fairfax's Devisee v. Hunter's Lessee, 524
Farkas v. Texas Instruments, Inc., 92
Farmer v. Philadelphia Electric Co. 92
Federal Energy Administration v. Algonquin SNG, Inc., 84, 571
Field v. Clark, 65, 76
Finnegan v. Matthews, 427
First National City Bank v. Banco Nacional de Cuba, 552
Flast v. Cohen, 444
Fletcher v. Peck, 125
Fleuti v. Rosenberg, 423
Flynt v. Weinberger, 670
Folsom v. Marsh, 212
Fong Yue Ting v. United States, 510
Foster v. Neilson, 524, 535
Foti v. INS, 125
FTC v. Owens-Corning Fiberglass Corp., 194

Ex Parte Garland, 440
Georgia v. National Democratic Party, 724, 727
Goldberg v. U.S. Dept. of State, 155
Goldwater v. Carter, 410, 418, 525, 537, 640
Gomez v. Toledo, 248
Gorin v. United States, 143
Gravel v. United States, 205, 247, 250
Gray v. Sanders, 731
Greenberg v. Bolger, 745
Grisar v. McDowell, 468
Guaranty Trust Co. v. United States, 546

Hadley v. Junior College Dist., 731
Haig v. Agee, 75, 561, 594, 595, 608
Halderman v. Pennhurst State School and Hospital, 479, 482
Halkin v. Helms, 172, 175, 180
Halperin v. Kissinger, 256
Hampton v. Mow Sun Wong, 85, 694
Harlow v. Fitzgerald, 242, 245, 251, 256

Harris v. McRae, 745
Hayburn's Case, 261, 478
Heckler v. Chaney, 365, 397, 429
Heckler v. Lopez, 427
In the matter of Hennen, 262, 449, 451
Hill v. U.S. Immigration and Naturalization Service, 426
Hines v. Davidowitz, 550
Hirabayashi v. United States, 681, 695
Hobson v. Hansen, 450
Hohri v. United States, 695
Hollingsworth v. Virginia, 123
Holtzman v. Schlesinger, 641
Hotel and Restaurant Employees Union v. Smith, 592
Human Resources Development Institute v. Donovan, 380
Humphrey's Executor v. United States, 122, 211, 265, 267, 300, 305, 308, 312, 315, 319, 324, 357, 402, 451, 528
Hutcheson v. United States, 194
Hutchinson v. Proxmire, 247

Illinois Central Railroad v. Bosworth, 440
Imbler v. Pachtman, 235, 330, 438, 461
Independent Gasoline Marketers Council v. Duncan, 571, 574
Independent Meat Packers Ass'n v. Butz, 101
Indian Towing Co. v. United States, 431, 433
Industrial Union Dept., AFL-CIO v. American Petroleum Inst., 85
INS v. Chadha, 104, 113, 115, 130, 216, 267, 305, 308, 311, 313, 316, 324, 336, 385, 389, 400, 406, 410, 413, 640, 649
INS v. Wang, 130
Itek Corporation v. First National Bank of Boston, 567
Ivanov v. United States, 500

Jean v. Nelson, 592
Jenness v. Fortson, 739, 744
Johnson v. Eisentrager, 639

Jones v. United States, 510
J.W. Hampton, Jr. & Co. v. United
    States, 66, 76

Katz v. United States, 251, 484, 486
Katzenbach v. Morgan, 741
Kendall v. United States ex rel. Stokes,
    44, 335, 379, 405
Kennedy v. Sampson, 110, 409, 413
Kent v. Dulles, 74, 84, 595, 598, 694
The King v. Baker et al., 36
Kissinger v. Reporters Committee for
    Freedom of the Press, 224
Kleindienst v. Mandel, 592
Kleppe v. New Mexico, 205
Koniag, Inc. v. Andrus, 135, 341
Korematsu v. United States, 680, 694

The Laura, 441
Light v. United States, 470
Linda R. S. v. Richard D., 438
Little v. Barreme, 42
Livingston v. Jefferson, 256
In the Matter of Longstaff, 426
Lopez v. Heckler, 427
Lubin v. Panish, 738
Ludecke v. Watkins, 700

McDonnell Douglas Corp. v. United
    States, 398
McGrain v. Daugherty, 192, 196, 266
McCulloch v. Maryland, 15, 127, 167,
    171, 264, 403, 736
Mahler v. Eby, 128
Manhattan-Bronx Postal Union v.
    Gronouski, 101
Marbury v. Madison, 31, 34, 37, 166,
    171, 191, 221, 243, 288, 298, 304,
    401, 415, 520, 539
Marcus v. Search Warrant, 488
Massachusetts v. Laird, 641
M'Clung v. Silliman, 41
Mead Data Cent., Inc. v. U.S.
    Department of Air Force, 204
Ex parte Merryman, 673
Ex parte Milligan, 55, 640, 674, 680
Mississippi v. Johnson, 44
Missouri v. Holland, 523

Missouri Highway Commission v.
    Volpe, 382
Missouri Pacific Ry. Co. v. Kansas,
    102
Mitchell v. Forsyth, 251, 255
Mitchell v. Laird, 641
Mitchell v. United States, 638
Moore v. United States House of
    Representatives, 410
Mora v. McNamara, 637, 641
Moscow Fire Ins. Co. v. Bank of New
    York & Trust Co., 546
Munro v. Socialist Workers Party, 746
Murphy v. Department of the Army,
    204
Myers v. United States, 50, 120, 129,
    262, 291, 300, 302, 305, 308,
    319, 324, 355, 401, 446, 451,
    528, 765

Nader v. Bork, 170, 444, 447
Nader v. Saxbe, 436
Nardone v. United States, 483
Nathan v. Smith, 457
National Association for the
    Advancement of Colored People v.
    Bell, 437
NAACP v. Levi, 434, 437
National Cable Television Ass'n v.
    United States, 84
National Council of Community
    Mental Health Centers, Inc. v.
    Weinberger, 405
National Treasury Employees Union v.
    Nixon, 45, 219
Natural Resources Defense Council v.
    Costle, 428
In re Neagle, 60, 62, 374, 436, 459,
    460, 465, 481, 650, 653
Near v. Minnesota, 140, 145, 147, 603
Neely v. Henkel, 534
New York Times v. United States, 138,
    147, 154, 465, 479, 609
Nixon v. Administrator of General
    Services, 124, 210, 216, 315, 410
Nixon v. Condon, 724
Nixon v. Fitzgerald, 234, 250, 255,
    323
Nixon v. Freeman, 217

Nixon v. Herndon, 724
Nixon v. Sirica, 44, 168, 209
NLRB v. Jones & Laughlin Steel
    Corp., 279
North v. Walsh, 456
Northern Securities Co. v. United
    States, 145
Norwegian Nitrogen Products Co. v.
    United States, 76

Oetjen v. Central Leather Co., 551
Ollman v. Evans, 418
Olmstead v. United States, 483
Orlando v. Laird, 641
Orvis v. Brownell, 558
O'Shea v. Littleton, 748
Ozonoff v. Berzak, 544

Pacific Legal Foundation v. Dept. of
    Transportation, 135
Panama Refining Co. v. Ryan, 69, 75,
    507, 512
Pan American World Airways, Inc. v.
    Civil Aeronautics Bd., 589
Patti v. Schweiker, 427
Pennhurst State School v. Halderman,
    482
Pennsylvania v. Lynn, 381, 419
Perkins v. Lukens Steel Co., 94
Petite v. United States, 438
Pierce v. Society of Sisters, 745
Pierson v. Ray, 235
Pillsbury Co. v. FTC, 207, 341
The Pocket Veto Case, 107
Powell v. McCormack, 209, 404
The Prize Cases, 610, 617, 639, 673
Process Gas Consumers Group v.
    Consumer Energy Council of
    America, 134
Propper v. Clark, 559
Public Citizen v. Burke, 397
Pugach v. Klein, 432

Ex parte Quirin, 680

Rainbow Navigation, Inc. v.
    Department of the Navy, 519
Ramirez de Arellano v. Weinberger,
    642

Ray v. Blair, 713, 719
Raymond v. Thomas, 680
Rayonier, Inc. v. United States, 430
Regan v. Wald, 595
Regional Rail Reorganization Act
    Cases, 565
Reid v. Covert, 523
Rendell-Baker v. Kohn, 725
Reynolds v. Sims, 733
Ripon Society v. National Republican
    Party, 724, 725
Rizzo v. Goode, 481
Roberts v. United States, 42
In re Robson and Will, 414
Roe v. Wade, 281
Rosario v. Rockefeller, 719
Russian Volunteer Fleet v. United
    States, 549

Sanchez-Espinoza v. Reagan, 642, 672
Sanders v. Gray, 731
Sangamon Valley Television Corp. v.
    United States, 337
Schenck v. United States, 140
Scheuer v. Rhodes, 235, 246, 248
In re Sealed Case, 456
Senate Select Committee on
    Presidential Campaign Activities
    v. Nixon, 186, 195, 202, 209
Service v. Dulles, 165, 446
Shakman v. Democratic Organization
    of Cook County, 749
Shanghai Power Co. v. United States,
    567
Shurtleff v. United States, 301
Sibbach v. Wilson, 118
Ex parte Siebold, 449, 706
Sierra Club v. Costle, 337, 343, 358,
    584
Simon v. Eastern Kentucky Welfare
    Rights Org., 748
Sinclair v. United States, 193, 205
Smith v. Allwright, 722, 724
Smith v. Jackson, 397
Smith v. United States, 429, 437
Snepp v. United States, 149, 154, 158,
    596
Southern Pacific v. Bell, 469

South Puerto Rico Sugar Co. Trading
    Corp. v. United States, 544
Spalding v. Vilas, 235, 246
Springer v. Philippine Islands, 261, 556
Sterling v. Constantin, 688
Steuart & Bro. v. Bowles, 698
Steward Machine Co. v. Davis, 94
Storer v. Brown, 724, 739
Stump v. Sparkman, 236
Sun Oil Company v. United States,
    205
Sweezy v. New Hampshire, 718
In re Surface Mining Regulation
    Litigation, 101
Synar v. United States, 307

Tashjian v. Republican Party of
    Connecticut, 724
Tenney v. Brandhove, 206, 235
Terry v. Adams, 722, 724
Terry v. Ohio, 490
Thomason v. Cooper, 703
Todok v. Union State Bank, 550
Toilet Goods Ass'n v. Gardner, 82
Train v. City of New York, 383
TVA v. Hill, 92, 98

Underhill v. Hernandez, 551
United States v.
    Allocco, 285
    American Bell Telephone Co., 478
    A. T. & T., 182, 184, 199, 203, 207
    Bank of New York & Trust Co.,
        545
    Batchelder, 438
    Belmont, 542, 546, 551
    Brand Jewelers, Inc., 479
    Brown, 124, 500
    Burr, 43, 168, 238, 242, 671
    Butenko, 500
    Butler, 366, 375, 737, 745
    California, 478
    City of Philadelphia, 472, 481
    Cox, 432, 452
    Curtiss-Wright Export Corp., 51,
        73, 79, 285, 507, 508, 518, 529,
        535, 539, 550, 584, 598
    El Paso Natural Gas Co., 427
    Ferreira, 261

    Frade, 592
    Germaine, 262, 448
    Grimaud, 76
    Guy W. Capps, 544, 551
    Haldeman, 193
    Hohri, 695
    I.C.C., 164
    Klein, 440
    Lovasco, 438
    Lovett, 402, 406
    Marchetti, 150, 153, 161
    Marzano, 447
    McDonnell Douglas Corp., 398
    Midwest Oil Co., 3, 51, 60, 466,
        471, 481, 553, 564
    Mitchell, 193
    Nixon, 44, 124, 162, 163, 170, 190,
        195, 202, 212, 216, 238, 243,
        323, 405, 445, 539
    Padelford, 440
    Peace Information Center, 594
    Percheman, 524, 535
    Pink, 544, 551, 561, 566
    Progressive, Inc., 147
    Ramirez, 671
    Reynolds, 168, 172, 180
    Russell, 688
    S.A. Empresa de Viacao Aerea Rio
        Grandense (Varig Airlines), 433
    San Jacinto Tin Corp., 478
    Solomon, 450, 479
    United States District Court (Keith),
        251, 485, 492, 500, 609
    United States House of
        Representatives, 180, 198
    Wilson, 440
    Woodley, 269, 283, 290
    Yoshida International, Inc., 569
United States ex rel. Accardi v.
    Shaughnessy, 165
United States ex rel. Chapman v. FPC,
    410
Universal Shipping Co. v. United
    States, 406
Urtetiqui v. D'Arcy, 599
U.S. House of Representatives v. FTC,
    134

Valley Forge Christian College v.
    Americans United for Separation
    of Church and State, 410

Vander Jagt v. O'Neill, 414
Vermont Yankee Nuclear Power Corp.
    v. Natural Resources Defense
    Council, Inc., 337, 341
Ex parte Virginia, 475
Vitarelli v. Seaton, 165, 446

Warth v. Seldin, 748
Watkins v. United States, 186, 192
Wayman v. Southard, 65
Wayte v. United States, 438
Weinberger v. Rossi, 544
Westinghouse Electric Corp. v. U.S.
    Nuclear Regulatory Commission,
    579, 584
Whitney v. Robertson, 525
Wiener v. United States, 265, 305,
    320, 357, 451
Ex parte William Wells, 440
Winpisinger v. Watson, 746
Wong Yang Sung v. McGrath, 83

Wood v. Strickland, 248
Woods v. Cloyd W. Miller Co., 700
Work v. Rives, 433
Wright v. United States, 108

Yakus v. United States, 73, 75, 122,
    307
Ex parte Young, 43, 82
Young v. United States ex rel. Vuitton
    et Fils S.A., 456, 466
Youngstown Sheet & Tube Co. v.
    Sawyer, 3, 45, 47, 61, 73, 84, 88,
    90, 122, 125, 129, 145, 148, 238,
    261, 307, 355, 358, 404, 458,
    462, 465, 471, 480, 520, 535,
    539, 553, 556, 570, 578, 584,
    591, 609, 640, 702

Zemel v. Rusk, 75, 79, 595, 597
Zittman v. McGrath, 558
Zweibon v. Mitchell, 501

Preface

This volume offers a set of cases and materials on law and the exercise of presidential power. Although thousands of books and articles exist on the Presidents and on the Presidency, we are aware of no other current volume of primary sources designed to permit lawyers, law students and political scientists a comprehensive review of the issues involved in the application of law to the President's functions. The book is innovative for law schools because its subject matter is not well covered by the mainstream curriculum. It is innovative for undergraduate and graduate courses on the Presidency because of its emphasis on primary materials at the expense of discursive secondary text.

As law teachers, we have found the value of this project for our students to be at least three-fold. First, despite the ever-increasing importance of all aspects of public law in our national life, legal curricula tend to focus on the operation of the courts. These materials, we hope, afford readers a clearer picture of how the executive branch of government operates and of how complex a process is the "execution of the laws." Although bits and pieces of the overall picture may appear in courses on constitutional law and international law, we find that a systematic overview of the Presidency better highlights and puts into context such processes as law enforcement, program administration, budgeting and accounting, and the implementation of foreign and military policy.

Second, as the ever-increasing number of legal cases involving the President attests, the subject of this work has become and is likely to remain a central national concern. The Nixon Presidency precipitated a major shift in legal attitude towards judicial oversight of the Presidency. Even if future administrations prove less troubled, however, the increasing burden that the executive branch shoulders for solving domestic and foreign problems will require citizens to concern themselves ever more with the issues surrounding executive effectiveness and accountability. These materials help to prepare students of law and political science to participate in that debate more knowledgeably.

Finally, a thorough exploration of the applicability of law to the President's functions highlights the crucial non-litigative role of legal counsel that, in all fields, legal curricula tend to underemphasize. Perhaps because most discussion materials in law school classes consist of reported cases, the impression is created that law is determined primarily in the courtroom and that arguing cases is what "real lawyers" do. Most hard legal questions facing the President must be decided, at least in the first instance, within the executive branch and on the basis of relatively little prior judicial guidance. The following materials thus rely substantially on sources other than judicial opinions to which the President's lawyers would resort in order to solve a difficult problem. We have also employed a problem-oriented approach to a number of issues, asking the reader: What would you advise the President on the issue if you were the President's lawyer? This orientation is intended to provide insights into the role of the President's legal counsel that will be useful to those who perform a counseling role in any large institutional setting.

The authors have found this work ideally suited for a three-hour second- or third-year law school course, although we have never attempted to cover each and every topic in class. Neither of us, for example, has found time to delve deeply into Chapter 8, on problems of presidential transitions. The book can be used successfully, however, even in a 2-hour course. Such a course, for example, might focus on the domestic Presidency, employing Chapters 1-5. Alternatively, omitting Chapters 4 and 5 and using Chapters 6 and 7 will produce a course focusing chiefly on the President's foreign affairs and military powers. Teachers interested in surveying all aspects of the Presidency in a 2-hour course may simply excise from each chapter those topics that seem to them least essential. The likeliest suggestions for excision, in our judgment, include Section B of Chapter 3, Sections A(2)-A(5) of Chapter 5, Sections D and E of Chapter 6, and Sections B(2) and C of Chapter 7, as well as Chapters 8 and 9.*

This work has profited greatly from the suggestions of students, friends, and colleagues. We would like to express our deep appreciation to Larry A. Hammond, Peter Raven-Hansen, Larry L. Simms, and especially to David A. Martin, who all offered helpful insights based on teaching the book in draft. We are also grateful to Jeffrey N. Shane, Deputy Assistant Secretary of State for International Transportation (and brother of one author) for his assistance in creating the case study of the now-defunct Civil Aeronautics Board. Among the students who made special contributions to this book are Greg Schwager, Kelly Schemenauer, David Stamp, Patrick Sullivan and Ruth Walz at Iowa, James Gattuso at UCLA, and Christopher Brancart and Michelle Hoogendam at Texas. We received exceptional typing assistance from Sally Laster and Phyllis Monaghan at Iowa, and from Sally Donaldson and Gretchen Woellner at Texas. Additionally, we owe thanks to our former colleagues at the Office of Legal Counsel at the U.S. Department of Justice for their innumerable insights that have shaped and deepened our thinking on the Presidency.

Three final notes on style: First, although we try to avoid using the masculine generic to describe all people, we continue to use "he" as an occasional pronoun for "the President" because of the historical circumstance that this country has not yet elected a woman to the Presidency. Second, although we have marked textual deletions in the excerpted materials, we often omit, without any printed signal, footnote material and citations to cases or other authorities that may appear in the excerpts. Third, in citing relevant secondary literature, we use forms of citation that are conventional among legal academics, but which may be unusual for political scientists and their students.

PMS
HHS
Iowa City, Iowa
Austin, Texas
January, 1988

---

*We have tried to organize the volume with sufficient clarity so that teachers using either a 2- or 3-hour format could also re-order the materials to fit their instructional tastes. One colleague, for example, has suggested teaching the impeachment materials in Chapter Eight together with the general materials on accountability in Chapter Three. Also, the executive privilege materials in Chapter Three could be delayed until students learned more of the substantive law surrounding presidential powers from Chapters Four through Seven. The pedagogically defensible permutations are undoubtedly endless.

THE LAW OF PRESIDENTIAL POWER:
Cases and Materials

Chapter 1
Introduction

The Constitution does not clearly define the powers of the President. The task that confronts anyone hoping to understand the law of presidential power was outlined eloquently by Justice Robert Jackson, himself a former Attorney General, in his famous concurrence in *Youngstown Sheet & Tube Co. v. Sawyer*, 343 U.S. 579, 634-35 (1952):

> A judge, like an executive adviser, may be surprised at the poverty of really useful and unambiguous authority applicable to concrete problems of executive power as they actually present themselves. Just what our forefathers did envision, or would have envisioned had they foreseen modern conditions, must be divined from materials almost as enigmatic as the dreams Joseph was called upon to interpret for Pharaoh. A century and a half of partisan debate and scholarly speculation yields no net result but only supplies more or less apt quotations from respected sources on each side of any question. They largely cancel each other.[1] And court decisions are indecisive because of the judicial practice of dealing with the largest questions in the most narrow way.

Article II of the Constitution, which creates and empowers the executive, is notoriously vague. As Edward S. Corwin observed in his classic book, The President, Office and Powers 1787-1984, 3-4 (5th rev. ed. 1984 by R. Bland, T. Hindson & J. Peltason): "To those who think that a constitution ought to settle everything beforehand it should be a nightmare; by the same token, to those who think that constitution makers ought to leave considerable leeway for the future play of political forces, it should be a vision realized." Section one states that "[t]he executive Power shall be vested in a President of the United States of America." Sections two and three designate him Commander in Chief of the armed forces, authorize him to appoint certain "Officers of the United States," and confer various foreign policy powers. Finally, he is charged to "take Care that the Laws be faithfully executed."

Questions of profound modern importance await anyone who would interpret the Constitution. What meaning should be given to various phrases in the text? What weight should the intent of the framers receive? What is the importance of historical practice under the Constitution? We will, of course, explore these questions throughout this book. We begin with a brief historical summary of matters that are often cited in current debates. Before we begin, however, some bibliographical notes are in order.

---

1. A Hamilton may be matched against a Madison. 7 The Works of Alexander Hamilton, 76-117; 1 Madison, Letters and Other Writings, 611-654. Professor Taft is counterbalanced by Theodore Roosevelt. Taft, Our Chief Magistrate and His Powers, 139-140; Theodore Roosevelt, Autobiography, 388-389. It even seems that President Taft cancels out Professor Taft. Compare his "Temporary Petroleum Withdrawal No. 5" of September 27, 1909, *United States v. Midwest Oil Co.*, 236 U.S. 459, with his appraisal of executive power in "Our Chief Magistrate and His Powers" 139-140.

Readers interested in consulting the primary materials in law and political philosophy that shaped the founding generation's ideas about executive power should see the five volume collection edited by P. Kurland & R. Lerner, The Founders' Constitution (1987), and 1 W. Goldsmith, The Growth of Presidential Power: A Documented History (1974). Good constitutional histories include L. Levy, Essays on the Making of the Constitution (2d ed. 1987); G. Wood, The Creation of the American Republic, 1776-1787 (1969); C. Thach, The Creation of the Presidency, 1775-1789 (1923).

Some of the best books on the Presidency, in addition to those cited above, are the following: J. Burns, Presidential Government: The Crucible of Leadership (1966); T. Cronin, The State of the Presidency (2d ed. 1980); M. Cunliffe, American Presidents and the Presidency (2d ed. 1976); L. Fisher, Constitutional Conflicts Between Congress and the President (1985); L. Koenig, The Chief Executive (3d ed. 1975); R. Neustadt, Presidential Power: The Politics of Leadership From FDR to Carter (2d ed. 1980); R. Pious, The American Presidency (1979); W. Taft, The President and His Powers (1916). The best starting bibliography is F. Greenstein, L. Berman & A. Felzenberg, Evolution of the Modern Presidency: A Bibliographical Survey (1977).

A. Constitutional History: The Creation of the Presidency

1. The Articles of Confederation

As the delegates to the Constitutional Convention met in Philadelphia in May, 1787, their stated task was to correct the defects found in the Articles of Confederation, the predecessor to the present Constitution. Written while the perceived abuses of George III were still fresh in the nation's memory, the Articles did not gather power in any one person. See Note, The United States and the Articles of Confederation: Drifting Toward Anarchy or Inching Toward Commonwealth?, 88 Yale L.J. 142 (1978). All executive as well as legislative power was vested in the Congress. While one member of the Congress was designated as the "President," this officer was not a head of government, but was equivalent to a modern Speaker of the House or President of the Senate.

The nearest thing to a separate executive office under the Articles was the "Committee of the States" (with one representative from each state), which was responsible for administering the government while Congress was out of session. While this body also had a "President," he was forbidden to serve for more than one year so that he would not gather too much power or prestige. Also, this body was authorized to take only limited actions, leaving the most important matters to the full Congress.

It soon became apparent that Congress could not effectively perform executive functions. As Alexander Hamilton complained (C. Thach, The Creation of the Presidency, 1775-1789, 64 (1923)):

> Congress have kept the power too much in their own hands and have meddled too much with details of every sort. Congress is, properly, a deliberative corps, and it forgets itself when it attempts to play the executive. It is impossible such a body, numerous as it is, and constantly fluctuating, can ever act with sufficient decision or with system.

These problems were also seen by such critics of centralized government as Thomas Jefferson. He wrote (*Id.* at 71):

> The want of a separate executive has been the source of more evil than we have experienced from any other cause. Nothing is so embarrassing as the details of execution. The smallest trifle of that kind occupies as long as the most important act of legislation, and takes place of everything else. Let any man recollect, or look over the files of congress, he will observe the most important propositions hanging over from week to week and month to month, till the occasion have past them and the thing never done.

While the defects of the existing system were thus apparent to most delegates to the Constitutional Convention, the proper solution was not. Few, if any, desired a return to monarchy, despite the fears of many outside the convention. Moreover, had a monarchy been proposed, it was unlikely to have been approved by the states. John Dickinson of Delaware, the nearest thing to a monarchist at the convention, said that while "a limited Monarchy be considered as *one* of the best Governments in the world," he believed it "was out of the question. The Spirit of the times—the state of our affairs, forbade the experiment, if it were desireable." (J. Madison, The Debates in the Federal Convention of 1787, 47 (1970).)

The convention was therefore committed to devising a republican form of executive authority. There were three sources of ideas upon which they could draw: republican governments in other nations, state governments established during the Revolution (which reflected colonial experience), and writings of the leading political philosophers.

2. *Republican Executives in Other Nations*

Historical experience with republics in other nations could not have given the delegates much encouragement. The ancient republics, such as Athens and Rome, had ended in failure. In the contemporary world, all but a handful of nations were ruled by hereditary monarchs. Among the exceptions was Switzerland, which had no national executive. (The Swiss cantons were ruled by small groups of wealthy families, and remained divided by religious disputes.) Holland had done without a monarch for several centuries, but was governed by a "Stadtholder" with near-monarchical powers. Poland had had an elective monarchy for over 150 years. The Kingship, however, was the subject of rampant intrigue and conspiracy before each election, both from within and without Poland. Jefferson had this example in mind in 1787 when he complained that the proposed American President "seems a bad edition of a Polish King." M. Cunliffe, American Presidents and the Presidency 20 (2d ed. 1976).

3. *State Governors*

A second source of models for the American executive was closer to home—governors under the newly written state constitutions. Unlike the Articles of Confederation, these constitutions generally created an executive distinct from the legislature, thus avoiding some of the disadvantages of having a legislature directly execute the laws.

The power of these chief executives, however, was usually severely limited. It was made clear in each state that the legislature was the supreme branch of government.

As James Wilson wrote of these governments, although three branches of government were created, "[t]he legislature was still discriminated by excessive partiality; and into its lap, every good and precious gift was profusely thrown." Thach, *supra*, at 27. Having just rid themselves of the Royal Governors, the legislatures were reluctant to create powerful new governors.

In eight of the states, the legislatures retained close control of the executive by electing him. In Pennsylvania, the "executive" consisted of the twelve members of the upper house of the legislature. In several others, the governor shared power with a "council of state" or "council of revision." Finally, in ten of the thirteen states, the governor was limited to a one-year term of office.

Although legislative supremacy prevented executive abuse of power, it fostered legislative excesses. Jefferson, no friend of a strong executive, complained (*Id.* at 30):

> All the powers of government, legislative, executive and judiciary, result to the legislative body. . . . But no barrier was provided between these several powers. The judiciary and executive members were left dependent for their subsistence in office, and some of them for their continuance in it. If therefore the legislature assumes executive and judiciary powers, no opposition is likely to be made; nor, if made, can it be effectual.

One exception to the general pattern of weak state governors was New York. Its Constitution, drafted in 1777 by John Jay with the assistance of Gouverneur Morris, granted the executive broad powers. First, he was elected by popular vote for a fixed term of three years, thus enjoying an independent source of support and security in office. In terms foreshadowing the federal Constitution, he was vested with "the supreme executive power and authority of [the] State," and had the duty to "take care that the Laws be faithfully executed." Also, he served as "commander-in-chief of all the militia, and admiral of the navy" of the state. He appointed all military officers, and could grant pardons and reprieves.

The Governor of New York also had substantial control over the legislature. As a member of a five-man "Council of Revision," he enjoyed a limited veto power. He could convene and disband the legislature for limited periods of time. Finally, the governor had a general duty to report to the legislature each year on the "condition of the state," and to recommend legislation.

The effectiveness of the New York governorship, especially during the term of George Clinton, the first governor, was noted throughout the nation. Several states, including Massachusetts, soon revised their own constitutions to provide for strong governors. Nor did New York's success escape the notice of the delegates at the federal convention. The example of New York was frequently discussed during the deliberations; its governor appears to have served as a significant model for the Presidency.

4. The Great Political Theorists

The delegates at Philadelphia drew upon abstract political theory in forming their conception of the Presidency. Most of the delegates were well read in political philosophy, and were familiar with the great contemporary political philosophers—notably Locke, Montesquieu, Blackstone, and Hume. *See* G. Wills, Explaining America: The Federalist (1981). While these writers differed in many ways, they shared a belief in a "balanced constitution," containing independent legislative and executive branches.

John Locke was among the first to expound this view. In his *Second Treatise on Government*, he asserted that the legislature is the supreme power of government, as it alone can impose laws upon the citizens. J. Locke, Two Treatises of Government, 384-85 (P. Laslett ed. 1967). He cautioned, however, that a separate and powerful executive is also essential for the proper execution of the laws. In describing the "prerogatives" of the executive, he wrote (*Id*. at 392):

> Where the Legislative and Executive Power are in distinct hands, (as they are in all moderated Monarchies, and well-framed Governments) there the good of the Society requires, that several things should be left to the discretion of him, that has the Executive Power. For the Legislators not being able to foresee, and provide, by Laws, for all, that may be useful to the Community, the Executor of the Laws, having the power in his hands, has by the common Law of Nature, a right to make use of it, for the good of the Society....

The concept of a constitution containing independent executive and legislative powers was more fully developed by the Baron de Montesquieu in his work *Spirit of the Laws*. Adding the judiciary as a third independent branch of government, he argued that each branch should be separate, and that none should be dependent upon another (Corwin, *supra*, at 9):

> When the legislative and executive powers are united in the same person, or in the same body of magistrates, there can be no liberty; because apprehensions may arise, lest the same monarch or senate enact tyrannical laws, and execute them in a tyrannical manner. Again, there is no liberty, if the judiciary power be not separated from the legislative and executive.... There would be an end of everything, were the same men or the same body ... to exercise those three powers, that of enacting laws, that of executing the public resolutions, and of trying the causes of individuals.

This evolving concept of a "separation of powers" was also described by Sir William Blackstone in his *Commentaries*. While, like Locke, Blackstone asserted the supremacy of the legislature (referring to the "omnipotence of Parliament"), he also defended the royal prerogative, especially in foreign and military affairs. (*Id*. at 9-10.)

A fourth major influence upon the delegates' vision of executive power was David Hume. Writing in the mid-18th century, Hume was nearly their contemporary. He asserted that there were only two "pure" forms of government—monarchy and republic. He depicted the current government of Great Britain as a mixture of these, a "mixed constitution." Power in this system was balanced between the King and Parliament, and within Parliament between Lords and Commons. Hume credited this division of authority with maintaining the existing balance between liberty and authority in Britain. J. Stewart, The Moral and Political Philosophy of David Hume, 235-36 (1963).

In his description of a "perfect commonwealth," Hume placed executive and judicial power in one house of his proposed legislature. Thus, his ideal constitution more closely resembled the modern British parliamentary system than one embodying a "separation of powers." Nevertheless, the idea of a "mixed" system appealed to many of his readers, both in Britain and in the colonies.

It is difficult to assess the impact that these theorists had upon the framers of the Constitution. It is unlikely that any particular decision turned solely on the basis of abstract political theory. Still, theory supported conclusions already drawn from the framers' practical experiences with government. After George III and the Confederation government, they were well aware of the difficulties that arose when either the executive or legislature became too powerful. Some kind of balance seemed necessary.

5. Deliberations of the Constitutional Convention

Our knowledge of the deliberations of the Constitutional Convention is less than wholly satisfactory. As everyone knows, its proceedings were held in secret. Notes of the participants, which were published many years later, are summary in form. The standard compilation is Max Farrand's four-volume The Records of the Federal Convention of 1787 (rev. ed. 1937). The description that follows is drawn largely from Madison, *supra*, who kept the most detailed notes, and from the valuable short history by Thach, *supra*.

As could be expected, delegates assembling in Philadelphia held a wide variety of views on executive power. At one extreme were "quasi-monarchists" such as John Dickinson of Delaware, who maintained that a "firm Executive could only exist in a limited monarchy." At the other extreme were such men as Roger Sherman of Connecticut, who considered the executive as "nothing more than an institution for carrying the will of the Legislature into effect."

It appears that a consensus existed from the beginning for a stronger and more effective national executive. Experience in state government had shown the potential for abuse of power by a dominant legislative branch. Similarly, experience under the Confederation had demonstrated that Congress should not execute the laws.

The major controversies concerning the Presidency at the convention concerned three or four issues. Elsewhere, a consensus already existed. For example, proposals for executive appointment of administrative officers, executive control of the military, and some separation from the legislature were virtually uncontested.

There remained, however, significant differences in opinion over the scope of presidential power. Many delegates, including Randolph and Sherman, saw the problems of the Confederation as administrative in nature. Thus, they could be solved by a manager who would be subordinate to Congress. This has been called the "administrative" principle of executive power. Others, such as Wilson and Morris, feared a repetition of the state experience, and maintained that the President must be independent and must enjoy his own source of power. This is known as the "political" principle. The specific issues that aroused controversy included the number of executives, the extent of the veto power (if any), the manner of election, the length of the term of office, and eligibility for re-election.

The first proposals made to the convention were introduced by Edmund Randolph of Virginia, as part of what became known as the "Virginia Plan" of government. It contemplated a weak executive of one or more men, clearly dependent upon Congress. It proposed that "a national Executive be instituted, to be chosen by the national Legislature—for the term of ____years . . . and to be ineligible a second time; and that besides a general authority to execute the National laws, it ought to enjoy the executive rights vested in Congress by the Confederation." At best, this executive would have had powers similar to a state governor of the time; at worst, it could have become little more than an executive committee of Congress.

Madison slightly expanded this definition by moving that the executive be granted power to "carry into effect the national laws, to appoint to offices in cases not otherwise provided for, and to execute such other powers not Legislative nor Judiciary in their nature as may from time to time be delegated by the national Legislature."

Soon after the introduction of this plan, James Wilson of Pennsylvania, a leading proponent of a strong executive, moved that the executive consist of a single individual. Wilson did not take this opportunity to contest the rather limited view of executive power contained in Madison's proposal. Instead he specifically rejected use of royal prerogatives as a guide. The only powers he saw as "strictly executive" were "executing the laws, and appointing officers." This suggestion evidently took the convention by surprise. As Madison noted, it was met with a "considerable pause." Many of the delegates shared the fears of Randolph, who described the idea as the "foetus of monarchy." Undaunted, Wilson stood his ground, arguing that a unitary executive would be the best safeguard against tyranny, as it would ensure "energy, dispatch, and responsibility." Wilson and the other supporters of a strong executive eventually won the day—the convention voted 7-3 for a single executive.

A second major question concerned the executive's opportunity to veto legislation. The Virginia Plan proposed a "Council of Revision," consisting of the executive and several members of the judiciary. Modeled on a similar body in New York, it would be authorized to veto any legislation not repassed by Congress. Elbridge Gerry, joined by Wilson, objected to this plan, arguing that the executive required greater power. He proposed exclusive executive control over the veto. Wilson also favored an absolute veto, to forestall constant legislative overrides. Wilson and Gerry won a partial victory. The Council of Revision was scrapped, leaving the executive in sole control of the veto. However, the power was made subject to override by a two-thirds vote of Congress. The strong-executive faction did not get all it wanted, but it did succeed in granting the President a major voice in legislation.

A third issue, the method of electing the executive, proved to be the most difficult for the delegates. The Virginia Plan proposed appointment by the legislature. Wilson called for direct election by the people. He envisioned the executive as a national leader, not an administrator for Congress, and thus felt that he should derive power directly from the people.

This proposal faced strong opposition. James Mason of Virginia probably best expressed the general sentiment when he argued that the average voter would have no way to know the qualifications of potential candidates. "It would be as unnatural to refer the choice of a proper character for chief Magistrate to the people," he said, "as it would to refer a trial of colours to a blind man." Others worried that voters would never give a majority of votes to any one candidate, because they would only support local favorites.

During these early debates, Gerry offered a compromise by which the President would be chosen not by the people, but by electors chosen by the people. The convention, however, was evidently not ready for the idea. On June 2d, resolutions were passed providing that the executive would be chosen by the legislature for a seven year term.

The delegates were still concerned, however, that the executive would become overly dependent on Congress. They feared that he would try to appease the legislature in hopes of reappointment. Therefore, they agreed to a single term of office, to remove any incentive "to intrigue with the Legislature for a re-appointment."

The Presidency outlined by these preliminary decisions of the convention was very different from the one eventually established. Appointed by the legislature, it was not yet a fully independent institution. Still, the strong-executive faction had made significant gains. The executive was to consist of a single person, who would enjoy an exclusive, though limited, veto power.

On July 24th, a Committee of Detail was set up to prepare a draft constitution incorporating the convention's decisions. When the Committee's draft was submitted, objections again arose over the mode of selection. Sentiment had grown to remove the legislature from the process. Madison and Hamilton, who earlier had been silent on this issue, now threw their weight in favor of election by popularly chosen electors.

The chief support for a change in the draft, however, now came from Robert Morris of Pennsylvania. Elaborating upon Wilson's concept of the executive as a protector of liberty, Morris declared that the office must "be a guardian of the people, even of the lower classes" against the tyranny of the "Great and the wealthy who in the course of things will necessarily compose the Legislative body."

Although these arguments swayed many delegates, the issue remained in doubt. A substantial minority, including Randolph, still opposed giving the President an independent base of support. The balance of power now fell to the delegates for the small states. To them, protection of their states' influence in the nation often seemed to overshadow all other considerations. Election of the executive by the legislature assured their states disproportionate influence, due to the composition of the Senate. Thus, the small states had resisted any plan for popular election. Their fears had to be calmed if the selection process were to be removed from the legislature. Ironically, then, final decisions on the Presidency hinged on a dispute between the large and the small states.

Deadlock over the mode of election continued until the closing days of the convention. Finally, on August 31st, the issue was delegated to a "Committee on Unfinished Business." After several days of discussion, the committee proposed an Electoral College, as Gerry had suggested earlier. To preserve the power of the small states, the Electors were to be apportioned to the states on the basis of their total representation in Congress. Thus, the small states would retain the advantages of equal representation in the Senate, even though Congress would not be involved in the election.

In addition, the President was made eligible for reelection an indefinite number of times, and the term of office was reduced from seven to four years. A tired convention quickly approved this compromise, and the executive article was complete.

The strong-executive faction had won most of its major objectives. The Presidency was to consist of a single person, elected independently of Congress, eligible for reelection, with a qualified power to veto legislation. Perhaps more important, few specific limitations upon the power of the President were imposed. From the beginning it appeared that the framers had a general concept of what "executive power" was, derived from political philosophy and the British and colonial experiences, and they did not attempt to define it further in the Constitution. The original Virginia Plan stated only that the executive shall "enjoy the Executive rights vested in Congress by the Confederation." Wilson, the principal proponent of enlarged executive powers, referred only to "those of executing the laws and appointing officers."

While specific powers of the President were enumerated in Sections two and three of Article II, these were not labeled as an exhaustive list of powers. Moreover, the enumeration was drafted by the Committee of Detail, and was never amended by the full convention, thus leaving specific purposes obscure. The actual drafting was performed by Wilson, who, not surprisingly, sketched presidential power in broad terms, often borrowing from the New York model. Because Wilson was only the draftsman, however, his intent cannot be imputed to the convention as a whole. It is probable that no consensus existed among the delegates even after four months in Philadelphia. While there was general agreement that a stronger executive was needed, conflict between "administrative" and "political" principles was never fully resolved.

Thus the convention established a Presidency with powers that resist definition. In the long run, this lack of definition may have had as much to do with the growth of the office as the issues which sparked debate at the time.

The ensuing task of persuading the state ratifying conventions to accept the proposed constitution led to production of The Federalist by Madison, Hamilton, and Jay. (The 1961 edition by B. Wright has a valuable introduction.) On the other side were the Anti-Federalists. For a concise introduction to their views, *see* H. Storing, What the Anti-Federalists Were *For*, the introductory essay to his seven-volume The Complete Anti-Federalist (1981). *See also* Nedelsky, Book Review, *Confining Democratic Politics: Anti-Federalists, Federalists, and the Constitution*, 96 Harv. L. Rev. 340 (1982).

When the proposed constitution was submitted to the states for ratification, the independence of the Presidency and the lack of a definition of its powers caused alarm. The office was heavily criticized as being too monarchical. Of particular concern to many Anti-Federalists was the lack of any prohibition on reelection. Thomas Jefferson maintained that " . . . the first magistrate will always be re-elected if the constitution permits it. He is then an officer for life." (Cunliffe, *supra*, at 13.) Another signer of the Declaration of Independence, Richard Henry Lee, shared this concern.[1] He argued that the President would have an undue interest in enlarging the powers of the office (M. Borden, The Antifederalist Papers 202 (1965)):

> [H]e will spare no artifice, no address, and no exertions, to increase the powers and importance of it. The servile supporters of his wishes will be placed in all offices, and tools constantly employed to aid his views and sound his praise.

Other opponents of the new constitution objected to the length of presidential terms, as well as their number. Clinton, citing Montesquieu, argued that the "greatness of the power" of the office, "must be compensated by the brevity of the duration." (*Id.* at 197.) Any term longer than one year, he concluded, would be dangerous to the liberties of a republic. A four-year term would only give the President the means and time to execute his ambitious designs.

Another Anti-Federalist objection was that the veto power violated separation of powers principles. If the President could reject legislation, it was argued, he has legislative power. (Although the British monarch had a theoretical veto power, it had

---

1. These Anti-Federalist fears of "presidents-for-life" did not materialize in fact, as Presidents confined themselves to two terms for the first 150 years of the Constitution. After the four terms of Franklin Roosevelt, however, concerns about reelection were rekindled. The Twenty-second Amendment, ratified in 1951, finally responded to the old Anti-Federalist concern by limiting the President to two terms of office.

not been exercised in almost 100 years.) Similarly, Anti-Federalists objected to the President's treaty-making power and the Vice-President's role as President of the Senate as violations of the separation of powers.

Finally, the Anti-Federalists attacked the Constitution's complicated plan for the indirect election of the President. Being generally more populist than the framers, they preferred a direct election. Also, it was widely believed that the Electoral College would rarely produce a majority, and that most elections would therefore be decided by the House of Representatives. Since the House could choose from among any of the top five candidates, and each state delegation would have an equal vote, opponents feared the House would choose candidates with little popular support.

Eventually, all thirteen states approved the new Constitution. Although the efforts of supporters and the sheer necessity of replacing the Articles of Confederation no doubt aided ratification, it appears that a great many fears about the Presidency were alleviated by the unspoken assumption that George Washington would be elected as the first President. Experience had shown that he could safely be entrusted with great power and responsibility—the chances of his becoming a tyrant seemed remote. Thus, even though it was recognized that the President's power as set out in the Constitution was vague and ambiguous, it was easier to accept the office because Washington would be the first to define its scope.

B. Competing Theories of the Presidency

One important source of competing theories of presidential power has been our Presidents themselves. We briefly introduce their main positions, down to Franklin Roosevelt and the creation of the modern Presidency. (The views of the more recent Presidents, often drawn from their predecessors, appear throughout this book.)

1. Washington

As he took office, George Washington was already a national hero, universally known as the commander of the victorious army during the Revolution. He had been unanimously elected by the Electoral College, giving him freedom to act above partisan politics. His influence on the Presidency would be magnified because he had no precedents to follow; instead, he would be creating precedent. He was well aware of his unique position in history (N. Small, Some Presidential Interpretations of the Presidency, 14 (1932)):

> In our progress toward political happiness my station is new, and if I may use the expression, I walk on untrodden ground. There is scarcely an action, the motive of which may not be subject to a double interpretation. There is scarcely any part of my conduct which may not hereafter be drawn into precedent. Under such a view of the duties inherent in my arduous office, I could not but feel a diffidence in myself on the one hand, and an anxiety for the community.

Washington consciously avoided important substantive tests of presidential power. The nation had just emerged from twenty years of turmoil, and the new government was just beginning to gain popular acceptance—now was not the time for such tests (Small, *supra*, at 14):

> [I]n this very early stage of affairs, and at a period so little removed from an exhausting war, the public welfare and safety evidently enjoin a conduct of circumspection, moderation, and forbearance.

Nevertheless, he asserted that (*Id.*):

> The powers of the executive of this country are more definite, and better understood, perhaps, than those of any other country; and my aim has been, and will continue to be, neither to stretch nor relax them in any instance whatever, unless compelled to it by imperious circumstances.

Although Washington himself struggled neither to "stretch nor relax" presidential powers, several important issues arose during his term of office. His 1793 "Proclamation of Neutrality" in the war between France and Britain raised serious questions regarding presidential power to make foreign policy. While Washington himself said little, debate erupted in the Cabinet between Treasury Secretary Hamilton and Secretary of State Jefferson. (*See* J. Roche & L. Levy, The Presidency 10-12 (1964)). Hamilton argued that the Proclamation was authorized by a grant of power in Article II:

> The second article of the constitution of the United States, section first, establishes this general proposition, "the EXECUTIVE POWER shall be vested in a president of the United States of America."
>
> The same article, in a succeeding section, proceeds to delineate particular cases of executive power....
>
> It would not consist with the rules of sound construction, to consider this enumeration of particular authorities, as derogating from the more comprehensive grant in the general clause, further than as it may be coupled with express restrictions or limitations.... The difficulty of a complete enumeration of all the cases of executive authority, would naturally dictate the use of general terms, and would render it improbable, that a specification of certain particulars was designed as a substitute for those terms, when antecedently used....
>
> The enumeration ought therefore to be considered, as intended merely to specify the principal articles implied in the definition of executive power; leaving the rest to flow from the general grant of that power....

James Madison, who fifteen years later was himself to become President, responded with the Jeffersonian position:

> If we consult, for a moment, the nature and operation of the two powers to declare war and to make treaties it will be impossible not to see that they can never fall within a proper definition of executive powers. The natural province of the executive magistrate is to execute laws, as that of the legislature is to make laws. All his acts, therefore, properly executive, must pre-suppose the existence of the laws to be executed. A treaty is not an execution of the laws; it does not pre-suppose the existence of laws. It is, on the contrary, to have itself the force of a *law*, and to be carried into *execution*, like all *other laws*, by the *executive magistrate*. To say then that the power of making treaties which are confessedly laws, belongs naturally to the department which is to execute laws, is to say, that the executive department naturally includes a legislative power. In theory this is an absurdity... in practice a tyranny....

Another important inference to be noted is, that the powers of making war and treaty being substantially of a legislative, not an executive nature, the rule of interpreting exceptions strictly, must narrow instead of enlarging executive pretensions on those subjects. . . .

These arguments are classic statements of broad and narrow views of constitutional interpretation. They echo the famous clash between Hamilton and Jefferson in 1791 over the constitutionality of the Bank of the United States. *See* G. Gunther, Constitutional Law, 83-87 (11th ed. 1985); Hurst, *Alexander Hamilton, Law Maker*, 78 Colum. L. Rev. 483 (1978). Hamilton's views persuaded Washington in both instances.

2. *Jefferson*

When Thomas Jefferson assumed the Presidency in 1801, it was widely assumed that, pursuant to his strict constructionist views, executive power would be severely restricted. Although Jefferson may have had an honest intention to reduce the President's role, his tenure expanded it.

The clearest example of this reversal is Jefferson's purchase of the Louisiana territory from France. He had, at first, felt that such a purchase exceeded the constitutional power of both the President and Congress: "To take a single step beyond the boundaries specifically drawn is to take possession of a boundless field of power, no longer susceptible of any definitions." (Small, *supra*, at 23.) But he also saw the territory as a great opportunity for the country, one which might be lost by waiting for congressional action or a constitutional amendment. Accordingly, he found a power in his office to act as a "guardian" or "steward" for the people, even for an action technically outside the Constitution (*Id.*):

The executive in seizing the fugitive occurrence, which so much advances the good of their country, has done an act beyond the Constitution. The Legislature in casting behind them metaphysical subtleties, and risking themselves like faithful servants, must ratify and pay for it, and throw themselves upon their country for doing for them unauthorized, what we know they would have done for themselves had they been in a situation to do it. It is the case of the guardian, investing the money of its ward in purchasing an important adjacent territory; and saying to him when of age, I did this for your good; I pretend to no right to bind you; you may disavow me and I must get out of the scrape as I can; I thought it my duty to risk myself for you. But we shall not be disavowed by the nation, and their act of indemnity will confirm and not weaken the Constitution by more strongly marking out its lines.

Jefferson continued to advocate a strict construction of the Constitution. His actions, however, set a precedent for a strong Presidency, one which would be taken to heart by several later executives.

3. *Jackson*

The next major expansion in the powers of the Presidency took place in the 1830s, under the administration of Andrew Jackson. Jackson, in many ways, was the first "popular" President. By his time, all but a few states were selecting presidential electors by popular vote, thus clearly tying the President directly to the people. Also, more than any previous President, Jackson was one of the "common people." Far from an aristocrat, he came from the backwoods of North Carolina, and achieved national fame as a hard-fighting general in wars against the British and the Indians.

Jackson became the first executive to appeal to the people over the heads of their legislative representatives. He claimed a role as the sole true representative of the people (A. Tourtellot, The Presidents on the Presidency 35 (1964)):

> We are *one people* in the choice of President and Vice-President. Here the States have no other agency than to direct the mode in which the votes shall be given. The candidates having the majority of all the votes are chosen. The electors of a majority of States may have given their votes to one candidate, and yet another may be chosen. The people, then, and not the States, are represented in the executive branch.

Jackson found many ways in which to exercise power. He fought the Bank of the United States, and succeeded in having it abolished. He battled Congress. Previous Presidents had wielded the veto power sparingly, usually on grounds that legislation was unconstitutional. Jackson vetoed any legislation with which he strongly disagreed. Also, he fought John Marshall and the Supreme Court. The story goes that, when the Court denied the states power to regulate Indian territory, Jackson mockingly declared, "Well, John Marshall has made his decision, now let him enforce it." (Roche & Levy, *supra*, at 13.)

Jackson consistently maintained that he could determine the constitutionality of legislation, regardless of what the Supreme Court ruled. He vetoed a bill to re-establish the Bank of the United States, after the constitutionality of its predecessor had been upheld in *McCulloch v. Maryland*, 17 U.S. (4 Wheat.) 316 (1819). He explained (Tourtellot, *supra*, at 268-69):

> The Congress, the Executive, and the Court must each for itself be guided by its own opinion of the Constitution. Each public officer who takes an oath to support the Constitution swears that he will support it as he understands it, and not as it is understood by others. It is as much the duty of the House of Representatives, of the Senate, and of the President to decide upon the constitutionality of any bill or resolution which may be presented to them for passage or approval as it is for the supreme judges when it may be brought before them for judicial decision. The opinion of the judges has no more authority over Congress than the opinion of Congress has over the judges, and on that point the President is independent of both. The authority of the Supreme Court must not, therefore, be permitted to control the Congress or the Executive when acting in their legislative capacities, but to have only such influence as the force of their reasoning may deserve.

4. Buchanan

After Jackson's retirement in 1836, the power of the Presidency receded dramatically. The period 1836-1861 saw mostly weak, short-lived Presidencies, as nine Presidents assumed office. At the same time, Congress was enjoying its Golden Age. Led by such men as Daniel Webster, Henry Clay, and John Calhoun, the legislature overshadowed the executive.

The administration of James Buchanan typified the Presidency during this period. In late 1860 and early 1861, as the southern states were announcing their secession from the Union, Buchanan maintained that there was little he could do to resolve the crisis. In his last State of the Union message he said of the Presidency (Tourtellot, *supra*, at 417):

> Wisely limited and restrained as is his power under our Constitution and laws, he alone can accomplish but little for good or for evil on such a momentous question.... From the very nature of his office, and its high responsibilities, he must necessarily be conservative. The stern duty of administering the vast and complicated concerns of this government affords in itself a guarantee that he will not attempt any violation of a clear constitutional right.
>
> After all, he is no more than the chief executive officer of the government. His province is not to make but to execute the laws....
>
> Apart from the execution of the laws, so far as this may be practicable, the Executive has no authority to decide what shall be the relations between the federal government and South Carolina.

5. Lincoln

Buchanan's successor, Abraham Lincoln, held an entirely different view of the President's power to respond to secession. Rejecting constitutional niceties concerning executive power, Lincoln maintained that his duty was to save the federal Union—and that he was justified in taking any action to achieve that end, even if it were otherwise unconstitutional. As he wrote to Samuel Chase: "These rebels are violating the Constitution to destroy the Union; I will violate the Constitution, if necessary, to save the Union; and I suspect, Chase, that our Constitution is going to have a rough time of it before we get done with this row." (*Id.* at 327.)

The Constitution did, in fact, have "a rough time of it" before the war was over. During his four years in office, Lincoln took a series of dramatic and constitutionally questionable steps. In the view of many, he assumed near-dictatorial powers over the country. Although no declaration of war had been made, troops were organized, a blockade against southern ports was ordered, and military action was begun. Basic civil liberties, including habeas corpus, were suspended. And in 1863 Lincoln unilaterally ordered the emancipation of all slaves within Confederate territory, without congressional approval.

Lincoln justified these extra-constitutional actions as measures necessary to save the Union. As he explained this "doctrine of necessity" (*Id.* at 399):

> [M]y oath to preserve the Constitution to the best of my ability imposed upon me the duty of preserving, by every indispensable means, that government.... Was it possible to lose the nation and yet preserve the Constitution? By general law, life and limb must be protected, yet often a limb must be amputated to save a life; but a life is never wisely given to save a limb. I felt that measures otherwise unconstitutional might become lawful by becoming indispensable to the preservation of the Constitution through the preservation of the nation. Right or wrong, I assumed this ground, and now avow it. I could not feel that, to the best of my ability, I had even tried to preserve the Constitution, if, to save slavery or any minor matter, I should permit the wreck of government, country, and Constitution all together.

6. *Wilson on the Post-Civil War Presidency*

The dramatic increase in executive power brought about by Lincoln was, however, not to continue beyond the Civil War. Although Andrew Johnson, Lincoln's successor, tried to exercise strong authority, he did not possess either the ability or popular support necessary to succeed. Congress reasserted its powers; Johnson soon faced an impeachment trial in the Senate for defying Congress. He escaped conviction by one vote, but the Presidency was not to recover fully. Beginning with the election of the famous but generally incompetent Ulysses Grant in 1868, weak and unassertive Presidents were to hold office for most of the rest of the century. The dominance of Congress, as in the antebellum years, had returned.

The sickly state of the Presidency during this era was noted in 1885 in Congressional Government: A Study in American Politics, by Woodrow Wilson, a doctoral candidate at Johns Hopkins University, and the future twenty-eighth President. Wilson believed that the "balance of powers" set up by the Constitution had been destroyed. Congress, in fact if not in theory, was the supreme branch of government (*Id.* at 6):

> The noble charter of fundamental law given us by the Convention of 1787 is still our Constitution; but it is now our *form of government* rather in name than in reality, the form of the Constitution being one of nicely adjusted, ideal balances, whilst the actual form of our present government is simply a scheme of congressional supremacy. . . .

Wilson urged solving the problem of legislative dominance by adoption of a system more like the British one, in which the President could act as a "Prime Minister." He rejected the idea, however, that the President could take extra-constitutional actions in times of crisis. Instead, the President should try to induce Congress to grant his requests. This could be done, he maintained, if the President became a leader of and spokesman for his party, and of the nation (W. Wilson, Constitutional Government in the United States 69 (1907)):

> He may be both the leader of his party and the leader of the nation, or he may be one or the other. If he lead the nation, his party can hardly resist him. His office is anything he has the sagacity and force to make it.

7. *Theodore Roosevelt and Taft*

Even before Wilson had the chance to implement his ideas in practice, the Presidency began to awake from its slumber. The revival began under William McKinley during the Spanish-American War. It crested when Theodore Roosevelt assumed office.

Roosevelt was an enthusiastic disciple of Lincoln's broad theory of presidential power. While Lincoln had been careful to justify his actions on the basis of wartime emergency, however, Roosevelt faced no such crisis. His views therefore exceeded the conceptions of presidential power held by any of his predecessors.

Roosevelt explicitly rejected the idea that a specific constitutional authorization was needed for a President to act. In his Autobiography he explained this "residuum of powers" theory (Tourtellot, *supra*, at 55-56):

> [I insisted] upon the theory that the executive power was limited only by specific restrictions and prohibitions appearing in the Constitution or imposed by the Congress under its Constitutional powers. My view was that every executive

officer . . . was a steward of the people bound actively and affirmatively to do all he could for the people, and not to content himself with the negative merit of keeping his talents undamaged in a napkin. I declined to adopt the view that what was imperatively necessary for the Nation could not be done by the President unless he could find some specific authorization to do it. My belief was that it was not only his right but his duty to do anything that the needs of the Nation demanded unless such action was forbidden by the Constitution or by the laws. . . . I did not usurp power, but I did greatly broaden the use of executive power.

Roosevelt did not hesitate to use the power he claimed. He took the initiative in foreign affairs by building the Panama Canal, intervening in Santo Domingo and Cuba, and—against the express wishes of Congress—by sending the U.S. fleet on a world-wide tour. Domestically, he became personally involved in everything from coal strikes to trust-busting. He was not deterred by those who criticized his use of power (*Id.* at 116):

While President I have *been* President, emphatically; I have used every ounce of power there was in the office and I have not cared a rap for the criticisms of those who spoke of my "usurpation of power"; for I knew that the talk was all nonsense and that there was no usurpation. I believe that the efficiency of this Government depends upon its possessing a strong central executive, and wherever I could establish a precedent for strength in the executive . . . I have felt not merely that my action was right in itself, but that . . . I was establishing a precedent of value.

When Roosevelt retired from the Presidency in 1908, he picked William Howard Taft to be his successor, apparently confident that Taft shared his views on the Presidency and would carry on his policies. Disappointment awaited, however. Taft, a future Chief Justice, not only did not share Roosevelt's broad view of the office—he held a nearly opposite view. He strongly opposed Roosevelt's theory that the President has a large, unspecific "residuum of powers." Directly addressing his arguments toward Roosevelt, he wrote in 1916 (Roche & Levy, *supra*, at 25):

My judgment is that the view of . . . Mr. Roosevelt, ascribing an undefined residuum of power to the President is an unsafe doctrine and that it might lead under emergencies to results of an arbitrary character, doing irremediable injustice to private right. The mainspring of such a view is that the Executive is charged with responsibility for the welfare of all the people in a general way, that he is to play the part of a Universal Providence and set all things right, and that anything that in his judgment will help the people he ought to do, unless he is expressly forbidden not to do it. The wide field of action that this would give to the Executive one can hardly limit.

Taft argued for a strict construction of Article II. The executive, he reasoned, should exercise only power that is expressly or impliedly granted by the Constitution (*Id.* at 23-24):

The true view of the Executive functions is, as I conceive it, that the President can exercise no power which cannot be fairly and reasonably traced to some specific grant of power or justly implied and included within such express grant as proper and necessary to its exercise. Such specific grant must be either in the Federal Constitution or in an act of Congress passed in pursuance thereof. There is no undefined residuum of power which he can exercise because it seems to him to be in the public interest.... The grants of Executive power are necessarily in general terms in order not to embarrass the Executive within a field of action plainly marked for him, but his jurisdiction must be justified and vindicated by affirmative constitutional or statutory provision, or it does not exist.

8. Franklin Roosevelt

In the decade following World War I, the Presidency again became less active. The country was enjoying a period of peace and prosperity, decreasing the need for a strong and active executive. Warren Harding and Calvin Coolidge seemed to fit the times, and served mostly non-controversial terms of office. The taciturn Coolidge said that "[t]he words of the President have an enormous weight and ought not to be used indiscriminately." (Tourtellot, *supra*, at 60.) Herbert Hoover took a more activist view of the office, but still supported limitations on its power.

The onset of the Great Depression and the election of Franklin Roosevelt led to a sudden expansion in the power of the presidential office. Although Roosevelt wrote very little on his theories of the Presidency, it is clear that he was willing to exercise power whenever he felt it necessary.

While Roosevelt apparently had no specific plan when he assumed office, he did feel that action of some sort was required. Within a year, Congress had approved his legislative proposals for programs and agencies, often controlled directly or indirectly by the President, that affected almost every aspect of economic life. Also, he frequently spoke directly to the nation through a series of press conferences and "fireside chats," thus developing an image of a national leader. His leadership role grew even more in 1941, with the outbreak of war.

In 1937, Roosevelt became the first President since Andrew Jackson to launch a major assault on the judicial branch, through his "court-packing" plan. In defending the plan, he described the government as a three-horse team (*Id.* at 429):

> The three horses are, of course, the three branches of government—the Congress, the Executive and the Courts. Two of the horses are pulling in unison today; the third is not. Those who have intimated that the President of the United States is trying to drive that team, overlook the simple fact that the President, as Chief Executive, is himself one of the three horses.

Nevertheless, many observers did not see things the same way, and felt that Roosevelt was trying to drive the team himself. Herbert Hoover, for example, warned that F.D.R. was amassing a dangerous amount of power (*Id.* at 123):

> There has been a gigantic and insidious building up of personal power of the President during these two terms [1933-1940]. The President himself admits these powers provide shackles upon liberty which may be dangerous. Many of these extraordinary powers have been obtained under claims of emergencies which proved not to exist or to have expired. Despite many promises, there has been no return of these dangerous powers or the unused powers, or those which proved futile or for which emergencies have passed. In building up these powers

the independence of the Supreme Court, the Congress and the local government has been degraded.

Whether or not Roosevelt assumed too much power, his administration permanently altered the role of the executive. At the end of his twelve years in office, the Presidency had much greater importance than ever before. To a large extent, he can be credited with the creation of the "modern Presidency."

C. The Institutional Presidency

Today the Presidency includes a substantial bureaucracy within the Executive Office of the President (EOP). It has not always been thus, according to S. Hess, Organizing The Presidency, 1-3 (1966):

> Presidents had been given vast emergency powers before the New Deal, always in anticipation of war or during its conduct. But the concept of the powerful Chief Executive was otherwise alien to the American ethic. According to the White House Chief Usher, before World War I Woodrow Wilson "worked but three or four hours a day and spent much of his time happily and quietly, sitting around with his family." Calvin Coolidge is reported to have "slept on an average of eleven hours per day." The pace of the White House was reflected in the modest size of its staff when Franklin Roosevelt took office. It soon became obvious, however, that the existing arrangements were inadequate to meet both the new responsibilities that Congress had given the President and the people's rising expectations of what they wished the federal government to do.
>
> There were three possibilities for reorganization. A "fourth branch" could be created to fill the gap between the executive and the rest of government, a solution that had been tried without great success since the 1870s through congressionally sanctioned and presidentially appointed commissions and agencies. The executive departments could be restructured by subdividing the departments into smaller units or by consolidating them into fewer and larger units, with the hope in either case that they would be more efficient and responsive. Or the presidential office could be enlarged.
>
> With Roosevelt's blessing, the President's Committee on Administrative Management, chaired by Louis Brownlow, chose the third option, urging the creation of an Executive Office of the President and additional all-purpose White House aides. Subsequent bodies of distinguished citizens proposed other ways to help the President. . . .
>
> World War II and its aftermath, the country's new role as a world leader, and national fears of economic dislocation, thrust additional burdens on the President and accelerated the trend toward White House centralization. Congress passed laws creating the President's Council of Economic Advisers (1946) and the National Security Council (1947). Later, Congress enlarged the Executive Office with the addition of an Office of Special Representative for Trade Negotiations (1963), a Council on Environmental Quality (1970), and a White House Office of Science and Technology Policy (1976).
>
> Thus the growth of the White House establishment reflects a conscious effort over four decades to impose a presidential presence on an executive conglom-

erate, which today is too vast for personal supervision. It also is a manifestation of the multiple roles that have been given to or assumed by Presidents: Commander in Chief, primary proposer of legislation and chief lobbyist, top executive in the executive branch, guardian of the economy, negotiator with other nations, head of state, party leader, and moral leader.

A President allots his time and organizes his administration along the lines of the diverse functions he must perform, hires different people to support him in his different duties, and organizes those around him to accommodate his perceptions of his task. Roosevelt constructed a circle with himself at the hub. Eisenhower designed a pyramid with himself at the apex. A President chooses the degree of tidiness or chaos that best supports his work habits. He chooses the amount of advice he wants to get from within government and how much he wants to receive from outside. He decides to give competing assignments and overlapping jurisdictions or to rely on aides with specific and tightly defined responsibilities. He selects between formal lines of command and informal arrangements. He chooses between the advice of specialists and generalists.

More detail about enduring problems in organizing the modern Presidency is provided from a congressional perspective, in Presidential Staffing—A Brief Overview, Subcomm. on Employee Ethics and Utilization, House Comm. on Post Office and Civil Service, 95th Cong., 2d Sess., 55-61 (1978):

The contemporary Chief Executive utilizes the services of a variety of assistants, their diversity and number perhaps being best reflected in the following consideration regarding presidential advisers:

Each President receives advice in the way he finds most congenial. Big meetings. Small meetings. No meetings. Long reports. Short memos. Each picks his own advice systems. He convenes conferences, commissions, task forces, and committees. He turns to Cabinet members, cronies, family, and staff. Each picks his own immediate subordinates, relying on lawyers and businessmen, generals and diplomats, scholars, union leaders, and party leaders. He seeks advice that is agreeable and advice that is representative. From blacks, westerners, Catholics, bankers. He seeks assistants who are loyal yet independent, free thinkers yet team players.[98]

The Cabinet continues to be available to every Chief Executive as a primary assistance institution. During the past few decades, a certain amount of support staff has been created for the President through the auxiliaries of Cabinet committees. Established to focus concentrated attention on pressing policy matters of concern to two or more departments, these temporary panels are usually launched at the direction of the President, chaired by a Cabinet member (sometimes the Vice President), and obtain personnel and operating resources through details and donations from the affected departments. President Johnson established the Cabinet Committee on the Environment and a Cabinet Task Force on Oil Import Control. President Nixon created similar such bodies to examine price stability and school desegregation. . . . Thus, on a temporary basis, the

98. Stephen Hess. Organizing the Presidency. Washington, The Brookings Institution, 1976, p.3.

Chief Executive can look to Cabinet-level advisory panels for both counsel and policy aides.

The President's principal source of assistants, however, continues to be the White House Office staff and the personnel of selected Executive Office agencies. These aides are the creation of the Brownlow Commission, envisioned as having "no power to make decisions or issue instructions in their own right" and "possessed of high competence, great vigor, and a passion for anonymity."[99] Commenting on the suggestion of establishing Executive assistants, a later analysis of the Commission's report noted:

> These men were to act as anonymous servants exercising no initiative independently of the President's wishes. No authority was delegated to them. Their function was to extend the President's power to listen wherever useful information could be gathered and to see whatever needed to be seen to provide the information required for decisions. In order to give them the utmost responsibility, to presidential will, as well as ultimate flexibility, their functions were not to be defined except as the President saw fit to define them. As such they would not constitute either an additional institution or certainly not an independent one, but rather an extension of the Presidency itself.[100]

In spite of these high hopes, White House assistants to succeeding presidents, since 1939, have become highly conspicuous, multiple in number, possessed of great power, and virtually unaccountable to anyone but the Chief Executive for their actions. The number of presidential advisers and policy aides within the White House Office and the larger Executive Office has exhibited generally steady growth, regardless of national or international events, changes of administration, or differing management styles of Chief Executives....

Managerial authority and program responsibility has been given over to presidential assistants because other coordinating and administrative guidance institutions, such as the Cabinet, have proven to be unsuitable for these functions. In this regard, one expert has commented:

> Whether manifested by a benign lack of interest or by purposeful competition, departmentalism operated to reduce the potentialities of the Cabinet as a coordinating mechanism. Yet in view of the extent to which executive decisionmaking must now be conducted across departmental boundaries, it does not seem too much to say that the Chief Executive's primary managerial task is precisely this one of coordination.... This, indeed, is the raison d'etre for the phenomenal proliferation of those staff organs with interdepartmental planning, operating, and advisory functions which now comprise the Executive Office of the President. The expansion of this Office ... must be considered in part as an inevitable response to the new dimensions of governmental activity, but also in part as an adverse reflection on the ability of the Cabinet in coping with the difficult problems of coordination involved.[101]

---

99. President's Committee on Administrative Management, [Reorganization of the Executive Departments, Sen. Doc. No. 8, 75th Cong., 1st Sess. (1937)], p. 5.

100. Karl, [Executive Reorganization and Reform in the New Deal (1963)], p. 241.

101. Fenno, [The President's Cabinet (1959)], pp. 141-142.

Thus, it is the White House Office and the Executive Office satellites which have come to better serve the President as coordinators of executive functions. And as managers of the Government, as well, they have come to play policy roles, refining policy suggestions and sometimes even the access of other policymakers to the Chief Executive. But, as Theodore Sorensen has noted, such a role carries with it certain dangers.

> A White House adviser may see a departmental problem in a wider context than a Secretary, but he also has less contact with actual operations and pressures, with Congress and interested groups. If his own staff grows too large, his office may become only another department, another level of clearances and concurrences instead of a personal instrument of the President. If his confidential relationship with the President causes either one to be too uncritical of the other's judgment, errors may go uncorrected. If he develops . . . a confidence in his own competence which outruns the fact, his contribution may be more mischievous than useful. If, on the other hand, he defers too readily to the authority of the renowned experts and Cabinet powers, then the President is denied the skeptical, critical service his staff should be providing.[102]

Of course, as presidential assistants move toward the possibility of the equivalent of departmental authority, whether such power be measured in fiscal or political influence terms, the wrath of official department heads can be, and often is, incurred. . . .

A short time ago, . . . former White House press secretary George Reedy made the following observation on the increasing authority of the White House staff and the significance of this development both in terms of information flow and accountability.

> At one time the White House staff was a relatively small group of people. They consisted of personal advisers to the President, and here you have the whole question of executive privilege which has been exercised, in my judgment, in an extremely legitimate form. I do not think that you should be able to pry loose from a President what he does not want to be pried loose. . . . But, because the authority lies within the White House, rather this ability lies within the White House, of exercising executive privilege, what has happened with the proliferation of White House staff members is that you are to the point where you are gradually getting a shift of the operating agencies into the White House itself.[104]

What may be approaching is a government controlled by Executive decisionmakers, untouchable by either Congress or perhaps even the departmental bureaucracy. . . . In the course of delivering a speech in San Jose, California, in May, 1971, Senator Ernest F. Hollings remarked:

---

102. Theodore C. Sorensen. Decision-Making in the White House. New York, Columbia University Press, 1963, pp. 71-72.

104. U.S. Congress. House. Committee on Government Operations. U.S. Government Information Policies and Practices—Administration and Operation of the Freedom of Information Act. Hearings, 92d Congress, 2d session. Washington, U.S. Govt. Print. Off., 1972, p. 1013.

It used to be that if I had a problem with food stamps, I went to see the Secretary of Agriculture, whose Department had jurisdiction over that program. Not any more. Now, if I want to learn the policy, I must go to the White House and consult John Price.

If I want the latest on textiles, I won't get it from the Secretary of Commerce, who has the authority and responsibility. No, I am forced to go to the White House and see Mr. Peter Flanigan. I shouldn't feel too badly. Secretary Stans has to do the same thing.[107] ...

The problem posed is not merely one of obtaining information from the Executive, but, more importantly, a matter of accountability.

The latest experiments with Cabinet government have been those of the Reagan administration. His first term saw the formation of seven domestic policy Cabinet councils, in which the secretaries of departments having related subject matter responsibilities met in efforts to coordinate policy. This structure proved unwieldy, however, and was replaced in the second term with two streamlined Cabinet councils, one for economics and one for all other domestic policy. Notwithstanding these elaborate structures, observers found that important issues often bypassed the councils in favor of direct decision by powerful officials such as Office of Management and Budget Director David Stockman. *See* Brownstein & Kirschten, *Cabinet Government*, 18 National Journal 1582 (June 28, 1986).

The phrase "the institutional Presidency" implies an institutional decisionmaking process, and that is what has arisen. The following outline of the process of presidential decisionmaking focuses on the President's implementation of his diverse statutory powers, but it applies to many decisions with constitutional overtones as well. Bruff, *Judicial Review and the President's Statutory Powers*, 68 Va. L. Rev. 1, 14-17 (1982):

Although the process that precedes a President's implementation of his statutory powers varies somewhat from administration to administration—indeed, from day to day—it follows an overall pattern. Few impending decisions reach the White House without previous, often extensive, analysis in one or more of the executive agencies. Thus, when the time comes for the President to exercise his discretion, an administrative record exists in the bureaucracy—a mass of raw data, analysis, and opinion from both within and without the government. This "record" is ordinarily far too massive and unwieldy for any actual transmittal to the White House; in any event, no one there would have either the time or the inclination to pore through it. Therefore, although statutes do not always require agencies to forward formal recommendations to the President prior to his decision, agencies normally do so, if only to summarize and evaluate the administrative record they have compiled. Moreover, any interested agency normally has a policy orientation that causes it to favor, either openly or subtly, a particular outcome. The White House staff, aware of the policy biases of the agencies, often attempts to compensate by subjecting their recommendations to

---

107. Dom Bonafede. Ehrlichman Acts As Policy Broker in Nixon's Formalized Domestic Council. National Journal, v. 3, June 12, 1971: 1240.

interagency review.[54] When several agencies having differing orientations are involved in a decision, there may be sharp disagreement, possibly multi-sided, over the best course of action.

Accompanying the policy materials that reach the White House is legal analysis, again from several sources. The interested agencies are likely to provide opinions from their general counsels' offices. Legal analysis from the agencies may conflict regarding the extent of the President's discretion in the matter. Moreover, the White House staff is likely to suspect that the general counsels' work product reflects the orientation of their clients. Accordingly, they turn to lawyers whose client is the President—the Counsel to the President, and, for "outside counsel," the Office of Legal Counsel in the Department of Justice.[55]

While the President's staff reviews and digests the policy and legal materials that were generated in the agencies, a somewhat separate process of policy and legal debate is likely to arise within the White House. Once it becomes known that a presidential decision is near, interested parties of all kinds—agency heads, Congressmen, private parties—may descend on those having an influence on the decision, including the President himself.

When the time arrives for a formal presidential decision, the mechanics are fairly simple, and essentially similar from administration to administration. The White House staff or an agency official prepares a decision memorandum for the President, in order to present concisely the major policy options or recommendations that have survived debate within the administration. It usually reflects, although it may not discuss, legal analysis of the extent of permissible discretion under the statute or statutes involved. Each option is likely to be accompanied by outlines of the arguments favoring and disfavoring its adoption. These arguments may be confined to a rather legalistic presentation of relevant policy concerns, or they may branch off into frank discussion of political considerations having little or no legal relevance to the decision. The President reads the memorandum, perhaps discusses it with his advisers, and then decides, usually initialing or marking the options memorandum to indicate his choice. His reasons for selecting a particular option may or may not be those presented by the memorandum, and they may or may not be revealed to his advisers.

Because this process is an informal one not governed by statutory procedures, it is subject to exceptions. Especially when there is pressure to reach a decision on short notice, the process often becomes an almost entirely oral one composed of hurried telephone conversations and meetings between the White House staff

---

54. For descriptions of a similar process of interagency review as applied to statutory decisions of the agencies, see ABA Comm'n on Law & the Economy, Federal Regulation: Roads to Reform 84-88 (1979).

55. When a presidential decision will be adopted by executive order or proclamation, an executive order requires it to be submitted in proposed form to the Attorney General "for his consideration as to both form and legality." 1 C.F.R. § 19.2(b) (1980). If disapproved by him, "it shall not thereafter be presented to the President unless it is accompanied by a statement of the reasons for such disapproval." Id. 19.2(e). The Attorney General's disapproval ordinarily is sufficient to halt any further processing of an executive order or proclamation. Within the Department of Justice, the review function has been delegated to the Assistant Attorney General for the Office of Legal Counsel, 28 C.F.R. § 0.25(b) (1980), who also aids the Attorney General in furnishing general legal advice to the President and the Cabinet. Id. § 0.25(a). See 28 U.S.C. § 511 (1976).

and their policy and legal advisers in the agencies. Whether from the press of events or otherwise, some presidential decisions occur without full consultation with the President's lawyers.[57] Indeed, there is sometimes an effort by the White House staff to prevent an interested agency—or even anyone outside a select group of presidential advisers—from knowing that a statutory decision is imminent. The usual motivation for such secrecy is to prevent opposition to, or widespread disclosure of, a policy initiative coming from within the White House. Thus, presidential decisions are sometimes made without knowledge of whether they are legal.

Overall, the process of presidential decisionmaking resembles the process that occurs within an agency as it considers a statutory decision not governed by special procedural constraints, such as those for adjudication. Agency heads reach their statutory decisions through a process of reading memoranda that summarize vast administrative records, consulting the agency's policy and legal staff, and considering the views of interested persons in the executive branch, Congress, and the private interest groups with which the agency deals. The principal difference in the process at the agency level is that the decisionmaker has a closer day-to-day relationship with the components of the agency that contribute to a decision—and closer administrative supervision over them—than the President can hope to enjoy with any particular agency that might participate in formulating his statutory decisions.

In the foregoing description, note the interplay—and the implied competition for influence—between the President's policy advisers and his legal advisers. The President has a number of kinds of legal advisers, not all working directly for him. The Counsel to the President, with a staff of fewer than ten lawyers, is in the White House. Many of the lawyers in the Office of Management and Budget are engaged in preparing advice or doing other legal work directly or indirectly for him. The Department of Justice, with its thousands of lawyers, is the major repository of "outside" legal advice for the White House. In the Department, the Office of Legal Counsel, with about twenty lawyers, has the principal responsibility for advising the Attorney General, the White House, and other agencies on questions of presidential power. And of course other executive branch agencies aid in performing this function.

The usual perspective of these materials is that of a legal adviser to the President. Consider the difference, if any, that this role should make in a lawyer's normal behavior? Is the relationship like any other lawyer/client one? Should the role of the "in-house" counsel to the President differ from that of "outside" counsel in the Department of Justice and elsewhere in the executive branch? If it seems to you that the oath to defend the Constitution that the President and all government lawyers take should affect the answer to these questions, consider how many concrete questions it is likely to answer.

---

57. For example, although the process for legal review of proposed executive orders and proclamations described in note 55 supra is followed most of the time, some of these documents are signed by the President without review by the Department of Justice.

D. Supreme Court Analysis of Separation of Powers Issues

The Supreme Court has displayed a number of different approaches to deciding separation of powers issues. The Court often mixes the approaches in a single case, and, in any event, the boundaries between them are often indistinct. Nevertheless, it should aid understanding and analysis to attempt a preliminary catalog here, so that you can apply it to the cases. We have identified at least the following categories of approaches, and principal questions that they raise, in the Court's opinions:

(1) *Textual.* Since it is a written constitution we are expounding, it is natural for the Court to lay at least some stress on the meaning of the text. You may be familiar with the interpretive stategies that are usually thought appropriate for the open-textured constitutional guarantees of due process and equal protection—should the same strategies apply to separation of powers issues? For arguments that different kinds of constitutional provisions should evoke different interpretive approaches, *see* Shane, *Conventionalism in Constitutional Interpretation and the Place of Administrative Agencies*, 36 Am. U. L. Rev. 573 (1987); Carter, *Constitutional Adjudication and the Indeterminate Text: A Preliminary Defense of an Imperfect Muddle*, 94 Yale L. J. 821 (1985); Schauer, *Easy Cases*, 58 S. Cal. L. Rev. 399 (1985).

As we saw at the outset of this chapter, Article II is sketchy and vague. This may help to explain why the cases place quite variant reliance on the text. Sometimes they purport to give it conclusive weight. Also, some of the cases employ canons of construction, with their notorious manipulability. If the text seems clear, to what extent should other techniques of analysis be employed? If the text seems ambiguous, how much should it confine decision, if at all? What kinds of implications should be drawn from the text?

(2) *Original intent.* We have enough constitutional history of the development of the text and the interpretations given it by the framers to tempt the Court to search for original intent. Indeed, one school of thought would confine the Court to analysis of the text and accompanying indicia of original intent. The controversial work of Professor Crosskey stands as the most elaborate example of this approach, *see* 3 W. Crosskey & W. Jeffrey, Politics and the Constitution in the History of the United States (1980); Krash, Book Review, *The Legacy of William Crosskey*, 93 Yale L.J. 959 (1984); *see also* Bork, *Neutral Principles and Some First Amendment Problems*, 47 Ind. L. J. 1 (1971); Rehnquist, *The Notion of a Living Constitution*, 54 Tex. L. Rev. 693 (1976); Meese, *Toward a Jurisprudence of Original Intention*, 2 Benchmark 1 (1986).

Advocates of an original intent approach face some obstacles. First, there are serious problems in imputing one intention to any product of group decisionmaking. Second, consider the outline of constitutional history *supra*. Many modern problems are simply not addressed there. Also, the records of the Constitutional Convention are far from a complete transcript of the proceedings, and serious doubt surrounds the accuracy of some of them. *See* Hutson, *The Creation of the Constitution: The Integrity of the Documentary Record*, 65 Tex. L. Rev. 1 (1986). Ironically, it appears that the framers rejected a jurisprudence of original intent. *See* Powell, *The Original Understanding of Original Intent*, 98 Harv. L. Rev. 885 (1985), arguing persuasively that the framers expected the Constitution to be interpreted according to its text and the general nature of the problems it was addressing, rather than by their own subjective understanding of its words.

Whose intent counts? The Court often credits the influential views of the authors of the Federalist Papers or records of the Constitutional Convention. Yet how do we discover and weigh the intent of the thirteen ratifying conventions in the states? The Court often gives special weight to the "contemporaneous construction" of the Constitution by the framers after ratification, especially in the First Congress. Yet perhaps these actions reflected perceived needs to depart from original intent in light of experience. (For example, Madison himself eventually abandoned his opposition to the constitutionality of the Bank of the United States, citing "repeated recognition . . . of [its] validity in acts of the legislative, executive, and judicial branches of the Government." Gunther, *supra*, at 89.)

Other puzzling questions remain. If history suggests an original meaning that seems inconsistent with the text, which should govern? If the original meaning seems inappropriate to present conditions, may it be disregarded?

The Court often decides separation of powers cases by using a process of reasoning logically from the text of the Constitution and what is known about the framers' intent. We call this formalism; notice that it tends to obscure the presence of any other reasons for decision, such as value preferences. *See* Bruff, *On the Constitutional Status of the Administrative Agencies*, 36 Am. U. L. Rev. 491 (1987).

(3) *Structure*. This process consists of reading the Constitution's provisions together in search of an overall pattern. *See* C. Black, Structure and Relationship in Constitutional Law (1969). A famous example of this technique, one not from separation of powers cases, is the development of privacy rights from the "penumbras" of the Bill of Rights.

Structural analysis seems especially apt for separation of powers issues. Yet it suffers serious problems of specificity and limits. For example, the Constitution creates separate branches for the three functions of legislation, execution, and judging. Does that imply rigid boundaries between them?

The activities of government are very diverse, and often resist easy characterization as purely one of the three classic functions. Is it necessary or even desirable to label government functions in this way in order to allocate responsibility for them? Are government entities that do not fit neatly in this tripartite scheme, such as independent agencies, forbidden? Perceived needs to allow diverse government structure, especially below the level of the three constitutional branches themselves, have led the Court to decide some cases by what we call a functional approach. It asks such questions as whether a particular institutional arrangement invades the "core functions" of one of the branches—if not, the Court upholds it. *See* Strauss, *The Place of Agencies in Government: Separation of Powers and the Fourth Branch*, 84 Colum. L. Rev. 573 (1984).

(4) *Institutional Competence*. This is a style of interpretation closely related to structural analysis. The three constitutional branches differ in their institutional nature. What does that suggest for the particular tasks that should be allocated to each branch? For example, the judiciary, enjoying life tenure and salary protections, is well situated to play a countermajoritarian role in American life. How far does that go in justifying judicial review as it now exists? Similarly, the Presidency enjoys the ad-

vantages in "energy, dispatch, and responsibility" that accrue to its unitary structure. What does that suggest for the allocation of foreign relations responsibilities between President and Congress?

(5) *Historical Practice*. Through their historically developed practices, the three branches have provided possible answers for many of the Constitution's ambiguities and silences. In what circumstances should the Court honor these? What if they seem to conflict with the text or original intent? What requisites such as duration, consistency, and visibility should be expected of a practice before it attains prescriptive weight? *See* Glennon, *The Use of Custom in Resolving Separation of Powers Disputes*, 64 B. U. L. Rev. 109 (1984). What if the other branches object or acquiesce? Of special interest here is the status of some legislation, such as the War Powers Resolution, that addresses the distribution of power that has developed incrementally, and tries to set enduring limits. These statutes, along with traditional practices, can achieve a kind of quasi-constitutional status even where a practice has not ripened into constitutional gloss.

(6) *Values*. This term is meant to cover a host of effects on decision that stem from values held by the Justices, but not obviously related to conventional methods of constitutional interpretation. *See generally* J. Ely, Democracy and Distrust: A Theory of Judicial Review (1980); P. Bobbitt, Constitutional Fate (1982). These values can, of course, have many sources, such as a sense of necessity in a particular situation or the Justice's personal political philosophy. The operative values are sometimes more obscure in separation of powers cases than in the individual rights cases where their presence and effects are so often openly debated.

Not surprisingly, value judgments inhere in the Court's efforts to draw the line between law and politics. Thus, the Court often pursues prudential values, whether explicitly or not, in deciding whether to reach the merits of separation of powers disputes. The doctrines of standing and political questions embody these values. *See* J. Choper, Judicial Review and the National Political Process: A Functional Reconsideration of the Role of the Supreme Court (1980).

On the merits, the Court often weighs comparative values of ambiguity and clarity in defining the powers of the branches. And individual Justices continue to engage in the ancient debates, traceable to Hamilton and Jefferson, between strict and loose construction of the Constitution, and between interpretations that favor a powerful executive and those that disperse the power of the national government. Similarly, in defining Presidential power, the Court weighs the comparative values of rules and discretion ("a government of laws, and not of men"). These tradeoffs can be quite complex and subtle. For example, even when recognizing discretion the Court can compensate by implying requirements for legal controls to assure accountability. And the Court can cloak any or all of these kinds of value judgments in neutral garb (such as textual analysis) or obfuscation (such as reference to undefined "inherent" powers). What are the appropriate sources of the Court's separation of powers values, and what role should they play in decision?

Chapter 2
Framework: The Separation and Confluence of Powers

When faced with a question whether the President is authorized to take some particular action, lawyers must interpret the Constitution and statutes. This task reflects the fact that ours is a government of limited powers. The limitations exist not only in the words of the Constitution, but in the distribution of powers among the legislative, executive, and judicial branches of government, each of which has power to help define the authorities of the other two by limiting or expanding them in practice.

The starting point for a study of the law of presidential power must thus be an examination of the executive's relationship to Congress and to the courts. Part A of this chapter examines those relationships most broadly. Part B, on delegation, concerns the power of Congress to confer authority on the executive. Part C, on executive orders, considers the President's ability to infer power from statutes and the Constitution. Part D examines the veto, the President's check on the legislative process, and Congress' attempt to limit the President's discretion through the "legislative veto."

A. Analytic Framework

1. The Executive and the Judiciary

We begin with *Marbury v. Madison*, a foundational case in both constitutional and administrative law. Of course, *Marbury* is best known for its assertion of judicial power to review the constitutionality of federal statutes, a question requiring the Court to determine its proper relationship to Congress. We do not pause to spill more ink on the legitimacy of judicial review. *See* G. Gunther, Constitutional Law 13-21 (11th ed. 1985). Instead, we focus on a less-noticed portion of the opinion, in which the Court considered its proper relationship to the executive. (At the time, this issue was the subject of heated controversy, fueling both the political antagonism of Federalists and Republicans and the profound personal antagonism of John Marshall and Thomas Jefferson.)

Before you read *Marbury*, we have some preliminary matters for you to consider. As we noted in Chapter One, proposed executive actions are usually reviewed for their legality by the Department of Justice. This process raises issues of professional responsibility that pervade this book. The following excerpt both provides some background on *Marbury* and, through an extended and very realistic hypothetical, presents recurring ethical dilemmas of the executive adviser. (Issues of litigation strategy also lurk there: consider how the case might best have been argued for the executive, and what effect a particular argument might have had on the Court's opinion.) As you read *Marbury*, then, consider your response to the following questions, put by Dean Norman Redlich in a symposium reported in Assn. of the Bar of the City of New York, Professional Responsibility of the Lawyer, The Murky Divide Between Right and Wrong 97-101 (1976):

> You may recall the facts that led up to *Marbury v. Madison*: Thomas Jefferson was elected President of the United States in November of 1800.... [O]n February 27th, 1801, just one week before the new administration was to take office, the old Congress passed a law creating some forty-two justices of the peace for the District of Columbia, with five-year terms. President Adams promptly appointed them all; they were promptly confirmed by the Senate, and the commissions were all signed by the then Secretary of State, John Marshall.... Now, imagine yourselves as the new Attorney General of the United States on the morning of March 5th, 1801. You, the new Attorney General, Levi Lincoln, are sitting in your office, ... and suddenly there is a knock at the door and in walks James Madison, the new Secretary of State.... Madison says, "You know, the darnedest thing happened. You won't believe this, but I came into my office this morning and ... I found ... [f]our commissions for justice of the peace signed by John Marshall. In his hurry to get out of here to be Chief Justice, he just left them here.... And one of them belongs to this fellow, Marbury, and you know how the President feels about Marbury! He's ... a political opponent, and I think you really ought not to send this commission to Marbury. I'd like your opinion as to what we ought to do."

> And so you go all out and research the question, and you legitimately reach the conclusion, based upon your best understanding of the law, that ... he is entitled to this job. You are about to inform your client, the Secretary of State, about this, when the President of the United States walks in and he says, "I understand that you've been asked for an opinion by Madison. Madison won't act without one, and I want you to advise Madison that he should withhold this commission. These are 'midnight' jobs; ... there is no reason why our opponents should get these lucrative jobs. I want this commission withheld and I want you to render an opinion which says that he has the right to withhold them." What does the Attorney General do under these circumstances? ...

> Next scene: You have not rendered your opinion.... The President and the Secretary of State turn to you as Attorney General and say to you, "Mr. Lincoln, we understand you're having a problem. We don't want to ask you to say anything you don't believe in; we are just going to withhold the commission anyway." And you say, "Why do you want to do that? I've told you ... Marbury has a clear right to this commission." "Well," says the President, "This is our chance to show that the courts can't control the executive branch of the Government. Suppose that Marshall *does* issue an order commanding us to give this commission to Marbury; how is he going to enforce it? This is our chance to show that the Federalist control of the judiciary can't push the people's representative—namely, the President—around." ...

> Next scene: The President and James Madison say, "Mr. Attorney General, we know you don't think we can win on the merits, but no one can be completely sure. Isn't that right? Besides, we think we should have a court decision on the question of whether someone is entitled to an appointment if all the steps in

the process have not been completed. And the final step in this process, namely, delivery of the commission, has not been completed. We think this is an important issue. We think that the courts have no business interfering in the process of appointment. We are not going to *defy* the courts if we are wrong; we are going to obey the court order; but we are saying that *you*, Mr. Attorney General, should not decide this issue; it's an issue that should be decided by the courts; it's too important to be decided by default." ...

My final scene in this drama comes up when you prepare the argument. The President and the Secretary of State call you in and say, "Mr. Attorney General, how are you preparing to handle this case?" Remember, you have refused to deliver the commission, Marbury has brought his lawsuit ... in the Supreme Court of the United States, claiming that the Supreme Court has original jurisdiction pursuant to an Act of Congress which, in the view of Mr. Marbury, gives the Court original jurisdiction to issue a mandamus to the Secretary of State to compel the delivery of the commission. That's the posture of the lawsuit.

You say, "Well, Mr. President, I am going to make [several] arguments. I've got them neatly laid out in the papers. Here they are: *One*: the Supreme Court has no jurisdiction to hear this case because Congress never gave the Supreme Court the power to issue writs of mandamus in this type of case. The only thing Congress did was to give the Supreme Court power to issue writs of mandamus in cases where they otherwise had jurisdiction, but there is no grant of jurisdiction to hear this case.... *Point number two*: If I have read the statute wrong, and if Congress *did* give the Supreme Court the power to issue a writ of mandamus in this case, it is unconstitutional because Congress cannot enlarge the original jurisdiction of the Supreme Court. If it did so, it is contrary to the Constitution and it is the obligation of the Supreme Court to declare the Act unconstitutional. My *third* argument is that if there is jurisdiction and if it comes out that what Congress did was constitutional, the Court has no right to interfere with the political power of the President. Nothing is more discretionary than appointment. This appointment was never completed. And so the Court has no right to order an appointment...."

The President and the Secretary of State listen to all this and they say, "Oh, no. It is perfectly all right to argue that the Congress never gave the Supreme Court jurisdiction—that is, the first argument—but we are not going to have you arguing that, if Congress *did* give them jurisdiction, the Court can declare it unconstitutional." You say, "Don't you want to win?" And they say, "Not on *that* ground. We'd much prefer that they decide against us, and let him try to enforce his order, than that we win because they say Congress didn't have the power to authorize the Supreme Court to push us around. Because Marshall is going to be in a position of being able to say that he not only has the power to tell the Congress what to do, but also has the power to tell *us* what to do, and we are not going to get into that situation."

The Attorney General says, "Look, Mr. President, what if the Court says, 'Mr. Attorney General, does the Congress have the power to enlarge the jurisdiction of the Supreme Court?' What do I say?" The President says, "You answer the question, 'Yes.' Because if you answer, 'No,' then you are going to give the Supreme Court the opportunity to declare this Act of Congress unconstitutional and I don't want that to happen."

Suppose you really think that the better argument is that Congress does *not* have the power to enlarge the jurisdiction of the Supreme Court, and you think it is very important for the country that at the outset of our national experience, the concepts of a limiting Constitution and of judicial review be established, do you still go in and handle this case in the Court in the way in which the President says you should?

Marbury v. Madison
5 U.S. (1 Cranch) 137 (1803)

Chief Justice MARSHALL delivered the opinion of the Court.

At the last term, on the affidavits then read and filed with the clerk, a rule was granted in this case, requiring the secretary of state to show cause why a mandamus should not issue, directing him to deliver to William Marbury his commission as a justice of the peace for the county of Washington, in the district of Columbia.

No cause has been shown, and the present motion is for a mandamus.... The first object of inquiry is, [h]as the applicant a right to the commission he demands?

His right originates in an act of congress passed in February 1801, concerning the district of Columbia. After dividing the district into two counties, the eleventh section of this law enacts, "that there shall be appointed in and for each of the said counties, such number of discreet persons to be justices of the peace as the president of the United States shall, from time to time, think expedient, to continue in office for five years." It appears from the affidavits, that in compliance with this law, a commission for William Marbury as a justice of peace for the county of Washington was signed by John Adams, then president of the United States; after which the seal of the United States was affixed to it; but the commission has never reached the person for whom it was made out.

In order to determine whether he is entitled to this commission, it becomes necessary to inquire whether he has been appointed to the office. For if he has been appointed, the law continues him in office for five years, and he is entitled to the possession of those evidences of office, which, being completed, became his property.... The last act to be done by the president, is the signature of the commission. He has then acted on the advice and consent of the senate to his own nomination. The time for deliberation has then passed. He has decided. His judgment, on the advice and consent of the senate concurring with his nomination, has been made, and the officer is appointed....

The commission being signed, the subsequent duty of the secretary of state is prescribed by law, and not to be guided by the will of the president. He is to affix the seal of the United States to the commission, and is to record it. This is not a proceeding which may be varied, if the judgment of the executive shall suggest one more eligible, but is a precise course accurately marked out by law, and is to be strictly pursued. It is the duty of the secretary of state to conform to the law, and in this he is an officer of the United States, bound to obey the laws. He acts, in this respect, as has been very properly stated at the bar, under the authority of law, and not by the instructions of the president. It is a ministerial act which the law enjoins on a particular officer for a particular purpose....

It is therefore decidedly the opinion of the court, that when a commission has been signed by the president, the appointment is made; and that the commission is complete when the seal of the United States has been affixed to it by the secretary of state. Where an officer is removable at the will of the executive, the circumstance which completes his appointment is of no concern; because the act is at any time revocable; and the commission may be arrested, if still in the office. But when the officer is not removable at the will of the executive, the appointment is not revocable and cannot be annulled. It has conferred legal rights which cannot be resumed.....

Mr. Marbury, then, since his commission was signed by the president and sealed by the secretary of state, was appointed; and as the law creating the office gave the officer a right to hold for five years independent of the executive, the appointment was not revocable; but vested in the officer legal rights which are protected by the laws of his country. To withhold the commission, therefore, is an act deemed by the court not warranted by law, but violative of a vested legal right.

This brings us to the second inquiry; which is, [i]f he has a right, and that right has been violated, do the laws of his country afford him a remedy? The very essence of civil liberty certainly consists in the right of every individual to claim the protection of the laws, whenever he receives an injury. One of the first duties of government is to afford that protection. In Great Britain the king himself is sued in the respectful form of a petition, and he never fails to comply with the judgment of his court.... The government of the United States has been emphatically termed a government of laws, and not of men. It will certainly cease to deserve this high appellation, if the laws furnish no remedy for the violation of a vested legal right.

If this obloquy is to be cast on the jurisprudence of our country, it must arise from the peculiar character of the case. It behooves us then to inquire whether there be in its composition any ingredient which shall exempt it from legal investigations, or exclude the injured party from legal redress....

Is it in the nature of the transaction? Is the act of delivering or withholding a commission to be considered as a mere political act belonging to the executive department alone, for the performance of which entire confidence is placed by our constitution in the supreme executive; and for any misconduct respecting which, the injured individual has no remedy? That there may be such cases is not to be questioned; but that every act of duty to be performed in any of the great departments of government constitutes such a case, is not to be admitted....

It follows then that the question, whether the legality of an act of the head of a department be examinable in a court of justice or not, must always depend on the nature of that act. If some acts be examinable, and others not, there must be some rule of law to guide the court in the exercise of its jurisdiction. In some instances there may be difficulty in applying the rule to particular cases; but there cannot, it is believed, be much difficulty in laying down the rule.

By the constitution of the United States, the president is invested with certain important political powers, in the exercise of which he is to use his own discretion, and is accountable only to his country in his political character, and to his own conscience. To aid him in the performance of these duties, he is authorized to appoint certain officers, who act by his authority and in conformity with his orders. In such cases, their acts are his acts; and whatever opinion may be entertained of the manner in which executive discretion may be used, still there exists, and can exist, no power to control that discretion. The subjects are political. They respect the nation, not individual rights, and being entrusted to the executive, the decision of the executive is conclusive. The application of this remark will be perceived by adverting to the act of congress for establishing the department of foreign affairs. This officer, as his duties were prescribed by that act, is to conform precisely to the will of the president. He is the mere organ by whom that will is communicated. The acts of such an officer, as an officer, can never be examinable by the courts.

But when the legislature proceeds to impose on that officer other duties; when he is directed peremptorily to perform certain acts; when the rights of individuals are dependent on the performance of those acts; he is so far the officer of the law; is amenable to the laws for his conduct; and cannot at his discretion sport away the vested rights of others....

If this be the rule, let us inquire how it applies to the case under the consideration of the court. The power of nominating to the senate, and the power of appointing the person nominated, are political powers, to be exercised by the president according to his own discretion. When he has made an appointment, he has exercised his whole power, and his discretion has been completely applied to the case....

The question whether a right has vested or not, is, in its nature, judicial, and must be tried by the judicial authority. If, for example, Mr. Marbury had taken the oaths of a magistrate, and proceeded to act as one; in consequence of which a suit had been instituted against him, in which his defence had depended on his being a magistrate; the validity of his appointment must have been determined by judicial authority. So, if he conceives that by virtue of his appointment he has a legal right either to the commission which has been made out for him or to a copy of that commission, it is equally a question examinable in a court, and the decision of the court upon it must depend on the opinion entertained of his appointment....

It is, then, the opinion of the Court,...[t]hat, having this legal title to the office, he has a consequent right to the commission; a refusal to deliver which is a plain violation of that right, for which the laws of his country afford him a remedy.

It remains to be inquired whether, [h]e is entitled to the remedy for which he applies. This depends on...[t]he nature of the writ applied for [a]nd...[t]he power of this court.

1st. The nature of the writ. Blackstone, in the third volume of his Commentaries, page 110, defines a mandamus to be, "a command issuing in the king's name from the court of king's bench, and directed to any person, corporation, or inferior court of judicature within the king's dominions, requiring them to do some particular thing therein specified which appertains to their office and duty, and which the court of king's bench has previously determined, or at least supposes, to be consonant to right and justice."

Lord Mansfield, in 3 Burrows, 1266, in the case of *The King v. Baker et al.*, states with much precision and explicitness the cases in which this writ may be used. "Whenever," says that very able judge, "there is a right to execute an office...(more especially if it be in a matter of public concern or attended with profit), and a person is kept out of possession,...and has no other specific legal remedy, this court ought to assist by mandamus."...

Still, to render the mandamus a proper remedy, the officer to whom it is to be directed, must be one to whom, on legal principles, such writ may be directed; and the person applying for it must be without any other specific and legal remedy. . . . The intimate political relation, subsisting between the president of the United States and the heads of departments, necessarily renders any legal investigation of the acts of one of those high officers peculiarly irksome, as well as delicate; and excites some hesitation with respect to the propriety of entering into such investigation. . . . The province of the court is, solely, to decide on the rights of individuals, not to inquire how the executive, or executive officers, perform duties in which they have a discretion. Questions, in their nature political, or which are, by the constitution and laws, submitted to the executive, can never be made in this court.

But, if this be not such a question; if so far from being an intrusion into the secrets of the cabinet, it respects a paper, which, according to law, is upon record, and to a copy of which the law gives a right, on the payment of ten cents; if it be no in-termeddling with a subject, over which the executive can be considered as having exercised any control; what is there in the exalted station of the officer, which shall bar a citizen from asserting, in a court of justice, his legal rights, or shall forbid a court to listen to the claim; or to issue a mandamus, directing the performance of a duty, not depending on executive discretion, but on particular acts of congress and the general principles of law? . . . It is not by the office of the person to whom the writ is directed, but the nature of the thing to be done, that the propriety or impro-priety of issuing a mandamus is to be determined. . . .

This, then, is a plain case of a mandamus, either to deliver the commission, or a copy of it from the record; and it only remains to be inquired, [w]hether it can issue from this court?

[Chief Justice MARSHALL concluded, in the remainder of the Court's unanimous opinion, that the writ of mandamus could not issue from the Supreme Court in this case because Congress could not constitutionally vest original jurisdiction in the Supreme Court to hear suits for mandamus against officers of the United States.]

---

1. First, let us return to the ethical questions with which we preceded *Marbury*. A response to some of Dean Redlich's questions comes from Fein, *Promoting the President's Policies Through Legal Advocacy: An Ethical Imperative of the Government Attorney*, 30 Fed. Bar News & J. 406, 408 (Sept./Oct. 1983):

> [T]he discovery by a government attorney of precedent that seemingly would condemn a Presidential policy does not ordain the conclusion that no responsible legal argument can be assembled to vindicate the policy. To the contrary, in most such situations, rational reasons can be adduced for modifying or reversing the adverse precedent, or distinguishing it, in order to effectuate the President's policy goal. The government attorney is ethically bound to develop when nec-essary plausible arguments for altering or overturning existing law. This duty is comparable to the ethical norm governing private attorneys that endorses advocacy of any non-frivolous constructions dependent on modification or re-versal of existing law, without regard to the attorney's professional opinion as to the likelihood that the construction will ultimately prevail. [See Canon EC-7-4, ABA Code of Professional Responsibility.] If a government attorney cannot ungrudgingly adhere to the ethical imperative requiring promotion of the Pres-ident's policies through legal advocacy, then he might seriously consider vol-untary resignation from the Executive Branch.

Do you agree? If Fein's advice seems appropriate for the conduct of government litigation, is it equally appropriate for the conduct of an executive adviser regarding a question that may never reach court? What would be the effect on the government if all advisers in the executive followed Fein's prescription? Compare the views of Shane, *Legal Disagreement and Negotiation in a Government of Laws: The Case of Executive Privilege Claims Against Congress*, 71 Minn. L. Rev. 461, 491-92 (1987):

> A government of laws...is a government in which officials feel obligated to look to legal points of reference to describe and justify official behavior. This obligation is treated as important, even if not always performed well and even if, because law and political interest may coincide, it is sometimes superfluous. It is deemed important that government officials at least exercise the self-discipline of questioning the legal significance of their acts and, often, of providing explicit justification for those acts in legal terms. It is the habitual commitment to this interpretive regime that perhaps most pervasively differentiates a government of laws from a government of unadorned power.

What does Shane's view mean in practice—for example, is the President entitled to the benefit of the doubt from his lawyers? A former Deputy Assistant Attorney General reports the views of a President (Letter from Larry A. Hammond to Peter M. Shane, Jan. 7, 1986):

> In many instances,...Jimmy Carter was not interested in playing the "lawmaker as advocate" game....Carter made it known, very clearly, that if there was a legal question in a policy paper, he wanted to know whether the options were lawful or not lawful....He knew that lawyers could "advocate" any position, but he wanted his Attorney General to tell him what the correct legal answer was, and he was prepared to live by it.

2. *Marbury* distinguished the executive's political discretion, which the courts could not control, from its statutory duties to individuals, which the courts could determine. What was Marshall's apparent source for these categories? Was he merely translating the traditional mandamus law distinction between ministerial and discretionary acts into a constitutional context? *See* G. Haskins & H. Johnson, Foundations of Power: John Marshall 1801-15 (2 History of the Supreme Court of the United States) (1981), arguing that the law/politics distinction was crucial to what the authors regard as Marshall's great achievement as Chief Justice: the establishment of the rule of law as the basis of Supreme Court jurisprudence. *See also* Haskins, *Law Versus Politics in the Early Years of the Marshall Court*, 130 U. Pa. L. Rev. 1 (1981).

Professor Haskins points out that eighteenth-century courts were viewed as an arm of the administration, and engaged in political as well as strictly legal activities. In *Marbury*, Marshall rejected that political role, yet claimed a vital legal role. (As elsewhere in the opinion, Marshall used a retreat in one direction to cover an advance in another.) Haskins concludes (Foundations, *supra*, at 406):

> In a sense the Court under Marshall had accepted a sharply diminished role in politics, but in so limiting its activities it had secured a better control of law, the jurisdiction to which it had undoubted entitlement. Removing itself from partisan politics, it entrenched itself as the constitutional guardian of individual rights against the excesses and vagaries of popular government in a disturbingly new egalitarian age. In beating a strategic retreat before the armies of Jeffer-

sonian legislators, the judges arrived at a delineation of judicial power such that even their detractors were forced to concede the validity of their pretensions, and Republican judges found incumbent Federalist judges to be of one mind with them. Upon this consensus was built the foundations of the Supreme Court of the United States as we know it today.

Marbury's line between law and politics is not self-defining. Instead, value questions inhere in deciding which issues of separation of powers or individual rights to remove from the sphere of democratic politics for resolution by the courts. *See* Nedelsky, *Confining Democratic Politics: Anti-Federalists, Federalists, and the Constitution*, 96 Harv. L. Rev. 340 (1982) (reviewing Haskins & Johnson). Therefore, we need to qualify Marshall's assertion (made in support of the power of judicial review) that "[i]t is emphatically the province and duty of the judicial department to say what the law is."

What deference was the executive bound to give to Marshall's dicta about the Court's power over the executive? Recall the quotation in Chapter One from a later President, Andrew Jackson, arguing that each branch "must be guided by its own opinion of the Constitution." If the executive is prepared to obey the order of a court having jurisdiction of a controversy, has it any broader duty to honor judicial statements of "what the law is"? *See generally* Symposium, *Perspectives on the Authoritativeness of Supreme Court Decisions*, 61 Tul. L. Rev. 977 (1987). We consider this issue in Chapter Five.

3. Both of the other branches routinely take positions on statutory and constitutional issues—to what extent should the courts defer to their views? This question pervades modern constitutional law in general, and separation of powers in particular, as we shall see. And it has an analogue in administrative law that is also pertinent throughout these materials. Reviewing courts generally defer to administrative interpretations of statutes, within the limits of reason and ascertainable legislative intent. *See Chevron, U.S.A., Inc. v. Natural Resources Defense Council, Inc.*, 467 U.S. 837 (1984); Starr, *Judicial Review in the Post-Chevron Era*, 3 Yale J. on Reg. 283 (1986). Should Marshall have given some deference to the executive's presumed interpretation of the pertinent statutes as making appointments complete only upon delivery of the commissions? *See generally* Monaghan, Marbury *and the Administrative State*, 83 Colum. L. Rev. 1 (1983).

Should Marshall have deferred *completely* to the executive's statutory interpretation, on grounds that it presented an unreviewable political question? That would have acknowledged the value content of the law/politics line, but it would have altered fundamentally the development of administrative law, according to Bruff, *Judicial Review and the President's Statutory Powers*, 68 Va. L. Rev. 1, 9-10 (1982):

> *Marbury* laid the foundation of American administrative law by affirming both the power of Congress to limit the President's discretion and the power of the courts to interpret and enforce those limits. The Court decided the latter issue without an analytic demonstration of the need for judicial intervention. The alternative of deferring to the executive would have required reliance in part on the executive's own constitutional duty to execute the laws faithfully, and in part on the opportunity for Congress to enter the fray. In *Marbury*, the Court appeared to find sufficient justification for its intervention in the need for judicial protection of individual rights against executive infringement.

There are additional reasons why it would be unwise to treat the President's statutory duties as political questions.[36] A government having two policymaking branches that are in constant competition needs an arbiter to identify the locus of responsibility in particular cases. The alternative would be to force Congress to work its will with the executive through means that would frequently be excessive[37] or unrelated to the controversy at hand.[38] This would introduce unnecessary inefficiencies into the operation of government. More seriously, it would accord Congress both too much and too little power to enforce its existing statutes. Congress would have insufficient power insofar as the President's role as head of his party would enable him to forestall effective legislative response. Congress would have excessive power in two ways. First, Congress could effectively alter existing statutes without following the constitutional process for amending them, simply by acceding to presidential decisions inconsistent with them. Second, the President would lose an important means of defending the legitimacy of his actions. A judicial determination that executive action is consistent with statutory authority enables a President to blunt charges that he has overstepped his role in defiance of the institutional interests of Congress.

4. Marshall states that every right, in the American constitutional system, must have legal redress. In his article on executive privilege (*supra*, at 490-91), Shane relates this concept to accountability:

> . . . The distribution of different powers among the branches, with the inevitability of some confrontation, makes unavoidable some occasions on which one branch can poignantly remind another of the importance of pursuing justification through legal reasoning. Justice Marshall's opinion in *Marbury v. Madison* can be read from just such a perspective. In statements that were technically dicta, Marshall constitutionalized the traditional distinction in the law of mandamus between judicially reviewable ministerial acts and unreviewable political acts for which a government officer is not accountable in court. He did so in the face of his undoubted awareness that presidential exercises of political discretion could result in constitutional violations which the courts, under *Marbury*, could not remedy. For example, it would presumably be unconstitutional for the President, with purely invidious motives, to veto those congressional enactments, and only those enactments, that had the effect of improving the social position of American Blacks. Yet, following Marshall's reasoning, no judicial sanction could enjoin such behavior. Indeed, no judicial sanction could compel Congress to override the President's vetoes, or to impeach him for his behavior.

Despite the potential for unjust results created by situations such as this, Marshall, without apparent irony, describes our government as a "government

---

36. For a provocative thesis that courts should regard constitutional (but not statutory) issues concerning the respective powers of Congress and the President as nonjusticiable political questions, see J. Choper, Judicial Review and the National Political Process 260-379 (1980). . . .

37. The ultimate congressional recourse of impeachment would be disproportionate for most statutory controversies. Congress might choose the alternative of removing all statutory authority for the program or shifting it to a subordinate officer who is subject to judicial control; either sanction could defeat Congress's overall purposes, however.

38. An example of an unrelated sanction would be denial of appropriations for one of the President's favorite programs.

of laws" in which the "laws" furnish a remedy for the violation of a "vested legal right." If "laws furnish[ing a] remedy," in Marshall's words, were interpreted simply to mean "courts furnishing mandatory relief," Marshall's characterization of our government as a government of laws would be wrong.[98]

It is possible, however, to interpret *Marbury* in a different light. Each branch of the government has a role in maintaining the ideal of the government of laws. The judicial branch, as *Marbury* illustrates, is not solely responsible for providing remedies for unconstitutional behavior. Prospectively, the allegiance of the executive branch to legal norms affords a kind of preliminary injunction against such behavior. That same sense of obligation may lead Congress, in the face of necessity, to vest jurisdiction in an appropriate court to review the Executive's acts. Failing that, an obligation to impeach may arise. Such remedies may not be perfect. As in Marbury's case, they may fail. They do, however, exist, and *Marbury* may be read as an exhortation to their use.[99]

Is Shane's view of the potential power of legal interpretation as a mechanism of accountability implausibly naive? How do you assess the significance of the extraordinary amount of interpretive activity that in fact goes on throughout the federal bureaucracy? As you read the various judicial opinions that follow, consider whether they lend credence to Shane's assertion that the branches often send messages to one another, reminding them of their obligations (even if unenforceable) under law. Is this an appropriate judicial function?

5. Could Marshall have persuasively characterized Marbury as not having a legal right under the facts presented, thus avoiding the question of remedy? For example, note the Court's assumptions about Marbury's removability from office. Would the case have been decided differently had the Court assumed that Marbury was removable by the President at will?

6. Was it proper for John Marshall, as the former Secretary of State who had received Marbury's commission, to have decided this case?

7. Had mandamus issued and had Madison failed to comply, could the Court have held him in contempt? What if he had been ordered to resist by President Jefferson? Should the Court's inability to execute such a sanction determine whether a legal right exists against the executive (or against Congress)?

---

98. *Marbury* itself would belie the "government of laws" claim because Marbury could not obtain judicial relief, despite Marshall's determination that Marbury had been denied his vested right in his commission. Marshall held the grant of mandamus jurisdiction to the Supreme Court unconstitutional. *Id.* at 175-76. No other federal court had original jurisdiction in a mandamus proceeding as of 1803. Judiciary Act of 1789, ch. 20, 1 Stat. 73. State courts could not constitutionally issue mandamus against federal officers. M'Clung v. Silliman, 19 U.S. (6 Wheat.) 598, 604 (1821).

99. Jefferson might have deduced this point from the discretion Marshall conspicuously exercised in choosing his rationale for decision and their shared, tacit recognition that the Court might exercise its discretion more forcefully against the President should more dire circumstances so require in the future. One conscientious response to *Marbury* might well have been not to deliver Marbury's commission—because Jefferson, as a matter of law, disclaimed any such obligation—but to execute and deliver a new commission to demonstrate Jefferson's intention to avoid even the appearance of injustice. Jefferson, in fact, did commission most of the justices of the peace appointed by Adams, whose commissions were not delivered.

8. Can Congress vest ministerial duties directly in the President? What would be the extent of judicial authority over the President should Congress vest a ministerial duty in him?

Note on Obtaining Judicial Review of Executive Actions

Marbury raised as many questions as it answered regarding methods of obtaining judicial review of presidential actions. Madison did not appear by counsel or in person in response to the Court's order to show cause—the Jeffersonians regarded it as an outrageous intrusion on executive authority. (*See* Haskins & Johnson, *supra*, at 183-86.) And, of course, Marshall's disposition of the constitutional question made it unnecessary for him to issue mandamus to an executive officer, although he asserted the power to do so. Therefore, questions lingered about the amenability of the President himself to judicial process, and about other limits to judicial power over the executive. It would be many years before definitive answers were provided to some of these questions.

First, notice the mode of review sought by Marbury—mandamus, one of the extraordinary writs in English law, brought into American law with the adoption of the common law. Marshall, to define the scope of the writ, sought ancient authority, where he found the traditional doctrine that mandamus will issue to compel an officer to perform a "ministerial" duty, but not to exercise discretion in a particular way. Thus, Marshall adapted a writ that was designed to control the King's officers in order to control the President and his officers.

This technique of adapting common law doctrines and remedies to American administrative law has continued to the present day. *See* G. Robinson, E. Gellhorn & H. Bruff, The Administrative Process, 135-40 (3d ed. 1986). For example, the Court later elaborated on the ministerial/discretionary distinction for mandamus, in *Roberts v. United States*, 176 U.S. 219, 231 (1900):

> Every statute to some extent requires construction by the public officer whose duties may be defined therein. Such officer must read the law, ... in order to form a judgment from its language what duty he is ... to perform. But that does not necessarily ... make the duty of the officer anything other than a purely ministerial one.
>
> If the law direct him to perform an act in regard to which no discretion is committed to him, and which, upon the facts existing, he is bound to perform, then that act is ministerial, although depending upon a statute which requires, in some degree, a construction of its language by the officer.

Today, 28 U.S.C. § 1361 codifies mandamus by granting federal jurisdiction "of any action in the nature of mandamus to compel an officer ... to perform a duty owed to the plaintiff."

Testing the implications of *Marbury* required exercising, rather than merely asserting, judicial power. The Court, and Marshall, soon found opportunities. In *Little v. Barreme*, 6 U.S. (2 Cranch) 170 (1804), decided a year later, the Court unanimously upheld an award of damages against a ship captain who, on orders of the President, seized a ship coming to the United States from France. Marshall's opinion said that the President might have power to seize ships without special statutory authority, but that the Nonintercourse Act had "prescribed ... the manner in which this law shall be carried into execution," and that a noncomplying seizure was illegal.

In *Little*, however, the Court issued no compulsory process to the President. A celebrated case soon gave Marshall that opportunity. Sitting on circuit in the treason trial of Aaron Burr, Marshall issued a subpoena to President Jefferson for evidence material to the case. *United States v. Burr*, 25 F. Cas. 30 (C.C. Va. 1807, No. 14,692-D). He rejected any absolute presidential immunity from judicial process (25 F. Cas. at 34):

> Of the many points of difference which exist between the first magistrate in England and the first magistrate of the United States, in respect to the personal dignity conferred on them by the constitutions of their respective nations, the court will only select and mention two. It is a principle of the English constitution that the king can do no wrong, that no blame can be imputed to him, that he cannot be named in debate. By the Constitution of the United States, the president, as well as any other officer of the government, may be impeached, and may be removed from office on high crimes and misdemeanors. By the constitution of Great Britain, the crown is hereditary, and the monarch can never be a subject. By that of the United States, the president is elected from the mass of the people, and, on the expiration of the time for which he is elected, returns to the mass of the people again. How essentially this difference of circumstances must vary the policy of the laws of the two countries, in reference to the personal dignity of the executive chief, will be perceived by every person.

Burr provided no definitive resolution, however. Jefferson "voluntarily" complied with the subpoena, protesting any obligation to do so. For the full story, see Freund, *Foreword: On Presidential Privilege, The Supreme Court, 1973 Term*, 88 Harv. L. Rev. 13, 23-30 (1974).

In the quoted passage from *Burr*, Marshall referred obliquely to the common law doctrine of sovereign immunity, that "the king can do no wrong." In *Cohens v. Virginia*, 19 U.S. (6 Wheat.) 264 (1821), he assumed that the doctrine applied to the United States. It was, he said, "the universally received opinion . . . that no suit can be commenced or prosecuted against the United States; that the judiciary act does not authorize such suits." (19 U.S. at 411). Despite this thin pedigree, sovereign immunity entered our law, and still forbids unconsented suits against the United States. *See* Scalia, *Historical Anomalies in Administrative Law*, Yearbook 1985, 103, 105.

In order to avoid having sovereign immunity bar review of the legality of ordinary administrative action, the courts had to evolve a fiction. Injunctive suits were brought against officers in their "personal" capacity, so that relief did not formally run against the government, although the point of the lawsuit was to produce that effect. *Ex Parte Young*, 209 U.S. 123 (1908). Eventually, Congress waived sovereign immunity for injunctive relief against the United States. 5 U.S.C. § 702. (Damages actions still require a specific statutory waiver.) Today, the standard method for challenging administrative action (absent a special statutory grant of review authority) is a suit invoking federal question jurisdiction under 28 U.S.C. § 1331 and seeking an injunction, perhaps coupled with a request for declaratory relief under 28 U.S.C. §§ 2201-02. And the mandamus statute provides another avenue for relief.

None of these statutes, however, specifically authorizes review of presidential action. Partly for that reason, Marbury's strategy of suing a subordinate officer who is executing the President's policies remains dominant. The first case to issue mandamus against an officer was *Kendall v. United States ex rel. Stokes*, 37 U.S. (12 Pet.) 524 (1838). A dispute arose between the Postmaster General and some contractors over amounts owing for the carriage of mail. Eventually, Congress passed a statute calling for another official to settle the claims and for the Postmaster to pay the amount awarded. The Postmaster declined to pay the full amount of the award; the contractors sought mandamus. It was clear to the Court that under ordinary mandamus principles, the Postmaster's action was purely ministerial—to pay whatever amount had been awarded. The only complicating factor was the breadth of the Postmaster's defense. There had been, said the Court, "a very extended range of argument on the independence and duties" of the executive. Nevertheless, the President did not stand in the way—he had notified Congress of the Postmaster's actions, without endorsing them. In that posture of the case, the Court upheld issuance of the writ. In an opinion by Justice Thompson, the Court responded to the argument that it had heard with some broad views of its own (37 U.S. at 612-13):

> It was urged at the bar, that the postmaster-general was alone subject to the direction and control of the president, with respect to the execution of the duty imposed upon him by this law; and this right of the president is claimed, as growing out of the obligation imposed upon him by the constitution, to take care that the laws be faithfully executed. This is a doctrine that cannot receive the sanction of this court. It would be vesting in the president a dispensing power, which has no countenance for its support, in any part of the constitution; and is asserting a principle, which, ... would be clothing the president with a power entirely to control the legislation of congress, and paralyze the administration of justice. To contend, that the obligation imposed on the president to see the laws faithfully executed, implies a power to forbid their execution, is a novel construction of the constitution, and entirely inadmissible.

A more serious challenge to presidential power followed the Civil War. Mississippi challenged the constitutionality of the Reconstruction Acts by seeking an injunction against presidential enforcement. Before the Supreme Court, Attorney General Stanbery argued that the courts could not issue an order to the President, because the power to do so would entail the power to punish his disobedience by contempt, and that sanction would effectively remove him from office, usurping the impeachment power of Congress. In *Mississippi v. Johnson*, 71 U.S. (4 Wall.) 475 (1866), the Court denied the injunction. Chief Justice Chase stressed that this facial attack on the Acts did not involve an effort to compel the President to perform a ministerial act. Characterizing the President's military duties under the Acts as "purely executive and political," the Court refused to intervene. Thus, the outcome in *Mississippi v. Johnson* probably turned on the presence of nonjusticiable political questions, and on the unripeness of the challenge, rather than on the amenability of the President to suit. It is one of a series of cases in which the Court successfully avoided ruling on the constitutionality of Reconstruction.

The Court finally held that the President is subject to judicial process in *United States v. Nixon*, 418 U.S. 683 (1974), excerpted in Chapter Three. Surprisingly, the *Nixon* Court made no direct analysis of the President's amenability to compulsory process, instead subsuming the question under the issue of the extent of his executive privilege to resist disclosure of confidential communications. The amenability issue did receive direct scrutiny, however, in an earlier stage of the litigation. In *Nixon v.*

Sirica, 487 F. 2d 700 (D.C. Cir. 1973), the court would not find the President immune from process (487 F. 2d at 710-12):

> Thus, to find the President immune from judicial process, we must read out of *Burr* and *Youngstown* [excerpted *infra*] the underlying principles that the eminent jurists in each case thought they were establishing. The Constitution makes no mention of special presidential immunities. Indeed, the Executive Branch generally is afforded none. This silence cannot be ascribed to oversight. James Madison raised the question of Executive privileges during the Constitutional Convention, and Senators and Representatives enjoy an express, if limited, immunity from arrest, and an express privilege from inquiry concerning "Speech and Debate" on the floors of Congress. Lacking textual support, counsel for the President nonetheless would have us infer immunity from the President's political mandate, or from his vulnerability to impeachment, or from his broad discretionary powers. These are invitations to refashion the Constitution, and we reject them. . . .
>
> Nor does the Impeachment Clause imply immunity from routine court process. . . . The order entered below . . . [does not] compete with the impeachment device by working a constructive removal of the President from office. The subpoena names in the alternate "any subordinate officer," and the tasks of compliance may obviously be delegated in whole or in part so as not to interfere with the President's official responsibilities. . . . That the Impeachment Clause may qualify the court's power to sanction non-compliance with judicial orders is immaterial. Whatever the qualifications, they were equally present in *Youngstown*: Commerce Secretary Sawyer, the defendant there, was an impeachable "civil officer," but the injunction against him was nonetheless affirmed. The legality of judicial orders should not be confused with the legal consequences of their breach; for the courts in this country always assume that their orders will be obeyed, especially when addressed to responsible government officials.

See also National Treasury Employees Union v. Nixon, 492 F. 2d 587 (D.C. Cir. 1974), holding that the President had violated a federal pay statute by refusing to grant certain pay raises, but withholding mandamus in favor of issuing a declaratory judgment "in order to show the utmost respect to the office of the Presidency and to avoid, if at all possible, direct involvement by the Courts in the President's constitutional duty to execute the laws and any clash between the judicial and executive branches of the Government." The President complied with the judgment.

An issue left open after *United States v. Nixon*, the availability of contempt against Cabinet officers, was litigated in *In re The Attorney General of the United States*, 596 F.2d 58 (2d Cir.), *cert. denied*, 444 U.S. 903 (1979). In 1973, the Socialist Workers Party (SWP) and others sued the Federal Bureau of Investigation (FBI), alleging that the plaintiffs had been subject to an unlawful investigation aimed at destroying their organizations. In the course of the litigation, the FBI refused to release 18 files under a discovery order by the District Court, on the ground of "informant privilege." The District Court consequently held the Attorney General in civil contempt. The Court of Appeals held, first, that the contempt order against the Attorney General was an interlocutory order that was not appealable. The court, per Judge Oakes, proceeded to hold, however, that the contempt order could appropriately be reviewed in a mandamus proceeding against the district judge. The court found that the SWP litigation met the test of "extraordinary significance" for considering mandamus. The court then held that contempt was inappropriate because of the availability of sanctions that were more reasonable in light of the consequences of contempt and the plaintiff's case. The court said (596 F. 2d at 65):

> We begin our analysis of the merits by stressing two considerations. The first is the nature of the contempt power itself. Just as, we trust, an Attorney General would not lightly invoke a privilege such as the one that he invokes here, so too the court must not lightly invoke its contempt power. For the exercise of that power is, even in the context of a private attorney, "awesome in its implications."
>
> Second, in an extraordinary case such as this, the significance of abuse of discretion is magnified. Here, as noted above, the contemnor is not simply an attorney but the chief law enforcement officer of the nation, [and] the principal attorney for another branch of government coequal to the judicial branch in constitutional function and design. Courts accordingly owe him respect as an official and, absent an abuse of power or misuse of office, the most careful and reasoned treatment as party or as litigant. Thus, holding the Attorney General of the United States in contempt to ensure compliance with a court order should be a last resort, to be undertaken only after all other means to achieve the ends legitimately sought by the court have been exhausted.
>
> Judged by these standards, the action of the trial court unfortunately falls short, for in our view the court insufficiently considered issue-related sanctions. The Federal Rules of Civil Procedure permit many sanctions other than contempt alternatives that the court did not sufficiently explore except to reject the Government's proposals.

In the SWP litigation, the Attorney General "interposed" himself as the defendant decisionmaker, after issuance of a court order to the FBI. Could the President have done so? Also, note that this case involved executive failure to comply with a court order based on a judicial rule, not an executive failure to execute a statute. In such a case, is it more or less appropriate for a court to hold a Cabinet officer in contempt? Does it make any difference? If the Attorney General had been held in contempt, what would have been the appropriate penalty? Incarceration? A fine? What do your answers to these questions suggest concerning the legitimacy or the utility of the contempt sanction?

Consider again whether, had mandamus issued against Secretary Madison, the Court could properly have held him in contempt. Could a court legitimately determine that the gravity of resistance to a court order in any one case outweighed the interference with the operation of the executive branch that incarcerating a Cabinet official—assuming a U.S. Marshal would do so—would entail?

Review the foregoing case law: what role should the prospect of litigation play in the process of legal interpretation by government lawyers? Do the courts have sufficient sanctions to earn the respect of those inclined to adhere to executive interpretations of law in the face of contrary judicial opinion?

Finally, consider in this context, as you will in many others, the extent to which this case law demonstrates that the success of the separation of powers depends on each branch avoiding a test of the utmost limits of its powers—a factor with profound significance for the way in which government actually works.

2. The Executive and Congress (as Mediated by the Courts)

The *Steel Seizure* case, portions of which follow, represents the modern Supreme Court's most thorough discussion of congressional restraints on presidential power.

Youngstown Sheet & Tube Co. v. Sawyer
343 U.S. 579 (1952)

Justice BLACK delivered the opinion of the Court.

We are asked to decide whether the President was acting within his constitutional power when he issued an order directing the Secretary of Commerce to take possession of and operate most of the Nation's steel mills. The mill owners argue that the President's order amounts to lawmaking, a legislative function which the Constitution has expressly confided to the Congress and not to the President. The Government's position is that the order was made on findings of the President that his action was necessary to avert a national catastrophe which would inevitably result from a stoppage of steel production, and that in meeting this grave emergency the President was acting within the aggregate of his constitutional powers as the Nation's Chief Executive and the Commander in Chief of the Armed Forces of the United States. The issue emerges here from the following series of events:

In the latter part of 1951, a dispute arose between the steel companies and their employees over terms and conditions that should be included in new collective bargaining agreements. Long-continued conferences failed to resolve the dispute. On December 18, 1951, the employees' representative, United Steelworkers of America, C.I.O., gave notice of an intention to strike when the existing bargaining agreements expired on December 31. The Federal Mediation and Conciliation Service then intervened in an effort to get labor and management to agree. This failing, the President on December 22, 1951, referred the dispute to the Federal Wage Stabilization Board to investigate and make recommendations for fair and equitable terms of settlement. This Board's report resulted in no settlement. On April 4, 1952, the Union gave notice of a nation-wide strike called to begin at 12:01 a.m. April 9. The indispensability of steel as a component of substantially all weapons and other war materials led the President to believe that the proposed work stoppage would immediately jeopardize our national defense and that governmental seizure of the steel mills was necessary in order to assure the continued availability of steel. Reciting these considerations for his action, the President, a few hours before the strike was to begin, issued Executive Order 10340.... The order directed the Secretary of Commerce to take possession of most of the steel mills and keep them running. The Secretary immediately issued his own possessory orders, calling upon the presidents of the various seized companies to serve as operating managers for the United States. They were directed to carry on their activities in accordance with regulations and directions of the Secretary. The next morning the President sent a message to Congress reporting his action. Twelve days later he sent a second message. Congress has taken no action.

Obeying the Secretary's orders under protest, the companies brought proceedings against him in the District Court. Their complaints charged that the seizure was not authorized by an act of Congress or by any constitutional provisions. The District Court was asked to declare the orders of the President and the Secretary invalid and to issue preliminary and permanent injunctions restraining their enforcement. Opposing the motion for preliminary injunction, the United States asserted that a strike disrupting steel production for even a brief period would so endanger the well-being and safety of the Nation that the President had "inherent power" to do what he had done—power "supported by the Constitution, by historical precedent, and by court decisions." The Government also contended that in any event no preliminary injunction should be issued because the companies had made no showing that their available legal remedies were inadequate or that their injuries from seizure would be irreparable. Holding against the Government on all points, the District Court on April 30 issued a preliminary injunction restraining the Secretary from "continuing the seizure and possession of the plants...and from acting under the purported authority of Executive Order No. 10340." 103 F.Supp. 569. On the same day the Court of Appeals stayed the District Court's injunction. Deeming it best that the issues raised be promptly decided by this Court, we granted certiorari on May 3 and set the cause for argument on May 12....

I.

[The Court first rejected the Government's argument that injunctive relief should be denied because damages were adequate to compensate for the harm suffered. The Court thought that difficulties in measuring and awarding damages justified a finding of irreparable injury.]

II.

The President's power, if any, to issue the order must stem either from an act of Congress or from the Constitution itself. There is no statute that expressly authorizes the President to take possession of property as he did here. Nor is there any act of Congress to which our attention has been directed from which such a power can fairly be implied. Indeed, we do not understand the Government to rely on statutory authorization for this seizure. There are two statutes which do authorize the President to take both personal and real property under certain conditions.[2] However, the Government admits that these conditions were not met and that the President's order was not rooted in either of the statutes. The Government refers to the seizure provisions of one of these statutes (§ 201(b) of the Defense Production Act) as "much too cumbersome, involved, and time-consuming for the crisis which was at hand."

Moreover, the use of the seizure technique to solve labor disputes in order to prevent work stoppages was not only unauthorized by any congressional enactment; prior to this controversy, Congress had refused to adopt that method of settling labor disputes. When the Taft-Hartley Act was under consideration in 1947, Congress rejected an amendment which would have authorized such governmental seizures in cases of emergency. Apparently it was thought that the technique of seizure, like that of compulsory arbitration, would interfere with the process of collective bargaining. Consequently, the plan Congress adopted in that Act did not provide for seizure under any circumstances. Instead, the plan sought to bring about settlements by use of the customary devices of mediation, conciliation, investigation by boards of inquiry, and public reports. In some instances temporary injunctions were authorized to provide cooling-off periods. All this failing, unions were left free to strike after a secret vote

---

2. The Selective Service Act of 1948, 62 Stat. 604, 625-627; the Defense Production Act of 1950, Tit. II, 64 Stat. 798, as amended, 65 Stat. 132.

by employees as to whether they wished to accept their employers' final settlement offer.

It is clear that if the President had authority to issue the order he did, it must be found in some provision of the Constitution. And it is not claimed that express constitutional language grants this power to the President. The contention is that presidential power should be implied from the aggregate of his powers under the Constitution. Particular reliance is placed on provisions in Article II which say that "The executive Power shall be vested in a President..."; that "he shall take Care that the Laws be faithfully executed"; and that he "shall be Commander in Chief of the Army and Navy of the United States."

The order cannot properly be sustained as an exercise of the President's military power as Commander in Chief of the Armed Forces. The Government attempts to do so by citing a number of cases upholding broad powers in military commanders engaged in day-to-day fighting in a theater of war. Such cases need not concern us here. Even though "theater of war" be an expanding concept, we cannot with faithfulness to our constitutional system hold that the Commander in Chief of the Armed Forces has the ultimate power as such to take possession of private property in order to keep labor disputes from stopping production. This is a job for the Nation's lawmakers, not for its military authorities.

Nor can the seizure order be sustained because of the several constitutional provisions that grant executive power to the President. In the framework of our Constitution, the President's power to see that the laws are faithfully executed refutes the idea that he is to be a lawmaker. The Constitution limits his functions in the lawmaking process to the recommending of laws he tninks wise and the vetoing of laws he thinks bad. And the Constitution is neither silent nor equivocal about who shall make laws which the President is to execute. The first section of the first article says that "All legislative Powers herein granted shall be vested in a Congress of the United States ...." After granting many powers to the Congress, Article I goes on to provide that Congress may "make all Laws which shall be necessary and proper for carrying into Execution the foregoing Powers and all other Powers vested by this Constitution in the Government of the United States, or in any Department or Officer thereof."

The President's order does not direct that a congressional policy be executed in a manner prescribed by Congress—it directs that a presidential policy be executed in a manner prescribed by the President.... The power of Congress to adopt such public policies as those proclaimed by the order is beyond question. It can authorize the taking of private property for public use. It can make laws regulating the relationships between employers and employees, prescribing rules designed to settle labor disputes, and fixing wages and working conditions in certain fields of our economy. The Constitution did not subject this law-making power of Congress to presidential or military supervision or control.

It is said that other Presidents without congressional authority have taken possession of private business enterprises in order to settle labor disputes. But even if this be true, Congress has not thereby lost its exclusive constitutional authority to make laws necessary and proper to carry out the powers vested by the Constitution "in the Government of the United States, or in any Department or Officer thereof."

The Founders of this Nation entrusted the law making power to the Congress alone in both good and bad times. It would do no good to recall the historical events, the fears of power and the hopes for freedom that lay behind their choice. Such a review would but confirm our holding that this seizure order cannot stand.

The judgment of the District Court is affirmed.

Justice FRANKFURTER, concurring.

. . . Congress in 1947 was . . . called upon to consider whether governmental seizure should be used to avoid serious industrial shutdowns. Congress decided against conferring such power generally and in advance, without special congressional enactment to meet each particular need. Under the urgency of telephone and coal strikes in the winter of 1946, Congress addressed itself to the problems raised by "national emergency" strikes and lockouts. The termination of wartime seizure powers on December 31, 1946, brought these matters to the attention of Congress with vivid impact. A proposal that the President be given powers to seize plants to avert a shutdown where the "health or safety" of the nation was endangered was thoroughly canvassed by Congress and rejected. No room for doubt remains that the proponents as well as the opponents of the bill which became the Labor Management Relations Act of 1947 clearly understood that as a result of that legislation the only recourse for preventing a shutdown in any basic industry, after failure of mediation, was Congress. . . .

But it is now claimed that the President has seizure power by virtue of the Defense Production Act of 1950 and its Amendments. And the claim is based on the occurrence of new events—Korea and the need for stabilization, etc.—although it was well known that seizure power was withheld by the Act of 1947 and although the President, whose specific requests for other authority were in the main granted by Congress, never suggested that in view of the new events he needed the power of seizure which Congress in its judgment had decided to withhold from him. The utmost that the Korean conflict may imply is that it may have been desirable to have given the President further authority, a freer hand in these matters. Absence of authority in the President to deal with a crisis does not imply want of power in the Government. Conversely the fact that power exists in the Government does not vest it in the President. . . .

No authority that has since been given to the President can by any fair process of statutory construction be deemed to withdraw the restriction or change the will of Congress as expressed by a body of enactments, culminating in the Labor Management Relations Act of 1947. . . .

Apart from his vast share of responsibility for the conduct of our foreign relations, the embracing function of the President is that "he shall take Care that the Laws be faithfully executed. . . . " Art. II, § 3. The nature of that authority has for me been comprehensively indicated by Mr. Justice Holmes. "The duty of the President to see that the laws be executed is a duty that does not go beyond the laws or require him to achieve more than Congress sees fit to leave within his power." Myers v. United States, 272 U.S. 52, 177. . . .

To be sure, the content of the three authorities of government is not to be derived from an abstract analysis. The areas are partly interacting, not wholly disjointed. The Constitution is a framework for government. Therefore the way the framework has consistently operated fairly establishes that it has operated according to its true nature. Deeply embedded traditional ways of conducting government cannot supplant the Constitution or legislation, but they give meaning to the words of a text or supply them. It is an inadmissibly narrow conception of American constitutional law to confine it to the words of the Constitution and to disregard the gloss which life has written upon them. In short, a systematic, unbroken, executive practice, long pursued to the knowledge of the Congress and never before questioned, engaged in by Presidents who have also sworn to uphold the Constitution, making as it were such exercise of power part of the structure of our government, may be treated as a gloss on "executive Power" vested in the President by § 1 of Art. II. . . .

Down to the World War II period, . . . the record is barren of instances comparable to the one before us. Of twelve seizures by President Roosevelt prior to the enactment of the War Labor Disputes Act in June, 1943, three were sanctioned by existing law, and six others were effected after Congress, on December 8, 1941, had declared the existence of a state of war. In this case, reliance on the powers that flow from declared war has been commendably disclaimed by the Solicitor General. Thus the list of executive assertions of the power of seizure in circumstances comparable to the present reduces to three in the six-month period from June to December of 1941. We need not split hairs in comparing those actions to the one before us, though much might be said by way of differentiation. Without passing on their validity, as we are not called upon to do, it suffices to say that these three isolated instances do not add up, either in number, scope, duration or contemporaneous legal justification, to the kind of executive construction of the Constitution revealed in the *Midwest Oil* case. [*United States v. Midwest Oil Co.*, 236 U.S. 459 (1915), excerpted in Chapter Five.] Nor do they come to us sanctioned by long-continued acquiescence of Congress giving decisive weight to a construction by the Executive of its powers . . . .

Justice JACKSON, concurring in the judgment and opinion of the Court.

. . . The actual art of governing under our Constitution does not and cannot conform to judicial definitions of the power of any of its branches based on isolated clauses or even single Articles torn from context. While the Constitution diffuses power the better to secure liberty, it also contemplates that practice will integrate the dispersed powers into a workable government. It enjoins upon its branches separateness but interdependence, autonomy but reciprocity. Presidential powers are not fixed but fluctuate, depending upon their disjunction or conjunction with those of Congress. We may well begin by a somewhat over-simplified grouping of practical situations in which a President may doubt, or others may challenge, his powers, and by distinguishing roughly the legal consequences of this factor of relativity.

1. When the President acts pursuant to an express or implied authorization of Congress, his authority is at its maximum, for it includes all that he possesses in his own right plus all that Congress can delegate.[2] In these circumstances, and in these only, may he be said (for what it may be worth), to personify the federal sovereignty. If his act is held unconstitutional under these circumstances, it usually means that the Federal Government as an undivided whole lacks power. A seizure executed by the President pursuant to an Act of Congress would be supported by the strongest of presumptions and the widest latitude of judicial interpretation, and the burden of persuasion would rest heavily upon any who might attack it.

---

2. It is in this class of cases that we find the broadest recent statements of presidential power, including those relied on here. *United States v. Curtiss-Wright Export Corp.*, 299 U.S. 304, involved, not the question of the President's power to act without congressional authority, but the question of his right to act under and in accord with an Act of Congress. The constitutionality of the Act under which the President had proceeded was assailed on the ground that it delegated legislative powers to the President. . . .

2. When the President acts in absence of either a congressional grant or denial of authority, he can only rely upon his own independent powers, but there is a zone of twilight in which he and Congress may have concurrent authority, or in which its distribution is uncertain. Therefore, congressional inertia, indifference or quiescence may sometimes, at least as a practical matter, enable, if not invite, measures on independent presidential responsibility. In this area, any actual test of power is likely to depend on the imperatives of events and contemporary imponderables rather than on abstract theories of law.[3]

3. When the President takes measures incompatible with the expressed or implied will of Congress, his power is at its lowest ebb, for then he can rely only upon his own constitutional powers minus any constitutional powers of Congress over the matter. Courts can sustain exclusive presidential control in such a case only by disabling the Congress from acting upon the subject. Presidential claim to a power at once so conclusive and preclusive must be scrutinized with caution, for what is at stake is the equilibrium established by our constitutional system.

Into which of these classifications does this executive seizure of the steel industry fit? It is eliminated from the first by admission, for it is conceded that no congressional authorization exists for this seizure. That takes away also the support of the many precedents and declarations which were made in relation, and must be confined, to this category.

Can it then be defended under flexible tests available to the second category? It seems clearly eliminated from that class because Congress has not left seizure of private property an open field but has covered it by three statutory policies inconsistent with this seizure. In cases where the purpose is to supply needs of the Government itself, two courses are provided: one, seizure of a plant which fails to comply with obligatory orders placed by the Government, another, condemnation of facilities, including temporary use under the power of eminent domain. The third is applicable where it is the general economy of the country that is to be protected rather than exclusive governmental interests. None of these were invoked. In choosing a different and inconsistent way of his own, the President cannot claim that it is necessitated or invited by failure of Congress to legislate upon the occasions, grounds and methods for seizure of industrial properties.

This leaves the current seizure to be justified only by the severe tests under the third grouping, where it can be supported only by any remainder of executive power after subtraction of such powers as Congress may have over the subject. In short, we can sustain the President only by holding that seizure of such strike-bound industries is within his domain and beyond control by Congress. Thus, this Court's first review of such seizures occurs under circumstances which leave presidential power most vulnerable to attack and in the least favorable of possible constitutional postures....

The Solicitor General seeks the power of seizure in three clauses of the Executive Article, the first reading, "The executive Power shall be vested in a President of the United States of America." Lest I be thought to exaggerate, I quote the interpretation

---

3. Since the Constitution implies that the writ of habeas corpus may be suspended in certain circumstances but does not say by whom, President Lincoln asserted and maintained it as an executive function in the face of judicial challenge and doubt. Congress eventually ratified his action. Habeas Corpus Act of March 3, 1863, 12 Stat. 755. See Hall, Free Speech in War Time, 21 Col.L.Rev. 526....

which his brief puts upon it: "In our view, this clause constitutes a grant of all the executive powers of which the Government is capable." If that be true, it is difficult to see why the forefathers bothered to add several specific items, including some trifling ones.[9]

The example of such unlimited executive power that must have most impressed the forefathers was the prerogative exercised by George III, and the description of its evils in the Declaration of Independence leads me to doubt that they were creating their new Executive in his image. Continental European examples were no more appealing. And if we seek instruction from our own times, we can match it only from the executive powers in those governments we disparagingly describe as totalitarian. I cannot accept the view that this clause is a grant in bulk of all conceivable executive power but regard it as an allocation to the presidential office of the generic powers thereafter stated.

The clause on which the Government next relies is that "The President shall be Commander in Chief of the Army and Navy of the United States...." These cryptic words have given rise to some of the most persistent controversies in our constitutional history. Of course, they imply something more than an empty title. But just what authority goes with the name has plagued presidential advisers who would not waive or narrow it by nonassertion yet cannot say where it begins or ends. It undoubtedly puts the Nation's armed forces under presidential command. Hence, this loose appellation is sometimes advanced as support for any presidential action, internal or external, involving use of force, the idea being that it vests power to do anything, anywhere, that can be done with an army or navy.

That seems to be the logic of an argument tendered at our bar—that the President having, on his own responsibility, sent American troops abroad derives from that act "affirmative power" to seize the means of producing a supply of steel for them. To quote, "Perhaps the most forceful illustrations of the scope of Presidential power in this connection is the fact that American troops in Korea, whose safety and effectiveness are so directly involved here, were sent to the field by an exercise of the President's constitutional powers." Thus, it is said he has invested himself with "war powers."

I cannot foresee all that it might entail if the Court should indorse this argument. Nothing in our Constitution is plainer than that declaration of a war is entrusted only to Congress. Of course, a state of war may in fact exist without a formal declaration. But no doctrine that the Court could promulgate would seem to me more sinister and alarming than that a President whose conduct of foreign affairs is so largely uncontrolled, and often even is unknown, can vastly enlarge his mastery over the internal affairs of the country by his own commitment of the Nation's armed forces to some foreign venture. I do not, however, find it necessary or appropriate to consider the legal status of the Korean enterprise to discountenance argument based on it.

---

9. "...he may require the Opinion, in writing, of the principal Officer in each of the executive Departments, upon any Subject relating to the Duties of their respective Offices...." U.S.Const. Art. II, § 2. He "...shall Commission all the Officers of the United States." U.S.Const. Art. II, § 3. Matters such as those would seem to be inherent in the Executive if anything is.

Assuming that we are in a war *de facto*, whether it is or is not a war *de jure*, does that empower the Commander in Chief to seize industries he thinks necessary to supply our army? The Constitution expressly places in Congress power "to raise and *support* Armies" and "to *provide* and *maintain* a Navy." (Emphasis supplied.) This certainly lays upon Congress primary responsibility for supplying the armed forces. Congress alone controls the raising of revenues and their appropriation and may determine in what manner and by what means they shall be spent for military and naval procurement. I suppose no one would doubt that Congress can take over war supply as a Government enterprise. On the other hand, if Congress sees fit to rely on free private enterprise collectively bargaining with free labor for support and maintenance of our armed forces, can the Executive because of lawful disagreements incidental to that process, seize the facility for operation upon Government-imposed terms? . . .

We should not use this occasion to circumscribe, much less to contract, the lawful role of the President as Commander in Chief. I should indulge the widest latitude of interpretation to sustain his exclusive function to command the instruments of national force, at least when turned against the outside world for the security of our society. But, when it is turned inward, not because of rebellion but because of a lawful economic struggle between industry and labor, it should have no such indulgence. His command power is not such an absolute as might be implied from that office in a militaristic system but is subject to limitations consistent with a constitutional Republic whose law and policy-making branch is a representative Congress. The purpose of lodging dual titles in one man was to insure that the civilian would control the military, not to enable the military to subordinate the presidential office. . . .

The third clause in which the Solicitor General finds seizure powers is that "he shall take Care that the Laws be faithfully executed. . . . " That authority must be matched against words of the Fifth Amendment that "No person shall be . . . deprived of life, liberty, or property, without due process of law . . . " One gives a governmental authority that reaches so far as there is law, the other gives a private right that authority shall go no farther. These signify about all there is of the principle that ours is a government of laws, not of men, and that we submit ourselves to rulers only if under rules.

The Solicitor General lastly grounds support of the seizure upon nebulous, inherent powers never expressly granted but said to have accrued to the office from the customs and claims of preceding administrations. The plea is for a resulting power to deal with a crisis or an emergency according to the necessities of the case, the unarticulated assumption being that necessity knows no law.

Loose and irresponsible use of adjectives colors all non-legal and much legal discussion of presidential powers. "Inherent" powers, "implied" powers, "incidental" powers, "plenary" powers, "war" powers and "emergency" powers are used, often interchangeably and without fixed or ascertainable meanings.

The vagueness and generality of the clauses that set forth presidential powers afford a plausible basis for pressures within and without an administration for presidential action beyond that supported by those whose responsibility it is to defend his actions in court. The claim of inherent and unrestricted presidential powers has long been a persuasive dialectical weapon in political controversy. While it is not surprising that counsel should grasp support from such unadjudicated claims of power, a judge cannot accept self-serving press statements of the attorney for one of the interested parties as authority in answering a constitutional question, even if the advocate was himself. But prudence has counseled that actual reliance on such nebulous claims stop short of provoking a judicial test. . . .

The appeal, however, that we declare the existence of inherent powers *ex necessitate* to meet an emergency asks us to do what many think would be wise, although it is something the forefathers omitted. They knew what emergencies were, knew the pressures they engender for authoritative action, knew, too, how they afford a ready pretext for usurpation. We may also suspect that they suspected that emergency powers would tend to kindle emergencies. Aside from suspension of the privilege of the writ of habeas corpus in time of rebellion or invasion, when the public safety may require it, they made no express provision for exercise of extraordinary authority because of a crisis.[19] I do not think we rightfully may so amend their work, and, if we could, I am not convinced it would be wise to do so, although many modern nations have forthrightly recognized that war and economic crises may upset the normal balance between liberty and authority. Their experience with emergency powers may not be irrelevant to the argument here that we should say that the Executive, of his own volition, can invest himself with undefined emergency powers.

Germany, after the First World War, framed the Weimar Constitution, designed to secure her liberties in the Western tradition. However, the President of the Republic, without concurrence of the Reichstag, was empowered temporarily to suspend any or all individual rights if public safety and order were seriously disturbed or endangered. This proved a temptation to every government, whatever its shade of opinion, and in 13 years suspension of rights was invoked on more than 250 occasions. Finally, Hitler persuaded President Von Hindenberg to suspend all such rights, and they were never restored. . . .

Great Britain also has fought both World Wars under a sort of temporary dictatorship created by legislation. As Parliament is not bound by written constitutional limitations, it established a crisis government simply by delegation to its Ministers of a larger measure than usual of its own unlimited power, which is exercised under its supervision by Ministers whom it may dismiss. This has been called the "highwater mark in the voluntary surrender of liberty," but, as Churchill put it, "Parliament stands custodian of these surrendered liberties, and its most sacred duty will be to restore them in their fullness when victory has crowned our exertions and our perseverance." Thus, parliamentary control made emergency powers compatible with freedom.

This contemporary foreign experience may be inconclusive as to the wisdom of lodging emergency powers somewhere in a modern government. But it suggests that emergency powers are consistent with free government only when their control is lodged elsewhere than in the Executive who exercises them. That is the safeguard that would be nullified by our adoption of the "inherent powers" formula. Nothing in my experience convinces me that such risks are warranted by any real necessity, although such powers would, of course, be an executive convenience.

In the practical working of our Government we already have evolved a technique within the framework of the Constitution by which normal executive powers may be considerably expanded to meet an emergency. Congress may and has granted ex-

---

19. I exclude, as in a very limited category by itself, the establishment of martial law. Cf. *Ex parte Milligan*, 4 Wall. 2; *Duncan v. Kahanamoku*, 327 U.S. 304.

traordinary authorities which lie dormant in normal times but may be called into play by the Executive in war or upon proclamation of a national emergency. In 1939, upon congressional request, the Attorney General listed ninety-nine such separate statutory grants by Congress of emergency or war-time executive powers. They were invoked from time to time as need appeared. Under this procedure we retain Government by law—special, temporary law, perhaps, but law nonetheless. The public may know the extent and limitations of the powers that can be asserted, and persons affected may be informed from the statute of their rights and duties.

In view of the ease, expedition and safety with which Congress can grant and has granted large emergency powers, certainly ample to embrace this crisis, I am quite unimpressed with the argument that we should affirm possession of them without statute. Such power either has no beginning or it has no end. If it exists, it need submit to no legal restraint. I am not alarmed that it would plunge us straightway into dictatorship, but it is at least a step in that wrong direction.

As to whether there is imperative necessity for such powers, it is relevant to note the gap that exists between the President's paper powers and his real powers. The Constitution does not disclose the measure of the actual controls wielded by the modern presidential office. That instrument must be understood as an Eighteenth-Century sketch of a government hoped for, not as a blueprint of the Government that is. Vast accretions of federal power, eroded from that reserved by the States, have magnified the scope of presidential activity. Subtle shifts take place in the centers of real power that do not show on the face of the Constitution.

Executive power has the advantage of concentration in a single head in whose choice the whole Nation has a part, making him the focus of public hopes and expectations. In drama, magnitude and finality his decisions so far overshadow any others that almost alone he fills the public eye and ear. No other personality in public life can begin to compete with him in access to the public mind through modern methods of communications. By his prestige as head of state and his influence upon public opinion, he exerts a leverage upon those who are supposed to check and balance his power which often cancels their effectiveness.

Moreover, rise of the party system has made a significant extraconstitutional supplement to real executive power. No appraisal of his necessities is realistic which overlooks that he heads a political system as well as a legal system. Party loyalties and interests, sometimes more binding than law, extend his effective control into branches of government other than his own and he often may win, as a political leader, what he cannot command under the Constitution. Indeed, Woodrow Wilson, commenting on the President as leader both of his party and of the Nation, observed, "If he rightly interpret the national thought and boldly insist upon it, he is irresistible.... His office is anything he has the sagacity and force to make it." I cannot be brought to believe that this country will suffer if the Court refuses further to aggrandize the presidential office, already so potent and so relatively immune from judicial review, at the expense of Congress....

[Justice DOUGLAS concurred, characterizing the presidential action as an unauthorized taking of property, which was legislative in nature and therefore invalid. Justices BURTON and CLARK also concurred, stating that Congress had specified methods for dealing with this kind of crisis, with which the President had not complied. Justice CLARK went on to say that in the absence of such legislation, "the President's independent power to act depends upon the gravity of the situation confronting the nation."]

Chief Justice VINSON, with whom Justice REED and Justice MINTON join, dissenting.

... In passing upon the question of presidential powers in this case, we must first consider the context in which those powers were exercised. Those who suggest that this is a case involving extraordinary powers should be mindful that these are extraordinary times. A world not yet recovered from the devastation of World War II has been forced to face the threat of another and more terrifying global conflict....

In 1950, when the United Nations called upon member nations "to render every assistance" to repel aggression in Korea, the United States furnished its vigorous support. For almost two full years, our armed forces have been fighting in Korea, suffering casualties of over 108,000 men. Hostilities have not abated.... Congressional support of the action in Korea has been manifested by provisions for increased military manpower and equipment and for economic stabilization, as hereinafter described....

Congress also directed the President to build up our own defenses. Congress, recognizing the "grim fact ... that the United States is now engaged in a struggle for survival" and that "it is imperative that we now take those necessary steps to make our strength equal to the peril of the hour," granted authority to draft men into the armed forces. As a result, we now have over 3,500,000 men in our armed forces.

Appropriations for the Department of Defense, which had averaged less than $13 billion per year for the three years before attack in Korea, were increased by Congress to $48 billion for fiscal year 1951 and to $60 billion for fiscal year 1952.... The bulk of the increase is for military equipment and supplies—guns, tanks, ships, planes and ammunition—all of which require steel....

Congress recognized the impact of these defense programs upon the economy. Following the attack in Korea, the President asked for authority to requisition property and to allocate and fix priorities for scarce goods. In the Defense Production Act of 1950, Congress granted the powers requested and, in *addition*, granted power to stabilize prices and wages and to provide for settlement of labor disputes arising in the defense program....

The President has the duty to execute the foregoing legislative programs. Their successful execution depends upon continued production of steel and stabilized prices for steel. Accordingly, when the collective bargaining agreements between the Nation's steel producers and their employees, represented by the United Steel Workers, were due to expire on December 31, 1951, and a strike shutting down the entire basic steel industry was threatened, the President acted to avert a complete shutdown of steel production....

[On] April 9, 1952, the President addressed the following Message to Congress:

"*To the Congress of the United States*:

"The Congress is undoubtedly aware of the recent events which have taken place in connection with the management-labor dispute in the steel industry. These events culminated in the action which was taken last night to provide for temporary operation of the steel mills by the Government.

"I took this action with the utmost reluctance. The idea of Government operation of the steel mills is thoroughly distasteful to me and I want to see it ended as soon as possible. However, in the situation which confronted me yesterday, I felt that I could make no other choice. The other alternatives appeared to be even worse—so much worse that I could not accept them.

"One alternative would have been to permit a shut-down in the steel industry. The effects of such a shut-down would have been so immediate and damaging with respect to our efforts to support our Armed Forces and to protect our national security that it made this alternative unthinkable.

"The only way that I know of, other than Government operation, by which a steel shut-down could have been avoided was to grant the demands of the steel industry for a large price increase. I believed and the officials in charge of our stabilization agencies believed that this would have wrecked our stabilization program. I was unwilling to accept the incalculable damage which might be done to our country by following such a course.

"Accordingly, it was my judgment that Government operation of the steel mills for a temporary period was the least undesirable of the courses of action which lay open. In the circumstances, I believed it to be, and now believe it to be, my duty and within my powers as President to follow that course of action.

"It may be that the Congress will deem some other course to be wiser. . . . I do not believe the Congress will favor any of these courses of action, but that is a matter for the Congress to determine. . . . On the basis of the facts that are known to me at this time, I do not believe that immediate congressional action is essential; but I would, of course, be glad to cooperate in developing any legislative proposals which the Congress may wish to consider. . . . "

Twelve days passed without action by Congress. On April 21, 1952, the President sent a letter to the President of the Senate in which he again described the purpose and need for his action and again stated his position that "The Congress can, if it wishes, reject the course of action I have followed in this matter." Congress has not so acted to this date.

Meanwhile, plaintiffs instituted this action in the District Court to compel defendant to return possession of the steel mills seized under Executive Order 10340. . . . We . . . assume without deciding that the courts may go behind a President's finding of fact that an emergency exists. But there is not the slightest basis for suggesting that the President's finding in this case can be undermined. Plaintiffs moved for a preliminary injunction before answer or hearing. Defendant opposed the motion, filing uncontroverted affidavits of Government officials describing the facts underlying the President's order. . . .

Accordingly, if the President has any power under the Constitution to meet a critical situation in the absence of express statutory authorization, there is no basis whatever for criticizing the exercise of such power in this case. . . .

In passing upon the grave constitutional question presented in this case, we must never forget, as Chief Justice Marshall admonished, that the Constitution is "intended to endure for ages to come, and consequently, to be adapted to the various crises of human affairs," and that "[i]ts means are adequate to its ends." Cases do arise presenting questions which could not have been foreseen by the Framers. In such cases, the Constitution has been treated as a living document adaptable to new situations. But we are not called upon today to expand the Constitution to meet a new situation. For, in this case, we need only look to history and time-honored principles of constitutional law—principles that have been applied consistently by all branches of the Government throughout our history. It is those who assert the invalidity of the Executive Order who seek to amend the Constitution in this case....

A review of executive action demonstrates that our Presidents have on many occasions exhibited the leadership contemplated by the Framers when they made the President Commander in Chief, and imposed upon him the trust to "take Care that the Laws be faithfully executed." With or without explicit statutory authorization, Presidents have at such times dealt with national emergencies by acting promptly and resolutely to enforce legislative programs, at least to save those programs until Congress could act. Congress and the courts have responded to such executive initiative with consistent approval....

[In support, the Chief Justice cited Washington's use of militia to quell domestic rebellion, the Proclamation of Neutrality, the Louisiana Purchase, the Monroe Doctrine, Jackson's removal of deposits from the Bank of the United States, various acts by Lincoln in prosecuting the Civil War, Hayes' use of federal troops during the 1877 railroad strike, Cleveland's use of troops in the 1895 Pullman strike, statements on presidential power by Theodore Roosevelt and Taft, Taft's withdrawal of public lands from private acquisition to prevent oil depletion, Wilson's War Labor Board, and FDR's bank holiday and World War II leadership, including wartime seizures of domestic property.]

Focusing now on the situation confronting the President on the night of April 8, 1952, we cannot but conclude that the President was performing his duty under the Constitution to "take Care that the Laws be faithfully executed"—a duty described by President Benjamin Harrison as "the central idea of the office."

The President reported to Congress the morning after the seizure that he acted because a work stoppage in steel production would immediately imperil the safety of the Nation by preventing execution of the legislative programs for procurement of military equipment. And, while a shutdown could be averted by granting the price concessions requested by plaintiffs, granting such concessions would disrupt the price stabilization program also enacted by Congress. Rather than fail to execute either legislative program, the President acted to execute both.

Much of the argument in this case has been directed at straw men. We do not now have before us the case of a President acting solely on the basis of his own notions of the public welfare. Nor is there any question of unlimited executive power in this case. The President himself closed the door to any such claim when he sent his Message to Congress stating his purpose to abide by any action of Congress, whether approving or disapproving his seizure action. Here, the President immediately made sure that Congress was fully informed of the temporary action he had taken only to preserve the legislative programs from destruction until Congress could act.

The absence of a specific statute authorizing seizure of the steel mills as a mode of executing the laws—both the military procurement program and the anti-inflation program—has not until today been thought to prevent the President from executing the laws. Unlike an administrative commission confined to the enforcement of the statute under which it was created, or the head of a department when administering a particular statute, the President is a constitutional officer charged with taking care that a "mass of legislation" be executed. Flexibility as to mode of execution to meet critical situations is a matter of practical necessity. This practical construction of the

"Take Care" clause, advocated by John Marshall, was adopted by this Court in *In re Neagle, In re Debs* and other cases cited *supra....*

There is no statute prohibiting seizure as a method of enforcing legislative programs. Congress has in no wise indicated that its legislation is not to be executed by the taking of private property (subject of course to the payment of just compensation) if its legislation cannot otherwise be executed. Indeed, the Universal Military Training and Service Act authorizes the seizure of any plant that fails to fill a Government contract or the properties of any steel producer that fails to allocate steel as directed for defense production. And the Defense Production Act authorizes the President to requisition equipment and condemn real property needed without delay in the defense effort. Where Congress authorizes seizure in instances not necessarily crucial to the defense program, it can hardly be said to have disclosed an intention to prohibit seizures where essential to the execution of that legislative program....

The President's action served the same purposes as a judicial stay entered to maintain the status quo in order to preserve the jurisdiction of a court.... In *United States v. Midwest Oil Co.*, 236 U.S. 459, this Court approved executive action where, as here, the President acted to preserve an important matter until Congress could act—even though his action in that case was contrary to an express statute. In this case, there is no statute prohibiting the action taken by the President in a matter not merely important but threatening the very safety of the Nation. Executive inaction in such a situation, courting national disaster, is foreign to the concept of energy and initiative in the Executive as created by the Founding Fathers. The Constitution was itself "adopted in a period of grave emergency.... While emergency does not create power, emergency may furnish the occasion for the exercise of power." The Framers knew, as we should know in these times of peril, that there is real danger in Executive weakness. There is no cause to fear Executive tyranny so long as the laws of Congress are being faithfully executed. Certainly there is no basis for fear of dictatorship when the Executive acts, as he did in this case, only to save the situation until Congress could act.

Plaintiffs place their primary emphasis on the Labor Management Relations Act of 1947, hereinafter referred to as the Taft-Hartley Act, but do not contend that that Act contains any provision prohibiting seizure. Under the Taft-Hartley Act, as under the Wagner Act, collective bargaining and the right to strike are at the heart of our national labor policy. Taft-Hartley preserves the right to strike in any emergency, however serious, subject only to an 80-day delay in cases of strikes imperiling the national health and safety....

Plaintiffs admit that the emergency procedures of Taft-Hartley are not mandatory. Nevertheless, plaintiffs apparently argue that, since Congress did provide the 80-day injunction method for dealing with emergency strikes, the President cannot claim that an emergency exists until the procedures of Taft-Hartley have been exhausted. This argument was not the basis of the District Court's opinion and, whatever merit the argument might have had following the enactment of Taft-Hartley, it loses all force when viewed in light of the statutory pattern confronting the President in this case.

In Title V of the Defense Production Act of 1950, Congress . . . authorized the President to initiate labor-management conferences and to take action appropriate to carrying out the recommendations of such conferences and the provisions of Title V. (§ 502) Due regard is to be given to collective bargaining practice and stabilization policies and no action taken is to be inconsistent with Taft-Hartley and other laws. (§ 503)....

The President authorized the Wage Stabilization Board (WSB), which administers the wage stabilization functions of Title IV of the Defense Production Act, also to deal with labor disputes affecting the defense program.... Aware that a technique separate from Taft-Hartley had been devised, members of Congress attempted to divest the WSB of its disputes powers. These attempts were defeated in the House, were not brought to a vote in the Senate, and the Defense Production Act was extended through June 30, 1952, without change in the disputes powers of the WSB. Certainly this legislative creation of a new procedure for dealing with defense disputes negatives any notion that Congress intended the earlier and discretionary Taft-Hartley procedure to be an exclusive procedure.

Accordingly, as of December 22, 1951, the President had a choice between alternate procedures for settling the threatened strike in the steel mills: one route created to deal with peacetime disputes; the other route specially created to deal with disputes growing out of the defense and stabilization program. There is no question of by-passing a statutory procedure because both of the routes available to the President in December were based upon statutory authorization. Both routes were available in the steel dispute....

When the President acted on April 8, he had exhausted the procedures for settlement available to him. Taft-Hartley was a route parallel to, not connected with, the WSB procedure. The strike had been delayed 99 days as contrasted with the maximum delay of 80 days under Taft-Hartley. There had been a hearing on the issues in dispute and bargaining which promised settlement up to the very hour before seizure had broken down. Faced with immediate national peril through stoppage in steel production on the one hand and faced with destruction of the wage and price legislative programs on the other, the President took temporary possession of the steel mills as the only course open to him consistent with his duty to take care that the laws be faithfully executed.

Plaintiffs' property was taken and placed in the possession of the Secretary of Commerce to prevent any interruption in steel production. It made no difference whether the stoppage was caused by a union-management dispute over terms and conditions of employment, a union-Government dispute over wage stabilization or a management-Government dispute over price stabilization. The President's action has thus far been effective, not in settling the dispute, but in saving the various legislative programs at stake from destruction until Congress could act in the matter.

---

1. Like many of the separation of powers cases in this book, *Youngstown* was litigated under great time pressure, and in the glare of intense national publicity. For a history of the case, *see* A. Westin, The Anatomy of a Constitutional Law Case (1958). Such trying circumstances can adversely affect the quality of the advocacy for both sides. A famous colloquy that haunted the government throughout occurred between Assistant Attorney General Baldridge and Judge Pine in the District Court (Westin, *supra*, at 64):

Mr. Baldridge: Section 1, Article II, of the Constitution reposes all of the executive power in the Chief Executive. I think that the distinction that the Constitution itself makes between the powers of the Executive and the powers of the legislative branch of the Government are significant and important. In so far as the Executive is concerned, all executive power is vested in the President. In so far as legislative powers are concerned, the Congress has only those powers that are specifically delegated to it, plus the implied power to carry out the powers specifically enumerated.

The Court: So, when the sovereign people adopted the Constitution, it ... limited the powers of the Congress and limited the powers of the judiciary, but it did not limit the powers of the Executive. Is that what you say?

Mr. Baldridge: That is the way we read Article II of the Constitution.

The Court: I see. . . .

Baldridge's argument produced an immediate storm of criticism. (Indeed, public and press reaction to the seizure was negative throughout.) President Truman himself issued a disclaimer (Westin, *supra*, at 67): "The powers of the President are derived from the Constitution, and they are limited, of course, by the provisions of the Constitution, particularly those that protect the rights of individuals." The government issued another disclaimer in the form of a "Supplemental Memorandum" that it filed in District Court, but the damage was done. The steel companies never tired of repeating Baldridge's assertion in their briefs.

2. What *were* the best arguments available to the Government in *Youngstown*? For the arguments actually made in the Supreme Court, review Chief Justice Vinson's dissent, which tracks parts of the government's briefs closely. (Apparently, Vinson played another, less savory role in the litigation. R. Donovan, Tumultuous Years, The Presidency of Harry S Truman 1949-53, 386-87 (1982), reports that Vinson, a close friend of Truman's, advised the President that it would be constitutional to seize the mills.) The government stressed the emergency nature of the seizure, and placed it against the background of other emergency actions by past Presidents. In his concurrence, Justice Clark suggested that courts can and should assess degrees of emergency. Do you agree? How should the government have argued the respective institutional competence of the branches on this point?

3. The government also stressed a series of cases in which the Court had upheld "inherent" presidential power to act without statutory authority or even contrary to a statute. There are three primary precedents, all of which we consider in more detail in Chapter Five. In *In re Neagle*, 135 U.S. 1 (1890), the Court upheld inherent presidential authority to assign a U.S. Marshal as a personal bodyguard for a Supreme Court Justice. In *In re Debs*, 158 U.S. 564 (1895), the Court upheld President Cleveland's inherent authority to seek an injunction to end the Pullman strike. And in *United States v. Midwest Oil Co.*, 236 U.S. 459 (1915), the Court allowed the President, contrary to statute, to withdraw public lands from private acquisition, on the basis of a longstanding executive practice acquiesced in by Congress. As a litigant or a judge in *Youngstown*, how much weight would you have assigned these precedents? Where does *Youngstown* leave the doctrine of inherent powers?

4. Justices Frankfurter and Jackson attached great significance to congressional rejection in 1947 of a proposal to confer seizure authority on the executive, which would have permitted actions such as President Truman's. Is this a legitimate approach? Should Congress, in rejecting a proposal, be deemed to legislate that the authority proposed is forbidden? Or, alternatively, is the fact that Congress knew of a proposal and rejected it simply part of a relevant "adjudicative context"? Should

it be persuasive for the government to argue that Congress did not foresee the particular emergency that arose in 1952, so that its rejection of advance seizure authority should not be construed as a blanket denial?

5. President Truman could have invoked the Taft-Hartley Act to stop the strike for eighty days, but declined to do so. He argued that there would be a temporary shutdown for a week or two while the Act's mechanism was engaged, and that the strike could resume after the "cooling-off period" if no settlement had been reached. Donovan, *supra*, at 385. What weight should the courts give to the availability of a statutory alternative to a presidential action, and to the President's reasons for eschewing it? Similarly, what weight should the courts have given to Truman's messages to Congress, inviting ratification of his action, and to congressional silence in response? If Congress has provided a statutory avenue for presidential action, must it also affirmatively negate other courses he might prefer, either in advance or in the event?

Can a court go behind a President's stated justifications to his "real" reasons for refusing to invoke statutory authority? In *Youngstown*, the underlying stakes were whether the union would receive a wage increase, and whether the steel companies would receive a compensating price increase. President Truman was a friend of labor and an enemy of the Taft-Hartley Act. He thought the unions deserved a wage increase (which they could be granted if the government could operate the mills), and that the companies should absorb the cost with little or no price increase. Is that a good reason to forego available statutory remedies?

6. Recall Justice Jackson's poignant observation, quoted at the beginning of this book, on "the poverty of really useful and unambiguous authority applicable to concrete problems of executive power as they actually present themselves." Can you crystallize "really useful" guidance for future problems from Jackson's concededly "over-simplified grouping of practical situations"?

Consider the following summary of Jackson's approach: there exist zones of exclusive executive power and of exclusive legislative power, which each branch may exercise without interference by the other, and:

> a twilight zone of concurrent power, [in which] either the President or Congress can act in the absence of initiative by the other. *If both attempt to act in ways that bring their wills into conflict, the deadlock must be resolved in favor of congressional action through valid legislation, which includes legislation passed over a presidential veto.*

Pollack, et al., Indochina: The Constitutional Crisis, Pt. II, 116 Cong. Rec. 16,478 (1978) (emphasis added). Is this accurate? In preparing legal advice to the President on a question of first impression, how do you think you would be influenced by this analysis?

7. Should the Court have avoided the ultimate constitutional issues by accepting the government's claim that "just compensation" under the Fifth Amendment would be available as a fully adequate remedy? On the complexities of this question, *see* P. Bator, P. Mishkin, D. Shapiro & H. Wechsler, Hart and Wechsler's The Federal Courts and the Federal System 1397-1406 (2d ed. 1973).

8. President Roosevelt's Attorney General throughout 1940 and during most of 1941 was Robert H. Jackson. In that role, he had supported controversial exercises

of presidential power in the transfer of over-age destroyers to Great Britain in exchange for air bases, *see* 39 Op. A.G. 484, and the seizure of the North American Aviation Plant. At 343 U.S. 649 & n.17, he distinguished that seizure from the one at bar, and remarked: "I do not regard it as a precedent for this, but, even if I did, I should not bind present judicial judgment by earlier partisan advocacy." Should a court disregard Attorney General opinions as merely an advocate's statements on behalf of a client? Do you think Attorneys General view their role that way?

9. As a Department of Justice lawyer, what advice would you render in the following circumstances: during a recess of Congress, natural disaster hits the State of Washington: a week's continuous rain makes air travel extremely hazardous; flooding makes main roads impassable. To save hundreds of lives in the flooded areas, the government must transport food and medical supplies. Only rail transportation can accomplish the task, and the relevant railroad is on strike. The President asks the Attorney General if he has authority to seize the railroad for 12 hours. No statute expressly permits or forbids a seizure; a previous administration had proposed the enactment of such authority and the proposal died in committee.

Would your advice differ if no proposal had been submitted? Would your advice differ if Congress had voted on the proposal and defeated it? Would it make a difference if the Secretary of Labor is arguing against a seizure on grounds that it will effectively end the strike and that weather reports indicate that air drops may be feasible sometime soon?

B. Congressional Delegation and Its Limits

In *Youngstown*, the parties argued over whether Congress had granted the President too *little* power to take action. Here we consider situations in which it is argued that Congress has granted the President too *much* power, thereby defaulting on its legislative responsibilities. The delegation doctrine, which states limits to the power of Congress to transfer broad authority to the executive, does not have a clear textual basis in the Constitution. True, Article I, section one, provides that "[a]ll legislative powers herein granted shall be vested in . . . Congress," but section eight authorizes Congress to "make all Laws . . . necessary and proper for carrying into Execution the foregoing Powers, and all other Powers vested by this Constitution in the Government of the United States, or in any Department or Officer thereof."

Both the assumption that Congress may grant the executive some measure of discretion and the concern that underlies the delegation doctrine surfaced at the Constitutional Convention. Madison moved that the President be authorized "to execute such other powers (not legislative nor judiciary in their nature) as may from time to time be delegated by the national Legislature." 1 M. Farrand, The Records of the Federal Convention of 1787, 67 (rev. ed. 1937) (Madison's notes). The suggestion was defeated after an argument that the phrase was surplusage to the general power to execute the laws; Madison demurred that it might "serve to prevent doubts and misconstructions." The parenthetical phrase, however, came not from Madison but from Pinckney, who proposed its addition to forestall any delegation of "improper powers."

Apparently, then, the framers thought that Congress would need to delegate discretion to the executive, but that somewhere there were limits. Both early congressional actions and the fragmentary case law of the framers' generation are consistent with such a general attitude. Between 1794 and 1810, Congress repeatedly authorized the President to lay or remove trade embargoes, amid some discussion whether the power to initiate or suspend a law was an exclusive legislative function that could not be delegated. Fisher, *Delegating Power to the President*, 19 Emory J. Public L. 251, 253-56 (1970). In *The Brig Aurora*, 11 U.S. (7 Cranch) 382 (1813), the Supreme Court gave the problem short shrift. The Court upheld a delegation to the President to lift embargoes when France and England "ceased to violate the neutral commerce of the United States." To an argument that Congress had unconstitutionally transferred its legislative power to the President, the Court (per Justice Johnson) responded that "we can see no sufficient reason, why the legislature should not exercise its discretion in reviving the [statute] either expressly or conditionally, as their judgment should direct."

Chief Justice Marshall's contribution to the subject occurred in *Wayman v. Southard*, 23 U.S. (10 Wheat.) 1 (1825), a case involving a delegation of power to the courts, not the executive. The Judiciary Act of 1789 had authorized the courts to make rules for the conduct of their business. Marshall rejected a challenge to the constitutionality of this provision (23 U.S. at 42-43, 46):

> It will not be contended that Congress can delegate to the Courts, or to any other tribunals, powers which are strictly and exclusively legislative. But Congress may certainly delegate to others, powers which the legislature may rightfully exercise itself.... The line has not been exactly drawn which separates these important subjects, which must be entirely regulated by the legislature itself, from those of less interest, in which a general provision may be made, and power given to those who are to act under such general provisions to fill up the details....

> The difference between the departments undoubtedly is, that the legislature makes, the executive executes, and the judiciary construes the law; but the maker of the law may commit something to the discretion of the other departments, and the precise boundary of this power is a subject of delicate and difficult inquiry, into which a Court will not enter unnecessarily.

Marshall was right—the limits of permissible delegation raise a "delicate and difficult inquiry," as later cases have shown. Until well into this century, the major delegation cases (except for *Wayman*) all involved direct grants of power to the President (rather than to subordinate officers) in the field of foreign relations. The Court displayed a willingness to uphold the delegations, perhaps because the need for executive discretion in foreign affairs is readily apparent. Yet, as we see in Marshall's gropings in *Wayman*, the Court was never very comfortable in its articulation of underlying theory.

A leading case, *Field v. Clark*, 143 U.S. 649 (1892), illustrates the problems. A statute allowed the President to suspend free import of certain goods if he found that the exporting country was not according American goods reciprocal treatment. For the Court, the first Justice Harlan stated a strict rule: "That Congress cannot delegate legislative power to the President is a principle universally recognized as vital to the integrity and maintenance of the system of government ordained by the Constitution." He then upheld the statute, however, by characterizing the President's role as limited to fact-finding, and therefore execution: "He was the mere agent of the law-making department to ascertain and declare the event upon which its expressed will was to take effect."

In *Field*, the Court essayed a functional distinction between legislative and executive power, between policymaking and factfinding. Of course, there is no clear line between these functions. *Field* itself illustrates this—the operative terms of the statute called on the President to act when he deemed foreign duties "reciprocally unequal and unreasonable." Plainly, a new doctrinal formulation was needed, one that would allow Congress to grant substantial policymaking discretion to the growing federal bureaucracy. Early in this century, the Court shifted to a requirement that legislation contain "standards" to limit the scope of executive discretion. A prominent case is *J. W. Hampton, Jr. & Co. v. United States*, 276 U.S. 394 (1928), in which the Court upheld another statute allowing the President to equalize tariff rates. The Court concluded that "if Congress shall lay down . . . an intelligible principle to which the [executive] is directed to conform, [that] is not a forbidden delegation of legislative power."

The standards requirement appeared to be an ideal marriage of principle with necessity. Congress cannot legislate in advance for every eventuality, and wisdom may lie in deferring to the executive's greater capacity to respond to unfolding events. Yet if an "intelligible principle" exists to guide the executive, the rule of law can be preserved. Nevertheless, the Court quickly began honoring the standards doctrine mainly in the breach, as it approved a series of extremely broad delegations to administrative agencies. (For example, the Court allowed railroad regulation under "just and reasonable rates," broadcast licensing in the "public interest, convenience, or necessity," and trade regulation of "unfair methods of competition.") To many observers, the doctrine seemed to lack teeth. The onset of the Great Depression in the 1930s would alter that perception, if temporarily.

The primary delegation cases of the 1930s involved the National Industrial Recovery Act of 1933 (NIRA), at one time President Roosevelt's flagship legislation. Like all major cases, they must be understood in historical context, and the context for these was truly extraordinary. It included FDR's war with the Court, which we consider with materials on judicial appointments and the ill-fated Court-packing plan (Chapter Four *infra*). It also included the explosion of legislative and executive activity, beginning with the "Hundred Days," that transformed both the face of American government and the Presidency.

In the depths of the economic emergency at Roosevelt's inauguration, the analogy to wartime crisis was easy to make. Early New Deal legislation borrowed government structure and procedure from emergency responses to World War I. Indeed, FDR's first official action, declaration of a bank holiday, rested for authority on the Trading with the Enemy Act of 1917. *See* Belknap, *The New Deal and the Emergency Powers Doctrine*, 62 Tex. L. Rev. 67, 73 (1983). It was hoped that judicial precedent accommodating the wartime actions could be relied on as well, but that was not to be.

An introduction to the times and to the NIRA is provided by James MacGregor Burns, in Roosevelt: The Lion and the Fox 166-93 (1956). As you read this history, consider what lessons it contains for Congress in delegating power in times of crisis, and for the executive in exercising it. Also, consider the effect of this background on the Supreme Court in its later consideration of the constitutional issues:

Summoned by the new President, Congress convened in special session on Thursday, March 9. While freshman members were still looking for their seats, the two houses hastily organized and received a presidential message asking for legislation to control resumption of banking. The milling representatives could hardly wait to act. By unanimous consent Democratic leaders introduced an emergency banking act to confirm Roosevelt's proclamation and to grant him new powers over banking and currency. Completed by the President and his advisers at two o'clock that morning, the bill was still in rough form. But even during the meager forty minutes allotted to the debate, shouts of "Vote! Vote!" echoed from the floor.... The House promptly passed the bill without a record vote; the Senate approved it a few hours later; the President signed it by nine o'clock....

Originally [FDR] had planned for Congress to adjourn after enacting the first set of bills, then to reassemble when permanent legislation was ready. But why not strike again and again while the mood of the country was so friendly? The leaders were willing to hold Congress in session; a host of presidential advisers were at work in a dozen agencies, in hotel rooms, anywhere they could find a desk, drawing up bills. The result was more of the fast and staccato action that would go down in history as the "Hundred Days."...

Roosevelt was following no master program—no "economic panaceas or fancy plans," as he later called them derisively.... The Chief Executive was Chief Legislator. It was only at the level of the presidential office that party interests, the crisscrossing legislative blocs, and the bustling bureaucrats were given some measure of integration in meeting national problems.... Nothing better exemplified this pragmatism—both in the manner it was drawn up and in its major provisions—than the National Industrial Recovery Act.... As the mainspring of the early New Deal, this measure for two years embodied its hopes and its liabilities....

[T]he NRA had its immediate origin with a number of persons working separately in Washington during the interregnum. Several congressmen introduced bills to modify antitrust laws in order to prevent "unfair and excessive" competition. Business representatives in Washington wanted to bring some order out of anarchy by establishing stronger associations or councils in the main sectors of industry, trade, and finance, with some power of self-government... . Some persons favored huge governmental loans to industry; others wanted to step up public works and direct relief....

The resulting bill did not have easy going in Congress. It was beset on all sides by groups asserting that antitrust laws must not be relaxed, or that the bill was a "sellout" to industry, or that it regimented industry too much, or that it failed to provide for currency inflation. Would Roosevelt's strategy of combining many disparate proposals, thereby gaining support from various elements in Congress, offset the voting strength of the opposition should the dissident groups combine against the bill? His strategy worked, but only because the great bulk of congressmen had an almost blind faith in him ... and because ticklish political issues were left to the President to decide by delegation of power....

The final act was a compromise among many groups and theories. Industrial councils could draw up codes of fair competition, but these had to be approved by the President. These codes were exempted from antitrust laws, but monop-olistic practices were still barred. The essence of the measure was voluntary self-government by industry.... [L]abor received a vague guarantee of the right to bargain collectively with employers through their own representatives, and equally vague provisions for wage and hour standards in the new codes. In an entirely different title of the bill, over three billion dollars were authorized for a huge spending effort through public works....

If the New Deal had circus-like qualities during the first years, the center ring was occupied by the National Recovery Administration, and the ringmaster presented a fresh new visage on the American scene. General Hugh S. Johnson looked like the old cavalry man that he was.... Johnson's main task was to induce businessmen to draw up codes of fair competition, which on the Pres-ident's approval had the full force of law. Administered under the general's supervision by a code authority in each industry, the codes were supposed to stop wasteful competition, to bring about more orderly pricing and selling policies, and to establish higher wages, shorter hours, and better working con-ditions for workers....

Within weeks the NRA burst on the American people like a national call to arms. The NRA eagle was suddenly in every shop window.... Almost at the start the President had virtually lost control of the NRA. He told the cabinet one day how Johnson... had rushed into his office, and handed the President three codes to sign. As Roosevelt was signing the last one, Johnson looked at his watch, said he had five minutes to catch his plane, and dashed out, the codes in his pocket. "He hasn't been seen since," Roosevelt added brightly. The Pres-ident was hardly more than a front man.... Johnson himself had to delegate huge policy-making powers to hastily summoned businessmen who might or might not be representative of the myriad interests in their industries. And in the first flush of enthusiasm the NRA coverage was extended so far that the machinery was nearly swamped....

By the end of 1933 the NRA eagle was fluttering through heavy weather. "N.R.A. is the worst law ever passed," some disillusioned Cleveland grocers wired the President.... [T]he President could not ignore the protests. In March 1934 he appointed a review board... which soon was reporting that the codes had allowed the more powerful interests to seize control or extend their control of industries. Roosevelt trimmed NRA's powers, limited its jurisdiction, eased Johnson out, and put a more domesticated chief, Donald Richberg, in his place. But by the time the Supreme Court [considered the NRA's constitutionality], it was near administrative and political collapse.

Against this backdrop, the Supreme Court decided two challenges to the NIRA. The first, in January 1935, assailed the "hot oil" code issued under section 9(c). The NIRA sought to protect the petroleum industry from a flood of newly discovered oil that was depressing the market. Section 9(c) provided (48 Stat. 200 (1933)):

> The President is authorized to prohibit the transportation in interstate and foreign commerce of petroleum... produced or withdrawn from storage in excess of the amount permitted... by any state law or valid regulation....

The President issued an executive order prohibiting the interstate shipment of oil violating state-imposed limits. Oil producers and refiners sought an injunction against the program. In *Panama Refining Co. v. Ryan*, 293 U.S. 388 (1935), the Supreme Court held section 9(c) unconstitutional, in an opinion by Chief Justice Hughes:

> Section 9(c) does not state whether, or in what circumstances or under what conditions, the President is to prohibit the transportation of the amount of petroleum ... produced in excess of the state's permission. It establishes no criterion to govern the President's course. It does not require any finding by the President as a condition of his action. The Congress in § 9(c) thus declares no policy as to the transportation of the excess production. So far as this section is concerned, it gives to the President an unlimited authority to determine the policy and to lay down the prohibition, or not to lay it down, as he may see fit. And disobedience to his order is made a crime punishable by fine and imprisonment.
>
> We examine the context to ascertain if it furnishes a declaration of policy or a standard of action, which can be deemed to relate to the subject of section 9(c) and thus to imply what is not here expressed.... But the other provisions of section 9 afford no ground for implying a limitation of the broad grant of authority in section 9(c).... We turn to the other provisions of Title I of the act. The first section is a "declaration of policy."[6] ... It is manifest that this broad outline is simply an introduction of the Act, leaving the legislative policy as to particular subjects to be declared and defined, if at all, by the subsequent sections.... [After further canvassing the statute, the Court found no limitations on the grant of authority in Section 9(c).]
>
> The Congress manifestly is not permitted to abdicate, or to transfer to others, the essential legislative functions with which it is ... vested. Undoubtedly legislation must often be adapted to complex conditions involving a host of details with which the national legislature cannot deal directly. The Constitution has never been regarded as denying to the Congress the necessary resources of flexibility and practicality which will enable it to perform its function in laying down policies and establishing standards, while leaving to select instrumentalities the making of subordinate rules within prescribed limits and the determination of facts to which the policy as declared by the legislature is to apply. Without capacity to give authorizations of that sort we should have the anomaly of a legislative power which in many circumstances calling for its exertion would be but a futility. But the constant recognition of the necessity and validity of such provisions, and the wide range of administrative authority which has been developed by means of them, cannot be allowed to obscure the limitations of the authority to delegate if our constitutional system is to be maintained.

---

6. The text of § 1 is as follows:

"Section 1.... It is hereby declared to be the policy of Congress to remove obstructions to the free flow of interstate and foreign commerce which tend to diminish the amount thereof; and to provide for the general welfare by promoting the organization of industry, for the purpose of cooperative action among trade groups to induce and maintain united action of labor and management under adequate governmental sanctions and supervision, to eliminate unfair competitive practices, to promote the fullest possible utilization of the present productive capacity of industries, to avoid undue restriction of production (except as may be temporarily required), to increase the consumption of industrial and agricultural products by increasing purchasing power, to reduce and relieve unemployment, to improve standards of labor, and otherwise to rehabilitate industry and to conserve natural resources."

The Court has had frequent occasion to refer to these limitations and to review the course of congressional action.... [I]n every case in which the question has been raised, the Court has recognized that there are limits on delegation which there is no constitutional authority to transcend. We think that § 9(c) goes beyond those limits. As to the transportation of oil products in excess of state permission, the Congress has declared no policy, has established no standard, has laid down no rule.... If § 9(c) were held valid, it would be idle to pretend that anything would be left of limitations upon the power of the Congress to delegate its law-making function....

Justice Cardozo dissented:

My point of difference with the majority of the court is narrow. I concede that to uphold the delegation there is need to discover in the terms of the act a standard reasonably clear whereby discretion must be governed. I deny that such a standard is lacking in respect of the prohibitions permitted by this section when the act with all its reasonable implications is considered as a whole. What the standard is becomes the pivotal inquiry.

As to the nature of the *act* which the President is authorized to perform there is no need for implication. That at least is definite beyond the possibility of challenge.... He is not left to roam at will among all the possible subjects of interstate transportation, picking and choosing as he pleases.... He has choice, though within limits, as to the occasion, but none whatever as to the means. The means have been prescribed by Congress. There has been no grant to the Executive of any roving commission to inquire into evils and then, upon discovering them, do anything he pleases. His act being thus defined, what else must he ascertain in order to regulate his discretion and bring the power into play? The answer is not given if we look to § 9(c) only, but it comes to us by implication from a view of other sections where the standards are defined. The prevailing opinion concedes that a standard will be as effective if imported into § 9(c) by reasonable implication as if put there in so many words. If we look to the whole structure of the statute, the test is plainly this, that the President is to forbid the transportation of the oil when he believes, in the light of the conditions of the industry as disclosed from time to time, that the prohibition will tend to effectuate the declared policies of the act—not merely his own conception of its policies, undirected by any extrinsic guide, but the policies announced by § 1 in the forefront of the statute as an index to the meaning of everything that follows....

A declared policy of Congress...is "to eliminate unfair competitive practices." Beyond question an unfair competitive practice exists when "hot oil" is transported in interstate commerce with the result that law-abiding dealers must compete with lawbreakers. Here is one of the standards set up in the act to guide the President's discretion. Another declared policy of Congress is "to conserve natural resources." Beyond question the disregard of statutory quotas is wasting the oil fields in Texas and other states, and putting in jeopardy of exhaustion one of the treasures of the nation.... Here is a second standard. Another declared policy of Congress is to "promote the fullest possible utilization of the present productive capacity of industries," and "except as may be temporarily required" to "avoid undue restriction of production."... The ascertainment of these facts at any time or place was a task too intricate and special to be performed by Congress itself through a general enactment in advance of the event. All that Congress could safely do was to declare the act to be done and the policies to be promoted, leaving to the delegate of its power the ascertainment of the shifting facts that would determine the relation between the doing of the act and the attainment of the stated ends. That is what it did. It said to the President, in substance: You are to consider whether the transportation of oil in excess of the statutory quotas is offensive to one or more of the policies enumerated in section 1 . . . If these standards or some of them have been flouted with the result of a substantial obstruction to industrial recovery, you may then by a prohibitory order eradicate the mischief.

I am not unmindful of the argument that the President has the privilege of choice between one standard and another, acting or failing to act according to an estimate of values that is individual and personal. To describe his conduct thus is to ignore the essence of his function. What he does is to inquire into the industrial facts as they exist from time to time. These being ascertained, he is not to prefer one standard to another in any subjective attitude of mind, in any personal or wilful way. He is to study the facts objectively, the violation of a standard impelling him to action or inaction according to its observed effect upon industrial recovery—the ultimate end . . . to which all the other ends are tributary and mediate.

Do you agree with the majority or with Justice Cardozo on the presence of a standard in section 9(c)? Is he guilty of picking and choosing among conflicting policies in section 1?

A challenge to the heart of the NIRA reached the Court in *A.L.A. Schechter Poultry Corp. v. United States*, 295 U.S. 495 (1935). Section 3 provided that trade associations could promulgate codes of "fair competition," which, upon approval by the President, would have the force of law. The President was authorized to approve a code only if he found that the trade association was representative of the industry, that the code was not designed to promote monopolies, and that the code would carry out the general policies of the Act. A trade group proposed a "poultry code"; the President approved it; the Schechters were convicted for violating it. They appealed.

In another opinion by Chief Justice Hughes, the Supreme Court invalidated the statute, on two grounds. First, the Court held that Congress had exceeded its powers to regulate interstate commerce. (Other New Deal legislation also fell for this reason, until the Court's famous "switch in time" that led to wholesale approval of New Deal legislation.) Second, the Court held that the code-making authority conferred by section 3 was an unconstitutional delegation of legislative power. Again the Chief Justice found no adequate standard in Title I of the Act. He then distinguished the recent cases that had upheld broad delegations of authority to administrative agencies:

The Federal Trade Commission Act (§ 5) introduced the expression "unfair methods of competition," which were declared to be unlawful. That was an expression new in the law. . . . What are "unfair methods of competition" are thus to be determined in particular instances, upon evidence, in the light of particular competitive conditions and of what is found to be a specific and substantial public interest. To make this possible, Congress set up a special procedure. A Commission, a quasi-judicial body, was created. Provision was made for formal complaint, for notice and hearing, for appropriate findings of fact supported by adequate evidence, and for judicial review to give assurance that the action of the Commission is taken within its statutory authority.

In providing for codes, the [NIRA] dispenses with this administrative procedure and with any administrative procedure of an analogous character. But the difference between the code plan of the Recovery Act and the scheme of the Federal Trade Commission Act lies not only in procedure but in subject matter. . . . The "fair competition" of the codes has a much broader range [than the FTC's delegation] and a new significance. . . .

Such a sweeping delegation of legislative power finds no support in the decisions upon which the Government relies. By the Interstate Commerce Act, Congress has itself provided a code of laws regulating the activities of the common carriers subject to the Act, in order to assure the performance of their services upon just and reasonable terms, with adequate facilities and without unjust discrimination. Congress from time to time has elaborated its requirements, as needs have been disclosed. To facilitate the application of the standards prescribed by the Act, Congress has provided an expert body. That administrative agency, in dealing with particular cases, is required to act upon notice and hearings, and its orders must be supported by findings of fact which in turn are sustained by evidence. . . .

Similarly, we have held that the Radio Act of 1927 established standards to govern radio communications and, in view of the limited number of available broadcasting frequencies, Congress authorized allocation and licenses. The authority of the [Federal Radio] Commission to grant licenses "as public convenience, interest or necessity requires" was limited by the nature of radio communications, and by the scope, character, and quality of the services to be rendered and the relative advantages to be derived through distribution of facilities. These standards established by Congress were to be enforced upon hearing, and evidence, by an administrative body acting under statutory restrictions adapted to the particular activity.

This time Justice Cardozo concurred:

The delegated power of legislation which has found expression in this code is not canalized within banks that keep it from overflowing. It is unconfined and vagrant . . . . Here, in the case before us, is an attempted delegation not confined to any [actions] identified or described by reference to a standard. Here in effect is a roving commission to inquire into evils and upon discovery correct them.

If codes of fair competition are codes eliminating "unfair" methods of competition ascertained upon inquiry to prevail in one industry or another, there is no unlawful delegation of legislative functions when the President is directed to inquire into such practices and denounce them when discovered. For many years a like power has been committed to the Federal Trade Commission with the approval of this court in a long series of decisions. Delegation in such circumstances is born of the necessities of the occasion. The industries of the country are too many and diverse to make it possible for Congress, in respect of matters such as these, to legislate directly with adequate appreciation of varying conditions. . . .

But there is another conception of codes of fair competition, [by which] a code is not to be restricted to the elimination of business practices that would be characterized by general acceptance as oppressive or unfair. It is to include whatever ordinances may be desirable or helpful for the well-being or prosperity of the industry affected.... What is fair, as thus conceived, is not something to be contrasted with what is unfair or fraudulent or tricky. The extension becomes as wide as the field of industrial regulation. If that conception shall prevail, anything that Congress may do within the limits of the commerce clause for the betterment of business may be done by the President upon the recommendation of a trade association by calling it a code. This is delegation running riot. No such plenitude of power is susceptible of transfer. The statute, however, aims at nothing less, as one can learn both from its terms and from the administrative practice under it. Nothing less is aimed at by the code now submitted to our scrutiny.

Do you agree with Justice Cardozo that § 1 of the NIRA provided a sufficient standard for banning contraband oil, but not for the industrial codes? The Court has often upheld broad delegations of power to the President in wartime (*see, e.g.*, Belknap, *supra*). Is there to be no way for Congress to grant peacetime emergency powers even when, in contrast to *Youngstown*, it wants to do so? This last question suggests the extent to which *Schechter Poultry* is inconsistent with the rest of the case law that you will see in this book. For example, compare a decision the next year—*United States v. Curtiss-Wright Export Corp.*, 299 U.S. 304 (1936) (excerpted in Chapter Six), in which the Court upheld a delegation of power to the President to prohibit arms sales to countries engaged in armed conflict in South America. The Court said that legislation in "the international field must often accord to the President a degree of discretion and freedom from statutory restriction which would not be admissible were domestic affairs alone involved." Might not the same be said for the difference between domestic emergencies and ordinary times?

In *Schechter Poultry*, notice the Court's emphasis on fair procedure to distinguish this delegation from other broad ones that it had approved. Is that a real distinction, or just a makeweight? Isn't the underlying concern of the delegation doctrine with congressional control of *substance*, and isn't fair procedure an independent requirement of due process or administrative law? In any event, the chaotic administration of the NRA certainly seemed to take its toll on the government's chances in *Schechter Poultry*. Congress later enacted a comprehensive code of federal administrative procedure, in the Administrative Procedure Act (APA) of 1946, 5 U.S.C. § 551 *et seq*. We will encounter the APA repeatedly in these materials.

Another major challenge to an economic control program involved World War II price controls, administered by the Office of Price Administration (OPA). This time the Supreme Court upheld the statute, in an opinion by Chief Justice Stone in *Yakus v. United States*, 321 U.S. 414 (1944):

That Congress has constitutional authority to prescribe commodity prices as a war emergency measure, and that the Act was adopted by Congress in the exercise of that power, are not questioned here....

Congress enacted the Emergency Price Control Act in pursuance of a defined policy and required that the prices fixed by the Administrator should further that policy and conform to standards prescribed by the Act. The boundaries of the field of the Administrator's permissible action are marked by the statute. It directs that the prices fixed shall effectuate the declared policy of the Act to stabilize commodity prices so as to prevent war-time inflation and its enumerated disruptive causes and effects. In addition the prices established must be fair and equitable, and in fixing them the Administrator is directed to give due consideration, so far as practicable, to prevailing prices during the designated base period, with prescribed administrative adjustments to compensate for enumerated disturbing factors affecting prices. . . .

The Act is unlike the National Industrial Recovery Act considered in Schechter Poultry Corp. v. United States, which proclaimed in the broadest terms its purpose "to rehabilitate industry and to conserve natural resources." It prescribed no method of attaining that end save by the establishment of codes of fair competition, the nature of whose permissible provisions was left undefined. It provided no standards to which those codes were to conform. The function of formulating the codes was delegated, not to a public official responsible to Congress or the Executive, but to private individuals engaged in the industries to be regulated. . . .

Acting within its constitutional power to fix prices it is for Congress to say whether the data on the basis of which prices are to be fixed are to be confined within a narrow or a broad range. In either case the only concern of courts is to ascertain whether the will of Congress has been obeyed. This depends not upon the breadth of the definition of the facts or conditions which the administrative officer is to find but upon the determination whether the definition sufficiently marks the field within which the Administrator is to act so that it may be known whether he has kept within it in compliance with the legislative will. . . . Only if we could say that there is an absence of standards for the guidance of the Administrator's action, so that it would be impossible in a proper proceeding to ascertain whether the will of Congress has been obeyed, would we be justified in overriding its choice of means for effecting its declared purpose of preventing inflation. The standards prescribed by the present Act, with the aid of the "statement of the considerations" required to be made by the Administrator, are sufficiently definite and precise to enable Congress, the courts and the public to ascertain whether the Administrator, in fixing the designated prices, has conformed to those standards. . . .

In *Yakus*, the Court mentioned congressional war powers as a basis for the statute. Yet did the Court's analysis and outcome seem to place any real reliance on the war powers? As we will see in the next principal case, *Yakus* now counterbalances *Schechter Poultry*. Indeed, *Yakus* initiated a string of decisions rejecting delegation doctrine challenges to domestic legislation that has continued unbroken to the present.

The doctrine has not been totally without effect during this period, however. Often a court invokes the doctrine to justify narrowly construing a statute. The classic example is *Kent v. Dulles*, 357 U.S. 116 (1958). The Secretary of State was denying passports to Communists. The Court avoided a direct civil liberties ground for decision by holding that the passport statute did not authorize the denial of passports for political beliefs. Reading the statute that broadly would encounter delegation doctrine perils, suggested the Court.

Another oblique use of the doctrine is illustrated by *Zemel v. Rusk*, 381 U.S. 1 (1965). In approving restrictions on travel to Cuba, the Court found standards in administrative practice—it held that the Act authorized "only those ... restrictions which it could fairly be argued were adopted by Congress in light of prior administrative practice." In a subsequent case, *Haig v. Agee*, 453 U.S. 280 (1981), excerpted in Chapter Six, the *Zemel* technique appeared again, amid a spirited dispute on the Court over whether the administrative practice in question was "sufficiently substantial and consistent" to warrant the conclusion that Congress had approved it.

Many of the themes that had been developing in the case law came together in a challenge to the economic control program of the early 1970s. The Economic Stabilization Act of 1970, 84 Stat. 799, certainly had the virtue of brevity. It authorized the President "to issue such orders and regulations as he may deem appropriate to stabilize prices, rents, wages, and salaries at levels not less than those prevailing on May 25, 1970," with such adjustments as might be necessary "to prevent gross inequities." The President was authorized to subdelegate the performance of any function under the Act; orders and regulations were enforceable by injunction, and willful violations were subject to penalties of up to $5,000.

On August 15, 1971, President Nixon went on nationwide television announcing a 90-day freeze on wages and prices while he worked out the details of a wage-price control program. His decision was implemented by Executive Order 11615, which directed that "[p]rices, rents, wages, and salaries ... be stabilized for a period of 90 days" at levels not greater than the highest of those actually in effect with respect to "a substantial volume of actual transactions" during the preceding thirty days. The Executive Order also established the Cost of Living Council as an agency of the United States and delegated to the Council "all the powers conferred on the President" by the Act.

A court challenge promptly appeared. The Meat Cutters Union sought a declaratory judgment of the unconstitutionality of the Act and injunctive relief against its enforcement. The Union also sought to require the major meat packing companies to grant wage increases in accordance with collective bargaining agreements which provided for such an increase effective September 6, 1971. In response to the claim of the companies that such an increase would violate the freeze order, the Union asserted the invalidity of the freeze. These actions were consolidated before a three-judge court, which issued a widely acclaimed opinion on the delegation doctrine.

Amalgamated Meat Cutters & Butcher Workmen v. Connally
337 F. Supp. 737 (D.D.C. 1971)

LEVENTHAL, Circuit Judge: ...

The matter has been argued to us on principle and precedent. The divergences in the principles perceived by the litigants are matched by divergences in the precedents they summon. The Government cites numerous authorities but relies most heavily on Yakus v. United States, 321 U.S. 414 (1944).... The Union particularly invokes the 1935 decisions in Schechter Corp. v. United States, 295 U.S. 495, and Panama Refining Co. v. Ryan, 293 U.S. 388....

We are of the view that the *Yakus* ruling and principles there applied provide the more meaningful guidance for the novel problem at hand, and that this constitutional assault cannot be sustained. We review the several interrelated considerations that lead us to this conclusion.

1. Permissibility of delegation of legislative power, within limits

We may usefully begin with the modest observation that the Constitution does not forbid every delegation of "legislative" power. This was recognized explicitly at least as long ago as Norwegian Nitrogen Products Co. v. United States, 288 U.S. 294, 305 (1933), where Justice Cardozo stated that the tariff provision under consideration involved "in substance a delegation, though a permissible one, of the legislative process."

There may thus be added to the outworn doctrines interred in the cause of wisdom the conception developed in Field v. Clark, 143 U.S. 649, 692-693 (1892), which centers the validity of a delegation by Congress to the President on whether he "was the mere agent of the law-making department to ascertain and declare the event upon which its expressed will was to take effect." That officials may lawfully be given far greater authority than the power to recognize a triggering condition was recognized within twenty years in the famous *Grimaud* case where a unanimous Court "admitted that it is difficult to define the line which separates legislative power to make laws, from administrative authority to make regulations." [*United States v. Grimaud*, 220 U.S. 506, 517 (1911), upholding a law that authorized the Secretary of Agriculture to make rules "to insure the objects" of the national forests.] There is no analytical difference, no difference in kind, between the legislative function—of prescribing rules for the future—that is exercised by the legislature or by the agency implementing the authority conferred by the legislature. The problem is one of limits.

An agency assigned to a task has its freedom of action circumscribed not only by the constitutional limitations that bind Congress but by the perimeters described by the legislature as hedgerows defining areas open to the agency. The question is the extent to which the Constitution limits a legislature that may think it proper and needful to give the agency broad flexibility to cope with the conditions it encounters.

2. Governing concepts of necessary flexibility and accountability for conformance to "intelligible principle" and legislative will

The legislative power granted to Congress by the Constitution includes the power to avail itself of "the necessary resources of flexibility and practicality . . . to perform its function." . . . Congress is free to delegate legislative authority provided it has exercised "the essentials of the legislative function"—of determining the basic legislative policy and formulating a rule of conduct. [quoting *Yakus*] . . . The key question is not answered by noting that the authority delegated is broad, or broader than Congress might have selected if it had chosen to operate within a narrower range. The issue is whether the legislative description of the task assigned "sufficiently marks the field within which the Administrator is to act so that it may be known whether he has kept within it in compliance with the legislative will."

The *Yakus* ruling . . . carries forward the doctrine earlier articulated . . . in *Hampton* that there is no forbidden delegation of legislative power "if Congress shall lay down by legislative act an intelligible principle" to which the official or agency must conform.

Concepts of control and accountability define the constitutional requirement. The principle permitting a delegation of legislative power, if there has been sufficient demarcation of the field to permit a judgment whether the agency has kept within the legislative will, establishes a principle of accountability under which compatibility with the legislative design may be ascertained not only by Congress but by the courts and the public. That principle was conjoined in *Yakus* with a recognition that the burden is on the party who assails the legislature's choice of means for effecting its purpose, a burden that is met "[o]nly if we could say that there is an absence of standards for the guidance of the Administrator's action, so that it would be impossible in a proper proceeding to ascertain whether the will of Congress has been obeyed." ...

[P]erhaps the broadest delegation yet sustained and the one closest to the case before us came in *Yakus*, for the ultimate standard in the 1942 statute was only that the maximum prices be "generally fair and equitable."

3. Standards of Act are sufficient, in context of history, to permit court to ascertain that 90-day "freeze" was in conformance to legislative will

... In some respects, ... Congress has been precise in its limitations. The President is given an authority to stabilize prices and wages by § 202(a) of the Act, but not at levels less than those prevailing on May 25, 1970.

Moreover the legislation is not as vulnerable as it would have been prior to the amendment adopted earlier in 1971, under which the President is precluded by § 202(b) from singling out "a particular industry or sector of the economy upon which to impose controls" unless he makes a specific finding that wages or prices in that industry or sector have increased at a rate disproportionate to the rate for the economy as a whole....

The limitation on the President's power to take action in particular industries or sectors made this authority more narrow than the authority over prices in the 1942 legislation. It also clarified the will of Congress. Congress gave the President broad authority to stabilize prices, rents, wages and salaries, but in effect it contemplated that controls to achieve broad stabilization would begin with a regulation applicable to the entire economy. While the subject matter was broad, the technique was relatively confined.... The House Banking and Currency Committee Report specifically envisaged a 3-month "freeze" to get "a handle on inflation."

This ascertainment of the contours of the power to "stabilize" is fortified by explicit legislative history. But even the text of the law, the starting point of analysis, must not be taken in a vacuum. [T]he Court has made clear that the standards of a statute are not to be tested in isolation and derive "meaningful content from the purpose of the Act, its factual background, and the statutory context."

The historical context of the 1970 law is emphasized in the Government's submission:

> In enacting the legislation in question here, Congress was, of course, acting against a background of wage and price controls in two wars. The administrative practice under both of those Acts was the subject of extensive judicial interpretation and review. This substantial background of prior law and practice provides a further framework for assessing whether the Executive has stayed within the bounds authorized by Congress and provides more than adequate standards for the exercise of the authority granted by the Act.

We think this contention is sound. The context of the 1970 stabilization law includes the stabilization statutes passed in 1942, and the stabilization provisions in ... the

Defense Production Act of 1950, and the "common lore" of anti-inflationary controls established by the agency approaches and court decisions. . . . We do not suggest that the 1970 law was intended as or constitutes a duplicate of the earlier laws. But those laws and their implementation do provide a validating context as against the charge that the later statute stands without any indication to the agencies and officials of legislative contours and contemplation.

The approaches and decisions under the earlier laws are certainly not "frozen" as guidelines for the present law. Indeed an ordinary agency is not precluded from modifying its policies. An agency "may switch rather than fight the lessons of experience." The present administration is entitled to a fresh approach. The fact that there are significant differences between the inflationary problems of 1970 and the inflationary problems of 1942 and 1950 provides additional reasons for differences in policies. Notwithstanding the permissible differences from prior approaches the historic context of government stabilization measures provides a starting point, within the broad contemplation of Congress, that negatives a conclusion that the whole program was set adrift without any rudder.

An undeniably prominent feature of the earlier stabilization programs was the adoption thereunder of across-the-board wage and price controls, typically with "freeze" and "hold-the-line" approaches, subject to relaxation for hardships and inequities under implementing standards. There can be no doubt that in its broad outlines the general freeze ordered by the President conforms to the legislative intention. Even a rudimentary recourse to available legal materials readily permits a court to ascertain at least to this extent the contours of the legislative will and the conformance of the Executive action to it. . . .

5. Delegation to President of "timing" of direct controls supported by legislative conclusions. . . .

We see no merit in the contention that the Act is constitutionally defective because the timing of the imposition of controls was delegated to the President. The House Report clarifies that this delegation was not an abdication by Congress, but the product of a reasoned analysis that only such delegation as to timing would further the legislative purpose of stabilization. . . .

Congress was acting in a setting where all were agreed on the need to control inflation but opinion was sharply divided on the optimum measures for the Government to use. As of 1970, the President was heeding the counsel of that substantial body of thought which advocated concentration on fiscal and monetary measures, the so-called indirect controls. Others were advocating an "incomes policy," with readiness to resort to direct controls, on the ground that wage-cost-price increases were so embedded in the structure of private decision-making that fiscal and monetary programs alone could not be successful in checking inflation without consequences of unemployment and recession that could not be tolerated.

The issue whether the delegation before us is excessive must be considered in the light of the unique situation, with the President not in accord with the conclusion of Congress as to the need or desirability of the power entrusted to him. Thus the Speaker, supporting the law, put it that the President and his advisers "are prescribing the wrong medicine for the particular inflationary virus now affecting the Nation," that restrictive fiscal and monetary policies are appropriate for combating traditional "demand-pull inflation" but the country was now beset by "cost-push inflation" for which direct controls were needed. It is not our place to review the merits of these differences. But the physician-virus metaphor is revealing. Viewing the President as a physician in charge, Congress could advise but not mandate his diagnosis. It sought in the national interest to have the right remedy available on a standby basis, if the President should wish to adopt that prescription, following his further reflection and taking into account future developments and experience.

We cannot say that this delegation was unreasoned, or a mere abdication to the President to do whatever he willed. It conferred an authority that Congress concluded, with reasons, had a substantial likelihood of being required....Finally the House Report takes cognizance, in support of delegation of "timing" to the President, that Congress might not be in session when action was requisite....

6. *Validity of delegation and of freeze not negatived by failure to require declaration of emergency, or by lack of sudden or sharp price movement in 1971*

... The Union [argues] that there was no emergency in fact, that the President himself, in his message of August 15, points out that the rate of inflation had declined from 6% to 4% per annum. It may be that the President concluded that the kind of fiscal and monetary controls that had permitted a reduction in the rate of inflation entailed consequences that would become so grievous, if relied on exclusively in the future, as to jeopardize the public interest. It may be that he concluded that fiscal and monetary controls alone could not arrive at the kind of reduction in rate of inflation, to a level under 4% or even 3%, that was necessary to offset the inflationary psychology that plagued the Nation. These are not matters for us to determine. It suffices that there are such possibilities, and that this court cannot say that the President's message either negatived any possible rational basis for his order, or offset the presumption of validity to which that order is entitled....

7. *Significance of international factors*

This is a suitable juncture to refer to the undoubted and substantial significance of the interrelation between the domestic wage and price controls and the actions taken by the President on August 15, 1971, in the field of international trade and monetary adjustments. The President's message identifies the existence of such an interrelation though not its exact nature. The House Report's recount of legislative policy includes its recital that the current inflation malady is significantly responsible for the balance-of-payments crisis and liquidity squeeze. This was a 1970 problem and a legislative objective not known at the time of the 1942 and 1950 legislation. The consequence for international trade, liquidity and monetary relationships, enhances the range of power Congress may permissibly delegate to the President. United States v. Curtiss-Wright Export Corp., 299 U.S. 304 (1936); Zemel v. Rusk, 381 U.S. 1, 17 (1965). And it particularly substantiates the legitimacy of delegating to the President the authority as to the timing for the blending of actions with international consequences.

8. *Limited duration of statute*

It is also material, though not dispositive, to note the limited time frame established by Congress for the stabilization authority delegated to the President. The Act as enacted on August 15, 1970, expired February 28, 1971, establishing a lifespan of about six months. Two subsequent extensions provided even shorter durations. When the current expiration date of April 30, 1972, was set on May 18, 1971, Congress rejected the administration request for a two-year extension. Thus, in the words of the Government's memorandum, Congress established a "close control." It conjoined flexibility in the President to act promptly with an obligation in Congress to undertake an affirmative review without prolonged delay, without the option of acquiescence by inaction.

9. Statute not subject to attack as delegating authority to be unfair and inequitable; law contains standard of broad fairness and avoidance of gross inequity

However, Congress cannot delegate unlimited authority to the Executive over prices and wages even for a period limited to say, the 8-9 months between the President's Order of August 15, 1971, and the April 30, 1972 expiration date.

The Union says that during this period the President has been given a "blank check" for internal affairs which is intolerable in our constitutional system. The Union notes that the order exempted from controls the prices charged for raw agricultural products without statutory authority for the exemption. It claims that the failure of Congress to require, as in the 1942 and 1950 legislation, that ongoing regulations be "fair and equitable" is tantamount to a delegation to the President of the power to be unfair and inequitable. The Union complains that there was a failure to provide a system for testing these orders, administratively and by judicial review, as in the earlier legislation....

We begin with the observation that we cannot stand on the analysis put to us by the Government. The Government does say, correctly, that the doors of the courts remain open. But the question is, whether the courts can appraise the claim that the stabilization actions do not conform to the legislative will, measured by an intelligible standard. If the courts are open only nominally, they would enhance rather than inhibit executive absolutism....

If the act gives the President authority to be unfair and inequitable, as the Union claims, this legislative vessel may indeed founder on a constitutional rock. But we do not reach this constitutional issue because we do not think the Act can be given the extremist interpretation offered by the Union. We take this view not only because of the doctrine that statutes are to be construed so as to avoid serious constitutional questions, but more directly because we do not think it can sensibly or fairly be said that this extremist approach was what was intended by the legislature....

The problem that now concerns us is whether the Act has sufficient specificity to avoid the constitutional condemnation, of excessive "blank check" authority to the President, as to the period following the initial general price-wage freeze. The legislative history records the hope of the House Committee that an initial freeze for two or three months would suffice to give a handle to control inflation, and could be followed by a termination of controls.... This country's experience with its prior stabilization programs fairly establishes as the contemplation of Congress that controls under the Act need not be continued in a perpetuation of the general freeze beyond a temporary opening period. A freeze is always arbitrary to some extent, and while such arbitrariness can be sustained for a relatively short-range initial period its prolongation in a country as vast as ours, with problems so various, runs the risk of betraying the concept of responsible government.

We do not think it can be said that the possibility of controls beyond the initial freeze was left without any standard other than the President's unfettered discretion, including the discretion to be unfair and inequitable. This is not a case where Congress indicated an intention to leave the matter wholly to the discretion of the President without any possibility of judicial review. The ultimate standard for follow-on controls replacing the freeze is a standard of fairness and equity. This standard of removal of "gross inequities" is voiced as an authority of the President in § 202 of the Act. We think there is fairly implicit in the Act the duty to take whatever action is required in the interest of broad fairness and avoidance of gross inequity, although presumably his range of discretion means there may be inequities that a President may remove that he is not compelled by law to remove.

This conclusion is supported by constitutional considerations and historic context. The 1942 statute on prices specifically articulated the "generally fair and equitable" standard. But the broad equity standard is inherent in a stabilization program.... Fairness and equity are also furthered by the requirement (see point 10) that the Executive develop implementing standards, with deliberate criteria replacing the fortuities of a freeze.... [However,] broad emergency price control measures need not entitle each particular seller to consideration of the equity of his position, for such an obligation would impose an administrative impracticability that would defeat the very purpose of the Act. Bowles v. Willingham, 321 U.S. 503 (1944)....

We ... rule that our judgment has two parts: first, that the statute does at least contain a standard of broad fairness and avoiding gross inequity—leaving to the future the implementation of that standard; second, that this statute is not unconstitutional as an excessive delegation of power by the legislature to the executive for the limited term of months contemplated by Congress to follow the initiating general freeze.

10. *Need for ongoing administrative standards as avoiding undue breadth of executive authority*

Another feature that blunts the "blank check" rhetoric is the requirement that any action taken by the Executive under the law, subsequent to the freeze, must be in accordance with further standards as developed by the Executive. This requirement, inherent in the Rule of Law and implicit in the Act, means that however broad the discretion of the Executive at the outset, the standards once developed limit the latitude of subsequent executive action....

The requirement of subsidiary administrative policy, enabling Congress, the courts and the public to assess the Executive's adherence to the ultimate legislative standard, is in furtherance of the purpose of the constitutional objective of accountability. This 1970 Act gives broadest latitude to the Executive. Certainly there is no requirement of formal findings. But there is an on-going requirement of intelligible administrative policy that is corollary to and implementing of the legislature's ultimate standard and objective....

In view of the administration of the prior two stabilization programs the Government cannot sensibly contend that the requirement of development of administrative standards is unattainable or would reduce to a futility the legislative objective of controlling inflation.

11. *Applicability of Administrative Procedure Act provisions on administrative rule-making and judicial review*

. . . The Government concedes and we agree that the Executive's actions under the 1970 Act are not immune from judicial review. There are occasions when Congress has so committed matters to executive discretion as to avoid judicial review or to remove judicial review for error of law, including abuse of discretion, restricting it to the narrow function of correcting flagrant disregard of a clear-cut legislative mandate. These occasions are, however, the rare exception arising only in such fields as foreign affairs and national defense, or where Congress has expressly or impliedly directed that the Executive proceed without statement of reasons because the functioning must rest on confidence or be conducted with extraordinary expedition, or where the legislature manifests an intent to avoid review in order to further its objective, as where a failure to exercise discretion to exempt is made non-reviewable in furtherance of the objective of narrow exemptions.

The Government's position rests on the proposition that since the Act provides for enforcement either by way of fine (§ 204), or by way of injunction restraining violations (§ 205), and the person charged with violation is able to obtain judicial review by inserting a defense to either type of enforcement proceeding, this provides ample judicial review for constitutional purposes.

We need not consider whether under conditions of modern life the Constitution permits a restriction to enforcement proceedings of judicial review of Executive discretion as broad in range and significant in impact as that provided by this law, requiring citizens with substantial doubts concerning the validity of the exercise of such broad discretion to run the risk of criminal proceedings. Compare Ex parte Young, 209 U.S. 123 (1908). It is our conclusion that in addition to the judicial reviews noted by the Government, challenges may be made under the provisions for judicial review in the Administrative Procedure Act, 5 U.S.C. §§ 701-706. These provisions contemplate an action for declaratory judgment or injunction, assuming pertinent requirements for these forms of action are met, as well as a defense in civil or criminal proceedings, see 5 U.S.C. § 703. They provide that a person suffering legal wrong because of agency action is entitled to review thereof, 5 U.S.C. § 702. Judicial review is provided for final agency action for which there is no other adequate remedy in court, 5 U.S.C. § 704.

When the impact of regulations is direct and immediate, so that the controversy is "ripe" for judicial resolution, these provisions of 5 U.S.C. §§ 701-706, permit pre-enforcement judicial review. There is a basic presumption of judicial review. The courts restrict access to judicial review only upon a showing of clear and convincing evidence of a contrary legislative intent. Abbott Laboratories v. Gardner, 387 U.S. 136, 140-141 (1967). Pre-enforcement judicial review may be withheld when regulations do not have an immediate impact on the complainant and only minimal adverse consequences will be involved if the regulation is challenged in an enforcement proceeding. Toilet Goods Ass'n v. Gardner, 387 U.S. 158, 164-166 (1967).

We have no occasion to expatiate on these familiar provisions and principles for judicial review of agency actions, or to determine what kinds of agency action under the 1970 Act may be classified as "final" and reviewable, or when some court remedy other than direct review may be "adequate." We merely note that we see no indication whatever, let alone the "clear and convincing evidence" required by the Supreme

Court decisions, that the actions taken under the 1970 Act are removed from the judicial review provisions of 5 U.S.C. §§ 701-706.

The term "agency" is defined broadly. See 5 U.S.C. § 701(b)(1): "agency" means each authority of the Government of the United States, whether or not it is within or subject to review by another agency, but does not include—[Congress or the courts]. The leading students of the APA . . . seem to be in agreement that the term "agency" in the APA includes the President—a conclusion fortified by the care taken to make express exclusion of "Congress" and "the courts."

But we need not consider whether an action for judicial review can be brought against the President *eo nomine*. Certainly such actions can be brought against the official who exercises functions vested by Congress in the President and delegated by the President to him. The Cost of Living Council is an "authority" of the United States and Executive Order 11615 was only recording the incontrovertible when it specified that the Council "shall act as an agency of the United States." . . .

By the same token actions under this 1970 Act are subject to the administrative procedure provisions of the Administrative Procedure Act, 5 U.S.C. § 551 ff. It may well be that the applicability of these provisions will have no practical consequence. The rule-making provisions of 5 U.S.C. § 553, requiring notice and opportunity for participation by interested persons, are subject to the provision in subsection (b) removing those requirements "(B) when the agency for good cause finds (and incorporates the finding and a brief statement of reasons therefor in the rules issued) that notice and public procedure thereon are impracticable, unnecessary, or contrary to the public interest." The adjudication provisions of 5 U.S.C. § 554 are applicable only when an agency hearing is required by the statute, or by compulsion of general law, *cf.* Wong Yang Sung v. McGrath, 339 U.S. 33 (1950). And *Yakus* upheld the validity of the failure to provide for such hearings in the 1942 maximum price law. . . .

In the context of the applicability of the general provisions of the Administrative Procedure Act, as amended, both as to administrative procedure and judicial review, it is hollow to say that the 1970 Act was void ab initio for failure to make provision for these matters. We have no basis or warrant for considering—or rather speculating—in this action whether the ongoing administration of the stabilization program may become subject to challenge for failure to provide reasonable and meaningful opportunity for interested persons to present objections or inequities that undercut the premise of broad equity, or for officials to take these into account, or for courts to discharge their function of judicial review. . . .

———————

1. Note the host of factors the court regards as relevant to determining the permissibility of a broad delegation, and the way it disposes of objections to uncertainties and the potential for unfairness in the application of the Act. If the court's analytical concern is not definitional, *i.e.*, whether the powers Congress has delegated are classifiably "legislative," what is the court's concern? Consider, in this connection, the relevance of the potential for judicial review under the Act and what the history of prior anti-inflationary statutes offers as a "validating context" for the Economic Stabilization Act of 1970. What does the court mean when it states that "[t]he problem is one of limits," and that Congress must exercise "the essentials of the legislative function?" Also, note that the court offers the executive a "fresh approach" under this statute, notwithstanding the guidance it draws from the history of earlier programs. How much of a "rudder" does this approach provide?

2. Does this opinion provide a reliable guide to factors that must or need not be present in order for a court to sustain a congressional delegation of power? As a government lawyer helping to draft an executive order or a covering legal opinion under some other equally broad delegating statute, how would you use this opinion in the drafting process?

3. Compare the court's treatment of the President's determination of extraordinary conditions in this case (¶6 of the opinion) with the Justices' treatment of Truman's "factfinding" in *Youngstown*. Why the difference in intensity of review? Is the difference justified? Should this difference strike a cautionary note with respect to the usefulness of judicial review under the 1970 Act—or is Leventhal's treatment of the applicability of the APA more revealing?

4. By exercising considerable creativity, the *Meat Cutters* court saved a delegation remarkable for both its substantive breadth and its lack of provision for such major details of implementation as administrative procedure and judicial review. A fundamental question remains: why should the courts go to such lengths to save a delegation so carelessly made?

5. Why *do* the federal courts usually strain so hard to find a sufficient standard, instead of following the lead of the New Deal cases and voiding broad delegations so that Congress must resolve fundamental policy issues? Consider a response once offered by the Supreme Court, in the process of approving a broad delegation to the Secretary of the Interior to apportion the water of the Colorado River, in *Arizona v. California*, 373 U.S. 546 (1963). The Court remarked that if the Secretary abused his broad powers, Congress could alter them by amending the statute. Is that an adequate control on broadly delegated powers? Does your answer change when the delegate is the President himself, in view of the likelihood that he will veto any restriction of previously granted powers? Consider this question in connection with the materials on presidential veto powers that appear later in this chapter.

The Supreme Court has not engaged in extensive analysis of delegation issues in recent years. For example, in *Federal Energy Administration v. Algonquin SNG, Inc.*, 426 U.S. 548 (1976), the Court rejected a challenge to the Trade Expansion Act, which authorized the President to restrict imports to protect "national security." In a brief discussion, the Court noted that the Act articulated a series of factors to be considered by the President; these, however, were very unconfining.

Still, the Court has continued to make indirect use of the delegation doctrine. In *National Cable Television Ass'n v. United States*, 415 U.S. 336 (1974), the Court considered the validity of certain assessments imposed by the Federal Communications Commission on cable television systems. The Court's concern was that the authorizing statute could be read to allow either a "fee" narrowly designed to recoup the Government's costs in providing regulatory services, or a "tax," which might involve broad policy judgments whether certain activities of regulated parties should be encouraged (by low assessments) or discouraged (by high ones). The latter possibility troubled the Court, because it "would be such a sharp break with our traditions to conclude the Congress had bestowed on a federal agency the taxing power." Accordingly, following the process of *Kent v. Dulles, supra*, and citing *Schechter*, the Court read the statute narrowly, "to avoid constitutional problems." The Court held that only a "fee" was authorized.

National Cable Television thus suggests that some congressional functions, such as the power to tax, may be nondelegable. James Freedman, in Crisis and Legitimacy: The Administrative Process and American Government 80-86 (1978), argues that nondelegability of the taxing function may stem from the "unique institutional competence of Congress for purposes of levying taxes." In brief, the idea is that the Constitution's framers relied on the direct political accountability of the members of Congress as our main protection against unfair or oppressive taxation. Of course, for such functions as taxes, a principle of nondelegability cannot be taken quite literally. (For some other functions such as impeachment, however, perhaps it can be taken literally, *see* Freedman, *supra*.)

And in a very curious decision, the Court has suggested that how power is distributed *within* the executive branch may receive constitutional scrutiny. In *Hampton v. Mow Sun Wong*, 426 U.S. 88 (1976), the Court invalidated a Civil Service rule excluding aliens from federal employment. Although the Court relied on due process, not the delegation doctrine, Justice Stevens' rationale had delegation overtones. He argued that proffered justifications for the restriction, such as to encourage naturalization, were remote from the responsibilities of the Commission. He admitted that both Congress and the President had apparently acquiesced in the rule. Nevertheless, he concluded that, if Congress or the President had imposed the restriction directly, such justifications might be credited, but not when the Government's personnel office formulated the rule. Do Congress and the President then have a duty to allocate decisions within the executive according to subject matter expertise? To date, the Court has not followed up on the implications of *Mow Sun Wong*.

There may be life in the delegation doctrine yet. In separate opinions, Justice Rehnquist has twice urged that the doctrine be applied to invalidate portions of the Occupational Safety and Health Act, 29 U.S.C. § 651 *et seq. Industrial Union Dept., AFL-CIO v. American Petroleum Inst.*, 448 U.S. 607 (1980); *American Textile Mfrs. Inst., Inc. v. Donovan*, 452 U.S. 490 (1981). His opinions urge the Court to "reshoulder the burden of ensuring that Congress itself make the critical policy decisions." Do you agree?

Naturally, the academics have joined the fray. A leading proponent of reviving the doctrine is Theodore Lowi. A representative sample of his views is The End of Liberalism; Ideology, Policy, and the Crisis of Public Authority 298-99 (1969), in which he indicts what he characterizes as "interest group liberalism," the distribution of positive government power among interest groups to the detriment of the general public interest and the "rule of law":

> Restoration of the *Schechter* rule would be dramatic because it would mean return to the practice of occasional Supreme Court invalidation of congressional acts. Nothing is more dramatic than the confrontation of these two jealous Branches, the more so due to its infrequent occurrence in recent years. But there is no reason to fear judicial usurpation. Under present conditions, when Congress delegates without a shred of guidance, the courts usually end up rewriting many of the statutes in the course of "construction." Since the Court's present procedure is always to try to find an acceptable meaning of a statute in order to avoid invalidating it, the Court is legislating constantly. A blanket invalidation under the *Schechter* rule is a Court order for Congress to do its own work. Therefore the rule of law is a restraint upon rather than an expansion of the judicial function.

There is also no reason to fear reduction of government power as a result of serious application of the *Schechter* rule.... Historically, rule of law, especially statute law, is the essence of positive government. A bureaucracy in the service of a strong and clear statute is more effective than ever. Granted, the rule-of-law requirement is likely to make more difficult the framing and passage of some policies. But why should any program be acceptable if the partisans cannot fairly clearly state purpose and means?

See also the debate in Symposium, *Delegation of Powers to Administrative Agencies*, 36 Am. U. L. Rev. 295-442 (1987); Schoenbrod, *The Delegation Doctrine: Could the Court Give it Substance*, 83 Mich. L. Rev. 1223 (1985); Aranson, Gellhorn & Robinson, *A Theory of Delegation*, 68 Corn. L. Rev. 1 (1982).

For critiques of the doctrine's utility, *see* Mashaw, *Prodelegation: Why Administrators Should Make Political Decisions*, 1 Yale J. of Law, Econ. & Org. 81 (1985); Bruff, *Judicial Review and the President's Statutory Powers*, 68 Va. L. Rev. 1, 25-29 (1982). Bruff argues:

In general, ... the delegation doctrine's present utility as a meaningful restraint on Congress is low. . . . Reviving the doctrine for statutes delegating power to the President would be unwise, however. Some of the reasons for this conclusion are relevant whether the delegation is to the President or to an agency. The courts are properly reluctant to employ the doctrine vigorously, in part because it involves a constitutional decision that overrides a congressional judgment regarding the amount of discretion that should be accorded the executive in a particular context. Moreover, the doctrine may foster judicial subjectivity, because no one has articulated neutral principles for deciding how specific a particular delegation should have to be. Finally, invocation of the doctrine to invalidate a statute invites a judicial confrontation with Congress, which may be unwilling or unable to articulate precise standards. In short, the delegation doctrine, which was designed to help maintain the separation of powers between Congress and the executive, fails because it requires courts to assume a role that they sense oversteps separation of powers limits on their own relationship with Congress.

A revived delegation doctrine would create special problems were courts to apply it to statutes granting power to the President. First, broad delegations to the President are often entirely appropriate or even necessary—his emergency statutory powers are an obvious example. Indeed, where the President has independent constitutional powers, as in foreign affairs, Congress may doubt its authority to bind him closely. Moreover, the accountability concerns at the center of the delegation doctrine are partially met when a grant of power is to the President himself, with his direct political responsibility. Although the doctrine's purpose of keeping policymaking in *Congress* is not met, at least delegations to the President do not transfer responsibility to an appointed bureaucrat. Furthermore, the ultimate power to intervene to correct overenthusiastic presidential initiatives remains with Congress.

It is possible to make too much of this point, however. The Constitution's checks on the legislative process are weakened if Congress may delegate power without restriction. The effect is to shift the burden of overcoming institutional inertia from the initial formation of policy through legislation to the generation of legislation to override a presidential initiative. Notwithstanding Congress's assent to it, this effect is deleterious to the policymaking process that the Constitution envisions. The Framers designed their checks on the legislative process not only to control Congress but also to minimize the amount of lawmaking to which the public would be subjected. By transferring broad authority to the executive, which has fewer internal impediments to forming decisions, Congress increases the amount of lawmaking that is likely to occur.

Nevertheless, the courts can do no more than to hold the delegation doctrine in reserve in case of a particularly egregious congressional abdication of power to the President, and to follow the lead of *Meat Cutters* in taking into account all available controls on executive discretion. Among these controls is statutory interpretation, a judicial function that is made both more important and more difficult to exercise by the delegation doctrine's failure to provide an effective means to force Congress to set policy standards for executive action.

Problem: The Limits of Delegated Power

The problem arises at a time in which there is a poor national economic climate. America's balance of trade is suffering. The imbalance is particularly noticeable with respect to natural resources such as coal, copper, oil, and uranium. There is also much evidence that state and local environmental regulations are interfering with the development of natural resources, particularly in the western United States. There is a perceived need to increase the development of resources on private and federal land. These issues lead to a year-long debate in Congress. There is a significant conflict between those who would encourage growth and those who fear that growth would despoil the environment. Although numerous hearings are held and several different bills are considered, none with any teeth can pass. The result is the following simple statute.

The bill has two sections. The first section contains a congressional "declaration of policy" which lists the background considerations mentioned above, and focuses particularly on the importance of developing resources, overcoming the trade deficit, pulling America out of its poor economic situation, and doing so while preserving the environment. The second section of the bill reads as follows:

> The President is authorized to establish such rules and regulations as he, in the exercise of his discretion, deems appropriate to achieve the orderly, efficient, and economic development of natural resources while taking due account of all considerations set forth in Section One of this act.

In implementing this statute, which the President signed without stating any constitutional reservation, the President issued an Executive Order establishing a special three-member natural resources development board composed of the Secretaries of Defense and the Interior, and the Administrator of EPA. He designated the Secretary of Interior to chair the board. The Executive Order is also quite a simple document. In addition to establishing the board, it simply empowers the commission to implement the legislation.

The three-member board issues and has published in the Federal Register a set of rules. The rules state that in carrying out the legislation and the Executive Order, the board will, upon appropriate request, consider exempting natural resource developers from those state and local environmental laws that interfere with the "orderly, efficient, and economic development of natural resources" as claimed and shown by any developer. Assume that no formal notice and comment procedures accompany or precede the issuance of the order and that no hearing process is established for granting these exemptions.

Anaconda Copper requests from the board, and obtains, an exemption from Arizona state environmental laws which have hindered the operation of copper plants in southern Arizona. The Attorney General of Arizona wishes to challenge the board's action.

What should the Arizona Attorney General do? If we assume that she files a suit to enjoin the implementation of the decision and contest the constitutionality of the statute, what arguments can she bring to bear in light of cases such as *Meat Cutters*? Also, does it make any difference that the board acts pursuant to an open-ended delegation from the President? Would the litigation result in a different conclusion if the President had been more precise in the issuance of his Executive Order? What about procedural niceties here? Would it make any difference if a notice and comment period had been included *before* the board issued its rules or if a hearing procedure were established *before* the board acted on particular requests?

C. Presidential "Legislation," or, the Other Side of Delegation: The Role of the Executive Order

When formally directing the executive branch in the fulfillment of a particular program, the President may implement his authority through an executive order. There is no clear distinction between such an order and a presidential proclamation. In general, however, it is customary that executive orders are directed to the President's subordinates, and proclamations address the public in general. *See generally* Levinson, *Presidential Self-Regulation Through Rulemaking: Comparative Comments on Structuring the Chief Executive's Constitutional Powers*, 9 Vand. J. Transnat'l L. 695, 710-12 (1976); Keenan, *Executive Orders: A Brief History of Their Use and the President's Power to Issue Them*, in Sen. Special Comm. on Nat'l Emergencies and Delegated Emergency Powers, 93d Cong., 2d Sess., Executive Orders in Times of War and National Emergency 20 (Comm. Print 1974); Neighbors, *Presidential Legislation by Executive Order*, 37 U. Colo. L. Rev. 105 (1964). For a compilation of many important executive orders, *see* Office of the Federal Register, Presidential Proclamations and Executive Orders, January 20, 1961—January 20, 1985 (1985).

As we have seen in *Youngstown* and *Meat Cutters*, Presidents use executive orders to implement many of their most important initiatives, basing them on any combination of constitutional and statutory authority that is thought to be available. Thus, these orders often dwell in Justice Jackson's zone of twilight, where authority is neither clearly present nor absent. Although interstitial, the programs involved may prove surprisingly durable. For a history of two prominent examples, orders promoting civil rights in government-related activities and orders seeking economic stabilization, *see* Fleishman & Aufses, *Law and Orders: The Problem of Presidential Legislation*, 40 Law & Contemp. Probs. 1 (1976). The principal case that follows, *AFL-CIO v. Kahn*, shows the interrelation of these two programs. Writing before *Kahn*, Fleishman & Aufses reported their overall conclusion as follows (at 5-6):

> Although the courts generally uphold executive orders, these orders have in some cases been of—at best—dubious constitutionality. On some occasions, Presidents have issued orders without specific statutory authority, only to have the courts find it for them. On others, Congress has delegated power to the executive so broadly that the President has lacked adequate standards with which to work. The subsequent executive orders have, accordingly, been without clear statutory basis.

How does the following case affect that conclusion? As you read it, consider the relationship of the authority issue to the delegation doctrine.

AFL-CIO v. KAHN
618 F. 2d 784 (D.C. Cir.) (en banc),
cert. denied, 443 U.S. 915 (1979)

J. SKELLY WRIGHT, Chief Judge:

This case presents the question whether Congress has authorized the President to deny Government contracts above $5 million to companies that fail or refuse to comply with the voluntary wage and price standards. We answer that question in the affirmative....

I. FACTS

On November 1, 1978 President Carter signed Executive Order 12092 directing the Council on Wage and Price Stability (Council) to establish voluntary wage and price standards for noninflationary behavior for the entire economy. For a business, the Order stated that noninflationary price increases would be no more than 0.5 percent less than that company's recent rate of average price increase; for workers, noninflationary wage increases were defined as no more than a seven percent annual rise. The President ordered the Chairman of the Council to monitor compliance with these standards and to publish the names of noncomplying companies. The Executive Order also instructed the head of each Executive agency and Military Department to require that all contractors certify that they are in compliance with the wage and price standards. The Office of Federal Procurement Policy (OFPP) was charged with implementation of the procurement aspect of the program. The initial wage and price standards announced by the Council ... [added a] provision that a company may be excepted from compliance in order to "avoid situations o[f] undue hardship or gross inequity."

OFPP issued a policy letter on January 4, 1979, requiring that Government contracts worth more than $5 million ... must include certification that the contractor is in compliance with the wage and price standards. The letter provides that if the Council finds that the standards have not been respected ... the relevant agency head may terminate the contract and the company may be ruled ineligible for future Government business. The policy letter established [certain] grounds for [waivers] .... The procurement compliance program is expected to reach 65 to 70 percent of all Government procurement dollars, or about $50 billion worth.

On March 31, 1979 plaintiff labor unions challenged the program in District Court as interfering with the exercise of the right to bargain collectively and as beyond the power of the President to initiate. The District Court granted the unions' motion for summary judgment on the latter ground on May 31, 1979, and enjoined the procurement compliance program. That injunction was stayed pending the outcome of this expedited appeal.

II

We note at the outset our disagreement with the contention that this case presents the same issue decided by the Supreme Court in *Youngstown.* . . . In arguing for the validity of Executive Order 12092, . . . the Government relies entirely upon authority said to be delegated by statute, and makes no appeal to constitutional powers of the Executive that have not been confirmed by legislation. . . . Appellees' challenge to the Executive Order is directed at the procurement aspect of the Order, not at the Council's authority under [the Council on Wage and Price Stability Act (COWPSA)] to promulgate voluntary standards. Thus the central issue in this case is whether the [Federal Property and Administrative Services Act of 1949 (FPASA)] indeed grants to the President the powers he has asserted.

A

The FPASA was a response to the recommendation of the Hoover Commission in 1949 that the Government's method of doing business be streamlined and modernized. The statute was designed to centralize Government property management and to introduce into the public procurement process the same flexibility that characterizes such transactions in the private sector. These goals can be found in the terms "economy" and "efficiency" which appear in the statute and dominate the sparse record of the congressional deliberations.

The most important provision of the Act for this case, Section 205(a), provides that the President "may prescribe such policies and directives, *not inconsistent with the provisions of this Act*, as he shall deem necessary *to effectuate the provisions of said Act.* . . . " Because this language is open-ended, it is important to examine its genesis. The initial Hoover Commission study of procurement recommended that a General Services Agency oversee Government acquisitions, and that the Agency be placed within the Executive Office of the President to bolster its authority and to ensure central direction of the bureaucracy. Congress, however, was reluctant to saddle the relatively small Executive Office with such a vast administrative burden, so it set up the General Services Administration as an independent agency. But in response to the Hoover Commission's concern that the strength of the presidency support the new agency, Congress added Section 205(a) to guarantee that "Presidential policies and directives shall *govern—not merely guide—*" the agencies under the FPASA. We believe that by emphasizing the leadership role of the President in setting Government-wide procurement policy on matters common to all agencies, Congress intended that the President play a direct and active part in supervising the Government's management functions.

To define the President's powers under Section 205(a), some content must be injected into the general phrases "not inconsistent with" the FPASA and "to effectuate the provisions" of the Act. The congressional declaration of policy for the FPASA sets forth the goal of an "economical and efficient system for . . . procurement and supply." Section 201 directs that the Administrator of General Services chart policy and procure supplies in a manner "advantageous to the Government in terms of *economy, efficiency*, or service, and with due regard to the program activities of the agencies concerned." This language recognizes that the Government generally must have some flexibility to seek the greatest advantage in various situations. "Economy" and "efficiency" are not narrow terms; they encompass those factors like price, quality, suitability, and availability of goods or services that are involved in all acquisition decisions. Similar concerns can be seen in the specific direction to contracting officers in Section 303(b) that contracts should be awarded to bidders whose terms "will be most advantageous to the Government, price and other factors considered."

Although the terms and legislative record of the FPASA are not unambiguous, the relationship of the Act to this case can be outlined. Section 205(a) grants the President particularly direct and broad-ranging authority over those larger administrative and management issues that involve the Government as a whole. And that direct presidential authority should be used in order to achieve a flexible management system capable of making sophisticated judgments in pursuit of economy and efficiency.

B

In light of the imprecise definition of presidential authority under the FPASA, it is useful to consider how the procurement power has been exercised under the Act. As the Commission on Government Procurement pointed out in its 1972 report, Congress itself has frequently imposed on the procurement process social and economic programs somewhat removed from a strict view of efficiency and economy.[25] More significant for this case, however, several Executive actions taken explicitly or implicitly under Section 205 of the FPASA have also imposed additional considerations on the procurement process. Of course, the President's view of his own authority under a statute is not controlling, but when that view has been acted upon over a substantial period of time without eliciting congressional reversal, it is "entitled to great respect." As the Supreme Court observed this Term, the "construction of a statute by those charged with its execution should be followed unless there are compelling indications that it is wrong."

In February 1964 President Johnson directed by Executive Order that federal contractors not "discriminate [against persons] because of their age except upon the basis of a bona fide occupational qualification, retirement plan, or statutory requirement...."[29] Since 1941, though, the most prominent use of the President's authority under the FPASA has been a series of anti-discrimination requirements for Government contractors. The early anti-discrimination orders were issued under the President's war powers and special wartime legislation,[32] but for the period from 1953 to 1964 only the FPASA could have provided statutory support for the Executive action.[33]

---

25. For example, the FPASA itself included a directive that a fair portion of Government purchases and contracts be placed with small businesses. Other prominent examples enacted since 1949 include directives that Government service contractors meet minimum standards for wages and working conditions, and that the Government not contract with any company that has been found in criminal violation of air pollution standards.

29. Executive Order 11141. Although the Order can now be justified under the Age Discrimination in Employment Act of 1967, 29 U.S.C. §§ 621-634 (1976), and the Age Discrimination Act of 1975, 42 U.S.C. §§ 6101-6107 (1976), for the first three years of its operation this Order was apparently based on only the FPASA. The Executive Order itself simply cites "the authority vested in [the President] by the Constitution and statutes of the United States."

32. President Franklin Roosevelt issued three Executive Orders dealing with fair em-

The anti-discrimination orders were not tested in the courts until 1964, when the Third Circuit held that they did not grant a private right of action to an employee alleging racial discrimination in work assignment. [*Farmer v. Philadelphia Electric Co.*, 329 F.2d 3 (3d Cir. 1964).] The court concluded that those orders were a proper exercise of presidential authority under Section 205 of the FPASA and the "declaration of policy" in the Defense Production Act of 1950. In a 1967 ruling on the private cause of action question, the Fifth Circuit observed that the FPASA supported President Kennedy's 1961 Order directing affirmative action by contractors to hire minority workers.

> We would be hesitant to say that the antidiscrimination provisions of Executive Order No. 10925 are so unrelated to the establishment of "an economical and efficient system for . . . the procurement and supply" of property and services, 40 U.S.C.A. § 471, that the order should be treated as issued without statutory authority. . . .

[*Farkas v. Texas Instruments, Inc.*, 375 F.2d 629, 632 n.1 (5th Cir.), *cert. denied*, 389 U.S. 977 (1967).] After pointing out that the parties did not contest the validity of the Order, the court added, "We, therefore, conclude that Executive Order No. 10925 was issued pursuant to statutory authority, and has the force and effect of law."

The only direct court holding on the validity of the anti-discrimination orders was provoked by a challenge to the "Philadelphia Plan," which required that bidders for federal or federally-assisted construction contracts submit an affirmative action program. In *Contractors Ass'n of Eastern Pennsylvania v. Secretary of Labor* [442 F.2d 159, 170 (3d Cir.), *cert. denied*, 404 U.S. 854 (1971)], the Court of Appeals rejected a claim that the President exceeded his powers in issuing the affirmative action Order. Judge Gibbons, writing for a unanimous panel, offered several alternative holdings. Although the vitality of two of the claimed bases of decision is subject to question,[40] we note as relevant to the instant case his view that the Orders were "authorized by the broad grant of procurement authority" under the FPASA. He stated, "[I]t is in the interest of the United States in all procurement to see that its suppliers are not over the long run increasing its costs and delaying its programs by excluding from the labor pool available minority workmen," and concluded that "[i]n the area of Government procurement Executive authority to impose non-discrimination contract

---

ployment practices. President Truman also signed three Executive Orders concerning fair employment practices which continued the policies embodied in President Roosevelt's Orders.

33. Two Eisenhower Executive Orders and one Kennedy Executive Order substantially continued the anti-discrimination policy, Executive Order 10479; Executive Order 10557; Executive Order 10925, but none of them referred to substantive statutes. President Kennedy extended the anti-discrimination policy to construction contracts, see Executive Order 11114. In the early 1970s Congress indicated its approval of the anti-discrimination orders. *See AFL-CIO v. Kahn*, 472 F.Supp. at 97.

40. Judge Gibbons suggested that, even if the FPASA did not apply, the President acted within his "implied authority," and that the Orders were impliedly ratified when Congress approved appropriations for construction projects covered by the Philadelphia Plan. Unlike the District Court in this case, we find that these portions of Judge Gibbons' opinion are not only of little relevance to the instant case, but also of doubtful force. The Supreme Court has recently criticized the interpretation of appropriations measures as implied approvals of substantive administrative action, see *TVA v. Hill*, 437 U.S. 153, 190 (1978), and much uncertainty attends any claim of "implied" or "inherent" presidential authority under the Constitution.

provisions [represents] action pursuant to the express or implied authorization of Congress."

C

This survey of the terms of the FPASA, its legislative history, and Executive practice since its enactment suggests that the District Court misapprehended the President's statutory powers in this case. Any order based on Section 205(a) must accord with the values of "economy" and "efficiency." Because there is a sufficiently close nexus between those criteria and the procurement compliance program established by Executive Order 12092, we find that program to be authorized by the FPASA.

The District Court was alarmed by the prospect of Government contracts being diverted from low bidders who are not in compliance with the wage and price standards to higher bidders. The result, it might seem, could be an unwarranted drain on the public fisc. Yet it is important to consider the procurement compliance program in its real-world setting. Much Government procurement takes place through the processes of negotiation rather than formal advertisement and competitive bidding. Military procurement, which is the largest single component of Government purchasing, is conducted almost exclusively through negotiated arrangements. In the context of a negotiated contract, the procurement program announced by Executive Order 12092 will likely have the direct and immediate effect of holding down the Government's procurement costs.

Moreover, to the extent that compliance with the wage and price standards is widespread a corresponding reduction (or more gentle increase) in Government expenses should take place.[45] There is every reason to anticipate general compliance throughout the economy. Executive officials have cited initial indications that most large companies will comply with the standards, and the inflation problem is too serious for businessmen and workers not to understand the importance of compliance. In addition, by setting standards for both wages and prices, Executive Order 12092 attempts to eliminate the need for either business or labor to seek price and wage increases. Finally, if the voluntary restraint program is effective in slowing inflation in the economy as a whole, the Government will face lower costs in the future than it would have otherwise.[47] Such a strategy of seeking the greatest advantage to the Government, both short- and long-term, is entirely consistent with the congressional policies behind the FPASA.

We do not deny that under Executive Order 12092 there may be occasional instances where a low bidder will not be awarded a contract. Nevertheless, we find no basis for rejecting the President's conclusion that any higher costs incurred in those trans-

---

45. *See* Currie affidavit:

Firms that meet the President's price and pay standards will be reducing their overall rate of increase in costs and prices. By directing procurement toward such firms an incentive will be provided to large numbers of Government suppliers to meet the standards. To the extent that this occurs, the inflationary element in overall Government procurement costs will be lessened, and the cost of procurement reduced.

47. *See* Currie affidavit:

[O]bservance of the [wage and price] standard[s] by large numbers of individual firms who supply the Government will put competitive pressure on other suppliers to do the same, tending to spread the cost-reducing consequences more broadly across the spectrum of procurement.

actions will be more than offset by the advantages gained in negotiated contracts and in those cases where the lowest bidder is in compliance with the voluntary standards and his bid is lower than it would have been in the absence of standards. Consequently, we conclude that Executive Order 12092 is in accord with the "economy and efficiency" touchstone of the FPASA. By acting to restrain procurement costs across the entire Government, the President was within his Section 205(a) powers.

We wish to emphasize the importance to our ruling today of the nexus between the wage and price standards and likely savings to the Government. As is clear from the terms and history of the statute and from experience with its implementation, our decision today does not write a blank check for the President to fill in at his will. The procurement power must be exercised consistently with the structure and purposes of the statute that delegates that power.[51]

III

The District Court concluded that the compliance program involved here was mandatory. As a result, that court found the program barred by this statement in Section 3(b) of COWPSA:

> Nothing in this Act . . . authorizes the continuation, imposition, or reimposition of any mandatory economic controls with respect to prices, rents, wages, salaries, corporate dividends, or any similar transfers. [12 U.S.C. § 1904 note (1976).]

We disagree with the District Court's conclusion. Although every denial of a benefit may be viewed in some sense as a sanction, we do not find in the procurement compliance program those elements of coercion and enforceable legal duty that are commonly understood to be part of any legally mandatory requirement. The situation in this case seems analogous to those federal programs that offer funds to state and local governments on certain conditions. The Supreme Court has upheld such conditional grants, observing on one occasion through Justice Cardozo that "to hold that motive or temptation is equivalent to coercion is to plunge the law in endless difficulties." [*Steward Machine Co. v. Davis*, 301 U.S. 548, 589-590 (1937).]

Further, any alleged mandatory character of the procurement program is belied by the principle that no one has a right to a Government contract. As the Supreme Court ruled in *Perkins v. Lukens Steel Co.*, [310 U.S. 113 (1940),] "[T]he Government enjoys the unrestricted power . . . to determine those with whom it will deal, and to fix the terms and conditions upon which it will make needed purchases." Those wishing to do business with the Government must meet the Government's terms; others need not.

---

51. *Amicus* argues that if the FPASA gives the President authority to adopt the procurement compliance program, the Act must run afoul of the constitutional prohibition against excessive delegation of legislative power to the President. . . . Although broad, [the FPASA's] standard can be applied generally to the President's actions to determine whether those actions are within the legislative delegation. At a more particular level, administrative standards exist to test the President's actions. . . . The standards for this program compare favorably with those found sufficient for purposes of judicial review of administrative action in *Amalgamated Meat Cutters & Butcher Workmen v. Connally*. That the procurement compliance program involves governmental contracting practices would not immunize actions under it from court challenge as arbitrary and capricious or contrary to law.

The question presented by this case, however, is not whether in some abstract sense President Carter's program is mandatory or voluntary, but whether it is barred by Section 3(b) of COWPSA. In our view, that provision refers to the sort of mandatory economic controls imposed during World War II, the Korean War, and the early 1970s. The statute covers "prices, rents, wages, salaries, [and] corporate dividends," a likely reference to a similar list in Section 203(a) of the Economic Stabilization Act Amendments of 1971 which established legally enforceable wage and price controls. Because COWPSA was enacted just a few months after the Economic Stabilization Act expired, it is reasonable to conclude that the language of Section 3(b) looks back to the provisions of the earlier Act. In addition, the standards in Executive Order 12092, which cover only wages and prices, are not as extensive as the list in Section 3(b). Consequently, we do not think the procurement compliance program falls within the coverage of Section 3(b), but rather is a halfway measure outside the contemplation of Congress in that enactment. This interpretation is reinforced by the fact that Executive Order 12092, unlike the earlier wage and price programs, makes no provision for civil or criminal penalties or injunctions.

Perhaps more important, Section 3(b) is irrelevant to the President's procurement compliance program. The statutory provision states that "[n]othing in *this* Act ... authorizes ... mandatory economic controls" (emphasis added). Executive Order 12092 relies on COWPSA for the Council's power to establish the voluntary wage and price standards, but the Order rests on the FPASA for implementation of the procurement compliance program. Since we think the procurement feature of the President's Order is supported by FPASA, it is of no concern that Section 3(b) may not also grant him that authority.

Finally, it is important to point out that just two months ago the Congress approved a one-year extension of COWPSA, a tripling of its budget, and a sixfold increase in its staff. The legislative history of this 1979 extension of COWPSA, which was approved while this suit was pending in the District Court, contains several assertions that Congress did not intend to make any statement on the issues raised in this case. Yet it strains credulity to maintain that COWPSA bars the procurement compliance program when Congress has just extended that statute knowing that the Council it established is charged with implementing the wage and price guidelines on which the procurement program is based. Congress can reverse incorrect Executive interpretations of its statutes and has used that power in the past. Congress, fully aware of the procurement program, renewed COWPSA without significant modification. In this context, a court could only in the most extreme case find that the Executive has violated the statute. . . .

Consequently, the order of the District Court is reversed and its injunction is vacated.[65]

[Judges BAZELON and TAMM filed brief concurrences relying on the "close nexus" between the order and the FPASA's purposes.]

---

65. We note our disagreement with the view taken by Judge MacKinnon in his lengthy dissent as to the role of Congress with respect to this case. We do not think it without any significance at all that the FPASA has not been revised in reaction to Executive Orders by Presidents Eisenhower, Kennedy, Johnson, and Nixon that explicitly or implicitly relied on the statute, and which deployed the procurement power in pursuit of ends that might not strictly be defined as economy or efficiency.

MacKINNON, Circuit Judge, dissenting:

. . . I can find no license in the President's important but modest powers under the 1949 Act [FPASA] to support his imposition of wage and price controls on federal government contractors. Moreover, I believe that were the majority's construction of section 205(a) correct, then the 1949 Act would amount to an unconstitutional delegation of legislative authority to the executive branch. Accordingly, I dissent. . . .

It is not necessary to wander beyond the specific context of Executive Order 12092 itself to discover that the majority's reasoning knows no bounds. Although the Executive Order confines its scope to government contractors and their first-tier sub-contractors and suppliers, and in any event to contracts in excess of $5 million, these limitations play no role in the majority's analysis. Accordingly under today's ruling the President could immediately extend the guidelines to any contractor or subcontractor regardless of the value of their contract. In addition, . . . there would be no reason why the President could not also immediately require as a condition of doing business with the government that all contractors now covered by his Order refuse to do business with any other entity not in compliance with the President's guidelines. Using only his section 205(a) power, then, the President could in effect impose a secondary boycott on any business that did not accept his wage and price "suggestions." . . .

Section 3(b) of the Council on Wage and Price Stability Act of 1974 provides that nothing therein authorizes the "continuation, imposition, or reimposition of *any mandatory economic controls* with respect to prices, rents, wages, salaries, [and] corporate dividends." . . . It is odd that the majority can rely on the 1979 extension of the Council on Wage and Price Stability Act of 1974 to support its interpretation of section 205(a), but rejects any reliance on the substantive provisions of the original enactment, though the latter established the mechanism the President is using to implement Executive Order 12092. Even recognizing that some restriction should be placed on the intent expressed in a statute, the intent expressed in section 3(b) is not "irrelevant" to our consideration of the President's procurement program. In analyzing what kinds of policies and directives the President can issue pursuant to his procurement power it is useful to examine other congressional enactments to explore whether Congress has expressly or impliedly intended to limit the President's options. Viewing section 3(b) from this perspective, I find inescapable the conclusion that the history of congressional control over and regulation of programs of wage and price stabilization, and especially its recent condemnations of such programs, indicate that Congress did not intend to permit the use of section 205(a) to establish the kinds of wage and price requirements the President has established here.

This conclusion emerges from the consistent pattern, stretching back over more than three decades, of complete and zealously guarded congressional control of wage and price stabilization. It exists in section 3(b) and its legislative history. I find it in Congress' refusal, after careful consideration and thorough debate, to extend the Economic Stabilization Act of 1971, an extension which would have permitted the President to order controls like those imposed pursuant to statutory authority by President Nixon in 1971. I find it in the Senate's adoption last September of a "Sense of the Senate" resolution—concededly not a complete expression of congressional intent—expressing the view that neither the 1949 Act nor any other statute sanctioned the imposition of wage and price standards. I find it in Congress' unequivocal statements that nothing in its recent extension of the Council on Wage and Price Stability

Act was to be in any way construed as an endorsement of the President's procurement program. H.R.Rep. No. 96-93, 96th Cong., 1st Sess. 3 (1979) (Conference Report).

The majority seeks solace in the last of this list, reasoning that Congress was by then aware of the President's procurement program and meant to display its approval of the program by extending the statute, tripling the Council's staff, and substantially increasing its budget. With clear and unambiguous statements to the contrary, it is a gross distortion of legislative intent to suggest that Congress' extension of the Council on Wage and Price Stability Act was a *sub silentio* endorsement of the President's procurement program. Even were the expressions of congressional intent less clear, and even were it appropriate to rely on the extension, the extension would still be insufficient to indicate an abrupt abdication of the authority to regulate wages and prices that Congress has so carefully and sparingly used over the past four decades. Similarly, I reject the majority's Rip Van Winkle theory that Congress' failure to overturn the President's program is an implied ratification of it. Congressional inaction does not strip courts of their responsibility to construe statutes. Congress was aware of the grave questions surrounding the President's use of the procurement power to promulgate Executive Order 12092, and it fully expected courts to fulfill their duty to resolve those questions. It is Congress' job to make law; it is the courts' job to say what the law is.

It is obvious to me that the President's procurement program falls within the species of *mandatory* controls that Congress has condemned in section 3(b) and elsewhere, and that therefore the Executive Order contradicts the expressed will of Congress.... For a program to be mandatory it need not compel every person in the Nation to conform to a particular requirement. It is sufficiently "mandatory" if those within its orbit are compelled to comply with the requirement under the pain of suffering a denial of some benefit that would have been open to them....

ROBB, Circuit Judge, dissenting:

... At the oral argument in this court counsel for the government rightly conceded that "[i]f the court were to conclude that these guidelines [established by the Executive Order] were an exercise of mandatory economic controls within the ... full meaning of that term ... the government would lose." In my opinion the government does lose, because the guidelines are mandatory. Contractors who fail to comply are threatened with the loss of contracts for the payment of millions, perhaps hundreds of millions of dollars. No amount of sophisticated or metaphysical argument can convince me that compliance under threat of such massive economic sanctions is voluntary. Accordingly, I think the government must fail on this ground alone....

———

1. On what did the court rely in finding that the President's program was reasonably related to the purposes of the Procurement Act? Should this have been enough? If judicial enforcement of the court's standard of review requires no more, is the standard of review likely to be a constraint on administrative behavior? For discussion of *Kahn*, see Note, *Presidential Power over Federal Contracts Under The Federal Property and Administrative Services Act: The Close Nexus Test of* AFL-CIO v. Kahn, 1980 Duke L. J. 205.

2. Was the court justified in giving so little weight to Congress' consistent practice of conferring or withdrawing wage-price authority explicitly by statute?

3. Was the court's literalist approach to COWPSA justified? Should Congress' appropriations decisions for COWPS be read as modifying the substantive legislation? *See TVA v. Hill*, 437 U.S. 153, 190-91 (1978):

> The doctrine disfavoring repeals by implication "applies with full vigor when ... the subsequent legislation is an *appropriations* measure." This is perhaps an understatement since it would be more accurate to say that the policy applies with even *greater* force when the claimed repeal rests solely on an Appropriations Act. We recognize that both substantive enactments and appropriations measures are "Acts of Congress," but the latter have the limited and specific purpose of providing funds for authorized programs. When voting on appropriations measures, legislators are entitled to operate under the assumption that the funds will be devoted to purposes which are lawful and not for any purpose forbidden. Without such an assurance, every appropriations measure would be pregnant with prospects of altering substantive legislation, repealing by implication any prior statute which might prohibit the expenditure. Not only would this lead to the absurd result of requiring Members to review exhaustively the background of every authorization before voting on an appropriation, but it would flout the very rules the Congress carefully adopted to avoid this need....
>
> Expressions of committees dealing with requests for appropriations cannot be equated with statutes enacted by Congress, particularly not in the circumstances presented by this case. First, the Appropriations Committees had no jurisdiction over the subject of endangered species, much less did they conduct the type of extensive hearings which preceded passage of the earlier Endangered Species Acts, especially the 1973 Act. We venture to suggest that the [committees having substantive jurisdiction] would be somewhat surprised to learn that their careful work on the substantive legislation had been undone by the simple—and brief—insertion of some inconsistent language in Appropriations Committees' Reports.

4. Presumably, the Procurement Act, if read broadly enough to permit wage-price measures, still does not violate the delegation doctrine. How does the relaxation of that doctrine affect the process of statutory interpretation in cases such as this?

5. Fleishman & Aufses, *supra*, proposed a variety of responses to the abuses they perceived in the issuance of executive orders. These included: narrower delegations of power by Congress (spurred by revival of the delegation doctrine), statutory and judicial requirements that orders specify their sources of authority, and greater judicial insistence that authority for orders actually exist. Do you agree with this overall prescription? Is it realistic? Is it wise?

Problem: Price Controls Under the Credit Control Act of 1969

As the court noted in *Meat Cutters*, President Nixon was opposed to legislative efforts to confer wage and price control authority on the President. Clearly, the Democratic Congress wished to insure that the President would have the broadest possible authority for fighting inflation, so that continued inflation could be blamed on the President, rather than on Congress.

In a similar spirit, but with far scantier legislative history, Congress also enacted the Credit Control Act of 1969, 12 U.S.C. §1901 *et seq.* In part, that act provides:

§ 1904. Credit controls

(a) Whenever the President determines that such action is necessary or appropriate for the purpose of preventing or controlling inflation generated by the extension of credit in an excessive volume, the President may authorize the [Board of Governors of the Federal Reserve System] to regulate and control any or all extensions of credit.

(b) The Board may, in administering this Act, utilize the services of the Federal Reserve banks and any other agencies, Federal or State, which are available and appropriate.

§ 1905. Extent of control

The Board, upon being authorized by the President under section 1904 of this title and for such period of time as he may determine, may by regulation

(1) require transactions or persons or classes of either to be registered or licensed.

(2) prescribe appropriate limitations, terms and conditions for any such registration or license.

(3) Provide for suspension of any such registration or license for violation of any provision thereof or of any regulation, rule, or order prescribed under this Act.

(4) prescribe appropriate requirements as to the keeping of records and as to the form, contents, or substantive provisions of contracts, liens, or any relevant documents.

(5) prohibit solicitations by creditors which would encourage evasion or avoidance of the requirements of any regulation, license, or registration under this Act.

(6) prescribe the maximum amount of credit which may be extended on, or in connection with, any loan, purchase, or other extension of credit.

(7) prescribe the maximum rate of interest, maximum maturity, minimum periodic payment, maximum period between payments, and any other specification or limitation of the terms and conditions of any extension of credit.

(8) prescribe the methods of determining purchase prices or market values or other bases for computing permissible extensions of credit or required downpayment.

(9) prescribe special or different terms, conditions, or exemptions with respect to new or used goods, minimum original cash payments, temporary credits which are merely incidental to cash purchase, payment or deposits usable to liquidate credits, and other adjustments or special situations.

(10) prescribe maximum ratios, applicable to any class of either creditors or borrowers or both, of loans of one or more types or of all types.

(A) to deposits of one or . . . all types.

(B) to assets of one or . . . all types.

(11) prohibit or limit any extensions of credit under any circumstances the Board deems appropriate.

§ 1907. Injunctions for compliance

Whenever it appears to the Board that any person has engaged, is engaged, or is about to engage in any acts or practices constituting a violation of any regulation under this chapter, it may in its discretion bring an action, in the proper district court of the United States ... to enjoin such acts or practices. ...

§1908. Civil penalties

(a) For each willful violation of any regulation under this chapter, the Board may assess upon any person to which the regulation applies, ... a civil penalty not exceeding $1,000.

(b) In the event of the failure of any person to pay any penalty assessed under this section, a civil action for the recovery thereof may, in the discretion of the Board, be brought in the name of the United States.

§ 1909. Criminal penalty

Whoever willfully violates any regulation under this chapter shall be fined not more than $1,000 or imprisoned not more than one year, or both.

You may note that, under the literal terms of this Act, several possibilities exist, given the requisite presidential determination, for the imposition of price guidelines throughout the economy. For example, one means of preventing or controlling "inflation generated by the extension of credit in an excessive volume" might be prohibiting sellers from extending credit to purchasers whenever the price of goods being sold exceeds some specified maximum. (Arguably, this would not amount to mandatory price control, because sellers could always sell their goods for cash at prices set above the guideline.) Alternatively, a system of price guidelines could be implemented by denying extensions of credit by financial institutions to those companies that sell goods above set prices.

Since the 1940s, credit controls have been imposed four times. Three times, all before 1969, the controls consisted of limitations on the availability of credit for particular purchases. In March, 1980, Secretary of the Treasury G. William Miller asked the Attorney General whether the President could lawfully authorize the Board of Governors of the Federal Reserve System, as he proposed to recommend, to regulate the extension of credit by requiring certain creditors, *i.e.*, consumer creditors and money market funds, to keep certain of their funds on deposit in non-interest-bearing Federal Reserve accounts. He further proposed that the President authorize the Board to require that commercial banks that do not belong to the Federal Reserve system keep in the same kind of accounts certain of the funds that such banks borrow on credit in the form of "managed liabilities." Such measures had never before been part of a government credit-control program. With the Attorney General's formal legal approval, 43 Op. A.G. No. 20 (1980), the President did authorize such controls, Exec. Order No. 12,201, 45 Fed. Reg. 17123 (1980), which the Board of Governors thereafter implemented. 45 Fed. Reg. 17927 (1980). The validity of the regulations was not tested in court.

In your view, does the Credit Control Act authorize the implementation of price guidelines? Would there be any delegation doctrine problem with the Act so interpreted?

In his formal opinion to the Secretary of the Treasury, concluding that these recommended measures, if adopted by the President, would constitute a proper exercise of his authority, the Attorney General stated:

Despite the flexibility of the authority vested both in the President and the Board of Governors of the Federal Reserve System, the Act does not transgress the constitutional prohibition against excessive delegations of legislative power. The determination required of the President, that action "is necessary or appropriate for the purpose of preventing or controlling inflation generated by the extension of credit in excessive volume," 12 U.S.C. §1904, provides an adequate standard against which the terms of the President's authorization and the Board's subsequent actions may be assessed [citing *AFL-CIO v. Kahn* and *Meat Cutters*].

Id. at 2-3 n. 2. Do you agree? Has the Attorney General dealt with the issue sufficiently?

Nothing in the legislative history of the Credit Control Act directly forbids the price guideline suggestions. Indeed, both proponents and opponents of the Act contended for a broad reading of its authorities. *See* 43 Op. A.G. No. 20, at 2 n. 1 (1980), and the legislative history there cited. Nonetheless, President Carter repeatedly denied during his administration that any statutory authority existed for the imposition of wage or price controls. Was his position well founded? Would it be relevant to a subsequent administration's or to a court's interpretation of the Credit Control Act?

Note: *Private Enforcement of Executive Orders*

In *In re Surface Mining Regulation Litigation*, 627 F.2d 1346 (D.C. Cir. 1980), the Court of Appeals reviewed a series of challenges to interim regulations issued by the Secretary of the Interior under the Surface Mining Control and Reclamation Act of 1977, 30 U.S.C. §1201 *et seq.* A number of coal mining companies and trade associations challenged the regulations because, among other things, the Secretary of the Interior assertedly failed to prepare a formal economic and inflationary impact analysis as required by Exec. Order No. 11,281. The court's response to this challenge provides a recent statement of the general rule concerning the private enforcement of obligations imposed on executive branch officials by executive orders (627 F.2d at 1357):

> Executive Order No. 11821, reprinted in 12 U.S.C. § 1904 note (1976), "require[s] that all major legislative proposals, regulations, and rules emanating from the executive branch of the Government include a statement certifying that the inflationary impact of such actions on the Nation has been carefully considered." OMB Circular No. A-107, which was issued to implement Executive Order No. 11821, directs agency heads to consider the effects of proposed regulations on inflation, employment, and energy supply and demand, and establishes criteria for identifying regulations that may have such an impact. In *Independent Meat Packers Ass'n v. Butz*, 526 F.2d 228, 236 (8th Cir. 1975), *cert. denied*, 424 U.S. 966 (1976), the . . . Eighth Circuit held that "Executive Order No. 11821 was intended primarily as a managerial tool for implementing the President's personal economic policies and not as a legal framework enforceable by private civil action" and, "therefore, that the district court erroneously set aside the revised [Department of Agriculture] regulations in their entirety because of alleged deficiencies in the impact statement." This court has also declared that executive orders without specific foundation in congressional action are not judicially enforceable in private civil suits. See *Manhattan-Bronx Postal*

Union v. Gronouski, 350 F.2d 451, 456-57 (1965), *cert. denied*, 382 U.S. 978 (1966) (Executive Order No. 10988). Thus, Executive Order No. 11821 and OMB Circular No. A-107 provide no basis for overturning the interim regulations.

D. Veto Powers

In this section we consider veto powers of various sorts. First, we explore the President's conditional power to veto legislation, and pause to note his related powers to initiate and press legislation within Congress. Then we introduce a special form of the presidential veto: the pocket veto, which occurs upon the adjournment of Congress. (We consider proposals for granting the President an item veto in Chapter Four, with the materials on federal spending to which it relates.) Finally, we turn to "legislative vetoes," devices for Congress to disapprove executive action, and to their invalidation by the Supreme Court.

1. *The President's Veto*

The key presidential check on the legislative process is the constitutional requirement, under Art. I, §7, that all actions of Congress having public effect, whatever their form, must be presented to the President for his approval. A bill or resolution may be enacted over the President's disapproval, or veto, only by a vote of two-thirds of each house of Congress (*i.e.*, by at least two-thirds of a quorum of each house, *Missouri Pacific Ry. Co. v. Kansas*, 248 U.S. 276 (1919)).

For *Some Thoughts on the Veto*, we turn to Professor Charles Black, 40 Law & Contemp. Prob. 87, 93-98 (1976), who emphasizes the great power the veto accords the President due to the difficulty of override:

> Let's take the House of Representatives.... The usual situation, where there is a general opposition between the President and the House, is where the President is of a different party from the House majority. Now the one simple factor that is steady is party loyalty, reenforced by patronage. Let us take a Congress much like the present one, with about 290 Democrats and about 145 Republicans— figures I pick for the exact two to one ratio—and with a Republican President. In our politics, this is about as high as the majority in the House is likely to get. We ought to assume, until some reason to the contrary appears, that equal percentages of Democrats and Republicans will, in the long run, defect, both as to Democrats supporting the President and as to Republicans voting to override. But if (in our 290-145 House) ten per cent of the Republicans and ten per cent of the Democrats switch sides, the override loses by something like 275-160, a ... failure of override by a wide margin.
>
> How big a Democratic majority would it take to get around this? The answer, of course, depends on the percentage of defection. Assuming, *pro forma*, the same 10 per cent defection across party fences both ways, you would need 308 Democrats and 127 Republicans to have a "veto-proof" Congress.... On a party vote, with defections in equal proportions, override loses heavily in any imaginable House of Representatives.
>
> Let us assume, since there is no reason not to, that the same situation exists in the Senate. And then (as reality requires, for a few overrides do occur) let

us soften our assumptions a bit, or the consequences drawn from them, as to both Houses, and say, again *pro forma*, that override in either House has, say, one chance in four. It is important to note that this would mean that override in both Houses has one chance in 4^2 or 16, which is not far from what we find through history. . . .

(Parenthetically, the situation is even worse where the majority party is the President's own, for in that case the party loyalty of the majority runs to the President, and against override. F. D. Roosevelt vetoed [372] bills; [9] were overridden.) . . .

What are the consequences for American politics? First and most obviously, the majorities, even quite large, in . . . the House and the Senate are powerless to fix American policy on anything, foreign or domestic, so long as Congress sticks to the forthright expression of policy judgment in a single bill, and attempts neither circumvention of the veto by "rider," nor reprisal. . . .

The result is, inevitably, that actual veto can be rather rare even now—the tip of the iceberg, to coin a phrase. For the practical task of the leadership of the House of Representatives and the Senate, in reality and as perceived by that leadership, is not to draft and pass a bill that seems good to strong working majorities in the House and Senate. It is to produce a bill, acceptable to those majorities, or reluctantly swallowed by those majorities, that may get by a veto.

I say and stress "may" because there is no means of compelling the President to announce in advance what his action will be on a bill, or what amendments it will take to buy his signature. Very often, the general direction of his views is known. But exactly how much movement toward those views will be necessary is normally not known.

I suppose here one begins to enter the field of force of games theory. . . . One player must move toward placating his opponent, while only the opponent knows what it will take to placate him—or perhaps has not yet decided what it will take. . . . Very often—perhaps typically— the result has to be a compromise which rests on no clear policy, which may be worse than the following-out of either policy—and which may be vetoed anyway. That is the real situation in which the veto power puts Congress, and every citizen should be brought to understand it. There is one way out, as matters now stand. That is for Congress to accept, virtually verbatim, whatever "recommendations" the President makes. . . .

Let me move on to a third and quite crucial point about the veto. [T]here is an asymmetry here: The President may veto any independent action of Congress—indeed, no independent action of Congress, having the force of law, exists, except for the possibility . . . of override. But Congress may not veto any independent action of the President, for the peculiar reason that its action in this regard would itself be subject to Presidential veto. . . . If the President believes that an Act of Congress encroaches upon his office, he may, under the strictest and most ancient standards, veto it; so, also, if he believes an Act of Congress unconstitutional. If Congress, however, believes that an action of the President encroaches on its powers, or is unconstitutional on other grounds, it may not veto it, because the congressional veto, to have effect as law, must be by concurrence of both Houses, and so, under Article I, § 7, is subject to Presidential veto. . . .

It is against this background that one must consider the oft-repeated formula . . . that the President's powers, insofar as they derive from the general "executive power," are interstitial and tentative, since Congress may undo what the President has done. True, in a sense. But not very important, since the disaffirming congressional action is subject to veto. Not true at all, if what one means is that majorities of, say, 65 per cent in each House—an enormous preponderance—may effectively disapprove and annul the presidential action. The result of this asymmetry is that the President, with what might be thought meager textual powers, is institutionally almost untrammeled, since he may veto disapproving action by the very body to which he is supposedly subject, while that body, textually empowered to an enormous degree, is institutionally bound toe and neck by the veto. This institutional reason for the development of Presidential power must be added to . . . the structural suitability of the Presidency for the exercise of power, as contrasted with the built-in manyheadedness of Congress.

Certainly the overall statistics confirm Black's argument that the veto is a powerful presidential weapon. By 1976, there had been 1367 regular vetoes, and 993 pocket vetoes, for a total of 2360. Of the regular vetoes, 92, or 6.7%, were overridden (pocket vetoes are absolute). J. S. Kimmitt, ed., Presidential Vetoes, 1789-1976 (U.S. Gov. Printing Office 1978). Still, might Black's case be somewhat overstated? He compares the veto to a game in which each side is uncertain of the other's strategy. In that situation, if the President wishes to avoid the considerable embarrassment of an override, he will have an incentive to favor bills that are clearly on the safe side, won't he? Also, Presidents have been known to swallow bills they detest rather than be punished with an override. Thus, it seems that President and Congress have reciprocal influence in the legislative process, and that raw statistics on overrides tell only part of a very rich story.

There is a longstanding controversy over the appropriate uses of the veto. Although The Federalist argued that the President could exercise his veto on either constitutional or policy grounds (see INS v. Chadha, infra), the first Presidents rarely exercised a veto and most of the early ones were constitutionally based (including the first one, Washington's 1791 veto of a bill apportioning representatives). Characteristically, Jefferson thought that the veto was solely a shield against congressional encroachment on the executive; Hamilton found it apt for a bill objectionable on any ground. See McGowan, The President's Veto Power: An Important Instrument of Conflict in Our Constitutional System, 23 San Diego L. Rev. 791, 798-806 (1986). Before Andrew Jackson's famous veto in 1832 of the rechartering of the Second Bank of the United States, there had been only 21 vetoes, 6 of which were based on other than constitutional grounds. R. Pious, The American Presidency 60 (1979).

Our increased reliance on legislation in modern times, and the accompanying veto opportunities, renew the question of the appropriate scope of the veto. Judge McGowan, supra at 806-08, sides with Hamilton:

There are . . . persuasive policy reasons for viewing the veto power as a broad tool of presidential review. At the Constitutional Convention, the Framers discussed and designed the veto as an integral component in our separation of powers scheme. But to be an effective check on the federal legislature, the veto need not and should not be limited to bills encroaching on the executive realm. The legislative branch can overreach without encroaching on the executive. Members of Congress often produce legislation that is the result of pressure employed by special interest groups. Indeed, while the legislative process is a model of compromise, the final product may be nothing more than an aggregation of narrow, special-interest proposals. . . . Even the Framers recognized that laws could be enacted in the heat of factionalism. It is both appropriate and desirable that interest groups have access to our lawmakers.

The presidency can be characterized in a similar fashion. All elective officals must necessarily be responsive to interest groups in today's political environment. But the President represents a more national voter constituency, as compared to a single legislator. A presidential veto can moderate legislation for the national good or skew legislation toward the President's personal agenda. Each of these results is desirable. Since the veto clearly contemplates presidential participation in the difficult task of legislating, there is no good reason why the President should don blinders and ignore the full range of his policy, and even political interests. . . . [I]f the President is a representative of *all* the people, there is no reason to limit his powers to respond to his constituency, at least in the absence of a clear, constitutional mandate to do so. There is certainly no *express* limitation on the veto power. . . .

Of course, it is important to recognize that a broad veto power enables a recalcitrant President to interfere with positive congressional programs. We often view the legislative branch as responsible for designing comprehensive solutions to our nation's problems. Without the support of the President, however, Congress' task can be far more difficult. . . . The fact that the President is often supported on veto overrides by his own political party (thus explaining the low override rate) does not cast his veto in a dark light. Rather it validates the political, and possibly popular acceptance of his position. Moreover, when Congress is populated by a majority of members of the opposite party, it is not defenseless against a systematic use of the veto. At some point, the President's reliance on a negative power in the face of continued congressional initiatives will produce untoward political consequences for the executive. Additionally, the President must work with Congress if he is to achieve his own agenda. Thus, Congress can use its role in other lawmaking to force a President to moderate particular vetoes, just as a President uses his vetoes to moderate Congress.

In addition to the veto power, the Constitution contemplates that the President will participate in the legislative process by "recommend[ing] to their Consideration such Measures as he shall judge necessary and expedient . . ." (Art. II, § 3). Judge McGowan's point that "the President must work with Congress if he is to achieve his own agenda" is one that some Presidents have grasped better than others. For a recent example, consider President Carter's relatively low—and his successor's relatively high—levels of interest and skill in congressional relations.

Critical as it is to his overall success, the President's role as legislative initiator and advocate is mostly in the province of political science rather than law. For overviews of the subject, *see* R. Pious, *supra*, Chs. 5-6; L. Fisher, The Politics of Shared Power, Congress and the Executive, Ch. 2 (1981). We deal with selected aspects of the President's role in the legislative process in Chapter Four, as it pertains to his powers to supervise the administrative establishment and to formulate the federal budget.

2. *Pocket Vetoes*

In one circumstance the President has what amounts to an absolute veto. Under Art. I, §7, the President must return vetoed legislation to the house from which it originated, with his objections, for possible override. If the President fails to return a bill within ten days, excepting Sundays, it becomes law, "unless Congress by their Adjournment prevent its Return, in which Case it shall not be a Law."[1] When the President prevents a bill from becoming law in this last way, it is called a "pocket veto," and Congress must pass an entirely new piece of legislation in its next session, which the President again may disapprove.

The limits of the President's pocket veto power were explored in a recent litigation. The question was whether "intersession" adjournments of Congress, which occur between the first and second sessions of each Congress, present an opportunity for a pocket veto. ("Intrasession" adjournments occur within a session, for example over holidays, and "final" adjournments conclude each Congress.) Various members of the House of Representatives sued for declaratory and injunctive relief to nullify President Reagan's attempted pocket veto of H.R. 4042, which restricted military assistance to El Salvador during the then current fiscal year. Both houses had passed the bill and adjourned *sine die* until the second session, but had authorized the Clerk of the House and the Secretary of the Senate to receive messages from the President in the interim.

A decision on the merits by the Court of Appeals was eventually vacated by the Supreme Court for mootness, because the bill in question had expired by its own terms. Nevertheless, we reproduce portions of the Court of Appeals' opinion here, to introduce you to the issues:

Barnes v. Kline

759 F.2d 21 (D.C. Cir. 1985), *vacated sub. nom.* Burke v. Barnes, 107 S.Ct. 734 (1987)

McGOWAN, Senior Circuit Judge:

. . . The question we confront is whether H.R. 4042 became law when the President failed to return it to the House of Representatives (where it originated) within the allotted time, or whether the bill expired because return was prevented by Congress's having adjourned its first session *sine die* on the day of presentment of the bill. We believe this question has a clear answer. Given that both the House of Representatives and the Senate had expressly arranged before adjourning for an agent specifically authorized to receive veto messages from the President during the adjournment, it is difficult to understand how Congress could be said to have prevented return of H.R. 4042 simply by adjourning. Rather, by appointing agents for receipt of veto messages, Congress affirmatively *facilitated* return of the bill in the eventuality that the President would disapprove it.

---

1. Despite an early presidential practice of going to the Capitol on the final day of each session of Congress to sign last minute bills, in order that all bills would be approved during Congress' session, it is now clear that a bill signed within ten days but during an adjournment of Congress becomes law. *Edwards v. United States*, 286 U.S. 482 (1932). *See* L. Tribe, American Constitutional Law 200 & n. 11 (1978).

The District Court held, however, that Congress's adjournment must be deemed to have "prevented" return of H.R. 4042 to the House, notwithstanding the existence of an agent authorized to receive the President's veto, and that H.R. 4042 thus expired through a pocket veto. The court rested the decision on its reading of the two Supreme Court opinions and the one opinion by this court that have construed the pocket veto clause. We believe that the District Court has misapplied these precedents and that its decision consequently frustrates the recognized purpose behind the pocket veto clause.

An examination of the Framers' intent with respect to the pocket veto clause is a natural place to begin our analysis. Nowhere in the records of the Federal Convention of 1787, however, is there any reference to the concept of a pocket veto, or, for that matter, to any of the specifics of the enactment process. Rather, the delegates were concerned with the broad issues of whether the President ought to have the power to veto legislation and, if so, whether Congress should be able to override a presidential veto. On these issues, however, the records speak plainly and decisively. The delegates were firmly convinced that the President must have some power to revise legislative acts. But an absolute veto, they equally strongly believed, was dangerous and un-warranted.... Thus, the delegates unanimously voted down an absolute veto....

The precise means of providing for a qualified presidential veto were devised by the Committee of Detail in what, with minor modifications, would ultimately constitute Article I, section 7, clauses 2 and 3 of the Constitution. The Committee's product reflects the recognition that to safeguard the qualified veto requires more than simply a set of rules directing Congress to present bills to the President and directing the President to approve or return such bills. For in the absence of any sanctions for violation of such rules, the President might simply decline to act upon a duly presented bill in order to block congressional reconsideration and thereby achieve through inaction what the Framers refused to permit him, namely, an absolute veto. The veto provision therefore mandates that a bill becomes law at the end of a ten-day period if not returned. Without more, however, Congress, which controls its own calendar, could in turn vitiate the President's qualified veto by cutting short or entirely eliminating, through adjournment, the period of time alloted the President to return a bill with his objections. It is that evil which the pocket veto clause forestalls by withholding the status of law from a bill whose return Congress prevented. The pocket veto clause thus is intended, not as an affirmative grant of power to the Executive, but rather as a limitation on the prerogative of Congress to reconsider a bill upon presidential disapproval, a limitation triggered when Congress "by their Adjournment prevent [the bill's] Return."

The manifest purpose of the pocket veto clause has guided application of the clause by the Supreme Court, as well as this circuit. In *The Pocket Veto Case*, 279 U.S. 655 (1929), the earliest judicial discussion of the pocket veto clause, the Supreme Court confronted the issue of whether return of a bill to the Senate, where it originated, had been prevented when the Sixty-ninth Congress adjourned its first session *sine die* fewer than ten days after presenting the bill to the President. Justice Sanford's opinion for the Court began by declaring that the term "adjournment" is used in the Constitution to refer to any occasion on which a house of Congress is not in session, and dismissed the contention that the term refers solely to final adjournments of a Congress:

We think that under the constitutional provision the determinative question in reference to an "adjournment" is not whether it is a final adjournment of Congress or an interim adjournment, such as an adjournment of the first session, but whether it is one that "prevents" the President from returning the bill to the House in which it originated within the time allowed.

. . . Because the veto provision specifies that the President must return a disapproved bill to its originating house, and because neither house was in session to receive delivery of the returned bill in that instance, the Court reasoned, return must be deemed to have been prevented.

Counsel for the House of Representatives had argued that, when the originating house is not in session, return may be made consistently with the constitutional provisions by delivering the bill, with the President's objections, to a proper agent of the house of origin, for subsequent delivery to that house when it reconvenes. Addressing itself to this argument, the Court noted first "the fact that Congress has never enacted any statute authorizing any officer or agent of either House to receive for it bills returned by the President during its adjournment, and that there is no rule to that effect in either House." Moreover, the Court stated, "delivery of the bill to such officer or agent, even if authorized by Congress itself, would not comply with the constitutional mandate." The Court explained its position thus:

> Manifestly it was not intended that, instead of returning the bill to the House itself, as required by the constitutional provision, the President should be authorized to deliver it, during an adjournment of the House, to some individual officer or agent not authorized to make any legislative record of its delivery, who should hold it in his own hands for days, weeks or perhaps months—not only leaving open possible questions as to the date on which it had been delivered to him, or whether it had in fact been delivered to him at all, but keeping the bill in the meantime in a state of suspended animation until the House resumes its sittings, with no certain knowledge on the part of the public as to whether it had or had not been seasonably delivered, and necessarily causing delay in its reconsideration which the Constitution evidently intended to avoid.

Two concerns thus led the Court to believe that return to an agent of the original house would not adequately guarantee the President the opportunity to exercise his qualified veto: (1) delivery to an agent unauthorized to make an official record of delivery would engender uncertainty over whether timely return had in fact been made and thus whether the bill had or had not become law; and (2) such a return would be followed by lengthy delay before possible reconsideration by the originating house.

That the Court was not categorically denying the use of agents for delivery of veto messages was made clear in the Court's next, and last, encounter with the pocket veto clause. In *Wright v. United States*, 302 U.S. 583 (1938), the Court was called upon to determine the effectiveness of the President's return of a bill on the tenth day after presentment, during a three-day adjournment by the originating house only. The Court, speaking through Chief Justice Hughes, held that return to that house had not been prevented and that, therefore, delivery of the veto message to the Secretary of the Senate constituted an effective return.

In the first place, the Court noted, the Senate alone had adjourned, not "the Congress." Under the pocket veto clause, only an adjournment by "the Congress" can prevent return of a bill. The Court then dismissed the notion that a bill cannot be returned by the President to the originating house if that house is in an intrasession adjournment. In this instance, the Court stated, there clearly was no "practical difficulty" in making return during the adjournment: "The organization of the Senate continued and was intact. The Secretary of the Senate was functioning and was able to receive, and did receive, the bill." More importantly, the Court held that "[i]n returning the bill to the Senate by delivery to its Secretary during the recess there was no violation of any express requirement of the Constitution. *The Constitution does not define what shall constitute a return of a bill or deny the use of appropriate agencies in effecting the return.*" *Id.* at 589 (emphasis added).

As the *Wright* Court explained, the *Pocket Veto Case* was not to the contrary. Although the opinion in the earlier case had expressed the view that return can only be made to a house that is actually assembled and not to an agent of the house, that view did not control this case because it was grounded in concerns that were wholly inapplicable to a brief, intrasession adjournment by the originating house:

> In such case there is no withholding of the bill from appropriate legislative record for weeks or perhaps months, no keeping of the bill in a state of suspended animation with no certain knowledge on the part of the public whether it was seasonably delivered, no causing of any undue delay in its reconsideration. When there is nothing but such a temporary recess the organization of the House and its appropriate officers continue to function without interruption, the bill is properly safeguarded for a very limited time and is promptly reported and may be reconsidered immediately after the short recess is over. The prospect that in such a case the public may not be promptly and properly informed of the return of the bill with the President's objections, or that the bill will not be properly safeguarded or duly recorded upon the journal of the House, or that it will not be subject to reasonably prompt action by the House, is we think wholly chimerical.

Given "the manifest realities of the situation," the Court held, return to an agent of the originating house was wholly effective. Moreover, other adjournments might well not prevent return, although the Court declined to speculate as to which would or would not.... Thus, the Court expressly left open the possibility that its analysis would apply to render return to an agent effective in adjournments other than brief, one-house, intrasession adjournments. The Court, however, did not leave future courts without guidance in applying the veto provisions, for it made clear that those provisions are to be interpreted in the light of their "two fundamental purposes."... On the one hand, the Court stated, the veto provisions are meant to ensure that "the President shall have suitable opportunity to consider the bills presented to him...." At the same time, the provisions ensure "that the Congress shall have suitable opportunity to consider his objections to bills and on such consideration to pass them over his veto provided there are the requisite votes."...

Wright thus has twofold significance. First, and most important, its rule of construction requires a court to find that the President was truly deprived of his opportunity to exercise his qualified veto power before it may hold that return was "prevented"; a court that fails in this responsibility ends up sacrificing, without justification, Congress's right to reconsider disapproved legislation. Second, *Wright* indisputably establishes that mere absence of the originating house does not prevent return if (1) there is an authorized agent to accept delivery of a veto message, and

(2) such a procedure would not entail the delay and uncertainty justly feared by the Court in the *Pocket Veto Case.*

Ten years ago, in *Kennedy v. Sampson*, 511 F.2d 430 (D.C. Cir. 1974), this circuit applied the teaching of *Wright* to hold that return is not prevented by an intrasession adjournment of any length by one or both houses of Congress, so long as the originating house arranged for receipt of veto messages. . . . As did the Court in *Wright*, this court demonstrated that the concerns that had led the Court in the *Pocket Veto Case* to disapprove return to a house not in session were simply unjustified in the context of the particular type of adjournment at issue. This court stated: "The modern practice of Congress with respect to intrasession adjournments creates neither of the hazards—long delay and public uncertainty—perceived in the *Pocket Veto Case.*" This court noted that, whereas at the time of the Pocket Veto Case "intersession adjournments of five or six months were still common," in the past decade Congress's intrasession adjournments have typically consisted of "several recesses of approximately five days for various holidays and a summer recess (or recesses) lasting about one month." . . .

As to the concern for public uncertainty, this court stated:

> Modern methods of communication make it possible for the return of a disapproved bill to an appropriate officer of the originating House to be accomplished as a matter of public record accessible to every citizen. The status of such a bill would be clear; it has failed to receive presidential approval but may yet become law if Congress, upon resumption of its deliberations, passes the bill again by a two-thirds majority. This state of affairs generates no more public uncertainty than does the return of a disapproved bill while Congress is in actual session.

Indeed, the *Sampson* court observed, "[t]he only possible uncertainty about this situation arises from the absence of a definitive ruling as to whether an intrasession adjournment 'prevents' the return of a vetoed bill. Hopefully, our present opinion eliminates that ambiguity."

In addressing ourselves to the issue in this appeal we are of course cognizant of the fact that the *Pocket Veto Case* remains the only decision concerning the opportunity *vel non* for a pocket veto during an intersession adjournment. It was the District Court's belief that the *Pocket Veto Case* is therefore "the only case directly in point." Emphasizing that *Wright* did not purport to approve of delivery to agents during anything other than a three-day adjournment and that even *Sampson*'s expansion of *Wright* did not reach beyond the line between intrasession and intersession adjournments, the District Court concluded that "neither *Wright* nor *Kennedy v. Sampson* give it license to depart from . . . *Pocket Veto.*" The court accordingly held, in essence, that intersession adjournments per se create an opportunity for a valid pocket veto.

We appreciate the District Court's desire to remain within the boundaries of precedent. We disagree, however, with its assessment of where those boundaries lie. Moreover, we believe that the District Court's holding fails to serve the essential purposes of the veto provisions.

The principle that we believe runs through *Pocket Veto* and *Wright* is a simple one: whenever Congress adjourns, return of a veto message to a duly authorized officer of the originating house will be effective only if, under the circumstances of that type of adjournment, such a procedure would not occasion undue delay or uncertainty over the returned bill's status. . . . Nor, we are convinced, do intersession adjournments pose either of those problems, for . . . such adjournments do not differ in any practical respect from the intrasession adjournments at issue in *Wright* and *Kennedy v. Sampson*. To be sure, an intersession adjournment delays possible reconsideration of a returned bill. But the delay is not substantial. In stark contrast to the five- or six-month intersession adjournments typical at the time of the *Pocket Veto Case*, intersession adjournments of the modern era have an average length of only four weeks, and are thus often even shorter than intrasession adjournments. . . .

The opportunity for immediate reconsideration after the intersession adjournment is guaranteed by the rules of each house of Congress, which mandate that all business unfinished at the end of the first session shall be resumed at the start of the second. Moreover, because in this case, as is typical, the adjournment resolution provided that Congress could be reassembled at any time, and because the rules of the two houses permit the convening of congressional committees during adjournments, reconsideration of a bill returned during an intersession adjournment is not necessarily delayed even the several weeks that such an adjournment lasts.

Uncertainty no more characterizes return during adjournment than does delay. As in the case of intrasession adjournments, the organization of each house of Congress remains unchanged, and their respective staffs continue to function uninterrupted. More importantly, neither house any longer lacks an authorized procedure for acceptance of veto messages during adjournment. The House of Representatives provides by rule that return may be made to the Clerk of the House; the Senate, by resolution, provides for acceptance of veto messages by the Senate Secretary. In both cases, the time of delivery is recorded on the journal of the respective house, and the message is retained by the authorized officer for presentation on the floor of the house immediately upon the house's reconvening. The return may thus "be accomplished as a matter of public record accessible to every citizen." *Kennedy v. Sampson*, 511 F.2d at 441. The status of a bill returned during an intersession adjournment therefore "would be clear; it has failed to receive presidential approval but may yet become law if Congress, upon resumption of its deliberations, passes the bill again by a two-thirds majority. This state of affairs generates no more public uncertainty than does the return of a disapproved bill while Congress is in actual session."

That intersession adjournments no longer present any real obstacle to the President's exercise of his qualified veto power was recognized by Presidents Ford and Carter, both of whom assumed the effectiveness of return vetoes made during such an adjournment. . . . For the line that divides the first session of a Congress from the second has ceased to have any practical significance. Were it not for the Article I, section 4, clause 2 requirement that "[t]he Congress shall assemble at least once in every Year," that line, it seems to us, would completely dissolve.

We fully recognize that clear rules respecting the pocket veto are vitally necessary in order that the status of bills in presidential disfavor be promptly resolved. In seeking clarity, we must be careful not to stray into arbitrariness by drawing an irrational line between intrasession and intersession adjournments. For we must be guided by the evident purpose of the pocket veto clause, which is simply to ensure that the President not be deprived of an opportunity to disapprove legislation. Manifestly, the president is no more deprived of that opportunity by a modern intersession adjournment than he was by the adjournments in *Wright* and *Sampson*. The line between intersession and intrasession adjournments, although a bright one, in no way furthers the intent behind the pocket veto clause, and it therefore fails to comport with the authorities interpreting the clause. Nothing is gained by drawing such a line. And what is lost is substantial, for a rule based on such a line deprives Congress of the final word on a significant portion of its legislation and grants the President an absolute veto, even though Congress has shown no disrespect for the President's role in the enactment process....

Appellees point out that the view that intersession adjournments do create an opportunity for a pocket veto has been accepted throughout most of the history of the Republic by both the President and Congress. Beginning with President Jefferson and continuing through President Nixon, twenty-five of the thirty Presidents who have exercised the pocket veto power at all have done so during intersession adjournments. In each of these pocket vetoes—272 in all—Congress has acquiesced. What is more, appellees argue, Congress in 1868 would have codified this practice of acquiescence into law with a bill to limit pocket vetoes to intersession adjournments, were it not for successful objections that so limiting *intra*session pocket vetoes would be unconstitutional. Clearly, however, neither the past practice of the Executive nor Congress's acquiescence in that practice is conclusive in this case. Nor is that practice particularly relevant here, given that it developed under adjournment conditions markedly different from those prevailing today....

The existence of an authorized receiver of veto messages, the rules providing for carryover of unfinished business, and the duration of modern intersession adjournments, taken together, satisfy us that when Congress adjourned its first session *sine die* on the day it presented H.R. 4042 to the President, return of that bill to the originating house was not prevented. We therefore hold that H.R. 4042 became law, and accordingly reverse and remand the decision of the District Court with instructions to enter summary declaratory judgment for appellants.

[Circuit Judge BORK dissented on grounds that members of Congress lack standing to litigate separation of powers cases. His opinion is excerpted in Chapter Five.]

————————

1. After the final demise of the *Barnes* litigation, how would you advise the President to treat various adjournments of Congress for pocket veto purposes?

2. In the present state of the law, the status of some legislation will be unknown if the President neither signs nor vetoes it during an adjournment. In light of that, should the Supreme Court have invoked the exception to mootness for cases that recur, to reach the merits?

3. Which position was more faithful to existing Supreme Court precedent, that of the District Court, or that of the Court of Appeals? *See* Note, Barnes v. Kline: *Picking the President's Pocket?*, 70 Minn. L. Rev. 1149 (1986).

4. Considering the evolution of congressional adjournment practices through the years and the modern methods for receiving messages from the President, what should a court's attitude toward the pocket veto be today? Is it an anachronistic exception to the overall grant of a qualified veto, whose scope should be minimized? Or is the pocket veto a legitimate tool of presidential politics, whose value the courts should recognize? *See* Note, *The Pocket Veto Reconsidered*, 72 Iowa L. Rev. 163 (1987).

3. ''Legislative Vetoes''

Most recent scholarly analysis of the significance of the President's veto powers has occurred in discussions of the so-called "legislative veto." Legislative veto is a shorthand phrase referring to any mechanism through which Congress employs a resolution of one or both of its houses to approve or disapprove executive exercise of delegated authority. These resolutions purport to have mandatory effect, although they are not submitted to the President for his consideration. For example, using a "one-house veto" Congress may delegate to an agency the authority to promulgate a rule, but provide that the rule shall not go into effect if it is "disapproved" by either house of Congress. Similarly, under a "committee approval" provision, Congress may delegate rulemaking authority to an agency, but provide that the rule shall not go into effect unless it is approved by the committees of the House and Senate having subject matter jurisdiction over the agency. A two-house veto takes the form of a *concurrent* resolution, which is a resolution of both houses not submitted to the President. (This should not be confused with a *joint* resolution, which is presented to the President and is essentially the same as ordinary legislation.) For a comprehensive history and typology of the legislative veto, *see* Watson, *Congress Steps Out: A Look at Congressional Control of the Executive*, 63 Calif. L. Rev. 983 (1975).

After decades of doubt and disagreement about the constitutionality of the legislative veto, the Supreme Court finally considered the issue in a landmark case, *INS v. Chadha*, which follows. Justice White's dissent in *Chadha* provides an introduction by recounting the variety of uses that Congress had found for the legislative veto, and the impetus that led to increasing reliance on it through the years:

> The prominence of the legislative veto mechanism in our contemporary political system and its importance to Congress can hardly be overstated. It has become a central means by which Congress secures the accountability of executive and independent agencies. Without the legislative veto, Congress is faced with a Hobson's choice: either to refrain from delegating the necessary authority, leaving itself with a hopeless task of writing laws with the requisite specificity to cover endless special circumstances across the entire policy landscape, or in the alternative, to abdicate its law-making function to the executive branch and independent agencies. To choose the former leaves major national problems unresolved; to opt for the latter risks unaccountable policymaking by those not elected to fill that role. Accordingly, over the past five decades, the legislative veto has been placed in nearly 200 statutes. The device is known in every field of governmental concern: reorganization, budgets, foreign affairs, war powers, and regulation of trade, safety, energy, the environment and the economy.

> The legislative veto developed initially in response to the problems of reorganizing the sprawling government structure created in response to the Depression. The Reorganization Acts established the chief model for the legislative veto. When President Hoover requested authority to reorganize the government in 1929, he coupled his request that the "Congress be willing to delegate its authority over the problem (subject to defined principles) to the Executive" with a proposal for legislative review. He proposed that the Executive "should act upon approval of a joint committee of Congress or with the reservation of power of revision by Congress within some limited period adequate for its consideration." Pub. Papers 432 (1929). Congress followed President Hoover's suggestion and authorized reorganization subject to legislative review. Act of June 30, 1932, ch. 314, § 407, 47 Stat. 382, 414.... Over the years, the provision was used extensively. Presidents submitted 115 reorganization plans to Congress of which 23 were disapproved by Congress pursuant to legislative veto provisions.

Shortly after adoption of the Reorganization Act of 1939, 54 Stat. 561, Congress and the President applied the legislative veto procedure to resolve the delegation problem for national security and foreign affairs. World War II occasioned the need to transfer greater authority to the President in these areas. The legislative veto offered the means by which Congress could confer additional authority while preserving its own constitutional role. During World War II, Congress enacted over thirty statutes conferring powers on the Executive with legislative veto provisions. President Roosevelt accepted the veto as the necessary price for obtaining exceptional authority.

Over the quarter century following World War II, Presidents continued to accept legislative vetoes by one or both Houses as constitutional, while regularly denouncing provisions by which Congressional committees reviewed Executive activity. The legislative veto balanced delegations of statutory authority in new areas of governmental involvement: the space program, international agreements on nuclear energy, tariff arrangements, and adjustment of federal pay rates.

During the 1970's the legislative veto was important in resolving a series of major constitutional disputes between the President and Congress over claims of the President to broad impoundment, war, and national emergency powers. The key provision of the War Powers Resolution authorizes the termination by concurrent resolution of the use of armed forces in hostilities. A similar measure resolved the problem posed by Presidential claims of inherent power to impound appropriations. Congressional Budget and Impoundment Control Act of 1974, 31 U.S.C. § 1403. In conference, a compromise was achieved under which permanent impoundments, termed "rescissions," would require approval through enactment of legislation. In contrast, temporary impoundments, or "deferrals," would become effective unless disapproved by one House. This compromise provided the President with flexibility, while preserving ultimate Congressional control over the budget. Although the War Powers Resolution was enacted over President Nixon's veto, the Impoundment Control Act was enacted with the President's approval. These statutes were followed by others resolving similar problems: the National Emergencies Act, 50 U.S.C. § 1622 (1976), resolving the longstanding problems with unchecked Executive emergency power; the Arms Export Control Act, 22 U.S.C. § 2776(b) (1976), resolving the problem of foreign arms sales; and the Nuclear Non-Proliferation Act of 1978, 42 U.S.C. §§ 2160(f), 2155(b), 2157(b), 2158, 2153(d) (Supp. IV. 1980), resolving the problem of exports of nuclear technology.

In the energy field, the legislative veto served to balance broad delegations in legislation emerging from the energy crisis of the 1970's. In the educational field, it was found that fragmented and narrow grant programs "inevitably lead to Executive-Legislative confrontations" because they inaptly limited the Commissioner of Education's authority. S.Rep. No. 763, 93d Cong., 2d Sess. 69 (1974). The response was to grant the Commissioner of Education rulemaking authority, subject to a legislative veto. In the trade regulation area, the veto preserved Congressional authority over the Federal Trade Commission's broad mandate to make rules to prevent businesses from engaging in "unfair or deceptive acts or practices in commerce."

Presidents from Franklin Roosevelt through Reagan resisted legislative veto provisions on both constitutional and policy grounds, often noting their reservations in signing bills containing veto provisions. Policy-based objections included the uncertainty veto provisions create in the administration of government programs, the opportunities they afford for undisclosed political pressure to influence administration (at the expense of meaningful public participation), the incentive that veto provisions provide for agencies to make policy through cumbersome adjudication, which is not vulnerable to legislative veto, and the difficulty of responsible congressional oversight of the details of the myriad government programs. Ironically, the veto, designed to increase congressional control of the executive, may actually have decreased that control whenever Congress did not give active review to an executive action, because it seems to have encouraged Congress to make broader delegations than it otherwise would, in hopes of checking policy as it formed at the implementing stage. *See* Bruff & Gellhorn, *Congressional Control of Administrative Regulation: A Study of Legislative Vetoes*, 90 Harv. L. Rev. 1369 (1977).

Immigration and Naturalization Service v. Chadha
462 U.S. 919 (1983)

Chief Justice BURGER delivered the opinion of the Court.

[This case] presents a challenge to the constitutionality of the provision in § 244(c)(2) of the Immigration and Nationality Act, 8 U.S.C. § 1254(c)(2), authorizing one House of Congress, by resolution, to invalidate the decision of the Executive Branch, pursuant to authority delegated by Congress to the Attorney General . . . to allow a particular deportable alien to remain in the United States.

I

Chadha is an East Indian who was born in Kenya and holds a British passport. He was lawfully admitted to the United States in 1966 on a nonimmigrant student visa. His visa expired on June 30, 1972. On October 11, 1973, the District Director of the Immigration and Naturalization Service ordered Chadha to show cause why he should not be deported for having "remained in the United States for a longer time than permitted." . . . [A] deportation hearing was held before an immigration judge [at which] Chadha conceded that he was deportable for overstaying his visa and the hearing was adjourned to enable him to file an application for suspension of deportation under § 244(a)(1) of the Act, [which] provides:

(a) . . . the Attorney General may, in his discretion, suspend deportation and adjust the status to that of an alien lawfully admitted for permanent residence, in the case of an alien who applies to the Attorney General for suspension of deportation and—

(1) is deportable under any law of the United States . . . and proves that . . . he was and is a person of good moral character; and is a person whose deportation would, in the opinion of the Attorney General, result in extreme hardship. . . .

After Chadha submitted his application . . . the deportation hearing was resumed. . . . On the basis of evidence adduced at the hearing, affidavits submitted with the application, and the results of a character investigation conducted by the INS, the immigration judge, on June 25, 1974, ordered that Chadha's deportation be suspended. The immigration judge found that Chadha met the requirements of § 244(a)(1)....

Pursuant to § 244(c)(1) of the Act, the immigration judge suspended Chadha's deportation and a report of the suspension was transmitted to Congress. Once the Attorney General's recommendation for suspension of Chadha's deportation was conveyed to Congress, Congress had the power under § 244(c)(2) of the Act to veto the Attorney General's determination that Chadha should not be deported. Section 244(c)(2) provides:

> (2) In the case of an alien specified in paragraph (1) of subsection (a) of this subsection—

> if... either the Senate or the House of Representatives passes a resolution stating in substance that it does not favor the suspension of such deportation, the Attorney General shall thereupon deport such alien or authorize the alien's voluntary departure at his own expense under the order of deportation in the manner provided by law. If, within the time above specified, neither the Senate nor the House of Representatives shall pass such a resolution, the Attorney General shall cancel deportation proceedings....

On December 12, 1975, Representative Eilberg, Chairman of the Judiciary Sub-committee on Immigration, Citizenship, and International Law, introduced a resolution opposing "the granting of permanent residence in the United States to [six] aliens," including Chadha. The resolution was referred to the House Committee on the Judiciary. On December 16, 1975, the resolution was discharged from further consideration by the House Committee... and submitted to the House of Representatives for a vote. The resolution had not been printed and was not made available to other Members of the House prior to or at the time it was voted on. So far as the record before us shows, the House consideration of the resolution was based on Representative Eilberg's statement from the floor that

> [i]t was the feeling of the committee, after reviewing 340 cases, that the aliens contained in the resolution [Chadha and five others] did not meet these statutory requirements, particularly as it relates to hardship; and it is the opinion of the committee that their deportation should not be suspended.

The resolution was passed without debate or recorded vote. Since the House action was pursuant to § 244(c)(2), the resolution was not treated as an Article I legislative act; it was not submitted to the Senate or presented to the President for his action.

After the House veto of the Attorney General's decision to allow Chadha to remain in the United States, the immigration judge reopened the deportation proceedings to implement the House order deporting Chadha. Chadha moved to terminate the proceedings on the ground that § 244(c)(2) is unconstitutional. The immigration judge held that he had no authority to rule on the constitutional validity of § 244(c)(2). On November 8, 1976, Chadha was ordered deported pursuant to the House action....

Chadha filed a petition for review of the deportation order in the United States Court of Appeals for the Ninth Circuit. The Immigration and Naturalization Service agreed with Chadha's position before the Court of Appeals and joined him in arguing that § 244(c)(2) is unconstitutional. In light of the importance of the question, the

Court of Appeals invited both the Senate and the House of Representatives to file briefs *amici curiae*.

After full briefing and oral argument, the Court of Appeals held that the House was without constitutional authority to order Chadha's deportation.... The essence of its holding was that § 244(c)(2) violates the constitutional doctrine of separation of powers. We granted certiorari...and we now affirm.

II

Before we address the important question of the constitutionality of the one-House veto provision of § 244(c)(2), we first consider several challenges to the authority of this Court to resolve the issue raised....

B

Severability

Congress...contends that the provision for the one-House veto in § 244(c)(2) cannot be severed from § 244. Congress argues that if the provision for the one-House veto is held unconstitutional, all of § 244 must fall. If § 244 in its entirety is violative of the Constitution, it follows that the Attorney General has no authority to suspend Chadha's deportation under § 244(a)(1) and Chadha would be deported. From this, Congress argues that Chadha lacks standing to challenge the constitutionality of the one-House veto provision because he could receive no relief even if his constitutional challenge proves successful.

Only recently this Court reaffirmed that the invalid portions of a statute are to be severed " '[u]nless it is evident that the Legislature would not have enacted those provisions which are within its power, independently of that which is not.' " *Buckley v. Valeo*, 424 U.S. 1, 108 (1976), quoting *Champlin Refining Co. v. Corporation Comm'n*, 286 U.S. 210 (1932). Here, however, we need not embark on that elusive inquiry since Congress itself has provided the answer to the question of severability in § 406 of the Immigration and Nationality Act, which provides:

> If any particular provision of this Act, or the application thereof to any person or circumstance, is held invalid, *the remainder of the Act and the application of such provision to other persons or circumstances shall not be affected thereby.* (Emphasis added.)

This language is unambiguous and gives rise to a presumption that Congress did not intend the validity of the Act as a whole, or of any part of the Act, to depend upon whether the veto clause of § 244(c)(2) was invalid.... Congress could not have more plainly authorized the presumption that the provision for a one-House veto in § 244(c)(2) is severable from the remainder of § 244 and the Act of which it is a part.

The presumption as to the severability of the one-House veto provision in § 244(c)(2) is supported by the legislative history of § 244. That section and its precursors supplanted the long established pattern of dealing with deportations like Chadha's on a case-by-case basis through private bills.... The [veto] proposal...was incorporated in the Immigration and Nationality Act of 1952, Pub. L. No. 414, 66 Stat. 163, 214. Plainly, Congress' desire to retain a veto in this area cannot be considered in isolation but must be viewed in the context of Congress' irritation with the burden of private immigration bills. This legislative history is not sufficient to rebut the presumption of severability raised by § 406 because there is insufficient evidence that Congress would have continued to subject itself to the onerous burdens of private bills had it known that § 244(c)(2) would be held unconstitutional.

A provision is further presumed severable if what remains after severance "is fully operative as a law." *Champlin Refining Co. v. Corporation Comm'n, supra,* 286 U.S., at 234. There can be no doubt that § 244 is "fully operative" and workable administrative machinery without the veto provision in § 244(c)(2). Entirely independent of the one-House veto, the administrative process enacted by Congress authorizes the Attorney General to suspend an alien's deportation under § 244(a). Congress' oversight of the exercise of this delegated authority is preserved since all such suspensions will continue to be reported to it under § 244(c)(1). Absent the passage of a bill to the contrary, deportation proceedings will be cancelled when the period specified in § 244(c)(2) has expired.[9] Clearly, § 244 survives as a workable administrative mechanism without the one-House veto....

III

A

We turn now to the question whether action of one House of Congress under § 244(c)(2) violates strictures of the Constitution. We begin, of course, with the presumption that the challenged statute is valid. Its wisdom is not the concern of the courts; if a challenged action does not violate the Constitution, it must be sustained....

By the same token, the fact that a given law or procedure is efficient, convenient, and useful in facilitating functions of government, standing alone, will not save it if it is contrary to the Constitution. Convenience and efficiency are not the primary objectives—or the hallmarks—of democratic government and our inquiry is sharpened rather than blunted by the fact that Congressional veto provisions are appearing with increasing frequency in statutes which delegate authority to executive and independent agencies:

> Since 1932, when the first veto provision was enacted into law, 295 congressional veto-type procedures have been inserted in 196 different statutes as follows: from 1932 to 1939, five statutes were affected; from 1940-49, nineteen statutes; between 1950-59, thirty-four statutes; and from 1960-69, forty-nine. From the year 1970 through 1975, at least one hundred sixty-three such provisions were included in eighty-nine laws. Abourezk, The Congressional Veto: A Contemporary Response to Executive Encroachment on Legislative Prerogatives, 52 Ind.L.Rev. 323, 324 (1977).

Justice White undertakes to make a case for the proposition that the one-House veto is a useful "political invention," and we need not challenge that assertion. We can even concede this utilitarian argument although the long range political wisdom

---

9. Without the one-House veto, § 244 resembles the "report and wait" provision approved by the Court in *Sibbach v. Wilson,* 312 U.S. 1 (1941). The statute examined in *Sibbach* provided that the newly promulgated Federal Rules of Civil Procedure "shall not take effect until they shall have been reported to Congress by the Attorney General at the beginning of a regular session thereof and until after the close of such session." This statute did not provide that Congress could unilaterally veto the Federal Rules. Rather, it gave Congress the opportunity to review the Rules ... and to pass legislation barring their effectiveness if the Rules were found objectionable....

of this "invention" is arguable. It has been vigorously debated and it is instructive to compare the views of the protagonists. But policy arguments supporting even useful "political inventions" are subject to the demands of the Constitution which defines powers and, with respect to this subject, sets out just how those powers are to be exercised.

Explicit and unambiguous provisions of the Constitution prescribe and define the respective functions of the Congress and of the Executive in the legislative process. Since the precise terms of those familiar provisions are critical to the resolution of this case, we set them out verbatim. Art. I provides:

> All legislative Powers herein granted shall be vested in a Congress of the United States, which shall consist of a Senate *and* a House of Representatives. Art. I, § 1. (Emphasis added).

> Every Bill which shall have passed the House of Representatives *and* the Senate, *shall*, before it becomes a Law, be presented to the President of the United States; ... Art. I, § 7, cl. 2. (Emphasis added).

> *Every* Order, Resolution, or Vote to which the Concurrence of the Senate and House of Representatives may be necessary (except on a question of Adjournment) *shall* be presented to the President of the United States; and before the Same shall take Effect, *shall* be approved by him, or being disapproved by him, *shall* be repassed by two thirds of the Senate and House of Representatives, according to the Rules and Limitations prescribed in the Case of a Bill. Art. I, § 7, cl. 3. (Emphasis added).

These provisions of Art. I are integral parts of the constitutional design for the separation of powers. We ... find that the purposes underlying the Presentment Clauses, Art. I, § 7, cls. 2, 3, and the bicameral requirement of Art. I, § 1 and § 7, cl. 2, guide our resolution of the important question presented in this case. The very structure of the articles delegating and separating powers under Arts. I, II, and III exemplify the concept of separation of powers and we now turn to Art. I.

B

The Presentment Clauses

The records of the Constitutional Convention reveal that the requirement that all legislation be presented to the President before becoming law was uniformly accepted by the Framers. Presentment to the President and the Presidential veto were considered so imperative that the draftsmen took special pains to assure that these requirements could not be circumvented. During the final debate on Art. I, § 7, cl. 2, James Madison expressed concern that it might easily be evaded by the simple expedient of calling a proposed law a "resolution" or "vote" rather than a "bill." 2 M. Farrand, The Records of the Federal Convention of 1787 301-302. As a consequence, Art. I, § 7, cl. 3, was added.

The decision to provide the President with a limited and qualified power to nullify proposed legislation by veto was based on the profound conviction of the Framers that the powers conferred on Congress were the powers to be most carefully circumscribed. It is beyond doubt that lawmaking was a power to be shared by both Houses and the President. In The Federalist No. 73, Hamilton focused on the President's role in making laws:

> If even no propensity had ever discovered itself in the legislative body to invade the rights of the Executive, the rules of just reasoning and theoretic propriety would of themselves teach us that the one ought not to be left to the mercy of the other, but ought to possess a constitutional and effectual power of self-defense.

See also The Federalist No. 51. In his Commentaries on the Constitution, Joseph Story makes the same point. 1 J. Story, Commentaries on the Constitution of the United States 614-615 (1858).

The President's role in the lawmaking process also reflects the Framers' careful efforts to check whatever propensity a particular Congress might have to enact oppressive, improvident, or ill-considered measures. The President's veto role in the legislative process was described later during public debate on ratification:

> It establishes a salutary check upon the legislative body, calculated to guard the community against the effects of faction, precipitancy, or of any impulse unfriendly to the public good which may happen to influence a majority of that body.... The primary inducement to conferring the power in question upon the Executive is to enable him to defend himself; the secondary one is to increase the chances in favor of the community against the passing of bad laws through haste, inadvertence, or design. The Federalist No. 73 (A. Hamilton).

The Court also has observed that the Presentment Clauses serve the important purpose of assuring that a "national" perspective is grafted on the legislative process:

> The President is a representative of the people just as the members of the Senate and of the House are, and it may be, at some times, on some subjects, that the President elected by all the people is rather more representative of them all than are the members of either body of the Legislature whose constituencies are local and not countrywide.... Myers v. United States, 272 U.S., at 123.

C

Bicameralism

The bicameral requirement of Art. I, §§ 1, 7 was of scarcely less concern to the Framers than was the Presidential veto and indeed the two concepts are interdependent. By providing that no law could take effect without the concurrence of the prescribed majority of the Members of both Houses, the Framers reemphasized their belief, already remarked upon in connection with the Presentment Clauses, that legislation should not be enacted unless it has been carefully and fully considered by the Nation's elected officials....

These observations are consistent with what many of the Framers expressed, none more cogently than Hamilton in pointing up the need to divide and disperse power in order to protect liberty:

> In republican government, the legislative authority necessarily predominates. The remedy for this inconveniency is to divide the legislature into different branches; and to render them, by different modes of election and different principles of action, as little connected with each other as the nature of their common functions and their common dependence on the society will admit. The Federalist No. 51.

However familiar, it is useful to recall that apart from their fear that special interests could be favored at the expense of public needs, the Framers were also concerned, although not of one mind, over the apprehensions of the smaller states. . . . It need hardly be repeated here that the Great Compromise, under which one House was viewed as representing the people and the other the states, allayed the fears of both the large and small states.

We see therefore that the Framers were acutely conscious that the bicameral requirement and the Presentment Clauses would serve essential constitutional functions. The President's participation in the legislative process was to protect the Executive Branch from Congress and to protect the whole people from improvident laws. The division of the Congress into two distinctive bodies assures that the legislative power would be exercised only after opportunity for full study and debate in separate settings. The President's unilateral veto power, in turn, was limited by the power of two thirds of both Houses of Congress to overrule a veto thereby precluding final arbitrary action of one person. See 1 M. Farrand, *supra*, at 99-104. It emerges clearly that the prescription for legislative action in Art. I, §§ 1, 7 represents the Framers' decision that the legislative power of the Federal government be exercised in accord with a single, finely wrought and exhaustively considered, procedure.

IV

The Constitution sought to divide the delegated powers of the new federal government into three defined categories, legislative, executive and judicial, to assure, as nearly as possible, that each Branch of government would confine itself to its assigned responsibility. The hydraulic pressure inherent within each of the separate Branches to exceed the outer limits of its power, even to accomplish desirable objectives, must be resisted.

Although not "hermetically" sealed from one another, the powers delegated to the three Branches are functionally identifiable. When any Branch acts, it is presumptively exercising the power the Constitution has delegated to it. When the Executive acts, it presumptively acts in an executive or administrative capacity as defined in Art. II. And when, as here, one House of Congress purports to act, it is presumptively acting within its assigned sphere.

Beginning with this presumption, we must nevertheless establish that the challenged action under § 244(c)(2) is of the kind to which the procedural requirements of Art. I, § 7 apply. Not every action taken by either House is subject to the bicameralism and presentment requirements of Art. I. Whether actions taken by either House are, in law and fact, an exercise of legislative power depends not on their form but upon "whether they contain matter which is properly to be regarded as legislative in its character and effect." S.Rep. No. 1335, 54th Cong., 2d Sess., 8 (1897).

Examination of the action taken here by one House pursuant to § 244(c)(2) reveals that it was essentially legislative in purpose and effect. In purporting to exercise power defined in Art. I, § 8, cl. 4 to "establish an uniform Rule of Naturalization," the House took action that had the purpose and effect of altering the legal rights, duties and relations of persons, including the Attorney General, Executive Branch officials and Chadha, all outside the legislative branch. Section 244(c)(2) purports to authorize one House of Congress to require the Attorney General to deport an individual alien whose deportation otherwise would be cancelled under § 244. The one-House veto operated in this case to overrule the Attorney General and mandate Chadha's deportation; absent the House action, Chadha would remain in the United States. Congress has *acted* and its action has altered Chadha's status.

The legislative character of the one-House veto in this case is confirmed by the character of the Congressional action it supplants. Neither the House of Representatives nor the Senate contends that, absent the veto provision in § 244(c)(2), either of them, or both of them acting together, could effectively require the Attorney General to deport an alien once the Attorney General, in the exercise of legislatively delegated authority,[16] had determined the alien should remain in the United States. Without the challenged provision in § 244(c)(2), this could have been achieved, if at all, only by legislation requiring deportation. Similarly, a veto by one House of Congress under § 244(c)(2) cannot be justified as an attempt at amending the standards set out in § 244(a)(1), or as a repeal of § 244 as applied to Chadha. Amendment and repeal of statutes, no less than enactment, must conform with Art. I.

The nature of the decision implemented by the one-House veto in this case further manifests its legislative character. After long experience with the clumsy, time consuming private bill procedure, Congress made a deliberate choice to delegate to the Executive Branch, and specifically to the Attorney General, the authority to allow deportable aliens to remain in this country in certain specified circumstances. It is not disputed that this choice to delegate authority is precisely the kind of decision that can be implemented only in accordance with the procedures set out in Art. I. Disagreement with the Attorney General's decision on Chadha's deportation—that is, Congress' decision to deport Chadha—no less than Congress' original choice to

---

16. Congress protests that affirming the Court of Appeals in this case will sanction "lawmaking by the Attorney General. . . . Why is the Attorney General exempt from submitting his proposed changes in the law to the full bicameral process?" To be sure, some administrative agency action—rule making, for example—may resemble "lawmaking." See 5 U.S.C. § 551(4), which defines an agency's "rule" as "the whole or part of an agency statement of general or particular applicability and future effect designed to implement, interpret, or prescribe *law* or policy. . . ." This Court has referred to agency activity as being "quasi-legislative" in character. *Humphrey's Executor v. United States*, 295 U.S. 602, 628 (1935). Clearly, however, "[i]n the framework of our Constitution, the President's power to see that the laws are faithfully executed refutes the idea that he is to be a lawmaker." *Youngstown Sheet & Tube Co. v. Sawyer*, 343 U.S. 579, 587 (1952). When the Attorney General performs his duties pursuant to § 244, he does not exercise "legislative" power. See *Ernst & Ernst v. Hochfelder*, 425 U.S. 185, 213-214 (1976). The bicameral process is not necessary as a check on the Executive's administration of the laws because his administrative activity cannot reach beyond the limits of the statute that created it—a statute duly enacted pursuant to Art. I, §§ 1, 7. The constitutionality of the Attorney General's execution of the authority delegated to him by § 244 involves only a question of delegation doctrine. The courts, when a case or controversy arises, can always "ascertain whether the will of Congress has been obeyed," *Yakus v. United States*, 321 U.S. 414, 425 (1944), and can enforce adherence to statutory standards. It is clear, therefore, that the Attorney General acts in his presumptively Art. II capacity when he administers the Immigration and Nationality Act. Executive action under legislatively delegated authority that might resemble "legislative" action in some respects is not subject to the approval of both Houses of Congress and the President for the reason that the Constitution does not so require. That kind of Executive action is always subject to check by the terms of the legislation that authorized it; and if that authority is exceeded it is open to judicial review as well as the power of Congress to modify or revoke the authority entirely. A one-House veto is clearly legislative in both character and effect and is not so checked; the need for the check provided by Art. I, §§ 1, 7 is therefore clear. Congress' authority to delegate portions of its power to administrative agencies provides no support for the argument that Congress can constitutionally control administration of the laws by way of a Congressional veto.

delegate to the Attorney General the authority to make that decision, involves determinations of policy that Congress can implement in only one way; bicameral passage followed by presentment to the President. Congress must abide by its delegation of authority until that delegation is legislatively altered or revoked.

Finally, we see that when the Framers intended to authorize either House of Congress to act alone and outside of its prescribed bicameral legislative role, they narrowly and precisely defined the procedure for such action. There are but four provisions in the Constitution, explicit and unambiguous, by which one House may act alone with the unreviewable force of law, not subject to the President's veto:

(a) The House of Representatives alone was given the power to initiate impeachments. Art. I, § 2, cl. 6;

(b) The Senate alone was given the power to conduct trials following impeachment on charges initiated by the House and to convict following trial. Art. I, § 3, cl. 5;

(c) The Senate alone was given final unreviewable power to approve or to disapprove presidential appointments. Art. II, § 2, cl. 2;

(d) The Senate alone was given unreviewable power to ratify treaties negotiated by the President. Art. II, § 2, cl. 2.

Clearly, when the Draftsmen sought to confer special powers on one House, independent of the other House, or of the President, they did so in explicit, unambiguous terms.[20] These carefully defined exceptions from presentment and bicameralism underscore the difference between the legislative functions of Congress and other unilateral but important and binding one-House acts provided for in the Constitution. These exceptions are narrow, explicit, and separately justified; none of them authorize the action challenged here. On the contrary, they provide further support for the conclusion that Congressional authority is not to be implied and for the conclusion that the veto provided for in § 244(c)(2) is not authorized by the constitutional design of the powers of the Legislative Branch.

Since it is clear that the action by the House under § 244(c)(2) was not within any of the express constitutional exceptions authorizing one House to act alone, and equally clear that it was an exercise of legislative power, that action was subject to the standards prescribed in Article I. . . .

V

We hold that the Congressional veto provision in § 244(c)(2) is severable from the Act and that it is unconstitutional. Accordingly, the judgment of the Court of Appeals is

Affirmed.

Justice POWELL, concurring in the judgment.

The Court's decision, based on the Presentment Clauses, Art. I, § 7, cls. 2 and 3, apparently will invalidate every use of the legislative veto. The breadth of this holding gives one pause. Congress has included the veto in literally hundreds of statutes, dating back to the 1930s. Congress clearly views this procedure as essential to con-

---

20. An exception from the Presentment Clauses was ratified in *Hollingsworth v. Virginia*, 3 Dall. 378 (1798). There the Court held presidential approval was unnecessary for a proposed constitutional amendment which had passed both Houses of Congress by the requisite two-thirds majority. See U.S. Const. Art. V.

trolling the delegation of power to administrative agencies. One reasonably may disagree with Congress' assessment of the veto's utility, but the respect due its judgment as a coordinate branch of Government cautions that our holding should be no more extensive than necessary to decide this case. In my view, the case may be decided on a narrower ground. When Congress finds that a particular person does not satisfy the statutory criteria for permanent residence in this country it has assumed a judicial function in violation of the principle of separation of powers. Accordingly, I concur only in the judgment.

I

A

The Framers perceived that "[t]he accumulation of all powers legislative, executive and judiciary in the same hands, whether of one, a few or many, and whether hereditary, self appointed, or elective, may justly be pronounced the very definition of tyranny." The Federalist No. 47 (J. Madison). Theirs was not a baseless fear. Under British rule, the colonies suffered the abuses of unchecked executive power that were attributed, at least popularly, to an hereditary monarchy. During the Confederation, the States reacted by removing power from the executive and placing it in the hands of elected legislators. But many legislators proved to be little better than the Crown. "The supremacy of legislatures came to be recognized as the supremacy of faction and the tyranny of shifting majorities. The legislatures confiscated property, erected paper money schemes, [and] suspended the ordinary means of collecting debts." Levi, 76 Colum.L.Rev., at 374-375.

One abuse that was prevalent during the Confederation was the exercise of judicial power by the state legislatures. The Framers were well acquainted with the danger of subjecting the determination of the rights of one person to the "tyranny of shifting majorities." . . .

It was to prevent the recurrence of such abuses that the Framers vested the executive, legislative, and judicial powers in separate branches. Their concern that a legislature should not be able unilaterally to impose a substantial deprivation on one person was expressed not only in this general allocation of power, but also in more specific provisions, such as the Bill of Attainder Clause, Art. I, § 9, cl. 3. As the Court recognized in *United States v. Brown*, 381 U.S. 437, 442 (1965), "the Bill of Attainder Clause was intended not as a narrow, technical . . . prohibition, but rather as an implementation of the separation of powers, a general safeguard against legislative exercise of the judicial function, or more simply—trial by legislature." This Clause, and the separation of powers doctrine generally, reflect the Framers' concern that trial by a legislature lacks the safeguards necessary to prevent the abuse of power.

B

The Constitution does not establish three branches with precisely defined boundaries. . . . But where one branch has impaired or sought to assume a power central to another branch, the Court has not hesitated to enforce the doctrine. See *Buckley v. Valeo, supra*, 424 U.S., at 123.

Functionally, the doctrine may be violated in two ways. One branch may interfere impermissibly with the other's performance of its constitutionally assigned function. See *Nixon v. Administrator of General Services*, 433 U.S. 425, 433 (1977); *United States v. Nixon*, 418 U.S. 683 (1974). Alternatively, the doctrine may be violated when one branch assumes a function that more properly is entrusted to another. See *Youngstown Sheet & Tube Co. v. Sawyer, supra,* 343 U.S., at 587 (1952). This case presents the latter situation.

II

... On its face, the House's action appears clearly adjudicatory. The House did not enact a general rule; rather it made its own determination that six specific persons did not comply with certain statutory criteria. It thus undertook the type of decision that traditionally has been left to other branches. Even if the House did not make a *de novo* determination, but simply reviewed the Immigration and Naturalization Service's findings, it still assumed a function ordinarily entrusted to the federal courts. See 5 U.S.C. § 704 (providing generally for judicial review of final agency action); *cf. Foti v. INS,* 375 U.S. 217 (1963) (holding that courts of appeals have jurisdiction to review INS decisions denying suspension of deportation)....

The impropriety of the House's assumption of this function is confirmed by the fact that its action raises the very danger the Framers sought to avoid—the exercise of unchecked power. In deciding whether Chadha deserves to be deported, Congress is not subject to any internal constraints that prevent it from arbitrarily depriving him of the right to remain in this country. Unlike the judiciary or an administrative agency, Congress is not bound by established substantive rules. Nor is it subject to the procedural safeguards, such as the right to counsel and a hearing before an impartial tribunal, that are present when a court or an agency adjudicates individual rights. The only effective constraint on Congress' power is political, but Congress is most accountable politically when it prescribes rules of general applicability. When it decides rights of specific persons, those rights are subject to "the tyranny of a shifting majority."

Chief Justice Marshall observed: "It is the peculiar province of the legislature to prescribe general rules for the government of society; the application of those rules would seem to be the duty of other departments." *Fletcher v. Peck,* 6 Cranch 87, 136 (1810). In my view, when Congress undertook to apply its rules to Chadha, it exceeded the scope of its constitutionally prescribed authority. I would not reach the broader question whether legislative vetoes are invalid under the Presentment Clauses.

Justice WHITE, dissenting.

Today the Court not only invalidates § 244(c)(2) of the Immigration and Nationality Act, but also sounds the death knell for nearly 200 other statutory provisions in which Congress has reserved a "legislative veto." For this reason, the Court's decision is of surpassing importance. And it is for this reason that the Court would have been well-advised to decide the case, if possible, on the narrower grounds of separation of powers, leaving for full consideration the constitutionality of other congressional review statutes operating on such varied matters as war powers and agency rulemaking, some of which concern the independent regulatory agencies....

The history of the legislative veto also makes clear that it has not been a sword with which Congress has struck out to aggrandize itself at the expense of the other branches—the concerns of Madison and Hamilton. Rather, the veto has been a means of defense, a reservation of ultimate authority necessary if Congress is to fulfill its designated role under Article I as the nation's lawmaker. While the President has often objected to particular legislative vetoes, generally those left in the hands of congressional committees, the Executive has more often agreed to legislative review as the price for a broad delegation of authority. To be sure, the President may have preferred unrestricted power, but that could be precisely why Congress thought it essential to retain a check on the exercise of delegated authority.

II

For all these reasons, the apparent sweep of the Court's decision today is regrettable. The Court's Article I analysis appears to invalidate all legislative vetoes irrespective of form or subject. Because the legislative veto is commonly found as a check upon rulemaking by administrative agencies and upon broad-based policy decisions of the Executive Branch, it is particularly unfortunate that the Court reaches its decision in a case involving the exercise of a veto over deportation decisions regarding particular individuals. Courts should always be wary of striking statutes as unconstitutional; to strike an entire class of statutes based on consideration of a somewhat atypical and more-readily indictable exemplar of the class is irresponsible....

III

...I agree with the Court that the President's qualified veto power is a critical element in the distribution of powers under the Constitution, widely endorsed among the Framers, and intended to serve the President as a defense against legislative encroachment and to check the "passing of bad laws through haste, inadvertence, or design." The Federalist No. 73 (A. Hamilton)....I also agree that the bicameral approval required by Art. I, §§ 1, 7 "was of scarcely less concern to the Framers than was the Presidential veto," and that the need to divide and disperse legislative power figures significantly in our scheme of Government. All of this, the Third Part of the Court's opinion, is entirely unexceptionable.

It does not, however, answer the constitutional question before us. The power to exercise a legislative veto is not the power to write new law without bicameral approval or presidential consideration. The veto must be authorized by statute and may only negative what an Executive department or independent agency has proposed. On its face, the legislative veto no more allows one House of Congress to make law than does the presidential veto confer such power upon the President....

A

The terms of the Presentment Clauses suggest only that bills and their equivalent are subject to the requirements of bicameral passage and presentment to the President.... Although [§ 7, cl. 3] does not specify the actions for which the concurrence of both Houses is "necessary," the proceedings at the Philadelphia Convention suggest its purpose was to prevent Congress from circumventing the presentation requirement in the making of new legislation.... The chosen language, Madison's comment, and the brevity of the Convention's consideration, all suggest a modest role was intended for the Clause and no broad restraint on Congressional authority was contemplated. This reading is consistent with the historical background of the Presentation Clause itself which reveals only that the Framers were concerned with limiting the methods for enacting new legislation.... There is no record that the Convention contemplated, let alone intended, that these Article I requirements would someday be invoked to restrain the scope of Congressional authority pursuant to duly-enacted law.

When the Convention did turn its attention to the scope of Congress' lawmaking power, the Framers were expansive. The Necessary and Proper Clause, Art. I, § 8, cl. 18, vests Congress with the power "to make all laws which shall be necessary and proper for carrying into Execution the foregoing Powers [the enumerated powers of § 8], and all other Powers vested by this Constitution in the government of the United States, or in any Department or Officer thereof." It is long-settled that Congress may "exercise its best judgment in the selection of measures, to carry into execution the constitutional powers of the government," and "avail itself of experience, to exercise its reason, and to accommodate its legislation to circumstances." *McCulloch v. Maryland*, 4 Wheat. 316, 415-416, 420 (1819).

B

The Court heeded this counsel in approving the modern administrative state. The Court's holding today that all legislative-type action must be enacted through the lawmaking process ignores that legislative authority is routinely delegated to the Executive branch, to the independent regulatory agencies, and to private individuals and groups.... This Court's decisions sanctioning such delegations make clear that Article I does not require all action with the effect of legislation to be passed as a law....

[T]hese cases establish that by virtue of congressional delegation, legislative power can be exercised by independent agencies and Executive departments without the passage of new legislation. For some time, the sheer amount of law—the substantive rules that regulate private conduct and direct the operation of government—made by the agencies has far outnumbered the lawmaking engaged in by Congress through the traditional process. There is no question but that agency rulemaking is lawmaking in any functional or realistic sense of the term. The Administrative Procedure Act, 5 U.S.C. § 551(4) provides that a "rule" is an agency statement "designed to implement, interpret, or prescribe law or policy." When agencies are authorized to prescribe law through substantive rulemaking, the administrator's regulation is not only due deference, but is accorded "legislative effect." These regulations bind courts and officers of the federal government, may pre-empt state law, and grant rights to and impose obligations on the public. In sum, they have the force of law.

If Congress may delegate lawmaking power to independent and executive agencies, it is most difficult to understand Article I as forbidding Congress from also reserving a check on legislative power for itself. Absent the veto, the agencies receiving delegations of legislative or quasi-legislative power may issue regulations having the force of law without bicameral approval and without the President's signature. It is thus not apparent why the reservation of a veto over the exercise of that legislative power must be subject to a more exacting test. In both cases, it is enough that the initial statutory authorizations comply with the Article I requirements.

Nor are there strict limits on the agents that may receive such delegations of legislative authority so that it might be said that the legislature can delegate authority to others but not to itself. While most authority to issue rules and regulations is given to the executive branch and the independent regulatory agencies, statutory delegations to private persons have also passed this Court's scrutiny.... Assuming [these cases] remain sound law, the Court's decision today suggests that Congress may place a "veto" power over suspensions of deportation in private hands or in the hands of an independent agency, but is forbidden from reserving such authority for itself. Perhaps this odd result could be justified on other constitutional grounds, such as the separation of powers, but certainly it cannot be defended as consistent with the Court's view of the Article I presentment and bicameralism commands.

The Court's opinion in the present case comes closest to facing the reality of administrative lawmaking in considering the contention that the Attorney General's action in suspending deportation under § 244 is itself a legislative act. The Court posits that the Attorney General is acting in an Article II enforcement capacity under § 244. This characterization is at odds with *Mahler v. Eby*, 264 U.S. 32, 40 (1924), where the power conferred on the Executive to deport aliens was considered a delegation of legislative power.... [T]he Court's reasoning does persuasively explain why a resolution of disapproval under § 244(c)(2) need not again be subject to the bicameral process. Because it serves only to check the Attorney General's exercise of the suspension authority granted by § 244, the disapproval resolution—unlike the Attorney General's action—"cannot reach beyond the limits of the statute that created it—a statute duly enacted pursuant to Article I."

More fundamentally, even if the Court correctly characterizes the Attorney General's authority under § 244 as an Article II Executive power, the Court concedes that certain administrative agency action, such as rulemaking, "may resemble lawmaking".... Such rules and adjudications by the agencies meet the Court's own definition of legislative action for they "alter[ ] the legal rights, duties, and relations of persons ... outside the legislative branch," and involve "determinations of policy." Under the Court's analysis, the Executive Branch and the independent agencies may make rules with the effect of law while Congress, in whom the Framers confided the legislative power, Art. I, § 1, may not exercise a veto which precludes such rules from having operative force. If the effective functioning of a complex modern government requires the delegation of vast authority which, by virtue of its breadth, is legislative or "quasi-legislative" in character, I cannot accept that Article I—which is, after all, the source of the non-delegation doctrine—should forbid Congress from qualifying that grant with a legislative veto.

C

The Court also takes no account of perhaps the most relevant consideration: However resolutions of disapproval under § 244(c)(2) are formally characterized, in reality, a departure from the status quo occurs only upon the concurrence of opinion among the House, Senate, and President. Reservations of legislative authority to be exercised by Congress should be upheld if the exercise of such reserved authority is consistent with the distribution of and limits upon legislative power that Article I provides....

The central concern of the presentation and bicameralism requirements of Article I is that when a departure from the legal status quo is undertaken, it is done with the approval of the President and both Houses of Congress—or, in the event of a presidential veto, a two-thirds majority in both Houses. This interest is fully satisfied by the operation of § 244(c)(2). The President's approval is found in the Attorney General's action in recommending to Congress that the deportation order for a given alien be suspended. The House and the Senate indicate their approval of the Executive's action by not passing a resolution of disapproval within the statutory period. Thus, a change in the legal status quo—the deportability of the alien—is consummated only with the approval of each of the three relevant actors. The disagreement of any one of the three maintains the alien's pre-existing status: the Executive may choose not to recommend suspension; the House and Senate may each veto the recommendation. The effect on the rights and obligations of the affected individuals and upon the legislative system is precisely the same as if a private bill were introduced but failed to receive the necessary approval....

Thus understood, § 244(c)(2) fully effectuates the purposes of the bicameralism and presentation requirements. I now briefly consider possible objections to the analysis.

First, it may be asserted that Chadha's status before legislative disapproval is one of nondeportation and that the exercise of the veto, unlike the failure of a private bill, works a change in the status quo. This position plainly ignores the statutory language. At no place in § 244 has Congress delegated to the Attorney General any final power to determine which aliens shall be allowed to remain in the United States. Congress has retained the ultimate power to pass on such changes in deportable status....

Second, it may be said that this approach leads to the incongruity that the two-House veto is more suspect than its one-House brother. Although the idea may be initially counter-intuitive, on close analysis, it is not at all unusual that the one-House veto is of more certain constitutionality than the two-House version. If the Attorney General's action is a proposal for legislation, then the disapproval of but a single House is all that is required to prevent its passage. Because approval is indicated by the failure to veto, the one-House veto satisfies the requirement of bicameral approval. The two-House version may present a different question....

Third, it may be objected that Congress cannot indicate its approval of legislative change by inaction. In the Court of Appeals' view, inaction by Congress "could equally imply endorsement, acquiescence, passivity, indecision or indifference," and the Court appears to echo this concern. This objection appears more properly directed at the wisdom of the legislative veto than its constitutionality. The Constitution does not and cannot guarantee that legislators will carefully scrutinize legislation and deliberate before acting. In a democracy it is the electorate that holds the legislators accountable for the wisdom of their choices. It is hard to maintain that a private bill receives any greater individualized scrutiny than a resolution of disapproval under § 244(c)(2). Certainly the legislative veto is no more susceptible to this attack than the Court's increasingly common practice of according weight to the failure of Congress to disturb an Executive or independent agency's action....

IV

... The legislative veto provision does not "prevent the Executive Branch from accomplishing its constitutionally assigned functions." First, it is clear that the Executive Branch has no "constitutionally assigned" function of suspending the deportation of aliens.... Nor can it be said that the inherent function of the Executive Branch in executing the law is involved. *The Steel Seizure Case* resolved that the Article II mandate for the President to execute the law is a directive to enforce the law which Congress has written. "The duty of the President to see that the laws be executed is a duty that does not go beyond the laws or require him to achieve more than Congress sees fit to leave within his power." *Myers v. United States,* 272 U.S., at 177 (Holmes, J., dissenting). Here, § 244 grants the executive only a qualified suspension authority and it is only that authority which the President is constitutionally authorized to execute.... In comparison to private bills, which must be initiated in the Congress and which allow a Presidential veto to be overriden by a two-thirds majority in both Houses of Congress, § 244 augments rather than reduces the executive branch's authority....

Nor does § 244 infringe on the judicial power, as Justice Powell would hold. Section 244 makes clear that Congress has reserved its own judgment as part of the statutory process. Congressional action does not substitute for judicial review of the Attorney General's decisions. The Act provides for judicial review of the refusal of the Attorney General to suspend a deportation and to transmit a recommendation to Congress. *INS v. Wang*, 450 U.S. 139 (1981) (per curiam). But the courts have not been given the authority to review whether an alien should be given permanent status; review is limited to whether the Attorney General has properly applied the statutory standards for essentially denying the alien a recommendation that his deportable status be changed by the Congress. Moreover, there is no constitutional obligation to provide any judicial review whatever for a failure to suspend deportation....

I do not suggest that all legislative vetoes are necessarily consistent with separation of powers principles. A legislative check on an inherently executive function, for example, that of initiating prosecutions, poses an entirely different question. But the legislative veto device here—and in many other settings—is far from an instance of legislative tyranny over the Executive. It is a necessary check on the unavoidably expanding power of the agencies, both executive and independent, as they engage in exercising authority delegated by Congress....

Justice REHNQUIST, with whom Justice WHITE joins, dissenting.

... Because I believe that Congress did not intend the one-House veto provision of § 244(c) (2) to be severable, I dissent. Section 244(c)(2) is ... severable only if Congress would have intended to permit the Attorney General to suspend deportations without it....

By severing § 244(c)(2), the Court permits suspension of deportation in a class of cases where Congress never stated that suspension was appropriate. I do not believe we should expand the statute in this way without some clear indication that Congress intended such an expansion. As the Court said in *Davis v. Wallace*, 257 U.S. 478, 484-485 (1922):

"Where an excepting provision in a statute is found unconstitutional, courts very generally hold that this does not work an enlargement of the scope or operation of other provisions with which that provision was enacted and which was intended to qualify or restrain...."

The Court finds that the legislative history of § 244 shows that Congress intended § 244(c)(2) to be severable because Congress wanted to relieve itself of the burden of private bills. But the history elucidated by the Court shows that Congress was unwilling to give the Executive Branch permission to suspend deportation on its own. Over the years, Congress consistently rejected requests from the Executive for complete discretion in this area. Congress always insisted on retaining ultimate control, whether by concurrent resolution, as in the 1948 Act, or by one-House veto, as in the present Act. Congress has never indicated that it would be willing to permit suspensions of deportation unless it could retain some sort of veto....

---

1. Both before and after *Chadha*, the topic of the legislative veto has produced a large volume of literature. Good examples of the various pre-*Chadha* positions include: Martin, *The Legislative Veto and the Responsible Exercise of Congressional Power*, 68 Va. L. Rev. 253 (1982); Javits & Klein, *Congressional Oversight and the Legislative Veto: A Constitutional Analysis*, 52 N.Y.U. L. Rev. 455 (1977); Dixon, *The Congres-*

sional Veto and Separation of Powers: The Executive on a Leash?, 56 N. C. L. Rev. 423 (1978). Also, *compare* 43 Op. A.G. No. 10 (1977) (approving legislative veto of proposed Reorganization Act) *with* 43 Op. A.G. No. 25 (1980) (denying constitutionality of legislative veto in General Education Provisions Act, 20 U.S.C. § 1232(d)). For analysis of *Chadha*, see Elliott, *INS v. Chadha: The Administrative Constitution, the Constitution, and the Legislative Veto*, 1983 Sup. Ct. Rev. 125; Tribe, *The Legislative Veto Decision: A Law by Any Other Name?*, 21 Harv. J. Legis. 1 (1984).

2. Which method of separation of powers analysis does the Court use in *Chadha*? Does the Court connect its conclusions to the purposes of bicameralism and presentation that it identifies? Elliott, *supra* at 134-35, 144-47, analyzes the Court's approach as follows:

> The core of the Court's reasoning is conceptual and formalistic: the legislative veto is "legislative" because it has the effect of "altering legal rights." The legislative veto "alters legal rights," however, only because the Court chooses to characterize its effect that way. The Court's manipulation of legal categories could just as easily be turned to support the opposite conclusion that the legislative veto does not alter legal rights....

> Even if it could be said that Chadha had acquired "legal rights," how were those rights "altered" by the House resolution? After all, the statute authorizing the Attorney General to suspend deportation on grounds of hardship also provided that either house of Congress could veto the Attorney General's action. Why was the nature of Chadha's legal rights not defined by the statute creating them?... These questions imply, not that the Court's analysis is incorrect, but that it is arbitrary....

> The underlying source of the problems is jurisprudential. The Court insists that the texts of the presentment clauses and the vesting of legislative power in a bicameral Congress dispose of the legislative veto *ex proprio vigore*. But constitutional texts do not apply themselves. Justice White is surely right that the Constitution is silent on the "precise question" of the legislative veto and neither "directly authorize[s]" nor "prohibit[s]" it. In order to treat the texts as dispositive, the Court must tacitly assume the postulate which should be under examination: whether the legislative veto is congressional action of the sort to which the requirements of bicameralism and presentment should apply. To answer this question necessarily requires a perspective from outside the system: "Syllogism" alone is incapable of resolving such questions....

> The second reason that the Court's approach in *Chadha* is unsatisfactory grows out of the first. The Court's linguistic arguments and analytical approach depend on dividing government power into three stark categories— legislative, executive, and judicial—and are troublesome because they are unpersuasive on their own terms. But the Court's approach is also troubling because it excludes other considerations that should be relevant. It is as if the Court were determined to avoid acknowledging what the case is really about....

> [To the Court, the] growth of the bureaucracy in the Executive branch and in agencies independent of presidential control is not of constitutional significance because it raises a nice point of classification that can be laid to rest once the Court decides whether the legal category "executive" or "legislative" is more

appropriate. Concern exists because of the reality that most of the federal law affecting most of the people most of the time is not made through the bicameral legislative process that the Court's opinion enshrines, but by administrative decisionmakers, who are not elected and who are not, by and large, subject to either effective presidential or judicial control.

The growth of lawmaking power in a vast administrative bureaucracy may be seen as a threat to the essence of the constitutional principle of separation of powers. Madison... summarized that fundamental constitutional principle in Federalist No. 51 as "contriving the interior structure of the government as that its several constituent parts may, by their mutual relations, be the means of keeping each other in their proper places." The "constant aim" of this strategy, Madison continues, "is to divide and arrange the several offices in such a manner as that each may be a check on the other." It is ironic that the Court in *Chadha*, in the name of the constitutional principles of checks and balances and separation of powers, ends up striking down one of the few existing checks on lawmaking by the bureaucracy.

Can you formulate a more complete rationale for the Court's decision? For one effort to do so, *see* Bruff, *Legislative Formality, Administrative Rationality*, 63 Tex.L.Rev. 207, 220-22 (1984):

The President's participation in the legislative process, both in proposing and supporting legislation and in exercising the veto power, dampens faction and increases the stability of legislation. The President's veto power is a more potent check on faction than is the bicameral structure of Congress, because the president's national constituency makes his calculus of the merits of a bill different from that of any congressman. He lacks the territorial representative's incentive to favor divisible local benefits. Also, because his constituency is an amalgam of all interest groups, he must weigh the benefits and costs of a bill directly against each other; Congress avoids doing so by combining provisions that benefit particular members but that are not justifiable in the aggregate. The coalitions that support the President may differ enough from the one promoting a particular bill to make a veto attractive; the smaller the coalition supporting a bill, the more likely is this disparity. Moreover, the mere threat of a veto can raise the size of the coalition necessary to push a bill through Congress and can affect the bill's substance.

When Congress passed statutes reserving legislative veto authority in one or both of its houses, the effect was to lower congressional decision costs [the difficulty of reaching agreement among those persons assigned to decide something] on particular issues, while necessarily increasing externalities [costs not borne by the deciders] both for members of Congress and ultimately for society as a whole. Decision costs were lowered in two ways. First, the statutes excluded the President (and often one of the two houses of Congress) from the consensus needed to override a regulation. Second, because veto resolutions were limited to invalidating regulations, it was easier to form a coalition of those opposed to a rule for various reasons than it would have been to enact a substitute policy. The external costs burdened those congressmen and citizens who stood to benefit from regulations that were either invalidated by a veto resolution or altered in response to more informal congressional pressures.

It is easy to see why Congress was tempted to replace the ordinary process of legislation with the legislative veto—Congress suffers all of the decision costs of legislation but only a portion of the external costs produced by more informal processes. The less formal process subverted primary controls on the fairness of legislation in two ways. The first was to vitiate the effectiveness of the bicameralism and presentation requirements in raising the size of coalitions needed for collective choice. Retention of veto authority systematically favored interest groups having advantages in one or both houses of Congress because of their distribution throughout the nation. Second, the veto device allowed Congress to select its decision rule [the rule that defines the necessary degree of consensus for a decision to be made in the future] at the operational stage of policymaking rather than at the constitutional stage. A check on the fairness of selecting decision rules is the difficulty of determining who will profit from their later use in specific cases. Yet at the operational stage it is much easier to predict the winners and losers from a change in the decision rules. In some cases, it might be possible to predict which particular faction would be aided by legislative veto authority.

The Framers expected that our constitutional structure, which makes it easier to block than to effect legislative change, would restrict the amount of legislation to which the people would be subject. The legislative veto, by circumventing the usual structure and creating an incentive for Congress to lower its decision costs by delegating power, tended to increase the size of government as a whole.

In contrast, Professor Shane has argued that the Court's justification was *more* elaborate than necessary. In *Conventionalism in Constitutional Interpretation and the Place of Administrative Agencies*, 36 Am. U. L. Rev. 573, 585-86 (1987), he argues that a textualist resolution of *Chadha* is sufficient:

> It is difficult to see how two-house vetoes, not presented to the President, can pass muster under [the Presentment Clauses]. . . . If that is true, then the question in *INS v. Chadha* was essentially, is there any reason to think that one-house vetoes are more permissible than two-house vetoes? . . . No matter what purpose is ascribed to article I, section 7, I cannot imagine an affirmative answer to that question.

In light of this argument, consider Justice White's admission that his view of the Constitution leads to the "counter-intuitive" conclusion that two-house vetoes are more vulnerable than the one-house form. Does that reveal a fundamental defect in his argument?

In Shane's view, what *does* require fuller explanation is the normative basis for conventional textualism as a mode of constitutional interpretation. He argues that, for provisions such as those in Articles I and II "which describe conventionally understood structures and processes," textualist interpretation is more accessible, more certain, and more likely to vindicate the Constitution's underlying functional premises than alternative approaches. *Id.* at 593-97. Additionally, *some* formalism in constitutional interpretation "gives voice to our aspirations for control and accountability as part of justice. It would be advantageous . . . if textualism in constitutional interpretation vis-a-vis administrative agencies passes the message to government officials that, sometimes, we just want them to do what they are told." *Id.* at 598. For a similar analysis, *see* Miller, *Independent Agencies*, 1986 Sup. Ct. Rev. 41, 52-58.

3. How broad is the scope of the *Chadha* ruling? Do you agree that it has swept away all forms of the legislative veto? *See generally* Strauss, *Was There a Baby in the Bathwater?, A Comment on the Supreme Court's Legislative Veto Decision*, 1983 Duke L.J. 789, for an argument that the Court should have distinguished legislative vetoes that directly address difficult separation of powers controversies between the branches from those governing ordinary administration. In your view, which is more vulnerable? We will consider the issue of the appropriate scope of *Chadha* in direct interbranch controversies twice below, in connection with legislative vetoes in the Impoundment Control Act (Chapter Four) and the War Powers Resolution (Chapter Seven).

4. Severability issues have proliferated after *Chadha*. *See* Note, *Severability of Legislative Veto Provisions: A Policy Analysis*, 97 Harv. L. Rev. 1182 (1984). How should the Department of Justice argue them? How should the courts dispose of them? What should Congress do?

In *Alaska Airlines, Inc. v. Brock*, 107 S. Ct. 1476 (1987), the Court decided its first post-*Chadha* severability case. In the course of holding that a legislative veto contained in the Airline Deregulation Act of 1978 was severable, the Court gave some general guidance. Regarding the part of the severability test that asks whether the statute is "fully operative" without the unconstitutional portion, the Court noted that "by its very nature" a legislative veto is separate from the substantive provisions, since it is contemplated that Congress will ordinarily refrain from employing it. From this the Court concluded that the statute's operability without the veto would "indicate little" about congressional intent regarding severability. The Court went on to say that

> The more relevant inquiry is whether the statute will function in a *manner* consistent with the intent of Congress.... [I]t is necessary to recognize that the absence of the veto necessarily alters the balance of powers between the Legislative and Executive Branches.... Thus, it is not only appropriate to evaluate the importance of the veto in the original legislative bargain, but also to consider the nature of the delegated authority that Congress made subject to a veto. Some delegations ... may have been so controversial or so broad that Congress would have been unwilling to make the delegation without a strong oversight mechanism. The final test ... is the traditional one: the unconstitutional provision must be severed unless the statute created in its absence is legislation that Congress would not have enacted.

Note that, as in *Chadha*, some statutes have severability clauses even when the legislative veto may have been essential to the "legislative bargain." Should a court ever ignore such a clause and hold that a legislative veto in a statute having one is nonseverable?

5. Review the Court's note 16. Do you agree that all executive activity is the same and that the independent agencies present no special considerations? After *Chadha*, the Court summarily affirmed decisions invalidating legislative vetoes applicable to rulemaking by independent agencies, *U.S. House of Representatives v. FTC*, 463 U.S. 1216 (1983); *Process Gas Consumers Group v. Consumer Energy Council of America*, *id*.

6. In the FTC case cited *supra*, the Court summarily affirmed a decision invalidating a two-house veto.

7. What steps should Congress take to oversee the executive in the wake of *Chadha*? Some in Congress have proposed a constitutional amendment to restore the veto. *See* DeConcini & Faucher, *The Legislative Veto: A Constitutional Amendment*, 21 Harv. J. Legis. 29 (1984). Of course, Congress retains its ordinary oversight devices, such as hearings with a view to altering legislation or appropriations. Some new devices have been proposed, such as subjecting executive action to joint resolutions of approval or disapproval before it becomes effective. *See* Kaiser, *Congressional Control of Executive Actions in the Aftermath of the Chadha Decision*, 36 Admin. L. Rev. 239 (1984). Of course, Congress may always alter delegated power by statute; these proposals add something new by changing the internal rules of Congress to ensure speedy floor consideration of the resolutions, without possibility of amendment. In that way, Congress can mimic the legislative veto without running afoul of *Chadha*. *See* Breyer, *The Legislative Veto After* Chadha, 72 Geo. L. J. 785 (1984). How would you advise Congress in this matter? When is it wise for Congress to forego its normal processes of committee deliberations and floor debate and amendment, in hopes of speedy review of executive action?

8. Does *Chadha* apply to appropriations decisions by Congress? Could Congress constitutionally limit an agency's use of its appropriations as follows: "No funds appropriated herein shall be used to implement any program, function, activity, or regulation that has been disapproved by Congress through any procedure authorized by statute?"

9. To what extent does Congress' exercise of a veto render vulnerable to judicial challenge any subsequently issued regulations on the same subject? Could it be argued that, in respecting a veto, an agency has violated some sort of administrative due process or has failed to execute properly its delegated authority? *See D.C. Federation of Civic Ass'ns v. Volpe*, 459 F.2d 1231 (D.C. Cir. 1972); *Koniag, Inc. v. Andrus*, 580 F.2d 601 (D.C. Cir. 1978); *Pacific Legal Foundation v. Dept. of Transportation*, 553 F.2d 1338 (D.C. Cir. 1979).

Chapter 3
Protecting the Exercise of Presidential Functions

Among the framers' most frequently repeated goals was the creation of an executive that could act with "energy" and "dispatch." They thought the advantages of the executive, as compared to Congress, lay in its smaller size and in its capacity for secrecy. This chapter considers the evolution of rules and practices aimed at fostering the energy, dispatch, and secrecy of the executive. Their wisdom and continuing vitality will, of course, be major questions.

Part A considers rules for protecting presidential privacy and resisting disclosure of executive branch information to the public, to Congress, and to courts. Part B considers protections for the President's "inner circle," and the immunities of federal officers from constitutional tort liability.

A. State Secrets, Executive Privilege, and Presidential Privacy

1. Resisting disclosure to the public

On June 13, 1971, the *New York Times* published its first installment of excerpts from a secret government study entitled *History of United States Decision Making Process on Vietnam Policy*. The study, better known as the Pentagon Papers, had been commissioned by Secretary of Defense Robert McNamara in June 1967 to present an "encyclopedic and objective" history of America's Vietnam policy between 1945 and 1968. Thirty-six historians, among them Daniel Ellsberg, researched for more than a year and a half to complete a massive document of several thousand pages in forty-seven volumes. Although classified "secret" and "top secret," the Pentagon Papers disclosed very little information that had not been publicly reported about the Vietnam War. But to Ellsberg, who leaked the Pentagon Papers to *The New York Times* and later *The Washington Post*, the study confirmed the growing impression that the government had failed at each escalation of the war to justify continued American involvement in Vietnam. He defended disclosure of the Pentagon Papers as an act of patriotism that served the national interest. To President Richard Nixon, however, it was an indefensible breach of national security.

The Justice Department moved quickly to enjoin further publication of the Pentagon Papers. (The Supreme Court's hurried disposition of the case appears below.) Meanwhile, the Nixon White House launched its own assault against Daniel Ellsberg and press leaks. President Nixon ordered his chief domestic advisor, John Ehrlichman, to form a Special Investigations Unit, dubbed the Plumbers. Ehrlichman assigned two White House staff members, Egil Krogh and David Young, to the Plumbers. They in turn hired Gordon Liddy and Howard Hunt, men trained in surveillance by the FBI and CIA. Their first objective was to discredit Daniel Ellsberg by leaking derogatory information to the press. On September 3, 1971, with Ehrlichman's approval and technical support from the CIA, Libby and Hunt led a burglary of the office of Ellsberg's psychiatrist. Taking Ellsberg's medical records back to the White House, Hunt drafted a damaging psychological profile of Ellsberg. Ehrlichman authorized Charles Colson, special counsel to the President, to leak the Ellsberg profile to the press.

Domestic espionage was not new to the Nixon White House. A year before the Pentagon Papers controversy, President Nixon had approved the "Huston Plan," under which White House employees wiretapped the private telephones of news reporters, infiltrated and disrupted anti-war groups, and mounted smear campaigns against the administration's detractors. The Plumbers, however, were much more threatening: once established, they enabled the President and his advisers to attempt ever more daring plots against their opponents.

Within a year of the Ellsberg break-in, the Plumbers, funded by Nixon campaign contributions, tried twice to bug the McGovern presidential campaign headquarters and successfully wiretapped some telephones at the Democratic National Committee Headquarters in the Watergate building. When former Attorney General John Mitchell, then serving as President Nixon's campaign director, complained that the wiretaps at the Watergate were useless, Liddy and Hunt reassembled the Ellsberg burglary team for a second Watergate break-in on June 17, 1972—this time to bug the telephone of Larry O'Brien, chair of the Democratic National Committee. The break-in was foiled, however, when police officers apprehended the burglars in O'Brien's office as they attempted to photograph documents.

Much of the Watergate affair following the June 17th arrests involved White House attempts to cover up the illegal activities of the Plumbers. John Dean, the President's Counsel, gave Hunt's psychological profile of Ellsberg to L. Patrick Gray, acting FBI director, who burned it along with other Plumbers' documents in the fireplace of his Connecticut home. FBI agents investigating the Watergate break-in traced checks in possession of the burglars to a slush fund maintained by the Committee to Reelect the President. Jailed for his part in the Watergate break-in, Hunt threatened to "bring down Ehrlichman" by revealing the Ellsberg break-in unless he received a substantial payment of "hush money." On March 21, 1973, President Nixon, in a taped conversation with John Dean in the oval office, planned the payment of hush money to the Watergate burglars in exchange for their silence about the Ellsberg break-in.

By 1974 President Nixon had resigned from the Presidency in the face of certain impeachment by the House of Representatives. His aides had been jailed or granted immunity for their parts in the Ellsberg and Watergate burglaries and for the obstruction of justice and perjury. American ground forces left Vietnam; the Republic of South Vietnam fell the next year.

New York Times Co. v. United States
403 U.S. 713 (1971)

PER CURIAM.

We granted certiorari in these cases in which the United States seeks to enjoin the New York Times and the Washington Post from publishing the contents of a classified study entitled "History of U.S. Decision-Making Process on Viet Nam Policy."

"Any system of prior restraints of expression comes to this Court bearing a heavy presumption against its constitutional validity." The Government "thus carries a heavy burden of showing justification for the imposition of such a restraint." The District Court[s] held that the Government had not met that burden. We agree.

[The Court summarily affirmed the District Courts.]

So ordered.

Justice BLACK, with whom Justice DOUGLAS joins, concurring.

I adhere to the view that the Government's case against the Washington Post should have been dismissed and that the injunction against the New York Times should have been vacated without oral argument when the cases were first presented to this Court. I believe that every moment's continuance of the injunctions against these newspapers amounts to a flagrant, indefensible, and continuing violation of the First Amendment. . . .

[T]he Government argues in its brief that in spite of the First Amendment, "[t]he authority of the Executive Department to protect the nation against publication of information whose disclosure would endanger the national security stems from two interrelated sources: the constitutional power of the President over the conduct of foreign affairs and his authority as Commander-in-Chief." . . .

The Government does not even attempt to rely on any act of Congress. Instead it makes the bold and dangerously far-reaching contention that the courts should take it upon themselves to "make" a law abridging freedom of the press in the name of equity, presidential power and national security, even when the representatives of the people in Congress have adhered to the command of the First Amendment and refused to make such a law.[5] To find that the President has "inherent power" to halt the publication of news by resort to the courts would wipe out the First Amendment and destroy the fundamental liberty and security of the very people the Government hopes to make "secure." No one can read the history of the adoption of the First Amendment without being convinced beyond any doubt that it was injunctions like those sought here that Madison and his collaborators intended to outlaw in this Nation for all time.

The word "security" is a broad, vague generality whose contours should not be invoked to abrogate the fundamental law embodied in the First Amendment. The guarding of military and diplomatic secrets at the expense of informed representative government provides no real security for our Republic. . . .

Justice DOUGLAS, with whom Justice BLACK joins, concurring.

. . . It should be noted at the outset that the First Amendment provides that "Congress shall make no law . . . abridging the freedom of speech, or of the press." That leaves, in my view, no room for governmental restraint on the press. There is, moreover, no statute barring the publication by the press of the material which the Times and

---

5. Compare the views of the Solicitor General with those of James Madison, the author of the First Amendment. When speaking of the Bill of Rights in the House of Representatives, Madison said: "If they [the first ten amendments] are incorporated into the Constitution, independent tribunals of justice will consider themselves in a peculiar manner the guardians of those rights; they will be an impenetrable bulwark against every assumption of power in the Legislative or Executive; they will be naturally led to resist every encroachment upon rights expressly stipulated for in the Constitution by the declaration of rights." 1 Annals of Cong. 439.

the Post seek to use. . . . So any power that the Government possesses must come from its "inherent power."

The power to wage war is "the power to wage war successfully." But the war power stems from a declaration of war. The Constitution by Art. I, § 8, gives Congress, not the President, power "[t]o declare War." Nowhere are presidential wars authorized. We need not decide therefore what leveling effect the war power of Congress might have.

These disclosures may have a serious impact. But that is no basis for sanctioning a previous restraint on the press. The Government says that it has inherent powers to go into court and obtain an injunction to protect the national interest, which in this case is alleged to be national security. *Near v. Minnesota*, 283 U.S. 697 (1931), repudiated that expansive doctrine in no uncertain terms.

The dominant purpose of the First Amendment was to prohibit the widespread practice of governmental suppression of embarrassing information. It is common knowledge that the First Amendment was adopted against the widespread use of the common law of seditious libel to punish the dissemination of material that is embarrassing to the powers-that-be. See T. Emerson, The System of Freedom of Expression, c. V (1970); Z. Chafee, Free Speech in the United States, c. XIII (1941). The present cases will, I think, go down in history as the most dramatic illustration of that principle. A debate of large proportions goes on in the Nation over our posture in Vietnam. That debate antedated the disclosure of the contents of the present documents. The latter are highly relevant to the debate in progress.

Secrecy in government is fundamentally anti-democratic, perpetuating bureaucratic errors. Open debate and discussion of public issues are vital to our national health. . . .

Justice BRENNAN, concurring.

. . . The error that has pervaded these cases from the outset was the granting of any injunctive relief whatsoever, interim or otherwise. The entire thrust of the Government's claim throughout these cases has been that publication of the material sought to be enjoined "could," or "might," or "may" prejudice the national interest in various ways. But the First Amendment tolerates absolutely no prior judicial restraints of the press predicated upon surmise or conjecture that untoward consequences may result. Our cases, it is true, have indicated that there is a single, extremely narrow class of cases in which the First Amendment's ban on prior judicial restraint may be overridden. Our cases have thus far indicated that such cases may arise only when the Nation "is at war," *Schenck v. United States*, 249 U.S. 47, 52 (1919), during which times "[n]o one would question but that a government might prevent actual obstruction to its recruiting service or the publication of the sailing dates of transports or the number and location of troops." *Near v. Minnesota*, 283 U.S. 697, 716 (1931). Even if the present world situation were assumed to be tantamount to a time of war, or if the power of presently available armaments would justify even in peacetime the suppression of information that would set in motion a nuclear holocaust, in neither of these actions has the Government presented or even alleged that publication of items from or based upon the material at issue would cause the happening of an event of that nature. . . . Thus, only governmental allegation and proof that publication must inevitably, directly, and immediately cause the occurrence of an event kindred to imperiling the safety of a transport already at sea can support even the issuance of an interim restraining order. In no event may mere conclusions be sufficient: for if the Executive Branch seeks judicial aid in preventing publication, it must inevitably submit the basis upon which that aid is sought to scrutiny by the judiciary. And therefore, every restraint issued in this case, whatever its form, has violated the First Amendment—and not less so because that restraint was justified as necessary to afford the courts an opportunity to examine the claim more thoroughly. Unless and until the Government has clearly made out its case, the First Amendment commands that no injunction may issue.

Justice STEWART, with whom Justice WHITE joins, concurring.

. . . If the Constitution gives the Executive a large degree of unshared power in the conduct of foreign affairs and the maintenance of our national defense, then under the Constitution the Executive must have the largely unshared duty to determine and preserve the degree of internal security necessary to exercise that power successfully. . . . [I]t is the constitutional duty of the Executive—as a matter of sovereign prerogative and not as a matter of law as the courts know law—through the promulgation and enforcement of executive regulations, to protect the confidentiality necessary to carry out its responsibilities in the fields of international relations and national defense.

This is not to say that Congress and the courts have no role to play. Undoubtedly Congress has the power to enact specific and appropriate criminal laws to protect government property and preserve government secrets. . . . But in the cases before us we are asked neither to construe specific regulations nor to apply specific laws. We are asked, instead, to perform a function that the Constitution gave to the Executive, not the Judiciary. We are asked, quite simply, to prevent the publication by two newspapers of material that the Executive Branch insists should not, in the national interest, be published. I am convinced that the Executive is correct with respect to some of the documents involved. But I cannot say that disclosure of any of them will surely result in direct, immediate, and irreparable damage to our Nation or its people. That being so, there can under the First Amendment be but one judicial resolution of the issues before us. I join the judgments of the Court.

Justice WHITE, with whom Justice STEWART joins, concurring.

I concur in today's judgments, but only because of the concededly extraordinary protection against prior restraints enjoyed by the press under our constitutional system. I do not say that in no circumstances would the First Amendment permit an injunction against publishing information about government plans or operations. Nor, after examining the materials the Government characterizes as the most sensitive and destructive, can I deny that revelation of these documents will do substantial damage to public interests. Indeed, I am confident that their disclosure will have that result. But I nevertheless agree that the United States has not satisfied the very heavy burden that it must meet to warrant an injunction against publication in these cases, at least in the absence of express and appropriately limited congressional authorization for prior restraints in circumstances such as these.

The Government's position is simply stated: The responsibility of the Executive for the conduct of the foreign affairs and for the security of the Nation is so basic that the President is entitled to an injunction against publication of a newspaper story whenever he can convince a court that the information to be revealed threatens "grave and irreparable" injury to the public interest; and the injunction should issue whether or not the material to be published is classified, whether or not publication would be lawful under relevant criminal statutes enacted by Congress, and regardless of the circumstances by which the newspaper came into possession of the information.

At least in the absence of legislation by Congress, based on its own investigations and findings, I am quite unable to agree that the inherent powers of the Executive and the courts reach so far as to authorize remedies having such sweeping potential for inhibiting publications by the press. Much of the difficulty inheres in the "grave and irreparable danger" standard suggested by the United States. If the United States were to have judgment under such a standard in these cases, our decision would be of little guidance to other courts in other cases, for the material at issue here would not be available from the Court's opinion or from public records, nor would it be published by the press....

It is not easy to reject the proposition urged by the United States and to deny relief on its good-faith claims in these cases that publication will work serious damage to the country. But that discomfiture is considerably dispelled by the infrequency of prior-restraint cases. Normally, publication will occur and the damage be done before the Government has either opportunity or grounds for suppression. So here, publication has already begun and a substantial part of the threatened damage has already occurred. The fact of a massive breakdown in security is known, access to the documents by many unauthorized people is undeniable, and the efficacy of equitable relief against these or other newspapers to avert anticipated damage is doubtful at best.

What is more, terminating the ban on publication of the relatively few sensitive documents the Government now seeks to suppress does not mean that the law either requires or invites newspapers or others to publish them or that they will be immune from criminal action if they do....

When the Espionage Act was under consideration in 1917, Congress eliminated from the bill a provision that would have given the President broad powers in time of war to proscribe, under threat of criminal penalty, the publication of various categories of information related to the national defense.[3] Congress at that time was unwilling to clothe the President with such far-reaching powers to monitor the press, and those opposed to this part of the legislation assumed that a necessary concomitant of such power was the power to "filter out the news to the people through some man." 55 Cong.Rec. 2008 (remarks of Sen. Ashurst). However, these same members of Congress appeared to have little doubt that newspapers would be subject to criminal prosecution if they insisted on publishing information of the type Congress had itself determined should not be revealed. Senator Ashurst, for example, was quite sure that the editor of such a newspaper "should be punished if he did publish information as to the movements of the fleet, the troops, the aircraft, the location of powder factories, the location of defense works, and all that sort of thing."

The Criminal Code contains numerous provisions potentially relevant to these cases. Section 797 makes it a crime to publish certain photographs or drawings of military

---

3. "Whoever, in time of war, in violation of reasonable regulations to be prescribed by the President, which he is hereby authorized to make and promulgate, shall publish any information with respect to the movement,... description,... or disposition of any of the armed forces... of the United States,... or any other information relating to the public defense calculated to be useful to the enemy, shall be punished by a fine... or by imprisonment...." 55 Cong.Rec. 2100.

installations. Section 798, also in precise language, proscribes knowing and willful publication of any classified information concerning the cryptographic systems or communication intelligence activities of the United States as well as any information obtained from communication intelligence operations. . . . I would have no difficulty in sustaining convictions under these sections on facts that would not justify the intervention of equity and the imposition of a prior restraint.

The same would be true under those sections of the Criminal Code casting a wider net to protect the national defense. Section 793(e) makes it a criminal act for any unauthorized possessor of a document "relating to the national defense" either (1) willfully to communicate or cause to be communicated that document to any person not entitled to receive it or (2) willfully to retain the document and fail to deliver it to an officer of the United States entitled to receive it. . . . Of course, in the cases before us, the unpublished documents have been demanded by the United States and their import has been made known at least to counsel for the newspapers involved. In *Gorin v. United States*, 312 U.S. 19, 28 (1941), the words "national defense" as used in a predecessor of § 793 were held by a unanimous Court to have "a well understood connotation"—a "generic concept of broad connotations, referring to the military and naval establishments and the related activities of national preparedness"—and to be "sufficiently definite to apprise the public of prohibited activities" and to be consonant with due process. Also, as construed by the Court in *Gorin*, information "connected with the national defense" is obviously not limited to that threatening "grave and irreparable" injury to the United States.

It is thus clear that Congress has addressed itself to the problems of protecting the security of the country and the national defense from unauthorized disclosure of potentially damaging information. It has not, however, authorized the injunctive remedy against threatened publication. It has apparently been satisfied to rely on criminal sanctions and their deterrent effect on the responsible as well as the irresponsible press. . . .

Justice MARSHALL, concurring.

. . . The issue is whether this Court or the Congress has the power to make law. In these cases there is no problem concerning the President's power to classify information as "secret" or "top secret." Congress has specifically recognized Presidential authority, which has been formally exercised in Exec. Order 10501 (1953), to classify documents and information. See, e.g., 18 U.S.C. § 798; 50 U.S.C. § 783. Nor is there any issue here regarding the President's power as Chief Executive and Commander in Chief to protect national security by disciplining employees who disclose information and by taking precautions to prevent leaks.

The problem here is whether in these particular cases the Executive Branch has authority to invoke the equity jurisdiction of the courts to protect what it believes to be the national interest. See *In re Debs*, 158 U.S. 564, 584 (1895). . . . It would . . . be utterly inconsistent with the concept of separation of powers for this Court to use its power of contempt to prevent behavior that Congress has specifically declined to prohibit. . . . The Constitution . . . did not provide for government by injunction in which the courts and the Executive Branch can "make law" without regard to the action of Congress. It may be more convenient for the Executive Branch if it need only convince a judge to prohibit conduct rather than ask the Congress to pass a law, and it may be more convenient to enforce a contempt order than to seek a criminal conviction in a jury trial. Moreover, it may be considered politically wise to get a court to share the responsibility for arresting those who the Executive Branch has probable cause to believe are violating the law. But convenience and political considerations of the moment do not justify a basic departure from the principles of our system of government.

In these cases we are not faced with a situation where Congress has failed to provide the Executive with broad power to protect the Nation from disclosure of damaging state secrets. Congress has on several occasions given extensive consideration to the problem of protecting the military and strategic secrets of the United States. This consideration has resulted in the enactment of statutes making it a crime to receive, disclose, communicate, withhold, and publish certain documents, photographs, instruments, appliances, and information.... Congress has provided penalties ranging from a $10,000 fine to death for violating the various statutes....

If the Government had attempted to show that there was no effective remedy under traditional criminal law, it would have had to show that there is no arguably applicable statute. Of course, at this stage this Court could not and cannot determine whether there has been a violation of a particular statute or decide the constitutionality of any statute. Whether a good-faith prosecution could have been instituted under any statute could, however, be determined....

It is true that Judge Gurfein found that Congress had not made it a crime to publish the items and material specified in § 793(e). He found that the words "communicates, delivers, transmits..." did not refer to publication of newspaper stories. And that view has some support in the legislative history and conforms with the past practice of using the statute only to prosecute those charged with ordinary espionage....

On at least two occasions Congress has refused to enact legislation that would have made the conduct engaged in here unlawful and given the President the power that he seeks in this case. In 1917 during the debate over the original Espionage Act, still the basic provisions of § 793, Congress rejected a proposal to give the President in time of war or threat of war authority to directly prohibit by proclamation the publication of information relating to national defense that might be useful to the enemy. The proposal provided that:

> "During any national emergency resulting from a war to which the United States is a party, or from threat of such a war, the President may, by proclamation, declare the existence of such emergency and, by proclamation, prohibit the publishing or communicating of, or the attempting to publish or communicate any information relating to the national defense which, in his judgment, is of such character that it is or might be useful to the enemy. Whoever violates any such prohibition shall be punished by a fine of not more than $10,000 or by imprisonment for not more than 10 years, or both: *Provided*, that nothing in this section shall be construed to limit or restrict any discussion, comment, or criticism of the acts or policies of the Government or its representatives or the publication of the same." 55 Cong.Rec. 1763.

Congress rejected this proposal after war against Germany had been declared even though many believed that there was a grave national emergency and that the threat of security leaks and espionage was serious.... [T]he Executive Branch comes to this Court and asks that it be granted the power Congress refused to give.

In 1957 the United States Commission on Government Security found that "[a]irplane journals, scientific periodicals, and even the daily newspaper have featured articles containing information and other data which should have been deleted in whole or in part for security reasons." In response to this problem the Commission proposed that "Congress enact legislation making it a crime for any person willfully to disclose without proper authorization, for any purpose whatever, information classified 'secret' or 'top secret,' knowing, or having reasonable grounds to believe, such information to have been so classified." Report of Commission on Government Security 619-620 (1957). After substantial floor discussion on the proposal, it was rejected. See 103 Cong.Rec. 10447-10450.... The Government is here asking this Court to remake that decision. This Court has no such power....

Justice HARLAN, with whom THE CHIEF JUSTICE and Justice BLACKMUN join, dissenting.

These cases forcefully call to mind the wise admonition of Mr. Justice Holmes, dissenting in *Northern Securities Co. v. United States*, 193 U.S. 197, 400-401 (1904):

> "Great cases, like hard cases, make bad law. For great cases are called great, not by reason of their real importance in shaping the law of the future, but because of some accident of immediate overwhelming interest which appeals to the feelings and distorts the judgment. These immediate interests exercise a kind of hydraulic pressure which makes what previously was clear seem doubtful, and before which even well settled principles of law will bend."

With all respect, I consider that the Court has been almost irresponsibly feverish in dealing with these cases.

Both the Court of Appeals for the Second Circuit and the Court of Appeals for the District of Columbia Circuit rendered judgment on June 23. The New York Times' petition for certiorari, its motion for accelerated consideration thereof, and its application for interim relief were filed in this Court on June 24 at about 11 a.m.... The briefs of the parties were received less than two hours before argument on June 26.

This frenzied train of events took place in the name of the presumption against prior restraints created by the First Amendment. Due regard for the extraordinarily important and difficult questions involved in these litigations should have led the Court to shun such a precipitate timetable. In order to decide the merits of these cases properly, some or all of the following questions should have been faced:

1. Whether the Attorney General is authorized to bring these suits in the name of the United States. Compare *In re Debs*, 158 U.S. 564 (1895), with *Youngstown Sheet & Tube Co. v. Sawyer*, 343 U.S. 579 (1952). This question involves as well the construction and validity of a singularly opaque statute—the Espionage Act, 18 U.S.C. § 793(e).

2. Whether the First Amendment permits the federal courts to enjoin publication of stories which would present a serious threat to national security. See *Near v. Minnesota*, 283 U.S. 697, 716 (1931) (dictum).

3. Whether the threat to publish highly secret documents is of itself a sufficient implication of national security to justify an injunction on the theory that regardless of the contents of the documents harm enough results simply from the demonstration of such a breach of secrecy.

4. Whether the unauthorized disclosure of any of these particular documents would seriously impair the national security.

5. What weight should be given to the opinion of high officers in the Executive Branch of the Government with respect to questions 3 and 4.

6. Whether the newspapers are entitled to retain and use the documents notwithstanding the seemingly uncontested facts that the documents, or the originals of which they are duplicates, were purloined from the Government's possession and that the newspapers received them with knowledge that they had been feloniously acquired.

7. Whether the threatened harm to the national security or the Government's possessory interest in the documents justifies the issuance of an injunction against publication in light of—

a. The strong First Amendment policy against prior restraints on publication;

b. The doctrine against enjoining conduct in violation of criminal statutes; and

c. The extent to which the materials at issue have apparently already been otherwise disseminated....

Forced as I am to reach the merits of these cases, I dissent from the opinion and judgments of the Court.... It is plain to me that the scope of the judicial function in passing upon the activities of the Executive Branch of the Government in the field of foreign affairs is very narrowly restricted. This view is, I think, dictated by the concept of separation of powers upon which our constitutional system rests.

In a speech on the floor of the House of Representatives, Chief Justice John Marshall, then a member of that body, stated: "The President is the sole organ of the nation in its external relations, and its sole representative with foreign nations." 10 Annals of Cong. 613. From that time, shortly after the founding of the Nation, to this, there has been no substantial challenge to this description of the scope of executive power.

From this constitutional primacy in the field of foreign affairs, it seems to me that certain conclusions necessarily follow. Some of these were stated concisely by President Washington, declining the request of the House of Representatives for the papers leading up to the negotiation of the Jay Treaty:

> "The nature of foreign negotiations requires caution, and their success must often depend on secrecy; and even when brought to a conclusion a full disclosure of all the measures, demands, or eventual concessions which may have been proposed or contemplated would be extremely impolitic; for this might have a pernicious influence on future negotiations, or produce immediate inconveniences, perhaps danger and mischief, in relation to other powers." 1 J. Richardson, Messages and Papers of the Presidents 194-195 (1896).

The power to evaluate the "pernicious influence" of premature disclosure is not, however, lodged in the Executive alone. I agree that, in performance of its duty to protect the values of the First Amendment against political pressures, the judiciary must review the initial Executive determination to the point of satisfying itself that the subject matter of the dispute does lie within the proper compass of the President's foreign relations power. Constitutional considerations forbid "a complete abandonment of judicial control." Moreover, the judiciary may properly insist that the determination that disclosure of the subject matter would irreparably impair the national security be made by the head of the Executive Department concerned—here the Secretary of State or the Secretary of Defense—after actual personal consideration by that officer. This safeguard is required in the analogous area of executive claims of privilege for secrets of state.

But in my judgment the judiciary may not properly go beyond these two inquiries and redetermine for itself the probable impact of disclosure on the national security. . . . Even if there is some room for the judiciary to override the executive determination, it is plain that the scope of review must be exceedingly narrow. I can see no indication in the opinions [below] that the conclusions of the Executive were given even the deference owing to an administrative agency, much less that owing to a co-equal branch of the Government operating within the field of its constitutional prerogative. . . .

Pending further hearings in each case conducted under the appropriate ground rules, I would continue the restraints on publication. I cannot believe that the doctrine prohibiting prior restraints reaches to the point of preventing courts from maintaining the status quo long enough to act responsibly in matters of such national importance as those involved here.

Justice BLACKMUN, dissenting.

I join Justice Harlan in his dissent. I also am in substantial accord with much that Justice White says, by way of admonition, in the latter part of his opinion. . . .

---

1. Garnering legal guidance from the *Pentagon Papers* case is not easy because the Court's nine opinions offer as many as seven different approaches to the case, differing in either nuance or overall theory. The terse *per curiam* opinion stresses the extraordinary threshold showing that the executive must make to justify a prior restraint. In this case, there were numerous sets of the papers, and they were no longer under any controlled custody. Indeed, the President had sent a set to Congress. Moreover, the material was entirely historical, recounting events up to 1968. Where does that leave us for prior restraints on material under a court's custody, relating to current secrets?

2. Justice Brennan cites the famous dictum from *Near v. Minnesota* that the government might prevent publication of such matters as troop locations in wartime. He argues that only proof of such direct threats to national security can justify a prior restraint, and that the courts can review the persuasiveness of the executive's factual submissions. Do you agree? What standard of judicial review would be appropriate? Compare Justice Harlan's argument that the courts should stop once they have ascertained that the subject matter pertains to the foreign relations power, and that the determination of necessity to suppress it has been made after "actual personal consideration" by an officer of appropriate rank. Would such a test sufficiently protect First Amendment values, in light of the incentives for government officers to resist disclosure of materials that are merely embarrassing?

In light of this debate, consider an extraordinary case that arose in 1979. A District Court granted the government a preliminary injunction against publication by *The Progressive* of an article detailing the basic design of the American hydrogen bomb. *U.S. v. Progressive, Inc.*, 467 F. Supp. 990 (W.D. Wis. 1979). The author, Howard Morland, deduced the information entirely from unclassified materials: interviews with government employees, visits to nuclear weapons facilities, and the study of government documents—all with the knowledge and consent of the U.S. Department of Energy. The government argued that the way this unclassified material was synthesized in the article could provide new insights to building an H-bomb.

Solely on the basis of affidavits and counsels' briefs and oral arguments, the District Court issued the injunction based on the *possibility* of "grave, direct, immediate and irreparable harm" to the national interest. Six months later, while the preliminary injunction was still in effect, the government moved to dismiss the case as moot after another author succeeded in publishing an article elsewhere with substantially the same information. *U.S. v. Progressive, Inc.*, 610 F. 2d 819 (7th Cir. 1979) (appeal dismissed without opinion). For a critical review of the court's rationale and its fact-finding procedure, *see* Note, United States v. Progressive, Inc.: *The Faustian Bargain and the First Amendment*, 75 Nw. U. L. Rev. 538 (1980).

Did the District Court apply the correct standard for reviewing the executive's claims? How can the executive address the "cat-out-of-the-bag" problem in these cases?

3. Justice White seemingly entertains little doubt that, consistent with the First Amendment, Congress may provide criminal liability for the publication of material that could not constitutionally be restrained prior to publication. Does this make sense? Why?

4. Is Justice Marshall correct that the *Pentagon Papers* case implicates not only First Amendment principles, but serious separation of powers questions as well? Note that both he and Justice White cite Congress' refusal to pass bills that would have made it a crime to publish information "relating to the national defense" in violation of presidential orders. Is this case like *Youngstown*, then? If the bills had been enacted, would they justify prior restraints? (And why, by the way, did Congress decline to pass these bills? Would it have been wise to enact them?) What result here if Congress had authorized the executive to sue for injunctive relief against the possible publication of materials, "the revelation of which will substantially damage the national security"?

For some ruminations on questions such as these, *see* Edgar & Schmidt, Curtiss-Wright *Comes Home: Executive Power and National Security Secrecy*, 21 Harv. Civ. Rts.-Civ. Lib. L. Rev. 349, 360-61 (1986):

> When the Nixon Administration sought to enjoin publication of the "Pentagon Papers" fifteen years ago, we were struck by what seemed the bizarre institutional premises of the Administration's main legal position. The government argued that without any statutory authorization, the President, in his role as commander-in-chief and steward of foreign relations, could create a legal norm of secrecy and enlist the injunctive powers of the federal courts to enforce his norm against publications that posed a "grave and irreparable danger" to national security. The government's brief in the Supreme Court did not even mention the statutory situation.
>
> Even if the Executive could sue for injunctive relief without statutory authorization, he cannot create the legal rule that he seeks to enforce in the domestic arena. Since Congress had made no law, what possible basis could there have been even to consider the first amendment?
>
> The absence of legislative authorization was noted in the questions at oral argument and in several of the Justices' opinions, although only Marshall argued that it should be decisive. Of the six Justices who concurred in the judgment against the government, all but Justice Brennan relied to some degree on the absence of statutory authority for injunctive relief. Moreover, considerable interest was expressed on the different issue of criminal sanctions for publication

of classified government documents. A number of the Justices volunteered readings of the espionage statutes in relation to hypothetical criminal proceedings against the publishers, reporters and information sources involved, even though such questions had not been briefed, were dreadfully difficult, and were quite unnecessary to a ruling about the injunction.

These speculative dicta addressing the potential capacity of the espionage statutes to criminalize publication of the "Pentagon Papers," when added to our own institutional predispositions, led us fifteen years ago to exaggerate the extent to which the Court accepted the premise of legislative hegemony over national security secrecy issues. [Edgar & Schmidt, *The Espionage Statutes and Publication of Defense Information*, 73 Colum. L. Rev. 929 (1973).] With hindsight, we now believe that the central theme of the *Pentagon Papers* opinions, at least in institutional terms, was the surprising willingness of many of the Justices to contemplate scenarios set in a statutory vacuum, where executive power backed by judicial support would govern issues of national security secrecy, at least so long as Congress remained a passive bystander.

Edgar & Schmidt explain the evolution of their views as follows (*id.* at 351):

> We [believed] that Congress should be the controlling institution in striking a tolerable balance between secrecy needs and the value of public debate about foreign and military policy. We . . . assumed that the Supreme Court in particular would see the virtues of legislative resolution of secrecy questions. Contrary to our predictions and prescriptions, the years since the *Pentagon Papers* have seen a considerable enhancement of executive power in areas of national security secrecy, an aggrandizement significantly assisted by the Supreme Court, with Congress noticeably absent from the discourse.

In Chapter Six, we will encounter several of the cases that led Edgar & Schmidt to change their view of *Pentagon Papers*. They also had in mind the following principal case:

Snepp v. United States
444 U.S. 507 (1980)

PER CURIAM. . . .

I

Based on his experiences as a CIA agent, [Frank] Snepp published a book [Decent Interval (1977)] about certain CIA activities in South Vietnam. Snepp published the account without submitting it to the Agency for prepublication review. As an express condition of his employment with the CIA in 1968, however, Snepp had executed an agreement promising that he would "not . . . publish . . . any information or material relating to the Agency, its activities or intelligence activities generally, either during or after the term of [his] employment . . . without specific prior approval by the Agency." The promise was an integral part of Snepp's concurrent undertaking "not to disclose any classified information relating to the Agency without proper authorization." Thus, Snepp had pledged not to divulge classified information and not to publish any information without prepublication clearance. The Government brought this suit to enforce Snepp's agreement. It sought a declaration that Snepp had breached the contract, an injunction requiring Snepp to submit future writings for prepublication review, and an order imposing a constructive trust for the Government's benefit on all profits that Snepp might earn from publishing the book in violation of his fiduciary obligations to the Agency.

The District Court found that Snepp had "willfully, deliberately and surreptitiously breached his position of trust with the CIA and the [1968] secrecy agreement" by publishing his book without submitting it for prepublication review [and] that publication of the book had "caused the United States irreparable harm and loss." The District Court therefore enjoined future breaches of Snepp's agreement and imposed a constructive trust on Snepp's profits.

The Court of Appeals . . . agreed that Snepp had breached a valid contract[3] [and] upheld the injunction against future violations of Snepp's prepublication obligation. The court, however, concluded that the record did not support imposition of a constructive trust. The conclusion rested on the court's perception that Snepp had a First Amendment right to publish unclassified information and the Government's concession—for the purposes of this litigation—that Snepp's book divulged no classified intelligence.[4] In other words, the court thought that Snepp's fiduciary obligation extended only to preserving the confidentiality of classified material. It therefore limited recovery to nominal damages and to the possibility of punitive damages if the Government—in a jury trial— could prove tortious conduct.

. . . We [conclude] that Snepp breached a fiduciary obligation and that the proceeds of his breach are impressed with a constructive trust.

II

Snepp's employment with the CIA involved an extremely high degree of trust. In the opening sentence of the agreement that he signed, Snepp explicitly recognized that he was entering a trust relationship. The trust agreement specifically imposed the obligation not to publish *any* information relating to the Agency without submitting the information for clearance. Snepp stipulated at trial that—after undertaking

---

3. . . . In his petition for certiorari, Snepp relies primarily on the claim that his agreement is unenforceable as a prior restraint on protected speech. When Snepp accepted employment with the CIA, he voluntarily signed the agreement that expressly obligated him to submit any proposed publication for prior review. He does not claim that he executed this agreement under duress. Indeed, he voluntarily reaffirmed his obligation when he left the Agency. We agree with the Court of Appeals that Snepp's agreement is an "entirely appropriate" exercise of the CIA Director's statutory mandate to "protec[t] intelligence sources and methods from unauthorized disclosure," 50 U.S.C. § 403(d)(3). Moreover, this Court's cases make clear that—even in the absence of an express agreement—the CIA could have acted to protect substantial government interests by imposing reasonable restrictions on employee activities that in other contexts might be protected by the First Amendment. The Government has a compelling interest in protecting both the secrecy of information important to our national security and the appearance of confidentiality so essential to the effective operation of our foreign intelligence service. The agreement that Snepp signed is a reasonable means for protecting this vital interest.

4. The Government's concession distinguished this litigation from *United States v. Marchetti*, 466 F.2d 1309 (CA4), cert. denied, 409 U.S. 1063 (1972) [upholding an injunction enforcing a prepublication clearance agreement]. There, the Government claimed that a former CIA employee intended to violate his agreement not to publish any *classified* information. *Marchetti* therefore did not consider the appropriate remedy for the breach of an agreement to submit *all* material for prepublication review. . . .

this obligation—he had been "assigned to various positions of trust" and that he had been granted "frequent access to classified information, including information regarding intelligence sources and methods."[6] Snepp published his book about CIA activities on the basis of this background and exposure. He deliberately and surreptitiously violated his obligation to submit all material for prepublication review. Thus, he exposed the classified information with which he had been entrusted to the risk of disclosure.

Whether Snepp violated his trust does not depend upon whether his book actually contained classified information. The Government does not deny—as a general principle—Snepp's right to publish unclassified information.... The Government simply claims that, in light of the special trust reposed in him and the agreement that he signed, Snepp should have given the CIA an opportunity to determine whether the material he proposed to publish would compromise classified information or sources....

Both the District Court and the Court of Appeals found that a former intelligence agent's publication of unreviewed material relating to intelligence activities can be detrimental to vital national interests even if the published information is unclassified. When a former agent relies on his own judgment about what information is detrimental, he may reveal information that the CIA—with its broader understanding of what may expose classified information and confidential sources—could have identified as harmful. In addition to receiving intelligence from domestically based or controlled sources, the CIA obtains information from the intelligence services of friendly nations and from agents operating in foreign countries. The continued availability of these foreign sources depends upon the CIA's ability to guarantee the security of information that might compromise them and even endanger the personal safety of foreign agents.

Undisputed evidence in this case shows that a CIA agent's violation of his obligation to submit writings about the Agency for prepublication review impairs the CIA's ability to perform its statutory duties. Admiral Turner, Director of the CIA, testified without contradiction that Snepp's book and others like it have seriously impaired the effectiveness of American intelligence operations. He said,

> "Over the last six to nine months, we have had a number of sources discontinue work with us. We have had more sources tell us that they are very nervous about continuing work with us. We have had very strong complaints from a number of foreign intelligence services with whom we conduct liaison, who have questioned whether they should continue exchanging information with us, for fear it will not remain secret. I cannot estimate to you how many potential sources or liaison arrangements have never germinated because people were unwilling to enter into business with us."[8]

---

6. Quite apart from the plain language of the agreement, the nature of Snepp's duties and his conceded access to confidential sources and materials could establish a trust relationship. Few types of governmental employment involve a higher degree of trust than that reposed in a CIA employee with Snepp's duties.

8. In questioning the force of Admiral Turner's testimony, Justice Stevens' dissenting opinion suggests that the concern of foreign intelligence services may not be occasioned by the hazards of allowing an agent like Snepp to publish whatever he pleases, but by the release of classified information or simply the disagreement of foreign agencies with our Government's

In view of this and other evidence in the record, both the District Court and the Court of Appeals recognized that Snepp's breach of his explicit obligation to submit his material—classified or not—for prepublication clearance has irreparably harmed the United States Government.

III

The decision of the Court of Appeals denies the Government the most appropriate remedy for Snepp's acknowledged wrong. Indeed, as a practical matter, the decision may well leave the Government with no reliable deterrent against similar breaches of security. No one disputes that the actual damages attributable to a publication such as Snepp's generally are unquantifiable. Nominal damages are a hollow alternative, certain to deter no one. The punitive damages recoverable after a jury trial are speculative and unusual. Even if recovered, they may bear no relation to either the Government's irreparable loss or Snepp's unjust gain.

The Government could not pursue the only remedy that the Court of Appeals left it without losing the benefit of the bargain it seeks to enforce. Proof of the tortious conduct necessary to sustain an award of punitive damages might force the Government to disclose some of the very confidences that Snepp promised to protect. The trial of such a suit, before a jury if the defendant so elects, would subject the CIA and its officials to probing discovery into the Agency's highly confidential affairs. Rarely would the Government run this risk. In a letter introduced at Snepp's trial, former CIA Director Colby noted the analogous problem in criminal cases. Existing law, he stated, "requires the revelation in open court of confirming or additional information of such a nature that the potential damage to the national security precludes prosecution." When the Government cannot secure its remedy without unacceptable risks, it has no remedy at all.

A constructive trust, on the other hand, protects both the Government and the former agent from unwarranted risks. This remedy is the natural and customary consequence of a breach of trust. It deals fairly with both parties by conforming relief to the dimensions of the wrong.... Since the remedy is swift and sure, it is tailored to deter those who would place sensitive information at risk. And since the remedy reaches only funds attributable to the breach, it cannot saddle the former agent with exemplary damages out of all proportion to his gain.... We therefore reverse the judgment of the Court of Appeals insofar as it refused to impose a constructive trust on Snepp's profits....

Justice STEVENS, with whom Justice BRENNAN and Justice MARSHALL join, dissenting.

---

classification policy. Justice Stevens' views . . . reflect a misapprehension of the concern reflected by Admiral Turner's testimony. . . . The problem is to ensure in advance, and by proper procedures, that information detrimental to national interest is not published. Without a dependable prepublication review procedure, no intelligence agency or responsible Government official could be assured that an employee privy to sensitive information might not conclude on his own—innocently or otherwise—that it should be disclosed to the world.

The dissent argues that the Court is allowing the CIA to "censor" its employees' publications. Snepp's contract, however, requires no more than a clearance procedure subject to judicial review. If Snepp . . . had submitted his manuscript for review and the Agency had found it to contain sensitive material, presumably . . . an effort would have been made to eliminate harmful disclosures. Absent agreement . . . the Agency would have borne the burden of seeking an injunction against publication.

... The rule of law the Court announces today is not supported by statute, by the contract, or by the common law. Although Congress has enacted a number of criminal statutes punishing the unauthorized dissemination of certain types of classified information, it has not seen fit to authorize the constructive trust remedy the Court creates today. Nor does either of the contracts Snepp signed with the Agency provide for any such remedy in the event of a breach....

[This] is an employment relationship in which the employee possesses fiduciary obligations arising out of his duty of loyalty to his employer. One of those obligations, long recognized by the common law even in the absence of a written employment agreement, is the duty to protect confidential or "classified" information. If Snepp had breached that obligation, the common law would support the implication of a constructive trust....

But Snepp did not breach his duty to protect confidential information. Rather, he breached a contractual duty, imposed in aid of the basic duty to maintain confidentiality, to obtain prepublication clearance. In order to justify the imposition of a constructive trust, the majority attempts to equate this contractual duty with Snepp's duty not to disclose, labeling them both as "fiduciary." I find nothing in the common law to support such an approach....

The Court has not persuaded me that a rule of reason analysis should not be applied to Snepp's covenant to submit to prepublication review. Like an ordinary employer, the CIA has a vital interest in protecting certain types of information; at the same time, the CIA employee has a countervailing interest in preserving a wide range of work opportunities (including work as an author) and in protecting his First Amendment rights. The public interest lies in a proper accommodation that will preserve the intelligence mission of the Agency while not abridging the free flow of unclassified information. When the Government seeks to enforce a harsh restriction on the employee's freedom, despite its admission that the interest the agreement was designed to protect—the confidentiality of classified information—has not been compromised, an equity court might well be persuaded that the case is not one in which the covenant should be enforced.

But even assuming that Snepp's covenant to submit to prepublication review should be enforced, the constructive trust imposed by the Court is not an appropriate remedy. ... [I]f Snepp had submitted the book to the Agency for prepublication review, the Government's censorship authority would surely have been limited to the excision of classified material. In this case, then, it would have been obliged to clear the book for publication in precisely the same form as it now stands.[11] Thus, Snepp has not gained any profits as a result of his breach; the Government, rather than Snepp, will be unjustly enriched if he is required to disgorge profits attributable entirely to his own legitimate activity....

The Court ... seems to suggest that the injury [to the government] stems from the Agency's inability to catch "harmful" but unclassified information before it is pub-

---

11. ... [T]he Court does not disagree with the Fourth Circuit's view in *Marchetti*, reiterated in *Snepp*, that a CIA employee has a First Amendment right to publish unclassified information. Thus, despite ... some ambiguity in the Court's reference to "detrimental" and "harmful" as opposed to "classified" information, I do not understand the Court to imply that the Government could obtain an injunction against the publication of unclassified information.

lished. I do not believe, however, that the Agency has any authority to censor its employees' publication of unclassified information on the basis of its opinion that publication may be "detrimental to vital national interests" or otherwise "identified as harmful." The CIA never attempted to assert such power over Snepp in either of the contracts he signed; rather, the Agency itself limited its censorship power to preventing the disclosure of "classified" information. Moreover, even if such a wide-ranging prior restraint would be good national security policy, I would have great difficulty reconciling it with the demands of the First Amendment....

In any event, to the extent that the Government seeks to punish Snepp for the generalized harm he has caused by failing to submit to prepublication review and to deter others from following in his footsteps, punitive damages is, as the Court of Appeals held, clearly the preferable remedy "since a constructive trust depends on the concept of unjust enrichment rather than deterrence and punishment."...

---

1. The Court decided *Snepp* summarily, on the basis of the government's conditional cross-petition for certiorari, without briefs or oral argument. Why the rush? And what accounts for the different approaches in *Pentagon Papers* and *Snepp*—that is, what justifies the *Snepp* Court in making law to protect executive confidences when the *Pentagon Papers* Court would not do so? Is it Snepp's contractual relationship with the government or his role as a CIA employee? Is it the government's cause of action (*i.e.*, that the CIA was not seeking an injunction against publication)?

2. Do you agree with the dissent that the government's interest in these cases is limited to protecting classified information? How do you interpret the majority's rejoinder, in footnote 8? The classified information of greatest concern to intelligence agencies is specially inventoried as "Sensitive Compartmented Information," or SCI. Consider what the executive would need to prove to justify a prepublication injunction pursuant to its SCI Nondisclosure Agreement, which requires the employee to submit for review

> all materials, including works of fiction... which contain...:
>
> (a) any SCI, any description of activities that produce or relate to SCI, or any information derived from SCI;
>
> (b) any classified information from intelligence reports or estimates; or
>
> (c) any information concerning intelligence activities, sources, or methods.

3. At what point after submitting his book for preclearance and rejecting the agency's suggested excisions could an author in Snepp's position publish the book anyway? Is the CIA constitutionally required to publish rules indicating the rights of employees upon a disagreement over preclearance? Can the CIA place the burden of seeking judicial review on the employee?

4. *Snepp* has received quite negative reviews, which argue that the Court gave unduly short shrift to First Amendment values. *See, e.g.*, Medow, *The First Amendment and the Secrecy State*: Snepp v. United States, 130 U. Pa. L. Rev. 775 (1982); Quint, *The Separation of Powers Under Carter*, 62 Tex. L. Rev. 785, 839-47 (1984); Edgar & Schmidt (1986), *supra*. What do you think?

Note on Classification of Government Documents

No statute sets overall government policy concerning the classification of documents. Instead, each administration has the opportunity to form its own policy by executive order. Substantial variations in government secrecy can result. For example, President Carter issued Executive Order No. 12,065, 3 C.F.R. 190 (1979), superseding earlier orders. The Carter order provided that information that otherwise would be classifiable was to be declassified if "the need to protect such information [is] outweighed by the public interest in disclosure. . . . " The order also instructed employees that declassification was favored in doubtful cases.

The Reagan administration revoked the Carter order in favor of its own, which was substantially more stringent. Exec. Order No. 12,356, 3 C.F.R. 166 (1983). The Reagan order deleted the balancing test of the Carter order and delegated more authority to classifiers to protect information. For example, it revoked a Carter requirement that the potential danger posed by release be "identifiable" before information may be classified, and allowed classification of information posing no danger in itself, if "in the context of other information," it might damage national security. *See generally* House Comm. on Government Operations, Security Classification Policy and Executive Order 12,356, H.R. Rept. No. 731, 97th Cong., 2d Sess. (1982); Note, *Developments Under the Freedom of Information Act—1982*, 1983 Duke L.J. 390, 394-401.

Once a document has been classified, the Freedom of Information Act (FOIA), 5 U.S.C. § 552, exempts it from the mandatory disclosure to which most agency records are subject, under certain conditions. Exemption 1 of FOIA, § 552(b)(1), protects documents that are "(A) specifically authorized under criteria established by an Executive order to be kept secret in the interest of national defense or foreign policy and (B) are in fact properly classified pursuant to such Executive order." The courts are authorized to review documents *in camera* as part of a *de novo* review of the agency's decision to withhold; the burden of proof is on the agency to justify classification on both substantive and procedural grounds. Courts are also authorized to order the release of information contained in classified documents if it is both nonclassifiable and segregable from protected portions of the documents. *See Goldberg v. U.S. Dept. of State*, 818 F.2d 71 (D.C. Cir. 1987); Comment, *A Nation Less Secure: Diminished Public Access to Information*, 21 Harv. Civ. Rts.-Civ. Lib. L. Rev. 409 (1986).

Agencies may also be able to protect documents under the authority of their governing statutes. Exemption 3 of FOIA allows the withholding of materials that are "specifically exempted from disclosure by statute." (§ 552(b)(3)) In *CIA v. Sims*, 105 S. Ct. 1881 (1985), the Court held that the National Security Act of 1947, by authorizing the CIA Director to protect "intelligence sources and methods," was an exempting statute for FOIA purposes. In addition, the Central Intelligence Agency Information Act, 50 U.S.C. §§ 431-32, protects CIA "operational files," with some limitations. *See* Winchester & Zirkle, *Freedom of Information and the CIA Information Act*, 21 U. Rich. L. Rev. 231 (1987). (Congress has also enacted the Intelligence Identities Protection Act, 50 U.S.C. §§ 421-26, which attaches criminal sanctions to the unauthorized disclosure of the names of covert agents.)

Thus the United States protects its secrets through a mosaic of statutes and executive orders. In 1986, Edgar & Schmidt recalled their 1973 review of the statutes discussed in the *Pentagon Papers* opinions, and concluded, *supra* at 357, that

> even though it is common knowledge that the current statutes are hopelessly muddled, Congress has found it impossible to enact more coherent general

legislation protecting national defense information against revelation. The effort to clarify would have required firm answers to too many difficult questions.

Still, sometimes a muddle is better than the alternatives. Unlike the British, we do not have a simple, comprehensive Official Secrets Act, criminalizing unauthorized release and possession of government information. *See* Wallach, *Executive Powers of Prior Restraint over Publication of National Security Information: the UK and USA Compared*, 32 Int'l & Comp. L.Q. 424 (1983). Would such a statute be consistent with the First Amendment?

If you were advising the President on ways to respond to the persistent problem of leaks of government information, what would you suggest? As the following presidential order and accompanying materials demonstrate, the executive has sought to take advantage of the *Snepp* precedent.

National Security Decision Directive 84

Safeguarding National Security Information[1]

As stated in Executive Order 12356, only that information whose disclosure would harm the national security interests of the United States may be classified. Every effort should be made to declassify information that no longer requires protection in the interest of national security.

At the same time, however, safeguarding against unlawful disclosures of properly classified information is a matter of grave concern and high priority for this Administration. In addition to the requirements set forth in Executive Order 12356, ... I direct the following:

1. Each agency of the Executive Branch that originates or handles classified information shall adopt internal procedures to safeguard against unlawful disclosures of classified information. Such procedures shall at a minimum provide as follows:

a. All persons with authorized access to classified information shall be required to sign a nondisclosure agreement as a condition of access. ...

b. All persons with authorized access to Sensitive Compartmented Information (SCI) shall be required to sign a nondisclosure agreement as a condition of access. ... All such agreements must include a provision for prepublication review to assure deletion of SCI and other classified information.

c. All [these] agreements ... must be in a form determined by the Department of Justice to be enforceable in a civil action brought by the United States. The Director, Information Security Oversight Office (ISOO), shall develop standardized forms that satisfy these requirements.

d. Appropriate policies shall be adopted to govern contacts between media representatives and agency personnel, so as to reduce the opportunity for negligent or deliberate disclosures of classified information. All persons with authorized access to classified information shall be clearly apprised of the agency's policies in this regard.

2. Each agency of the Executive branch that originates or handles classified information shall adopt internal procedures to govern the reporting and investigation of

---

1. Reprinted in National Security Decision Directive 84, Hearing Before the Senate Comm. on Governmental Affairs, 98th Cong., 1st Sess. 85-86 (1983).

unauthorized disclosures of such information. Such procedures shall at a minimum provide that: . . .

b. The agency shall conduct a preliminary internal investigation. . . .

e. Persons determined by the agency to have knowingly made such disclosures or to have refused cooperation with investigations of such unauthorized disclosures will be denied further access to classified information and subjected to other administrative sanctions as appropriate.

3. Unauthorized disclosures of classified information shall be reported to the Department of Justice and the Information Security Oversight Office. . . . The Department of Justice shall . . . determine whether FBI investigation is warranted. . . . The FBI is authorized to investigate such matters as constitute potential violations of federal criminal law, even though administrative sanctions may be sought instead of criminal prosecution. . . .

5. The Office of Personnel Management and all departments and agencies with employees having access to classified information are directed to revise existing regulations and policies, as necessary, so that employees may be required to submit to polygraph examinations, when appropriate, in the course of investigations of unauthorized disclosures of classified information. As a minimum, such regulations shall permit an agency to decide that appropriate adverse consequences will follow an employee's refusal to cooperate with a polygraph examination that is limited in scope to the circumstances of the unauthorized disclosure under investigation. Agency regulations may provide that only the head of the agency, or his delegate, is empowered to order an employee to submit to a polygraph examination. Results of polygraph examinations should not be relied upon to the exclusion of other information obtained during investigations. . . .

––––––––––

Consider the constitutionality and the wisdom of NSDD-84 as you read the following excerpts from an oversight hearing concerning it. They include a common oversight device, a written question-and-answer colloquy between the branches. As you read it, consider whether, if you were on the committee's staff, you would find this device satisfactory. Are the executive's answers responsive and complete? Also consider how you would formulate answers for the executive. How much would you want to say? To what extent would your answers bind your discretion later?

National Security Decision Directive 84
Hearing Before the Senate Comm. on Governmental Affairs, 98th Cong., 1st Session 23-30 (1983)
Prepared Statement of Richard K. Willard

. . . This directive . . . was based on the recommendations of an interdepartmental group convened by the Attorney General. I served as chairman of this group, which also included representatives designated by the Secretaries of State, the Treasury, Defense, Energy and the Director of Central Intelligence. Copies of the report of this group, which is unclassified, have been furnished to the Committee.

The protection of national security information is a fundamental constitutional responsibility of the President. This responsibility is derived from the President's powers as Chief Executive, Commander-in-Chief, and the principal instrument of

United States foreign policy. Since the days of the Founding Fathers, we have recognized the need to protect military and diplomatic secrets.

Since at least 1940, Presidents have provided for the protection of national security information by promulgating Executive orders providing for a system of classification. President Reagan's Executive Order limits the use of classification to information which "reasonably could be expected to cause damage to the national security" if released without proper authorization. This Executive Order also prohibits the use of classification to conceal violations of law, inefficiency or administrative error, or to prevent embarrassment to a government agency or employee.

The unauthorized disclosure of classified information has been specifically prohibited by each of the Executive Orders on this subject. Such disclosures also violate numerous more general standards of conduct for government employees based on statutes and regulations. Moreover, in virtually all cases the unauthorized disclosure of classified information potentially violates one or more federal criminal statutes.

Notwithstanding the clear illegality of this practice, unauthorized disclosures of classified information appear in the media with startling frequency. Such disclosures damage national security by providing valuable information to our adversaries, by hampering the ability of our intelligence agencies to function effectively, and by impairing the conduct of American foreign policy. . . .

A significant aspect of implementing NSDD-84 has been the development of two new nondisclosure agreement forms for government-wide use. These forms have been reviewed by the Department of Justice, which has determined that they would be enforceable in civil litigation initiated by the United States. . . .

Prepublication review agreements have been used at CIA for a number of years, and in 1980 the Supreme Court approved their use in *Snepp v. United States*. The sole purpose of prepublication review is to permit deletion of classified information before it is made public. This program does not permit the government to censor material because it is embarrassing or critical. . . .

Responses of Mr. Willard to Written Questions
Submitted by Senator Mathias

Question 1. What are the disclosures to which the pre-clearance requirement extends? . . . [D]oesn't it . . . extend beyond published writings? For example, does the pre-clearance requirement of . . . the SCI agreement extend to reports or correspondence that a former employee might prepare in the course of his business? Does it cover lecture notes of a former official who enters the academic world?

Answer. The agreement not to disclose classified information extends to any method by which such information can be communicated, including oral disclosures. The prepublication review obligation extends only to "materials" that contain or purport to contain certain kinds of information. This could include reports, correspondence or lecture notes. Implementing regulations recognize that oral statements cannot be subject to prepublication review in the same manner as writings.

Question 2. Admiral Gayler testified that . . . long-term protection is justified only in very special cases having to do with intelligence methods. You yourself pointed out that while intelligence does become stale, intelligence sources and methods do not. Given the substantial agreement on this point, shouldn't a . . . short-term prepublication review requirement be ample for the other categories of information?

Answer. Although information concerning intelligence sources and methods (including SCI) is likely to have long-term sensitivity, the same may also be true of certain information from intelligence reports or concerning intelligence activities. Of course, once particular information no longer requires protection in the interest of national security, then it must be declassified and cannot be deleted from materials submitted for prepublication review. . . .

Question 4. The report of the interdepartment group . . . recommended the enactment of a general criminal statute prohibiting the unauthorized disclosure of classified information. Some observers, including former CIA Director William Colby, feel that criminal sanctions would be the most effective way to punish unauthorized disclosures, and would be more workable than prepublication review and other measures contained in the directive. . . . Has the interdepartmental group's recommendation been accepted by the administration?

Answer. Nearly all unauthorized disclosures of classified information potentially violate one or more existing criminal statutes. . . . [I]t is unlikely that criminal prosecution would ever by itself be a satisfactory response to most unauthorized disclosures. We believe that a realistic prospect of administrative sanctions can effectively deter most unauthorized disclosures. Of course, criminal prosecution can and will be considered where circumstances warrant.

Question 5. Some portions of the SCI Agreement appear to sweep very broadly. In particular, a former official is required to pre-clear any materials that contain "any information about intelligence activities, sources or methods"—whether or not the information is classified. This broad language appears to include information about intelligence activities of all nations and all times. The "escape clause" . . . of the SCI Agreement does not completely solve this problem, since it excludes . . . only information obtained by an official when he is out of office. Thus it would not protect an official who learned about intelligence activities during the War of 1812 through his leisure reading while in office, and wanted to write about that subject after leaving office. Might the Agreement be interpreted to cover such a situation, and if so, shouldn't it be more narrowly tailored to avoid sweeping in such obviously harmless material?

Answer. The term "intelligence sources and methods" is found in the National Security Act, 50 U.S.C. § 403(d)(3). The term "intelligence activities" is defined in Executive Order 12333, § 3.4(e). Together, these terms comprise a category of information that must be considered for classification under Executive Order 12356, § 1.3(a)(4). We believe the terms are sufficiently precise as to be understood by persons who sign the SCI Nondisclosure Agreement, although it would certainly be appropriate for agencies to provide further explanations in their implementing regulations. . . .

We will interpret the protection of the "escape clause" as extending to published information that is generally available to the public, even if the employee may have consulted the publication during the time he was employed. Thus in your hypothetical question, the employee would not be required to submit his manuscript for review. . . .

However, it is important to recognize that former employees cannot speak or write in a manner that expressly or impliedly confirms the accuracy of classified information that may have entered the public domain as the consequence of an unauthorized disclosure. Any such confirmation of the accuracy of published information thus [is] a separate disclosure, which is subject to prepublication review if it otherwise falls within the terms of the agreement.

Finally, the Attorney General's decision to authorize the filing of litigation to enforce the prepublication review requirement for a manuscript that did not actually contain classified information would depend on all the facts and circumstances of the particular situation.

Question 6. At the hearing, you indicated that an objective standard would be used to determine whether an individual had complied with his obligations to submit materials for prepublication review. However, you went on to say that the usual objective standard—objectively reasonable belief—would not apply. Instead, the standard would effectively be one of absolute liability, since an honest and reasonable mistake would not provide a defense. Given this absolute liability standard, won't the only safe course be to submit every manuscript that would conceivably be thought to be covered by the agreement?

Answer. The SCI nondisclosure agreement, like most contracts, is enforceable according to its terms. Employees who are uncertain whether material must be submitted are encouraged to consult with designated officials who are authorized to express the view of the government on the interpretation and application of the agreement....

Question 9. With regard to the reference in ... the SCI nondisclosure agreement to "any other Executive Order or statute that prohibits the unauthorized disclosure of information in the interest of national security," is this an attempt to incorporate by reference future executive orders and statutes (e.g., any successor to E.O. 12356), or is it intended to refer to executive orders and statutes currently in existence? ...

Answer. This reference ... is intended to refer to future executive orders and statutes as well as those currently existing....

Question 10. ... Is the government asserting a property interest in [classified] information, or in the documents or other formats in which it is embodied? If the former, what is the legal basis for this assertion? Is there any inconsistency with 17 U.S.C. 105, prohibiting a copyright in government works? If the former, what about government information which enters the public domain? Does it "remain the property of the U.S. Government"? To what extent, if any, does this assertion affect the rights of persons not signatory to the SCI nondisclosure agreement?

Answer. We believe that the government has a property interest in classified information itself, which is not limited to ownership of the tangible medium in which the information is embodied. This property interest is a consequence of statutes and Executive orders that establish a government monopoly in the creation and use of classified information.... [W]e are prepared to argue in an appropriate case that its property interest in classified information is entitled to common law protection. The United States would lose any property interest in classified information when it is declassified pursuant to Executive Order 12356. The ability of the government to bring a prosecution under 18 U.S.C. § 641 for theft of government property is not determined by the provisions of a nondisclosure agreement and, in any event, has not been definitively decided by the courts....

Question 16. ... Under what circumstances would the Justice Department seek a prior restraint of a publication assertedly subject to the prepublication review [or] ... non-disclosure agreement? In the Justice Department's view, what standard should a court apply in ruling upon an application for a prior restraint ... ?

Answer.... The Department of Justice would seek to enjoin a publication in violation of the nondisclosure agreements only with the approval of the Attorney General, based upon a determination that the facts and circumstances of the case warranted this remedy. The courts have approved the issuance of injunctions to compel individuals to comply with secrecy agreements, including provisions for prepublication review. *United States v. Marchetti*; *Agee v. CIA*, 500 F.Supp. 506 (D.D.C. 1980). There is, however, an unresolved question as to the legal standard that should be applied....

Question 19. What would be the standard of judicial review in a lawsuit in which an author challenged the censorship of his manuscript by his former agency?

Answer. We believe the standard of review would as a practical matter be the same as under the Freedom of Information Act. See *Alfred A. Knopf, Inc. v. Colby*, 509 F.2d 1362, 1367-70 (4th Cir. 1974), cert. denied, 421 U.S. 892 (1975)....

Responses of Mr. Willard to Written Questions
Submitted by Senator Levin

... *Question 2.* [T]he Sensitive Compartmented Information (SCI) nondisclosure agreement requires that a person with SCI or classified information access submit for pre-disclosure/publication review any material, including "works of fiction", containing "information concerning intelligence activities, sources or methods", which such person contemplates disclosing to the public or persons "not authorized to have such information". [T]he agreement [also] requires that an individual forfeit any proceeds resulting from the unauthorized "disclosure, publication or revelation of information inconsistent with the terms of the agreement." Would you please tell the Committee whether an author would be required to forfeit the proceeds from his or her work if the author did not submit the work for prepublication review, and subsequently a court determined that the work contains a description of "intelligence activities, sources or methods", but does not contain any SCI or classified information?

Answer. Failure to submit material for prepublication review as provided in paragraphs 5-7 would subject the employee to forfeiture as provided in paragraph 9, regardless of whether the material actually contained SCI or classified information. See *Snepp v. United States*, 444 U.S. 507, 511-513 (1980).

---

1. Is NSDD-84 constitutional on its face? Would it be constitutional as applied if it were administered in accordance with Assistant Attorney General Willard's interpretation? Would either the President or Willard have been wise to adopt a narrower strategy?

2. For (unfavorable) analysis of NSDD-84, *see* Cheh, *Judicial Supervision of Executive Secrecy: Rethinking Freedom of Expression for Government Employees and the Public Right of Access to Government Information*, 69 Corn. L. Rev. 690 (1984); Powe, *The Constitutional Implications of President Reagan's Censorship* Directive 84, 17 The Center Magazine 2 (1984).

3. The polygraph requirements of NSDD-84 raise issues under the Fourth Amendment. *See* Note, *Reagan's Polygraph Order and the Fourth Amendment: Subjecting Federal Employees to Warrantless Searches*, 69 Corn. L. Rev. 896 (1984). Considering the notorious unreliability of polygraphs, would you have included provision for them in the order?

4. NSDD-84 received a hostile reaction in Congress, which legislated to delay implementation of both the prepublication clearance and polygraph provisions of the order. The administration subsequently suspended the order, with a view to its possible later reinstatement. The story is told in Comment, *The Constitutionality of Expanding Prepublication Review of Government Employees' Speech*, 72 Calif. L. Rev. 962, 973-74 (1984). Could you redraft NSDD-84 to make it more palatable to Congress, while still meeting security needs?

5. Subsequently, the administration promulgated Standard Form 189, which all government employees and contractors with access to classified information must sign, on pain of losing their security classifications—and their jobs. The form's signatories are bound never to divulge in a "direct or indirect" fashion "classified or classifiable" data. "Classifiable" information is that which "as a result of negligence, time constraints, error, or lack of opportunity or oversight has not been marked as classified information," and disclosures violate SF 189 if the person "knew or reasonably should have known" that material was classifiable. 52 Fed. Reg. 28802 (1987). Any information to which signatories gain access is to remain government property "forever." Is SF 189 legally valid? How does your analysis differ from that concerning NSDD-84?

2. Resisting disclosure in court

Throughout our history, the executive branch has resisted disclosure of certain information to private parties or to other branches of government, based on a series of justifications typically grouped under the label "executive privilege." Executive privilege is not, however, a clear or unitary concept. It has encompassed claims of varying kinds, some of them having statutory support.

Among the most important variables in assessing a claim of privilege are the nature of the information sought, the level of government at which the information was developed, the government's asserted interest in nondisclosure, the availability of the information from other sources, and the impact of nondisclosure on private rights.

The three varieties of privilege most commonly asserted are for state secrets, for information the disclosure of which would jeopardize law enforcement activities (*e.g.*, names of informers), and for intra-branch deliberative communications. In *United States v. Nixon*, which follows, the President claimed a privilege to protect the confidentiality of all his personal communications. This, of course, is potentially a much broader privilege than one based on state secrets or the protection of particular executive branch functions.

Unavoidably present in these cases is the question: who decides the scope of the asserted privilege? Whether information should be disclosed could be regarded as a question committed to the discretion of the executive, and unreviewable in court under the "political question" doctrine. Not surprisingly, President Nixon raised this issue when his claim of privilege reached the Supreme Court. In 1974, the Court had yet to decide whether the Constitution affords the President an executive privilege, what its scope might be, and who decides its coverage. As you read *Nixon*, consider how persuasively and completely the Court handled these issues.

United States v. Nixon
418 U.S. 684 (1974)

Chief Justice BURGER delivered the opinion of the Court.

... On March 1, 1974, a grand jury of the United States District Court for the District of Columbia returned an indictment charging seven named individuals[3] with various offenses, including conspiracy to defraud the United States and to obstruct justice. Although he was not designated as such in the indictment, the grand jury named the President, among others, as an unindicted coconspirator. On April 18, 1974, upon motion of the Special Prosecutor, a subpoena duces tecum was issued pursuant to Rule 17(c) to the President.... This subpoena required the production, ... of certain tapes, memoranda, papers, transcripts or other writings relating to certain precisely identified meetings between the President and others. The Special Prosecutor was able to fix the time, place, and persons present at these discussions because the White House daily logs and appointment records had been delivered to him. On April 30, the President publicly released edited transcripts of 43 conversations; portions of 20 conversations subject to subpoena in the present case were included. On May 1, 1974, the President's counsel filed a "special appearance" and a motion to quash the subpoena under Rule 17(c). This motion was accompanied by a formal claim of privilege....

On May 20, 1974, the District Court denied the motion to quash.... 377 F.Supp. 1326. It further ordered "the President or any subordinate officer, official, or employee with custody or control of the documents or objects subpoenaed," to deliver to the District Court ... the originals of all subpoenaed items, as well as an index and analysis of those items, together with tape copies of those portions of the subpoenaed recordings for which transcripts had been released to the public by the President on April 30....

I

JURISDICTION

The threshold question presented is whether the May 20, 1974, order of the District Court was an appealable order.... [The Court had granted certiorari immediately following appeal of the order to the Court of Appeals.] The Court of Appeals' jurisdiction under 28 U.S.C. § 1291 encompasses only "final decisions of the district courts."... The finality requirement of 28 U.S.C. § 1291 embodies a strong congressional policy against piecemeal reviews, and against obstructing or impeding an ongoing judicial proceeding by interlocutory appeals....

Here ... the traditional contempt avenue to immediate appeal is peculiarly inappropriate due to the unique setting in which the question arises. To require a President of the United States to place himself in the posture of disobeying an order of a court merely to trigger the procedural mechanism for review of the ruling would be un-

---

3. The seven defendants were John N. Mitchell, H. R. Haldeman, John D. Ehrlichman, Charles W. Colson, Robert C. Mardian, Kenneth W. Parkinson, and Gordon Strachan. Each had occupied either a position of responsibility on the White House staff or the Committee for the Re-election of the President.

seemly, and would present an unnecessary occasion for constitutional confrontation between two branches of the Government. Similarly, a federal judge should not be placed in the posture of issuing a citation to a President simply in order to invoke review. The issue whether a President can be cited for contempt could itself engender protracted litigation. ... These considerations lead us to conclude that the order of the District Court was an appealable order. ...

II

JUSTICIABILITY

[T]he President's counsel argue[s] that the Court lacked jurisdiction to issue the subpoena because the matter was an intra-branch dispute between a subordinate and superior officer of the Executive Branch and hence not subject to judicial resolution [and] that the dispute does not present a "case" or "controversy" which can be adjudicated in the federal courts. ... Since the Executive Branch has exclusive authority and absolute discretion to decide whether to prosecute a case, it is contended that a President's decision is final in determining what evidence is to be used in a given criminal case. Although his counsel concedes that the President has delegated certain specific powers to the Special Prosecutor, he has not "waived nor delegated to the Special Prosecutor the President's duty to claim privilege as to all materials ... which fall within the President's inherent authority to refuse to disclose to any executive officer." The Special Prosecutor's demand for the items therefore presents, in the view of the President's counsel, a political question under *Baker v. Carr*, 369 U.S. 186 (1962), since it involves a "textually demonstrable" grant of power under Art. II.

The mere assertion of a claim of an "intra-branch dispute," without more, has never operated to defeat federal jurisdiction; justiciability does not depend on such a surface inquiry. In *United States v. ICC*, 337 U.S. 426 (1949), the Court observed, "courts must look behind names that symbolize the parties to determine whether a justiciable case or controversy is presented." Our starting point is the nature of the proceeding for which the evidence is sought—here a pending criminal prosecution. ... Under the authority of Art. II, § 2, Congress has vested in the Attorney General the power to conduct the criminal litigation of the United States Government. 28 U.S.C. § 516. It has also vested in him the power to appoint subordinate officers to assist him in the discharge of his duties. 28 U.S.C. §§ 509, 510, 515, 533. Acting pursuant to those statutes, the Attorney General has delegated the authority to represent the United States in these particular matters to a Special Prosecutor with unique authority and tenure.[8] The regulation gives the Special Prosecutor explicit power to

---

8. The regulation issued by the Attorney General pursuant to his statutory authority, vests in the Special Prosecutor plenary authority to control the course of investigations and litigation related to "all offenses arising out of the 1972 Presidential Election for which the Special Prosecutor deems it necessary and appropriate to assume responsibility, allegations involving the President, members of the White House staff, or Presidential appointees, and any other matters which he consents to have assigned to him by the Attorney General." 38 Fed. Reg. 30739, as amended by 38 Fed. Reg. 32805. In particular, the Special Prosecutor was given full authority, *inter alia*, "to contest the assertion of 'Executive Privilege' ... and handl[e] all aspects of any cases within his jurisdiction." The regulation then goes on to provide:

"In exercising this authority, the Special Prosecutor will have the greatest degree of independence that is consistent with the Attorney General's statutory accountability for all matters falling within the jurisdiction of the Department of Justice. The Attorney General will not countermand or interfere with the Special Prosecutor's decisions or actions. ... In accordance

contest the invocation of executive privilege in the process of seeking evidence deemed relevant to the performance of these specially delegated duties.

So long as this regulation is extant it has the force of law. In *United States ex rel. Accardi v. Shaughnessy*, 347 U.S. 260 (1954), regulations of the Attorney General delegated certain of his discretionary powers to the Board of Immigration Appeals and required that Board to exercise its own discretion on appeals in deportation cases. The Court held that so long as the Attorney General's regulations remained operative, he denied himself the authority to exercise the discretion delegated to the Board even though the original authority was his and he could reassert it by amending the regulations. *Service v. Dulles*, 354 U.S. 363, 388 (1957), and *Vitarelli v. Seaton*, 359 U.S. 535 (1959), reaffirmed the basic holding of *Accardi*.

Here, as in *Accardi*, it is theoretically possible for the Attorney General to amend or revoke the regulation defining the Special Prosecutor's authority. But he has not done so. So long as this regulation remains in force the Executive Branch is bound by it, and indeed the United States as the sovereign composed of the three branches is bound to respect and to enforce it. Moreover, the delegation of authority to the Special Prosecutor in this case is not an ordinary delegation by the Attorney General to a subordinate officer: with the authorization of the President, the Acting Attorney General provided in the regulation that the Special Prosecutor was not to be removed without the "consensus" of eight designated leaders of Congress.

The demands of and the resistance to the subpoena present an obvious controversy in the ordinary sense, but that alone is not sufficient to meet constitutional standards. In the constitutional sense, controversy means more than disagreement and conflict; rather it means the kind of controversy courts traditionally resolve. Here at issue is the production or nonproduction of specified evidence deemed by the Special Prosecutor to be relevant and admissible in a pending criminal case. It is sought by one official of the Executive Branch within the scope of his express authority; it is resisted by the Chief Executive on the ground of his duty to preserve the confidentiality of the communications of the President. . . . The independent Special Prosecutor with his asserted need for the subpoenaed material in the underlying criminal prosecution is opposed by the President with his steadfast assertion of privilege against disclosure of the material. This setting assures there is "that concrete adverseness which sharpens the presentation of issues upon which the court so largely depends for illumination of difficult constitutional questions". *Baker v. Carr*, 369 U.S. at 204. Moreover, since the matter is one arising in the regular course of a federal criminal prosecution, it is within the traditional scope of Art. III power.

IV
THE CLAIM OF PRIVILEGE

A

[W]e turn to the claim that the subpoena should be quashed because it demands "confidential conversations between a President and his close advisors that it would

---

with assurances given by the President to the Attorney General that the President will not exercise his Constitutional powers to effect the discharge of the Special Prosecutor or to limit the independence that he is hereby given, the Special Prosecutor will not be removed from his duties except for extraordinary improprieties on his part and without the President's first consulting the Majority and the Minority Leaders and Chairmen and ranking Minority Members of the Judiciary Committees of the Senate and House of Representatives and ascertaining that their consensus is in accord with his proposed action."

be inconsistent with the public interest to produce." The first contention is a broad claim that the separation of powers doctrine precludes judicial review of a President's claim of privilege. The second contention is that if he does not prevail on the claim of absolute privilege, the court should hold as a matter of constitutional law that the privilege prevails over the subpoena duces tecum.

In the performance of assigned constitutional duties each branch of the Government must initially interpret the Constitution, and the interpretation of its powers by any branch is due great respect from the others. The President's counsel . . . reads the Constitution as providing an absolute privilege of confidentiality for all Presidential communications. Many decisions of this Court, however, have unequivocally reaffirmed the holding of *Marbury v. Madison*, 1 Cranch 137 (1803), that "[i]t is emphatically the province and duty of the judicial department to say what the law is."

[O]ther exercises of power by the Executive Branch and the Legislative Branch have been found invalid as in conflict with the Constitution. In a series of cases, the Court interpreted the explicit immunity conferred by express provisions of the Constitution on Members of the House and Senate by the Speech or Debate Clause, U.S. Const. Art. I, § 6. . . . And in *Baker v. Carr*, 369 U.S. at 211, the Court stated:

> "[D]eciding whether a matter has in any measure been committed by the Constitution to another branch of government, or whether the action of that branch exceeds whatever authority has been committed, is itself a delicate exercise in constitutional interpretation, and is a responsibility of this Court as ultimate interpreter of the Constitution."

Notwithstanding the deference each branch must accord the others, the "judicial Power of the United States" vested in the federal courts by Art. III, § 1, of the Constitution can no more be shared with the Executive Branch than the Chief Executive, for example, can share with the Judiciary the veto power. . . . Any other conclusion would be contrary to the basic concept of separation of powers and the checks and balances that flow from the scheme of a tripartite government. The Federalist No. 47. We therefore reaffirm that it is the province and duty of this Court "to say what the law is" with respect to the claim of privilege presented in this case.

B

In support of his claim of absolute privilege, the President's counsel urges two grounds, one of which is common to all governments and one of which is peculiar to our system of separation of powers. The first ground is the valid need for protection of communications between high Government officials and those who advise and assist them in the performance of their manifold duties; the importance of this confidentiality is too plain to require further discussion. Human experience teaches that those who expect public dissemination of their remarks may well temper candor with a concern for appearances and for their own interests to the detriment of the decisionmaking process.[15] Whatever the nature of the privilege of confidentiality of Presidential communications in the exercise of Art. II powers, the privilege can be said

---

15. There is nothing novel about governmental confidentiality. The meetings of the Constitutional Convention in 1787 were conducted in complete privacy [and] all records of those meetings were sealed for more than 30 years. . . . Most of the Framers acknowledged that without secrecy no constitution of the kind that was developed could have been written. C. Warren, The Making of the Constitution 134-139 (1937).

to derive from the supremacy of each branch within its own assigned area of constitutional duties. Certain powers and privileges flow from the nature of enumerated powers;[16] the protection of the confidentiality of Presidential communications has similar constitutional underpinnings.

The second ground asserted by the President's counsel in support of the claim of absolute privilege rests on the doctrine of separation of powers. Here it is argued that the independence of the Executive Branch within its own sphere insulates a President from a judicial subpoena in an ongoing criminal prosecution, and thereby protects confidential Presidential communications.

However, neither the doctrine of separation of powers, nor the need for confidentiality of high-level communications, without more, can sustain an absolute, unqualified Presidential privilege of immunity from judicial process under all circumstances. The President's need for complete candor and objectivity from advisers calls for great deference from the courts. However, when the privilege depends solely on the broad, undifferentiated claim of public interest in the confidentiality of such conversations, a confrontation with other values arises. Absent a claim of need to protect military, diplomatic, or sensitive national security secrets, we find it difficult to accept the argument that even the very important interest in confidentiality of Presidential communications is significantly diminished by production of such material for in camera inspection with all the protection that a district court will be obliged to provide.

The impediment that an absolute, unqualified privilege would place in the way of the primary constitutional duty of the Judicial Branch to do justice in criminal prosecutions would plainly conflict with the function of the courts under Art. III. In designing the structure of our Government and dividing and allocating the sovereign power among three co-equal branches, the Framers of the Constitution sought to provide a comprehensive system, but the separate powers were not intended to operate with absolute independence. . . . To read the Art. II powers of the President as providing an absolute privilege as against a subpoena essential to enforcement of criminal statutes on no more than a generalized claim of the public interest in confidentiality of nonmilitary and nondiplomatic discussions would upset the constitutional balance of "a workable government" and gravely impair the role of the courts under Art. III.

C

Since we conclude that the legitimate needs of the judicial process may outweigh Presidential privilege, it is necessary to resolve those competing interests in a manner that preserves the essential functions of each branch. . . .

The expectation of a President to the confidentiality of his conversations and correspondence, like the claim of confidentiality of judicial deliberations, for example, has all the values to which we accord deference for the privacy of all citizens and, added to those values, is the necessity for protection of the public interest in candid, objective, and even blunt or harsh opinions in Presidential decisionmaking. A President and those who assist him must be free to explore alternatives in the process of shaping

---

16. The Special Prosecutor argues that there is no provision in the Constitution for a Presidential privilege . . . corresponding to the . . . Speech or Debate Clause. But the silence of the Constitution on this score is not dispositive. . . . *McCulloch v. Maryland*, 4 Wheat 316, [held] that that which was reasonably appropriate and relevant to the exercise of a granted power was to be considered as accompanying the grant. . . .

policies and making decisions and to do so in a way many would be unwilling to express except privately. These are the considerations justifying a presumptive privilege for Presidential communications. The privilege is fundamental to the operation of Government and inextricably rooted in the separation of powers under the Constitution. In *Nixon v. Sirica*, 487 F.2d 700 (1973), the Court of Appeals held that such Presidential communications are "presumptively privileged," and this position is accepted by both parties in the present litigation. We agree with Chief Justice Marshall's observation, therefore, that "[i]n no case of this kind would a court be required to proceed against the president as against an ordinary individual." *United States v. Burr*, 25 F.Cas., at 192.

But this presumptive privilege must be considered in light of our historic commitment to the rule of law.... To ensure that justice is done, it is imperative to the function of courts that compulsory process be available for the production of evidence needed either by the prosecution or by the defense.... The privileges ... are designed to protect weighty and legitimate competing interests. Thus, the Fifth Amendment to the Constitution provides that no man "shall be compelled in any criminal case to be a witness against himself." And, generally, an attorney or a priest may not be required to disclose what has been revealed in professional confidence. These and other interests are recognized in law by privileges against forced disclosure, established in the Constitution, by statute, or at common law. Whatever their origins, these exceptions to the demand for every man's evidence are not lightly created nor expansively construed, for they are in derogation of the search for truth.

In this case the President challenges a subpoena served on him as a third party requiring the production of materials for use in a criminal prosecution; he does so on the claim that he has a privilege against diclosure of confidential communications. He does not place his claim of privilege on the ground they are military or diplomatic secrets. As to these areas of Art. II duties the courts have traditionally shown the utmost deference to Presidential responsibilities.... In *United States v. Reynolds*, 345 U.S. 1 (1953), dealing with a claimant's demand for evidence in a Tort Claims Act case against the Government, the Court said:

> "It may be possible to satisfy the court, from all the circumstances of the case, that there is a reasonable danger that compulsion of the evidence will expose military matters which, in the interest of national security, should not be divulged. When this is the case, the occasion for the privilege is appropriate, and the court should not jeopardize the security which the privilege is meant to protect by insisting upon an examination of the evidence, even by the judge alone, in chambers."

No case of the Court, however, has extended this high degree of deference to a President's generalized interest in confidentiality. Nowhere in the Constitution ... is there any explicit reference to a privilege of confidentiality, yet to the extent this interest relates to the effective discharge of a President's powers, it is constitutionally based.

The right to the production of all evidence at a criminal trial similarly has constitutional dimensions. The Sixth Amendment explicitly confers upon every defendant in a criminal trial the right "to be confronted with the witnesses against him" and "to have compulsory process for obtaining witnesses in his favor." Moreover, the Fifth Amendment also guarantees that no person shall be deprived of liberty without due process of law. It is the manifest duty of the courts to vindicate those guarantees, and to accomplish that it is essential that all relevant and admissible evidence be produced.

In this case we must weigh the importance of the general privilege of confidentiality of Presidential communications in performance of the President's responsibilities against the inroads of such a privilege on the fair administration of criminal justice.[19] The interest in preserving confidentiality is weighty indeed and entitled to great respect. However, we cannot conclude that advisers will be moved to temper the candor of their remarks by the infrequent occasions of disclosure because of the possibility that such conversations will be called for in the context of a criminal prosecution.

On the other hand, the allowance of the privilege to withhold evidence that is demonstrably relevant in a criminal trial would cut deeply into the guarantee of due process of law and gravely impair the basic function of the courts. . . . The President's broad interest in confidentiality of communications will not be vitiated by disclosure of a limited number of conversations preliminarily shown to have some bearing on the pending criminal cases.

We conclude that when the ground for asserting privilege as to subpoenaed materials sought for use in a criminal trial is based only on the generalized interest in confidentiality, it cannot prevail over the fundamental demands of due process of law in the fair administration of criminal justice. The generalized assertion of privilege must yield to the demonstrated, specific need for evidence in a pending criminal trial.

D

. . . If a President concludes that compliance with a subpoena would be injurious to the public interest he may properly, as was done here, invoke a claim of privilege on the return of the subpoena. Upon receiving a claim of privilege from the Chief Executive, it became the further duty of the District Court to treat the subpoenaed material as presumptively privileged and to require the Special Prosecutor to demonstrate that the Presidential material was "essential to the justice of the [pending criminal] case." *United States v. Burr*, 25 Fed.Cas., at 192. Here the District Court treated the material as presumptively privileged, proceeded to find that the Special Prosecutor had made a sufficient showing to rebut the presumption, and ordered an *in camera* examination of the subpoenaed material. On the basis of our examination of the record we are unable to conclude that the District Court erred in ordering the inspection. Accordingly we affirm the order of the District Court that subpoenaed materials be transmitted to that court. We now turn to the important question of the District Court's responsibilities in conducting the *in camera* examination of Presidential materials. . . .

E

Statements that meet the test of admissibility and relevance must be isolated; all other material must be excised. . . . It is elementary that *in camera* inspection of evi-

---

19. We are not here concerned with the balance between the President's generalized interest in confidentiality and the need for relevant evidence in civil litigation, nor with that between the confidentiality interest and congressional demands for information, nor with the President's interest in preserving state secrets. We address only the conflict between the President's assertion of a generalized privilege of confidentiality and the constitutional need for relevant evidence in criminal trials.

dence is always a procedure calling for scrupulous protection against any release or publication of material not found by the court, at that stage, probably admissible in evidence and relevant to the issues of the trial for which it is sought.…

Moreover, a President's communications and activities encompass a vastly wider range of sensitive material than would be true of any "ordinary individual." It is therefore necessary… to afford Presidential confidentiality the greatest protection consistent with the fair administration of justice. The need for confidentiality even as to idle conversations with associates in which casual reference might be made concerning political leaders within the country or foreign statesmen is too obvious to call for further treatment.… [O]nce the decision is made to excise, the material is restored to its privileged status and should be returned under seal to its lawful custodian.…

Affirmed.

Justice REHNQUIST took no part in… these cases.

————

1. As Professor Freund put it, in *Foreword: On Presidential Privilege, The Supreme Court, 1973 Term*, 88 Harv. L. Rev. 13 (1974), the *Nixon* case came to the Court "trailing clouds of jurisdictional and procedural issues." Should the Court have invoked one of them to avoid the merits?

(a) Review the materials in Chapter Two on the amenability of the President to judicial process, where we note that, although *Nixon* includes no direct analysis of the issue, related litigation probed it extensively. Obviously, the Court held that the President must comply with a subpoena in at least some circumstances. Does the Court state or imply limits to his amenability to process? What about congressional subpoenas (*see* the Court's note 19), or those of civil litigants, or those of state courts? Could the President be ordered to give a deposition, or be subjected to criminal prosecution? How might the requisite preliminary showing of need vary in these instances?

(b) Do you agree with the Court that this was not just a nonjusticiable family quarrel within the executive? The Court's note 8 quotes the regulation creating the office of Special Prosecutor, which reveals the extraordinary promise of independence that the President had made. The Court then relies on the general doctrine that agencies must obey their own regulations. See Note, *Violations by Agencies of Their Own Regulations*, 87 Harv. L. Rev. 629 (1974). It is unclear that this doctrine is of constitutional dimension, however (*see* G. Robinson, E. Gellhorn & H. Bruff, The Administrative Process 200-02 (3d ed. 1986)). Is it then a sufficient response? If the President could rescind the regulation and fire the Prosecutor anytime, is there an Article III "case or controversy" here? And is the President competent to bargain away his constitutional power to remove his subordinates? (We will return to these questions in Chapters Four and Five when we consider powers of removal and statutory special prosecutors. You may wish to refer now to *Nader v. Bork* in Chapter Five, holding that President Nixon's earlier dismissal of Special Prosecutor Cox was illegal.)

Professor Van Alstyne, in *A Political and Constitutional Review of* United States v. Nixon, 22 U.C.L.A. L. Rev. 116 (1974), suggests that the Court's analysis threatens an unjustifiable fragmentation of executive power. Given that successful prosecution and the confidentiality of presidential communications can both be viewed as "executive" interests, can a court justifiably permit a subordinate official to override the President's determination as to the relative weight of those interests in a particular instance? Would your answer be different if the President were not an unindicted co-conspirator in the case?

(c) To the President's argument that the executive should decide claims of privilege, the Court responds with a cite to *Marbury*'s assertion that it is the province of the courts to say what the law is. Is that a sufficient answer? *See* Gunther, *Judicial Hegemony and Legislative Autonomy: The* Nixon *Case and the Impeachment Process*, 22 U.C.L.A. 30, 34 (1974): "[T]here is nothing in *Marbury* . . . that precludes a constitutional interpretation that gives final authority to another branch." What would be the consequences for our government if the Court had held that the executive has sole power to resolve executive privilege claims? For a probing critique of the Court's handling of the "who decides?" issue in *Nixon, see* Van Alstyne, *supra*.

2. Turning to the merits of the sufficiency of the President's claim of privilege, what is the holding of *Nixon*? If a presidential communication is relevant and admissible in a criminal trial, should the generalized interest in confidentiality alone ever override the interest in disclosure? If not, does this case involve *ad hoc* balancing, or a categorical judgment of comparative institutional needs?

Is the Court's balancing persuasive in *Nixon*? Why is there a threat to due process if the trial court could dismiss the prosecution for unfairness? Note that the defendants are not seeking the evidence, and that privileges *per se* (attorney-client; husband-wife) are allowed in criminal trials.

3. What is the constitutional basis for the Court's theory of executive privilege? See note 16: is *McCulloch* correctly cited? Doesn't it stand for the proposition that, under the "necessary and proper" clause, *Congress* can exercise powers "reasonably appropriate and relevant" to its granted powers? What has that to do with implied presidential powers? Is the Court's ground for privilege one of necessity for the functioning of the Presidency? Of reasonableness? Can Congress promulgate statutory procedures for the exercise of executive privilege?

4. We have remarked above that the Court's great cases must be read in historical context. To what extent is the Court's approach in *Nixon* a product of the extraordinary historical circumstances of a case whose outcome produced the resignation of a President? *See* Mishkin, *Great Cases and Soft Law: A Comment on United States v. Nixon*, 22 U.C.L.A. L. Rev. 76 (1974), explaining various defects and mysteries in the Court's opinion as "dictated by the self-defensive needs of the Court as an institution." For more analysis of *Nixon*, see the other articles in *Symposium*, United States v. Nixon, 22 U.C.L.A. L. Rev. 4 (1974); Cox, *Executive Privilege*, 122 U. Pa. L. Rev. 1383 (1974); Freund, *supra*.

Note on the State Secrets Privilege

The state secrets privilege enables a federal executive to bar discovery of evidence whose disclosure may prejudice national security. The origins of the privilege are unclear. Chief Justice Marshall, sitting on circuit, recognized the government's authority to withhold secrets in the treason trial of Aaron Burr (*see* Freund, *supra*). Wigmore later observed magisterially that the existence of a state secrets privilege "has never been doubted" (8 J. Wigmore, Evidence § 2378 at 794 (McNaughten rev.

1961)). Still, the Supreme Court did not establish the modern formulation of the privilege until it decided *United States v. Reynolds*, 345 U.S. 1 (1952).

Reynolds was a wrongful death action under the Federal Tort Claims Act, brought for the death of civilians in the crash of an Air Force bomber. Plaintiffs sought production of the official crash report. The government resisted, claiming in a public affidavit by the Secretary of the Air Force that the state secrets privilege barred discovery of the report. Instead, the Secretary offered to produce the surviving crew members for depositions about unclassified matters. The Court upheld the claim of privilege. Although a statute and regulations supported the Secretary's claim of privilege in this case, Chief Justice Vinson noted that the ultimate source of a state secrets privilege is "an inherent executive power which is protected in the constitutional system of separation of power." His opinion went on (345 U.S. at 7-11):

> The privilege belongs to the Government and must be asserted by it; it can neither be claimed nor waived by a private party. It is not to be lightly invoked. There must be a formal claim of privilege, lodged by the head of the department which has control over the matter, after actual personal consideration by that officer. The court itself must determine whether the circumstances are appropriate for the claim of privilege, and yet do so without forcing a disclosure of the very thing the privilege is designed to protect. . . .
>
> Judicial control over the evidence in a case cannot be abdicated to the caprice of executive officers. Yet we will not go so far as to say that the court may automatically require a complete disclosure to the judge before the claim of privilege will be accepted in any case. It may be possible to satisfy the court, from all the circumstances of the case, that there is a reasonable danger that compulsion of the evidence will expose military matters which, in the interest of national security, should not be divulged. When this is the case, the occasion for the privilege is appropriate, and the court should not jeopardize the security which the privilege is meant to protect by insisting upon an examination of the evidence, even by the judge alone, in chambers. . . .
>
> In each case, the showing of necessity which is made will determine how far the court should probe in satisfying itself that the occasion for invoking the privilege is appropriate. Where there is a strong showing of necessity, the claim of privilege should not be lightly accepted, but even the most compelling necessity cannot overcome the claim of privilege if the court is ultimately satisfied that military secrets are at stake. A fortiori, where necessity is dubious, a formal claim of privilege . . . will have to prevail. Here, necessity was greatly minimized by an available alternative [examination of the surviving crew members]. By their failure to pursue that alternative, respondents have posed the privilege question for decision with the formal claim of privilege set against a dubious showing of necessity.

Since *Reynolds*, the government has raised the state secrets privilege to bar discovery in constitutional tort actions by plaintiffs seeking to recover for warrantless surveillance. Whether the privilege strikes an appropriate balance between the government's need for secrecy and protection of individual constitutional rights was considered in *Halkin v. Helms*, 598 F.2d 1 (D.C. Cir. 1978). Individuals and organizations who had actively opposed the Vietnam War sued the former and present directors of the National Security Agency, Central Intelligence Agency, Defense Intelligence Agency,

Federal Bureau of Investigation, and Secret Service, claiming that the defendants had violated their statutory and constitutional rights. Specifically, plaintiffs alleged that the National Security Agency (NSA) conducted warrantless interceptions of their international communications at the request of the other defendants. In addition to damages, plaintiffs sought declaratory and injunctive relief against further illegal surveillance by the government.

The suit was filed in October 1975, after the President's Commission on CIA Activities Within the United States revealed that defendants had conducted illegal surveillance of anti-war activists. The Commission disclosed that NSA had furnished other agencies reports of the foreign communications of Americans, to assist investigations of possible foreign influence over domestic peace groups. NSA obtained the intelligence by scanning electronic communications worldwide. Its computers were programmed with "watchlists," words or phrases designed to identify communications of intelligence interest. Using this technique, NSA established two surveillance operations: MINARET, to intercept foreign communications, and SHAMROCK, to intercept communications entering or leaving the United States. Between 1967 and 1973, NSA added the names of approximately 1,200 Americans to its watchlists under these operations. The acquired communications were disseminated in 2,000 reports to other intelligence agencies.

Plaintiffs sought to discover whether their communications had been intercepted by NSA and disseminated to other defendants. Defendants responded with a motion to dismiss based on a formal claim of the state secrets privilege. In a public affidavit to the District Court, the Secretary of Defense asserted: "Civil discovery or a responsive pleading which would (1) confirm the identity of individuals or organizations whose foreign communications were acquired by NSA, (2) disclose the dates and contents of such communications, or (3) divulge the methods and techniques by which the communications were acquired by NSA, would severely jeopardize the intelligence collection mission of NSA by identifying present communications collection and analysis capabilities." The Secretary also submitted a classified affidavit and gave ex parte testimony for *in camera* examination by the court. On the basis of this information, the court upheld the claim of privilege for operation MINARET, but denied the privilege with respect to operation SHAMROCK because extensive public disclosure of operation SHAMROCK had defeated the purpose behind the privilege.

On appeal, the Court of Appeals held that both NSA operations were privileged as state secrets. A panel of the court, per Judge Robb, rejected plaintiff's argument that it would not reveal state secrets to discover whether NSA had acquired their communications, without more. The panel ruled that a standard of "utmost deference" should guide any assessment of the executive's claim of the state secrets privilege. Despite the plaintiffs' strong showing of need, the panel held that the District Court's *in camera* examination of the basis for the claim of privilege satisfied the scrutiny required by *Reynolds*.

The panel applied the *Reynolds* test whether "there is a reasonable danger that compulsion of the evidence will expose military matters which, in the interest of national security, should not be divulged." The test of "reasonable danger" in this case, the panel posited, was whether discovery would reveal "useful information to a sophisticated analyst." This standard gave the Secretary's claim of privilege a presumption of validity. The panel found that the

[p]laintiffs' argument is naive. A number of inferences flow from the confirmation or denial of acquisition of a particular individual's communications. What may seem trivial to the uninformed, may appear of great moment to one who has a broad view of the scene and may put the questioned item of information in its proper context. The courts, of course, are ill-equipped to become sufficiently steeped in foreign intelligence matters to serve effectively in the review of secrecy classifications in that area.

The panel also rejected plaintiffs' contention that their case was indistinguishable from prior disclosures of similar information, which had not been held to endanger national security. "The government is not estopped from concluding in one case that disclosure is permissive while in another case it is not." Nor was the panel persuaded by the District Court's finding that "congressional committees investigating intelligence matters had revealed so much information about SHAMROCK that such a disclosure would pose no threat to the NSA mission." Instead, the panel concluded that further disclosures could pose a reasonable danger to national security.

The Court of Appeals denied a motion for rehearing en banc. Circuit Judge Bazelon, joined by Chief Judge Wright, stated his reasons for voting in favor of a rehearing. He found two serious flaws in the panel's review of the government's claim. First, the panel slighted the teachings of *U.S. v. Reynolds*, which requires measuring any claim of privilege against the plaintiff's need for the suppressed information. "It is difficult to imagine a stronger instance of need than this case [because the privilege] precludes all judicial scrutiny of the signals intelligence operations of NSA, regardless of the degree to which such activity invades the protections of the Fourth Amendment."

Judge Bazelon argued that because of the weight of the plaintiffs' claim, *Reynolds* required the panel to examine both the necessity for disclosure to maintenance of the suit (which the panel considered and rejected), and the necessity for disclosure "to assure that simply because private communications become entangled with sophisticated intelligence gathering methods, the constitutional protection for those communications are not unlawfully and cavalierly tossed aside"—which the panel neglected. Consequently, the panel exhibited "a total disregard of the Fourth Amendment . . . [and neglected] the significance of . . . firm limits on the authority of the Executive to conduct warrantless surveillance, even in the name of national security." Judge Bazelon concluded: "The panel employs an evidentiary privilege to carve out an exception to this basic principle of constitutional limitations on government."

Judge Bazelon also argued that the panel erred in according "utmost deference" to the Secretary of Defense's submission, because *Reynolds* was to the contrary, and because this standard amounted to abdicating "judicial control over the evidence in a case . . . to the caprice of executive officers." Instead, the state secrets privilege should be subjected to the same de novo scrutiny required for assessing the government's assertion of the "national security exemption" under the Freedom of Information Act (FOIA). The panel's deference

> produces the anomalous result that a FOIA requester, who may have no special need for the requested information, is given broader access to government information than a plaintiff who requires the information in order to pursue remedies for violation of constitutional rights. Thus, far from taking into account the plaintiffs' need for information, as required by *Reynolds*, the panel has stood

Reynolds on its head and penalized the plaintiffs precisely because their needs differ from that of the public at large.

This error led the panel to the wrong result. Since it failed to review de novo the claim of privilege, the panel could disregard the significance of operation SHAMROCK's publicity and previous disclosures by NSA. Judge Bazelon concluded that previous public disclosures of this kind contradicted the government's argument that any further disclosure of the SHAMROCK operation would pose a danger to national security.

On remand, plaintiffs amended their complaint to expand its allegations of unwarranted surveillance. They averred that, in addition to NSA's interception of their international communications, the CIA had engaged in unwarranted surveillance of Americans under operation CHAOS, an intelligence project designed to determine whether foreign governments influenced domestic anti-war activists. Operation CHAOS employed three methods of surveillance. First, it enlisted the aid of foreign intelligence agencies to spy on American dissidents traveling abroad. Second, it infiltrated foreign and domestic anti-war groups. Third, the CIA expanded its existing projects to obtain intelligence about American dissidents. Project MERRIMAC infiltrated domestic anti-war and radical groups believed to pose a threat to CIA property or personnel. Project RESISTANCE gathered information about the activities of anti-war groups without infiltration. The Director of the CIA moved to block further discovery under the state secrets privilege. The District Court granted the motion and dismissed the complaint.

Appealing again, plaintiffs challenged the adequacy of the CIA's justification for raising the state secrets privilege to bar discovery of operation CHAOS. *Halkin v. Helms*, 690 F.2d 977 (D.C. Cir. 1982). They argued that the CIA's public affidavit invoking the privilege was too vague, and also that the District Court's reliance on the agency's *in camera* affidavit unfairly deprived them of the opportunity to litigate the legality of the CIA's position. The panel, per Judge MacKinnon, ruled that the CIA's public affidavit satisfied the *Reynolds* test and therefore found no need to address plaintiffs' second contention. Ironically, the panel enlisted one of plaintiffs' own arguments—that public disclosure of operation CHAOS had defeated any justification for the privilege—to uphold the District Court's decision to grant the CIA immunity from discovery. The panel thought that new discovery of operation CHAOS, coupled with prior public disclosure, would pose a reasonable danger to American diplomatic interests:

> It is self-evident that the disclosures sought here pose a "reasonable danger" to the diplomatic and military interests of the United States. Revelation of particular instances in which foreign governments assisted the CIA in conducting surveillance of dissidents could strain diplomatic relations in a number of ways—by generally embarrassing foreign governments who may wish to avoid or may even explicitly disavow allegations of CIA or United States involvements, or by rendering foreign governments or their officials subject to political or legal action by those among their own citizens who may have been subjected to surveillance in the course of dissident activity.

Discovery would also endanger CIA agents: "the identities of CIA operatives who contributed information to CHAOS . . . are self-evidently the sort of information which if disclosed could harm national security or diplomatic interests."

Plaintiffs also argued that the requirements for withholding documents under FOIA apply to discovery under the state secrets privilege. The panel, however, distinguished FOIA on the ground that it serves a fundamentally different purpose from the privilege:

> The most important difference is that the claim of the state secrets privilege is a decision of policy made at the highest level of the executive branch after consideration of the facts of the particular case. The *Reynolds* requirements compel that it fullfil these requisites. Consequently, the risk of permitting relatively unaccountable "invisible" bureaucratic decisions as to the national security value of information (specifically, the decisions to classify information that trigger FOIA Exemption 1) to bar disclosure of information on a wholesale basis is not presented in a state secrets case.

The court said that, although FOIA and the privilege are distinguishable in purpose, both bar disclosure of the sort of information sought here. Since the information fit within FOIA's national security exemption, the panel concluded that there was no reason to order the CIA further to justify the redactions in documents it had produced for plaintiffs.

Once the panel had upheld the CIA's invocation of the state secrets privilege, it turned to the question of available remedies. Plaintiffs sought injunctive and declaratory relief against submission of their names by the CIA to watchlists for interception by NSA. The panel held that plaintiffs lacked standing to seek this relief. Since submission of names to a watchlist is not a violation of the Fourth Amendment, and since plaintiffs were barred from discovering whether their communications were actually intercepted (*Halkin I*), they could not show the requisite injury for standing:

> Without evidence of the detailed circumstances in which the CIA forwarded [plaintiffs'] names to NSA, the contents of communications intercepted as a result..., the duration of the [plaintiffs'] stays on the watchlists, and like matters—in short, "the essential information on which the legality of executive action [in foreign intelligence surveillance] turns"—it would be inappropriate to resolve the extremely difficult and important fourth amendment issue presented.

Plaintiffs' only recourse was congressional legislation.

> In the present context, where the Constitution compels the subordination of [plaintiffs'] interest in the pursuit of their claims to the executive's duty to preserve our national security, this means that remedies for constitutional violations that cannot be proven under existing legal standards, if there are to be such remedies, must be provided by Congress. That is where the government's power to remedy wrongs is ultimately reposed. Consequently, that is where the responsibility for compensating those injured in the course of pursuing the ends of state must lie.

The panel also concluded that plaintiffs lacked standing to seek an injunction against implementation of two new executive orders that authorized foreign intelligence operations similar to those under CHAOS.

Since the CIA admitted to spying on several of the plaintiffs under operation CHAOS, plaintiffs could allege injury from operation CHAOS to establish standing. But what relief was appropriate? The panel held that because plaintiffs could not satisfy the "traditional burden of proving the threat of imminent, specific, and irreparable harm," they could not obtain an injunction against future CIA spying. Declaratory relief does not pose such burdens. The panel, however, held that a declaration of the illegality of past CIA conduct was inapposite because the controversy was moot. The panel thought that the plaintiffs "confuse the injury-in-fact requirement necessary to standing with the 'liveness' showing necessary to avoid a dismissal for mootness. Both are constitutional conditions on the exercise of federal court jurisdiction. Thus, [plaintiffs'] assertion that 'the necessary case or controversy exists because defendant's actions have affected plaintiffs adversely' demonstrates only a necessary, not a sufficient, condition for maintaining their action." Accordingly, the panel affirmed the judgment of the District Court.

Another prominent state secrets case is *Ellsberg v. Mitchell*, 709 F.2d 51 (D.C. Cir. 1983). Daniel Ellsberg and others sued for damages for warrantless electronic surveillance by various federal officials. Plaintiffs sought to discover the identity of the official who authorized the wiretaps. Defendants admitted that plaintiffs had been overheard on wiretaps, but claimed that the state secrets privilege barred further discovery. The District Court upheld the claim of privilege and dismissed plaintiffs' claim. On appeal, the judgment was affirmed in part and reversed in part. The court, per Judge Edwards, said (at 56-60):

> It is now well established that the United States, by invoking its state secrets privilege, may block discovery in a lawsuit of any information that, if disclosed, would adversely affect national security. Prior to World War Two, the government rarely had occasion to exercise this prerogative, and, consequently, the scope of the privilege remained somewhat in doubt. In recent years, however, the state secrets privilege has been asserted in a growing number of cases, and the resultant bevy of judicial decisions assessing the legitimacy of its invocation has brought its lineaments into reasonably sharp focus. The following principles may be distilled from the case law.
>
> The privilege may be asserted only by the government itself; neither a private party nor an individual official may seek its aid. Furthermore, in order to invoke it, "[t]here must be a formal claim of privilege, lodged by the head of the department which has control over the matter, after actual personal consideration by that officer." Possibly because the state secrets doctrine pertains generally to *national security* concerns, the privilege has been viewed as both expansive and malleable. The various harms, against which protection is sought by invocation of the privilege, include impairment of the nation's defense capabilities, disclosure of intelligence-gathering methods or capabilities, and disruption of diplomatic relations with foreign governments.
>
> When properly invoked, the state secrets privilege is absolute. No competing public or private interest can be advanced to compel disclosure of information found to be protected by a claim of privilege. However, because of the broad sweep of the privilege, the Supreme Court has made clear that "[i]t is not to be lightly invoked." Thus, the privilege may not be used to shield any material not strictly necessary to prevent injury to national security; and, whenever possible, sensitive information must be disentangled from nonsensitive information to allow for the release of the latter.

It has been argued that certain limitations on the capacity of the judicial branch safely and reliably to evaluate invocations of the state secrets privilege should induce the courts to renounce any role in this area, *i.e.*, to accept without question a privilege claim made by a ranking executive officer. Such an extreme solution, however, would have grave drawbacks. As noted by Professor Mc-Cormick [Handbook of the Law of Evidence (E. Cleary ed. 1972)]:

> The head of an executive department can appraise the public interest of secrecy as well (or perhaps in some cases better) than the judge, but his official habit and leaning tend to sway him toward a minimizing of the interest of the individual. Under the normal administrative routine the question will come to him with recommendations from cautious subordinates against disclosure and in the press of business the chief is likely to approve the recommendation about such a seemingly minor matter without much independent consideration.

Sensitive to these concerns, the Supreme Court has declared that "[j]udicial control over the evidence in a case cannot be abdicated to the caprice of executive officers." Thus, to ensure that the state secrets privilege is asserted no more frequently and sweepingly than necessary, it is essential that the courts continue critically to examine instances of its invocation.

Although there can be no abdication of a judicial role in connection with proposed applications of the state secrets doctrine, it is nevertheless frequently noted that the trial judge should accord considerable deference to recommendations from the executive department. Moreover, it is recognized that the government need not demonstrate that injury to the national interest will inevitably result from disclosure; a showing of "reasonable danger" that harm will ensue is sufficient. Finally, when assessing claims of a state secrets privilege, a trial judge properly may rely on affidavits and other secondary sources more often than he might when evaluating assertions of other evidentiary privileges.

Whether (and in what spirit) the trial judge in a particular case should examine the materials sought to be withheld depends upon two critical considerations. First, the more compelling a litigant's showing of need for the information in question, the deeper "the court should probe in satisfying itself that the occasion for invoking the privilege is appropriate." Second, the more plausible and substantial the government's allegations of danger to national security, in the context of all the circumstances surrounding the case, the more deferential should be the judge's inquiry into the foundations and scope of the claim. Neither of these two factors can affect the judge's response, however, if he is "ultimately satisfied" that disclosure of the material *would* damage national security.

With these principles in mind, we turn to the objections made by the plaintiffs to the positions taken by the defendants, the government, and the District Court. The plaintiffs' first argument—a challenge to the scope of the privilege claim—is necessarily somewhat vague. Ignorant of what in fact has been withheld, they are able to say only that "too much" has been shielded. The tasks of posing and answering more specific questions therefore devolve on us.

We have examined all of the various affidavits and exhibits submitted to the District Court for *in camera* inspection. For the most part, the documents contained therein indicate what the defendants' responses to the plaintiffs' interrogatories would be, and why such responses cannot be made public. With regard to almost all of the material, we find that the District Court was correct in concluding that invocation of the state secrets privilege was proper. In other words, we conclude that there is a "reasonable danger" that revelation of the information in question would either enable a sophisticated analyst to gain insights into the nation's intelligence-gathering methods and capabilities or would disrupt diplomatic relations with foreign governments.

In one important respect, however, we find that the government and the District Court went too far. In their interrogatories, the plaintiffs requested the defendants to state, among other things, "by what . . . form of authority such surveillance was conducted, and if in written form, . . . the name of the person who signed the authorization." In their public affidavits submitted in support of the government's privilege claims, Kleindienst and Bell acknowledged that the wiretaps were "authorized by the Attorney General pursuant to the power delegated to him by the President." However, albeit without justification, neither the defendants nor the representatives of the United States have been willing to specify *which* Attorneys General authorized the surveillance.

At oral argument, counsel for the defendants conceded that none of the *in camera* exhibits or accompanying public affidavits submitted by the government explain why the identities of the authorizing officials must be concealed. . . . We cannot see, and the government does not even purport to explain, how any further disruption of diplomatic relations or undesirable education of hostile intelligence analysts would result from naming the responsible officials. . . .

The panel went on to discuss the effect of its partial reversal:

The effect of the government's successful invocation of the state secrets privilege, when the government is not itself a party to the suit in question, is well established: "[T]he result is simply that the evidence is unavailable, as though a witness had died, and the case will proceed accordingly, with no consequences save those resulting from the loss of the evidence." Likewise, it is now settled that, when the government is a defendant in a civil suit, its invocation of the privilege results in no alteration of pertinent substantive or procedural rules; the effect is the same, in other words, as if the government were not involved in the controversy. The rationale for this doctrine is that the United States, while waiving its sovereign immunity for many purposes, has never consented to an *increase* in its exposure to liability when it is compelled, for reasons of national security, to refuse to release relevant evidence. . . .

Under these conditions, dismissal of the relevant portion of the suit would be proper only if the plaintiffs were manifestly unable to make out a *prima facie* case without the requested information. Are the plaintiffs thus incapacitated? With regard to those whom the government has not admitted overhearing, the answer is clearly yes. An essential element of each plaintiff's case is proof that he himself has been injured. . . . Dismissal of the claims of those parties was therefore proper.

With regard to the five plaintiffs whom the government has conceded overhearing, the answer is far less obvious. Unlike their colleagues, they can demonstrate injury to themselves. On remand, they will be informed . . . of the identities of the Attorneys General who authorized the taps during which they were overheard. And the defendants have acknowledged that none of those taps was instituted pursuant to a warrant. Is this complex of facts sufficient to establish a *prima facie* case of violation of the plaintiffs' constitutional rights?

The court concluded that:

> the burden is on those seeking an exemption from the Fourth Amendment warrant requirement to show the need for it. Accordingly, to make out a *prima facie* case of a constitutional violation, the plaintiffs need not disprove the defendants' allegation that their actions are excused by the "foreign agent" exemption; rather, the defendants must prove their contention. As the defendants have not yet made such a showing in the instant case, dismissal of the claims of the five plaintiffs whom the defendants have acknowledged overhearing would be improper.

What conclusions do you draw from these cases? The plaintiffs in *Halkin I* and *II*, denied standing because they could not prove the injuries that they sought to discover, might have perceived a Catch-22. Was the Court of Appeals faithful to the *Reynolds* formula? Does *Ellsberg* take a significantly different tack?

For more analysis, *see* Note, *The Military and State Secrets Privilege: Protection for the National Security or Immunity for the Executive*, 91 Yale L.J. 570 (1982); Quint, *The Separation of Powers Under Carter*, 62 Tex. L. Rev. 785, 875-80 (1984). Viewing the *Halkin* litigation with dismay, Quint concludes that "the privilege ordinarily should not defeat liability in the absence of a specific authorizing statute [which] would represent a balancing of individual constitutional interests with executive secrecy interests, a balancing that the Executive cannot undertake objectively and that the judiciary has declined to perform." Would it make sense to award damages to any plaintiff who is met by a state secrets defense? How would you draft a statutory codification of the privilege?

3. Resisting disclosure to Congress

Of particular political, as well as legal, sensitivity are executive branch refusals to disclose requested information to Congress. Judicial decisions on the scope of executive privilege against Congress are rare, because the executive finds it difficult to mount court challenges to congressional demands for information, as *United States v. United States House of Representatives*, below, illustrates. Ordinarily, to obtain judicial review, an executive official must accept a citation for contempt of Congress and await court action to enforce it. (Prior to 1857, Congress, in citing persons for contempt, set the punishment on an *ad hoc* basis. In 1857, Congress enacted the original version of 2 U.S.C. § 192, imposing criminal liability for refusing any congressional demand for information.) To avoid extreme "brinksmanship" on the part of both branches, most disputes over requested information are resolved through negotiation, without a formal privilege claim.

Executive privilege disputes between President and Congress have a substantial history. For a brief review and appraisal, we turn to Professor—and former Watergate Special Prosecutor—Archibald Cox, in *Executive Privilege*, 122 U. Pa. L. Rev. 1383, 1395-1405 (1974):

> Senate and House Committees and less often the Senate and House themselves have been demanding information from the Executive Branch since the admin-

istration of George Washington. Nearly always the requests were satisfied, but one finds interspersed through history occasions on which Presidents declined to comply with congressional requests. Some of the refusals were accompanied by messages asserting a very broad presidential discretion to withhold any papers or other material the President thinks it in the public interest to withhold. Some Attorneys General gave opinions supporting the claim. Some Senators and Representatives and some committee reports acquiesced in the claim. Others resisted it...

Historians, judges and lawyers differ over the proper description and analysis of these incidents. All ended inconclusively because there was not in the past and may not be today any method of resolving the conflict short of impeachment. One gets a useful picture of the kinds of occasions on which information has been withheld by Chief Executives, however, by classifying each of the twenty-seven occasions listed in a purportedly complete compilation of prior claims of executive privilege made by the Department of Justice under President Eisenhower, not by what was said, but by what was done. [Memorandum by Attorney General Rogers, reprinted in Hearing on S. 921 Before the Subcomm. on Constitutional Rights of the Sen. Comm. on the Judiciary, 85th Cong., 2d Sess., at 33-146 (1958).]

At the very outset four of the seventeen Presidents and five of the twenty-seven instances compiled must be stricken from the list upon the ground that the congressional request explicitly stated that the President should decide whether furnishing the papers would be in the public interest. In these instances there was no need for a claim of constitutional right because there was no resistance to a congressional demand. President Jefferson, for example, is often said to have claimed executive privilege in withholding from the House information regarding the Burr conspiracy. The House request shows on its face that the House asked for information "except such as [the President] may deem the public welfare to require not to be disclosed."...

A number of Presidents withheld information from the Senate or House as a method of challenging the power of the particular body to deal with the subject matter upon which the information was said to bear. Analytically, these cases have no bearing upon any possible privilege of executive secrecy with respect to matters admittedly within the jurisdiction of the House making the demand. The most notable example is George Washington's firm declination in 1796 to deliver to the House of Representatives documents pertaining to the negotiation of the Jay Treaty. Washington relied in his rebuff of the House, not upon the need for secrecy but upon the principle that the Constitution assigns no role to the House in relation to treaties. All the papers requested by the House were "in fact... laid before the Senate," to aid that body in the performance of its legitimate role in the treaty-making function.

[Cox includes in the same category presidential refusals to produce information regarding removals of executive officers. He then identifies a category of presidential withholding of investigative files.] All nine instances can honestly be described as assertions of the confidentiality of papers in the Executive Branch, but it is equally plain that the claim was not based upon an undifferentiated interest in preserving confidentiality among executive officials.... The chief purpose of the withholding was to protect possibly innocent persons...

against disclosure of the rumors and loose allegations often found in investigative reports. [Citing 40 Op. A.G. 45 (1941)(Jackson).] . . .

If this reading of history is fair, four conclusions follow:

(1) Over a period of a century and a half thirteen Presidents found a total of twenty occasions on which to refuse to turn over information demanded by an arm of Congress. Sometimes Presidents bespoke a broad discretion. Attorneys General wrote broad opinions to support them. Commentators often accepted their views.

(2) If one looks at what was done and confines the words to the events, nothing appears which even approaches a solid historical practice of recognizing claims of executive privilege based upon an undifferentiated need for preserving the secrecy of internal communications within the Executive Branch. Only two Presidents, Andrew Jackson and Theodore Roosevelt, can be said to have withheld information under circumstances in which the withholding could not easily be justified upon some other, specialized ground.

(3) So far as one can judge from the history of past occasions for claiming power to withhold, President Nixon would have not done the slightest damage to the Presidency by an immediate, full disclosure. President Jackson, surely a strong Chief Executive, wrote that if the Congress could

> point to any case where there is the slightest reason to suspect corruption or abuse of trust, no obstacle which I can remove shall be interposed to prevent the fullest scrutiny by all legal means. The offices of all the departments will be opened to you, and every proper facility furnished for this purpose.

(4) There is no settled executive practice of giving Congress whatever it wishes from the Executive Branch.

The materials that follow are used to illuminate the processes by which legal and policy issues involved in a dispute over Congress' right to executive branch information are resolved. We begin with the current executive branch policy statement concerning the invocation of executive privilege. Judge Leventhal's opinion in *United States v. A.T. & T.*, which follows, asserts that the Constitution contemplates a process of good faith negotiation and compromise between the branches in such a dispute. The case study involving EPA Administrator Anne Gorsuch and Secretary of the Interior James Watt shows the rough road that negotiation sometimes takes.

As you read the materials, note, among other things, the competing traditions of legal interpretation in Congress and the executive branch. How well does the process you see here comport with the ideal of a "government of laws"?

a. Executive Branch Procedure for Invoking Executive Privilege

Executive branch procedures for responding to congressional requests for information were most recently set forth in the following memorandum issued by President Reagan (reprinted in H.R. Rept. No. 435, 99th Cong., 1st Sess. 1106 (1985)):

November 4, 1982

MEMORANDUM FOR THE HEADS OF EXECUTIVE
DEPARTMENTS AND AGENCIES

SUBJECT: Procedures Governing Responses to Congressional Requests for Information

The policy of this Administration is to comply with Congressional requests for information to the fullest extent consistent with the constitutional and statutory obligations of the Executive Branch. While this Administration, like its predecessors, has an obligation to protect the confidentiality of some communications, executive privilege will be asserted only in the most compelling circumstances, and only after careful review demonstrates that assertion of the privilege is necessary. Historically, good faith negotiations between Congress and the Executive Branch have minimized the need for invoking executive privilege, and this tradition of accommodation should continue as the primary means of resolving conflicts between the Branches. To ensure that every reasonable accommodation is made to the needs of Congress, executive privilege shall not be invoked without specific Presidential authorization.

The Supreme Court has held that the Executive Branch may occasionally find it necessary and proper to preserve the confidentiality of national security secrets, deliberative communications that form a part of the decision-making process, or other information important to the discharge of the Executive Branch's constitutional responsibilities. Legitimate and appropriate claims of privilege should not thoughtlessly be waived. However, to ensure that this Administration acts responsibly and consistently in the exercise of its duties, with due regard for the responsibilities and prerogatives of Congress, the following procedures shall be followed whenever Congressional requests for information raise concerns regarding the confidentiality of the information sought:

1. Congressional requests for information shall be complied with as promptly and as fully as possible, unless it is determined that compliance raises a substantial question of executive privilege. A "substantial question of executive privilege" exists if disclosure of the information requested might significantly impair the national security (including the conduct of foreign relations), the deliberative processes of the Executive Branch or other aspects of the performance of the Executive Branch's constitutional duties.

2. If the head of an executive department or agency ("Department Head") believes, after consultation with department counsel, that compliance with a Congressional request for information raises a substantial question of executive privilege, he shall promptly notify and consult with the Attorney General through the Assistant Attorney General for the Office of Legal Counsel, and shall also promptly notify and consult with the Counsel to the President. If the information requested of a department or agency derives in whole or in part from information received from another department or agency, the latter entity shall also be consulted as to whether disclosure of the information raises a substantial question of executive privilege.

3. Every effort shall be made to comply with the Congressional request in a manner consistent with the legitimate needs of the Executive Branch. The Department Head, the Attorney General and the Counsel to the President may, in the exercise of their discretion in the circumstances, determine that executive privilege shall not be invoked and release the requested information.

4. If the Department Head, the Attorney General or the Counsel to the President believes, after consultation, that the circumstances justify invocation of executive privilege, the issue shall be presented to the President by the Counsel

to the President, who will advise the Department Head and the Attorney General of the President's decision.

5. Pending a final Presidential decision on the matter, the Department Head shall request the Congressional body to hold its request for the information in abeyance. The Department Head shall expressly indicate that the purpose of this request is to protect the privilege pending a Presidential decision, and that the request itself does not constitute a claim of privilege.

6. If the President decides to invoke executive privilege, the Department Head shall advise the requesting Congressional body that the claim of executive privilege is being made with the specific approval of the President.

Any questions concerning these procedures or related matters should be addressed to the Attorney General, through the Assistant Attorney General for the Office of Legal Counsel, and to the Counsel to the President.

Ronald Reagan

The Reagan memorandum is the first new presidential directive on the subject since a March 24, 1969, memorandum by President Nixon. The primary changes made by Reagan are: the inclusion of the second unnumbered prefatory paragraph, a requirement in paragraph 2 that the head of a department concerned about privilege consult White House counsel in addition to the Attorney General, and the addition of the White House counsel to the decisionmaking process outlined in paragraphs 3 and 4. What do you think these changes are meant to accomplish? Do they pose potential problems for the President? As an adviser to an incoming administration, would you suggest altering the policy?

b. A Constitutional Requirement of Compromise?

United States v. American Telephone & Telegraph Co.
567 F.2d 121 (D.C. Cir. 1977)

[This dispute arose when the Subcommittee on Oversight and Investigations of the House Interstate and Foreign Commerce Committee subpoenaed documents from A.T. & T. pertaining to certain warrantless wiretapping that the United States, with the assistance of A.T. & T., assertedly conducted for national security reasons. The Department of Justice sued A.T. & T. to enjoin compliance with the subpoena on the ground that public disclosure of the Attorney General's letters requesting foreign intelligence surveillance of particular targets would harm the national security. The chair of the House subcommittee intervened, on behalf of the House, as the real party defendant.

Rather than resolve the dispute on its merits, the Court of Appeals, when the case first reached it, remanded with a suggestion that the parties negotiate a settlement under guidelines proposed by the court. The Justice Department then proceeded— unsuccessfully—to attempt to negotiate a procedure under which, instead of receiving the Attorney General's letters, the subcommittee would receive expurgated copies of the backup memoranda upon which the Attorney General based his decisions to authorize wiretaps. Information identifying the wiretap targets would be replaced by generic descriptive language fashioned by the Department. Negotiations broke down, however, over the proper procedure for assuring the subcommittee of the accuracy of the generic descriptions. The Department of Justice would permit subcommittee staff to inspect a substantial sample of unexpurgated memoranda for purposes of comparison, but, for fear of a leak, would neither turn over to the subcommittee the unexpurgated memos themselves, nor notes that the subcommittee staff might take upon inspecting the memos.

When the case returned to the Court of Appeals, it ordered a procedure that, although closer to the executive's "final offer," represented a genuine compromise of the two branches' positions. Judge Leventhal justified his concededly delicate balancing approach as follows:]

As Judge Friendly recalled in his 1976 Bicentennial lecture, it is one of the major strengths of the Constitution, and far from a weakness, that conflicting viewpoints have been resolved through intermediate positions. Much of this spirit of compromise is reflected in the generality of language found in the Constitution—generality which allows for dispute as to which of the coordinate branches may exercise authority in a particular fact situation.

The framers, rather than attempting to define and allocate all governmental power in minute detail, relied, we believe, on the expectation that where conflicts in scope of authority arose between the coordinate branches, a spirit of dynamic compromise would promote resolution of the dispute in the manner most likely to result in efficient and effective functioning of our governmental system. Under this view, the coordinate branches do not exist in an exclusively adversary relationship to one another when a conflict in authority arises. Rather, each branch should take cognizance of an implicit constitutional mandate to seek optimal accommodation through a realistic evaluation of the needs of the conflicting branches in the particular fact situation. This aspect of our constitutional scheme avoids the mischief of polarization of disputes. Professor Freund has cautioned that "[i]n the eighteenth-century Newtonian universe that is the Constitution, an excessive force in one direction is apt to produce a corresponding counterforce." [Freund, *supra*, at 20.]

The present dispute illustrates the danger of polarization, as well as the road to mediation. The positions of the parties are closer now than they were initially. Nevertheless, agreement has not been reached, and it is necessary for this Court to consider the conflicting claims of the parties to absolute authority. Both claims are put in absolute terms, to run without limit; and neither can be accepted as put.

The executive would have it that the Constitution confers on the executive absolute discretion in the area of national security. This does not stand up. While the Constitution assigns to the President a number of powers relating to national security, including the function of commander in chief and the power to make treaties and appoint ambassadors, it confers upon Congress other powers equally inseparable from the national security, such as the powers to declare war, raise and support armed forces and, in the case of the Senate, consent to treaties and the appointment of ambassadors.

More significant, perhaps, is the fact that the Constitution is largely silent on the question of allocation of powers associated with foreign affairs and national security. These powers have been viewed as falling within a "zone of twilight" in which the President and Congress share authority or in which its distribution is uncertain. The present dispute illustrates this uncertainty. The concern of the executive that public disclosure of warrantless wiretapping data may endanger national security is, of course, entirely legitimate. But the degree to which the executive may exercise its discretion in implementing that concern is unclear when it conflicts with an equally legitimate assertion of authority by Congress to conduct investigations relevant to its legislative functions.

The Subcommittee has pressed a different argument, that judicial interference with its actions in this dispute is barred by the Constitution. Reliance is placed on the Speech or Debate Clause, which provides that "for any Speech or Debate in either House, [Senators or Representatives] shall not be questioned in any other Place."

In *Eastland v. United States Servicemen's Fund*, 421 U.S. 491 (1975), the Supreme Court had occasion to scrutinize the role of the Speech or Debate Clause in immunizing a congressional subpoena from judicial interference. There, a Senate Subcommittee investigating internal security matters issued a subpoena directing a bank to produce bank records of an organization suspected of subversive activity. The organization, arguing that its First Amendment rights were being infringed, sued members of the Subcommittee to enjoin implementation of the subpoena. The Supreme Court held that where the actions of members of Congress fall within the "sphere of legitimate legislative activity," the Speech or Debate Clause is an absolute bar to judicial interference. This broad language must, however, be examined in the context of other decisions concerning the congressional investigatory power.

In *Eastland* itself, the Supreme Court acknowledged its earlier holdings that, in a criminal prosecution for refusal to answer congressional inquiries, defendants could assert as a defense the claimed infringement of their First Amendment rights, and the Court would balance this against the public interest in the congressional investigation going forward. *See Watkins v. United States*, 354 U.S. 178 (1957); *Barenblatt v. United States*, 360 U.S. 109 (1959).

Another instance of judicial balancing of executive and legislative interests emerged when the Senate Committee investigating improper activities in the 1972 presidential campaign issued a subpoena directing the President to deliver certain relevant tapes and documents. The President declined on the ground of executive privilege. The Committee sought to enforce the subpoena. This court weighed the public interest protected by the President's claim of privilege against the interest that would be served by disclosure to the Committee, and declined to enforce the congressional subpoena. *Senate Select Committee on Presidential Campaign Activities v. Nixon*, 498 F.2d 725 (D.C. Cir. 1974).

It appears from *Watkins, Barenblatt* and *Senate Select Committee* that individual members of Congress are not impermissibly "questioned in any other place" regarding their investigatory activities merely because the validity and permissibility of their activities are adjudicated. In these cases, unlike *Eastland*, the challenge to congressional investigatory activity was raised as a defense. The distinction should not be dismissed as merely procedural, since it sheds light on the nature and purpose of the protection afforded by the Speech or Debate Clause. The Clause was intended to protect legislators from executive and judicial harassment. "[L]egislators acting within the sphere of legitimate legislative activity 'should be protected not only from the consequences of litigation's results but also from the burden of defending themselves.' " 421 U.S. at 503. As is clear from *Watkins, Barenblatt*, and *Senate Select Committee*, however, the Clause does not and was not intended to immunize congressional investigatory actions from judicial review. Congress' investigatory power is not, itself, absolute. *Barenblatt v. United States*, 360 U.S. 109, 111-12 (1959). And the fortuity that documents sought by a congressional subpoena are not in the hands of a party claiming injury from the subpoena should not immunize that subpoena from challenge by that party.

If the request letters were only in the hands of the Justice Department, it could have refused to comply with the legislative demand, citing *Senate Select Committee*. The fact that the request letters are available from AT&T as well as from the Justice Department does not make the legislative authority unreviewable in court, for AT&T could have refused to comply and insisted on an ultimate court decision to avoid prosecution. The fact that the Executive is not in a position to assert its claim of constitutional right by refusing to comply with a subpoena does not bar the challenge so long as members of the Subcommittee are not, themselves, made defendants in a suit to enjoin implementation of the subpoena.

The approach by which the Executive here achieves judicial consideration of its challenge is not properly subject to reproach as exalting form over substance. The role of the court often turns on matters of procedure. The contrary position of the Subcommittee is itself an exercise in procedural refinement: The Subcommittee argues that the court can act only if AT&T itself initiates a challenge to the subpoena; so long as AT&T merely awaits a court ruling on the Executive's challenge, the court must abstain. It would be strange indeed if the Constitution made judicial consideration available to one who defies the legislature outright, but not to one like AT&T, who seeks an orderly resolution of a disputed question.

---

1. For analysis of this case, *see* Comment, United States v. AT&T: *Judicially Supervised Negotiation and Political Questions*, 77 Colum. L. Rev. 466 (1977). The author concludes that in the presence of constitutional conflict, "the constitutional scheme would seem to require no less than that the line between [the branches] be drawn at the point of optimal accommodation." Assuming that Professor Pareto is not available to draw such a line, how is a court to do so?

2. Without judicial prodding, what would you suppose is the likelihood of the branches successfully achieving, in Judge Leventhal's words, "optimal accommodation through a realistic evaluation of the needs of the conflicting branches in the particular fact situation?" What factors would likely affect the success of negotiations? What factors would you recommend should shape the executive's negotiating strategy? Consider the following case studies.

c. Case Studies: Executive Response to Congressional Subpoenas

Anne Gorsuch, President Reagan's first Administrator of the Environmental Protection Agency, became in 1982 the first executive official to be held in contempt of Congress while in office. The impetus for the contempt citation was her refusal to divulge certain documents to the Investigations and Oversight Subcommittee ("the Levitas subcommittee") of the House Committee on Public Works and Transportation, in connection with that subcommittee's investigation of EPA's administration of the so-called Superfund for the cleanup of hazardous waste dumping sites.

The Comprehensive Environmental Response, Compensation and Liability Act of 1980, 42 U.S.C. § 9601-57, commonly known as the Superfund Act, created a $1.6

billion trust fund to be used for financing the cleanup of hazardous waste sites and spills of hazardous chemicals. Among other things, the Act authorizes the government to act to control a hazardous waste situation when a responsible party either cannot be identified timely, or cannot act. Parties responsible for hazardous waste or chemical spill sites are required to reimburse the government for cleanup costs and damages to natural resources; noncooperating parties may be fined treble damages.

In 1982, several House subcommittees undertook investigations of various aspects of EPA's Superfund enforcement. The Levitas subcommittee, in March, 1982, commenced a general investigation of hazardous and toxic waste control, focusing on the impact of wastes on ground and surface water resources. Of special concern were an EPA decision to suspend its prior restriction on disposing containerized liquid wastes in landfills that might permit the migration of such wastes to ground surface waters, and allegations that the EPA was not adequately enforcing the Superfund provisions against parties responsible for hazardous waste sites. In September, subcommittee staff requested access to EPA's files on enforcement of the Superfund Act and related statutes in "Region II." Despite an early assurance of access, EPA subsequently informed the subcommittee that it would not make available certain materials in enforcement files connected with active cases.

At almost the same time as the Levitas subcommittee staff requested access to EPA files on Region II, the Oversight and Investigations Subcommittee ("the Dingell subcommittee") of the House Committee on Energy and Commerce requested documents relating to several hazardous waste sites outside Region II, on which the subcommittee's own investigation of enforcement effectiveness was focusing. Although this subcommittee's investigation did not spawn any contempt citations of its own, the coexistence of different EPA oversight hearings and demands for access to enforcement files was critically important to the dynamics of the subsequent interbranch negotiation. The broader range of interested parties made negotiation more difficult because of the greater number of persons to satisfy and the greater likelihood that congressional access to EPA files would undermine executive control over the outflow of information on Superfund investigations.

After the Levitas subcommittee staff's demand for access to EPA enforcement files, two weeks of unsuccessful negotiations ensued at the staff level. EPA offered to permit staff access to its files, subject to prescreening by an EPA official to maintain the confidentiality of sensitive documents. The offer was declined. On September 30, 1982, the subcommittee authorized subpoenas to issue for the requested documents.

Throughout most of October, 1982, service of the subpoenas was postponed under EPA assurances of cooperation. EPA continued to assert confidentiality for a limited class of litigation-related documents, but then reverted to its position of protecting all "enforcement sensitive" documents—apparently as a reaction to the issuance of a subpoena by the Dingell subcommittee for similar information. On November 22, 1982, the Levitas subcommittee served a broad subpoena on Gorsuch, demanding the documents and her testimony on December 2, 1982.

On November 30, 1982, Attorney General Smith released a letter to Rep. Dingell, justifying the Administration's refusal to comply with a subpoena for "sensitive open law enforcement investigative files." Smith forwarded the letter also to Rep. Levitas, to explain EPA's refusal to comply fully with the latter's subpoena. On the same day, President Reagan issued a memorandum to Gorsuch directing that she not divulge documents from "open investigative files, [which] are internal deliberative materials containing enforcement strategy and statements of the Government's position on various legal issues which may be raised in enforcement actions...."

The documents that follow are Smith's letter to Dingell, an analysis prepared by a lawyer for the House of Representatives, and a surrebuttal prepared within the Department of Justice. After reading these documents, how do you assess the merits of the two branches' respective legal and policy positions?

CONTEMPT OF CONGRESS

H.R. Rept. No. 968, 97th Cong., 2d Sess. 37-41, 58-64, 82-90 (1982).

Office of the Attorney General
November 30, 1982

Hon. John D. Dingell,
Chairman, Subcommittee on Oversight and Investigations,
Committee on Energy and Commerce, House of Representatives,
Washington, D.C.

Dear Mr. Chairman: This letter responds to your letter to me of November 8, 1982, in which you ... continue to seek to compel the production to your Subcommittee of copies of sensitive open law enforcement investigative files ... of the Environmental Protection Agency.... I shall reiterate at some length in this letter the longstanding position of the Executive Branch with respect to such matters. I do so with the knowledge and concurrence of the President....

[I]t has been the policy of the Executive Branch throughout this Nation's history generally to decline to provide committees of Congress with access to or copies of law enforcement files except in the most extraordinary circumstances. Attorney General Robert Jackson, subsequently a Justice of the Supreme Court, restated this position to Congress over forty years ago:

"It is the position of [the] Department [of Justice], restated now with the approval of and at the direction of the President, that all investigative reports are confidential documents of the executive department of the Government, to aid in the duty laid upon the President by the Constitution to 'take care that the laws be faithfully executed,' and that congressional or public access to them would not be in the public interest.

"Disclosure of the reports could not do otherwise than seriously prejudice law enforcement. Counsel for a defendant or prospective defendant, could have no greater help than to know how much or how little information the Government has, and what witnesses or sources of information it can rely upon. This is exactly what these reports are intended to contain."

This policy does not extend to all material contained in investigative files. Depending upon the nature of the specific files and the type of investigation involved, much of the information contained in such files may and is routinely shared with Congress in response to a proper request. Indeed, in response to your Subcommittee's request, considerable quantities of documents and factual data have been provided to you. The EPA estimates that approximately 40,000 documents have been made available for your Subcommittee and its staff to examine relative to the three hazardous waste sites in which you have expressed an interest. The only documents which have been withheld are those which are sensitive memoranda or notes by EPA attorneys and investigators reflecting enforcement strategy, legal analysis, lists of potential witnesses, settlement considerations and similar materials the disclosure of which might adversely affect a pending enforcement action, overall enforcement policy, or the rights of individuals.

I continue to believe, as have my predecessors, that unrestricted dissemination of law enforcement files would prejudice the cause of effective law enforcement and,... I see no reason to depart from the consistent position of previous presidents and attorneys general. As articulated by former Deputy Assistant Attorney General Thomas E. Kauper over a decade ago: "the Executive cannot effectively investigate if Congress is, in a sense, a partner in the investigation. If a congressional committee is fully apprised of all details of an investigation as the investigation proceeds, there is a substantial danger that congressional pressures will influence the course of the investigation."

Other objections to the disclosure of law enforcement files included the potential damage to proper law enforcement which would be caused by the revelation of sensitive techniques, methods or strategy, concern over the safety of confidential informants and the chilling effect on sources of information if the contents of files are widely disseminated, [and] sensitivity to the rights of innocent individuals who may be identified in law enforcement files but who may not be guilty of any violation of law. ... Our policy is premised in part on the fact that the Constitution vests in the President and his subordinates the responsibility to "take Care that the Laws be faithfully executed." The courts have repeatedly held that "the Executive Branch has exclusive authority and absolute discretion to decide whether to prosecute a case"... *United States v. Nixon*, 418 U.S. 683, 693 (1974).

The policy which I reiterate here was first expressed by President Washington and has been reaffirmed by or on behalf of most of our Presidents, including Presidents Jefferson, Jackson, Lincoln, Theodore Roosevelt, Franklin Roosevelt, and Eisenhower. I am aware of no President who has departed from this policy regarding the general confidentiality of law enforcement files.

I also agree with Attorney General Jackson's view that promises of confidentiality ... do not remove the basis for the policy of nondisclosure of law enforcement files. As [he] observed in writing [the] Chairman of the House Committee on Naval Affairs, in 1941:

> "I ... have no doubt that this pledge would be kept and that you would weigh every consideration before making any matter public. Unfortunately, however, a policy cannot be made anew because of personal confidence of the Attorney General in the integrity and good faith of a particular committee chairman. We cannot be put in the position of discriminating between committees or of attempting to judge between them, and their individual members, each of whom has access to information once placed in the hands of the committee."

Deputy Assistant Attorney General Kauper articulated additional considerations in explaining why congressional assurances of confidentiality could not overcome concern over the integrity of law enforcement files:

> "[S]uch assurances have not led to a relaxation of the general principle that open investigative files will not be supplied to Congress, for several reasons. First, to the extent the principle rests on the prevention of direct congressional

influence upon investigations in progress, dissemination to the Congress, not by it, is the critical factor. Second, there is the always present concern, often factually justified, with 'leaks.' Third, members of Congress may comment or publicly draw conclusions from such documents, without in fact disclosing their contents."

... We are confident that your Subcommittee and other congressional committees would guard...documents carefully. Nor do I mean to imply that any particular committee would necessarily "leak" documents improperly although, as you know, that phenomenon has occasionally occurred. Concern over potential public distribution of the documents is only a part of the basis for the Executive's position. At bottom, the President has a responsibility vested in him by the Constitution to protect the confidentiality of certain documents which he cannot delegate to the Legislative Branch.

With regard to the assurance of confidential treatment contained in your November 8, 1982 letter, I am sensitive to Rule XI, cl. 2, § 706c of the Rules of the House of Representatives which provides that "[a]ll committee hearings, records, data, charts, and files...shall be the property of the House and *all Members of the House shall have access thereto....*" In order to avoid the requirements of this rule regarding access to documents by all Members of the House, your November 8 letter offers to receive these documents in "executive session" pursuant to Rule XI, cl. 2, § 712.... But...the only protection given such materials by that section...is that they shall not be made public, in your own words, "without the consent of the Subcommittee."...

[N]either a congressional committee nor the House (or Senate, as the case may be) has the right under the Constitution to receive such disputed documents from the executive and sit in final judgment as to whether it is in the public interest for such documents to be made public....It is not up to a congressional subcommittee but to the courts ultimately " 'to say what the law is' with respect to the claim of privilege present in [any particular] case." *United States v. Nixon*, 418 U.S. at 705, *quoting Marbury v. Madison*, 1 Cranch 137, 177 (1803).

The crucial point is not that your Subcommittee, or any other subcommittee, might wisely decide not to make public sensitive information contained in law enforcement files. Rather, it is that the President has the constitutional responsibility to take care that the laws are faithfully executed; if the President believes that certain types of information in law enforcement files are sufficiently sensitive that they should be kept confidential, it is the President's constitutionally required obligation to make that determination.

These principles will not be employed to shield documents which contain evidence of criminal or unethical conduct by agency officials from proper review. However, no claims have been advanced that this is the case with the files at issue here. As you know, your staff has examined many of the documents which lie at the heart of this dispute to confirm that they have been properly characterized. These arrangements were made in the hope that that process would aid in resolving this dispute. Furthermore, I understand that you have not accepted Assistant Attorney General McConnell's offer to have the documents at issue made available to the Members of your Subcommittee at the offices of your Subcommittee for an inspection under conditions which would not have required the production of copies and which, in this one instance, would not have irreparably injured our concerns over the integrity of the law enforcement process. Your apparent rejection of that offer would appear to leave no room for further compromise of our differences on this matter....

I hope you will appreciate the historical perspective from which these views are now communicated to you and that this assertion of a fundamental right by the Executive will not, as it should not, impair the ongoing and constructive relationship that our two respective Branches must enjoy in order for each of us to fulfill our different but equally important responsibilities under our Constitution.

Sincerely,

WILLIAM FRENCH SMITH,
Attorney General.

OFFICE OF THE CLERK,
U.S. HOUSE OF REPRESENTATIVES,
December 8, 1982.

Re Attorney General's Letter Concerning Subpoena...

To: Honorable Elliott H. Levitas, Chairman, Subcommittee...

From: Stanley M. Brand, General Counsel to the Clerk.

... Regarding the Attorney General's first premise that Congress cannot subpoena material in law enforcement files, the Attorney General's opinion cites no caselaw to support this proposition; indeed, he could not because none exists to support him. Nothing is better established than that Congress' investigative power "encompasses inquiries concerning the administration of existing laws as well as proposed or possibly needed statutes.... [I]t comprehends probes into departments of the Federal Government to expose corruption, inefficiency or waste." *Watkins v. United States*, 354 U.S. 178, 187 (1957).

Of particular importance here is the history of legislative oversight of the Justice Department and its enforcement of the law. Indeed, past congressional investigations have focused on the Department's efforts in particular cases, rather than general or abstract policies. In *McGrain v. Daugherty*, 273 U.S. 135 (1926) a Senate committee investigated charges that the Department of Justice had failed to prosecute public corruption, antitrust and other matters.

The Supreme Court expressly recognized congressional authority to examine and inquire into specific enforcement decisions by the Department of Justice whether to prosecute as an incident of the legislative function:

> The subject to be investigated was the administration of the Department of Justice—whether its functions were being properly discharged or were being neglected or misdirected, and particularly *whether the Attorney General and his assistants were performing or neglecting their duties in respect of the institution and prosecution of proceedings*...the subject...would be materially aided by the information [sought]...the functions of the Department of Justice, the powers and duties of the Attorney General and the duties of his assistants, are all subject to regulation by congressional legislation, and...the department is maintained and its activities are carried on under such appropriations as in the judgment of Congress are needed from year to year. (273 U.S. at 177-78.) (Emphasis added.)

... The Attorney General does not discuss the congressional reach of investigatory power established by *McGrain*, and he does not distinguish it from the situation here. Instead, he argues that special principles, hitherto raised by the Justice Department primarily to defend nondisclosure of *criminal investigations* of the Justice Department itself, should be extended to contexts such as EPA's preparations for civil suits and settlements ... [which] do not raise the concerns involved in release of Justice Department criminal investigation files, such as the danger that prejudicial pretrial publicity will deny criminal defendants a fair trial or that the safety of FBI informants will be jeopardized. The Attorney General's opinion places its principal reliance on the 1941 opinion of Attorney General Jackson concerning nondisclosure of the FBI's investigative files. Yet the Attorney General cites no precedent for extending the policy regarding FBI criminal investigation files, with their special concerns, throughout the government whenever any matter may relate to civil suits—an enormous extension of secrecy.

Even where ... FBI intelligence gathering has been at issue, Congress has not foregone its power of inquiry in appropriate circumstances. Yet here, those weightier concerns are not even present. In their absence, the Attorney General would block congressional inquiry on the basis of two much weaker arguments.

First, concern is expressed that congressional inquiry is somehow inconsistent with the absolute prosecutorial discretion vested in the Executive branch, a point not in dispute. The Attorney General has once again confused congressional oversight with interference in prosecutorial decisionmaking. By reviewing these records, the committee seeks not to influence individual enforcement decisions, but rather to review the integrity and effectiveness of EPA's enforcement program and to evaluate the adequacy of existing law.

Second, concern is expressed that congressional oversight calls for information which reflects the government's strategy or the methods or weaknesses of its investigations. Yet if this type of concern were recognized as blocking congressional inquiry, it would end a major portion of all such inquiry. Congressional inquiry into foreign affairs and military matter calls for information on strategy and weaknesses in national security matters; congressional inquiry into waste, fraud, and inefficiency, *Watkins v. United States, supra*, in domestic operations calls for information on strategy and weaknesses in combating these. Congress does not forego inquiry simply because it may produce information on the government's strategies and weaknesses; the only way to correct either bad law or bad administration is to examine these matters.

Nor does the fact that these matters may be the subject of civil suit mean that congressional inquiry should be blocked. There is unbroken precedent that Congress may investigate subjects relevant to its legislative function which are concurrently the subject matter of pending suit or likely to come before the courts. ... See *McGrain v. Daugherty, supra* at 180; *Sinclair v. United States*, 279 U.S. 263, 295 (1929)(authority of Senate "to require pertinent disclosures in aid of its own constitutional power is not abridged because the information sought to be elicited may also be of use in such suits").

In any event, claims by litigants that concurrent congressional investigations violate constitutional precepts of fairness of due process, also an apparent concern of the Attorney General, have largely been rejected. *United States v. Mitchell*, 397 F. Supp. 166, 179-180 (D.D.C. 1974), *aff'd sub. nom. United States v. Haldeman*, 559 F. 2d

31 (D.D.C. 1976), *cert. denied*, 431 U.S. 933 (1977); *United States v. Mitchell*, 372 F. Supp. 1239, 1259-60 (S.D.N.Y. 1973).

The Attorney General's second premise is that the Subcommittee's offer to receive information in executive session is not a legal basis for providing that information. The Attorney General argues that providing the Subcommittee with that material would mean the executive had "lost control" over the material. . . . However, there is extensive judicial, statutory, and historic precedent for disclosure of the most sensitive material to congressional committees in executive session. . . . The Framers anticipated that Congress would need to receive sensitive information requiring secret treatment, and provided expressly for it in the Journal Clause, Art. I, § 5, Cl. 3, which requires the Senate and House to keep and publish Journals, "except such parts as may in their judgment require secrecy." . . . The very reason the Framers conferred this authority on Congress to keep its record secret was so that it could receive sensitive information, such as information about "negotiations about treaties," from the executive. *See generally*, Kaye, *Congressional Papers, Judicial Subpoenas, and The Constitution*, 24 U.C.L.A. L. Rev. 523, 533 (1977) (secrecy clause protects Congress' proceedings concerning negotiation of treaties and planning of military operations in wartime).

. . . Private parties have frequently objected . . . to receipt by congressional committees of information from law enforcement agencies; their objections relied on the ground urged by the Attorney General, that a committee might subsequently use executive session material in public. The courts have uniformly given this objection short shrift, holding that disclosure to congressional committees is not tantamount to public disclosure. *Exxon Corp. v. FTC*, 589 F.2d 582, 589 (D.C. Cir. 1978), *cert. denied*, 441 U.S. 943 (1979). The courts "presume that the committees of Congress will exercise their powers responsibly and with due regard for the rights of affected parties." *FTC v. Owens-Corning Fiberglass Corp.*, 626 F.2d 966, 970 (D.C. Cir. 1980).

Similarly, a leading Supreme Court case notes the importance of executive session as a basis for receiving testimony when there is parallel litigation. In *Hutcheson v. United States*, [369 U.S. 599 (1962)], the Court ruled that Congress could obtain testimony even from a defendant facing a pending state criminal case. As Justice Brennan noted in his seminal concurring opinion, "Surely it cannot be said that a fair criminal trial and a full power of [congressional] inquiry are interests that defy accommodation. . . . [by means such as] postponement of inquiry until after an immediately pending trial, *or the taking of testimony in executive session*—or that the State grant a continuance in the trial."

Three examples directly contradict the Attorney General's view that the availability of executive session is not a basis for providing sensitive information. First, both the House and Senate receive extensive secret intelligence material through their intelligence committees, precisely because both the House and Senate have rules that such material shall be kept secret by the committees. Second, authorized House and Senate committees receive confidential tax information, precisely because they receive it in executive session. Third, the Justice Department itself has disclosed confidential information to House and Senate committees, such as wiretap information from a pension fraud and bribery investigation, based on the receipt of such information in executive session and commitments concerning nondisclosure.

In sum, the spectre raised by the Attorney General that Congress compromises the prosecution of cases by concurrently investigating the subject matter, even in advance of any decision to make public the information it obtains, is unfounded. It is also inconsistent with the prior position of the Department of Justice. For example, in 1979, the representatives of the Department testified in connection with an investigation into fraudulent oil pricing and Congress requested access to open civil litigation files in a specific case. The Department stated it has "[n]o objection, except that we would ask that because of the pending litigation that they not be made public at this juncture, *unless the committee has some compelling need.*"

Thus, there is ample precedent for congressional inquiries into the conduct by the Executive of investigations and litigation. There is ample precedent for receipt in executive session as a basis for providing sensitive material. There is no reason for extending the secrecy principles hitherto reserved for FBI criminal investigative files to the entire government.

U.S. DEPARTMENT OF JUSTICE,
OFFICE OF LEGAL COUNSEL,
December 14, 1982.

MEMORANDUM FOR THE ATTORNEY GENERAL

Re Response to Legal Memorandum of the General Counsel to the Clerk of the House of Representatives Regarding Executive Privilege.

. . . Before responding to the specific points raised by the General Counsel Memorandum, certain general observations are in order. First, although [it] relies on or cites to 13 separate court decisions in support of the various propositions asserted, not a single one of those authorities deals with an assertion of Executive privilege by the President in response to a subpoena issued by a congressional committee or even a claim of Executive privilege against a Judicial Branch subpoena. For some reason not disclosed in the General Counsel Memorandum, it does not even mention the major judicial authorities which do treat the subject of Executive Privilege. Thus, as is often our experience in these situations, the legal argument put forward by a congressional entity to counter the Executive's legal position on this issue fails to grapple with the extant judicial authority that is either directly in point, e.g., *Senate Select Committee on Presidential Campaign Activities v. Nixon*, 498 F.2d 725 (1974), or is highly relevant to the issues at hand, e.g., *United States v. Nixon*, 418 U.S. 683 (1974). . . .

Second, [never have we] questioned in any way that Congress may appropriately empower its committees to investigate the Executive Branch's conduct of its duties and responsibilities. The challenge and responsibility in situations involving competing interests and obligations of the two coequal Branches is to attempt, to the extent possible, to balance the competing interests of the two Branches. The General Counsel Memorandum neither recognizes the Executive's constitutional prerogative nor attempts to balance the competing interests. . . .

Third, the General Counsel Memorandum contains no discussions of, and reflects no appreciation for, the principle of separation of powers which is fundamental to our Constitution and, of course, to the most basic understanding of the concept of Executive Privilege. [I]t proceeds from the unstated premise that congressional power to investigate and to demand and receive documents in the possession of the Executive

Branch is unlimited... The Framers of our Constitution... were particularly concerned about the threat of combining the power to legislate and the power to execute the law. They agreed with Montesquieu that "there can be no liberty" "when the legislative and executive powers are united in the same person or body."...

The General Counsel Memorandum states that your position is "that the information is beyond the reach of congressional subpeona power because it is 'sensitive' material in 'law enforcement files...,' " and that your premise is that "Congress cannot subpoena material in law enforcement files." However, your position is much more limited—that the information at issue here is of a peculiar and special nature such that its disclosure would impair the President's ability to enforce the law and that such information need not be disclosed by the Executive absent extraordinary circumstances.

The only interest which has been asserted by the Legislature in seeing the material in such sensitive segments of files is identified... as a "right to see how the laws it passes are being administered...." The authority relied upon by the General Counsel Memorandum on this point, *McGrain v. Daugherty*, 273 U.S. 135 (1926), involved a subpoena issued to the brother of a former Attorney General. Nowhere in that case did the Supreme Court suggest that the subpoena... could have been used to obtain production of documents in open law enforcement files. Furthermore, the Court was careful to point out that the congressional investigation... was based on highly specific alleged acts of criminal misconduct and malfeasance in office by that former Attorney General....

[N]owhere does the Memorandum challenge your position that once the documents are provided to a Committee, the President in fact and in law loses control to the extent that the Committee has, from that time forward, the unilateral right to make any use of the documents it sees fit to make.... The... Memorandum appears to suggest that the fact that material over which the President could assert privilege is often turned over to Congress establishes an unrestricted right in Congress to receive all information in the possession of the Executive Branch over the objection of the President. The argument is nothing less than an assertion that the customary attitude of the Executive Branch in attempting to... avoid needless friction between the two Branches has effectively destroyed Executive Privilege itself....

At several points, the General Counsel Memorandum suggests that your reliance on Attorney General Jackson's letter to Chairman Vinson, 40 Op. A.G. 45 (1941), is misplaced because . . . that opinion was limited to "nondisclosure of the FBI's criminal investigative files."... The specific request for information to which Attorney General Jackson responded covered investigations of both "alleged violations of law" and investigations to gather "intelligence" information, the latter decidedly noncriminal and the former not... necessarily confined to criminal matters....

Another example is Attorney General Brownell's [response to] requests for documents by congressional committees[;] the Attorney General distinguished only between open and closed cases. The order applied to all cases over which the Department of Justice had enforcement responsibility and, with regard to open cases, the policy was [nondisclosure].

Finally, we would observe that the limitation placed on... open investigative files by Attorneys General Jackson and Brownell,... are, if anything, far greater than the policy adopted by President Reagan in his November 30, 1982 Memorandum to

Administrator Gorsuch. Under both the Jackson and Brownell views, for example, congressional committees were to receive no documents found in open investigative files in criminal or civil actions; under current policy much effort will be expended by Executive Branch personnel to segregate out from these files only sensitive, deliberative documents.... The policy of this Administration is less restrictive than its predecessors.

The General Counsel Memorandum strives at great length to establish the proposition that the constitutional rights of potential targets of enforcement actions will not be endangered unacceptably by the documents being made available to congressional committees. It is, of course, not surprising that the courts have been generally reluctant to reverse the convictions of criminal defendants because of pre-trial publicity generated by congressional inquiry into specific cases. That reluctance, however, in no way establishes the proposition... that a Nation constitutionally committed to fair and impartial administration of criminal and civil justice would or should tolerate trial by congressional committee....

[A]ny policy in this area must assume ... the possibility of misuse along with proper use of sensitive information and, if the information is very important to a pending or developing case, it should not be disseminated beyond those directly involved in the enforcement process.... [I]f the tactical materials will not make a critical contribution to the legislative process and are primarily useful to law enforcement officials (and the potential defendant), proper attention to the faithful execution of the law requires that the circle of access to the open law enforcement file be kept as narrow as possible....

[T]he Legislative Branch was not empowered by the Constitution to participate directly and intimately in the enforcement of the law. Cf. *Buckley v. Valeo*, 424 U.S. 1, 138-43 (1976). [The Memorandum does not say] why access to open law enforcement files is necessary in order for the committee to perform its legitimate legislative duties.... [U]ntil the committee can establish that its access to the files in closed cases coupled with the many other means by which it may inquire into this issue, including the testimony of high EPA officials [is insufficient]... there is no reason... why the committee should have sensitive material turned over to it.... "The sufficiency of the Committee's showing must depend solely on whether the subpoenaed evidence is *demonstrably critical* to the responsible fulfillment of the committee's functions." *Senate Select Committee v. Nixon, supra*, 498 F.2d at 731 (emphasis added).

Following his subcommittee's hearing, Rep. Levitas met with administration officials to attempt a settlement. His offer was: subcommittee staff would review and designate for copying or delivery all EPA documents relative to the waste sites at issue. If EPA or the Justice Department designated any document as sensitive, it would remain at EPA for inspection there. If actual delivery to the subcommittee of any of these documents proved necessary, further subpoenas might issue. All information disclosed would be treated as confidential.

The Attorney General declined the settlement offer, reiterating EPA's original offer of access subject to EPA prescreening. The only concession was that documents would be withheld only after broad-based and high-level review in the executive branch. The full Public Works and Transportation Committee responded by recommending, in a party-lines vote, that the House hold Gorsuch in contempt.

Six days later, the House overwhelmingly approved a resolution to certify Gorsuch's "contumacious conduct" to the U.S. Attorney for the District of Columbia. Prior to the actual certification, the Justice Department filed an extraordinary suit in federal district court to enjoin further action to enforce the subpoena, on the ground of its unconstitutionality.

As you read the court's opinion, which follows, consider whether the suit was appropriate. Should the Attorney General have considered himself bound to prosecute Gorsuch forthwith after the House vote? Could Congress constitutionally so bind the Attorney General?

United States v. House of Representatives of the United States
556 F. Supp. 150 (D.D.C. 1983)

JOHN LEWIS SMITH, Jr., District Judge.

The United States of America and [Administrator Gorsuch] bring this action under the Declaratory Judgment Act, 28 U.S.C. § 2201. Plaintiffs ask the Court to declare that Administrator Gorsuch acted lawfully in refusing to release certain documents to a congressional subcommittee. Defendants in the action are: The House of Representatives of the United States; The ... Subcommittee on Investigations and Oversight of the Committee on Public Works and Transportation; The Honorable Elliott J. Levitas, Chairman of the Subcommittee ... The Honorable Thomas P. O'Neill, Speaker of the House of Representatives; Edmund L. Henshaw, Jr., Clerk of the House of Representatives; Jack Russ, Sergeant at Arms of the House of Representatives; and James T. Molloy, Doorkeeper of the House of Representatives.... The case is now before the Court on defendants' motion to dismiss.

The essential facts are undisputed. On November 22, 1982, a subpoena was served upon Anne Gorsuch by the Subcommittee [requiring her] to ... produce ... the following documents:

> all books, records, correspondence, memorandums, papers, notes and documents drawn or received by the Administrator and/or her representatives since December 11, 1980, ... for those sites listed as national priorities pursuant to Section 105(8)(B) of P.L. 96-510, the "Comprehensive Environmental Response, Compensation and Liability Act of 1980."

On November 30, 1982, President Reagan sent a Memorandum to Administrator Gorsuch instructing her to withhold ... open law enforcement files.... The full House cited Administrator Gorsuch for contempt of Congress on December 16, 1982. The initial complaint in this case was filed on the same day, one day before the contempt resolution was certified to the United States Attorney for the District of Columbia for presentment to the grand jury. To date, the United States Attorney has not presented the contempt citation to the grand jury for its consideration.

Section 192 of Title 2 of the United States Code provides that a subpoenaed witness who refuses "to produce papers upon any matter under inquiry before either House ... or any committee of either House of Congress", shall be guilty of a misdemeanor "punishable by a fine of not more than $1,000 nor less than $100 and imprisonment in a common jail for not less than one month nor more than twelve months." Once an individual has been found in contempt by either House of Congress, [the U.S. Attorney is] required to bring the matter before the grand jury. [2 U.S.C. § 194] . . .

Defendants raise several challenges to the propriety of plaintiffs' cause of action. Included among defendants' grounds for dismissal are lack of subject matter jurisdiction, lack of standing, and the absence of a "case or controversy" as required by Article III, § 2 of the United States Constitution. In addition, defendants claim that they are immune from suit under the Speech and Debate Clause, Article I, § 6, cl. 1. Plaintiffs have addressed and opposed each of these threshold challenges.

. . . If these two co-equal branches maintain their present adversarial positions, the Judicial Branch will be required to resolve the dispute by determining the validity of the Administrator's claim of executive privilege. Plaintiffs request the Court to provide immediate answers, in this civil action . . . . Defendants, however, have indicated a preference for established criminal procedures in their motion to dismiss this case. Assuming there are no jurisdictional bars to this suit, therefore, the Court must initially determine whether to resolve the constitutional controversy in the context of a civil action, or defer to established statutory procedures for deciding challenges to congressional contempt citations.

The statutory provisions concerning penalties for contempt of Congress constitute "an orderly and often approved means of vindicating constitutional claims arising from a legislative investigation." Under these provisions, constitutional claims and other objections to congressional investigatory procedures may be raised as defenses in a criminal prosecution. Courts have been extremely reluctant to interfere with the statutory scheme by considering cases brought by recalcitrant witnesses seeking declaratory or injunctive relief. *See, e.g., Eastland v. United States Servicemen's Fund*, 421 U.S. 491 (1975). Although the Court of Appeals for this Circuit has entertained one civil action seeking to block compulsory legislative process, that action was brought by the Executive Branch to prevent a private party from complying with a congressional subpoena. *See United States v. American Telephone and Telegraph Company*, 551 F.2d 384 (D.C. Cir. 1976). Significantly, therefore, in that case the Executive Branch was not able to raise its claim of executive privilege as a defense to criminal contempt proceedings.

Courts have a duty to avoid unnecessarily deciding constitutional issues. When constitutional disputes arise concerning the respective powers of the Legislative and Executive Branches, judicial intervention should be delayed until all possibilities for settlement have been exhausted. Judicial restraint is essential to maintain the delicate balance of powers among the branches established by the Constitution. Since [this case] clearly raises difficult constitutional questions in the context of an intragovernmental dispute, the Court should not address these issues until circumstances indicate that judicial intervention is necessary.

The gravamen of plaintiffs' complaint is that executive privilege is a valid defense to congressional demands for sensitive law enforcement information from the EPA. Plaintiffs have, thus, raised this executive privilege defense as the basis for affirmative relief. Judicial resolution of this constitutional claim, however, will never become necessary unless Administrator Gorsuch becomes a defendant in either a criminal contempt proceeding or other legal action taken by Congress. The difficulties apparent in prosecuting Administrator Gorsuch for contempt of Congress should encourage the two branches to settle their differences without further judicial involvement. Compromise and cooperation, rather than confrontation, should be the aim of the parties. The Court, therefore, finds that to entertain this declaratory judgment action would be an improper exercise of the discretion granted by the Declaratory Judgment Act. In light of this determination, the Court will not address the additional grounds for dismissal raised by defendants.

Accordingly, defendants' motion to dismiss is granted.

After the case was dismissed, Representative Levitas and President Reagan reached agreement that the subcommittee would receive edited copies of all relevant documents and a briefing on their contents, and then would be permitted to review any requested unedited documents in closed session.

Although the settlement resolved the Levitas dispute, it did not end the imbroglio. Still pending were subpoenas from the Dingell subcommittee, which now asserted that its investigation was focusing on specific allegations of misconduct by EPA officials. Rita Lavelle, the Superfund administrator and the most prominent of these officials, was dismissed on February 7, 1983, by the President amid allegations of her perjury to Congress and improper administration of the trust fund.

Following the agreement with Levitas, further disclosures of possible criminal conduct at EPA made prolonged resistance to the Dingell subpoenas politically impossible. On March 9, 1983, Anne Gorsuch resigned as EPA administrator, and the White House agreed to deliver all subpoenaed documents to the Dingell subcommittee, subject to certain limited protections for the confidentiality of enforcement-sensitive materials. For Gorsuch's view of the affair, see Anne Gorsuch Burford, Are You Tough Enough? (1986).

In assessing the foregoing history, it is helpful to recall that the Department of Justice had taken a nearly contemporaneous formal stance on executive privilege in its unsuccessful defense of confidentiality in a dispute involving Interior Secretary James Watt. The "actors" in the Gorsuch dispute were well aware of the earlier history because, in large part, the same people were involved. As you read the Attorney General's opinion on the Watt matter and the House response, do you view the Watt privilege claim as more or less credible (and credibly presented) than the Gorsuch claim? How do the claims of the two branches differ when the material sought involves general policy debate and foreign affairs, rather than specific law enforcement decisions?

CONTEMPT OF CONGRESS

H.R. Rept. No. 898, 97th Cong., 2d Sess. 42-56 (1982).

OFFICE OF THE ATTORNEY GENERAL,
October 13, 1981.

THE PRESIDENT,
The White House,
Washington, D.C.

DEAR MR. PRESIDENT: You have requested my advice concerning the propriety of an assertion of executive privilege in response to a subpoena issued by the Subcommittee on Oversight and Investigations of the House Committee on Energy and Commerce.... It seeks "All documents relative to the determination of reciprocity under the Mineral Lands Leasing Act, 30 U.S.C. § 181, including documents relating to the general matter of reciprocity and the specific question of the status of Canada, utilized or written by officials and staff of the Department of Interior on or before September 1, 1981." [The Act disqualifies citizens of a country which denies "like privileges" to Americans from obtaining an interest in a lease.] The Office of Legal Counsel . . . has examined documents embraced by the subpoena . . . and has concluded that a proper claim of privilege may be asserted [for certain documents]. I concur in that conclusion.

I.

. . . [T]he Department of the Interior supplied the Subcommittee with a large number of the materials presently demanded by the subpoena, including a list of 36 published sources and copies of 143 documents. Once the subpoena was issued, the Department . . . in consultation with other Departments having an interest in the matter, . . . once again reviewed the documents which had not previously been provided to the Subcommittee. In an effort to make every reasonable accommodation to the legitimate needs of the Legislative Branch, the Department of the Interior released an additional 31 documents . . . In addition, the Subcommittee was provided with a written list and oral description of the 31 documents which had been withheld. The Subcommittee staff was permitted to ask questions concerning the nature of those documents, a procedure designed to provide the Subcommittee with enough information to assure itself that the documents are not essential to the conduct of the Subcommittee's legislative business. . . .

All of the documents in issue are either necessary and fundamental to the deliberative process presently ongoing in the Executive Branch or relate to sensitive foreign policy considerations. Several of the documents reflect views of officials of the Canadian Government transmitted in confidence to United States officials as well as statements regarding the status of Canada by officials of the Department of State. Other documents, . . . are predecisional, deliberative memoranda which have been considered by officials at the highest levels of government [to] prepare recommendations for Presidential action . . . . Finally, a large portion of the documents being withheld reflect internal deliberations within the Department of the Interior regarding the status of Canada under the Act. Some of these documents are staff level advice to policymakers containing recommendations regarding decisions which have not yet become final. . . . Still other documents reflect tentative legal judgments regarding questions arising under the Act. In addition, the subpoena encompasses preliminary drafts of congressional testimony by the Secretary of the Interior. These latter documents, although generated at levels below that of the Cabinet and subcabinet, are of a highly deliberative nature and involve an on-going decisional process of considerable sensitivity.

II.

. . . These documents are quintessentially deliberative, predecisional materials. Each of the agencies which generated the documents has stated that their release to the Subcommittee would seriously interfere with or impede the deliberative process of government and, in some cases, the Nation's conduct of its foreign policy. Because the policy options considered in many of these documents are still under review in the Executive Branch, disclosure to the Subcommittee at the present time could distort that decisional process by causing the Executive Branch officials to modify policy positions they would otherwise espouse because of actual, threatened, or anticipated congressional reaction. Moreover, even if the decision at issue had already been made, disclosure to Congress could still deter the candor of future Executive Branch deliberations, because officials at all levels would know that they could someday be called by Congress to account for the tentative policy judgments which they had earlier advanced in the councils of the Executive Branch. As the Supreme Court has noted, "human experience teaches that those who expect dissemination of their remarks may well temper candor with a concern for appearances and for their own interests to the detriment of the decisionmaking process." *United States v. Nixon*, 418 U.S. 683, 705 (1974). You must have access to complete and candid advice in order to provide the soundest basis for presidential decisions. I have concluded that release of these documents would seriously impair the deliberative process and the conduct of foreign policy. There is, therefore, a strong public interest in withholding the documents from congressional scrutiny at this time.

Against this strong public interest I must consider the interest of Congress in obtaining these documents. The Subcommittee ... stated that it was conducting a "legislative oversight inquiry" into the impact of Canadian energy policies upon American companies. ... Congress does have a legitimate interest in obtaining information to assist it in enacting, amending or repealing legislation. This interest extends beyond information bearing on specific proposals for legislation; it includes, as well, the congressional "oversight" function of being informed regarding the manner in which the Executive Branch is executing the laws which Congress has passed. Such oversight enables the Legislative Branch to identify at an early stage shortcomings or problems in the execution of the law which can be remedied through legislation.

[T]he interest of Congress in obtaining information for oversight purposes is, I believe, considerably weaker than its interest when specific legislative proposals are in question. At the stage of oversight, the congressional interest is a generalized one of ensuring that the laws are well and faithfully executed and of proposing remedial legislation if they are not. The information requested is usually broad in scope and the reasons for the request correspondingly general and vague. In contrast, when Congress is examining specific proposals for legislation, the information which Congress needs ... is usually quite narrow in scope and the reasons for obtaining that information correspondingly specific. A specific, articulated need for information will weigh substantially more heavily in the constitutional balancing than a generalized interest in obtaining information. *See United States v. Nixon, supra; Senate Select Committee on Presidential Campaign Activities v. Nixon*, 498 F.2d 725, 730-33 (D.C. Cir. 1974) (*en banc*).

... When such "oversight" is used as a means of participating directly in an ongoing process of decision within the Executive Branch, it oversteps the bounds of the proper legislative function. [Oversight] can almost always be properly conducted with reference to information concerning decisions which the Executive Branch has already reached. Congress will have a legitimate need to know the preliminary positions taken by Executive Branch officials during internal deliberations only in the rarest of circumstances. Congressional demands, under the guise of oversight, for such preliminary positions and deliberative statements raise at least the possibility that the Congress has begun to go beyond the legitimate oversight function and has impermissibly intruded on the Executive Branch's function of executing the law. At the same time the interference with the President's ability to execute the law is greatest while the decisionmaking process is ongoing.

Applying the balancing process required by the Supreme Court, it is my view that the Executive Branch's interests in safeguarding the integrity of its deliberative processes and its conduct of the Nation's foreign policy outweigh the stated interest of the Subcommittee in obtaining this information for oversight purposes. It is, therefore, my view that these documents may properly be withheld from the Subcommittee at the present time.

III.

Finally, a brief word is in order concerning the negotiations between the Department of the Interior and the Subcommittee during this dispute. [T]he courts have referred to the obligation of each Branch to accommodate the legitimate needs of the other. *See United States v. American Tel. & Tel. Co.*, 567 F.2d 121, 127, 130 (D.C. Cir. 1977); *see generally United States v. Nixon, supra.* The accommodation required is not simply an exchange of concessions or a test of political strength. It is an obligation of each Branch to make a principled effort to acknowledge, and if possible to meet, the legitimate needs of the other Branch.

It is my view that the Executive Branch has made such a principled effort at accommodation in the present case.... In contrast, the Subcommittee has not to date shown itself sensitive to the legitimate needs of the Executive Branch. As noted, it has never formally stated its need for the materials beyond a generalized interest in "oversight." To date, the Subcommittee has shown little interest in accommodating legitimate interests of the Executive Branch in safeguarding the privacy of its deliberative processes and conducting the Nation's foreign policy. This lack of accommodation on the Subcommittee's part lends further support to my conclusion that the documents in question may properly be withheld....

Sincerely,

WILLIAM FRENCH SMITH,
Attorney General.

––––––––––

U.S. HOUSE OF REPRESENTATIVES,
OFFICE OF THE CLERK,
November 10, 1981.

MEMORANDUM

Re Attorney General's letter concerning claim of executive privilege for Department of Interior documents.

HON. JOHN DINGELL,
Chairman, Subcommittee on Oversight and Investigations,
U.S. House of Representatives.

... The Attorney General's letter seeking to justify an assertion of executive privilege is based on one fundamental premise: that such a privilege can be asserted for material anywhere within the executive branch, even when it has been created and communicated within or between one of the departments.... The claim that documents generated within the Department of Interior are within the privilege, including "staff level advice to policymakers," concerning duties devolved upon the Secretary by statute is unfounded.... [I]n *In re Attorney General of the United States*, 596 F.2d 58 (2d Cir. 1979), the court rejected the claim advanced by the Department that records generated within the executive branch were not subject to civil subpoena and distinguished *United States v. Nixon*.

> Moreover, in *Nixon* the President claimed a privilege as to his personal papers. Here the Attorney General seeks to protect from disclosure official records that he holds or has under supervision in *his official capacity only*. 596 F.2d at 62 (emphasis added).

Likewise here records under the control of the Secretary of Interior, generated pursuant to duties devolved upon him by statute, are neither "personal" to the President nor subject to a claim of privilege. "Finally, and most important, the executive responsibilities and constitutional status of the Attorney General, do not compare to those of the President." Of course, the same is true of the Department of Interior, and as the court further declared the "Attorney General has no greater statutory authority over his department's official records than does any other cabinet officer."

The Attorney General's position that Congress has a legitimate need to acquire preliminary, predecisional documents from the executive "during internal deliberations only in the rarest of circumstances," is unsupported by any citation of authority. What case law there is concerning executive "pre-decisional" materials arises in a totally inapposite context. The Attorney General attempts, in effect, to assert Exemption 5 of the Freedom of Information Act [5 U.S.C. § 552(b)(5)(exempting from disclosure those matters that are "intra-agency memorandums or letters which would not be available by law to a party other than an agency in litigation with the agency")] against a congressional request for information. Of course, Congress decided not to allow the exemptions in that the Act to be used as a basis for withholding documents from the Congress. *Id.* § 552(c). Moreover, while the Congress recognized the interest in full and frank exchange of ideas during agency decisionmaking in adopting Exemption 5, its "decision that certain information falls within Exemption 5 therefore rests fundamentally on the conclusion that, unless protected from public disclosure, information of that type would not flow freely within the agency." *Mead Data Cent., Inc. v. U.S. Department of Air Force*, 566 F.2d 242, 256 (D.C. Cir. 1977)(emphasis added). And as one court has concluded in construing Exemption 5:

> The same policy considerations which favor a narrow construction of the exemptions—desirability of maximum access to government information and minimum secrecy— support a broad interpretation of *the provision which safeguards unimpeded congressional access*... Congress, whether as a body, *through its committees*, or otherwise, *must have the widest possible access to executive branch information* if it is to perform its manifold responsibilities effectively. *Murphy v. Department of the Army*, 613 F.2d 1151, 1158 (D.C. Cir. 1979) (emphasis added).

In addition, Exemption 5 "incorporates the governmental privilege developed in discovery cases" to protect documents used in formulating policy, *id.*, and the courts have already held since *United States v. Nixon*, 418 U.S. 683 (1974), that civil litigants can overcome the President's presumptive privilege upon a proper showing and obtain, for purposes of discovery, even documents constituting communications to the President from his advisors and communications among his closest White House advisors.

Dellums v. Powell, 561 F.2d 242, 245-46 (D.C. Cir.) *cert. denied*, 434 U.S. 880 (1977). *Sun Oil Company v. United States*, 514 F.2d 1020, 1026 (Ct. Cl. 1975)(subpoena for White House papers relevant to plaintiff oil company's claim that government breached its contract for off-shore oil exploration by denying permission to construct platform for development of lease based not on environmental reasons but on basis of political decision forced on Secretary of Interior by White House). Since civil litigants can overcome Presidential privilege, then clearly Congress can.

The Attorney General's letter asserts *ex cathedra* and without citation of a single authority that "the interest of Congress in obtaining information for oversight purposes is, I believe, considerably weaker than its interest when specific legislative proposals are in question" and that "congressional oversight of Executive Branch actions is justifiable only as a means of facilitating the legislative task of enacting, amending or repealing laws." In arriving at these baseless conclusions, the Attorney General ignores an unbroken line of Supreme Court precedents to the contrary, many of which were decided in the very context of legislative reviews of executive action.

In fact, in *Sinclair v. United States*, 279 U.S. 263 (1929), the Senate conducted an investigation into fraudulent oil and gas leases of government property after the executive branch instituted suit for recovery and applied to empanel a special grand jury. The Court rejected the recalcitrant witness' contention that the Congress had departed from its legislative mooring and instead affirmed that Congress may "through its committees,... require pertinent disclosures in aid of its own constitutional power [notwithstanding that] the information sought to be elicited may also be of use in [judicial] suits."... It can hardly be argued this late in the day, in light of the Supreme Court's holding that Congress' power over public lands "is without limitations," *Kleppe v. New Mexico*, 426 U.S. 529, 539 (1976) that congressional requests for information on determinations of reciprocity relating to federal lands are beyond legislative reach.

Indeed, a review of the intent of the Framers of the Constitution shows that Congress' power to conduct oversight was far clearer in their minds than Congress' power to investigate in aid of legislation. "An examination of pre-constitutional history reveals that both the English Parliament and the colonial legislatures engaged in examinations of executive conduct and asserted the right to executive information. As William Pitt the elder stated in 1742 regarding the powers of Parliament, 'We are called the Grand Inquest of the Nation, and as such it is our duty to inquire into every step of public management, either abroad or at home, in order to see that nothing has been done amiss.' " J. Hamilton, *The Power to Probe*, 172 (1976). The first congressional investigation, the inquiry into General St. Clair's defeat by the Indians in 1792, was not in aid of specific legislation. 3 Annals of Cong. 490-494 (1792). Congress has since that time inquired into executive administration of the law without necessarily framing legislation based on the investigation. For example, the House inquired into whether General Jackson misapplied funds appropriated for the support of the army. 35 Annals of Cong. 717 (1819). Although the Committee found the disbursements under investigation were "irregular and unauthorized," H.R. Rep. No. 72, 16th Cong., 1st Sess. 12 (1820), the committee declined to devise specific "legislative remedies against recurrence of these disorders"....

The courts have repeatedly and consistently instructed the executive branch that it cannot unilaterally determine what is relevant to Congress, or how to interpret its internal rules.... *Gravel v. United States*, 408 U.S. 606 (1972). The Court has made it clear that the judiciary will "not go beyond the narrow confines of determining that a committee's inquiry may be fairly deemed within its province." *Tenney v. Brandhove*, 341 U.S. 367, 378 (1951).... Similarly, any disputes regarding the jurisdiction of the parent committee over the subject matter, or the relevance of the documents to bills pending before it, are determinations to be made within the Congress and are not reasons for non-compliance.

As the Court has recognized, "... the investigative function—like any research ... takes the searchers up some 'blind alleys' and into nonproductive enterprises. To be a valid legislative inquiry there need be no predictable end result." *Eastland v. United States Servicemen's Fund*, 421 U.S. 491, 509 (1975)(emphasis added).

Subsidiary to this assertion is the Attorney General's claim that oversight which is used as a means of participating in the executive's decision making process ... constitutes "interference" with execution of the law.... Legislative information gathering simply is not, and has never been construed by the courts to constitute interference in the administration of laws. The Subcommittee, by issuance of a subpoena, does not direct the Secretary to act in any particular manner....

The final position of the Attorney General, without citation of authority, is that the subpoenaed documents regarding implementation of a statute enacted by Congress "relate to sensitive foreign policy considerations" and are therefore outside congressional purview.... By express constitutional grant, the Congress has authority "[t]o regulate Commerce with foreign Nations," U.S. Const., art. I, §8, cl. 3.... "One of the most important functions of the President in the conduct of American foreign relations has always been as agent of Congress to effectuate the purposes and administer the details of legislative policy." The Congress has announced its policy in ... the Mineral Lands Leasing Act and to the extent that the President participates in effectuation of that policy through the Secretary of Interior, Congress clearly has the power to review the Secretary's implementation of statutes it passes.

> STANLEY M. BRAND,
> General Counsel to the Clerk,
> U.S. House of Representatives

A vote by the full House on Watt's contempt was averted on March 18, 1982, when President Reagan relented and permitted inspection of the papers withheld. Rep. Dingell had proposed a last-ditch compromise on March 5: the Secretary would permit the subcommittee members and their staffs to review the documents for 8 hours in the subcommittee hearing room. The compromise that the White House offered was 4 hours' review for the members only—which was accepted. Representative Dingell reserved, in writing, all rights of the subcommittee under its subpoena, but no further enforcement was undertaken.

---

1. First, some overall questions about the two case studies: given the outcomes, what was the relative success of the branches in these disputes? Do the case studies show that Congress will ultimately obtain what it wants if the committees have enough tenacity, and enough support from their houses? Both sides staked out broad legal positions. Consider why they did so, and whether narrower arguments would have been more responsible and effective. How could the negotiation process be improved?

2. In the Gorsuch controversy, the Department expressed a fear of congressional pressure on prosecutorial discretion if law enforcement files were revealed. Is that a realistic fear? Would the rights of suspects be seriously at risk? Note that outright congressional intervention in law enforcement can lead to a due process violation. *See Pillsbury Co. v. FTC*, 354 F.2d 952 (5th Cir. 1966)(condemning pressure on administrative adjudication, exerted in open committee hearings). How is the situation different if pressure may occur behind the scenes? Is it enough to say that the executive has the constitutional responsibility to resist improper intervention from any source?

3. The Department also expressed the fear that the committees would leak sensitive material submitted to them. As we will see in later chapters, this is a frequent argument for executive secrecy in foreign affairs and war powers controversies. Preliminarily, do you think this is a serious problem, considering the frequency of leaks from within the executive itself? What of the Attorney General's point that the Rules of Congress ensure access to committee materials by every member of the house, including those bitterly opposed to the administration in power?

4. The Attorney General argues that control over law enforcement files is a non-delegable responsibility of the President. On this and other points, consider the historical summary by Professor Cox, *supra*. Does the historical record support the Attorney General's position? What compromises can he make in a particular instance without waiving claims to executive power by muddying the historical record? On this score, note Mr. Brand's allegation that the Department had been inconsistent in its approach to executive privilege, and his citation of an instance in which it had been more forthcoming. What incentive does that argument from Congress give the Attorney General in future cases?

5. Consider the Department's attempt to obtain a declaratory judgment in the Gorsuch imbroglio. Was it the best course of action? What were the alternatives? And were the congressional defendants all amenable to suit? Review the treatment of this issue in *U.S. v. A.T.&T.*, *supra*.

6. In the Watt case, the Attorney General takes a broad view of the need for deliberative confidentiality in the executive. Do you concur? Note that this aspect of executive privilege is always contingent at best—it is qualified at the outset by the prospect of leaks by those involved, and it is eroded over time by the production of memoirs, the activity of historians, and the availability of the official records of Presidents and other senior officials. Why, then, does the executive think it so important to shield debate from Congress? Is it less a matter of principle than of practical politics, that control of access to information closely equates with power to determine policy? And for Congress, note the advantages in oversight if policy alternatives and their fate can be drawn directly from the participants. The credibility and wisdom of official positions can be much more readily assessed. To this, the executive can rejoin that political accountability should attend positions adopted by officers assigned to make them, and not tentative or rejected ideas from the staff. Where do you come out on all this?

7. In the case quoted in the Brand memorandum to Chairman Dingell, is the *Nixon* case accurately characterized? Did it deal with his personal conversations, not official ones? And do you think that *Nixon* establishes an executive privilege only for the Oval Office, as Brand contends, or for the entire executive branch, as the Attorney General would have it?

8. Where do we go from here? For an extensive analysis of the competing views of the three branches on executive privilege, and a critical assessment of the executive's handling of the Gorsuch and Watt episodes, *see* Shane, *Legal Disagreement and Negotiation in a Government of Laws: The Case of Executive Privilege Claims Against Congress*, 71 Minn. L. Rev. 461 (1987). Shane argues that the political branches should establish a *modus vivendi* to permit the maximum resolution of these disputes through "problem-solving negotiation," rather than through "hard bargaining" or resort to the courts. In a June, 1987, resolution, the Administrative Law Section of the American Bar Association recommended that the ABA endorse this approach.

In the complete version of a 1976 statement to Congress that is excerpted in Chapter Five, below, Assistant Attorney General Rex Lee suggested the creation of jurisdiction in the federal courts to hear civil actions for the enforcement of congressional subpoenas. For a similar proposal, *see* Hamilton & Grabow, *A Legislative Proposal for Resolving Executive Privilege Disputes Precipitated by Congressional Subpoenas*, 21 Harv. J. Legis. 145 (1984); *see also* Note, *The Conflict Between Executive Privilege and Congressional Oversight: The Gorsuch Controversy*, 1983 Duke L.J. 1333. For an argument that a criminal enforcement provision is preferable, and that Congress should have resort to independent counsel to enforce its subpoenas, *see* Brand & Connelly, *Constitutional Confrontations: Preserving a Prompt and Orderly Means By Which Congress May Enforce Investigative Demands Against Executive Branch Officials*, 36 Cath. U. L. Rev. 71 (1986).

As counsel to the House Judiciary Committee, consider what legislation you might recommend to expedite resolution of executive privilege disputes with Congress. Imagine a meeting among congressional staff and White House and Justice Department lawyers concerning such legislation. What concerns, legal and political, would you raise in such a discussion?

Note on the Political Question Doctrine

Among interbranch conflicts, executive privilege controversies present the courts with especially serious problems of justiciability, as the preceding materials reveal. Therefore, we pause to sketch existing views of the "political question" doctrine, under which most courts address the justiciability of separation of powers issues. We will encounter these problems again repeatedly in the foreign affairs and war powers chapters below.

Modern political question analysis customarily begins with *Baker v. Carr*, 369 U.S. 186 (1962), in which the Court held that equal protection challenges to legislative districting schemes are justiciable. Justice Brennan's majority opinion delineated six factors that identify the presence of a political question:

> Prominent on the surface of any case held to involve a political question is found a textually demonstrable constitutional commitment of the issue to a coordinate political department; or a lack of judicially discoverable and manageable standards for resolving it; or the impossibility of deciding without an initial policy determination of a kind clearly for nonjudicial discretion; or the impossibility of a court's undertaking independent resolution without expressing lack of the respect due coordinate branches of government; or an unusual need for unquestioning adherence to a political decision already made; or the potentiality

of embarrassment from multifarious pronouncements by various departments on one question.

Subsequently, in *Powell v. McCormack*, 395 U.S. 486 (1969), the Court held that a congressional decision to exclude a member was justiciable. The Court gave great weight to the first of the *Baker* factors—whether there is "a textually demonstrable constitutional commitment of the issue to a coordinate political department." The Court said that, in order to determine whether such a commitment exists, "we must interpret the Constitution," and proceeded to examine the clause in Article I, § 5, that grants Congress the power to judge the qualifications of its members. The Court read the clause narrowly, as allowing exclusion only for failure to meet the Constitution's stated qualifications of age, citizenship, and residence. So viewed, the clause was not a broad grant of power to Congress to exclude members without judicial review.

The Court's decision in *Powell* led observers to suggest that the "commitment" issue is the core of the political question doctrine, and that the doctrine itself is almost indistinguishable from the merits. *See generally* Symposium, *Comments on* Powell v. McCormack, 17 U.C.L.A. L. Rev. 1 (1969). Professor Sandalow concluded, *id.* at 172-73:

> Having begun by asking the right question, whether there was a "constitutional commitment of the issue" to the House, the Court proceeded to answer a quite different one, whether the "qualifications" which Article I, Section 5 authorized the House to "judge" were only those specified in [the Constitution]. The opinion reflects, in short, a classic instance of confusion between "jurisdiction"—the power to decide—and "the merits"—the correctness of decisions.
>
> The source of this confusion, it seems fairly clear, is the Court's assumption that it bears "responsibility . . . to act as the ultimate interpreter of the Constitution." [quoting the Court, 395 U.S. at 549.] On that premise, it is but a short step to the conclusion that the Court is obligated to intervene when another branch of government acts in a manner prohibited by the Constitution.

See also Henkin, *Is There a "Political Question" Doctrine?*, 85 Yale L. J. 597 (1976). Professor Henkin argues that the judiciary does not need to be blind to any part of the Constitution. He argues that many of the political question cases could as easily have held that the action in question was within constitutional limits, and therefore was open only to political challenge.

For the contrasting view that courts should regard constitutional issues concerning the respective powers of Congress and the President as nonjusticiable, *see* J. Choper, Judicial Review and the National Political Process 260-379 (1980), *reviewed by* McGowan, *Constitutional Adjudication: Deciding When to Decide*, 79 Mich. L. Rev. 616 (1980); Monaghan, *Book Review*, 94 Harv. L. Rev. 296 (1980).

After the *Nixon* case, *supra*, we noted the Court's cursory treatment of the "who decides" issue. Can you sketch a fuller analysis for executive privilege cases? The lower courts have dealt with the issue in the cases involving congressional subpoenas. In *Senate Select Committee on Presidential Compaign Activities v. Nixon*, 498 F. 2d 725 (D.C. Cir. 1974), the court, relying on its earlier decision in *Nixon v. Sirica*, 487 F.2d 700 (D.C. Cir. 1973), rejected a claim that the dispute between the Senate Watergate Committee and Nixon was a nonjusticiable political question. The same result was reached in *United States v. A. T. & T. Co., supra*, where the court said (567 F.2d at 126):

> The simple fact of a conflict between the legislative and executive branches over a congressional subpoena does not preclude judicial resolution. ... Normally, when the court abstains on political question grounds it acquiesces in a "commitment of the issue" to one of the political branches for resolution of the merits. ... That branch is recognized as having the constitutional authority to make a decision that settles the dispute. Where the dispute consists of a clash of authority between two branches, however, judicial abstention does not lead to orderly resolution of the dispute. No one branch is identified as having final authority in the area of concern.

Finding that there were manageable standards for resolution of the controversy, the court concluded: "In our view, neither the traditional political question doctrine nor any close adaptation thereof is appropriate where neither of the conflicting political branches has a clear and unequivocal constitutional title." Do you agree that interbranch conflicts create a special need for judicial umpiring?

4. Congressional regulation of access to presidential documents

Until the Nixon Presidency, it was the custom of Presidents leaving office to collect their papers and to dispose of them as they liked. The following case reveals an abrupt change in that practice:

Nixon v. Administrator of General Services
433 U.S. 425 (1977)

[Following his resignation as President, Richard Nixon reached an agreement with the Administrator of General Services, governing access to and care and storage of 42 million pages of presidential papers and nearly 900 tape recordings of presidential conversations. Under the agreement, Nixon retained title to the documents with the express purpose of eventually donating them to the United States. The tapes were to remain on deposit for five years, after which the U.S. would take title, but Nixon could direct that certain tapes be destroyed, and, in any event, the tapes would be destroyed at the time of his death or on September 1, 1984, whichever came first.

Largely to abrogate this agreement, Congress, within months, enacted the Presidential Recordings and Materials Preservation Act, note following 44 U.S.C. § 2111, directing the Administrator to "receive, obtain, or retain ... complete possession and control" over the Nixon materials, and to promulgate regulations governing public access to them, taking account of the following factors:

> (1) the need to provide the public with the full truth, at the earliest reasonable date, of the abuses of governmental power popularly identified under the generic term "Watergate";
>
> (2) the need to make such recordings and materials available for use in judicial proceedings; ...

(5) the need to protect any party's opportunity to assert any legally or constitutionally based right or privilege which would prevent or otherwise limit access
to such recordings and materials; . . . and;

(7) the need to give to Richard M. Nixon, or his heirs, for his sole custody and
use, tape recordings and other materials which are not likely to be related to
the need described in paragraph (2) and are not otherwise of general historical
significance.

Nixon sued to enjoin the enforcement of the Act and its implementing regulations.
The three-judge District Court considered and rejected only facial challenges to the
Act; regulations were yet to be drafted. The Supreme Court, in an opinion by Justice
BRENNAN, affirmed the judgment:]

IV
Claims Concerning the Autonomy of the Executive Branch

A
Separation of Powers

We reject at the outset appellant's argument that the Act's regulation of the disposition of Presidential materials within the Executive Branch constitutes, without
more, a violation of the principle of separation of powers. Neither President Ford nor
President Carter supports this claim. The Executive Branch became a party to the
Act's regulation when President Ford signed the Act into law, and the administration
of President Carter . . . vigorously supports affirmance of the District Court's judgment
sustaining its constitutionality. Moreover, the control over the materials remains in
the Executive Branch. The Administrator of General Services, who must promulgate
and administer the regulations that are the keystone of the statutory scheme, is himself
an official of the Executive Branch, appointed by the President. The career archivists
appointed to do the initial screening for the purpose of selecting out and returning
to appellant his private and personal papers similarly are Executive Branch employees.

Appellant's argument is in any event based on an interpretation of the separation-
of-powers doctrine inconsistent with the origins of that doctrine, recent decisions of
the Court, and the contemporary realities of our political system. True, it has been
said that "each of the three general departments of government [must remain] entirely
free from the control or coercive influence, direct or indirect, of either of the others
. . . ," *Humphrey's Executor v. United States*, 295 U.S. 602, 629 (1935), and that
"[t]he sound application of a principle that makes one master in his own house
precludes him from imposing his control in the house of another who is master there."
Id., at 630.

But the more pragmatic, flexible approach of Madison in the Federalist Papers and
later of Justice Story[5] was expressly affirmed by this Court only three years ago in

---

5. Madison in The Federalist No. 47, reviewing the origin of the separation-of-powers
doctrine, remarked that Montesquieu, the "oracle" always consulted on the subject, "did not
mean that these departments ought to have no *partial agency* in, or no *controul* over the acts
of each other. His meaning, as his own words import . . . can amount to no more than this,
that where the *whole* power of one department is exercised by the same hands which possess
the *whole* power of another department, the fundamental principles of a free constitution, are

United States v. Nixon, supra. There ... the Court squarely rejected the argument that the Constitution contemplates a complete division of authority between the three branches. ... [W]e therefore find that appellant's argument rests upon an "archaic view of the separation of powers as requiring three airtight departments of government."

Rather, in determining whether the Act disrupts the proper balance between the coordinate branches, the proper inquiry focuses on the extent to which it prevents the Executive Branch from accomplishing its constitutionally assigned functions. *United States v. Nixon*, 418 U.S., at 711-712. Only where the potential for disruption is present must we then determine whether that impact is justified by an overriding need to promote objectives within the constitutional authority of Congress.

It is therefore highly relevant that the Act provides for custody of the materials in officials of the Executive Branch. ... For it is clearly less intrusive to place custody and screening of the materials within the Executive Branch itself than to have Congress or some outside agency perform the screening function. While the materials may also be made available for use in judicial proceedings, this provision is expressly qualified by any rights, defense, or privileges that any person may invoke including, of course, a valid claim of executive privilege. Similarly, although some of the materials may eventually be made available for public access, the Act expressly recognizes ... defenses or privileges available to appellant or the Executive Branch. ...

Thus, whatever are the future possibilities for constitutional conflict in the promulgation of regulations respecting public access to particular documents, nothing contained in the Act renders it unduly disruptive of the Executive Branch and, therefore, unconstitutional on its face. And, of course, there is abundant statutory precedent for the regulation and mandatory disclosure of documents in the possession of the Executive Branch. *See, e.g.,* the Freedom of Information Act, 5 U.S.C. § 552; the Privacy Act of 1974, 5 U.S.C. § 552a; the Government in the Sunshine Act, 5 U.S.C. § 552b; the Federal Records Act, 44 U.S.C. § 2101 *et seq.* Such regulation of material generated in the Executive Branch has never been considered invalid as an invasion of its autonomy.[8] Similar congressional power to regulate Executive Branch documents

---

subverted." (emphasis in original).

Similarly, Justice Story wrote:

"[W]hen we speak of a separation of the three great departments of government, and maintain that that separation is indispensable to public liberty, we are to understand this maxim in a limited sense. It is not meant to affirm that they must be kept wholly and entirely separate and distinct, and have no common link of connection or dependence, the one upon the other, in the slightest degree." 1 J. Story, Commentaries on the Constitution § 525 (M. Bigelow, 5th ed. 1905).

8. We see no reason to engage in the debate whether appellant has legal title to the materials. ... [E]ven if legal title is his, the materials are not thereby immune from regulation. It has been accepted at least since Justice Story's opinion in *Folsom v. Marsh*, 9 Fed.Cas. 342, 347 (No. 4,901) (CC Mass. 1841), that regardless of where legal title lies, "from the nature of the public service, or the character of documents, embracing historical, military, or diplomatic information, it may be the right, and even the duty, of the government, to give them publicity, even against the will of the writers." ... Significantly, ... although indicating a view that the materials belonged to appellant, the [Attorney General's opinion to President Ford] acknowledged that "Presidential materials" without qualification "are peculiarly affected by a public interest" which may justify subjecting "the absolute ownership rights" to certain "limitations directly related to the character of the documents as records of government activity." 43 Op.Atty.Gen. No. 1 (1974). ...

exists in this instance, a power that is augmented by the important interests that the Act seeks to attain.

B
Presidential Privilege

[W]e next consider appellant's more narrowly defined claim that the Presidential privilege shields these records from archival scrutiny. We start with what was established in *United States v. Nixon, supra*—that the privilege is a qualified one. . . . [T]his case initially involves appellant's assertion of a privilege against the very Executive Branch in whose name the privilege is invoked. The nonfederal appellees rely on this apparent anomaly to contend that only an incumbent President can assert the privilege of the Presidency. . . . Nevertheless, we think that the Solicitor General states the sounder view, and we adopt it:

> " . . . Unless he can give his advisers some assurance of confidentiality, a President could not expect to receive the full and frank submissions of facts and opinions upon which effective discharge of his duties depends. The confidentiality necessary to this exchange cannot be measured by the few months or years between the submission of the information and the end of the President's tenure; the privilege is not for the benefit of the President as an individual, but for the benefit of the Republic. Therefore the privilege survives the individual President's tenure."

At the same time, however, the fact that neither President Ford nor President Carter supports appellant's claim detracts from the weight of his contention that the Act impermissibly intrudes into the executive function and the needs of the Executive Branch. . . .

The appellant may legitimately assert the Presidential privilege, of course, only as to those materials whose contents fall within the scope of the privilege. . . . [In *Nixon*,] the Court held that the privilege is limited to communications "in performance of [a President's] responsibilities," . . . "of his office," . . . and made "in the process of shaping policies and making decisions." Of the estimated 42 million pages of documents and 880 tape recordings whose custody is at stake, the District Court concluded that the appellant's claim of Presidential privilege could apply at most to the 200,000 items with which the appellant was personally familiar.

The appellant bases his claim of Presidential privilege in this case on the assertion that the potential disclosure of communications given to the appellant in confidence would adversely affect the ability of future Presidents to obtain the candid advice necessary for effective decision-making. We are called upon to adjudicate that claim, however, only with respect to the process by which the materials will be screened and catalogued by professional archivists. For any eventual public access will be governed by the guidelines of § 104, which direct the Administrator to take into account "the need to protect any party's opportunity to assert any . . . constitutionally based right or privilege," § 104(a)(5), and the need to return purely private materials to the appellant, § 104(a)(7).

In view of these specific directions, there is no reason to believe that the restriction on public access ultimately established by regulation will not be adequate to preserve executive confidentiality. An absolute barrier to all outside disclosure is not practically or constitutionally necessary. . . . [T]here has never been an expectation that the confidences of the Executive Office are absolute and unyielding. All former Presidents from President Hoover to President Johnson have deposited their papers in Presidential libraries (an example appellant has said he intended to follow) for governmental preservation and eventual disclosure.[12] The screening processes for ... these libraries also involved comprehensive review by archivists, often involving materials upon which access restrictions ultimately have been imposed. The expectation of the confidentiality of executive communications thus has always been limited and subject to erosion over time after an administration leaves office....

The screening constitutes a very limited intrusion by personnel in the Executive Branch sensitive to executive concerns. These very personnel have performed the identical task in each of the Presidential libraries without any suggestion that such activity has in any way interfered with executive confidentiality. Indeed, in light of this consistent historical practice, past and present executive officials must be well aware of the possibility that, at some time in the future, their communications may be reviewed on a confidential basis by professional archivists....

Moreover, adequate justifications are shown for this limited intrusion into executive confidentiality comparable to those held to justify the *in camera* inspection of the District Court sustained in *United States v. Nixon*.... The legislative history of the Act clearly reveals that ... Congress acted to ... deal with the perceived need to preserve the materials for legitimate historical and governmental purposes. An incumbent President should not be dependent on happenstance or the whim of a prior President when he seeks access to records of past decisions that define or channel current governmental obligations. Nor should the American people's ability to reconstruct and come to terms with their history be truncated by an analysis of Presidential privilege that focuses only on the needs of the present. Congress can legitimately act to rectify the hit-or-miss approach that has characterized past attempts to protect these substantial interests by entrusting the materials to expert handling by trusted and disinterested professionals.

Other substantial public interests that led Congress to seek to preserve appellant's materials were the desire to restore public confidence in our political processes by ... facilitating a full airing of the events leading to appellant's resignation, and Congress' need to understand how those political processes had in fact operated in order to gauge the necessity for remedial legislation. Thus by preserving these materials, the Act may be thought to aid the legislative process and thus to be within the scope of Congress' broad investigative power. And, of course, the Congress repeatedly referred to the importance of the materials to the Judiciary in the event that they shed light upon issues in civil or criminal litigation, a social interest that cannot be doubted.

In light of these objectives, the scheme adopted by Congress for preservation of the appellant's Presidential materials cannot be said to be overbroad. It is true that among the voluminous materials to be screened by archivists are some materials that bear no relationship to any of these objectives (and whose prompt return to appellant

---

12. [I]n the Hoover Library there are no restrictions on Presidential papers, ... and in the Roosevelt Library, less than 0.5% of the materials is restricted. There is no evidence in the record as to the ... Truman or Eisenhower Libraries, but in the Kennedy Library, 85% of the materials has been processed, and of the processed materials, only 0.6% is under donor (as distinguished from security-related) restriction. In the Johnson Library, ... more than 99% of all nonsecurity classified materials is unrestricted. In each of the Presidential libraries, provision has been made for the removal of the restrictions with the passage of time.

is therefore mandated by § 104(a)(7)). But these materials are commingled with other materials whose preservation the Act requires, for the appellant, like his predecessors, made no systematic attempt to segregate official, personal, and private materials. . . .

Thus, as in the Presidential libraries, the intermingled state of the materials requires the comprehensive review and classification contemplated by the Act if Congress' important objectives are to be furthered. . . . [G]iven the safeguards built into the Act . . . and the minimal nature of the intrusion into the confidentiality of the Presidency, we believe that the claims of Presidential privilege clearly must yield to the important congressional purposes of preserving the materials and maintaining access to them for lawful governmental and historical purposes. . . . If the broadly written protections of the Act should nevertheless prove inadequate to safeguard appellant's rights or to prevent usurpation of executive powers, there will be time enough to consider that problem in a specific factual context. For the present, we hold, in agreement with the District Court, that the Act on its face does not violate the Presidential privilege. . . .

VI
First Amendment

During his Presidency appellant served also as head of his national political party and spent a substantial portion of his working time on partisan political matters. Records arising from his political activities, like his private and personal records, are not segregated from the great mass of materials. He argues that the Act's archival screening process therefore necessarily entails invasion of his constitutionally protected rights of associational privacy and political speech. . . .

It is, of course, true that involvement in partisan politics is closely protected by the First Amendment, *Buckley v. Valeo*, 424 U.S. 1 (1976), and that "compelled disclosure, in itself, can seriously infringe on privacy of association and belief guaranteed by First Amendment." But a compelling public need that cannot be met in a less restrictive way will override those interests, "particularly when the 'free functioning of our national institutions' is involved." *Buckley v. Valeo*. Since no less restrictive way than archival screening has been suggested as a means for identification of materials to be returned to appellant, the burden of that screening is presently the measure of his First Amendment claim. The extent of any such burden, however, is speculative in light of the Act's terms protecting appellant from improper public disclosures and guaranteeing him full judicial review before any public access is permitted. As the District Court concluded, the First Amendment claim is clearly outweighed by the important governmental interests promoted by the Act.

For the same reasons, we find no merit in appellant's argument that the Act's scheme for custody and archival screening of the materials "necessarily inhibits [the] freedom of political activity [of future Presidents] and thereby reduces the 'quantity and diversity' of the political speech and association that the Nation will be receiving from its leaders." It is significant, moreover, that this concern has not deterred President Ford from signing the Act into law, or President Carter from urging this Court's affirmance of the judgment of the District Court.

VII
Bill of Attainder Clause

Finally, we address appellant's argument that the Act constitutes a bill of attainder proscribed by Art. I, § 9, of the Constitution. His argument is that Congress acted on the premise that he had engaged in "misconduct," was an "unreliable custodian" of his own documents, and generally was deserving of a *"legislative judgment* of blameworthiness." Thus, he argues, the Act is pervaded with the key features of a bill of attainder: a law that legislatively determines guilt and inflicts punishment upon an identifiable individual without provision of the protections of a judicial trial.

[The Court concluded that the Act did not constitute a bill of attainder because no feature of the Act constituted legislative punishment as historically understood, the Act served legitimate purposes in maintaining evidence for criminal trials and assuring the preservation of historical records, and no punitive intent appeared from the legislative history.

Six justices wrote separate opinions as follows:

Justice STEVENS concurred on the ground that Nixon resigned his office "under unique circumstances," that provided "a legitimate justification for the specificity of the statute."

Justice WHITE concurred in the judgment and, except for the majority's discussion of the Bill of Attainder issue, in the Court's opinion. He would have found the statute valid under the Bill of Attainder Clause because it imposed no "punishment."

Justice POWELL, concurring in the judgment, joined the Court's opinion, except for its treatment of the separation of powers and privacy questions. He argued that the Act fell within the ambit of Congress's "broad authority to investigate, to inform the public, and, ultimately, to legislate against suspected corruption and abuse of power in the Executive Branch." It avoided usurping any inherently executive function by entrusting enforcement of its provisions solely to executive officers. Powell thought that executive interests were reduced by President Carter's representation that "the Act is consistent with 'the effective discharge of the President's powers,' " the same position President Ford took in signing the Act.

Justice BLACKMUN, although generally agreeing with Justice Powell, thought that President Ford's approval of the Act did not dispose of the separation-of-powers questions. "The fact that [he] signed the Act does not mean that he necessarily approved of its every detail. Political realities often guide a President to a decision not to veto."

Chief Justice BURGER dissented, arguing that the Act violated the separation of powers principle by coercing the president in his disposition of presidential papers, that the act usurped exclusively presidential functions of controlling presidential files, records, and papers, and that it violated the President's privilege in confidential communications. He further argued that the Act amounted to a "Bill of Attainder" by singling out a class of one for detrimental treatment.

Justice REHNQUIST dissented because the Act would "restrain the necessary free flow of information to and from the present President and future Presidents," and that so substantial an intrusion upon the effective discharge of presidential duties violated the separation of powers.]

---

1. Note the majority's separation of powers analysis in *Nixon v. GSA*. The Court defines the issue as whether the executive is prevented "from accomplishing its constitutionally assigned functions." The Court then appears to balance the Act's intrusion on executive functions against the justifications advanced for them. Is this "functional" analysis similar to the Court's approach in *United States v. Nixon*? Compare the Court's use of formalist analysis in cases such as *Chadha*. What outcome would

a formalist approach produce here? Presumably, functional analysis allows more mixing of the powers of the branches than does formalism. Is one of these approaches better for all cases, or only some of them? If the latter, which ones?

2. Do you agree with Justice Powell that the positions of Presidents Ford and Carter should be dispositive on the question of the executive interests at stake in this case?

3. Advise the Attorney General on the constitutionality of proposed legislation requiring that, 15 years after issuance, all unclassified government documents shall be available for public inspection.

4. Final regulations under the Presidential Recordings and Materials Preservation Act were promulgated on December 16, 1977. The D.C. Circuit upheld summary judgment for GSA in President Nixon's legal challenge to the regulations. *Nixon v. Freeman*, 670 F.2d 346 (D.C. Cir.), *cert. denied*, 459 U.S. 1035 (1982).

5. In 1978, President Carter signed the Presidential Records Act, 44 U.S.C. § 2201-07, which provides for government ownership of presidential records, except for the private papers of the President. There are restrictions on access to certain categories of information (such as classified material and the President's deliberations with his advisers) for not more than 12 years. Thereafter, access is permitted under the Freedom of Information Act, but exemption 5, shielding policy deliberations, is not available. The Department of Justice testified in support of the constitutionality of the Act. Presidential Records Act of 1978, Hearings on H.R. 10998 and Related Bills Before a Subcomm. of the House Comm. on Government Operations, 95th Cong., 2d Sess. (1978).

B. Legal Accountability of the President and His "Inner Circle"

The preceding materials, concerning Congress' access to executive communications and its power to regulate the disposition of presidential documents, revealed ways of fostering the legal and political accountability of the President and his advisers. Two other legislative means to this end are: extending administrative procedure statutes to the President and his advisers (considered in subsection B-1 below), and subjecting the President's advisers to congressional oversight through confirmation and post-appointment hearings (subsection B-2).

Arguably, the "energy" and "dispatch" of the executive would be enhanced if the President's closest advisers were shielded from the rules of procedural regularity and accountability that Congress has applied to subordinate federal officers and agencies. Whether or not the Constitution affords any such protection, whether Congress should so limit itself is a matter of regular and heated debate.

Subsection B-3 considers the tradeoff between unfettered executive action and legal accountability that is implicit in doctrines immunizing certain executive officials from tort liability for their official acts.

While reading the following materials, consider the plausibility of constitutional arguments that would limit Congress' power to (1) provide for judicial review of presidential acts, (2) require Senate approval for presidential appointments, or (3) remove the immunity from damages that is otherwise available to senior executive officials.

1. *Applicability of administrative procedure statutes*
a. Administrative Procedure Act

Most day-to-day questions of presidential power depend in large part on statutory authority. Here we consider how the courts should approach statutory issues.

Bruff, Judicial Review and the President's Statutory Powers
68 Va. L. Rev. 1, 17-24, 50-60 (1982)

Substantively, presidential actions implementing statutes fall into two broad functional categories, law-making and law-applying. [Although the line between them is indistinct, the essential difference is that law-making actions establish a general policy to govern a class of persons or situations; law-applying actions determine how a general policy should apply to a particular set of facts.] Presidential law-making is functionally similar to administrative rulemaking, for which the [Administrative Procedure Act, 5 U.S.C. § 551 *et seq.*] provides minimum procedural prerequisites. An agency must usually notify the public of a proposed rulemaking, afford an opportunity for written comment on the proposed rule, and accompany the rule it finally adopts with a statement of its basis and purpose. [§ 553] In practice, these simple requirements have developed into a rather elaborate and time-consuming process that tends to produce a massive public record of information, analysis, and opinion, and that culminates in a detailed explanation of the factual basis and policy rationale for the final rule. In contrast, Presidents perform their rulemaking activities simply by issuing executive orders or proclamations, without any prior public procedure, and often without any accompanying explanation.

Presidential law-applying is functionally similar to "informal" decisionmaking by administrative officials (so called because the APA requires no special procedures for administrative actions other than rulemaking and adjudication). Agencies, under the pressure of judicial review, normally accompany announcements of their informal statutory decisions with explanations similar to those used for rulemaking. Presidents sometimes furnish contemporaneous explanations of their law-applying decisions, but there is no consistent practice.

The Applicability of the Administrative Procedure Act to the President

The presidential actions of interest here are procedurally and functionally similar to decisions of cabinet-level administrative officers, for which the APA provides both minimum procedural requirements and a well-understood standard for judicial review. Yet no court has ever held that the President is subject to the APA's requirements. Before analyzing whether the APA should be applied to the President, it is necessary to sketch its pertinent requisites for agencies.

Under the APA, a court reviewing agency action must first decide whether the action is reviewable at all. The Supreme Court has established a "basic presumption of review," under which "only upon a showing of 'clear and convincing evidence' of a contrary legislative intent should the courts restrict access to judicial review." [*Abbott Laboratories v. Gardner*, 387 U.S. 136, 141 (1967).] Where review occurs, a court examines agency action for its constitutionality, statutory authorization, procedural regularity, and substantive rationality. [APA § 706(2)(A)-(D).] The APA's standard of judicial review for rulemaking and for informal agency actions is much the same, except for procedural issues relating to rulemaking.

Constitutional and procedural issues aside, the courts focus on the presence of statutory authority for a challenged action and on the rationality of the judgments of fact and policy that underlie it. On issues of statutory authority, courts often state—but do not always follow—a doctrine that they should defer to an administrator's statutory interpretation within the bounds of reason and ascertainable legislative intent. This deference is based on the administrator's presumed expertise and a related notion that Congress commits these leeway issues (which are intermixed with policy concerns) to the agency and not to the courts.

On issues of fact and policy, the APA requires courts to set aside agency actions that are "arbitrary, capricious, [or] an abuse of discretion." [§ 706(2)(A).] The Supreme Court has parsed this terminology to require a "searching and careful" inquiry into the agency's judgments, although a reviewing court is not to "substitute its judgment for that of the agency." [*Citizens to Preserve Overton Park, Inc. v. Volpe*, 401 U.S. 402, 416 (1971).] The effort is to ensure that agency actions are "based on a consideration of the relevant factors" and have a "rational basis" in fact.

Courts exercise this review for statutory authority and rationality by comparing any formal explanation adopted at the time of the decision with the "administrative record" on which the agency based the decision. Substantial indeterminacies attend this process, however. First, administrative records are not self-defining, because there are often no formal agency procedures for determining in advance which documents will be considered in reaching a final decision. Accordingly, efforts to link the morass of documents in an agency with a final decision usually require a process of post hoc reconstruction.

Second, an agency may not provide a formal explanation that suffices to reveal the factual and policy judgments that underlie its decision. The APA does not require formal findings and reasons for informal actions, although it does require the equivalent for rulemaking, in a statement of basis and purpose. To facilitate review, courts frequently have implied requirements for findings and reasons from particular program statutes. Where they have done so, or where administrators have furnished explanations on their own initiative, courts have restricted review to a comparison of the formal explanation with the administrative record. Absent particular indications of "bad faith or improper behavior," the court does not inquire further into the "actual" basis of decision. If the explanation does not sufficiently justify the action on the basis of the administrative record, the usual remedy is a remand to the agency for further consideration.

Scholars have concluded that the APA governs the President;[81] their analysis focuses on the desirability of ensuring judicial review of his actions. That goal can be met without reliance on the APA for authority, however, because Congress meant the Act's judicial review chapter to be a restatement of existing law, not a new departure. The APA did not alter the basic availability and scope of the traditional "nonstatutory" remedies of mandamus, injunction, and declaratory judgment. The United States Court of Appeals for the District of Columbia Circuit has held that mandamus may issue against the President, although the court, in appropriate deference to the Presidency, confined itself to a more politic declaratory judgment. [*National Treasury Employees Union v. Nixon*, 492 F.2d 587 (D.C. Cir. 1974).] The principal elements

---

81. Berger, *Administrative Arbitrariness: A Synthesis*, 78 Yale L.J. 965, 997 (1969); Davis, *Administrative Arbitrariness—A Postscript*, 114 U.Pa.L.Rev. 823, 832 (1966).

of nonstatutory review (mandamus in particular) parallel those contained in the APA: conformity to substantive constitutional and statutory limits, compliance with required procedures, and rationality. Indeed, the drafters of the APA drew these requisites from existing practice.

Whether the APA should apply to the President depends on the extent to which the Presidency is comparable to an administrative agency for purposes of statutory decisionmaking. Certainly some close parallels appear. Many of the decisions that Congress delegates directly to the President could be assigned as appropriately to an agency,[86] and the process preceding a presidential decision is quite similar to that of an agency. Yet there are important differences that legal analysis must take into account: the President's constitutional powers, the multifarious responsibilities of his office, and his direct political accountability as the only elected official with a national constituency.

The President bears substantially more direct political accountability for his own statutory decisions than for those of agency officials. It is true that the President nominates the agency officials to whom the APA applies, and bears responsibility for the overall performance of the executive branch. Nevertheless, the extent to which the President may lawfully supervise a decision allocated by statute to another officer is uncertain, even when the officer is removable at the President's pleasure. Furthermore, as a practical matter no President can hope to give close supervision to all executive branch decisionmaking. Accordingly, his political accountability for any particular agency decision is quite attenuated.

Because of the President's limited accountability for the actions of appointed officials, concern about the legitimacy of subjecting the public to their decisions has long been a central theme in administrative law. It has appeared in such diverse manifestations as the judicial doctrine that Congress may not delegate unrestricted lawmaking power to an agency and Congress's imposition of procedural constraints on the agencies in order to ensure that the public can participate in and influence agency decisions. Because both Congress and the courts have responded to the indirectness of the agencies' political accountability in their efforts to control agency action, existing law merits careful appraisal before it is applied to the President.

Neither the terminology[93] nor the legislative history[94] of the APA compels the conclusion that it governs the President. Application of the APA to the President might

---

86. The President's statutory authority to delegate his statutory powers to other officials recognizes this. Congress does not appear to follow any consistent theory when it decides whether to delegate power to the President or to an agency.

93. The APA applies to each "agency," a term that ordinarily does not include the President. 5 U.S.C. §§ 551(1), 701(b)(1) (1976).... The APA does, however, define agency to mean "each authority of the Government of the United States, whether or not it is within or subject to review by another agency," and it specifically excludes Congress and the courts, which suggests that the President is not excepted. The legislative history of this terminology, however, reveals that the purpose of the definition is to include subdivisions of agencies (e.g., the Social Security Administration).

94. The legislative history of the APA nowhere mentions a purpose to bind the President. Indeed, the Final Report of the Attorney General's Committee on Administrative Procedure, which was influential in the genesis of the APA, concluded that a generally applicable statute should not include the President:

From the earliest times Congress has conferred upon the President powers which differ

have some unfortunate consequences, because the APA and its judicial gloss do not take account of the special character of the Presidency. As a result, every major aspect of judicial review as it has evolved under the APA seems inappropriate when applied to the President. First, judicial review under the APA does not directly confront the President's constitutional executive privilege, although analogous concepts apply. Second, case law that erects a broad presumption of reviewability for agency action must be narrowed to conform to the cases that directly analyze the substantive reviewability of presidential action. Third, the process of statutory interpretation acquires unique features when the President is involved, due to interrelationships between issues of statutory and constitutional power. Fourth, application of the APA to the President would subject him to procedural requisites designed to ensure responsiveness of appointed officials to the public. Finally, courts reviewing agency actions for substantive rationality often employ a "hard look" doctrine that closely analyzes the persuasiveness of the agency's judgments of fact and policy on the basis of the administrative record. This substantial gloss on the underlying principle that executive action must have a rational basis may be inappropriate for presidential actions, in view of the burdens on the decisionmaking process that it imposes and the lesser need for close substantive review of a politically accountable official.

Rather than risk creating distortions in the case law for both the President and the agencies by subjecting them to the same procedures and standard of review, it seems best to fashion a method for review of presidential decisions that is expressly tailored to the unique character of his office. The courts can find the necessary justification for his enterprise in the set of traditional principles for judicial review of executive action that trace from *Marbury*. Prescribing a standard for judicial review of the President's statutory actions thus requires consideration of each of the techniques that courts have used to conform executive action to law. Because of the similarities between presidential and agency actions and the roots of the APA in existing law, a process similar but not identical to that found in the APA cases should emerge....

Establishing a Rational Basis For Presidential Action

Under the APA, courts reviewing informal agency decisions ordinarily require the Government to establish the rationality of the decision on the basis of the administrative record. The issue here is the suitability of this mode of review for presidential decisions. It might be argued that courts should eschew any attempt to probe the basis of presidential decisions—that they should uphold any presidential action for which they can imagine a rational basis, whether or not it actually existed and was relied on by the President. Such an approach would be analogous to the process by which federal courts review the rationality of most legislation. The argument would be that the President, as the head of a coordinate branch of government, is entitled to the same degree of deference as Congress receives for its actions. In particular, because the President's law-making activities can be as readily analogized to legislation

---

importantly from those [of the agencies].... Instead of being simply one of continuous, integrated regulation, such as most of the regulatory bureaus and commissions undertake, [the President's powers] involve isolated or temporary authority to deal with emergency situations and often the determination of high matters of state.... [T]he very emergency character of the situations makes inapplicable the procedures evolved for dealing with the normal regulations promulgated by administrative agencies in the performance of their duties.

S. Doc. No. 8, 77th Cong., 1st Sess. 100-01 (1941).

as to administrative rulemaking, perhaps they should be reviewed as legislation would be.

Such an approach would be unsuited to review of presidential action. First, a primary reason for judicial willingness to suppose a rational basis for legislation is that, unlike execution, legislative action need not be taken to promote specific, prescribed aims. It is sufficient for legislation to serve as a rational means to any legitimate end; execution, on the other hand, must serve as a rational means to the particular ends sought by the statute. Unless the courts ensure that executive action rationally serves statutory ends, they will allow the erosion of Congress's constitutional power to direct the course of execution.

Nevertheless, some may argue that when Congress delegates power directly to the President, it impliedly intends that judicial review be especially deferential. Indeed, this article has concluded that courts should not employ either the delegation doctrine or statutory interpretation in a fashion that will artificially constrain congressional grants of broad discretion to the President. Yet, for this very reason, a meaningful constraint must exist somewhere, in order to enforce whatever limits Congress does set. Otherwise, if the President could take any action that is compatible on its face with a statutory purpose, the practical consequence would be the adoption of Theodore Roosevelt's expansive theory that the President may take any action not forbidden by law. In view of the facial breadth of most statutory delegations of power to the President, this approach either would foster an undue concentration of power in the executive or would impel Congress to shackle execution by imposing more conditions in advance than it might deem wise. Moreover, a method of judicial review that examined only the facial validity of presidential actions would encourage Presidents to issue opaque decisions, deterring the present practice of explaining some (if not all) presidential actions.

In defining judicial review of the substance of presidential decisions, courts should begin with the traditional "rational basis" requirement of nonstatutory review.... [T]he rational basis standard is not self-defining. This characteristic, however, may be an advantage in that the courts can adapt its application to the nature of each presidential decision under review.... Here it is only possible to articulate some factors for the courts to consider in defining their role. On the one hand, review should be relatively deferential when the President's independent constitutional powers are present in the case, or when the substantive judgments involved approach nonreviewability. ... On the other hand, review should be relatively close when the President's action nears the substantive constitutional or statutory limits on his power....

The administrative record against which a court should compare a President's decision usually is generated principally in one or more executive agencies; White House materials are likely to be mostly policy memoranda that are protected by executive privilege. Therefore, a central task for the courts is to see that appropriate links exist between a record developed in one place and a decision reached in another. Performed correctly, judicial review can help to ensure bureaucratic regularity, with particular tasks being performed at appropriate levels in the bureaucracy. The primary effect on executive branch decisionmaking should be to force the White House to consult with agencies having relevant program responsibilities, and with counsel. The agencies may already possess an administrative record pertinent to an upcoming decision; at any rate, they—not the White House—are the appropriate place to compile one. The function of compiling and reviewing an administrative record within an agency is to discover, and explain to the ultimate policymakers, the limits of defensible discretion. Similarly, the role of the President's counsel is to render opinions on the permissibility of postulated policy choices, given certain fact assumptions and the terms and legislative history of the relevant statute.

If legal review of a proposed decision reveals that certain factual judgments or policy rationales must underlie a decision if it is to be legal, these matters ought to accompany the proposal all the way to the President's desk. The effect, however, should never be to increase the work load of the President himself. All that need reach the President is an indication in the options memorandum (or in oral discussion) that a particular decision would require certain fact and policy underpinning, a summary of those conclusions, and a statement that the appropriate officials believe them to be adequately supported. The President's selection of a particular option will then also select the basis for it that will be advanced on judicial review. As a matter of mechanics, the White House staff can structure presidential decision memoranda to separate the policy analysis from an attached formal document that is prepared for signature and release to the public.

Judicial requirements for the identification of a legally sufficient rationale for presidential action cannot guarantee that no ulterior purposes for it exist. The same is true, however, for judicial review of administrative action pursuant to the APA, in which formal findings and reasons may not be penetrated absent special circumstances. If no formal explanation accompanies a presidential decision, a court can require affidavits describing the rationale and can check their veracity through in camera procedures.

Judicial review of the President's proffered rationale for a decision under a rational basis standard offers special institutional advantages for the courts. It allows them to exercise a role that is appropriately limited, because to require identification of the basis of a decision does not prevent deferential review of the judgments involved. Especially when statutes delegate power without meaningful standards, a wide range of fact and policy bases of decision may be available. Moreover, this mode of review would free the courts to accord the President the latitude his office deserves on the other issues in the case, such as statutory interpretation. Thus, the doctrine that courts should defer to reasonable administrative interpretations of statutes is in part a function of explanation requirements.

In recent years, courts reviewing administrative action have employed explanation requirements as a substitute for the delegation doctrine. This development implicitly recognizes that an officer's accountability to Congress and the public is ensured if he or she must demonstrate that a statutory decision is based on judgments of fact and policy that are rational and within statutory parameters. If, for example, announcement of a rationale that is politically unpalatable is a legally necessary precondition to a particular option, another option may be selected. Moreover, from the standpoint of the President's political accountability to Congress and the public, a requirement that he reveal his rationale for a decision clearly is preferable to a system that would allow him to select an option without explanation, leaving all concerned to speculate on the reasons for it. Thus, if the courts exercise their review function in a way that makes the President take responsibility for an action by stating a legally sufficient rationale for it, they will have done all they can to clarify the respective responsibilities of the two policymaking branches of government. Congressional oversight of the President's decision will be easier to exercise; if Congress chooses not to intervene with legislation that alters the President's authority, the executive practice in question will gather legitimacy from the precedent.

Explanation requirements can also increase the efficacy of executive branch checks on presidential action. The President bears a constitutional responsibility to ensure the legality of his actions, which is discharged by the ordinary processes of bureaucratic review that precede his decisions. Thus, the bureaucracy constitutes an important check on both the policy and legal bases of presidential action. Although administrative officials ordinarily are prepared to judge both the facts and the law in a fashion that is sympathetic to known presidential desires, there are limits to what they will approve. If the responsible agency officials and lawyers are consulted in advance of a presidential decision, they can urge caution or advance alternatives without having to threaten to refuse their assent to a proposed decision until it is necessary to do so. After the fact, the situation changes radically—especially for the President's lawyers, who are left with the unappetizing question of whether they should refuse to defend in court an action they would not have approved in advance. Of course, bureaucratic checks on presidential action are by no means an unalloyed benefit. An agency that is not in sympathy with a presidential initiative can attempt to confine him by narrowing his policy or legal options in ways that the White House is hard pressed to identify. For the courts, however, it is enough to accord the President the kinds of deference on law and policy that are described above, in order to give full play to his policymaking role.

―――――――

b. Freedom of Information Act

―――――――

Kissinger v. Reporters Committee for Freedom of the Press
445 U.S. 136 (1980)

[During his tenure as Assistant to the President for National Security Affairs (1969-1975) and as Secretary of State (1973-1977), Henry Kissinger followed the practice of having his secretaries monitor all of his telephone conversations and record their contents by shorthand or on tape. The notes or tapes were used to prepare detailed summaries or verbatim transcripts of the conversations, and then destroyed. In late 1976, while still Secretary of State, Kissinger arranged—without consulting the Department of State office responsible for record maintenance and disposal—to move the telephone notes from his State Department office to the New York estate of Nelson Rockefeller.

In December, 1976, Kissinger donated the notes to the Library of Congress under an agreement substantially delaying public access to them. Several weeks later, a Kissinger aide extracted portions of the notes for the Department of State files, indicating "significant policy decisions or actions not otherwise reflected in the Department's records." Kissinger declined, however, to subject the notes themselves to inspection by the Government Archivist to determine which, if any, were properly Department records.

This case involved three Freedom of Information Act requests for the notes. The plaintiffs asked the District Court to require the Library of Congress, not an "agency" under the FOIA, to return the notes to the Department of State with directions to process them for FOIA disclosure. The District Court granted most of the relief requested. In an opinion by Justice REHNQUIST, the Supreme Court held that no statute authorized an order to produce the materials that had been donated to the Library of Congress:]

II

. . . The question must be, of course, whether Congress has conferred jurisdiction on the federal courts to impose this remedy. Two statutory schemes are relevant to this inquiry. First, if Congress contemplated a private right of action under the Federal Records Act and the Federal Records Disposal Act, this would in itself justify the remedy imposed if Kissinger in fact wrongfully removed the documents. In the alternative, the lower court order could be sustained if authorized by the FOIA.

A

The Federal Records Act of 1950, 44 U.S.C. §§ 2901 et seq., authorizes the "head of each Federal agency" to establish a "records management program" and to define the extent to which documents are "appropriate for preservation" as agency records. The records management program requires that adequate documentation of agency policies and procedures be retained. The Records Disposal Act, a complementary records management Act, provides the exclusive means for record disposal. 44 U.S.C. § 3314.

Under the Records Disposal Act, once a document achieves the status of a "record" as defined by the Act, it may not be alienated or disposed of without the consent of the Administrator of General Services, who has delegated his authority in such matters to the Archivist of the United States. 44 U.S.C. §§ 3303, 3303a, 3308-3314. Thus if Kissinger's telephone notes were "records" within the meaning of the Federal Records Act, a question we do not reach, then Kissinger's transfer might well violate the Act since he did not seek the approval of the Archivist prior to transferring custody to himself and then to the Library of Congress. We assume such a wrongful removal arguendo for the purposes of this opinion.

But the Federal Records Act establishes only one remedy for the improper removal of a "record" from the agency. The head of the agency is required under 44 U.S.C. § 3106 to notify the Attorney General if he determines or "has reason to believe" that records have been improperly removed from the agency. The Administrator of General Services is obligated to assist in such actions. 44 U.S.C. § 2905. At the behest of these administrators, the Attorney General may bring suit to recover the records.

The Archivist did request return of the telephone notes from Kissinger on the basis of his belief that the documents may have been wrongfully removed under the Act. Despite Kissinger's refusal to comply with the Archivist's request, no suit has been instituted against Kissinger to retrieve the records under 44 U.S.C. § 3106.

Plaintiff requesters effectively seek to enforce these requirements of the Acts by seeking the return of the records to State Department custody. No provision of either Act, however, expressly confers a right of action on private parties. Nor do we believe that such a private right of action can be implied. . . . Congress expressly recognized the need for devising adequate statutory safeguards against the unauthorized removal of agency records, and opted in favor of a system of administrative standards and enforcement. See U.S. Commission on Organization of the Executive Branch of the Government, Task Force Report on Records Management 27 (1949)....

B

... [FOIA] authorizes federal courts to ensure private access to requested materials when three requirements have been met. Under 5 U.S.C. § 552(a)(4)(B) federal jurisdiction is dependent upon a showing that an agency has (1) "improperly"; (2) "withheld"; (3) "agency records." Judicial authority to devise remedies and enjoin agencies can only be invoked... if the agency has contravened all three components of this obligation. We find it unnecessary to decide whether the telephone notes were "agency records" since we conclude that a covered agency—here the State Department—has not "withheld" those documents from the plaintiffs. We also need not decide the full contours of a prohibited "withholding." We do decide, however, that Congress did not mean that an agency improperly withholds a document which has been removed from the possession of the agency prior to the filing of the FOIA request. In such a case, the agency has neither the custody or control necessary to enable it to withhold.... An agency's failure to sue a third party to obtain possession is not a withholding under the Act....

The conclusion that possession or control is a prerequisite to FOIA disclosure duties is reinforced by an examination of the purposes of the Act. The Act does not obligate agencies to create or retain documents; it only obligates them to provide access to those which it in fact has created and retained. It has been settled by decision of this Court that only the Federal Records Act, and not the FOIA, requires an agency to actually create records, even though the agency's failure to do so deprives the public of information which might have otherwise been available to it....

[Other materials, however, raised a different issue:]

III

The Safire request raises a separate question. At the time when Safire submitted his request for certain notes of Kissinger's telephone conversations, all the notes were still located in Kissinger's office at the State Department.... We conclude that the Safire request sought disclosure of documents which were not "agency records" within the meaning of the FOIA.

Safire's request sought... all transcripts of telephone conversations made by Kissinger from his White House office between January 21, 1969, and February 12, 1971, in which (1) Safire's name appeared; or (2) in which Kissinger discussed the subject of information "leaks" with General Alexander Haig, Attorney General John Mitchell, President Richard Nixon, J. Edgar Hoover, or any other official of the FBI.

The FOIA does render the "Executive Office of the President" an agency subject to the Act. 5 U.S.C. § 552(e). The legislative history is unambiguous, however, in explaining that the "Executive Office" does not include the Office of the President. The Conference Report for the 1974 FOIA Amendments indicates that "the President's immediate personal staff or units in the Executive Office whose sole function is to advise and assist the President" are not included within the term "agency" under the FOIA. H. R. Conf. Rep. No. 93-1380, p. 15 (1974). Safire's request was limited to a period of time in which Kissinger was serving as Assistant to the President. Thus these telephone notes were not "agency records" when they were made.

The RCFP requesters have argued that since some of the telephone notes made while Kissinger was adviser to the President may have related to the National Security Council they may have been National Security Council records and therefore subject to the Act. See H. R. Rep. No. 93-876, p. 8 (1974), U.S. Code Cong. & Admin. News 1974, p. 6267, indicating that the National Security Council is an executive agency to which the FOIA applies. We need not decide when records which, in the words of the RCFP requesters, merely "relate to" the affairs of an FOIA agency become records of that agency. To the extent Safire sought discussions concerning information leaks which threatened the internal secrecy of White House policymaking, he sought conversations in which Kissinger had acted in his capacity as a Presidential adviser, only. . . .

The RCFP requesters nevertheless contend that if the transcripts of telephone conversations made while adviser to the President were not then "agency records," they acquired that status under the Act when they were removed from White House files and physically taken to Kissinger's office at the Department of State. We simply decline to hold that the physical location of the notes of telephone conversations renders them "agency records." The papers were not in the control of the State Department at any time. They were not generated in the State Department. They never entered the State Department's files, and they were not used by the Department for any purpose. If mere physical location of papers and materials could confer status as an "agency record" Kissinger's personal books, speeches, and all other memorabilia stored in his office would have been agency records subject to disclosure under the FOIA. It requires little discussion or analysis to conclude that the lower courts correctly resolved this question in favor of Kissinger. . . .

[Justices BRENNAN and STEVENS concurred in part and dissented in part. Justices MARSHALL and BLACKMUN took no part in the case.]

---

1. In his separate opinion, Justice Stevens lamented the effect of the Court's decision in creating "an incentive for outgoing agency officials to remove potentially embarrassing documents from their files in order to frustrate future FOIA requests." He would have defined "withholding" to include documents that an agency "has a legal right to possess or control." Do you agree? Note that after the 1978 legislation concerning presidential records, subordinate officers may be able to exert more control over their official records than the President can. Is that appropriate?

2. In the National Archives and Records Administration Act of 1984, Pub. L. No. 98-497, codified at 44 U.S.C. § 2101 et seq., Congress established an independent National Archives and Records Administration, and transferred to it the record-keeping functions previously exercised by the GSA. Congress hoped to ensure professional rather than political records management. The legislative history noted the Kissinger imbroglio; in response, Congress authorized the Archivist to seek the initiation of action by the Attorney General to recover improperly removed records, with notice to Congress. Does that solve the problem?

3. Is FOIA's inapplicability to the President and his immediate advisers compelled by the constitutional executive privilege? If so, is the scope of the FOIA exception correctly drawn? On the other hand, in view of the FOIA exemptions we have seen so far—for example, for classified documents and policy deliberations—did Congress need to create any special blanket exception for the President?

c. Internal Management of the Executive Branch (National Environmental Policy Act; Government in the Sunshine Act)

In *Andrus v. Sierra Club*, 442 U.S. 347 (1979), the Supreme Court held that §102(2)(C) of the National Environmental Policy Act (NEPA), 42 U.S.C. § 4321-4370a, which requires that environmental impact statements ("EIS's") be included in recommendations or reports of federal agencies on "proposals for legislation and other major Federal actions significantly affecting the quality of the human environment," does not require agencies to file EIS's with their appropriations requests, which are considered and processed originally by the Office of Management and Budget (OMB), part of the Executive Office of the President. At the time of the Court of Appeals decision, which had gone the other way, guidelines issued by the Council on Environmental Quality (CEQ), another part of the Executive Office of the President, included a contrary interpretation of NEPA. CEQ reversed its position in 1978, in the process of re-promulgating the guidelines as regulations to be binding on government agencies, arguing that not requiring EIS's for appropriations requests was consistent with traditional procedural distinctions in the handling of appropriations and substantive legislation. The Supreme Court accepted this reading of NEPA, on statutory grounds. Perhaps significantly, however, there was no hint in the Court's opinion of any constitutional limitation on Congress' power to regulate the process by which agencies prepare policy recommendations for presidential review.

In *Common Cause v. Nuclear Regulatory Commission*, 674 F. 2d 921 (D.C. Cir. 1982), the Court of Appeals held that the Government in the Sunshine Act, 5 U.S.C. §552b, which generally requires meetings of multi-member federal agencies to be open to the public, does not exempt agency budget deliberations from its requirements. Although an independent agency, the NRC is required to participate in OMB's centralized budget review process. The Commission, in arguing for a blanket exemption for budget deliberations, relied partly on the "[l]ongstanding practice of confidentiality for Executive Branch discussions leading to the formulation of the President's budget," and partly on the President's statutory rulemaking authority for budget preparation. The court rejected both these arguments, stating that the President's statutory rulemaking authority was limited by other applicable statutes, including the Sunshine Act, and that public disclosure of agency deliberations did not, on its face, interfere with the President's ability to revise agency requests and prepare a unified budget. The court did recognize "that specific items discussed at Commission budget meetings might be exempt from the open meetings requirement of the act," 674 F.2d at 936, and expressed "no view with regard to any constitutional issue of Executive privilege, a question," according to the court, "which is narrower than the . . . general claim based on separation of powers." The court added that only the President, and not an agency, may assert presidential privilege.

2. Accessibility of the ''inner circle'' to congressional oversight

Although the question has not been adjudicated, the executive has historically taken the position that the separation of powers bars Congress from demanding the testimony of the President's Cabinet and special assistants. The general practice, however, has been to permit such persons to testify "voluntarily." Should questions arise that might require divulging privileged information, the testifying official can assert privilege as to particular answers.

Partly in order to secure greater cooperation from the President's advisers in congressional testimony, Congress has considered subjecting particular advisers to appointment with the Senate's advice and consent. Nominees to such positions could then be questioned during confirmation hearings about their willingness to supply information to Congress. For example, in 1974 the Director and Deputy Director of OMB were made subject to advice and consent. Similar legislation has been proposed regarding the Assistant to the President for National Security Affairs. Following are excerpts from the Senate report in support of the OMB bill and a statement by former Deputy Secretary of State Warren Christopher in opposition to altering the status of the National Security Adviser.

Senate Confirmation of Director and Deputy Director of the Office of Management and Budget
S. Rept. No. 93-7, 93d Cong., 1st Sess. (1973)

S. 518 would require that, ... appointments by the President to fill the offices of Director and Deputy Director of the Office of Management and Budget be subject to the advice and consent of the Senate. ... The objective of the bill is to afford the Senate an opportunity to inquire into the qualifications, background, and fitness of these officials in the same manner as is required for virtually all other policy-making officials in the executive branch.

Prior to 1921, no machinery existed in the National Government to handle the formulation of a single, consolidated statement of the prospective revenues and the estimated expenditure needs of the Government to guide the Congress in determining the policies and programs to be approved and adopted. Congress sought to meet this deficiency by enacting the Budget and Accounting Act, 1921, which, among other things, established a national budget system and a Bureau of the Budget to advise and assist the President in developing a unified budget for submission to the Congress. ... [The Conference Committee deleted a requirement] that appointments to the offices of Director and Assistant Director of the Bureau of the Budget should be subject to Senate confirmation, ... on the theory that these positions were personal to the President and that he should be allowed to "appoint men whom he believed he could trust to do his will in the preparation of the budget." ...

Since 1939, vast changes have occurred in the structure, responsibilities and authority of the Office of Management and Budget (the name was changed from Bureau of the Budget by Reorganization Plan No. 2 of 1970). With a current staff of nearly 700 persons, this agency, originally established by the Congress as a management tool and institutional aid for the President, has developed into a super department with enormous authority over all of the activities of the Federal Government. Its Director has become, in effect, a Deputy President who exercises vital Presidential powers.

OMB determines line by line budget limitations for each agency, including the regulatory commissions. Following authorization by the Congress of programs and activities, and the funding of such activities, the Office of Management and Budget develops impoundment actions, limiting the expenditures of funds for programs approved by law to those falling within the President's priorities, rather than those established by the Congress. By statute, the Director of OMB has authority to apportion appropriations, approve agency systems for the control of appropriated funds and establish reserves....

Under numerous ... statutes, or by Presidential delegations, the Director of OMB has been given a vast number of additional functions.... The Director ... exercises control over the nature and types of questionnaires, surveys, reports, and forms which may be issued and utilized by Government agencies.... Finally, the Director and his staff exercise oversight and control over the management of, and expenditures for, national security programs, international programs, defense expenditures, natural resources programs, and many others having a direct impact upon the economy and security of the Nation....

Senate confirmation has, since the earliest days of the Nation, been required for appointments to every major policy-making position in the executive branch, and in the regulatory agencies. Even in the Executive Office of the President, where the principal officers of agencies placed therein serve as staff advisers to the President, as well as heads of operating agencies, in many instances, Senate confirmation has been required....

The committee does not take issue with the President's requirement for an institutional aid to assist him in exercising management and control over the executive branch. It believes, however, that such requirement must be balanced with the Constitutional role of the Congress in the formulation and finalization of national policy.

The committee has concluded that the reasons which were the bases for the immunity from Senate confirmation of the Director and Deputy Director of this agency no longer exist, and that persons chosen by the President to fill these offices should be subject to the same scrutiny by the Senate as is required for all other nominees to policy-making positions in the Government....

The National Security Adviser: Role and Accountability

Hearing Before the Senate Comm. on Foreign Relations, 96th Cong., 2d Sess. (1980)

Prepared Statement of Hon. Warren Christopher

... As part of these hearings, I understand that the committee is once again considering whether the positions of Assistant and Deputy Assistant to the President for National Security Affairs should be subject to the advice and consent of the Senate.

Let me state our position at the outset. As the President indicated in his letter to Senator Church last year, the Administration opposes this proposal. We believe it would intrude upon the authority of the President in international affairs and complicate the conduct of our foreign relations. It would do so without significant compensating value to the Congress.

Let me begin my discussion by reviewing briefly the development of the position of the National Security Adviser and its relationship to the National Security Council. [The NSC] was created ... to coordinate the many strands of national policy set by various departments, all of which bore upon our global posture. The [National Security Act] specified statutory members of the National Security Council, including the President and the Secretaries of State and Defense, and it provided for a civilian staff headed by an executive secretary. There was no mention of an Assistant to the

President for National Security Affairs. That position was created by Presidential statement in 1953.

I do not propose to trace the intervening history in any depth. From it, however, some broad observations emerge. First, the function of the NSC and its staff has varied widely, depending primarily on the needs and preferences of the President in office. During the Eisenhower Administration, for example, the Council structure was highly developed and extensively used. President Kennedy, by contrast, preferred a less formal approach.

Second, the requirement which inspired the creation of the National Security Council—for interdepartmental coordination on foreign affairs—remains its most important role. Indeed, the breadth of today's foreign policy concerns—reaching from such traditional areas as defense and trade to newer concerns such as communications and energy—could not have been foreseen 30 years ago....

Within the NSC system, the National Security Adviser has a dual responsibility. First, at the President's request, he provides advice on foreign and defense policy. He also directs the NSC system in order to bring options to the President's attention and to assure that the President's decisions are appropriately followed.

Finally, like all Presidential advisers, the National Security Adviser performs additional duties, such as conducting fact-finding missions, on behalf of the President and at his direction.

Against this background, I would like now to turn to the proposal of Senator Zorinsky. [We agree] with the principle that the Congress has a vital role in American foreign policy, both in helping to guide its direction and in monitoring its implementation. Those responsibilities have taken on new meaning in recent years as we have worked to build a post-Vietnam consensus on our international priorities. The Administration recognizes that the United States can have an effective and durable foreign policy only if the Congress is fully informed and involved.

. . . [W]e also believe there is agreement that the President of the United States requires a personal and confidential staff of his own choosing. He must be able to draw upon advisers who, within the law, answer only to him. He must be able to hear a wide range of views and consider all possible options when he makes his decisions. The availability of the unfettered advice of persons the President trusts serves not just the convenience of the President, but the interests of the country as well.

In outlining the agreement on these central propositions, I have defined the interests that are most directly touched by the proposal before this Committee: the oversight interest of the Congress; the national interest in a sound structure for conducting our international relations; and the Presidential interest in managing his own office and responsibilities. In our judgment the proposed legislation is not necessary for achieving the first of these interests, and it would tend to be inconsistent with the other two....

State Department officials have been readily available for formal testimony and have conducted countless informal briefings and consultations. You hear regularly from the Secretary as well as from me, from the Under Secretaries, from the Assistant Secretaries and their deputies, from the directors of offices and the administrators of agencies, and from our ambassadorial nominees. This access reaches two of the four statutory members of the National Security Council, the Secretary of State and the Secretary of Defense, and all its statutory advisers and their principal assistants.

These are the officials with direct responsibility for our policy and our programs in the world. Either through designation by statute, or through delegation from the President or Secretary of State, they have the direct authority to shape and implement our policy, and the specific obligation to account for public funds.

By contrast, the Assistant to the President for National Security Affairs does not administer statutory programs. He does not expend public funds. Rather, the principal roles of the National Security Adviser are to provide confidential advice to the President and to coordinate foreign policy. His appearance to testify on the Hill would impinge upon the President's right to obtain confidential advice from individuals responsible only to him.

Thus, the Zorinsky proposal would provide the Congress with, at most, a redundant source of information. At the same time, the proposal would compromise crucial interests by hindering the capacity of the Executive Branch to represent effectively the nation's interests in the world. First, the proposal would inevitably, if unintentionally, diminish the authority of the Secretary of State. If our own Congress were to look explicitly to another source for authoritative descriptions of American policy, then governments elsewhere would be inspired to do the same. This alteration in our foreign policy structure would confuse foreign governments and complicate our foreign relations.

The simple truth is that the focus of American foreign policy, under the President's direction, must reside in one person, the Secretary of State. As chief officer of the Department which implements foreign policy, he is uniquely situated to comprehend all the interests that must be weighed when national policy is formed. . . .

Let me turn now to the final and most compelling reason for opposing the proposal of Senator Zorinsky. It would directly impinge upon the Office of the President by limiting his necessary flexibility in foreign policy. . . . In the post-Vietnam period the involvement of the Congress in foreign policy decisions has, of course, increased through such steps as the War Powers Act, notifications on executive agreements and intelligence activities, review of conventional arms sales, and others. These initiatives, however, have been designed to help the Congress to perform better its own Constitutional duties. Now, in my view, we are presented with something quite different: a step that bears no strong legislative purpose, but which would inhibit the President in the performance of functions that are clearly assigned to him. . . .

As the chief architect of American foreign policy, the President must be able to choose his personal and confidential advisers without the searching inquiry that confirmation hearings entail. It is inappropriate for the Senate to pass on the qualifications of intimate Presidential advisers. For only the President is in a position to adjudge the needs of his immediate office and to decide what, if any, advice he requires and who, if anyone will provide it. Just as it is unthinkable that the selection of personal aides of Senators would be subject to outside scrutiny, it is equally unthinkable that the appointment of the President's personal advisers should be subject to the advice and consent of the Senate. . . . Moreover, as the Nation's chief diplomat, the President should have flexibility to decide the level and formality of our contacts with other countries, including the use of personal emissaries when he deems it appropriate. So long as the Congress is informed and the Administration is answerable for the results, the prerogatives of the Congress are in no way impaired.

Our system provides ample opportunity to question and challenge the President's decisions. But if our government is to operate effectively, it must accord the President breathing space.... The proposal under consideration is an unwarranted intrusion by the Congress that will needlessly hamper future Presidents.

----

1. Has the President a constitutional right, in the exercise of his "core functions," to some advisers and agents of his own selection, not subject to senatorial advice and consent and not ordinarily amenable to congressional subpoenas? If so, how many and for which functions?

2. Unfortunately, providing for Senate confirmation does not ensure its effectiveness. As part of its valuable six-volume Study on Federal Regulation (95th Cong., 1st Sess. 1977), the Senate Committee on Government Operations examined the process of appointing and confirming federal regulators, and reported its findings and recommendations in volume 1, The Regulatory Appointments Process. It reported that "[f]or much of the past fifteen years, neither the White House nor the Senate has demonstrated a sustained commitment to high quality regulatory appointments." (xxxi) Still, "[i]n recent years, the Senate confirmation process has become more vigorous and more thorough." (xxxii). The Committee made a series of recommendations to the Senate, calling for more thorough background investigations and hearings. (xxvii-xxix). In short, the Committee hoped that its house would advise and not merely consent to presidential appointments.

3. In the wake of the Iran/Contra scandal, calls for subjecting the National Security Adviser to confirmation were made anew. The President's Special Review Board (Tower Commission), however, took essentially the same position in 1987 as had Warren Christopher in his testimony. The Board's Recommendation 2 was: "We urge the Congress not to require Senate confirmation of the National Security Adviser." In explanation, the Board urged that

> confirmation is inconsistent with the role the National Security Adviser should play. He should not decide, only advise. He should not engage in policy implementation or operations. He should serve the President, with no collateral and potentially diverting loyalties. Confirmation would tend to institutionalize the natural tension that exists between the Secretary of State and the National Security Adviser. Questions would increasingly arise about who really speaks for the President in national security matters.... Several [officials we interviewed] suggested that [requiring confirmation] could induce the President to turn to other internal staff or to people outside government to play that role.

3. *Immunities of Executive Officers from Civil Liability*

In this section we consider whether senior executive officials, including the President, should be amenable to damages for their unlawful actions. Congress has never created a cause of action for such lawsuits. In contrast, Congress long ago subjected *state* officials to liability for actions under color of law that deprive persons of their "rights, ... secured by the Constitution and laws." 42 U.S.C. § 1983. The Supreme Court filled the gap in *Bivens v. Six Unknown Named Agents of Federal Bureau of Narcotics*, 403 U.S. 388 (1971). The victim of an arrest and search claimed to be violative of the Fourth Amendment sued the responsible federal agents for damages. The Court, stating that "[h]istorically, damages have been regarded as the ordinary remedy for an invasion of personal interests in liberty," implied a cause of action for damages from the Fourth Amendment. Justice Harlan, concurring, pointed out that traditional injunctive remedies against illegal conduct are useless where a citizen not accused of any crime has been subjected to a completed constitutional violation: in such cases, "it is damages or nothing."

Bivens reserved the question whether federal defendants could assert qualified or absolute immunities from damages in at least some circumstances. The Court has since been busily about that task, as the following three cases reveal. Note that in limning immunities for federal officers, the Court has had a body of law to draw on—the immunities it had implied for state officers sued under § 1983.

Nixon v. Fitzgerald
457 U.S. 731 (1982)

Justice POWELL delivered the opinion of the Court.

The plaintiff in this lawsuit seeks relief in civil damages from a former President of the United States. The claim rests on actions allegedly taken in the former President's official capacity during his tenure in office. The issue before us is the scope of the immunity possessed by the President of the United States.

I

In January 1970 the respondent A. Ernest Fitzgerald lost his job as a management analyst with the Department of the Air Force. Fitzgerald's dismissal occurred in the context of a departmental reorganization and reduction in force, in which his job was eliminated. In announcing the reorganization, the Air Force characterized the action as taken to promote economy and efficiency in the Armed Forces.

Respondent's discharge attracted unusual attention in Congress and in the press. Fitzgerald had attained national prominence approximately one year earlier, during the waning months of the Presidency of Lyndon B. Johnson. On November 13, 1968, Fitzgerald appeared before the Subcommittee on Economy in Government of the Joint Economic Committee of . . . Congress. To the evident embarrassment of his superiors in the Department of Defense, Fitzgerald testified that cost-overruns on the C-5A transport plane could approximate $2 billion. . . .

Concerned that Fitzgerald might have suffered retaliation for his congressional testimony, the Subcommittee . . . convened public hearings on Fitzgerald's dismissal. The press reported those hearings prominently. . . . At a news conference on December 8, 1969, President Richard Nixon was queried about Fitzgerald's impending separation from Government service. The President responded by promising to look into the matter. Shortly after the news conference the petitioner asked White House Chief of Staff H. R. Haldeman to arrange for Fitzgerald's assignment to another job within the administration. . . .

Fitzgerald's proposed reassignment encountered resistance within the administration. In an internal memorandum of January 20, 1970, White House aide Alexander Butterfield reported to Haldeman that "Fitzgerald is no doubt a top-notch cost expert, but he must be given very low marks in loyalty; and after all, loyalty is the name of the game." Butterfield therefore recommended that "[w]e should let him bleed, for a while at least." There is no evidence of White House efforts to reemploy Fitzgerald subsequent to the Butterfield memorandum. . . .

At a news conference on January 31, 1973, the President [assumed] personal responsibility for Fitzgerald's dismissal:

"I was totally aware that Mr. Fitzgerald would be fired or discharged or asked to resign. . . . No, this was not a case of some person down the line deciding he should go. It was a decision that was submitted to me. I made it and I stick by it."

A day later, however, the White House press office issued a retraction of the President's statement. According to a press spokesman, the President had confused Fitzgerald with another former executive employee. On behalf of the President, the spokesman asserted that Mr. Nixon had not had "put before him the decision regarding Mr. Fitzgerald." . . .

III

A

This Court consistently has recognized that government officials are entitled to some form of immunity from suits for civil damages. In *Spalding v. Vilas*, 161 U.S. 483 (1896), the Court considered the immunity available to the Postmaster General in a suit for damages based upon his official acts. Drawing upon principles of immunity developed in English cases at common law, the Court concluded that "[t]he interests of the people" required a grant of absolute immunity to public officers. In the absence of immunity, the Court reasoned, executive officials would hesitate to exercise their discretion in a way "injuriously affect[ing] the claims of particular individuals," even when the public interest required bold and unhesitating action. Considerations of "public policy and convenience" therefore compelled a judicial recognition of immunity from suits arising from official acts. . . .

Decisions subsequent to *Spalding* have extended the defense of immunity to actions besides those at common law. In *Tenney v. Brandhove*, 341 U.S. 367 (1951), the Court considered whether the passage of 42 U.S.C. § 1983, which made no express provision for immunity for any official, had abrogated the privilege accorded to state legislators at common law. *Tenney* held that it had not. . . . Similarly, the decision in *Pierson v. Ray*, 386 U.S. 547 (1967), involving a § 1983 suit against a state judge, recognized the continued validity of the absolute immunity of judges for acts within the judicial role. . . . The Court in *Pierson* also held that police officers are entitled to a qualified immunity protecting them from suit when their official acts are performed in "good faith."

In *Scheuer v. Rhodes*, 416 U.S. 232 (1974), the Court considered the immunity available to state executive officials in a § 1983 suit alleging the violation of constitutional rights. In that case we rejected the officials' claim to absolute immunity under the doctrine of *Spalding v. Vilas*, finding instead that state executive officials possessed a "good faith" immunity from § 1983 suits alleging constitutional violations. . . . *Scheuer* established a two-tiered division of immunity defenses in § 1983 suits. To most executive officers *Scheuer* accorded qualified immunity. For them the scope of the defense varied in proportion to the nature of their official functions and the range of decisions that conceivably might be taken in "good faith." This "functional" approach also defined a second tier, however, at which the especially sensitive duties of certain officials—notably judges and prosecutors—required the continued recognition of absolute immunity. *See, e.g., Imbler v. Pachtman*, 424 U.S. 409 (1976) (state prosecutors possess absolute immunity with respect to the initiation and pursuit of prosecutions); *Stump v. Sparkman*, 435 U.S. 349 (1978) (state judge possesses absolute immunity for all judicial acts).

This approach was reviewed in detail in *Butz v. Economou*, 438 U.S. 478 (1978), when we considered for the first time the kind of immunity possessed by *federal* executive officials who are sued for constitutional violations.[25] In *Butz* the Court rejected an argument, based on decisions involving federal officials charged with common-law torts, that all high federal officials have a right to absolute immunity from constitutional damages actions. [W]e held that federal officials generally have the same qualified immunity possessed by state officials in cases under § 1983.... In *Butz* itself we upheld a claim of absolute immunity for administrative officials engaged in functions analogous to those of judges and prosecutors....

B

Our decisions concerning the immunity of government officials from civil damages liability have been guided by the Constitution, federal statutes, and history. Additionally, at least in the absence of explicit constitutional or congressional guidance, our immunity decisions have been informed by the common law. This Court necessarily also has weighed concerns of public policy, especially as illuminated by our history and the structure of our government....

Because the Presidency did not exist through most of the development of common law, any historical analysis must draw its evidence primarily from our constitutional heritage and structure. Historical inquiry thus merges almost at its inception with the kind of "public policy" analysis appropriately undertaken by a federal court. This inquiry involves policies and principles that may be considered implicit in the nature of the President's office in a system structured to achieve effective government under a constitutionally mandated separation of powers.

IV

Here a former President asserts his immunity from civil damages claims of two kinds. He stands named as a defendant in a direct action under the Constitution and in two statutory actions under federal laws of general applicability. In neither case has Congress taken express legislative action to subject the President to civil liability for his official acts.[27]

Applying the principles of our cases to claims of this kind, we hold that petitioner, as a former President of the United States, is entitled to absolute immunity from damages liability predicated on his official acts. We consider this immunity a functionally mandated incident of the President's unique office, rooted in the constitutional

---

25. *Spalding v. Vilas* was distinguished on the ground that the suit...had asserted a common-law—and not a constitutional—cause of action.

27. [W]e therefore are presented only with "implied" causes of action, and we need not address directly the immunity question as it would arise if Congress expressly had created a damages action against the President of the United States. ...[W]e assume...that private causes of action may be inferred both under the First Amendment and the two statutes on which respondent relies. But it does not follow that we must—in considering a *Bivens* remedy or interpreting a statute in light of the immunity doctrine—assume that the cause of action runs against the President of the United States.... Consequently, our holding today need only be that the President is absolutely immune from civil damages liability for his official acts in the absence of explicit affirmative action by Congress....

tradition of the separation of powers and supported by our history. Justice Story's analysis remains persuasive:

> "There are ... incidental powers, belonging to the executive department, which are necessarily implied from the nature of the functions, which are confided to it. Among these, must necessarily be included the power to perform them. . . . The president cannot, therefore, be liable to arrest, imprisonment, or detention, while he is in the discharge of the duties of his office; and for this purpose his person must be deemed, in civil cases at least, to possess an official inviolability." 3 J. Story, Commentaries on the Constitution of the United States § 1563, pp. 418-419 (1st ed. 1833).

A

The President occupies a unique position in the constitutional scheme. Article II, § 1, of the Constitution provides that "[t]he executive Power shall be vested in a President of the United States. . . . " This grant of authority establishes the President as the chief constitutional officer of the Executive Branch, entrusted with supervisory and policy responsibilities of utmost discretion and sensitivity. These include the enforcement of federal law—it is the President who is charged constitutionally to "take Care that the Laws be faithfully executed"; the conduct of foreign affairs—a realm in which the Court has recognized that "[i]t would be intolerable that courts, without the relevant information, should review and perhaps nullify actions of the Executive taken on information properly held secret"; and management of the Executive Branch—a task for which "imperative reasons requir[e] an unrestricted power [in the President] to remove the most important of his subordinates in their most important duties."

In arguing that the President is entitled only to qualified immunity, the respondent relies on cases in which we have recognized immunity of this scope for governors and cabinet officers. We find these cases to be inapposite. The President's unique status under the Constitution distinguishes him from other executive officials.[31] Be-

---

31. Noting that the Speech and Debate Clause provides a textual basis for congressional immunity, respondent argues that the Framers must be assumed to have rejected any similar grant of executive immunity. This argument is unpersuasive. First, a specific textual basis has not been considered a prerequisite to the recognition of immunity. No provision expressly confers judicial immunity. Yet the immunity of judges is well settled. Second, this Court already has established that absolute immunity may be extended to certain officials of the Executive Branch. Third, there is historical evidence from which it may be inferred that the Framers assumed the President's immunity from damages liability. At the Constitutional Convention several delegates expressed concern that subjecting the President even to impeachment would impair his capacity to perform his duties of office. See 2 M. Farrand, Records of the Federal Convention of 1787, p. 64 (1911) (remarks of Gouverneur Morris); id., at 66 (remarks of Charles Pinckney). The delegates of course did agree to an Impeachment Clause. But nothing in their debates suggests an expectation that the President would be subjected to the distraction of suits by disappointed private citizens. And Senator Maclay has recorded the views of Senator Ellsworth and Vice President John Adams—both delegates to the Convention—that "the President, personally, was not the subject to any process whatever. . . . For [that] would . . . put it in the power of a common justice to exercise any authority over him and stop the whole machine of Government." Journal of William Maclay 167 (E. Maclay ed. 1890). Justice Story, writing in 1833, held it implicit in the separation of powers that the President must be permitted to discharge his duties undistracted by private lawsuits. 3 J. Story, Commentaries on the Constitution of the United States § 1563, pp. 418-419 (1st ed. 1833). Thomas Jefferson also argued

cause of the singular importance of the President's duties, diversion of his energies by concern with private lawsuits would raise unique risks to the effective functioning of government. As is the case with prosecutors and judges—for whom absolute immunity now is established—a President must concern himself with matters likely to "arouse the most intense feelings." Yet, as our decisions have recognized, it is in precisely such cases that there exists the greatest public interest in providing an official "the maximum ability to deal fearlessly and impartially with" the duties of his office. This concern is compelling where the officeholder must make the most sensitive and far-reaching decisions entrusted to any official under our constitutional system. Nor can the sheer prominence of the President's office be ignored. In view of the visibility of his office and the effect of his actions on countless people, the President would be an easily identifiable target for suits for civil damages. Cognizance of this personal vulnerability frequently could distract a President from his public duties, to the detriment of not only the President and his office but also the Nation that the Presidency was designed to serve.

B

Courts traditionally have recognized the President's constitutional responsibilities and status as factors counseling judicial deference and restraint. For example, while courts generally have looked to the common law to determine the scope of an official's evidentiary privilege, we have recognized that the Presidential privilege is "rooted in the separation of powers under the Constitution." It is settled law that the separation-of-powers doctrine does not bar every exercise of jurisdiction over the President of the United States. But our cases also have established that a court, before exercising jurisdiction, must balance the constitutional weight of the interest to be served against the dangers of intrusion on the authority and functions of the Executive Branch. When judicial action is needed to serve broad public interests—as when the Court acts, not in derogation of the separation of powers, but to maintain their proper balance, cf. *Youngstown Sheet & Tube Co. v. Sawyer*, or to vindicate the public interest in an ongoing criminal prosecution, see *United States v. Nixon*—the exercise

---

that the President was not intended to be subject to judicial process. When Chief Justice Marshall held in *United States v. Burr*, 25 F.Cas. 30 (No. 14,692d) (CC Va.1807), that a subpoena duces tecum can be issued to a President, Jefferson protested strongly:... "The leading principle of our Constitution is the independence of the Legislature, executive and judiciary of each other ... But would the executive be independent of the judiciary, if he were subject to the *commands* of the latter, & to imprisonment for disobedience; if the several courts could bandy him from pillar to post, keep him constantly trudging from north to south & east to west, and withdraw him entirely from his constitutional duties?... " 10 The Works of Thomas Jefferson 404 n. (P. Ford ed. 1905). See also 5 D. Malone, Jefferson and His Time: Jefferson the President 320-325 (1974).

In light of the fragmentary character of the most important materials reflecting the Framers' intent, we do think that the most compelling arguments arise from the Constitution's separation of powers and the Judiciary's historic understanding of that doctrine. But our primary reliance on constitutional structure and judicial precedent should not be misunderstood. The best historical evidence clearly supports the Presidential immunity we have upheld. Justice White's dissent cites some other materials, including ambiguous comments made at state ratifying conventions and the remarks of a single publicist. But historical evidence must be weighed as well as cited.... Other powerful support derives from the actual history of private lawsuits against the President. Prior to the litigation explosion commencing with this Court's 1971 *Bivens* decision, fewer than a handful of damages actions ever were filed against the President. None appears to have proceeded to judgment on the merits.

of jurisdiction has been held warranted. In the case of this merely private suit for damages based on a President's official acts, we hold it is not.

C

In defining the scope of an official's absolute privilege, this Court has recognized that the sphere of protected action must be related closely to the immunity's justifying purposes. Frequently our decisions have held that an official's absolute immunity should extend only to acts in performance of particular functions of his office. But the Court also has refused to draw functional lines finer than history and reason would support. In view of the special nature of the President's constitutional office and functions, we think it appropriate to recognize absolute Presidential immunity from damages liability for acts within the "outer perimeter" of his official responsibility.

Under the Constitution and laws of the United States the President has discretionary responsibilities in a broad variety of areas, many of them highly sensitive. In many cases it would be difficult to determine which of the President's innumerable "functions" encompassed a particular action. In this case, for example, respondent argues that he was dismissed in retaliation for his testimony to Congress—a violation of 5 U.S.C. § 7211 and 18 U.S.C. § 1505. The Air Force, however, has claimed that the underlying reorganization was undertaken to promote efficiency. Assuming that petitioner Nixon ordered the reorganization in which respondent lost his job, an inquiry into the President's motives could not be avoided under the kind of "functional" theory asserted both by respondent and the dissent. Inquiries of this kind could be highly intrusive.

Here respondent argues that petitioner Nixon would have acted outside the outer perimeter of his duties by ordering the discharge of an employee who was lawfully entitled to retain his job in the absence of "such cause as will promote the efficiency of the service." 5 U.S.C. § 7512(a). . . . [He argues that] no federal official could, within the outer perimeter of his duties of office, cause Fitzgerald to be dismissed without satisfying this standard in prescribed statutory proceedings.

This construction would subject the President to trial on virtually every allegation that an action was unlawful, or was taken for a forbidden purpose. Adoption of this construction thus would deprive absolute immunity of its intended effect. It clearly is within the President's constitutional and statutory authority to prescribe the manner in which the Secretary will conduct the business of the Air Force. Because this [includes] the authority to prescribe reorganizations and reductions in force, we conclude that petitioner's alleged wrongful acts lay well within the outer perimeter of his authority.

V

A rule of absolute immunity for the President will not leave the Nation without sufficient protection against misconduct on the part of the Chief Executive. There remains the constitutional remedy of impeachment. In addition, there are formal and informal checks on Presidential action that do not apply with equal force to other executive officials. The President is subjected to constant scrutiny by the press. Vigilant oversight by Congress also may serve to deter Presidential abuses of office, as well as to make credible the threat of impeachment. Other incentives to avoid misconduct may include a desire to earn reelection, the need to maintain prestige as an element of Presidential influence, and a President's traditional concern for his historical stature.

The existence of alternative remedies and deterrents establishes that absolute immunity will not place the President "above the law." For the President, as for judges and prosecutors, absolute immunity merely precludes a particular private remedy for alleged misconduct in order to advance compelling public ends. . . .

Chief Justice BURGER, concurring.

I join the Court's opinion, but I write separately to underscore that the Presidential immunity . . . is mandated by the constitutional doctrine of separation of powers. . . . Absolute immunity for a President . . . is either to be found in the constitutional separation of powers or it does not exist. The Court today holds that the Constitution mandates such immunity and I agree.

Justice WHITE, with whom Justice BRENNAN, Justice MARSHALL, and Justice BLACKMUN join, dissenting.

. . . The Court now [holds that a] President, acting within the outer boundaries of what Presidents normally do, may, without liability, deliberately cause serious injury to any number of citizens even though he knows his conduct violates a statute or tramples on the constitutional rights of those who are injured. Even if the President in this case ordered Fitzgerald fired by means of a trumped-up reduction in force, knowing that such a discharge was contrary to the civil service laws, he would be absolutely immune from suit. . . . He would be immune regardless of the damage he inflicts, regardless of how violative of the statute and of the Constitution he knew his conduct to be, and regardless of his purpose. . . .

We have not taken such a scatter-gun approach in other cases. *Butz* held that absolute immunity did not attach to the office held by a member of the President's Cabinet but only to those specific functions performed by that officer for which absolute immunity is clearly essential. Members of Congress are absolutely immune under the Speech or Debate Clause of the Constitution, but the immunity extends only to their legislative acts. . . . Members of Congress, for example, repeatedly importune the executive branch and administrative agencies outside hearing rooms and legislative halls, but they are not immune if in connection with such activity they deliberately violate the law. . . . Judges are absolutely immune from liability for damages, but only when performing a judicial function, and even then they are subject to criminal liability. The absolute immunity of prosecutors is likewise limited to the prosecutorial function. A prosecutor who directs that an investigation be carried out in a way that is patently illegal is not immune. . . . The Court . . . makes no effort to distinguish categories of Presidential conduct that should be absolutely immune from other categories of conduct that should not qualify for that level of immunity.

I

. . . [This decision] has all the earmarks of a constitutional pronouncement—absolute immunity for the President's office is mandated by the Constitution. Although the Court appears to disclaim this, ante at n. 27, it is difficult to read the opinion coherently as standing for any narrower proposition: Attempts to subject the President to liability either by Congress through a statutory action or by the courts through a *Bivens* proceeding would violate the separation of powers. Such a generalized absolute immunity cannot be sustained when examined in the traditional manner and in light of the traditional judicial sources. . . .

A

The Speech or Debate Clause, Art. I, § 6, guarantees absolute immunity to Members of Congress; nowhere, however, does the Constitution directly address the issue of Presidential immunity.... The debate at the Convention on whether or not the President should be impeachable did touch on the potential dangers of subjecting the President to the control of another branch, the Legislature. Gouverneur Morris, for example, complained of the potential for dependency and argued that "[the President] can do no criminal act without Coadjutors who may be punished. In case he should be re-elected, that will be sufficient proof of his innocence." Colonel Mason responded to this by asking if "any man [shall] be above Justice" and argued that this was least appropriate for the man "who can commit the most extensive injustice." Madison agreed that "it [is] indispensable that some provision should be made for defending the Community against the incapacity, negligence or perfidy of the chief Magistrate." Pinckney responded on the other side, believing that if granted the power, the Legislature would hold impeachment "as a rod over the Executive and by that means effectually destroy his independence." ...

[T]he Convention debate did not focus on wrongs the President might commit against individuals, but rather on whether there should be a method of holding him accountable for what might be termed wrongs against the state. Thus, examples of the abuses that concerned delegates were betrayal, oppression, and bribery; the delegates feared that the alternative to an impeachment mechanism would be "tumults & insurrections" by the people in response to such abuses. 2 Farrand 67. The only conclusions that can be drawn from this debate are that the independence of the Executive was not understood to require a total lack of accountability to the other branches and that there was no general desire to insulate the President from the consequences of his improper acts.

Much the same can be said in response to petitioner's reliance on The Federalist No. 77. In that essay, Hamilton [noted that the Constitution] subjected the President to both the electoral process and the possibility of impeachment, including subsequent criminal prosecution. Petitioner concludes from this that these were intended to be the exclusive means of restraining Presidential abuses. This, by no means follows. Hamilton was concerned in The Federalist No. 77, as were the delegates at the Convention, with the larger political abuses—"wrongs against the state"—that a President might commit. He did not consider what legal means might be available for redress of individualized grievances....

The second piece of historical evidence cited by petitioner is an exchange at the first meeting of the Senate, involving Vice President Adams and Senators Ellsworth and Maclay. The debate started over whether or not the words "the President" should be included at the beginning of federal writs, similar to the manner in which English writs ran in the King's name. Senator Maclay thought that this would improperly combine the executive and judicial branches.... Senator Ellsworth and Vice President Adams defended the proposition that

> "the President, personally, was not subject to any process whatever; could have no action, whatever, brought against him; was above the power of all judges, justices, &c. For [that] would ... put it in the power of a common justice to exercise any authority over him, and stop the whole machine of government."

In their view the impeachment process was the exclusive form of process available against the President. Senator Maclay ardently opposed this view and put the case of a President committing "murder in the street." In his view, in such a case . . . there was "loyal justice." . . . Again, nothing more can be concluded from this than that the proper scope of Presidential accountability, including the question whether the President should be subject to judicial process, was no clearer then than it is now. . . .

From the history discussed above, . . . all that can be concluded is that absolute immunity from civil liability for the President finds no support in constitutional text or history, or in the explanations of the earliest commentators. This is too weak a ground to support a declaration by this Court that the President is absolutely immune from civil liability, regardless of the source of liability or the injury for which redress is sought. This much the majority implicitly concedes since history and text, traditional sources of judicial argument, merit only a footnote in the Court's opinion.

B

No bright line can be drawn between arguments for absolute immunity based on the constitutional principle of separation of powers and arguments based on what the Court refers to as "public policy." This necessarily follows from the Court's functional interpretation of the separation-of-powers doctrine. . . . Petitioner argues that public policy favors absolute immunity because absent such immunity the President's ability to execute his constitutionally mandated obligations will be impaired. The convergence of these two lines of argument is superficially apparent from the very fact that in both instances the approach of the Court has been characterized as a "functional" analysis.

The difference is only one of degree. While absolute immunity might maximize executive efficiency and therefore be a worthwhile policy, lack of such immunity may not so disrupt the functioning of the Presidency as to violate the separation-of-powers doctrine. Insofar as liability in this case is of congressional origin, petitioner must demonstrate that subjecting the President to a private damages action will prevent him from "accomplishing [his] constitutionally assigned functions." Insofar as liability is based on a *Bivens* action, perhaps a lower standard of functional disruption is appropriate. Petitioner has surely not met the former burden; I do not believe that he has met the latter standard either. . . .

The President has been held to be subject to judicial process at least since 1807. *United States v. Burr*. . . . If there is a separation-of-powers problem here, it must be found in the nature of the *remedy* and not in the *process* involved.

We said in *Butz v. Economou*, that "it is not unfair to hold liable the official who knows or should know he is acting outside the law, and . . . insisting on an awareness of clearly established constitutional limits will not unduly interfere with the exercise of official judgment." Today's decision in *Harlow v. Fitzgerald*, [*infra*] makes clear that the President, were he subject to civil liability, could be held liable only for an action that he knew, or as an objective matter should have known, was illegal and a clear abuse of his authority and power. In such circumstances, the question that must be answered is who should bear the cost of the resulting injury—the wrongdoer or the victim.

The principle that should guide the Court in deciding this question was stated long ago by Chief Justice Marshall: "The very essence of civil liberty certainly consists in the right of every individual to claim the protection of the laws, whenever he receives an injury." *Marbury v. Madison*, 1 Cranch, at 163. Much more recently, the Court considered the role of a damages remedy in the performance of the courts' traditional function of enforcing federally guaranteed rights: "Historically, damages have been regarded as the ordinary remedy for an invasion of personal interests in liberty." *Bivens v. Six Unknown Fed. Narcotics Agents*, 403 U.S., at 395. To the extent that the Court denies an otherwise appropriate remedy, it denies the victim the right to be made whole and, therefore, denies him "the protection of the laws." ...

The possibility of liability may, in some circumstances, distract officials from the performance of their duties and influence the performance of those duties in ways adverse to the public interest. But when this "public policy" argument in favor of absolute immunity is cast in these broad terms, it applies to all officers, both state and federal: All officers should perform their responsibilities without regard to those personal interests threatened by the possibility of a lawsuit. Inevitably, this reduces the public policy argument to nothing more than an expression of judicial inclination as to which officers should be encouraged to perform their functions with "vigor," although with less care. ...

II

The functional approach to the separation-of-powers doctrine and the Court's more recent immunity decisions converge on the following principle: The scope of immunity is determined by function, not office. The wholesale claim that the President is entitled to absolute immunity in all of his actions stands on no firmer ground than did the claim that all Presidential communications are entitled to an absolute privilege, which was rejected in favor of a functional analysis, by a unanimous Court in *United States v. Nixon*. Therefore, whatever may be true of the necessity of such a broad immunity in certain areas of executive responsibility, the only question that must be answered here is whether the dismissal of employees falls within a constitutionally assigned executive function, the performance of which would be substantially impaired by the possibility of a private action for damages. I believe it does not.

Respondent has so far proceeded in this action on the basis of three separate causes of action: two federal statutes—5 U.S.C. § 7211 and 18 U.S.C. § 1505—and the First Amendment. ... Assuming the correctness of the lower court's determination that the two federal statutes create a private right of action, I find the suggestion that the President is immune from those causes of action to be unconvincing. ... The first of these statutes, 5 U.S.C. § 7211, states that "[t]he right of employees ... to ... furnish information to either House of Congress, or to a committee or Member thereof, may not be interfered with or denied." The second, 18 U.S.C. § 1505, makes it a crime to obstruct congressional testimony.

It does not take much insight to see that at least one purpose of these statutes is to assure congressional access to information in the possession of the Executive Branch, which Congress believes it requires in order to carry out its responsibilities. Insofar as these statutes implicate a separation-of-powers argument, I would think it to be just the opposite of that suggested by petitioner and accepted by the majority. In enacting these statutes, Congress sought to preserve its own constitutionally mandated functions in the face of a recalcitrant Executive. ... It is no response to this to say that such a cause of action would disrupt the President in the furtherance of his responsibilities. That approach ... assumes that Presidential functions are to be valued over congressional functions.

The argument that Congress, by providing a damages action under these statutes (as is assumed in this case), has adopted an unconstitutional means of furthering its ends, must rest on the premise that Presidential control of executive employment decisions is a constitutionally assigned Presidential function with which Congress may not significantly interfere. This is a frivolous contention.... [W]ith respect to those who fill traditional bureaucratic positions, restrictions on executive authority are the rule and not the exception....

Absolute immunity is appropriate when the threat of liability may bias the decisionmaker in ways that are adverse to the public interest. But as the various regulations and statutes protecting civil servants from arbitrary executive action illustrate, this is an area in which the public interest is demonstrably on the side of encouraging less "vigor" and more "caution" on the part of decisionmakers.... Absolute immunity would be nothing more than a judicial declaration of policy that directly contradicts the policy of protecting civil servants reflected in the statutes and regulations....

It is, of course, theoretically possible that the President should be held to be absolutely immune because each of the functions for which he has constitutional responsibility would be substantially impaired by the possibility of civil liability. I do not think this argument is valid for the simple reason that the function involved here does not have this character. On which side of the line other Presidential functions would fall need not be decided in this case....

I do not believe that subjecting the President to a *Bivens* action would create separation-of-powers problems or "public policy" problems different from those involved in subjecting the President to a statutory cause of action. Relying upon the history and text of the Constitution, as well as the analytic method of our prior cases, I conclude that these problems are not sufficient to justify absolute immunity for the President in general, nor under the circumstances of this case in particular.

III

... The [majority] opinion suffers from serious ambiguity even with respect to the most fundamental point: How broad is the immunity granted the President? The opinion suggests that its scope is limited by the fact that under none of the asserted causes of action "has Congress taken express legislative action to subject the President to civil liability for his official acts." We are never told, however, how or why congressional action could make a difference. It is not apparent that any of the propositions relied upon by the majority to immunize the President would not apply equally to such a statutory cause of action; nor does the majority indicate what new principles would operate to undercut those propositions....

Focusing on the actual arguments the majority offers for its holding of absolute immunity for the President, one finds surprisingly little.... First, the majority informs us that the President occupies a "unique position in the constitutional scheme," including responsibilities for the administration of justice, foreign affairs, and management of the Executive Branch. True as this may be, it says nothing about why a "unique" rule of immunity should apply to the President. The President's unique role may indeed encompass functions for which he is entitled to a claim of absolute immunity. It does not follow from that, however, that he is entitled to absolute immunity either in general or in this case in particular....

Second, the majority contends that because the President's "visibility" makes him particularly vulnerable to suits for civil damages, a rule of absolute immunity is required. The force of this argument is surely undercut by the majority's admission that "there is no historical record of numerous suits against the President." Even granting that a *Bivens* cause of action did not become available until 1971, in the 11 years since then there have been only a handful of suits. Many of these are frivolous and dealt with in a routine manner by the courts and the Justice Department. There is no reason to think that, in the future, the protection afforded by summary judgment procedures would not be adequate to protect the President, as they currently protect other executive officers from unfounded litigation.... Even if judicial procedures were found not to be sufficient, Congress remains free to address this problem if and when it develops.

Finally, the Court suggests that potential liability "frequently could distract a President from his public duties." ... [I]n no instance have we previously held legal accountability in itself to be an unjustifiable cost.... The caution that comes from requiring reasonable choices in areas that may intrude on individuals' legally protected rights has never before been counted as a cost....

Justice BLACKMUN, with whom Justice BRENNAN and Justice MARSHALL join, dissenting.

I join Justice White's dissent. For me, the Court leaves unanswered his unanswerable argument that no man, not even the President of the United States, is absolutely and fully above the law.... Nor can I understand the Court's holding that the absolute immunity of the President is compelled by separation-of-powers concerns, when the Court at the same time expressly leaves open, ante n. 27, the possibility that the President nevertheless may be fully subject to congressionally created forms of liability. These two concepts, it seems to me, cannot coexist....

Harlow & Butterfield v. Fitzgerald
457 U.S. 800 (1982)

Justice POWELL delivered the opinion of the Court.

The issue in this case is the scope of the immunity available to the senior aides and advisers of the President of the United States in a suit for damages based upon their official acts.

I

In this suit for civil damages petitioners Bryce Harlow and Alexander Butterfield are alleged to have participated in a conspiracy to violate the constitutional and statutory rights of the respondent A. Ernest Fitzgerald ... in their capacities as senior White House aides to former President Richard M. Nixon.... Respondent claims that Harlow joined the conspiracy in his role as the Presidential aide principally responsible for congressional relations.... As evidence of Harlow's conspiratorial activity respondent relies heavily on a series of conversations in which Harlow discussed Fitzgerald's dismissal with Air Force Secretary Robert Seamans.... Disputing Fitzgerald's contentions, Harlow ... contends that he took all his actions in good faith.

Petitioner Butterfield also is alleged to have entered the conspiracy not later than May 1969. Employed as Deputy Assistant to the President and Deputy Chief of Staff to H. R. Haldeman, Butterfield circulated a White House memorandum in that month in which he claimed to have learned that Fitzgerald planned to "blow the whistle" on some "shoddy purchasing practices" by exposing these practices to public view. Fitzgerald characterizes this memorandum as evidence that Butterfield had commenced efforts to secure Fitzgerald's retaliatory dismissal.... In a subsequent memorandum emphasizing the importance of "loyalty," Butterfield counseled against offering Fitzgerald another job in the administration at that time....

Together with their codefendant Richard Nixon, petitioners Harlow and Butterfield moved for summary judgment.... In denying the motion the District Court upheld the legal sufficiency of Fitzgerald's *Bivens* claim under the First Amendment and his "inferred" statutory causes of action under 5 U.S.C. § 7211 and 18 U.S.C. § 1505. The court found that genuine issues of disputed fact remained for resolution at trial. It also ruled that petitioners were not entitled to absolute immunity.... The Court of Appeals dismissed the appeal without opinion. Never having determined the immunity available to the senior aides and advisers of the President of the United States, we granted certiorari.

I

... For executive officials in general, ... our cases make plain that qualified immunity represents the norm. In *Scheuer v. Rhodes*, we acknowledged that high officials require greater protection than those with less complex discretionary responsibilities. Nonetheless, we held that a governor and his aides could receive the requisite protection from qualified or good-faith immunity. In *Butz v. Economou*, we extended the approach of *Scheuer* to high federal officials of the Executive Branch. [We balanced] competing values: not only the importance of a damages remedy to protect the rights of citizens, but also "the need to protect officials who are required to exercise their discretion and the related public interest in encouraging the vigorous exercise of official authority." Without discounting the adverse consequences of denying high officials an absolute immunity from private lawsuits alleging constitutional violations—consequences found sufficient in *Spalding v. Vilas*, to warrant extension to such officials of absolute immunity from suits at common law—we emphasized our expectation that insubstantial suits need not proceed to trial:

> "Insubstantial lawsuits can be quickly terminated by federal courts alert to the possibilities of artful pleading. Unless the complaint states a compensable claim for relief..., it should not survive a motion to dismiss. Moreover, the Court recognized in *Scheuer* that damages suits... can be terminated on a properly supported motion for summary judgment based on the defense of immunity.... [F]irm application of the Federal Rules of Civil Procedure will ensure that federal officials are not harassed by frivolous lawsuits."...

III

A

Petitioners argue that they are entitled to a blanket protection of absolute immunity as an incident of their offices as Presidential aides. In deciding this claim we do not write on an empty page. In *Butz v. Economou*, the Secretary of Agriculture—a Cabinet official directly accountable to the President—asserted a defense of absolute official immunity from suit for civil damages. We rejected his claim. In so doing we did not question the power or the importance of the Secretary's office. Nor did we doubt the importance to the President of loyal and efficient subordinates in executing his duties of office. Yet we found these factors, alone, to be insufficient to justify absolute immunity. "[T]he greater power of [high] officials," we reasoned, "affords a greater potential for a regime of lawless conduct." ...

Having decided in *Butz* that Members of the Cabinet ordinarily enjoy only qualified immunity from suit, we conclude today that it would be equally untenable to hold absolute immunity an incident of the office of every Presidential subordinate based in the White House. Members of the Cabinet are direct subordinates of the President, frequently with greater responsibilities, both to the President and to the Nation, than White House staff. The considerations that supported our decision in *Butz* apply with equal force to this case....

B

In disputing the controlling authority of *Butz*, petitioners rely on the principles developed in *Gravel v. United States*, 408 U.S. 606 (1972). In *Gravel* we endorsed the view that "it is literally impossible ... for Members of Congress to perform their legislative tasks without the help of aides and assistants" and that "the day-to-day work of such aides is so critical to the Members' performance that they must be treated as the latter's alter egos.... " Having done so, we held the Speech and Debate Clause derivatively applicable to the "legislative acts" of a Senator's aide that would have been privileged if performed by the Senator himself.

Petitioners contend that the rationale of *Gravel* mandates a similar "derivative" immunity for the chief aides of the President of the United States. Emphasizing that the President must delegate a large measure of authority to execute the duties of his office, they argue that recognition of derivative absolute immunity is made essential by all the considerations that support absolute immunity for the President himself.

Petitioners' argument is not without force. Ultimately, however, it sweeps too far. If the President's aides are derivatively immune because they are essential to the functioning of the Presidency, so should the Members of the Cabinet—Presidential subordinates some of whose essential roles are acknowledged by the Constitution itself—be absolutely immune. Yet we implicitly rejected such derivative immunity in *Butz*. Moreover, in general our cases have followed a "functional" approach to immunity law. We have recognized that the judicial, prosecutorial, and legislative functions require absolute immunity. But this protection has extended no further than its justification would warrant. In *Gravel*, for example, we emphasized that Senators and their aides were absolutely immune only when performing "acts legislative in nature," and not when taking other acts even "in their official capacity." See *Hutchinson v. Proxmire*, 443 U.S. 111, 125-133 (1979)....

C

Petitioners also assert an entitlement to immunity based on the "special functions" of White House aides. This form of argument accords with the analytical approach of our cases. For aides entrusted with discretionary authority in such sensitive areas as national security or foreign policy, absolute immunity might well be justified to protect the unhesitating performance of functions vital to the national interest. But a "special functions" rationale does not warrant a blanket recognition of absolute immunity for all Presidential aides in the performance of all their duties. This conclusion too follows from our decision in *Butz*, which establishes that an executive official's claim to absolute immunity must be justified by reference to the public interest in the special functions of his office, not the mere fact of high station.

Butz also identifies the location of the burden of proof. The burden of justifying absolute immunity rests on the official asserting the claim.... [T]he general requisites are familiar in our cases. In order to establish entitlement to absolute immunity a Presidential aide first must show that the responsibilities of his office embraced a function so sensitive as to require a total shield from liability. He then must demonstrate that he was discharging the protected function when performing the act for which liability is asserted.

Applying these standards to the claims advanced by petitioners Harlow and Butterfield, we cannot conclude on the record before us that either has shown that "public policy requires [for any of the functions of his office] an exemption of [absolute] scope." Nor, assuming that petitioners did have functions for which absolute immunity would be warranted, could we now conclude that the acts charged in this lawsuit—if taken at all—would lie within the protected area....

IV

Even if they cannot establish that their official functions require absolute immunity, petitioners [argue for] the qualified immunity standard that would permit the defeat of insubstantial claims without resort to trial. We agree.

A

... In identifying qualified immunity as the best attainable accommodation of competing values, in *Butz*, as in *Scheuer*, we relied on the assumption that this standard would permit "[i]nsubstantial lawsuits [to] be quickly terminated." Yet petitioners advance persuasive arguments that the dismissal of insubstantial lawsuits without trial ... requires an adjustment of the "good faith" standard established by our decisions.

B

Qualified or "good faith" immunity is an affirmative defense that must be pleaded by a defendant official. *Gomez v. Toledo*, 446 U.S. 635 (1980). Decisions of this Court have established that the "good faith" defense has both an "objective" and a "subjective" aspect. The objective element involves a presumptive knowledge of and respect for "basic, unquestioned constitutional rights." *Wood v. Strickland*, 420 U.S. 308, 322 (1975). The subjective component refers to "permissible intentions." Characteristically the Court has defined these elements by identifying the circumstances in which qualified immunity would *not* be available. Referring both to the objective and subjective elements, we have held that qualified immunity would be defeated if an official *"knew or reasonably should have known* that the action he took within his sphere of official responsibility would violate the constitutional rights of the [plaintiff], *or if he took the action with the malicious intention* to cause a deprivation of constitutional rights or other injury ... " (emphasis added).

The subjective element of the good-faith defense frequently has proved incompatible with our admonition in *Butz* that insubstantial claims should not proceed to trial. Rule 56 of the Federal Rules of Civil Procedure provides that disputed questions of fact ordinarily may not be decided on motions for summary judgment. And an official's subjective good faith has been considered to be a question of fact that some courts have regarded as inherently requiring resolution by a jury.

In the context of *Butz'* attempted balancing of competing values, it now is clear that substantial costs attend the litigation of the subjective good faith of government officials. Not only are there the general costs of subjecting officials to the risks of trial—distraction of officials from their governmental duties, inhibition of discretionary action, and deterrence of able people from public service. There are special costs to "subjective" inquiries of this kind. Immunity generally is available only to officials performing discretionary functions. In contrast with the thought processes accompanying "ministerial" tasks, the judgments surrounding discretionary action almost inevitably are influenced by the decisionmaker's experiences, values, and emotions. These variables explain in part why questions of subjective intent so rarely can be decided by summary judgment. Yet they also frame a background in which there often is no clear end to the relevant evidence. Judicial inquiry into subjective motivation therefore may entail broad-ranging discovery and the deposing of numerous persons, including an official's professional colleagues. Inquiries of this kind can be peculiarly disruptive of effective government.

Consistently with the balance at which we aimed in *Butz*, we conclude today that bare allegations of malice should not suffice to subject government officials either to the costs of trial or to the burdens of broad-reaching discovery. We therefore hold that government officials performing discretionary functions generally are shielded from liability for civil damages insofar as their conduct does not violate clearly established statutory or constitutional rights of which a reasonable person would have known. . . .

Where an official could be expected to know that certain conduct would violate statutory or constitutional rights, he should be made to hesitate; and a person who suffers injury caused by such conduct may have a cause of action. But where an official's duties legitimately require action in which clearly established rights are not implicated, the public interest may be better served by action taken "with independence and without fear of consequences."

C

In this case petitioners have asked us to hold that the respondent's pretrial showings were insufficient to survive their motion for summary judgment. We think it appropriate, however, to remand the case to the District Court for its reconsideration of this issue in light of this opinion. . . .

Justice BRENNAN, with whom Justice MARSHALL and Justice BLACKMUN join, concurring.

I agree with the substantive standard announced by the Court today, imposing liability when a public-official defendant "knew or should have known" of the constitutionally violative effect of his actions. This standard would not allow the official who *actually knows* that he was violating the law to escape liability for his actions, even if he could not "reasonably have been expected" to know what he actually did know. Thus the clever and unusually well-informed violator of constitutional rights will not evade just punishment for his crimes. . . . I write separately only to note that given this standard, it seems inescapable to me that some measure of discovery may sometimes be required to determine exactly what a public-official defendant did "know" at the time of his actions. . . .

Justice REHNQUIST, concurring.

At such time as a majority of the Court is willing to re-examine our holding in *Butz v. Economou*, I shall join in that undertaking with alacrity. But until that time comes, I agree that the Court's opinion in this case properly disposes of the issues presented, and I therefore join it.

Chief Justice BURGER, dissenting.

... In this case the Court decides that senior aides of the President do not have derivative immunity from the President. I am at a loss, however, to reconcile this conclusion with our holding in *Gravel v. United States*.... We very properly recognized in *Gravel* that the central purpose of a Member's absolute immunity would be "diminished and frustrated" if the legislative aides were not also protected by the same broad immunity.... [W]ithout absolute immunity for these "elbow aides," who are indeed "alter egos," a Member could not effectively discharge all of the assigned constitutional functions of a modern legislator.

The Court has made this reality a matter of our constitutional jurisprudence. How can we conceivably hold that a President of the United States, who represents a vastly larger constituency than does any Member of Congress, should not have "alter egos" with comparable immunity? To perform the constitutional duties assigned to the Executive would be "literally impossible, in view of the complexities of the modern [Executive] process, ... without the help of aides and assistants." These words reflect the precise analysis of *Gravel*, and this analysis applies with at least as much force to a President. The primary layer of senior aides of a President—like a Senator's "alter egos"—are literally at a President's elbow, with offices a few feet or at most a few hundred feet from his own desk. The President, like a Member of Congress, may see those personal aides many times in one day. They are indeed the President's "arms" and "fingers" to aid in performing his constitutional duty to see "that the laws [are] faithfully executed." Like a Member of Congress, but on a vastly greater scale, the President cannot personally implement a fraction of his own policies and day-to-day decisions....

Precisely the same public policy considerations on which the Court now relies in *Nixon v. Fitzgerald*, and that we relied on only recently in *Gravel*, are fully applicable to senior Presidential aides.... In addition, exposure to civil liability for official acts will result in constant judicial questioning, through judicial proceedings and pretrial discovery, into the inner workings of the Presidential Office beyond that necessary to maintain the traditional checks and balances of our constitutional structure....

The *Gravel* Court took note of the burdens on congressional aides: the stress of long hours, heavy responsibilities, constant exposure to harassment of the political arena. Is the Court suggesting the stresses are less for Presidential aides? By construing the Constitution to give only qualified immunity to senior Presidential aides we give those key "alter egos" only lawsuits, winnable lawsuits perhaps, but lawsuits nonetheless, with stress and effort that will disperse and drain their energies and their purses....

Butz v. Economou does not dictate that senior Presidential aides be given only qualified immunity. *Butz* held only that a Cabinet officer exercising discretion was not entitled to absolute immunity; we need not abandon that holding. A senior Presidential aide works more intimately with the President on a daily basis than does a Cabinet officer, directly implementing Presidential decisions literally from hour to hour....

The Court's analysis in *Gravel* demonstrates that the question of derivative immunity does not and should not depend on a person's rank or position in the hierarchy, but on the *function* performed by the person and the relationship of that person to the superior.... The function of senior Presidential aides, as the "alter egos" of the President, is an integral, inseparable part of the function of the President....

Mitchell v. Forsyth
472 U.S. 511 (1985)

Justice WHITE delivered the opinion of the Court.

This is a suit for damages stemming from a warrantless wiretap authorized by petitioner, a former Attorney General of the United States. The case presents [the question] whether the Attorney General is absolutely immune from suit for actions undertaken in the interest of national security....

I

In 1970, the Federal Bureau of Investigation learned that members of an antiwar group known as the East Coast Conspiracy to Save Lives (ECCSL) had made plans to blow up heating tunnels linking federal office buildings in Washington, D.C., and had also discussed the possibility of kidnaping then National Security Adviser Henry Kissinger. On November 6, 1970, acting on the basis of this information, the then Attorney General John Mitchell authorized a warrantless wiretap on the telephone of William Davidon, a Haverford College physics professor who was a member of the group. According to the Attorney General, the purpose of the wiretap was the gathering of intelligence in the interest of national security.

[T]he Government intercepted three conversations between Davidon and respondent Keith Forsyth. The record before us does not suggest that the intercepted conversations, which appear to be innocuous, were ever used against Forsyth in any way.... [Revelation of the tap to Forsyth in other litigation was accompanied by an] affidavit, sworn to by then Attorney General Richard Kleindienst, averring that the surveillance to which Forsyth had been subjected was authorized "in the exercise of [the President's] authority relating to the national security...."

Shortly thereafter, this Court ruled that the Fourth Amendment does not permit the use of warrantless wiretaps in cases involving domestic threats to the national security. *United States v. United States District Court*, 407 U.S. 297 (1972) (*Keith*). In the wake of the *Keith* decision, Forsyth filed this lawsuit.... Forsyth alleged that the surveillance to which he had been subjected violated both the Fourth Amendment and Title III of the Omnibus Crime Control and Safe Streets Act, 18 U.S.C. §§ 2510-2520, which sets forth comprehensive standards governing the use of wiretaps and electronic surveillance by both governmental and private agents. He asserted that both the constitutional and statutory provisions provided him with a private right of action; he sought compensatory, statutory, and punitive damages....

The District Court rejected Mitchell's argument that under [the *Harlow*] standard he should be held immune from suit for warrantless national security wiretaps authorized before this Court's decision in *Keith*: that decision was merely a logical extension of general Fourth Amendment principles and in particular of the ruling in *Katz v. United States*, 389 U.S. 347 (1967), in which the Court held for the first time that electronic surveillance unaccompanied by physical trespass constituted a search subject to the Fourth Amendment's warrant requirement. Mitchell and the Justice Department, the court suggested, had chosen to "gamble" on the possibility that this Court would create an exception to the warrant requirement if presented with a case involving national security. Having lost the gamble, Mitchell was not entitled to complain of the consequences. The court therefore denied Mitchell's motion for summary judgment, granted Forsyth's motion for summary judgment on the issue of liability, and scheduled further proceedings on the issue of damages....

II

We first address Mitchell's claim that the Attorney General's actions in furtherance of the national security should be shielded from scrutiny in civil damage actions by an absolute immunity similar to that afforded the President, judges, prosecutors, witnesses, and officials performing "quasi-judicial" functions, ... We conclude that the Attorney General is not absolutely immune from suit for damages arising out of his allegedly unconstitutional conduct in performing his national security functions.

As the Nation's chief law enforcement officer, the Attorney General provides vital assistance to the President in the performance of the latter's constitutional duty to "preserve, protect, and defend the Constitution of the United States." U.S. Const., Art. II, § 1, cl. 8. Mitchell's argument, in essence, is that the national security functions of the Attorney General are so sensitive, so vital to the protection of our Nation's well-being, that we cannot tolerate any risk that in performing those functions he will be chilled by the possibility of personal liability for acts that may be found to impinge on the constitutional rights of citizens....

Our decisions in this area leave no doubt that the Attorney General's status as a Cabinet officer is not in itself sufficient to invest him with absolute immunity.... Mitchell's claim, then, must rest not on the Attorney General's position within the Executive Branch, but on the nature of the functions he was performing in this case. Because Mitchell was not acting in a prosecutorial capacity in this case, the situations in which we have applied a functional approach to absolute immunity questions provide scant support for blanket immunization of his performance of the "national security function."

First, in deciding whether officials performing a particular function are entitled to absolute immunity, we have generally looked for a historical or common-law basis for the immunity in question.... Mitchell points to no analogous historical or common-law basis for an absolute immunity for officers carrying out tasks essential to national security.

Second, the performance of national security functions does not subject an official to the same obvious risks of entanglement in vexatious litigation as does the carrying out of the judicial or "quasi-judicial" tasks that have been the primary wellsprings of absolute immunities. The judicial process is an arena of open conflict, and in virtually every case there is, if not always a winner, at least one loser. It is inevitable that many of those who lose will pin the blame on judges, prosecutors, or witnesses and will bring suit against them in an effort to relitigate the underlying conflict. National security tasks, by contrast, are carried out in secret; open conflict and overt winners and losers are rare. Under such circumstances, it is far more likely that actual abuses will go uncovered than that fancied abuses will give rise to unfounded and burdensome litigation. Whereas the mere threat of litigation may significantly affect the fearless and independent performance of duty by actors in the judicial process, it is unlikely to have a similar effect on the Attorney General's performance of his national security tasks.

Third, most of the officials who are entitled to absolute immunity from liability for damages are subject to other checks that help to prevent abuses of authority from going unredressed. Legislators are accountable to their constituents, and the judicial process is largely self-correcting: procedural rules, appeals, and the possibility of collateral challenges obviate the need for damage actions to prevent unjust results. Similar built-in restraints on the Attorney General's activities in the name of national security, however, do not exist. And despite our recognition of the importance of those activities to the safety of our Nation and its democratic system of government, we cannot accept the notion that restraints are completely unnecessary. . . .

We emphasize that the denial of absolute immunity will not leave the Attorney General at the mercy of litigants with frivolous and vexatious complaints. Under the standard of qualified immunity articulated in *Harlow v. Fitzgerald*, the Attorney General will be entitled to immunity so long as his actions do not violate "clearly established statutory or constitutional rights of which a reasonable person would have known." . . . We do not believe that the security of the Republic will be threatened if its Attorney General is given incentives to abide by clearly established law.

III

. . . [*Harlow*'s concerns] are not limited to liability for money damages; they also include "the general costs of subjecting officials to the risks of trial—distraction of officials from their governmental duties, inhibition of discretionary action, and deterrence of able people from public service." Indeed, *Harlow* emphasizes that even such pretrial matters as discovery are to be avoided if possible, as "(i)nquiries of this kind can be peculiarly disruptive of effective government." . . .

Accordingly, we hold that a district court's denial of a claim of qualified immunity, to the extent that it turns on an issue of law, is an appealable "final decision" within the meaning of 28 U.S.C. § 1291 notwithstanding the absence of a final judgment.

IV

. . . Under *Harlow v. Fitzgerald*, Mitchell is immune unless his actions violated clearly established law. Forsyth complains that in November, 1970, Mitchell authorized a warrantless wiretap aimed at gathering intelligence regarding a domestic threat to national security—the kind of wiretap that the Court subsequently declared to be illegal. *Keith*. The question of Mitchell's immunity turns on whether it was clearly established in November, 1970, well over a year before *Keith* was decided, that such wiretaps were unconstitutional. We conclude that it was not. . . .

As of 1970, the Justice Departments of six successive administrations had considered warrantless domestic security wiretaps constitutional. Only three years earlier, this Court had expressly left open the possibility that this view was correct. Two Federal District Courts had accepted the Justice Department's position, and although the Sixth Circuit later firmly rejected the notion that the Fourth Amendment countenanced warrantless domestic security wiretapping, this Court found the issue sufficiently doubtful to warrant the exercise of its discretionary jurisdiction. In framing the issue before it, the *Keith* Court explicitly recognized that the question was one that had yet to receive the definitive answer that it demanded. . . .

The District Court's conclusion that Mitchell is not immune because he gambled and lost on the resolution of this open question departs from the principles of *Harlow*. Such hindsight-based reasoning on immunity issues is precisely what *Harlow* rejected. The decisive fact is not that Mitchell's position turned out to be incorrect, but that the question was open at the time he acted. Hence, in the absence of contrary directions from Congress, Mitchell is immune from suit for his authorization of the Davidon wiretap notwithstanding that his actions violated the Fourth Amendment....

Justice STEVENS, concurring in the judgment.

. . . The absolute immunity of the President of the United States rests, in part, on the absence of any indication that the authors of either the constitutional text or any relevant statutory text intended to subject him to damages liability predicated on his official acts.

The practical consequences of a holding that no remedy has been authorized against a public official are essentially the same as those flowing from a conclusion that the official has absolute immunity. Moreover, similar factors are evaluated in deciding whether to recognize an implied cause of action or a claim of immunity. In both situations, when Congress is silent, the Court makes an effort to ascertain its probable intent. In my opinion, when Congress has legislated in a disputed area, that legislation is just as relevant to any assertion of official immunity as to the analysis of the question whether an implied cause of action should be recognized.

In Title III of the Omnibus Crime Control and Safe Streets Act of 1968, Congress enacted comprehensive legislation regulating the electronic interception of wire and oral communications. See 18 U.S.C. §§ 2510-2520. One section of that Act, § 2511(3), specifically exempted "any wire or oral communication intercepted by authority of the President" for national security purposes. In *United States v. United States District Court (Keith)*, 407 U.S. 297 (1972), the Court held that certain wiretaps authorized by the Attorney General were covered by the proviso in § 2511(3) and therefore exempt from the prohibitions in Title III....

The Court's determination ... that Attorney General Mitchell was exercising the discretionary "power of the President" in the area of national security when he authorized these episodes of surveillance, inescapably leads to the conclusion that absolute immunity attached to the special function then being performed by Mitchell. In *Harlow v. Fitzgerald*, the court explicitly noted that absolute immunity may be justified for Presidential "aides entrusted with discretionary authority in such sensitive areas as national security or foreign policy ... to protect the unhesitating performance of functions vital to the national interest." In "such 'central' Presidential domains as foreign policy and national security" the President can not "discharge his singularly vital mandate without delegating functions nearly as sensitive as his own."

Here, the President expressly had delegated the responsibility to approve national security wiretaps to the Attorney General. The Attorney General determined that the wiretap in this case was essential to gather information about a conspiracy that might be plotting to kidnap a Presidential adviser and sabotage essential facilities in government buildings. That the Attorney General was too vigorous in guaranteeing the personal security of a Presidential aide and the physical integrity of important government facilities does not justify holding him personally accountable for damages in a civil action that has not been authorized by Congress.

When the Attorney General, the Secretary of State, and the Secretary of Defense make erroneous decisions on matters of national security and foreign policy, the primary liabilities are political. Intense scrutiny, by the people, by the press, and by Congress, has been the traditional method for deterring violations of the Constitution by these high officers of the Executive Branch. Unless Congress authorizes other remedies, it presumably intends the retributions for any violations to be undertaken by political action. Congress is in the best position to decide whether the incremental deterrence added by a civil damages remedy outweighs the adverse effect that the exposure to personal liability may have on governmental decision making. . . .

The availability of qualified immunity is hardly comforting when it took 13 years for the federal courts to determine that the plaintiff's claim in this case was without merit. If the Attorney General had violated the provisions of Title III, . . . he would have no immunity. Congress, however, had expressly refused to enact a civil remedy against cabinet officials exercising the President's powers described in § 2511(3). In that circumstance, I believe the cabinet official is entitled to the same absolute imm unity as the President of the United States. Indeed, it is highly doubtful whether the rationale of *Bivens v. Six Unknown Federal Narcotics Agents*, 403 U.S. 388 (1971), even supports an implied cause of action for damages after Congress has enacted legislation comprehensively regulating the field of electronic surveillance but has specifically declined to impose a remedy for the national security wiretaps described in § 2511(3). . . .

[Justices POWELL and REHNQUIST took no part in the decision. Chief Justice BURGER concurred; he thought the Attorney General was "entitled to absolute immunity for . . . his exercise of the discretionary power of the President in the area of national security." Justice O'CONNOR concurred, emphasizing that the denial of immunity comes within a "small class" of immediately appealable interlocutory orders. Justices BRENNAN and MARSHALL concurred that qualified immunity was the correct standard, but dissented from the holding that denials of immunity are immediately appealable.]

---

1. The majority in *Nixon v. Fitzgerald* reserves the question whether Congress could create a statutory damages remedy against the President. What do you think? Consider Chief Justice Burger's statement that "[a]bsolute immunity for a President . . . is either to be found in the constitutional separation of powers or it does not exist. The Court today holds that the Constitution mandates such immunity and I agree."

2. As an alternative ground of decision, the Court could have declined to imply a cause of action against the President under *Bivens*, noting that Congress had legislated to forbid obstructing congressional testimony, but had provided no damages remedy, suggesting that it had decided to eschew one. (Compare Justice Stevens' similar argument regarding the wiretap laws in *Mitchell*.) Would the Court have been wise to take this tack, inviting Congress to legislate if it cared to?

Should the Court have held instead that the *separation of powers* precludes judicial implication of a *Bivens*-style damages remedy against the President, given the textual commitment to Congress of power to discipline Presidents? *See* Carter, *The Political Aspects of Judicial Power: Some Notes on the Presidential Immunity Decision*, 131 U. Pa. L. Rev. 1341, 1366-68 (1983):

The balance of powers among the three branches of the federal government is a delicate construct, and if any one of the branches is empowered to create new checks on the others that branch will be in the position to upset the very balance that it purports to protect.... That is why the federal courts cannot create a cause of action for damages running against a President....

3. Note the *Fitzgerald* Court's rejection (in note 31) of a structural argument against presidential immunity, based on the presence of congressional immunity. Is Justice White right when he chides the majority for giving arguments from text and history short shrift?

In note 31, the Court remarks on the paucity of pre-*Bivens* suits against the President for damages. Which way does that cut? The best-known precedent is *Livingston v. Jefferson*, 15 F. Cas. 660 (No. 8,411)(C.C. Va. 1811). An old enemy of Jefferson's, who claimed land in New Orleans, sued the former President for damages for having secured possession for the United States by sending in the U.S. Marshal. The suit was dismissed by the ubiquitous John Marshall (pursuant to his circuit duties) because it was not brought where the land was. The story is engagingly told by Degnan, *Livingston v. Jefferson—A Freestanding Footnote*, 75 Calif. L. Rev. 115 (1987).

4. Is Justice White correct in characterizing the Court's approach to separation of powers questions in *Fitzgerald* as "functional," and closely akin to public policy analysis? If so, does Powell or White have the better of the functional argument? For example, are you persuaded that the protections against presidential misconduct catalogued by Justice Powell in Part V of his opinion are sufficient to preserve individual rights?

5. Under a functional analysis, what weight should be given to congressional attempts to ensure that the executive branch operates in compliance with law? Fitzgerald was a prominent example of a "whistleblower," someone who exposes illegality or at least mismanagement in government programs. Congress has since expanded protection for whistleblowers, forbidding reprisals for disclosures of information reasonably believed to evidence a violation of law or regulation, mismanagement, and the like. 5 U.S.C. § 2302(b)(8). *See* Vaughn, *Statutory Protection of Whistleblowers in the Federal Executive Branch*, 1982 U. Ill. L. Rev. 615. Alas, there are signs that employees still decline to reveal waste and illegality out of fear of reprisal. U.S. Merit Systems Protection Board, Blowing the Whistle in the Federal Government 24 (1984). If the Court were informed of all this, should it imply a damages remedy to help Congress achieve its manifest aims?

6. Part IV of *Harlow* recognizes that, to be of use, qualified immunity must defeat insubstantial claims without going to trial. Is the Court's reformulation of the immunity in *Harlow* likely to achieve that end? Unhappily, as then-Judge Scalia has pointed out, whether conduct violates clearly established rights "often, if not invariably, depends on the intent with which the conduct is performed." *Halperin v. Kissinger*, 807 F.2d 180, 184 (D.C. Cir. 1986). Thus, the legality of the wiretap involved in *Halperin* depended on whether its purpose was to obtain foreign intelligence. After noting that *Harlow* was "to say the least, unclear" about how to handle such problems, Scalia concluded:

> [A]t least where ... the officials claiming immunity purported at the time ... to have been motivated by national security concerns, a purely objective inquiry into the pretextuality of the purpose is appropriate. That is to say, if the facts

establish that the purported national security motivation would have been reasonable, the immunity defense will prevail.

See also Note, *Qualified Immunity for Government Officials: The Problem of Unconstitutional Purpose in Civil Rights Litigation,* 95 Yale L. J. 126 (1985).

7. Why does the *Harlow* Court deny the executive the benefit of the "alter ego" immunity that congressional aides enjoy? Is it so that presidential aides will have an incentive to resist, and ultimately to refuse, presidential orders that they consider illegal?

8. A further complication exists for government lawyers trying these cases. Sometimes the terms of an agency's appropriations may be broad enough to permit the agency to settle a lawsuit against an employee sued in his or her individual capacity, although the agency would be precluded from indemnifying the employee for damages awarded after a trial. In such a case, if the Department of Justice provides representation for the employee, it is problematic whether the employee's true adversary is the plaintiff or the employee's own agency. The Department does sometimes provide for retention of private defense counsel. *See* Senate Subcomm. on Administrative Practice and Procedure, Comm. on the Judiciary, Justice Department Retention of Private Legal Counsel to Represent Federal Employees in Civil Lawsuits, 95th Cong., 2d Sess. (Comm. Print 1978).

9. After *Mitchell,* what specific functions of presidential aides are likely to receive absolute immunity? What about those relating to defense and foreign policy? Are they sharply different from the national security functions involved in *Mitchell*?

10. Should Congress waive sovereign immunity for constitutional torts of executive officers, in exchange for conferring absolute immunity on government employees? For the Carter administration's proposals to this effect, *see* Bell, *Proposed Amendments to the Federal Tort Claims Act,* 16 Harv. J. Legis. 1 (1979); *see also* Madden, Allard & Remes, *Bedtime for* Bivens: *Substituting the United States as Defendant in Constitutional Tort Suits,* 20 Harv. J. Legis. 469 (1983). It has been argued that existing law provides strong incentives for risk-averse officials to avoid vigorous discharge of their duties, out of fear of liability, or at least litigation. P. Schuck, Suing Government (1983); Cass, *Damage Suits Against Public Officers,* 129 U. Pa. L. Rev. 1110 (1981). How would you advise Congress on this subject? Would your advice to the executive be different?

Chapter 4

The President as Chief Administrator

Among the President's institutional roles, the most familiar is that of chief administrator, the head of the executive branch. In this chapter, we consider the powers through which he fulfills that role: the appointment and removal of officers, the organization and direction of government agencies, and, on the financial side, control of the executive budget process and the spending of appropriations. With respect to many problems connected with this role of the President, courts and commentators have given analytical weight to various interpretations of the "faithful execution" clause. You will have to consider the degree to which this clause both vests a duty and implies additional powers.

A. Appointments

1. Executive officers

Buckley v. Valeo
424 U.S. 1 (1976)

[In a long per curiam opinion, the Court decided a series of constitutional challenges to the Federal Election Campaign Act of 1971, which was a comprehensive attempt to reform the processes of electing federal officials by limiting political contributions and expenditures, establishing public funding for campaigns, and requiring financial recordkeeping and disclosures by candidates and political committees. After considering these features of the Act, the Court turned to the constitutionality of the structure and operation of the Federal Election Commission, created by Congress to administer the Act:]

IV. The Federal Election Commission

The 1974 amendments to the Act create an eight-member Federal Election Commission, and vest in it primary and substantial responsibility for administering and enforcing the Act. The question ... is whether, in view of the manner in which a majority of its members are appointed, the Commission may under the Constitution exercise the powers conferred upon it. ... It will suffice for present purposes to describe what appear to be representative examples of its various powers.

Beyond ... recordkeeping, disclosure, and investigative functions, ... the Commission is given extensive rulemaking and adjudicative powers. ... [2 U.S.C.] Section

437d(a)(9) authorizes it to "formulate general policy with respect to the administration of this Act" and enumerated sections of Title 18's Criminal Code, as to all of which provisions the Commission "has primary jurisdiction with respect to [their] civil enforcement." § 437c(b). The Commission is authorized ... to render advisory opinions with respect to activities possibly violating the Act, the Title 18 sections, or the campaign funding provisions of Title 26; [those relying on advisory opinions are] presumed to be in compliance with the [statutory provision] with respect to which such advisory opinion is rendered." ...

The Commission's enforcement power is both direct and wide ranging. It may institute a civil action for [declaratory or injunctive relief to enforce the campaign laws.] ... If after the Commission's ... audit of candidates ... it finds an overpayment, it is empowered to seek repayment of all funds due the Secretary of the Treasury. In no respect do the foregoing civil actions require the concurrence of or participation by the Attorney General; conversely, the decision not to seek judicial relief in the above respects would appear to rest solely with the Commission. With respect to the referenced Title 18 sections, § 437g(a)(7) provides that if, after notice and opportunity for a hearing before it, the Commission finds an actual or threatened criminal violation, the Attorney General "upon request by the Commission ... shall institute a civil action for relief." Finally, as "[a]dditional enforcement authority," § 456(a) authorizes the Commission, after notice and opportunity for hearing, to make "a finding that a person ... failed to file" a required report of contributions or expenditures. [The candidate is thereby disqualified from seeking federal office for a year.] ...

The body in which this authority is reposed consists of eight members. The Secretary of the Senate and the Clerk of the House of Representatives are ex officio members of the Commission without the right to vote. Two members are appointed by the President pro tempore of the Senate "upon the recommendations of the majority leader of the Senate and the minority leader of the Senate." Two more are to be appointed by the Speaker of the House of Representatives, likewise upon the recommendations of its respective majority and minority leaders. The remaining two members are appointed by the President. Each of the six voting members of the Commission must be confirmed by the majority of both Houses of Congress, and each of the three appointing authorities is forbidden to choose both of their appointees from the same political party. ...

B. The Merits

Appellants urge that since Congress has given the Commission wide-ranging rulemaking and enforcement powers with respect to the substantive provisions of the Act, Congress is precluded under the principle of separation of powers from vesting in itself the authority to appoint those who will exercise such authority. Their argument is based on the language of Art. II, § 2, cl. 2, of the Constitution. ... Appellants' argument is that this provision is the exclusive method by which those charged with executing the laws of the United States may be chosen. ...

Appellee Commission and amici in support of the Commission urge that the Framers of the Constitution, while mindful of the need for checks and balances among the three branches of the National Government, had no intention of denying to the Legislative Branch authority to appoint its own officers. Congress, either under the Appointments Clause or under its grants of substantive legislative authority and the

Necessary and Proper Clause in Art. I, is in their view empowered to provide for the appointment to the Commission in the manner which it did because the Commission is performing "appropriate legislative functions." . . .

1. Separation of Powers

. . . Our inquiry of necessity touches upon the fundamental principles of the Government established by the Framers of the Constitution, and all litigants and all of the courts which have addressed themselves to the matter start on common ground in the recognition of the intent of the Framers that the powers of the three great branches of the National Government be largely separate from one another.

James Madison, writing in the Federalist No. 47, defended the work of the Framers against the charge that these three governmental powers were not *entirely* separate from one another in the proposed Constitution. He asserted that while there was some admixture, the Constitution was nonetheless true to Montesquieu's well-known maxim that the legislative, executive, and judicial departments ought to be separate and distinct:

> "The reasons on which Montesquieu grounds his maxim are a further demonstration of his meaning. 'When the legislative and executive powers are united in the same person or body,' says he, 'there can be no liberty, because apprehensions may arise lest *the same* monarch or senate should *enact* tyrannical laws to *execute* them in a tyrannical manner.' Again: 'Were the power of judging joined with the legislative, the life and liberty of the subject would be exposed to arbitrary control, for *the judge* would then be *the legislator*. Were it joined to the executive power, *the judge* might behave with all the violence of *an oppressor. . . .* ' " (emphasis in original)

Yet it is also clear from the provisions of the Constitution itself, and from the Federalist Papers, that the Constitution by no means contemplates total separation of each of these three essential branches of Government. The President is a participant in the law-making process by virtue of his authority to veto bills enacted by Congress. The Senate is a participant in the appointive process by virtue of its authority to refuse to confirm persons nominated to office by the President. The men who met in Philadelphia in the summer of 1787 were practical statesmen, experienced in politics, who viewed the principle of separation of powers as a vital check against tyranny. But they likewise saw that a hermetic sealing off of the three branches of Government from one another would preclude the establishment of a Nation capable of governing itself effectively. . . . The Framers regarded the checks and balances that they had built into the tripartite Federal Government as a self-executing safeguard against the encroachment or aggrandizement of one branch at the expense of the other. . . .

The Court has held that executive or administrative duties of a nonjudicial nature may not be imposed on judges holding office under Art. III of the Constitution. *United States v. Ferreira*, 54 U.S. (13 How.) 40 (1852); *Hayburn's Case*, 2 U.S. (2 Dall.) 409 (1792). The Court has held that the President may not execute and exercise legislative authority belonging only to Congress. *Youngstown Sheet & Tube Co. v. Sawyer*. . . . More closely in point to the facts of the present case is this Court's decision in *Springer v. Philippine Islands*, 277 U.S. 189 (1928), where the Court held that the legislature of the Philippine Islands could not provide for legislative appointment to executive agencies.

2. The Appointments Clause

The principle of separation of powers was not simply an abstract generalization in the minds of the Framers: it was woven into the document that they drafted in Philadelphia in the summer of 1787. Article I, § 1, declares: "All legislative Powers herein granted shall be vested in a Congress of the United States." Article II, § 1, vests the executive power "in a President of the United States of America," and Art. III, § 1, declares that "The judicial Power of the United States, shall be vested in one supreme Court, and in such inferior Courts as the Congress may from time to time ordain and establish." The further concern of the Framers of the Constitution with maintenance of the separation of powers is found in the so-called "Ineligibility" and "Incompatibility" Clauses contained in Art. I, § 6. . . .

It is in the context of these cognate provisions of the document that we must examine the language of Art. II, § 2, cl. 2, which appellants contend provides the only authorization for appointment of those to whom substantial executive or administrative authority is given by statute. . . . The Appointments Clause could, of course, be read as merely dealing with etiquette or protocol in describing "Officers of the United States," but the drafters had a less frivolous purpose in mind. This conclusion is supported by language from *United States v. Germaine*, 99 U.S. 508, 509-510 (1879):

> "The Constitution for purposes of appointment very clearly divides all its officers into two classes. The primary class requires a nomination by the President and confirmation by the Senate. But foreseeing that when offices became numerous, and sudden removals necessary, this mode might be inconvenient, it was provided that, in regard to officers inferior to those specially mentioned, Congress might by law vest their appointment in the President alone, in the courts of law, or in the heads of departments. *That all persons who can be said to hold an office under the government about to be established under the Constitution were intended to be included within one or the other of these modes of appointment there can be but little doubt.*" (Emphasis supplied.)

We think that the term "Officers of the United States" as used in Art. II, defined to include "all persons who can be said to hold an office under the government" in *United States v. Germaine*, is a term intended to have substantive meaning. We think its fair import is that any appointee exercising significant authority pursuant to the laws of the United States is an "Officer of the United States," and must, therefore, be appointed in the manner prescribed by § 2, cl. 2, of that Article. . . . If a postmaster first class, *Myers v. United States*, 272 U.S. 52 (1926), and the clerk of a district court, *Ex parte Hennen*, 38 U.S. 225, 13 Pet. 230 (1839), are inferior officers of the United States within the meaning of the Appointments Clause, as they are, surely the Commissioners before us are at the very least such "inferior Officers" within the meaning of that Clause.[162]

---

162. "Officers of the United States" does not include all employees of the United States, but there is no claim made that the Commissioners are employees of the United States rather than officers. Employees are lesser functionaries subordinate to officers of the United States, see *Auffmordt v. Hedden*, 137 U.S. 310, 327 (1890); *United States v. Germaine*, 99 U.S. 508 (1897), whereas the Commissioners, appointed for a statutory term, are not subject to the control or direction of any other executive, judicial, or legislative authority.

Although two members of the Commission are initially selected by the President, his nominations are subject to confirmation not merely by the Senate, but by the House of Representatives as well. The remaining four voting members of the Commission are appointed by the President pro tempore of the Senate and by the Speaker of the House. While the second part of the Clause authorizes Congress to vest the appointment of the officers described in that part in "the Courts of Law, or in the Heads of Departments," neither the Speaker of the House nor the President pro tempore of the Senate comes within this language.

The phrase "Heads of Departments," used as it is in conjunction with the phrase "Courts of Law," suggests that the Departments referred to are themselves in the Executive Branch or at least have some connection with that branch. While the Clause expressly authorizes Congress to vest the appointment of certain officers in the "Courts of Law," the absence of similar language to include Congress must mean that neither Congress nor its officers were included within the language "Heads of Departments" in this part of cl. 2.

Thus with respect to four of the six voting members of the Commission, neither the President, the head of any department, nor the Judiciary has any voice in their selection. The Appointments Clause specifies the method of appointment only for "Officers of the United States" whose appointment is not "otherwise provided for" in the Constitution. But there is no provision of the Constitution remotely providing any alternative means for the selection of the members of the Commission or for anybody like them. Appellee Commission has argued, . . . that the Appointments Clause of Art. II should not be read to exclude the "inherent power of Congress" to appoint its own officers to perform functions necessary to that body as an institution. But there is no need to read the Appointments Clause contrary to its plain language in order to reach [that] result. . . . Ranking nonmembers, such as the Clerk of the House of Representatives, are elected under the internal rules of each House and are designated by statute as "officers of the Congress." . . . [N]othing in our holding with respect to Art. II, § 2, cl. 2, will deny to Congress "all power to appoint its own inferior officers to carry out appropriate legislative functions."

Appellee Commission and amici contend somewhat obliquely that because the Framers had no intention of relegating Congress to a position below that of the coequal Judicial and Executive Branches of the National Government, the Appointments Clause must somehow be read to include Congress or its officers as among those in whom the appointment power may be vested. But the debates of the Constitutional Convention, and the Federalist Papers, are replete with expressions of fear that the Legislative Branch of the National Government will aggrandize itself at the expense of the other two branches. The debates during the Convention, and the evolution of the draft version of the Constitution, seem to us to lend considerable support to our reading of the language of the Appointments Clause itself.

An interim version of the draft Constitution had vested in the Senate the authority to appoint Ambassadors, public Ministers, and Judges of the Supreme Court, and the language of Art. II as finally adopted is a distinct change in this regard. We believe that it was a deliberate change made by the Framers with the intent to deny Congress any authority itself to appoint those who were "Officers of the United States." The debates on the floor of the Convention reflect at least in part the way the change came about.

On Monday, August 6, 1787, the Committee on Detail to which had been referred the entire draft of the Constitution reported its draft to the Convention, including the following two articles that bear on the question before us:

Article IX, § 1: "The Senate of the United States shall have power...to appoint Ambassadors, and Judges of the Supreme Court."

Article X, § 2: "[The President] shall commission all the officers of the United States; and shall appoint officers in all cases not otherwise provided for by this Constitution."

It will be seen from a comparison of these two articles that the appointment of Ambassadors and Judges of the Supreme Court was confided to the Senate, and that the authority to appoint—not merely nominate, but to actually appoint—all other officers was reposed in the President....

[O]n Friday, August 31, a motion had been carried without opposition to refer such parts of the Constitution as had been postponed or not acted upon to a Committee of Eleven. Such reference carried with it both Arts. IX and X. The following week the Committee of Eleven made its report to the Convention, in which the present language of Art. II, § 2, cl. 2, dealing with the authority of the President to nominate is found, virtually word for word, as § 4 of Art. X. The same Committee also reported a revised article concerning the Legislative Branch to the Convention. The changes are obvious. In the final version, the Senate is shorn of its power to appoint Ambassadors and Judges of the Supreme Court. The President is given, not the power to *appoint* public officers of the United States, but only the right to *nominate* them, and a provision is inserted by virtue of which Congress may require Senate confirmation of his nominees.

It would seem a fair surmise that a compromise had been made. But no change was made in the concept of the term "Officers of the United States," which since it had first appeared in Art. X had been taken by all concerned to embrace all appointed officials exercising responsibility under the public laws of the Nation.

Appellee Commission and amici urge that because of what they conceive to be the extraordinary authority reposed in Congress to regulate elections, this case stands on a different footing than if Congress had exercised its legislative authority in another field. There is, of course, no doubt that Congress has express authority to regulate congressional elections, by virtue of the power conferred in Art. I, § 4. This Court has also held that it has very broad authority to prevent corruption in national Presidential elections. *Burroughs v. United States*, 290 U.S. 534 (1934). But Congress has plenary authority in all areas in which it has substantive legislative jurisdiction, *McCulloch v. Maryland*, 17 U.S. 316, 4 Wheat. 316 (1819), so long as the exercise of that authority does not offend some other constitutional restriction. We see no reason to believe that the authority of Congress over federal election practices is of such a wholly different nature from the other grants of authority to Congress that it may be employed in such a manner as to offend well-established constitutional restrictions stemming from the separation of powers.

The position that because Congress has been given explicit and plenary authority to regulate a field of activity, it must therefore have the power to appoint those who are to administer the regulatory statute is both novel and contrary to the language of the Appointments Clause. Unless their selection is elsewhere provided for, all Officers of the United States are to be appointed in accordance with the Clause.

Principal officers are selected by the President with the advice and consent of the Senate. Inferior officers Congress may allow to be appointed by the President alone, by the heads of departments, or by the Judiciary. No class or type of officer is excluded because of its special functions. The President appoints judicial as well as executive officers. Neither has it been disputed and apparently it is not now disputed that the Clause controls the appointment of the members of a typical administrative agency even though its functions, as this Court recognized in *Humphrey's Executor v. United States*, 295 U.S. 602, 624 (1935), may be "predominantly quasi-judicial and quasi-legislative" rather than executive. The Court in that case carefully emphasized that although the members of such agencies were to be independent of the Executive in their day-to-day operations, the Executive was not excluded from selecting them. . . .

We are also told by appellees and amici that Congress had good reason for not vesting in a Commission composed wholly of Presidential appointees the authority to administer the Act, since the administration of the Act would undoubtedly have a bearing on any incumbent President's campaign for re-election. While one cannot dispute the basis for this sentiment as a practical matter, it would seem that those who sought to challenge incumbent Congressmen might have equally good reason to fear a Commission which was unduly responsive to members of Congress whom they were seeking to unseat. But such fears, however rational, do not by themselves warrant a distortion of the Framers' work.

Appellee Commission and amici finally contend . . . that whatever shortcomings the provisions for the appointment of members of the Commission might have under Art. II, Congress had ample authority under the Necessary and Proper Clause of Art. I to effectuate this result. We do not agree. The proper inquiry when considering the Necessary and Proper Clause is not the authority of Congress to create an office or a commission, which is broad indeed, but rather its authority to provide that its own officers may make appointments to such office or commission. . . .

Congress could not, merely because it concluded that such a measure was "necessary and proper" to the discharge of its substantive legislative authority, pass a bill of attainder or ex post facto law contrary to the prohibitions contained in § 9 of Art. I. No more may it vest in itself, or in its officers, the authority to appoint officers of the United States when the Appointments Clause by clear implication prohibits it from doing so.

The trilogy of cases from this Court dealing with the constitutional authority of Congress to circumscribe the President's power to *remove* officers of the United States is entirely consistent with this conclusion. In *Myers v. United States*, 272 U.S. 52 (1926), the Court held that Congress could not by statute divest the President of the power to remove an officer in the Executive Branch whom he was initially authorized to appoint. . . . In the later case of *Humphrey's Executor*, where it was held that Congress could circumscribe the President's power to remove members of independent regulatory agencies, the Court was careful to note that it was dealing with an agency intended to be independent of executive authority "*except in its selection.*" 295 U.S., at 625 (emphasis in original). *Wiener v. United States*, 357 U.S. 349 (1958), which applied the holding in *Humphrey's Executor* to a member of the War Claims Commission, did not question in any respect that members of independent agencies are not independent of the Executive with respect to their appointments. . . .

3. The Commission's Powers

Thus, on the assumption that all of the powers granted in the statute may be exercised by an agency whose members have been appointed in accordance with the Appointments Clause, the ultimate question is which, if any, of those powers may be exercised by the present voting Commissioners, none of whom was appointed as provided by that Clause. Our previous description of the statutory provisions disclosed that the Commission's powers fall generally into three categories: functions relating to the flow of necessary information—receipt, dissemination, and investigation; functions with respect to the Commission's task of fleshing out the statute—rulemaking and advisory opinions; and functions necessary to ensure compliance with the statute and rules—informal procedures, administrative determinations and hearings, and civil suits.

Insofar as the powers confided in the Commission are essentially of an investigative and informative nature, falling in the same general category as those powers which Congress might delegate to one of its own committees, there can be no question that the Commission as presently constituted may exercise them. As this Court stated in *McGrain* [*v. Daugherty*], 273 U.S., at 175:

> "A legislative body cannot legislate wisely or effectively in the absence of information respecting the conditions which the legislation is intended to affect or change; and where the legislative body does not itself possess the requisite information—which not infrequently is true—recourse must be had to others who do possess it...."

But when we go beyond this type of authority to the more substantial powers exercised by the Commission, we reach a different result. The Commission's enforcement power, exemplified by its discretionary power to seek judicial relief, is authority that cannot possibly be regarded as merely in aid of the legislative function of Congress. A lawsuit is the ultimate remedy for a breach of the law, and it is to the President, and not to the Congress, that the Constitution entrusts the responsibility to "take Care that the Laws be faithfully executed." Art. II, § 3.

Congress may undoubtedly under the Necessary and Proper Clause create "offices" in the generic sense and provide such method of appointment to those "offices" as it chooses. But Congress' power under that Clause is inevitably bounded by the express language of Art. II, § 2, cl. 2, and unless the method it provides comports with the latter, the holders of those offices will not be "Officers of the United States." They may, therefore, properly perform duties only in aid of those functions that Congress may carry out by itself, or in an area sufficiently removed from the administration and enforcement of the public law as to permit their being performed by persons not "Officers of the United States."...

We hold that these provisions of the Act, vesting in the Commission primary responsibility for conducting civil litigation in the courts of the United States for vindicating public rights, violate Art. II, § 2, cl. 2, of the Constitution. Such functions may be discharged only by persons who are "Officers of the United States" within the language of that section.

All aspects of the Act are brought within the Commission's broad administrative powers: rulemaking, advisory opinions, and determinations of eligibility for funds and even for federal elective office itself. These functions, exercised free from day-to-day supervision of either Congress or the Executive Branch, are more legislative and judicial in nature than are the Commission's enforcement powers, and are of kinds usually performed by independent regulatory agencies or by some department in the Executive Branch under the direction of an Act of Congress. Congress viewed these broad powers as essential to effective and impartial administration of the entire substantive framework of the Act. Yet each of these functions also represents the performance of a significant governmental duty exercised pursuant to a public law. While the President may not insist that such functions be delegated to an appointee of his removable at will, *Humphrey's Executor v. United States*, none of them operates merely in aid of congressional authority to legislate or is sufficiently removed from the administration and enforcement of public law to allow it to be performed by the present Commission. These administrative functions may therefore be exercised only by persons who are "Officers of the United States." . . .

1. The *Buckley* Court says that anyone "exercising significant authority pursuant to the laws of the United States" is an Officer of the United States, and must be appointed in conformity with Article II. The Court then provides some further definition by distinguishing investigative and informative functions, which Congress may perform itself or through its agents, from enforcement powers, exercised through litigation, administrative adjudication, and rulemaking, which must be performed by Officers of the United States because they constitute "the performance of a significant governmental duty exercised pursuant to a public law." Note the Court's unwillingness to characterize some administrative functions, such as adjudication and rulemaking, as other than "executive" in nature (compare the Court's similar approach in footnote 16 in *Chadha, supra* Chapter Two). Also, note the Court's attempts to distinguish its earlier cases concerning *removal* of officers. We will explore these matters in connection with the removal cases below.

2. Which mode of separation of powers analysis does *Buckley* employ? There are formalist elements—the Court starts with the text of the appointments clause, adds a premise about what officers do, and concludes that Congress may not share this power. Yet there are functional elements also, in the sense that the Court distinguishes activities that must be assigned to the executive from those congressional agents may perform. But the Court does not ask the question usually associated with functional analysis: whether core executive functions are threatened. The Court could easily have written a purely functionalist opinion, because the President would have little control of administration if Congress could place ordinary regulation in the hands of its own agents. So the choice of analytic method probably did not affect the outcome. In that case, why did the Court employ formalism? Which method would aid later application by lower courts? And should Congress retain some authority to appoint officers having clearly executive responsibilities, where "core" presidential powers are not threatened?

3. What is the scope of the *Buckley* holding? Consider the case of the United States Commission on Civil Rights. Under 42 U.S.C. § 1975c, the Commission's duties are to "study and collect information" and to "appraise the laws and policies of the Federal Government" concerning civil rights violations, and to report its findings to Congress and the President. Following a controversy over President Reagan's removal of several Commission members, the Commission was reconstituted by Congress. *See* Comment, *The Rise and Fall of the United States Commission on Civil Rights*, 22 Harv. Civ. Rt.-Civ. Lib. L. Rev. 449 (1987). Under 42 U.S.C. § 1975(b)(1), four

members are appointed by the President, two by the President *pro tem.* of the Senate, and two by the Speaker of the House. Is this statute constitutional? Even though the Commission's activities are investigative, has the President a good argument that he should be able to appoint all the members of a body that functions as a watchdog over federal civil rights enforcement? Or is that a good reason for the current composition of the Commission?

4. How effectively do Presidents employ their appointment power? Not very well, according to Sen. Comm. on Government Operations, The Regulatory Appointments Process, 1 Study on Federal Regulation, 95th Cong., 1st Sess. (1977). The Committee concluded (xxxi):

> Generally speaking, Presidents have not displayed much continued interest in the appointments process: often the process has been set up with little or no thought, and then relegated to middle level status in the White House; criteria, either on a specific selection or more generally, are rarely enunciated; and Presidents have frequently not insisted on the most able appointees....

The Committee made a number of recommendations to improve the process, including a more systematic and open White House recruitment process, the formation of informal, broad-based advisory committees to recommend candidates, more thorough investigation of candidates, and—especially important—greater presidential interest in and support for the appointment of outstanding persons (xxvi-xxvii). (In short, the buck stops there.) *See also* J.Graham & V. Kramer, Appointments to the Regulatory Agencies: The FCC and the FTC (1949-74), Sen. Commerce Comm., 94th Cong., 2d Sess. (Comm. Print 1976); Gellhorn & Freer, *Assuring Competence in Federal Agency Appointments*, 65 A.B.A.J. 218 (1979), recommending a panel to screen executive nominees, similar to that employed by the ABA for judges (described below).

5. Article II, § 2, clause 3 authorizes the President to "fill up all Vacancies that may happen during the Recess of the Senate, by granting Commissions which shall expire at the End of their next Session." Our primary consideration of the recess appointments power is below, in connection with the appointment of judges, where most controversy centers. There is, however, some controversy regarding recess appointments of executives. Does the clause apply only to vacancies that *occur* while the Senate is in recess, or to those that *exist* then, even if they occurred while the Senate was in session, and could have considered nominees?

The importance of the issue is that the broader interpretation of the clause could allow a President to circumvent confirmation, for example by making a series of recess appointments or by appointing persons who could not win confirmation, and who might have a substantial period in which to form and execute policy before the expiry of the session of the Senate. *See* Comment, *Constitutional Restrictions on the President's Power to Make Recess Appointments*, 79 Nw. U. L. Rev. 191 (1984) (arguing for a narrow view of the clause). Would you advise a President to ignore the Senate's views in his exercise of the recess appointments power? Has the Senate no powers of retribution?

Congress has enacted 5 U.S.C. § 5503, which forbids paying unconfirmed recess appointees for their services if the vacancy existed while the Senate was in session, unless (1) the vacancy arose within 30 days of the end of the session, (2) at the recess, a nomination for the office was pending before the Senate, or (3) a nomination was rejected by the Senate within 30 days of the end of the session and someone other than the rejected nominee receives the recess appointment. Is this statute constitutional? *See* the discussion of the scope of the President's power in *United States v. Woodley, infra.*

Note on Presidential Authority and the Civil Service

Presidents are not always impressed with their power over the bureaucracy. On leaving office, Truman remarked that former General Eisenhower would encounter some surprises: "He'll sit there . . . and he'll say, 'Do this! Do that!' And nothing will happen. Poor Ike—it won't be a bit like the Army." S. Opotowsky, The Kennedy Government 27 (1961). Perhaps Truman had forgotten his Army service, but the fact remains that Presidents and the rather small cadre of their direct appointees sit atop a pyramid of a much larger, semi-permanent federal bureacracy. *See generally* R. Pious, The American Presidency, Ch. 7 (1979). Indeed, modern presidential candidates often run against the sins of the establishment (even when they are in it).

The proportions of political appointees to merit-based civil servants vary somewhat. Recent decades have seen an increase in the numbers of political appointees: there were 71 executive branch positions requiring Senate confirmation in 1933, and 523 in 1984. There are also larger numbers of political appointees in the middle-management positions that are described below. *See* Pfiffner, *Political Appointees and Career Executives: The Democracy-Bureaucracy Nexus in the Third Century*, 47 Pub. Admin. Rev. 57 (1987), arguing that the capacity of the White House is being strained—and the effectiveness of government reduced—by increasing numbers of inexperienced political appointees.

The past one hundred years or so has seen the creation of the civil service as a professional cadre of bureaucrats who have some insulation from politics. *See generally Developments in the Law—Public Employment*, 97 Harv. L.Rev. 1611, 1619-76 (1984); H. Heclo, A Government of Strangers: Executive Politics in Washington (1977); P. Van Riper, History of the United States Civil Service (1958).

In the early years of the nation the federal service was perceived primarily as a rather patrician meritocracy. "Fitness of character" was emphasized because of a fear of the "excesses of democracy." Not surprisingly, it was Jackson who replaced this concept by introducing a policy of removing prior political appointees from office. In fact, Jackson did not remove as large a proportion of the prior administration's officers as had Jefferson, but Jackson was the first to make removal a matter of political principle—that of promoting democratic responsibility. Unfortunately, this principle degenerated into a "spoils system" of patronage and cronyism. The spoils system flourished for a half-century, as each new administration filled the federal service with its partisans. Reformers began calling for merit-based selections and political neutrality after the Civil War. Eventually, the Pendleton Act was passed in 1883 in the wake of the assassination of Garfield by a disappointed office-seeker.

The Pendleton Act created a bipartisan Civil Service Commission responsible for establishing competitive examinations and issuing civil service rules. Initially, only about ten percent of the federal service was "classified," but the classified service grew over the years, to over seventy percent by 1919. The Act established no criteria for removal of classified employees, however. In 1912 the Lloyd-La Follette Act established the present standard by providing that removal from the civil service might occur "only for such cause as will promote the efficiency of the service," codifying a series of executive orders that began in 1897. The Act further required that an employee sought to be removed must be given notice of charges and an opportunity to reply; hearing requirements have since expanded.

In 1978 the Civil Service Reform Act, 92 Stat. 1111 (codified in scattered sections of 5, 10, 15, 28, 31, 38, 39 and 42 U.S.C.), made a number of major changes in the civil service. It abolished the Civil Service Commission, transferring its managerial and administrative duties to a new Office of Personnel Management and its review functions to a separate Merit Systems Protection Board. The Office of Special Counsel within the MSPB investigates and prosecutes before the MSPB charges of prohibited personnel practices, including reprisals against "whistleblowers." *See generally Developments in the Law, supra*, at 1632-50.

Today, the federal civil service is organized around a series of classifications reflecting different degrees of political accountability, policymaking responsibility, and other functional criteria. The current classifications are as follows (*see* Office of Personnel Management, Federal Managers Guide to Washington (1980)):

> *Executive Levels I through V*: This group, numbering approximately 500 persons, includes all executive department and other agency heads, and subordinate positions created by statute (including, for example, deputies, under-secretaries, assistant secretaries and positions of comparable rank). These are the top political positions, appointed by the President and subject to Senate confirmation.

> *Senior Executive Service*: This classification, established by the Civil Service Reform Act of 1978, includes managerial, supervisory, and political policy makers in positions equivalent to GS-16 through Executive Level IV. Appointments are made by agency heads. SES members give up routine increases in pay, in return for those based on performance evaluations. An SES official can be removed at any time for "less than fully successful executive performance." There are currently about 6,300 executives in SES positions, in several types of appointments. Career appointments (no less than 85% of SES) are competitive. (The Career Service consists of approximately 1.7 million employees, ranging from the top of the Senior Executive Service down to GS-1.) Noncareer appointments (no more than 10%) do not require competition, but appointees must meet certain qualifications. Some positions may only be filled by career appointees.

> *Schedule C*: This classification embraces the largest group of positions in the so-called "excepted service," appointment to which is not subject to competition. Included are persons in grades GS-15 and below who are in policymaking positions or positions that involve close personal relations with the head of an agency or other key appointed officials. Also included in this schedule are positions in the Foreign Service, the FBI, and the intelligence agencies. These excepted positions plus those excepted by the Office of Personnel Management in Schedules A and B constitute the "excepted service," which includes about 1.1 million positions.

> *Schedule A*: This classification includes positions for which it is not practicable to hold any examinations and which are not of a confidential or policy-deter-

mining nature. Attorneys are placed in this schedule, which includes about 100,000 positions.

Schedule B: There are a small (about 16,000) number of positions for which competitive exams are deemed impracticable, but the person must pass a noncompetitive examination.

The increasing number of political appointees available to Presidents has been accompanied by increasingly close White House control. As the above summary shows, many important appointments are made not by the President but by agency heads. As late as 1965, these appointments were made through a decentralized process in which selection was delegated to the agency heads. Subsequently, control has shifted to the White House. The Reagan administration has been the most aggressive in this regard. The Director of its Personnel Office, Pendleton James, announced: "We handled all the appointments: boards, commissions, Schedule C's, ambassadorships, judgeships. . . . If you are going to run the government, you've got to control the people that come into it." Pfiffner, *supra*, at 59.

2. Judges

The power of judicial appointment allows a President to work an enduring influence on the course of American government. Yet this power is subject to very little law. Aspirants even to the Supreme Court, unlike presidential, vice-presidential, and congressional candidates, are not subject to any constitutional limitations regarding age, citizenship, or residency. Indeed, no judge or Justice need even be a lawyer. Congress has considered bills to limit Supreme Court appointments to persons under a particular age or with prior judicial experience, but no limitation has been enacted. The history of judicial appointments is consequently one of presidential discretion, limited formally only by the Senate confirmation process, which also proceeds without direct constitutional guidance.

For the most part, we do not consider legal issues here. Instead, we seek to round out the picture of the President's functions and to surface a variety of policy questions that attend the judicial appointments process.

We begin with a brief discussion of presidential criteria for choosing Supreme Court Justices, and of the processes for identifying, evaluating, and confirming nominees. We then examine the controversy that surrounded President Franklin D. Roosevelt's court-packing plan of 1937. We also note current debate over the appropriate nature of Senate inquiry into the ideology of Supreme Court nominees. Turning to the lower courts, we summarize an innovative Carter administration process for the selection of Court of Appeals judges. Finally, we consider the permissibility and appropriateness of presidential use of the recess appointment power for judges.

a. Appointments to the Supreme Court

Note: Identifying, Evaluating, and Confirming Supreme Court Candidates.

All but four Presidents have appointed at least one Supreme Court Justice. Presidents have sometimes made their purported criteria explicit; more often, the criteria have been tacit and ad hoc. Nonetheless, based on the history of 103 appointments (counting those who actually served, through Scalia), it is possible to catalogue several factors that are likely to count in virtually all nominations. *See generally* H. Abraham, Justices and Presidents: A Political History of Appointments to the Supreme Court (2d ed. 1985).

Ability and character. Every President, in explaining nominations publicly, has cited ability and character among his criteria for selection. The appropriate measure of merit, however, may well vary with the needs of the country and of the Court when a vacancy occurs. Sometimes, the Court's greatest need may be an exceptional intellectual leader. At other times, a catalytic administrator or effective advocate may be better. In any event, because there is always a surplus of highly capable individuals for the available vacancies, rarely has a candidate's outstanding ability seemed to have decided the nomination (Holmes and Cardozo may be examples). Indeed, a few of the nation's greatest justices appear to have been chosen without primary regard for their intellectual capacity. For example, James Madison nominated Joseph Story to the Court only after two confirmed appointees declined the position and a third nominee had been rejected by the Senate. It is uncertain what led Madison to Story, although it is known that Story's uncle and Madison were close friends.

An obvious potential measure of merit is prior distinguished judicial experience. About 60 per cent of the Justices have had prior judicial experience; in the twentieth century, Republican Presidents have appointed proportionately more former judges than have Democrats. All but one Justice, however, reached the Court only after a substantial career in politics or public service of some sort. Some history of functioning in a high-pressure environment may help to assure that public criticism or the magnitude of a Justice's tasks will not compromise the nominee's judicial effectiveness and independence.

Political and legal philosophy. A *sine qua non* for nomination is likely to be the acceptability to the President of a candidate's personal philosophy. As with merit, however, the precise measure of acceptability may vary with other political considerations, the President's attitude toward the Court, and on a candidate's fitness in other respects.

On occasion, the importance of a single issue to the nation's welfare or to a President's program may loom so large that a candidate's position on it becomes the litmus test of acceptability. Examples include the cause of the Union under Lincoln, the constitutionality of paper money under Grant, and the legitimacy of federal regulation of the economy under Franklin Roosevelt. At other times, acceptability may be measured more in terms of general party affiliation.

Even if either partisan identification or single-issue politics predominates, however, the Justice's performance may not be predictable. Examples of Justices whose rulings have been at odds with the philosophies of their appointing Presidents include James McReynolds, whom Woodrow Wilson appointed based largely on McReynolds' fervent antitrust position, and Earl Warren, whom Eisenhower appointed based largely on Warren's political service to Eisenhower and the Republican Party. Such disappointments may convince a President of the importance of examining a nominee's overall pattern of values and opinions as closely as possible.

One reason why a Justice's performance may surprise the appointing President is possible confusion, in the recruitment process, between a candidate's political and legal philosophies. Felix Frankfurter was, in terms of political philosophy, the ardent New Dealer that Franklin Roosevelt had expected. The central theme of Frankfurter's judicial philosophy, however, was one of judicial restraint, thus distinguishing his Court performance dramatically from those of other FDR appointees such as Douglas, Black, and Murphy.

Enhancing the Representativeness of the Court. In narrowing the pool of potential nominees, Presidents have frequently sought individuals who would enhance public perceptions of the representativeness of the Court. The primary measure of representativeness has been geographical—especially in the Nineteenth Century—although partisan affiliation and, more recently, religion, race, and gender have entered as considerations. Of the 103 Justices to date, 102 have been men, 102 have been white, 96 have been of Anglo-Saxon descent, 96 have been native-born, and 91 have been Protestant. Since 1894, at least one seat on the Court has been held by a Catholic (except for the period 1949-1956), and at least one seat was held by a Jew from 1916 to 1969.

Other criteria. Additional criteria for selection have included age, health, friendship, the elimination of a potential opponent from electoral politics, placating political opposition, and securing political support. The presence of such motives need not correlate with the unsuitability of a candidate on other grounds. Among the Justices appointed in part because of close personal friendship with a President are Taney, Field, Stone, and Frankfurter, all of whom would have been qualified under any likely set of criteria.

Identifying and Evaluating Potential Nominees. Potential sources of the names of prospects for the Court are almost endless. Solicited or unsolicited suggestions may come from the President's advisers, members of Congress, sitting judges or Justices, legal scholars, state bar representatives, concerned private citizens, and from candidates themselves.

Once potential nominees are identified, someone must evaluate the serious contenders. A tradition has arisen of active Department of Justice participation in the process of assessing Supreme Court candidates. The Department may initiate its own study of potential candidates, and plays a leading role in marshalling assessments from private groups and individuals, most notably—since the Eisenhower Administration—of the American Bar Association Standing Committee on the Federal Judiciary.

Although FBI "full-field" checks on proposed nominees are routine, the mode of ABA participation may vary. The ABA-Justice Department relationship was especially stormy during the Nixon Administration. For undisclosed reasons, Nixon initially abandoned his predecessors' practice of consulting the ABA prior to announcing nominees. The ABA wound up in the embarrassing posture of favorably evaluating two Nixon nominees whom the Senate refused to confirm. When the Administration changed policy in 1971 and asked the ABA for its views on two candidates prior to their public designation, the ABA returned the embarrassment by reviewing the candidates unfavorably and disclosing its report to the press.

Such extensive ABA participation has led to some criticism that an organization that is not responsible to any public political process is exercising undue influence in the appointments process. The presumed benefit of ABA review is its potential for nonpartisan professional evaluation of a nominee.

Senate Confirmation. Once the President nominates, he submits his choice for the "advice and consent" of the Senate. During the first half of this century, the Senate seldom materially influenced the selection of a Justice. Since the conditional resignation of Earl Warren in 1968, however, four presidential nominations for the Court have either been defeated by the Senate or have been withdrawn in part because of Senate pressure.

Whether a nominee can secure the support of a majority of the Senate may depend on a host of factors, none of which need necessarily relate to the President's criteria for making an appointment. Typically the reasons for rejection include doubts about a candidate's ability or good character, dislike of a nominee's partisanship or ideology, or disfavor due to a candidate's prior identification with the unpopular side of a significant popular controversy. Most recently, the Senate opposed Judge Harrold Carswell's nomination because of his alleged lack of ability and apparent insensitivity to civil rights concerns; Judge Clement Haynesworth, because of his participation in lower court cases in which he arguably had or had created a financial conflict of interest; and Justice Abe Fortas (to become Chief Justice), because while on the Court, he accepted paid employment by a university, maintained a close advisory relationship with the President, and received fees from a private foundation.

Politics, like law, has precedents that confine later decisions. Some modern limits to a President's ability to shape the Supreme Court through use of the appointments power are demonstrated by the history of FDR's ill-fated "Court-packing" plan in 1937. The full story is told in J. Burns, Roosevelt: The Lion and the Fox, Ch. 15 (1956); *see also* Leuchtenburg, *The Origins of Franklin D. Roosevelt's "Court-Packing Plan,"* 1966 Sup. Ct. Rev. 347. We provide excerpts from the President's argument to the nation in favor of the plan, and the Senate Judiciary Committee's adverse report on it.

The Coming Crisis in Recovery and What Can Be Done About It

President Roosevelt, by Radio from
Washington, March 9, 1937

S. Rept. No. 711, 75th Cong., 1st Sess. 41-45 (1937)

... Tonight, sitting at my desk in the White House, I make my first radio report to the people in my second term of office. ... The American people have learned from the depression. For in the last three national elections an overwhelming majority of them voted a mandate that the Congress and the President begin the task of providing [a program of] protection—not after long years of debate, but now.

The courts, however, have cast doubts on the ability of the elected Congress to protect us against catastrophe, by meeting squarely our modern social and economic conditions. We are at a crisis in our ability to proceed with that protection. It is a quiet crisis. There are no lines of depositors outside closed banks. But to the far-sighted it is far-reaching in its possibilities of injury to America. ... [Here the President made his analogy of the government to a three-horse team, with one of the horses—the Court—not pulling in unison, which we quoted in Chapter One.]

I hope that you have re-read the Constitution of the United States. Like the Bible, it ought to be read again and again. It is an easy document to understand when you remember that it was called into being because the Articles of Confederation under which the original thirteen States tried to operate after the Revolution showed the need of a national government with power enough to handle national problems.... But the framers went further. Having in mind that in succeeding generations many other problems then undreamed of would become national problems, they gave to the Congress the ample broad powers "to levy taxes ... and provide for the common defense and general welfare of the United States."...

[S]ince the rise of the modern movement for social and economic progress through legislation, the Court has more and more often and more and more boldly asserted a power to veto laws passed by the Congress and State Legislatures.... In the last four years the sound rule of giving statutes the benefit of all reasonable doubt has been cast aside. The Court has been acting not as a judicial body but as a policy-making body.

When the Congress has sought to stabilize national agriculture, to improve the conditions of labor, to safeguard business against unfair competition, to protect our national resources, and in many other ways to serve our clearly national needs, the majority of the Court has been assuming power to pass on the wisdom of these acts of Congress—and to approve or disapprove the public policy written into these laws. That is not only my accusation. It is the accusation of most distinguished justices of the present Supreme Court. I have not the time to quote to you all the language used by dissenting justices in many of these cases.... [I]t is perfectly clear, that as Chief Justice Hughes has said: "We are under a Constitution but the Constitution is what the judges say it is."

The Court ... has improperly set itself up as a third house of the Congress—a super-legislature, as one of the justices has called it—reading into the Constitution words and implications which are not there, and which were never intended to be there. We have, therefore, reached the point as a nation where we must take action to save the Constitution from the Court and the Court from itself. We must find a way to take an appeal from the Supreme Court to the Constitution itself. We want a Supreme Court which will do justice under the Constitution—not over it. In our courts we want a government of laws and not of men....

When I commenced to review the situation ... I [decided] that short of amendments the only method which was clearly constitutional, and would at the same time carry out other much-needed reforms, was to infuse new blood into all our courts. We must have men worthy and equipped to carry out impartial justice. But, at the same time, we must have judges who will bring to the courts a present-day sense of the Constitution—judges who will retain in the courts the judicial functions of a court and reject the legislative powers which the courts have today assumed.

In forty-five out of the forty-eight States of the Union, judges are chosen not for life but for a period of years. In many States judges must retire at the age of 70. Congress has provided financial security by offering life pensions at full pay for Federal judges on all courts who are willing to retire at 70.... But all Federal judges, once appointed, can, if they choose, hold office for life, no matter how old they may get to be.

What is my proposal? It is simply this: Whenever a judge or justice of any Federal court has reached the age of 70 and does not avail himself of the opportunity to retire on a pension, a new member shall be appointed by the President then in office, with the approval, as required by the Constitution, of the Senate of the United States. That plan has two chief purposes. By bringing into the judicial system a steady and continuing stream of new and younger blood I hope, first, to make the administration of all Federal justice speedier and, therefore, less costly; secondly, to bring to the decision of social and economic problems younger men who have had personal experience and contact with modern facts and circumstances under which average men have to live and work. This plan will save our national Constitution from hardening of the judicial arteries....

If, for instance, any one of the six Justices of the Supreme Court now over the age of 70 should retire as provided under the plan, no additional place would be created. Consequently, although there never can be more than fifteen, there may be only fourteen, or thirteen, or twelve. And there may be only nine. There is nothing novel or radical about this idea.... It has been discussed and approved by many persons of high authority ever since a similar proposal passed the House of Representatives in 1869....

Those opposing this plan have sought to arouse prejudice and fear by crying that I am seeking to "pack" the Supreme Court and that a baneful precedent will be established.... If by that phrase, "packing the court," it is charged that I wish to place on the bench spineless puppets who would disregard the law and would decide specific cases as I wished them to be decided, I make this answer—that no President fit for his office would appoint, and no Senate of honorable men fit for their office would confirm, that kind of appointees to the Supreme Court.

But, if by that phrase the charge is made that I would appoint and the Senate would confirm justices worthy to sit beside present members of the Court who understand those modern conditions—that I will appoint justices who will not undertake to override the judgment of the Congress or legislative policy—... if the appointment of such justices can be called "packing the courts," then I say that I and with me the vast majority of the American people favor doing just that thing—now.

Is it a dangerous precedent for the Congress to change the number of the justices? The Congress has always had, and will have, that power. The number of justices has been changed several times before—in the administrations of John Adams and Thomas Jefferson, both signers of the Declaration of Independence—Andrew Jackson, Abraham Lincoln and Ulysses S. Grant....

We think it so much in the public interest to maintain a vigorous judiciary that we encourage the retirement of elderly judges by offering them a life pension at full salary.... But chance and the disinclination of individuals to leave the Supreme bench have now given us a court in which five justices will be over seventy-five years of age before next June and one over seventy. Thus a sound public policy has been defeated....

During the past half century the balance of power between the three great branches of the Federal Government has been tipped out of balance by the courts in direct contradiction of the high purposes of the framers of the Constitution. It is my purpose to restore that balance. You who know me will accept my solemn assurance that in a world in which democracy is under attack I seek to make American democracy succeed.

Reorganization of the Federal Judiciary
S. Rept. No. 711, 75th Cong., 1st Sess. (1937)

The Committee on the Judiciary, to whom was referred the bill (S. 1392) to re-organize the judicial branch of the Government, after full consideration,... hereby report the bill adversely with the recommendation that it do not pass.... The bill... may be summarized in the following manner:

By section 1(a) the President is directed to appoint an additional judge to any court of the United States when and only when three contingencies arise:

(a) That a sitting judge shall have attained the age of 70 years;

(b) That he shall have held a Federal judge's commission for at least 10 years;

(c) That he has neither resigned nor retired within 6 months after the happening of the two contingencies first named....

By section 1(b) it is provided that in event of the appointment of judges under the provisions of section 1(a), then the size of the court to which such appointments are made is "permanently" increased by that number. But... [r]egardless of the age or service of the members of the Federal judiciary,... the Supreme Court may not be increased beyond 15 members; no circuit court of appeals... may be increased by more than 2 members; and... the number of judges now authorized to be appointed for any district or group of districts may not be more than doubled....

The next question is to determine to what extent "the persistent infusion of new blood" may be expected from this bill. It will be observed that the bill before us does not and cannot compel the retirement of any judge.... It will be remembered that the mere attainment of three score and ten by a particular judge does not, under this bill, require the appointment of another... unless he has served as a judge for 10 years. In other words, age itself is not penalized; the penalty falls only when age is attended with experience.... [T]he introduction of old and inexperienced blood into the courts is not prevented by this bill....

Take the Supreme Court as an example. As constituted at the time this bill was presented to the Congress, there were six members of that tribunal over 70 years of age. If all six failed to resign or retire... then the Supreme Court would consist of 15 members. These 15 would then serve, regardless of age, at their own will, during good behavior, in other words, for life. Though as a result we had a court of 15 members 70 years of age or over, nothing could be done about it under this bill, and there would be no way to infuse "new" blood or "young" blood except by a new law further expanding the Court, unless, indeed, Congress and the Executive should be willing to follow the course defined by the framers of the Constitution for such a contingency and submit to the people a constitutional amendment limiting the terms of Justices or making mandatory their retirement at a given age.

It thus appears that the bill before us does not with certainty provide for increasing the personnel of the Federal judiciary, does not remedy the law's delay, does not serve the interest of the "poorer litigant" and does not provide for the "constant" or "persistent infusion of new blood" into the judiciary. What does it do?

The answer is clear. It applies force to the judiciary. It is an attempt to impose upon the courts a course of action, a line of decision which, without that force, without that imposition, the judiciary might not adopt.... Increasing the personnel is not the object of this measure; infusing young blood is not the object; for if either one of these purposes had been in the minds of the proponents, the drafters would not have written the following clause...: "*Provided*, That no additional judge shall be appointed hereunder if the judge who is of retirement age dies, resigns, or retires prior to the nomination of such additional judge."

Let it also be borne in mind that the President's message submitting this measure contains the following sentence: "If, on the other hand, any judge eligible for retirement should feel that his Court would suffer because of an increase of its membership, he may retire or resign under already existing provisions of law if he wishes to do so."...

Can reasonable men by any possibility differ about the constitutional impropriety of such a course?... That judges should hold office during good behavior is the prescription. It is founded upon historic experience of the utmost significance. Compensation at stated times, which compensation was not to be diminished during their tenure, was also ordained. Those comprehensible terms were the outgrowths of experience which was deep-seated.... [The framers] sought to correct an abuse and to prevent its recurrence....

Age and behavior have no connection; they are unrelated subjects. By this bill, judges who have reached 70 years of age may remain on the bench and have their judgment augmented if they agree with the new appointee, or vetoed if they disagree. This is far from the independence intended for the courts by the framers of the Constitution.... The effect of this bill is not to provide for an increase in the number of Justices composing the Supreme Court. The effect is to provide a forced retirement or, failing in this, to take from the Justices affected a free exercise of their independent judgment.

The President... in his address to the Nation of March 9... [makes] the frank acknowledgment that neither speed nor "new blood" in the judiciary is the object of this legislation, but a change in the decisions of the Court—a subordination of the views of the judges to the views of the executive and legislative, a change to be brought about by forcing certain judges off the bench or increasing their number.

Let us, for the purpose of the argument, grant that the Court has... substituted its will for the congressional will in the matter of legislation. May we nevertheless safely punish the Court? Today it may be the Court which is charged with forgetting its constitutional duties. Tomorrow it may be the Congress. The next day it may be the Executive. If we yield to temptation now to lay the lash upon the Court, we are only teaching others how to apply it to ourselves and to the people when the occasion seems to warrant. Manifestly, if we may force the hand of the Court to secure our interpretation of the Constitution, then some succeeding Congress may repeat the process to secure another and a different interpretation and one which may not sound so pleasant in our ears as that for which we now contend.

There is a remedy for usurpation or other judicial wrongdoing. If this bill be supported by the toilers of this country upon the ground that they want a Court which will sustain legislation limiting hours and providing minimum wages, they must remember that the procedure employed in the bill could be used in another administration to lengthen hours and to decrease wages.... When members of the Court usurp legislative powers or attempt to exercise political power, they lay themselves open to the charge of having lapsed from that "good behavior" which determines the period of their official life. But, if you say, the process of impeachment is difficult and uncertain, the answer is, the people made it so when they framed the Constitution....

But, if the fault of the judges is not so grievous as to warrant impeachment, if their offense is merely that they have grown old, and we feel, therefore, that there should be a "constant infusion of new blood", then obviously the way to achieve that result is by constitutional amendment fixing definite terms for the members of the judiciary or making mandatory their retirement at a given age. Such a provision would indeed provide for the constant infusion of new blood, not only now but at all times in the future. The plan before us is but a temporary expedient which operates once and then never again, leaving the Court as permanently expanded to become once more a court of old men, gradually year by year falling behind the times.... But, if you say the process of reform by amendment is difficult and uncertain, the answer is, the people made it so when they framed the Constitution....

---

1. What is your assessment of FDR's Court-packing plan? Do you agree with the Committee that it was unconstitutional? Does your answer depend on the motive behind the plan? If so, was Roosevelt's error merely one of how he structured and explained the plan?

2. Apart from the crisis that stemmed from the Court's repeated invalidation of New Deal legislation, is there a real need for "a steady and continuing stream of new and younger blood" on the Court? In short, did FDR pick a bad time to advance a good idea? If so, what measures would be appropriate, and by what process (legislation or constitutional amendment) should they be adopted?

3. What is the enduring historical lesson of the Court-packing plan? Is it that the Court is sacrosanct from blatant political manipulation by the President? Or is the message exactly to the contrary—Roosevelt eventually abandoned the plan, but it may have spurred the Court's rather abrupt switch to approving New Deal legislation. (E.g., *NLRB v. Jones & Laughlin Steel Corp.*, 301 U.S. 1 (1937), decided while the debate raged.) Was Roosevelt correct in his later assessment that he lost the battle but won the war?

How closely should the Senate question prospective Justices about their positions on particular legal or political issues? Consider the views of Professor Clinton, in *Judges Must Make Law: A Realistic Appraisal of the Judicial Function in a Democratic Society*, 67 Iowa L. Rev. 711 (1982):

> The appropriate role of courts in a democratic society was again brought to public attention by the Senate confirmation hearings involving the appointment of Justice Sandra Day O'Connor.... Under the slogan "Judges should interpret, not make, law," the Senate Judiciary Committee repeatedly probed Justice O'-Connor about her judicial attitudes and her views about specific legal and political issues. Indeed, Attorney General William French Smith, in explaining the criteria used by the United States Justice Department for the screening of potential Supreme Court appointees, indicated that this test of judicial attitude was a prime criterion. Senator Grassley of Iowa and others repeatedly used this phrase or some variant of it in their public statements about the appointment and their questioning of the appointee during the hearings.... Nevertheless, no observation about judicial behavior could be further from the truth. The plain

and simple fact is that judges, of necessity, must from time to time make, rather than interpret, law and that they are perfectly justified in so doing. Indeed, no clear line actually can be drawn between making and interpreting law and the distinction is therefore illusory. . . .

In the adversary system . . . the system itself tends to produce at least two sides to every argument about a legal question. If an issue of law is so clear that reasonable people could not disagree about the applicable standard, the legal issue will disappear from the case long before formal appellate court action on the question. . . . Indeed, legislatures sometimes use intentionally vague or broad language in order to delegate to judges the authority to refine the meaning of a statute in the context of applying it to specific cases. . . .

[T]he observed distinctions between liberals and conservatives or between activists and proponents of self-restraint on the bench are actuated by a judge's personal perceptions of the society and by personal values. These differences indicate that it is vital that such matters be explored in the process of selecting and approving justices of the United States Supreme Court and judges of any other court. Aside from the impeachment process, which has never successfully been used to oust a justice of the United States Supreme Court,[66] the appointment and confirmation processes are, after all, the only check short of constitutional amendment that the Constitution provides for assuring the quality and direction of federal judiciary. . . .

Thus, while many decried the Reagan "litmus test" of adherence to family values articulated in the republican platform during the 1980 presidential campaign as a touchstone for federal judicial appointment, the use of such inquiries into social and political views of a potential nominee . . . seems constitutionally appropriate and justified. . . . Presidents Franklin Roosevelt, Johnson, Nixon, and Ford all applied such criteria in seeking nominees to the United States Supreme Court. Furthermore, President Carter no doubt applied similar criteria in the selection process for lower federal court judges. Indeed, during the last half of this century, only Presidents Truman, Eisenhower, and Kennedy seem to have made judicial appointments without extensive inquiry into the political and social orientation of their candidates. Often their appointments represented pay-offs of past political debts. Not unexpectedly, these presidents sometimes found themselves surprised by the orientation of their appointees, as, for example, President Eisenhower was with Chief Justice Earl Warren and Justice William Brennan. . . .

To suggest that an in-depth exploration of a potential nominee's social, political, and moral values is appropriate is not to suggest, however, that the President or the Senate should or can secure iron-clad guarantees as to how judicial nominees will decide particular cases in the future. Such efforts are simply inappropriate. The judicial process is a deliberative one in which the judges are requested to suspend judgment until they have heard the arguments

---

66. A bill of impeachment was voted against Justice Samuel Chase in 1804 but the Senate failed to convict, in part because no crimes other than the merits of his judicial conduct were put at issue by the bill of impeachment and the Senate recognized the importance of maintaining an independent judiciary even if it disliked the political orientation it had shown. *See* G. Haskins & H. Johnson, 2 History of the Supreme Court of The United States, 1801-15, at 215-34, 238-45 (1981).

on both sides of the case. . . . Because the argument between two adverse parties, each having an important stake in the controversy, often illuminates the policy considerations that underlie constitutional decisionmaking, federal courts are constitutionally prohibited from rendering advisory opinions. Similarly, a nominee for the federal bench is justified in refusing to answer or evading questions about how he or she would in the future decide particular issues or cases. Thus, Justice Sandra Day O'Connor is to be applauded for her dogged efforts to resist such questioning. . . .

On the other hand, because some inquiry into the social, political, and moral values of a nominee is appropriate and necessary, it may be that Justice O'Connor legitimately can be criticized, insofar as she refused to respond to specific questions dealing with her political philosophy, which were framed in a manner that could not implicate a case that could come before the Court. For example, there is an important difference between asking a judge, "Would you vote to overrule the decision in *Roe v. Wade?*" and asking the nominee to respond to the following question: "If constitutionally permissible, would you as a legislator vote to prohibit abortions in all cases or, possibly, except in cases of rape or incest?" While the former question is plainly inappropriate, the latter question, while hypothetical, does test the nominee's political and social value structure in a context divorced from any potential judicial decisionmaking and, for that reason, seems justified and appropriate. . . . [S]uch information is vital to the Senate if it is effectively to exercise one of the few democratic checks available in our system of government to shape the course and direction of the federal judiciary.

Does Clinton endorse questioning nominees about matters unrelated to judging ("If you were a legislator, . . ."), while excluding questions that *are* related to the job? Should a nominee be expected to answer whether he or she thought a particular case had been correctly decided? ("How would you have voted in *Roe v. Wade?*") How far could such probing extend without calling for a promised vote in a future case? *See also* Rees, *Questions for Supreme Court Nominees at Confirmation Hearings: Excluding the Constitution,* 17 Ga. L. Rev. 913 (1983).

b. Appointments to the Court of Appeals.

Executive Order 12059   May 11, 1978

United States Circuit Judge Nominating Commission

By virtue of the authority vested in me as President by the Constitution and statutes of the United States of America, . . . it is hereby ordered as follows:

SECTION 1. *Establishment of the Commission.* There is hereby established the United States Circuit Judge Nominating Commission. . . . The Commission shall be composed of thirteen panels [one for the D.C. Circuit, and one each for the other circuits, except two for the Ninth] each of which shall, upon the request of the President, recommend for nomination as circuit judges persons whose character, experience, ability and commitment to equal justice under law, fully qualify them to serve in the Federal judiciary. . . .

SECTION 2. *Membership.* (a) The membership of the Commission shall consist of the combined memberships of the panels. The President may appoint a member of the Commission as its Chairman, with such duties as the President may assign.

(b) A panel shall be composed of a Chairman and such other members as the President may appoint;

(c) Each panel shall include members of both sexes and members of minority groups, and each panel shall include at least one lawyer from each State within a panel's area of responsibility.

(d) All members of the panel for the District of Columbia Circuit shall be persons residing within the District of Columbia or with twenty miles of its boundaries.

SECTION 3. *Functions of Panels.* (a) A panel shall begin functioning when the President or his designee notifies its Chairman that the President desires the panel's assistance in aid of his constitutional responsibility and discretion to select a nominee to fill a vacancy or vacancies on a United States Court of Appeals. Upon such notification, the panel shall:

(1) Give public notice of the vacancy or vacancies within the relevant geographic area, inviting suggestions as to potential nominees;

(2) Conduct inquiries to identify potential nominees;

(3) Conduct inquiries to identify those persons among the potential nominees who are well qualified to serve as a United States Circuit Judge; and

(4) Report to the President, within the time specified in the notification of the vacancy or vacancies, the results of its activities, including its recommendations as to the persons whom the panel considers best qualified to fill the vacancy or vacancies. . . .

SECTION 4. *Standards of Selection of Proposed Nominees.* (a) Before transmitting to the President the names of the persons it deems best qualified to fill an existing vacancy or vacancies, a panel shall have determined:

(1) That those persons are members in good standing of at least one state bar, or the District of Columbia bar, and members in good standing of any other bars of which they may be members;

(2) That they possess, and have reputations for, integrity and good character;

(3) That they are of sound health;

(4) That they possess, and have demonstrated, outstanding legal ability and commitment to equal justice under law; and

(5) That their demeanor, character, and personality indicate that they would exhibit judicial temperament if appointed to the position of United States Circuit Judge.

(b) In selecting persons whose names will be transmitted to the President, a panel shall consider whether the training, experience, or expertise of certain of the well qualified individuals would help to meet a perceived need of the court of appeals on which the vacancy or vacancies exist.

(c) To implement the above standards, a panel may adopt such additional criteria or guidelines as it considers appropriate for the identification of potential nominees and the selection of those best qualified to serve as United States Circuit Judges.

(d) Each panel is encouraged to make special efforts to seek out and identify well qualified women and members of minority groups as potential nominees.

SECTION 5. *Ineligibility of Commission Members.* No person shall be considered by a panel as a potential nominee while serving as a Commission member or for a period of one year after termination of such service. . . .

President Reagan revoked the order. Do you agree or disagree with the Carter approach? If you agree, would you extend the approach to the appointment of District Court judges or would you preserve the current system, which gives the key influence in the recruitment of District Court candidates to the Senators of the relevant state?

c. Recess Appointments of Judges

As we noted above, Article II, § 2, authorizes the President to fill vacancies during recesses of the Senate, by granting commissions that expire at the end of the session. Does this power to make temporary appointments include federal judges, who are guaranteed life tenure by Article III?

United States v. Woodley
751 F.2d 1008 (9th Cir. 1985) (en banc),
cert. denied, 106 S. Ct. 1269 (1986)

BEEZER, Circuit Judge:

We take this case en banc to address the constitutionality of a practice followed by the Executive for nearly 200 years. The question before us is whether the President of the United States may constitutionally confer temporary federal judicial commissions during a recess of the Senate pursuant to article II, section 2 of the Constitution.

I

On February 28, 1980, Walter Heen was nominated to fill a judicial vacancy in the United States District Court for Hawaii. The Senate Judiciary Committee began confirmation hearings on his nomination on September 25, 1980. When the Senate recessed on December 16, 1980, testimony and hearings on the nomination were complete, but the nomination did not come before the full Senate for its advice and consent. During the Senate's recess, on December 31, 1980, President Carter conferred a commission on Judge Heen pursuant to the recess appointment clause of article II of the United States Constitution. Heen then took his oath and assumed his duties as district court judge. On January 21, 1981, Heen's nomination was withdrawn by President Reagan. Heen continued sitting as a district judge pursuant to his recess commission until December 16, 1981, when the 97th Congress ended its First Session.

On September 18, 1981, while Heen was sitting out his commission, appellant Janet Woodley was indicted on three counts of narcotics violations. Woodley filed a motion to suppress evidence, which was denied by Heen. Judge Heen then presided over a bench trial on stipulated facts and found Woodley guilty as charged in the indictment.

Woodley appealed the denial of her motion to suppress. A panel of this court . . . vacated Woodley's conviction [on grounds that Heen could not preside]. The court having convened en banc, we hold that the recess appointment clause extends to judicial officers and that a recess appointee to the federal bench can exercise the judicial power of the United States.

II

. . . Woodley contends that under generally accepted principles of statutory construction, the more specific language of article III governs over the general language of the recess appointment clause. She concludes therefore that article III forbids interim judicial recess appointments. We reject this argument.... [W]hile article III speaks specifically about the tenure of federal judges, article II is equally specific in addressing the manner of their appointment. There is therefore no reason to favor one Article over the other.

The language of the recess appointment clause explicitly provides that the President has the power to fill all vacancies during the recess of the Senate. The *Federalist* papers clarify the meaning of the recess clause, stating that it "is to be considered as supplementary to the [clause] which precedes" and that the vacancies referred to "must be construed to relate to the 'officers' described in the preceding [clause]." The Federalist No. 67 (A. Hamilton). The preceding clause ... [is the appointments clause, whose] language further underscores that there is no basis upon which to carve out an exception from the recess power for federal judges. Particularly relevant in this context is Alexander Hamilton's statement that "[a]s to the mode of appointing the judges: This is the same with that of appointing the officers of the union in general...." The Federalist No. 78.

III

Woodley also argues that there is no historical evidence that the Framers intended the recess provision to apply to the judiciary. This argument is not only refuted by the express language of the recess clause, which ... refers to all vacancies, but it is also refuted by legislative history, as well as historical practice, consensus, and acquiescence.

Although the recess appointment clause was adopted without debate, 2 Farrand, Records of the Federal Convention 533, 540 (1911), there is evidence that it was not entirely uncontroversial. Edmund Randolph, the governor of Virginia, initially declined to sign the Constitution, in part because the recess provision gave the Executive the power to confer judicial commissions during the recess of the Senate.

In 1789, shortly after ratification of the Constitution, George Washington, who had served as President of the Constitutional Convention, exercised his power under the recess provision. During the recess between the sessions of the First Congress, he conferred three recess district judge commissions.... Moreover, the district court judges were confirmed upon the return of the Senate without objection to their recess appointments. It is further noteworthy that President Washington's recess appointments of Justice Johnson in 1791 and of Chief Justice Rutledge in 1795 went unchallenged. One commentator has aptly noted that "the most significant historical fact is that by the end of 1823, there had been five recess appointments to the Supreme Court. During this period, when those who wrote the Constitution were alive and active, not one dissenting voice was raised against the practice." Note, *Recess Appointments to the Supreme Court—Constitutional But Unwise?*, 10 Stan.L.Rev. 124, 132 (1957).

The actions of the three branches of our government have consistently confirmed the President's power to make recess appointments. The Executive Branch has made extensive use of the recess power. Approximately 300 judicial recess appointments have been made in our nation's history. Presidents Eisenhower and Kennedy alone made fifty-three such appointments during their Administrations. *See* H. Chase, Federal Judges The Appointing Process 86-88, 114-15 (1972).

The Legislative Branch has consistently confirmed judicial recess appointees without dissent. Moreover, Congress has passed legislation providing for the salaries of recess appointees, without excluding judges. 5 U.S.C. § 5503.

Finally, we turn to the Judicial Branch. The only direct challenge, prior to the present action, to the President's power to make judicial recess appointments was rejected by the Second Circuit in *United States v. Allocco*, 305 F.2d 704 (2d Cir. 1962), *cert. denied*, 371 U.S. 964 (1963). Although the United States Supreme Court has never passed on the issue, numerous Justices have been recess appointees. Chief Justice Rutledge sat as a recess appointee for six months and participated in two decisions.... Altogether, fifteen recess appointments have been made to the Supreme Court. Staff of House Comm. on the Judiciary, 86th Cong., 1st Sess., Recess Appointments of Federal Judges 40 (Comm. Print 1959). Of these, at least four appointees sat on the Court prior to their confirmation. There is no evidence that any member of the Supreme Court ever objected to this practice on constitutional grounds.

IV

... The United States Supreme Court has made clear that considerable weight is to be given to an unbroken practice, which has prevailed since the inception of our nation and was acquiesced in by the Framers of the Constitution when they were participating in public affairs. *See, e.g., United States v. Curtiss-Wright Export Corp.*, 299 U.S. 304, 322 (1936)....

V

Woodley [argues] that the language of the recess clause giving the President the power to fill all vacancies that "may happen during the Recess of the Senate," means that only those vacancies that occur during the recess itself can be filled by Presidential appointment. She reasons therefore that Judge Heen's appointment is invalid, because the vacancy which he filled did not occur during a recess of the Senate.... [That] interpretation would lead to the absurd result that all offices vacant on the day the Senate recesses would have to remain vacant at least until the Senate reconvenes....

VI

... [T]he recess appointment clause ... prevents the Executive from being incapacitated during the recess of the Senate. This in turn prevents extended judicial vacancies, which can cause the denial of the important right of access to the courts. The Framers considered the recess appointment clause sufficiently important to include it in the Constitution. In the early days of the Republic, travel time was measured in days, not hours, and extended congressional recesses were expected. The advent of modern jet travel, instant communication, and present day prolonged sessions of Congress do not justify characterizing the recess appointment clause merely as a housekeeping measure.

A recess appointee lacks life tenure and is not protected from salary diminution. As a result, such an appointee is in theory subject to greater political pressure than a judge whose nomination has been confirmed. Yet our Constitution has bestowed upon the Executive the power to make interim judicial appointments. This power is not unfettered, however, but is subject to its own limitations and safeguards. It may only be invoked when the Senate is in recess, and recess commissions expire at the end of the next congressional session. We must therefore view the recess appointee not as a danger to the independence of the judiciary, but as the extraordinary exception to the prescriptions of article III. The judicial recess appointee, who has sworn to uphold the Constitution, fills a void left by those preceding in office, thereby permitting the unbroken orderly functioning of our judicial system. . . .

VII

. . . Accordingly, we hold that Judge Heen, as a recess appointee to the federal bench, could exercise the judicial power of the United States. . . .

NORRIS, Circuit Judge, with whom FLETCHER, FERGUSON and REINHARDT, Circuit Judges, join, dissenting.

Article III of the Constitution provides that "[t]he judicial Power of the United States" shall be exercised by judges whose independence from the political branches of government is assured by guarantees of life tenure and undiminished compensation. Today, our Court carves out an exception to this explicit and unqualified constitutional command. . . .

I agree with the majority that there is a direct conflict between the Recess Appointments Clause of Article II and the tenure and salary provisions of Article III of the Constitution. I also agree with the majority that in deciding which clause should prevail, we must look beyond the Constitution itself. . . .

My major point of disagreement with the majority is its reliance upon the executive's practice of making recess judicial appointments as virtually the sole basis for its conclusion that the practice is constitutional. In my view, the majority skips what I believe should be a crucial step in the constitutional inquiry: evaluating and balancing the competing constitutional values at stake. Because of its uncritical acceptance of the historical practice as determinative of the constitutional issue, the majority fails to make any serious comparative analysis of the concerns for governmental efficiency underlying the Recess Appointments Clause and the principle of judicial independence underlying the tenure and salary provisions of Article III.

We need only look to recent history to appreciate that there is genuine tension between the values underlying the two opposing constitutional provisions. President Eisenhower's recess appointments to the Supreme Court of Chief Justice Earl Warren in 1953 and Justice Brennan in 1956 both created controversy about the legitimacy of recess appointments to that Court. Senator Joseph McCarthy's public interrogation of Justice Brennan while the latter was a sitting Justice of the Court tells its own cautionary tale:

> Senator McCarthy. You, of course, I assume, will agree with me and a number of the members of the committee—that communism is not merely a political way of life, it is a conspiracy designed to overthrow the United States Government.

> Mr. Brennan. Will you forgive me an embarrassment, Senator. You appreciate that I am a sitting Justice of the Court. There are presently pending before the Court some cases in which I believe will have to be decided the question what is communism, at least in the frame of reference in which those particular cases have come before the Court.

> I know, too, that you appreciate that having taken an oath of office it is my obligation not to discuss any of those pending matters. With that qualification, whether the label communism or any other label, any conspiracy to overthrow the Government of the United States is a conspiracy that I not only would do

anything appropriate to aid suppressing, but a conspiracy which, of course, like every American, I abhor.

Senator McCarthy. Mr. Brennan, I don't want to press you unnecessarily, but the question was simple. You have not been confirmed yet as a member of the Supreme Court. There will come before that Court a number of questions involving the all-important issue of whether or not communism is merely a political party or whether it represents a conspiracy to overthrow this Government.

I believe that the Senators are entitled to know how you feel about that and you won't be prejudicing then any cases by answering the question.

Hearings Before the Senate Committee on the Judiciary on Nomination of William Joseph Brennan, Jr., 85th Cong., 1st Sess., 17-18 (1957).

Even before Justice Brennan's ordeal, the recess appointment of Chief Justice Warren provoked what seems to have been the first scholarly comment concerning the constitutionality of such appointments. The Warren appointment occurred after *Brown v. Board of Education*, 347 U.S. 483 (1954), was originally argued to the Supreme Court but before reargument actually took place. In response to the Warren appointment, the eminent constitutional scholar Professor Henry M. Hart, Jr. warned that for Warren to take his seat and decide cases before his confirmation by the Senate would "violate the spirit of the Constitution, and possibly also its letter." Harvard Law School Record, October 8, 1953, p. 2, col. 2. Professor Hart noted that Warren's permanent appointment would be

> subject to three future contingencies: (1) the decision of the President to forward his nomination to the Senate; (2) the decision of the President not to withdraw the nomination before it has been acted upon; and (3) the decision of the Senate to confirm the nomination. The Senate will be entirely free . . . to postpone its action until near the close of the session in order to see how the new nominee is going to vote.

Hart then stated, "I cannot believe that the Constitution contemplates that any Federal judge . . . should hold office, and decide cases, with all these strings tied to him." Recognizing that, as the majority here stresses, recess appointments had been made in the past and that Attorneys General had assumed such appointments to be valid, Hart stressed that "occasional practice backed by mere assumption cannot settle a basic question of constitutional principle." Looking to "the spirit and purpose of the Constitution," Hart observed,

> the impropriety [of recess appointments to the federal judiciary] becomes unmistakable. On few other points in the Constitutional Convention were the framers in such complete accord as on the necessity of protecting judges from every kind of extraneous influence upon their decisions.

Hart concluded, a judge

> cannot possibly have this independence if his every vote, indeed his every question from the bench, is subject to the possibility of inquiry in later committee hearings and floor debates to determine his fitness to continue in judicial office.

The majority today all but ignores the careful analysis of constitutional purposes and values that Professor Hart obviously believed was critical to resolution of the tension between Article III and the Recess Appointments Clause.

To be sure, the executive's practice of vesting recess appointees with Article III power has a long and impressive historical pedigree, but the majority indiscriminately defers to this practice as dispositive of its constitutionality. In my view, such uncritical acceptance of a practice as a basis for judging its constitutionality is inconsistent with the judiciary's historic role as the final arbiter of the constitutionality of the actions of the political branches of government. *Marbury v. Madison*, 5 U.S. (1 Cranch) 137 (1803)....

I. THE CONSTITUTIONAL TEXT

The Constitution presents us with two separate and contradictory clauses, one in Article II and one in Article III, each clear and unambiguous on its face....

II. THE CONTEMPORANEOUS WRITINGS

The contemporaneous writings of the Framers are virtually barren of any references to the Recess Appointments Clause. Although the record contains a few scattered references to the Clause, it was never explained, debated or discussed in any meaningful way. Other than the text of Article II, Section 2 itself, all we know is that the Clause was proposed just ten days before the end of the Constitutional Convention and was adopted without debate....

In contrast to the paucity of comments on the Recess Appointments Clause by the Framers, the historical record is a cornucopia of references to the principle of life tenure enshrined in Article III. History makes absolutely clear the supreme importance the Framers attached to an independent judiciary as a vital corollary to the fundamental concept of the constitutional plan, the separation of powers.

The experience of the Framers with the colonial judiciary had not been a happy one. The signers of the Declaration of Independence charged that the King "obstructed the Administration of Justice by refusing his Assent to Laws for establishing Judiciary Powers. He has made Judges dependent on his Will alone for the tenure of their office and the amount and payment of their salaries." The Declaration of Independence para. 11-12 (U.S.1776).

... Thus, the letter as well as the spirit and guiding intention of Article III is inconsistent with the exercise of judicial power by recess appointees whose tenure is dependent upon both political branches of government....

For all the record shows, the Framers' attention was never focused on the conflict. If it did occur to them, it was not mentioned in the debates. As one commentator concludes, "The legislative history of article III and of the recess appointments clause reveals no specific intent on the part of the framers regarding how the two provisions would interact."

III. CONSTITUTIONAL VALUES

... The threat of institutional destabilization posed by recess appointments is not purely hypothetical. History informs us that during the civil rights struggle of the 1960's, political pressures induced recess appointees to avoid politically sensitive cases. A writer of contemporary history has recounted some of the events of that turbulent period:

[Griffin] Bell and [Walter] Gewin both began service on the Fifth Circuit on October 6, 1961, with interim appointments so they could begin work on the overloaded backlog of cases. But their appointments would not become final until after confirmation.... At an initial meeting with [Chief Judge Elbert] Tuttle, Bell suggested that the sensitivity of race cases was such that they might create problems for Gewin at the confirmation hearings. Tuttle agreed and said he would not assign such cases to Gewin until after confirmation and for the same reason would also withhold such assignments from Bell.

J. Bass, Unlikely Heroes 164 (1981). The difficulty with such judicial accommodation to political pressure is that it requires the assignment process itself to depart from strict neutrality and enter the realm of political machination. Yet, a fundamental purpose of Article III was to isolate the judiciary from just such political entanglements.

The strain on judicial independence and the threat to the appearance of independence exemplified by the Fifth Circuit's experience during the struggle for civil rights and the confrontation of Justice Brennan by Senator McCarthy are but two examples of the potentially pernicious effects of departing from the Article III mandate that judicial power be exercised only by judges with permanent tenure and protection against diminution of salary. We have no way of knowing how many other recess appointees may have been shunted away from controversial cases because they were vulnerable to political retaliation for unpopular decisions. Nor do we have any way of knowing if a judge privately succumbs to intense pressure and decides a case in a manner that ensures his confirmation rather than according to the dictates of legal principle and precedent. What we do know is that the constitutional plan of separation of powers rests on clear institutional protections for judicial independence.

The concerns for efficiency, convenience, and expediency that underlie the Recess Appointments Clause pale in comparison. The purpose served by the President's power to fill judicial vacancies during a recess of the Senate is obviously to avoid delay in the administration of justice in federal courts.... There are ways, however, of coping with pressing caseloads without compromising the principle of judicial independence. Because district and circuit judges are largely interchangeable, interdistrict or intercircuit assignments provide an expedient and effective way of dealing with a short term problem....

Thus, could we set historical practice aside, I believe our decision today would be relatively easy. Given that the language of the two clauses is in conflict and that the intentions of the Framers are unclear, the principles that animate the salary and tenure provisions of Article III—judicial independence and separation of powers—clearly outweigh the concerns of expediency and efficiency that underlie the Recess Appointments Clause....

IV. HISTORICAL PRACTICE

... [O]ur task is to evaluate critically the historical practice of recess judicial appointments.... President Washington's use of the recess appointment power to confer interim judicial commissions is not accompanied by a record of considered deliberation that gives us meaningful insight into the intentions of the Framers.... There is a ready explanation as to why the public record does not reflect that President Washington's recess judicial appointments were subject to ... careful scrutiny.... [T]he use of the recess appointment power ... involves the unilateral action of individual Presidents. Although Congress may ultimately confirm a recess appointee, it has no authority or opportunity to review the President's exercise of his recess appointment power because an interim commission is simply not subject to Senate approval. . . .

If the Framers adopted a practice carelessly or without attention to a possible constitutional infirmity, then the lineage is entitled to little weight in constitutional analysis. . . .

[I]t could still be argued that the judiciary should defer to the executive's longstanding practice on the theory that it constitutes a "structural accommodation" between the various branches of government. . . . In the case at hand, two reasons emerge for concluding [to the contrary]. First, judicial silence cannot be interpreted as acquiescence in the constitutionality of a practice because Article III courts cannot react to an encroachment on their separate powers until presented with the issue in a concrete case or controversy. Second, because Article III's tenure and salary provisions are designed as safeguards of individual as well as institutional interests, the courts have a duty to prevent erosion of those safeguards that transcends the structural importance of an independent judiciary. . . .

---

1. If *Woodley* had reached the Supreme Court, how should it have been decided? *See* Note, *Recess Appointments to Article III Courts: The Use of Historical Practice in Constitutional Interpretation*, 84 Colum. L. Rev. 1758 (1984).

2. Assuming that the recess appointments power applies to judges, how would you advise a President regarding the wisdom of its use?

B. Removals (Herein of Independent Agencies)

1. Separation of powers considerations

The Supreme Court has decided a series of important cases on the power of the President to remove inferior officers, three of which appear below. The prominence of these cases stems partly from the fact that the Court has not directly addressed the President's power to supervise executive officers; therefore, whether he can dismiss them is generally thought to determine whether he may direct their behavior in office. There may, however, be differences between removal and supervision—keep the distinction in mind as you read the cases, and we will explore it later.

The prominence of the removal cases has another, related source: the Court has taken the occasion to spin broad theories about the separation of powers, which have important implications in many other contexts. Yet the theories of the next three cases contain marked inconsistencies. As you read them, notice the modes of separation of powers analysis that the Justices employ, and try to identify the vision of executive power that seems to lie behind each of the various positions.

Before any of these cases arose, a removal controversy eventuated in our first impeachment of a President. Andrew Johnson was impeached by the House, and came within one vote of conviction in the Senate, for defying the Tenure of Office Act of 1867. The Act forbade presidential removal of certain cabinet members without the consent of the Senate; Johnson removed Secretary of War Stanton, amid a battle over Reconstruction. Although disputed at the time, the constitutionality of the Act was not resolved by the courts. Sixty years later, successor legislation finally produced a case that reached the Supreme Court. Although the official removed was minor—a postmaster—the Court gave extensive and scholarly attention to the underlying issues. The result must have comforted the ghost of Andrew Johnson.

Myers v. United States
272 U.S. 52 (1926)

Chief Justice TAFT delivered the opinion of the Court.

This case presents the question whether under the Constitution the President has the exclusive power of removing executive officers of the United States whom he has appointed by and with the advice and consent of the Senate.

Myers . . . was on July 21, 1917, appointed by the President, by and with the advice and consent of the Senate, to be a postmaster of the first class at Portland, Oregon, for a term of four years. On January 20, 1920, Myers' resignation was demanded. He refused the demand. On February 2, 1920, he was removed from office by order of the Postmaster General, acting by direction of the President. . . . On April 21, 1921, he brought this suit in the Court of Claims for his salary from the date of his removal . . . . The Court of Claims gave judgment against Myers and this is an appeal from that judgment. . . .

By the sixth section of the Act of Congress of July 12, 1876, 19 Stat. 80, 81, under which Myers was appointed with the advice and consent of the Senate as a first-class postmaster, it is provided that "Postmasters of the first, second, and third classes shall be appointed and may be removed by the President by and with the advice and consent of the Senate, and shall hold their offices for four years unless sooner removed or suspended according to law."

The Senate did not consent to the President's removal of Myers during his term. If this statute . . . is valid, the appellant . . . is entitled to recover his unpaid salary. . . . The government maintains that the requirement is invalid, for the reason that . . . the President's power of removal of executive officers appointed by him with the advice and consent of the Senate is full and complete without consent of the Senate. If this view is sound, the removal of Myers by the President without the Senate's consent was legal. . . . We are therefore confronted by the constitutional question and cannot avoid it. . . .

The question where the power of removal of executive officers . . . was vested, was presented early in the first session of the First Congress. There is no express provision respecting removals in the Constitution, except as section 4 of Article II . . . provides for removal from office by impeachment. The subject was not discussed in the Constitutional Convention. . . .

In the House of Representatives of the First Congress, on Tuesday, May 18, 1789, Mr. Madison moved in the committee of the whole that there should be established three executive departments, one of Foreign Affairs, another of the Treasury, and a third of War, at the head of each of which there should be a Secretary, to be appointed by the President by and with the advice and consent of the Senate, and to be removable by the President. The committee agreed to the establishment of a Department of Foreign Affairs, but a discussion ensued as to making the Secretary removable by the

President. "The question was now taken and carried, by a considerable majority, in favor of declaring the power of removal to be in the President." 1 Annals of Congress, 383.

On June 16, 1789, the House resolved itself into a committee of the whole on a bill proposed by Mr. Madison for establishing an executive department to be denominated the Department of Foreign Affairs, [the head of which was] "to be removable from office by the President of the United States." After a very full discussion the question was put: Shall the words "to be removable by the President" be struck out? It was determined in the negative—yeas 20, nays 34.

On June 22, in the renewal of the discussion: Mr. Benson moved to amend the bill ... so as to imply the power of removal to be in the President alone.... "Mr. Benson stated that his objection to the clause 'to be removable by the President' arose from an idea that the power of removal by the President hereafter might appear to be exercised by virtue of a legislative grant only, and consequently be subjected to legislative instability, when he was well satisfied in his own mind that it was fixed by a fair legislative construction of the Constitution."

Mr. Madison admitted the objection.... He said: "They certainly may be construed to imply a legislative grant of the power. He wished everything like ambiguity expunged, ... and therefore seconded the motion. Gentlemen have all along proceeded on the idea that the Constitution vests the power in the President....

Mr. Benson's first amendment to alter the second clause by the insertion of the italicized words, made that clause read as follows:

"That there shall be in the State Department an inferior officer ... to be called the chief clerk ... *and who, whenever the principal officer shall be removed from office by the President of the United States*, or in any other case of vacancy, shall ... have charge and custody of all records, books and papers appertaining to said department."

The first amendment was then approved by a vote of 30 to 18. Mr. Benson then moved to strike out in the first clause the words "to be removable by the President," in pursuance of the purpose he had already declared, and this second motion of his was carried by a vote of 31 to 19. The bill as amended ... was then passed by a vote of 29 to 22....

After the bill as amended had passed the House, it was sent to the Senate, where it was discussed in secret session, without report. The critical vote there was upon the striking out of the clause recognizing and affirming the unrestricted power of the President to remove. The Senate divided by 10 to 10, requiring the deciding vote of the Vice President, John Adams, who voted against striking out, and in favor of the passage of the bill as it had left the House. Ten of the Senators had been in the Constitutional Convention, and of them 6 voted that the power of removal was in the President alone. The bill, having passed as it came from the House, was signed by President Washington and became a law. Act of July 27, 1789, 1 Stat. 28....

Mr. Madison insisted that Article II by vesting the executive power in the President was intended to grant to him the power of appointment and removal of executive officers except as thereafter expressly provided in that article.... He said: " ... If there is any point in which the separation of the legislative and executive powers ought to be maintained with great caution, it is that which relates to officers and offices." 1 Annals of Congress, 581....

[T]he...reasonable construction of the Constitution must be that the branches should be kept separate in all cases in which they were not expressly blended, and the Constitution should be expounded to blend them no more than it affirmatively requires.... The vesting of the executive power in the President was essentially a grant of the power to execute the laws. But the President alone and unaided could not execute the laws. He must execute them by the assistance of subordinates.... As he is charged specifically to take care that they be faithfully executed, the reasonable implication, even in the absence of express words, was that as part of his executive power he should select those who were to act for him under his direction in the execution of the laws. The further implication must be, in the absence of any express limitation respecting removals, that as his selection of administrative officers is essential to the execution of the laws by him, so must be his power of removing those for whom he cannot continue to be responsible. It was urged that the natural meaning of the term "executive power" granted the President included the appointment and removal of executive subordinates. If such appointments and removals were not an exercise of the executive power, what were they? They certainly were not the exercise of legislative or judicial power in government as usually understood....

The requirement of the second section of Article II that the Senate should advise and consent to the presidential appointments, was to be strictly construed.... The executive power was given in general terms, strengthened by specific terms where emphasis was regarded as appropriate, and was limited by direct expressions where limitation was needed, and the fact that no express limit was placed on the power of removal by the executive was convincing indication that none was intended. This is the same construction of Article II as that of Alexander Hamilton....

The history of the clause by which the Senate was given a check upon the President's power of appointment makes it clear that it was not prompted by any desire to limit removals.... [T]he important purpose of those who brought about the restriction was to lodge in the Senate, where the small states had equal representation with the larger states, power to prevent the President from making too many appointments from the larger states.... The formidable opposition to the Senate's veto on the President's power of appointment indicated that in construing its effect, it should not be extended beyond its express application to the matter of appointments....

It was pointed out in this great debate that the power of removal, though equally essential to the executive power, is different in its nature from that of appointment. A veto by the Senate—a part of the legislative branch of the government—upon removals is a much greater limitation upon the executive branch, and a much more serious blending of the legislative with the executive, than a rejection of a proposed appointment. It is not to be implied. The rejection of a nominee of the President for a particular office does not greatly embarrass him in the conscientious discharge of his high duties...because the President usually has an ample field from which to select for office, according to his preference, competent and capable men. The Senate has full power to reject newly proposed appointees whenever the President shall remove the incumbents. Such a check enables the Senate to prevent the filling of offices with bad or incompetent men, or with those against whom there is tenable objection.

The power to prevent the removal of an officer who has served under the President is different from the authority to consent to or reject his appointment. When a nomination is made, it may be presumed that the Senate is, or may become, as well advised as to the fitness of the nominee as the President, but in the nature of things the defects in ability or intelligence or loyalty in the administration of the laws of one who has served as an officer under the President are facts as to which the President, or his trusted subordinates, must be better informed than the Senate, and the power to remove him may therefore be regarded as confined for very sound and practical reasons, to the governmental authority which has administrative control. . . .

Another argument urged against the constitutional power of the President alone to remove executive officers . . . is that, in the absence of an express power of removal granted to the President, power to make provision for removal of all such officers is vested in the Congress by section 8 of Article I. Mr. Madison, mistakenly thinking that an argument like this was advanced by Roger Sherman, took it up and answered it as follows:

> "He seems to think . . . that the power of displacing from office is subject to legislative discretion, because, it having a right to create, it may limit or modify as it thinks proper. . . . [W]hen I consider that the Constitution clearly intended to maintain a marked distinction between the legislative, executive and judicial powers of government, and when I consider that, if the Legislature has a power such as is contended for, they may subject and transfer at discretion powers from one department of our government to another, they may, on that principle, exclude the President altogether from exercising any authority in the removal of officers, they may . . . vest it in the whole Congress, or they may reserve it to be exercised by this house. When I consider the consequences of this doctrine, and compare them with the true principles of the Constitution, I own that I cannot subscribe to it. . . ." 1 Annals of Congress, 495, 496.

. . . The constitutional construction that excludes Congress from legislative power to provide for the removal of superior officers finds support in the second section of Article II. . . . This is "but the Congress may by law vest the appointment of such inferior officers, as they think proper, in the President alone, in the Courts of Law, or in the Heads of Departments." These words, it has been held by this court, give to Congress the power to limit and regulate removal of such inferior officers by heads of departments when it exercises its constitutional power to lodge the power of appointment with them. . . . By the plainest implication it excludes Congressional dealing with appointments or removals of executive officers not falling within the exception and leaves unaffected the executive power of the President to appoint and remove them. . . .

It could never have been intended to leave to Congress unlimited discretion to vary fundamentally the operation of the great independent executive branch of government and thus most seriously to weaken it. It would be a delegation by the convention to Congress of the function of defining the primary boundaries of another of the three great divisions of government. . . . It is reasonable to suppose also that had it been intended to give to Congress power to regulate or control removals in the manner suggested, it would have been . . . specifically enumerated. . . .

The difference between the grant of legislative power under Article I to Congress, which is limited to powers therein enumerated, and the more general grant of the executive power to the President under Article II is significant. The fact that the executive power is given in general terms strengthened by specific terms where emphasis is appropriate, and limited by direct expressions where limitation is needed and that no express limit is placed on the power of removal by the executive, is a convincing indication that none was intended.

It is argued that the denial of the legislative power to regulate removals in some way involves the denial of power to prescribe qualifications for office, or reasonable classification for promotion, and yet that has been often exercised. We see no conflict between the latter power and that of appointment and removal, provided of course that the qualifications do not so limit selection and so trench upon executive choice as to be in effect legislative designation. As Mr. Madison said in the First Congress:

> "The powers relative to offices are partly legislative and partly executive. The Legislature creates the office, defines the powers, limits its duration, and annexes a compensation. This done, the legislative power ceases. They ought to have nothing to do with designating the man to fill the office. That I conceive to be of an executive nature...."

Mr. Madison and his associates pointed out with great force the unreasonable character of the view that the convention intended, without express provision, to give to Congress or the Senate, in case of political or other differences, the means of thwarting the executive in the exercise of his great powers and in the bearing of his great responsibility by fastening upon him, as subordinate executive officers, men who by their inefficient service under him, by their lack of loyalty to the service, or by their different views of policy might make his taking care that the laws be faithfully executed most difficult or impossible.

As Mr. Madison said in the debate in the First Congress:

> "Vest this power in the Senate jointly with the President, and you abolish at once that great principle of unity and responsibility in the executive department, which was intended for the security of liberty and the public good. If the President should possess alone the power of removal from office, those who are employed in the execution of the law will be in their proper situation, and the chain of dependence be preserved; the lowest officers, the middle grade, and the highest will depend, as they ought, on the President, and the President on the community." 1 Annals of Congress, 499....

Made responsible under the Constitution for the effective enforcement of the law, the President needs as an indispensable aid to meet it the disciplinary influence upon those who act under him of a reserve power of removal. But it is contended that executive officers appointed by the President with the consent of the Senate are bound by the statutory law, and are not his servants to do his will, and that his obligation to care for the faithful execution of the laws does not authorize him to treat them as such. The degree of guidance in the discharge of their duties that the President may exercise over executive officers varies with the character of their service as prescribed in the law under which they act. The highest and most important duties which his subordinates perform are those in which they act for him. In such cases they are exercising not their own but his discretion. This field is a very large one. It is sometimes described as political. Each head of a department is and must be the President's alter ego in the matters of that department where the President is required by law to exercise authority....

But this is not to say that there are not strong reasons why the President should have a like power to remove his appointees charged with other duties than those above described. The ordinary duties of officers prescribed by statute come under the general administrative control of the President by virtue of the general grant to him of the executive power, and he may properly supervise and guide their construction of the statutes under which they act in order to secure that unitary and uniform execution of the laws which Article II of the Constitution evidently contemplated in vesting general executive power in the President alone. Laws are often passed with specific provision for adoption of regulations by a department or bureau head to make the law workable and effective. The ability and judgment manifested by the official thus empowered, as well as his energy and stimulation of his subordinates, are subjects which the President must consider and supervise in his administrative control. Finding such officers to be negligent and inefficient, the President should have the power to remove them. Of course there may be duties so peculiarly and specifically committed to the discretion of a particular officer as to raise a question whether the President may overrule or revise the officer's interpretation of his statutory duty in a particular instance. Then there may be duties of a quasi judicial character imposed on executive officers and members of executive tribunals whose decisions after hearing affect interests of individuals, the discharge of which the President cannot in a particular case properly influence or control. But even in such a case he may consider the decision after its rendition as a reason for removing the officer, on the ground that the discretion regularly entrusted to that officer by statute has not been on the whole intelligently or wisely exercised. Otherwise he does not discharge his own constitutional duty of seeing that the laws be faithfully executed....

For the reasons given, we must therefore hold that the provision of the law of 1876 by which the unrestricted power of removal of first-class postmasters is denied to the President is in violation of the Constitution and invalid. This leads to an affirmance of the judgment of the Court of Claims....

The separate opinion of Justice McREYNOLDS.

... Nothing short of language clear beyond serious disputation should be held to clothe the President with authority wholly beyond congressional control arbitrarily to dismiss every officer whom he appoints except a few judges. There are no such words in the Constitution, and the asserted inference conflicts with the heretofore accepted theory that this government is one of carefully enumerated powers under an intelligible charter.... If the phrase "executive power" infolds the one now claimed, many others heretofore totally unsuspected may lie there awaiting future supposed necessity, and no human intelligence can define the field of the President's permissible activities. "A masked battery of constructive powers would complete the destruction of liberty."...

The Legislature may create post offices and prescribe qualifications, duties, compensation, and term. And it may protect the incumbent in the enjoyment of his term unless in some way restrained therefrom. The real question, therefore, comes to this: Does any constitutional provision definitely limit the otherwise plenary power of Congress over postmasters, when they are appointed by the President with the consent of the Senate?...

Congress, in the exercise of its unquestioned power, may deprive the President of the right either to appoint or to remove any inferior officer, by vesting the authority to appoint in another.... He must utilize the force which Congress gives. He cannot, without permission, appoint the humblest clerk or expend a dollar of the public funds.

It is well to emphasize that our present concern is with the removal of an "inferior officer," within Article II, § 2, of the Constitution, which the statute positively prohibits without consent of the Senate. . . . We are not dealing with an ambassador, public minister, consul, judge, or "superior officer." . . . From its first session down to the last one Congress has consistently asserted its power to prescribe conditions concerning the removal of inferior officers. The executive has habitually observed them, and this court has affirmed the power of Congress therein. . . .

Congress may vest the power to appoint and remove [postmasters] in the head of a department and thus exclude them from presidential authority. From 1789 to 1836 the Postmaster General exercised these powers, as to all postmasters. . . . For 40 years the President functioned . . . without the semblance of power to remove any postmaster. So I think the supposed necessity and theory of government are only vapors. . . .

The Constitution empowers the President to appoint ambassadors, other public ministers, consuls, judges of the Supreme Court and superior officers, and no statute can interfere therein. But Congress may authorize both appointment and removal of all inferior officers without regard to the President's wishes—even in direct opposition to them. . . .

[I]f it were possible to spell out of the debate and action of the first Congress on the bill to establish the Department of Foreign Affairs some support for the present claim of the United States, this would be of little real consequence, for the same Congress on at least two occasions took the opposite position, and time and time again subsequent Congresses have done the same thing. It would be amazing for this court to base the interpretation of a constitutional provision upon a single doubtful congressional interpretation, when there have been dozens of them extending through 135 years, which are directly to the contrary effect. . . .

Congress has long and vigorously asserted its right to restrict removals and there has been no common executive practice based upon a contrary view. The President has often removed, and it is admitted that he may remove, with either the express or implied assent of Congress; but the present theory is that he may override the declared will of that body. This goes far beyond any practice heretofore approved or followed; it conflicts with the history of the Constitution, with the ordinary rules of interpretation, and with the construction approved by Congress since the beginning and emphatically sanctioned by this court. To adopt it would be revolutionary. . . . It is beyond the ordinary imagination to picture 40 or 50 capable men, presided over by George Washington, vainly discussing, in the heat of a Philadelphia summer, whether express authority to require opinions in writing should be delegated to a President in whom they had already vested the illimitable executive power here claimed. . . .

The Federalist, Article LXXVI, by Mr. Hamilton, says:

> "It has been mentioned as one of the advantages to be expected from the cooperation of the Senate, in the business of appointments, that it would contribute to the stability of the administration. The consent of that body would be necessary to displace as well as to appoint. A change of the Chief Magistrate, therefore, would not occasion so violent or so general a revolution in the officers of the government as might be expected, if he were the sole disposer of offices. Where a man in any station had given satisfactory evidence of his fitness for it, a new President would be restrained from attempting a change in favor of a person more agreeable to him, by the apprehension that a discountenance of

the Senate might frustrate the attempt, and bring some degree of discredit upon himself. Those who can best estimate the value of a steady administration will be most disposed to prize a provision, which connects the official existence of public men with the approbation or disapprobation of that body, which, from the greater permanency of its own composition, will in all probability be less subject to inconstancy than any other member of the government." ...

The claim advanced for the United States is supported by no opinion of this court, and conflicts with *Marbury v. Madison*. ... The court must have appreciated that, unless it found Marbury had the legal right to occupy the office irrespective of the President's will, there would be no necessity for passing upon the much-controverted and far-reaching power of the judiciary to declare an act of Congress without effect. ...

If the framers of the Constitution had intended "the executive power," ... to include all power of an executive nature, they would not have added the carefully defined grants of section 2. ... That the general words of a grant are limited, when followed by those of special import, is an established canon; and an accurate writer would hardly think of emphasizing a general grant by adding special and narrower ones without explanation. ...

Those who maintain that Art. II § 1, was intended as a grant of every power of executive nature not specifically qualified or denied must show that the term "executive power" had some definite and commonly accepted meaning in 1787. This court has declared that it did not include all powers exercised by the King of England; and, considering the history of the period, none can say that it had then (or afterwards) any commonly accepted and practical definition. If any one of the descriptions of "executive power" known in 1787 had been substituted for it, the whole plan would have failed. Such obscurity would have been intolerable to thinking men of that time. ...

Justice BRANDEIS, dissenting:

... The separation of the powers of government did not make each branch completely autonomous. It left each in some measure, dependent upon the others. ... Obviously the President cannot secure full execution of the laws, if Congress denies to him adequate means of doing so. Full execution may be defeated because Congress declines to create offices indispensable for that purpose. Or, because Congress having created the office, declines to make the indispensable appropriation. ... If, in any such way, adequate means are denied to the President, the fault will lie with Congress. The President performs his full constitutional duty, if, with the means and instruments provided by Congress and within the limitations prescribed by it, he uses his best endeavors to secure the faithful execution of the laws enacted.

Checks and balances were established in order that this should be a "government of laws and not of men." As White said in the House in 1789, an uncontrollable power of removal in the Chief Executive "is a doctrine not to be learned in American governments." Such power had been denied in Colonial Charters, and even under Proprietary Grants and Royal Commissions. It had been denied in the thirteen States before the framing of the Federal Constitution. The doctrine of the separation of powers was adopted by the Convention of 1787 not to promote efficiency but to preclude the exercise of arbitrary power. The purpose was not to avoid friction, but, by means of the inevitable friction incident to the distribution of the governmental powers among three departments, to save the people from autocracy. In order to prevent arbitrary executive action, the Constitution provided in terms that presidential appointments be made with the consent of the Senate, unless Congress should otherwise provide; and this clause was construed by Alexander Hamilton in The Federalist, No. 77, as requiring like consent to removals. . . .

Justice HOLMES, dissenting:

. . . We have to deal with an office that owes its existence to Congress and that Congress may abolish tomorrow. Its duration and the pay attached to it while it lasts depend on Congress alone. Congress alone confers on the President the power to appoint to it and at any time may transfer the power to other hands. With such power over its own creation, I have no more trouble in believing that Congress has power to prescribe a term of life for it free from any interference than I have in accepting the undoubted power of Congress to decree its end. I have equally little trouble in accepting its power to prolong the tenure of an incumbent until Congress or the Senate shall have assented to his removal. The duty of the President to see that the laws be executed is a duty that does not go beyond the laws or require him to achieve more than Congress sees fit to leave within his power.

---

1. The Court's opinion by Chief Justice Taft, himself a former President, has always been a favorite of the executive in briefs and Attorney General opinions. Do you see why? Taft's approach is quite formalist: no branch should have implied powers to participate in functions assigned by the Constitution to another; because removal is an executive function, the Senate may not share it. Therefore the President has an illimitable power to remove those executive officers whom he has appointed.

As is typical of formalism, however, much remains unanswered. *Why* is removal an exclusively executive function (it is not mentioned in the Constitution, except for Congress' power to impeach)? Taft answers that the President needs removal power in order to perform his own constitutional duties, for which he must have loyal subordinates. Surely there is a core of truth to this, but *which* subordinates must he control, and for *what* executive functions? In short, why does the President need a removal power that extends down the hierarchy to the Portland postmaster?

The approach of the dissenters resembles a modern functional one. They argue that the President does not need a removal power that extends to this level of government in order to discharge his responsibilities. They point out that Congress often places appointment power in the heads of departments, and then limits removal through the civil service laws. They also stress Congress' undoubted power to define the term and powers of offices and to determine appropriations for them. The majority thinks that Senatorial participation in a removal is different—do the dissents adequately answer that point? (With the next case, consider whether statutory requirements of cause for presidential removal should be distinguished from reserving the power to advise and consent after the fact.)

2. The Court lavishes attention on the "decision of 1789." What do you think it stands for? For example, was the Tenure of Office Act of 1867 unconstitutional as applied to the Secretary of War?

3. Taft appears to have a vision of a unitary executive branch, organized hierarchically under the President. He says, in language dear to the heart of later executive advisers, that the President may "supervise and guide" subordinates in pursuit of a

"unitary and uniform" execution of the laws. Taft then includes a dictum that apparently refers to regulatory commissions such as the Interstate Commerce Commission and the Federal Trade Commission. He says that the President might not be able to overrule matters "committed to the discretion of a particular officer." (How are we to identify those?) And he refers to "quasi judicial" activities as beyond the President's influence. Nevertheless, Taft would allow the President to remove such officers afterwards, for their unwisdom. He views that as a necessary component of the President's duty to "take Care that the Laws be faithfully executed." Do you agree? As you read the next case, see whether you think the Court adequately responds to Taft.

The *Myers* dissenters seemed to have a much more fragmentary view of the executive. This view is captured in the quote from Hamilton's *Federalist No. 77*, which seemed to envision a semipermanent bureaucracy at the highest levels, which the President could not unilaterally displace. Do you agree with Hamilton that the "stability of the administration" that would result would be beneficial? What if the Cabinet were composed of a group having little sympathy for the President or for each other? Do you agree with the apparent position of the dissenters that Congress should be able to organize the executive largely as it pleases, under the grant of power in the "necessary and proper" clause?

The Court's next removal case occurred at the height of its war with Franklin D. Roosevelt, who removed an FTC Commissioner on the advice that *Myers* meant that Congress could not restrict the President's power to discharge presidential appointees. The Court unanimously rebuked the President in an opinion issued the same day as its invalidation of the NIRA in *Schechter Poultry, supra* Chapter Two. Viewing the juxtaposition, the future Justice Scalia wrote that "the same mistrust of New Deal executive freewheeling aroused by the truly sweeping NRA proposals addressed in *Schechter* colored the companion case as well." (*Historical Anomalies in Administrative Law*, Yearbook 1985, 103, 108.) As you will see, the Court's hostility produced a broad opinion that contrasted sharply with *Myers*. To what extent does the Court state principles that should govern today?

Humphrey's Executor v. United States
295 U.S. 602 (1935)

Justice SUTHERLAND delivered the opinion of the Court.

... William E. Humphrey, the decedent, ... was nominated by President Hoover to succeed himself as a member of the Federal Trade Commission, and was confirmed by the United States Senate ... for a term of seven years. ... On July 25, 1933, President Roosevelt addressed a letter to the commissioner asking for his resignation, on the ground "that the aims and purposes of the Administration with respect to the work of the Commission can be carried out most effectively with personnel of my own selection," but disclaiming any reflection upon the commissioner personally or upon his services. [Subsequently,] the President on August 31, 1933, wrote the commissioner expressing the hope that the resignation would be forthcoming, and saying: "You will, I know, realize that I do not feel that your mind and my mind go along together on either the policies or the administering of the Federal Trade Commission, and, frankly, I think it is best for the people of this country that I should have a full confidence."

The commissioner declined to resign; [the President removed him.] Humphrey never acquiesced in this action.... [His executor sued for his salary from the date of removal to the date of death.] Upon these facts, ... the following questions are certified:

"1. Do the provisions of section 1 of the Federal Trade Commission Act, stating that 'any commissioner may be removed by the President for inefficiency, neglect of duty, or malfeasance in office', restrict or limit the power of the President to remove a commissioner except upon one or more of the causes named?

"If the foregoing question is answered in the affirmative, then—

"2. If the power of the President to remove a commissioner is restricted or limited as shown by the foregoing interrogatory and the answer made thereto, is such a restriction or limitation valid under the Constitution of the United States?"

The Federal Trade Commission Act, 15 U.S.C. §§ 41, 42, creates a commission of five members to be appointed by the President by and with the advice and consent of the Senate, ... In exercising [its power under § 5 of the Act to prevent "unfair methods of competition"], the commission must issue a complaint stating its charges and giving notice of hearing.... A person, partnership, or corporation proceeded against is given the right to appear ... and show cause why an order to cease and desist should not be issued.... If the commission finds the method of competition is one prohibited by the act, it is directed to [state] its findings as to the facts, and to issue and cause to be served a cease and desist order. If the order is disobeyed, the commission may apply to the appropriate Circuit Court of Appeals for its enforcement. The party subject to the order may seek and obtain a review in the Circuit Court of Appeals in a manner provided by the act....

First. The question ... is whether, by the provisions of section 1 of the [Act], the President's power is limited to removal for the specific causes enumerated therein. The negative contention of the government is based principally upon the decision of this court in *Shurtleff v. United States*, 189 U.S. 311. That case involved the power of the President to remove a general appraiser of merchandise appointed under [a statute providing that appraisers] "may be removed from office at any time by the President for inefficiency, neglect of duty, or malfeasance in office." The President removed Shurtleff without assigning any cause therefor. The Court [noted] that no term of office was fixed by the act and that, with the exception of judicial officers provided for by the Constitution, no civil officer had ever held office by life tenure since the foundation of the government.... [It declined to grant] the appraiser the right to hold office during his life or until found guilty of some act specified in the statute....

The situation here presented is plainly and wholly different. The statute fixes a term of office, in accordance with many precedents.... But if the intention of Congress that no removal should be made during the specified term except for one or more of the enumerated causes were not clear upon the face of the statute, as we think it is, it would be made clear by a consideration of the character of the commission and the legislative history which accompanied and preceded the passage of the act.

The commission is to be nonpartisan; and it must, from the very nature of its duties, act with entire impartiality. It is charged with the enforcement of no policy except the policy of the law. Its duties are neither political nor executive, but predominantly quasi-judicial and quasi-legislative. Like the Interstate Commerce Commission, its members are called upon to exercise the trained judgment of a body of experts "appointed by law and informed by experience." ...

Thus, the language of the act, the legislative reports, and the general purposes of the legislation as reflected by the debates, all combine to demonstrate the congressional intent to create a body of experts who shall gain experience by length of service; a body which shall be independent of executive authority, *except in its selection*, and free to exercise its judgment without the leave or hindrance of any other official or any department of the government. To the accomplishment of these purposes, it is clear that Congress was of opinion that length and certainty of tenure would vitally contribute. And to hold that, nevertheless, the members of the commission continue in office at the mere will of the President, might be to thwart, in large measure, the very ends which Congress sought to realize by definitely fixing the term of office.

We conclude that the intent of the act is to limit the executive power of removal to the causes enumerated, the existence of none of which is claimed here; and we pass to the second question.

Second. To support its contention that the removal provision of section 1, as we have just construed it, is an unconstitutional interference with the executive power of the President, the government's chief reliance is *Myers v. United States.* ... Nevertheless, the narrow point actually decided was only that the President had power to remove a postmaster of the first class, without the advice and consent of the Senate as required by act of Congress. In the course of the opinion of the court, expressions occur which tend to sustain the government's contention, but these are beyond the point involved and, therefore, do not come within the rule of stare decisis. In so far as they are out of harmony with the views here set forth, these expressions are disapproved. ...

The office of a postmaster is so essentially unlike the office now involved that the decision in the *Myers* case cannot be accepted as controlling our decision here. A postmaster is an executive officer restricted to the performance of executive functions. He is charged with no duty at all related to either the legislative or judicial power. The actual decision in the *Myers* case finds support in the theory that such an officer is merely one of the units in the executive department and, hence, inherently subject to the exclusive and illimitable power of removal by the Chief Executive, whose subordinate and aid he is. Putting aside dicta, ... the necessary reach of the decision goes far enough to include all purely executive officers. It goes no farther; much less does it include an officer who occupies no place in the executive department and who exercises no part of the executive power vested by the Constitution in the President.

The Federal Trade Commission is an administrative body created by Congress to carry into effect legislative policies embodied in the statute in accordance with the legislative standard therein prescribed, and to perform other specified duties as a legislative or as a judicial aid. Such a body cannot in any proper sense be characterized as an arm or an eye of the executive. Its duties are performed without executive leave and, in the contemplation of the statute, must be free from executive control. In administering the provisions of the statute in respect of "unfair methods of competition,"—that is to say, in filling in and administering the details embodied by that general standard—the commission acts in part quasi-legislatively and in part quasi-judicially. In making investigations and reports thereon for the information of Congress under section 6, in aid of the legislative power, it acts as a legislative agency. Under section 7, which authorizes the commission to act as a master in chancery under rules prescribed by the court, it acts as an agency of the judiciary. To the extent that it exercises any executive function, as distinguished from executive power in the constitutional sense, it does so in the discharge and effectuation of its quasi-legislative or quasi-judicial powers, or as an agency of the legislative or judicial departments of the government.

If Congress is without authority to prescribe causes for removal of members of the trade commission and limit executive power of removal accordingly, that power at once becomes practically all-inclusive in respect of civil officers with the exception of the judiciary provided for by the Constitution. The Solicitor General, at the bar, apparently recognizing this to be true, with commendable candor, agreed that his view in respect of the removability of members of the Federal Trade Commission necessitated a like view in respect of the Interstate Commerce Commission and the Court of Claims. We are thus confronted with the serious question whether not only the members of these quasi-legislative and quasi-judicial bodies, but the judges of the legislative Court of Claims, exercising judicial power, continue in office only at the pleasure of the President.

We think it plain under the Constitution that illimitable power of removal is not possessed by the President in respect of officers of the character of those just named. The authority of Congress, in creating quasi-legislative or quasi-judicial agencies, to require them to act in discharge of their duties independently of executive control, cannot well be doubted; and that authority includes, as an appropriate incident, power to fix the period during which they shall continue, and to forbid their removal except for cause in the meantime. For it is quite evident that one who holds his office only during the pleasure of another cannot be depended upon to maintain an attitude of independence against the latter's will.

The fundamental necessity of maintaining each of the three general departments of government entirely free from the control or coercive influence, direct or indirect, of either of the others, has often been stressed and is hardly open to serious question. So much is implied in the very fact of the separation of the powers of these departments by the Constitution; and in the rule which recognizes their essential coequality. The sound application of a principle that makes one master in his own house precludes him from imposing his control in the house of another who is master there. . . . Justice Story, in the first volume of his work on the Constitution, 4th ed. § 530, citing No. 48 of the Federalist, said that neither of the departments in reference to each other "ought to possess, directly or indirectly, an overruling influence in the administration of their respective powers."

The power of removal here claimed for the President falls within this principle, since its coercive influence threatens the independence of a commission, which is not only wholly disconnected from the executive department, but which, as already fully appears, was created by Congress as a means of carrying into operation legislative and judicial powers, and as an agency of the legislative and judicial departments.

In the light of the question now under consideration, we have re-examined the precedents referred to in the *Myers case*, and find nothing in them to justify a conclusion contrary to that which we have reached. . . . [In the "decision of 1789," regarding the Secretary of State, the office] was not only purely executive, but the officer one who was responsible to the President, and to him alone, in a very definite sense.

A reading of the debates shows that the President's illimitable power of removal was not considered in respect of other than executive officers. And it is pertinent to observe that when, at a later time, the tenure of office for the Comptroller of the Treasury was under consideration, Mr. Madison quite evidently thought that, since the duties of that office were not purely of an executive nature but partook of the judiciary quality as well, a different rule in respect of executive removal might well apply. 1 Annals of Congress, cols. 611-612.

In *Marbury v. Madison*, it is made clear that Chief Justice Marshall was of opinion that a justice of the peace for the District of Columbia was not removable at the will of the President; and that there was a distinction between such an officer and officers appointed to aid the President in the performance of his constitutional duties. In the latter case, the distinction he saw was that "their acts are his acts" and his will, therefore, controls; and, by way of illustration, he adverted to the act establishing the Department of Foreign Affairs, which was the subject of the "decision of 1789."

The result of what we now have said is this: Whether the power of the President to remove an officer shall prevail over the authority of Congress to condition the power by fixing a definite term and precluding a removal except for cause will depend upon the character of the office; the *Myers* decision, affirming the power of the President alone to make the removal, is confined to purely executive officers; and as to officers of the kind here under consideration, we hold that no removal can be made during the prescribed term for which the officer is appointed, except for one or more of the causes named in the applicable statute.

To the extent that, between the decision in the *Myers* case, . . . and our present decision . . . there shall remain a field of doubt, we leave such cases as may fall within it for future consideration and determination as they may arise.

In accordance with the foregoing, the questions submitted are answered: [Yes].

---

1. Notice why the Court construes the FTC Act to forbid removal for reasons other than the statutory grounds. It reads the Act as embodying a premise associated with the Progressive movement, that regulation should be a neutral and expert process, above the unseemly strife of politics. For the Court, itself in sympathy with the Progressive view, it was then only a short step to the conclusion that it is constitutional for Congress to minimize the political influence of the President on the regulators. Yet the independent agencies have never been totally isolated from politics—consider, for example, the nature of *congressional* oversight. Today, the Progressive view seems both an impossible and an undesirable dream. Inescapably, regulation is rife with politics. Indeed, political oversight is crucial to the legitimacy of regulation by un-elected bureaucrats. Thus, the Court's opinion now rests partly on discredited political science.

2. If the Court's theory of administrative expertise seems too unrealistic today to justify the Court's conclusions, is there another available basis? The case seems to rest in large part on a procedural value, the need to recognize congressional power to protect officers engaged in adjudication from summary removal without cause. This is a clearly appropriate ground for restrictions on presidential intervention, isn't it? Indeed, concepts of due process and statutes codifying them (e.g., 5 U.S.C. § 557(d)) forbid ex parte intervention in administrative adjudication by anyone. And compare the Court's emphasis on fair process in its delegation doctrine analysis in its contemporaneous decision in *Schechter Poultry*. So perhaps Chief Justice Taft was

wrong to opine that the President should be able to fire an adjudicator for decisions he disapproves. (If the President's views on a matter in adjudication are known in advance, there would be a risk of influence on the outcome of the case.) But what about rulemaking and other informal executive actions, for which neither due process nor statutes forbid ex parte contacts? We will consider this issue in connection with presidential supervision of executive branch policymaking.

3. Procedural values appeared again in *Wiener v. United States*, 357 U.S. 349 (1958). Congress established the War Claims Commission to "adjudicate according to law" certain claims arising from enemy action in World War II. The Commissioners were presidential appointees; there was no provision regarding their removal. President Eisenhower, asserting a need to complete the Commission's task "with personnel of my own selection," removed Commissioner Myron Wiener, who then sued for lost salary. Justice Frankfurter's opinion for a unanimous Court found that Congress intended the Commission to decide claims on the merits, entirely free of influence from any other branch of government. Wiener's removal was illegal because Congress would not want the Commissioners to fear "the Damocles' sword of removal by the President for no reason other than that he preferred to have...men of his own choosing."

4. What is the precise holding of *Humphrey's Executor*? Is it that Congress may constitutionally forbid presidential removals of FTC Commissioners without cause? If so, and considering that specific cause was not asserted in any of the removal cases, what is the meaning of the typical statutory formulation of "inefficiency, neglect of duty, or malfeasance in office"? We consider this issue below, with presidential supervision of agency policymaking.

5. *Humphrey's Executor* is responsible for the oft-asserted special constitutional status of the independent agencies. In dicta, the Court accords them a position entirely outside the executive branch, without textual support in the Constitution for doing so. For justification, the Court points to the "quasi-judicial" and "quasi-legislative" functions performed by the FTC, and distinguishes them from activities performed by "purely executive officers." This attempt to draw a functional distinction is, however, belied by practice: executive branch agencies often perform "quasi-judicial" and "quasi-legislative" functions. (For example, the Food and Drug Administration issues many rules, and the Social Security Administration performs many adjudications. Both are within the Department of Health and Human Services.) Similarly, independent agencies often perform such executive duties as prosecution (for example, the FTC has concurrent jurisdiction to enforce the antitrust laws with the Department of Justice). Thus, the Court's constitutional distinction is highly oversimplified and unrealistic. Can you supply a better basis for protecting some functions from presidential interference? Which ones should qualify?

Whatever the soundness of these dicta in *Humphrey's Executor*, Congress has embraced them with a fervor equal to the executive's attachment to *Myers*. Congressional committees never tire of reminding nominees to the independent agencies that they are "arms of Congress." Scalia, *supra* at 110, laments that "the holding of the case has been expanded to embrace its entire rationale... [it] continues to induce the Executive to leave the policy control of the independent agencies to congressional committees, and fastidiously to avoid any appearance of influence in those entities."

6. Times may be changing. Have the Court's subsequent decisions in *Buckley* and *Chadha* undercut the rationale of *Humphrey's Executor*? Recall the *Buckley* Court's

statement that although the FEC's rulemaking and adjudicative functions "are more legislative and judicial in nature than are the Commission's enforcement powers," they must be performed by presidential appointees because "none of them operates merely in aid of congressional authority to legislate or is sufficiently removed from the administration and enforcement of public law to allow it to be performed by the present Commission." Still, the *Buckley* Court insisted that its decision was "entirely consistent" with the removal cases. Do you agree? If these activities are not purely executive, why need they be performed by Officers of the United States?

As for *Chadha*, review the Court's characterization of administrative functions in its footnote 16. The Court would not create a special preserve for the legislative veto either for the independent agencies or for rulemaking. Isn't that inconsistent with *Humphrey's Executor*? We will have more to say on these matters, but first we turn to the Court's latest removal case.

Bowsher v. Synar
106 S.Ct. 3181 (1986)

Chief Justice BURGER delivered the opinion of the Court.

The question presented by these appeals is whether the assignment by Congress to the Comptroller General of the United States of certain functions under the Balanced Budget and Emergency Deficit Control Act of 1985 violates the doctrine of separation of powers.

I
A

On December 12, 1985, the President signed into law the Balanced Budget and Emergency Deficit Control Act of 1985, 2 U.S.C. § 901 et seq. (Supp.1986), popularly known as the "Gramm-Rudman-Hollings Act." The purpose of the Act is to eliminate the federal budget deficit. To that end, the Act sets a "maximum deficit amount" for federal spending for each of fiscal years 1986 through 1991. The size of that maximum deficit amount progressively reduces to zero in fiscal year 1991. If in any fiscal year the federal budget deficit exceeds the maximum deficit amount by more than a specified sum, the Act requires across-the-board cuts in federal spending to reach the targeted deficit level, with half of the cuts made to defense programs and the other half made to non-defense programs. The Act exempts certain priority programs from these cuts.

These "automatic" reductions are accomplished through a rather complicated procedure, spelled out in § 251, the so-called "reporting provisions" of the Act. Each year, the Directors of the Office of Management and Budget (OMB) and the Congressional Budget Office (CBO) independently estimate the amount of the federal budget deficit for the upcoming fiscal year. If that deficit exceeds the maximum targeted deficit amount for that fiscal year by more than a specified amount, the Directors of OMB and CBO independently calculate, on a program-by-program basis, the budget reductions necessary to ensure that the deficit does not exceed the maximum deficit amount. The Act then requires the Directors to report jointly their deficit estimates and budget reduction calculations to the Comptroller General.

The Comptroller General, after reviewing the Directors' reports, then reports his conclusions to the President. § 251(b). The President in turn must issue a "sequestration" order mandating the spending reductions specified by the Comptroller General. § 252. There follows a period during which Congress may by legislation reduce spending to obviate, in whole or in part, the need for the sequestration order. If such reductions are not enacted, the sequestration order becomes effective and the spending reductions included in that order are made.

Anticipating constitutional challenge to these procedures, the Act also contains a "fallback" deficit reduction process to take effect "[i]n the event that any of the reporting procedures described in section 251 are invalidated." § 274(f). Under these provisions, the report prepared by the Directors of OMB and the CBO is submitted directly to a specially-created Temporary Joint Committee on Deficit Reduction, which must report in five days to both Houses a joint resolution setting forth the content of the Directors' report. Congress then must vote on the resolution under special rules, which render amendments out of order. If the resolution is passed and signed by the President, it then serves as the basis for a Presidential sequestration order.

B

Within hours of the President's signing of the Act, Congressman Synar, who had voted against the Act, filed a complaint seeking declaratory relief that the Act was unconstitutional.... A virtually identical lawsuit was also filed by the National Treasury Employees Union. The Union alleged that its members had been injured as a result of the Act's automatic spending reduction provisions, which have suspended certain cost-of-living benefit increases to the Union's members.

A three-judge District Court, appointed pursuant to 2 U.S.C. § 922(a)(5), invalidated the reporting provisions. Synar v. United States, 626 F.Supp. 1374 (DC 1986) (Scalia, Johnson, Gasch, JJ.).... The District Court... rejected appellees' challenge that the Act violated the delegation doctrine. The court expressed no doubt that the Act delegated broad authority, but delegation of similarly broad authority has been upheld in past cases. The District Court observed that in *Yakus v. United States*, 321 U.S. 414, 420 (1944), this Court upheld a statute that delegated to an unelected "Price Administrator" the power "to promulgate regulations fixing prices of commodities." Moreover, in the District Court's view, the Act adequately confined the exercise of administrative discretion. The District Court concluded that "the totality of the Act's standards, definitions, context, and reference to past administrative practice provides an adequate 'intelligible principle' to guide and confine administrative decisionmaking."

Although the District Court concluded that the Act survived a delegation doctrine challenge, it held that the role of the Comptroller General in the deficit reduction process violated the constitutionally imposed separation of powers.... Appeals were taken directly to this Court pursuant to § 274(b) of the Act.... We affirm....

III

... The declared purpose of separating and dividing the powers of government, of course, was to "diffus[e] power the better to secure liberty." *Youngstown Sheet & Tube Co. v. Sawyer*, 343 U.S. 579, 635 (1952) (Jackson, J., concurring). Justice Jackson's words echo the famous warning of Montesquieu, quoted by James Madison in The Federalist No. 47, that " 'there can be no liberty where the legislative and executive powers are united in the same person, or body of magistrates'.... " Unlike parliamentary systems such as that of Great Britain, no person who is an officer of the United States may serve as a Member of the Congress. Art. I, § 6. Moreover, unlike parliamentary systems, the President, under Article II, is responsible not to the Congress but to the people, subject only to impeachment proceedings which are exercised by the two Houses as representatives of the people. Art. II, § 4....

The Constitution does not contemplate an active role for Congress in the supervision of officers charged with the execution of the laws it enacts. The President appoints "Officers of the United States" with the "Advice and Consent of the Senate..." Article II, § 2. Once the appointment has been made and confirmed, however, the Constitution explicitly provides for removal of Officers of the United States by Congress only upon impeachment by the House of Representatives and conviction by the Senate [which] can rest only on "Treason, Bribery or other high Crimes and Misdemeanors." A direct congressional role in the removal of officers charged with the execution of the laws beyond this limited one is inconsistent with separation of powers....

This Court first directly addressed this issue in *Myers v. United States*, 272 U.S. 52 (1925).... Chief Justice Taft, writing for the Court, declared the statute [requiring advice and consent to removal] unconstitutional on the ground that for Congress to "draw to itself, or to either branch of it, the power to remove or the right to participate in the exercise of that power... would be... to infringe the... separation of governmental powers." A decade later, in *Humphrey's Executor v. United States*, 295 U.S. 602 (1935),... a Federal Trade Commissioner who had been removed by the President sought back pay. *Humphrey's Executor* involved an issue not presented either in the *Myers* case or in this case—i.e., the power of Congress to limit the President's powers of removal of a Federal Trade Commissioner.[4]... The Court distinguished *Myers*, reaffirming its holding that congressional participation in the removal of executive officers is unconstitutional....

In light of these precedents, we conclude that Congress cannot reserve for itself the power of removal of an officer charged with the execution of the laws except by impeachment. To permit the execution of the laws to be vested in an officer answerable only to Congress would, in practical terms, reserve in Congress control over the execution of the laws. As the District Court observed, "Once an officer is appointed, it is only the authority that can remove him, and not the authority that appointed him, that he must fear and, in the performance of his functions, obey." The structure of the Constitution does not permit Congress to execute the laws; it follows that Congress cannot grant to an officer under its control what it does not possess.

Our decision in *INS v. Chadha*, 462 U.S. 919 (1983), supports this conclusion. In *Chadha*, we struck down a one house "legislative veto" provision by which each House of Congress retained the power to reverse a decision Congress had expressly authorized the Attorney General to make:

---

4. Appellants therefore are wide of the mark in arguing that an affirmance in this case requires casting doubt on the status of "independent" agencies because no issues involving such agencies are presented here. The statutes establishing independent agencies typically specify either that the agency members are removable by the President for specified causes, or else do not specify a removal procedure, *see, e.g.*, 2 U.S.C. § 437c (Federal Election Commission). This case involves nothing like these statutes, but rather a statute that provides for direct Congressional involvement over the decision to remove the Comptroller General. Appellants have referred us to no independent agency whose members are removable by the Congress for certain causes short of impeachable offenses, as is the Comptroller General.

"Disagreement with the Attorney General's decision on Chadha's deportation—that is, Congress' decision to deport Chadha—no less than Congress' original choice to delegate to the Attorney General the authority to make that decision, involves determinations of policy that Congress can implement in only one way; bicameral passage followed by presentment to the President. Congress must abide by its delegation of authority until that delegation is legislatively altered or revoked."

To permit an officer controlled by Congress to execute the laws would be, in essence, to permit a congressional veto. Congress could simply remove, or threaten to remove, an officer for executing the laws in any fashion found to be unsatisfactory to Congress. This kind of congressional control over the execution of the laws, *Chadha* makes clear, is constitutionally impermissible. . . .

IV

Appellants urge that the Comptroller General performs his duties independently and is not subservient to Congress. We agree with the District Court that this contention does not bear close scrutiny. The critical factor lies in the provisions of the statute defining the Comptroller General's office relating to removability. Although the Comptroller General is nominated by the President from a list of three individuals recommended by the Speaker of the House of Representatives and the President pro tempore of the Senate, see 31 U.S.C. § 703(a)(2), and confirmed by the Senate, he is removable only at the initiative of Congress. He may be removed not only by impeachment but also by Joint Resolution of Congress "at any time" resting on any one of the following bases:

"(i) permanent disability;
"(ii) inefficiency;
"(iii) neglect of duty;
"(iv) malfeasance; or
"(v) a felony or conduct involving moral turpitude."

31 U.S.C. § 703(e)(1). This provision was included, as one Congressman explained in urging passage of the Act, because Congress "felt that [the Comptroller General] should be brought under the sole control of Congress, so that Congress at the moment when it found he was inefficient and was not carrying on the duties of his office as he should and as the Congress expected, could remove him without the long, tedious process of a trial by impeachment." 61 Cong.Rec. 1081 (1921). . . .

The statute permits removal for "inefficiency," "neglect of duty," or "malfeasance." These terms are very broad and, as interpreted by Congress, could sustain removal of a Comptroller General for any number of actual or perceived transgressions of the legislative will. The Constitutional Convention chose to permit impeachment of executive officers only for "Treason, Bribery, or other high Crimes and Misdemeanors." It rejected language that would have permitted impeachment for "maladministration," with Madison arguing that "[s]o vague a term will be equivalent to a tenure during pleasure of the Senate." 2 Farrand 550. . . .

Justice White, however, assures us that "[r]ealistic consideration" of the "practical result of the removal provision," reveals that the Comptroller General is unlikely to be removed by Congress. The separated powers of our government can not be permitted to turn on judicial assessment of whether an officer exercising executive power is on good terms with Congress. The Framers recognized that, in the long term, structural protections against abuse of power were critical to preserving liberty. In constitutional terms, the removal powers over the Comptroller General's office dictate that he will be subservient to Congress.

This much said, we must also add that the dissent is simply in error to suggest that the political realities reveal that the Comptroller General is free from influence by Congress. The Comptroller General heads the General Accounting Office, "an instrumentality of the United States Government independent of the executive departments," 31 U.S.C. § 702(a), which was created by Congress in 1921 as part of the Budget and Accounting Act of 1921, 42 Stat. 23. Congress created the office because it believed that it "needed an officer, responsible to it alone, to check upon the application of public funds in accordance with appropriations." H. Mansfield, The Comptroller General: A Study in the Law and Practice of Financial Administration 65 (1939).

It is clear that Congress has consistently viewed the Comptroller General as an officer of the Legislative Branch. The Reorganization Acts of 1945 and 1949, for example, both stated that the Comptroller General and the GAO are "a part of the legislative branch of the Government." Similarly, in the Accounting and Auditing Act of 1950, Congress required the Comptroller General to conduct audits "as an agent of the Congress." Over the years, the Comptrollers General have also viewed themselves as part of the Legislative Branch. . . .

Against this background, we see no escape from the conclusion that, because Congress has retained removal authority over the Comptroller General, he may not be entrusted with executive powers. The remaining question is whether the Comptroller General has been assigned such powers in the Balanced Budget and Emergency Deficit Control Act of 1985.

V

The primary responsibility of the Comptroller General under the instant Act is the preparation of a "report." This report must contain detailed estimates of projected federal revenues and expenditures. The report must also specify the reductions, if any, necessary to reduce the deficit to the target for the appropriate fiscal year. The reductions must be set forth on a program-by-program basis.

In preparing the report, the Comptroller General is to have "due regard" for the estimates and reductions set forth in a joint report submitted to him by the Director of CBO and the Director of OMB, the President's fiscal and budgetary advisor. However, the Act plainly contemplates that the Comptroller General will exercise his independent judgment and evaluation with respect to those estimates. The Act also provides that the Comptroller General's report "shall explain fully any differences between the contents of such report and the report of the Directors."

Appellants suggest that the duties assigned to the Comptroller General in the Act are essentially ministerial and mechanical so that their performance does not constitute "execution of the law" in a meaningful sense. On the contrary, we view these functions as plainly entailing execution of the law in constitutional terms. Interpreting a law enacted by Congress to implement the legislative mandate is the very essence of "execution" of the law. Under § 251, the Comptroller General must exercise judgment concerning facts that affect the application of the Act. He must also interpret the provisions of the Act to determine precisely what budgetary calculations are required. Decisions of that kind are typically made by officers charged with executing a statute.

The executive nature of the Comptroller General's functions under the Act is revealed in § 252(a)(3) which gives the Comptroller General the ultimate authority to determine the budget cuts to be made. Indeed, the Comptroller General commands the President himself to carry out, without the slightest variation (with exceptions not relevant to the constitutional issues presented), the directive of the Comptroller General as to the budget reductions:

> "The [Presidential] order *must provide* for reductions in the manner specified in section 251(a)(3), *must incorporate* the provisions of the [Comptroller General's] report submitted under section 251(b), and *must be consistent with such report in all respects*. The President *may not modify or recalculate any of the estimates, determinations, specifications, bases, amounts, or percentages* set forth in the report submitted under section 251(b) in determining the reductions to be specified in the order with respect to programs, projects, and activities, or with respect to budget activities, within an account...." § 252(a)(3) (emphasis added).

Congress of course initially determined the content of the Balanced Budget and Emergency Deficit Control Act; and undoubtedly the content of the Act determines the nature of the executive duty. However, as *Chadha* makes clear, once Congress makes its choice in enacting legislation, its participation ends. Congress can thereafter control the execution of its enactment only indirectly—by passing new legislation. By placing the responsibility for execution of the Balanced Budget and Emergency Deficit Control Act in the hands of an officer who is subject to removal only by itself, Congress in effect has retained control over the execution of the Act and has intruded into the executive function. The Constitution does not permit such intrusion....

We conclude the District Court correctly held that the powers vested in the Comptroller General under § 251 violate the command of the Constitution that the Congress play no direct role in the execution of the laws. Accordingly, the judgment and order of the District Court are affirmed. Our judgment is stayed for a period not to exceed 60 days to permit Congress to implement the fallback provisions.

Justice STEVENS, with whom Justice MARSHALL joins, concurring in the judgment.

... I disagree with the Court... on the reasons why the Constitution prohibits the Comptroller General from exercising the powers assigned to him by... the Act. It is not the dormant, carefully circumscribed congressional removal power that represents the primary constitutional evil. Nor do I agree with the conclusion of both the majority and the dissent that the analysis depends on a labeling of the functions assigned to the Comptroller General as "executive powers." Rather, I am convinced that the Comptroller General must be characterized as an agent of Congress because of his longstanding statutory responsibilities; that... when Congress, or a component or an agent of Congress, seeks to make policy that will bind the Nation, it must follow the procedures mandated by Article I of the Constitution....

I

The fact that Congress retained for itself the power to remove the Comptroller General is important evidence supporting the conclusion that he is a member of the

Legislative Branch of the Government. Unlike the Court, however, I am not persuaded that the congressional removal power is either a necessary, or a sufficient, basis for concluding that his statutory assignment is invalid. . . .

The notion that the removal power at issue here automatically creates some kind of "here-and-now subservience" of the Comptroller General to Congress is belied by history. There is no evidence that Congress has ever removed, or threatened to remove, the Comptroller General for reasons of policy. Moreover, the President has long possessed a comparable power to remove members of the Federal Trade Commission, yet it is universally accepted that they are independent of, rather than subservient to, the President in performing their official duties. Thus, . . . in *Humphrey's Executor*, . . . the Court stressed the independence of the Commission from the President. There was no suggestion that the retained Presidential removal powers—similar to those at issue here—created a subservience to the President. . . .

The fact that Congress retained for itself the power to remove the Comptroller General thus is not necessarily an adequate reason for concluding that his role in the Gramm-Rudman-Hollings budget reduction process is unconstitutional. It is, however, a fact that lends support to my ultimate conclusion that, in exercising his functions under this Act, he serves as an agent of the Congress.

II

In assessing the role of the Comptroller General, it is appropriate to consider his already existing statutory responsibilities. . . . In the statutory section that identifies the Comptroller General's responsibilities for investigating the use of public money, four of the five enumerated duties specifically describe an obligation owed to Congress. . . . The statutory provision detailing the Comptroller General's role in evaluating programs and activities of the United States Government similarly leaves no doubt regarding the beneficiary of the Comptroller General's labors. The Comptroller General may undertake such an evaluation for one of three specified reasons: (1) on his own initiative; (2) "when either House of Congress orders an evaluation"; or (3) "when a committee of Congress with jurisdiction over the program or activity requests the evaluation." 31 U.S.C. § 717(b). In assessing a program or activity, moreover, the Comptroller General's responsibility is to "develop and recommend *to Congress* ways to evaluate a program or activity the Government carries out under existing law." § 717(c) (emphasis added). . . .

The Comptroller General's current statutory responsibilities on behalf of Congress are fully consistent with the historic conception of the Comptroller General's office. The statute that created the Comptroller General's office—the Budget and Accounting Act of 1921—provided that four of the five statutory responsibilities given to the Comptroller General be exercised on behalf of Congress, three of them exclusively so. On at least three occasions since 1921, moreover, in considering the structure of government, Congress has defined the Comptroller General as being a part of the Legislative Branch. . . .

This is not to say, of course, that the Comptroller General has no obligations to the Executive Branch, or that he is an agent of the Congress in quite so clear a manner as the Doorkeeper of the House. . . . The Comptroller General must "give the President information on expenditures and accounting the President requests." 31 U.S.C. § 719(f). . . . Historically, as well, the Comptroller General has had some relationship to the Executive Branch. [I]n the 1921 Act, one of the Comptroller General's specific responsibilities was to provide information to the Bureau of the Budget. In fact, when the Comptroller General's office was created, its functions, personnel, records, and even furniture derived from a previous Executive office.

Thus, the Comptroller General retains certain obligations with respect to the Executive Branch. Obligations to two Branches are not, however, impermissible and the presence of such dual obligations does not prevent the characterization of the official with the dual obligations as part of one branch. It is at least clear that, in most, if not all, of his statutory responsibilities, the Comptroller General is properly characterized as an agent of the Congress.

III

Everyone agrees that the powers assigned to the Comptroller General by ... the Gramm-Rudman-Hollings Act are extremely important. They require him to exercise sophisticated economic judgment concerning anticipated trends in the Nation's economy, projected levels of unemployment, interest rates, and the special problems that may be confronted by the many components of a vast federal bureaucracy. His duties are anything but ministerial—he is not merely a clerk wearing a "green eye shade" as he undertakes these tasks. Rather, he is vested with the kind of responsibilities that Congress has elected to discharge itself under the fallback provision that will become effective if and when § 251(b) and § 251(c)(2) are held invalid....

The Court concludes that the Gramm-Rudman-Hollings Act impermissibly assigns the Comptroller General "executive powers." The dissent agrees that "the powers exercised by the Comptroller under the Act may be characterized as 'executive' in that they involve the interpretation and carrying out of the Act's mandate." This conclusion is not only far from obvious but also rests on the unstated and unsound premise that there is a definite line that distinguishes executive power from legislative power....

One reason that the exercise of legislative, executive, and judicial powers cannot be categorically distributed among three mutually exclusive branches of government is that governmental power cannot always be readily characterized with only one of those three labels. On the contrary, as our cases demonstrate, a particular function, like a chameleon, will often take on the aspect of the office to which it is assigned. ... The *Chadha* case itself illustrates this basic point. The governmental decision that was being made was whether a resident alien who had overstayed his student visa should be deported. From the point of view of the administrative law judge who conducted a hearing on the issue—or as Justice Powell saw the issue in his concurrence—the decision took on a judicial coloring. From the point of view of the Attorney General ... to whom Congress had delegated the authority to suspend deportation of certain aliens, the decision appeared to have an executive character. But, as the Court held, when the House of Representatives finally decided that Chadha must be deported, its action "was essentially legislative in purpose and effect."

The powers delegated to the Comptroller General by § 251 of the Act before us today have a similar chameleon-like quality. The District Court persuasively explained why they may be appropriately characterized as executive powers. But, when that delegation is held invalid, the "fallback provision" provides that the report that would otherwise be issued by the Comptroller General shall be issued by Congress itself. In the event that the resolution is enacted, the congressional report will have the same legal consequences as if it had been issued by the Comptroller General. In that event, moreover, surely no one would suggest that Congress had acted in any capacity other than "legislative." . . .

Under the District Court's analysis, and the analysis adopted by the majority today, it would therefore appear that the function at issue is "executive" if performed by the Comptroller General but "legislative" if performed by the Congress. In my view, however, the function may appropriately be labeled "legislative" even if performed by the Comptroller General or by an executive agency. [I]t is far from novel to acknowledge that independent agencies do indeed exercise legislative powers. . . . Thus, I do not agree that the Comptroller General's responsibilities under the Gramm-Rudman-Hollings Act must be termed "executive powers," or even that our inquiry is much advanced by using that term. For, whatever the label given the functions to be performed by the Comptroller General under § 251—or by the Congress under § 274—the District Court had no difficulty in concluding that Congress could delegate the performance of those functions to another branch of the Government. If the delegation to a stranger is permissible, why may not Congress delegate the same responsibilities to one of its own agents? That is the central question before us today.

IV

. . . The Gramm-Rudman-Hollings Act assigns to the Comptroller General the duty to make policy decisions that have the force of law. The Comptroller General's report is, in the current statute, the engine that gives life to the ambitious budget reduction process. It is the Comptroller General's report that "provide[s] for the determination of reductions" and that "contain[s] estimates, determinations, and specifications for all of the items contained in the report" submitted by the Office of Management and Budget and the Congressional Budget Office. It is the Comptroller General's Report that the President must follow and that will have conclusive effect. It is, in short, the Comptroller General's report that will have a profound, dramatic, and immediate impact on the government and on the Nation at large.

Article I of the Constitution specifies the procedures that Congress must follow when it makes policy that binds the Nation: its legislation must be approved by both Houses of Congress and presented to the President. . . . If Congress were free to delegate its policymaking authority to one of its components, or to one of its agents, it would be able to evade "the carefully crafted restraints spelled out in the Constitution." That danger—congressional action that evades constitutional restraints—is not present when Congress delegates lawmaking power to the executive or to an independent agency. . . .

In my opinion, Congress itself could not exercise the Gramm-Rudman-Hollings functions through a concurrent resolution. The fact that the fallback provision in § 274 requires a joint resolution rather than a concurrent resolution indicates that Congress endorsed this view. I think it equally clear that Congress may not simply delegate those functions to an agent such as the Congressional Budget Office. Since I am persuaded that the Comptroller General is also fairly deemed to be an agent of Congress, he too cannot exercise such functions. . . .

In short, even though it is well settled that Congress may delegate legislative power to independent agencies or to the Executive, and thereby divest itself of a portion of its lawmaking power, when it elects to exercise such power itself, it may not authorize a lesser representative of the Legislative Branch to act on its behalf. It is for this reason that I believe § 251(b) and § 251(c)(2) of the Act are unconstitutional. . . .

Justice WHITE, dissenting.

. . . Before examining the merits of the Court's argument, I wish to emphasize what it is that the Court quite pointedly and correctly does not hold: namely, that "executive" powers of the sort granted the Comptroller by the Act may only be exercised by officers removable at will by the President. The Court's apparent unwillingness to accept this argument, which has been tendered in this Court by the Solicitor General, is fully consistent with the Court's longstanding recognition that it is within the power of Congress under the "Necessary and Proper" Clause, Art. I, § 8, to vest authority that falls within the Court's definition of executive power in officers who are not subject to removal at will by the President and are therefore not under the President's direct control. In an earlier day, in which simpler notions of the role of government in society prevailed, it was perhaps plausible to insist that all "executive" officers be subject to an unqualified presidential removal power, but with the advent and triumph of the administrative state and the accompanying multiplication of the tasks undertaken by the Federal Government, the Court has been virtually compelled to recognize that Congress may reasonably deem it "necessary and proper" to vest some among the broad new array of governmental functions in officers who are free from the partisanship that may be expected of agents wholly dependent upon the President.

The Court's recognition of the legitimacy of legislation vesting "executive" authority in officers independent of the President does not imply derogation of the President's own constitutional authority—indeed, duty—to "take Care that the Laws be faithfully executed," Art. II, § 3, for any such duty is necessarily limited to a great extent by the content of the laws enacted by the Congress. As Justice Holmes put it, "The duty of the President to see that the laws be executed is a duty that does not go beyond the laws or require him to achieve more than Congress sees fit to leave within his power." Justice Holmes perhaps overstated his case, for there are undoubtedly executive functions that, regardless of the enactments of Congress, must be performed by officers subject to removal at will by the President. Whether a particular function falls within this class or within the far larger class that may be relegated to independent officers "will depend upon the character of the office." *Humphrey's Executor.* In determining whether a limitation on the President's power to remove an officer performing executive functions constitutes a violation of the constitutional scheme of separation of powers, a court must "focu[s] on the extent to which [such a limitation] prevents the Executive Branch from accomplishing its constitutionally assigned functions." *Nixon v. Administrator of General Services*, 433 U.S. 425, 443 (1977). "Only where the potential for disruption is present must we then determine whether that impact is satisfied by an overriding need to promote objectives within the constitutional authority of Congress." This inquiry is, to be sure, not one that will beget easy answers; it provides nothing approaching a bright-line rule or set of rules. Such an inquiry, however, is necessitated by the recognition that "formalistic and unbending rules" in the area of separation of powers may "unduly constrict Congress' ability to take needed and innovative action pursuant to its Article I powers." *Commodity Futures Trading Commission v. Schor*, 106 S.Ct. 3245 (1986).

It is evident (and nothing in the Court's opinion is to the contrary) that the powers exercised by the Comptroller General under the Gramm-Rudman Act are not such that vesting them in an officer not subject to removal at will by the President would in itself improperly interfere with Presidential powers. Determining the level of spending by the Federal Government is not by nature a function central either to the exercise of the President's enumerated powers or to his general duty to ensure execution of the laws; rather, appropriating funds is a peculiarly legislative function, and one expressly committed to Congress by Art. I, § 9, which provides that "[n]o Money shall be drawn from the Treasury, but in Consequence of Appropriations made by Law." In enacting Gramm-Rudman, Congress has chosen to exercise this legislative power to establish the level of federal spending by providing a detailed set of criteria for reducing expenditures below the level of appropriations in the event that certain conditions are met. Delegating the execution of this legislation—that is, the power to apply the Act's criteria and make the required calculations—to an officer independent of the President's will does not deprive the President of any power that he would otherwise have or that is essential to the performance of the duties of his office. Rather, the result of such a delegation, from the standpoint of the President, is no different from the result of more traditional forms of appropriation: under either system, the level of funds available to the Executive branch to carry out its duties is not within the President's discretionary control....

II

If, as the Court seems to agree, the assignment of "executive" powers under Gramm-Rudman to an officer not removable at will by the President would not in itself represent a violation of the constitutional scheme of separated powers, the question remains whether, as the Court concludes, the fact that the officer to whom Congress has delegated the authority to implement the Act is removable by a joint resolution of Congress should require invalidation of the Act. The Court's decision ... is based on a syllogism: the Act vests the Comptroller with "executive power"; such power may not be exercised by Congress or its agents; the Comptroller is an agent of Congress because he is removable by Congress; therefore the Act is invalid. I have no quarrel with the proposition that the powers exercised by the Comptroller under the Act may be characterized as "executive" in that they involve the interpretation and carrying out of the Act's mandate. I can also accept the general proposition that although Congress has considerable authority in designating the officers who are to execute legislation, the constitutional scheme of separated powers does prevent Congress from reserving an executive role for itself or for its "agents." *Buckley v. Valeo*. I cannot accept, however, that the exercise of authority by an officer removable for cause by a joint resolution of Congress is analogous to the impermissible execution of the law by Congress itself, nor would I hold that the congressional role in the removal process renders the Comptroller an "agent" of the Congress, incapable of receiving "executive" power....

That a joint resolution removing the Comptroller General would satisfy the requirements for legitimate legislative action laid down in *Chadha* does not fully answer the separation of powers argument, for it is apparent that even the results of the constitutional legislative process may be unconstitutional if those results are in fact destructive of the scheme of separation of powers. The question to be answered is whether the threat of removal of the Comptroller General for cause through joint resolution ... renders the Comptroller sufficiently subservient to Congress that investing him with "executive" power can be realistically equated with the unlawful retention of such power by Congress itself; more generally, the question is whether there is a genuine threat of "encroachment or aggrandizement of one branch at the expense of the other," *Buckley v. Valeo*, 424 U.S., at 122. Common sense indicates that the existence of the removal provision poses no such threat to the principle of separation of powers.

The statute does not permit anyone to remove the Comptroller at will; removal is permitted only for specified cause, with the existence of cause to be determined by Congress following a hearing. Any removal under the statute would presumably be subject to post-termination judicial review to ensure that a hearing had in fact been held and that the finding of cause for removal was not arbitrary. These procedural and substantive limitations on the removal power militate strongly against the characterization of the Comptroller as a mere agent of Congress by virtue of the removal authority. Indeed, similarly qualified grants of removal power are generally deemed to protect the officers to whom they apply and to establish their independence from the domination of the possessor of the removal power. Removal authority limited in such a manner is more properly viewed as motivating adherence to a substantive standard established by law than as inducing subservience to the particular institution that enforces that standard. That the agent enforcing the standard is Congress may be of some significance to the Comptroller, but Congress' substantively limited removal power will undoubtedly be less of a spur to subservience than Congress' unquestionable and unqualified power to enact legislation reducing the Comptroller's salary, cutting the funds available to his department, reducing his personnel, limiting or expanding his duties, or even abolishing his position altogether.

More importantly, the substantial role played by the President in the process of removal through joint resolution reduces to utter insignificance the possibility that the threat of removal will induce subservience to the Congress. [A] joint resolution must be presented to the President and is ineffective if it is vetoed by him, unless the veto is overridden by the constitutionally prescribed two-thirds majority of both Houses of Congress. The requirement of presidential approval obviates the possibility that the Comptroller will perceive himself as so completely at the mercy of Congress that he will function as its tool. If the Comptroller's conduct in office is not so unsatisfactory to the President as to convince the latter that removal is required under the statutory standard, Congress will have no independent power to coerce the Comptroller unless it can muster a two-thirds majority in both Houses—a feat of bipartisanship more difficult than that required to impeach and convict. The incremental *in terrorem* effect of the possibility of congressional removal in the face of a presidential veto is therefore exceedingly unlikely to have any discernible impact on the extent of congressional influence over the Comptroller.

The practical result of the removal provision is not to render the Comptroller unduly dependent upon or subservient to Congress, but to render him one of the most independent officers in the entire federal establishment. Those who have studied the office agree that... dislodging him against his will [is] practically impossible. As one scholar put it nearly fifty years ago, "Under the statute the Comptroller General, once confirmed, is safe so long as he avoids a public exhibition of personal immorality, dishonesty, or failing mentality." H. Mansfield, The Comptroller General 75-76 (1939). The passage of time has done little to cast doubt on this view: of the six Comptrollers who have served since 1921, none has been threatened with, much less subjected to, removal. Recent students of the office concur that "[b]arring resignation, death, physical or mental incapacity, or extremely bad behavior, the Comptroller General is assured his tenure if he wants it, and not a day more." F. Mosher, The

GAO 242 (1979). The threat of "here-and-now subservience" is obviously remote indeed.

Realistic consideration of the nature of the Comptroller General's relation to Congress thus reveals that the threat to separation of powers conjured up by the majority is wholly chimerical. The power over removal retained by the Congress is not a power that is exercised outside the legislative process as established by the Constitution, nor does it appear likely that it is a power that adds significantly to the influence Congress may exert over executive officers through other, undoubtedly constitutional exercises of legislative power and through the constitutionally guaranteed impeachment power. . . .

The majority's contrary conclusion rests on the rigid dogma that, outside of the impeachment process, any "direct congressional role in the removal of officers charged with the execution of the laws . . . is inconsistent with separation of powers." Reliance on such an unyielding principle to strike down a statute posing no real danger of aggrandizement of congressional power is extremely misguided and insensitive to our constitutional role. The wisdom of vesting "executive" powers in an officer removable by joint resolution may indeed be debatable—as may be the wisdom of the entire scheme of permitting an unelected official to revise the budget enacted by Congress— but such matters are for the most part to be worked out between the Congress and the President through the legislative process, which affords each branch ample opportunity to defend its interests. The Act vesting budget-cutting authority in the Comptroller General represents Congress' judgment that the delegation of such authority to counteract ever-mounting deficits is "necessary and proper" to the exercise of the powers granted the Federal Government by the Constitution; and the President's approval of the statute signifies his unwillingness to reject the choice made by Congress. Under such circumstances, the role of this Court should be limited to determining whether the Act so alters the balance of authority among the branches of government as to pose a genuine threat to the basic division between the lawmaking power and the power to execute the law. Because I see no such threat, I cannot join the Court in striking down the Act.

Justice BLACKMUN, dissenting.

. . . Appellees have not sought invalidation of the 1921 provision that authorizes Congress to remove the Comptroller General by joint resolution; indeed, it is far from clear they would have standing to request such a judgment. The only relief sought in this case is nullification of the automatic budget-reduction provisions of the Deficit Control Act, and that relief should not be awarded even if the Court is correct that those provisions are constitutionally incompatible with Congress' authority to remove the Comptroller General by joint resolution. Any incompatibility, I feel, should be cured by refusing to allow congressional removal—if it ever is attempted—and not by striking down the central provisions of the Deficit Control Act. However wise or foolish it may be, that statute unquestionably ranks among the most important federal enactments of the past several decades. I cannot see the sense of invalidating legislation of this magnitude in order to preserve a cumbersome, 65-year-old removal power that has never been exercised and appears to have been all but forgotten until this litigation.

---

1. The *Bowsher* Court remarks in passing that the Comptroller General is nominated by the President from a list of three individuals recommended by the Speaker of the

House and the President *pro tem.* of the Senate. Does that infringe the President's appointments power under *Buckley*, in view of the severely limited choice available to the President? Recall that in *Myers* the Court remarked that the Senate's rejection of a nominee "does not greatly embarrass" the President's discharge of his constitutional duties, "because [he] usually has an ample field from which to select for office, according to his preference, competent and capable" replacements. Is that true in this situation?

2. Would the Court have been well advised to accept Justice Blackmun's invitation to strike down the removal provision rather than the Deficit Control Act? In the wake of *Bowsher*, doubts now surround the GAO's other statutory functions. (*See, e.g.*, Comment, *The New Separation of Powers Jurisprudence and the Comptroller General: Does He "Execute the Law" Under the Federal Employees' Retirement Act?*, 9 Geo. Mason U. L. Rev. 35 (1986); we will encounter one such controversy, involving government contract bid procedures, in Chapter Five.) Should Congress now amend the removal provision to make the Comptroller removable by the President for cause? *See* Verkuil, *The Status of Independent Agencies After* Bowsher v. Synar, 1986 Duke L. J. 779, 802-04. Would that radically alter the Comptroller's relationships with the two branches?

3. Note that the removal statute involved in *Bowsher* contains the core provisions usually found in statutes restricting *presidential* removal: "inefficiency, neglect of duty, malfeasance." The Court says that "[t]hese terms are very broad and, as interpreted by Congress, could sustain removal . . . for any number of actual or perceived transgressions of the legislative will." Does that mean that the President has broad discretion under the cognate statutes? That certainly isn't what *Humphrey's Executor* suggests.

At this point, we pause to examine three illustrative statutory provisions on presidential removal. As you read each, consider how much guidance you can infer regarding permissible grounds for removal and the President's managerial prerogatives over the agency:

Nuclear Regulatory Commission (42 U.S.C. § 5841(e)):

> Any member of the commission may be removed by the President for inefficiency, neglect of duty, or malfeasance in office. No member of the Commission shall engage in any business, vocation, or employment other than that of serving as a member of the Commission.

Consumer Product Safety Commission (15 U.S.C. § 2053(a)):

> An independent regulatory commission is hereby established, to be known as the Consumer Product Safety Commission, consisting of five Commissioners who shall be appointed by the President, by and with the advice and consent of the Senate. *The Chairman shall be appointed by the President, by and with the advice and consent of the Senate, from among the members of the Commission. An individual may be appointed as a member of the Commission and as Chairman at the same time.* Any member of the Commission may be removed by the President for neglect of duty or malfeasance in office but for no other cause.

(Emphasis added). Section 2 of the Act of Nov. 10, 1978, Pub. L. No. 95-631, amended this subsection by adding the underlined language. The immediately preceding sentence originally read: "Senate, one of whom shall be designated by the President as Chairman." The next sentence, which the amendment deleted, read:

> The Chairman, when so designated, shall act as Chairman until the expiration of his term of office as Commissioner.

See Act of Oct. 27, 1972, Pub. L. No. 92-573, Sec. 4(a), 86 Stat. 1210.

Environmental Protection Agency (5 U.S.C. App., Reorg. Plan No. 3 of 1970, l(b)):

> There shall be at the head of the Agency the Administrator of the Environmental Protection Agency ... The Administrator shall be appointed by the President, by and with the advice and consent of the Senate....

How do you interpret those statutes that explicitly require cause for removal? Can a member of the Nuclear Regulatory Commission be dismissed for drunkenness at NRC meetings? For taking bribes? For handing in decisions tardily, *i.e.*, "inefficiently?" For interpreting the law contrary to an opinion on point issued by the Attorney General?

Do limited removability and agency independence go hand in hand? Do you infer from the absence of express limitations on the President's power to remove the Administrator of EPA that it is meant to be less "independent" than the Consumer Product Safety Commission? Notice the amendment to the CPSC statute. The chair of a multi-member agency normally has substantial managerial responsibilities within the agency, for example the power to hire important staff members. For some independent agencies, the practice is for the President to designate or demote a chair at will. What implication do you draw from the amendment changing the process for designating the CPSC chair?

4. In its footnote 4, the *Bowsher* Court denies that its holding casts doubt on the constitutional status of the independent agencies—the case involves "nothing like" the statutes qualifying presidential removal, because the statute at hand involves congressional removal. Do you agree? The Court approvingly quotes the District Court's conclusion that "[o]nce an officer is appointed, it is only the authority that can remove him ... that he must fear, and, in the performance of his functions, obey." The Court later says that "[i]n constitutional terms, the removal powers over the Comptroller General's office dictate that he will be subservient to Congress." If control follows removability for constitutional purposes, may the President now control the independent agencies? The answer depends on how one reads the removal provisions. That leads to a trap, doesn't it: if *Humphrey's Executor* still means that these agencies are independent of the President "except in their selection," what are they doing executing the law?

Recall the Court's decision in *Wiener*, in which it implied restrictions on removal from a statute that contained none, because of the adjudicative functions of the officers. Does *Bowsher* suggest that the courts should avoid implying removal restrictions in order to minimize Article II concerns? Consider the U.S. Commission on Civil Rights, around which controversy has swirled during the Reagan administration. In the notes following *Buckley, supra*, we raised questions about the way the Commission is appointed under a statutory reconstitution in 1983. Previously, its members were all presidential appointees and there was no statutory restriction on their removal. In an effort to reshape the Commission to accord with his views, President Reagan removed three of its members. (The full story is told in Comment, *The Rise and Fall of the United States Commission on Civil Rights*, 22 Harv. Civ. Rt.-Civ. Lib. L. Rev. 449, 476-80 (1987).) They obtained a preliminary injunction against the removal, *Berry v. Reagan*, 32 Empl. Prac. Dec. (CCH) ¶ 33,898 (D.D.C.), *vacated as moot*, 732 F.2d 949 (D.C. Cir. 1983). The District Court concluded that Congress intended the Commission to be free of presidential control, because "[w]hen performing its fact-finding, investigatory, and monitoring functions . . . the Commission is often required to criticize the policies of the Executive that are contrary to existing civil rights legislation." Does *Bowsher* undermine this result, or is there special reason to insulate "watchdog" functions within the executive? We return to this question when we consider "special prosecutors" in Chapter Five.

Plainly, footnote 4 to the contrary, bigger game is afoot than the *Bowsher* Court wishes to hunt. Academics have filled the air with potshots. *See generally* Symposium, *The Uneasy Constitutional Status of the Administrative Agencies*, 36 Am. U. L. Rev. 277 (1987); Symposium, Bowsher v. Synar, 72 Corn. L. Rev. 421 (1987); Currie, *The Distribution of Powers After* Bowsher, 1986 Sup. Ct. Rev. 19; Verkuil, *supra*; Entin, *The Removal Power and the Federal Deficit: Form, Substance, and Administrative Independence*, 75 Ky. L.J. 699 (1987).

5. Consider the constitutionality of the United States Sentencing Commission. It is established as "an independent commission in the judicial branch" by 28 U.S.C. § 991(a). Its function is to promulgate guidelines to determine the range of sentences that federal judges may impose. It has seven members, appointed by the President and removable by him "only for neglect of duty or malfeasance in office or for other good cause shown." At least three of the members are to be federal judges, selected from a list submitted by the Judicial Conference.

What does *Bowsher* tell us about this entity? If the promulgation of guidelines is legislative or executive, can the commission do it? Can federal judges sit on the commission? *See* Note, *The Constitutional Infirmities of the United States Sentencing Commission*, 96 Yale L. J. 1363 (1987); *see also* Comment, *Separation of Powers and Judicial Service on Presidential Commissions*, 53 U. Chi. L. Rev. 993 (1986).

6. The Court has provided some further explanation of *Bowsher*. In a decision issued the same day, *Commodity Futures Trading Commission v. Schor*, 106 S. Ct. 3245 (1986), the Court upheld allocation of potential Article III adjudicative authority (over a counterclaim arising under state law) to an administrative agency rather than to a federal court. The Court employed functional analysis, in sharp contrast to the formalism of *Bowsher*. Justice O'Connor explained:

> Unlike *Bowsher*, this case raises no question of the aggrandizement of congressional power at the expense of a coordinate branch. Instead, the separation of powers question presented in this case is whether Congress impermissibly undermined, without appreciable expansion of its own power, the role of the Judicial Branch. . . . [W]e have also been faithful to our Article III precedents, which counsel that bright line rules cannot effectively be employed to yield broad principles applicable in all Article III inquiries.

Is "aggrandizement" then the key to the Court's choice of approach—and outcome? Professor Peter Strauss, in *Formal and Functional Approaches to Separation-of-Powers Questions—A Foolish Inconsistency?*, 72 Corn. L. Rev. 488, 492-94, 519-21 (1987), summarizes his own functional approach, adopted in a fine earlier article, *The Place of Agencies in Government: Separation of Powers and the Fourth Branch*, 84 Colum. L. Rev. 573 (1984):

> The Constitution does not define the administrative, as distinct from the political, organs of the federal government; it leaves that *entirely* to Congress. What the Constitution describes instead are three generalist national institutions (Congress, President, and Supreme Court) which, together with the states, serve as the principal heads of political and legal authority. Each of these three generalist institutions serves as the ultimate authority for a distinctive governmental authority-type (legislative, executive, or judicial). Each may be thought of as having a paradigmatic relationship, characterized by that authority-type, with the working government that Congress creates.
>
> Although these heads of government serve distinct functions, employing distinctive procedures, . . . the same cannot be said of the administrative level of government. Virtually every part of the government Congress has created—the Department of Agriculture as well as the Securities and Exchange Commission—exercises *all three* of the governmental functions the Constitution so carefully allocates among Congress, President, and Court. These agencies adopt rules having the shape and impact of statutes, mold governmental policy through enforcement decisions and other initiatives, and decide cases in ways that determine the rights of private parties. If in 1787 such a merger of function was unthinkable, in 1987 it is unavoidable given Congress's need to delegate at some level the making of policy for a complex and interdependent economy, and the equal incapacity (and undesirability) of the courts to resolve all matters appropriately characterized as involving "adjudication." A formal theory of separation of powers that says these functions cannot be joined is unworkable; that being so, a theory that locates each agency "in" one or another of the three conventional "branches" of American government, according to its activities, fares no better. . . .
>
> Rather than describe agencies in terms of branches, in other words, the analysis suggested one could examine their relationships with each of the three named heads of government, to see whether those relationships undermine the intended distribution of authority *among those three*. . . . [T]his analysis of separation-of-powers issues proposes examining the quality of relationships between an agency and each of the three named heads of government. It is not necessary to insist that there be particular relationships between an agency and any of the named constitutional actors (beyond the few specified in the constitutional text) in order to require relationships of a certain overall character or quality. . . .
>
> [Regarding *Bowsher*, it] is not simply that Congress chose a particular mechanism for protecting the "independence" and "objectivity" of the Comptroller General . . . . The Comptroller General's relationships with the President, from the proposing of his appointment onward, are strikingly weaker than those that characterize other agencies; the President and the courts both are utterly divorced from participating in the control of the particular functions under review; and the relationship between Congress and the Comptroller General is far more embracive and proprietary than the relationships that characterize the rest of government. Here one could fairly describe Congress as having appropriated to itself the President's characteristic functions (and made nugatory those of the courts). Functionalist and formalist could be equally concerned with these out-

comes; that the Court chose a formalist analysis speaks to possible rhetorical advantages, but not to outcome.

Viewing "aggrandizement" in terms of the full set of relationships among agency, Congress, President, and courts rather than in terms of a single "talismanic" feature of one of those relationships is, of course, precisely what the *Bowsher* Court failed to do.... If the right question is whether the arrangements under challenge threaten to aggrandize one of the three named constitutional actors at the expense of another, thus imperiling the balance of American government and the performance of core functions by the weakened actor, then that question requires a broader view.

Note that the question asks nothing directly about the agency empowered to act—the GAO or the CFTC—but rather asks about the impact of the challenged arrangements on the three named heads of constitutional government and the relationships among them. Although one can easily agree with the *Schor* majority that empowering the CFTC to entertain counterclaims under state common law entails no such consequences, the equation in *Bowsher* is not as clear. In *Bowsher*, aggrandizement *is* present: what the President loses in the way of ordinary controls over the tenure of government officials, Congress has asserted for itself.... Congress could be excused much in its own relationship with the GAO if it recognized conventional presidential and judicial relationships with that agency. Its insistence on an exclusive relationship, a device which if successful could indeed propel Congress into a general position of dominance over the national government, is the differentiating feature....

Professor Bruff, in *On the Constitutional Status of the Administrative Agencies*, 36 Am. U. L. Rev. 491, 493-94 (1987), begins by arguing that "the optimal level of specificity for constitutional rules that organize the government is low," because

[t]he government is vast and diverse; perforce, even statutes that have government-wide effect are cast in generalities. Moreover, predicting the effects of rules on institutions is hazardous, even in the short run. Also, the obstacles to altering constitutional rules are considerable, even when they are generated by the courts. Not only does constitutional ambiguity serve these needs for flexibility, it also aids the operation of government. Mutual uncertainties about the limits of power foster cooperation between the branches. Where there is clarity, the incentive to compromise disappears.

In that case, what justifies formalism? Bruff identifies a principle of political accountability as a possible explanation for the Court's choice of analytic method:

In [cases such as *United States v. Nixon* and *Nixon v. Fitzgerald,*] the Court may have been drawn to functional analysis by the absence of pertinent constitutional text on which to base a formalist approach. There were also important benefits of flexibility. For both executive privilege and immunity, the Court was defining the power of its own branch regarding the President. Functional analysis allowed the Court to create protection for the executive and to limit it at the same time. Moreover, the Court decided these cases in the absence of statutory guidance. The functional approach avoided disabling Congress from legislating in a way that the Court might later approve.

This view of *Nixon* and *Fitzgerald* suggests that the Court's choice of analytic approach may be result-oriented. Formalism minimizes the sharing of power by the branches; functionalism maximizes it. When the Court perceives aggrandizement, it issues a formalist opinion insisting on the separation of powers. Examples would be *Myers, Buckley, Chadha,* and *Bowsher.* When the blending of power presents no such threat, a functional opinion allows it. In addition to the cases involving President Nixon, one could cite *Humphrey's Executor,* in which the Court thought that allowing Congress to share control of the removal of officers would prevent *presidential* aggrandizement.

Hence, constitutional analysis might be improved by a direct focus on the presence or absence of aggrandizement. Assessments of the relative power of the branches, however, are inherently subjective. For example, the New Deal Court's fear of executive arbitrariness seems exaggerated today. Similarly, before *Chadha* there was a spirited debate over the legislative veto: was Congress meddling in executive matters, or imposing a necessary check on a runaway executive? The *Chadha* Court noted the debate in passing and avoided it by employing formalism. Thus, aggrandizement lies in the eye of the beholder.

Both formalism and functionalism have serious problems of scope and predictability. Because formalism employs syllogistic reasoning, there is no obvious terminus to its logic, as *Myers* illustrates. Its predictability is low because the Court's underlying rationale is obscure. Functional analysis, focusing on difficult and subjective fact inquiries, also resists consistent application. The Court needs a criterion for decision that does not depend on imponderables and that has sufficient legitimacy to be discussed openly in the cases. A theory of political accountability can provide such a criterion....

The Supreme Court's recent separation of powers cases have clarified political responsibility for administration. The Court has consistently rejected schemes that would have given Congress power to share in administrative decisions without full political responsibility for doing so. If *Buckley* had allowed both presidential and congressional appointments to regulatory agencies, neither branch would answer for the agencies' decisions. If *Chadha* had upheld the legislative veto, neither branch would be solely responsible for regulation that did take effect. If *Bowsher* had upheld the role of the Government Accounting Office (GAO) in the Gramm-Rudman Act, it would be difficult to identify the branch that was determining whether sequestration was needed.

Thus the Court's formalism may rest on a value judgment that accountability for administration should be centered in the executive branch. Such a judgment does not necessarily answer *where* in the executive authority should lie, but it does create an essentially unitary executive with regard to Congress. Imagine the shape of the government if *Buckley, Chadha,* and *Bowsher* had reached opposite results. Congress could appoint some officers and could forbid the President to remove at least some of his appointees without a joint resolution. All officers would act subject to legislative veto. We would truly have "congressional government."

Formalism that is guided by value judgments about accountability has the advantage of avoiding difficult fact issues. In *Bowsher,* the Court's constitutional equation of removal power with control was not an assertion of fact that could stand scrutiny. No one has tried to remove a Comptroller General. Nor do

Presidents readily remove members of the independent agencies. The Court's conclusion can be understood, and justified, only as an assignment of responsibility.

Congressional partisans might respond that under the rejected schemes, both branches would be responsible, with the necessary cooperation between them providing an *increase* in political accountability. I think that the Court has been silently rejecting such a notion, and properly so. Congress was not required to endorse executive policy in a way that carried clear responsibility. The presence of some congressional appointees on a commission would not tie its every action to Congress. Failure to pass a legislative veto resolution, it was often asserted in Congress, would not endorse an executive action, but would only indicate that it was not wholly unacceptable. Under the Gramm-Rudman Act, three differently composed entities were to generate estimates; it would be difficult to place the final product at anyone's door. Still, it could be argued that congressional accountability was increased under these schemes even if it was divided with the executive. Yet any gains for Congress were offset by losses for the executive as the ultimate responsibility for decisions became blurred. Each branch could point to the other as the author of defective policy.

Perhaps hopes for clarity in political accountability are dashed by the practical interdependence that permeates modern government. Surely the Court is aware that Congress retains many avenues of informal influence even when the formal sharing of power is forbidden. Examples abound. Although Congress may not displace the President's appointment power, nominees are screened in advance through the informal practice of senatorial courtesy. Judicial invalidation of the legislative veto does not prevent congressional committees from pressuring agencies in hearings and other informal ways. And notwithstanding *Humphrey's Executor*, the independent agencies are dependent on the executive in a myriad of ways. Nevertheless, a scheme of independent authority that is open to influence is fundamentally different from one with shared responsibility. A branch possessing formal authority is politically accountable for a decision no matter how vigorous outside pressure may be. Such clarity does not exist when the power to decide is shared.

A constitutional separation of powers doctrine that emphasizes clear accountability can be anchored in the framers' goals. *The Federalist Papers* are replete with emphasis on the need to ensure public knowledge of accountability for particular actions. The Constitution incorporates this value most prominently in the choice of a single executive. . . .

The Court has recently employed an additional kind of formalism, which I will call procedural formality to distinguish it from the Court's formalist style of logical reasoning. A number of recent cases, most prominently *Chadha*, have required Congress to act through full, formal legislative procedures to control the executive. Accountability values may also explain this procedural formality. The political responsibility of members of Congress is mostly individual. True, each may bear some diffuse liability for the performance of the institution as a whole, but the record of individual actions certainly dominates reelection campaigns. Indeed, incumbents often run against Congress. Consequently, Congress is accountable as a branch of government only when it acts as a whole in legislation. . . .

If the Court had employed functional analysis in these cases, it might not have drawn clear lines of accountability. Focusing only on whether a branch is disrupting the core functions of another would result in a much more mixed set of outcomes than does formalism.

Bruff concludes that the Court should restrict its use of formalism to situations needing clear lines of political responsibility. Thus, in *Schor*, the Court was correct to employ functional analysis for allocations of adjudicative authority, where the need for political supervision is weakest.

7. Where does all this leave the special constitutional status of the independent agencies? Bruff, *supra*, concludes that principles of accountability provide no justification for granting independent agencies *constitutional* status different from executive agencies with respect to presidential oversight. The effect, Bruff argues, of treating all agencies as having equivalent constitutional status subordinate to the President is "to prevent Congress from denying the President a supervisory role that is appropriate to the function involved." This distinction between independent *agencies* and independent *functions* runs through the analysis of several commentators. *See, e.g.*, Professor Strauss' Columbia article, *supra*, in which he argues that limits on presidential policy-based removals of agency heads are constitutional if they do not disturb the overall parity of political influence on administration between Congress and the President. That is, under a rule of parity, both political branches may oversee a particular function if either may do so.

One reason why it is difficult to pinpoint the constitutional status of independent agencies is that Congress has employed no grand theory in creating them, but rather has followed a pragmatic course that has made a mess of the government's organization chart. Indeed, Professor Shane, in *Presidential Policymaking and the Faithful Execution of the Laws* (forthcoming), explains that the very phrase "independent agency" is misleading:

> Federal agencies do not come in two discrete models, one "executive" and one "independent," that are recognizable by clearly differentiated characteristics. ... The reasons why some agencies are informally denominated "independent agencies" is that certain of their features are designed to mitigate the degree to which partisan politics can dominate their decisionmaking. These features may, but need not include the adoption of collegial decisionmaking, staggered terms for the agency's prime decisionmakers, terms of office that are longer than the four-year presidential term, and quotas on the number of agency members who may belong to either of the major parties. ...
>
> The [most controversial] aspect of some agencies' independence ... is the supposed immunity from removal of agency heads who refuse to follow the policy directives of the President. That is, although all administrators are apparently removable "for cause," it is frequently understood that it is not cause for removal that an administrator declines to follow the President's policy preferences in favor of other policy directives which the administrator prefers and which are also within the administrator's lawful discretion.

Professor Geoffrey Miller, in *Independent Agencies*, 1986 Sup. Ct. Rev. 41, 44-45, assails this understanding directly:

The thesis of this article is that Congress may not constitutionally deny the President the power to remove a policy-making official who has refused an order of the President to take an action within the officer's statutory authority. This thesis rests on a model of the President's relationship to the federal administrative state. Congress, in this model, has power to create federal agencies, to vest substantial discretion in agency heads, and to provide that action by the agency head is a necessary precondition to the effective exercise of the authority in question. The President retains the constitutional power to direct the officer to take particular actions within his or her discretion or to refrain from acting when the officer has discretion not to act. Such presidential directives can either be specific to the action in question or general programmatic instruction applicable to a range of actions or agencies. Congress may not constitutionally restrict the President's power to remove officials who fail to obey these presidential instructions, but may prohibit the President from removing officers for other reasons, such as personal animus or refusing to obey an order to do something outside the officer's statutory authority.

This thesis—that the President may not be denied the power to remove an officer who has failed to comply with a presidential directive to take an action within the scope of the officer's discretion—may sound revolutionary. In fact, the thesis could be implemented without wholesale invalidation of federal statutes. Most statutes establishing independent agencies can easily be construed as including disobedience of the President's lawful instructions within the varieties of "cause" for which presidential removal is already authorized. In the relatively infrequent cases where the statutes cannot be so construed, the unconstitutionality of the removal provision would not ordinarily invalidate the agency's substantive and enforcement powers.

The foregoing introduces our exploration of various aspects of agency independence. In materials below, we examine presidential supervision of administrative policymaking. Subsequently, we consider the allocation of two functions to independent administrators: spending of appropriated funds (as in *Bowsher*), and the conduct of civil or criminal litigation to enforce the laws of the United States (in Chapter Five).

2. First Amendment limitations

The Supreme Court has recently begun placing First Amendment limitations on executive power to discharge non-civil service employees on party allegiance grounds under traditional patronage practices. The cases have arisen in state governments; their application to the federal executive has yet to be delineated. In *Elrod v. Burns*, 427 U.S. 347 (1976), the Court forbade a newly elected Democratic Sheriff to discharge several Republican employees (three process servers and a bailiff and security guard). The scope of the holding was unclear. Justice Brennan's plurality opinion concluded that patronage dismissals must be limited to "policymaking positions." Justice Stewart's concurrence would not accept all of the plurality's analysis, but similarly concluded that a "nonpolicymaking, nonconfidential" employee could not be discharged solely for political beliefs. Four years later, the Court attempted to refine and clarify its mandate:

Branti v. Finkel
445 U.S. 507 (1980)

[A newly-appointed Democratic head of a county public defender office notified Republican assistant public defenders of their impending termination. They sued to enjoin the discharges; Justice STEVENS delivered the Court's opinion affirming issuance of the injunction.]

II

Both opinions in *Elrod* recognize that party affiliation may be an acceptable requirement for some types of government employment. Thus, if an employee's private political beliefs would interfere with the discharge of his public duties, his First Amendment rights may be required to yield to the State's vital interest in maintaining governmental effectiveness and efficiency. In *Elrod*, it was clear that the duties of the employees—the chief deputy of the process division of the sheriff's office, a process server and another employee in that office, and a bailiff and security guard at the Juvenile Court of Cook County—were not of that character, for they were, as Justice Stewart stated, "nonpolicymaking, nonconfidential" employees.

As Justice Brennan noted in *Elrod*, it is not always easy to determine whether a position is one in which political affiliation is a legitimate factor to be considered. Under some circumstances, a position may be appropriately considered political even though it is neither confidential nor policymaking in character. As one obvious example, if a State's election laws require that precincts be supervised by two election judges of different parties, a Republican judge could be legitimately discharged solely for changing his party registration. That conclusion would ... simply rest on the fact that party membership was essential to the discharge of the employee's governmental responsibilities.

It is equally clear that party affiliation is not necessarily relevant to every policy-making or confidential position. The coach of a state university's football team formulates policy, but no one could seriously claim that Republicans make better coaches than Democrats, or vice versa, no matter which party is in control of the state government. On the other hand, it is equally clear that the Governor of a State may appropriately believe that the official duties of various assistants who help him write speeches, explain his views to the press, or communicate with the legislature cannot be performed effectively unless those persons share his political beliefs and party commitments. In sum, the ultimate inquiry is not whether the label "policymaker" or "confidential" fits a particular position; rather, the question is whether the hiring authority can demonstrate that party affiliation is an appropriate requirement for the effective performance of the public office involved.

Having thus framed the issue, it is manifest that the continued employment of an assistant public defender cannot properly be conditioned upon his allegiance to the political party in control of the county government. The primary, if not the only, responsibility of an assistant public defender is to represent individual citizens in controversy with the State.... Thus, whatever policymaking occurs in the public defender's office must relate to the needs of individual clients and not to any partisan political interests.... [I]t would undermine, rather than promote, the effective performance of an assistant public defender's office to make his tenure dependent on his allegiance to the dominant political party....

Justice STEWART, dissenting.

... The analogy [between the office of the Rockland County Public Defender and] a firm of lawyers in the private sector is a close one, and I can think of few occupational relationships more instinct with the necessity of mutual confidence and trust than that kind of professional association. I believe that the ... Public Defender was not constitutionally compelled to enter such a close professional and necessarily confidential association with the respondents if he did not wish to do so.

Justice POWELL with whom Justice REHNQUIST joins, and with whom Justice STEWART joins as to Part I, dissenting.

The Court today continues the evisceration of patronage practices begun in *Elrod v. Burns*, 427 U.S. 347 (1976). With scarcely a glance at almost 200 years of American political tradition, the Court further limits the relevance of political affiliation to the selection and retention of public employees. Many public positions previously filled on the basis of membership in national political parties now must be staffed in accordance with a constitutionalized civil service standard that will affect the employment practices of federal, state, and local governments. Governmental hiring practices long thought to be a matter of legislative and executive discretion now will be subjected to judicial oversight. Today's decision is an exercise of judicial lawmaking that "represents a significant intrusion into the area of legislative and policy concerns."

I

The Court contends that its holding is compelled by the First Amendment. In reaching this conclusion, the Court largely ignores the substantial governmental interests served by patronage. Patronage is a long-accepted practice[1] that never has been eliminated totally by civil service laws and regulations. The flaw in the Court's opinion lies not only in its application of First Amendment principles, but also in its promulgation of a new, and substantially expanded, standard for determining which governmental employees may be retained or dismissed on the basis of political affiliation....

The standard articulated by the Court is framed in vague and sweeping language certain to create vast uncertainty. Elected and appointed officials at all levels who now receive guidance from civil service laws, no longer will know when political affiliation is an appropriate consideration in filling a position. Legislative bodies will

---

1. When Thomas Jefferson became the first Chief Executive to succeed a President of the opposing party, he made substantial use of appointment and removal powers. Andrew Jackson, the next President to follow an antagonistic administration, used patronage extensively when he took office. The use of patronage in the early days of our Republic played an important role in democratizing American politics. President Lincoln's patronage practices and his reliance upon the newly formed Republican Party enabled him to build support for his national policies during the Civil War. See E. McKitrick, Party Politics and the Union and Confederate War Efforts, in The American Party System 117, 131-133 (W. Chambers & W. Burnham eds. 1967). Subsequent patronage reform efforts were "concerned primarily with the corruption and inefficiency that patronage was thought to induce in civil service and the power that patronage practices were thought to give the 'professional' politicians who relied on them." As a result of these efforts, most federal and state civil service employment was placed on a nonpatronage basis. A significant segment of public employment has remained, however, free from civil service constraints.

not be certain whether they have the final authority to make the delicate line-drawing decisions embodied in the civil service laws. Prudent individuals requested to accept a public appointment must consider whether their predecessors will threaten to oust them through legal action.

One example at the national level illustrates the nature and magnitude of the problem created by today's holding. The President customarily has considered political affiliation in removing and appointing United States attorneys. Given the critical role that these key law enforcement officials play in the administration of the Department of Justice, both Democratic and Republican Attorneys General have concluded, not surprisingly, that they must have the confidence and support of the United States attorneys. And political affiliation has been used as one indicator of loyalty.

Yet, it would be difficult to say, under the Court's standard, that "partisan" concerns properly are relevant to the performance of the duties of a United States attorney. This Court has noted that " '[t]he office of public prosecutor is one which must be administered with courage and independence.' " *Imbler v. Pachtman*, 424 U.S. 409, 423 (1976). Nevertheless, I believe that the President must have the right to consider political affiliation when he selects top ranking Department of Justice officials. The President and his Attorney General, not this Court, are charged with the responsibility for enforcing the laws and administering the Department of Justice. The Court's vague, overbroad decision may cast serious doubt on the propriety of dismissing United States attorneys, as well as thousands of other policymaking employees at all levels of government, because of their membership in a national political party....[5]

III

Patronage appointments help build stable political parties by offering rewards to persons who assume the tasks necessary to the continued functioning of political organizations. "As all parties are concerned with power they naturally operate by placing members and supporters into positions of power. Thus there is nothing derogatory in saying that a primary function of parties is patronage." J. Jupp, Political Parties 25-26 (1968)....

Strong political parties also aid effective governance after election campaigns end. Elected officials depend upon appointees who hold similar views to carry out their policies and administer their programs. Patronage—the right to select key personnel and to reward the party "faithful"—serves the public interest by facilitating the

---

5. The Court notes that prosecutors hold "broader public responsibilities" than public defenders. The Court does not suggest, however, that breadth of responsibility correlates with the appropriateness of political affiliation as a requirement for public employment. Indeed, such a contention would appear to be inconsistent with the Court's assertion that the "ultimate inquiry is not whether the label 'policymaker' ... fits a particular position ...."

I do not suggest that the Constitution requires a patronage system. Civil service systems have been designed to eliminate corruption and inefficiency not to protect the political beliefs of public employees. Indeed, merit selection systems often impose restrictions on political activities by public employees. D. Rosenbloom, Federal Service and the Constitution: The Development of the Public Employment Relationship 83-86 (1971); see *CSC v. Letter Carriers*, 413 U.S. 548 (1973). Of course, civil service systems further important governmental goals, including continuity in the operation of government. A strength of our system has been the blend of civil service and patronage appointments, subject always to oversight and change by the legislative branches of government.

implementation of policies endorsed by the electorate. The Court's opinion casts a shadow over this time-honored element of our system. It appears to recognize that the implementation of policy is a legitimate goal of the patronage system and that some, but not all, policymaking employees may be replaced on the basis of their political affiliation. But the Court does not recognize that the implementation of policy often depends upon the cooperation of public employees who do not hold policymaking posts.... The growth of the civil service system already has limited the ability of elected politicians to effect political change. Public employees immune to public pressure "can resist changes in policy without suffering either the loss of their jobs or a cut in their salary." Such effects are proper when they follow from legislative or executive decisions to withhold some jobs from the patronage system....

Although the Executive and Legislative Branches of Government are independent as a matter of constitutional law, effective government is impossible unless the two Branches cooperate to make and enforce laws. Over the decades of our national history, political parties have furthered—if not assured—a measure of cooperation between the Executive and Legislative Branches. A strong party allows an elected executive to implement his programs and policies by working with legislators of the same political organization. But legislators who owe little to their party tend to act independently of its leadership. The result is a dispersion of political influence that may inhibit a political party from enacting its programs into law. The failure to sustain party discipline, at least at the national level, has been traced to the inability of successful political parties to offer patronage positions to their members or to the supporters of elected officials.

The breakdown of party discipline that handicaps elected officials also limits the ability of the electorate to choose wisely among candidates. Voters with little information about individuals seeking office traditionally have relied upon party affiliation as a guide to choosing among candidates. With the decline in party stability, voters are less able to blame or credit a party for the performance of its elected officials....

Broad-based political parties supply an essential coherence and flexibility to the American political scene. They serve as coalitions of different interest that combine to seek national goals. The decline of party strength inevitably will enhance the influence of special interest groups whose only concern all too often is how a political candidate votes on a single issue. The quality of political debate, and indeed the capacity of government to function in the national interest, suffer when candidates and officeholders are forced to be more responsive to the narrow concerns of unrepresentative special interest groups than to overarching issues of domestic and foreign policy....

———————

1. Review the summary of the division between political and civil service appointments in the federal government in the *Note on Presidential Authority and the Civil Service, supra*. Does *Branti* jeopardize any of the current categories of political appointments? What about Schedule C, for example? What about United States Attorneys?

2. Consider the arguments among the Justices over the justifications for patronage. Do any of the arguments apply differently to the federal government than to state and local governments?

C. Supervision of Executive Branch Policymaking

1. The formative years: groping for principles

The President's obligation to "take Care that the Laws be faithfully executed" raises a series of questions relating to his role in managing government (we consider the clause more broadly in Chapter Five). Is the President responsible for the lawfulness of the acts of his subordinates? If so, may he direct administrative actions to the extent necessary to ensure their legality? An affirmative answer to these questions leads to further inquiries about the extent of permissible presidential control of policymaking discretion in the agencies. We begin with two early efforts to sketch principles applicable to these issues. They raise themes that are with us yet.

The President and Accounting Officers
1 Op. A.G. 624 (1823).

[President Monroe asked Attorney General William Wirt whether Monroe could legally and properly revise the Treasury Department's settlement of the account of Major Joseph Wheaton for the period of his tenure in the Quartermaster's Department. Before concluding that Major Wheaton's case was inappropriate for presidential intervention, the Attorney General opined that the President was powerless to review the Department's decision:]

The constitution of the United States requires the President, in general terms, to take care that the laws be faithfully executed: that is, it places the officers engaged in the execution of the laws under his general superintendence: he is to see that they do their duty faithfully; and on their failure, to cause them to be displaced, prosecuted, or impeached, according to the nature of the case. In case of forcible resistance to the laws, too, so as to require the interposition of the power of the government to overcome the illegal resistance, he is to see that that power be furnished. But it could never have been the intention of the constitution, in assigning this general power to the President to take care that the laws be executed, that he should in person execute the laws himself. . . .

To interpret this clause of the constitution so as to throw upon the President the duty of a personal interference in every specific case of an alleged or defective execution of the laws, and to call upon him to perform such duties himself, would be not only to require him to perform an impossibility himself, but to take upon himself the responsibility of all the subordinate executive officers of the government—a construction too absurd to be seriously contended for. But the requisition of the constitution is, that he shall *take care* that the *laws* be executed. If the laws, then, require a particular officer by name to perform a duty, not only is that officer bound to perform it, but no other officer can perform it without a violation of the law; and were the President to perform it, he would . . . be violating [the law] himself. The constitution assigns to Congress the power of designating the duties of particular officers: the President is only required to take care that they execute them faithfully. . . .

It would be strange, indeed, if it were otherwise. The office of President is ordained for very different purposes than that of settling individual accounts. The constitution has committed to him the care of the great interests of the nation, in all its foreign and domestic relations. . . . How will it be possible for the President to perform these great duties, if he is also to exercise the appellate power of revising and correcting the settlement of all the individual accounts which pass through the hands of the accounting officers? . . .

My opinion is, that the settlement made of the accounts of individuals by the accounting officers appointed by law is final and conclusive, so far as the executive department of the government is concerned. If an individual conceives himself injured by such settlement, his recourse must be one of the other two branches of government—the legislative or judicial. If a balance be found against him, by the disallowance of credits which he deems just, he may refuse payment and abide a suit; in which case, he will have the benefit of the opinion of a court and jury. If a balance be found in his favor, but smaller than he thinks himself entitled to, his appeal is to Congress, where the representatives of the people will pass upon his claim.

------

1. Does the Attorney General provide a satisfactory account of the President's responsibility for the lawfulness of the acts of subordinate officers? Do you think that Wirt's concerns about the practicability of presidential review identify limits on presidential authority?

2. Other than reviewing his subordinates' decisions or dismissing the incompetent, what can the President do to "take Care that the Laws be faithfully executed"? If there are alternatives to a power of removal that would help the President to keep discipline, should they be regarded as part of the President's constitutional power?

A point of view rather different from Wirt's emerges in an opinion rendered eight years later, by Attorney General (later Chief Justice) Roger B. Taney to Andrew Jackson's Secretary of State.

The Jewels of the Princess of Orange
2 Op. A.G. 482 (1831)

[Apparently on behalf of the President, the Secretary of State asked Taney whether the President could direct the United States Attorney in New York to discontinue the prosecution of an action to condemn certain stolen jewels brought into the United States in violation of the revenue laws. The true owner, the Princess of Orange, a member of the royal family of the Netherlands, had asked for their return. After concluding that the jewels were not liable to forfeiture, Taney turned to the questions whether the proceeding could be terminated, and whether the President could so direct. Taney concluded that a United States Attorney had legal authority to discontinue any suit when termination would be in the interest of the U.S. Attorney's client, the United States:]

Assuming that the district attorney possesses the power to discontinue a prosecution, the next inquiry is, Can the President lawfully direct him, in any case, to do so? . . . I think the President does possess the power. The interest of the country and the purposes of justice manifestly require that he should possess it; and its existence is necessarily implied by the duties imposed upon him in that clause of the constitution . . . which enjoins him to take care that the laws be faithfully executed. . . .

There is no specific grant of power in the constitution which authorizes the President to order the discontinuance of a prosecution against the public property of a foreign nation; and the circumstances that such a prosecution would endanger the peace of the United States, would not confer on the President the right to interfere, although it would be a strong reason for exercising the power if he possessed it. And if he does possess it in such cases, and it is not specifically granted by the constitution, it must be derived from the general supervisory powers which belong to his office, and which are necessary to enable him to perform the duty imposed upon him, of seeing that the law is faithfully executed. . . .

If it should be said that, the district attorney having the power to discontinue the prosecution, there is no necessity for inferring a right in the President to direct him to exercise it, I answer, that the direction of the President is not required to communicate any new authority to the district attorney, but to direct him or aid him in the execution of the power he is admitted to possess. It might, indeed, happen that a district attorney was prosecuting a suit in the name of the United States, against their interest and against justice, and for the purpose of oppressing an individual; such a prosecution would not be a faithful execution of the law; and upon the President being satisfied that the forms of law were abused for such a purpose, and being bound to take care that the law was faithfully executed, it would become his duty to take measures to correct the procedure. And the most natural and proper measure to accomplish that object would be, to order the district attorney to discontinue the prosecution. The district attorney might refuse to obey the President's order; and if he did refuse, the prosecution, while he remained in office, would still go on; because the President could give no order to the court or the clerk to make any particular entry. He could only act through his subordinate officer, the district attorney, who is responsible to him, and who holds his office at his pleasure. And if that officer still continued a prosecution which the President was satisfied ought to be discontinued, the removal of the disobedient officer, and the substitution of one more worthy in his place, would enable the President, through him, faithfully to execute the law. And it is for this, among other reasons, that the power of removing the district attorney resides in the President. . . .

The dismissal of a prosecution by the district attorney, in which the public are interested, is always a matter of great delicacy; and in justice to himself, the power ought never to be exercised upon his own responsibility, where the subject of the controversy is important, or any doubt can be supposed to exist as to the propriety of the measure. And if Mr. Hamilton and the court were both convinced that the prosecution in question was groundless and unjust, yet, as matters now stand, they could not, with propriety, act on their own judgment, without previously understanding the views entertained by the Executive; and the prosecution must go on, even if, in point of fact, it is groundless and unjust, unless the President may lawfully interfere, and authorize and direct the district attorney to strike it off.

The district attorney stands in relation to the President on very different grounds from that of the court. The judicial power is wholly independent of the Executive. The President's direction or approbation would be no justification for their acts. He has no right to interfere with their proceedings; and if they misbehave themselves in office, they are not responsible to him. . . . Upon the whole, I consider the district attorney as under the control and direction of the President, . . . and that it is within the legitimate power of the President to direct him to institute or to discontinue a pending suit, and to point out to him his duty, whenever the interest of the United States is directly or indirectly concerned. And I find, on examination, that the practice of the government has conformed to this opinion; and that, in many instances where the interference of the Executive was asked for, the cases have been referred to the

Attorney General, and, in every case, the right to interfere and direct the district attorney is assumed or asserted.

It may be said that . . . the authority to remit for the violation of the revenue laws being given to the Secretary of the Treasury, it cannot afterwards be exercised by the President. . . . [I]f this case were clearly embraced in the powers given to the Treasury Department, it would not, and could not, deprive the President of the powers which belong to him under the Constitution. The power conferred on the Secretary, by the law of Congress, would be merely in aid of the President, and to lighten the labors of his office. It could not restrain his constitutional powers.

[I]t follows that a prosecution for a forfeiture incurred by a breach of the revenue laws stands on the same principles with a forfeiture occasioned by a breach of any other law of the United States, and is equally under the control and the direction of the President.

---

1. Why do you think the Secretary of State requested Attorney General Taney's opinion?

2. Why do you think Taney eschews a foreign affairs basis for his opinion? Do you infer that Taney agrees or disagrees with the Wirt opinion above?

3. Does Taney suggest that Congress may not deprive the President of power to direct his subordinates even in the exercise of nondiscretionary duties? The Supreme Court, seven years after the Taney opinion, rejected the notion that the President could forbid a subordinate to perform a ministerial task vested in the officer by Congress. *Kendall v. United States ex rel. Stokes*, 37 U.S. (12 Pet.) 524 (1838), discussed in the *Note on Obtaining Judicial Review of Executive Actions* in Chapter Two. In *Kendall*, the Court issued a famous dictum: "To contend, that the obligation imposed on the president to see the laws faithfully executed, implies a power to forbid their execution, is a novel construction of the constitution, and entirely inadmissible." Does this ringing statement beg the important question—what if the President and his subordinate disagree on what the law requires? For example, suppose the United States Attorney and the President disagree over whether the forfeiture action may legally be dismissed—whose will should prevail?

2. The President's statutory powers to manage the executive branch

A number of statutes confer managerial authority on the President. Their existence feeds the current debate over the President's power to control executive policymaking in statutory interstices. We will examine the most important of these statutory powers, relating to the budgetary and spending processes of the government, in section D of this chapter. We need to mention them here, however, to make the overall picture complete and because they relate to arguments about the President's implied statutory powers.

Since enactment of the Budget and Accounting Act of 1921, the President has been responsible for compiling the yearly budget for the federal government and submitting it to Congress for its consideration. In general, OMB controls both the budgetary and legislative requests of federal agencies, including the independent agencies. Congress has occasionally granted an exception from one or both of these requirements, however (e.g., 15 U.S.C. § 2076k, Consumer Product Safety Commission). The procedures for submittal and clearance of agency requests are set forth in OMB Circular A-19 (rev. 1979).

Thus, Congress has recognized both the need for coordination of government policy and the President's unique capacity to provide it. As a practical matter, OMB derives considerable leverage from its power to review the agencies' requests to Congress. As we shall see, OMB has not been loath to exercise this leverage in pursuit of the President's policy agenda.

OMB also has power to control the agencies' demands for information from the public, under the Paperwork Reduction Act of 1980, Pub. L. No. 96-511, 94 Stat. 2812 (codified in scattered sections of 5, 20, 30, 42, and 44 U.S.C.). The independent agencies may overrule OMB directives under this statute by majority vote. 44 U.S.C. § 3507(c). The component of OMB that administers the Paperwork Reduction Act, the Office of Information and Regulatory Affairs (OIRA), also administers the executive order programs for coordinating policymaking that we explore below. Stormy relations between OIRA and Congress due to the executive orders have led Congress to subject the head of the office to advice and consent (Pub. L. No. 99-591, Oct. 30, 1986).

Since the New Deal, Congress has authorized the President to prepare government reorganization plans, which, within certain limits, may transfer, consolidate, or abolish agency functions. 5 U.S.C. § 901 *et seq.* The current statute, for example, forbids abolishing or transferring all the functions of an executive department or independent regulatory agency. For many years, Congress subjected presidential reorganization plans to legislative veto (recall Justice White's historical summary in *Chadha*). In 1984, Congress amended the statute to require the plans to be approved by joint resolution. 5 U.S.C. §§ 908-12. This continuing congressional desire to keep a close control on reorganization authority recognizes that it is not just a matter of pigeonholing government functions. Instead, the placement of a function in one agency rather than another can have important effects on substantive policy. *See generally* Karl, *Executive Reorganization and Presidential Power*, 1977 Sup. Ct. Rev. 1. For example, the Environmental Protection Agency was created by reorganization plan in 1970. What difference do you think it makes that pesticide regulation resides in EPA rather than the Agriculture Department?

Finally, some statutes vest substantive authority directly in the President. Under 3 U.S.C. § 301, he may subdelegate these powers to any agency in the executive branch, "[p]rovided, That nothing contained herein shall relieve the President of his responsibility . . . for the acts of any such . . . official." For an example of such subdelegation, see *Meat Cutters* in Chapter Two. The legislative history of the statute recognized that "the President cannot delegate many functions because delegation would be inappropriate due to their character." (S. Rept. No. 1867, 81st Cong., 2d Sess. (1950)). Which statutory functions should the President exercise directly?

The foregoing is not an exhaustive catalogue of the President's statutory powers to manage the government. For more detail, *see* Strauss, *The Place of Agencies in Government: Separation of Powers and the Fourth Branch*, 84 Colum. L. Rev. 573, 587-91 (1984), reminding us of such managerial powers as the Department of Justice's control of most government litigation and the Office of Personnel Management's employment functions.

3. *Supervising the exercise of discretionary administrative authority*
a. Participation in administrative rulemaking

Sierra Club v. Costle
657 F.2d 298 (D.C. Cir. 1981)

[In an extensive opinion, the court reviewed and upheld the Environmental Protection Agency's new source performance standards for coalfired power plants. The standards, issued pursuant to the Clean Air Act, are intended to reduce sulfur dioxide and particulate emissions from new facilities through the use of expensive "scrubber" technology. After rejecting substantive challenges to the standards by both industry and environmental groups, including the Environmental Defense Fund (EDF), the court turned to procedural issues concerning EPA's rulemaking. Here it considered the legality of meetings between EPA officials and private groups, White House officials, and members of Congress, which occurred after the formal period for public comment on the proposed rules had ended.

Section 553 of the Administrative Procedure Act, which governs most agency rulemaking, contains no ban on "ex parte" contacts between rulemakers and interested persons, occurring outside the "administrative record" that is compiled for judicial review. (Other statutes, such as the Clean Air Act, sometimes modify the APA's basic procedures.) Nevertheless, case law in the late 1970's began evincing concerns that the administrative record faithfully reflect the facts and policy arguments actually available to the agency, and that all interested persons be treated fairly. *See* G. Robinson, E. Gellhorn & H. Bruff, The Administrative Process 367-84 (3d ed. 1986). Here a complicating factor was the Supreme Court's decision in *Vermont Yankee Nuclear Power Corp. v. Natural Resources Defense Council, Inc.*, 435 U.S. 519 (1978), which emphasized that lower courts must not require agencies to follow procedures not mandated by statute, but which reaffirmed the duty of courts to review the substantive adequacy of the administrative record to support the agency's rule. How ex parte contacts stood under this distinction was (and is), to say the least, unclear. *Sierra Club* is an important development in this line of cases, and is of special interest here because of its consideration of contacts from the executive branch and Congress. Excerpts from Judge WALD's opinion follow.]

2. *Meetings Held With Individuals Outside EPA*

The [Clean Air Act] does not explicitly treat the issue of post-comment period meetings with individuals outside EPA. Oral face-to-face discussions are not prohibited anywhere, anytime, in the Act. The absence of such prohibition may have arisen from the nature of the informal rulemaking procedures Congress had in mind. Where agency action resembles judicial action, where it involves formal rulemaking, adjudication, or quasi-adjudication among "conflicting private claims to a valuable privilege,"[499] the insulation of the decisionmaker from ex parte contacts is justified by basic notions of due process to the parties involved. But where agency action involves informal rulemaking of a policymaking sort, the concept of ex parte contacts is of more questionable utility.

---

499. *Sangamon Valley Television Corp. v. United States*, 269 F.2d 221, 224 (D.C.Cir.

Under our system of government, the very legitimacy of general policymaking performed by unelected administrators depends in no small part upon the openness, accessibility, and amenability of these officials to the needs and ideas of the public from whom their ultimate authority derives, and upon whom their commands must fall. As judges we are insulated from these pressures because of the nature of the judicial process in which we participate; but we must refrain from the easy temptation to look askance at all face-to-face lobbying efforts, regardless of the forum in which they occur, merely because we see them as inappropriate in the judicial context.[503] Furthermore, the importance to effective regulation of continuing contact with a regulated industry, other affected groups, and the public cannot be underestimated. Informal contacts may enable the agency to win needed support for its program, reduce future enforcement requirements by helping those regulated to anticipate and shape their plans for the future, and spur the provision of information which the agency needs. The possibility of course exists that in permitting ex parte communications with rulemakers we create the danger of "one administrative record for the public and this court and another for the Commission." Under the Clean Air Act procedures, however, "[t]he promulgated rule may not be based (in part or whole) on any information or data which has not been placed in the docket. . . ." Thus EPA must justify its rulemaking solely on the basis of the record it compiles and makes public.

Regardless of this court's views on the need to restrict all post-comment contacts in the informal rulemaking context, however, it is clear to us that Congress has decided not to do so in the statute which controls this case. As we have previously noted:

> . . . If Congress wanted to forbid or limit ex parte contact in every case of informal rulemaking, it certainly had a perfect opportunity of doing so when it enacted the Government in the Sunshine Act, Pub.L. No. 94-409, 90 Stat. 1241 (Sept. 13, 1976). . . . That it did not extend the ex parte contact provisions of the amended section 557 [which governs adjudication] to section 553—even though such an extension was urged upon it during the hearing—is a sound indication that Congress still does not favor a per se prohibition or even a "logging" requirement in all such proceedings.

. . . It still can be argued, however, that if oral communications are to be freely permitted after the close of the comment period, then at least some adequate summary of them must be made in order to preserve the integrity of the rulemaking docket, which under the statute must be the sole repository of material upon which EPA intends to rely. The statute does not require the docketing of all post-comment period conversations and meetings, but we believe that a fair inference can be drawn that in some instances such docketing may be needed in order to give practical effect to

---

1959) (FCC channel assignment proceeding involved claims of this sort, and "basic fairness requires such proceeding to be carried on in the open").

503. See Remarks of Carl McGowan (Chief Judge, U.S. Court of Appeals, D.C. Circuit), Ass'n of Amer. Law Schools, Section on Admin. Law (San Antonio, Texas, Jan. 4, 1981):

> I think it likely that ambivalence will continue to pervade the ex parte contact problem until we face up to the question of whether legislation by informal rulemaking under delegated authority is, in terms of process, to be assimilated to lawmaking by the Congress itself, or to the adversary trial carried on in the sanitized and insulated atmosphere of the courthouse. . . . The customs, the traditions, the mores, if you please, of the processes of persuasion, are emphatically not the same. . . .

section 307(d)(4)(B)(i), which provides that all *documents* "of central relevance to the rulemaking" shall be placed in the docket as soon as possible after their availability. This is so because unless oral communications of central relevance to the rulemaking are also docketed in some fashion or other, information central to the justification of the rule could be obtained without ever appearing on the docket, simply by communicating it by voice rather than by pen, thereby frustrating the command of section 307 that the final rule not be "based (in part or whole) on any information or data which has not been placed in the docket...."

(a) *Intra-Executive Branch Meetings*

We have already held that a blanket prohibition against meetings during the post-comment period with individuals outside EPA is unwarranted, and this perforce applies to meetings with White House officials. We have not yet addressed, however, the issue whether such oral communications with White House staff, or the President himself, must be docketed on the rulemaking record, and we now turn to that issue. The facts, as noted earlier, present us with a single undocketed meeting held on April 30, 1979, at 10:00 a.m., attended by the President, White House staff, other high ranking members of the Executive Branch, as well as EPA officials, and which concerned the issues and options presented by the rulemaking.

We note initially that section 307 makes specific provision for including in the rulemaking docket the...drafts of the final rule submitted to an executive review process prior to promulgation, as well as all "written comments," "documents," and "written responses" resulting from such interagency review process....[519] This specific requirement does not mention informal meetings or conversations concerning the rule which are not part of the initial or final review processes, nor does it refer to oral comments of any sort. Yet it is hard to believe Congress was unaware that intra-executive meetings and oral comments would occur throughout the rulemaking process. We assume, therefore, that unless expressly forbidden by Congress, such intra-executive contacts[520] may take place, both during and after the public comment period; the only real issue is whether they must be noted and summarized in the docket.

The court recognizes the basic need of the President and his White House staff to monitor the consistency of executive agency regulations with Administration policy.

---

519. These materials, although docketed, are excluded from the "record for judicial review." 42 U.S.C. § 7607(d)(7)(A). The logic of this exclusion of final draft comments from the agency's "record for judicial review" is not completely clear, but we believe it evinces a Congressional intent for the reviewing court to judge the rule solely upon the data, information, and comments provided in the public docket, as well as the explanations EPA provides when it promulgates the rule, and not to concern itself with who in the Executive Branch advised whom about which policies to pursue.

520. In this case we need not decide the effect upon rulemaking proceedings of a failure to disclose so-called "conduit" communications, in which administration or inter-agency contacts serve as mere conduits for private parties in order to get the latter's off-the-record views into the proceeding.... We note that the Department of Justice Office of Legal Counsel has taken the position that it may be improper for White House advisers to act as conduits for outsiders. It has therefore recommended that Council of Economic Advisers officials summarize and place in rulemaking records a compilation of all written or oral comments they receive relevant to particular proceedings. EDF has given us no reason to believe that a policy similar to this was not followed here, or that unrecorded conduit communications exist in this case.

. . .

He and his White House advisers surely must be briefed fully and frequently about rules in the making, and their contributions to policymaking considered. The executive power under our Constitution, after all, is not shared—it rests exclusively with the President. The idea of a "plural executive," or a President with a council of state, was considered and rejected by the Constitutional Convention. Instead the Founders chose to risk the potential for tyranny inherent in placing power in one person, in order to gain the advantages of accountability fixed on a single source. To ensure the President's control and supervision over the Executive Branch, the Constitution—and its judicial gloss—vests him with the powers of appointment and removal, the power to demand written opinions from executive officers, and the right to invoke executive privilege to protect consultative privacy. In the particular case of EPA, Presidential authority is clear since it has never been considered an "independent agency," but always part of the Executive Branch.

The authority of the President to control and supervise executive policymaking is derived from the Constitution; the desirability of such control is demonstrable from the practical realities of administrative rulemaking. Regulations such as those involved here demand a careful weighing of cost, environmental, and energy considerations.[526] They also have broad implications for national economic policy. Our form of government simply could not function effectively or rationally if key executive policymakers were isolated from each other and from the Chief Executive. Single mission agencies do not always have the answers to complex regulatory problems. An overworked administrator exposed on a 24-hour basis to a dedicated but zealous staff needs to know the arguments and ideas of policymakers in other agencies as well as in the White House.

We recognize, however, that there may be instances where the docketing of conversations between the President or his staff and other Executive Branch officers or rulemakers may be necessary to ensure due process. This may be true, for example, where such conversations directly concern the outcome of adjudications or quasi-

---

526. *See generally* C. Schultze, The Public Use of Private Interest 9-10 (1977):

In the field of energy and the environment the generally accepted objectives of national policy imply a staggeringly complex and interlocking set of actions, directly affecting the production and consumption decisions of every citizen and every business firm. Consider for a moment the chain of collective decisions and their effects just in the case of electric utilities. Petroleum imports can be conserved by switching from oil-fired to coal-fired generation. But barring other measures, burning high-sulfur Eastern coal substantially increases pollution. Sulfur can be "scrubbed" from coal smoke in the stack, but at a heavy cost, with devices that turn out huge volumes of sulfur wastes that must be disposed of and about whose reliability there is some question. Intermittent control techniques (installing high smokestacks and switching off burners when meteorological conditions are adverse) can, at lower cost, reduce local concentrations of sulfur oxides in the air, but cannot cope with the growing problem of sulfates and widespread acid rainfall. Use of low-sulfur Western coal would avoid many of these problems, but this coal is obtained by strip mining. Strip-mining reclamation is possible, but substantially hindered in large areas of the West by lack of rainfall. Moreover, in some coal-rich areas the coal beds form the underground aquifer and their removal could wreck adjacent farming or ranching economies. Large coal-burning plants might be located in remote areas far from highly populated urban centers in order to minimize the human effects of pollution. But such areas are among the few left that are unspoiled by pollution and both environmentalists and the residents (relatively few in number compared with those in metropolitan localities but large among the voting population in the particular states) strongly object to this policy. Fears, realistic or imaginary, about safety and about accumulation of radioactive waste have increasingly hampered the nuclear option.

adjudicatory proceedings; there is no inherent executive power to control the rights of individuals in such settings. Docketing may also be necessary in some circumstances where a statute like this one *specifically requires* that essential "information or data" upon which a rule is based be docketed. But in the absence of any further Congressional requirements, we hold that it was not unlawful in this case for EPA not to docket a face-to-face policy session involving the President and EPA officials during the post-comment period, since EPA makes no effort to base the rule on any "information or data" arising from that meeting. Where the President himself is directly involved in oral communications with Executive Branch officials, Article II considerations—combined with the strictures of *Vermont Yankee*—require that courts tread with extraordinary caution in mandating disclosure beyond that already required by statute.

The purposes of full-record review which underlie the need for disclosing ex parte conversations in some settings do not require that courts know the details of every White House contact, including a Presidential one, in this informal rulemaking setting. After all, any rule issued here with or without White House assistance must have the requisite *factual support* in the rulemaking record, and under this particular statute the Administrator may not base the rule in whole or in part on any *"information or data"* which is not in the record, no matter what the source. The courts will monitor all this, but they need not be omniscient to perform their role effectively. Of course, it is always possible that undisclosed Presidential prodding may direct an outcome that *is* factually based on the record, but different from the outcome that would have obtained in the absence of Presidential involvement. In such a case, it would be true that the political process did affect the outcome in a way the courts could not police. But we do not believe that Congress intended that the courts convert informal rulemaking into a rarified technocratic process, unaffected by political considerations or the presence of Presidential power. In sum, we find that the existence of intra-Executive Branch meetings during the post-comment period, and the failure to docket one such meeting involving the President, violated neither the procedures mandated by the Clean Air Act nor due process.

(b) *Meetings Involving Alleged Congressional Pressure*

Finally, EDF challenges the rulemaking on the basis of alleged Congressional pressure, citing principally two meetings with Senator Byrd. EDF asserts that under the controlling case law the political interference demonstrated in this case represents a separate and independent ground for invalidating this rulemaking. But among the cases EDF cites in support of its position,[533] only *D.C. Federation of Civic Associ-*

---

533. EDF relies heavily upon *Pillsbury Co. v. FTC*, 354 F.2d 952 (5th Cir. 1966), and *Koniag, Inc. v. Andrus*, 580 F.2d 601 (D.C.Cir.), *cert. denied*, 439 U.S. 1052 (1978). Neither case is apposite to the facts here. In *Pillsbury*, several Senators on [a] Subcommittee of the Senate Judiciary Committee expressed strong opinions on a key issue in the *Pillsbury* case then pending before the FTC. In its subsequent decision, the FTC ruled as the members of the Senate committee had suggested. The court, basing its holding on the fact that the agency was carrying out "its judicial function," found that the "private litigants" in the case had a right "to a fair trial" and "to the appearance of impartiality" when the agency was acting in such capacity. Therefore procedural due process required a reversal of the agency's decision.

In *Koniag*, a letter was sent from a Congressman to the Secretary of the Interior about an adjudicatory, adversary proceeding which concerned the eligibility of certain Alaskan villages to take land and revenues under the Alaskan Native Claims Settlement Act. The letter requested

ations v. Volpe [459 F.2d 1231 (D.C. Cir. 1971), *cert. denied*, 405 U.S. 1030 (1972)] seems relevant to the facts here.

In *D.C. Federation* the Secretary of Transportation, pursuant to applicable federal statutes, made certain safety and environmental findings in designating a proposed bridge as part of the interstate highway system. Civic associations sought to have these determinations set aside for their failure to meet certain statutory standards, and because of possible tainting by reason of improper Congressional influence. Such influence chiefly included public statements by the Chairman of the House Subcommittee on the District of Columbia, Representative Natcher, indicating in no uncertain terms that money earmarked for the construction of the District of Columbia's subway system would be withheld unless the Secretary approved the bridge. [A] majority of this court ... [agreed] on the controlling principle of law: "that the decision [of the Secretary] would be invalid if based in whole or in part on the pressures emanating from Representative Natcher." ... The court remanded ... so that the Secretary could make this decision strictly and solely on the basis of considerations made relevant by Congress in the applicable statute.

D.C. Federation thus requires that two conditions be met before an administrative rulemaking may be overturned simply on the grounds of Congressional pressure. First, the content of the pressure upon the Secretary is designed to force him to decide upon factors not made relevant by Congress in the applicable statute. Representative Natcher's threats were of precisely that character, since deciding to approve the bridge in order to free the "hostage" mass transit appropriation was not among the decisionmaking factors Congress had in mind when it enacted the highway approval provisions of Title 23 of the United States Code. Second, the Secretary's determination must be affected by those extraneous considerations.

In the case before us, there is no persuasive evidence that either criterion is satisfied. Senator Byrd requested a meeting in order to express "strongly" his already well-known views that the SO_2 standards' impact on coal reserves was a matter of concern to him. EPA initiated a second responsive meeting to report its reaction to the reserve data submitted by the NCA. In neither meeting is there any allegation that EPA made any commitments to Senator Byrd. The meetings did underscore Senator Byrd's deep concerns for EPA, but there is no evidence he attempted actively to use "extraneous" pressures to further his position. Americans rightly expect their elected representatives to voice their grievances and preferences concerning the administration of our laws. We believe it entirely proper for Congressional representatives vigorously to represent the interests of their constituents before administrative agencies engaged in informal, general policy rulemaking, so long as individual Congressmen do not frustrate the intent of Congress as a whole as expressed in statute, nor undermine applicable rules of procedure. Where Congressmen keep their comments focused on the substance of the proposed rule—and we have no substantial evidence to cause us to believe Senator Byrd did not do so here—administrative agencies are expected to balance Congressional pressure with the pressures emanating from all other sources. To hold otherwise would deprive the agencies of legitimate sources of information and call into question the validity of nearly every controversial rulemaking. ...

---

the Secretary to postpone his decision on the cases pending a review and opinion by the Comptroller General, because it "appears from the testimony [at the hearings] ... that certain villages should not have been certified as eligible for land selections under ANCSA." This court found that the letter compromised the appearance of the Secretary's impartiality. Both *Pillsbury* and *Koniag* are easily distinguishable [because this is rulemaking].

1. Declining to require disclosure of the White House meeting, the court says that it is permissible for "undisclosed Presidential prodding" to "direct an outcome that *is* factually based on the record, but different from the outcome that would have obtained" otherwise. Do you agree? Has the court taken sufficient account of the concerns apparently underlying § 307 of the Clean Air Act Amendments? In general, what is the significance of a statutory delegation directly to an agency, rather than to the President? One could argue that, when Congress delegates power to an executive agency rather than an independent one, it contemplates presidential supervision. On the other hand, perhaps a delegation to EPA is meant to take advantage of both the expertise and the political orientation of that agency.

2. Could Congress, consistent with the President's executive privilege, require disclosure of White House-agency contacts in rulemaking? If such a statute would be constitutional, would it improve the administrative process? How should it deal with the problem of "conduit" communications, explained in the court's note 520?

3. *Sierra Club* is the fullest judicial discussion to date of ad hoc presidential intervention in rulemaking. For more analysis of the issues, *see Symposium on Presidential Intervention in Administrative Rulemaking*, 56 Tul. L. Rev. 811 (1982); Bruff, *Presidential Power and Administrative Rulemaking*, 88 Yale L. J. 451 (1979). It is easy to see what drew the President's attention in *Sierra Club* (and that of Senator Byrd). This was a very high-stakes rulemaking, with millions of dollars, large aggregate environmental effects, and perhaps thousands of jobs in the balance. It also had implications for a highly complex and wide-ranging set of national policy issues about energy and the environment. *See* the excerpt from Charles Schultze's perceptive book in the court's note 526. This should help you to understand why recent Presidents have been unwilling to rely on occasional "jawboning" in a particular controversy, and have sought means for overall coordination of federal regulation. We now turn to that topic.

b. Coordinating the regulatory process

Each President since Nixon has tried to achieve some systematic coordination of rulemaking by executive branch agencies, to make it more responsive to the President's policy concerns. The Ford, Carter, and Reagan efforts all took the form of executive orders. Before considering the Reagan order, which is the most ambitious, we provide some background. First, we outline efforts through the years to identify the causes of, and solutions to, the imperfections of government regulation. (The French are said to define regulation as "the substitution of error for chance.") Then we turn to competing arguments concerning the need for greater executive coordination of policy.

Various study commissions, most of them presidential, have analyzed the administrative "malaise" and have recommended cures. They reveal a surprising (and depressing) similarity of perceptions about the problems and necessary reforms. First came the "Brownlow Commission" in the New Deal, famous for its condemnation of independent agencies as a "headless 'fourth branch' of Government, a haphazard deposit of irresponsible agencies and uncoordinate powers." President's Comm. on Administrative Management, Report 40 (1937). Shortly thereafter, The Final Report of the Attorney General's Committee, S. Doc. No. 8, 77th Cong., 1st Sess. (1941), laid the basis for the federal APA. Alone among the study groups, it could claim landmark results.

In 1955, the Hoover Commission recommended the creation of an administrative court to hear and decide enforcement actions. Commission on the Organization of the Executive Branch of the Government, Legal Services and Procedure (1955). Its views were repeated in part by the Ash Council in 1971. The President's Advisory Council on Executive Organization, A New Regulatory Framework (1971). (*But see* R. Noll, Reforming Regulation (1971)). Thus observers have repeatedly called for a separation of adjudicative from policymaking functions in the agencies. W. Cary, Politics and the Regulatory Agencies 125-34 (1967). Agency independence has been attacked as the villain by some and defended by others; some skeptics have argued that it is unclear that it makes very much of a difference whether regulation is formally independent or within an executive department, without regard to whether the difference is beneficial. *See* Robinson, *On Reorganizing the Independent Regulatory Agencies*, 57 Va. L. Rev. 947 (1971).

In 1960, James Landis, a former dean of the Harvard Law School, Chairman of the CAB, and member of the FTC, prepared a report for the new President examining alleged internal deficiencies of the agencies—delay, costs, personnel, ethics, policy coordination and formulation, and administrative organization. Report on Regulatory Agencies to the President-Elect, reprinted in Sen. Comm. on the Judiciary, 86th Cong., 2d Sess. (Comm. Print 1960).

Almost twenty years later agencies were still being criticized for taking too much time, for adopting inconsistent or otherwise counterproductive requirements, for ignoring elementary requirements of fairness, and so forth. *See generally* Sen. Comm. on Governmental Affairs, Study on Federal Regulation, 95th Cong., 1st Sess., vols. I-V (1977). Nevertheless, as we will see below, the Committee did not think that increased presidential management was the answer to regulation's problems.

Most recently, the American Bar Association created a prestigious Commission on Law and the Economy, whose final report, Federal Regulation: Roads to Reform (1979), contained a series of recommendations on improving federal regulation. The Commission favored stronger presidential management of the regulatory process to achieve policy coordination and to avoid unnecessary cost, duplication, and conflict. The Commission said (at 68):

> Our government has adopted a wide variety of national goals. Many of these goals—checking inflation, spurring economic growth, reducing unemployment, protecting our national security, assuring equal opportunity, increasing social security, cleaning up the environment, improving energy sufficiency—conflict with one another, and all of them compete for the same resources. One of the central tasks of modern democratic government is to make wise balancing choices among courses of action that pursue one or more of these conflicting and competing objectives.
>
> While Congress establishes the goals, it cannot legislate the details of every action taken in pursuit of each goal, or make the balancing choices that each such decision requires. It has therefore delegated this task to the regulatory agencies. But we have given each of the regulatory agencies one set of primary goals, with only limited responsibility for balancing a proposed action in pursuit of its own goals against adverse impacts on the pursuit of other goals. For most of these agencies, no effective mechanisms exist for coordinating the decisions of one agency with those of other agencies, or conforming them to the balancing

judgments of elected generalists, such as the President and Congress. Appointed rather than elected, specialist rather than generalist, regulatory agency officials enjoy an independence from the political process—and from one another—that weakens the national ability to make balancing choices, or to hold anyone politically accountable when choices are made badly or not at all.

To illustrate the problem, the Commission noted that, as of 1979, at least 16 federal agencies bore regulatory responsibilities that directly affected the price and supply of energy. This diffusion of policymaking authority persisted despite the earlier consolidation of several energy-oriented agencies into a Department of Energy. Similar multiplicity problems present themselves with respect to antitrust, equal employment, industrial safety, and natural resources policymaking. From this, the Commission concluded (at 73):

> Congress cannot perform these [balancing] tasks by legislating the details of one regulation after another; that is why Congress delegated rulemaking power to the agencies in the first place, and gave them a wide degree of discretion as to the content of the rules to be issued. The President is the elected official most capable of making the needed balancing decisions as critical issues arise, while the most appropriate and effective role for Congress is to review and, where necessary, to curb unwise presidential intervention.

Accordingly, the Commission recommended passage of a statute authorizing the President to direct agencies to decide certain "critical" regulatory issues, and to order changes in their decisions. *See also* Cutler & Johnson, *Regulation and the Political Process*, 84 Yale L. J. 1395 (1975). Congress has not accepted the invitation; presidential coordination has proceeded, as before, by executive order.

For a congressional perspective, one markedly less receptive to presidential coordination, we utilize the Study on Federal Regulation, *supra*, which has a thorough analysis that cites the best of the voluminous literature on this subject.

Regulatory Organization
5 Study on Federal Regulation, Senate Comm. on Governmental
Affairs, 95th Cong., 1st Sess. 6-7, 67-81 (1977)

Few beliefs about Government have enjoyed greater durability than the notion that somehow the structure of Government is rife with "duplication and overlap," a deplorable situation preventing the "efficient" administration of programs. While instances of "duplication and overlap" may be found . . . it is our view that a certain degree of "redundancy" is not only natural, but also necessary for sound regulatory administration. . . .

Our study of antitrust enforcement suggests that in a politically sensitive and complex area such as antitrust, it makes sense to have more than one agency involved, especially where there is adequate coordination and where one agency is "independent" (the FTC) and the other is part of an executive department (the Antitrust Division of the Department of Justice). On the other hand, our study of food regulation by the Food and Drug Administration and the Department of Agriculture finds that divided responsibility has resulted in a regulatory program which is often duplicative, sometimes contradictory, and undeniably costly and overly complex.

In the case of food regulation, neither agency is independent yet there appears to be a failure in coordination. Similarly, in the area of worker protection and product safety protection, there are instances of failure of coordination and regulatory gaps or statutory mandates lacking sufficient precision which result in failures to protect the consumer against potential risks of bodily harm or injury to health. In the area of banking regulation, our study suggests that jurisdictional overlap among the three federal banking agencies should be remedied by consolidation in a new Federal Banking Commission.

One of the primary reasons for the creation of the Department of Energy, as our study of energy regulation demonstrates, was to prevent similar failures of coordination and duplication of effort by consolidating most energy activities in a single executive agency. It was also hoped that the creation of a cabinet level department would provide the mechanism for comprehensive policy development and planning for national energy goals. The inclusion of the Federal Power Commission, a formerly independent regulatory commission, in the new department was a unique effort to provide some measure of executive policy guidance and initiative in an area previously beyond the control of the President. At the same time, it was recognized (and strenuous efforts were made to insure) that the adjudicatory functions of Federal Energy Regulatory Commission remain insulated from political direction. . . .

Freedom from executive domination was . . . the prime motivating force for the creation by Congress of the independent regulatory commissions. More than anything else, they were intended to be independent of the White House. That mainspring, expressed often in terms of the "arm of Congress" idea, also emphasized the special relationship of the commissions to Congress. . . .

As a general proposition, Presidents have respected the independent status of the commissions. There is an expectation that, in discharging their adjudicatory functions in particular, those agencies should be free of interference or direction from the White House. . . . Communications to those commissions from the White House have always been viewed as sensitive matters. In the 1950s a major scandal, which led to the resignation of a top Presidential advisor [Sherman Adams], involved improper White House communication to an independent agency on a pending matter. Not unsimilar attempts at undue influence also occurred in the early 1970s, one of which contributed to the departure of a chairman of the Securities and Exchange Commission. In this area, appearance is as important as reality; and the President must be and appear to be at an arm's length distance from these quasi-judicial commissions. . . .

For years the commission form has been bombarded with . . . criticisms. . . . [M]uch of the coordination that presently exists can be traced to the Roosevelt area: executive control of budgets and legislative recommendations, supervision of information gathering plans, and the power to reorganize these bodies in whole or part all first occurred during his presidency. . . .

In the 1950s Marver Bernstein viewed efficient coordination of policy in an independent setting as improbable [Regulating Business by Independent Commission, 144 (1955)]:

> In an age which throws upon the President an unmanageable burden of political leadership and administrative management, the survival of islands of administrative independence, however qualified, only serves to increase the difficulties of integration.

On the eve of the Kennedy Administration, James Landis in less stringent terms raised the same question of accountability and coordination in his report to the President-elect. And as recently as 1970, the Ash Council reported to President Nixon that multi-member commissions precluded effective regulatory action [President's Advisory Council on Executive Organization, A New Regulatory Framework, Report on Selected Independent Regulatory Agencies, 40 (1971)]:

> The overseeing of economic regulation by responsible public officials, necessary to assure effective discharge of agency responsibilities, cannot exist if the decisionmakers are immune from public concerns as expressed through their elected representatives ... commissioners [have] a degree of independence that may serve to protect them from improper influence but was not intended to allow them to become unresponsive.

What is needed, according to a leading member of the bar, is "*continuous* political monitoring of all government regulation to ensure its responsiveness to the changing economic and social needs that the political process reflects." [Cutler & Johnson, *Regulation and the Political Process*, 84 Yale L.J. 1395, 1397 (1975).] Independence of course precludes that monitoring by the Executive Branch.

Independence, it has also been argued, weakens the agencies, by removing them from the benefits of Presidential support and making them more vulnerable to domination by the regulated industries. Marver Bernstein viewed the private sector as the major beneficiary of the independent form:

> ... Maintenance of the myth of commission independence represents a conscious effort by regulated groups to confine regulatory authority to an agency that is somewhat more susceptible than an executive department to influence, persuasion, and, eventually, capture and control.

Originally independence from partisan control was considered to be a guarantee of strong regulatory policy; has the reverse occurred? ...

According to opponents of independence, there are other negative impacts of isolation from the President: the more these agencies are removed from the budget process, the less Administration support they receive on this important matter. The result may be commissions that are budgetarily weak; which again works to the advantage of those private interests that have no enthusiasm for vigorous regulatory activities. [See Roger Noll, Reforming Regulation: An Evaluation of Ash Council Proposals, pp. 6-7 (1972). In short the theory goes that independence from the President means that the agencies lack a champion—a void that, at no small cost, is filled by the regulated industries.

But shouldn't that be the responsibility of Congress, which after all created these agencies and vested them with quasi-judicial and quasi-legislative powers? And aren't the agencies guided by statutory terms that outline their regulatory mission? Opponents of the independent form have considered and rejected those propositions.... The Ash Council ... thought the answer did not lie with Congress:

> Congressional statements of policy are understandably general, leaving to commissions the task of making specific policy to implement those [statutory] objectives. One result is that the commissions, in the course of time, have developed policies affecting the economy without sufficient guidance or check by Congress.

Thus, since the President is by law prohibited from coordinating these bodies and Congress is by nature incapable of supplying the guidance they need, the independent commissions are as a result held accountable to no one.... Those who favor abandonment of the independent form conclude there is but one answer. And that is, greater integration of these agencies into the executive branch. In no other way, it is thought, will there be clear lines of accountability and effective coordination of national policies on regulation.

The foregoing arguments against the independent form are, at first blush, considerable. But does a far too close association with the regulated industries, or a lack of systematic Congressional oversight, necessarily suggest abandonment of the independent form? We think not. The private sector carefully monitors the work of these commissions, very simply because it has so much at stake. Would not the same resources and energy be expended, regardless of where these agencies were located? And what is there—in fact, not supposition—to suggest that executive departments or agencies are any less independent from the sustained efforts of those interests? We wonder whether, in that regard, there are any significant differences between an independent commission and a Presidential regulatory agency, such as OSHA or NHTSA. Every regulatory body, wherever it is located, will be subject to pressure from the regulated industries.

To be sure, changing the status of the commissions will not address the problems of Congressional oversight. Indeed opponents of independence bypass that issue altogether, dismissing it in favor of closer executive branch oversight. In our opinion the answers to both problems lie outside the question of independence: we have proposed a series of recommendations to improve Congressional oversight and increase the agencies' responsiveness to the public interest. We are convinced that the remedies will be more likely found in that direct approach to those problems.

Congress can be faulted for its lack of interest in these quasi-legislative agencies. But the executive branch has also failed to effectively utilize the powers it has to properly influence these commissions. That fact is most apparent in the power of appointment, often considered to be the major executive opportunity to affect the course of regulatory policy. Have Presidents used this power wisely to place able appointees with vigorous regulatory objectives on these bodies? We answered that question in volume I of this study [quoted earlier in this Chapter. Presidential] disinterest, which has marked so many regulatory appointments for such a long time, surely constitutes one of the major disabilities of the independent commission.

In other regards, the degree of interest displayed by Presidents in the regulatory agencies does not appear to be high. In the scheme of things, it is understandable that the President and his top advisors have more pressing concerns to occupy their time. As Judge Friendly has pointed out [The Federal Administrative Agencies: The Need for Better Definition of Standards 154 (1962)]:

> The spectacle of a chief executive, burdened to the limit of endurance with decisions on which the very existence of mankind may depend, personally taking on the added task of determining to what extent newspapers should be allowed to own television stations or whether railroads should be allowed to reduce rates only to or somewhat below the truck level, is pure mirage.

In point of fact, Presidential concern over such matters, when it exists at all, is delegated to often middle-level White House assistants. And the relatively hum-drum issues that mark day-to-day regulation rarely capture the attention to top advisors to the President. In addition to the press of other business, it is also probably true that there is very little political gain for Presidents from properly-functioning regulatory agencies. ... Therefore it is something short of accurate to characterize independence as a barrier to a continuing Presidential interest in the commissions.

Much of what there is has not been competently used by either legislative or executive branch to coordinate the independent agencies. There is truth in Professor Cary's assertion that the independent commissions are really "stepchildren whose custody is contested by both the Congress and the Executive, but without very much affection from either one." The dispute over structure, over where these agencies fit in the federal scheme, is really a diversion from a much more difficult issue; again to cite Cary, the real problem is the development of coherent national policies on regulation itself. In that quandary, neither legislative nor executive branches have shown much sustained interest.

At present the greatest degree of systematic attention the agencies receive from Congress and the President occurs in the budget process. The budget is the single oversight mechanism the agencies can expect on a regular basis from either Congress or the White House. The Office of Management and Budget does deliberately and carefully review agency funding requests, and the same is true of the appropriation committees of Congress.... OMB and Congressional review is expected to remain as searching as it is at present.

In addition there is nothing, to our knowledge, which prevents the President from taking a greater interest either in the independent commission or broad regulatory policy. As President Kennedy, in his regulatory message to Congress in 1961, asserted an affirmative duty to oversee the proper functioning of federal agencies, whether independent or otherwise ["Regulatory Agencies—Message from the President of the United States", *Congressional Record*, April 13, 1961, p. 5357]:

> ... The President's responsibilities require him to know and evaluate how efficiently these agencies dispatch their business, including any lack of prompt decision of the thousands of cases they are called upon to decide, any failure to evolve policy in areas where they have been charged by the Congress to do so, or any other difficulties that militate against the performance of their statutory duties.

In a more coherent fashion than in the past, Congress could also display greater interest. Since such efforts have not been systematically made in the past, who can say that the commissions would turn a deaf ear?

What are the problems, in specific terms, that justify abandonment of the independent commission? Much of the response to that question has come in sweeping generalizations. Assertions regarding the extent of conflict between the commissions and the executive branch are often phrased in vague terms. Indeed the study which formed the basis of the Brownlow Committee report in 1937 conceded that the problem was something short of critical:

> The President and the Commissions have had their disagreements, but they are not chronically at loggerheads, and the commission can probably be counted upon to cooperate with the President most of the time. The important fact is, however, that they do not need to cooperate unless they wish, and the President cannot therefore, depend on that cooperation.

In other words, *potentially* the commissions could be obstinate and obstructive. Of course the independent commissions will have disagreements with the White House and Congress; is that not true of the Department of Agriculture, or the Environmental Protection Agency? But it is upon that kind of slender reed that Congress is asked to reverse its long-standing inclination toward the independent form.

On the grounds that the case had not been proved, the Administrative Conference in 1971 resisted the recommendation of the Ash Council that the independent form be abandoned. According to the [Conference], whatever deficiencies may exit "cannot be attributed solely or primarily to faulty structure", and the view that greater Executive integration "would solve regulatory problems is simplistic, unsupported by empirical data, and overlooks other plausible explanations of regulatory ills...."

In point of fact the argument against independence, as a Hoover Commission task force observed in 1949, frequently is "based mainly on theoretical or doctrinal grounds and not on actual failures of coordination or conflicts among agencies." Coordination is not of course a commandment, and instead is required only when it is justified. Coordination is necessary only to the extent that there are direct unresolved conflicts between, or unnecessary duplication of, agency functions. To a substantial extent, independent commissions exercise functions that are not closely related to the rest of government, and that require no extensive coordination. For example the regulation of security exchanges and issuance of new securities can be carried on by the Securities and Exchange Commission without active coordination by any other Federal department or agency. The same is true of other independent commissions.

The functions these commissions perform also lend justification to their independent status. These agencies, it is important to note, are themselves coordinating bodies for certain purposes.... For instance the matter of communications affects government very extensively; and the Federal Communications Commission is charged, not only with the responsibility of regulating the private sector in that regard, but also with overseeing federal uses of the airwaves. FCC coordinates the use of communications for the entire government.

Are these commissions in fact unaccountable, a kind of "miniature independent government" adrift without guidance or purpose? Our examination suggests that is not the case. As previously discussed, there are a series of formal limitations upon the independent status of the commissions: Congress charts their regulatory mandate in the statutes; OMB and the President examine and typically revise their budgets, which in turn are subject to adoption by Congress; OMB also reviews their recommendation concerning legislative action; [OMB] screens their information-gathering plans; the Justice Department coordinates, even conducts, their litigation; and the President with the advice and consent of the Senate appoints their commissioners. Indeed, unlike almost all top-level Executive Branch officials, agency chairmen are appointed solely by the President without Senate concurrence, and may be removed from that office for any reason by the White House. Thus the top official of the independent commissions is very much accountable to the President. As such, how much accuracy is there in the assertion that these agencies constitute a "headless 'fourth branch'"? To be sure, there is room for improvement. For example Congressional delegation of authority could be more narrow, and Congressional oversight could be more consistent and effective. The agencies could also be prompted,... toward more systematic review of their regulations and procedures. And... there may be appropriate mechanisms to assure Executive involvement without major infringements on agency independence. But the problems, such as they are, do not warrant radical measures. The situation does not, in our opinion, justify plans to integrate the commissions into the Executive Branch. . . .

Independence does have its positive advantages. First, and perhaps most important, these commissions exercise quasi-judicial functions in that they adjudicate and reach decisions on particular cases. That alone is sufficient justification for a status somewhat removed from direct control by the executive branch. Insulation from politics, a major historical justification for this form, remains today a further reason for independent status. Adjudicatory decisions should be made absolutely on the merits, without regard to partisan considerations and priorities. The White House should not be empowered to direct decisions on who should receive a public license, or privilege or whether a certain regulation ought to be enforced. . . .

In addition Presidential commissions would necessarily mean that the policies of those bodies would change with the occupant of the White House; regulation, affecting as it does major aspects of the economy, ought not be subject to such abrupt changes. The multiple membership of these agencies, with terms expiring at staggered intervals, does tend to serve as a buffer against Presidential control and direction. Finally the notion of government officials gaining expertise as a result of comparatively lengthy terms is not without validity. The turnover for commissions . . . is considerably less frequent than that of executive officials serving at the pleasure of the President. Experience gained from that longer service undoubtedly serves the public interest.

In 1972, Congress was convinced of the advantages of the independent form when it created the Consumer Product Safety Commission, the first independent regulatory commission to be established by legislation since the New Deal. . . . The decision for an independent commission, according to the House Interstate and Foreign Commerce Committee, reflected the belief—

> . . . that an independent agency can better carry out the legislative and judicial functions contained in this bill with the cold neutrality that the public has a right to expect of regulatory agencies formed for its protection. [The independent form] will tend to provide greater insulation from political and economic pressures than is possible or likely in a cabinet-level department.

A new agency lodged within an existing department was not considered the most effective approach. To the contrary, "creation of a new independent agency," the House committee declared, "will assure that the regulatory program contained in this bill will be highly visible to get off to a firm and vigorous start." The committee doubted whether the Administration's proposal [to place it in the executive branch] would accomplish that objective:

> . . . it has been the committee's experience that when regulatory programs are placed in Executive Departments which have broad and diverse responsibilities, the regulatory effort has typically suffered from a lack of adequate funding and staffing. This has often been the result of the regulatory program's inability to compete effectively with other deserving programs within the Department or to gain public attention and support.

. . . With all that said, however, there may be particular instances where a greater degree of regular executive coordination is both appropriate and necessary. Executive *control* may be advisable when regulatory policy significantly affects foreign policy matters. As regards certain regulatory functions, this is already the case. For example, the actions of the International Trade Commission are required to be regularly presented to the President for his consideration. To cite another example, the Nuclear Non-Proliferation Act of 1977 requires Presidential involvement in the export licensing process of the Nuclear Regulatory Commission, to assure that a proposed export would not be inimical to the common defense and security. Thus regulatory action, which has a direct and substantial relationship to foreign policy, may appropriately be subject to Presidential review and direction....

What are the appropriate circumstances for the creation of an independent regulatory commission? It is a question that admits of no definite answer outside the context of a given situation. Even strictly regulatory tasks involving quasi-judicial functions need not necessarily be vested in an independent collegial structure. The Agriculture Department as well as other executive agencies, such as the EPA, are proof of that proposition. In no small part it depends on who is creating the structure: Presidents have generally tended toward a single administrator form, while Congress has an inclination favoring multimember commissions; but neither branch has consistently favored one structure over the other. A decision on structure is after all a political issue, very much influenced by the prevailing political situation. And that situation can neither be quantified nor predicted.

Yet, there are general guidelines drawn from past experience which do merit consideration in such structural decisions. Chief among them is the relative importance to be attached to group decision-making. A commission form obviously requires a majority vote for adoption of policy. Necessarily one commissioner must convince his fellow members of the desirability of a course of action—a process that usually and properly involves compromise and accommodation of varying viewpoints and opinions. On the other hand, a single administrator does not need the approval, as such, of other members of his agency in order to act.... In certain situations group deliberation in a nonpartisan setting requires a commission form. One obvious example is federal supervision of communications. There it is generally agreed that the commission form is appropriate. Even the Ash Council, which argued forcefully for abolition of the commission, conceded that a collegial form was needed for communications oversight. Under the heading, "A Structure for Impartiality," the Council concluded:

> A single administrator for the Federal Communications Commission would be in an exceptionally vulnerable position which, because of its appearances, could impair public trust. The public is entitled to assume that the information it obtains through the broadcast media is not distorted by the political perspectives of the party in favor.

Other responsibilities suggest the appropriateness of the commission form. For example the power to award long-term licenses among competing applicants, or to set rates and prices for commodities is often thought to require a collegial body; group decision-making is considered appropriate for that authority. The rate-fixing consideration was of pivotal importance in the recent decision by Congress to establish the new Federal Energy Regulatory Commission. As this Committee's report on that measure stated, "No single official should have sole responsibility for both proposing and setting such prices" for oil and natural gas....

In summary the Committee believes that the independent status of the regulatory commissions should be continued.

However, the situation concerning the characteristics of independence is, at present, confusing. In a patchwork, even haphazard fashion, certain independent regulatory commissions have been excepted, sometimes for only specific purposes, from certain requirements of central coordination. That is the case with budget clearance, legislative message review, and the process by which top staff officials of those agencies are selected. It has required a detailed study to determine which of those agencies are subject to which requirements. In only one area, the gathering of information from the public, is an exception given to the commissions as a group.

We believe the situation warrants a single piece of legislation. To as great an extent as possible, that legislation should apply at least to the eleven independent regulatory commissions [Board of Governors of the Federal Reserve System; Civil Aeronautics Board; Commodity Futures Trading Commission; Consumer Product Safety Commission; Federal Communications Commission; Federal Maritime Commission; Federal Energy Regulatory Commission; Federal Trade Commission; Interstate Commerce Commission; Nuclear Regulatory Commission; and the Securities and Exchange Commission]. . . .

The major components of that proposal would include:

(1) The selection by the independent regulatory commissions of individuals for positions classed as schedule "C" or Noncareer Executive Assignments would not be subject to clearance or approval by any executive branch official. . . .

(2) Independent regulatory commissions located outside executive departments should concurrently transmit to Congress any budget request, testimony or comments, intended for the legislative branch, at the same time they are submitted to an official or agency of the executive department.

(3) Legislative messages originating with independent regulatory commissions and intended for submission to Congress should be exempted from prior clearance by any official or agency of the executive branch.

(4) The independent regulatory commissions should be authorized to sue and be sued, in their own name and by their own attorneys, in any civil actions brought in connection with their jurisdiction and functions. That authority should apply to all civil cases, other than those before the Supreme Court.

---

1. Who has the better of the argument, the proponents of consolidation or those of independence? Or is each right some of the time?

2. Do the Senate Committee's justifications for independence rise to *constitutional* distinctions? Put another way, what is the *minimum* residuum of executive control required by the Constitution? Appointment only?

3. How do removal powers bear on issues of supervision? Does the President's "faithful execution" obligation encompass more than a duty to assure the sobriety and punctuality of federal officers? Is removal, in any event, a good management tool? Putting aside the imposition of policy, how should the President react when a commission puts out sloppily reasoned decisions after prolonged and unjustified delays? Should he remove some or all of the commissioners? Demote the chair? What if he considers the delays unjustified, but the results good, or vice versa?

Among recent presidential efforts to impose some overall coordination on regulation, the Reagan Administration has adopted the most ambitious program, as explained by Professor Shane, in *Presidential Regulatory Oversight and the Separation of Powers: The Constitutionality of Executive Order No. 12,291*, 23 Ariz. L.Rev. 1235, 1235-42 (1981):

> Executive Order No. 12,291, "Federal Regulation," requires executive agencies, to the extent permitted by statute, to observe cost-benefit principles in implementing regulations. In order to assure agency compliance for regulations that have a significant effect on the economy, the order requires executive agencies also to evaluate proposed "major rules" according to a prescribed "regulatory impact analysis." ... [W]ith the Reagan order, the President has finally both articulated a set of overarching policy principles to guide the regulatory process and explicitly required his subordinates to be bound by those principles to the extent permitted by law. The order is not a break with the past in that, through it, the President attempts to assert significant control over administrative rulemaking. Rather, the key innovations of Executive Order No. 12,291 are the mandatory character of the requirements it imposes and the comprehensive management system that the order creates to effect the President's goals. ... The most notable of the new provisions are the requirements in section 3 of the order for agencies to issue preliminary and final Regulatory Impact Analyses (RIA's) in connection with "major rules." An RIA must include statements of the anticipated costs and benefits of the proposed major rule, the anticipated incidence of those costs and benefits, the net anticipated benefits of the regulation, and other potentially more cost-effective regulatory possibilities, with an explanation, if appropriate, of the legal reasons why the most cost-effective means of achieving the anticipated benefits cannot be adopted. The cost-benefit analysis mandated by the order expressly requires the inclusion of beneficial or adverse regulatory effects that cannot be quantified in monetary terms. ...
>
> A second category of requirements, appearing in section 2 of the order, is most clearly substantive in nature. [S]ection 2 requires agencies, to the extent permitted by law, to "adhere" to five general principles "[i]n promulgating new regulations, reviewing existing regulations, and developing legislative proposals concerning regulation." These principles require agencies to base administrative decisions on "adequate information concerning the need for and consequences of proposed government action" and to set regulatory objectives, order regulatory priorities, and undertake regulatory action in a way that will maximize the net benefits to society when costs and benefits are compared.
>
> These provisions, as drafted, do not dictate particular regulatory decisions. Even in a particular context, they may do no more than set a range of permissible options, rather than pointing to a necessary result. The terms "cost" and "benefit" are not defined by the order, and the mandatory inclusion of even unquantifiable costs and benefits in the required calculus can afford agencies significant leeway in exercising their own policy judgment in identifying the beneficial or adverse effects of regulation.
>
> The section 2 principles are, however, expressly intended to require agencies to weigh competing values in a particular direction and to be prepared to justify regulatory decisions according to a generally prescribed form of analysis. In this sense, section 2 is not neutrally "procedural." Its requirements would ob-

viously be of no effect if agencies did not treat them as foreclosing at least some regulatory possibilities....

[A]n agency must transmit each proposed major rule, together with a preliminary RIA, to the Director of OMB sixty days prior to the publication of any notice of proposed rulemaking. The Director then has sixty days to review such a submission, and may require the agency to consult with him concerning the preliminary RIA and notice of proposed rulemaking, and to refrain, subject to judicial or statutory deadlines, from publishing its proposal until the Director's review is concluded.... The prospects of protracted high-level "jawboning" and delay in the regulatory process may be effective sanctions to procure agency compliance with OMB regulatory policy. The potential exists, in particular cases, for the Director to abuse his discretion and overstep his legal authority despite the order's general provision that the Director's review powers shall not "be construed as displacing the agencies' responsibilities delegated by law."

See also Sunstein, *Cost-Benefit Analysis and the Separation of Powers*, 23 Ariz. L.Rev. 1267 (1981).

Before the executive order was issued, the Assistant Attorney General for the Office of Legal Counsel issued the following opinion, on February 12, 1981, concluding that the proposed order was legal on its face, and could be applied to the independent agencies if the President chose to do so (which he did not):

Memorandum for Honorable David Stockman Director, Office of Management and Budget

Re: Proposed Executive Order on Federal Regulation

. . . I. *Legal Authority: Executive Branch Agencies*

The President's authority to issue the proposed Executive Order derives from his constitutional power to "take Care that the Laws be faithfully executed." U.S. Const., Art. II. § 3. It is well established that this provision authorizes the President, as head of the Executive Branch, to "supervise and guide" Executive officers in "their construction of the statutes under which they act in order to secure that unitary and uniform execution of the laws which Article II of the Constitution evidently contemplated in vesting general executive power in the President alone." *Myers v. United States*, 272 U.S. 52, 135 (1926).[1]

The supervisory authority recognized by *Myers* is based on the distinctive constitutional role of the President. The "take Care" clause charges the President with the function of coordinating the execution of many statutes simultaneously: "Unlike an administrative commission confined to the enforcement of the statute under which it was created ... the President is a constitutional officer charged with taking care that a 'mass of legislation' be executed," *Youngstown Sheet & Tube Co. v. Sawyer*, 343 U.S. 579, 702 (1952) (Vinson, C.J., dissenting). Moreover, because the President is the only elected official who has a national constituency, he is uniquely situated to

---

1. In *Buckley v. Valeo*, 424 U.S. 1, 140-41 (1976), the Supreme Court held that any "significant governmental duty exercised pursuant to a public law" must be performed by an "Officer of the United States," appointed by the President or the Head of a Department pursuant to Art. II, § 2, cl. 2. We believe that this holding recognizes the importance of preserving the President's supervisory powers over those exercising statutory duties, subject of course to the power of Congress to confine presidential supervision by appropriate legislation.

design and execute a uniform method for undertaking regulatory initiatives that responds to the will of the public as a whole. In fulfillment of the President's constitutional responsibilities, the proposed Order promotes a coordinated system of regulation, ensuring a measure of uniformity in the interpretation and execution of a number of diverse statutes. If no such guidance were permitted, confusion and inconsistency could result as agencies interpreted open-ended statutes in differing ways.

Nevertheless, it is clear that the President's exercise of supervisory powers must conform to legislation enacted by Congress.[3] In issuing directives to govern the Executive Branch, the President may not, as a general proposition, require or permit agencies to transgress boundaries set by Congress. *Youngstown Sheet & Tube Co. v. Sawyer*, 343 U.S. 579 (1952). It is with these basic precepts in mind that the proposed Order must be approached.

We believe that an inquiry into congressional intent in enacting statutes delegating rulemaking authority will usually support the legality of presidential supervision of rulemaking by Executive Branch agencies. When Congress delegates legislative power to Executive Branch agencies, it is aware that those agencies perform their functions subject to presidential supervision on matters of both substance and procedure. This is not to say that Congress never intends in a specific case to restrict presidential supervision of an Executive agency; but it should not be presumed to have done so whenever it delegates rulemaking power directly to a subordinate Executive Branch official rather than the President. Indeed, after *Myers* it is unclear to what extent Congress may insulate Executive Branch agencies from presidential supervision. Congress is also aware of the comparative insulation given to the independent regulatory agencies, and it has delegated rulemaking authority to such agencies when it has sought to minimize presidential interference. By contrast, the heads of non-independent agencies hold their positions at the pleasure of the President, who may remove them from office for any reason. It would be anomalous to attribute to Congress an intention to immunize from presidential supervision those who are, by force of Art. II, subject to removal when their performance in exercising their statutory duties displeases the President.... This Office has often taken the position that the President may consult with those having statutory decisionmaking responsibilities, and may require them to consider statutorily relevant matters that he deems appropriate, as long as the President does not divest the officer of ultimate statutory authority. Of course, the President has the authority to inform an appointee that he will be discharged if he fails to base his decisions on policies the President seeks to implement....

We believe that the President would not exceed any limitations on his authority by authorizing the ... Director to supervise agency rulemaking as the Order would provide. The Order does not empower the Director ... to displace the relevant agencies in discharging their statutory functions or in assessing and weighing the costs and benefits of proposed actions. The function of the Director would be supervisory in nature. It would include such tasks as the supplementation of factual data, the development and implementation of uniform systems of methodology, the identification of incorrect statements of fact, and the placement in the administrative record of a statement disapproving agency conclusions that do not appear to conform to the

---

3. In certain circumstances, statutes could invade or intrude impermissibly upon the President's "inherent" powers, but that issue does not arise here.

principles expressed in the President's Order. Procedurally, the Director . . . would be authorized to require an agency to defer rulemaking while it responded to . . . statements of disapproval of proposed agency action. This power of consultation would not, however, include authority to reject an agency's ultimate judgment, delegated to it by law, that potential benefits outweigh costs, that priorities under the statute compel a particular course of action, or that adequate information is available to justify regulation. . . .

II. *Independent Regulatory Commissions*

We now consider whether the proposed Order may legally be applied to the independent regulatory commissions in certain respects. Principally, the Order would require independent agencies to prepare RIA's and would authorize the Director or the Task Force to exercise limited supervision over the RIA's. For reasons stated below, we believe that, under the best view of the law, these and some other requirements of the Order can be imposed on the independent agencies. We would emphasize, however, that an attempt to exercise supervision of these agencies through techniques such as those in the proposed Order would be lawful only if the Supreme Court is prepared to repudiate certain expansive dicta in the leading case on the subject, and that an attempt to infringe the autonomy of the independent agencies is very likely to produce a confrontation with Congress, which has historically been jealous of its prerogatives with regard to them. . . .

The holding of *Humphrey's Executor* is that Congress may constitutionally require cause for the removal of an FTC Commissioner; the Court's opinion, however, contains broad dicta endorsing a perceived congressional purpose to insulate the FTC almost entirely from Presidential supervision. . . .

If the dicta of *Humphrey's Executor* are taken at face value, the President's constitutional power to supervise the independent agencies is limited to his power of appointment, and none of the proposed Order's requirements may legally be applied to the independent agencies. We believe, however, that there are several reasons to conclude that the Supreme Court would today retreat from these dicta. First, the Court in *Humphrey's Executor* and *Wiener* focused primarily on the inappropriateness of Presidential interference in agency adjudication, a concern not pertinent to supervision of rulemaking. Second, insofar as the Court was concerned about rulemaking, it did not take account of the fact that Executive Branch and independent agencies engage in rulemaking in a functionally indistinguishable fashion. Third, the Court espoused what is now an outmoded view about the "apolitical" nature of regulation. It is now recognized that rulemaking may legitimately reflect political influences of certain kinds from a number of sources, including Congress and the affected public. Fourth, the President has today a number of statutory powers over the independent agencies, which recognize the legitimacy of his influence in their activities. . . .

We believe that the foregoing constitutional and statutory analysis supports the application to the independent agencies of those portions of the Order that would be extended to them. The principal requirement is that independent agencies prepare RIA's. These analyses would have only an indirect effect on substantive discretion, since the identification of costs and benefits and the particular balance struck would be for the agency to make. It should also be possible for OMB to prescribe criteria for independent agencies to follow in preparing their RIA's, to consult with them in the process, and to disagree with an independent agency's analysis on the administrative record. None of these actions would directly displace the agencies' ultimate discretion to decide what rule best fulfills their statutory responsibilities....

1. Is Executive Order No. 12,291 lawful on its face? What constitutional support exists for the reportorial requirements of Sections 4 and 5 of the order? For the substantive provisions of Section 2? For analyses of the legal issues surrounding the executive order, *see* Symposium, *Cost-Benefit Analysis and Agency Decision-Making: An Analysis of Executive Order No. 12,291*, 23 Ariz. L.Rev. 1195 (1981). The debate continues: *compare* Morrison, *OMB Interference with Agency Rulemaking: The Wrong Way to Write a Regulation*, 99 Harv. L. Rev. 1059 (1986), *with* DeMuth & Ginsburg, *White House Review of Agency Rulemaking, id.* at 1075.

2. Note that, if lawful, the order would be most potent in application to programs operating under broad delegations. For an argument favoring broad statutory delegations precisely because they facilitate political accountability to the President, *see* Mashaw, *Prodelegation: Why Administrators Should Make Political Decisions*, 1 Yale J. of Law, Econ. & Org. 81 (1985).

3. Could the order be applied to independent agencies? (The definition of "agency" in §1(d) of the final version of the order excludes what are commonly considered the independent regulatory commissions from its purview.) Here, consider the views of Professor Miller, quoted *supra* after *Bowsher*, that the President may order members of the independent agencies to take any action within their statutory authority. Is he right? If so, were OLC and the President too timid? What advice would you give the President on whether he *should* apply the order to the independent agencies, assuming that he has the power to do so?

4. The implementation of the order involves considerable intra-branch ex parte contacts. To what extent are these legally problematic after *Sierra Club v. Costle*? What advice would you give OMB regarding ex parte contacts with agencies before, during, and after the comment period in informal rulemaking? *See* Verkuil, *Jawboning Administrative Agencies: Ex Parte Contacts by the White House*, 80 Colum. L. Rev. 943 (1980).

5. In analyzing the order under *Youngstown*, what weight should be given to Congress' statutory decisions to vest regulatory authority under various programs in officers other than the President? Of what relevance is it that the APA does not provide for any centralized presidential review of executive agency rulemaking? On these questions, *see* Shane, *supra*, at 1255-62. Would a court deem it relevant to constitutional analysis that, since issuance of the order, Congress has—without questioning the order—exempted an administrative decision from its requirements? Marine Mammal Protection Act of 1972 Amendments, § 4(d)(2), Pub. L. No. 97-58, 95 Stat. 984 (1981). What is the relevance of continuing appropriations for the administering office of OMB, the OIRA?

6. In assessing the wisdom of the order, it is necessary to consider the institutional capacity of the Executive Office of the President to oversee executive branch regulatory activity. George Eads, a member of President Carter's Council of Economic Advisers and chairman of the Regulatory Analysis Review Group established under Exec. Order No. 12,044, offered a skeptical early view in *Harnessing Regulation: The Evolving Role of White House Oversight*, Regulation, May-June 1981, at 19. Eads questioned whether OMB has the staff resources to muster the kind of analytical capability

necessary to monitor agency performance, overcome agency bias, coordinate rules according to a set of national economic priorities, and raise important new issues for agency consideration. Eads expressed concern also with OMB's credibility in providing regulatory analysis independent of foregone political conclusions, as well as with the potential strain on agency resources and the likely flowering of ex parte contacts at the expense of meaningful public input.

7. A wide range of policymakers, by 1980, had come to question whether many federal economic and social regulatory schemes were well-structured to achieve useful ends at the lowest possible cost. To the extent this criticism is justified, of course, regulatory reform efforts aimed merely at better coordinating executive branch rule-making under existing programs would be insufficient to accomplish the more substantive objectives of Executive Order No. 12,291. Indeed, one commentator feared that White House concentration on administrative reform, and the Reagan administration's insistence on publicly focusing on the usefulness of regulatory "relief" for business, may have squandered political opportunities for achieving substantive legislative change—the key to long-run regulatory reform. Crandall, *Has Reagan Dropped the Ball?*, Regulation, Sep./Oct. 1981, at 15.

8. Section 9 of the order provides that it "is intended only to improve the internal management of the Federal government, and is not intended to create any right or benefit, substantive or procedural, enforceable at law...." Review the *Note: Private Enforcement of Executive Orders* in Chapter Two. Should the President be allowed to control whether his subordinates' compliance with his directions is judicially reviewable? What is the source of existing limitations on judicial review of compliance with executive orders—the Constitution, prudential concerns, or a reading of presidential intent? For an argument in favor of limited judicial review, *see* Raven-Hansen, *Making Agencies Follow Orders: Judicial Review of Agency Violations of Executive Order 12,291*, 1983 Duke L.J. 285. Assuming that no statute expressly authorizes the order, could the President have authorized courts to invalidate rules found to be inconsistent with its requirements?

9. Notice that the OLC memorandum makes a series of assumptions about the nature of the program's actual operation. Are these assumptions critical to the legality of the program as applied, on either statutory or constitutional grounds? For analysis of the program in operation and its place in the Reagan administration's overall approach to regulation, *see* G. Eads & M. Fix, Relief or Reform? Reagan's Regulatory Dilemma (1984). *See also* Olson, *The Quiet Shift of Power: Office of Management & Budget Supervision of Environmental Protection Agency Rulemaking Under Executive Order 12,291*, 4 Va. J. of Nat'l Res. L. 1 (1984).

Subsequently, Executive Order No. 12,498 was promulgated to establish a "regulatory planning process." The order requires the head of each executive agency to send OMB a "draft regulatory program" that describes "all significant regulatory actions" to be undertaken within the next year. OMB reviews the plan for consistency with administration policy, and a final plan is published. *See* Note, *Presidential Policy Management of Agency Rules Under Reagan Order 12,498*, 38 Admin. L. Rev. 63 (1986). As seen by Strauss & Sunstein, *The Role of the President and OMB in Informal Rulemaking*, 38 Ad. L. Rev. 181, 187-88 (1986), Executive Order 12,498 supplements the earlier order by giving agency heads and OMB more power over the early stages of the regulatory process, thus diminishing the capacity of agency staff components to develop a regulatory initiative to the point that it develops a constituency—and a life—of its own:

> [The orders respond to the] perception that agency heads are, to an undesirable degree, the captives of their own staffs rather than politically powerful managers of agency business. Courts have created a number of techniques to attempt to respond to this problem, including review to ensure that the benefits of regulation are roughly commensurate with the costs. The value of such techniques is, however, severely diminished by institutional limits of the courts, which are not well-equipped to calculate the costs and benefits of regulatory initiatives and are incapable of imposing a hierarchical or coordinative structure. The orders represent an effort to deal with the general problem of uncoordinated and insufficiently accountable administrative decisions.
>
> While the orders on their surface mark a major enhancement of presidential authority, a significant element of their attractiveness lies in their potential to expand the effective authority, accountability, and oversight capacity of the agency head. This potential is particularly strong for Executive Order 12,498. Requiring the development of an agency regulatory plan should have the same effect on the regulatory side as requiring agency presentation of a budget request does for fiscal planning. It will provide an annual opportunity for the agency head to focus on the work of her agency in a planning rather than a reactive mode, stressing broad vision and priority setting, and involving her early enough that one may expect her to have a significant impact on options considered. Fewer staff deals will have been cut. The requirement of early disclosure of plans—through ventilation of alternatives (in the case of Executive Order 12,291) and annual statement of the regulatory plan (in the case of Executive Order 12,498)—is thus a means of ensuring that regulatory policy is set by agency heads rather than staffs. In this respect, the two orders may be understood, not only as efforts to enhance presidential or OMB power as against agencies, but also as a means of enhancing the agency head's effective control over her staff.

How have the executive orders worked in practice? Here is the appraisal of a panel of the National Academy of Public Administration, which conducted a study.

Presidential Management of Rulemaking in Regulatory Agencies

National Academy of Public Administration 25-28, 33-35 (1987)

The federal district court for the District of Columbia, in ruling on a 1985 challenge to OMB review of EPA regulations, . . . concluded that OMB's use of its review powers to "withhold approval until the acceptance of certain content in the promulgation of any new EPA regulation, thereby encroaching upon the independence and expertise of EPA" was "incompatible with the will of Congress and cannot be sustained as a valid exercise of the President's Article II powers" (*Environmental Defense Fund v. Thomas*, 627 F.Supp. 566, D.D.C. 1986, at 570).

Critics of OMB argue that it has displaced agency authority to make the final decisions on regulations, in violation of congressional mandates. They contrast the broad statutory language of Congress that champions aggressive regulatory intervention with OMB's bias against new regulations, its preoccupation with regulatory costs and burdens, and its emphasis on regulatory relief. Defenders of OMB respond by referring to the language in E.O. 12291 (Sec. 3(f)(3)) declaring that OMB's role shall not be "construed as displacing the agencies' responsibilities delegated by law." The Department of Justice filed a brief in *Environmental Defense Fund v. Thomas* arguing that OMB review under E.O. 12291 was advisory only and agencies were free to ignore OMB, although in practice it does not appear that agencies are really in a position to do so.

. . . [W]e have had to reach a judgment based on staff interviews with participants at all levels of the regulatory review process. From these discussions, we conclude that reality lies somewhere in the middle [of the opposing claims]. OMB arguments are more than advisory but still less than mandatory. The review process is more one of negotiation and accommodation than of agency initiatives being overruled by OMB demands. Agencies are not monolithic, and political appointees frequently differ with career employees. While rule-writers may believe that agency management has caved into OMB pressure, the situation may be more complex. Senior administrators may acquiesce to OMB concerns for a variety of reasons. They may simply agree with OMB's analysis of costs and benefits. They may wish to appear supportive of the administration's position. They may find that a management perspective requires that they take into account a broader range of factors than those considered by agency scientists. Agency economists involved in internal regulatory review efforts may also agree with OMB's analyses of costs and benefits.

OMB officials emphasize the limitations on their power. Robert Bedell, who has served as Deputy Administrator of OIRA, argues that, "If we try to push something that is not authorized in the statute or is precluded, the agencies will say no; they have batteries of lawyers and are quick to tell us. Ninety percent of the time they are wrong. . . . The final resolution will be by the Department of Justice. . . . However, if we tell the agency head not to do something, it is his decision as to what to do. He can go ahead and do it. He can appeal it to the Cabinet Council; he can appeal to [OMB Director] Jim Miller; he can talk to us and ask us what we mean. The authority to proceed is the agency head's." Former OIRA head James Tozzi agrees: "OMB does not have extreme power. . . . OMB has a heavy burden to state why we disagree; an agency outnumbers OMB by an order of magnitude in resources; they outgun us on data and research money. . . . Constituent groups and the press provide external pressure." Miller, however, has also characterized OIRA as "the toughest kid on the block" and he has been known to remind agency officials of the considerable power of OMB behind the regulatory review process.

Many agency officials reject the idea that OMB forces them to take illegal actions. As one official put it, "The department is not doing something that is illegal or not what it wants. . . . No agency will do anything it thinks is wrong. It just tries to balance a lot of things. After we beat our heads against the wall, we are not forced to do anything we don't want to do. At higher levels, reasonable heads prevail." Mid-level agency officials argue that while changes in regulations may only be made officially by administrators, the impetus for the change comes from OMB rather than from agency determinations.

Officials at the agency level agreed on OMB's political power but disagreed on whether it has been abused. One agency official said, "It is a myth that OMB's 'heavy hand' is directing the agencies...." Others thought OMB powerhungry: "OMB's shadow is over all government operations." Several agency officials believed that OMB simply opposed all new rulemaking activity, regardless of what a particular rule might do....

Speaking for OMB, Deputy Director Joseph R. Wright justified the process in terms of the president's responsibility for policy leadership:

> We are trying to change the way people have been operating for years, and people don't like it.... The fact is, there's no management system; Congress orders money to be spent before a management system is in effect.... Look at history. We have not been able to control ourselves as a federal government. There is need for institutionalizing the reform. Political appointees need to make an impact on how career people operate and then institutionalize the changes or they won't last....

Different perspectives produce differing descriptions of the process. Is OMB biased against regulations or just asking questions? OMB officials indicate that both are happening. They want to improve the quality of the analysis, but also assume that agencies are too regulatory-minded and need to be reined in. Wendy Gramm, administrator of OIRA, has argued that,

> There are so many pressures to take care of special interests. The job of the bureaucracy [and Congress] is to take care of special interests. The president, in contrast, is elected to represent the people. He can take competing demands and balance them.... [OIRA's] task is to provide a management backstop to agency heads....

OIRA's critics argue, in response, that OIRA's review efforts are susceptible to special-interest intervention and provide opportunities for representatives of regulated industries to circumvent the rulemaking process.

One agency official described the difficulty of disagreeing with OMB when there is no outside support: "We are not too willing to challenge OMB. Agencies are political creatures in a political environment.... If Congress comes along with a bill, we would be more willing to take on OMB. But there is a tacit acquiescence by Congress and the courts, so we go along."...

Others find themselves torn because they want to be "team players" yet still carry out their agency's traditional mission. The result is compromise: "A couple of times, OMB has been burned—[the Secretary] has gone over their heads. But [the Secretary] wants to support the administration and is hesitant to do that.... We try to cooperate and work things out and avoid confrontation... Sometimes rules [provide less protection] than they would have without OMB, but some things are not worth fighting."...

Gramm and Bedell see the review process in a different light. Bedell said, "Because of the review process, [agency heads and senior officials in the departments] can give a rule a different level of attention, analysis and thought. They can give it the judgment that the President and Congress expect. They need to exercise their political judgment and we are better off when they do that. The system makes it better. The further the decision making is from the head of an agency, the more parochial the judgment becomes. At the top level, they are driven by the pure weighing of the record against their exercise of judgment. They are more accountable than those down in the program areas." Gramm believes the real cause of dissension might be that regulatory review deals with rules that allow special interests to "collect rents through governmental action." Regulatory review is a strong management tool to protect the broad public interest when congressional and agency intent is to accommodate special interests.

An independent agency official who has extensive dealings with Congress pointed to the difficulties arising from the legislative-executive struggle: "The whole process makes policy-making so much more difficult. If you assume each decision will be litigated, is it a decision or a first offer in a political forum?" He described unified "congressional intent" as an illusion:

> We have two oversight committees on subject matter and they don't hesitate to get involved. Individual Congressmen also write letters and say their view is the view of the Congress.... The Senate and House will pass one statute and it is binding. Then we get the views of one subcommittee as to what the views should be or murky legislation we have to interpret. What are we to do? Each can say we are defying the will of Congress.... We can be held hostage on the budget. Or they can put 'shall not do' in appropriations language or put language in committee reports....

This view, in essence, was shared by an agency official: "The big question is who is your boss? Agencies are caught between Congress—statutes—and the President—OMB."...

Other comments indicate that... the agency does what it really wants to so long as it holds out: "The problem is not results but process. Substantive questions are eventually dealt with. OMB can balk at certain areas and the agency will have to endure. If you endure long enough, you can get what you want. If you endure, that shows the thing was important."...

An OMB staff member described the process as merely reasonable: "OMB dilutes agency authority and requires another set of compromises. But the purpose is important—to represent the President's point of view."... One agency official spoke for others when she described the reality of the process: "There is always some give and take in any negotiations process. Tradeoffs are done on the margin. We [OMB and the agency] both have several issues and we need to come to closure and have to compromise. I am determined to have two things and will compromise on the third. ... They [OMB] do the same kind of compromising.... We discuss, then go back to the agency, and decide on our points. I sometimes tell OMB that they have to give in or escalate. In some cases we give in and in others they give in. OMB's role is somewhere between advisory and mandating...."

A second kind of threat to statutory integrity and the rule of law lies in the possibility that the principles serving as the basis of OMB review of regulations conflict with statutory provisions. Executive Order 12291 establishes several requirements that agencies must satisfy "to the extent permitted by law." Regulatory actions are to be based on a consideration of alternative regulatory approaches that "maximize the net benefits to society," rely on the "alternative involving the least net cost to society," and have "potential benefits that outweigh the potential costs to society."

These criteria have the potential for conflicting with some statutes in the area of environmental, health, and safety regulation. The primary source of conflict is determining when agencies can consider compliance costs in formulating regulations. In a relatively few cases, such as the Delaney clause of the Food and Drug Act and section 112 of the Clean Air Act, the statutes clearly mandate regulatory action for substances that are shown to be harmful to animal or human life without considerations of cost. Critics of such statutes argue that dramatic advances in the ability to detect increasingly minute levels of dangerous substances render these legal mandates obsolete or unrealistic.

In other cases, statutes discuss health and protection concerns but are silent on costs. The EPA, for example, in regulating stationary sources of pollution, is directed by law to issue regulations that provide "an ample margin of safety to protect public health." . . . It is not clear to what extent agencies can consider factors neither expressly mandated or prohibited by law. . . .

Executive Order 12498 emphasizes the idea that the president can order agencies to give primary attention to economic considerations in regulatory decisionmaking even more explicitly than does E.O. 12291. . . . The regulatory program prepared each year by agencies is to "explain how each new activity will carry out the regulatory policies of this Administration and specify the agency's plan for reviewing and revising existing regulatory programs to bring them into accord with Administration policies." OMB review of the regulatory program is to "focus on consistency with general Administration policy." Absent is the qualifier that the review process is to be limited "to the extent permitted by law." Regulations are to be formulated with an eye to the goals of the administration as well as those of the statutes.

Critics have argued that OMB, in practice, dictates the contents of the Regulatory Program rather than accepting the recommendations of the agency heads. They point to numerous examples where agency submissions for studies and data collection were rejected by OMB without public discussion and debate over the need for the information. . . .

The OMB regulatory review process raises the potential for conflict with the idea of due process and specific provisions of the APA. . . . [True,] the review process permits at least a technical compliance with the formal standards of the law. The agency still takes full legal responsibility for the ultimate action. If OMB criticisms and complaints cause the agency to issue regulations that differ from what it would have done absent the OMB review, the agency must still provide justification for its final rule in the rulemaking record. . . . As long as agencies are acting within the discretion given them by law, the relative influence of OMB and other factors is neither possible to define nor legally significant. It is possible, however, that OMB might pressure agencies to take into account factors that are inconsistent with those mandated by statute. While OMB officials deny that this occurs, critics disagree. If there is an adequate rulemaking record, reviewing courts can compare the statutorily-mandated factors with those provided by the agency.

OMB pressure that results in changes in a regulation can to some extent defeat the purpose of the rulemaking record. That record is designed to trace the reasoning and analysis that led to the agency action, but a record that is written to justify the original agency proposal may not fully explain the factors that were the subject of negotiation with OMB and are the basis for the amended decision. Perhaps it is unrealistic to expect that the rulemaking record will reflect perfectly the actual evaluation of a regulation, even absent OMB review, but the review may operate to push agency practices even further from the ideal. . . .

A second problem posed by OMB review is that the arguments raised by OMB officials themselves or by others who transmit them through OMB are not always made part of the rulemaking record or provided early enough for interested parties to enter their comments and response. Since OMB-agency interaction is largely oral, and may take place after the close of the public comment period, those wishing to respond to the claims raised by OMB are unable to do so. If the OMB review process causes an agency to take no action, there is no rulemaking record, no formal means of monitoring OMB's intervention. When OMB refuses to approve agency proposals submitted under E.O. 12498, affected parties have no legal recourse to challenge OMB actions, which leaves them only the option of suing the agency for failing to act. But the Supreme Court has ruled that agency decisions to not initiate a rulemaking effort that are "committed to agency discretion by law" are immune from judicial review (*Heckler v. Chaney*, 84 L. Ed. 2d. 714, 1985)....

In June 1986, OMB announced refinements in regulatory review procedures to address some of these concerns. OIRA would henceforth make available copies of draft advance notice of proposed rulemakings (ANPRMs), notice of proposed rulemakings (NPRMs), and final rules that are submitted to OIRA for review under E.O. 12291 and copies of all correspondence between OIRA and agency heads related to that review following publication of the ANPR, the NPRM, or final rule in the *Federal Register*. It agreed to send agencies copies of "all written material" concerning regulations received "from persons who are not employees of the federal government," would advise agencies of all "oral communications" concerning their rules received from persons outside the federal government, and would invite agency personnel to attend meetings with such persons concerning their rules. OIRA would provide on request copies of agency submissions under E.O. 12498, following publication of the final Regulatory Agenda, and lists, at the end of each calendar month, of all draft ANPRM's, NPRMs, and final rules for which OMB had completed review under E.O. 12291. It would make available in its public reading room written materials and lists of pertinent meetings and communications involving persons outside the federal government.

These new procedures ameliorate some, but not all, of the conflicts between OMB review and the APA-based standards of due process. OMB disapprovals of proposed pre-rulemaking actions, for example, are not documented; hence no judicial review is possible nor is the decision subjected to debate and discussion involving outside groups. The new procedures, according to one congressional subcommittee analysis, continue to fall short. They fail to, for example, (1) require a summary of oral communication between agency and OMB officials on draft rules or the agency's draft regulatory agenda; (2) require the disclosure of draft rules which are returned for reconsideration following OMB review or withdrawn by an agency following OMB review; (3) require the disclosure of communications between OMB and industry officials or other outside parties on the agency's draft regulatory agenda; and (4) require the disclosure of written correspondence between OMB and agency officials relating to the Agency's regulatory agenda. Moreover, ... OMB can continue to comment after the rulemaking record has closed while other interested parties are denied a similar opportunity.

Bringing OMB review and planning efforts under the requirements of the Administrative Procedure Act to the extent that, for example, agency submissions to OMB for the Regulatory Program, under E.O. 12498, and proposed rules, under E.O.

12291, would be published at the same time in the Federal Register, would do much to reduce the tension between the APA and regulatory management. This should be the subject of attention by Congress as it provides by statute the specific elements of the regulatory management process.

———————

1. Does this summary of how the process has worked alter your judgment about its legality? Should procedural controls be imposed in addition to those OIRA has accepted? Strauss & Sunstein, *supra* at 206-07, reproduce the recommendations of the Administrative Law Section of the ABA concerning the executive order program. Although generally supportive of both the legality and appropriateness of the program, the recommendations urge OMB to make agency submissions to OMB, and responsive OMB documents, available to relevant congressional committees after the rulemaking activity is complete.

2. What would be your advice to the President-elect in 1988 concerning a regulatory management program? Would your advice differ if you were employed by a congressional committee?

D. Budget and Spending Processes

No picture of executive-legislative relations is complete without a rudimentary sketch of the way that the federal government spends money. Usually, there are three important stages (we mention exceptions below). First, the executive branch furnishes Congress a budget for the government. Second, Congress translates the budget into appropriations of funds. Third, actual expenditures occur in the daily operations of the agencies. *See generally* G. Mills & J. Palmer, eds., Federal Budget Policy in the 1980s (1984).

This section of the chapter begins with an overview of budget and spending processes. (Of course, we have already encountered them in *Bowsher v. Synar* earlier in this chapter, which you should review for its discussion of the budget statutes.) Next we examine the nature of—and constitutional limits to—congressional controls on executive expenditures. We then examine executive control of spending, and the contentious question of impoundment of appropriated funds. Finally, we note proposals for constitutional reforms of these processes, with emphasis on a perennial presidential favorite, the item veto.

1. Overview

The Constitution gives Congress the authority to tax and spend "for the common Defence and general Welfare of the United States." (Art. I, § 8, cl. 1) In *United States v. Butler*, 297 U.S. 1 (1936), the Supreme Court settled a longstanding controversy by holding that the power to tax and spend is not limited to implementation of other substantive powers of Congress, such as the commerce clause, but is a freestanding power to pursue the "general welfare." Madison had contended for the narrow view of the clause, stressing that ours is a government of limited and enumerated powers; the Court sided with Hamilton, who, later buttressed by Story, advanced the broad view. (Nevertheless, the *Butler* Court struck down the statute at bar for invading the rights of the states reserved by the Tenth Amendment—not a likely outcome today.) In subsequent years, the Court has realized the promise of *Butler* by approving a vast range of federal expenditures. In the absense of important substantive limits to the power to tax and spend, congressional process takes on special importance. For an able overview (now somewhat dated), see A. Schick, Congress and Money (1980).

Rules of both the House and Senate require that legislation authorizing a substantive program be enacted before any appropriations are made. Assuming the existence of authorizations, appropriations bills traditionally begin in the House Appropriations Committee. This very powerful committee is divided into thirteen functional sub-committees, such as Agriculture and Defense, each of which submits its own appro-priations bill. Formulated in a subcommittee and amended by the full committee, a bill then proceeds to the floor of the House. Once passed by the House, it goes to the Senate Appropriations Committee. Due to constraints of time and energy, the Senate committee traditionally acts as an appellate forum. Changes may also be made, of course, when the bills reach the Senate floor, or in conference with the House.

Today, the central procedural question is how these separate spending decisions should be aggregated into a national fiscal policy, a budget. Through the end of the nineteenth century, customs revenues were large enough, and federal expenditures small enough, that budgets were not a major problem. Prior to World War I, neither Congress nor the President had a comprehensive budgeting system. The Budget and Accounting Act of 1921 reformed the financial machinery of the executive branch by setting up the Bureau of the Budget and the General Accounting Office. (As we saw in *Bowsher*, the Act grants the GAO broad powers to investigate all matters relating to the use of public funds, and requires it to report annually to Congress the results of its audits.) The creation of the Bureau of the Budget centralized executive branch fiscal management under the President. Previously, federal agencies had made direct requests to Congress for appropriations. The Act required all agencies to submit their appropriations proposals to the Bureau of the Budget. (As we noted above, Congress has sometimes granted ad hoc exceptions to this requirement, especially for the independent agencies.) Under the Nixon Administration, the Bureau was reorganized and renamed the Office of Management and Budget (OMB).

A *congressional* budget procedure was introduced by the Congressional Budget and Impoundment Control Act of 1974, Pub. L. No. 93-344, 88 Stat. 297. For the first time, the Act required Congress to review overall expenditures and revenues systematically, and to determine what actions its appropriations and revenue com-mittees should take to meet broad fiscal goals. Previously, taxing and spending bills percolated up through the various subcommittees and committees, with no procedure to force Congress to decide between another dollar for butter and another dollar for guns.

Indeed, by 1974, only about 60% of federal spending was subject to annual ap-propriations procedure at all. The rest either did not require yearly appropriations or created obligations that Congress felt obligated to meet. Such "backdoor spending" is accomplished through several devices, such as authorizing agencies to borrow or to enter contracts in advance of appropriations, through permanent or multi-year appropriations, or through entitlement programs in which Congress makes payments to individuals mandatory through fixed formulas. These methods have the potential of eliminating the authority of the appropriations committees. In 1965, the committees had been given the power to designate the maximum amount to be spent. The 1974 Act added more controls to backdoor spending. New borrowing authority and contract authority must now be approved by the appropriations committees, and entitlement programs are subject to tighter committee review.

In hopes of instilling fiscal discipline, the Act set a detailed timetable for passing a legislative budget. Congress has since modified it twice, in 1985 and 1987. Unfortunately, none of these self-regulatory efforts have forced Congress to balance the federal budget, or even to engage in an orderly weighing of choices. *See* A. Schick, Crisis in the Budget Process (1986). Congressional budgeting still tends to be a last-minute, chaotic process in which only some of the 13 regular appropriations bills are passed on time—or at all. (We explore some of the consequences below.) Thus, although Congress can help itself to frame the issues involved in budgeting, making the hard underlying choices remains as painful as ever.

The 1974 Act established a two-stage budgeting process, by which Congress was to adopt a first resolution each spring, setting broad targets for the individual appropriations bills, and then a second resolution on the eve of the new fiscal year (which begins on October 1st), making final decisions in light of the bills as they had passed, and ordering reconciliation of the bills with its overall budget. This process, however, proved cumbersome and unrealistic. Congress considered various reforms; *see, e.g.*, House Comm. on Rules, Report of the Task Force on the Budget Process, 98th Cong., 2d Sess. (Comm. Print 1984). With the 1985 "Gramm-Rudman-Hollings Act" that was partly invalidated in *Bowsher*, Congress simplified the timetable by providing for a single budget resolution in the spring and deficit estimates in the summer, with presidential sequestration orders if necessary to meet the Act's targets. See House Committee on the Budget, The Congressional Budget Process: A General Explanation, 99th Cong., 2d Sess. (Comm. Print 1986).

In 1987, responding to *Bowsher*, Congress passed the "Balanced Budget and Emergency Deficit Control Reaffirmation Act of 1987," Pub. L. No. 100-xx, 101 Stat. xxx. The Act restores the automatic deficit-reduction features of the 1985 legislation, with some modifications. The yearly target figures are altered somewhat, and the ultimate goal of a zero deficit is delayed until fiscal year 1993. The Comptroller General is removed from the sequestration process. A presidential order is to be triggered by a report from the OMB Director, who is to give "due regard" to deficit estimates from CBO. A constitutional issue remains, however: may Congress delegate such broad power over spending to *anyone?* Considering the 1985 Act, Congressman Brooks argued not, in *Gramm-Rudman: Can Congress and the President Pass This Buck?*, 64 Tex. L. Rev. 131 (1985).

2. *Congressional control of spending*

Congress has never managed, since the passage of the 1974 budget act, to enact all of its 13 regular appropriations bills by the start of the fiscal year. As a result, Congress has had to rely on "continuing resolutions," *i.e.*, joint resolutions that contain budget authority for agencies, designed to serve during the interim between the start of the fiscal year and the passage of a regular appropriations bill. Political pressures often become so intense in connection with these emergency spending measures that Congress has occasionally been unable to prevent a lapse in appropriations from occurring because of a missed deadline. How should the executive respond to such lapses?

Authority for the Continuance of Governmental Functions During a Temporary Lapse in Appropriations
43 Op. A.G. No. 29 (1981)

My Dear Mr. President:

You have asked my opinion concerning the scope of currently existing legal and constitutional authorities for the continuance of government functions during a temporary lapse in appropriations, such as the Government sustained on October 1, 1980. As you know, some initial determination ... had to be made in the waning hours of the last fiscal year in order to avoid extreme administrative confusion that might have arisen from Congress' failure timely to enact 11 of the 13 anticipated regular appropriations bills, or a continuing resolution to cover the hiatus between regular appropriations. The resulting guidance ... appeared in a memorandum ... on September 30, 1980. Your request, in effect, is for a close and more precise analysis of the issues raised by the September 30 memorandum.

... I think it useful to place this opinion in the context of my April 25, 1980 opinion to you concerning the applicability of the Antideficiency Act, 31 U.S.C. § 665, upon lapses in appropriations. That opinion set forth two essential conclusions. First, if, after the expiration of an agency's appropriations, Congress has enacted no appropriation for the immediately subsequent period, the agency may make no contracts and obligate no further funds except as authorized by law. Second, because no statute generally permits federal agencies to incur obligations without appropriations for the pay of employees, agencies are not, in general, authorized by law to employ the services of their employees upon a lapse in appropriations. My interpretation of the Antideficiency Act in this regard is based on its plain language, its history, and its manifest purposes.

... Upon determining that the blanket prohibition expressed in § 665(a) against unauthorized obligations in advance of appropriations is to be applied as written, the opinion added only that the Antideficiency Act does permit agencies that are ceasing their functions to fulfill certain legal obligations connected with the orderly termination of agency operations. The opinion [which dealt with a lapse in appropriations for the FTC] did not consider the more complex legal questions posed by a general congressional failure to enact timely appropriations, or the proper course of action to be followed when no prolonged lapse in appropriations in such a situation is anticipated.

... Under the terms of the Antideficiency Act, the authorities upon which the Government may rely for the continuance of functions despite a lapse in appropriations implicate two fundamental questions. Because the proscription of § 665(a) excepts obligations in advance of appropriations that are "authorized by law," it is first necessary to consider which functions this exception comprises. Further, given that § 665(b) expressly permits the Government to employ the personal service of its employees in "cases of emergency involving the safety of human life or the protection of property," it is necessary to determine how this category is to be construed. I shall address these questions in turn, bearing in mind that the ... [correct response] must, in each case, be determined in light of all the circumstances surrounding a particular lapse in appropriations.

I

... Under the language of § 665(a) ... when an agency's regular appropriation lapses, that agency may not enter contracts or create other obligations unless the agency has legal authority to incur obligations in advance of appropriations. Such authority, in some form, is not uncommon in the Government. For example, notwithstanding the lapse of regular appropriations, an agency may continue to have available to it particular funds that are subject to a multi-year or no-year appropriation. A lapse in authority to spend funds under a one-year appropriation would not affect such other authorities.

A more complex problem of interpretation, however, may be presented with respect to obligational authorities that are not manifested in appropriations acts. In a few cases, Congress has expressly authorized agencies to incur obligations without regard to available appropriations. More often, it is necessary to inquire under what circumstances statutes that vest particular functions in government agencies imply authority to create obligations for the accomplishment of those functions despite the lack of current appropriations. This, of course, would be the relevant legal inquiry even if Congress had not enacted the Antideficiency Act; the second phrase of § 665(a) clearly does no more than codify what, in any event and not merely during lapses in appropriations, is a requirement of legal authority for the obligation of public funds.

Previous Attorneys General and the Comptrollers General have had frequent occasion to address, directly or indirectly, the question of implied authority. Whether the broader language of all of their opinions is reconcilable may be doubted, but the conclusions of the relevant opinions fully establish the premise upon which my April 25, 1980 memorandum to you was based: statutory authority to incur obligations in advance of appropriations may be implied as well as express, but may not ordinarily be inferred, in the absence of appropriations, from the kind of broad, categorical authority, standing alone, that often appears, for example, in the organic statutes of government agencies. The authority must be necessarily inferable from the specific terms of those duties that have been imposed upon, or of those authorities that have been invested in, the officers or employees purporting to obligate funds on behalf of the United States.

Thus, for example, when Congress specifically authorizes contracts to be entered into for the accomplishment of a particular purpose, the delegated officer may negotiate such contracts even before Congress appropriates all the funds necessary for their fulfillment. On the other hand, when authority for the performance of a specific function rests on a particular appropriation that proves inadequate to the fulfillment of its purpose, the responsible officer is not authorized to obligate further funds for that purpose in the absence of additional appropriations.

This rule prevails even though the obligation of funds that the official contemplates may be a reasonable means for fulfilling general responsibilities that Congress has delegated to the official in broad terms, but without conferring specific authority to enter into contracts or otherwise obligate funds in advance of appropriations. For example, Attorney General McReynolds concluded, in 1913, that the Postmaster General could not obligate funds in excess of appropriations for the employment of temporary and auxiliary mail carriers to maintain regular service, notwithstanding his broad authorities for the carrying of the mails. 30 Op. A.G. 157. Similarly, in 1877, Attorney General Devens concluded that the Secretary of War could not, in the absence of appropriations, accept "contributions" of materiel for the army, *e.g.*, ammunition and medical supplies, beyond the Secretary's specific authorities to contract in advance of appropriations. 15 Op. A.G. 209.

Ordinarily, then, should an agency's regular one-year appropriation lapse, the "authorized by law" exception to the Antideficiency Act would permit the agency to continue the obligation of funds to the extent that such obligations are: (1) funded by moneys, the obligational authority for which is not limited to one year, e.g., multi-year appropriations; (2) authorized by statutes that expressly permit obligations in advance of appropriations; or (3) authorized by necessary implication from the specific terms of duties that have been imposed on, or of authorities that have been invested in, the agency. A nearly Government-wide lapse, however, such as occurred on October 1, 1980, implicates one further question of Executive authority.

Unlike his subordinates, the President performs not only functions that are authorized by statute, but functions authorized by the Constitution as well. To take one obvious example, the President alone, under Art. II, § 2, cl. 1 of the Constitution, "shall have Power to grant Reprieves and Pardons for Offenses against the United States, except in Cases of Impeachment." Manifestly, Congress could not deprive the President of this power by purporting to deny him the minimum obligational authority sufficient to carry this power into effect. Not all of the President's powers are so specifically enumerated, however, and the question must consequently arise, upon a Government-wide lapse in appropriations, whether the Antideficiency Act should be construed as depriving the President of authority to obligate funds in connection with those initiatives that would otherwise fall within the President's powers.

In my judgment, the Antideficiency Act should not be read as necessarily precluding exercises of executive power through which the President, acting alone or through his subordinates, could have obligated funds in advance of appropriations had the Antideficiency Act not been enacted. With respect to certain of the President's functions, as illustrated above, such an interpretation could raise grave constitutional questions. It is an elementary rule that statutes should be interpreted, if possible, to preclude constitutional doubts, *Crowell v. Benson*, 285 U.S. 22, 62 (1932), and this rule should surely be followed in connection with a broad and general statute, such as 31 U.S.C. § 665(a), the history of which indicates no congressional consideration at all of the desirability of limiting otherwise constitutional presidential initiatives.

The President, of course, cannot legislate his own obligational authorities; the legislative power rests with Congress.... [T]he Antideficiency Act is not the only source of law or the only exercise of congressional power that must be weighed in determining whether the President has authority for an initiative that obligates funds in advance of appropriations. The President's obligational authority may be strengthened in connection with initiatives that are grounded in the peculiar institutional powers and competency of the President. His authority will be further buttressed in connection with any initiative that is consistent with statutes—and thus with the exercise of legislative power in an area of concurrent authority—that are more narrowly drawn than the Antideficiency Act and that would otherwise authorize the President to carry out his constitutionally assigned tasks in the manner he contemplates....

Unfortunately, no catalogue is possible of those exercises of presidential power that may properly obligate funds in advance of appropriations. Clearly, such an exercise of power could most readily be justified if the functions to be performed would assist the President in fulfilling his peculiar constitutional role, and Congress has otherwise authorized those or similar functions to be performed within the control of the President.[10] Other factors to be considered would be the urgency of the initiative and the likely extent to which funds would be obligated in advance of appropriations.

In sum, I construe the 'authorized by law' exception contained within 31 U.S.C. § 665(a) as exempting from the prohibition enacted by the second clause of that section not only those obligations in advance of appropriations for which express or implied authority may be found in the enactments of Congress, but also those obligations necessarily incident to presidential initiatives undertaken within his constitutional powers.

II

In addition to regulating generally obligations in advance of appropriations, the Antideficiency Act further provides, in 31 U.S.C. § 665(b):

> No officer or employee of the United States shall accept voluntary service for the United States or employ personal service in excess of that authorized by law, except in cases of emergency involving the safety of human life or the protection of property.

Despite the use of the term "voluntary service," the evident concern underlying this provision is not government agencies' acceptance of the benefit of services rendered without compensation. Rather, the original version of § 665(b) was enacted as part of an urgent deficiency appropriation act in 1884, Act of May 1, 1884, ch. 37, 23 Stat. 17, in order to avoid claims for compensation arising from the unauthorized provision of services to the Government by non-employees, and claims for additional compensation asserted by government employees performing extra services after hours. That is, under § 665(b), government officers and employees may not involve the Government in contracts for *employment*, *i.e.*, for compensated labor, except in emergency situations. 30 Op. A.G. 129 (1913).

Under § 665(b), it is thus crucial, in construing the Government's authority to continue functions in advance of appropriations, to interpret the phrase "emergencies involving the safety of human life or the protection of property." Although the legislative history of the phrase sheds only dim light on its precise meaning, this history, coupled with an administrative history—of which Congress is fully aware—of the interpretation of an identical phrase in a related budgeting context, suggests two rules for identifying those functions for which government officers may employ personal services for compensation in excess of legal authority other than § 665(b) itself. First, there must be some reasonable and articulable connection between the function to be performed and the safety of human life or the protection of property. Second, there must be some reasonable likelihood that the safety of human life or the protection of property would be compromised, in some degree, by delay in the performance of the function in question.

---

10. One likely category into which certain of these functions would fall would be "the conduct of foreign relations essential to the national security," referred to in the September 30, 1980 memorandum.

As originally enacted in 1884, the provision forbade unauthorized employment "except in cases of *sudden* emergency involving the *loss* of human life or the *destruction* of property." (Emphasis supplied.) The [legislative history] ... confirms what the originally enacted language itself suggests, namely, that Congress initially contemplated only a very narrow exception to what is now § 665(b), to be employed only in cases of dire necessity.

In 1950, however, Congress enacted the modern version of the Antideficiency Act and accepted revised language for 31 U.S.C. § 665(b) [to its present form].... Consequently, we infer from the plain import of the language of their amendments that the drafters intended to broaden the authority for emergency employment. In essence, they replaced the apparent suggestion of a need to show absolute necessity with a phrase more readily suggesting the sufficiency of a showing of reasonable necessity in connection with the safety of human life or the protection of property in general.

This interpretration is buttressed by the history of interpretation by the Bureau of the Budget and its successor, the Office of Management and Budget, of 31 U.S.C. § 665(e), which prohibits the apportionment or reapportionment of appropriated funds in a manner that would indicate the need for a deficiency or supplemental appropriation, except in, among other circumstances, "emergencies involving the safety of human life, [or] the protection of property...." § 665(e)(1)(B). Directors ... have granted dozens of deficiency reapportionments under this subsection in the last 30 years, and have apparently imposed no test more stringent than the articulation of a reasonable relationship between the funded activity and the safety of human life or the protection of property. Activities for which deficiency apportionments have been granted on this basis include FBI criminal investigations, legal services rendered by the Department of Agriculture in connection with state meat inspection programs and ... the investigation of aircraft accidents by the National Transportation Safety Board.... Most important, under § 665(e)(2), each apportionment or reapportionment indicating the need for a deficiency or supplemental appropriation has been reported contemporaneously to both Houses of Congress, and, in the face of these reports, Congress has not acted in any way to alter the relevant 1950 wording of § 665(e)(1)(B), which is, in this respect, identical to § 665(b).

... To erect the most solid foundation for the Executive branch's practice ... I would recommend that, in preparing contingency plans for periods of lapsed appropriations, each government department or agency provide for the Director of the Office of Management and Budget some written description, that could be transmitted to Congress, of what the head of the agency, assisted by its General Counsel, considers to be the agency's emergency functions.

In suggesting the foregoing principles to guide the interpretation of § 665(b), I must add my view that, in emergency circumstances in which a government agency may employ personal service in excess of legal authority other than § 665(b), it may also, under the authority of § 665(b), incur obligations in advance of appropriations for material to enable the employees involved to meet the emergency successfully.... Congress has contemplated expressly, in enacting § 665(b), that emergencies will exist that will justify incurring obligations for employee compensation in advance of appropriations; it must be assumed that, when such an emergency arises, Congress would intend those persons so employed to be able to accomplish their emergency functions with success. Congress, for example, having allowed the Government to hire firefighters must surely have intended that water and firetrucks would be available to them.

III

. . . As the law is now written, the nation must rely initially for the efficient operation of government on the timely and responsible functioning of the legislative process. The Constitution and the Antideficiency Act itself leave the Executive leeway to perform essential functions and make the government "workable." Any inconvenience that this system, in extreme circumstances, may bode is outweighed, in my estimation, by the salutary distribution of power that it embodies.

Respectfully,

BENJAMIN R. CIVILETTI
Attorney General

-----

1. The Antideficiency Act was adopted at a time when budgetary oversight was simpler and Congress' performance in enacting timely appropriations was better. Does the language of the Antideficiency Act leave room for a coherent interpretation with less drastic potential consequences, given Congress' current budgeting difficulties, than the Civiletti interpretation? If not, should Congress enact a permanent appropriations act, providing that upon any lapse in regular appropriations, funds are appropriated for an agency at the same level as under its most recent authority, until the passage of a subsequent appropriations bill? Would this undermine the "salutary distribution of power" to which Civiletti refers?

2. Although Civiletti's view of the Antideficiency Act is determined by the plain meaning of the statute, he does find implied authority for the administration of entitlements programs, certain presidential initiatives, "orderly shutdown" expenses, and material for emergency government functions. Are these conclusions based on sound statutory construction? With respect to the President, Civiletti states that the Act would "raise grave constitutional questions" if interpreted to preclude all exercises of executive power through which the President could have obligated funds in advance of appropriations had the Antideficiency Act not been enacted. Which functions would raise the most serious questions?

Note that the Civiletti opinion does not cite cases defining "inherent" constitutional powers of the President. When you read the *Neagle* and *Debs* cases in Chapter Five, consider whether you would have relied on them here.

3. Is Congress constitutionally required to provide any funds whatsoever for the operation of the executive branch, aside from the President's salary? Professor Charles Black, in *Some Thoughts on the Veto*, 40 L. & Contemp. Probs. 87, 89 (1976), presents a vision that

> arose from my asking myself, "To what state could Congress, without violating the Constitution, reduce the President?" I arrived at a picture of a man living in a modest apartment, with perhaps one secretary to answer mail; that is where one appropriation bill could put him, at the beginning of a new term.

Do you share this vision of a President constitutionally shorn of all the trappings and implements of office? If not, what is the minimum Congress must provide, and who could force them to provide it?

A recurrent constitutional question surrounds congressional restrictions on executive use of appropriations. We know that Congress has, after *Butler* and its progeny, wide discretion over spending. Does that mean that Congress has *more* power to control executive action through the technique of conditioning appropriations than it would have through a direct limitation on a substantive grant of power? The following case shows how these problems arise.

Brown v. Califano
627 F.2d 1221 (D.C. Cir. 1980)

BAZELON, Senior Circuit Judge:

Darryl and David Brown and sixteen other public school children, the appellants, challenge the constitutionality of amendments that restrict federal methods for assuring nondiscrimination in public schools receiving federal support. The amendments essentially prevent the Department of Health, Education, and Welfare (HEW) from requiring "the transportation of any student to a school other than the school which is nearest the student's home." The district court found that the existence of an alternative federal avenue to effect transportation remedies saves these amendments from constitutional challenge on their face. The district court explicitly left open the possibility of future challenges to the amendments as applied. For the reasons described below, we affirm.

I. BACKGROUND

... Title VI of the [Civil Rights] Act prohibits discrimination on the ground of race, color, or national origin under any program receiving federal financial assistance. [42 U.S.C. § 2000d] ... [T]he Act permits the Executive to avoid providing support to noncomplying public school districts, and to use the threat of fund-termination to persuade or induce recipients to dismantle vestiges of segregation.

Through agreement with other executive departments, HEW assumed responsibility for Title VI enforcement with respect to most federal financial assistance to elementary, secondary and higher education and other specified health and social welfare activities. Between the passage of the Act and March of 1970, HEW diligently followed rules it promulgated under Title VI and brought some six hundred administrative proceedings against noncomplying districts. Then, between March 1970 and February 1971, HEW brought no enforcement proceedings. At the same time, HEW continued to advance federal funds to schools HEW found in violation of Title VI.

Based on factual findings of this sort, Judge Pratt in *Adams v. Richardson* [356 F. Supp. 92 (D.D.C. 1973)] and Judge Sirica in the earlier proceedings in this case ordered declaratory and injunctive relief requiring HEW to resume enforcement under Title VI. Those decisions disapproved of HEW's conduct but left its regulations in place to guide future enforcement. Under these regulations, HEW requires elementary and secondary school applicants and recipients to provide assurances of their compliance with desegregation plans. ... Upon finding apparent violation of the assured compliance, HEW must notify the recipient and seek voluntary compliance. If voluntary compliance cannot be secured, HEW can pursue enforcement through fund termination proceedings within the agency, or through other means under law. The regulations specify the primary alternative to fund-termination: referral to the Department of Justice with a recommendation of appropriate legal action....

Enacted as floor amendments to appropriation bills, the amendments challenged here lack careful explanation or description of their intended effect on HEW's enforcement procedures under Title VI. Their general purpose, however, is clear. Congress wanted to ensure that no student would be transported beyond the school nearest his home because of an HEW requirement.

Of course, as members of Congress were aware, HEW never had the authority to order any particular remedial plan. Its enforcement authority permits it only to require assurances of compliance from applicants, and to seek enforcement through fund-termination proceedings or referral to the Department of Justice. Nonetheless, as the legislative debates also acknowledge, the power to threaten fund-termination—the power that attaches strings to financial assistance—can often work coercively. Thus, Congress explicitly intended that HEW could not use this power to require, "directly or indirectly," student transportation beyond the school closest to their home....

Although the sponsors maintained that HEW retains Title VI enforcement authority under the amendments, the extent of that authority is not entirely apparent. On the one hand, it is clear that the amendments leave intact HEW's entire administrative enforcement process, including fund-termination, for violations not calling for transportation remedies. But the legislative debates do not identify when and through what procedures HEW can avoid funding schools known to violate the Constitution and Title VI. Congress apparently intended HEW to retain the power to refer cases to the Department of Justice for appropriate legal action. Congress neglected, however, to specify the steps HEW may take before a referral....

II. THE AMENDMENTS AND EFFECTIVE DESEGREGATION ENFORCEMENT

The amendments here at issue make no classification along impermissible lines, but that does not prevent an equal protection challenge. Interference with the remedies necessary to implement the promise of *Brown v. Board of Education*, 347 U.S. 483 (1954), could well rise to the level of impermissible discriminatory effect and purpose. ... Appellants argue that, by restricting HEW's ability to require busing remedies, the amendments demonstrate discriminatory intent to interfere with desegregation. Presumably, this claim attaches to HEW's statutory obligation under Title VI to achieve equality in federally-funded schools and to the Executive's duty to "take care that the Laws [are] faithfully executed."

Thus, appellants assert that the amendments...violate the fifth amendment by eliminating "the single, proven, and most effective remedy for desegregating schools receiving federal aid." There are actually two prongs to this claim: the amendments will effectively inhibit desegregation and thereby dilute the guarantees of the fifth amendment; and the amendments reflect an impermissible legislative motivation to inhibit desegregation. Because the amendments on their face leave open many apparently effective avenues for desegregation, we are not persuaded by either argument.

A. *Construing the Amendments*

The traditional judicial practice of reaching statutory issues before constitutional ones, combined with deference to Congress, supports application here of the general rule that legislation "should be interpreted, if fairly possible, in such a way as to free it from not insubstantial constitutional doubts." The amendments can be interpreted here to advance a permissible purpose, with no general inhibition of desegregation. Although individual supporters broadly attacked busing as a desegregation remedy, we do not find these statements expressive of the entire legislature's intent. Were they representative, we would be confronted with grave constitutional difficulties. Instead, we recognize the primary focus of the congressional debates on the role of HEW as an enforcement agency. An explicit, major purpose of the amendments was to take "HEW out of the busing business." In other words, Congress wanted to ensure that mandatory busing orders derive either from local school officials or federal courts.

Accordingly, the amendments only restrain HEW from using its fund-termination authority to induce school districts to require student transportation beyond schools closest to their homes. They do not in any way restrict HEW's authority to threaten or actually terminate funds with respect to any other desegregation remedy which would suffice. Thus, HEW can reject fund applications which fail to provide for magnet schools, faculty desegregation, school construction or school closings that enhance desegregation, or other nontransportation remedies it deems necessary for compliance with Title VI and the Constitution.

For those noncomplying school districts which HEW believes require transportation remedies, the amendments clearly eliminate use of the fund-termination option to induce busing. At the same time, nothing in their language or legislative history ... precludes HEW from referring such cases to the Department of Justice, with recommendations for appropriate legal action. ...

Appellants contest the sufficiency of this referral option by claiming that time-consuming litigation will impermissibly forestall the requisite remedy. This is an issue which clearly requires concrete development, and is not susceptible to resolution in the abstract. ... Thus, as a facial challenge to the amendments, appellants' argument cannot succeed. Further, the Department of Justice is not limited to a litigative strategy; it may conduct negotiations and seek settlements, where appropriate. Finally, the Department is under a strict obligation to avoid delay. This obligation to guard against delay applies with equal force to HEW when it seeks to procure compliance. The government argues that the amendments do not prevent HEW from threatening referral to the Department of Justice in order to increase HEW's leverage in persuading offending districts to "voluntarily" reassign students. We agree, with this proviso: HEW cannot delay in taking necessary steps to bring about compliance. ...

B. *Dilution of Equal Protection Guarantees*

The amendments would be constitutionally flawed if they diluted rather than enforced equal protection guarantees. ... [Since they allow fund-termination except to induce busing and since] the amendments also leave in place the enforcement options at the Department of Justice, we cannot find that on their face they "restrict, abrogate, or dilute" the guarantee of equal protection. Where a choice of alternative enforcement routes is available, and the one preferred is not demonstrably less effective, Congress has the power to exercise its preference.

C. *Legislative Motivation*

Absent discriminatory effect, judicial inquiry into legislative motivation is unnecessary, as well as undesirable. Obviously, the foreseeable effect of these amendments is increased litigation for court-ordered desegregation, and settlements supervised by HEW and the courts—not unremedied segregation. Thus, statements by individual congressmen that reveal opposition to busing or to student assignment to achieve desegregation, do not by themselves establish constitutional flaws in the amendments.

III. PROHIBITION AGAINST GOVERNMENT SUPPORT FOR SEGREGATION

More problematic is appellants' charge that the amendments interfere with the government's obligation not to support segregated schools. . . . Distinct from its duty to enforce the law, the Executive must not itself participate in unlawful discrimination. This prohibition is embodied in Title VI and in numerous subsequent statutory schemes. To avoid the cloud of constitutional doubt, we must assume that Congress did not intend the amendments to force federal financial support of illegal discrimination.

Thus, the amendments cannot be read to prevent HEW from fulfilling its obligation to assure no federal moneys support segregated schools. HEW has an obligation, as a government agency, not to participate in unlawful discrimination. In particular instances, HEW may be required to 1) refer a case to the Department of Justice for appropriate action; 2) terminate funds through HEW's administrative procedures; or 3) alert the President that a case may require Executive impoundment of funds.[90] Appellants and other private individuals certainly are not barred from challenging HEW's failure to take any such steps.

. . . We agree . . . with the district court that the record does not establish sufficient factual evidence to permit a review of the amendments as applied. Therefore, we affirm the district court's judgment that the amendments survive facial challenge. . . .

Affirmed.

---

1. From either a political or constitutional point of view, was Congress better advised to limit busing through the appropriations process rather than through substantive or jurisdictional legislation?

2. Is there any constitutional obstacle to appropriations limitations that allow the Department of Justice to bring certain lawsuits but attempt to control how such lawsuits shall be tried? Should any such congressional directives be viewed as posing ethical problems for government lawyers? At the time of the *Brown* litigation, how would you have advised the federal agencies involved on the nature of their legal obligations?

3. Would it be unconstitutional for Congress to permit tax exemptions for racially discriminatory private schools? (In *Bob Jones University v. United States*, 461 U.S. 574 (1983), the Court held that Congress had authorized the IRS to deny exemptions for such schools, and could constitutionally do so.) Assuming that Congress *must* deny such exemptions, may it nevertheless deny funds to the IRS to investigate the racially discriminatory practices of tax-exempt institutions?

4. Notice one option the court identifies for preventing government funds from aiding discriminatory activity: presidential impoundment (see note 90 and accompanying text). Does the existence of this option cast doubt on the constitutional

---

90. The President's authority to impound funds derives from his duty to "take care that the laws [are] faithfully executed," article II, § 3 of the Constitution, and from specific statutory provisions. Impoundment takes on special importance where the Executive believes the expenditure would violate a constitutional provision. . . .

necessity for authorizing Department of Justice lawsuits, or must the impoundment option be shown to be realistic? As you read the materials in the next section of this chapter, consider the soundness of the court's view of impoundment.

Note that, in order to avoid funding racially discriminatory schools, the President need not actually impound funds—the executive branch could simply shift funds from racially discriminatory school districts to nondiscriminatory districts, without actually spending any less money. If the President has the power to order such shifting, what administrative protections would need to be afforded the purportedly discriminatory school districts? Could Congress expressly deny the President power to alter the administrative allotment of federal grant funds in order to require busing? What if the Supreme Court squarely held that, in particular cases, busing is essential to the vindication of individual rights under the Constitution?

5. The potential for governmental havoc posed by appropriations disputes illustrates again an essential truth of the separation of powers: the success of our government depends largely on each branch's willingness not to press what arguably are its powers to their logical extreme.

3. Executive control of spending (herein, of impoundment)

For appropriations, as for substantive statutory actions, Congress bounds executive discretion within varying limits. At one extreme is a lump sum for a broadly defined purpose; at the other is an appropriation broken down by "line items," each for a specific use. The nation's experience while governed by those who had framed the Constitution illustrates the scope of the possible variations. (The story is told in a good general introduction to the issues in this section, L. Fisher, Presidential Spending Power 60-61 (1975)). The first appropriations act in 1789 simply provided lump sums for four general categories of expenditures, for example, $137,000 for the War Department. A period of much greater itemization soon followed, however. By 1793, appropriations had descended to such minutiae as $450 for the Treasurer's office supplies. This trend was actually encouraged by the newly inaugurated Jefferson, who urged Congress to appropriate "specific sums to every specific purpose susceptible of definition." (Hamilton trenchantly termed this "preposterous.") Experience soon convinced Jefferson, however, that at least from the standpoint of the executive, "too minute a specification has its evil as well as a too general one." Congress, he had come to believe, should repose a temporary trust in the executive, which could be "put an end to if abused." Congress has subsequently displayed an appreciation for the principles that Jefferson eventually adopted. In applying them, Congress has varied the specificity of its appropriations greatly, according to the subject matter, the temper of the times, and the degree of trust reposed in the President.

It has long been accepted that Congress may direct expenditure in at least some circumstances. That is the principle established by *Kendall v. United States ex rel. Stokes*, 37 U.S. 524 (1838), discussed in Chapter Two, in which the Court upheld issuance of mandamus to the Postmaster General to pay government contractors an award for their services as determined by an arbitrator. A statute had set up the arbitration procedure and had commanded payment of the award.

Notwithstanding implications that might be taken from *Kendall*, federal spending is not a purely mechanical function, but one invested with varying degrees of executive discretion. Despite the surface precision of appropriations, expressed as they are in numbers, they do not necessarily confer less executive discretion than do substantive delegations. There is often a respectable argument that a particular appropriation is a ceiling on expenditure, not a specific directive, as our discussion of impoundment will reveal. Also, the executive possesses a number of techniques for manipulating spending, which can convert appropriations from one purpose to another. Moreover, the delegation doctrine, which purports to restrain the breadth of substantive delegations of power, has only rarely been applied to appropriations. (For a summary rejection of an argument that an appropriation violated the delegation doctrine, *see Cincinnati Soap Co. v. United States*, 301 U.S. 308, 321 (1937); judicial review of federal spending is often barred by such doctrines as standing.)

It may be useful to distinguish positive from negative executive spending decisions. Positive discretion results in expenditure. It includes shifting appropriations among budgeted accounts within one statutory category of appropriations (reprogramming), timing expenditures to affect the availability or amount of appropriations, and obligating funds that have yet to be appropriated. The extent of executive discretion concerning such matters has never been authoritatively determined, although the effect can be to alter substantially the expenditure patterns anticipated in both executive budgets and congressional appropriations. Negative discretion, which refers to decisions that result in withholding appropriated amounts from expenditure, also takes numerous forms, which tend to be lumped together under the general term "impoundment." Examples include the formation of reserves and the withholding of contract authority. A practical difference between positive and negative discretion may favor implying broader executive authority for the latter—impounded funds remain available for Congress to appropriate to the purpose of its choice.

Broad, lump sum appropriations are common in periods of war or economic crisis. (Smaller contingency funds of diverse sorts are scattered in appropriations in ordinary times.) At times, the consequence has been to grant a President virtually unfettered control over large sums. For example, at the end of Franklin Roosevelt's first term, it was estimated that Congress had given him discretionary authority over $15.4 billion, as compared to $1.6 billion for all previous Presidents.

The more common practice, however, has been for Congress to itemize sufficiently to produce executive branch grumbling through the years. Often the executive can draw support from public administration school theories of budgeting, which have traditionally favored executive responsibility for spending decisions. Whether in response to these pressures or from felt needs of its own, Congress has moved somewhat toward broader "program" budgeting in recent decades. In doing so, Congress has increased its needs to monitor spending as it occurs, instead of specifying acceptable uses of money in advance.

Not all congressional controls on spending appear in the appropriations statutes themselves. Instructions appear in the committee reports, hearings, and floor debates. These latter controls, however, may not be enforceable in court. *See Human Resources Development Institute v. Donovan*, 587 F. Supp. 617 (D.D.C. 1983), refusing to limit the Secretary of Labor's discretion over budgetary apportionment to conform with instructions in the Conference Report accompanying the appropriation. Nevertheless, if congressional wishes are ignored, or if the promises implied by the executive's budget requests are not met, Congress can retaliate the next year with cutbacks, restrictive conditions, and line itemization. Because many of the operative promises are negotiated between the executive and the committees, and do not appear in the appropriations bills, the appropriations committees enjoy substantial power of their own in controlling spending. This is not to say that the system lacks flexibility, however. Budgets are prepared far enough in advance of actual expenditure that a perfect fit cannot be expected. Accordingly, the committees are prepared to tolerate a certain amount of reprogramming of funds within statutory accounts, and of executive impoundments. (There is also authority to transfer funds from one statutory account to another. It is conferred exclusively, and sometimes broadly, by statute.) The problem is one of limits.

Although Presidents have probably impounded funds since the first administration, few controversies arose in the early years. *See generally* Stanton, *History and Practice of Executive Impoundment of Appropriated Funds*, 53 Neb. L. Rev. 1 (1974). It quickly became clear that the nature of the appropriations process required some kinds of executive impoundments. First, since predictions of cost are always somewhat uncertain even if the goods or services are precisely identified, the executive can sometimes fulfill Congress's purpose for less than the amount appropriated. Second, in the interval between appropriation and expenditure, changing circumstances may remove the original reason for the appropriation. In a famous early example, Jefferson declined to spend an amount appropriated for gunboats because a "favorable and peaceable turn of affairs" on the Mississippi had rendered the expenditure unnecessary. (Fisher, *supra*, at 150.) Thus, perhaps every appropriation carries an implied authorization to impound the money if to spend it would not advance the original purpose. (We consider this question in connection with *Pennsylvania v. Lynn*, discussed in Chapter Five.) Third, the process of apportionment, by which the timing of spending a year's appropriation is scheduled to avoid deficiencies at the end, can produce a surplus as readily as a shortfall. This process can include the conscious sequestration of a reserve for unforeseen requirements.

The first controversial impoundment occurred when President Grant refused to spend river and harbor funds for "works of purely private interest," as opposed to national interests. The pork barrel aspects of public works legislation have led several Presidents to delete some projects authorized by Congress while executing others. Congress has not always reacted vigorously. For example, although Grant's action produced some incandescent rhetoric in the House of Representatives ("Upon what meat hath this our Caesar fed?"), the House later accepted the President's position that the appropriation was not mandatory.

A few court decisions in the late 19th century mentioned impoundments, but they offered no guidance as to the lawfulness of the practice. Four Attorney General opinions rendered during this period, however, all asserted that the President's impoundment power depended upon the intent of Congress. The Attorneys General did not rely entirely on Congress' appropriations language to determine legislative intent. For example, Attorney General Lamont, in 1896, opined that a sum that Congress indicated "shall be expended" for a specified project did not have to be expended if the project could be completed for less. He asserted that economizing would accord with Congress' intent.

In the modern era, extensive impoundments began when Franklin Roosevelt withheld public works and other funds in response to emergency conditions created by the depression and World War II. Notwithstanding some dissatisfaction with Roosevelt's actions, Congress amended the Antideficiency Act in 1950 to authorize the President to establish reserves "to provide for contingencies, or to effect savings whenever savings are made possible by or through changes in requirements, greater efficiency of operations, or other developments subsequent to" the appropriation.

After the war, Presidents continued to impound funds, sometimes in large amounts. Much of the controversy concerned defense appropriations for weapons systems. Here the President's power as Commander in Chief was offered as a constitutional justification for impoundment. Also, the executive's special informational advantages in national security and foreign affairs helped to thwart congressional opposition. Not surprisingly, Presidents usually prevailed, although considerable maneuvering was sometimes required. President Johnson broadened the argument to include inherent authority to impound funds for domestic programs.

Although Congress has long been prepared to allow routine "programmatic" impoundments (such as to prevent waste), other impoundments have raised much more controversy because they appeared to negate the policy decisions made by appropriations. These "policy impoundments," which fall into several categories, are for the most part a phenomenon of the last fifty years. They have engendered arguments over whether such broad statutory language as the Antideficiency Act's "other developments" phrase should be read to authorize policy impoundments.

The impoundment issue finally became acute when President Nixon impounded unprecedented proportions of appropriations, as much as 20% of "controllable" federal expenditures. A number of programs were to be terminated outright. Again, however, Congress did not respond unambiguously. For example, in 1972 the Department of Agriculture announced a change that effectively terminated one class of rural development loans and replaced them with loans made available at somewhat higher interest rates and under more stringent qualification standards. Congress reacted by considering legislation completely restoring the loan program. Yet the compromise measure that eventually passed did not mandate the spending of any funds, and the administrator was given unprecedented statutory discretion in return for an informal promise to make the funds available under the program for at least three years.

Reasons advanced for the Nixon impoundments were usually general ones of fiscal integrity, such as the need to control inflation. Where particular projects were to be deleted, as in public works, there was usually no effort to justify the choices as the result of any criteria other than presence in the President's budget. Accompanying legal arguments consisted of a distortion of the historical record through claims that nothing new was occurring, and an oversimplification of previous constitutional arguments in support of a conclusion that the President could impound essentially without limitation. See Abascal & Kramer, *Presidential Impoundment Part I: Historical Genesis and Constitutional Framework*, 62 Geo. L.J. 1549 (1974); *Part II: Judicial and Legislative Responses*, 63 Geo. L.J. 149 (1974).

The Nixon impoundments finally provoked both judicial and legislative response. Neither, however, produced a definitive resolution of the permissible extent of impoundment. A series of lower court cases challenging particular impoundments generally produced defeats for the executive. For example, in *Missouri Highway Commission v. Volpe*, 479 F.2d 1099 (8th Cir. 1973), the court held that the Secretary of Transportation could not lawfully refuse to obligate highway funds which had been allocated to the state of Missouri on the ground that such expenditures would aggravate inflationary pressures in the economy. The court held that even if the governing statute were not mandatory, the Secretary lacked power to impound funds for reasons not related to the program being administered.

The Supreme Court's only foray into the issues occurred in *Train v. City of New York*, 420 U.S. 35 (1975). In 1972, Congress amended the Federal Water Pollution Control Act to provide federal financing for municipal sewage treatment works, in the form of 75% grants. The amendments authorized the appropriation of amounts "not to exceed" $5 billion for the program's first year, with greater amounts thereafter. The bill provided that the authorized sums "shall be allotted" to the states by EPA according to a formula, whereupon grant applications for the amounts allotted, once approved, would become contractual obligations of the United States. President Nixon vetoed the bill as "budget-wrecking;" Congress promptly overrode the veto. The President than instructed EPA to allot no more than $2 billion in the first year of the program, with further large reductions in subsequent years. The City of New York sued for a declaration that EPA was required to allot the full amount of the authorization, and prevailed.

The case reached the Supreme Court in the wake of the Nixon resignation. The executive had abandoned broad claims of constitutional impoundment power; only statutory issues remained. The executive now claimed only discretion as to the timing of expenditure. Therefore the Court was not deciding a contested issue when it read the legislative history to mandate "a firm commitment of substantial sums" to meet water pollution problems, one not subject to a "seemingly limitless" power to withhold funds. The Court considered the effect of two changes to the statutory language that had been added in conference in hopes of avoiding a veto. These eliminated a requirement that "all" sums be allotted, and added "not to exceed" to the sum authorized for expenditure. The changes had been explained in Congress as allowing some flexibility consistent with the basic commitment involved. (Similar ambiguity attended the veto override.) The Court decided that whatever discretion there was should be exercised at the later obligation stage, not for allotments.

Thus, the Court was able to sidestep the important issue of the amount of spending discretion conferred by the statute, because that issue would arise at a later stage of administration. Surely, the Court was correct to invalidate the President's impoundment at the allotment stage, because it amounted to an effort to ignore congressional authorization of the program. That was an issue on which the President had exercised his veto and had been overridden. To uphold that impoundment would have accorded the President an absolute veto, not a conditional one. Therefore, *Train* appears to delineate at least some role for the courts in reviewing impoundments—otherwise, Presidents could terminate congressionally mandated programs by withholding their funding. Still, the Court left the thorniest issues open: what the limits to policy impoundment might be, and how a court could draw the lines.

In *Train*, then, the President's action was not at the late stages of program implementation, involving project selection and funding. If he had impounded funds for particular projects on grounds of the inefficiency that is so typical of pork barrel appropriations, a different issue would have been presented. Similarly, if the impoundment had been at a program-wide level, for example 10% of all program funds, but had occurred after enough time had passed since the authorization to allow an argument for changed circumstances (such as unanticipated budgetary developments or actual waste in the administration of the program), an issue distinguishable from *Train* would be presented. In either case, a court faced with a suit to compel expenditure could stay its hand in favor of a "remand to Congress" to allow the President to test support for his action. An advantage of this approach for the courts would be that it would minimize their inquiry into issues of degree surrounding the permissibility of policy impoundments. How do you think the courts should address these problems?

Congress responded to the impoundment crisis of the Nixon administration with the Congressional Budget and Impoundment Control Act of 1974, Pub. L. No. 93-344, 88 Stat. 297, which set up a procedure for impoundments. Proposals to rescind appropriations entirely were to be submitted to Congress, where they would be without effect unless approved by a bill passed within a specified period. Proposals to defer spending temporarily within the fiscal year were to be valid unless disapproved by a one-house legislative veto. Congress avoided any constitutional confrontation over the Act, however, by including a disclaimer that it was not to be construed as "asserting or conceding the constitutional powers or limitations of either the Congress or the President." At the same time, Congress deleted the Antideficiency Act's authorization to create reserves in response to "other developments."

The passage of the 1974 Act has not stilled impoundment controversies, as the following case reveals.

City of New Haven v. United States
809 F.2d 900 (D.C. Cir. 1987)

HARRY T. EDWARDS, Circuit Judge:

In this case, we are called upon to decide the extent of the President's *statutory* authority to delay (or "defer") the expenditure of funds appropriated by Congress. Under section 1013 of the Impoundment Control Act of 1974 ("ICA" or the "Act"), 2 U.S.C. § 684 (1982), the President must indicate his intention to defer a congressional appropriation by sending a "special message" to Congress. In that message, the President is required to justify the deferral and specify its amount, its intended length and its probable fiscal consequences. Under the Act, if either House of Congress passes an "impoundment resolution" disapproving the "proposed" deferral, the President is required to make the funds available for obligation. If neither House acts, the deferral takes effect automatically, although it may not last beyond the end of the fiscal year.

The majority of proposed deferrals are routine "programmatic" deferrals, by which the Executive Branch attempts to meet the inevitable contingencies that arise in administering congressionally-funded agencies and programs. Occasionally, however, the President will seek to implement "policy" deferrals, which are intended to advance the broader fiscal policy objectives of the Administration. The critical distinction between "programmatic" and "policy" deferrals is that the former are ordinarily intended to *advance* congressional budgetary policies by ensuring that congressional programs are administered efficiently, while the latter are ordinarily intended to *negate* the will of Congress by substituting the fiscal policies of the Executive Branch for those established by the enactment of budget legislation.[2]

---

2. As a hypothetical example, one might consider a congressional appropriation of

In the instant case, the President invoked section 1013 as authority for implementing four separate policy deferrals. In particular, the President deferred the expenditure of funds earmarked for four housing assistance programs to be administered by the Department of Housing and Urban Development ("HUD"). The appellees—various cities, mayors, community groups, members of Congress, associations of mayors and municipalities and disappointed expectant recipients of benefits under the four programs—brought these consolidated actions challenging the authority of the President to implement policy deferrals pursuant to section 1013. That challenge was based on the inclusion in the statute of a legislative veto provision of the type held unconstitutional by the Supreme Court in *Immigration and Naturalization Service v. Chadha*, 462 U.S. 919 (1983). According to the appellees, the unconstitutional legislative veto provision contained in section 1013 rendered the *entire* section invalid, leaving the President without statutory authority on which to base the deferrals in question. The appellees requested a declaratory judgment that section 1013 was void in its entirety and an injunction . . . to release the funds appropriated by Congress for the four HUD programs.

. . . [W]e hold that the unconstitutional legislative veto provision in section 1013 is inseverable from the remainder of that section. We therefore affirm the District Court's declaratory judgment striking down section 1013 in its entirety. We hold, however, that the request for injunctive relief is now moot. [The President had subsequently signed legislation releasing the funds.]

I. Background

In November of 1985, President Reagan signed HUD's fiscal year 1986 appropriations bill. Included in that bill were appropriations for four programs administered by HUD: the Community Development Block Grant Program, under which HUD makes grants to state and local governments for community development projects; the Section 8 Housing Assistance Payments Program, under which HUD provides subsidies (through public housing agencies) to low-income families to enable them to obtain low-cost housing; the Section 312 program, under which HUD lends money (typically to cities or local public agencies) to be used to rehabilitate residential property in low-income neighborhoods; and the Section 202 program, under which HUD lends money to rehabilitate low-cost rental units for the handicapped and the elderly. In February of 1986, the President sent impoundment notices to Congress pursuant to section 1013 announcing his intention to defer the expenditure of funds for these four programs. One of the reasons provided by the President for the deferrals was to bring 1986 spending levels into line with the Administration's 1987 proposed budget. Previously, the President had failed in his efforts to convince Congress to drastically reduce these expenditures in its 1986 budget. Thus, it is not disputed that the deferrals were made for "policy" reasons.

Because the President relied solely on section 1013 as authority for the deferrals, the District Court was faced squarely with the question whether the unconstitutional legislative veto provision in section 1013 is severable from the remainder of that section. . . . [T]he court was required to consider what Congress *would have done* had it known

---

$10,000,000 to construct a new highway between Washington, D.C. and New York. If inclement weather threatened completion of the construction project, the President might seek to defer the expenditure of the appropriated funds for "programmatic" reasons. However, if the President believed that the project was inflationary, he might attempt to delay the expenditure of the funds for "policy" reasons.

at the time it passed section 1013 that the legislative veto provision was unconstitutional. Would Congress nonetheless have conferred deferral authority on the President, even though it could not exercise control over that authority by means of a legislative veto? Or would Congress have refused to confer deferral authority on the President, preferring "no statute[ ] at all" to a statute that permitted the President to defer funds without the check of a legislative veto?

. . . [T]he District Court had little difficulty concluding that Congress would have preferred no statute at all to a statute that conferred unchecked deferral authority on the President. . . . [T]he court found that the "raison d'etre" of the entire legislative effort was to wrest control over the budgetary process from what Congress perceived as a usurping Executive:

> Control—how to regain and retain it—was studied and debated at length, on the floor and in committee, over a period of years by a Congress virtually united in its quest for a way to reassert its fiscal prerogative. A clearer case of congressional intent—obsession would be more accurate—is hard to imagine.

. . . [The] overwhelming evidence of congressional intent, the court concluded, conclusively demonstrated that Congress—had it known that it could not disapprove unwanted impoundments by means of a legislative veto—would never have enacted a statute that *conceded* impoundment authority to the President. Indeed, it could be said with "conviction" that Congress

> would have preferred no statute to one without the one-House veto provision, for with no statute at all, the President would be remitted to such pre-ICA authority as he might have had for particular deferrals which, in Congress' view (and that of most of the courts having passed upon it) was not much.

Having found that the legislative veto provision in section 1013 was inseverable from the remainder of the section . . . the court . . . declared section 1013 void in its entirety. . . .

II. Analysis

. . . The appellants concede, as they must, that the legislative veto provision in section 1013 is unconstitutional under the Supreme Court's decision in *Immigration and Naturalization Service v. Chadha*, 462 U.S. 919 (1983). . . . [O]n the record in this case we must affirm the District Court's judgment . . . that Congress would not have enacted section 1013 had it known that the legislative veto provision was unconstitutional. Indeed, to the extent that section 1013 is "operable" absent the legislative veto provision, it operates in a manner wholly inconsistent with the intent of Congress in enacting deferral legislation. . . .

[T]he ICA was passed at a time when Congress was united in its furor over presidential impoundments and intent on reasserting its control over the budgetary process. Although the Senate and House initially differed over the precise means for reasserting congressional prerogatives, the legislation that eventually emerged from Congress contained several strong measures expressly designed to limit the President's ability to impound funds appropriated by Congress. For permanent impoundments (or "rescissions"), Congress adopted the Senate approach, which required prior legislative approval of proposed impoundments. *See* 2 U.S.C. § 683 (1982). For temporary impoundments (or "deferrals"), Congress adopted the House approach, which allowed impoundments to become effective without prior approval *if* neither House of Congress passed a resolution disapproving the impoundment. *See* 2 U.S.C. § 684 (1982). Importantly, Congress also amended the Anti-Deficiency Act to preclude the President from relying on that Act as authority for implementing policy impoundments.[18]

It is abundantly clear from both the statute and its legislative history that the overriding purpose of the deferral provision was to permit either House of Congress to veto any deferral proposed by the President—particularly policy deferrals. The title of the statute itself—"*Disapproval of proposed deferrals of budget authority*"—makes it plain that Congress was preoccupied with assuring for itself a ready means of disapproving proposed deferrals. The House Report accompanying H.R. 7130—from which the deferral provision was drawn—expressly states that the "basic purpose" of the bill was to provide each House an opportunity to veto an impoundment. The Conference Committee Report also emphasizes that the bill was designed to provide Congress with an effective system of impoundment control.

When the numerous statements of individual legislators urging the passage of legislation to control presidential impoundments are also considered, the evidence is incontrovertible that the "basic purpose" of section 1013 was to provide each House of Congress with a veto power over deferrals. Yet, the appellants would have us hold that Congress, had it foreseen *Chadha*, would nevertheless have gone ahead and enacted section 1013 *without* a legislative veto provision. As difficult (and precarious) as it may be at times to reconstruct what a particular Congress might have done had it been apprised of a particular set of facts, we refuse to entertain this remarkable proposition.... It is simply untenable to suggest that a Congress precluded from achieving this goal would have turned around and ceded to the President the very power it was determined to curtail.

... Here, rather than adding the legislative veto provision as somewhat of an afterthought, as in *Alaska Airlines* [discussed after *Chadha* in Chapter Two], Congress focused almost exclusively on the means for asserting control over presidential impoundments.... The appellants [emphasize] the distinction drawn in the Act between rescissions and deferrals. As noted earlier, the original bill passed by the House would have permitted both rescissions and deferrals to go into effect automatically, subject of course to a legislative veto. The House Report explained that the Committee favored a legislative veto mechanism because

> [i]n the normal process of apportionment, the executive branch necessarily withholds funds on hundreds of occasions during the course of a fiscal year. If Congress adopts a procedure requiring it to approve every necessary impoundment, its legislative process would be disrupted by the flood of approvals that would be required for the normal and orderly operation of the government. The

---

18. Before it was amended, the Anti-Deficiency Act authorized the President to "apportion[ ]" funds where justified by "other developments subsequent to the date on which such appropriation was made available." 31 U.S.C. § 665(c)(2) (1970). This open-ended language was amended to limit apportionments to three specified situations: "to provide for contingencies," "to achieve savings made possible by or through changes in requirements or greater efficiency of operations" or "as specifically provided by law." 31 U.S.C. § 1512(c)(1) (1982). The purpose of the amendment was to preclude the President from invoking the Act as authority for implementing "policy" impoundments, while preserving the President's authority to implement routine "programmatic" impoundments. President Nixon had attempted to use the Act as an instrument for shaping fiscal policy....

negative mechanism . . . will permit Congress to focus on critical and important matters, and save it from submersion in a sea of trivial ones.

In the final analysis, however, the House approach prevailed only for deferrals; for rescissions, Congress adopted the Senate approach, which required prior congressional approval before a rescission could go into effect. According to the appellants, this distinction is critical, for it demonstrates that Congress' intent in enacting section 1013 was to render deferrals "presumptively valid." Because Congress did not want to trouble itself by approving deferrals in advance, they argue, Congress would have authorized the President to implement deferrals even had it known that it could not maintain oversight over those deferrals by means of a legislative veto.

This argument completely misreads the above-quoted passage and is completely at odds with Congress' expressed intention to *control* rather than *authorize* presidential deferrals. First, the quoted passage plainly speaks to "trivial," everyday *programmatic* deferrals. It is these "trivial" impoundments relating to the "normal and orderly operation of the government" that Congress expected to present little controversy. Congress most certainly did not mean to suggest that impoundments designed to negate congressional budgetary policies would be "presumptively valid." It is precisely this sort of impoundment that Congress was determined to forestall.

Second, the quoted passage proves only that Congress preferred a system in which it need not enact legislation approving deferrals *because it could easily disapprove them* by the relatively simple expedient of the one-House veto. Nowhere in the legislative history is there the slightest suggestion that the President be given statutory authority to defer funds without the possible check of at least a one-House veto. Indeed, the House Report completely refutes the notion that Congress would have granted the President statutory authority to implement deferrals, thereby forcing itself to reenact an appropriations bill each time it disapproved of a deferral:

> [The one-House veto] is suggested on the ground that the impoundment situation established by the bill involves a presumption *against* the President's refusing to carry out the terms of an already considered and enacted statute. To make Congress go through a procedure involving agreement between the two Houses on an already settled matter would be to require both, in effect, to reconfirm what they have already decided.

Yet, a finding of severability would create a presumption in favor of deferrals and require Congress to legislate a second time in order to effectuate its budgetary policies. We cannot conceive of a result more contrary to congressional intent.

The appellants further argue that Congress' more permissive treatment of deferrals suggests that the congressional furor over "impoundments" was principally a dissatisfaction with rescissions. Again, this contention has absolutely no basis in the legislative history. Although Congress certainly distinguished between rescissions and deferrals, it spoke in general terms of the need to control "impoundments," which it defined as "withholding or *delaying* the expenditure or obligation of budget authority . . . and the termination of authorized projects or activities for which appropriations have been made." The appellants can point to nothing in the legislative history to suggest that members of Congress were disturbed with rescissions but tolerant of deferrals. Indeed, to the extent that Congress expressed any tolerance of deferrals at all, it was referring to routine programmatic deferrals, not policy deferrals.

("[T]he Committee recognizes that a brief delay in expending or obligating funds may sometimes be legitimately necessary for purely administrative reasons.")

We cannot emphasize enough in this context the critical distinction between programmatic and policy deferrals. As the appellants concede, our holding in this case will not impair the President's ability to implement routine programmatic deferrals. When Congress amended the Anti-Deficiency Act in the ICA, it did not disturb the President's authority to "impound" funds for purely administrative purposes. Thus, the President may still invoke the Anti-Deficiency Act as authority for implementing programmatic deferrals. By amending the Anti-Deficiency Act, however, Congress intended to foreclose the President from relying on that Act as separate statutory authority for *policy* deferrals. Congress intended to permit policy deferrals only under section 1013, and only if it could ensure itself a ready means of overturning policy deferrals with which it disagreed. Had Congress known it could not employ such a mechanism, it most assuredly would not have nullified its own amendment to the Anti-Deficiency Act by creating new statutory authority for policy deferrals.

Finally, the appellants contend that if we invalidate section 1013 in its entirety, we must also strike down the ICA's other "deferral-related provision"—*i.e.*, Congress' amendment to the Anti-Deficiency Act. We find this argument to be wholly specious. As noted earlier, a court's duty in a severability case is to preserve as much of the statute as it can consistent with congressional intent.... The amendment to the Anti-Deficiency Act ... is fully consistent with the expressed intent of Congress to control presidential impoundments. Thus, there is absolutely no basis for overturning Congress' amendment to the Anti-Deficiency Act.

III. Conclusion

... [W]e affirm the judgment of the District Court invalidating section 1013 in its entirety.

So ordered.

------

1. Is the *New Haven* court's ruling on severability correct under the criteria of *Alaska Airlines* (which is quoted in the notes following *Chadha*)? If so, how should Congress reformulate the Act? *See* Note, *Addressing the Resurgence of Presidential Budgetmaking Initiative: A Proposal to Reform the Impoundment Control Act of 1974*, 63 Tex. L. Rev. 693 (1984).

2. The court makes a sharp distinction between programmatic and policy impoundments—is the difference that clear? Consider the court's hypothetical in its note 2: what if the President impounds the portion of the highway funds that would pay construction worker wage increases, on grounds that the increases both render the project no longer cost-effective and contribute to general inflation?

3. The court also emphasizes that the case concerns only statutory issues. What is the constitutional status of impoundment? Consider the history of interbranch conflict through 1974, and the disclaimer in the Act. Would it be constitutional for Congress to require particular amounts of money to be spent for foreign affairs or military purposes? Does the "take Care" clause give the President some residual constitutional authority even for domestic spending?

4. In its 1987 legislation restoring automatic deficit reduction procedures, Congress included a provision designed to codify *New Haven*. The Act prohibits policy deferrals

and allows programmatic deferrals only (1) for contingencies, (2) for efficiency, or (3) as specifically provided for by law. Does that solve the problems?

5. In light of the preceding materials on congressional and presidential spending powers, reconsider *Bowsher*. Recall that the Gramm-Rudman-Hollings Act placed discretion to make the critical deficit estimates in various officers, not all of whom are responsible to the President (CBO is not, OMB is, GAO may be after the Court's ruling). Was it constitutional for Congress to reduce the President's role in controlling spending to this degree? *See* Elliott, *Regulating the Deficit After* Bowsher v. Synar, 4 Yale J. on Reg. 317 (1987). (Recall that the 1987 legislation shifted GAO's role to OMB, removing this objection.)

4. Constitutional reform (herein, of the item veto)

The persisting inability of the federal government to balance its budget has led to serious proposals for constitutional reform of the process. Some have called for a constitutional amendment requiring a balanced budget. For a sampling of the diverse views on the wisdom of this step, *see* The Constitution and the Budget (W. Moore & R. Penner, eds. 1980); Elliott, *Constitutional Conventions and the Deficit*, 1985 Duke L. J. 1077; Foster, *The Balanced Budget Amendment and Economic Thought*, 2 Const. Commentary 353 (1985); Note, *The Balanced Budget Amendment: An Inquiry into Appropriateness*, 96 Harv. L. Rev. 1600 (1983); Constitutional Amendments Seeking to Balance the Budget and Limit Federal Spending, Hearings Before the Subcomm. on Monopolies of the House Comm. on the Judiciary, 97th Cong., 1st & 2d Sess. (Ser. No. 84, 1982).

Proposals for a constitutional amendment to grant the President a line-item veto have received consideration in Congress. *See* Line-Item Veto, Hearing Before the Subcomm. on the Constitution, Sen. Comm. on the Judiciary, 98th Cong., 2d Sess. (1984). Presidents have sought this authority for many years; they point to the fact that governors of most of the states have it. We review the arguments for and against the item veto, because they relate closely to preceding materials on spending.

The Line-Item Veto: An Appraisal

House Comm. on the Budget
98th Cong., 2d Sess. 13-16 (Comm. Print 1984)

Debate over the institution of a Presidential line-item veto has given rise to a number of arguments both favoring and opposing the concept. Those arguments are summarized below. . . .

Balance of powers: For

It would restore the veto power to the President. The line-item veto would reestablish the constitutionally provided system of checks and balances. Appropriation bills almost invariably are composed of items necessary for the public welfare as well as items not necessarily in the public interest. At present, the President has no choice but to approve all or disapprove all, thus risking delay or discontinuance of necessary functions and work on needed projects. The existing veto power has been eroded by omnibus appropriations and late passage of bills.

Against

It would give the President legislative authority not envisioned by the Constitution. The veto power is legislative in nature. It is inappropriate for the President to substitute his judgment for that of the legislature. Such a move would mix the powers of executive and legislative departments in a way that was never intended by the framers of the Constitution.

The device would violate the principle of separation of powers embodied in the Constitution. The item veto would practically destroy the only power Congress now has over the President other than impeachment. The power of coercion would be removed by this device thus making the legislature subservient to the will of the Executive.

It would defeat the legislative intent of Congress. In exercising his line-item veto, the President would be proposing to give an independent appropriation to individual objects, a proposal upon which the will of Congress has never been expressed. The President would thereby originate an appropriation, not suggested by Congress, and make it law, if more than one-third of either House agrees with him, thus eroding the principle of majority rule. Congress would be forbidden to make dependent appropriations.

Most recently Congress has tended toward a system of omnibus appropriations bills. Each of these measures represents a statement of policy—the provisions taken as a whole representing the congressional will for the coordinated operation and management of a program based on a broad theme. To afford the President power of a line-item veto would be to allow the Executive to thwart the congressional will in legislating public policy.

Reducing deficits: For

It would help to reduce deficits. The item veto power would bring the President into the budget process to a greater degree to help reduce deficits without undermining the congressional power of the purse.

Against

Item veto power would not lead to a major and timely reduction in the deficit. Two major causes of high deficits, defense spending growth and certain taxes, are often supported by the Executive and would not be addressed under the power. The vehicle could only be used to control discretionary spending—a relatively small portion of the Federal budget.

The proposal is a political move rather than a substantive approach to deal with Federal deficits. The item veto cannot reach the enormous sums provided for entitlement programs and most proposals are silent on the subject of addressing tax expenditures.

Even if the item veto power were used to address the Federal deficit, adoption of a constitutional amendment would take several years. Record deficits choking off this Nation's economy are today's problem.

The President already has the tools to cut spending in individual line items. The Congressional Budget and Impoundment Control Act of 1974 granted power to the President to propose rescissions and deferrals of budget authority. In his first 2 years in office, Congress allowed more than 75 percent of President Reagan's rescission requests under that authority, resulting in more than $20 billion in lower appropriated spending in fiscal years 1981 and 1982.

Congressional timetable: For

It would force early congressional consideration of appropriations. Veto of an entire bill near the end of a session necessitates prolongation of the session as, in the absence of a veto override, a new bill must pass the House and the Senate and go to conference prior to final enactment. The item veto power would expedite completion of the legislative program so that specific vetoed items could be reconsidered prior to the beginning of the fiscal year.

Against

It would delay the timely consideration of appropriations. As has been the case in a number of States, the legislature would be reluctant to send appropriations measures forward to the President prior to extensive negotiation on his use of the line-item veto. The Appropriations Committees would hold back all of their bills until agreement could be reached on a myriad of details. If compromise is not arrived at, the real threat would be a shutdown of Government services on a broad scale.

Addressing omnibus appropriations: For

It would work to curb the effectiveness of logrolling and discourage pork-barrel appropriations and would reduce extravagance in public expenditures. The item veto would allow the President to focus attention on items he believes to be wasteful, inappropriate, or unwise without holding hostage portions of appropriations to which he does not object.

Against

It would lessen the responsibility of Congress. The item veto would allow one branch of Government to pass the buck to the other. Members of Congress could put all of their pet projects in a bill, letting the President take the heat for vetoing fiscally irresponsible yet district-pleasing projects. As President Taft said, in 1916, "It is wiser to leave the remedy ... to the action of the people in condemning at the polls the party which becomes responsible for such riders than to give, in such a powerful instrument, a temptation to its sinister use by a President eager for continued political success."

Power of persuasion: For

It would provide a useful tool of persuasion to the President. The item veto threat would be effective in persuading Congress to modify legislation before presenting it to the President for signature.

Against

In recent years the President has become so closely in touch with legislation as it progresses through each House that he can make his opposition to particular items or provisions known before the bill is presented to him for signature. By personal consultation with party leaders, by his use of liaison officers, by his supervision over the budget, by special messages to Congress, or even by radio and television appeals to the people, the President can exercise influence over details in appropriations.

The experience of the States in use of the line-item veto: For

Governors and State legislators alike have called exercise of the item veto favorable in completing budgetary policy in their States. They claim the device has been used with wise judgment and discretion to check unnecessary or unsound expenditures, to delete legislative riders, and to prevent pork-barrel appropriations.

Against

While the item veto was adopted by many States as a corrective measure for the mistakes of legislatures which met irregularly and had little knowledge about programs, Congress meets constantly and, based on the responsibility given it in Article I of the Constitution, makes the major decisions about the expenditures of public funds. Furthermore, some Governors have privately questioned the effectiveness of their own line-item veto power.

Other arguments: For

Unwise action by the President would be combatted. Congress would almost certainly override unwise action by the President vetoing a recognizedly vital project or function.

Against

It would be an uncertain grant of power. The language of the usual amendments designed to confer on the President the power to veto items or provisions in appropriation bills has been given varying interpretations in the several States. The Pennsylvania Supreme Court has construed the expression "to disapprove any item" to include the right "to reduce any item." Were the U.S. Supreme Court to interpret similar language the same way, the President could modify legislative appropriations almost at will; he could delete some items; he could reduce others; he could approve the remainder. This would, in effect, shift control of the purse strings of the Government from Congress to the Executive.

---

1. Considering not only the immediately preceding materials on federal spending, but also those in Chapter Two on the President's veto, where do you come out on the desirability of the item veto? For more of the debate, *see* Symposium on the Line-Item Veto, 1 Notre Dame J. of Law, Ethics & Public Policy 157 (1985); Fisher & Devins, *How Successfully Can the States' Item Veto be Transferred to the President?*, 75 Geo. L. J. 159 (1986).

2. Impoundment has long offered Presidents a functional analogue to the item veto, hasn't it? (Indeed, impoundment is more flexible than some variants of the item veto, because it allows reducing rather than wholly eliminating categories of spending.) What effect does the impoundment controversy have on your view of the desirability of an item veto?

3. In an effort to avoid constitutional change, with its long-term effects, some have suggested that Congress grant the President a *statutory* item veto, to be withdrawn if abused. Would that be constitutional? *See* Gressman, *Is the Item Veto Constitutional?*, 64 N.C. L. Rev. 819 (1986)("no"); Note, *Is a Presidential Item Veto Constitutional?*, 96 Yale L.J. 838 (1987) ("no"). Recall that the President's veto power applies to "bills." Could Congress avoid constitutional problems by altering its internal rules to divide each appropriations measure into as many bills as there are items, at least if each such "bill" then receives separate formal passage by both houses? Constitutionality aside, how would you advise Congress on the wisdom of such a proposal?

Chapter 5

The President and the Faithful Execution of the Laws

One of the most striking aspects of article II is how little of it appears to confer significant power on the President regarding domestic affairs. Some such powers could be read into the general category of "executive power" vested in the President, but the article II vesting clause has generally been regarded as encompassing only those domestic powers granted explicitly or implicitly by the remainder of the article. Besides the vesting clause, the only other broad charge to the President in domestic affairs is the obligation to "take Care that the Laws be faithfully executed." This chapter considers the roles, responsibilities, and powers that have been associated with the faithful execution obligation.

In a sense, the importance that the faithful execution clause has taken on as a potential source of presidential power is ironic. The clause was hardly debated during the framing or ratification of the Constitution. In all probability, it was generally understood as a ministerial obligation to enforce the laws and a prohibition against their suspension. *See generally* the documents excerpted in 4 The Founders' Constitution (P. B. Kurland & R. Lerner, eds. 1987). Yet, the bare phrasing of the clause seems to carry more import than that. The fact that the President is to "take Care" that the laws be executed implies a supervisory relationship with subordinate officials. It is an easy jump to argue that the President must be able to discharge subordinate officials who are not themselves faithfully executing the laws. Reading the faithful execution clause literally, therefore, has provided successful arguments for presidential power that are not closely tied to the historical origins of the clause.

This chapter considers the President as executor of the law, taking "law" in its commonly understood sense. We will explore the President's power, in relation to the other branches, to determine and enforce public policy in domestic affairs, or to resist its enforcement, on behalf of the United States. You have already seen from Chapter Two that Congress, in at least a certain class of cases, is entitled to the implementation of its legislative decisions irrespective of the President's legal or policy views. That principle, however, leaves a host of important questions unanswered. Among them:

1. Must the executive enforce laws that the President determines to be unconstitutional? Does it make a difference that he or a predecessor approved them?

2. Must the executive enforce a law if the President or his subordinate determines that enforcement would not accomplish, or would perhaps undermine, Congress' purpose in enacting the law?

3. Must the executive defend in court a law that it determines is unworkable or unconstitutional? Do the same rules apply to both trial and appellate challenges?

4. What is the scope of the executive's policymaking prerogatives with respect to enforcing laws that cannot, in any event, be enforced in all cases, for example, the criminal laws?

5. To what extent does the President have constitutional power that does not need statutory support to enforce public policies? What significance, if any, attaches to Congress' silence in the face of presidential initiatives?

6. To what extent may Congress remove from the President's control law enforcement functions that are not truly ministerial, but instead require the exercise of discretion in interpreting and implementing statutes?

This chapter reviews these questions, plus the President's pardoning power, an express check on the lawmaking and interpretive powers of the other governmental branches. *See generally* Ledewitz, *The Uncertain Power of the President to Execute the Laws*, 46 Tenn. L. Rev. 757 (1979).

A. Discretionary "Non-Execution" of the Laws

1. Unconstitutional Laws

a. Implementation

An obvious source of tension in the President's duty to "take Care that the Laws be faithfully executed" lies in the scope of the word "Laws." Does "Laws" include the Constitution? Does the President's oath of office suggest an answer? If the President is obligated to enforce the Constitution, how should he react to legislative enactments he deems to be unconstitutional? What if his interpretation of the Constitution conflicts with a Supreme Court decision?

The proposition that the President need not enforce an unconstitutional law was voiced early by Thomas Jefferson, with respect to the Alien and Sedition Laws. In a letter to Abigail Adams, he wrote:

> You seem to think it devolved on the judges to decide on the validity of the sedition law. But nothing in the Constitution has given them a right to decide for the Executive, more than to the Executive to decide for them. Both magistracies are equally independent in the sphere of action assigned to them. The judges, believing the law constitutional, had a right to pass a sentence of fine and imprisonment; because that power was placed in their hands by the Constitution. But the Executive, believing the law to be unconstitutional, was bound to remit the execution of it; because that power has been confided to him by the Constitution. That instrument meant that its co-ordinate branches should be checks on each other. But the opinion which gives to the judges the right to decide what laws are constitutional, and what not, not only for themselves in their own sphere of action, but for the Legislature & Executive also, in their spheres, would make the judiciary a despotic branch.

VIII Writings of Thomas Jefferson 310 (P. Ford ed. 1897).

Do you agree with Jefferson's stance? Note that the executive branch is generally presumed to have plenary discretion over prosecutions—including decisions based on virtually any reason not to prosecute potential criminal defendants. *Cf. Heckler v. Chaney*, 470 U.S. 821 (1985) (holding nonenforcement decision by Food and Drug Administration judicially unreviewable). Given that point, does Jefferson's example of constitutional disagreement leave harder questions on the President's relationship with Congress unanswered? What if, for example, Congress orders the President to take measures he regards as unconstitutional, and the President does not have any obvious source of constitutionally based discretion to decline to enforce Congress's commands?

In October, 1986, Attorney General Edwin Meese III delivered a speech at Tulane University, which addressed the relationship between the executive and the Supreme Court on constitutional issues. In terms reminiscent of Jefferson's letter, Meese asserted: "[C]onstitutional interpretation is not the business of the Court only, but also properly the business of all branches of government." Meese, *The Law of the Constitution*, 61 Tulane L. Rev. 979, 985 (1987). He argued that there is a "necessary distinction between the Constitution and constitutional law." *Id.* at 981. The former, the document itself, is the nation's supreme law. The latter, "constitutional law," is "that body of law that has resulted from the Supreme Court's adjudications involving disputes over constitutional provisions or doctrines." *Id.* at 982. The distinction, Meese argued, must be recognized in order to preserve the possibility that each branch of government, including the Supreme Court, may appeal to the Constitution as a source of authority for correcting past errors in the law: "If a constitutional decision is not the same as the Constitution itself, if it is not binding in the same way that the Constitution is, we as citizens may respond to a decision with which we disagree." *Id.* at 985. In illustration of the point, Meese cited Abraham Lincoln's stance on *Dred Scott v. Sandford*, 60 U.S. (19 How.) 393 (1856). Although agreeing that the decision bound the parties to the immediate case, Lincoln said:

> We nevertheless do oppose [*Dred Scott*] . . . as a political rule which shall be binding on the voter, to vote for nobody who thinks it wrong, which shall be binding on the members of Congress or the President to favor no measure that does not actually concur with the principles of that decision.

3 Collected Works of Abraham Lincoln 255 (R. Basler, ed. 1953).

The Meese address was widely interpreted in the press as part of an Administration assault on the Supreme Court, which, despite the addition of two Reagan appointees by 1987, did not seem poised to reverse any of the major Warren or Burger Court rulings with which the Administration had vocally disagreed. Was that a fair assessment of Meese's actual remarks? *See generally* Symposium, *Perspectives on the Authoritativeness of Supreme Court Decisions*, 61 Tulane L. Rev. 977 (1987); Greenawalt, *Constitutional Decisions and the Supreme Law*, 58 U. Colo. L. Rev. 145 (1987). Was it a fair reaction to politics at the Justice Department? *Compare* L. Caplan, The Tenth Justice (1987), *with* Lauber, *An Exchange of Views: Has the Solicitor's Office Become Politicized?* Legal Times, Nov. 2, 1987, at 22.

CASE STUDY: "STAY" PROVISIONS OF THE COMPETITION IN CONTRACTING ACT

It is generally recognized that the Attorney General, through the power to issue formal opinions of law, may constrain executive agencies to follow those opinions unless they are withdrawn or overruled in court. *Smith v. Jackson*, 246 U.S. 388, 390-91 (1918); *Public Citizen v. Burke*, 655 F.Supp. 318, 321-22 (D.D.C. 1987).

Nonetheless, despite Jefferson's opinion on independent executive authority to construe the Constitution, Attorneys General traditionally refrain from rendering opinions as to the constitutionality of statutes once they are enacted, whether or not those statutes had the approval of the President. As Attorney General Cummings said in 1937, the head of an administrative agency is:

> under no duty to question or to inquire into the constitutional power of the Congress.... Assuming, therefore, that in the administrative branch of the Government only the President ordinarily can have proper interest in questioning the validity of a measure passed by the Congress, and that such interest ceases when he has expressed his approval or disapproval, it necessarily follows that there rarely can be proper occasion for the rendition of an opinion by the Attorney General upon its constitutionality after it has become law.

39 Op. Att'y Gen. 12, 13-14 (1937). *See generally* Note, *The Authority of Administrative Agencies to Consider the Constitutionality of Statutes*, 90 Harv. L. Rev. 1682 (1977). The one exception noted by Cummings encompasses laws that involve "conflict between the prerogatives of the legislative department and those of the executive department," that is, acts that may violate the separation of powers. 39 Op. Att'y Gen. at 16. That position was recently amplified by Attorney General Civiletti as follows: "[T]he Executive's duty faithfully to execute the law embraces a duty to enforce the fundamental law set forth in the Constitution as well as a duty to enforce the law founded in the Acts of Congress, and cases arise in which the duty to the one precludes the duty to the other." In such cases, according to Civiletti, enforcement of the unconstitutional acts "would constitute an abdication of the responsibility of the Executive Branch, as an equal and coordinate branch of Government with the Legislative Branch, to preserve the integrity of its functions against constitutional encroachment." 43 Op. Att'y Gen. No. 25 at 11-12 (June 5, 1980).

Whether the executive branch has authority to suspend the execution of laws that assertedly violate the separation of powers is a question recently highlighted by a dispute between Congress and the executive branch over the powers of the Comptroller General. The importance of the dispute to the executive branch is best understood if one appreciates, as a threshold matter, the importance that the Department of Justice has always attached to the centralization of all government litigation authority in the Attorney General.

To prevent fragmentation of the Government's legal position, the Attorney General has always resisted congressional efforts to permit any agency outside the Department of Justice to go to court independently. The fear of independent litigation authority is heightened with respect to the Comptroller General, who is head of the General Accounting Office, traditionally regarded by Justice as a legislative agency. (Recall the Supreme Court's endorsement of this view in *Bowsher v. Synar*, discussed in Chapter Four.) When Congress, in the General Accounting Office Act of 1980, gave the Comptroller General independent power to enforce subpoenas in district court against private parties, the Justice Department failed in its efforts to persuade courts that such independent litigation authority violated the President's exclusive power to take care that the laws be faithfully executed. *See United States v. McDonnell Douglas Corp.*, 751 F.2d 220 (8th Cir. 1984); *McDonnell Douglas Corp. v. United States*, 754 F.2d 365 (Fed. Cir. 1985). These decisions undoubtedly persuaded the Department of Justice of the importance of opposing any further congressional efforts to give what are ordinarily deemed executive powers to the Comptroller General.

The most recent dispute involves the so-called "stay provisions" of the Competition in Contracting Act of 1984 (CICA), Pub. L. No. 98-369, Title VII, 98 Stat. 1175 (1984). The CICA establishes procedures for disappointed bidders on contracts with executive branch agencies to file bid protests before the General Accounting Office. In the case of a bid protest before a contract is awarded, the act prohibits awarding a contract while the protest is pending, except in urgent circumstances. Additionally, if a protest is made within ten days after a contract is awarded, the awarding agency must direct the contractor to suspend its performance pending resolution of the protest. Ultimately, GAO's decisions on the bid protest are subject to judicial review. The act authorizes the Comptroller General to award filing and attorneys fees plus the cost of preparing a bid and proposal to deserving parties if the Comptroller General determines that an award did not comply with applicable statutes or regulations.

In October, 1984, the Office of Legal Counsel of the Department of Justice prepared an opinion for the Attorney General asserting the unconstitutionality of the stay provisions on separation of powers grounds. OLC concluded that the constitutional role of the Comptroller General must be limited "to those duties that could constitutionally be performed by a congressional committee." Memorandum for the Attorney General Re: Implementation of the Bid Protest Provisions of the Competition in Contracting Act, at 14 (Oct. 17, 1984), *reprinted in* Constitutionality of GAO's Bid Protest Function, Hearings Before the Legislation and National Security Subcomm. of the House Comm. on Gov't Operations, 99th Cong., 1st. Sess. 615, 628 (1985) ["GAO Bid Protest Hearings"].

As a consequence, the Office of Management and Budget instructed executive agencies to take no action based upon the contested provisions of the CICA. Specifically, OMB told agencies to proceed with their procurement processes as though no such provisions were contained in the Act. That, of course, still permitted agencies to agree voluntarily to stay procurements pending the resolution of bid protests, so long as such stays were otherwise authorized by law. Agencies were told, however, not to comply with declarations of awards of costs, including attorneys fees or bid preparation costs, made by the Comptroller General.

The OMB order triggered an uproar in Congress. *See generally* GAO Bid Protest Hearings, cited above. Although Congress disputed the executive branch's constitutional analysis, its wrath was provoked mainly by the refusal of the Department of Justice and OMB to enforce the statute. We reproduce from the hearings a letter from Attorney General Smith to the chair of the House Judiciary Committee defending the Department of Justice position, and a response prepared by the Congressional Research Service on the duty of the executive branch to enforce the laws. Decide for yourself, as you read the contending positions, which is better founded. Does it make a difference in your view that executive branch noncompliance with the CICA was probably not necessary in order to provoke a judicial challenge to the constitutionality of the act? That is, judicial resolution of the constitutional issue might well have been available even if the executive branch enforced the law it thought was unconstitutional. Should this make a difference in the executive branch's posture? Consider, in this respect, the stance of the Department of Justice with respect to defending or opposing the legislative veto, discussed in Chapter Two, above.

Constitutionality of GAO's Bid Protest Function

Hearings Before the Legislation and National Security Subcomm. of the
House Comm. on Gov't Operations, 99th Cong., 1st. Sess. 432-39,
544-59 (1985)

Letter from Attorney General William French Smith
Honorable Peter W. Rodino, Jr., Chairman, House Judiciary Committee,
on the Competition in Contracting Act (Feb. 22, 1985)

Dear Chairman Rodino:

Thank you for your letter of January 31, 1985, . . . [which] requested reports concerning the legal precedent and authority for the Department's directing agencies to refrain from complying with [certain] provisions of the statute and the Department's expressed intention to refrain from defending the validity of those aspects of the statute in future litigation. You also requested lists of all instances in which the Department has determined not to execute or not to defend a statute. Because the legal theories and precedents underlying the Executive Branch's decisions not to execute or not to defend a statute are inextricably intertwined, I have combined in the following paragraphs the discussion of the historical practice and [known] precedents in this area. . . .

My determination that the bid protest provisions at issue should neither be defended nor executed by the Executive Branch is inextricably bound up in the substantive constitutional defects of those provisions. . . . [I]t would be plainly unconstitutional under the Supreme Court's decision in *INS v. Chadha*, 103 S. Ct. 2764 (1983), to vest in the Comptroller General the power to lift the "stay" automatically imposed by the CICA whenever a bid protest is filed because that action would affect the legal rights, duties, and relations of Executive Branch officials. After *Chadha*, the Comptroller General, as an arm of Congress, can no more be assigned veto power than can a committee of Congress. Likewise, the provisions of the CICA purporting to authorize the Comptroller General to assess reasonable attorneys' fees and bid preparation costs are unconstitutional. These provisions would give the Comptroller General the authority to bind the Executive Branch and therefore are clearly inconsistent with the principles of *Chadha*.

I turn now to the legal precedent and authority for the decision not to execute or to defend the CICA. This position is based upon the fact that in addition to the duty of the President to uphold the Constitution in the context of the enforcement of Acts of Congress, the President also has a constitutional duty to protect the Presidency from encroachment by the other branches. He takes an oath to "preserve, protect and defend" the Constitution. An obligation to take action to resist encroachments on his institutional authority by the legislature may be implied from that oath, especially when he may determine it prudent to present his point of view in court. In this regard, we believe that the President must, in appropriate circumstances, resist measures which would impermissibly weaken the Presidency: "The hydraulic pressure inherent within each of the separate Branches to exceed the outer limits of its power, even to accomplish desirable objectives, *must* be resisted." *INS v. Chadha*, 103 S. Ct. at 2784 (emphasis added).

The President's veto power is usually adequate to express and implement his judgment that an Act of Congress is unconstitutional. By exercising his veto power, the President may fulfill his responsibility under the Constitution and also impose a check on the power of Congress to enact statutes that violate the Constitution. On some occasions, however, the exercise by the President of his veto power may not be feasible. For example, an unconstitutional provision may be a part of a larger and vitally necessary piece of legislation. The Supreme Court has held that the President's failure to veto a measure does not prevent him subsequently from challenging the Act in court, nor does presidential approval of an enactment cure constitutional defects. *See INS v. Chadha, supra*, 103 S. Ct. 2764 (1983); *Myers v. United States*, 272 U.S. 52 (1926).

The following words of President Andrew Johnson's counsel in an early recorded statement[3] specifically address the President's responsibilities:

> If the law be upon its very face in flat contradiction of plain expressed provisions of the Constitution, as if a law should forbid the President to grant a pardon in any case, or if the law should declare that he should not be Commander-in-Chief, or if the law should declare that he should take no part in the making of a treaty, I say the President, without going to the Supreme Court of the United States, maintaining the integrity of his department, which for the time being is entrusted to him, is bound to execute no such legislation; and he is cowardly and untrue to the responsibility of his position if he should execute it.

2 *Trial of Andrew Johnson* 200 (Washington 1868). This statement, of course, was made in the context of the attempt to impeach President Johnson for, *inter alia*, having refused to obey the Tenure in Office Act, an act "which he believed with good reason ... to be unconstitutional...." 38 Op. A.G. 252, 255 (1935).

This duty to preserve the institution of the Presidency, captured in the words of President Andrew Johnson's counsel, was articulated eloquently and more authoritatively by Chief Justice Chase, who presided over the trial in the Senate of President Johnson. Chief Justice Chase declared that the President had no duty to execute a statute that:

> directly attacks and impairs the executive power confided in him by [the Constitution]. In that case it appears to me to be the clear duty of the President to disregard the law, so far at least as it may be necessary to bring the question of its constitutionality before the judicial tribunals.

. . .

> How can the President fulfill his oath to preserve, protect, and defend the Constitution, if he has no *right* to *defend* it against an act of Congress, sincerely believed by him to have passed in violation of it?[4]

---

3. Years earlier, President Jefferson, believing that Congress had no constitutional power to grant authority to the courts to control executive officers through the issuance of writs of mandamus, refused to have his Attorney General appear, except as a reluctant witness, and defend the constitutionality of a statute in the case of *Marbury v. Madison*, 1 Cranch 137 (1803), an original action before the Supreme Court. The Court ultimately held the statute unconstitutional.

4. R. Warden, *An Account of the Private Life and Public Services of Salmon Portland Chase* 685 (1874). Chief Justice Chase's comments were made in a letter written the day after the Senate had voted to exclude evidence that the entire cabinet had advised President Johnson that the Tenure of Office Act was unconstitutional. *Id. See* M. Benedict, *The Impeachment and Trial of Andrew Johnson* 154-55 (1973). Ultimately, the Senate admitted evidence that the President had desired to initiate a court test of the law. *Id.* at 156.

(Emphasis in original.) If the President does not resist intrusions by Congress into his sphere of power, Congress may not only successfully shift the balance of power in the particular case but may succeed in destroying the presidential authority and effectiveness that would otherwise act as a check of Congress's exercise of power in other circumstances.

The major historical examples of refusals by the Executive to enforce or defend an Act of Congress have been precipitated for the most part by Congress's attempt to alter the distribution of constitutional power by arrogating to itself a power which the Executive believes the Constitution does not confer on Congress but, instead, reposes in him. In such situations, a fundamental conflict arises between the two Branches, and this conflict has generally resulted in Attorneys General presenting to the courts the Executive's view of what the Constitution requires. The potential for such a conflict arising was expressly recognized by Attorney General Palmer in 1919 when he opined that the general duty of the Attorney General to enforce a statute did not apply in the case of a conflict between the executive and the legislature. *See* 31 Op. A.G. 475, 476 (1919).

Seven years later, this exception to the general rule was applied when the President acted contrary to a statute prohibiting the removal of a postmaster. That act led to the Executive challenging successfully the Act's constitutionality in litigation brought by the removed postmaster. *Myers v. United States*, 272 U.S. 52 (1926). *Myers* appears to be the first case to reach the Supreme Court in which the Executive acted contrary to and then directly challenged the constitutionality of a federal statute in court:

> In the 136 years that have passed since the Constitution was adopted, there has come before this Court for the first time, so far as I am able to determine a case in which the government, through the Department of Justice, questions the constitutionality of its own act.

Id. at 57 (condensation of oral argument for counsel for appellant Myers).

[*Humphrey's Executor* and *Buckley v. Valeo* are additional examples. Also, in 1946,] the Executive carried out, but then refused to defend when sued, and indeed successfully challenged the constitutionality of, a statute which directed that the salaries of certain federal employees not be paid. *United States v. Lovett*, 328 U.S. 303 (1946)....

In addition to these examples, there have been a number of cases in which the Executive has challenged the constitutionality of legislative veto devices. *See, e.g., INS v. Chadha.* As is true of the other cases discussed above, the *Chadha* Court never suggested that there was any impropriety in the Executive's conduct in contesting Acts of Congress he believed trenched on his constitutional prerogatives.

Although I believe that the decision of Attorney General Bell to enforce the legislative veto device at issue in *Chadha* until held unconstitutional by the courts was not inappropriate, I note that in 1955, almost three decades before *Chadha* was decided, President Eisenhower instructed the Secretary of Defense to ignore another legislative veto device contained in the Department of Defense Appropriation Act, a so-called "committee approval" provision, by stating in a signing statement that that provision "will be regarded as invalid by the Executive Branch of the Government... unless otherwise determined by a court of competent jurisdiction." *Public Papers of the Presidents: Dwight D. Eisenhower* 689 (1955). [Presidents Kennedy and Johnson similarly refused to honor committee approval devices.]...

My decision that the Executive Branch would not implement or defend certain provisions of the Competition in Contracting Act is completely consistent with the Supreme Court's decision in *Chadha* and the publicly stated position of this Administration that the Executive would, subsequent to *Chadha*, observe only the constitutional "report and wait" features of legislative veto devices. This decision also had the coincidental and desirable effect of enhancing the potential for judicial review of the constitutional issues.

As I stated in my letter of November 21, 1984, notifying Congress that the Department had determined that federal agencies should not execute certain provisions of CICA, it is doubtful that anyone would have standing to raise the important constitutional issues presented by the disputed provisions if the Executive Branch were to execute them fully. It may be possible, as you suggest in your letter, that if the Executive Branch were to execute the disputed provisions a case might eventually arise in which a court might find that a party had standing to raise those constitutional issues. On the other hand, the disputed provisions might well never reach the courts, especially given the likelihood that such cases would become moot before judicial determination, and the Executive would then be implementing indefinitely provisions that it believes trench on the President's constitutional prerogatives. The foregoing authorities establish that the President is not required to execute such an act provisionally against the day that it is declared unconstitutional by the courts. *See Myers v. United States, supra*, 272 U.S. 52. Moreover, my advice to Executive Branch agencies not to implement the disputed provisions has the beneficial byproduct of increasing the likelihood of a prompt judicial resolution. Thus, far from unilaterally nullifying an Act of Congress, the Department's actions are fully consistent with the allocation of judicial power by the Constitution to the courts. . . .

R. Celada, *Congressional Research Service Memorandum to the House Committee on Government Operations Concerning "The Executive's Duty to Enforce the Laws" (Feb. 6, 1985)*

. . . The refusal to implement the bid protest provisions of the law, as best we can determine, rests ultimately on an assertion of an assumed presidential power. In other words, prosecutorial discretion [and] the distinction between mandatory or directory statutes and ministerial or discretionary duties . . . are not involved here. . . . While the law confers some discretion on the CG and other officials, . . . these conferrals go to the manner of execution, not to whether the law should be implemented.

The Administration's position on the bid protest provisions of the law is neither unprecedented nor unparalleled. Although there has been no consistent pattern of behavior with respect to the implementation or execution of laws various Presidents considered to be unconstitutional, some Executives have declared an intent to disregard law on these grounds. In apparent frustration over congressional proliferation of the legislative veto device to control executive action, President Carter stated that he would "give [congressional concern] serious consideration, but we will not under our reading of the Constitution, consider it legally binding." 124 Cong. Rec. H. 5880 (daily ed. June 21, 1978).

President Jackson in 1832 vetoed a bill providing for a recharter of the National Bank on the ground of unconstitutionality notwithstanding that in the case of *McCulloch v. Maryland*, 4 Wheat. (17 U.S.) 316 (1819), this institution was held constitutional. [Ed.: See the Jackson veto message, reprinted in Chapter One, *su-pra*.] . . .

Another well known instance of a presidential refusal to execute the law, albeit decisional rather than statutory law, was the refusal to release Merryman from confinement in disobedience to a writ of habeas corpus issued by Chief Justice Taney while on circuit. "The officer in charge of the prisoner having declined to obey the writ on the ground that he was authorized by the President to suspend the writ of habeas corpus for the public safety, Taney at once issued an attachment for contempt. Its service . . . [was] prevented by the military. . . ." Warren, 2 *The Supreme Court in United States History* 368-369 (1926). See, Douglas, J., concurring, *Youngstown Co. v. Sawyer*, 343 U.S. 579, 631 note 1 (1952).

However, a number of Presidents have yielded to the legislative will despite serious constitutional misgivings. Thus, for example, President Roosevelt, while condemning as "unwise and discriminatory [and] unconstitutional" a rider to an appropriations bill forbidding the use of money appropriated therein to pay the salaries of three named persons whom the House of Representatives wished discharged because they were deemed to be "subversive," submitted to the legislative will. See *United States v. Lovett*, 328 U.S. 303 (1946), where the provision was held to be a bill of attainder. On the other hand, President Andrew Johnson refused to be bound by the Federal Tenure of Office Act and discharged Secretary of War Stanton contrary thereto. His subsequent impeachment largely rested on this action which it was contended constituted a violation of the constitutional duty to "take care that the laws be faithfully executed."

The Jackson precedent is distinguishable from the present situation since his alleged flouting of the law occurred in justifying his exercise of a veto, not in defiance of a validly enacted and effective law.

The mentioned FDR and Andrew Johnson precedents, in our view, are more in accord with the dictates of the separation of powers principle. The former allowed for resolution of the constitutional question in the judicial forum; the latter effectively and not without some inkling of the likely consequences, allowed his impeachment trial to clarify the congressional intent behind the Federal Tenure of Office Act.

The fact that other Presidents have refused on the basis of personal constitutional scruple to implement a law is not determinative of the constitutionality of either those or current actions. "That an unconstitutional action has been taken before surely does not render the same action any less unconstitutional at a later date." *Powell v. McCormack*, 395 U.S. 486, 547 (1969).

In the absence of a fundamental change in the scheme of government devised by the Framers and barring any change in directions clearly stated or implied by the Supreme Court, it would appear that such broad claims to power as are implied by the December 17, 1984 OMB instructions to the Federal agencies cannot be sanctioned "without reading Article II as giving the President not only the power to execute the laws but to make [and unmake] some." Douglas, J., concurring, *Youngstown Co. v. Sawyer*, 343 U.S. at 633. . . .

Is it part of the executive power to make the laws? Does either the grant of executive authority or the obligations imposed by the Take Care Clause permit the President to suspend the law? Do any of these sources of presidential power admit of authoritative executive determinations as to what the Constitution ultimately means? These questions, or so it seems, virtually answer themselves....

The power to execute the law starts and ends with the laws Congress has enacted. The nature of the authority conferred by the Take Care Clause was comprehensively stated by Justice Holmes. "The duty of the President to see that the laws be executed is a duty that does not go beyond the laws or require him to achieve more than Congress sees fit to leave within his power." *Myers v. United States*, 272 U.S. 52, 177 (1926).

The refusal of the President to execute the law is indistinguishable from the power to suspend the laws. That power, as is true of the power to amend or to revive an expired law, is a legislative power....

The legislative nature of the action taken by the Administration in instructing the Federal agencies to disregard the bid protest provisions of the law seems clear. In so doing the President has effectively suspended its operation across the board, an action which entails lawmaking. Moreover, in presuming to act in this manner because of the law's asserted unconstitutionality, the President arguably has violated the separation of powers by intruding into the judicial sphere. "... [i]t is emphatically the province and duty of the judicial department to say what the law is." *United States v. Nixon*, 418 U.S. at 705, citing *Marbury v. Madison*, 1 Cranch 137 (1803)....

The courts have rejected the assertion that the President has any inherent power to deny the execution of laws imposing purely ministerial duties, such as halting congressionally authorized expenditures. *Kendall v. United States*, 12 Pet. (37 U.S.) 524 (1838)....In line with the *Kendall* decision is the series of consistent rulings overturning efforts by the Nixon Administration to prevent the spending of appropriated funds. Termed an impoundment, this effective substitution of presidential policy choices regarding spending for those established by congressional appropriations was justified as part and parcel of the President's authority to see to the faithful execution of the law. The courts denied that the President had either constitutional or statutory power to decline to spend or obligate funds.... Expressly or impliedly, the courts in these cases rejected the claim of "inherent constitutional power in the Executive to decline to spend in the face of a clear statutory intent and directive to do so." *National Council of Community Mental Health Centers, Inc. v. Weinberger*, 361 F. Supp. 897, 901 (D.D.C. 1973). It follows that if Congress can by eliminating discretion prevent administrative refusals to implement or carry statutes into effect, executive claims to the contrary cannot be constitutionally based....

---

1. Do you agree in general with the proposition that the executive branch is entitled to suspend execution of laws that violate the separation of powers? Would it matter that a President had signed a disputed enactment? Consider the Attorney General's argument that an unconstitutional provision "may be a part of a larger and vitally necessary piece of legislation." Should it matter whether the provision is central or peripheral to the legislation, or whether Congress has provided that the legislation is severable? Should it matter whether the President who signed the legislation objected to it during the legislative process or in his signing statement? On the relevance of signing statements to subsequent statutory interpretation, *see* Garber and Wimmer, *Presidential Signing Statements as Interpretations of Legislative Intent: An Executive Aggrandizement of Power*, 24 Harv. J. on Legis. 363 (1987). Is the case stronger for allowing the President to waive the constitutional prerogatives of the executive branch

than for allowing the President to waive objections to infringements on individual rights?

2. The early efforts of the Department of Justice to persuade the federal courts of its constitutional position have been unsuccessful. *See Ameron, Inc. v. United States Army Corps of Engineers*, 809 F.2d 979 (3d Cir. 1986); *Universal Shipping Co. v. United States*, 652 F. Supp. 668 (D.D.C. 1987). *See also* Note, *GAO Bid Protest Procedures Under the Competition in Contracting Act: Constitutional Implications After* Buckley *and* Chadha, 34 Cath. U.L. Rev. 485 (1985). Does it make a difference in your assessment of the executive branch's position on nonenforcement that the stay provisions, even if unconstitutional, were not patently so?

3. On May 14, 1985, the House Government Operations Committee voted along party lines to recommend withholding funds from the Department of Justice and OMB until the CICA was enforced; the House Judiciary Committee had earlier approved a similar proposal for the Justice Department. On June 3, 1985, Attorney General Meese ordered agencies to comply with the law, at least until appellate review of the constitutional issues involved.

4. Compare with the CICA experience the executive branch's handling of *United States v. Lovett*, 328 U.S. 303 (1946). *Lovett* arose from an appropriations rider that prohibited the payment of salary to three government employees who had been accused informally of disloyalty; they could be paid only if they were reappointed to office with the advice and consent of the senate. The Department of Justice successfully contested the constitutionality of the statute, but the executive branch, in part to produce a justiciable controversy, did enforce the statute in order not to moot the litigation. See Ely, United States vs. Lovett: *Litigating the Separation of Powers*, 10 Harv. C. R.-C. L. L. Rev. 1 (1975). Recall that the same tactic worked in *Chadha*, discussed in Chapter Two.

b. Defending Congress in Court

The *Lovett* episode underscores a possible distinction between the executive branch's duty to enforce a law and its responsibilities once the statute is challenged in court. That is, even if it is assumed that the executive is presumptively required—and that the presumption is a strong one—to implement the enactments of Congress, there might not be an equal presumption that the executive must defend a statute attacked in court as unconstitutional. Indeed, the position of executive branch lawyers as "officers of the Court" might suggest a wholly different role.

This issue arose in connection with *Buckley v. Valeo*, 424 U.S. 1 (1976), a case challenging the constitutionality of the Federal Election Commission. The Justice Department refused in *Buckley*, on separation of powers grounds, to defend Congess' authority to appoint four of the Commission's six voting members. (See Chapter Four, above.) Consider, as you read the following statements offered at a Congressional hearing spurred by Justice's position, whether the Attorney General must defend every law the government carries out. Could he be obligated to defend a law that the executive branch refuses to implement on constitutional grounds? Consider also, if the executive branch is prepared to concede a statute's unconstitutionality, how Congress might defend itself. The following excerpted statements addressing these issues were offered by former Assistant Attorney General (later Solicitor General) Rex Lee and Simon Lazarus, later a member of the Domestic Policy Staff under President Carter.

Representation of Congress and Congressional Interests in Court

Hearings Before the Subcomm. on Separation of Powers of the Senate
Comm. on the Judiciary, 94th Cong., 2d Sess 4-6, 150-52 (1976).

Statement of Rex Lee

... The defense of statutes attacked on constitutional grounds is an important part of the Justice Department's work. There are essentially two situations in which the Department will not defend the constitutionality of a statute. The first situation involves those cases in which upholding the statute would have the effect of limiting the President's constitutional powers or prerogatives. It is neither shocking nor surprising that the Congress in enacting legislation occasionally takes a different view from that of the President concerning the President's rights. It is equally clear that the President is entitled to a defense of his perceived rights.

The litigation now before the Supreme Court in *Buckley v. Valeo* is illustrative.... The Attorney General is ... a named party in that case. On his own behalf and as counsel for the Federal Election Commission, he is defending the constitutionality of the Federal Election Campaign laws as amended by the Federal Election Campaign Act Amendments of 1974, 88 Stat. 1263, insofar as those statutes are being challenged under the first, fourth, or ninth amendments, or the due process clause of the fifth amendment. However, the brief the Department has filed for the Federal Election Commission does not address any of the issues arising out of the law enforcement powers of the Commission. With respect to these, the Attorney General has filed a separate brief urging the Supreme Court not to decide the constitutionality of the Commission's enforcement powers. The separate brief urges that this issue is not ripe for adjudication. Should the Court reach it, however, our position is that the statute unconstitutionally vests in the Federal Election Commission, as essentially an arm of the Congress, enforcement responsibilities reserved by article II of the Constitution to the executive branch. On this aspect of the case the Commission is represented by its own special counsel.

The second situation in which the Department will not defend against a claim of unconstitutionality involves cases where the Attorney General believes, not only personally as a matter of conscience, but also in his official capacity as the chief legal officer of the United States, that a law is so patently unconstitutional that it cannot be defended. Such a situation is thankfully most rare. In fact, the only instance of which I am aware is the case of *United States v. Lovett*. The statute in that case, in effect, dismissed three named executive officials. There were two grounds on which the Department declined to defend its constitutionality, first, that it unconstitutionally infringed on the President's control over executive personnel, and second, that it worked a bill of attainder. The House of Representatives hired special counsel to defend the statute. A majority of the Senate also believing it to be unconstitutional had passed the bill only because it was a rider to a necessary appropriations bill and after several conferences the House refused to recede. The United States Supreme Court unanimously held the statute unconstitutional.

These situations should not be confused with situations in which the Department defends the constitutionality of a statute unsuccessfully in lower courts but does not seek an appeal. The Supreme Court cannot and will not give plenary review to every lower court decision declaring a statute unconstitutional. By limiting the cases in which review is sought, the Solicitor General is more likely to obtain plenary review in those cases where it is most important. The decision not to appeal a finding that a law is unconstitutional is, of course, not made lightly. In both of these contexts— congressional representation and defense of constitutionality—the factor which dictates non-participation of the Department of Justice is a conflict of interest. The result of this disqualification of Justice Department lawyers is not that congressional defendants are unrepresented, or that the constitutionality of congressional legislation is not vigorously and ably asserted. In either situation, outside counsel is always available. . . .

Testimony of Simon Lazarus, Arnold and Porter
Law Firm, Washington, D.C.

. . . My purpose this morning is to discuss the question of the obligation, if there is one, of the Department of Justice to uphold the constitutionality of statutes passed by Congress and signed by the President when they are challenged in court and to consider whether it is appropriate or when it is appropriate for the Department to fail to support the constitutionality of Federal laws, what problems that raises, and what remedies there might be, and in particular, whether there is reason for concern that the interests of Congress are not adequately being represented by the manner in which this problem is dealt with now. . . .

I don't think that one can legitimately construe any of the various provisions of the United States Code defining the Attorney General's obligations and authority or any provision of the Constitution to require the Attorney General or the Solicitor General to support the constitutionality of laws that are challenged in the courts.

However, I think that it has always been understood, as a matter of practice, that that is what the Solicitor General is there for. He is there to be a responsible and distinguished advocate for the interests of the U.S. Government, which is generally understood to include the Congress, as well as the executive branch. And I think this is reflected in our practice. . . . The Department, and the Solicitor General's Office, in particular, does not always blindly push for the narrow interests of the agency it happens to be defending at a particular moment and that's also understood.

However, the standard by which the Department and the Solicitor General's Office has historically determined whether it should uphold the position that has been taken by an executive agency or an administrative agency has always been, according to Robert L. Stern, who is one of the most eminent authorities on the Solicitor General's Office, that the position taken by the agency would be supportive unless there was "no respectable argument" in favor of the agency's position.

If that standard were applied to the Federal Election Campaign Act, I think it's quite clear that the Justice Department would have taken a position in support of the law, because there's no question that even the most vulnerable provisions of the Federal Election Campaign Act could be supported by very respectable, if not very strong, arguments. . . .

What would be the consequences, if it were understood that it was part of the Attorney General's function when he thought a constitutional issue was important enough to simply go to court and say, "These are my views" and represent that those views are the views of the United States.

The amicus curiae brief that was filed in the Supreme Court [in *Buckley v. Valeo*]— which, in effect, revealed that the Justice Department was taking at one and the same time an advocate's and a neutral position on the law—was filed in the name of the United States. And I think that that is a very disturbing issue. To be sure it's perfectly clear what authority the Attorney General has when he comes to court to defend an action of the Government, such as the passage of a law. It's even reasonably clear what authority he has to come in and represent the interests of the executive branch, if they conflict with the law, which is a very rare occurrence, I would say.

But I see no basis for coming into court and simply giving an opinion which is a personal opinion, such as he might express in a law review article, where it would be perfectly appropriate for him to express such an opinion....

Note on Congressional Standing

According to Rex Lee, one reason why Congress need not be unduly concerned by occasional refusals by the executive branch to defend statutes is that Congress has independent means of litigating constitutional issues. As part of the Ethics in Government Act of 1978, passed two years after Lee's statement, Congress established the Office of Senate Legal Counsel. *See* 2 U.S.C. § 288 *et seq.* Congress is also able to hire private counsel to defend itself. In the House of Representatives, the Office of the Clerk of the House handles litigation involving house members, officers, and staff. Perhaps most remarkably, however, individual members of Congress have increasingly sought standing in federal court to challenge executive branch actions. An example is the most recent pocket veto case, discussed in Chapter Two, above, which provoked a heated panel dialogue on the standing issue. (Indeed, although the Supreme Court vacated the suit for mootness, it was widely assumed that the writ of certiorari had been provoked by the standing issue, not by the substantive issue of the pocket veto.) As you review the contending opinions, note that they offer not only different conclusions, but different approaches to analysis of the constitutional problem presented. Consider whether Judge McGowan responds fully to Judge Bork's historical analysis. Should historical analysis carry the day, or should this issue be resolved according to the court's conscientious judgment as to its ability to manage its "equitable discretion" so as to avoid the practical problems with congressional standing that Judge Bork foresees?

Barnes v. Kline

759 F.2d 21 (D.C. Cir. 1985),
vacated sub nom. Burke v. Barnes, 107 S. Ct. 734 (1987)

McGOWAN. Senior Circuit Judge:

... Before examining the merits of this dispute, we address the question of whether appellants have standing to come before a federal court for resolution of the claims they press in the present litigation. In *Kennedy v. Sampson,* [511 F.2d 430 (D.C. Cir. 1974),] this court held that a single United States Senator had standing to challenge an unconstitutional pocket veto on the ground that it had nullified his original vote in favor of the legislation in question.[11] At the same time, the court stated that either

---

11. The Senator himself characterized the injury as a deprivation of his constitutional

house of Congress clearly would have had standing to challenge the injury to its participation in the lawmaking process, since it is the Senate and the House of Representatives that pass legislation under Article I, and improper exercise of the pocket veto power infringes that right more directly than it does the right of individual members to vote on proposed legislation.

In the present action, the thirty-three individual Representatives allege an injury identical to that of the individual lawmaker in *Kennedy v. Sampson.* The House Bipartisan Leadership Group and the United States Senate assert an injury of the second, more direct type described in that opinion, that is, an injury to the lawmaking powers of the two houses of Congress.[12] Under the law of this circuit,[13] therefore, all the appellants are properly before this court.

In a wide-ranging dissent from this panel's decision on standing, Judge Bork propounds the view that neither individual congressmen nor the houses of Congress may challenge in federal court the President's invocation of the pocket veto power. More broadly, the dissent reads Article III to bar *any* governmental official or body from pursuing in federal court any claim, the gravamen of which is that another governmental official or body has unlawfully infringed the official powers or prerogatives of the first.... Courts[, however,] may not avoid resolving genuine cases or controversies—those "of a type which are traditionally justiciable"—simply because one or both parties are coordinate branches. As Justice Rehnquist has stated:

> Proper regard for the complex nature of our constitutional structure requires neither that the Judicial Branch shrink from a confrontation with the other two coequal branches of the Federal Government, nor that it hospitably accept for adjudication claims of constitutional violation by other branches of government where the claimant has not suffered cognizable injury.

Valley Forge Christian College v. Americans United for Separation of Church and State, Inc., 454 U.S. 464, 474 (1982). Thus, Supreme Court precedent contradicts the dissent's sweeping view that Article III bars any governmental plaintiff from litigating a claim of infringement of lawful function. See *Immigration & Naturalization Service v. Chadha,* 462 U.S. 919 (1983) ; *Nixon v. Administrator of General Services,* 433 U.S. 425, 439 (1977); *United States ex rel. Chapman v. FPC,* 345 U.S. 153, 154-56 (1953) (Secretary of Interior had standing to press a claim against the Federal Power Commission for alleged infringement of the Secretary's role).

In congressional lawsuits against the Executive Branch, a concern for the separation of powers has led this court consistently to dismiss actions by individual congressmen whose real grievance consists of their having failed to persuade their fellow legislators of their point of view, and who seek the court's aid in overturning the results of the legislative process. Similarly, in *Goldwater v. Carter,* 444 U.S. 996 (1979), Justice

---

the opportunity to override never arose because the President had not attempted a return veto. Under either characterization, however, the result of the President's inaction was a diminution of the Senator's power to participate in the enactment of legislation through voting on proposed or returned bills.

12. The Senate has intervened in this action [in support of the House plaintiffs.] ...

13. *See also Moore v. United States House of Representatives,* 733 F.2d 946, 950-54 (D.C.Cir.1984), *cert. denied,* —U.S.— (1985) (holding that individual members of House of Representatives have standing to sue for declaration that a tax law was unconstitutional because it originated in the Senate rather than the House).

Powell, concurring in the judgment, would have dismissed as unripe a claim by several members of Congress that the President's action in terminating a treaty infringed their constitutional role: "Congress has taken no official action. In the present posture of this case, we do not know whether there ever will be an actual controversy between the Legislative and Executive Branches." As Justice Powell also stated, however, a dispute between Congress and the President *is* ready for judicial review when "each branch has taken action asserting its constitutional authority"—when, in short, "the political branches reach a constitutional impasse."

There could be no clearer instance of "a constitutional impasse" between the Executive and the Legislative Branches than is presented by this case. Congress has passed an Act; the President has failed to sign it, and has declared it not to be a law; Congress has challenged the validity of that declaration. The court is not being asked to provide relief to legislators who failed to gain their ends in the legislative arena. Rather, the legislators' dispute is solely with the Executive Branch. And it cannot be said that Congress is asking for an advisory judicial opinion on a hypothetical question of constitutional law; Congress is seeking a declaration, not about the legal possibility of pocket vetoes during intersession adjournments, but about the validity of a particular purported veto. Congress has raised a claim that is founded on a specific and concrete harm to its powers under Article I, section 7—a "[d]eprivation of a constitutionally mandated process of enacting law" that has actually occurred. *Moore*, 733 F.2d at 951. That such injury is judicially cognizable has been clear since the Supreme Court held in *Coleman v. Miller*, 307 U.S. 433 (1939), that state legislators had standing to litigate the question of whether the legislature had ratified a constitutional amendment, within the meaning of Article V.... As the Executive Branch itself concedes, Congress clearly has standing to litigate the specific constitutional question presented.

The dissent believes, however, that the separation of powers would be better served in this case by remitting the question involved to a political solution, rather than a judicial one. The dissent understandably leaves unspecified the precise course of events contemplated: a "political solution" would at best entail repeated, time-consuming attempts to reintroduce and repass legislation, and at worst involve retaliation by Congress in the form of refusal to approve presidential nominations, budget proposals, and the like. That sort of political cure seems to us considerably worse than the disease, entailing, as it would, far graver consequences for our constitutional system than does a properly limited judicial power to decide what the Constitution means in a given case.... By defining the respective roles of the two branches in the enactment process, this court will help to preserve, not defeat, the separation of powers....

BORK, Circuit Judge, dissenting:

... With a constitutional insouciance impressive to behold, various panels of this court, without approval of the full court, have announced that we have jurisdiction to entertain lawsuits about governmental powers brought by congressmen against Congress or by congressmen against the President.... [T]he jurisdiction asserted is flatly inconsistent with the judicial function designed by the Framers of the Constitution....

It is clear ... that appellants are suing not because of any personal injury done them but solely to have the courts define and protect their governmental powers. Until this circuit permitted such actions eleven years ago, this suit would have been impossible. Indeed, for most of our history this suit would have been inconceivable. The respective constitutional powers of Congress and the President could have been given judicial definition only when a private party, alleging a concrete injury, actual or threatened, brought those powers necessarily into question. No doubt it appears more "convenient" to let congressmen sue directly and at once; in actuality, that convenience is purchased at the cost of subverting the constitutional roles of our political institutions.[1]

. . . [T]he rationale which underlies congressional standing doctrine also demands that members of the Executive and the Judicial Branches be granted standing to sue when their official powers are allegedly infringed by another branch or by others within the same branch. In addition, states would have standing to protect their powers of governance against the national government on the same theory. The consequences of this expansion of standing, which will bring an enormous number of inter- and intra-government disputes into the federal courts (usually, one supposes, into this physically convenient court) will be nothing short of revolutionary. . . .

I.

. . . [T]he jurisdictional requirement of standing keeps courts out of areas that are not properly theirs. It is thus an aspect of democratic theory. Questions of jurisdiction are questions of power, power not merely over the case at hand but power over issues and over other branches of government. . . . Among the most important limitations is that expressed in section 2 of article III, confining our jurisdiction to "Cases" and "Controversies." The meaning of those terms, however, is decided by federal courts. It follows that judges can determine the extent of their own power within American government by how they define cases and controversies. It is for this reason that the proper definition of those terms is crucial to the maintenance of the separation of powers that is central to our constitutional structure. . . .

A critical aspect of the idea of standing is the definition of the interests that courts are willing to protect through adjudication. A person may have an interest in receiving money supposedly due him under law. Courts routinely regard an injury to that interest as conferring upon that person standing to litigate. Another person may have an equally intensely felt interest in the proper constitutional performance of the United States government. Courts have routinely regarded injury to that interest as not conferring standing to litigate. The difference between the two situations is not the reality or intensity of the injuries felt but a perception that according standing in the latter case would so enhance the power of the courts as to make them the dominant branch of government. There would be no issue of governance that could not at once be brought into the federal courts for conclusive disposition. . . .

The first problem with this court's doctrine of congressional standing is that, on the terms of its own rationale, the concept is uncontrollable. Congress is not alone

---

1. The Executive Branch conceded at oral argument that the Senate has standing to sue in this suit. . . . That concession does not, of course, remove the issue from this dispute, for it is axiomatic that parties cannot confer subject matter jurisdiction by waiver. No reason appears why the Executive should oppose standing for individual legislators but concede as to a House. The constitutional problems would seem to be identical. More important is the misunderstanding of the importance of the issue that underlies this concession. According to counsel, the Executive Branch is pursuing decision on the merits to vindicate its governmental interest in constitutional governance. While this is undoubtedly true, I suggest that, given this concern, appellees have misordered the priorities. By conceding the standing issue appellees endanger a constitutional principle far more momentous than the scope of the pocket veto power, especially since the latter issue can arise and be decided later in a private suit.

in having governmental powers created or contemplated by the Constitution. This means that the vindication-of-constitutional-powers rationale must confer standing upon the President and the judiciary to sue other branches just as much as it does upon Congress. "Congressional standing" is merely a subset of "governmental standing." This rationale would also confer standing upon states or their legislators, executives, or judges to sue various branches of the federal government. Indeed, no reason appears why the power or duty being vindicated must derive from the Constitution. One would think a legal interest created by statute or regulation would suffice to confer standing upon an agency or official who thought that interest had been invaded.[2] ...

No avoidance of these implications is possible unless courts lay down fiats, resting upon no discernible principle, that arbitrarily limit those institutions whose members may vindicate constitutional and legal interests. Because the implications of what is being done here are unfamiliar, it will be well to offer a few examples of governmental standing that flow directly from the majority's rationale. We may begin with Congress. Members of Congress, dissatisfied with the President's performance, need no longer proceed, as historically they always have, by oversight hearings, budget restrictions, political struggle, appeals to the electorate, and the like, but may simply come to the district court down the hill from the Capitol and obtain a ruling from a federal judge. ... Members of Congress would have standing to sue the President whenever he committed troops, as in Lebanon, on the allegation that there had been a violation of the War Powers Resolution or of Congress' power to declare war under article I, section 8. Members could sue the President about his law enforcement policies and priorities, claiming that their power to make laws under article I, section 8, and his duty, arising under article II, section 3 to "take Care that the Laws be faithfully executed," had both been infringed. ...

But the transformation this court has wrought in its own powers necessarily runs much farther than that. If Congress, its Houses, or its members can sue the President for a declaration of abstract legal right, it must follow that the President may, by the same token, sue Congress. For example, Presidents at least since Franklin Roosevelt have objected to the device known as the congressional veto on the grounds of its unconstitutionality. Had they understood our constitutional system as this court now understands it, these Presidents need not have waited for a private person to raise the issue in *INS v. Chadha*, 462 U.S. 919 (1983), to obtain a declaration of the unconstitutionality of that device, but could have sued Congress at any time. This court may become a potent supplement to the checks and balances the Constitution provides. Under the majority's reasoning, whenever the President vetoes a bill that, in his judgment, requires him to execute an unconstitutional law or invades his legitimate constitutional powers and Congress overrides his veto, the President may

---

2. Indeed, this court has so held, on the authority of *Kennedy v. Sampson. AFGE v. Pierce*, 697 F.2d 303, 305 (D.C.Cir.1982).... The case was taken as an emergency expedited appeal, and the panel, on which I sat, held that Congressman Sabo did not have standing as a member of the House of Representatives, but did have standing as a member of the Appropriations Committee. Id. at 305.... My vote in *Pierce* is, of course, inconsistent with the position I adopt in this dissent.... I overlooked the latent separation-of-powers issues in that case, which was my first encounter with this court's congressional standing doctrine, and in which, because of the emergency nature of the appeal, the opinion was released one day after oral argument. *See Pierce*, 697 F.2d at 303.

sue before the ink is dry for a judicial declaration of unconstitutionality. We will become not only a part of the legislative process but perhaps the most important part.

Indeed, if unlawful interference with one's official powers is enough to confer standing I do not know why members of the judiciary should not join in the game, with the added advantage, of course, that one federal judge's lawsuit claiming a right to powers denied would be heard and decided by other federal judges. Thus, when Congress limited the habeas corpus jurisdiction of the District Court for the District of Columbia, there is no reason, under the majority's rationale, why a district court judge, or a judge of this court who had lost appellate jurisdiction, should not have sued Congress and the President for a declaration of unconstitutionality. . . .

Intra-branch disputes also must succumb to this court's plenary interpretation of its own powers. Individual legislators now have standing to sue each other, the Houses of Congress, other bodies composed of legislators, such as committees and caucuses, and so on. Virtually every internal rule, custom, or practice by which the internal operations of Congress are regulated is reviewable at the discretion of this court at the behest of disgruntled legislators. That means, for example, that the opponents of a filibuster have standing to sue for an injunction directing the filibuster to cease. Legislators who were not selected to serve on the committees of their choice have standing to challenge the manner in which the selection process was conducted. Indeed, this court has so held. *Vander Jagt v. O'Neill*, 699 F.2d 1166, 1170 (D.C. Cir. 1983), *cert. denied,__U.S.__ (1983). . . .*

The same reasoning, of course, applies to disputes within the Executive and Judicial Branches. . . . Presumably, a district judge whose jurisdiction had been limited by a court of appeals decision could seek rehearing *en banc* or petition the Supreme Court for a writ of certiorari. According to this court's rationale, I should be able to petition the Supreme Court for a writ of certiorari or of mandamus to overturn the result in this case because it unconstitutionally alters my duties and powers as an article III judge.[5]

Nor must it be forgotten that the Constitution contemplates areas of authority for the states, areas in which the national government is not to impinge. Should Congress enact a law that arguably is beyond its powers and that has an impact upon citizens of the several states, it would seem, under this court's reasoning, that members of a state legislature, whose jurisdiction had been ousted, would have standing to sue the national executive to enjoin enforcement of that law. Certainly the State itself would have standing. States, after all, have constitutional functions and powers as surely as Congress does. . . .

II.

It is easily demonstrated from several different lines of cases that the doctrine of congressional standing is ruled out by binding Supreme Court precedent. . . .

---

5. Lest this be regarded as fantasy or burlesque, it should be noted that this very sort of litigation within the judicial branch is being attempted. *See In re Robson and Will, petition for mandamus or in the alternative for cert. filed,* 53 U.S.L.W. 3552 (U.S. Feb. 5, 1985) (No. 84-1127) (United States District Judges seeking relief against Court of Appeals on grounds that Court of Appeals improperly substituted its discretion for that of the District Court, and exceeded its authority by ordering a remedy that is contrary to law). The possibilities seem boundless.

B.

The Supreme Court's decisions about suits over "generalized grievances" . . . require [dismissal for lack of standing]. The merits of the dispute offered us turn upon the interpretation of article I, section 7, clause 2 of the Constitution. That is a task for which courts are suited, and I would have no hesitation in reaching and deciding the substantive question if this were a suit by a private party who had a direct stake in the outcome. . . . This is an action by representatives of people who themselves have no concrete interest in the outcome but only a "generalized grievance" about an allegedly unconstitutional operation of government. It is well settled that citizens, whose interest is here asserted derivatively, would have no standing to maintain this action. That being so, it is impossible that these representatives should have standing that their constituents lack. The Supreme Court has repeatedly rejected the proposition that one who sues as a citizen or taxpayer, alleging nothing more than that the government is acting unconstitutionally, has standing to sue. . . . Yet, the legislators on whom this court has bestowed standing have alleged only two things—an unconstitutional act and an impairment of their constitutional powers as a result of that act. It is clear that the citizens and taxpayers these legislators represent would not have standing if they alleged that the same unconstitutional act had impaired the official powers of their representatives. . . . The only possible [ground for congressional standing] is that elected representatives have a separate private right, akin to a property interest, in the powers of their offices. But that is a notion alien to the concept of a republican form of government. It has always been the theory, and it is more than a metaphor, that a democratic representative holds his office in trust, that he is nothing more nor less than a fiduciary of the people. . . .

C.

. . . [I]t is the necessity to decide a case that creates a court's duty to "say what the law is." *Marbury v. Madison*, 5 U.S. (1 Cranch) 137, 177 (1803). In the new view [of the majority in this case], it is the court's desire to pronounce upon the law that leads to the necessity to create a case. . . . In this respect, the standing requirement is like the requirement of ripeness, another of the traditional aspects of dispute resolution through the judicial process. . . .

D.

. . . A firm standing concept . . . decreases the number of occasions upon which courts will frame constitutional principles to govern the behavior of other branches and of states. There will thus be fewer constitutional principles of that sort in the system. That, too, is a benefit. The business of government is intensely practical and much is accomplished by compromise and accommodation. The powers of the branches with respect to one another, as well as the reciprocal powers of the federal and state governments, ebb and flow as the exigencies of changing circumstances suggest. It is proper and healthful that this should be so. These matters should not be always settled at the outset by declarations of abstract principle from an isolated judiciary not familiar with the very real and multitudinous problems of governing. . . .

Our democracy requires a mixture of both principle and expediency. As Professor Bickel put the matter:

> [T]he absolute rule of principle is . . . at war with a democratic system. . . . No society, certainly not a large and heterogeneous one, can fail in time to explode

if it is deprived of the arts of compromise, if it knows no ways of muddling through. No good society can be unprincipled; and no viable society can be principle-ridden.

A. Bickel, The Least Dangerous Branch 64 (1962)....

[E]xcept where a conventional lawsuit requires a judicial resolution, much of the allocation of powers is best left to political struggle and compromise. Indeed, it was to facilitate and safeguard such a continuing process that the checks and balances of the Constitution were created. It was to allow room for the evolution of the powers of various offices and branches that the Constitution's specification of those powers was made somewhat vague. The Framers contemplated organic development, not a structure made rigid at the outset by rapid judicial definition of the entire subject as if from a blueprint. The majority finds this plan inadequate and the idea of political struggle between the political branches distasteful, at best "time-consuming," at worst involving "retaliation." Just so. That is what politics in a democracy is and what it involves. It is absurd to say, as the majority does, that a "political cure seems to us considerably worse than the disease, entailing, as it would, far graver consequences for our constitutional system than does a properly limited judicial power to decide what the Constitution means in a given case." That is a judgment about how the Constitution might better have been written and it is not a judgment this or any other court is free to make. Moreover, I know of no grave consequences for our constitutional system that have flowed from political struggles between Congress and the President. This nation got along with that method of resolving matters between the branches for 185 years, until this court discerned that the nation would be better off if we invented a new role for ourselves....

III.

Though we are obligated to comply with Supreme Court precedent, the ultimate source of constitutional legitimacy is compliance with the intentions of those who framed and ratified our Constitution. The doctrine of congressional or governmental standing is doubly pernicious, therefore, because it flouts not only the rules enunciated and applied by the Supreme Court but the historical meaning of our basic document as well....

[T]he members of the Convention repeatedly defeated the proposal for a Council of Revision.... [T]he effect the Council would have had upon our constitutional arrangements and upon the role of the courts [would have been] ... remarkably similar to those that would result from the final adoption of this circuit's doctrine of governmental standing....

[T]he Convention drafted article III of the Constitution in a way that does not contemplate suits directly between the branches of government. Article III extends "judicial power" to various categories of "cases" and "controversies," which itself indicates the Framers had in mind a role for the judiciary similar to the common-law function with which they were familiar. It is perhaps more noteworthy that article III creates ... specific, independent categories of federal judicial power.... Given that listing, it is incredible that Framers who intended to extend judicial power to direct controversies between Congress and the President failed to include so important a category in their recitation.

The drafters, moreover, singled out especially sensitive categories of judicial power for the original jurisdiction of the Supreme Court.... Had they contemplated that the federal courts would regularly supervise relationships between Congress and the President, the Framers would undoubtedly have placed that class of cases within the Supreme Court's original jurisdiction.... The Framers simply cannot have contemplated that disputes directly between Congress and the President would be decided in the first instance in any of the thirteen existing state court systems....

The intentions of the Framers need not be derived entirely from the records of the Constitutional Convention, nor even from the structure and language of the document itself. Courts may and frequently do look to evidence of what was said and done immediately after the original act of composition.... [T]he only discussion in The Federalist of possible judicial involvement in disputes between the President and Congress comes in connection with the impeachment power.... The task of umpiring disputes between the coordinate branches which this court has agreed to undertake is no more suited to judicial competence than trial by impeachment, and raises the same or greater dangers of repeated and head-on confrontation with the other branches that underlie Hamilton's objections [to giving the courts jurisdiction over impeachment trials].

A similar point may be made about Hamilton's discussion of the President's veto power in *The Federalist* No. 73.... [I]f this court's governmental standing doctrine is correct, Hamilton has described a power that is largely superfluous. The President would not need to defend himself through the veto power—he could at once challenge any "vote[s]" or "resolutions" that endangered his "constitutional rights" as President in the courts....

IV.

To make its standing doctrine more palatable this court has adopted a doctrine of remedial or equitable discretion. This doctrine permits the court to say that a congressional plaintiff has standing, and hence that the court has jurisdiction, and yet refuse to hear the case because the court is troubled by the separation-of-powers implications of deciding on the merits. We have no such equitable discretion, however, for "[w]e have no more right to decline the exercise of jurisdiction which is given, than to usurp that which is not given." *Cohens v. Virginia*, 19 U.S. (6 Wheat.) 264, 404 (1821). By claiming that discretion, the court has created for itself a kind of certiorari jurisdiction—which it took an act of Congress to create for the Supreme Court. There would be no need to violate the settled principle of federal jurisprudence that a court with jurisdiction may not decline it if the article III limits on this court's jurisdiction were adhered to.[13] The introduction of discretion into the standing inquiry is therefore an attempt to change the very nature of that doctrine....

The limits that standing places upon judicial power do not mean that many important questions of constitutional power will forever escape judicial scrutiny. Many of the constitutional issues that congressional or other governmental plaintiffs could be expected to litigate would in time come before the courts in suits brought by private plaintiffs who had suffered a direct and cognizable injury. That is entirely appropriate, and it belies the argument that this court's governmental standing doctrine is necessary to preserve our basic constitutional arrangements.

---

13. The standing requirements of article III are jurisdictional—discretion plays no part in their application. The prudential standing requirements are no less jurisdictional. I am aware of no case in which the Court has held that a lower federal court may decide that those requirements need not be satisfied if the court thinks it would be inequitable to deny standing.

At bottom, equitable discretion is a lawless doctrine that is the antithesis of the "principled decisionmaking" that was invoked to justify its manufacture....Ultimately, the doctrine of equitable discretion makes cases turn on nothing more than the sensitivity of a particular trio of judges.... The combination of congressional standing and equitable discretion will very probably prove to have been but a way-station to general, continual, and intrusive judicial superintendence of the other institutions in which the Framers chose to place the business of governing.

VI.

... There is not one shred of support for what the majority has done, not in the Constitution, in case law, in logic, or in any proper conception of the relationship of courts to democracy....

I dissent.

---

1. A major thrust of Judge Bork's dissent is that the court's recognition of congressional standing makes irresistible the recognition of standing in a host of supposedly absurd intragovernmental cases. Is he persuasive? Do threshold doctrines other than standing, such as ripeness or the political question doctrine, provide any measure of assurance in this respect? *See* the opinions of Justices Rehnquist and Powell in *Goldwater v. Carter*, discussed in Chapter Six. What about Judge McGowan's invocation of "equitable discretion" as a source of power to monitor the appropriate functioning of the court? Does the fact, as Judge Bork recognizes in his note 13, that certain standing rules are "prudential"—that is, judge-made and discretionary—belie his argument? To what degree is discretion involved in the application of all the "threshold" doctrines?

2. Of the various examples Judge Bork offers of intolerable lawsuits, which are likely? Which do you think are undesirable?

3. Judge Bork notes that a person entitled to the payment of money under a particular law would have standing to challenge a presidential pocket veto of that law. Should a court be more willing to adjudicate an issue of constitutional process on behalf of such a plaintiff than on behalf of a plaintiff, such as a member of Congress, with a long-run stake in the operation of the legislative system? One policy typically associated with the Supreme Court's elaboration of standing rules is the Court's desire to secure the best possible plaintiff to bring a concrete, well-focused dispute. Who—the disappointed payee or the member of Congress—is likely to be the more useful litigant in this respect?

4. Judge Bork's dissent exemplifies a particularistic view of constitutional originalism as a method of interpretation. That is, Judge Bork defends his conclusion as the conclusion "the Framers" would have reached had they been asked the question of congressional standing. Is this method helpful? Does Judge Bork employ it persuasively?

In this connection, consider Judge Bork's separate concurrence in a first amendment case decided four months earlier, *Ollman v. Evans*, 750 F.2d 970, 993 (D.C. Cir. 1984) (en banc), *cert. denied*, 471 U.S. 1127 (1985). A majority in *Ollman* held that two conservative columnists were immune to a libel suit brought by a Marxist political scientist. They concluded that the defendants' denigration of the plaintiff's professional reputation was a constitutionally protected statement of opinion, not a statement of purported fact that may be actionable under the first amendment. Judge (now Justice)

Scalia dissented on the ground that the columnists' statement was a "classic . . . libel," 750 F.2d at 1036, and argued that Judge Bork's concurring opinion represented an instance of judicial creativity based unduly on "subjective judgment." *Id.* at 1038. Judge Bork replied:

> Judges given stewardship of a constitutional provision . . . whose core is known but whose outer reach and contours are ill-defined, face the never-ending task of discerning the meaning of the provision from one case to the next. . . . In a case like this, it is the task of the judge in this generation to discern how the framers' values, defined in the context of the world they knew, apply to the world we know.

Id. at 995.

Did Judge Bork adhere in *Barnes* to the version of originalism he espoused in *Ollman*? Are not the references in article III to "cases" and "controversies," constitutional provisions "whose core is known but whose outer reach and contours are ill-defined?" If they are, should Judge Bork have employed a more value-oriented "originalism?" Judge Bork, in *Barnes*, recognizes an "original" desire for political solutions to political disputes. Should he have also considered the weight attached by the founding generation to the President's adherence to constitutional process? To Congress' primacy in the legislative process? To the role of the courts in construing the Constitution? Should he, on this basis, have come to a different result? What limits, if any, does this level of interpretive uncertainty reveal concerning originalism as an interpretive technique? *See generally* Powell, *Rules for Originalists*, 73 Va. L. Rev. 659 (1987).

2. Laws "Unjustified" in Fact

Having considered whether the President, or his subordinates, may decline to enforce a statute based on an executive interpretation of the Constitution, consider now whether the executive branch may decline to enforce a statute based on its view of legislative intent. That is, if Congress has expressed its statutory purpose, may the executive decline to enforce a statute if it independently determines that enforcement of the statute will not accomplish and perhaps will undermine the legislative goal? Relatedly, what should happen if the executive determines that Congress' enactment of a statute was based on certain factual assumptions that the executive is prepared to determine are no longer, if they ever were, true?

Note: Commonwealth of Pennsylvania v. Lynn

The leading case on the "non-execution" of a statutory program is *Commonwealth of Pa. v. Lynn*, 501 F.2d 848 (D.C. Cir. 1974), overturning a grant of summary judgment requiring the Secretary of the Department of Housing and Urban Development (HUD) to resume accepting, processing, and approving applications for federal subsidies under three different housing programs he had suspended on the ground that they were not accomplishing Congress' intended purposes.

The three programs involved were as follows:

Section 101 of the National Housing Act, 12 U.S.C. § 1701s, enacted in 1965, which established a rent supplement program under which the federal government agreed to make rent payments on behalf of qualified tenants in housing erected under other government programs;

Section 235 of the Act, 12 U.S.C. § 1715z, which was enacted in 1968 to assist lower-income families in purchasing their own homes by providing mortgage subsidies for single-family homes built under the program; and

Section 236 of the Act, 12 U.S.C. § 1715z-1, also enacted in 1968, which was intended to assist lower-income renters by subsidizing mortgages for rental housing approved under the program.

HUD Secretary Lynn, in early 1973, ordered the suspension of these programs and announced that HUD would conduct a study and evaluation of them. It was undisputed that the Secretary suspended the programs for reasons related to the feasibility of accomplishing their express objectives ("program-related reasons") and not for reasons of policy extrinsic to the operation of the programs (for example, political opposition to government intervention in the housing market).

Plaintiffs in the case were proposed sponsors of Section 235 or Section 236 projects. The District Court had certified a class suit on behalf of the named plaintiffs and other potential sponsors, and went on to hold that the Secretary was not vested with any discretion to suspend the disputed programs. 362 F. Supp. 1363 (D.D.C. 1973). The Court of Appeals characterized the issue before it as the narrow question whether the Secretary had statutory discretion to withhold the exercise of authority Congress gave him for specific purposes in the National Housing Act in order to determine whether those purposes would be achieved or frustrated by HUD's continued exercise of that authority under existing circumstances. The Court of Appeals analysis proceeded in two stages. First, the court considered whether Congress gave the Secretary any discretion in administering these programs to decide on their suspension. Second, the court determined whether any such discretion was abused.

The court initially concluded that the mix of instructions given to the Secretary by Sections 101, 235, and 236 of the National Housing Act—some seemingly permissive and some seemingly mandatory—precluded any reliance on the text of those sections alone to determine the scope of the Secretary's discretion. The court, in deciding on the scope of the Secretary's authority, relied primarily on provisions of other housing statutes that supported Secretary Lynn's claim of discretion. Aspects of the Housing Act of 1949 and the HUD Act of 1968, as well as the explicit purposes of Sections 101, 235, and 236 all led to the conclusion that the Secretary was bound to administer the programs so as to assist the intended beneficiaries. The court thus inferred that the Secretary had limited discretion to suspend the programs when he had adequate reason to believe that they were frustrating national housing policy and not serving Congress's express statutory purposes to aid low-income persons.

The Court of Appeals drew further support for the Secretary's position from congressional response to the Secretary's decision to suspend the programs. The court's rationale for relying on this response, however, was not entirely clear. In the House of Representatives, neither the committee with oversight responsibility for the suspended programs, nor the Committee on Appropriations took any action expressly challenging the legality of the suspensions. Senate committees were clear in expressing their disagreement with the wisdom of the suspensions, but likewise did not question their legality. The congressional response, the court concluded, was corroborative of the inference of discretion drawn from the relevant statutes:

> We emphasize that Congress's failure to enact mandatory spending legislation in response to the Executive's decision to withhold authorized funds is not and

cannot be the basis, in any degree, for an inference that it did not intend in the first instance to preclude executive discretion to suspend the programs. Congress may make its adherence to an original intent unmistakable by further legislation, or by overriding a presidential veto, but it cannot be put to the necessity of acting twice before it is taken to mean what it said in duly enacted legislation. We have examined Congress's response to the executive action here challenged only for the light it might shed on its original intent in establishing these three housing programs.

That response is corroborative of the inference of discretion in the Secretary reasonably to be drawn from the statutes and their contexts; and we hold that, in the circumstances revealed by this record, the Secretary is not without authority to suspend the Section 235, 236 and 101 programs.

501 F.2d at 861.

Before determining whether the Secretary abused this discretion, the court noted that, during the pendency of the appeal, the program evaluation study initiated by the Secretary was completed. The court held that, although not available to the Secretary when the programs were suspended, the report would now be relevant in determining whether the suspensions were an "abuse of discretion."

The court's threshold issue in reviewing the program suspensions, as in every case of judicial review of administrative action, was the identification of the proper legal standard for evaluating the administrator's behavior. Because of the great potential for abuse of any program-suspension power, the court determined that it had to find more than the "rational basis" usually required to validate informal administrative decisions in order to sustain the Secretary's actions. The court would determine, instead, the "reasonableness" of the challenged actions. Thus, the court perceived the issue before it as whether the Secretary, "having [Congress's] policies in mind and considering the consequences to be expected from continuing the [disputed] programs," acted "reasonably" in discontinuing them.

The court posed two questions as to each program in making its determination of reasonableness:

(1) Was the program consistent with the national housing policies and purposes for which Congress enacted it?

(2) If not, was the inconsistency reasonably attributable to the program's structural features as opposed to the manner of its administration? (It would not be reasonable for the Secretary to terminate programs on the basis of administrative failings he had the power to correct.)

The court identified a number of significant problems associated with Section 235 and Section 236 housing projects, which led to results inconsistent with Congressional policy. Under Section 235, for example, the statutory maximum amount for mortgage subsidies led to an overconcentration—relative to the population of poor persons—of Section 235 housing in regions of the country where construction costs were low. The Section 235 formula for calculating the amount of mortgage subsidy had the additional seemingly perverse result of increasing the amount of subsidy for beneficiary families with relatively higher incomes. Similarly, the Section 236 formula for mortgage subsidies for rental housing had the effect of encouraging the building of projects for relatively higher-income tenants who could afford higher rents.

With regard to Section 235, the court concluded there was limited potential for administrative correction of the program short of suspension. The links between the program's unintended results and its structural features had already led one congressional study to recommend legislative reconsideration. The court held that the Secretary had not acted unreasonably in terminating rather than continuing the program.

Although the court concluded that some problems of the Section 236 program were not rooted in the statute, enough problems associated with Section 236 were likewise sufficiently structural to sustain the Secretary's suspension order. The court held that the Secretary had not acted unreasonably in terminating the Section 236 program on the ground that he could not administer it consistently with congressional intent.

Finally, the court noted that Section 101 rent programs are triggered only in conjunction with housing projects constructed under other programs. The vitality of the Section 101 program would therefore be dependent upon the continued operation of the underlying construction programs. Because the only potential landlords belonging to the class certified by the district court were potential sponsors of Section 236 projects and the Section 236 program was reasonably suspended, the court of appeals held that it was reasonable to suspend the Section 101 program as to such sponsors. The case did not present any other issue concerning section 101.

———————

1. Part of the court's analytic methodology seems quite straightforward, that is, its consideration whether the Housing Acts of 1949 and 1968 imply executive authority to impose the moratorium at issue. What is the relevance to the court's holding, however, of Congress's response to the moratorium? Should a recent Congress's acquiescence in an administrative decision be relevant to interpreting an earlier Congress's intent as to that decision?

2. As General Counsel to the Department of Education, how would you go about advising the Secretary if extensive studies developed substantial evidence that, despite Congress' continued funding of such programs, the Department's preschool reading development programs were not promoting literacy, and the Secretary wanted to suspend those programs?

CASE STUDY: ENFORCING THE STATUTORY EXCLUSION OF ALIEN HOMOSEXUALS

In the preceding case, the court of appeals accepted the argument that the Secretary of HUD could suspend a program upon determining that the program was not fulfilling Congress' intended purpose. Is it likewise reasonable to suspend a program if an administrator determines that, although the enforcement of a statute would accomplish Congress' original purpose, common understanding of the factual context involved would now lead to the conclusion that Congress erred in adopting such a purpose?

Under the Immigration and Nationality Act of 1952, Congress required the exclusion from the United States of aliens "afflicted with psychopathic personality, epilepsy, or a mental defect." The legislative history of this provision unambiguously indicated Congress' intent to include homosexuals within the class of persons "afflicted with psychopathic personality."

Notwithstanding the legislative history, the Ninth Circuit, in 1962, held the exclusionary provision inapplicable to homosexuals because "psychopathic personality" would be an unconstitutionally vague reference to homosexuals. *Fleuti v. Rosenberg*, 302 F.2d 652 (9th Cir. 1962). Congress responded, in 1965, by substituting "sexual deviation" for "epilepsy" in the exclusionary clause, and reiterating its intent to exclude homosexual aliens. As it turns out, this response proved unnecessary. A pre-1965 case involving the phrase "psychopathic personality" reached the Supreme Court, and, in 1967, the Court held (a) that the void-for-vagueness protection does not apply to nonadmitted aliens, and (b) that Congress, in 1952, clearly intended to include homosexuals within the "psychopathic personality" category. *Boutilier v. INS*, 387 U.S. 118 (1967).

This ruling, however, did not end legal attempts to eviscerate or eliminate the requirement that homosexual aliens be excluded. Under the Act, administrative responsibility for enforcing the exclusionary provisions is divided between the Immigration and Naturalization Service (INS), which is the lead agency, and the Public Health Service (PHS), which assists the INS. The PHS is responsible for such physical and mental health examinations as the Act may require; the INS handles all other examinations. If the INS suspected an alien of homosexuality, and the alien would not voluntarily withdraw his or her application for admission, the INS ordinarily would refer the alien to the PHS for a mental health examination. A PHS finding of homosexuality would inevitably lead to the alien's exclusion because the Act provides that a PHS certificate, unlike an INS inspector's assessment, is dispositive of any health issue in dispute.

After the American Psychiatric Association in 1974 removed homosexuality from the list of psychiatric disorders in its Diagnostic and Statistical Manual, the leading accepted classification, opponents of the exclusion provision increased their pressure on the Surgeon General, as head of the Public Health Service, to stop certifying "homosexuality" as a mental defect. On August 2, 1979, the Surgeon General finally issued such an order resting, first, on the change in psychiatric understanding of homosexuality, and, second, on the contention that the determination of homosexuality is not made through a medical diagnostic procedure.

This order inevitably required INS to reevaluate its enforcement policy. On August 13, 1979, it requested an opinion from the Office of Legal Counsel of the Department of Justice concerning the authority of the Surgeon General to decline examinations based on suspected homosexuality and, in any event, the INS's statutory obligation to exclude homosexual aliens. OLC responded that the Surgeon General could not legally decline to certify homosexuality as a mental defect based on new medical opinion, but that OLC could not evaluate the Surgeon General's seeming contention that medical diagnosis of homosexuality was, as a matter of fact, impossible. It further argued, however, that INS remained responsible for enforcing the exclusion and that it could do so based on nonmedical evidence.

Following the OLC opinion, lawyers for several gay rights groups were invited to brief the Department of Justice on the disputed issue. Protracted discussions followed between the private attorneys and the Department on the precise legal question whether INS was empowered to exclude an alien on the ground of "psychopathic personality" or "sexual deviation" based on nonmedical evidence. The Department concluded, finally, that the INS was so empowered, which apparently obviated what might otherwise have been the necessity to challenge the Surgeon General's order within the Administration. The Department did, however, adopt a high evidentiary threshold and a liberal policy with respect to homosexual exclusions.

The documents that follow present the Department's eventual enforcement policy. After reviewing them, consider the notes and questions that follow:

DEPARTMENT OF JUSTICE PRESS RELEASE OF SEPT. 9, 1980

The Department of Justice has concluded it has the legal obligation to exclude homosexuals from entering the United States, but it will be done solely upon the voluntary admission by the alien that he or she is homosexual.

David Crosland, acting Commissioner of the Immigration and Naturalization Service (INS) said the policy, is effective immediately. "It fulfills the Justice Department's and INS's responsibility to enforce the laws of the United States," Crosland said. "It also strives to apply a uniform policy to protect the privacy of individuals."

On August 2, 1979 the Public Health Service announced it would no longer certify that homosexuality is a mental disease or defect. The agency advised INS it should no longer refer aliens suspected of only being homosexuals to the PHS for certification of mental disease or defect.

Under the new policy, Mr. Crosland said persons will be excluded without a medical examination when non-medical evidence establishes an individual is a homosexual.

To ensure a uniform and fair enforcement policy and to prevent invasion of personal privacy, INS inspectors have been directed not to ask aliens questions concerning their sexual preference during the initial inspection process. However, if an alien makes an unsolicited, unambiguous admission of homosexuality he or she will undergo a secondary inspection.

Also, if a third party who has arrived at the same time identifies an alien as a homosexual, the alien will undergo a secondary inspection.

In the secondary inspection the alien will be asked in private if he or she is a homosexual. If the response is negative the alien will be allowed to enter the country; if it is positive, the alien will be advised of the right to appear before an immigration judge for an exclusion hearing. No other questions concerning sexual preference will be asked of the alien.

Since August 1979, suspected alien homosexuals have been allowed to enter the country on a "deferred inspection" basis. About 50 persons entered on that basis, and nearly all have left the country, Mr. Crosland said. Those who have not left will be asked to submit to a secondary inspection.

The Justice Department is presently supporting legislation which would eliminate homosexuality as a ground for exclusion.

# # # #

JUSTICE DEPARTMENT BACKGROUND PAPER ON HOMOSEXUAL EXCLUSION POLICY

. . . After a detailed analysis, the Department of Justice has concluded that it has a legal obligation to enforce the exclusion of homosexuals and that where non-medical evidence establishes that the individual is a homosexual the INS may exclude the alien without referring him or her to the Public Health Service for a medical examination.

The establishment of non-medical evidence sufficient to support exclusion raises substantial enforcement problems. First, there is no generally agreed-upon definition of homosexuality and no generally accepted diagnostic technique for determining homosexuality. Second, reliance upon subjective indicia (such as attire or mannerisms) is likely to produce a non-uniform and unfair enforcement policy. Third, in-depth questioning of an alien regarding his or her sexual preference is a severe invasion of personal privacy. Fourth, INS has no expertise in determining whether an alien is a homosexual. . . .

This policy, effective immediately, fulfills the Department's responsibility to enforce the laws of the United States. It also strives to apply a uniform policy that protects the privacy of individuals. The Department is presently supporting legislation which would eliminate homosexuality as a ground for exclusion.

---

1. Was the Surgeon General's order proper? Which, if any, of the following should the Surgeon General have regarded as rationales sufficient to sustain the order: (1) it is not possible, as a practical matter, to diagnose homosexuality medically; (2) Congress would not include homosexuals within the class of medically excludable aliens if it were to address that issue today; (3) the exclusion of persons from the United States based solely on their associational preferences is reprehensible policy; (4) notwithstanding Supreme Court precedent, exclusion of gays from the United States is, under the better view, unconstitutional?

2. If you were an OLC attorney, and it appeared to you that the ultimate legal question of the INS's authority to proceed on nonmedical evidence is close, would you entertain a presumption that the law should be interpreted so as to permit enforcement? How should you, as an executive adviser, determine the facts relevant to a proper resolution of the legal issue? Would you ignore the statute if you could find a way to do so? Would you, as Attorney General, ask the Secretary of Health and Human Services, or the President, to reverse the Surgeon General?

3. A number of gay rights groups and private lawyers presented material to the Justice Department designed to show arbitrariness in the then-current enforcement of the law, and the asserted intractability of recognizing and defining homosexuality. To show arbitrariness, the lawyers related a series of recent enforcement episodes that clients had brought to their attention. Among the allegations was that immigration officials, during the weekend of August 23-25, 1979, stopped 55 Canadian women en route to the "Fourth Annual Michigan Women's Festival." On no more than the assumption that the festival attracts lesbian women, the officials allegedly confronted the Canadians with crassly offensive questions concerning their sexual practices and their enjoyment of sex. To show the impossibility of enforcing the law nonarbitrarily, the lawyers cited a variety of medical experts for the propositions that (a) no clear definition of homosexuality exists; and (b) "homosexuality," as commonly understood, embraces a wide variety of behaviors and motivations, many of which exist within the self-identified heterosexual population, and many of which may change within the life of a single individual. *See* Memorandum from Gay Rights Advocates, Inc., et al. to the United States Department of Justice and Acting Associate Attorney General John H. Shenefield Re: Formulation of Department of Justice Policy as to the Enforcement of Title 8, section 1182(a)(4) of the United States Code (Jan. 24, 1979). Assuming the accuracy of this presentation, did the Justice Department policy appropriately reflect its implications? Do these arguments persuade you that the INS's final enforcement policy is "arbitrary" or "capricious" as a legal matter?

4. Does the final Department policy represent "faithful execution of the laws?" Do you perceive real differences between this policy and a seemingly more straightforward position that the law is unenforceable?

5. The courts of appeals are now divided on the legal issue that OLC addressed. The Ninth Circuit, without reaching the question whether homosexuals should still be deemed excludable, held that an alien could not be excluded on the ground of homosexuality by the INS alone; a PHS health certificate was statutorily required. *Hill v. Immigration and Naturalization Service*, 714 F.2d 1470 (9th Cir. 1983). The Fifth Circuit, however, held that the INS properly deemed an alien barred from naturalization on the ground that his self-declaration of homosexuality—even without PHS certification—indicated that his initial admittance for permanent residence was unlawful. *In the Matter of Longstaff*, 716 F.2d 1439 (5th Cir. 1983), *cert. denied*, 467 U.S. 1219 (1984). Note that the United States declined to petition for certiorari after losing in the Ninth Circuit, but opposed the alien's petition for certiorari in the later Fifth Circuit cases. Were these appropriate decisions by the Solicitor General?

6. Should the legal or policy analysis of the foregoing set of problems be affected by the AIDS epidemic? Would your answer depend on whether aliens carrying AIDS-related viruses are otherwise excludable as persons "afflicted with [a] dangerous contagious disease?" 8 U.S.C. § 1182(a)(6)?

3. Civil Litigation and Faithful Execution of the Laws

The question of what constitutes faithful execution of the laws is made considerably more complicated by private parties' use of litigation against the government to enforce the government's putative statutory obligations.

For example, to what extent is the Attorney General—as head of the Department of Justice and as executive branch lawyer—bound by the statutes of another agency in settling private litigation against that agency? The Attorney General enjoys broad statutory power to conduct litigation in furtherance of "the interests of the United States." 28 U.S.C. § 518 (1982). Attorneys General have claimed that, under this power, they have plenary authority to compromise disputes against the United States. The only admitted "limitation" upon this power is that it be "exercised with wise discretion and resorted to only to promote the Government's best interest or to prevent flagrant injustice...." 38 Op. Att'y Gen. 98, 102 (1934).

Is such a broad inference of settlement authority consistent with the faithful execution of the laws? Suppose that Congress has authorized mineral leases on public lands only under certain conditions, and that the Department of the Interior has disqualified a particular applicant on statutory grounds. If the Attorney General determines that the private applicant is otherwise a qualified lessee, that the statutory disability is of little consequence, and that the government's defense of a lawsuit would be unduly expensive, may he waive the statutory requirement as part of his settlement of a lawsuit for the lease? Would recognition of such authority create too great a likelihood of "sweetheart deals" between private parties and the Department of Justice, to the detriment of a faithful execution of Congress's intended policies? Or, because Congress could presumably limit the Attorney General's settlement discretion by statute, should it be assumed that, unless Congress has done so explicitly, it intends the Attorney General's authority to be as broad as the language of 28 U.S.C. § 518 implies?

This knotty question is made all the thornier once a court has become involved. In *Cascade Natural Gas Corp. v. El Paso Natural Gas Co.*, 386 U.S. 129 (1967), the Supreme Court held the Department of Justice may not use its settlement authority to circumscribe the power of the courts to see that their orders are carried out. In a prior decision, *United States v. El Paso Natural Gas Co.*, 376 U.S. 651 (1964), the Supreme Court had held that the acquisition of Pacific Northwest Pipeline Corporation by the El Paso Natural Gas Company violated Section 7 of the Clayton Act, and it directed the District Court "to order the divestiture without delay." Subsequent to this decision, the United States agreed to a settlement of the litigation that would have permitted interests aligned with El Paso to obtain stock in the newly formed company. The Supreme Court, in rejecting the "settlement" decree, said: "We do not question the authority of the Attorney General to settle suits after, as well as before, they reach here. The Department of Justice, however, by stipulation or otherwise has no authority to circumscribe the power of the courts to see that our mandate is carried out. No one, except this court, has authority to alter or modify our mandate." 386 U.S. at 136.

Should the Department of Justice understand from this opinion that its settlement authority after a judicial decree is more circumscribed than when a case is first filed? That is, would the agreement by the United States to the settlement decree in *Cascade Natural Gas Corp.* have been more acceptable before the Supreme Court "educated" the executive branch as to the proper interpretation of the Clayton Act in the context of this particular case? Or, assuming that the United States thought the acquisition unlawful, should it have thought itself barred at all times from settling the lawsuit in a way that would permit a reacquisition of the disputed assets by the putative antitrust violator?

Of closely related interest is the recent controversy over the government's so-called nonacquiescence policy regarding judicial decisions. Under this policy, for example, the Internal Revenue Service has routinely declined to follow Court of Appeals decisions on statutory interpretations when the IRS disagrees with those decisions and hopes to elicit more favorable decisions from other circuits, and ultimately from the Supreme Court.

The legitimacy of this policy has been heatedly argued in light of a dispute between the Ninth Circuit and the U.S. Department of Health and Human Services (HHS). In two decisions, in 1981 and 1982, the Ninth Circuit disapproved two HHS policies designed to help eliminate ineligible recipients from the federal disability rolls. *Finnegan v. Matthews*, 641 F.2d 1340 (9th Cir. 1981); *Patti v. Schweiker*, 669 F.2d 582 (9th Cir. 1982). HHS reacted by indicating that, although it would follow the Ninth Circuit decisions in the two individual cases, it did not consider itself bound by those decisions in any other eligibility determinations. Instead, HHS deemed itself bound to modify its procedures only to conform to Supreme Court decisions. The Ninth Circuit subsequently affirmed an injunction in a class action, requiring HHS to reinstate, as eligible persons, all those residents of the Ninth Circuit whose disability payments had been terminated by HHS as a result of its nonacquiescence policy. *Lopez v. Heckler*, 713 F.2d 1432 (9th Cir. 1983). Justice Rehnquist subsequently stayed the judgment in part on the ground that the order significantly interfered "with the distribution between administrative and judicial responsibility for enforcement of the Social Security Act which Congress has established." *Heckler v. Lopez*, 463 U.S. 1328, 1331 (1983). Without shedding further light on the separation of powers issues involved, the Supreme Court ultimately granted certiorari and vacated the judgment, with directions that the district court remand the cases of unnamed class members to the Secretary of HHS for an exhaustion of administrative remedies. 469 U.S. 1082 (1984).

Is the nonacquiescence policy consistent with the faithful execution of the laws? Does the executive branch's disagreement with a lower court's statutory interpretation justify noncompliance? Alternatively, should a lower court decree be deemed binding on a coequal branch of the government beyond the particular case adjudicated? For further discussion of these issues see R. Pierce, S. Shapiro, and P. Verkuil, Administrative Law and Process 413-417 (1985); Eichel, *"Respectful Disagreement": Nonacquiescence by Federal Administrative Agencies in United States Courts of Appeals Precedents*, 18 Colum. J. L. & Soc. Probs. 463 (1985); Note, *Administrative Agency Intracircuit Nonacquiescence*, 85 Colum. L. Rev. 582 (1985).

An issue that recently focused unusual attention on Justice Department settlement policy involves so-called discretion-binding consent decrees. These decrees typically include settlement promises by the United States involving budgeting, the allocation of law enforcement resources, or decisions whether to issue or amend administrative regulations—areas over which administrative agencies usually enjoy unreviewable discretion. For example, in one controversial instance, the Environmental Protection Agency settled a lawsuit that charged it with using improper criteria in deciding which toxic pollutants to regulate, by agreeing on "a detailed, comprehensive regulatory program for implementation ... of the toxic pollutant control and pretreatment objectives" of the Federal Water Pollution Control Act (now called the Clean Water Act, 33 U.S.C. § 1251 [1982]). *Natural Resources Defense Council v. Costle*, 12 Env't Rptr. Cas. (BNA) 1833, 1834 (D.D.C. 1979). *See Citizens for a Better Environment v. Gorsuch*, 718 F.2d 1117 (D.C. Cir. 1983) (upholding settlement against separation of powers challenge).

On March 13, 1986, Attorney General Meese issued a set of guidelines purporting to forbid Justice Department attorneys from agreeing to such decrees. The Attorney General asserted that such decrees in the past had:

> forfeited the prerogatives of the Executive in order to preempt the exercise of those prerogatives by a subsequent Administration. These errors sometimes have resulted in an unwarranted expansion of the powers of [the] judiciary— often with the consent of government parties—at the expense of the executive and legislative branches.

Memorandum from Attorney General Edwin Meese, III to All Assistant Attorneys General and All United States Attorneys Re: Department Policy Regarding Consent Decrees and Settlement Agreements 1 (Mar. 13, 1986), *reprinted in* Review of Nixon Presidential Materials Access Regulations, Hearing Before a Subcomm. of the House Comm. on Gov't Operations, 99th Cong., 2d Sess. 180 (1986). Some observers, however, regarded the guidelines simply as an attempt to deter agencies from settling litigation brought against them by public interest groups seeking the vigorous enforcement of regulatory legislation to which the Reagan Administration is hostile.

The Attorney General's Guidelines are puzzling for two reasons. First, the Attorney General asserts that discretion-limiting consent decrees violate the constitutional separation of powers, but seemingly purports to retain authority to approve them in certain circumstances. Second, the Attorney General expressly permits Justice Department attorneys to approve certain discretion-limiting settlement agreements, that is, settlements not embodied in judicial orders, even though such agreements are also judicially enforceable, and thus equally binding on the executive branch.

For a full review of the fairly arcane issues surrounding the constitutional limits on discretion-binding consent decrees, see Symposium, *Consent Decrees: Practical Problems and Legal Dilemmas*, 1987 U. Chi. Legal F. 241-351 (articles by Shane, McConnell, and Percival).

4. Enforcing the Criminal Law

Notwithstanding the constitutional requirement of faithful execution of the laws, all criminal law enforcement displays a traditional—and largely unquestioned—practice of discretionary nonenforcement. Police and prosecutors at all levels of government routinely decline to investigate or prosecute all possible violations of all the positive criminal laws in force. This practice, however, may surely be questioned—both on policy grounds, and as a matter of constitutional values. Kenneth Culp Davis, for example, has written extensively on discretionary nonenforcement, arguing vehemently for a more principled exercise of discretion in order to prevent discrimination. See 2 Davis, Administrative Law Treatise Ch. 9 (2d ed. 1979). Writing on police nonenforcement, one commentator has said: [T]he use of rulemaking by the police to limit the scope of the substantive criminal law . . . is inconsistent with our theory of government. . . . " R. Allen, *The Police and Substantive Rulemaking: Reconciling Principle and Expediency*, 125 U. Pa. L. Rev. 62, 69 (1976). Does "the faithful execution of the laws" legally permit federal prosecutors to determine, as a matter of priority, never to enforce certain laws? How should an executive counsel's advice on such a question be affected by the presumptive nonreviewability of most nonenforcement decisions? *Heckler v. Chaney*, 470 U.S. 821 (1985). What are proper grounds, as a general matter or in particular cases, for nonenforcement? Is the separation of powers relevant to this debate?

Smith v. United States
375 F.2d 243 (5th Cir. 1967)

GOLDBERG, Circuit Judge.

We have here another facet of the Albany, Georgia, imbroglio. Alex Carl Smith, the plaintiff, lives in Albany, and at the time relevant to this action owned a grocery store there. Smith alleges that the clientele of this store was about 98 per cent Negro.

In early April 1963, Smith was summoned to serve as a juror in the United States District Court for the Middle District of Georgia, Albany Division. Smith sat on the jury in the case of Ware v. Johnson, which, Smith alleges, was a "civil rights damage suit in which the plaintiff Ware was colored, and the defendant Johnson was the duly elected sheriff of Baker County, Georgia." The jury returned a verdict for the defendant Johnson on April 12.

Smith alleges that on about April 15, because of his participation in the jury verdict, certain "militant and activist" civil rights groups conspired to retaliate against him by picketing his grocery business with the aim of inducing a boycott of it.

On April 20, the picketing began. Smith alleges that in furtherance of the conspiracy, would-be customers were "physically carried" from his store. Sensing that the boycott was becoming effective, Smith requested the United States Attorney and the Federal Bureau of Investigation in Albany to investigate and prosecute the boycotters for intimidation of a federal juror. Smith alleges that the FBI investigated only to the extent of determining that C. B. King, the attorney for Ware, was not part of the conspiracy. Upon this determination, the FBI refused to act further, despite repeated requests from Smith.

Smith alleges that the boycott resulting from the picketing completely destroyed his business. He filed suit against the United States under the Federal Tort Claims Act, 28 U.S.C. § 1346 [reprinted in appendix], claiming that the government failed to arrest or prosecute the persons injuring his business. The government moved to dismiss for failure to state a claim, and this motion was granted. Smith appeals, and we affirm.

This case tests the meaning of vital sections of the Federal Tort Claims Act: 28 U.S.C. §§ 1346(b), 2674, and 2680(a) [reprinted in appendix].

Smith argues here first that the government owes an affirmative duty to its citizens to investigate and prosecute crime, and that where, as here, there is a "clear violation" of a federal statute, the government may not rely on the discretionary function exception of § 2680(a) to avoid liability for failure to prosecute. Second, Smith argues that even if the failure to act complained of was discretionary, once an investigation is started by the government, the operation changes from the "planning" stage to the "operational" stage, and that discretionary functions on the "operational" stage are not within the exception of § 2680(a).

The government answers by arguing that the government's duty to prosecute crime does not run to the victim of the crime but to the nation as a whole, and that a victim's only remedy in tort is to sue the criminal. It argues further that the aspects of investigation and prosecution complained of here are discretionary functions within the exception of § 2680(a).

While we believe that the facts of the present case compellingly uphold the government's immunity from liability, we are also concerned lest we make some comment which would impede in other cases the full extension of the Act to its proper purpose, which includes waiving "the Government's traditional all-encompassing immunity from tort actions and * * * [establishing] novel and unprecedented governmental liability." Rayonier, Inc. v. United States, 1957, 352 U.S. 315, 319. We therefore have undertaken to set out the precise ground for our decision that the government activity complained of here was discretionary within the meaning of § 2680(a).

I.

Each party recognizes, of course, that the major case interpreting the Act in this area is *Dalehite v. U.S.*, 1953, 346 U.S. 15. In *Dalehite*, the United States was sought to be held liable for the catastrophic explosion in Texas City, Texas, of nitrate fertilizers manufactured by the government for shipment to Europe. The plaintiffs there could show no negligence by specific individuals in handling the material: therefore they claimed that the government was liable for having allowed manufacture and shipment of inherently dangerous fertilizers without either warning of the danger or demanding safe procedures for their handling. The Supreme Court rejected this claim, holding that any governmental misfeasance was protected because it was part of governmental discretion, and excepted from liability by § 2680(a):

"It is unnecessary to define, apart from this case, precisely where discretion ends. It is enough to hold, as we do, that the 'discretionary function or duty' that cannot form a basis for suit under the Tort Claims Act includes more than the initiation of programs and activities. It also includes determinations made by executives or administrators in establishing plans, specifications or schedules of operations. Where there is room for policy judgment and decision there is discretion. It necessarily follows that acts of subordinates in carrying out the operations of government in accordance with official directions cannot be actionable. If it were not so, the protection of § 2680(a) would fail at the time it would be needed, that is, when a subordinate performs or fails to perform a causal step, each action or nonaction being directed by the superior, exercising, perhaps abusing, discretion." 346 U.S. at 35-36.

Smith contends that this holding has been rejected or so completely diluted by the holdings in *Indian Towing Co. v. United States*, 1955, 350 U.S. 61 and *Rayonier*, supra, that it is no longer authoritative.

The government brushes off this suggestion with a quotation from *Blaber v. United States*, 2 Cir. 1964, 332 F.2d. 629, 631:

"These cases [*Indian Towing* and *Rayonier*] did enlarge the scope of the United States' liability as it might have been thought to exist after *Dalehite*, but they did not affect the scope of the discretionary function immunity."

We cannot agree with this statement. The description of a discretionary function in *Dalehite* permits the interpretation that any federal official vested with decision-making power is thereby invested with sufficient discretion for the government to withstand suit when those decisions go awry. Most conscious acts of any person whether he works for the government or not, involve choice. Unless government officials (at no matter what echelon) make their choices by flipping coins, their acts involve discretion in making decisions.

If the Tort Claims Act is to have the corpuscular vitality to cover anything more than automobile accidents in which government officials were driving, the federal courts must reject an absolutist interpretation of *Dalehite*, and that interpretation is rejected by *Indian Towing* and especially by *Rayonier*. In the latter case, the Court held that the government could be liable for substandard firefighting by the Forest Service. The facts of the case make it clear that the negligence lay in part in the decision to withdraw a major part of the firefighting force before the blaze was truly extinguished. This is perhaps a minor decision when compared to some made in the government, but it is a decision nonetheless, made by an official exercising some discretion. Cases under the Act therefore put courts to the question of what sorts of decisions can be classified as resulting from discretion within the meaning of § 2680(a). It is not a sufficient defense for the government merely to point out that some decision-making power was exercised by the official whose act was questioned. Answering these questions, a difficult process, is not aided by importation of the planning stage-operational stage standard as argued for by Smith. Such a distinction is specious. It may be a makeweight in easy cases where of course it is not needed, but in difficult cases it proves to be another example of a distinction "so finespun and capricious as to be almost incapable of being held in the mind for adequate formulation." Mr. Justice Frankfurter for the Court in *Indian Towing*, supra, 350 U.S. at 68. Such nonstatutory "aids" to construction tend to obscure, to limit, or even to replace the standards whose meaning they are supposed to clarify. It must be remembered that the question at hand here is the nature and quality of the discretion involved in the acts complained of.

II.

The President of the United States is charged in Article 2, Section 3, of the Constitution with the duty to "take care that the laws be faithfully executed * * *" The Attorney General is the President's surrogate in the prosecution of all offenses against the United States. 5 U.S.C.A. § 291 et seq., 28 U.S.C.A. § 507. The discretion of the Attorney General in choosing whether to prosecute or not to prosecute, or to abandon a prosecution already started, is absolute. We held in United States v. Cox, 5 Cir. 1965, 342 F.2d 167, 171:

> "The discretionary power of the attorney for the United States in determining whether a prosecution shall be commenced or maintained may well depend upon matters of policy wholly apart from any question of probable cause. Although as a member of the bar, the attorney for the United States is an officer of the court, he is nevertheless an executive official of the Government, and it is as an officer of the executive department that he exercises a discretion as to whether or not there shall be a prosecution in a particular case. It follows, as an incident of the constitutional separation of powers, that the courts are not to interfere with the free exercise of the discretionary powers of the attorneys of the United States in their control over criminal prosecutions."

This discretion is required in all cases. The present case provides, however, a most compelling example of the soundness of the rule. "All must be aware now that there are times when the interests of the nation require that a prosecution be foregone." Concurring opinion of Judge Brown in United States v. Cox, supra, 342 F.2d at 182.

The national wellbeing has been in balance during the recent struggle for racial equality, of which the present action is a piece. The federal government's decisions concerning enforcement of its criminal statutes comprise a part of its pursuit of national policy. If the government could be held liable for prosecuting or failing to prosecute such a case, its choices in this area could quite conceivably be affected by such a suit. Thus, a policy decision of the federal government might be influenced by a plaintiff with no governmental responsibility.

We emphasize that this discretion, exercised in even the lowliest and least consequential cases, can affect the policies, duties, and success of a function placed under the control of the Attorney General by our Constitution and statutes. For example, in order to keep from congesting the courts and wasting the prosecutors' time with many ordinary cases, in some areas the government must choose to prosecute only impressive test cases with a high potential of success. Further, many defendants who commit federal crimes of a comparatively lowly order (such as transportation of stolen automobiles in interstate commerce, and narcotics and gambling violations) simultaneously commit similar state offenses. The decision to prosecute in federal court or to defer to state prosecution must therefore be made. Such decisions involve considerations of federalism and cooperation between the federal government and the states. These are fundamental questions. Decisions which must be made in run of the mill cases reflect "[j]udgment reached primarily by balancing the public interest in effective law enforcement against the growing rights of the accused...." *Pugach v. Klein*, S.D.N.Y. 1961, 193 F. Supp. 630, 635.

III.

We therefore hold that § 2680(a) exempts the government from liability for exercising the discretion inherent in the prosecutorial function of the Attorney General, no matter whether these decisions are made during the investigation or prosecution of offenses. Another holding could diffuse the government's control over policies committed to it by the Constitution, and irrationally concentrate political responsibility in fortuitous lawsuits.

Whatever else § 2680(a) may do, its discretionary function exception prevents this diffusion of governmental power into private hands. The United States is immune from liability in the present case not because of the mere fact that government officials made choices, but because the choices made affected the political (not merely the monetary) interests of the nation. The Act is intended to spread monetary losses in certain cases among the taxpayers; it is not intended to affect the distribution of political responsibility. Mr. Justice Jackson, dissenting in *Dalehite*, recognized this:

> "When an official exerts governmental authority in a manner which legally binds one or many, he is acting in a way which no private person could. Such activities do and are designed to affect, often deleteriously, the affairs of individuals, but courts have long recognized the public policy that such official shall be controlled solely by the statutory or administrative mandate and not by the added threat of private damage suits. For example, the Attorney General will not be liable for false arrest in circumstances where a private person performing the same act would be liable, and such cases could be multiplied. The official's act might inflict just as great an injury and might be just as wrong as that of the private person, but the official is not answerable." 346 U.S. at 59, 60.

The present case falls easily into the exception. It is easy to think of future cases which will be more difficult, but prosecutorial discretion has long been recognized as sacrosanct. It here withstands the questioning of complaining critics. The judgment of the Department of Justice is an important aspect of governmental policy, and it makes no difference here that the Department was allegedly negligent or wrongful....

Affirmed.

---

1. Would Smith have done any better seeking mandamus against the local U.S. attorney, 28 U.S.C. § 1361, or would proper implementation of the distinction between "ministerial" acts subject to the writ and unreviewable "discretionary" acts have produced the same result? *See* Byse and Fiocca, *Section 1361 of the Mandamus and Venue Act of 1962 and "Nonstatutory" Judicial Review of Federal Administrative Action*, 81 Harv. L. Rev. 308 (1967); *Work v. Rives*, 267 U.S. 175 (1925).

2. The Supreme Court recently reaffirmed the *Dalehite* doctrine in *United States v. S.A. Empresa de Viacao Aerea Rio Grandense (Varig Airlines)*, 467 U.S. 797 (1984), holding that the Federal Aviation Administration was not subject to tort liability for improperly certifying aircraft that did not meet federal safety standards, and which subsequently crashed due to aircraft defects. The Court expressly rejected the argument that *Dalehite* was undermined by the Court's holding in *Indian Towing Co. v. United States*, 350 U.S. 61 (1955), noting that the Government, in *Indian Towing*, conceded the inapplicability of the discretionary function exception to the FTCA. While again eschewing any attempt at defining the discretionary function exception comprehensively, the Court said: "[W]hatever else the discretionary function exception

may include, it plainly was intended to encompass the discretionary acts of the Government acting in its role as a regulator of the conduct of private individuals." 467 U.S. at 813-14.

3. Judge Goldberg says the purpose of the FCTA is "to spread monetary losses in certain cases among the taxpayers; ... not ... to affect the distribution of political responsibility." Can these two impacts be separated? For an argument in favor of overhauling the rules governing government liability to increase compensation for tort, *see* P. Schuck, Suing Government: Citizen Remedies for Official Wrongs (1983).

NAACP v. Levi
418 F.Supp. 1109 (D.D.C. 1976)

PARKER, District Judge:

This proceeding presents troublesome questions of standing and prosecutorial discretion. They arise in connection with a citizen's death from gunshot wounds while in custody of Arkansas law enforcement officers. The plaintiffs allege that Federal officers failed to conduct an affirmative and exhaustive investigation of the incident and that they acted arbitrarily, capriciously and in a racially discriminatory manner to determine if the citizen's constitutionally guaranteed and other rights provided by Federal law had been violated.

... [T]he defendants present ... a motion to dismiss. For the reasons detailed below, the Court concludes that ... this proceeding should advance to trial.

The plaintiffs are the National Association for the Advancement of Colored People (NAACP), Mrs. Clementine Russ, widow of Carnell Russ and the Russ minor children. The defendants are Edward Levi, the Attorney General of the United States, Clarence Kelley, the Director of the Federal Bureau of Investigation (FBI or Bureau) and certain FBI agents assigned to the Little Rock, Arkansas, office....

In an amended complaint seeking declaratory, injunctive and other equitable relief, plaintiffs assert violations of the constitutional and civil rights of Carnell Russ, deceased, a citizen of Arkansas. They seek this Court's aid compelling the defendants to undertake a thorough and meaningful investigation into his fatal shooting. The shooting took place at the Lincoln County Courthouse, Star City, Arkansas, while Russ was in the custody of Arkansas law enforcement officers.

... [The defendants] move to dismiss the complaint and assert: that the plaintiffs ... have failed to state a claim upon which relief can be granted....

FACTUAL BACKGROUND

On May 31, 1971, Carnell Russ, a 24 year old black, while operating his motor vehicle on an Arkansas highway, was arrested for an alleged speeding violation by Jerry Mac Green, a white state trooper. Russ was accompanied by his wife, their minor children and an adult cousin. The trooper directed him to the County Courthouse. Russ complied and upon arrival, parked his vehicle and was escorted into the Courthouse by the arresting trooper and two other white law enforcement officers, Charles Ratliff and Norman Draper. Minutes later, Russ returned to the vehicle where his family awaited. He requested and received from his wife sufficient money to post the necessary collateral. He then joined the three officers who were close by observing his actions. The four retraced their steps with Russ again in custody.

A short time thereafter, Mrs. Russ first observed two of the officers leave and minutes later an ambulance depart from the rear of the Courthouse area where her husband had just entered in the officers' custody. She later learned that Mr. Russ, while under detention, had been shot in the center of his forehead by Ratliff and then transported to a hospital. Green and Draper were the sole witnesses to the shooting. Her husband died from the gunshot wound within hours.

The Governor of Arkansas ordered an immediate investigation of the incident by the State Police. In less than one week Ratliff was indicted for voluntary manslaughter. Plaintiffs allege that minutes or transcripts of the grand jury proceedings were not maintained. Ratliff was tried in January, 1972. The jurors' deliberations consumed less than 15 minutes and in that period they selected a foreperson, reviewed and considered the evidence and returned a verdict of "not guilty." Ratliff's weapon was not offered in evidence during his criminal trial. There was no evidence or testimony that Carnell Russ possessed or had access to a weapon while in custody. Indeed, the testimony was to the contrary.

The shooting triggered the attention of both the national and Arkansas branches of the NAACP. Immediately, those organizations embarked upon a campaign importuning the Justice Department to undertake an independent investigation to determine whether Federal laws had been violated in any manner. Several months following the acquittal of the state trooper, Assistant Attorney General David L. Norman of the Civil Rights Division of the Justice Department wrote to the General Counsel of the NAACP:

> After careful examination of the [Ratliff trial] transcript, as well as materials previously submitted by the Federal Bureau of Investigation, this Division has determined that this incident lacks prosecutive merit under federal criminal civil rights statutes. Therefore, we are closing our file.

The plaintiffs allege that subsequent events and disclosures led them to believe that the Department's investigation was superficial, less than thorough and meaningless. The substance of their claim is that the FBI abdicated its responsibility and in effect applied a "whitewash" to the incident; that the Bureau deferred to and relied principally upon a report of the Criminal Investigation Division of the Arkansas State Police; and that the policy to rely solely on the state and local criminal justice system for vindication of a citizen's rights was unreasonable, improper, arbitrary and without a rational basis. Fairly read, the complaint alleges that the defendants acted in an arbitrary, capricious and discriminatory manner by failing to investigate the Russ shooting to determine if his constitutional rights and Federal statutes had been violated by Arkansas law enforcement authorities. . . .

THE MOTION TO DISMISS

The Question of Standing

[The Court concluded that both the NAACP and the individual plaintiffs had standing to bring suit.]

Failure to State a Claim and Prosecutorial Discretion

A prosecutor's chief responsibility is to see that the laws are faithfully executed and enforced in order to maintain the rule of law. He has an affirmative responsibility to investigate prudently suspected illegal activity when it is not adequately pursued by other agencies.... Federal courts have traditionally acquiesced in discretionary decisions of the United States Attorney not to prosecute persons against whom a complaint of criminal conduct is made. The rule in this circuit is not otherwise. Even though judicial restraint is generally observed, an unfettered discretion is questionable when it fails to promote the ends of justice and denies rights conferred upon a citizen by the Constitution and by Federal law.

In *Nader v. Saxbe*[13] our Court of Appeals was concerned with an application for a mandatory injunction against the Attorney General and others to exercise their discretion to initiate prosecutions against violators of the Federal Corrupt Practices Act.[14] The plaintiffs were an individual citizen and a nonprofit corporation. The Act was enacted in 1925. While many violations had been committed, only one prosecution, a test case, had been brought. The Attorney General had exercised his prosecutorial discretion of nonenforcement.

The case was mooted by the repeal of the statute during the course of the litigation. However, Circuit Judge J. Skelly Wright suggested that prosecutorial discretion was not totally free from judicial review:

> The instant complaint does not ask the court to assume the essentially Executive function of deciding whether a particular alleged violator should be prosecuted. Rather, the complaint seeks a conventionally judicial determination of whether certain fixed policies allegedly followed by the Justice Department and the United States Attorney's office lie outside the constitutional and statutory limits of 'prosecutorial discretion.' 497 F.2d at 679.

In a continuing footnote he further commented:

> The Executive's constitutional duty to 'take Care that the Laws be faithfully executed,' Art. II, § 3, applies to all laws, not merely to criminal statutes, *see In re Neagle*, 135 U.S. 1, 63-64 (1890). It would seem to follow that the exercise of prosecutorial discretion, like the exercise of Executive discretion generally, is subject to statutory and constitutional limits enforceable through judicial review (citations omitted). The law has long recognized the distinction between judicial usurpation of discretionary authority and judicial review of the statutory and constitutional limits to that authority (citations omitted). Judicial review of the latter sort is normally available unless Congress has expressly withdrawn it (citations omitted) 497 F.2d at 679, 680, fn. 19.

The judiciary has the responsibility of assuring that the purpose and intent of congressional enactments are not negated and frustrated by arbitrary conduct of government officials.... The amended complaint, together with supporting affidavits and memoranda [allege]... arbitrary and racially discriminatory conduct by Federal officials. They should be afforded an opportunity to support these allegations....

---

13. 497 F.2d 676 (1974).
14. 43 Stat. 1070, et seq., 2 U.S.C. former §§ 241-256.

NAACP v. Bell

76 F.R.D. 134 (D.D.C. 1977)

BARRINGTON D. PARKER, District Judge.

On July 12, 1977, the parties to this litigation moved jointly to dismiss these proceedings without prejudice to renewal by the plaintiffs. The basis of this request was an announced policy of the Honorable Griffin B. Bell, Attorney General of the United States, dealing with federal prosecution for violation of criminal civil rights statutes. The primary objective of the plaintiffs in this cause of action was to ensure that the United States Department of Justice did not fail to vindicate federally protected interests by not prosecuting local law enforcement officers alleged to have violated federal criminal civil rights statutes simply because state or local authorities had already prosecuted those officers for state or local offenses arising from the same conduct. The Attorney General, however, has recently issued a memorandum that states that federal prosecution will be instituted whenever necessary to vindicate federally protected interests, regardless of whether prior state prosecution has occurred. Since this memorandum is in accord with the policy objectives which underlie this suit and, in any event, may have rendered this cause of action moot, the parties have concluded that no useful purpose would be served by the continued litigation of this lawsuit. . . .

Exhibit A

MEMORANDUM TO ALL UNITED STATES ATTORNEYS AND ALL HEADS OF OFFICES, DIVISIONS, BUREAUS AND BOARDS OF THE DEPARTMENT OF JUSTICE

SUBJECT: Dual Prosecution Policy in Cases Involving Violations of Civil Rights

By memorandum dated April 6, 1959, former Attorney General Rogers set forth Department of Justice policy guidelines regarding federal prosecution of an individual where there has already been a state prosecution of that individual for substantially the same act or acts.

I have reviewed this policy as it applies to cases involving the violation of federal statutes pertaining to civil rights. It is my belief that these statutes protect interests which merit enforcement in their own right, regardless of whatever related enforcement action has been taken by the states. Accordingly, the policy which I shall follow in considering recommendations from U.S. Attorneys regarding separate federal prosecutions is that each and every allegation of a violation of the civil rights laws shall be evaluated on its own merits, with the determining factor being whether or not a federal prosecution is likely to vindicate rights sought to be protected by those laws. The April 6, 1959 guidelines are hereby modified to the extent they are inconsistent with this policy.

/s/ GRIFFIN B. BELL, Attorney General

1. Do you agree with the courts' decisions (a) in *Smith*, to approve the Department of Justice's nonprosecution decision and (b) in the Russ cases, not to dismiss a complaint seeking mandatory relief against the Department in another instance of

nonprosecution? Are the decisions reconcilable other than in their common solicitude for minority interests? Consider:

A. Should the court review more or less intensely a nonprosecution decision based on law enforcement program concerns or a nonprosecution decision based on non-program-related social values? Do the results in these cases accord with your view?

B. Should the court review more or less intensely a nonprosecution decision based on a preexisting written policy or an *ad hoc* nonprosecution decision? Do the results in these cases accord with your view?

C. Is it irrational for the Department of Justice, in the ordinary case, to decline to pursue a federal prosecution when a state, apparently in good faith, has prosecuted the persons involved for the same acts that are potentially punishable under federal law? (State and federal prosecutions for the same offense have been held not to violate the constitutional bar to double jeopardy because of the separate state and federal "sovereignties.") Indeed, is not such a policy—commonly referred to as the *Petite* policy because it was approved in *Petite v. U.S.*, 361 U.S. 529 (1960)—a salutary implementation of Fifth Amendment values? Does this affect your view of the Russ cases? (The Department of Justice policy on Dual and Successive Federal Prosecutions appears at 9 U.S. Att'ys' Manual § 9-2.142.)

2. Assuming a nonprosecution decision in the Russ cases would be actionable in a suit for mandamus, would damages be available for nonprosecution as well? Recall the discussion of the Federal Tort Claims Act in *Smith*.

3. If you think the result in *Smith* may be justified, are there facts not stated in the opinion that you hypothesize may have led to the nonprosecution decision? Have you weighed in your policy analysis any potential effects of federal failure to protect federal jurors from postverdict harassment?

Note: Prosecutorial Discretion, Due Process, and the Separation of Powers

The *Smith* case, above, is fairly representative of the deferential stance of the federal judiciary toward prosecutorial decision making. The Supreme Court has regarded prosecutorial discretion as all but nonreviewable in a host of contexts, for example: (1) discretion to prosecute only a subclass of all suspected violators of a federal law, *Wayte v. United States*, 470 U.S. 598 (1985); (2) discretion to prosecute under the more punitive of two statutes under which the same conduct could be prosecuted, *United States v. Batchelder*, 442 U.S. 114 (1979); (3) discretion to delay prosecution for strategic reasons, *United States v. Lovasco*, 431 U.S. 783 (1977). The Court has further limited the judicial role in reviewing prosecutorial discretion by restricting plaintiff standing to challenge nonprosecution decisions, *Linda R. S. v. Richard D.*, 410 U.S. 614 (1973), and by granting prosecutors absolute immunity from personal damages liability for actions performed within the scope of their prosecutorial duties, *Imbler v. Pachtman*, 424 U.S. 409 (1976).

It is generally perceived that the federal courts' deference towards federal prosecutors stems, at least in part, from separation of powers concerns. The question is, what are they? To understand the problem, it is necessary to distinguish between two distinct sets of concerns, both served by the separation of powers, which have different implications for prosecutorial decision making and its review.

One set of issues might be called "separation of powers proper," that is, a concern that the core "legislative," "executive," and "judicial" powers each be retained by the respective branch involved. It might be argued, for example, that criminal prosecution is a core executive function, and that judicial deference is required to avoid usurpation of prerogatives that belong categorically within the executive branch.

A different set of concerns is usually captured in the phrase, "separation of functions." These concerns, closely related to concepts of due process, focus on the unfairness of melding the powers to make rules, to enforce rules, to interpret rules, and to impose sanctions for rule violations all in the same actor. Because modern administrative agencies typically exercise each of these functions somewhere within each agency, structural protections such as guaranteed tenure for adminstrative law judges are used to assure fairness. What is critical from this point of view is not that the executive branch have plenary discretion regarding prosecution, but that article III judges who may be finders of fact, adjudicators of law, and sentencers do not become unduly involved in the decisions whether and with what to charge individuals in the first place.

In the cases cited above, it would seem to make little difference whether the Court's animating concern was the separation of powers proper or a separation of functions. Either concern would have yielded deferential judicial review. If the Court's philosophy is one of separation of powers proper, however, that would make a difference on other issues—for example, whether Congress could vest in the courts the power to appoint special prosecutors, as discussed in section B of this chapter, below. If criminal prosecution is a core executive function, such a legislative initiative is clearly more problematic than if the relevant legal theory is only separation of functions, which might permit judicial appointment of prosecutors, albeit with limited judicial oversight of their performance.

As discussed in section B, the case that criminal prosecution was understood in 1787 as a core executive power is quite dubious. It is a position, however, frequently advanced by the executive branch, and supported by some Supreme Court dicta. It is also true that, since the First Congress, Congress has always reposed primary prosecutorial appointment power in the President. As you read the following materials, consider whether criminal prosecution should be treated as necessarily an executive function under the Constitution. If you conclude otherwise, do you think the Court has entertained more deference towards prosecutors than a "separation of functions" theory warrants? After all, the separation of functions is intended chiefly as a protection against governmental unfairness towards individual defendants. How far should a court go, in the name of fairness produced by a separation of functions, in *not* policing more particularized claims that a prosecutor has behaved unfairly?

5. Pardons and Reprieves

An express presidential power with the potential to override Congress' exercise of legislative judgment and the courts' exercise of judicial power in particular cases is the power "to Grant Reprieves and Pardons for Offenses against the United States, except in cases of impeachment." Art. II, § 3. The pardon power:

> embraces all "offenses against the United States," except cases of impeachment, and includes the power to remit fines, penalties, and forfeitures, except as to

money covered into the Treasury or paid an informer,[1] the power to pardon absolutely or conditionally, and the power to commute sentences.[2] ... It was early assumed [but not adjudicated until after the Civil War* that the power included the power to pardon specified classes or communities wholesale, in short, the power of amnesty, which is usually exercised by proclamation. General amnesties were issued by Washington in 1795, by Adams in 1800, by Madison in 1815, by Lincoln in 1863, by Johnson in 1865, 1867, and 1868, and by the first Roosevelt—to Aguinaldo's followers—in 1902.[4]

The Constitution of the United States of America: Analysis and Interpretation, S. Doc. No. 82, 92d Cong., 2d Sess. 476 (1973) [hereafter, "Library of Congress Analysis"].

Chief Justice Marshall declared in *United States v. Wilson*, 32 U.S. 150, 160-161 (1833), that the legal nature of federal pardons would be determined according to the usages of English common law. On that basis, the Court early regarded the pardon as an "act of grace," *id.*, which might be declined by its intended recipient. *Burdick v. United States*, 236 U.S. 79 (1915). This view has been modified, however, at least with respect to the commutation of sentences. In *Biddle v. Perovich*, 274 U.S. 480 (1927), the Court sustained the right of the President to commute a sentence of death to one of life imprisonment, against the will of the prisoner. "A pardon in our days," the Court said, "is not a private act of grace from an individual happening to possess power. It is a part of the Constitutional scheme. When granted it is the determination of the ultimate authority that the public welfare will be better served by inflicting less than what the judgment fixed." *Id.* at 486.

Ex parte Garland, 71 U.S. 333 (1867), is the leading case on the effect of a pardon:

By an act passed in 1865 Congress had prescribed that before any person should be permitted to practice in a federal court he must take oath asserting that he had never voluntarily borne arms against the United States, had never given aid or comfort to enemies of the United States, and so on. Garland, who had been a Confederate sympathizer and so was unable to take the oath, had however received from President Johnson the same year "a full pardon 'for all offenses by him committed, arising from participation, direct or implied, in the Rebellion,' ... " The question before the Court was whether, armed with this pardon, Garland was entitled to practice in the federal courts despite the act of Congress just mentioned. Said Justice Field for a divided Court: "The inquiry arises as to the effect and operation of a pardon, and on this point all the authorities concur. A pardon reaches both the punishment prescribed for the offence and the guilt of the offender; and when the pardon is full, it releases the punishment

---

1. 23 *Ops. Atty. Gen.* 360, 363 (1901); *Illinois Central Railroad v. Bosworth*, 133 U.S. 92 (1890).

2. *Ex parte William Wells*, 18 How. (59 U.S.) 307 (1856). For the contrary view, *see* some early opinions of the Attorney General, 1 *Ops. Atty. Gen.* 341 (1820); 2 *Ops. Atty. Gen.* 275 (1829); 5 *Ops. Atty. Gen.* 687 (1795); *cf.* 4 *Ops. Atty. Gen.* 458 (1845); *United States v. Wilson*, 7 Pet. (32 U.S.) 150, 161 (1833).

* *United States v. Klein*, 13 Wall. (80 U.S.) 128, 147 (1872). *See also United States v. Padelford*, 9 Wall. (76 U.S.) 531 (1870).

4. *See* 1 J. Richardson, Messages and Papers of the Presidents, (Washington: 1897), 173, 293; 2 id., 543; 7 id., 3414, 3508; 8 id., 3853; 14 id., 6690.

and blots out of existence the guilt, so that in the eye of the law the offender is as innocent as if he had never committed the offence. If granted before conviction, it prevents any of the penalties and disabilities consequent upon conviction from attaching [thereto]; if granted after conviction, it removes the penalties and disabilities, and restores him to all his civil rights; it makes him, as it were, a new man, and gives him a new credit and capacity."[12] . . .

[Further,] Congress cannot limit the effects of a presidential amnesty. Thus the act of July 12, 1870, making proof of loyalty necessary to recover property abandoned and sold by the Government during the Civil War, notwithstanding any executive proclamation, pardon, amnesty, or other act of condonation or oblivion, was pronounced void. [Under the 1870 Act, acceptance of pardon for offenses connected with participation in the Confederate war effort was to be treated as conviction for treason, disqualifying the recipient from recovering property seized during the Civil War. In *United States v. Klein*, a case challenging the Act,] Chief Justice Chase [said]: " . . . [T]he legislature cannot change the effect of such a pardon any more than the executive can change a law. Yet this is attempted by the provision under consideration. The Court is required to receive special pardons as evidence of guilt and to treat them as null and void. It is required to disregard pardons granted by proclamation on condition, though the condition has been fulfilled, and to deny them their legal effect. This certainly impairs the executive authority and directs the Court to be instrumental to that end."[18] On the other hand, Congress itself, under the necessary and proper clause, may enact amnesty laws remitting penalties incurred under the national statutes.[19]

Library of Congress Analysis, at 477-80.

It would, we assume, be implausible to characterize any exercise of the President's pardon power as a violation of his duty to take care that the laws be faithfully executed. The impact of a pardon on law enforcement may, however, be considerable, extending beyond the particular case addressed. Intriguingly, among the early acts of each of the three most recent Presidents has been a controversial pardon raising significant public policy issues.

On September 8, 1974, President Gerald Ford granted his predecessor, Richard Nixon, "a full, free, and absolute pardon . . . for all offenses against the United States which he, Richard Nixon, has committed or may have committed or taken part in

---

12. 71 U.S. (4 Wall.) at 380. [*But see Carlesi v. New York*, 233 U.S. 51 (1914): "Carlesi had been convicted several years before of committing a federal offense. In the instant case the prisoner was being tried for a subsequent offense committed in New York. He was convicted as a second offender, although the President had pardoned him for the earlier offense. In other words, the fact of prior conviction by a federal court was considered in determining the punishment for a subsequent state offense. This conviction and sentence were upheld by the Supreme Court. While this case involved offenses against different sovereignties, the Court declared by way of dictum that its decision 'must not be understood as in the slightest degree intimating that a pardon would operate to limit the power of the United States in punishing crimes against its authority to provide for taking into consideration past offenses committed by the accused as a circumstance of aggravation even although for such past offenses there had been a pardon granted.' " Library of Congress Analysis, at 478.]

18. *United States v. Klein*, 80 U.S. (13 Wall.) 128, 143, 148 (1872).

19. *The Laura*, 114 U.S. 411 (1985).

during the period from January 20, 1969 through August 9, 1974." Proclamation No. 4311, 3A C.F.R. 66 (1974). He explained the pardon as follows:

> [The Nixons'] is an American tragedy in which we all have played a part. It could go on and on and on, or someone must write the end to it. I have concluded that only I can do that, and if I can, I must.
>
> There are no historic or legal precedents to which I can turn in this matter, none that precisely fit the circumstances of a private citizen who has resigned the Presidency of the United States. But it is common knowledge that serious allegations and accusations hang like a sword over our former President's head, threatening his health as he tries to reshape his life, a great part of which was spent in the service of this country and by the mandate of its people.
>
> After years of bitter controversy and divisive national debate, I have been advised, and I am compelled to conclude that many months and perhaps more years will have to pass before Richard Nixon could obtain a fair trial by jury in any jurisdiction of the United States under governing decisions of the Supreme Court....
>
> The facts, as I see them, are that a former President of the United States, instead of enjoying equal treatment with any other citizen accused of violating the law, would be cruelly and excessively penalized either in preserving the presumption of his innocence or in obtaining a speedy determination of his guilt in order to repay a legal debt to society.
>
> During this long period of delay and potential litigation, ugly passions would again be aroused. And our people would again by polarized in their opinions. And the credibility of our free institutions of government would again be challenged at home and abroad.
>
> In the end, the courts might well hold that Richard Nixon had been denied due process, and the verdict of history would even more be inconclusive with respect to those charges arising out of the period of his Presidency, of which I am presently aware.
>
> But it is not the ultimate fate of Richard Nixon that most concerns me, though surely it deeply troubles every decent and every compassionate person. My concern is the immediate future of this great country....
>
> My conscience tells me clearly and certainly that I cannot prolong the bad dreams that continue to reopen a chapter that is closed. My conscience tells me that only I, as President, have the constitutional power to firmly shut and seal this book. My conscience tells me it is my duty, not merely to proclaim domestic tranquility but to use every means that I have to insure it....
>
> Finally, I feel that Richard Nixon and his loved ones have suffered enough and will continue to suffer, no matter what I do, no matter what we, as a great and good Nation, can do together to make his goal of peace come true.

Pub. Papers: Gerald R. Ford, 101 (1974).

On the first day of his Administration, January 21, 1977, President Jimmy Carter granted "a full, complete and unconditional pardon" to all persons other than agents, officers, or employees of the Military Selective Service system (1) who may have committed any nonviolent offense between August 4, 1964 and March 28, 1973 in violation of the Military Selective Service Act or any rule or regulation promulgated thereunder; or (2) who were convicted, irrespective of the date of conviction, of any nonviolent offense committed between August 4, 1964 and March 28, 1973 in violation of the Military Selective Service Act, or any rule or regulation promulgated thereunder. Proclamation No. 4483, 3 C.F.R. 4 (1978). *See also* Executive Order No. 11967, 3 C.F.R. 91 (1978), implementing the pardon.

Four years later, Carter's successor, President Ronald Reagan, issued a "full and unconditional pardons to W. Mark Felt and Edward S. Miller," two former FBI agents convicted for unlawful "black-bag jobs" or break-ins at the homes of people thought to be connected in the 1970's with the Weather Underground. On signing the pardon, Reagan stated:

> [Felt's and Miller's] convictions ... grew out of their good-faith belief that their actions were necessary to preserve the security interests of our country. The record demonstrates that they acted not with criminal intent, but in the belief that they had grants of authority reaching to the highest levels of government.
>
> America was at war in 1972, and Messrs. Felt and Miller followed procedures they believed essential to keep the Director of the FBI, the Attorney General, and the President of the United States advised of the activities of hostile foreign powers and their collaborators in this country. They have never denied their actions, but, in fact, came forward to acknowledge them publicly in order to relieve their subordinate agents from criminal actions.
>
> Four years ago, thousands of draft evaders and others who violated the Selective Service laws were unconditionally pardoned by my predecessor. America was generous to those who refused to serve their country in the Vietnam war. We can be no less generous to two men who acted on high principle to bring an end to the terrorism that was threatening our Nation.

Pub. Papers: Ronald Reagan 358 (1981).

What is your assessment of the appropriateness, as a matter of policy, of the Ford, Carter, and Reagan pardons? For intriguing data on the more general recent use of the pardon power, *see* Clark, "Reagan Parsimonious in Use of Pardon Power," Cong. Q. Weekly Rpt. 2878 (1984).

B. Does Congress Need the President? Herein, of Special Prosecutors and Congressional Authority to Remove Execution of the Laws from Presidential Control

The discussion following *Bowsher v. Synar* in Chapter Four introduced a variety of constitutional issues concerning so-called "independent agencies." A common theme among the cited commentators is that the question, "Are independent agencies constitutional?" is too broad. With respect to any officer charged with some aspect of implementing the laws of the United States, constitutional analysis compels more focused attention on (a) the precise functions the officer is discharging, and (b) the precise ways in which the officer's relationships with Congress, the President, and the courts are structured.

An example of just such a narrowly focused controversy is the dispute concerning the constitutionality of court-appointed special prosecutors, now called "independent counsels," who are charged with investigating and possibly prosecuting high-level executive branch and presidential campaign officials in cases where serious criminal misconduct is alleged. The issue is to what degree the vesting of executive power in the President, the appointments clause, and the constitutional specification that the President take care that the laws be faithfully executed, require Congress to rely exclusively on the President or on his subordinates for the implementation of criminal statutes.

The issue of the appropriateness of federal criminal law enforcement independent of presidential direction was first joined squarely in connection with the investigation of Richard Nixon's involvement in the Watergate affair. The independence of the first Watergate Special Prosecutor, Archibald Cox, existed under Justice Department regulations, not by virtue of statute. The consequences are discussed in the following case:

Nader v. Bork
366 F. Supp. 104 (D.D.C. 1973)

GESELL, District Judge.

This is a declaratory judgment and injunction action arising out of the discharge of Archibald Cox from the office of Watergate Special Prosecutor. Defendant Robert H. Bork was the Acting Attorney General who discharged Mr. Cox....

All injunctive relief...was denied from the bench. The effect of the injunctions sought would have been to reinstate Mr. Cox as Watergate Special Prosecutor and to halt the Watergate investigation until he had reassumed control. It appeared to the Court that Mr. Cox's participation in this case was required before such relief could be granted. *See* Rule 19(a) of the Federal Rules of Civil Procedure. Yet Mr. Cox has not entered into this litigation, nor has he otherwise sought to be reinstated as Special Prosecutor. On the contrary, his return to prior duties at Harvard has been publicly announced. Moreover, a new Watergate Special Prosecutor was sworn in on November 5, 1973, and the Court felt that the public interest would not be served by placing any restrictions upon his on-going investigation of Watergate-related matters.

Plaintiffs continue to press for a declaratory judgment on the only remaining issue to be resolved: the legality of the discharge of Mr. Cox and of the temporary abolition of the Office of Watergate Special Prosecutor. To this end, it must initially be determined whether plaintiffs have standing and whether a justiciable controversy still exists.

Defendant Bork contends that the congressional plaintiffs lack standing[1] and that the controversy is moot. This position is without merit. [The court allowed the congressional plaintiffs standing because a declaration as to the legality of Cox's discharge would inform ongoing legislative efforts to insulate the special prosecutor's

---

1. At the injunction hearing, the Court dismissed Mr. Nader as a plaintiff from the bench, it being abundantly clear that he had no legal right to pursue these claims. Flast v. Cohen, 392 U.S. 83, 102.

office, and "would bear upon the duties of plaintiffs to consider whether to impeach" the President.]

. . . [D]efendant Bork suggests that the instant case has been mooted by subsequent events and that the Court as a discretionary matter should refuse to rule on the legality of the Cox discharge. This view of the matter is more academic than realistic, and fails to recognize the insistent demand for some degree of certainty with regard to these distressing events which have engendered considerable public distrust of government. There is a pressing need to declare a rule of law that will give guidance for future conduct with regard to the Watergate inquiry.

While it is perfectly true that the importance of the question presented cannot alone save a case from mootness, the congressional plaintiffs before the Court have a substantial and continuing interest in this litigation. It is an undisputed fact that pending legislation may be affected by the outcome of this dispute and that the challenged conduct of the defendant could be repeated with regard to the new Watergate Special Prosecutor if he presses too hard,[3] an event which would undoubtedly prompt further congressional action. This situation not only saves the case from mootness, but forces decision. . . .

Turning then to the merits, the facts are not in dispute and must be briefly stated to place the legal discussion in the proper context.

The duties and responsibilities of the Office of Watergate Special Prosecutor were set forth in a formal Department of Justice regulation,[4] as authorized by statute. This regulation gave the Watergate Special Prosecutor very broad power to investigate and prosecute offenses arising out of the Watergate break-in, the 1972 Presidential election, and allegations involving the President, members of the White House staff or presidential appointees. Specifically, he was charged with responsibility to conduct court proceedings and to determine whether or not to contest assertions of Executive privilege. He was to remain in office until a date mutually agreed upon between the Attorney General and himself, and it was provided that "The Special Prosecutor will not be removed from his duties except for extraordinary improprieties on his part."

On the same day that this regulation was promulgated, Archibald Cox was designated as Watergate Special Prosecutor. Less than four months later, Mr. Cox was fired by defendant Bork. It is freely admitted that he was not discharged for an extraordinary impropriety. Instead, Mr. Cox was discharged on the order of the President because he was insisting upon White House compliance with a Court Order which was no longer subject to further judicial review. After the Attorney General had resigned rather than fire Mr. Cox on this ground and the Deputy Attorney General had been discharged for refusing to do so, defendant Bork formally dismissed Mr. Cox on October 20, 1973. . . . Thereafter, on October 23, Mr. Bork rescinded the

---

3. The regulation from which the present Watergate Special Prosecutor, Mr. Leon Jaworski, derives his authority and his independence from the Executive branch is virtually identical to the original regulation at issue in this case. [See *United States v. Nixon*, excerpted in Chapter Three, *supra*.] It is therefore particularly desirable to enunciate the rule of law applicable if attempts are made to discharge him.

4. 38 F.R. 14688 (June 4, 1973). The terms of this regulation were developed after negotiations with the Senate Judiciary Committee and were submitted to the Committee during its hearings on the nomination of Elliot Richardson for Attorney General. Hearings Before the Senate Comm. on the Judiciary, 93rd Cong., 1st Sess. 144-46 (1973).

underlying Watergate Special Prosecutor regulation, retroactively, effective as of October 21.

The issues presented for declaratory judgment are whether Mr. Cox was lawfully discharged by defendant on October 20, while the regulation was still in existence, and, if not, whether the subsequent cancellation of the regulation lawfully accomplished his discharge. Both suppositions will be considered.

It should first be noted that Mr. Cox was not nominated by the President and did not serve at the President's pleasure. As an appointee of the Attorney General, Mr. Cox served subject to congressional rather than Presidential control. *See Myers v. United States*, 272 U.S. 52 (1926). The Attorney General derived his authority to hire Mr. Cox and to fix his term of service from various Acts of Congress. Congress therefore had the power directly to limit the circumstances under which Mr. Cox could be discharged, and to delegate that power to the Attorney General. Had no such limitations been issued, the Attorney General would have had the authority to fire Mr. Cox at any time and for any reason. However, he chose to limit his own authority in this regard by promulgating the Watergate Special Prosecutor regulation previously described. It is settled beyond dispute that under such circumstances an agency regulation has the force and effect of law, and is binding upon the body that issues it. . . .

Even more directly on point, the Supreme Court has twice held that an Executive department may not discharge one of its officers in a manner inconsistent with its own regulations concerning such discharge. *See Vitarelli v. Seaton*, 359 U.S. 535 (1959); *Service v. Dulles*, 354 U.S. 363 (1957). The firing of Archibald Cox in the absence of a finding of extraordinary impropriety was in clear violation of an existing Justice Department regulation having the force of law and was therefore illegal.

Defendant suggests that, even if Mr. Cox's discharge had been unlawful on October 20, the subsequent abolition of the Office of Watergate Special Prosecutor was legal and effectively discharged Mr. Cox at that time. This contention is also without merit. It is true that an agency has wide discretion in amending or revoking its regulations. However, we are once again confronted with a situation in which the Attorney General voluntarily limited his otherwise broad authority. The instant regulation contains within its own terms a provision that the Watergate Special Prosecutor (as opposed to any particular occupant of that office) will continue to carry out his responsibilities until he consents to the termination of that assignment.[12] This clause can only be read as a bar to the total abolition of the Office of Watergate Special Prosecutor without the Special Prosecutor's consent, and the Court sees no reason why the Attorney General cannot by regulation impose such a limitation upon himself and his successors.

Even if the Court were to hold otherwise, however, it could not conclude that the defendant's Order of October 23 revoking the regulation was legal. An agency's power to revoke its regulations is not unlimited—such action must be neither arbitrary nor unreasonable. In the instant case, the defendant abolished the Office of Watergate Special Prosecutor on October 23, and reinstated it less than three weeks later under

---

12. *See* 38 F.R. 14688 (June 4, 1973): "The Special Prosecutor will carry out these responsibilities with the full support of the Department of Justice, until such time as, in his judgment, he has completed them or until a date mutually agreed upon between the Attorney General and himself."

a virtually identical regulation.[13] It is clear that this turnabout was simply a ruse to permit the discharge of Mr. Cox without otherwise affecting the Office of the Special Prosecutor—a result which could not legally have been accomplished while the regulation was in effect under the circumstances presented in this case. Defendant's Order revoking the original regulation was therefore arbitrary and unreasonable, and must be held to have been without force or effect....

Plaintiffs have emphasized that over and beyond these authorities the Acting Attorney General was prevented from firing Mr. Cox by the explicit and detailed commitments given to the Senate, at the time of Mr. Richardson's confirmation, when the precise terms of the regulation designed to assure Mr. Cox's independence were hammered out. Whatever may be the moral or political implications of the President's decision to disregard those commitments, they do not alter the fact that the commitments had no legal effect. Mr. Cox's position was not made subject to Senate confirmation, nor did Congress legislate to prevent illegal or arbitrary action affecting the independence of the Watergate Special Prosecutor.

The Court recognizes that this case emanates in part from congressional concern as to how best to prevent future Executive interference with the Watergate investigation. Although these are times of stress, they call for caution as well as decisive action. The suggestion that the Judiciary be given responsibility for the appointment and supervision of a new Watergate Special Prosecutor, for example, is most unfortunate. Congress has it within its own power to enact appropriate and legally enforceable protections against any effort to thwart the Watergate inquiry. The Courts must remain neutral. Their duties are not prosecutorial. If Congress feels that laws should be enacted to prevent Executive interference with the Watergate Special Prosecutor, the solution lies in legislation enhancing and protecting that office as it is now established and not by following a course that places incompatible duties upon this particular Court. As Judge Learned Hand warned in United States v. Marzano, 149 F.2d 923, 926 (2 Cir. 1945):

> Prosecution and judgment are two quite separate functions in the administration of justice; they must not merge....

FINAL ORDER AND DECLARATORY JUDGMENT

On the basis of findings of fact and conclusions of law set forth in an accompanying Memorandum filed this day, it is hereby

Ordered and Decreed that:...

(5) The Court declares that Archibald Cox, appointed Watergate Special Prosecutor pursuant to 28 C.F.R. § 0.37 (1973), was illegally discharged from that office.

---

1. Was *Nader v. Bork* properly decided? Did the court issue an advisory opinion in a moot case? Should Congress have standing to procure judicial declarations as to the scope of Congress's legislative responsibilities?

---

13. The two regulations are identical, except for a single addition to the new regulation which provides that the Special Prosecutor may not even be discharged for extraordinary improprieties unless the President determines that it is the "consensus" of certain specified congressional leaders that discharge is appropriate. *Compare* 38 F.R. 30738 (Nov. 9, 1973) *with* 38 F.R. 14688 (June 4, 1973).

2. Assuming Congress could not require by statute that an executive appointee be dismissed only with the acquiescence of congressional leaders, should a court view as binding on the executive a self-imposed regulation that accomplishes the same result? Recall the delegation doctrine, which prevents Congress from abdicating the core of the legislative function. Is there an analogous limit on executive abdications of constitutional functions? Was it implicated by this case?

3. Was the President bound to accomplish the discharge of Archibald Cox through the Attorney General? Could the President lawfully override the regulation implemented by his subordinate and discharge the special prosecutor directly?

4. Partly in reaction to Watergate, Congress, in 1978, provided by statute for the court appointment of special prosecutors to investigate alleged wrongdoing by the President and high-level officials—contrary to Judge Gesell's sentiments expressed in *Nader v. Bork*. The relevant provisions, as amended, appear in the Appendix. Review the Act, together with the following excerpts from (a) the House Judiciary Committee report on an early version of the Act, (b) Acting Attorney General (now Judge) Bork's testimony against the original bill, and (c) a brief essay defending the constitutionality of the Act.

Independent Special Prosecutor
H.R. Rept. No. 660, 93d Cong., 1st Sess. 6-11 (1973)
Constitutional Considerations

A question has been raised as to the constitutionality of providing for a court appointed Special Prosecutor. The Subcommittee on Criminal Justice called and examined a number of witnesses on that specific question.... Only Acting Attorney General Bork and Dean Roger C. Cramton of the Cornell University Law School questioned the constitutionality of providing for a court appointed Special Prosecutor.

I. *The Appointing Power*

A. Article II, section 2, clause 2 of the Constitution is the primary underpinning which supports the approach of H.R. 11401. This provision reads as follows:

> He [the President] shall ... nominate, and by and with the Advice and Consent of the Senate, shall appoint ... all ... Officers of the United States, whose Appointments are not herein otherwise provided for, and which shall be established by Law: *but the Congress may by Law vest the Appointment of such inferior Officers, as they think proper, in the President alone, in the Courts of Law, or in the Heads of Departments.* (Emphasis added)

(1) *The Special Prosecutor is an "inferior officer" within the meaning of Article II, Section 2, Clause 2.*

In *United States v. Germaine*, 99 U.S. 508 (1878), the Supreme Court said:

> The Constitution for purposes of appointment very clearly divides all its officers into two classes. The primary class requires a nomination by the President and confirmation by the Senate. But foreseeing that when offices become numerous, and sudden removals necessary, this mode might be inconvenient, it was provided that, in regard to officers inferior to those specifically mentioned, Congress might by law vest their appointment in the President alone, in the Courts of law, or in the heads of departments. That all persons who can be said

to hold an office under the government about to be established under the Constitution were intended to be included within one or the other of these modes of appointment there can be little doubt.

This case has never been reversed.

(2) *Vesting the appointment of the Special Prosecutor in a court of law is a valid exercise of this Congressional power to provide for the appointment of inferior officers.*

In sustaining the appointment of supervisors of Congressional elections by courts of law, pursuant to legislation enacted by the Congress, the Supreme Court said in *Ex Parte Siebold*, 100 U.S. 371 (1879), at pages 397-398:

> Finally, it is objected that the act of Congress imposes upon the Circuit Court duties not judicial, in requiring them to appoint the supervisors of election, whose duties, it is alleged, are entirely executive in their character. It is contended that no power can be conferred upon the courts of the United States to appoint officers whose duties are not connected with the judicial department of the government.
>
> . . . It is no doubt usual and proper to vest the appointment of inferior officers in that department of the government, executive or judicial, or in that particular executive department to which the duties of such officers appertain. But there is no absolute requirement to this effect in the Constitution; and, if there were, it would be difficult in many cases to determine to which department an office properly belonged. Take that of marshal, for instance. He is an executive officer, whose appointment, in ordinary cases, is left to the President and Senate. But if Congress should, as it might, vest the appointment elsewhere, it would be questionable whether it should be in the President alone, in the Department of Justice, or in the courts. The marshal is pre-eminently the officer of the courts; and, in case of a vacancy, Congress has in fact passed a law bestowing the temporary appointment of the marshal upon the justice of the [local] circuit. . . .
>
> But as the Constitution stands, the selection of the appointing power, as between the functionaries named, is a matter resting in the discretion of Congress. And, looking at the subject in a practical light, it is perhaps better that it should rest there, than that the country should be harassed by the endless controversies to which a more specific direction on this subject might have given rise. The observation in the case of Hennen,* . . . that the appointing power in the clause referred to "was no doubt intended to be exercised by the department of the government to which the official to be appointed most appropriately belonged," was not intended to define the constitutional power of Congress in this regard, but rather to express the law or rule by which it should be governed. The cases in which the courts have declined to exercise certain duties imposed by Congress, stand upon a different consideration from that which applies in the present case. The law of 1792, which required the circuit courts to examine claims to revolutionary pensions, and the law of 1849, authorizing the district judge of Florida to examine and adjudicate upon claims for injuries suffered by the inhabitants of Florida from the American army in 1812, were rightfully held

---

* [Ed. note: In *Ex Parte Hennen*, 38 U.S. 230 (1839), the Supreme Court held that the presiding judge of a federal district court could, without Senate approval, dismiss a clerk whom he had appointed.]

to impose upon the courts powers not judicial, and were, therefore, void. But the duty to appoint inferior officers, when required thereto by law, is a constitutional duty of the courts; and in the present case there is no such incongruity in the duty required as to excuse the courts from its performance, or to render their acts void. It cannot be affirmed that the appointment of the officers in question could, with any greater propriety, and certainly not with equal regard to convenience, have been assigned to any other depositary of official power capable of exercising it. Neither the President, nor any head of department, could have been equally competent to the task.

In our judgment, Congress had the power to vest the appointment of the supervisors in question in the circuit courts.

The *Siebold* case has never been reversed, nor has the Supreme Court ever watered down its decision; rather the opinion has often been cited with approval. The *Siebold* case stands clearly and unequivocally for the following:

(a) Congress can empower the courts to appoint officers whose duties are not judicial.

(b) It is impractical to attempt to restrict the power of appointment by a test based on some sort of functional relationship between the appointor and the appointee.

(c) The duty to appoint inferior officers when required by law to do so, is a constitutional duty from which a court may be excused only if there is such an "incongruity" in the required duty that the court should or must be excused. In the instant case there clearly is no such incongruity; but there would be an incongruity in the Executive making the appointment of a Special Prosecutor charged with investigating and prosecuting the Executive. In the words of *Siebold*, "Neither the President, nor any head of department, could have been equally competent to the task."

(3) *Other instances of appointments by the courts of non-judicial officers.*

(*a*) Section 546 of title 28, United States Code, provides for the appointment by the courts of United States attorneys. Sustained in *United States v. Solomon*, 216 F. Supp. 836 (S.D.N.Y. 1963).

(*b*) Section 565 of title 28, United States Code, provides for the appointment by the courts of United States marshals. See *Ex Parte Siebold*, 100 U.S. 371, 397 (1879).

(*c*) D.C. Code § 31-101 (1973 ed) empowers the courts to fill vacancies on the District of Columbia Board of Education. Sustained in *Hobson v. Hansen*, 265 F. Supp. 902 (D.D.C. 1967), appeal dismissed 393 U.S. 801 (1968).

(*d*) The courts regularly appoint defense counsel pursuant to the provisions of the Criminal Justice Act of 1964, as amended (78 Stat 552; 18 U.S.C. 3006A).

(4) *Article I, Section 8, Clause 18, of the Constitution also supports the legislation.*

. . . If, for argument's sake, it is assumed that the prosecution of criminal offenses is an exclusive power of the President, or of the Department of Justice, and they are disabled by conflict of interest from exercising that power, then Congress under the plain language of [the necessary and proper] clause has full authority to take remedial legislative action. The power is to "make all laws", which should disabuse any argument that the sole Congressional remedy is impeachment and should further support providing for the appointment of the Special Prosecutor by the courts of law under Article II, Section 2, Clause 2....

II. The Removal Power

Giving the Special Prosecutor independence from the President has been analyzed in terms of "separation of powers", in terms of "checks and balances", and in terms of "conflict of interest". What these analyses all come down to, however, is the issue whether the President ought to be able to control the persons responsible for investigating and prosecuting some of his closest and most trusted associates, and perhaps even himself. If Congress determines that it is necessary and proper to restrict the President's removal power in order to assure that the Special Prosecutor will be able to carry out his functions promptly, thoroughly, and fairly, can it validly do so?

The doctrine of separation of powers is not explicitly provided for in the text of the Constitution, but it is considered one of the premises upon which our constitutional system of government rests. The doctrine does not contemplate the complete separation of the different branches of government, but rather it contemplates the sharing of power among them. The doctrine does not demand the creation of three "watertight compartments", but aims to avoid a concentration in one branch of government of power that could be exercised tyrannically (See *United States v. Solomon*, 216 F. Supp. 835, 838-9 (S.D.N.Y. 1963) for an excellent, extended discussion.) The proposed Special Prosecutor Act of 1973 is consistent with this concept.

The power to remove an official, in the absence of statutory specification, generally goes with the power to appoint. *In the matter of Hennen*, 13 Pet. 230 (1839). In 1926, however, the Supreme Court limited this rule on the ground that its application to postmasters violated the doctrine of separation of powers....

While the decision in ... [*Myers v. United States*, 272 U.S. 52 (1926)] seemed to preclude restricting the President's removal power in a broad area of appointments, subsequent Supreme Court decisions narrowed the area within which the President can exercise unfettered discretion.... [U]nder the doctrine of separation of powers developed by the Supreme Court in the *Myers*, *Humphrey's Executor*, and *Wiener* cases, Congress may restrict the President's removal power if (1) the Special Prosecutor's functions are not exclusively executive, or (2) the Special Prosecutor's functions require freedom from executive branch interference.

The prosecutorial function in Anglo-American jurisprudence is not, and has not been, purely an executive branch function. At the time of the adoption of the Constitution, private citizens both here and in England, could prosecute criminal charges. The federal government's role in prosecuting violations of federal criminal laws was established by statute, not by the Constitution. See 1 Stat. 92. Further, Congress has also authorized criminal prosecutions by private persons. See, for example, 1 Stat. 112. See also L. White, *The Federalists* 415-16 (1948). That the prosecutorial function is not purely executive is further illustrated by the grand jury system. The grand jury exists outside the executive branch to act as a buffer between private citizens and the executive branch. Unless the grand jury votes to return an indictment charging a crime, a felony prosecution of a private citizen cannot take place (unless, of course, the citizen waives indictment). The Special Prosecutor Act of 1973 gives the Special Prosecutor functions and duties with regard to the grand jury.

The background of events leading to the introduction of H.R. 11401 makes it evident the allegations about violations of federal criminal laws by high officials of the executive branch cannot be fully, impartially and thoroughly investigated by a prosecutor who does not have freedom from executive branch interference. It is just as important to insulate a prosecutor responsible for investigating and prosecuting high executive branch officials from interference by the executive branch, as it is to insulate a member of the War Claims Commission from such interference.

One further element of separation of powers is that, within his sphere of discretion, the Special Prosecutor must be free from judicial (as well as executive) control of his decisions. In *United States v. Cox*, 342 F.2d 167 (5th Cir. 1965), the Court of Appeals for the Fifth Circuit held that a court could not compel a United States attorney to sign an indictment when by law the United States attorney was free to decide whether or not he wanted to sign. The Special Prosecutor Act of 1973 does not provide for any supervision of the Special Prosecutor by the district court for the District of Columbia. The Act gives the Special Prosecutor complete freedom of action within his jurisdiction—freedom from judicial as well as executive control.

Special Prosecutor

Hearings Before the Senate Comm. on the Judiciary, 93d Cong., 1st
Sess. 449-53 (1973).

Testimony of Robert H. Bork, Acting Attorney General

... The question is whether congressional legislation appointing a Special Prosecutor outside the executive branch or empowering courts to do so would be constitutionally valid and whether it would provide significant advantages that make it worth taking a constitutionally risky course. I am persuaded that such a course would almost certainly not be valid and would, in any event, pose more problems than it would solve....

The constitutional problem arises, of course, because the Constitution of the United States makes prosecution of criminal offenses an executive branch function. The Constitution distributes the powers of the three branches of Government and the only reference to prosecutorial powers is in article II, section 3, which states that the President "shall take care that the laws be faithfully executed." Article II, section 2, gives the President "Power to Grant Reprieves and Pardons for Offenses against the United States." This power, too, indicates that the Constitution lodges in the executive branch complete control over criminal prosecutions. As Professor Roger Cramton has stated, although "the nature and extent of this power has been disrupted, there can be little doubt that functions placed in the four original Federal departments—conduct of foreign relations, command of the military, enforcement of the law, and collection of taxes—are at the core of the Executive's authority."

This conclusion was emphatically affirmed by the Fifth Circuit Court of Appeals, sitting *en banc*, in *United States v. Cox*, 342 F. 2d 167 (1965). A Federal grand jury handed up a perjury indictment against two black witnesses on the basis of their testimony in a civil rights case. At the direction of Acting Attorney General Katzenbach, the U.S. attorney refused to sign the indictment and the district court cited him for contempt. The Fifth Circuit reversed, holding that prosecution is placed by the Constitution under the control of the executive branch, not the judiciary. The majority opinion said:

It follows, as an incident of the constitutional separation of powers, that the courts are not to interfere with the free exercise of the discretionary powers of the attorneys of the United States in their control over criminal prosecution. (342 F.2d at 171).

Judge Wisdom, concurring specially, further noted:

The prosecution of offenses against the United States is an executive function within the exclusive prerogative of the Attorney General. (342 F.2d at 190.)

And, further:

The functions of prosecutor and judge are incompatible. (342 F.2d 192.)

The Supreme Court declined to review the *Cox* decision....

The bill before this committee attempts to rebut this traditional understanding of the Constitution by relying upon [the] constitutional powers of Congress....I shall examine these powers in turn to suggest why I do not think the power to lodge prosecutorial powers outside the executive branch is fairly contained in any of them.

Article II, section 2, grants wide powers to the President with respect to ... the nomination or appointment of various officers of the United States.... It seems as clear as such matters ever can be that the Framers intended to give Congress the power to vest in the courts to the power to appoint "inferior officers" such as clerks, bailiffs, and similar functionaries necessary to the functioning of courts, just as they intended "Heads of Departments" to be able to appoint most of their subordinates without troubling the President in every case. The power is clearly one to enhance convenience of administration, not to enable Congress to destroy the separation of powers by transferring the powers of the Executive to the Judiciary or, for the matter of that, transferring the powers of the Judiciary to the Executive....

Much the same argument applies to Congress's powers under [the necessary and proper clause] ... I take it that no one suggests the power to create a Special Prosecutor outside the executive branch is found among the enumerated powers such as the power to regulate commerce or to lay and collect taxes. The theory, therefore, must be that the power to make laws necessary and proper for the enforcement of the laws includes the power to remove law enforcement from the executive branch.

If the Necessary and Proper Clause were read in that fashion it would be a power lodged in Congress that swallows up much of the rest of the Constitution. Under this theory, for example, there could have been no doubt of the constitutionality of the plan to pack the Supreme Court in the 1930's.... No one has ever suspected before that the Necessary and Proper Clause was a power to amend the Constitution that makes wholly unnecessary the specific procedures for amendment provided by article V.

The Necessary and Proper clause must be read as a means of making the exercise of powers by the various branches effective, not as a means of shifting powers between the branches of government. Thus Congress may create or abolish various positions within the Department of Justice. It may provide or take away jurisdiction. It may pass or repeal substantive laws. It may appropriate funds or not as it sees fit. But all of this does not add up to a theory that it can keep the laws but forbid the executive branch to enforce them and transfer the enforcement function to itself or to the courts....

It is particularly important in times of crisis and deepseated unease that we adhere to the constitutional system that has sustained us for so long. It is all too easy to say that this is an emergency and we will only violate the Constitution this one time. But that kind of expediency is habit forming. Bad precedents, once established, are easily used in the future.

P. Shane, Special Prosecutor Post Will Survive Legal Test

Des Moines Register, Mar. 25, 1987, at 7A, col. 3.

. . . [T]he President does not need either to appoint all criminal prosecutors or to control potentially all prosecutorial discretion in order to "take care that the laws be faithfully executed." The only authority he needs for this purpose is the authority to remove criminal prosecutors who are themselves not faithfully executing the laws, whether because of incapacity or malfeasance. Congress has delegated just this power over the current special prosecutors to the Attorney General, who is entirely subordinate to the President.

. . . [O]pponents of special prosecutors . . . hope[] to rely on several recent Supreme Court decisions that struck down important congressional initiatives on highly formalistic constitutional grounds. These cases overturned so-called "legislative vetoes" and the powers granted originally to the Comptroller General under the Gramm-Rudman budget balancing law. Both decisions, however, involved procedural issues addressed by the Constitution with a fair degree of specificity—how Congress may enact legislation or remove officers of the United States. The Constitution does not provide any similarly explicit guidance on the issue of special prosecutors.

On questions like the special prosecutor issue, where constitutional text is plainly ambiguous, the Supreme Court routinely applies a functional test to determine whether the act of any branch of the government contravenes the intended separation of powers. The first question posed by the Court is whether the challenged act of one branch— here, Congress—poses the potential for disrupting the constitutionally assigned functions of another branch—here, the executive. If it does, then the Court inquires whether that impact is nonetheless "justified by an overriding need to promote objectives within the constitutional authority of Congress" to protect.

In assessing the special prosecutor provisions of the Ethics in Government Act, a court could quite properly conclude that the Act does not pose even the potential for disrupting the President's constitutionally assigned functions. It is true that a court appoints each special prosecutor, but the court may do so only if the Attorney General requests the appointment. Congress has given the Attorney General unreviewable discretion to decline to regard allegations of high-level misconduct as serious enough to warrant investigation. Even if the Attorney General investigates, Congress has delegated unreviewable discretion to him or her to decline to request the appointment of a special prosecutor.

Nor is the special prosecutor, once appointed, a renegade officer. The Ethics in Government Act provides that the prosecutor "shall, except where not possible, comply with the written or other established policies of the Department of Justice respecting enforcement of the criminal laws." Furthermore, the Attorney General may, under the Act, remove a special prosecutor "for good cause, physical disability, mental incapacity, or any other condition that substantially impairs the performance" of the prosecutor's duties. These statutory provisions greatly mitigate any prospect that the special prosecutor will intrude on the executive's legitimate policy-making discretion in any respect.

Even if a court perceives that the Ethics in Government Act does present the potential for disrupting the executive's assigned role, a persuasive argument exists that the intrusion is justified by an overwhelming public interest. The special prosecutor process comes into play only with respect to the highest government officials or presidential campaign officers. The blatant conflict of interest confronting the President whenever an official of this stature is accused of serious wrongdoing threatens to undermine not only justice in the particular case, but public confidence generally in the fair administration of justice. The Supreme Court has characterized the avoidance of government corruption or its appearance as legislative interests of the highest order. . . .

Notes and Questions on Independent Counsel

1. Congess' 1982 reauthorization of the special prosecutor statute included several changes from the original act. These included (a) changing the name of the "special prosecutor" to "independent counsel"; (b) changing the standard that triggers a preliminary investigation of covered officials to allow the Attorney General to consider the credibility of the accuser and the specificity of the information received; and (c) permitting the Attorney General to remove independent counsel for "good cause," instead of only for "extraordinary impropriety" or mental and physical disability. The 1982 amendments further required the appointment of independent counsel only when the Attorney General "finds reasonable grounds to believe that further investigation or prosecution is warranted." This language replaced a more stringent earlier standard, which required a special prosecutor unless the information received "is so unsubstantiated that no further investigation is warranted." A final change of considerable importance was permitting the Attorney General, in determining whether reasonable grounds exist to warrant further investigation or prosecution, to "comply with the written or other established policies of the Department of Justice with respect to the enforcement of criminal law." Under this last provision, for example, the Attorney General could forbear from appointing an independent counsel in an undisputed case of illicit drug possession by a high level executive branch official, if the Department of Justice has a preexisting policy not to prosecute possession offenses unless the quantity of substance involved is greater than present in the particular case. In your view, did these changes represent sensible law enforcement policy or an undue relaxation of congressional vigilance over high level executive branch officials?

Despite constitutional misgivings, President Reagan, in December, 1987, signed another five-year reauthorization of the special prosecutor process. Congress moved this time to restrict the Attorney General's discretion and to buttress the autonomy of the independent counsel. The reauthorization, for example, requires a preliminary investigation "whenever the Attorney General receives information sufficient to constitute grounds to investigate whether any person [covered by the act] *may have* committed a violation of any Federal criminal law other than a petty offense." The earlier acts triggered investigations only when the information received suggested that a person covered by the Act "has committed" a serious criminal violation. Further, the reauthorization would forbid the Attorney General to rely "upon a determination that [a] person lacked the state of mind required for the violation of criminal law" as a reason for not having a preliminary investigation or not applying for the appointment of an independent counsel.

Although the Administration had threatened to veto the reauthorization on constitutional grounds, Congress appeared poised for an override. The Senate vote approving the measure was 85 to 7; the House vote was 322 to 90. For the original bills, *see* H.R. 2939, 100th Cong., 1st Sess. (1987), *reprinted at* 133 Cong. Rec. H8871-74, 8891 (Lungren amendment), 8892 (Frank amendment), 8808-09 (Shaw amendment) (daily ed. Oct. 21, 1987); S. 1293, 100th Cong., 1st Sess. (1987), *reprinted at* 133 Cong. Rec. S15646-50 (daily ed. Nov. 3, 1987).

2.   The United States Court of Appeals for the District of Columbia recently held the 1982 independent counsel statute unconstituional. *In re Sealed Case*, Nos. 87-5261, 5264, and 5265 (D.C. Cir. Jan. 22, 1988), *rev'g*, 665 F.Supp. 56 (D.D.C. 1987). *But see Deaver v. Seymour*, 656 F.Supp. 900 (D.D.C. 1987) (denying preliminary injunction); *North v. Walsh*, 656 F.Supp. 414 (D.D.C. 1987). Prompt Supreme Court review of this judgment seems likely.

What is your assessment of the constitutionality of the independent counsel provisions of the Ethics in Government Act? Do you agree with Shane that the legislative veto and Gramm-Rudman Act cases can be distinguished? Does Shane underestimate the potential for disruption of the executive branch's discharge of its constitutionally assigned duties? Does the history of criminal prosecution demonstrate that limitations on executive power to control criminal prosecution do not implicate the executive's constitutional authority? (Recall, for example, then-Acting Attorney General Bork's argument that the President's pardon power "indicates that the Constitution lodges in the executive branch complete control over criminal prosecutions." Is it relevant that the pardon has always been a royal prerogative in England, even though the Crown does *not* control criminal prosecutions?) Note that, in his functional analysis, Shane mentions several features of the current act that minimize its intrusiveness into executive branch policymaking. Do you think any or all of these features are required to preserve the constitutionality of the act?

3. A recent decision that potentially foreshadows the Supreme Court's position on the constitutionality of independent prosecution is *Young v. United States ex rel. Vuitton et Fils S.A.*, 107 S.Ct. 2124 (1987). The petitioners had been convicted of criminal contempt for violating an injunction barring their further infringement of the trademark of Louis Vuitton, S.A., a French handbag manufacturer. To prosecute the criminal contempt, the U.S. district court had appointed two private attorneys, both counsel to Vuitton. The Supreme Court held that such appointments were within the inherent power of the judiciary, but, in a split vote, reversed the petitioners' convictions. Four members of the Court regarded it as impermissible to appoint counsel for an interested party as contempt prosecutors. Four members of the Court regarded the practice as disfavored, but harmless in *Vuitton*. Justice Scalia, the deciding vote, was the only Justice to argue that judicial appointment of the prosecutors was impermissible.

Because the *Vuitton* prosecutions involved the judicial vindication of *judicial* orders, not criminal laws of general applicability, the appointment authority upheld in *Vuitton* is distinguishable from the special prosecutor situation. It is striking, however, that Justice Scalia articulated a separation of powers position clearly broad enough to invalidate special prosecutors, 107 S.Ct. at 2141-47 (Scalia, J., concurring), and no other Justice joined it.

4. The lower courts that have addressed the issue have held Attorney General decisions under the Ethics in Government Act to be immune from judicial review. In *Banzhaf v. Smith*, 737 F.2d 1167 (D.C. Cir. 1984) (en banc), the D.C. Circuit held that the act precludes judicial review, at the behest of members of the public, of Attorney General decisions not to investigate particular allegations and not to seek appointment of independent counsel. *See also Nathan v. Smith*, 737 F.2d 1069 (D.C. Cir. 1984). In *Dellums v. Smith*, 797 F.2d 817 (9th Cir. 1986), the court of appeals reversed a lower court holding [577 F. Supp. 1449 (N.D. Cal. 1984)] that judicial review does exist to compel the Attorney General to conduct a preliminary investigation if the information presented by plaintiffs to trigger investigation was sufficiently specific and from a sufficiently credible source. In *Dellums*, the plaintiffs—including a member of Congress—provided information to the Attorney General supporting allegations that the President, the Secretary of State, the Secretary of Defense, and other federal executive officers violated the Neutrality Act, 18 U.S.C. § 960 (1982), by supporting paramilitary operations against Nicaragua. The district court had concluded that, even if the Department of Justice had a policy in place providing for the nonprosecution of officials for Neutrality Act violations, such a policy could be implemented only subsequent to the preliminary investigation compelled by the act. 577 F.Supp. at 454-5.

As you review the language of the Act (*see* Appendix), does it give you any basis for firm inferences about Congress' intent with respect to judicial review, or about the right of private parties to compel Attorney General action? Should it be decisive that Congress failed to adopt at least two predecessor bills that would have specifically included provisions for judicial review at the behest of private parties? Do separation of powers considerations militate for or against judicial review in this context? *See* Comment, Banzhaf v. Smith: *Judicial Review Under the Independent Counsel Provisions of the Ethics in Government Act*, 70 Iowa L. Rev. 1339 (1985).

5. For a perspective on the special prosecutor process offered by the subject of an investigation, *see* H. Jordan, Crisis 237-293 (1982).

6. Even if the current statutory provisions governing independent counsels (and other independent agencies) are constitutional, Congress may generate a variety of practical problems by bifurcating enforcement of the civil and criminal provisions of the same Act between an independent agency and the Department of Justice. For example, a dispute arose in 1980 between the Justice Department and the Securities and Exchange Commission (SEC) concerning whether to render advisory opinions under the antibribery provisions of the Foreign Corrupt Practices Act (FCPA). Specifically, the Department of Justice established an FCPA Review Procedure, which permitted companies to obtain guidance concerning the applicability of the FCPA's bribery prohibitions to particular transactions. Under that procedure, a company could request a review of a proposed transaction and a statement whether the Department would take enforcement action if the transaction were carried out in the manner described. Justice promised not to disclose any information exempt from mandatory public disclosure under the Freedom of Information Act that was submitted as part of a review request.

To publicize its enforcement policies further, Justice promised that it would issue public releases with respect to review requests, which would describe the nature of reviewed transactions in general terms and set forth the Department's advice with respect to those transactions. Justice also issued a statement of its enforcement priorities with respect to the bribery prohibitions, identifying a number of factors that would increase the likelihood of investigation or prosecution.

The SEC, which is responsible for civil enforcement under the FCPA, chose not to participate in the Justice Department's FCPA Review Procedure because of its view that determinations with respect to the applicability of the FCPA to particular fact patterns often would turn on judgments concerning motivation and intent. It concluded that many transactions do not easily lend themselves to guidance on the basis of a written description, and that questions concerning the FCPA could, in the first instance, better be resolved by corporate officials and their professional advisers, who have better access to the relevant facts.

Nonetheless, the SEC felt constrained to state publicly that it would not commence an enforcement action alleging violations of the FCPA in any case in which a public company sought clearance for a proposed transaction under the FCPA Review Procedure and received a letter from the Department of Justice, prior to May 31, 1981, stating that the Department did not intend to take enforcement action based on the facts and circumstances presented. The SEC explained that it viewed the review procedure as an experiment that might serve to provide a greater measure of predictability as to how the bribery prohibitions would be applied, and might provide a needed source of reliable data concerning the impact and operation of the bribery prohibitions. Commenters suggested to the SEC that the possibility of SEC enforcement action, despite a favorable review letter from Justice, might deter some public companies from making use of the advisory procedure. *See* Statement of Commission Policy Concerning Section 30A of the Securities Exchange Act of 1934, 45 Fed. Reg. 59,001 (1980).

Under what circumstances, if any, is the Department of Justice's use of resources to provide advice on potential criminal liability arising from private activity justifiable? Do you agree with the SEC's rationale for not entering into such an advisory process? If so, do you perceive that the SEC had any responsible alternative to what was effectively its acquiescence in the Justice Department process?

C. Does the President Need Congress? Herein, Of Inherent Presidential Authority to Execute the Law

The preceding sections considered the nature of the President's power to execute the laws in instances in which Congress had also exercised its power; the issue, in essence, was how much flexibility the President retains after Congress has enacted a particular public policy. You will recall that the majority in *Youngstown* viewed this as the core issue in that case.

This section considers the scope of the President's powers when Congress has not legislated. To what extent is the faithful execution clause, with or without additional textual support in the Constitution, a sufficient legal basis for a presidential initiative in domestic affairs? Consider especially how, if the legal questions presented in the materials that follow were presented to you in your planning role as legal counsel, you would approach the analysis.

1. General Considerations

In Re Neagle
135 U.S. 1 (1890)

[*In re Neagle* is invariably cited in Department of Justice legal memoranda as legitimating a broad implied power to take all steps necessary and proper for the enforcement of federal law, even in the face of apparent conflict with state law obligations.

Neagle was an appeal by California of a successful federal habeas corpus petition brought by a deputy U.S. Marshal, who had been charged with killing one Judge Terry. Neagle killed Terry while assigned to protect Supreme Court Justice Field, whose life, after a bizarre series of events, Terry had threatened. The uncontradicted evidence showed that Neagle killed Terry after Terry physically assaulted Justice Field, and in the reasonable belief that Terry was about to draw a gun. After his arrest, Neagle sought release under a federal habeas statute on the statutory ground that he was being held "in custody for an act done . . . in pursuance of a law of the United States." California argued that the statute was inapplicable, because no federal statute had authorized Neagle's protection of Justice Field or an assault in the discharge of his duties.

Writing for the majority, Justice Miller reasoned:]

It is not supposed that any special act of Congress exists which authorizes the marshals or deputy marshals of the United States in express terms to accompany the judges of the Supreme Court through their circuits, and act as a body-guard to them, to defend them against malicious assaults against their persons. But we are of opinion that this view of the statute is an unwarranted restriction of the meaning of a law designed to extend in a liberal manner the benefit of the writ of *habeas corpus* to persons imprisoned for the performance of their duty. And we are satisfied that if it was the duty of Neagle, under the circumstances, a duty which could only arise under the laws of the United States, to defend Mr. Justice Field from a murderous attack upon him, he brings himself within the meaning of the section we have recited. . . .

In the view we take of the Constitution of the United States, any obligation fairly and properly inferrible from that instrument, or any duty of the marshal to be derived from the general scope of his duties under the laws of the United States, is "a law" within the meaning of this phrase. It would be a great reproach to the system of government of the United States, declared to be within its sphere sovereign and supreme, if there is to be found within the domain of its powers no means of protecting the judges, in the conscientious and faithful discharge of their duties, from the malice and hatred of those upon whom their judgments may operate unfavorably. . . .

Where, then, are we to look for the protection which we have shown Judge Field was entitled to when engaged in the discharge of his official duties? Not to the courts of the United States; because, as has been more than once said in this court, in the division of the powers of government between the three great departments, executive, legislative and judicial, the judicial is the weakest for the purposes of self-protection and for the enforcement of the powers which it exercises. The ministerial officers through whom its commands must be executed are marshals of the United States, and belong emphatically to the executive department of the government. They are appointed by the President, with the advice and consent of the Senate. They are removable from office at his pleasure....

The legislative branch of the government can only protect the judicial officers by the enactment of laws for that purpose, and the argument we are now combating assumes that no such law has been passed by Congress.

If we turn to the executive department of the government, we find a very different condition of affairs. The Constitution, section 3, Article 2, declares that the President "shall take care that the laws be faithfully executed," and he is provided with the means of fulfilling this obligation by his authority to commission all the officers of the United States, and, by and with the advice and consent of the Senate, to appoint the most important of them and to fill vacancies. He is declared to be commander-in-chief of the army and navy of the United States. The duties which are thus imposed upon him he is further enabled to perform by the recognition in the Constitution, and the creation by acts of Congress, of executive departments, which . . . aid him in the performance of the great duties of his office, and represent him in a thousand acts to which it can hardly be supposed his personal attention is called, and thus he is enabled to fulfil the duty of his great department, expressed in the phrase that "he shall take care that the laws be faithfully executed."

Is this duty limited to the enforcement of acts of Congress or of treaties of the United States according to their *express terms*, or does it include the rights, duties and obligations growing out of the Constitution itself, our international relations, and all the protection implied by the nature of the government under the Constitution? . . .

We cannot doubt the power of the President to take measures for the protection of a judge of one of the courts of the United States, who, while in the discharge of the duties of his office, is threatened with a personal attack which may probably result in his death, and we think it clear that where this protection is to be afforded through the civil power, the Department of Justice is the proper one to set in motion the necessary means of protection. . . .

To the objection made in argument, that the prisoner is discharged by this writ from the power of the state court to try him for the whole offence, the reply is, that if the prisoner is held in the state court to answer for an act which he was authorized to do by the law of the United States, which it was his duty to do as marshal of the United States, and if in doing that act he did no more than what was necessary and proper for him to do, he *cannot* be guilty of a crime under the law of the State of California. When these things are shown, it is established that he is innocent of any crime against the laws of the State, or of any other authority whatever. There is no occasion for any further trial in the state court, or in any court.

---

1. One can confidently assert that *Neagle* proscribes, under the supremacy clause, any state criminal liability for the performance by a United States employee of a function derived from the general scope of the employee's duties. How far beyond its facts, however, can *Neagle*'s holding be extended? Does it stand for the proposition that the "faithful execution" clause confers inherent authority on the President to enforce "the rights, duties, and obligations growing out of the Constitution itself, our international relations, and all the protection implied by the nature of the government under the Constitution?" Would you cite *Neagle* for the proposition that the president has constitutional power to use the armed forces to rescue "Americans

illegally detained abroad?" *See* Legal Opinion of May 9, 1980, by Lloyd Cutler, the President's Counsel, on War Powers Consultation Relative to the Iran Rescue Mission, which appears in Chapter Seven.

2. The issue raised in *Neagle* arises regularly in the planning of federal undercover law enforcement investigations. That is, the FBI is required to consider routinely the circumstances in which it is lawful for federal law enforcement officers, in the course of an investigation, to violate criminal statutes of general applicability. Government officials, even when immune from civil liability, may not be beyond criminal liability for the same actions. *Imbler v. Pachtman*, 424 U.S. 409, 429 (1976).

It is the Department of Justice's understanding, following *Neagle*, that federal law enforcement statutes authorize undercover investigators to violate state law so long as the state law violations are reasonable and justified by the social interests at stake in a particular investigation. Obvious factors in reaching such a judgment include the number and seriousness of federal offenses that could reasonably be expected to occur if investigating officers did not violate any state criminal statutes during an investigation; the social harms that official participation in crime would cause; and the prospects that a contemplated investigation will be successful. Although the Department of Justice does not have precise guidelines for making these determinations, the FBI and Office of Legal Counsel typically consult in difficult cases to determine if the government's participation in crime is justified. For a proposed codification of an operating policy on the use of criminal participation in law enforcement investigation, see Dix, *Undercover Investigations and Police Rulemaking*, 53 Tex. L. Rev. 203-86 (1975).

3. Between 1981 and 1983, Congress turned special attention to the problems of overseeing FBI undercover investigations after press reports in 1980 revealed Operation ABSCAM. ABSCAM was a "sting" operation in which FBI agents, posing as business people and Arab sheiks, successfully bribed seven members of Congress for various forms of legislative assistance. Following a nine-month study, a Senate Select Committee concluded in 1981 that none of the ABSCAM targets was chosen on the basis of partisan political considerations, but urged tighter legislative control over such undercover law enforcement operations generally. Specifically, the panel called for the statutory codification of Justice Department guidelines on undercover operations, and for tightening the appropriate standard for targeting suspects of undercover investigations. *See* S. Rept. No. 682, 97th Cong., 2d Sess. (1982). Although bills were introduced in the Senate in 1983 which would have provided statutory guidance on undercover operations, required "reasonable suspicion" in the choice of investigative targets, provided compensation for innocent victims of sting operations, and required additional notice of undercover operations to Congress, no such legislation has been enacted.

In Re Debs

158 U.S. 564 (1895)

[*In re Debs* grew out of the famous Pullman strike of 1894, during which railroad workers refused to service Pullman cars until the Pullman Company agreed to arbitrate its differences with labor. Eugene Debs was personally enjoined from communicating with railway employees concerning the strike, and his arrest succeeded in breaking the strikers' morale. The eventual criminal prosecution against Debs for conspiracy to obstruct the mails was dismissed when one juror became ill, and the government declined to press its case further. Consider, in relation to *Youngstown*, what limits exist to the executive authority conferred in *Debs*. Must emergency circumstances exist? As determined by whom? What is the relevance of Congress' legislative silence? Of Congress' rejection of express statutory authority for the measures taken?]

JUSTICE BREWER . . . delivered the opinion of the court.

The case presented by the bill is this: The United States, finding that the interstate transportation of persons and property, as well as the carriage of the mails, is forcibly obstructed, and that a combination and conspiracy exists to subject the control of such transportation to the will of the conspirators, applied to one of their courts, sitting as a court of equity, for an injunction to restrain such obstruction and prevent carrying into effect such conspiracy. Two questions of importance are presented: First. Are the relations of the general government to interstate commerce and the transportation of the mails such as authorize a direct interference to prevent a forcible obstruction thereof? Second. If authority exists, as authority in governmental affairs implies both power and duty, has a court of equity jurisdiction to issue an injunction in aid of the performance of such duty.

First. What are the relations of the general government to interstate commerce and the transportation of the mails? They are those of direct supervision, control, and management. While under the dual system which prevails with us the powers of government are distributed between the State and the Nation, and while the latter is properly styled a government of enumerated powers, yet within the limits of such enumeration it has all the attributes of sovereignty, and, in the exercise of those enumerated powers, acts directly upon the citizen, and not through the intermediate agency of the State. . . .

As, under the Constitution, power over interstate commerce and the transportation of the mails is vested in the national government, and Congress by virtue of such grant has assumed actual and direct control, it follows that the national government may prevent any unlawful and forcible interference therewith. But how shall this be accomplished? Doubtless, it is within the competency of Congress to prescribe by legislation that any interference with these matters shall be offenses against the United States, and prosecuted and punished by indictment in the proper courts. But is that the only remedy? Have the vast interests of the nation in interstate commerce, and in the transportation of the mails, no other protection than lies in the possible punishment of those who interfere with it? To ask the question is to answer it. . . . [I]f . . . the national government had no other way to enforce the freedom of interstate commerce and the transportation of the mails than by prosecution and punishment for interference therewith, the whole interests of the nation in these respects would be at the absolute mercy of a portion of the inhabitants of that single State [because of the possibility of jury nullification].

But there is no such impotency in the national government. The entire strength of the nation may be used to enforce in any part of the land the full and free exercise of all national powers and the security of all rights entrusted by the Constitution to its care. The strong arm of the national government may be put forth to brush away all obstructions to the freedom of interstate commerce or the transportation of the mails. If the emergency arises, the army of the Nation, and all its militia, are at the service of the Nation to compel obedience to its laws.

But passing to the second question, is there no other alternative than the use of force on the part of the executive authorities whenever obstructions arise to the freedom of interstate commerce or the transportation of the mails? Is the army the only instrument by which rights of the public can be enforced and the peace of the nation preserved? Grant that any public nuisance may be forcibly abated either at the instance of the authorities, or by any individual suffering private damage therefrom, the existence of this right of forcible abatement is not inconsistent with nor does it destroy the right of appeal in an orderly way to the courts for a judicial determination, and an exercise of their powers by writ of injunction and otherwise to accomplish the same result. . . .

So, in the case before us, the right to use force does not exclude the right of appeal to the courts for a judicial determination and for the exercise of all their powers of prevention. Indeed, it is more to the praise than to the blame of the government, that, instead of determining for itself questions of right and wrong on the part of these petitioners and their associates and enforcing that determination by the club of the policeman and the bayonet of the soldier, it submitted all those questions to the peaceful determination of judicial tribunals, and invoked their consideration and judgment as to the measure of its rights and powers and the correlative obligations of those against whom it made complaint. And it is equally to the credit of the latter that the judgment of those tribunals was by the great body of them respected, and the troubles which threatened so much disaster terminated.

Neither can it be doubted that the government has such an interest in the subject-matter as enables it to appear as party plaintiff in this suit. It is said that equity only interferes for the protection of property, and that the government has no property interest. A sufficient reply is that the United States have a property in the mails, the protection of which was one of the purposes of this bill. . . .

We do not care to place our decision upon this ground alone. Every government, entrusted, by the very terms of its being, with powers and duties to be exercised and discharged for the general welfare, has a right to apply to its own courts for any proper assistance in the exercise of the one and the discharge of the other, and it is no sufficient answer to its appeal to one of those courts that it has no pecuniary interest in the matter. The obligations which it is under to promote the interest of all, and to prevent the wrongdoing of one resulting in injury to the general welfare, is often of itself sufficient to give it a standing in court. . . .

[W]hile it is not the province of the government to interfere in any mere matter of private controversy between individuals, or to use its great powers to enforce the rights of one against another, yet, whenever the wrongs complained of are such as affect the public at large, and are in respect of matters which by the Constitution are entrusted to the care of the Nation, and concerning which the Nation owes the duty to all the citizens of securing to them their common rights, then the mere fact that the government has no pecuniary interest in the controversy is not sufficient to exclude it from the courts, or prevent it from taking measures therein to fully discharge those constitutional duties.

The national government, given by the Constitution power to regulate interstate commerce, has by express statute assumed jurisdiction over such commerce when carried upon railroads. It is charged, therefore, with the duty of keeping those highways of interstate commerce free from obstruction, for it has always been recognized as one of the powers and duties of a government to remove obstructions from the highways under its control. . . .

That the bill filed in this case alleged special facts calling for the exercise of all the powers of the court is not open to question. The picture drawn in it of the vast interests involved, not merely of the city of Chicago and the State of Illinois, but of all the States, and the general confusion into which the interstate commerce of the country was thrown; the forcible interference with that commerce; the attempted exercise by individuals of powers belonging only to government, and the threatened continuance of such invasions of public right, presented a condition of affairs which called for the fullest exercise of all the powers of the courts. If ever there was a special exigency, one which demanded that the court should do all that courts can do, it was disclosed by this bill, and we need not turn to the public history of the day, which only reaffirms with clearest emphasis all its allegations. . . .

[I]t is objected that it is outside of the jurisdiction of a court of equity to enjoin the commission of crimes. This, as a general proposition, is unquestioned. A chancellor has no criminal jurisdiction. Something more than the threatened commission of an offence against the laws of the land is necessary to call into exercise the injunctive powers of the court. . . .

The law[, however,] is full of instances in which the same act may give rise to a civil action and a criminal prosecution. . . . So here, the acts of the defendants may or may not have been violations of the criminal law. If they were, that matter is for inquiry in other proceedings. The complaint made against them in this is of diso- bedience to an order of a civil court, made for the protection of property and the security of rights. . . .

Nor is there in this any invasion of the constitutional right of trial by jury. . . . [T]he power of a court to make an order carries with it the equal power to punish for a disobedience of that order, and the inquiry as to the question of disobedience has been, from time immemorial, the special function of the court. . . .

[I]t is said by counsel in their brief:

"No case can be cited where such a bill in behalf of the sovereign has been entertained against riot and mob violence, though occurring on the highway. It is not such fitful and temporary obstruction that constitutes a nuisance. The strong hand of executive power is required to deal with such lawless demonstrations.

"The courts should stand aloof from them and not invade executive prerogative, nor even at the behest or request of the executive travel out of the beaten path of well-settled judicial authority. A mob cannot be suppressed by injunction; nor can its leaders be tried, convicted, and sentenced in equity.

"It is too great a strain upon the judicial branch of the government to impose this essentially executive and military power upon courts of chancery."

We do not perceive that this argument questions the jurisdiction of the court, but only the expediency of the action of the government in applying for its process. It surely cannot be seriously contended that the court has jurisdiction to enjoin the obstruction of a highway by one person, but that its jurisdiction ceases when the obstruction is by a hundred persons. . . . It is doubtless true that *inter arma leges silent*, and in the throes of rebellion or revolution the processes of civil courts are of little avail, for the power of the courts rests on the general support of the people and their recognition of the fact that peaceful remedies are the true resort for the correction of wrongs. But does not counsel's argument imply too much? Is it to be assumed that these defendants were conducting a rebellion or inaugurating a revolution, and that they and their associates were thus placing themselves beyond the reach of the civil process of the courts? We find in the opinion of the Circuit Court a quotation from the testimony given by one of the defendants before the United States Strike Commission, which is sufficient answer to this suggestion:

> "As soon as the employees found that we were arrested, and taken from the scene of action, they became demoralized, and that ended the strike. It was not the soldiers that ended the strike. It was not the old brotherhoods that ended the strike. It was simply the United States courts that ended the strike. Our men were in a position that never would have been shaken, under any circumstances, if we had been permitted to remain upon the field among them. Once we were taken from the scene of action, and restrained from sending telegrams or issuing orders or answering questions, then the minions of the corporations would be put to work.... Our headquarters were temporarily demoralized and abandoned, and we could not answer any messages. The men went back to work, and the ranks were broken, and the strike was broken up, ... not by the army, and not by any other power, but simply and solely by the action of the United States courts in restraining us from discharging our duties as officers and representatives of our employees."

Whatever any single individual may have thought or planned, the great body of those who were engaged in these transactions contemplated neither rebellion nor revolution, and when in the due order of legal proceedings the question of right and wrong was submitted to the courts, and by them decided, they unhesitatingly yielded to their decisions. The outcome, by the very testimony of the defendants, attests the wisdom of the course pursued by the government, and that it was well not to oppose force simply by force, but to invoke the jurisdiction and judgment of those tribunals to whom by the Constitution and in accordance with the settled conviction of all citizens is committed the determination of questions of right and wrong between individuals, masses, and States.

It must be borne in mind that this bill was not simply to enjoin a mob and mob violence. It was not a bill to command a keeping of the peace; much less was its purport to restrain the defendants from abandoning whatever employment they were engaged in. The right of any laborer, or any number of laborers, to quit work was not challenged. The scope and purpose of the bill was only to restrain forcible obstructions of the highways along which interstate commerce travels and the mails are carried. And the facts set forth at length are only those facts which tended to show that the defendants were engaged in such obstructions....

The petition for a writ of *habeas corpus* is *Denied*.

----

1. Have *Neagle* and *Debs* been undermined by the Court's later decisions in *Youngstown* and *New York Times*? If so, do they remain valuable, if limited precedents, or should they be regarded as no more than products of their times and places without continuing force? That is, is *Debs* anything more than the artifact of nineteenth century judicial hostility to the labor movement, and *Neagle* anything more than a period piece out of the Old West?

2. What do you think of the Court's argument in *Debs* that the greater power to use force justifies the lesser power to seek injunctive relief? Is it always true that the availability of force justifies lesser action? Should courts be friendly to executive requests for injunctions not rooted in statutory authority in order to forestall the executive's use of force?

3. Assuming *Debs* fairly reflects the arguments of Debs' counsel, are there better arguments that could have been brought to bear?

4. Seventy-three years after *Debs*, the Supreme Court overruled its holding that courts have inherent power to punish criminal contempt *summarily*. *Bloom v. Illinois*, 391 U.S. 194 (1968). The Court recently held, however, that *Bloom*'s procedural ruling did not diminish the power of courts to protect their own authority through contempt prosecutions. *Young v. United States ex rel. Vuitton et Fils S.A.*, 107 S.Ct. 2124, 2132 n.8 (1987).

2. Case Studies

a. Public Lands

United States v. Midwest Oil Co.
236 U.S. 459 (1915)

Justice LAMAR delivered the opinion of the court.

All public lands containing petroleum or other mineral oils and chiefly valuable therefor, have been declared by Congress to be "free and open to occupation, exploration and purchase by citizens of the United States . . . under regulations prescribed by law." Act of February 11, 1897, c. 216, 29 Stat. 526; R.S. 2319, 2329.

As these regulations permitted exploration and location without the payment of any sum, and as title could be obtained for a merely nominal amount, many persons availed themselves of the provisions of the statute. Large areas of California were explored; and petroleum having been found, locations were made, not only by the discoverer but by others on adjoining land. And, as the flow through the well on one lot might exhaust the oil under the adjacent land, the interest of each operator was to extract the oil as soon as possible so as to share what would otherwise be taken by the owners of nearby wells.

The result was that oil was so rapidly extracted that on September 7, 1909, the Director of the Geological Survey made a report to the Secretary of the Interior which, with enclosures, called attention to the fact that, while there was a limited supply of coal on the Pacific coast and the value of oil as a fuel had been fully demonstrated, yet at the rate at which oil lands in California were being patented by private parties it would "be impossible for the people of the United States to continue ownership of oil lands for more than a few months. After that the Government will be obliged to repurchase the very oil that it has practically given away . . . " "In view of the increasing use of fuel by the American Navy there would appear to be an immediate necessity for assuring the conservation of a proper supply of petroleum for the Government's own use . . . " and "pending the enactment of adequate legislation on this subject, the filing of claims to oil lands in the State of California should be suspended."

This recommendation was approved by the Secretary of the Interior. Shortly afterwards he brought the matter to the attention of the President who, on September 27, 1909, issued the following Proclamation:

"Temporary Petroleum Withdrawal No. 5."

"In aid of proposed legislation affecting the use and disposition of the petroleum deposits on the public domain, all public lands in the accompanying lists are hereby temporarily withdrawn from all forms of location, settlement, selection, filing, entry, or disposal under the mineral or nonmineral public-land laws. All locations or claims existing and valid on this date may proceed to entry in the usual manner after field investigation and examination."

The list attached described an area aggregating 3,041,000 acres in California and Wyoming—though, of course, the order only applied to the public lands therein, the acreage of which is not shown.

On March 27, 1910, six months after the publication of the Proclamation, William T. Henshaw and others entered upon a quarter section of this public land in Wyoming so withdrawn. They made explorations, bored a well, discovered oil and thereafter assigned their interest to the Appellees, who took possession and extracted large quantities of oil. On May 4, 1910, they filed a location certificate.

As the explorations by the original claimants, and the subsequent operation of the well, were both long after the date of the President's Proclamation, the Government filed, in the District Court of the United States for the District of Wyoming, a Bill in Equity against the Midwest Oil Company and the other Appellees, seeking to recover the land and to obtain an accounting for 50,000 barrels of oil alleged to have been illegally extracted. The court sustained the defendant's demurrer and dismissed the bill. Thereupon the Government took the case to the Circuit Court of Appeals of the Eighth Circuit which . . . certified certain questions to this court. . . .

On the part of the Government it is urged that the President, as Commander-in-Chief of the Army and Navy, had power to make the order for the purpose of retaining and preserving a source of supply of fuel for the Navy, instead of allowing the oil land to be taken up for a nominal sum, the Government being then obliged to purchase at a great cost what it had previously owned. It is argued that the President, charged with the care of the public domain, could, by virtue of the executive power vested in him by the Constitution (Art. 2, § 1), and also in conformity with the tacit consent of Congress, withdraw, in the public interest, any public land from entry or location by private parties.

The Appellees, on the other hand, insist that there is no dispensing power in the Executive and that he could not suspend a statute or withdraw from entry or location any land which Congress had affirmatively declared should be free and open to acquisition by citizens of the United States. They further insist that the withdrawal order is absolutely void since it appears on its face to be a mere attempt to suspend a statute—supposed to be unwise,—in order to allow Congress to pass another more in accordance with what the Executive thought to be in the public interest.

1. We need not consider whether, as an original question, the President could have withdrawn from private acquisition what Congress had made free and open to occupation and purchase. The case can be determined on other grounds and in the light of the legal consequences flowing from a long continued practice to make orders like

the one here involved. For the President's proclamation of September 27, 1909, is by no means the first instance in which the Executive, by a special order, has withdrawn land which Congress, by general statute, had thrown open to acquisition by citizens. And while it is not known when the first of these orders was made, it is certain that "the practice dates from an early period in the history of the government." *Grisar* v. *McDowell*, 6 Wall. 381. Scores and hundreds of these orders have been made; and treating them as they must be, as the act of the President, an examination of official publications will show that...he has during the past 80 years, without express statutory authority—but under the claim of power so to do—made a multitude of Executive Orders which operated to withdraw public land that would otherwise have been open to private acquisition. They affected every kind of land—mineral and nonmineral. The size of the tracts varied from a few square rods to many square miles and the amount withdrawn has aggregated millions of acres. The number of such instances cannot, of course, be accurately given, but the extent of the practice can best be appreciated by a consideration of what is believed to be a correct enumeration of such Executive Orders mentioned in public documents.

They show that prior to the year 1910 there had been issued

> 99 Executive Orders establishing or enlarging Indian Reservations;
>
> 109 Executive Orders establishing or enlarging Military Reservations and setting apart land for water, timber, fuel, hay, signal stations, target ranges and rights of way for use in connection with Military Reservations;
>
> 44 Executive Orders establishing Bird Reserves.

In the sense that these lands may have been intended for public use, they were reserved for a public purpose. But they were not reserved in pursuance of law or by virtue of any general or special statutory authority. For, it is to be specially noted that there was no act of Congress providing for Bird Reserves or for these Indian Reservations. There was no law for the establishment of these Military Reservations or defining their size or location. There was no statute empowering the President to withdraw any of these lands from settlement or to reserve them for any of the purposes indicated.

But when it appeared that the public interest would be served by withdrawing or reserving parts of the public domain, nothing was more natural than to retain what the Government already owned. And in making such orders, which were thus useful to the public, no private interest was injured. For prior to the initiation of some right given by law the citizen had no enforceable interest in the public statute and no private right in land which was the property of the people. The President was in a position to know when the public interest required particular portions of the people's lands to be withdrawn from entry or location; his action inflicted no wrong upon any private citizen, and being subject to disaffirmance by Congress, could occasion no harm to the interest of the public at large. Congress did not repudiate the power claimed or the withdrawal orders made. On the contrary it uniformly and repeatedly acquiesced in the practice and, as shown by these records, there had been, prior to 1910, at least 252 Executive Orders making reservations for useful, though nonstatutory purposes.

This right of the President to make reservations,—and thus withdraw land from private acquisition,—was expressly recognized in *Grisar v. McDowell*, 6 Wall. 364 (9), 381 (1867), where it was said that "from an early period in the history of the

Government it has been the practice of the President to order, from time to time, as the exigencies of the public service required, parcels of land belonging to the United States to be reserved from sale and set apart for public uses."

But notwithstanding this decision and the continuity of this practice, the absence of express statutory authority was the occasion of doubt being expressed as to the power of the President to make these orders. The matter was therefore several times referred to the law officers of the Government for an opinion on the subject. One of them stated (1889) (19 Op. 370) that the validity of such orders rested on "a long-established and long-recognized power in the President to withhold from sale or settlement, at discretion, portions of the public domain." [The Court cited two similar attorney general opinions from 1881.]

Similar views were expressed by officers in the Land Department. Indeed, one of the strongest assertions of the existence of the power is the frequently quoted statement of Secretary Teller made in 1881:

> "That the power resides in the Executive from an early period in the history of the country to make reservations has never been denied either legislatively or judicially, but on the contrary has been recognized. It constitutes in fact a part of the Land Office Law, exists *ex necessitati rei*, is indispensable to the public weal and in that light, by different laws enacted as herein indicated, has been referred to as an existing undisputed power too well settled ever to be disputed." 1 L.D., 338 (1881-3).

2. It may be argued that while these facts and rulings prove a usage they do not establish its validity. But government is a practical affair intended for practical men. Both officers, law-makers and citizens naturally adjust themselves to any long-continued action of the Executive Department—on the presumption that unauthorized acts would not have been allowed to be so often repeated as to crystallize into a regular practice. That presumption is not reasoning in a circle but the basis of a wise and quieting rule that in determining the meaning of a statute or the existence of a power, weight shall be given to the usage itself—even when the validity of the practice is the subject of investigation....

3 ... [D]ecisions [supporting the Court's conclusion] do not, of course, mean that private rights could be created by an officer withdrawing for a Rail Road more than had been authorized by Congress in the land grant act. *Southern Pacific v. Bell*, 183 U.S. 685; *Brandon v. Ard*, 211 U.S. 21. Nor do these decisions mean that the Executive can by his course of action create a power. But they do clearly indicate that the long-continued practice, known to and acquiesced in by Congress, would raise a presumption that the withdrawals had been made in pursuance of its consent or of a recognized administrative power of the Executive in the management of the public lands. This is particularly true in view of the fact that the land is property of the United States and that the land laws are not of a legislative character in the highest sense of the term (Art. 4, § 3) "but savor somewhat of mere rules prescribed by an owner of property for its disposal." *Butte City Water Co. v. Baker*, 196 U.S. 126.

These rules or laws for the disposal of public land are necessarily general in their nature. Emergencies may occur, or conditions may so change as to require that the agent in charge should, in the public interest, withhold the land from sale; and while no such express authority has been granted, there is nothing in the nature of the power exercised which prevents Congress from granting it by implication just as could be done by any other owner of property under similar conditions. The power of the Executive, as agent in charge, to retain that property from sale need not necessarily be expressed in writing.

For it must be borne in mind that Congress not only has a legislative power over the public domain, but it also exercises the powers of the proprietor therein. Congress "may deal with such lands precisely as a private individual may deal with his farming property. It may sell or withhold them from sale." *Camfield v. United States*, 167 U.S. 524; *Light v. United States*, 220 U.S. 536. Like any other owner it may provide when, how and to whom its land can be sold. It can permit it to be withdrawn from sale. Like any other owner, it can waive its strict rights, as it did when the valuable privilege of grazing cattle on this public land was held to be based upon an "implied license growing out of the custom of nearly a hundred years." *Buford v. Houtz*, 133 U.S. 326. So too, in the early days the "Government, by its silent acquiescence, assented to the general occupation of the public lands for mining." *Atchison v. Peterson*, 20 Wall. 512. If private persons could acquire a privilege in public land by virtue of an implied congressional consent, then for a much stronger reason, an implied grant of power to preserve the public interest would arise out of like congressional acquiescence.

The Executive, as agent, was in charge of the public domain; by a multitude of orders extending over a long period of time and affecting vast bodies of land, in many States and Territories, he withdrew large areas in the public interest. These orders were known to Congress, as principal, and in not a single instance was the act of the agent disapproved. Its acquiescence all the more readily operated as an implied grant of power in view of the fact that its exercise was not only useful to the public but did not interfere with any vested right of the citizen.

4. The appellees, however, argue that the practice thus approved, related to Reservations—to cases where the land had been reserved for military or other special public purposes—and they contend that even if the President could reserve land for a public purpose or for naval uses, it does not follow that he can withdraw land in aid of legislation.

When analyzed, this proposition, in effect, seeks to make a distinction between a Reservation and a Withdrawal—between a Reservation for a purpose, not provided for by existing legislation, and a Withdrawal made in aid of future legislation. It would mean that a Permanent Reservation for a purpose designated by the President, but not provided for by a statute, would be valid, while a merely Temporary Withdrawal to enable Congress to legislate in the public interest would be invalid. It is only necessary to point out that, as the greater includes the less, the power to make permanent reservations includes power to make temporary withdrawals....

5. ... [T]hat the existence of this power was recognized and its exercise by the Executive assented to by Congress, is emphasized by the fact that the above-mentioned withdrawals were issued after the Report which the Secretary of the Interior made in 1902, in response to a resolution of the Senate calling for information "as to what, if any, of the public lands have been withdrawn from disposition under the settlement or other laws by order of the Commissioner of the General Land Office and *what, if any, authority of law exists for such order of withdrawal.*"

The answer to this specific inquiry was returned March 3, 1902, (Senate Doc. 232, 57th Cong., 1st Sess., Vol. 17). On that date the Secretary transmitted to the Senate the elaborate and detailed report of the Commissioner of the Land Office.... This report refers to *Withdrawals* and not to *Reservations*. It is most important in connection with the present inquiry as to whether Congress knew of the practice to make temporary withdrawals and knowingly assented thereto. It will be noted that the Resolution called on the Department to state the extent of such withdrawals and the authority by which they were made. The officer of the Land Department in his answer shows that there have been a large number of withdrawals made for good but for non-statutory reasons. He shows that these 92 orders had been made by virtue of a long-continued practice and under claim of a right to take such action in the public interest "as exigencies might demand . . ." Congress with notice of this practice and of this claim of authority, received the Report. Neither at that session nor afterwards did it ever repudiate the action taken or the power claimed. Its silence was acquiescence. Its acquiescence was equivalent to consent to continue the practice until the power was revoked by some subsequent action by Congress.

6. Nor is the position of the appellees strengthened by the act of June 25, 1910 (36 Stat. 847), [passed after the withdrawals contested in this case] to authorize the President to make withdrawals of public lands and requiring a list of the same to be filed with Congress. . . . The legislative history of the statute shows that there was no . . . intent and no purpose to make the Act retroactive or to disaffirm what the agent in charge had already done. . . .

The case is therefore remanded to the District Court with directions that the decree dismissing the Bill be

Reversed.

Justice MCREYNOLDS took no part in the decision of this case.

———

1. It is familiar enough doctrine that courts will defer to reasonable contemporaneous executive interpretations of statutes. The interpreting agency, after all, may have helped to draft the statute, and the language and history of a statute allow judicial review to constrain extreme interpretations. How far beyond this does *Midwest Oil* go in deferring to longstanding executive branch interpretations of the Constitution? Does anything justify a nonstatutory acquiescence doctrine in domestic affairs?

2. If the *Midwest Oil* dispute were presented today, could you hypothesize a rationale for the result that would rest on statutory interpretation or that could be confined to public lands management?

3. Review the kinds of evidence proffered by the Court for its conclusion that Congress authorized temporary withdrawals in aid of legislation. Are all equally probative? Is any actually necessary to the Court's conclusion?

4. How strong a precedent do you think *Midwest Oil* is after *Youngstown*? See the Court's discussion of *Midwest Oil* in *Dames & Moore v. Regan*, reprinted in Chapter Six.

5. Perhaps the boldest act of presidential land management was President Carter's 1978 decision to reserve about 55 million acres of land in Alaska from development by creating or enlarging national monuments on those lands. Carter implemented his decision through 17 proclamations issued under the authority of the Antiquities Act of 1906, 16 U.S.C. § 431 (1982). The Antiquities Act authorizes the president:

> to declare by public proclamation historic landmarks, historic and pre-historic structures, and other objects of historic or scientific interest that are situated

upon the lands owned or controlled by the Government of the United States to be national monuments, and may reserve as a part thereof parcels of land, the limits of which in all cases shall be confined to the smallest area compatible with the proper care and management of the objects to be protected.

Although the statutory language most readily calls to mind such phenomena as Indian burial mounds and surrounding lands the Act had been used previously for "objects" as large as the Grand Canyon. Carter's decision to invoke the Act to protect 55 million acres of land, however, went far beyond any previous presidential proclamations in scope.

The President acted following Congress's failure to pass various legislative proposals on the disposition of these largely wilderness lands. Some of the lands had been withdrawn from development by earlier administrative orders that were soon to expire, and Carter acted in large part to maintain the status quo on the lands pending eventual congressional resolution of their proper treatment. Congress ultimately did decide on the status of the lands through the Alaska National Interest Lands Conservation Act, Pub. L. No. 96-487, 94 Stat. 2371 (1980).

The Anaconda Copper Company and other parties, including the state of Alaska, challenged the creation of the monuments on the ground that the President exceeded his authority under the Antiquities Act. A federal district court determined that Presidents had consistently interpreted the terms "historic or scientific interest" broadly, that the Supreme Court had approved that practice, and that Congress, aware of the executive practice, had at least acquiesced in it. *Anaconda Copper Company v. Andrus*, 14 Env't Rep. Cas. (BNA) 1853 (D. Alaska 1980). In a related suit, the district court had held that the environmental impact statement requirements of the National Environmental Policy Act do not apply to presidential actions under the Antiquities Act. *Alaska v. Carter*, 462 F. Supp. 1155 (D. Alaska 1978). See generally Bruff, *Judicial Review and the President's Statutory Powers*, 68 Va. L. Rev. 1, 36-39 (1982).

b. Vindicating Fourteenth Amendment Rights

United States v. City of Philadelphia
644 F.2d 187 (3d Cir. 1980)

ALDISERT, Circuit Judge.

The primary question in this appeal is whether the United States has implied authority to sue a city and its officials for an injunction against violations of the fourteenth amendment rights of individuals. The government argues that both the criminal provisions of the Civil Rights Acts of 1866 and 1870, 18 U.S.C. §§ 242 and 241, and the fourteenth amendment itself give rise to an implied right of action. We also must decide whether the government has stated a claim for relief under the Omnibus Crime Control and Safe Streets Act of 1968, 42 U.S.C. § 3789d, or the State and Local Fiscal Assistance Act of 1972 (the "Revenue Sharing Act"), 31 U.S.C. § 1242. In a pair of published opinions, the district court held that the Attorney General has no standing to advance the civil rights of third persons absent an express statutory grant of the necessary authority, and that the complaint did not allege claims under the two funding statutes with sufficient specificity; and accordingly it dismissed the complaint. *United States v. City of Philadelphia*, 482 F.Supp. 1248 and 1274 (E.D.Pa.1979). We affirm.

I.

[The court stated that, because of the procedural posture of this case, it would assume as true the allegations of the complaint that (1) Philadelphia police officers engaged in a widespread practice of violating the rights of persons they encountered on the streets and elsewhere in the city, and (2) the high-ranking city and Police Department officials had deliberately encouraged such illegal practices through the policies and procedures they established for investigating complaints of illegal police activity, and further, they had deliberately encouraged discriminatory police treatment of blacks and Hispanics.]

In its prayer for relief, the government asks for a declaration "that the acts, practices, policies and procedures alleged herein violate the Constitution and laws of the United States." It also asks the court to enjoin "the defendants, their agents, employees, successors in office, and all those acting in concert or participation with them" from engaging in the conduct alleged, "from failing or refusing to correct the effects" of that conduct, "from failing or refusing to ensure" that such conduct will not recur, "and from receiving, expending, or failing to make restitution for previously expended federal funds, unless and until defendants cease such acts, policies, practices, and procedures and correct their effects."

II.

We first address the contention that the two criminal statutes, 18 U.S.C. §§ 241 and 242, implicitly grant the United States a right of action for injunctive relief....

Between 1865 and 1871 Congress drafted the thirteenth, fourteenth, and fifteenth amendments and enacted a comprehensive statutory scheme for their enforcement. It gave extensive consideration to the creation of remedies to enforce the amendments. It provided several criminal and civil actions. In § 9 of the Civil Rights Act of 1866, 14 Stat. 29, repealed by § 122 of the Civil Rights Act of 1957, Pub.L.No. 85-315, 71 Stat. 637, it even authorized the President to call out the military "to prevent the violation and enforce the due execution of this Act." The Attorney General discusses the legislative history at length, but he fails to draw the obvious inference: that the extensive congressional consideration of the problem of enforcement and the comprehensive legislative program that it developed simply foreclose the possibility that it implicitly created an additional remedy without ever mentioning its existence in either the statutes or the debates. There certainly is no evidence of congressional intent to create an additional remedy with the incredible breadth and scope of this one. The responsible answer to this question, and indeed, the overarching answer to this appeal, is that Congress never intended to grant a civil action to the Attorney General.

The same conclusion is supported by an examination of three express refusals of modern Congresses to grant the Executive general injunctive powers in this field, which not only demonstrates explicit congressional intent not to create the power claimed here by the Attorney General but also reveals an understanding, unanimously shared by members of Congress and Attorneys General, that no such power existed....

We conclude, therefore, that the history of the Reconstruction era legislation reveals an implicit legislative intent, and that the modern history demonstrates an explicit intent, to deny the government the right of action asserted here....

IV.

The Attorney General's second theory for maintaining this lawsuit rests on the fourteenth amendment itself and on the President's duty under Article II, § 3 to "take Care that the Laws be faithfully executed." His premise is that because the national government is the "guarantor" of the rights of individuals, we must provide him with a remedy under the Constitution. Relying on *Carlson v. Green*, 446 U.S. 14 (1980), *Davis v. Passman*, 442 U.S. 228 (1979), and *Bivens v. Six Unknown Federal Narcotics Agents*, 403 U.S. 388 (1971), he argues that he has a right of action even though Congress has not exercised its power under § 5 of the fourteenth amendment to create one.

Carlson, Davis, and *Bivens* do not support the government's case. Those decisions rest on the principle that

> the class of those litigants who allege that their own constitutional rights have been violated, and who at the same time have no effective means other than the judiciary to enforce these rights, must be able to invoke the existing jurisdiction of the courts for the protection of their justiciable constitutional rights.

Davis, 442 U.S. at 242. That principle does not apply to the government's action in this case. The appellant is not a member of the class whose rights have been violated, but an officer of the federal government seeking to vindicate the constitutional rights of citizens. To allow this action to proceed under the "constitutional tort" theory of *Bivens* and its progeny would be to ignore, not merely to extend, the *ratio decidendi* of those decisions.

In addition, we note that the Supreme Court has held that a cause of action that otherwise would be recognized under the *Bivens* theory "may be defeated . . . in two situations."

> The first is when defendants demonstrate "special factors counselling hesitation in the absence of affirmative action by Congress." [*Bivens*,] 403 U.S., at 396; *Davis v. Passman*, 442 U.S. 228, 245 (1979). The second is when defendants show that Congress has provided an alternative remedy which it explicitly declared to be a *substitute* for recovery directly under the Constitution and viewed as equally effective. *Bivens, supra*, at 397; *Davis v. Passman*, 442 U.S., at 245-247.

Carlson, 446 U.S. at 18-19. The second test cannot be applied literally in this case, but we think it weighs against the government's action because Congress has enacted a comprehensive remedial scheme while deliberately refusing to create the right of action asserted here. More important, however, and by itself sufficient to require rejection of the government's *Bivens* theory if it were valid otherwise, this case involves important "special factors counselling hesitation in the absence of affirmative action by Congress." Recognition of the asserted right of action would violate the constitutional scheme of separation of powers as exemplified and embodied in § 5 of the fourteenth amendment and would trample on important constitutional principles that underlie and give life to our federal system.

Section 5 of the fourteenth amendment confers on Congress, not on the Executive or the Judiciary, the "power to enforce, by appropriate legislation, the provisions of this article." The Supreme Court has repeatedly recognized the central role of Congress in establishing appropriate mechanisms to enforce the fourteenth amendment. "It is not said the *judicial power* of the general government shall extend to enforcing the prohibitions and to protecting the rights and immunities guaranteed.... It is the power of Congress which has been enlarged." *Ex parte Virginia*, 100 U.S. 339, 345 (1879). Congress has exercised its power to "enforc[e] the prohibitions" on many occasions, but it has refused to grant the Executive and the Judiciary the authority that now is asserted....

In addition, the Supreme Court in the last decade has repeatedly recognized the importance of a proper respect for the independent roles of state and local governments in our federal system. Judge Ditter wrote eloquently and persuasively for the court below that to permit this action to proceed "would be to vest an excessive and dangerous degree of power in the hands of the Attorney General":

> ... Quite literally, there would be no end to the local and state agencies, bureaus, offices, departments, or divisions whose day-to-day operating procedures could be challenged by suit, and changed by injunction.
>
> It is well to remember that this case does not present an attack on brutality, *per se*. Rather, the challenge here is to policies, practices and procedures of the police department that are said to violate constitutional rights because they *foster* brutality. The conceivable variations on this lawsuit are practically infinite.

United States v. City of Philadelphia, 482 F.Supp. at 1268....

The Attorney General's apparent (albeit oblique) response is that the asserted right of action will be limited to "exceptional" cases involving "widespread and continuing" violations, for which the remedies expressly provided are not "adequate." There are several problems with this argument. First, the asserted standards are so vague as to lack real content. Second, the fundamental objection is to permitting the federal executive to assume authority over state and local governments. If that power is once granted, it will take an active judiciary indeed to confine it within principled limits. Third, even if the government's authority could be confined to "exceptional" cases, judicial assertion of the power to compel drastic and far-reaching changes in local governments would be inconsistent with a proper division of power in a federal system.

We hold, therefore, that the fourteenth amendment does not implicitly authorize the United States to sue to enjoin violations of its substantive prohibitions.

V.

Our conclusion, that neither §§ 241 and 242 nor the fourteenth amendment create in the government a right to maintain this action for an injunction, is bolstered by an additional consideration: the longstanding and uniform agreement of all concerned that no such right of action has ever existed. Our discussion of the modern legislative history ... demonstrates that neither Attorneys General nor Congress between 1956 and 1964 believed that either Congress or the Constitution had created this power *sub silentio*....

We note also that as recently as two years ago, only eight months before the complaint initiating this action was filed, Assistant Attorney General Drew S. Days, III, head of the Civil Rights Division, who argued for the government in this case, publicly stated his opinion that §§ 241 and 242 do not give the Justice Department authority to seek injunctions against violations of civil rights. Addressing the short-comings of criminal prosecutions under §§ 241 and 242 as a means of deterring police brutality, Mr. Days stated:

> A prosecution for police misconduct does not address itself to the activities of a police department as such or of a city administration per se, but only to the actions of one or more officers in a given circumstance, framed by and limited to the wording of the criminal indictment. Moreover, criminal prosecutions are reactive litigations involving only the calling to account of individuals who have already engaged in acts of misconduct. Any conscious effort to anticipate instances of police misconduct and head them off before they occur must arise from *some other source than the Federal criminal code.*

Police Practices and the Preservation of Civil Rights, A Consultation Sponsored by the United States Commission on Civil Rights, Washington, D.C., December 12-13, 1978, at 141 (emphasis added). We agree with Mr. Days' 1978 statement that the criminal code does not authorize the Justice Department to seek prospective relief.

In sum, the Attorney General argues that he possesses implied authority under the Civil Rights Acts and under the fourteenth amendment to request far-reaching mandatory injunctions, notwithstanding three separate refusals of Congress to grant him this authority and a widely-shared understanding that the authority does not exist. He also has looked to the courts, and applications similar to this have been rejected in the fourth, seventh, and ninth circuits. Unabashed, he has continued to shop for a forum that will lend its ear. He will not find it here. . . .

VI.

Appellant's remaining claims rest on allegations of racial discrimination in the administration of certain federally funded programs. The district court held that the Attorney General has explicit statutory authority to bring suit against discriminatory administration of federal funds, 482 F.Supp. at 1259, but it subsequently granted appellee's motion to dismiss these claims for failure to plead with sufficient specificity. *Id.* at 1274. Although the district court offered it "a reasonable opportunity to file an amended complaint," *id.* at 1279, the government declined the offer and moved for entry of final judgment, stating that "it is in the interest of the United States not to amend the complaint." App. at 154. We now must determine whether the district court erred in requiring a more specific complaint. . . .

We conclude . . . that the complaint was correctly dismissed. Its allegations of racial discrimination can only be characterized as vague, conclusory, and inconsistent. It fails to identify the specific "program or activity" of the Police Department which has expended federal funds in an illegal manner. It does not in any manner allege facts showing a nexus between acts of racial discrimination and the named individual defendants or between the expenditure of federal funds and incidents of police abuse, nor does it indicate how the city *qua* city practiced discrimination. We hold, therefore, that the complaint neither provides "fair notice of what the plaintiff's claim is and the grounds upon which it rests" nor "show[s] that the pleader is entitled to relief" against any defendant. . . .

[F]undamental principles of comity and federalism demand that federal court intervention in the orderly procedures of state and local governments be limited to serious cases presenting some realistic basis for believing that the plaintiff will be able to produce evidence of violations of federal law. These principles have even greater weight in this case because federal court intervention is sought by the federal Executive even though Congress has explicitly stated its determination to place strict limits on federal executive interference with local police departments. Before being permitted to proceed to discovery, with its attendant potential for disrupting local government activities, the United States should have filed a complaint providing fair notice that there were substantial issues of unlawful racial discrimination related to particular federal programs, practiced by the City and the named defendants, for which a federal court could provide a remedy.

In sum, we will hold the Attorney General to the same pleading requirements we demand of a private litigant who brings an action under the Civil Rights Acts. The appellant failed to satisfy these standards, and it deliberately rejected an opportunity to amend its complaint. We find no error in the district court's disposition of this case.

VII.

The judgment of the district court will be affirmed in all respects.

Gibbons, Circuit Judge, dissenting from an order denying rehearing.

. . . Article II section 3 of the Constitution charges the Executive to "take care that the Laws be faithfully executed." Independent of any explicit statutory grant of authority, provided Congress has not expressly limited its authority, the Executive has the inherent constitutional power and duty to enforce constitutional and statutory rights by resort to the courts. When Federal courts have upheld executive standing without explicit congressional authority, they have looked to other provisions of the Constitution, such as the commerce clause and the fourteenth amendment, and to a general statutory scheme defining federal rights but lacking the specific remedy of executive suit. In addition, 28 U.S.C. § 518(b) affords the Attorney General statutory authority to "conduct and argue any case in a court of the United States in which the United States is interested." The Supreme Court has held that this statute confers on the Executive general authority to initiate suits "to safeguard national interests." Moreover, the Supreme Court has held that the Executive's general constitutional duty to protect the public welfare "is often of itself sufficient to give it standing in court."

A review of the caselaw construing executive authority to bring suit helps set this suit in context. Prior cases show that the district court's arguments for denying standing because of congressional inaction to afford explicit standing or because of a threat of abuse of executive power have already been rehearsed and rejected.

From the beginning of the nineteenth century, the Supreme Court has recognized the nonstatutory authority of the executive to sue to protect the United States' contractual and proprietary interests.

After the civil war, with the creation of the Justice Department, An Act to Establish the Department of Justice, 16 Stat. 162 ch. 150 (June 22, 1870), the scope of the Attorney General's statutory and nonstatutory authority to conduct litigation in which the United States had an interest expanded. The 1870 Justice Department Act, part of the Reconstruction Congress' efforts to implement and to secure enforcement of the 13th, 14th and 15th amendments, *see generally*, H. Cummings & C. McFarland, *Federal Justice*, 218-249 (1937), broadened the Attorney General's authority to appear in federal court to present the interests of the United States.[13] ... The Justice Department Act, if it did not automatically grant standing (a latter-day concept with which the legislators of 1870, accustomed to practice under the Process Act, would hardly be familiar), did authorize the Attorney General, or his designees, to sue in the lower federal courts.

In *United States v. San Jacinto Tin Co.*, [125 U.S. 273 (1888)], the Attorney General sued to revoke a fraudulently obtained land patent. Although the United States had a proprietary interest in the action, for if the patent were revoked the land would have reverted to the United States, the Court's concerns focused more on protecting the integrity of the land patents scheme than on any pecuniary interest of the United States.... It is important to note that this early non-statutory action afforded the Supreme Court the opportunity to reflect on, and to reject, the argument that executive resort to the courts without congressional authority threatened the balance of power among the coordinate branches of the federal government....

In *United States v. American Bell Telephone Co.*, 128 U.S. 315 (1888), the Supreme Court expanded on the public protection theme announced in *San Jacinto*. In this case, the United States had no pecuniary interest, for the Attorney General was suing, without Congressional authority, to revoke a fraudulently obtained inventor's patent. ... In effect, the Executive was filling in the interstices of a statutory scheme whose policy was clear. Congress' failure specifically to provide for this mode of enforcing patent policy did not prevent the Executive from taking its own steps to effect the general statutory goal of awarding a monopoly only to those inventions meeting the statutory criteria of unique originality. Even accepting this more narrow reading of *United States v. American Bell Telephone*, this case falls within it, for there is a pervasive federal statutory policy protecting civil rights.

In *In re Debs*, 158 U.S. 564 (1895), the Attorney General sought an injunction against the activities of Eugene V. Debs and other leaders of the Pullman railway workers.... While one might attempt to limit *Debs* to its facts of extreme crisis, or to suggest that extensive congressional regulation of interstate commerce made *Debs*, like *Bell Telephone*, an example of filling in remedial interstices, *see* Note, *Nonstatutory Executive Authority to Bring Suit*, 85 Harv.L.Rev. at 1569-70, the Court's express language goes well beyond these interpretations. While in 1895 there might have been differences in the Court as to the appropriate standard of conduct, even then the Court would not have suggested that the interests protected by the thirteenth, fourteenth and fifteenth amendments were less "entrusted to the care of the nation" than were those protected by the commerce clause.

In *United States v. California*, 332 U.S. 19 (1946), the dispute concerned legal title to oil-rich land under three-mile belt off the California shore. California maintained the Attorney General had no standing to assert the United States' claim.... The Court's examination of the legislative history of Congress' two failures to grant express standing to the Executive to initiate a suit to confirm the United States' title, 332 U.S. at 28 n.4, did not lead the Court to conclude that Congressional failure to authorize the suit therefore meant Congress forbade the action. The broad statutory

---

13. Section 35 of the first judiciary act, Act of Sept. 24, 1789, c. 20 § 35, 1 Stat. 92, had granted the Attorney General such authority only with respect to suits before the Supreme Court, *see Hayburn's Case*, 2 U.S. 408, 2 Dall. 409 (1792); 1 C. Warren, The Supreme Court in United States History (1926) 78; J. Goebel, I History of the Supreme Court: Antecedents and Beginnings 562-64 (1971). In other courts, until 1870, local district attorneys appeared.

authority invested in the Attorney General to argue the interests of the United States supplied ample standing. . . .

More recently, the civil rights movement of the late fifties and early sixties also occasioned nonstatutory executive resort to the federal courts. Courts in the Fifth Circuit, addressing the activities of the Ku Klux Klan against the "freedom riders," and segregation in bus and airline terminals, applied the *Debs* precedent to hold that the Executive had a nonstatutory right of action to sue to enjoin burdens on interstate commerce. While some of these decisions find statutory standing under interstate commerce acts and under the Federal Aviation Act, all explicitly also ground the Attorney General's right of action in the duty to enforce the commerce clause of the Constitution. It must be acknowledged that between 1877 and the late fifties, instances of Executive Branch civil actions to enforcement of rights protected by the post Civil War amendments cannot be found. The reason, however, is not lack of standing. Any kind of Executive Branch enforcement of those amendments was almost non-existent. The question was not lack of standing, but lack of initiative.

In *United States v. Brand Jewelers, Inc.*, 318 F.Supp. 1293 (S.D.N.Y.1970), Judge Marvin Frankel, relying on *Debs* and its Fifth Circuit progeny, held that the Attorney General had nonstatutory authority to sue to enjoin the New York "sewer service" practice. . . . In addition to the burden on interstate commerce this practice engendered, Judge Frankel found the practice resulted in "large-scale denials of due process," 318 F.Supp. at 1300. The court held "the United States may maintain this action because it has standing to sue to end widespread deprivation (i.e. deprivation affecting many people) of property through 'state action' without due process of law," *id.* at 1299. . . .

The following year, in *New York Times Co. v. United States*, 403 U.S. 713 (1971), the Supreme Court heard and ruled on the Executive's nonstatutory action seeking an injunction against publication of the "Pentagon Papers." In his dissent, Justice Harlan argued the Court should have faced the question whether "the Attorney General is authorized to bring these suits in the name of the United States," 403 U.S. at 753. The rest of the court assumed the United States could sue.

VI. THE EXECUTIVE AS PLAINTIFF-INTERVENOR AND AS PARTY IN CHARGE OF THE CONDUCT OF THE SUIT

In addition to initiating suits to protect the public from "large-scale deprivations of due process," burdens on interstate commerce, and fraud, and to assert its federal sovereign interests, the Executive has successfully intervened in civil rights actions. . . . This circuit, en banc, has recently affirmed the Attorney General's nonstatutory right of intervention in civil rights cases. In *Halderman v. Pennhurst State School and Hospital*, 612 F.2d 84 (3d Cir. 1979), rev'd and remanded on other grounds,—- U.S.—- (1981), this court reviewed and rejected the Fourth Circuit's decision in *United States v. Solomon*, 563 F.2d 1121 (4th Cir. 1977), which had denied the Attorney General standing to initiate an action to enjoin civil rights violations in a state hospital for the mentally retarded. . . .

This Circuit has also construed the statutes authorizing the Attorney General's appearance in a pending federal court suit "to attend to the interests of the United States," 28 U.S.C. § 517, and to "conduct and to argue any case in a court of the United States in which the United States is interested," 28 U.S.C. § 518, to permit the Attorney General to represent a private citizen in a civil damages action implicating the United States' interests. *Brawer v. Horowitz*, 535 F.2d 830 (3d Cir. 1976) (Aldisert,

J.). In *Brawer v. Horowitz*, the government undertook the defense representation of a criminal informer whose testimony at a prior trial resulted in plaintiff's conviction. . . . The court found the United States' interest in enforcing the criminal laws, including the protection of informers, met the *Debs* standard.

Thus statutory and Third Circuit caselaw authority present the following picture: when a private action implicates the United States' interests, the Attorney General may 1) intervene; and 2) take over the conduct of the litigation with respect to issues involving the United States' interests. It is difficult to perceive a qualitatively different "threat" to separation of powers, or to local autonomy, when the Attorney General intervenes and conducts the injunctive action, and when he initiates the action. Clearly, had the United States joined a class or even individual private plaintiffs in this action, the Attorney General's standing would be indisputable. To hold the absence of private plaintiffs denies the Attorney General standing seems an exercise in piercing the substance to uncover the form.[23] . . .

VIII. SEPARATION OF POWERS

Separation of powers afforded a second ground for the district court's bewailing of nonstatutory executive activity. . . . [A]s this court recognized in *Halderman*, [however,] executive action to secure an injunction is by its nature not an overweening exercise of power. A suit for an injunction is not a naked exercise of executive authority. Unlike the steel seizure in *Youngstown Sheet & Tube*, the Executive can do nothing here without the concurrence of the federal judiciary. And, because the United States is in effect suing as class representative for the citizens of Philadelphia, the Executive is entitled to no more relief than would be accorded the class members.

. . . [D]espite its fear that this action would violate separation of powers, the district court failed to articulate a congressional purpose or intent that the Executive's non-statutory action would undermine. What are the identifiable congressional interests this action threatens? Congress cannot intend to insulate defendants from enforcement of the fourteenth amendment. At most, Congress might prefer that Justice Department energies and resources be expended in some other way. Congress has not so declared, however, and were it to announce such an intent, an attempt to enforce it might itself implicate separation of powers. While the Executive may not decline to follow a congressional mandate within its proper legislative competence, it is questionable, to say the least, whether Congress may compel the Executive not to enforce the fourteenth amendment or the commerce clause. The Executive's Article II § 3 duty to enforce the laws may override certain congressionally imposed limitations on executive authority. But in any event, because Congress has not here attempted to forbid the Executive from carrying out its constitutional obligations, the question whether such an endeavor would violate separation of powers need not be reached.

Finally, the general problem of suits by the Executive to protect the public welfare should be confronted. While the potential of unbridled executive initiation of suits in the "national interest" understandably may evoke visceral fears of executive power run rampant, careful analysis of the Attorney General's action in this case reveals

---

23. If the *Halderman* and *Brawer* opinions authorizing the United States to intervene in and conduct a lawsuit by a private party are left unimpaired, the power of the Executive Branch to prevent future violations of civil rights may not be seriously diminished, since it is quite likely that cooperative private plaintiffs can be found. . . .

those fears to be baseless. . . . Before any court upholds the exercise of executive resort to it without explicit statutory standing, . . . the court should determine what kind of right the Executive is seeking to enforce. Is the Executive endeavoring to protect its contractual and proprietary rights? To fill in the remedial interstices of a statutory scheme? To enforce a judicially recognized constitutional right? Or is the Executive instead attempting to create a new right that may conflict with statutory or judicial precedent? When, as here, the Attorney General can substantiate the "national interest" and "public welfare" by reference to clearly articulated legislative policies or judicial precedent, the danger of untoward exercise of executive power is fanciful. Thus viewed, this case does not pose a threat of limitless definition of executive authority to bring suit. In this action, the Attorney General seeks to enjoin the pattern or practice of police brutality in Philadelphia. The Attorney General can point to at least four statutes specifically enacted to prohibit concerted and official deprivations of civil rights by physical abuse, 42 U.S.C. §§ 1983 and 1985 and 18 U.S.C. §§ 241 and 242. In addition, the Attorney General has invoked a host of other statutes guaranteeing civil rights, as well as the fourteenth amendment. Thus, this action does not involve the creation of new rights conflicting with legislative and judicial precedent in the "national interest." Rather, it falls comfortably into the category of decisions upholding nonspecific statutory authority to supply a new remedy for an established scheme of rights. . . .

––––––––––

1. Are you persuaded by the majority or the dissent in the Philadelphia case? For a vigorous defense of an executive role in enforcing fourteenth amendment rights, *see* Ledewitz, *The Power of the President to Enforce the Fourteenth Amendment*, 52 Tenn. L. Rev. 605 (1985). Why does the majority omit any mention of *Debs*? Do the facts of *Debs* or *City of Philadelphia* present a stronger case for reading the faithful execution clause broadly? Which set of facts better illustrates the dangers of an expansive interpretation of inherent executive power?

2. Faced with the Third Circuit's opinion, would you, as an attorney in the Civil Rights Division of the Department of Justice, recommend that the Solicitor General seek Supreme Court review of the case?

3. Are *Debs*, *Midwest Oil* and the Philadelphia case reconcilable with *Youngstown*? *Youngstown* implies that judicial scrutiny of independent presidential initiatives will be intensified to the degree Congress has manifested its intent not to confer legislative authority for the challenged act. Could it be argued that, in *Midwest Oil*, Congress should be regarded as *not* having done enough, given that the President's acts posed no threat to fundamental liberties and given the President's historic role as Congress' land agent? Is there some ground in the Philadelphia case for deciding Congress *has* done enough to require strict judicial scrutiny of the Executive's claim of power? Is that ground federalism? Is the Philadelphia case consistent with *Neagle* in that respect?

4. The federalism concerns that apparently animated the majority in the Philadelphia case echo throughout many important Supreme Court opinions of the last decade. Indeed, a central event precipitating the Justice Department's involvement in the litigation was the Supreme Court's decision in *Rizzo v. Goode*, 423 U.S. 362 (1976), overturning a lower court order that would have required the Philadelphia Police Department to draft a "comprehensive program for dealing adequately with civilian complaints." *Rizzo*, like the Philadelphia case, centered on accusations that super-

visory officials in the Police Department either did nothing to respond to complaints of unlawful police treatment of civilians, or so structured the complaint process as to preclude meaningful relief. The Court first stated doubts whether any article III case or controversy existed to sustain an injunctive suit because the individual plaintiffs did not claim any particular likelihood of future harm to themselves sufficient for standing. The Court proceeded to decide, however, that, even if a case or controversy existed, the plaintiff's proof fell short of demonstrating a "pattern or practice" of unlawfulness sufficient to sustain an action under 42 U.S.C. § 1983. Finally, the Court said that considerations of federalism argued against any broad structural relief in a case such as *Rizzo*: "Where, as here, the exercise of authority by state officials is attacked, federal courts must be constantly mindful of the 'special delicacy of the adjustment to be preserved between federal equitable power and State administration of its own law.' " 423 U.S. at 378.

Based on *Rizzo*, the Justice Department reasoned: (1) it was in the best position because of its litigation resources to mount the proof of a pattern and practice of police unlawfulness sufficient to sustain a suit under § 1983, and (2) it was in the best position to demonstrate the essential national interest at stake in the enforcement of the fourteenth amendment, itself a dramatic restructuring of the federal system. Was the Department wrong? Should federal courts in similar cases prefer Justice Department suits to individual suits, which presumably represent a less efficient mechanism for the vindication of constitutional rights? Should courts consider the greater potential for the intimidation of plaintiffs in individual suits? After *City of Philadelphia*, can anyone effectively seek judicial relief for a pattern and practice of unconstitutional police conduct?

In another case arising from the Third Circuit, the Supreme Court held in *Pennhurst State School v. Halderman*, 451 U.S. 1 (1981), that the Developmentally Disabled Assistance and Bill of Rights Act of 1965 did not create substantive rights enforceable by private citizens against programs for the care and treatment of the mentally retarded. The Court held that, on federalism grounds, it would not infer the imposition of affirmative federal statutory obligations on state institutions absent a clear statutory statement imposing those obligations. In footnote, Justice Rehnquist expressed some doubt whether Congress could impose such obligations at all pursuant to section 5 of the fourteenth amendment unless the obligations were designed to enforce judicially declared constitutional rights of the mentally retarded.

5. Should courts be wary of granting structural injunctive relief because of the judicial role that enforcement of such orders may necessitate? Would the supervision of a police department involve the courts in functions uncomfortably similar to executive functions? Are they functions courts are well equipped to perform? These are questions on which an immense literature exists. *See, e.g.*, D. Horowitz, The Courts and Social Policy (1977); Chayes, *The Role of the Judge in Public Law Litigation*, 89 Harv. L. Rev. 1281 (1976); Diver, *The Judge as Political Pawnbroker: Superintending Structural Change in Public Institutions*, 65 Va. L. Rev. 43 (1979); Eisenberg and Yeazell, *The Ordinary and the Extraordinary in Institutional Litigation*, 93 Harv. L. Rev. 465 (1980); Note, *Implementation Problems in Institutional Reform Litigation*, 91 Harv. L. Rev. 428 (1977); Special Project, *The Remedial Process in Institutional Reform Litigation*, 78 Colum. L. Rev. 784 (1978).

c. Protecting National Security

1.) *History of Electronic Surveillance*

FOREIGN INTELLIGENCE SURVEILLANCE ACT OF 1977*

S. Rept. No. 604, 95th Cong., 1st Sess. (1977)

In 1928, the Supreme Court in *Olmstead v. United States* [5] held that wiretapping was not within the coverage of the Fourth Amendment. Three years later, Attorney General William D. Mitchell authorized telephone wiretapping, upon the personal approval of bureau chiefs, of syndicated bootleggers and in "exceptional cases where the crimes are substantial and serious, and the necessity is great and [the bureau chief and the Assistant Attorney General] are satisfied that the persons whose wires are to be tapped are of the criminal type." These general guidelines governed the Department's practice through the thirties and telephone wiretapping was considered to be an important law enforcement tool.

Congress placed the first restrictions on wiretapping in the Federal Communications Act of 1934, which made it a crime for any person "to intercept and divulge or publish the contents of wire and radio communications."[7] The Supreme Court construed this section to apply to Federal agents and held that evidence obtained from the interception of wire and radio communications, and the fruits of that evidence, were inadmissible in court.[8] However, the Justice Department did not interpret the Federal Communications Act or the *Nardone* decision as prohibiting the interception of wire communications *per se*; rather only the interception and divulgence of their contents outside the Federal establishment was considered to be unlawful. Thus, the Justice Department found continued authority for its national security wiretaps.

In 1940, President Roosevelt issued a memorandum to the Attorney General stating his view that electronic surveillance would be proper under the Constitution where "grave matters involving defense of the nation" were involved. The President authorized and directed the Attorney General "to secure information by listening devices [directed at] the conversation or other communications of persons suspected of subversive activities against the Government of the United States, including suspected spies." The Attorney General was requested "to limit these investigations so conducted to a minimum and to limit them insofar as possible as to aliens."

This practice was continued in successive administrations. In 1946, Attorney General Tom C. Clark sent President Truman a letter informing him of President Roo-

---

* Congress did not pass legislation on electronic surveillance for foreign intelligence purposes until 1978. Foreign Intelligence Act of 1978, Pub. L. No. 95-511, 92 Stat. 1783, *codified at* 50 U.S.C. § 1801 *et seq.* There is substantial continuity, however, between the 1977 and 1978 bills and legislative reports. *See* H.R. Rept. No. 1283, 95th Cong., 2d Sess. (1978); S. Rept. No. 701, 95th Cong., 2d Sess. (1978); H.R. Rept. No. 1720, 95th Cong., 2d Sess. (1978) (conference report).

5. 277 U.S. 468.

7. 47 U.S.C. 605 (1964 ed.), 48 Stat. 1103.

8. *Nardone v. United States*, 302 U.S. 379 (1937); 308 U.S. 338 (1939).

sevelt's directive. Clark's memorandum, however, omitted the portion of President Roosevelt's directive limiting wiretaps "insofar as possible to aliens." Instead, he recommended that the directive "be continued in force" in view of the "increase in subversive activities" and "a very substantial increase in crime." President Truman approved.[10]

In the early fifties, however, Attorney General J. Howard McGrath took the position that he would not approve or authorize the installation of microphone surveillances by means of trespass. This policy was quickly reversed by Attorney General Herbert Brownell in 1954 in a sweeping memorandum to FBI Director Hoover instructing him that the Bureau was indeed authorized to conduct such trespassory surveillances regardless of the fact of surreptitious entry, and without the need to first acquire the Attorney General's authorization. Such surveillance was simply authorized whenever the Bureau concluded that the "national interest" so required. The Brownell memorandum is instructive:

> It is my opinion that the department should adopt that interpretation which will permit microphone coverage by the FBI in a manner most conducive to our national interest. I recognize that for the FBI to fulfill its important intelligence function, considerations of internal security and the national interest are paramount; and, therefore, may compel the unrestricted use of this technique in the national interest.

From the relatively limited authorization of warrantless electronic surveillance under President Roosevelt, then, the mandate for the FBI was quickly expanded to the point where the only criterion was the FBI's subjective judgment that the "national interest" required the electronic surveillance....

In *Katz v. United States*, 389 U.S. 347 (1967), the Supreme Court finally discarded the *Olmstead* doctrine and held that the Fourth Amendment's warrant provision did apply to electronic surveillance. The Court explicitly declined, however, to extend its holding to cases "involving the national security." 389 U.S. at 358, n. 23. The next year, Congress followed suit: responding to the *Katz* case, Congress enacted the Omnibus Crime Control and Safe Streets Act (18 U.S.C. sections 2510-2520).[14] Title III of that Act established a procedure for the judicial authorization of electronic surveillance for the investigation and prevention of specified types of serious crimes and the use of the product of such surveillance in court proceedings. It prohibited wiretapping and electronic surveillance by persons other than duly authorized law enforcement officers, personnel of the Federal Communications Commission, or communication common carriers monitoring communications in the normal course of their employment. Title III, however, disclaimed any intention of legislating in the national security area....

---

10. In 1950, aides to President Truman discovered Clark's incomplete quotation, and the President considered returning to the terms of the original 1940 authorization. However, the 1946 directive was never rescinded.

14. See also, S. Rept. 1097, *Senate Committee on the Judiciary, Omnibus Crime Control and Safe Streets Act of 1967*; 90th Cong., 2d sess. (1968).

2.) *Electronic Surveillance and National Security Investigations Generally*

United States v. United States District Court (Keith)
407 U.S. 297 (1972).

Justice POWELL delivered the opinion of the Court.

The issue before us is an important one for the people of our country and their Government. It involves the delicate question of the President's power, acting through the Attorney General, to authorize electronic surveillance in internal security matters without prior judicial approval. Successive Presidents for more than one-quarter of a century have authorized such surveillance in varying degrees, without guidance from the Congress or a definitive decision of this Court. This case brings the issue here for the first time. Its resolution is a matter of national concern, requiring sensitivity both to the Government's right to protect itself from unlawful subversion and attack and to the citizen's right to be secure in his privacy against unreasonable Government intrusion.

This case arises from a criminal proceeding in the United States District Court for the Eastern District of Michigan, in which the United States charged three defendants with conspiracy to destroy Government property in violation of 18 U.S.C. § 371. One of the defendants, Plamondon, was charged with the dynamite bombing of an office of the Central Intelligence Agency in Ann Arbor, Michigan.

During pretrial proceedings, the defendants moved to compel the United States to disclose certain electronic surveillance information and to conduct a hearing to determine whether this information "tainted" the evidence on which the indictment was based or which the Government intended to offer at trial. In response, the Government filed an affidavit of the Attorney General, acknowledging that its agents had overheard conversations in which Plamondon had participated. The affidavit also stated that the Attorney General approved the wiretaps "to gather intelligence information deemed necessary to protect the nation from attempts of domestic organizations to attack and subvert the existing structure of the Government." The logs of the surveillance were filed in a sealed exhibit for *in camera* inspection by the District Court.

On the basis of the Attorney General's affidavit and the sealed exhibit, the Government asserted that the surveillance was lawful, though conducted without prior judicial approval, as a reasonable exercise of the President's power (exercised through the Attorney General) to protect the national security. The District Court held that the surveillance violated the Fourth Amendment, and ordered the Government to make full disclosure to Plamondon of his overheard conversations. 321 F. Supp. 1074 (ED Mich. 1971).

The Government then filed in the Court of Appeals for the Sixth Circuit a petition for a writ of mandamus to set aside the District Court order, which was stayed.... [T]hat court held that the surveillance was unlawful and that the District Court had properly required disclosure of the overheard conversations, 444 F.2d 651 (1971).

I

Title III of the Omnibus Crime Control and Safe Streets Act, 18 U.S.C. §§ 2510-2520, authorizes the use of electronic surveillance for classes of crimes carefully specified in 18 U.S.C. § 2516. Such surveillance is subject to prior court order. Section 2518 sets forth the detailed and particularized application necessary to obtain such an order as well as carefully circumscribed conditions for its use. The Act represents a comprehensive attempt by Congress to promote more effective control of crime while protecting the privacy of individual thought and expression. Much of Title III was drawn to meet the constitutional requirements for electronic surveillance enunciated by this Court in *Berger v. New York*, 388 U.S. 41 (1967), and *Katz v. United States*, 389 U.S. 347 (1967).

Together with the elaborate surveillance requirements in Title III, there is the following proviso, 18 U.S.C. § 2511 (3):

> "Nothing contained in this chapter or in section 605 of the Communications Act of 1934 (48 Stat. 1143; 47 U.S.C. 605) shall limit the constitutional power of the President to take such measures as he deems necessary to protect the Nation against actual or potential attack or other hostile acts of a foreign power, to obtain foreign intelligence information deemed essential to the security of the United States, or to protect national security information against foreign intelligence activities. *Nor shall anything contained in this chapter be deemed to limit the constitutional power of the President to take such measures as he deems necessary to protect the United States against the overthrow of the Government by force or other unlawful means, or against any other clear and present danger to the structure or existence of the Government.* The contents of any wire or oral communication intercepted by authority of the President in the exercise of the foregoing powers may be received in evidence in any trial hearing, or other proceeding only where such interception was reasonable, and shall not be otherwise used or disclosed except as is necessary to implement that power."
> (Emphasis supplied.)

The Government relies on § 2511 (3). It argues that "in excepting national security surveillances from the Act's warrant requirement Congress recognized the President's authority to conduct such surveillances without prior judicial approval." Brief for United States 7, 28. The section thus is viewed as a recognition or affirmance of a constitutional authority in the President to conduct warrantless domestic security surveillance such as that involved in this case.

We think the language of § 2511 (3), as well as the legislative history of the statute, refutes this interpretation. The relevant language is that:

> "Nothing contained in this chapter ... shall limit the constitutional power of the President to take such measures as he deems necessary to protect ... "

against the dangers specified. At most, this is an implicit recognition that the President does have certain powers in the specified areas. Few would doubt this, as the section refers—among other things—to protection "against actual or potential attack or other hostile acts of a foreign power." But so far as the use of the President's electronic surveillance power is concerned, the language is essentially neutral.

Section 2511 (3) certainly confers no power, as the language is wholly inappropriate for such a purpose. It merely provides that the Act shall not be interpreted to limit or disturb such power as the President may have under the Constitution. In short, Congress simply left presidential powers where it found them....

[I]t would have been incongruous for Congress to have legislated with respect to the important and complex area of national security in a single brief and nebulous paragraph. This would not comport with the sensitivity of the problem involved or with the extraordinary care Congress exercised in drafting other sections of the Act. We therefore think the conclusion inescapable that Congress only intended to make clear that the Act simply did not legislate with respect to national security surveillances.

The legislative history of § 2511 (3) supports this interpretation.... [V]iewing § 2511 (3) as a congressional disclaimer and expression of neutrality, we hold that the statute is not the measure of the executive authority asserted in this case. Rather, we must look to the constitutional powers of the President.

II

It is important at the outset to emphasize the limited nature of the question before the Court. This case raises no constitutional challenge to electronic surveillance as specifically authorized by Title III of the Omnibus Crime Control and Safe Streets Act of 1968. Nor is there any question or doubt as to the necessity of obtaining a warrant in the surveillance of crimes unrelated to the national security interest. *Katz v. United States*, 389 U.S. 347 (1967); *Berger v. New York*, 388 U.S. 41 (1967). Further, the instant case requires no judgment on the scope of the President's surveillance power with respect to the activities of foreign powers, within or without this country. The Attorney General's affidavit in this case states that the surveillances were "deemed necessary to protect the nation from attempts of *domestic organizations* to attack and subvert the existing structure of Government" (emphasis supplied). There is no evidence of any involvement, directly or indirectly, of a foreign power.[8]

Our present inquiry, though important, is therefore a narrow one. It addresses a question left open by *Katz, supra*, at 358 n. 23:

> "Whether safeguards other than prior authorization by a magistrate would satisfy the Fourth Amendment in a situation involving the national security..."

The determination of this question requires the essential Fourth Amendment inquiry into the "reasonableness" of the search and seizure in question, and the way in which that "reasonableness" derives content and meaning through referent to the warrant clause.

... [T]he President of the United States has the fundamental duty, under Art. II, § 1, of the Constitution, to "preserve, protect and defend the Constitution of the United States." Implicit in that duty is the power to protect our Government against those who would subvert or overthrow it by unlawful means. In the discharge of this

---

8. Section 2511 (3) refers to "the constitutional power of the President" in two types of situations: (i) where necessary to protect against attack, other hostile acts or intelligence activities of a "foreign power"; or (ii) where necessary to protect against the overthrow of the Government or other clear and present danger to the structure or existence of the Government. Although both of the specified situations are sometimes referred to as "national security" threats, the term "national security" is used only in the first sentence of § 2511 (3) with respect to the activities of foreign powers. This case involves only the second sentence of § 2511 (3), with the threat emanating—according to the Attorney General's affidavit—from "domestic organizations." Although we attempt no precise definition, we use the term "domestic organization" in this opinion to mean a group or organization (whether formally or informally constituted) composed of citizens of the United States and which has no significant connection with a foreign power, its agents or agencies. No doubt there are cases where it will be difficult to distinguish between "domestic" and "foreign" unlawful activities directed against the Government of the United States where there is collaboration in varying degrees between domestic groups or organizations and agents or agencies of foreign powers. But this is not such a case.

duty, the President—through the Attorney General—may find it necessary to employ electronic surveillance to obtain intelligence information on the plans of those who plot unlawful acts against the Government. The use of such surveillance in internal security cases has been sanctioned more or less continuously by various Presidents and Attorneys General since July 1946.[10] ...

Though the Government and respondents debate their seriousness and magnitude, threats and acts of sabotage against the Government exist in sufficient number to justify investigative powers with respect to them. The covertness and complexity of potential unlawful conduct against the Government and the necessary dependency of many conspirators upon the telephone make electronic surveillance an effective investigatory instrument in certain circumstances. The marked acceleration in technological developments and sophistication in their use have resulted in new techniques for the planning, commission, and concealment of criminal activities. It would be contrary to the public interest for Government to deny to itself the prudent and lawful employment of those very techniques which are employed against the Government and its law-abiding citizens. ...

But a recognition of these elementary truths does not make the employment by Government of electronic surveillance a welcome development—even when employed with restraint and under judicial supervision. There is, understandably, a deep-seated uneasiness and apprehension that this capability will be used to intrude upon cherished privacy of law-abiding citizens. We look to the Bill of Rights to safeguard this privacy. Though physical entry of the home is the chief evil against which the wording of the Fourth Amendment is directed, its broader spirit now shields private speech from unreasonable surveillance. Our decision in *Katz* refused to lock the Fourth Amendment into instances of actual physical trespass. Rather, the Amendment governs "not only the seizure of tangible items, but extends as well to the recording of oral statements ... without any 'technical trespass under ... local property law.' " ...

National security cases, moreover, often reflect a convergence of First and Fourth Amendment values not present in cases of "ordinary" crime. Though the investigative duty of the executive may be stronger in such cases, so also is there greater jeopardy to constitutionally protected speech. "Historically the struggle for freedom of speech and press in England was bound up with the issue of the scope of the search and seizure power," *Marcus v. Search Warrant*, 367 U.S. 717, 724 (1961). History abundantly documents the tendency of Government—however benevolent and benign its motives—to view with suspicion those who most fervently dispute its policies. Fourth Amendment protections become the more necessary when the targets of official surveillance may be those suspected of unorthodoxy in their political beliefs. The danger to political dissent is acute where the Government attempts to act under so vague a concept as the power to protect "domestic security." Given the difficulty of defining

---

10. In that month Attorney General Tom Clark advised President Truman of the necessity of using wiretaps "in cases vitally affecting the domestic security." In May 1940 President Roosevelt had authorized Attorney General Jackson to utilize wiretapping in matters "involving the defense of the nation," but it is questionable whether this language was meant to apply to solely domestic subversion. The nature and extent of wiretapping apparently varied under different administrations and Attorneys General, but, except for the sharp curtailment under Attorney General Ramsey Clark in the latter years of the Johnson administration, electronic surveillance has been used both against organized crime and in domestic security cases at least since the 1946 memorandum from Clark to Truman. Brief for United States 16-18; Brief for Respondents 51-56; 117 Cong. Rec. 14056.

the domestic security interest, the danger of abuse in acting to protect that interest becomes apparent....

III

As the Fourth Amendment is not absolute in its terms, our task is to examine and balance the basic values at stake in this case: the duty of Government to protect the domestic security, and the potential danger posed by unreasonable surveillance to individual privacy and free expression. If the legitimate need of Government to safeguard domestic security requires the use of electronic surveillance, the question is whether the needs of citizens for privacy and free expression may not be better protected by requiring a warrant before such surveillance is undertaken. We must also ask whether a warrant requirement would unduly frustrate the efforts of Government to protect itself from acts of subversion and overthrow directed against it.

Though the Fourth Amendment speaks broadly of "unreasonable searches and seizures," the definition of "reasonableness" turns, at least in part, on the more specific commands of the warrant clause.... [W]here practical, a governmental search and seizure should represent both the efforts of the officer to gather evidence of wrongful acts and the judgment of the magistrate that the collected evidence is sufficient to justify invasion of a citizen's private premises or conversation. Inherent in the concept of a warrant is its issuance by a "neutral and detached magistrate." The further requirement of "probable cause" instructs the magistrate that baseless searches shall not proceed.

These Fourth Amendment freedoms cannot properly be guaranteed if domestic security surveillances may be conducted solely within the discretion of the Executive Branch. The Fourth Amendment does not contemplate the executive officers of Government as neutral and disinterested magistrates. Their duty and responsibility are to enforce the laws, to investigate, and to prosecute. But those charged with this investigative and prosecutorial duty should not be the sole judges of when to utilize constitutionally sensitive means in pursuing their tasks. The historical judgment, which the Fourth Amendment accepts, is that unreviewed executive discretion may yield too readily to pressures to obtain incriminating evidence and overlook potential invasions of privacy and protected speech.

It may well be that, in the instant case, the Government's surveillance of Plamondon's conversations was a reasonable one which readily would have gained prior judicial approval. But this Court "has never sustained a search upon the sole ground that officers reasonably expected to find evidence of a particular crime and voluntarily confined their activities to the least intrusive means consistent with that end." The Fourth Amendment contemplates a prior judicial judgment, not the risk that executive discretion may be reasonably exercised. This judicial role accords with our basic constitutional doctrine that individual freedoms will best be preserved through a separation of powers and division of functions among the different branches and levels of Government. The independent check upon executive discretion is not satisfied, as the Government argues, by "extremely limited" post-surveillance judicial review. Indeed, post-surveillance review would never reach the surveillances which failed to result in prosecutions. Prior review by a neutral and detached magistrate is the time-tested means of effectuating Fourth Amendment rights.

It is true that there have been some exceptions to the warrant requirement. But those exceptions are few in number and carefully delineated; in general, they serve the legitimate needs of law enforcement officers to protect their own well-being and preserve evidence from destruction. Even while carving out those exceptions, the Court has reaffirmed the principle that the "police must, whenever practicable, obtain advance judicial approval of searches and seizures through the warrant procedure," *Terry v. Ohio*, 392 U.S. 1, 20 (1968).

The Government argues that the special circumstances applicable to domestic security surveillances necessitate a further exception to the warrant requirement. It is urged that the requirement of prior judicial review would obstruct the President in the discharge of his constitutional duty to protect domestic security. We are told further that these surveillances are directed primarily to the collecting and maintaining of intelligence with respect to subversive forces, and are not an attempt to gather evidence for specific criminal prosecutions. It is said that this type of surveillance should not be subject to traditional warrant requirements which were established to govern investigation of criminal activity, not ongoing intelligence gathering.

The Government further insists that courts "as a practical matter would have neither the knowledge nor the techniques necessary to determine whether there was probable cause to believe that surveillance was necessary to protect national security." These security problems, the Government contends, involve "a large number of complex and subtle factors" beyond the competence of courts to evaluate.

As a final reason for exemption from a warrant requirement, the Government believes that disclosure to a magistrate of all or even a significant portion of the information involved in domestic security surveillances "would create serious potential dangers to the national security and to the lives of informants and agents. . . . Secrecy is the essential ingredient in intelligence gathering; requiring prior judicial authorization would create a greater 'danger of leaks . . . , because in addition to the judge, you have the clerk, the stenographer and some other officer like a law assistant or bailiff who may be apprised of the nature' of the surveillance."

. . . There is, no doubt, pragmatic force to the Government's position. But we do not think a case has been made for the requested departure from Fourth Amendment standards. The circumstances described do not justify complete exemption of domestic security surveillance from prior judicial scrutiny. Official surveillance, whether its purpose be criminal investigation or ongoing intelligence gathering, risks infringement of constitutionally protected privacy of speech. Security surveillances are especially sensitive because of the inherent vagueness of the domestic security concept, the necessarily broad and continuing nature of intelligence gathering, and the temptation to utilize such surveillances to oversee political dissent. We recognize, as we have before, the constitutional basis of the President's domestic security role, but we think it must be exercised in a manner compatible with the Fourth Amendment. In this case we hold that this requires an appropriate prior warrant procedure.

We cannot accept the Government's argument that internal security matters are too subtle and complex for judicial evaluation. Courts regularly deal with the most difficult issues of our society. There is no reason to believe that federal judges will be insensitive to or uncomprehending of the issues involved in domestic security cases. Certainly courts can recognize that domestic security surveillance involves different considerations from the surveillance of "ordinary crime." If the threat is too subtle or complex for our senior law enforcement officers to convey its significance to a court, one may question whether there is probable cause for surveillance.

Nor do we believe prior judicial approval will fracture the secrecy essential to official intelligence gathering. The investigation of criminal activity has long involved imparting sensitive information to judicial officers who have respected the confidentialities involved. Judges may be counted upon to be especially conscious of security requirements in national security cases. Title III of the Omnibus Crime Control and Safe Streets Act already has imposed this responsibility on the judiciary in connection with such crimes as espionage, sabotage, and treason, §§ 2516 (1)(a) and (c), each of which may involve domestic as well as foreign security threats. Moreover, a warrant application involves no public or adversary proceedings: it is an *ex parte* request before a magistrate or judge. Whatever security dangers clerical and secretarial personnel may pose can be minimized by proper administrative measures, possibly to the point of allowing the Government itself to provide the necessary clerical assistance.

Thus, we conclude that the Government's concerns do not justify departure in this case from the customary Fourth Amendment requirement of judicial approval prior to initiation of a search or surveillance. Although some added burden will be imposed upon the Attorney General, this inconvenience is justified in a free society to protect constitutional values. Nor do we think the Government's domestic surveillance powers will be impaired to any significant degree. A prior warrant establishes presumptive validity of the surveillance and will minimize the burden of justification in post-surveillance judicial review. By no means of least importance will be the reassurance of the public generally that indiscriminate wiretapping and bugging of law-abiding citizens cannot occur.

IV

. . . [W]e do not hold that the same type of standards and procedures prescribed by Title III are necessarily applicable to this case. We recognize that domestic security surveillance may involve different policy and practical considerations from the surveillance of "ordinary crime." The gathering of security intelligence is often long range and involves the interrelation of various sources and types of information. The exact targets of such surveillance may be more difficult to identify than in surveillance operations against many types of crime specified in Title III. Often, too, the emphasis of domestic intelligence gathering is on the prevention of unlawful activity or the enhancement of the Government's preparedness for some possible future crisis or emergency. Thus, the focus of domestic surveillance may be less precise than that directed against more conventional types of crime.

Given these potential distinctions between Title III criminal surveillances and those involving the domestic security, Congress may wish to consider protective standards for the latter which differ from those already prescribed for specified crimes in Title III. Different standards may be compatible with the Fourth Amendment if they are reasonable both in relation to the legitimate need of Government for intelligence information and the protected rights of our citizens. For the warrant application may vary according to the governmental interest to be enforced and the nature of citizen rights deserving protection. . . .

We . . . hold . . . that prior judicial approval is required for the type of domestic security surveillance involved in this case and that such approval may be made in accordance with such reasonable standards as the Congress may prescribe.

V

As the surveillance of Plamondon's conversations was unlawful, because conducted without prior judicial approval, the courts below correctly held that *Alderman* v.

United States, 394 U.S. 165 (1969), is controlling and that it requires disclosure to the accused of his own impermissibly intercepted conversations. As stated in *Alderman*, "the trial court can and should, where appropriate, place a defendant and his counsel under enforceable orders against unwarranted disclosure of the materials which they may be entitled to inspect."

The judgment of the Court of Appeals is hereby
Affirmed.

---

1. Justice Powell purports to limit the foregoing decision to domestic national security threats, reserving questions as to the scope of inherent presidential authority with respect to gathering national security information on foreign powers and the standards that might govern implementation of the warrant clause, if it applies. How easy a distinction is this for government agents to implement, especially before they have received the information they seek to obtain?

2. In the wake of *Keith*, Congress sought to preempt the constitutional questions concerning foreign intelligence gathering by enacting the Foreign Intelligence Surveillance Act of 1978 (FISA), 50 U.S.C. § 1801 *et seq.* (1982). That Act established warrant requirements to govern certain instances of foreign intelligence gathering, and a process for assembling a panel of judges, now called the Foreign Intelligence Surveillance Court, to enforce them. The warrant procedure of FISA is unusual. The Foreign Intelligence Surveillance Court operates in secret, and, in cases in which a warrant is challenged, the court may "review in camera and ex parte the [warrant] application, order, and such other materials ... as may be necessary to determine whether the surveillance ... was lawfully authorized and conducted." 50 U.S.C. § 1806(f). Was this wise? Given the competing interests involved in structuring national security investigations, how far should Congress go in regulating the executive branch? (As you analyze the description of the Act below, consider, alternatively, whether Congress went far enough.) For an appreciation of the political atmosphere in which Congress adopted FISA, some further history of intelligence gathering and its oversight is helpful:

Note: Presidential and Congressional Oversight Of CIA and FBI Intelligence Gathering

No area of government activity has raised more profound questions of delegated authority and effective oversight than the enterprise of intelligence gathering. Since its creation in 1947, the Central Intelligence Agency has conducted its activities under a very broad statutory mandate, subject to the general direction of the National Security Council. National Security Act of 1947, § 102(d), 61 Stat. 497 (1947), *codified with amendments at* 50 U.S.C. §§403(A) (1982). *See generally* Note, *The Central Intelligence Agency: Present Authority and Proposed Legislative Change*, 62 Va. L. Rev. 332 (1976). More remarkably, the Federal Bureau of Investigation (FBI) has never been subject to any substantive statutory restrictions at all as to the scope of its permissible intelligence activities; the Bureau derives its investigative authority entirely from the general statutory powers of the Attorney General regarding investigations. 28 U.S.C. §533 (1982). *See generally* Elliff, *The Attorney General's Guidelines for FBI Investigations*, 69 Cornell L. Rev. 785 (1984).

For nearly 30 years, congressional oversight of the intelligence community was practically nonexistent. Between 1947 and 1975, Congress either rejected or ignored

200 legislative proposals to increase its oversight over the CIA. In 1975, however, that immunity from oversight came to an abrupt end. (*See generally* 1975 Cong. Q. Almanac 361-412; 1976 Cong. Q. Almanac 294-308, 415-421.) The CIA, FBI, and other intelligence-gathering units within the executive branch became the focus of intense governmental investigations chiefly because of a series of *New York Times* articles disclosing massive, illegal domestic intelligence operations during the Nixon administration. The alleged activities, in apparent violation of the National Security Act, were aimed at antiwar and dissident groups. The newspaper's startling disclosures followed close upon the heels of alleged CIA links to the Watergate scandal and allegations of CIA efforts to "destabilize" the government of deposed Chilean President Salvador Allende, episodes which had likewise spurred calls for deeper scrutiny.

Reports of CIA abuse provoked responses from both the President and Congress. On January 5, 1975, following the resignation of James Angleton, the CIA counterintelligence chief, President Ford named an eight-member commission (including future President Reagan) under Vice President Rockefeller ("Rockefeller Commission") to investigate alleged CIA statutory violations.

On January 15, CIA Director William Colby sent a lengthy report to the Senate Appropriations Intelligence Operations Subcommittee, acknowledging that the CIA had carried out surveillance of journalists and political activists, opened the mail of U.S. citizens, infiltrated domestic protest groups and gathered information for secret files on more than 10,000 Americans. Twelve days later, the Senate established an eleven-member select committee under Senator Franch Church ("Church Committee") to investigate the activities of the CIA, FBI, and other law enforcement and intelligence agencies to determine if they had engaged in any illegal or unethical intelligence activities during the Vietnam period. (A parallel study was later undertaken in the House of Representatives, under Rep. Otis G. Pike, of New York.)

The Rockefeller Commission reported that, although most CIA intelligence operations were within statutory bounds, some were "plainly unlawful and constituted improper invasions upon the rights of Americans." The commission revealed the existence from 1962-72 of a special group within the CIA called Operation CHAOS, charged with collecting information on dissident groups within the United States. CHAOS developed a computerized index with the names of more than 300,000 persons and organizations, and compiled files on 7,200 Americans. The Commission found further that the CIA exceeded its authority by investigating journalists and American citizens who had no relationship with the Agency. In five instances, the CIA investigated American newsmen to identify their sources of classified information.

The CIA also provided "supplies" (alias documents, tape recorder and photography equipment) to former CIA employee E. Howard Hunt, Jr., who had used some of these in his Watergate activities. Additionally, the CIA turned over classified information to President Nixon for use towards political ends.

The Commission reported numerous incidents of improper wiretapping, bugging, break-ins, obtaining federal tax returns, and opening mail. From the late 1940's until 1967, the CIA had conducted an illegal drug experimentation program on persons without their consent. In addition, the Agency participated in law enforcement activities, such as recruitment for the Bureau of Narcotics and Dangerous Drugs, which are prohibited by the CIA charter. In addition to the 7,200 CHAOS files, the CIA kept 57,000 open files on United States citizens.

The Rockefeller Commission made some thirty recommendations to prevent future abuses. It was recommended that the practice of gathering intelligence on domestic activities by the CIA be generally prohibited, with exceptions for the domestic monitoring of U.S. citizens who pose a "clear threat" to the agency's facilities or personnel, of citizens suspected of espionage, and of persons currently or formerly affiliated with the CIA or CIA applicants. The Rockefeller Commission recommended that the 1947 National Security Act be amended to define "foreign intelligence" as information concerning the activities and intentions of foreign nations, *wherever* that information might be found, and that the CIA not be able to infiltrate organizations in the United States in the absence of written approval by the Director after a determination that such action is necessary to meet a clear danger.

The revelations of the Rockefeller Commission were but a hint, however, of the more comprehensive findings to be reported by the Church Committee. On September 16, 1975, CIA Director William E. Colby admitted in public hearings that agency employees had violated a 1970 presidential order requiring the destruction of two deadly poisons. Other testimony revealed the existence of a twenty-year mail surveillance program undertaken by the CIA even though the Agency knew it to be illegal and regarded it as of little value. The mail included correspondence of several prominent figures including Richard Nixon, Senators Edward Kennedy and Hubert Humphrey, Martin Luther King, Jr., Federal Reserve Board Chairman Arthur Burns, and even Senator Church. Between 1970 and 1972 alone, the CIA examined about 2 million pieces of mail a year.

In relation to foreign policy, the CIA's involvement in attempts to assassinate foreign leaders was no longer speculation. The Committee reported plots to kill Fidel Castro of Cuba and Patrice Lumumba of the Congo (now Zaire). The CIA also conducted covert operations against General Raphael Trujillo of the Dominican Republic and President Ngo Dinh Diem of South Vietnam. Although both were eventually assassinated, no direct links connected the CIA to their deaths. The CIA also supported groups in Chile attempting to kidnap Chilean General Rene Schneider. Schneider was killed in 1970 but by an unrelated group.

The aid to Chilean insurgents went far beyond aid to the group trying to kidnap Schneider. Massive intervention was reportedly aimed at overthrowing the government of President Salvador Allende.

The Church Committee also revealed extraordinary FBI abuses. The FBI had employed blackmail, bugging, and intimidation tactics in a campaign initiated by former director J. Edgar Hoover to discredit Martin Luther King, Jr. Sixteen separate bugs were placed in hotel rooms used by King during 1964-65. Wiretaps were placed in the offices of King's Southern Christian Leadership Conference in Atlanta and New York from 1963-66. In 1964, just before King was to receive the Nobel Peace Prize, FBI agents sent him an anonymous letter containing compromising transcripts from the hotel bugging and suggesting the only way out for him was suicide. During a sanitation strike in Memphis, which included a boycott of white-owned businesses, the bureau leaked information to the press that King was staying at a white-owned hotel. King moved to a black-owned hotel where he was later assassinated.

Even after King's death the harassment tactics continued. The Bureau devised a plan to prevent congressional support for a national holiday on King's birthday. The testimony before the Committee did not reveal whether this plan was ever implemented.

The Church Committee reported numerous FBI break-ins in connection with the Bureau's counterintelligence operations. From 1942 to 1968, the Bureau conducted 238 burglaries against "domestic subversive targets" and kept records of such break-ins in secret files. In addition, surveillance of prominent figures was undertaken during the 1964 Democratic National Convention. During the 1970's, campus surveillance was also expanded to disrupt political movements. During some point in the history of campus surveillance, the FBI had an actual plan to disrupt leftist college groups. Some of the techniques suggested were starting rumors that student leaders were FBI informants, sending letters to members' parents or employers, and harassing students through narcotics enforcement.

The FBI also tried "divide and conquer" tactics against dissident groups. The Bureau, for example, tried to promote tensions between two black militant groups in Chicago by anonymously tipping the leader of the Blackstone Rangers that the Black Panthers planned on having him killed. On another occasion, the FBI sent letters to suspected Mafia-owned businesses, chastising them for allegedly discriminatory employment practices and then forging a suspected Communist's name to the letters, apparently hoping for reprisals against him.

The Ku Klux Klan was one of the FBI's main targets. In order to infiltrate the Klan effectively, however, the Bureau allowed (but did not instruct) its agents to participate in violence against blacks and civil rights activists.

The Committee reported widespread use of the FBI by past Presidents for personal political ends. The Committee concluded that Presidents Roosevelt, Truman, Eisenhower, Kennedy, Johnson, and Nixon had all received reports from the FBI on journalists, political opponents, and critics of administration policy. Although the practice began in the Roosevelt Administration, the committee reported that it "grew to unprecedented" dimensions during the Johnson and Nixon eras.

According to Senator Church, the lack of congressional oversight was a basic reason for the intelligence community's failures and misdeeds. The committee set out ninety-six recommendations, most intended to be included in legislation improving congressional oversight of intelligence gathering. The committee proposed to allow only limited activity within the United States by the CIA and to centralize domestic activities under the FBI. *See generally* Commission on CIA Activities Within the United States, Report to the President (1975) ["Rockefeller Report"]; Final Report of the Senate Select Comm. to Study Governmental Operations with Respect to Intelligence Activities, S. Rep. No. 755, 94th Cong., 2d Sess. (1976) (6 vols.) ["Church Committee Report"].

Despite the calls for increased oversight, Congress has yet to provide any substantive charter for the FBI or to revise the CIA's statutory mandate to clarify the permissible bounds of intelligence activities. The most significant legislative reform was the reorganization of legislative oversight of intelligence pursuant to provisions included in the Fiscal 1981 Intelligence Authorization Act, Pub. L. No. 96-450, 94 Stat. 1975 (1980). That Act created a single intelligence oversight committee in each House of Congress, and required the executive branch to keep each committee "fully and currently informed" of all current intelligence activities. 50 U.S.C. §413 (1982). Each committee was specifically to be notified of all covert operations, although the President, in extraordinary circumstances, could limit notification to the chair and ranking members, plus the House Speaker and minority leader, and the majority and minority leaders of the Senate.

More significant reform of intelligence operations occurred, however, under executive order. Responding modestly to the Rockefeller and Church investigations, President Ford issued an order in 1976 intended to clarify the responsibilities of the various investigative agencies of government with respect to intelligence gathering, all of which would be coordinated by a Committee on Foreign Intelligence, chaired by the Director of Central Intelligence (DCI), and an Operations Advisory Group. Although placing no new restrictions on foreign covert operations, the Order did seek to clarify the scope of domestic intelligence activities the President regarded as unlawful. Exec. Order No. 11,905, 3 C.F.R. 90 (1977).

Less than two years later, President Carter overhauled the executive order process, providing much more extensive substantive guidance on proscribed intelligence-gathering techniques. Carter created an Intelligence Oversight Board consisting of advisors from outside the government to assist him in overseeing the intelligence agencies. He abolished the Committee on Foreign Intelligence and the Operations Advisory Group, instead coordinating policy through committees of the National Security Council. The Carter order provided additional detail on the respective duties of the various intelligence agencies, and created a central role for the Attorney General to ensure legal compliance in the conduct of all intelligence activities. Exec. Order No. 12,036, 3 C.F.R. 112 (1979).

In December, 1981, President Reagan replaced the Carter order with a new order intended to streamline executive branch oversight. The Order eliminated much of the Carter order's codification of restricted or prohibited intelligence practices, and greatly reduced the Attorney General's express role in intelligence oversight. Exec. Order No. 12,333, 3 C.F.R. 200 (1982). These moves were controversial, especially because Congress, in enacting the Foreign Intelligence Surveillance Act of 1978, had foregone the regulation of some aspects of intelligence gathering because of assurances that the executive branch would establish and implement effective internal guidelines.

Paralleling these developments, Attorney General William French Smith, in 1983, issued new guidelines for FBI domestic security investigations, replacing the 1976 guidelines implemented by Attorney General Levi, which were followed throughout the Carter Administration, as well. There was substantial continuity, however, between the two sets of guidelines. Perhaps the main difference is that the newer standards permit a full domestic security investigation based on a "reasonable indication" of political action based on violence and a violation of federal laws, while the former standards required "specific and articulable facts giving reason" to suspect such activity. The Carter Administration, however, had recommended that the broader standard be adopted for domestic security investigations in a statutory FBI charter. The changes are described in detail in Elliff, *The Attorney General's Guidelines for FBI Investigations*, 69 Cornell L. Rev. 785 (1984).

Congressional and public oversight of the intelligence agencies has undoubtedly been impeded by ambiguities in the substantive missions of the intelligence agencies, and the reluctance of any decisionmaker to appear to be impeding efforts to protect national security. Yet, lurking behind this complex story is another uncertainty that has likely impeded effective oversight—uncertainty as to the constitutional locus of authority for intelligence gathering and national security generally. As you review the next two chapters, on the President's foreign affairs and military powers, you will become further acquainted with executive branch claims of inherent powers in these areas. Are you persuaded by these claims? Do the arguments persuade you that there are limits, either constitutional or policy-based, to the appropriate role of Congress in overseeing intelligence operations?

For further information on the intelligence agencies and the issues relating to oversight, *see* American Bar Association Working Group on Intelligence Oversight and Accountability, Oversight and Accountability of the U.S. Intelligence Agencies: An Evaluation (1985); S. Turner, Secrecy and Democracy: The CIA in Transition (1985); J. Bamford, The Puzzle Palace: A Report on America's Most Secret Agency (1982); and S. Ungar, FBI: An Uncensored Look Behind the Walls (1976).

3.) *Investigations Under the Foreign Intelligence Surveillance Act of 1978*

FOREIGN INTELLIGENCE SURVEILLANCE ACT OF 1977
S. Rept. No. 604, 95th Cong., 1st Sess. (1977)
GENERAL STATEMENT
I. SUMMARY OF THE LEGISLATION

. . . The purpose of the bill is to provide a procedure under which the Attorney General can obtain a judicial warrant authorizing the use of electronic surveillance in the United States for foreign intelligence purposes. If enacted, this legislation would require a judicial warrant authorizing the following for foreign intelligence purposes:

(a) The acquisition of a wire or radio communication sent to or from the United States by intentionally targeting a known United States person in the United States under circumstances in which the person has a reasonable expectation of privacy and a warrant would be required for law enforcement purposes.

(b) A wiretap in the United States to intercept a wire communication, such as a telephone or telegram communication;

(c) The acquisition of a private radio transmission in which all of the communicants are located within the United States; or

(d) The use in the United States of any electronic, mechanical or other surveillance device to acquire information other than a wire communication or radio communication under circumstances in which the person has a reasonable expectation of privacy and a warrant would be required for law enforcement purposes.

S. 1566 authorizes the Chief Justice of the United States to designate seven district court judges, any one of whom may hear applications for and grant orders approving electronic surveillance for foreign intelligence purposes. The bill further provides that the Chief Justice shall designate three judges from the United States district courts or courts of appeals to sit as a special Court of Appeals to hear appeals by the United States from denials of applications made by any one of the seven district court judges. The United States may further appeal from this special court to the Supreme Court.

Under S. 1566, a judge may issue a warrant authorizing electronic surveillance within the United States only if he finds that: the President has authorized the Attorney General to approve applications for such electronic surveillance; the application has been approved by the Attorney General; on the basis of the facts submitted to the court, there is probable cause to believe that the target of the surveillance is a foreign power or an agent of a foreign power; the place at which the surveillance is directed is being used or about to be used by that foreign power or agent; minimization procedures to be followed are reasonably designed to minimize the acquisition and retention of information relating to Americans that is not foreign intelligence information; Executive certification that the information sought is foreign intelligence information which cannot reasonably be obtained by normal investigative techniques; and, if the target of the surveillance is a United States person, such certification is not clearly erroneous. The order may approve the electronic surveillance for no longer than 90 days with respect to all natural persons and some foreign powers, but extensions of up to 90 days may be granted upon an application and after the same findings as required for the original order. With respect to official "foreign powers," as defined in the legislation, the approval may be for as long as one year.

In the event that an emergency arises and resort to a court is not possible, the Attorney General is authorized to approve electronic surveillance. Such an emergency surveillance cannot continue for more than 24 hours without a judge's approval; a judge must be immediately notified of the emergency surveillance; and an application must be made to the judge within 24 hours of approval of that emergency surveillance.

The bill would limit the use of information concerning United States citizens and lawful resident aliens acquired from electronic surveillances to matters properly related to foreign intelligence and the enforcement of criminal law. No information obtained from an electronic surveillance could be used or disclosed against any person except for lawful purposes. A judge may order the notification of a person under electronic surveillance if an emergency surveillance was authorized but subsequently disapproved by a judge.

S. 1566 provides for annual reports by the Attorney General to the Congress and the Administrative Office of the United States Courts containing statistical information relating to surveillances during the preceding year.

The bill does not provide statutory authorization for the use of any technique other than electronic surveillance, and, combined with chapter 119 of title 18, it constitutes the exclusive means by which electronic surveillance, as defined, and the interception of domestic wire and oral communications may be conducted; the bill recognizes no inherent power of the President in this area.

In three major respects S. 1566 increases the protections for United States citizens and lawful resident aliens over those contained in S. 3197. First, the definition of electronic surveillance has been expanded to include the targeting of United States persons in their international communications. . . . Second, when a United States citizen or lawful resident alien is the target of an electronic surveillance, the judge is required to review the Executive Branch certification to determine if it is clearly erroneous. . . . Finally, S. 1566 spells out that the Executive cannot engage in electronic surveillance within the United States without a prior judicial warrant. This is accomplished by repealing the so-called executive "inherent power" disclaimer clause currently found in section 2511 (3) of Title 18, United States Code. S. 1566 provides instead that its statutory procedures (and those found in chapter 119 of title 18) "shall be the exclusive means" for conducting electronic surveillance, as defined in the legislation, in the United States. The highly controversial disclaimer has often been cited as evidence of a congressional ratification of the President's inherent constitutional power to engage in electronic surveillance in order to obtain foreign intelligence information essential to the national security. Despite the admonition of the Supreme Court that the language of the disclaimer was "neutral" and did not reflect any such congressional recognition of inherent power, the section has been a major source of controversy. By repealing section 2511 (3) and expressly stating that the statutory warrant procedures spelled out in the law must be followed in conducting electronic surveillance in the United States, this legislation ends the eight-year debate over the meaning and scope of the inherent power disclaimer clause.

. . . S. 1566 goes a long way in striking a fair and just balance between protection of national security and protection of personal liberties. It is a recognition by both the Executive Branch and the Congress that the statutory rule of law must prevail in the area of foreign intelligence surveillance.

The need for such statutory safeguards has become apparent in recent years. This legislation is in large measure a response to the revelations that warrantless electronic surveillance in the name of national security has been seriously abused. These abuses were initially illuminated in 1973 during the investigation of the Watergate break-in. Since that time, however, the Senate Select Committee to Study Government Operations with Respect to Intelligence Activities, chaired by Senator Church (hereafter referred to as the Church Committee), has concluded that every President since Franklin D. Roosevelt asserted the authority to authorize warrantless electronic surveillance and exercised that authority. While the number of illegal or improper national security taps and bugs conducted during the Nixon administration may have exceeded those in previous administrations, the surveillances were regrettably by no means atypical. In summarizing its conclusions that surveillance was "often conducted by illegal or improper means," the Church committee wrote:

> Since the 1930's, intelligence agencies have frequently wiretapped and bugged American citizens without the benefit of judicial warrant. . . . [P]ast subjects of these surveillances have included a United States Congressman, Congressional staff member, journalists and newsmen, and numerous individuals and groups who engaged in no criminal activity and who posed no genuine threat to the national security, such as two White House domestic affairs advisers and an anti-Vietnam War protest group. (vol. 2, p. 12)
>
> *   *   *   *   *
>
> The application of vague and elastic standards for wiretapping and bugging has resulted in electronic surveillances which, by any objective measure, were improper and seriously infringed the Fourth Amendment Rights of both the targets and those with whom the targets communicated. The inherently intrusive nature of electronic surveillance, moreover, has enabled the Government to generate vast amounts of information—unrelated to any legitimate government interest—about the personal and political lives of American citizens. The collection of this type of information has, in turn, raised the danger of its use for partisan political and other improper ends by senior administration officials. (vol. 3, p. 32.)

. . . S. 1566 is designed . . . to curb the practice by which the Executive Branch may conduct warrantless electronic surveillance on its own unilateral determination that national security justifies it. At the same time, however, this legislation does not prohibit the legitimate use of electronic surveillance to obtain foreign intelligence information. As the Church committee pointed out:

> Electronic surveillance techniques have understandably enabled these agencies to obtain valuable information relevant to their legitimate intelligence missions. Use of these techniques has provided the Government with vital intelligence, which would be difficult to acquire through other means, about the activities and intentions of foreign powers and has provided important leads in counter-espionage cases. (vol. 2, p. 274)

Safeguarding national security against the intelligence activities of foreign agents remains a vitally important Government purpose. Few would dispute the fact that we live in a dangerous world in which hostile intelligence activities in this country are still carried on to our detriment....

The committee believes that the Executive Branch of Government should have, under proper circumstances and with appropriate safeguards, authority to acquire important foreign intelligence information by means of electronic surveillance. The committee also believes that the past record and the state of the law in the area make it desirable that the Executive Branch not be the sole or final arbiter of when such proper circumstances exist. S. 1566 is designed to permit the Government to gather necessary foreign intelligence information by means of electronic surveillance but under limitations and according to procedural guidelines which will better safeguard the rights of individuals.

... Whether the President has so-called "inherent power" to engage in or authorize warrantless electronic surveillance and, if such power exists, what limitations, if any, restrict the scope of that power, are issues which have troubled constitutional scholars for decades. The history of warrantless electronic surveillance offers support to both proponents and critics of the concept of "inherent power" and clearly highlights the need for passage of S. 1566....

Since the *Keith* case [*United States v. United States District Court*, excerpted *supra*], three circuit courts of appeals have addressed the question the Supreme Court reserved [concerning the surveillance of foreign powers and their agents]. The Fifth Circuit in *United States v. Brown*, 484 F.2d 418 (5th Cir. 1973), cert. denied, 415 U.S. 960 (1974), upheld the legality of a surveillance in which the defendant, an American citizen, was incidentally overheard as a result of a warrantless wiretap authorized by the Attorney General for foreign intelligence purposes. The court found that on the basis of "the President's constitutional duty to act for the United States in the field of foreign affairs, and his inherent power to protect national security in the conduct of foreign affairs... the President may constitutionally authorize warrantless wiretaps for the purpose of gathering foreign intelligence."[25]

In *United States v. Butenko*, 494 F.2d 593 (3d Cir. 1974) (en banc), cert. denied *sub nom. Ivanov v. United States*, 419 U.S. 881 (1974), the Third Circuit similarly held that electronic surveillance conducted without a warrant would be lawful so long as the primary purpose was to obtain foreign intelligence information. The court found that such surveillance would be reasonable under the Fourth Amendment without a warrant even though it might involve the overhearing of conversations.

---

25. 484 F.2d at 426.

However, in *Zweibon v. Mitchell*, 516 F.2d 594 (D.C.Cir. 1975), cert. denied, 425 U.S. 944 (1976), the Circuit Court of Appeals for the District of Columbia, in the course of an opinion requiring that a warrant must be obtained before a wiretap is installed on a domestic organization that is neither the agent of, nor acting in collaboration with, a foreign power, questioned whether any national security exception to the warrant requirement would be constitutionally permissible.

Although the holding of *Zweibon* was limited to the case of a domestic organization without ties to a foreign power, the plurality opinion of the court—in legal analysis closely patterned on *Keith*—concluded "that an analysis of the policies implicated by foreign security surveillance indicates that, absent exigent circumstances, all warrantless electronic surveillance is unreasonable and therefore unconstitutional." . . .

S. 1566 would alter the current debate arising out of the uncertainty of the present law by completing an exclusive charter for the conduct of electronic surveillance in the United States. It would relegate to the past the wire-tapping abuses brought to light during the committee hearings by providing, for the first time, effective substantive and procedural statutory controls over foreign intelligence electronic surveillance.

The basis for this legislation is the understanding—concurred in by the Attorney General—that even if the President has an "inherent" constitutional power to authorize warrantless surveillance for foreign intelligence purposes, Congress has the power to regulate the exercise of this authority by legislating a reasonable warrant procedure governing foreign intelligence surveillance.

The bill provides external and internal checks on the executive. The external check is found in the judicial warrant procedure which requires the executive branch to secure a warrant before engaging in electronic surveillance for purposes of obtaining foreign intelligence information. Such surveillance would be limited to a "foreign power" and "agent of a foreign power." United States citizens and lawful resident aliens could be targets of electronic surveillance only if they are: (1) knowingly engaged in "clandestine intelligence activities which involve or will involve a violation" of the criminal law; (2) knowingly engaged in activities "that involve or will involve sabotage or terrorism for or on behalf of a foreign power"; or (3) "pursuant to the direction of an intelligence service or intelligence network of a foreign power" are knowingly or secretly collecting or transmitting foreign intelligence in a manner harmful to the security of the United States. All other persons—such as illegal aliens or foreign visitors—could also be targets if they are: (1) either officers or employees of a foreign power; or (2) are "knowingly engaging in clandestine intelligence activities for or on behalf of a foreign power under circumstances which indicate that such activities would be harmful to the security of the United States." For such surveillance to be undertaken, a judicial warrant must be secured on the basis of a showing of "probable cause" that the target is a "foreign power" or an "agent of a foreign power." Thus the courts for the first time will ultimately rule on whether such foreign intelligence surveillance should occur.

Before a warrant can be requested, a designated Executive Branch official must first certify in writing to the court that the information sought to be obtained is "foreign intelligence information" as defined, and that the purpose of the surveillance is to obtain such information. Moreover the Attorney General is required to make a finding that the requirements for a warrant application have been met before he authorizes the application. These provisions provide an internal check on applications for electronic surveillance by establishing a method of written accountability within the Executive Branch.

Other procedural safeguards assure that the Government will not engage in illegitimate eavesdropping or misuse of information so acquired. The bill requires that each order include a detailed procedure to minimize the extraneous or irrelevant information that might otherwise be obtained; information acquired concerning United States citizens or lawful resident aliens can be used and disclosed only for foreign intelligence purposes or in connection with the enforcement of the criminal law; even if the target is not a United States citizen or lawful resident alien information acquired can only be used for "lawful purposes"; detailed provisions safeguard the right of the criminal defendant to challenge the validity and propriety of the surveillance; if the target is an individual or specified types of foreign powers the application for a warrant must state the means by which the surveillance will be effected; when the target is an "official" foreign power, as defined, the application must still designate the type of electronic surveillance to be used and whether or not physical entry will be used to effect the surveillance; finally, the Attorney General is required to transmit to the Congress annually certain statistics concerning the surveillances engaged in during the preceding year.

Most importantly, the disclaimer in 18 U.S.C. § 2511 (3) is replaced by provisions that assure that this bill, together with chapter 119, will be the *exclusive* means by which electronic surveillance covered by this bill, and the interception of wire and oral communications, may be conducted.

A difficult issue posed during committee deliberations was whether foreign intelligence electronic surveillance should be limited to situations involving the commission of a crime.... This bill authorizes electronic surveillance in a limited number of noncriminal situations only under the twin safeguards of an independent review by a neutral judge and his application of a "probable cause standard."

It is important to note that the committee's favorable recommendation of this legislation in no way reflects any judgment that it would also be appropriate to depart from the standard of criminal activity as the basis for using other intrusive investigative techniques. The bill does not impliedly authorize departure from the standard of criminality in other aspects of national security investigations or intelligence collection directed at Americans without the safeguards of judicial review and probable cause. It remains to determine, in fashioning a charter for the use of informants, physical surveillance and other investigative procedures, whether the departure from a criminal standard is an acceptable basis for investigating United States citizens on grounds of national security....

---

1. Note the difficulty in prescribing precise substantive standards to guide the conduct of national security investigations. How does this difficulty affect the role of congressional oversight committees as a mechanism for assuring that intelligence agencies follow the law?

2. As noted in the report, FISA "does not provide authorization for the use of any technique other than electronic surveillance." Was the failure to cover physical searches of real and personal property a wise omission? What approach would Congress likely take today in considering a proposed charter to govern "the use of informants, physical surveillance and other investigative procedures?" Consider the next opinion—the only public opinion of the Foreign Intelligence Surveillance Court:

In the Matter of the Application of the United States for an Order Authorizing the Physical Search of Nonresidential Premises and Personal Property

Unnumbered Slip Opinion
(U. S. Foreign Intelligence Surveillance Court, Jun. 11, 1981).

Before HART, Presiding Judge.

The United States has applied for an order authorizing the physical search of certain real and personal property. I have decided that as a designated judge of the United States Foreign Intelligence Surveillance Court (FISC) I have no authority to issue such an order. I am authorized to state that the other designated judges of the FISC concur in this judgment.

The FISC was established by the Foreign Intelligence Surveillance Act (FISA), 92 Stat. 1783, 50 U.S.C. 1801. It consists (sec. 103(a)) of seven United States district court judges designated by the Chief Justice "who shall constitute a court which shall have jurisdiction to hear applications for and grant orders approving electronic surveillance anywhere within the United States under the procedures set forth in this Act." As an inferior court established by Congress pursuant to Article III of the Constitution, the FISC has only such jurisdiction as the FISA confers upon it and such ancillary authority as may fairly be implied from the powers expressly granted to it.

Obviously, the instant application implicates a question of the jurisdiction of the FISC under the terms of the FISA. Here, as in any case involving statutory interpretation, "...the meaning of the statute must, in the first instance, be sought in the language in which the act is framed, and if that is plain...the sole function of the courts is to enforce it according to its terms." *Caminetti v. United States*, 242 U.S. 470, 485 (1917). In my opinion, the language of the FISA clearly limits the authority of the judges designated to sit as judges of the FISC to the issuance of orders approving "electronic surveillance" as that term is defined in the act....

The reference throughout this subsection is to "electronic, mechanical or other surveillance device." The purpose is the "*acquisition*" of "*the contents*" of a wire or radio communication or monitoring (par. 4) to "*acquire information*, other than from a wire or radio communication." (Emphasis added.) Clearly, the thrust is a search, by the use of surveillance devices, for words or other sounds to acquire "foreign intelligence information" as that term is defined in sec. 101(e). There is not a word in the definitions of "electronic surveillance" even remotely indicating that the term encompasses a physical search of premises or other objects for tangible items.[2]

---

2. Paragraph (4) of sec. 101(f) provides for the "installation or use" of a surveillance device "for monitoring to acquire information." "This is intended to include the acquisition of oral communications." H. Rep. 95-1283, p. 52. By implication, it encompasses the means necessary to make an installation. This is made clear by the requirement that an application to a judge of the FISC state "whether physical entry is required to effect the surveillance" (sec. 104(a)(8)) and the provision that an order approving an electronic surveillance shall specify "whether physical entry will be used to effect the surveillance." Sec. 105(b)(1)(D). But all that is authorized is "physical entry." Such an authorization cannot be bootstrapped into authority to search entered premises for tangible items. The "search" in such a situation is limited to such observation of the premises as may be necessary to make an effective installation of the surveillance device.

The limiting terms of sec. 101(f) apply, of course, throughout the FISA. As noted above, FISC "shall have jurisdiction to hear applications for and grant orders approving electronic surveillance anywhere within the United States under the procedures set forth in this Act" (sec. 103(a)); an "application for an order approving electronic surveillance shall be made," etc. (sec. 104(a)); "the judge shall enter an ex parte order as requested or as modified approving the electronic surveillance if he finds," etc. (sec. 105(a)).

The legislative history of the FISA confirms what the statutory language so plainly teaches: the FISC has no jurisdiction in the area of physical searches. The committee reports deal specifically with the subjects of physical searches and the opening of mail; they make the same distinction between such searches and searches by electronic surveillance as is so clearly drawn in the very terms of the FISA. H. Rep. 95-1283 of the House Intelligence Committee puts the distinction sharply (p. 53):

> The committee does not intend the term "surveillance device" as used in paragraph (4) [of sec. 101(f)] to include devices which are used incidentally as part of a physical search, or the opening of mail, but which do not constitute a device for monitoring. Lock picks, still cameras, and similar devices can be used to acquire information, or to assist in the acquisition of information, by means of physical search. So-called chamfering devices can be used to open mail. This bill does not bring these activities within its purview. Although it may be desirable to develop legislative controls over physical search techniques, the committee has concluded that these practices are sufficiently different from electronic surveillance so as to require separate consideration by the Congress. The fact that the bill does not cover physical searches for intelligence purposes should not be viewed as congressional authorization for such activities. In any case, any requirements of the fourth amendment would, of course, continue to apply to this type of activity.

At the end of the paragraph the committee dropped a footnote stating: "It should be noted that Executive Order 12036, Jan. 24, 1978, places limits on physical searches and the opening of mail." That order (43 Fed. Reg. 3674, 3685) governs the conduct of physical searches without judicial warrant for foreign intelligence purposes pursuant to the constitutional authority of the President.

Thus, the clearly expressed view of the House Intelligence Committee was (1) that the FISA does not authorize physical searches or the opening of mail for foreign intelligence purposes and (2) that until Congress legislates in those areas, the executive branch is relegated to the President's inherent authority in such matters or the procedures of F. R. Cr. P. 41.

The same view was articulated by the Senate Intelligence Committee in its earlier S. Rep. 95-701, p. 38. The language there is virtually the same as the language of the House Intelligence Committee quoted above. In addition, the Senate committee referred to the bill S. 2525, 95th Cong., the National Intelligence Reorganization and Reform Act of 1978, which, it said, "addresses the problem of physical searches within the United States or directed against U.S. persons abroad for intelligence purposes."[3] In the same vein, the Senate Judiciary Committee said (S. Rep. 95-604, p. 6): "the

---

3. S. 2525 was a precursor of S. 2284, 96th Cong., the National Intelligence Act of 1980, discussed below.

bill does not provide statutory authorization for the use of any technique other than electronic surveillance...."

We have seen that Congress decided to consider separately the subject of physical searches, including the opening of mail. This subject was covered by S. 2284 in the last Congress. Since it would have amended and supplemented the FISA, it must be considered as part of the legislative materials bearing on our question.

Title VIII of S. 2284, entitled, "Physical Searches Within the United States" (Cong. Rec., daily ed., Feb. 8, 1980, pp. S1325 - S1327), was the vehicle for the promised separate consideration of that subject. The section-by-section analysis stated that the "court order procedures of the [FISA] are extended to 'physical search,' defined as any search of property located in the United States and any opening of mail in the United States or in the U.S. postal channels, under circumstances in which a person has a reasonable expectation of privacy and a warrant would be required for law enforcement purposes." Id., p. S1333. In a statement joining in the introduction of S. 2284 (id., p. S1334), then chairman Bayh of the Intelligence Committee said (id., p. S1335):

> ... But perhaps the best way to bring overseas surveillance and search powers under the rule of law and within the constitutional system of checks and balances is through this Act. We must carefully consider these issues in the weeks to come.
>
> The same is true for the provisions that bring physical search in the United States within the framework of the Foreign Intelligence Surveillance Act of 1978. Current restrictions on physical search under the Executive order procedures are very stringent. Thus, the charter could result in the lifting of certain limitations. However, without the requirement in law to obtain a court order under a criminal standard for searches of Americans in this country, a future administration could abandon the Executive order procedures and assert "inherent power" to search the homes and offices of citizens without effective checks.

Title VIII contained 57 amendments of the FISA, beginning with the insertion of the words, "physical searches and" in the statement of purpose, so as to read, "To authorize physical searches and electronic surveillance to obtain foreign intelligence information," and changing the title of the Act to "Foreign Intelligence Search and Surveillance Act." Id., p. S1325. The other amendments would have added similar appropriate language to nearly every section of the FISA.

The foregoing review of the language of the FISA and the reports of the three committees which gave the legislation exhaustive consideration demonstrates that the FISC has no jurisdiction to authorize physical searches or the opening of mail. This conclusion is buttressed by the fact that Congress subsequently gave active consideration to the deferred question whether the FISA should be amended to extend the procedures of the Act to cover physical searches. That question has not yet been resolved by amending or other legislation.

In view of the clearly expressed intent of Congress to withhold authority to issue orders approving physical searches, it would be idle to consider whether a judge of the FISC nevertheless has some implied or inherent authority to do so. Obviously, where a given authority is denied it cannot be supplied by resort to principles of inherent, implied or ancillary jurisdiction.

1. Are you persuaded by Judge Hart's reasoning? Why would it be "idle" to speculate as to inherent judicial power to approve warrants for physical searches? Is abandonment of a judicial check wise?

2. Could the executive branch seek a warrant for a physical search from an ordinary U.S. district court, citing *Debs*? If so, must it do so? If not, what should the executive branch conclude about its authority to conduct warrantless physical searches for foreign intelligence purposes?

3. May Congress deny the President all authority to conduct surveillance for non-criminally-related national security matters? What about authority for "black bag jobs?" Any investigations at all?

Chapter 6
The President and Foreign Policy

After an initial, broad look at the theory of separation of powers, we have now considered a variety of presidential powers and functions in the domestic context. It remains to be considered whether the insights we have thus far developed apply to the President's functions in dealing with other nations.

Several of his constitutionally specified functions imply that the President must have a crucial role in our foreign affairs. He is designated Commander in Chief of the Army and Navy, empowered to make treaties (with the concurrence of the Senate), and to appoint and to receive ambassadors and other public ministers. As with the President's domestic powers, however, the import and scope of foreign affairs functions are not delimited by the constitutional text alone. For example, the unadorned constitutional text does not clearly signal whether the President alone may recognize the government of another nation; yet early precedent and subsequent history have ratified this interpretation of article II.

For purposes of our examination, we have separated the President's non-military foreign affairs functions, which are considered in this chapter, from his military functions—both foreign and domestic—which are considered in the next. Section A looks broadly at separation of powers in foreign policy-making. Sections B and C consider the President's powers respecting agreements with other nations. Section D considers further how the legislative process and the delegation of particular functions to administrative agencies may shape and limit the President's role in foreign affairs. The final section considers the government's "monopoly" on foreign policy-making, and its implications for individual rights.

The President's role in foreign affairs can be appreciated most fully in the context of international law and legal processes, subjects which cannot be treated comprehensively in this book. Readers seeking additional background can usefully consult L. Henkin, Foreign Affairs and the Constitution (1972); H. Steiner and D. Vagts, Transnational Legal Problems (2d ed. 1976); and T. Franck and M. Glennon, Foreign Relations and National Security Law (1987).

A. Analytic Framework: the President's Role in Foreign Affairs

The following case, *United States v. Curtiss-Wright Corp.*, was decided within two years of *Panama Refining Co. v. Ryan*, 293 U.S. 388 (1935), and *Schechter Poultry Corp. v. United States*, 295 U.S. 495 (1935), the only two Supreme Court decisions ever to overturn federal statutes as overbroad delegations of legislative authority to the federal executive branch. Because of those earlier decisions, the delegation question presented in *Curtiss-Wright* loomed as a serious issue; today, in light of the cases reviewed in Chapter Two, it would not. Although much of Justice Sutherland's discourse on the President's foreign affairs powers thus today appears to be dictum, it merits close analysis because, for reasons that will become apparent, the opinion is a favorite among executive branch lawyers. Why would the Court be so much more supportive here than in the context of domestic regulation of broad delegations of policymaking power?

United States v. Curtiss-Wright Corp.
299 U.S. 304 (1936)

Justice SUTHERLAND delivered the opinion of the Court.

. . . [A]n indictment was returned in the court below, the first count of which charges that appellees . . . conspired to sell in the United States certain arms of war, namely fifteen machine guns, to Bolivia, a country then engaged in armed conflict in the Chaco, in violation of the Joint Resolution of Congress approved May 28, 1934, and the provisions of a proclamation issued on the same day by the President of the United States pursuant to authority conferred by § 1 of the resolution. . . . The Joint Resolution (c. 365, 48 Stat. 811) follows:

> " . . . [I]f the President finds that the prohibition of the sale of arms and munitions of war in the United States to those countries now engaged in armed conflict in the Chaco may contribute to the reëstablishment of peace between those countries, and if after consultation with the governments of other American Republics and with their coöperation, as well as that of such other governments as he may deem necessary, he makes proclamation to that effect, it shall be unlawful to sell, except under such limitations and exceptions as the President prescribes, any arms or munitions of war in any place in the United States to the countries now engaged in that armed conflict . . . until otherwise ordered by the President or by Congress.
>
> "Sec. 2. Whoever sells any arms or munitions of war in violation of section 1 shall, on conviction, be punished by a fine not exceeding $10,000 or by imprisonment not exceeding two years, or both."

The President's proclamation (48 Stat. 1744), after reciting the terms of the Joint Resolution, declares:

> "Now, therefore, I, Franklin D. Roosevelt, President of the United States of America, acting under and by virtue of the authority conferred in me by the said joint resolution of Congress, do hereby declare and proclaim that I have found that the prohibition of the sale of arms and munitions of war in the United States to those countries now engaged in armed conflict in the Chaco may contribute to the reëstablishment of peace between those countries, and that I have consulted with the governments of other American Republics . . . ; and I do hereby admonish all citizens of the United States and every person to abstain from every violation of the provisions of the joint resolution. . . . [The President delegated to the Secretary of State his power to prescribe exceptions and limitations to the application of the joint resolution.]

Appellees severally demurred to the first count of the indictment on the grounds ... first, that the joint resolution effects an invalid delegation of legislative power to the executive; second, that the joint resolution never became effective because of the failure of the President to find essential jurisdictional facts;....

The court below sustained the demurrers.... The government appealed to this court [under a statute authorizing a direct government appeal in any criminal case in which a court invalidates the statute on which an indictment was founded.]

First. It is contended that by the Joint Resolution, the going into effect and continued operation of the resolution was conditioned (a) upon the President's judgment as to its beneficial effect upon the reestablishment of peace between the countries engaged in armed conflict in the Chaco; (b) upon the making of a proclamation, which was left to his unfettered discretion, thus constituting an attempted substitution of the President's will for that of Congress; (c) upon the making of a proclamation putting an end to the operation of the resolution, which again was left to the President's unfettered discretion; and (d) further, that the extent of its operation in particular cases was subject to limitation and exception by the President, controlled by no standard. In each of these particulars, appellees urge that Congress abdicated its essential functions and delegated them to the Executive.

Whether, if the Joint Resolution had related solely to internal affairs it would be open to the challenge that it constituted an unlawful delegation of legislative power to the Executive, we find it unnecessary to determine. The whole aim of the resolution is to affect a situation entirely external to the United States, and falling within the category of foreign affairs.... In other words, assuming (but not deciding) that the challenged delegation, if it were confined to internal affairs, would be invalid, [the question this Court faces is] may it nevertheless be sustained on the ground that its exclusive aim is to afford a remedy for a hurtful condition within foreign territory?

It will contribute to the elucidation of the question if we first consider the differences between the powers of the federal government in respect of foreign or external affairs and those in respect of domestic or internal affairs....

The two classes of powers are different, both in respect of their origin and their nature. The broad statement that the federal government can exercise no powers except those specifically enumerated in the Constitution, and such implied powers as are necessary and proper to carry into effect the enumerated powers, is categorically true only in respect of our internal affairs. In that field, the primary purpose of the Constitution was to carve from the general mass of legislative powers *then possessed by the states* such portions as it was thought desirable to vest in the federal government, leaving those not included in the enumeration still in the states. That this doctrine applies only to powers which the states had, is self evident. And since the states severally never possessed international powers, such powers could not have been carved from the mass of state powers but obviously were transmitted to the United States from some other source. During the colonial period, those powers were possessed exclusively by and were entirely under the control of the Crown. By the Declaration of Independence, "the Representatives of the United States of America" declared the United [not the several] Colonies to be free and independent states, and as such to have "full Power to levy War, conclude Peace, contract Alliances, establish Commerce and to do all other Acts and Things which Independent States may of right do."

As a result of the separation from Great Britain by the colonies acting as a unit, the powers of external sovereignty passed from the Crown not to the colonies severally, but to the colonies in their collective and corporate capacity as the United States of America. Even before the Declaration, the colonies were a unit in foreign affairs, acting through a common agency—namely the Continental Congress, composed of delegates from the thirteen colonies. That agency exercised the powers of war and peace, raised an army, created a navy, and finally adopted the Declaration of Independence. Rulers come and go; governments end and forms of government change; but sovereignty survives. A political society cannot endure without a supreme will somewhere. Sovereignty is never held in suspense. When, therefore, the external sovereignty of Great Britain in respect of the colonies ceased, it immediately passed to the Union. That fact was given practical application almost at once....

The Union existed before the Constitution, which was ordained and established among other things to form "a more perfect Union." Prior to that event, it is clear that the Union, declared by the Articles of Confederation to be "perpetual," was the sole possessor of external sovereignty and in the Union it remained without change save in so far as the Constitution in express terms qualified its exercise. The Framers' Convention was called and exerted its powers upon the irrefutable postulate that though the states were several their people in respect of foreign affairs were one. Compare *The Chinese Exclusion Case*, 130 U.S. 581, 604, 606. In that convention, the entire absence of state power to deal with those affairs was thus forcefully stated by Rufus King:

> "The states were not 'sovereigns' in the sense contended for by some. They did not possess the peculiar features of sovereignty,—they could not make war, nor peace, nor alliances, nor treaties. Considering them as political beings, they were dumb, for they could not speak to any foreign sovereign whatever. They were deaf, for they could not hear any propositions from such sovereign. They had not even the organs or faculties of defence or offence, for they could not of themselves raise troops, or equip vessels, for war." 5 Elliott's Debates 212.[1]

It results that the investment of the federal government with the powers of external sovereignty did not depend upon the affirmative grants of the Constitution. The powers to declare and wage war, to conclude peace, to make treaties, to maintain diplomatic relations with other sovereignties, if they had never been mentioned in the Constitution, would have vested in the federal government as necessary concomitants of nationality. Neither the Constitution nor the laws passed in pursuance of it have any force in foreign territory unless in respect of our own citizens; and operations of the nation in such territory must be governed by treaties, international understandings and compacts, and the principles of international law. As a member of the family of nations, the right and power of the United States ... are equal to the right and power of the other members of the international family. Otherwise, the United States is not completely sovereign. The power to acquire territory by discovery and occupation (*Jones v. United States*, 137 U.S. 202, 212), the power to expel undesirable aliens (*Fong Yue Ting v. United States*, 149 U.S. 698, 705 *et seq.*), the power to make such international agreements as do not constitute treaties in the constitutional sense, none of which is expressly affirmed by the Constitution, nevertheless exist as inherently

---

1. In general confirmation of the foregoing views, see 1 Story on the Constitution, 4th ed., §§ 198-217, and especially §§ 210, 211, 213, 214, 215 (p. 153), 216.

inseparable from the conception of nationality. This the court recognized, and in each of the cases cited found the warrant for its conclusions not in the provisions of the Constitution, but in the law of nations.

Not only, as we have shown, is the federal power over external affairs in origin and essential character different from that over internal affairs, but participation in the exercise of the power is significantly limited. In this vast external realm, with its important, complicated, delicate and manifold problems, the President alone has the power to speak or listen as a representative of the nation. He *makes* treaties with the advice and consent of the Senate; but he alone negotiates. Into the field of negotiation the Senate cannot intrude; and Congress itself is powerless to invade it. As Marshall said in his great argument of March 7, 1800, in the House of Representatives, "The President is the sole organ of the nation in its external relations, and its sole representative with foreign nations." Annals, 6th Cong., col. 613. The Senate Committee on Foreign Relations at a very early day in our history (February 15, 1816), reported to the Senate, among other things, as follows:

> "The President is the constitutional representative of the United States with regard to foreign nations. He manages our concerns with foreign nations and must necessarily be most competent to determine when, how, and upon what subjects negotiation may be urged with the greatest prospect of success. For his conduct he is responsible to the Constitution. The committee consider this responsibility the surest pledge for the faithful discharge of his duty. They think the interference of the Senate in the direction of foreign negotiations calculated to diminish that responsibility and thereby to impair the best security for the national safety. The nature of transactions with foreign nations, moreover, requires caution and unity of design, and their success frequently depends on secrecy and dispatch."

U.S. Senate, Reports, Committee on Foreign Relations, vol. 8, p. 24.

It is important to bear in mind that we are here dealing not alone with an authority vested in the President by an exertion of legislative power, but with such an authority plus the very delicate, plenary and exclusive power of the President as the sole organ of the federal government in the field of international relations—a power which does not require as a basis for its exercise an act of Congress, but which, of course, like every other governmental power, must be exercised in subordination to the applicable provisions of the Constitution. It is quite apparent that if, in the maintenance of our international relations, embarrassment—perhaps serious embarrassment—is to be avoided and success for our aims achieved, congressional legislation which is to be made effective through negotiation and inquiry within the international field must often accord to the President a degree of discretion and freedom from statutory restriction which would not be admissible were domestic affairs alone involved. Moreover, he, not Congress, has the better opportunity of knowing the conditions which prevail in foreign countries, and especially is this true in time of war. He has his confidential sources of information. He has his agents in the form of diplomatic, consular and other officials. Secrecy in respect of information gathered by them may be highly necessary, and the premature disclosure of it productive of harmful results. Indeed, so clearly is this true that the first President refused to accede to a request to lay before the House of Representatives the instructions, correspondence and documents relating to the negotiation of the Jay Treaty—a refusal the wisdom of which was recognized by the House itself and has never since been doubted. In his reply to the request, President Washington said:

> "The nature of foreign negotiations requires caution, and their success must often depend on secrecy; and even when brought to a conclusion a full disclosure of all the measures, demands, or eventual concessions which may have been proposed or contemplated would be extremely impolitic; for this might have a pernicious influence on future negotiations, or produce immediate inconveniences, perhaps danger and mischief, in relation to other powers. The necessity of such caution and secrecy was one cogent reason for vesting the power of making treaties in the President, with the advice and consent of the Senate, the principle on which that body was formed confining it to a small number of members. To admit, then, a right in the House of Representatives to demand and to have as a matter of course all the papers respecting a negotiation with a foreign power would be to establish a dangerous precedent."

1 Messages and Papers of the Presidents, p. 194....

When the President is to be authorized by legislation to act in respect of a matter intended to affect a situation in foreign territory, the legislator properly bears in mind the important consideration that the form of the President's action—or, indeed, whether he shall act at all—may well depend, among other things, upon the nature of the confidential information which he has or may thereafter receive, or upon the effect which his action may have upon our foreign relations. This consideration, in connection with what we have already said on the subject, discloses the unwisdom of requiring Congress in this field of governmental power to lay down narrowly definite standards by which the President is governed....

In the light of the foregoing observations, it is evident that this court should not be in haste to apply a general rule which will have the effect of condemning legislation like that under review as constituting an unlawful delegation of legislative power. The principles which justify such legislation find overwhelming support in the unbroken legislative practice which has prevailed almost from the inception of the national government to the present day....

Practically every volume of the United States Statutes contains one or more acts or joint resolutions of Congress authorizing action by the President in respect of subjects affecting foreign relations, which either leave the exercise of the power to his unrestricted judgment, or provide a standard far more general than that which has always been considered requisite with regard to domestic affairs....

We had occasion to review these embargo and kindred acts in connection with an exhaustive discussion of the general subject of delegation of legislative power in a recent case, *Panama Refining Co. v. Ryan*, 293 U.S. 388, 421-422, and in justifying such acts, pointed out that they confided to the President "an authority which was cognate to the conduct by him of the foreign relations of the government."

The result of holding that the joint resolution here under attack is void and unenforceable as constituting an unlawful delegation of legislative power would be to stamp this multitude of comparable acts and resolutions as likewise invalid. And while this court may not, and should not, hesitate to declare acts of Congress, however many times repeated, to be unconstitutional if beyond all rational doubt it finds them to be so, an impressive array of legislation such as we have just set forth, enacted by nearly every Congress from the beginning of our national existence to the present day, must be given unusual weight in the process of reaching a correct determination of the problem. . . .

The uniform, long-continued and undisputed legislative practice just disclosed rests upon an admissible view of the Constitution which, even if the practice found far less support in principle than we think it does, we should not feel at liberty at this late day to disturb.

We deem it unnecessary to consider, *seriatim*, the several clauses which are said to evidence the unconstitutionality of the Joint Resolution as involving an unlawful delegation of legislative power. It is enough to summarize by saying that, both upon principle and in accordance with precedent, we conclude there is sufficient warrant for the broad discretion vested in the President to determine whether the enforcement of the statute will have a beneficial effect upon the reestablishment of peace in the affected countries; whether he shall make proclamation to bring the resolution into operation; whether and when the resolution shall cease to operate and to make proclamation accordingly; and to prescribe limitations and exceptions to which the enforcement of the resolution shall be subject. . . .

The judgment of the court below must be reversed and the cause remanded for further proceedings in accordance with the foregoing opinion.

Reversed.

Justice McREYNOLDS does not agree. He is of opinion that the court below reached the right conclusion and its judgment ought to be affirmed.

Justice STONE took no part in the consideration or decision of this case.

Chicago & Southern Airlines, Inc. v. Waterman Steamship Corp.
333 U.S. 103 (1948)

JUSTICE JACKSON delivered the opinion of the Court.

The question of law which brings this controversy here is whether § 1006 of the Civil Aeronautics Act, 49 U.S.C. § 646, authorizing judicial review of described orders of the Civil Aeronautics Board, includes those which grant or deny applications by citizen carriers to engage in overseas and foreign air transportation which are subject to approval by the President under § 801 of the Act.

By proceedings not challenged as to regularity, the Board, with express approval of the President, issued an order which denied Waterman Steamship Corporation a certificate of convenience and necessity for an [overseas and foreign] air route and granted one to Chicago & Southern Air Lines, a rival applicant. . . . Waterman filed a petition for review under § 1006 of the Act with the Circuit Court of Appeals for the Fifth Circuit. Chicago & Southern intervened. Both the latter and the Board moved to dismiss, the grounds pertinent here being that because the order required and had approval of the President, under § 801 of the Act, it was not reviewable. The Court of Appeals disclaimed any power to question or review either the President's approval or his disapproval, but it regarded any Board order as incomplete until court review, after which "the completed action must be approved by the President as to citizen air carriers in cases under Sec. 801." . . .

Congress has set up a comprehensive scheme for regulation of common carriers by air. . . . All air carriers by similar procedures must obtain from the Board certificates of convenience and necessity by showing a public interest in establishment of the route and the applicant's ability to serve it. But when a foreign carrier asks for any permit, or a citizen carrier applies for a certificate to engage in any overseas or foreign air transportation, a copy of the application must be transmitted to the President before hearing; and any decision, either to grant or to deny, must be submitted to the President before publication and is unconditionally subject to the President's approval. Also the statute subjects to judicial review "any order, affirmative or negative, issued by the Board under this Act, except any order in respect to any foreign air carrier subject to the approval of the President as provided in section 801 of this Act." It grants no express exemption to an order such as the one before us, which concerns a citizen carrier but which must have Presidential approval because it involves overseas and foreign air transportation. The question is whether an exemption is to be implied. . . . [W]e do not subject to judicial control orders which, from their nature, from the context of the Act, or from the relation of judicial power to the subject-matter, are inappropriate for review.

The Waterman Steamship Corporation urges that review of the problems involved in establishing foreign air routes are of no more international delicacy or strategic importance than those involved in routes for water carriage. . . . From this premise it reasons that we should interpret this statute to follow the pattern of judicial review adopted in relation to orders affecting foreign commerce by rail, or communications by wire, or by radio; and it likens the subject-matter of aeronautics legislation to that of Title VI of the Merchant Marine Act of 1936, 46 U.S.C. § 1171, and the function of the Aeronautics Board in respect to overseas and foreign air transportation to that of the Maritime Commission to such commerce when water-borne.

We find no indication that the Congress either entertained or fostered the narrow concept that air-borne commerce is a mere outgrowth or overgrowth of surface-bound transport. Of course, air transportation, water transportation, rail transportation, and motor transportation all have a kinship in that all are forms of transportation and their common features of public carriage for hire may be amenable to kindred regulations. But these resemblances must not blind us to the fact that legally, as well as literally, air commerce, whether at home or abroad, soared into a different realm than any that had gone before. . . . A way of travel which quickly escapes the bounds of local regulative competence called for a more penetrating, uniform and exclusive regulation by the nation than had been thought appropriate for the more easily controlled commerce of the past. . . . However useful parallels with older forms of transit may be in adjudicating private rights, we see no reason why the efforts of the Congress to foster and regulate development of a revolutionary commerce that operates in three dimensions should be judicially circumscribed with analogies taken over from two-dimensional transit.

The "public interest" that enters into awards of routes for aerial carriers, who in effect obtain also a sponsorship by our government in foreign ventures, is not confined to adequacy of transportation service, as we have held when that term is applied to railroads. That aerial navigation routes and bases should be prudently correlated with facilities and plans for our own national defenses and raise new problems in conduct of foreign relations, is a fact of common knowledge. . . .

In the regulation of commercial aeronautics, the statute confers on the Board many powers conventional in other carrier regulation under the Congressional commerce power. They are exercised through usual procedures and apply settled standards with only customary administrative finality.... Those orders which do not require Presidential approval are subject to judicial review to assure application of the standards Congress has laid down.

But when a foreign carrier seeks to engage in public carriage over the territory or waters of this country, or any carrier seeks the sponsorship of this Government to engage in overseas or foreign air transportation, Congress has completely inverted the usual administrative process. Instead of acting independently of executive control, the agency is then subordinated to it. Instead of its order serving as a final disposition of the application, its force is exhausted when it serves as a recommendation to the President.... Nor is the President's control of the ultimate decision a mere right of veto. It is not alone issuance of such authorizations that are subject to his approval, but denial, transfer, amendment, cancellation or suspension, as well. And likewise subject to his approval are the terms, conditions and limitations of the order. Thus, Presidential control is not limited to a negative but is a positive and detailed control over the Board's decisions, unparalleled in the history of American administrative bodies.

Congress may of course delegate very large grants of its power over foreign commerce to the President. The President also possesses in his own right certain powers conferred by the Constitution on him as Commander-in-Chief and as the Nation's organ in foreign affairs. For present purposes, the order draws vitality from either or both sources. Legislative and Executive powers are pooled obviously to the end that commercial strategic and diplomatic interests of the country may be coordinated and advanced without collision or deadlock between agencies.

These considerations seem controlling on the question whether the Board's action on overseas and foreign air transportation applications by citizens are subject to revision or overthrow by the courts.

It may be conceded that a literal reading of § 1006 subjects this order to re-examination by the courts. It also appears that the language was deliberately employed by Congress, although nothing indicates that Congress foresaw or intended the consequences ascribed to it by the decision of the Court below. The letter of the text might with equal consistency be construed to require any one of three things: first, judicial review of a decision by the President; second, judicial review of a Board order before it acquires finality through Presidential action, the court's decision on review being a binding limitation on the President's action; third, a judicial review before action by the President, the latter being at liberty wholly to disregard the court's judgment. We think none of these results is required by usual canons of construction.

In this case, submission of the Board's decision was made to the President, who disapproved certain portions of it and advised the Board of the changes which he required. The Board complied and submitted a revised order and opinion which the President approved. Only then were they made public, and that which was made public and which is before us is only the final order and opinion containing the President's amendments and bearing his approval....

While the changes made at direction of the President may be identified, the reasons therefor are not disclosed beyond the statement that "because of certain factors relating to our broad national welfare and other matters for which the Chief Executive has special responsibility, he has reached conclusions which require" changes in the Board's opinion.

The court below considered, and we think quite rightly, that it could not review such provisions of the order as resulted from Presidential direction. The President, both as Commander-in-Chief and as the Nation's organ for foreign affairs, has available intelligence services whose reports are not and ought not to be published to the world. It would be intolerable that courts, without the relevant information, should review and perhaps nullify actions of the Executive taken on information properly held secret. Nor can courts sit *in camera* in order to be taken into executive confidences. But even if courts could require full disclosure, the very nature of executive decisions as to foreign policy is political, not judicial. Such decisions are wholly confided by our Constitution to the political departments of the government, Executive and Legislative. They are delicate, complex, and involve large elements of prophecy. They are and should be undertaken only by those directly responsible to the people whose welfare they advance or imperil. They are decisions of a kind for which the Judiciary has neither aptitude, facilities nor responsibility and which has long been held to belong in the domain of political power not subject to judicial intrusion or inquiry. We therefore agree that whatever of this order emanates from the President is not susceptible of review by the Judicial Department.

The court below thought that this disability could be overcome by regarding the Board as a regulatory agent of Congress to pass on such matters as the fitness, willingness and ability of the applicant, and that the Board's own determination of these matters is subject to review.... The legal incongruity of interposing judicial review between the action by the Board and that by the President are as great as the practical disadvantages. The latter arise chiefly from the inevitable delay and obstruction in the midst of the administrative proceedings. The former arises from the fact that until the President acts there is no final administrative determination to review. The statute would hardly have forbidden publication before submission if it had contemplated interposition of the courts at this intermediate stage. Nor could it have expected the courts to stay the President's hand after submission while they deliberate on the inchoate determination. The difficulty is manifest in this case. Review could not be sought until the order was made available, and at that time it had ceased to be merely the Board's tentative decision and had become one finalized by Presidential discretion.

Until the decision of the Board has Presidential approval, it grants no privilege and denies no right.... The dilemma faced by those who demand judicial review of the Board's order is that before Presidential approval it is not a final determination even of the Board's ultimate action, and after Presidential approval the whole order, both in what is approved without change as well as in amendments which he directs, derives its vitality from the exercise of unreviewable Presidential discretion.

The court below considered that after it reviewed the Board's order its judgment would be submitted to the President, that his power to disapprove would apply after as well as before the court acts, and hence that there would be no chance of a deadlock and no conflict of function. But if the President may completely disregard the judgment of the court, it would be only because it is one the courts were not authorized to render. Judgments within the powers vested in courts by the Judiciary Article of the

Constitution may not lawfully be revised, overturned or refused faith and credit by another Department of Government.

To revise or review an administrative decision which has only the force of a recommendation to the President would be to render an advisory opinion in its most obnoxious form—advice that the President has not asked, tendered at the demand of a private litigant, on a subject concededly within the President's exclusive, ultimate control....

We conclude that orders of the Board as to certificates for overseas or foreign air transportation are not mature and are therefore not susceptible of judicial review at any time before they are finalized by Presidential approval. After such approval has been given, the final orders embody Presidential discretion as to political matters beyond the competence of the courts to adjudicate. This makes it unnecessary to examine the other questions raised....

Judgment reversed.

Justice DOUGLAS, with whom Justice BLACK, Justice REED and Justice RUTLEDGE concur, dissenting.

Congress has specifically provided for judicial review of orders of the Civil Aeronautics Board of the kind involved in this case. That review can be had without intruding on the exclusive domain of the Chief Executive. And by granting it we give effect to the interests of both the Congress and the Chief Executive in this field.

The Commerce Clause of the Constitution grants Congress control over interstate and foreign commerce. Art. I, § 8. The present Act is an exercise of that power. Congress...expressly made subject to judicial review orders of the Board granting or denying certificates to citizens and withheld judicial review where the applicants are not citizens....

But Congress did not leave the matter entirely to the Board. Recognizing the important role the President plays in military and foreign affairs, it made him a participant in the process.... Since his decisions in these matters are of a character which involves an exercise of his discretion in foreign affairs or military matters, I do not think Congress intended them to be subject to judicial review.

But review of the President's action does not result from reading the statute in the way it is written. Congress made reviewable by the courts only orders "issued by the Board under this Act." Those orders can be reviewed without reference to any conduct of the President, for that part of the orders which is the work of the Board is plainly identifiable. The President is presumably concerned only with the impact of the order on foreign relations or military matters. To the extent that he disapproves action taken by the Board, his action controls. But where that is not done, the Board's order has an existence independent of Presidential approval, tracing to Congress' power to regulate commerce. Approval by the President under this statutory scheme has relevance for purposes of review only as indicating *when* the action of the Board is reviewable. When the Board has finished with the order, the administrative function is ended. When the order fixes rights, on clearance by the President, it becomes reviewable. But the action of the President does not broaden the review. Review is restricted to the action of the Board and the Board alone.

The statute, as I construe it, contemplates that certificates issued will rest on orders of the Board which satisfy the standards prescribed by Congress. Presidential approval cannot make valid invalid orders of the Board. His approval supplements rather than supercedes Board action. Only when the Board has acted within the limits of its authority has the basis been laid for issuance of certificates. The requirement that a valid Board order underlie each certificate thus protects the President as well as the litigants and the public interest against unlawful Board action. . . .

In this petition for review, the respondent charged that the Board has no substantial evidence to support its findings that Chicago & Southern Air Lines was fit, willing and able to perform its obligations under the certificate; and it charged that when a change of conditions as to Chicago & Southern Air Lines' ability to perform was called to the attention of the Board, the Board refused to reopen the case. I do not know whether there is merit in those contentions. But no matter how substantial and important the questions, they are now beyond judicial review. Today a litigant tenders questions concerning the arbitrary character of the Board's rulings. Tomorrow those questions may relate to the right to notice, adequacy of hearings, or the lack of procedural due process of law. But no matter how extreme the action of the Board, the courts are powerless to correct it under today's decision. Thus the purpose of Congress is frustrated. . . .

---

1. *Curtiss-Wright* gave Justice Sutherland the opportunity to propound as law a theory of U.S. foreign relations powers he first put forth as a Senator. Sutherland, The Internal and External Powers of the National Government, S. Doc. No. 417, 61st Cong., 2d Sess. (1910); G. Sutherland, Constitutional Power and World Affairs (1919). For further background on *Curtiss-Wright*, see Lofgren, United States v. Curtiss-Wright Export Corporation: *An Historical Reassessment*, 83 Yale L. J. 1 (1973).

2. Sutherland argues in *Curtiss-Wright* that the government's foreign affairs powers derive not from the states, but from the nature of national sovereignty. (His argument that sovereignty never rested in state governments is forcefully challenged in Levitan, *The Foreign Relations Power: An Analysis of Mr. Sutherland's Theory*, 55 Yale L. J. 467 (1946).) Would it follow, even if Sutherland is correct, that the executive branch is the sole repository of those sovereign powers? Sutherland notes that, in some respects, the Constitution limits Congress' participation in foreign affairs decision-making. Congress' enumerated powers, however, include several with undeniable foreign affairs implications. How far, therefore, is Congress limited in its regulation of the President in his capacity as "sole organ of the federal government in the field of international relations?" If Congress, under its foreign trade power, prohibits strategic U.S. military goods from being sold to a country the President now wishes to befriend, would he have constitutional power to disregard the legislative prohibition? (See section D-1 of this chapter, below.) How critical to the persuasiveness of Sutherland's legal views is the correctness of his history?

3. Despite Justice Sutherland's description of the President as "the sole organ of the federal government in the field of international relations," Congress is not always reluctant to "get into the act." A nightmarish (but not wholly unprecedented) example, from the executive point of view, occurred during October, 1987, when the Senate, in four days, voted 86 floor amendments to the State Department authorization bill, many of them controversial, all affecting foreign affairs. Among the controversial amendments adopted without hearings or more than a few minutes' debate were a cancellation of two U.S.-Soviet embassy site agreements, the imposition of travel restrictions on Communist diplomats, and a ban on the PLO office in New York, notwithstanding the provisions of the United Nations Headquarters agreement pro-

tecting that office. Oberdorfer and Dewar, *The Capitol Hill Broth Is Being Seasoned By a Lot of Cooks: The Senate makes 'sausage' of the State Department*, Wash. Post Weekly Edition, Oct. 26, 1987, at 12. Yet another recent controversial example of congressional initiative was the involvement of House Speaker Jim Wright in November, 1987, in attempting to facilitate peace talks between the competing forces in Nicaragua. Felton, *Nicaragua Peace Process Moves to Capitol Hill*, 45 Cong. Q. 2789 (1987). As you review the materials in this chapter, consider both the scope of Congress' formal powers to legislate with respect to foreign affairs and the potential for conflict through informal congressional participation in foreign relations. Is the current set of institutional relationships and legal understandings between Congress and the President sufficient to facilitate the development of coherent foreign policy? Are helpful reforms possible? *See generally* Christopher, *Ceasefire Between the Branches: A Compact in Foreign Affairs*, 60 Foreign Affairs 989 (1982).

4. May Congress vest regulatory authority with the potential to affect our foreign relations in an official subordinate to the President, and legislatively proscribe presidential supervision of that authority? Consider the material in section D-2 of this chapter on foreign policy and administrative agencies.

5. The executive branch typically cites references in *Curtiss-Wright* to the delicacy of foreign policy and a concern for secrecy in its implementation to buttress claims of inherent presidential authority to protect national security. For critical assessments of such claims, see Edgar and Schmidt, Curtiss-Wright *Comes Home: Executive Power and National Security Secrecy*, 21 Harv. C.R.-C.L. L. Rev. 349 (1986); Paust, *Is the President Bound by the Supreme Law of the Land?—Foreign Affairs and National Security Reexamined*, 9 Hastings Const. L. Q. 719 (1982).

6. Putting aside Justice Jackson's strangely infelicitous (and geometrically unsound) discussion of the "two-dimensionality" of rail, water, and motor transportation, why, in *Waterman Steamship*, is the Court precluded from reviewing the CAB's order to determine its conformity with legislative authorization? Does the President possess constitutional power to grant or deny certificates of convenience or necessity for air routes? If not, why did his approval of such a grant or denial by the CAB make the order unreviewable? Did the Act provide that any CAB decision shall be deemed lawful, if, in his unreviewable discretion, the President agrees with that decision? Could the President legalize an otherwise unlawful decision by the CAB by deciding it accorded with our foreign policy interests? *See Rainbow Navigation, Inc. v. Department of the Navy*, 620 F.Supp. 534 (D.D.C. 1985), *aff'd*, 783 F.2d 1072 (D.C. Cir. 1986) (Secretary of the Navy could not, on foreign affairs grounds, prefer Icelandic vessels to U.S. shipper for military supplies when Congress precluded foreign affairs criteria from influencing preference for U.S. shippers). *See also* Hochman, *Judicial Review of Administrative Processes in Which the President Participates*, 74 Harv. L. Rev. 684 (1961), and on unreviewability generally, Saferstein, *Nonreviewability: A Functional Analysis of "Committed to Agency Discretion,"* 82 Harv. L. Rev. 367 (1968).

7. Assuming Congress makes some category of administrative orders judicially unreviewable because those orders are potentially based in part on presidential assessments of foreign affairs, should a President be able to render an order reviewable by informing a court that, in fact, a particular order does not rest on foreign affairs

considerations? For a negative answer, *see Braniff Airways, Inc. v. CAB*, 581 F.2d 846 (D.C. Cir. 1978).

8. Congress has amended the Civil Aeronautics Act to permit the President to disapprove CAB decisions for foreign policy reasons; if he approves of a decision, however, that decision is now, by statute, judicially reviewable. Is this amendment constitutional?

9. Our introductory domestic cases, *Marbury* and *Youngstown*, might be thought to have established two critical analytical principles:

> a. Courts may ordinarily review the legality of presidential actions, unless those actions are constitutionally committed to the President's political discretion;

> b. Only the President or Congress may act within their respective spheres of exclusive authority, but either may act in areas of arguably concurrent authority, unless both act in contrary ways, in which case Congress prevails.

Does it follow, in contrast to these principles in domestic policymaking, that all presidential foreign policy decisions are unreviewable? Do *Curtiss-Wright* and *Waterman Steamship* erect a presumption opposite to the last clause of "Principle (b)" in foreign policy matters? In other words, if congressional and presidential initiatives with foreign policy impact conflict, does the President always prevail? Presumptively prevail? Ever prevail? Does the outcome depend on the "specificity" of the foreign policy power on which the President's initiative assertedly rests? In other words, to what extent does Justice Jackson's *Youngstown* opinion provide authoritative guidance in foreign as well as domestic policy contexts?

B. Treaty Powers

1. Overview

Powers of the President and Senate

The Constitution states that the President shall have the power to make treaties, provided two-thirds of the members of the Senate present advise and consent in each case. U.S. Const., art. I, sec. 2, par. 2. The requirement for a two-thirds vote testifies to an apparent wariness of international entanglements; recall that advice and consent to Presidential appointments requires only a bare majority.

Although the treaty-making power is thus expressly shared between the Senate and the President, the precise boundaries of each participant's responsibilities are unclear. Treaty-making consists of negotiation, approval, ratification, the exchange of ratifications and proclamation. Although the last two steps may be considered merely administrative requirements for the formal completion of an international pact, the Constitution is silent as to how the first and critical discretionary step—negotiation—is conducted. Historically, the President has acquired the task of negotiating treaties, while the Senate has played a more passive role, entering the process at the approval stage. The Senate has managed to continue to be influential in treaty-making, however, by refusing approval, placing restrictions on treaties, or purporting to aid the President in treaty interpretation. *See generally* Congressional Research Service (for the Senate Comm. on Foreign Relations), 98th Cong., 2d Sess., Treaties and Other International Agreements: The Role of the United States Senate (Comm. Print 1984).

President Washington originally interpreted the Senate's "advise and consent" power to mean that, before a treaty is negotiated, the Senate's advice must be sought on a preliminary basis. The Senate rejected the system as unworkable, as have later Presidents. The Senate now does not formally advise on treaties before or during negotiations. Instead, the President appoints and instructs the negotiators and follows their progress in negotiations. If he approves what they have negotiated and obtains the advice and consent of the Senate, he may "ratify" or "make" the treaty. Because ratification is thus a discretionary power of the President, he may decline to make a treaty even after obtaining the Senate's consent.

This is not to minimize the extraordinary potential impact of the Senate approval process. The lack of consent to a treaty has played havoc in more than a few Presidents' foreign policy plans. An important example is the Senate's rejection of the Treaty of Versailles. President Wilson referred to the Senate thereafter as the "graveyard of treaties."

The Senate, of course, is not constrained to base its approval or disapproval decisions on any particular criteria. Thus, the Senate may deny its consent not because it thinks a proposed treaty would contravene the national interest, but because, for example, of partisan politics.

The Senate has also managed to forestall some potential agreements through inaction. A familiar example is the International Convention on the Prevention and Punishment of the Crime of Genocide, which was placed before the Senate in 1949, but not consented to until 1986. In fact, the United States still has not ratified the convention because the Senate conditioned final ratification on the enactment of implementing legislation, which has not yet been passed. *See* 132 Cong. Rec. 51377-78 (daily ed. Feb. 19, 1986).

The Senate may modify a treaty through the use of reservations, giving it another important source of influence in the treaty-making process. A reservation is a unilateral statement purporting to exclude or modify the legal effect of certain treaty provisions as they might be applied to the United States. International law permits such reservations unless expressly precluded by treaty or "incompatible with the object or the purpose of the treaty." *See* Vienna Convention on the Law of Treaties, arts. 2, 17-23, U.N. Doc. No. A/Conf. 39/27, *reprinted in* 63 Am. J. Int. L. 875 (1969). The constitutional authority of the Senate to impose reservations has not been questioned seriously. If the Senate may give or withhold consent, it is thought to follow that the Senate may also give its consent based on the condition that changes be made.

Conditions may be imposed not only to modify international obligations of a treaty but also to control its effect in the United States. Such reservations, for example, include Senate insistence that a treaty not take effect or that action not be taken under it by United States officials without the approval of Congress. Other reservations have required the President to perform some domestic act to affect the treaty's impact. For example, the Senate Reservation to the Reciprocal Military Service Convention with Great Britain, June 3, 1918, 40 Stat. 1620, required the President, before ratifying the Convention, to issue a general certificate exempting from military service citizens of the United States in Great Britain who were outside the ages of military service specified in United States laws. He fulfilled his obligation through an exchange of diplomatic notes.

For international purposes, the President determines the United States' position as to the meaning of a treaty, but domestically, Congress also contributes. Congress interprets a treaty when it considers implementing legislation or other legislation on the same subject. The result is that, even though Congress admits to giving the executive interpretation "great weight," Congress does claim an independent right of interpretation.

A current controversy exists concerning the relevance to treaty interpretation of the Senate's understanding of a treaty at the time it gave its consent, when that understanding was not codified in a series of conditions or reservations. In 1972, the United States concluded an Antiballistic Missile (ABM) treaty with the Soviet Union, Treaty on the Limitation of Anti-Ballistic Missile Systems, May 26, 1972, United States-U.S.S.R., 23 U.S.T. 3435, T.I.A.S. No. 7503. That treaty was then interpreted as imposing a perpetual ban on the development, testing, or deployment of mobile or space-based ABM systems. Notwithstanding this view, the Defense Department, in late 1985, began to argue that the treaty did not ban the testing and development of exotic, so-called "Star Wars" space-based defense systems. The interpretation, supported by State Department Legal Adviser Abraham Sofaer, precipitated strong dissent both within the Administration and Congress. Critics, including all but one of the eight key negotiators of the ABM treaty, charged first that the text and negotiating record of the treaty simply did not support the Sofaer view. Morrison, *Rereading ABM*, 19 Nat'l J. 2304 (1987); S. Rep. No. 164, 100th Cong., 1st Sess. 28-36 (1987). Equally important, Senators insisted that, even if records of secret negotiations did support the Sofaer view, the executive could not constitutionally reinterpret the treaty in a manner that differed from the executive's original presentation of the treaty to the Senate. Any such power of unilateral reinterpretation, it was argued, would undermine the contemplated role of the Senate in consenting to a treaty before it could be formally made and ratified. As of fall, 1987, several legislative measures were underway in an effort to prevent the Administration from implementing its reinterpretation. After both the House and Senate adopted amendments to the 1988 defense authorization bill that would have required U.S. adherence to the traditional interpretation of the ABM treaty, White House advisers and congressional leaders agreed on a compromise. Without naming the ABM treaty, the compromise act prohibits for one year those specific Star Wars tests that would be in violation of the traditional interpretation, and the purchase of hardware necessary to conduct those tests. National Defense Authorization Act for Fiscal Years 1988 and 1989, Pub. L. No. 100-180, § 225, 101 Stat. 1019, 1056 (1987). For a challange to the Reagan Administration ABM interpretation by one of the treaty's negotiators, see R. L. Garthoff, Policy Versus the Law: The Reinterpretation of the ABM Treaty (1987). *See also Review of ABM Treaty Interpretation Dispute and SDI: Hearing Before the Subcomm. on Arms Control, Int'l Security and Science of the House Comm. on Foreign Relations,* 100th Cong., 1st Sess. (1987).

At different times, the power to terminate a treaty has been claimed for the President, for the President and Senate jointly, and for Congress alone. Presidents have claimed authority, presumably under their foreign affairs powers, to act for the United States to terminate treaties, whether in accordance with their terms or in violation of international law. In some situations, a President has invited another party to terminate a treaty, achieving the same result.

Whether or not Congress has any treaty termination power as a formal matter, it does have the capacity effectively to breach treaties. It can accomplish termination by refusing to pass legislation necessary to the implementation of treaty obligations, passing legislation inconsistent with a treaty, or seeking indirectly to compel the President to terminate a treaty or induce another party to do so.

Permissible Scope of Treaties

The Constitution does not expressly impose substantive limits on the treaty power, nor does it directly imply that any exist. The Supreme Court has not held any provision of any treaty unconstitutional, and few have been seriously challenged there. It is likely, however, that treaties are subject to the constitutional limitations that apply to all exercises of federal power, principally the prohibitions contained in the Bill of Rights. The leading case is *Reid v. Covert*, 354 U.S. 1 (1957), involving overseas courts-martial for civilian wives for killing their serviceman husbands. Military jurisdiction assertedly rested, in part, on executive agreements providing military jurisdiction over civilian dependents of U.S. servicepeople overseas. A Supreme Court plurality said: "[W]e reject the idea that when the United States acts against citizens abroad it can do so free of the Bill of Rights. The United States is entirely a creature of the Constitution. Its power and authority have no other source." *Id*. at 5-6. Therefore: "It would be manifestly contrary to the...Constitution...to...[permit] the United States to exercise power under an international agreement without observing constitutional prohibitions." *Id*. at 17. The holding of *Reid*, however, was that the asserted jurisdiction was unauthorized, not that the executive agreement was unconstitutional.

In addition to the Bill of Rights, it has been argued that structural provisions of the Constitution likewise limit the treaty power. For example, although the Constitution does not give the states any role in the treaty-making process, the claim was made early in this century that the tenth amendment protects the states by forbidding treaties to be made on subjects constitutionally reserved to the states. This argument was rejected by the Supreme Court in *Missouri v. Holland*, 252 U.S. 416 (1920), involving a treaty between Canada and the United States to protect migratory birds through hunting regulations. Although this subject matter would today not be viewed as reserved to the states even vis-a-vis Congressional enactments, Justice Holmes went so far as to imply that, even if the tenth amendment were a limit on Congress' regulatory power, it would not similarly limit the treaty power.[1]

Similarly, members of the House of Representatives have argued that treaties may not be used to dispose of federal property because article IV of the Constitution expressly vests the property disposition power in both Houses of Congress. In a suit seeking to block the transfer of federal property to Panama under treaties negotiated by President Carter, the U.S. Court of Appeals rejected that position. *Edwards v. Carter*, 580 F.2d 1055 (D.C. Cir. 1978), *cert. denied*, 436 U.S. 907 (1978).

Legal Impact of Treaties

The laws of nations differ as to the domestic legal status of a treaty invoked as the source of governing law in a lawsuit. England regards treaties as only international

---

1. During the early 1950s, there was a concerted effort led by Senator Bricker to amend the Constitution in order to "overrule" *Missouri v. Holland*. The Bricker Amendment would have provided, in part: "A treaty shall become effective as internal law in the United States only through legislation which would be valid in the absence of a treaty." Even if adopted, it is doubtful the amendment would now have much force given the breadth of congressional regulatory power sanctioned by the Supreme Court over the last half century. G. Gunther, Constitutional Law 226-27 (11th ed. 1985).

obligations, without effect as domestic law unless so implemented by Parliament. Other countries may regard most treaties as providing rules of decision in domestic cases without further legislative action.

The supremacy clause of the U.S. Constitution includes treaties among the sources of law that represent "the supreme Law of the Land." Art. VI, par. 2. Article VI was designed principally to assure the supremacy of treaties to state law, but it has also been interpreted to mean that treaties may become domestic law upon ratification, if they are "self-executing."

The distinction between "self-executing" and "non-self-executing" treaties recognizes that, although treaties bind the United States internationally, U.S. courts may not always implement the treaties directly as sources of decisional rules in relevant domestic cases. A non-self-executing treaty is not a source of domestic law without implementing legislation. To determine whether or not a treaty is self-executing, courts purport to examine the intent of the negotiating parties. In fact, courts may give predominant consideration to whether regarding a treaty as self-executing will prove impracticable or derogate from Congress's legislative authority. T. Buergenthal & H. Maier, Public International Law in a Nutshell 194-200 (1985); *see also* Iwasawa, *The Doctrine of Self-Executing Treaties in the United States: A Critical Analysis*, 26 Va. J. Int'l L. 627 (1986). Chief Justice Marshall, in *Foster v. Neilson*, 27 U.S. (2 Pet.) 253 (1829), *overruled on other grds., United States v. Percheman*, 32 U.S. (7 Pet.) 51 (1833), recognized that a treaty must be regarded as equivalent to an act of legislation, when the treaty operates of itself without the aid of any legislative provision. Thus, for example, the Peace Treaty of 1783 and the Jay Treaty of 1794 were self-executing in restoring Tory land rights. *Fairfax's Devisee v. Hunter's Lessee*, 11 U.S. (7 Cranch) 603 (1813). Marshall said, however: "[W]hen the terms of the stipulation import a contract—when either of the parties engages to perform a particular act, the treaty addresses itself to the political, not the judicial department; and the legislature must execute the contract before it can become a rule for the court." *Id.* at 314.

Because of our constitutional distribution of power, there are presumably some measures which cannot be authorized by a self-executing treaty. A treaty may not appropriate funds; the Constitution expressly provides: "No money shall be drawn from the Treasury, but in Consequence of Appropriations made by Law." Art. I, sec. 9, par. 7. Therefore, any financial undertaking by the United States will require appropriation by Congress. A treaty likewise may not enact criminal law; only Congress may prescribe penal sanctions. It has also been said that the United States cannot declare war by treaty; Congress must declare it.

A treaty of any kind lacks status as law if it is not binding internationally, it is invalid under international law, or if expired, or terminated, or destroyed by breach.

Congress presumably has power to do what is "necessary and proper" to implement a treaty even if its actions are otherwise not within its expressly enumerated powers. There is still debate as to whether Congress is constitutionally and morally obligated to implement treaties once made. It has been urged that the House of Representatives may not refuse to execute a treaty because the treaty amounts to a national pledge—although such refusal would surely be judicially unreviewable. The opposing viewpoint is that the House of Representatives must use its own judgment as to what is most conducive to the public good. This debate still exists in principle, although Congress has not yet failed to carry out international obligations in practice, at least at the time of original commitment. Although Congress may later enact legislation inconsistent with an old treaty, it typically goes no farther following ratification than shaping and limiting important details of implementation, sometimes not giving the President the precise authorities or as much money as he may urge that a treaty requires.

Because treaties are law and often deal with matters within the purview of congressional legislation, it has sometimes happened that a treaty and an act of Congress are inconsistent. The legal consequences have long been settled by the Supreme Court. In *Whitney v. Robertson*, 124 U.S. 190, 194 (1888) the Court held that a treaty is on the same footing as legislation; because both are the supreme law of the land, if the two are inconsistent, the more recent controls.

2. Treaty Termination by the President

As noted earlier, the President is now regarded by all branches of government as having exclusive power to establish (or break) diplomatic relations with other nations. E.S. Corwin, The President: Office and Powers, 1787-1957 177-93 (4th ed. 1957). Establishing diplomatic relations, however, typically requires attention to a variety of additional problems, such as the resolution of outstanding claims by U.S. nationals against the nationals of the other country, and vice versa, or adjustments in our foreign policy with regard to third countries. As you review the following case and the cases on claims settlement through executive agreement, consider how far the President's exclusive power over diplomatic recognition should be deemed to imply exclusive power over other aspects of foreign affairs implicated in the recognition process.

Goldwater v. Carter
617 F.2d 697 (D.C. Cir. 1979) (en banc)
vacated, 444 U.S. 996 (1979)

PER CURIAM:

The court *en banc* has before it for review the judgment of the District Court that the notice of termination given by the President pursuant to the terms of the Mutual Defense Treaty with the Republic of China is ineffective absent either (1) a manifestation of the consent of the Senate to such termination by a two-thirds vote or (2) an approving majority vote therefor by both houses of Congress. The preliminary questions we confront are, first, whether the District Court was without jurisdiction because appellees lacked standing, and, second, whether it should in any event have declined to exercise jurisdiction by reason of the political nature of the question it was called upon to decide. Since a majority of the court does not exist to dispose of the appeal on either of these bases,[1] we reach the merits and reverse.

In doing so, however, we think it important at the outset to stress that the Treaty, as it was presented to the Senate in 1954 and consented to by it, contained an explicit provision for termination by either party on one year's notice. The Senate, in the

---

1. In a separate concurring opinion, Judges Wright and Tamm have limited their consideration to the question of standing; and, finding that none exists, vote to reverse the District Court. There are no votes to reverse founded upon the political question doctrine.

course of giving its consent, exhibited no purpose and took no action to reserve a role for itself—by amendment, reservation, or condition—in the effectuation of this provision. Neither has the Senate, since the giving of the notice of termination, purported to take any final or decisive action with respect to it, either by way of approval or disapproval. The constitutional issue we face, therefore, is solely and simply the one of whether the President in these precise circumstances is, on behalf of the United States, empowered to terminate the Treaty in accordance with its terms. It is our view that he is, and that the limitations which the District Court purported to place on his action in this regard have no foundation in the Constitution.

BACKGROUND

In the aftermath of the Chinese Revolution and the Korean War, the United States and the Republic of China (ROC) negotiated a Mutual Defense Treaty, primarily directed against the perceived threat from the People's Republic of China (PRC). The Treaty was signed by representatives of both nations on December 2, 1954. It was approved by the Senate, and finally signed by the President on February 11, 1955. Article V of the Treaty provided that, in the event of an attack on Taiwan, the Pescadores, or United States territories in the western Pacific, each nation "would act to meet the common danger in accordance with its constitutional processes." Article X of the Treaty provided that it would remain in force "indefinitely," but said that "[e]ither Party may terminate it one year after notice has been given to the other Party."

At that time both the ROC and PRC claimed—and still claim—to be the sole legitimate government of China; both considered Taiwan a part of China. Since then over 100 nations, including all of our NATO allies[,] Japan, [and the United Nations] have officially recognized the PRC as the sole government of China, breaking off relations with Taiwan. . . .

In the early 1970's the United States began to pursue a policy of closer relations with the PRC. . . . The PRC stipulated that full mutual diplomatic recognition was preconditioned on United States agreement to cease all diplomatic and other official relations with the ROC, to withdraw United States military units from Taiwan, and to terminate the Mutual Defense Treaty with the ROC.

In September 1978 Congress passed and the President signed the International Security Assistance Act of 1978, Pub.L.No. 95-384, 92 Stat. 746. Section 26 of that Act, called the "Dole-Stone Amendment," provided:

> It is the sense of the Congress that there should be prior consultation between the Congress and the executive branch on any proposed policy changes affecting the continuation in force of the Mutual Defense Treaty of 1954.

On December 15, 1978 President Carter announced that the United States would recognize the PRC as the sole government of China, effective January 1, 1979, and would simultaneously withdraw recognition from the ROC. In addition, the United States announced that the ROC would be notified that "the Mutual Defense Treaty is being terminated in accordance with the provisions of the Treaty." . . .

While severing all official ties with the ROC, the United States has sought to preserve "extensive, close, and friendly commercial, cultural, and other relations between the people of the United States and the people on Taiwan." The Taiwan Relations Act,

Pub.L.No.96-8, 93 Stat. 14, signed into law on April 10, 1979, established the statutory framework for such relations.[4] It provided:

> For all purposes, including actions in any court in the United States, the Congress approves the continuation in force of all treaties ... entered into by the United States and the governing authorities on Taiwan recognized by the United States as the Republic of China prior to January 1, 1979, and in force between them on December 31, 1978, unless and until terminated in accordance with law.

Id. § 4(c).

On December 22, 1978 plaintiffs-appellees filed this suit in District Court, seeking declaratory and injunctive relief to prevent termination of the Treaty without senatorial or congressional consent. The complaint ... asserted that the President has no unilateral power under the Constitution to abrogate treaties, and that the United States, not the President, is the party invested by Article X of the Treaty with the power of termination.

On June 6, 1979 the District Court dismissed the suit, without prejudice, for lack of standing. The court observed that three resolutions then pending in the Senate might resolve the controversy without need for judicial intervention. ...

Within hours of the District Court order the Senate called up Senate Resolution 15 which, as amended by the Foreign Relations Committee, would have recognized some fourteen grounds that would justify unilateral action by the President to terminate treaty obligations of the United States.[6] By a vote of 59 to 35 the Senate substituted for its consideration an amendment drafted by Senator Harry Byrd, Jr.:

> That it is the sense of the Senate that approval of the United States Senate is required to terminate any mutual defense treaty between the United States and another nation.

125 Cong.Rec. S7015, S7038-S7039 (daily ed. June 6, 1979). Later that day, during the course of debate on the amended resolution, a dispute arose among the Senators over whether the resolution would have retrospective, or merely prospective effect. No final vote was ever taken on the resolution, and the Majority Leader returned the resolution to the calendar.

On June 12, 1979, after the Byrd amendment was voted on, the plaintiffs-appellees filed a motion in District Court for alteration or amendment of the June 6 order of dismissal. They contended that the Senate's action on the Byrd amendment [created] a justiciable controversy. On October 17, 1979 the District Court granted this motion, ruling that the plaintiffs had suffered the requisite injury in fact because of the denial of their right to be consulted and to vote on treaty termination. ... Reaching the

---

4. Section 3 of the Act authorizes the United States to provide defense material to Taiwan, and says that "[t]he President and the Congress shall determine the nature and quantity of such defense articles and services based solely upon their judgment of the needs of Taiwan." It further directs the President to report to the Congress on "any threat to the security or the social or economic system of the people on Taiwan and any danger to the interests of the United States arising therefrom." The President and the Congress than "shall determine * * * appropriate action by the United States in response to any such danger." *Id.* § 3.

6. Among other grounds, the Committee version would have recognized the right of the President to terminate treaties containing termination clauses like Article X of the 1954 Treaty.

constitutional question, the court granted plaintiffs' cross-motion for summary judgment. This appeal followed.

II

Various considerations enter into our determination that the President's notice of termination will be effective on January 1, 1980. The result we reach draws upon their totality, but in listing them hereinafter we neither assign them hierarchical values nor imply that any one factor or combination of factors is determinative.

1. We turn first to the argument, embraced by the District Court, drawn from the language of article II, § 2, of the Constitution. It is that, since the President clearly cannot enter into a treaty without the consent of the Senate, the inference is inescapable that he must in all circumstances seek the same senatorial consent to terminate that treaty. As a matter of language alone, however, the same inference would appear automatically to obtain with respect to the termination by the President of officers appointed by him under the same clause of the Constitution and subject to Senate confirmation. But the Supreme Court has read that clause as not having such an inevitable effect in any and all circumstances. *Compare Myers v. United States*, 272 U.S. 52 (1926) *with In re Humphrey's Executor v. United States*, 295 U.S. 602 (1935). In the area of foreign relations in particular, where the constitutional commitment of powers to the President is notably comprehensive, it has never been suggested that the services of Ambassadors—appointed by the President, confirmed by the Senate, and of critical importance as they are to the successful conduct of our foreign relations—may not be terminated by the President without the prior authorization of that body.

Expansion of the language of the Constitution by sequential linguistic projection is a tricky business at best. Virtually all constitutional principles have unique elements and can be distinguished from one another. As the Supreme Court has recognized with respect to the clause in question, it is not abstract logic or sterile symmetry that controls, but a sensible and realistic ascertainment of the meaning of the Constitution in the context of the specific action taken.

2. The District Court's declaration, in the alternative, that the necessary authority in this instance may be granted by a majority of each house of Congress presumably has its source in the Supremacy Clause of Article VI. The argument is that a treaty, being a part of the "supreme Law of the Land," can only be terminated at the least by a subsequent federal statute.

The central purpose of the Supremacy Clause has been accepted to be that of causing each of the designated supreme laws—Constitution, statute, and treaty—to prevail, for purposes of domestic law, over state law in any form. Article VI speaks explicitly to the judges to assure that this is so. But these three types of supreme law are not necessarily the same in their other characteristics, any more than are the circumstances and terms of their creation the same. Certainly the Constitution is silent on the matter of treaty termination. And the fact that it speaks to the common characteristic of supremacy over state law does not provide any basis for concluding that a treaty must be unmade either by (1) the same process by which it was made, or (2) the alternative means by which a statute is made or terminated.

3. The constitutional institution of advice and consent of the Senate, provided two-thirds of the Senators concur, is a special and extraordinary condition of the exercise by the President of certain specified powers under Article II. It is not lightly to be

extended in instances not set forth in the Constitution. Such an extension by implication is not proper unless that implication is unmistakably clear.

The District Court's absolutist extension of this limitation to termination of treaties, irrespective of the particular circumstances involved, is not sound. The making of a treaty has the consequences of an entangling alliance for the nation. Similarly, the amending of a treaty merely continues such entangling alliances, changing only their character, and therefore also requires the advice and consent of the Senate. It does not follow, however, that a constitutional provision for a special concurrence (two-thirds of the Senators) prior to entry into an entangling alliance necessarily applies to its termination in accordance with its terms.

4. The Constitution specifically confers no power of treaty termination on either the Congress or the Executive. We note, however, that the powers conferred upon Congress in Article I of the Constitution are specific, detailed, and limited, while the powers conferred upon the President by Article II are generalized in a manner that bespeaks no such limitation upon foreign affairs powers. "Section 1. The executive power shall be vested in a President..."[17] Although specific powers are listed in Section 2 and Section 3, these are in many instances not powers necessary to an Executive, while "The executive Power" referred to in Section 1 is nowhere defined. There is no required two-thirds vote of the Senate conditioning the exercise of any power in Section 1.

In some instances this difference is reflective of the origin of the particular power in question. In general, the powers of the federal government arise out of specific grants of authority delegated by the states—hence the enumerated powers of Congress in Article I, Section 8. The foreign affairs powers, however, proceed directly from the sovereignty of the Union. "[I]f they had never been mentioned in the Constitution, [they] would have vested in the federal government as necessary concomitants of nationality." *United States v. Curtiss-Wright Export Corp.*, 299 U.S. 304, 318 (1936).

The President is the constitutional representative of the United States with respect to external affairs. It is significant that the treaty power appears in Article II of the Constitution, relating to the executive branch, and not in Article I, setting forth the powers of the legislative branch. It is the President as Chief Executive who is given the constitutional authority to enter into a treaty; and even after he has obtained the consent of the Senate it is for him to decide whether to ratify a treaty and put it into effect. Senatorial confirmation of a treaty concededly does not obligate the President to go forward with a treaty if he concludes that it is not in the public interest to do so.

Thus, in contrast to the lawmaking power, the constitutional initiative in the treaty-making field is in the President, not Congress. It would take an unprecedented feat of judicial construction to read into the Constitution an absolute condition precedent of congressional or Senate approval for termination of all treaties, similar to the specific one relating to initial approval. And it would unalterably affect the balance of power between the two Branches laid down in Articles I and II.

5. Ultimately, what must be recognized is that a treaty is *sui generis*. It is not just another law. It is an international compact, a solemn obligation of the United States and a "supreme Law" that supersedes state policies and prior federal laws. For clarity

---

17. Contrastingly, Article I, Section 1, provides: "All legislative Powers *herein granted* shall be vested in a Congress of the United States..." (emphasis supplied).

of analysis, it is thus well to distinguish between treaty-making as an international act and the consequences which flow domestically from such act. In one realm the Constitution has conferred the primary role upon the President; in the other, Congress retains its primary role as lawmaker. The fact that the Constitution, statutes, and treaties are all listed in the Supremacy Clause as being superior to any form of state law does not mean that the making and unmaking of treaties can be analogized to the making and unmaking of domestic statutes any more than it can be analogized to the making or unmaking of a constitutional amendment.

The recognized powers of Congress to implement (or fail to implement) a treaty by an appropriation or other law essential to its effectuation, or to supersede for all practical purposes the effect of a treaty on domestic law, are legislative powers, not treaty-making or treaty termination powers. The issue here, however, is not Congress' legislative powers to supersede or affect the domestic impact of a treaty; the issue is whether the Senate (or Congress) must in this case give its prior consent to discontinue a treaty which the President thinks it desirable to terminate in the national interest and pursuant to a provision in the treaty itself. The existence, in practical terms, of one power does not imply the existence, in constitutional terms, of the other.

6. If we were to hold that under the Constitution a treaty could only be terminated by exactly the same process by which it was made, we would be locking the United States into all of its international obligations, even if the President and two-thirds of the Senate minus one firmly believed that the proper course for the United States was to terminate a treaty. Many of our treaties in force, such as mutual defense treaties, carry potentially dangerous obligations. These obligations are terminable under international law upon breach by the other party or change in circumstances that frustrates the purpose of the treaty. In many of these situations the President must take immediate action. The creation of a constitutionally obligatory role in all cases for a two-thirds consent by the Senate would give to one-third plus one of the Senate the power to deny the President the authority necessary to conduct our foreign policy in a rational and effective manner.

7. Even as to the formal termination of treaties, as the District Court pointed out, "a variety of means have been used to terminate treaties."[18] There is much debate among the historians and scholars as to whether in some instances the legislature has been involved at all; they are agreed that, when involved, that involvement with the President has taken many different forms. It appears moreover that the Senate may wish to continue to determine the nature of its involvement on a case by case basis.

The District Court concluded that the diversity of historical precedents left an inconclusive basis on which to decide the issue of whether the President's power to terminate a treaty must always be "shared" in some way by the Senate or Congress. We agree. Yet we think it is not without significance that out of all the historical

---

18. Since the first treaty to which the United States was a party was terminated in 1798 by an act of Congress, a variety of means have been used to terminate treaties: by statute directing the President to deliver notice of termination; by the President acting pursuant to a joint resolution of Congress or otherwise acting with the concurrence of both houses of Congress; by the President acting with senatorial consent; and by the President acting alone.
Goldwater v. Carter, 481 F.Supp. at 959 (D.D.C. 1979) (footnotes omitted).

precedents brought to our attention, in no situation has a treaty been continued in force over the opposition of the President.

There is on the other hand widespread agreement that the President has the power as Chief Executive under many circumstances to exercise functions regarding treaties which have the effect of either terminating or continuing their vitality.[19] Prominent among these is the authority of the President as Chief Executive (1) to determine whether a treaty has terminated because of a breach, *Charlton v. Kelly*, 229 U.S. 447, 473-476 (1913); and (2) to determine whether a treaty is at an end due to changed circumstances.

In short, the determination of the conduct of the United States in regard to treaties is an instance of what has broadly been called the "foreign affairs power" of the President. We have no occasion to define that term, but we do take account of its vitality. The *Curtiss-Wright* opinion, written by a Justice who had served in the United States Senate, declares in oft-repeated language that the President is "the sole organ of the federal government in the field of international relations." That status is not confined to the service of the President as a channel of communication, as the District Court suggested, but embraces an active policy determination as to the conduct of the United States in regard to a treaty in response to numerous problems and circumstances as they arise.

8. How the vital functions of the President in implementing treaties and in deciding on their viability in response to changing events can or should interact with Congress' legitimate concerns and powers in relating to foreign affairs is an area into which we

---

19.   The Senate Committee on Foreign Relations after careful consideration of the matter came to the conclusion that there were 14 different bases on which the President could terminate a treaty in the course of his executive function. The grounds identified are the following:

(1) in conformity with the provisions of the treaty;

(2) by consent of all the parties after consultation with the other contracting states.

(3) where it is established that the parties intended to admit the possibility of denunciation or withdrawal;

(4) where a right of denunciation or withdrawal may be implied by the nature of the treaty;

(5) where it appears from a later treaty concluded with the same party and relating to the same subject matter that the matter should be governed by that treaty;

(6) where the provisions of the later treaty are so far incompatible with those of the earlier one that the two treaties are not capable of being applied at the same time;

(7) where there has been a material breach by another party;

(8) where the treaty has become impossible to perform;

(9) where there has been a fundamental change of circumstances;

(10) where there has been a severance of diplomatic or consular relations and such relations are indispensable for the application of the treaty;

(11) where a new peremptory norm of international law emerges which is in conflict with the treaty;

(12) where an error was made regarding a fact or situation which was assumed by that state to exist at the time when the treaty was concluded and formed an essential basis of its consent to be bound;

(13) where a state has been induced to conclude a treaty by the fraudulent conduct of another state; and

(14) where a state's consent to be bound has been procured by the corruption or coercion of its representatives or by the threat or use of force.

S.Rep.No.119, 96th Cong., 1st Sess. 10 (1979).

should not and do not prematurely intrude. History shows us that there are too many variables to lay down any hard and fast constitutional rules.

We cannot find an implied role in the Constitution for the Senate in treaty termination for some but not all treaties in terms of their relative importance. There is no judicially ascertainable and manageable method of making any distinction among treaties on the basis of their substance, the magnitude of the risk involved, the degree of controversy which their termination would engender, or by any other standards. We know of no standards to apply in making such distinctions. The facts on which such distinctions might be drawn may be difficult of ascertainment; and the resolution of such inevitable disputes between the two Branches would be an improper and unnecessary role for the courts. To decide whether there was a breach or changed circumstances, for example, would involve a court in making fundamental decisions of foreign policy and would create insuperable problems of evidentiary proof. This is beyond the acceptable judicial role. All we decide today is that two-thirds Senate consent or majority consent in both houses is not necessary to terminate this treaty in the circumstances before us now.

9. The circumstances involved in the termination of the Mutual Defense Treaty with the Republic of China include a number of material and unique elements. Prominent is assertion by the officials of both the Republic of China and the People's Republic of China that each of them is the government of China, intending the term China to comprehend both the mainland of China and the island of Taiwan. . . . It is in this context that the recent Joint Communique set forth as of January 1, 1979 that the United States recognizes the People's Republic of China as "the sole legal government of China." This action made reference to "the people of Taiwan," stating that the peoples of the United States and Taiwan "will maintain cultural, commercial and other unofficial relations." This formulation was confirmed by the Taiwan Relations Act.

It is undisputed that the Constitution gave the President full constitutional authority to recognize the PRC and to derecognize the ROC. What the United States has evolved for Taiwan is a novel and somewhat indefinite relationship, namely, of unofficial relations with the people of Taiwan. The subtleties involved in maintaining amorphous relationships are often the very stuff of diplomacy—a field in which the President, not Congress, has responsibility under our Constitution. The President makes a responsible claim that he has authority as Chief Executive to determine that there is no meaningful vitality to a mutual defense treaty when there is no recognized state. That is not to say that the recognition power automatically gives the President authority to take any action that is required or requested by the state being recognized. We do not need to reach this question. Nevertheless, it remains an important ingredient in the case at bar that the President has determined that circumstances have changed so as to preclude continuation of the Mutual Defense Treaty with the ROC; diplomatic recognition of the ROC came to an end on January 1, 1979, and now there exists only "cultural, commercial and other unofficial relations" with the "people on Taiwan."

10. Finally, and of central significance, the treaty here at issue contains a termination clause. The existence of Article X of the ROC treaty, permitting termination by either party on one year's notice, is an overarching factor in this case, which in effect enables all of the other considerations to be knit together.

Without derogating from the executive power of the President to decide to act contrary to the wording of a treaty—for example, because of a breach by the other party, or because of a doctrine of fundamental change of circumstances ... —the President's authority as Chief Executive is at its zenith when the Senate has consented to a treaty that expressly provides for termination on one year's notice, and the President's action is the giving of notice of termination.

As already noted, we have no occasion to decide whether this factor would be determinative in a case lacking other factors identified above, *e.g.*, under a notice of withdrawal from the NATO treaty unaccompanied by derecognition of the other signatories. No specific restriction or condition on the President's action is found within the Constitution or this treaty itself. The termination clause is without conditions and without designation as to who shall act to terminate it. No specific role is spelled out in either the Constitution or this treaty for the Senate or the Congress as a whole. That power consequently devolves upon the President, and there is no basis for a court to imply a restriction on the President's power to terminate not contained in the Constitution, in this treaty, or in any other authoritative source.

While under the termination clause of this and similar treaties the power of the President to terminate may appear theoretically absolute, to think that this is so would be to ignore all historical practices in treaty termination and past and current reciprocal relationships between the Chief Executive and Congress. The wide variety of roles played by the Executive and the Congress (or the Senate alone) in the past termination of treaties teaches us nothing conclusive as to constitutional theory, but it instructs us as to what may fairly be contemplated as to the President's future exercise of the treaty termination power. Treaty termination is a political act, but political acts are not customarily taken without political support. Even if formal advice and consent is not constitutionally required as a prerequisite to termination, it might be sought. If the Congress is completely ignored, it has its arsenal of weapons, as previous Chief Executives have on occasion been sharply reminded.

Thus, the court is not to be taken as minimizing the role of the legislature in foreign affairs. The legislature's powers, including prominently its dominant status in the provision of funds, and its authority to investigate the Executive's functioning, establish authority for appropriate legislative participation in foreign affairs. The question of whether the Senate may be able to reserve to itself in particular treaties, at the time of their original submission, a specific role in their termination is not presented by the record in this appeal and we decide nothing with respect to it. The matter before us is solely one of whether the Constitution nullifies the procedure followed by the President in this instance. We find the President did not exceed his authority when he took action to withdraw from the ROC treaty, by giving notice under Article X of the Treaty, without the consent of the Senate or other legislative concurrences.

III

... *Reversed.*

MacKINNON, Circuit Judge, dissenting in part and concurring in part.

I concur in the decision of a majority of my colleagues that the Senators and Representatives who are the plaintiffs in this action possess standing. ... I disagree, however, with the majority's conclusion on the merits that the Constitution confers the absolute power on the President, *acting alone*, to terminate this Mutual Defense

Treaty. No prior President has ever claimed the absolute power to terminate such a treaty.

The majority in effect holds that the President has the absolute power to terminate *this* treaty but their decision indicates it is not to be considered as a binding precedent that future Presidents could terminate treaties in similar circumstances. This advance attempt to minimize its harmful effect for the future is accomplished by stating that the opinion is "narrow" and could not necessarily be relied upon to confer the same absolute power to terminate the NATO treaty, which has a similar termination provision. History will not deal kindly with such an obviously expedient decision.

My interpretation is based on the admitted fact that the termination of treaties is not one of the enumerated powers of the Constitution. Rather it is an implied power vested in the government. As such, under the "Necessary and Proper" clause of Article I, Section 8, which the majority decision avoids like the plague, power is conferred upon "*[t]he Congress*" to pass a law to terminate treaties. Since the Constitution makes treaties along with other laws the "Law of the Land", Article II, Section 2, a treaty is to be terminated in the same manner as any other "law"—by a formal act of Congress approved by the President. The language of the Constitution, its interpretation by the Framers, and historical precedent overwhelmingly support such a conclusion.

This is thus *not* a case where, as the President contends: "[t]here are no judicially discoverable and manageable standards for determining the extent of constitutionally required legislative participation in treaty termination." Appellant's Brief, p. 14. The judicial standards are easily discoverable in the Constitution.

I *The Enumerated Powers of the Constitution and the Power to Terminate Treaties.*

... While the power to "make treaties" is a constitutionally enumerated power, the power to repeal or terminate treaties is *not* one of the enumerated powers. Yet it is manifest that the termination of treaties is frequently necessary. It must thus be recognized that the power to terminate treaties is one of the *implied powers* that the Constitution implicitly vested in the *Government* when it provided for the "making" of treaties. . . . *Neely v. Henkel*, 180 U.S., 120 (1901), . . . [unanimously] held . . . that the necessary and proper clause applied to the treaty power and treaties executed thereunder. . . . This clearly recognizes the power of Congress to enact legislation pursuant to the termination clause that President Eisenhower had inserted in the Taiwan Treaty. . . .

It is . . . submitted that since the exercise of the power to terminate treaties, which have the status of law of the land, requires passage of a repealing law, it is Congress' responsibility under the Necessary and Proper Clause to do so. . . . When Congress passes an act terminating a treaty, it *makes a law*, as is illustrated by the Act of July 7, 1798, the first instance of treaty termination by the United States.

It is significant that Thomas Jefferson interpreted the Constitution as placing the power to terminate treaties in Congress and so declared in his "Manual," which as a guide for Congressional procedure persists to this day:

> Treaties being declared, equally with the laws of the United States, to be the supreme law of the land, it is understood that an act of the legislature *alone* can declare them infringed and rescinded. This was accordingly the process adopted in the case of France in 1798.

Jefferson's Manual, Rules and Practices, House of Representatives, 96th Congress, §
599, at 274 (1979). (Emphasis added)....

In 1829 Chief Justice Marshall interpreted Article II, Section 2 of the Constitution
as having the following effect:

> "Our constitution declares a treaty to be the law of the land. It is, consequently,
> to be regarded in courts of justice, as *equivalent to an act of legislature*, whenever
> it operates of itself, without the aid of any legislative provision."

Foster v. Neilson, 2 Pet. (27 U.S.) 253, 314-15 (1829) (Emphasis added), *overruled
on other grounds, United States v. Percheman*, 7 Pet. (32 U.S.) 51, 89 (1833).

These interpretations and our historical practice... consider treaties and statutes
to be of equal dignity....

IV *Foreign Affairs within the Constitutional Scheme*

A. *The Curtiss-Wright Case.*

The President asks this court to provide him with *absolute power to terminate all
treaty obligations of the United States.* This claim of absolute Presidential power is
of the same breadth as the power to seize the steel mills that President Truman claimed
and was denied in *Youngstown.* President Carter argues that this unchecked power
is a necessary incident of his power to recognize foreign governments, and is consistent
with the panoply of foreign affairs powers that the Supreme Court in *United States
v. Curtiss-Wright Export Corp.*, 299 U.S. 304 (1936) held that he was authorized to
exercise.... Neither the *Curtiss-Wright* decision nor the President's constitutional authority in foreign affairs should be construed to infringe upon Congress' exercise of
its constitutional right to exercise "all legislative powers... granted" by the Constitution, or allowed to undermine our constitutional scheme of checks and balances.

... Commentators in the years since the *Curtiss-Wright* decision, considering on
the one hand the decision's expansion of Presidential international powers, and on
the other, the powers over foreign affairs vested by the Constitution in Congress, have
puzzled over appropriate apportionment of international powers among the two
branches. Professor Henkin, for example, remarks:

> [W]e are not told how the undifferentiated bundle of powers inherent in sov-
> ereignty is distributed among the federal branches. It seems to have been assumed
> that they are distributed "naturally", those that are "legislative in character"
> to the Congress, those "executive" to the President....[59]

... The President's authority in foreign affairs is that of head of state. Through
his office the actual contacts involved in international relations are carried out. But
this power, as Justice Sutherland stated in *Curtiss-Wright*, "must be exercised in
subordination to the applicable provisions of the Constitution." Hence, when in the
conduct of foreign affairs, a legislative function is implicated, the President's power
must be accommodated to a congressional exercise of power. The negotiation of
treaties, being an executive function by the Constitution, is within the presidential
prerogative, subject to Senate approval, or possible amendment. So too, the negotiation to end treaties, if negotiations there be, may be a presidential function. Yet when
the negotiations, or other determinations, lead to a presidential decision to terminate

---

59. L. Henkin, Foreign Affairs and the Constitution 27 (1972).

a treaty, a law is necessary and thus the next required step is legislative. As law of the land, a treaty must be repealed by *Congress* as the body charged by our Constitution with the legislative function. . . .

B. *The Recognition of Foreign Governments.*

The President maintains that it would be an interference with his power to "receive Ambassadors and other public Ministers" were he not given the absolute right, *alone*, to terminate the Mutual Defense Treaty with Taiwan without any advice or consent of the Senate or any congressional action. Had the Republic of China (Taiwan) violated the treaty he might have the same right to give notice of the termination of abrogated treaties that other presidents have exercised, but Taiwan has not violated our treaty in any respect.

The President argues that the termination was necessary to his recognition of the People's Republic of China. In making that argument, the President, in effect, asks the courts of this nation to choose between upholding his right to recognize foreign governments and Congress' right to approve the termination of United States' treaties.

I am not persuaded that the court need view these distinctly separate Constitutional powers as necessarily bound together, nor need we elevate one power over the other. As the termination of a treaty is an independent legislative act under our Constitution, termination requires an independent legislative exercise. To the extent that Congress thereby becomes involved in the conduct of foreign relations, it does so in a strictly legislative sense, its approval being required for the repeal of any law.

The President's objective can be achieved merely by inviting Congress to pass a Joint Resolution authorizing the termination of the Taiwan Treaty. Or he can receive the Ambassador from the Peoples [sic] Republic of China without the treaty being terminated. There is nothing inherent in the President's constitutional power to receive the Ambassador from the People's Republic that compels terminating the Taiwan Treaty. What creates the complication that bothers the President is that there are *actually* two Chinas. The President wants to act in some respects as though there is only one China and in other respects, as indicated by the Taiwan Relations Act, as though there are two. This attempt to carry water on both shoulders is the basic cause of the President's problem and he asks this court to distort the Constitution to accomplish his objective without Congressional approval. . . .

C. *The Termination Provision of the Treaty.*

In several places the majority opinion makes an argument that is essentially based on a play on words and has no legal validity. An example of this is the statement that "notice of termination [was] given by the President *pursuant to the terms of the Mutual Defense Treaty . . .*" This is designed to give the impression that the Treaty provides that "the *President*" is specifically authorized to give the "notice of termination." Such is *not* the fact. The Treaty provision provides:

> Article X: This Treaty shall remain in force indefinitely. Either *Party* may terminate one year after notice has been given to the other *Party*.

TIAS 3178. (Emphasis added)

Clearly the *parties* referred to are "the United States of America and the Republic of China". . . . The sole issue in this case is who can act for the United States; that issue is not determined by the Treaty but by the Constitution of the United States. . . .

Goldwater v. Carter
444 U.S. 996 (1979)

ORDER

Dec. 13, 1979. The petition for a writ of certiorari is granted. The judgment of the Court of Appeals is vacated and the case is remanded to the District Court with directions to dismiss the complaint.

Justice MARSHALL concurs in the result. . . .

Justice WHITE and Justice BLACKMUN join in the grant of the petition for a writ of certiorari but would set the case for argument and give it plenary consideration. . . .

Justice POWELL, concurring.

Although I agree with the result reached by the Court, I would dismiss the complaint as not ripe for judicial review.

I

This Court has recognized that an issue should not be decided if it is not ripe for judicial review. Prudential considerations persuade me that a dispute between Congress and the President is not ready for judicial review unless and until each branch has taken action asserting its constitutional authority. Differences between the President and the Congress are commonplace under our system. The differences should, and almost invariably do, turn on political rather than legal considerations. The Judicial Branch should not decide issues affecting the allocation of power between the President and Congress until the political branches reach a constitutional impasse. Otherwise, we would encourage small groups or even individual Members of Congress to seek judicial resolution of issues before the normal political process has the opportunity to resolve the conflict.

In this case, a few Members of Congress claim that the President's action in terminating the treaty with Taiwan has deprived them of their constitutional role with respect to a change in the supreme law of the land. Congress has taken no official action. In the present posture of this case, we do not know whether there ever will be an actual confrontation between the Legislative and Executive Branches. . . . If the Congress chooses not to confront the President, it is not our task to do so. I therefore concur in the dismissal of this case.

II

Justice Rehnquist suggests, however, that the issue presented by this case is a nonjusticiable political question which can never be considered by this Court. I cannot agree. In my view, reliance upon the political-question doctrine is inconsistent with our precedents. As set forth in the seminal case of *Baker v. Carr*, 369 U.S. 186, 217 (1962), the doctrine incorporates three inquiries: (i) Does the issue involve resolution of questions committed by the text of the Constitution to a coordinate branch of Government? (ii) Would resolution of the question demand that a court move beyond areas of judicial expertise? (iii) Do prudential considerations counsel against judicial intervention? In my opinion the answer to each of these inquires would require us to decide this case if it were ready for review.

First, the existence of "a textually demonstrable constitutional commitment of the issue to a coordinate political department," *ibid.*, turns on an examination of the constitutional provisions governing the exercise of the power in question. No constitutional provision explicitly confers upon the President the power to terminate treaties. Further, Art. II, § 2, of the Constitution authorizes the President to make treaties with the advice and consent of the Senate. Article VI provides that treaties shall be a part of the supreme law of the land. These provisions add support to the view that the text of the Constitution does not unquestionably commit the power to terminate treaties to the President alone.

Second, there is no "lack of judicially discoverable and manageable standards for resolving" this case; nor is a decision impossible "without an initial policy determination of a kind clearly for nonjudicial discretion." *Baker v. Carr*, 369 U.S. at 217. We are asked to decide whether the President may terminate a treaty under the Constitution without congressional approval. Resolution of the question may not be easy, but it only requires us to apply normal principles of interpretation to the constitutional provisions at issue. The present case involves neither review of the President's activities as Commander in Chief nor impermissible interference in the field of foreign affairs. Such a case would arise if we were asked to decide, for example, whether a treaty required the President to order troops into a foreign country. But "it is error to suppose that every case or controversy which touches foreign relations lies beyond judicial cognizance." *Baker v. Carr*, 369 U.S., at 211. This case "touches" foreign relations, but the question presented to us concerns only the constitutional division of power between Congress and the President.

A simple hypothetical demonstrates the confusion that I find inherent in Justice Rehnquist's opinion concurring in the judgment. Assume that the President signed a mutual defense treaty with a foreign country and announced that it would go into effect despite its rejection by the Senate. Under Justice Rehnquist's analysis that situation would present a political question even though Art. II, § 2, clearly would resolve the dispute. Although the answer to the hypothetical case seems self-evident because it demands textual rather than interstitial analysis, the nature of the legal issue presented is no different from the issue presented in the case before us. In both cases, the Court would interpret the Constitution to decide whether congressional approval is necessary to give a Presidential decision on the validity of a treaty the force of law. Such an inquiry demands no special competence or information beyond the reach of the Judiciary.

Finally, the political-question doctrine rests in part on prudential concerns calling for mutual respect among the three branches of Government. Thus, the Judicial Branch should avoid "the potentiality of embarrassment [that would result] from multifarious pronouncements by various departments on one question." Similarly, the doctrine restrains judicial action where there is an "unusual need for unquestioning adherence to a political decision already made." *Baker v. Carr*, 369 U.S., at 217.

If this case were ripe for judicial review, none of these prudential considerations would be present. Interpretation of the Constitution does not imply lack of respect for a coordinate branch. If the President and the Congress had reached irreconcilable positions, final disposition of the question presented by this case would eliminate, rather than create, multiple constitutional interpretations. The specter of the Federal Government brought to a halt because of the mutual intransigence of the President and the Congress would require this Court to provide a resolution pursuant to our duty "'to say what the law is.'" *United States v. Nixon*, 418 U.S. 683, 703 (1974), quoting *Marbury v. Madison*, 1 Cranch 137, 177 (1803).

III

In my view, the suggestion that this case presents a political question is incompatible with this Court's willingness on previous occasions to decide whether one branch of our Government has impinged upon the power of another.... If the Congress, by appropriate formal action, had challenged the President's authority to terminate the treaty with Taiwan, the resulting uncertainty could have serious consequences for our country. In that situation, it would be the duty of this Court to resolve the issue.

Justice REHNQUIST, with whom THE CHIEF JUSTICE, Justice STEWART, and Justice STEVENS join, concurring in the judgment.

I am of the view that the basic question presented by the petitioners in this case is "political" and therefore nonjusticiable because it involves the authority of the President in the conduct of our country's foreign relations and the extent to which the Senate or the Congress is authorized to negate the action of the President. In *Coleman v. Miller*, 307 U.S. 433, a case in which members of the Kansas Legislature brought an action attacking a vote of the State Senate in favor of the ratification of the Child Labor Amendment, ... Chief Justice Hughes' opinion concluded that "Congress in controlling the promulgation of the adoption of a constitutional amendment has the final determination of the question whether by lapse of time its proposal of the amendment had lost its vitality prior to the required ratifications."

I believe it follows *a fortiori* from *Coleman* that the controversy in the instant case is a nonjusticiable political dispute that should be left for resolution by the Executive and Legislative Branches of the Government. Here, while the Constitution is express as to the manner in which the Senate shall participate in the ratification of a treaty, it is silent as to that body's participation in the abrogation of a treaty. In this respect the case is directly analogous to *Coleman, supra.* ... In light of the absence of any constitutional provision governing the termination of a treaty, and the fact that different termination procedures may be appropriate for different treaties, the instant case in my view also "must surely be controlled by political standards."

I think that the justifications for concluding that the question here is political in nature are even more compelling than in *Coleman* because it involves foreign relations—specifically a treaty commitment to use military force in the defense of a foreign government if attacked.

The present case differs in several important respects from *Youngstown Sheet & Tube Co. v. Sawyer*, 343 U.S. 579 (1952), cited by petitioners as authority both for reaching the merits of this dispute and for reversing the Court of Appeals. In *Youngstown*, private litigants brought a suit contesting the President's authority under his war powers to seize the Nation's steel industry, an action of profound and demonstrable domestic impact. Here, by contrast, we are asked to settle a dispute between coequal branches of our Government, each of which has resources available to protect and assert its interests, resources not available to private litigants outside the judicial forum.[1] Moreover, as in *Curtiss-Wright*, the effect of this action, as far as we can tell,

---

1. As observed by Chief Judge Wright in his concurring opinion below:

"Congress has initiated the termination of treaties by directing or requiring the President to give notice of termination, without any prior presidential request. Congress has annulled

is "entirely external to the United States, and [falls] within the category of foreign affairs." Finally, as already noted, the situation presented here is closely akin to that presented in *Coleman*, where the Constitution spoke only to the procedure for ratification of an amendment, not to its rejection.... Since the political nature of the questions presented should have precluded the lower courts from considering or deciding the merits of the controversy, the prior proceedings in the federal courts must be vacated, and the complaint dismissed.

[The opinion of Justice BLACKMUN is omitted.]

Justice BRENNAN, dissenting.

I ... would affirm the judgment of the Court of Appeals insofar as it rests upon the President's well-established authority to recognize, and withdraw recognition from, foreign governments.

In stating that this case presents a non-justiciable "political question," Justice Rehnquist, in my view, profoundly misapprehends the political-question principle as it applies to matters of foreign relations. Properly understood, the political-question doctrine restrains courts from reviewing an exercise of foreign policy judgment by the coordinate political branch to which authority to make that judgment has been "constitutional[ly] commit[ted]." *Baker v. Carr*, 369 U.S. 186, 211-213 (1962). But the doctrine does not pertain when a court is faced with the *antecedent* question whether a particular branch has been constitutionally designated as the repository of political decisionmaking power. The issue of decisionmaking authority must be resolved as a matter of constitutional law, not political discretion; accordingly, it falls within the competence of the courts.

The constitutional question raised here is prudently answered in narrow terms. Abrogation of the defense treaty with Taiwan was a necessary incident to Executive recognition of the Peking Government, because the defense treaty was predicated upon the now-abandoned view that the Taiwan Government was the only legitimate political authority in China. Our cases firmly establish that the Constitution commits to the President alone the power to recognize, and withdraw recognition from, foreign regimes. That mandate being clear, our judicial inquiry into the treaty rupture can go no further.

---

1. There are a host of plausible positions as to where the Constitution assigns treaty-termination power. Which of the following is most persuasive:

a. The constitutional requirement of Senate treaty approval implies a requirement of Senate approval for treaty termination?

---

treaties without any presidential notice. It has conferred on the President the power to terminate a particular treaty, and it has enacted statutes practically nullifying the domestic effects of a treaty and thus caused the President to carry out termination....

"Moreover, Congress has a variety of powerful tools for influencing foreign policy decisions that bear on treaty matters. Under Article I, Section 8 of the Constitution, it can regulate commerce with foreign nations, raise and support armies, and declare war. It has power over the appointment of ambassadors and the funding of embassies and consulates. Congress thus retains a strong influence over the President's conduct in treaty matters.

"As our political history demonstrates, treaty creation and termination are complex phenomena rooted in the dynamic relationship between the two political branches of our government. We thus should decline the invitation to set in concrete a particular constitutionally acceptable arrangement by which the President and Congress are to share treaty termination." (footnote omitted).

b. The President's constitutional foreign policy powers include the power of treaty termination:

(1) Always?

(2) When treaty termination is a necessary incident to the recognition of a foreign government?

(3) Unless the treaty expressly reserves to the legislature a role in termination?

(4) As long as treaty termination does not implicate our participation in a congressionally approved military alliance?

c. The only constitutional language that could be thought to cover termination expressly is the necessary and proper clause, and, therefore, treaty termination requires ordinary legislation?

2. Treaty termination conceivably poses at least two separate questions: first, whether the treaty was terminated by the branch of government with power to terminate treaties; second, whether the terminating branch acted on permissible grounds. Does Rehnquist persuade you that the latter question is a political question? Would Powell disagree? What about the former question?

3. Note that, following President Carter's announcement that the United States would recognize the PRC, Congress enacted legislation to govern future U.S. relations with Taiwan. Should it be relevant to a federal court's decision whether to adjudicate any legal issue regarding treaty termination that Congress did not take the occasion of that statute to object to the termination of the Mutual Defense Treaty of 1954?

4. The Court of Appeals majority coyly refused to rank in importance those factors that yielded its conclusion as to the lawfulness of President Carter's action. How do you rank those factors in importance? Assuming the case correctly resolves the merits as to the particular treaty at issue, how far should it be thought to extend? Was it proper for the court to reach the merits only because, as treaty terminations go, the facts here presented an easy case?

5. Could a two-thirds vote of each House of Congress constitutionally prevent the President's termination of a treaty? How could or should Congress resist if a President were unilaterally to withdraw from NATO without the derecognition of any signatory to the NATO treaty?

6. For historical perspectives on the treaty termination power, see Bestor, *Respective Roles of Senate and President in the Making and Abrogation of Treaties—The Original Intent of the Framers of the Constitution Historically Examined*, 55 Wash. L. Rev. 1 (1979); Berger, *The President's Unilateral Termination of the Taiwan Treaty*, 75 Nw. U. L. Rev. 577 (1980).

C. Executive Agreements

Note: International Non-Treaty Agreements

Although the Constitution does not mention executive agreements, the instrument was known even in President Washington's day, and has become the predominant form of international agreement for the U.S. Its use has been vastly expanded by practice and judicial sanction. As of 1981, 6,188 such agreements were in force, as compared to 967 treaties. Even Congress has recognized the constitutionality of negotiating executive agreements by enacting the Case Act, 1 U.S.C. § 112b (1982), which requires the Secretary of State to transmit the text of agreements other than treaties to each chamber for informational purposes.

There are three types of executive agreement: treaty-based executive agreements, congressional-executive agreements and unilateral-executive agreements.

Treaty-based executive agreements, made, as the term implies, pursuant to treaties, enjoy the same legal status as the treaties that authorize them so long as they are consistent with and within the scope of those treaties.

Congressional-executive agreements are those authorized by statute. On some particular subjects, such as postal relations, reciprocal trade, and foreign assistance, Congress has authorized the President in advance to negotiate and conclude executive agreements. Congress has also authorized the President to conclude certain agreements that have already been negotiated, as in the case of the Headquarters Agreement with the United Nations and various multilateral agreements establishing international organizations, e.g., UNRA, the International Bank and the International Monetary Fund, and the International Refugee Organization. There is no express constitutional basis for such interbranch collaboration. The Constitution expressly prescribes the treaty procedure, but does not mention other methods for negotiating foreign relations.

No branch of government seems to have been much troubled by theoretical objections to the executive agreement mechanism. It is now widely accepted that the congressional-executive agreement is a complete alternative to a treaty; instead of seeking approval from the Senate only, approval is sought from both houses of Congress. Like a treaty, such an agreement becomes the law of the land, superseding inconsistent state laws as well as inconsistent provisions in earlier treaties, other international agreements or acts of Congress.

The appeal behind using the congressional-executive agreement as an alternative to a treaty has several facets. Because such agreements may be approved by a simple majority of both houses, the Senate cannot veto an executive agreement by the one-third-plus-one vote sufficient to defeat a treaty. Another important element is the inclusion of the House. Many international agreements require legislative implementation, if only the appropriation of funds. If approval of an agreement is sought from both houses before ratification, the danger that the House of Representatives might later refuse to join in the agreement is all but eliminated.

Executive agreements may also be made solely under the President's authority. While no one has doubted that the President has the power to make some such executive agreements, there has been constitutional controversy surrounding others. It is accepted, for example, that the President, as commander-in-chief, may make armistice agreements; viewed broadly, his commander-in-chief power might support many other agreements as well, including war-time commitments on territorial and political issues for the post-war era, as at Yalta and Potsdam. The President also has sole responsibility for the recognition of foreign governments, and the Supreme Court has held this power sufficient to authorize unilateral-executive agreements to settle issues that are necessary to establish diplomatic relations. *See United States v. Belmont*, 301 U.S. 324 (1937). Additionally, it is sometimes suggested that executive agreements, unlike treaties, do not involve long-term relationships or obligations. *See* Acquisition of Naval

Air Bases in Exchange for Over-Age Destroyers, 39 Op. Att'y Gen. 484, 487 (1940) (purporting to differentiate executive agreements from treaties, which "involve commitments as to the future which would carry an obligation to exercise powers vested in the Congress").

It is unclear, however, that any principled line identifies in practice those unilateral executive agreements that do not improperly trespass on the Senate's role. Historical practice alone does not establish that the President is constitutionally free to make any agreement on any matter involving our relations with another country. This would remove the express "check" of Senate consent to treaties that appears in article II.

The Supreme Court has not yet held any executive agreement ultra vires for lack of Senate consent, nor has it given other guidelines that might define the President's power to act alone. Members of the Senate have periodically charged presidential usurpation, but have not articulated plausible limits to presidential power. *See, e.g., Dole v. Carter*, 444 F. Supp. 1065 (D. Kan. 1977) (denying Senator's petition to enjoin return to Hungary, absent a treaty, of Hungarian coronation regalia). Presidential practice, too, has not reflected any principle of limitation. Numerous agreements have been made ranging over the entire field of foreign relations.

Although there are thus few limitations on when a President may use an executive agreement rather than a treaty, the State Department has attempted to set standards for some functional accommodation between the branches in this area. State Dept. Circular 175, "Procedures on Treaties and Other International Agreements," 11 F.A.M. 700. Written in 1974, the text notes that deviation from its provisions will not invalidate actions taken by government officers nor affect the validity of negotiations engaged in or of treaties or other agreements concluded.

The Circular's general objectives are to make sure that treaties and other international agreements for the United States are carried out within constitutional and other appropriate limits. It cites three constitutional authorities for the negotiation of executive agreements: (1) the President may conclude an executive agreement pursuant to a treaty brought into force with the advice and consent of Senate; (2) the President may conclude an executive agreement on the basis of existing legislation or subject to legislation to be enacted by the Congress; and (3) the President may conclude agreements to implement his own inherent powers, including: (a) the President's authority as Chief Executive to represent the nation in foreign affairs; (b) the President's authority to receive ambassadors and other public ministers; (c) the President's authority as "commander-in-Chief" and (d) the President's authority "to take care that the laws be faithfully executed." In order to decide which constitutionally authorized procedure for international agreement ought to be chosen, other guidelines mention: (a) the extent to which the agreement involves commitments or risks affecting the nation as a whole; (b) whether the agreement is intended to affect state laws; and (c) whether the agreement may be given effect without the enactment of subsequent legislation by the Congress. Other variables include the formality needed, the anticipated duration of the agreement and past practice. Most of all, the State Department attempts in its guidelines to enhance communication between the President and Congress, asking the President to consult Congress before making an international agreement.

It is possible to identify at least one likely limitation on the unilateral executive agreement power that does not apply to treaties. Unless an executive agreement may be connected to at least implicit statutory authorization, it is probable that, unlike a treaty, it may not override prior statutes. Thus, in *United States v. Guy W. Capps*, 204 F.2d 655 (4th Cir. 1953), *aff'd on other grounds*, 348 U.S. 296 (1955), the court refused to give effect to an executive agreement regulating the export of potatoes from Canada to the United States. The court regarded the agreement, effecting a regulation of interstate and foreign commerce, as not within Presidential authority alone, but also within Congress's power to regulate such trade. Because the agreement conflicted with provisions of the Agricultural Act of 1948, the Court held that the agreement was invalid; the President's inherent foreign affairs powers were insufficient to permit him to override Congress's determinations as to trade. *Cf. South Puerto Rico Sugar Co. Trading Corp. v. United States*, 334 F.2d 622 (Ct. Cl. 1964), *cert. denied*, 379 U.S. 964 (1965).

This requirement that Presidents respect prior statutes has not, however, been thought to prevent Presidents altogether from making executive agreements as to matters on which Congress could legislate, but has not. In some circumstances, the domestic legal impact of an executive agreement may be identical to that of an article II treaty. *See, e.g., Weinberger v. Rossi*, 456 U.S. 25 (1982) (construing "treaty" exception to antidiscrimination statute as extending to executive agreements).

If an executive agreement is within the President's power, there seem to be no formal requirements as to how it must be made. It may be signed by the President or on his behalf; it may be made by Secretaries of State, ambassadors or lesser authorized officials; and there is no reason why it must be formal or even written.

Finally, it should be noted that executive agreements—like treaties—may not contravene constitutional protections for individual rights. *Ozonoff v. Berzak*, 744 F.2d 224 (1st Cir. 1984) (prohibiting loyalty check of World Health Organization physician under executive order, the terms of which violated the First Amendment).

For additional discussion, see L. Margolis, Executive Agreements and Presidential Power in Foreign Policy (1986).

United States v. Pink
315 U.S. 203 (1942)

Justice DOUGLAS delivered the opinion of the Court.

This action was brought by the United States to recover the assets of the New York branch of the First Russian Insurance Co. which remained in the hands of respondent after the payment of all domestic creditors....

The First Russian Insurance Co., organized under the laws of the former Empire of Russia, established a New York branch in 1907. It deposited with the Superintendent of Insurance, pursuant to the laws of New York, certain assets to secure payment of claims resulting from transactions of its New York branch. By certain laws, decrees, enactments and orders, in 1918 and 1919, the Russian Government nationalized the business of insurance and all of the property, wherever situated, of all Russian insurance companies (including the First Russian Insurance Co.), and discharged and cancelled all the debts of such companies and the rights of all shareholders in all such property. The New York branch of the First Russian Insurance Co. continued to do business in New York until 1925. At that time, respondent, pursuant to an order of the Supreme Court of New York, took possession of its assets for a determination and report upon the claims of the policyholders and creditors in the United States. Thereafter, all claims of domestic creditors, *i.e.*, all claims arising out of the business of the New York branch, were paid by respondent, leaving a balance in his hands of more than $1,000,000. In 1931, the New York Court of Appeals directed respondent to dispose of that balance as follows: first, to pay claims of foreign creditors who had filed attachment prior to the commencement of the liquidation proceeding. . .; and second, to pay any surplus to a quorum of the board of directors of the company. Pursuant to that mandate, respondent proceeded with the liquidation of the claims of the foreign creditors. Some payments were made thereon. The major portion of the allowed claims, however, were not paid, a stay having been granted pending disposition of the claim of the United States. On November 16, 1933, the United States recognized the Union of Soviet Socialist Republics as the *de jure* Government of Russia and as an incident of that recognition accepted an assignment (known as the Litvinov Assignment) of certain claims. The Litvinov Assignment was in the form of a letter, dated November 16, 1933, to the President of the United States from Maxim Litvinov, People's Commissar for Foreign Affairs, reading as follows:

> "Following our conversations I have the honor to inform you that the Government of the Union of Soviet Socialist Republics agrees that . . . the Government of the Union of Soviet Socialist Republics will not take any steps to [litigate] . . . for the amounts admitted to be due or that may be found to be due it, as the successor of prior Governments of Russia, or otherwise, from American nationals, including corporations, . . . does hereby release and assign all such amounts to the Government of the United States, the Government of the Union of Soviet Socialist Republics to be duly notified in each case of any amount realized . . . from such release and assignment.
>
> "The Government of the Union of Soviet Socialist Republics further agrees . . . not to make any claims with respect to:
>
> "(a) judgments rendered or that may be rendered by American courts in so far as they relate to property, or rights, or interests therein, in which the Union of Soviet Socialist Republics or its nationals may have had or may claim to have an interest; or, "(b) acts done or settlements made by or with the Government of the United States, or public officials in the United States, or its nationals, relating to property, credits, or obligations of any Government of Russia or nationals thereof."

This was acknowledged by the President on the same date. The acknowledgment, after setting forth the terms of the assignment, concluded:

> "I am glad to have these undertakings by your Government and I shall be pleased to notify your Government in each case of any amount realized by the Government of the United States from the release and assignment to it of the amounts admitted to be due, or that may be found to be due, the Government of the Union of Soviet Socialist Republics. . . . "

On November 14, 1934, the United States brought an action in the federal District Court for the Southern District of New York, seeking to recover the assets in the hands of respondent. This Court held in *United States v. Bank of New York & Trust Co.*, 296 U.S. 463, that . . . " . . . the jurisdiction of the state court should be respected"; and that, whatever might be "the effect of recognition" of the Russian

Government, it did not terminate the state proceedings. The United States was remitted to the state court for determination of its claim, no opinion being intimated on the merits. . . .

Thereafter, the present suit was instituted in the Supreme Court of New York. The defendants, other than respondent, were certain designated policyholders and other creditors who had presented in the liquidation proceedings claims against the corporation. The complaint prayed, *inter alia*, that the United States be adjudged to be the sole and exclusive owner entitled to immediate possession of the entire surplus fund in the hands of the respondent.

Respondent's answer denied the allegations of the complaint that title to the funds in question passed to the United States and that the Russian decrees had the effect claimed. It also set forth various affirmative defenses—that the order of distribution pursuant to the decree in 255 N.Y. 415, 175 N.E. 114, could not be affected by the Litvinov Assignment; . . . that the Russian decrees had no extraterritorial effect, according to Russian law; that if the decrees were given extraterritorial effect, they were confiscatory and their recognition would be unconstitutional and contrary to the public policy of the United States and of the State of New York; and that the United States, under the Litvinov Assignment, acted merely as a collection agency for the Russian Government and hence was foreclosed from asserting any title to the property in question.

The answer was filed in March, 1938. In April, 1939, the New York Court of Appeals decided *Moscow Fire Ins. Co. v. Bank of New York & Trust Co.*, 280 N.Y. 286, 20 N.E. 2d 758. . . . The New York Court of Appeals held in the *Moscow* case that the Russian decrees in question had no extraterritorial effect. If that is true, it is decisive of the present controversy. For the United States acquired, under the Litvinov Assignment, only such rights as Russia had. *Guaranty Trust Co. v. United States*, 304 U.S. 126, 143. If the Russian decrees left the New York assets of the Russian insurance companies unaffected, then Russia had nothing here to assign. But that question of foreign law is not to be determined exclusively by the state court. The claim of the United States based on the Litvinov Assignment raises a federal question. *United States v. Belmont*, 301 U.S. 324. This Court will review or independently determine all questions on which a federal right is necessarily dependent. Here, title obtained under the Litvinov Assignment depends on a correct interpretation of Russian law. As in cases arising under the full faith and credit clause, these questions of foreign law on which the asserted federal right is based are not peculiarly within the cognizance of the local courts. While deference will be given to the determination of the state court, its conclusion is not accepted as final.

We do not stop to review all the evidence in the voluminous record of the *Moscow* case bearing on the question of the extraterritorial effect of the Russian decrees of nationalization, except to note that the expert testimony tendered by the United States gave great credence to its position. Subsequently to the hearings in that case, however, the United States, through diplomatic channels, requested the Commissariat for Foreign Affairs of the Russian Government to obtain an official declaration by the Commissariat for Justice of the R.S.F.S.R. which would make clear, as a matter of Russian law, the intended effect of the Russian decree nationalizing insurance companies upon the funds of such companies outside of Russia. The official declaration, dated November 28, 1937, [certified that all property of the insurance companies had been nationalized, wherever located].

The referee in the *Moscow* case found, and the evidence supported his finding, that the Commissariat for Justice has power to interpret existing Russian law. That being true, this official declaration is conclusive so far as the intended extraterritorial effect of the Russian decree is concerned.

We hold that, so far as its intended effect is concerned, the Russian decree embraced the New York assets of the First Russian Insurance Co.

The question of whether the decree should be given extraterritorial effect is, of course, a distinct matter. One primary issue raised in that connection is whether, under our constitutional system, New York law can be allowed to stand in the way.

The decision of the New York Court of Appeals in the *Moscow* case is unequivocal. It held that "under the law of this State such confiscatory decrees do not affect the property claimed here" .... It is one thing to hold, as was done in *Guaranty Trust Co. v. United States, supra*, 304 U.S. at p. 142, that under the Litvinov Assignment the United States did not acquire "a right free of preexisting infirmity," such as the running of the statute of limitations against the Russian Government, its assignor. Unlike the problem presented here and in the *Moscow* case, that holding in no way sanctions the asserted power of New York to deny enforcement of a claim under the Litvinov Assignment because of an overriding policy of the State which denies validity in New York of the Russian decrees on which the assigned claim rest. That power was denied New York in *United States v. Belmont, supra*, 301 U.S. 324. With one qualification, to be noted, the *Belmont* case is determinative of the present controversy.

That case involved the right of the United States under the Litvinov Assignment to recover, from a custodian or stakeholder in New York, funds which had been nationalized and appropriated by the Russian decrees.

This Court, speaking through Justice Sutherland, held that the conduct of foreign relations is committed by the Constitution to the political departments of the Federal Government; that the propriety of the exercise of that power is not open to judicial inquiry; and that recognition of a foreign sovereign conclusively binds the courts and "is retroactive and validates all actions and conduct of the government so recognized from the commencement of its existence." It further held (p. 330) that recognition of the Soviet Government, the establishment of diplomatic relations with it, and the Litvinov Assignment were "all parts of one transaction, resulting in an international compact between the two governments." After stating that, "in respect of what was done here, the Executive had authority to speak as the sole organ" of the national government, it added: "The assignment and the agreements in connection therewith did not, as in the case of treaties, as that term is used in the treaty making clause of the Constitution (Art. II, § 2), require the advice and consent of the Senate." It held that the "external powers of the United States are to be exercised without regard to state laws or policies. The supremacy of a treaty in this respect has been recognized from the beginning." And it added that "all international compacts and agreements" are to be treated with similar dignity for the reason that "complete power over international affairs is in the national government and is not and cannot be subject to any curtailment or interference on the part of the several states." This Court did not stop to inquire whether in fact there was any policy of New York which enforcement of the Litvinov Assignment would infringe since "no state policy can prevail against the international compact here involved."

The New York Court of Appeals, in the *Moscow* case (280 N.Y. 309, 20 N.E. 2d 758), distinguished the *Belmont* case on the ground that it was decided on the sufficiency of the pleadings, the demurrer to the complaint admitting that under the Russian decree the property was confiscated by the Russian Government and then transferred to the United States under the Litvinov Assignment. But, as we have seen, the Russian decree in question was intended to have an extraterritorial effect and to embrace funds of the kind which are here involved. Nor can there by an serious doubt that claims of the kind here in question were included in the Litvinov Assignment. It is broad and inclusive. It should be interpreted consonantly with the purpose of the compact to eliminate all possible sources of friction between these two great nations. Strict construction would run counter to that national policy. For, as we shall see, the existence of unpaid claims against Russia and its nationals, which were held in this country, and which the Litvinov Assignment was intended to secure, had long been one impediment to resumption of friendly relations between these two great powers.

The holding in the *Belmont* case is therefore determinative of the present controversy, unless the stake of the foreign creditors in this liquidation proceeding and the provision which New York has provided for their protection call for a different result.

The *Belmont* case forecloses any relief to the Russian corporation. For this Court held in that case (301 U.S. at p. 332): "... our Constitution, laws and policies have no extraterritorial operation, unless in respect of our own citizens.... What another country has done in the way of taking over property of its nationals, and especially of its corporations, is not a matter for judicial consideration here. Such nationals must look to their own government for any redress to which they may be entitled."

But it is urged that different considerations apply in case of the foreign creditors to whom the New York Court of Appeals ordered distribution of these funds. The argument is that their rights in these funds have vested by virtue of the New York decree; that to deprive them of the property would violate the Fifth Amendment which extends its protection to aliens as well as to citizens; and that the Litvinov Assignment cannot deprive New York of its power to administer the balance of the fund in accordance with its laws for the benefit of these creditors.

At the outset, it should be noted that, so far as appears, all creditors whose claims arose out of dealing with the New York branch have been paid. Thus we are not faced with the question whether New York's policy of protecting the so-called local creditors by giving them priority in the assets deposited with the State should be recognized within the [full faith and credit interpretation] of *Clark v. Williard*, 294 U.S. 211, or should yield to the Federal policy expressed in the international compact or agreement. We intimate no opinion on that question. The contest here is between the United States and creditors of the Russian corporation who, we assume, are not citizens of this country and whose claims did not arise out of transactions with the New York branch. The United States is seeking to protect not only claims which it holds but also claims of its nationals. H. Rep. No. 865, 76th Cong., 1st Sess. Such claims did not arise out of transactions with this Russian corporation; they are, however, claims against Russia or its nationals. The existence of such claims and their non-payment had for years been one of the barriers to recognition of the Soviet regime by the Executive Department. The purpose of the discussions leading to the policy of recognition was to resolve "all questions outstanding" between the two nations. Settlement of all American claims against Russia was one method of removing some of the prior objections to recognition based on the Soviet policy of nationalization. The Litvinov Assignment was not only part and parcel of the new policy of recognition, it was also the method adopted by the Executive Department for alleviating in this country the rigors of nationalization. Congress tacitly recognized that policy. Acting in anticipation of the realization of funds under the Litvinov Assignment (H. Rep. No. 865, 76th Cong., 1st Sess.), it authorized the appointment of a Commissioner to determine the claims of American nationals against the Soviet Government. Joint Resolution of August 4, 1939, 53 Stat. 1199.

If the President had the power to determine the policy which was to govern the question of recognition, then the Fifth Amendment does not stand in the way of giving full force and effect to the Litvinov Assignment. To be sure, aliens as well as citizens are entitled to the protection of the Fifth Amendment. *Russian Volunteer Fleet v. United States*, 282 U.S. 481. A State is not precluded, however, by the Fourteenth Amendment from according priority to local creditors as against creditors who are nationals of foreign countries and whose claims arose abroad. *Disconto Gesellschaft v. Umbreit*, 208 U.S. 570. By the same token, the Federal Government is not barred by the Fifth Amendment from securing for itself and our nationals priority against such creditors. And it matters not that the procedure adopted by the Federal Government is globular and involves a regrouping of assets. There is no Constitutional reason why this Government need act as the collection agent for nationals of other countries when it takes steps to protect itself or its own nationals on external debts. There is no reason why it may not, through such devices as the Litvinov Assignment, make itself and its nationals whole from assets here before it permits such assets to go abroad in satisfaction of claims of aliens made elsewhere and not incurred in connection with business conducted in this country. The fact that New York has marshaled the claims of the foreign creditors here involved and authorized their payment does not give them immunity from that general rule.

If the priority had been accorded American claims by treaty with Russia, there would be no doubt as to its validity. The same result obtains here. The powers of the President in the conduct of foreign relations included the power, without consent of the Senate, to determine the public policy of the United States with respect to the Russian nationalization decrees. "What government is to be regarded here as representative of a foreign sovereign state is a political rather than a judicial question, and is to be determined by the political department of the government." *Guaranty Trust Co. v. United States, supra*, 304 U.S. at p. 137. That authority is not limited to a determination of the government to be recognized. It includes the power to determine the policy which is to govern the question of recognition. Objections to the underlying policy as well as objections to recognition are to be addressed to the political department and not to the courts. As we have noted, this Court in the *Belmont* case recognized that the Litvinov Assignment was an international compact which did not require the participation of the Senate. It stated: "There are many such compacts, of which a protocol, a modus vivendi, a postal convention, and agreements like that now under consideration are illustrations." Recognition is not always absolute; it is sometimes conditional. 1 Moore, International Law Digest (1906), pp. 73-74; 1 Hackworth, Digest of International Law (1940), pp. 192-195. Power to remove such obstacles to full recognition as settlement of claims of our nationals (Levitan, Executive Agreements, 35 Ill. L. Rev. 365, 382-385) certainly is a modest implied power of the President who is the "sole organ of the federal government in the field of international relations." *United States v. Curtiss-Wright Corp.*, *supra*, p. 320. Effectiveness in handling the delicate problems of foreign relations requires no less. Unless such a power exists, the power of recognition might be thwarted or seriously diluted. No such obstacle can be placed in the way of rehabilitation of relations between this country and another nation, unless the historic conception of the powers and responsibilities of the President in the conduct of foreign affairs is to be drastically revised. It was the judgment of the political department that full recognition of the Soviet Government required the settlement of all outstanding problems including the claims of our nationals. Recognition and the Litvinov Assignment were interdependent. We would usurp the executive function if we held that that decision was not final and conclusive in the courts.

"All constitutional acts of power, whether in the executive or in the judicial department, have as much legal validity and obligation as if they proceeded from the legislature,..." The Federalist, No. 64. A treaty is a "Law of the Land" under the supremacy clause (Art. VI, Cl. 2) of the Constitution. Such international compacts and agreements as the Litvinov Assignment have a similar dignity. *United States v. Belmont*, *supra*, 301 U.S. at p. 331. See Corwin, The President, Office & Powers (1940), pp. 228-240.

It is, of course, true that even treaties with foreign nations will be carefully construed so as not to derogate from the authority and jurisdiction of the States of this nation unless clearly necessary to effectuate the national policy. *Guaranty Trust Co. v. United States*, *supra*, p. 143 and cases cited. For example, in *Todok v. Union State Bank*, 281 U.S. 449, this Court took pains in its construction of a treaty, relating to the power of an alien to dispose of property in this country, not to invalidate the provisions of state law governing such dispositions. Frequently the obligation of a treaty will be dependent on state law. But state law must yield when it is inconsistent with, or impairs the policy or provisions of, a treaty or of an international compact or agreement. Then, the power of a State to refuse enforcement of rights based on foreign law which runs counter to the public policy of the forum must give way before the superior Federal policy evidenced by a treaty or international compact or agreement.

Enforcement of New York's policy as formulated by the *Moscow* case would collide with and subtract from the Federal policy, whether it was premised on the absence of extraterritorial effect of the Russian decrees, the conception of the New York branch as a distinct juristic personality, or disapproval by New York of the Russian program of nationalization. For the *Moscow* case refuses to give effect or recognition in New York to acts of the Soviet Government which the United States by its policy of recognition agreed no longer to question. Enforcement of such state policies would indeed tend to restore some of the precise impediments to friendly relations which the President intended to remove on inauguration of the policy of recognition of the Soviet Government....

We recently stated in *Hines v. Davidowitz*, 312 U.S. 52, 68, that the field which affects international relations is "the one aspect of our government that from the first has been most generally conceded imperatively to demand broad national authority"; and that any state power which may exist "is restricted to the narrowest of limits." There, we were dealing with the question as to whether a state statute regulating aliens survived a similar federal statute. We held that it did not. Here, we are dealing with an exclusive federal function. If state laws and policies did not yield before the exercise of the external powers of the United States, then our foreign policy might be thwarted. These are delicate matters. If state action could defeat or alter our foreign policy, serious consequences might ensue. The nation as a whole would be held to answer if a State created difficulties with a foreign power. Certainly, the conditions for "enduring friendship" between the nations, which the policy of recognition in this instance was designed to effectuate, are not likely to flourish where, contrary to national policy, a lingering atmosphere of hostility is created by state action.

Such considerations underlie the principle of *Oetjen v. Central Leather Co.*, 246 U.S. 297, 302-303, that when a revolutionary government is recognized as a *de jure* government, "such recognition is retroactive in effect and validates all the actions and conduct of the government so recognized from the commencement of its existence." They also explain the rule expressed in *Underhill v. Hernandez*, 168 U.S. 250, 252, that "the courts of one country will not sit in judgment on the acts of the government of another done within its own territory." ...

We hold that the right to the funds or property in question became vested in the Soviet Government as the successor to the First Russian Insurance Co.; that this right has passed to the United States under the Litvinov Assignment; and that the United States is entitled to the property as against the corporation and the foreign creditors.

The judgment is reversed and the cause is remanded to the Supreme Court of New York for proceedings not inconsistent with this opinion.

Reversed.

Justice REED and Justice JACKSON did not participate in the consideration or decision of this case.

[Justice FRANKFURTER wrote a separate concurrence. Justice STONE dissented.]

---

1. Among the more instructive aspects of the *Pink* case is the hint it gives of the factual and legal complexity of claims settlement litigation. Can you summarize the procedural history of this litigation and the question that differentiates this case from *Belmont*?

2. The court holds that the executive agreement at issue, accepting the Litvinov Assignment, did not require Senate consent. Does *Pink* cast doubt on the statement in *U.S. v. Guy W. Capps, Inc.*, 204 F.2d 655 (4th Cir. 1953), *aff'd on other grounds*, 348 U.S. 296 (1955), cited earlier, that the President may not enter into executive agreements inconsistent with prior federal legislation? What if the agreement is part and parcel of the United States' recognition of another country?

3. Claims litigation often involves a challenge to the expropriatory or other injurious acts of foreign governments in foreign territory. In the United States, as well as in other countries, litigants raising such claims may find adjudication barred by the so-called Act of State Doctrine, a judicially-imposed rule of self-restraint, by which courts do not inquire into the validity of acts of other governments within their own territory. The doctrine, given modern explanation in *Banco Nacional de Cuba v. Sabbatino*, 376 U.S. 398 (1964), respects the separation of powers because it seeks to prevent courts from undermining the political branches. The contours of the doctrine are not always clear, however. Both Congress and the executive branch, for example, may try to prevent its application. In 1964, Congress enacted the Hickenlooper Amendment, 22 U.S.C. § 2370(e)(2) (1982), seeking to limit the use of the doctrine, unless the President determines and suggests to a court that, because of U.S.

foreign policy interests, the doctrine ought to be applied.* The Amendment has been strictly construed by the courts, and has not always prevented courts from following the Act of State doctrine on their own initiative.

In 1972, three of the five majority Justices in *First National City Bank v. Banco Nacional de Cuba*, 406 U.S. 759, expressed approval of the so-called *Bernstein* exception [based on *Bernstein v. N.V. Nederlandsche-Amerikaansche Stoomvaart-Maatschappij*, 210 F.2d 375 (2d Cir. 1954)] to the doctrine. In *Bernstein*, the Court of Appeals, on separation of powers grounds, respected a request from the State Department to refrain from applying the doctrine and examine the legal issues raised by an otherwise protected foreign sovereign act. Six of the 9 Justices disapproved of the exception, however, and it is not followed as law. Nonetheless, courts may give some weight to the Department of State's views in deciding, in a particular case, whether invocation of the doctrine is appropriate.

This tortuous history raises several separation of powers puzzles. First, should the Act of State doctrine be regarded as a judicial statement that the validity of other governments' acts in their own territory is a question constitutionally committed to the political branches of government to determine? If so, the doctrine would then appear to be a branch of the political question doctrine, and the political branches presumably could not delegate their constitutionally vested decisionmaking authority to the courts. Alternatively, should the doctrine be viewed as a prudential practice to avoid undermining foreign relations in particular cases? If so, then assurances in a particular case that foreign relations would not be adversely affected by judicial inquiry into another government's acts should have weight. Perhaps, given that the courts have no foreign affairs powers, they should be determinative. But, from whom may those assurances come—from the President or from Congress? May Congress limit the President's ability to command either the application or nonapplication of the doctrine? Must Congress authorize such commands?

For a more thorough exploration of the Act of State doctrine, see H. Steiner & D. Vagts, Transnational Legal Problems: Materials and Text 672-728 (1976); T. Franck and M. Glennon, Foreign Relations and National Security Law 202-214 (1987).

4. For further discussion of the separation of powers implications of international claims settlements, see Note, *The Executive Claims Settlement Power: Constitutional Authority and Foreign Affairs Applications*, 85 Colum. L. Rev. 155 (1985).

Dames & Moore v. Regan
453 U.S. 654 (1981)

[In the waning hours of the Carter Administration, executive branch officials worked feverishly to reach a settlement of the Iranian hostage crisis, which began in November,

---

* In a variety of contexts, the State Department provides courts with specific "suggestions" or instructions as to U.S. foreign policy. Such suggestions, for example, are used to inform courts as to the U.S. recognition policy with respect to a particular foreign government. The State Department may supply its views on its own initiative and, in rare cases, a court may seek them *sua sponte*; typically, however, they are sought by one of the parties to pending litigation. With respect to recognition, the current judicial practice is to rely on these views conclusively.

1979. As a part of a deal for the hostages' release, President Carter agreed both to nullify certain attachments that courts had awarded U.S. creditors against assets of the Iranian government, and to suspend certain claims against Iran pending their resolution in an international claims tribunal. Only the former action purported to rest on statutory authority. Carter's agreement did not involve our recognition of Iran. Although the U.S. recognized the revolutionary government in 1979, we subsequently broke diplomatic relations (which did not affect the prior recognition). As you read this decision, consider how you would have advised President Carter in advance regarding the legality of the settlement. Which sources of authority would you have invoked, with what weight for each? Also, consider the decision's effect on precedent. Does this case breathe new life into *Midwest Oil*? What guidance does Justice Rehnquist derive from *Youngstown*?]

Justice REHNQUIST delivered the opinion of the Court.

The questions presented by this case touch fundamentally upon the matter in which our Republic is to be governed. Throughout the nearly two centuries of our Nation's existence under the Constitution, this subject has generated considerable debate.... As [various] writings reveal it is doubtless both futile and perhaps dangerous to find any epigrammatical explanation of how this country has been governed. Indeed, as Justice Jackson noted, "[a] judge...may be surprised at the poverty of really useful and unambiguous authority applicable to concrete problems of executive power as they actually present themselves." *Youngstown Sheet & Tube Co. v. Sawyer*, 343 U.S. 579, 634 (1952) (concurring opinion).

Our decision today will not dramatically alter this situation, for the Framers "did not make the judiciary the overseer of our government." *Id.*, at 594 (Frankfurter, J., concurring). We are confined to a resolution of the dispute presented to us. That dispute involves various Executive Orders and regulations by which the President nullified attachments and liens on Iranian assets in the United States, directed that these assets be transferred to Iran, and suspended claims against Iran that may be presented to an International Claims Tribunal. This action was taken in an effort to comply with an Executive Agreement between the United States and Iran. We granted certiorari before judgment in this case, and set an expedited briefing and argument schedule, because lower courts had reached conflicting conclusions on the validity of the President's actions and, as the Solicitor General informed us, unless the Government acted by July 19, 1981, Iran could consider the United States to be in breach of the Executive Agreement.

But before turning to the facts and law which we believe determine the result in this case, we stress that the expeditious treatment of the issues involved by all of the courts which have considered the President's actions makes us acutely aware of the necessity to rest decision on the narrowest possible ground capable of deciding the case. This does not mean that reasoned analysis may give way to judicial fiat. It does mean that the statement of Justice Jackson—that we decide difficult cases presented to us by virtue of our commissions, not our competence—is especially true here. We attempt to lay down no general "guidelines" covering other situations not involved here, and attempt to confine the opinion only to the very questions necessary to decision of the case.

Perhaps it is because it is so difficult to reconcile the foregoing definition of Art. III judicial power with the broad range of vitally important day-to-day questions regularly decided by Congress or the Executive, without either challenge or interference by the Judiciary, that the decisions of the Court in this area have been rare, episodic, and afford little precedential value for subsequent cases....

As we now turn to the factual and legal issues in this case, we freely confess that we are obviously deciding only one more episode in the never-ending tension between the President exercising the executive authority in a world that presents each day some new challenge with which he must deal and the Constitution under which we all live and which no one disputes embodies some sort of system of checks and balances.

I

On November 4, 1979, the American Embassy in Tehran was seized and our diplomatic personnel were captured and held hostage. In response to that crisis, President Carter, acting pursuant to the International Emergency Economic Powers Act, 91 Stat. 1626, 50 U.S.C. §§ 1701-1706 (hereinafter IEEPA), declared a national emergency on November 14, 1979,[1] and blocked the removal or transfer of "all property and interests in property of the Government of Iran, its instrumentalities and controlled entities and the Central Bank of Iran which are or become subject to the jurisdiction of the United States...." Exec. Order No. 12170.[2] President Carter authorized the Secretary of the Treasury to promulgate regulations carrying out the blocking order. On November 15, 1979, the Treasury Department's Office of Foreign Assets Control issued a regulation providing that "[u]nless licensed or authorized... any attachment, judgment, decree, lien, execution, garnishment, or other judicial process is null and void with respect to any property in which on or since [November 14, 1979,] there existed an interest of Iran." 31 CFR § 535.203(e) (1980). The regulations also made clear that any licenses or authorizations granted could be "amended, modified, or revoked at any time." § 535.805.

On November 26, 1979, the President granted a general license authorizing certain judicial proceedings against Iran but which did not allow the "entry of any judgment or of any decree or order of similar or analogous effect..." On December 19, 1979, a clarifying regulation was issued stating that "the general authorization for judicial proceedings contained... includes pre-judgment attachment." § 535.418.

On December 19, 1979, petitioner Dames & Moore filed suit in the United States District Court for the Central District of California against the Government of Iran, the Atomic Energy Organization of Iran, and a number of Iranian banks. In its complaint, petitioner alleged that its wholly owned subsidiary... was a party to a written contract with the Atomic Energy Organization.... [T]he subsidiary was to conduct site studies for a proposed nuclear power plant in Iran. As provided in the terms of the contract, the Atomic Energy Organization terminated the agreement for its own convenience on June 30, 1979. Petitioner contended, however, that it was

---

1. Title 50 U.S.C. § 1701(a) states that the President's authority under the Act "may be exercised to deal with any unusual and extraordinary threat, which has its source in whole or substantial part outside the United States, to the national security, foreign policy, or economy of the United States, if the President declares a national emergency with respect to such threat." Petitioner does not challenge President Carter's declaration of a national emergency.

2. Title 50 U.S.C. § 1702(a)(1)(B) empowers the President to

"investigate, regulate, direct and compel, nullify, void, prevent or prohibit, any acquisition, holding, withholding, use, transfer, withdrawal, transportation, importation or exportation of, or dealing in, or exercising any right, power, or privilege with respect to, or transactions involving, any property in which any foreign country or a national thereof has any interest..."

owed $3,436,694.30 plus interest for services performed under the contract prior to the date of termination. The District Court issued orders of attachment directed against property of the defendants, and the property of certain Iranian banks was then attached to secure any judgment that might be entered against them.

On January 20, 1981, the Americans held hostage were released by Iran pursuant to an Agreement entered into the day before and embodied in two Declarations of the Democratic and Popular Republic of Algeria. The Agreement stated that "[i]t is the purpose of [the United States and Iran]... to terminate all litigation as between the Government of each party and the nationals of the other, and to bring about the settlement and termination of all such claims through binding arbitration." In furtherance of this goal, the Agreement called for the establishment of an Iran-United States Claims Tribunal which would arbitrate any claims not settled within six months. Awards of the Claims Tribunal are to be "final and binding" and "enforceable... in the courts of any nation in accordance with its laws." Under the Agreement, the United States is obligated

> "to terminate all legal proceedings in United States courts involving claims of United States persons and institutions against Iran and its state enterprises, to nullify all attachments and judgments obtained therein, to prohibit all further litigation based on such claims, and to bring about the termination of such claims through binding arbitration."

In addition, the United States must "act to bring about the transfer" by July 19, 1981, of all Iranian assets held in this country by American banks. One billion dollars of these assets will be deposited in a security account in the Bank of England, to the account of the Algerian Central Bank, and used to satisfy awards rendered against Iran by the Claims Tribunal.

On January 19, 1981, President Carter issued a series of Executive Orders implementing the terms of the agreement. Exec. Orders Nos. 12276-12285, 46 Fed.Reg. 7913-7932. These Orders revoked all licenses permitting the exercise of "any right, power, or privilege" with regard to Iranian funds, securities, or deposits; "nullified" all non-Iranian interests in such assets acquired subsequent to the blocking order of November 14, 1979; and required those banks holding Iranian assets to transfer them "to the Federal Reserve Bank of New York, to be held or transferred as directed by the Secretary of the Treasury."

On February 24, 1981, President Reagan issued an Executive Order in which he "ratified" the January 19th Executive Orders. Exec. Order No. 12294, 46 Fed.Reg. 14111. Moreover, he "suspended" all "claims which may be presented to the... Tribunal" and provided that such claims "shall have no legal effect in any action now pending in any court of the United States." The suspension of any particular claim terminates if the Claims Tribunal determines that it has no jurisdiction over that claim; claims are discharged for all purposes when the Claims Tribunal either awards some recovery and that amount is paid, or determines that no recovery is due.

Meanwhile, on January 27, 1981, petitioner moved for summary judgment in the District Court[, which]... awarded petitioner the amount claimed under the contract plus interest.... The District Court [later] ordered that all prejudgment attachments obtained against the Iranian defendants be vacated and that further proceedings against the bank defendants be stayed in light of the Executive Orders discussed above.

... [P]etitioner [subsequently] filed this action in the District Court for declaratory and injunctive relief against the United States and the Secretary of the Treasury, seeking to prevent enforcement of the Executive Orders and Treasury Department regulations implementing the Agreement with Iran. In its complaint, petitioner alleged that the actions of the President and the Secretary of the Treasury implementing the Agreement with Iran were beyond their statutory and constitutional powers and, in any event, were unconstitutional to the extent they adversely affect petitioner's final judgment against the Government of Iran and the Atomic Energy Organization, its execution of that judgment in the State of Washington, its prejudgment attachments, and its ability to continue to litigate against the Iranian banks. On May 28, 1981, the District Court denied petitioner's motion for a preliminary injunction and dismissed petitioner's complaint for failure to state a claim upon which relief could be granted. Prior to the District Court's ruling, the United States Courts of Appeals for the First and the District of Columbia Circuits upheld the President's authority to issue the Executive Orders and regulations challenged by petitioner. See *Chas. T. Main Int'l, Inc. v. Khuzestan Water & Power Authority*, 651 F.2d 800 (CA1 1981); *American Int'l Group, Inc. v. Islamic Republic of Iran*, 211 U.S. App.D.C. 468, 657 F.2d 430 (1981).

On June 3, 1981, petitioner filed a notice of appeal from the District Court's order, and the appeal was docketed in the United States Court of Appeals for the Ninth Circuit. On June 4, the Treasury Department amended its regulations to mandate "the transfer of bank deposits and certain other financial assets of Iran in the United States to the Federal Reserve Bank of New York by noon, June 19." The District Court, however, entered an injunction pending appeal prohibiting the United States from requiring the transfer of Iranian property that is subject to "any writ of attachment, garnishment, judgment, levy, or other judicial lien" issued by any court in favor of petitioner. Arguing that this is a case of "imperative public importance," petitioner then sought a writ of certiorari before judgment. See 28 U.S.C. § 2101(e); this Court's Rule 18. Because the issues presented here are of great significance and demand prompt resolution, we granted the petition for the writ, adopted an expedited briefing schedule, and set the case for oral argument on June 24, 1981. 452 U.S. 932 (1981).

II

The parties and the lower courts, confronted with the instant questions, have all agreed that much relevant analysis is contained in *Youngstown Sheet & Tube Co. v. Sawyer*, 343 U.S. 579 (1952). Justice Black's opinion for the Court in that case, involving the validity of President Truman's effort to seize the country's steel mills in the wake of a nationwide strike, recognized that "[t]he President's power, if any, to issue the order must stem either from an act of Congress or from the Constitution itself." Justice Jackson's concurring opinion elaborated in a general way the consequences of different types of interaction between the two democratic branches in assessing Presidential authority to act in any given case....

Although we have in the past found and do today find Justice Jackson's classifications of executive actions into three general categories analytically useful, we should be mindful of Justice Holmes' admonition, ... that "[t]he great ordinances of the Constitution do not establish and divide fields of black and white." *Springer v. Philippine Islands*, 277 U.S. 189, 209 (1928) (dissenting opinion). Justice Jackson himself recognized that his three categories represented "a somewhat over-simplified grouping," and it is doubtless the case that executive action in any particular instance falls, not neatly in one of three pigeonholes, but rather at some point along a spectrum running from explicit congressional authorization to explicit congressional prohibition. This is particularly true as respects cases such as the one before us, involving responses to international crises the nature of which Congress can hardly have been expected to anticipate in any detail.

III

In nullifying post-November 14, 1979, attachments and directing those persons holding blocked Iranian funds and securities to transfer them to the Federal Reserve Bank of New York for ultimate transfer to Iran, President Carter cited five sources of express or inherent power. The Government, however, has principally relied on § 203 of the IEEPA, 50 U.S.C. § 1702(a)(1), as authorization for these actions. Section 1702(a)(1) provides in part:

> "At the times and to the extent specified in section 1701 of this title, the President may, under such regulations as he may prescribe, by means of instructions, licenses, or otherwise—

> "(A) investigate, regulate, or prohibit—

> "(i) any transactions in foreign exchange,

> "(ii) transfers of credit or payments between, by, through, or to any banking institution, to the extent that such transfers or payments involve any interest of any foreign country or a national thereof,

> "(iii) the importing or exporting of currency or securities, and

> "(B) investigate, regulate, direct and compel, nullify, void, prevent or prohibit, any acquisition, holding, withholding, use, transfer, withdrawal, transportation, importation or exportation of, or dealing in, or exercising any right, power, or privilege with respect to, or transactions involving, any property in which any foreign country or a national thereof has any interest;

> "by any person, or with respect to any property, subject to the jurisdiction of the United States."

The Government contends that the acts of "nullifying" the attachments and ordering the "transfer" of the frozen assets are specifically authorized by the plain language of the above statute. The two Courts of Appeals that have considered the issue agreed with this contention. In *Chas. T. Main Int'l, Inc. v. Khuzestan Water & Power Authority*, the Court of Appeals for the First Circuit explained:

> "The President relied on his IEEPA powers in November 1979, when he 'blocked' all Iranian assets in this country, and again in January 1981, when he 'nullified' interests acquired in blocked property, and ordered that property's transfer. The President's actions, in this regard, are in keeping with the language of IEEPA: initially he 'prevent[ed] and prohibit[ed]' 'transfers' of Iranian assets; later he 'direct[ed] and compel[led]' the 'transfer' and 'withdrawal' of the assets, 'nullify[ing]' certain 'rights' and 'privileges' acquired in them.

> "Main argues that IEEPA does not supply the President with power to override judicial remedies, such as attachments and injunctions, or to extinguish 'interests' in foreign assets held by United States citizens. But we can find no such limitation in IEEPA's terms. The language of IEEPA is sweeping and unqualified.

It provides broadly that the President may void or nullify the 'exercising [by *any* person of] *any* right, power or privilege with respect to ... any property in which any foreign country has any interest. ...' 50 U.S.C. § 1702(a)(1)(B)."

651 F.2d, at 806-807 (emphasis in original). In *American Int'l Group, Inc. v. Islamic Republic of Iran*, the Court of Appeals for the District of Columbia Circuit employed a similar rationale in sustaining President Carter's action. ...

Petitioner contends that we should ignore the plain language of this statute because an examination of its legislative history as well as the history of § 5(b) of the Trading With the Enemy Act (hereinafter TWEA), 40 Stat. 411, as amended, 50 U.S.C. App. § 5(b) (1976 ed. and Supp. III), from which the pertinent language of § 1702 is directly drawn, reveals that the statute was not intended to give the President such extensive power over the assets of a foreign state during times of national emergency. According to petitioner, once the President instituted the November 14, 1979, blocking order, § 1702 authorized him "only to continue the freeze or to discontinue controls."

We do not agree and refuse to read out of § 1702 all meaning to the words "transfer," "compel," or "nullify." Nothing in the legislative history of either § 1702 or § 5(b) of the TWEA requires such a result. To the contrary, we think both the legislative history and cases interpreting the TWEA fully sustain the broad authority of the Executive when acting under this congressional grant of power. See, *e.g.*, *Orvis v. Brownell*, 345 U.S. 183 (1953).[5] Although Congress intended to limit the President's emergency power in peacetime, we do not think the changes brought about by the enactment of the IEEPA in any way affected the authority of the President to take the specific actions taken here. We likewise note that by the time petitioner instituted this action, the President had already entered the freeze order. Petitioner proceeded against the blocked assets only after the Treasury Department had issued revocable licenses authorizing such proceedings and attachments. The Treasury Regulations provided that "unless licensed" any attachment is null and void, 31 CFR § 535.203(e) (1980), and all licenses "may be amended, modified, or revoked at any time." §

---

5.   Petitioner argues that under the TWEA the President was given two powers: (1) the power temporarily to freeze or block the transfer of foreign-owned assets; and (2) the power summarily to seize and permanently vest title to foreign-owned assets. It is contended that only the "vesting" provisions of the TWEA gave the President the power *permanently* to dispose of assets and when Congress enacted the IEEPA in 1977 it purposefully did not grant the President this power. According to petitioner, the nullification of the attachments and the transfer of the assets will permanently dispose of the assets and would not even be permissible under the TWEA. We disagree. Although it is true the IEEPA does not give the President the power to "vest" or to take title to the assets, it does not follow that the President is not authorized under both the IEEPA and the TWEA to otherwise permanently dispose of the assets in the manner done here. Petitioner errs in assuming that the only power granted by the language used in both § 1702 and § 5(b) of the TWEA is the power temporarily to freeze assets. As noted above, the plain language of the statute defies such a holding. Section 1702 authorizes the President to "direct and compel" the "transfer, withdrawal, transportation, ... or exportation of ... any property in which any foreign country ... has any interest. ..."

We likewise reject the contention that *Orvis v. Brownell* and *Zittman v. McGrath*, 341 U.S. 446 (1951), grant petitioner the right to retain its attachments on the Iranian assets. To the contrary, we think *Orvis* supports the proposition that an American claimant may not use an attachment that is subject to a revocable license and that has been obtained after the entry of a freeze order to limit in any way the actions the *President* may take under § 1702 respecting the frozen assets. An attachment so obtained is in every sense subordinate to the President's power under the IEEPA.

535.805. As such, the attachments obtained by petitioner were specifically made subordinate to further actions which the President might take under the IEEPA. Petitioner was on notice of the contingent nature of its interest in the frozen assets.

This Court has previously recognized that the congressional purpose in authorizing blocking orders is "to put control of foreign assets in the hands of the President...." *Propper v. Clark*, 337 U.S. 472, 493 (1949). Such orders permit the President to maintain the foreign assets at his disposal for use in negotiating the resolution of a declared national emergency. The frozen assets serve as a "bargaining chip" to be used by the President when dealing with a hostile country. Accordingly, it is difficult to accept petitioner's argument because the practical effect of it is to allow individual claimants throughout the country to minimize or wholly eliminate this "bargaining chip" through attachments, garnishments, or similar encumbrances on property. Neither the purpose the statute was enacted to serve nor its plain language supports such a result.[6]

Because the President's action in nullifying the attachments and ordering the transfer of the assets was taken pursuant to specific congressional authorization, it is "supported by the strongest of presumptions and the widest latitude of judicial interpretation, and the burden of persuasion would rest heavily upon any who might attack it." *Youngstown*, 343 U.S., at 637 (Jackson, J., concurring). Under the circumstances of this case, we cannot say that petitioner has sustained that heavy burden. A contrary ruling would mean that the Federal Government as a whole lacked the power exercised by the President, and that we are not prepared to say.

IV

Although we have concluded that the IEEPA constitutes specific congressional authorization to the President to nullify the attachments and order the transfer of Iranian assets, there remains the question of the President's authority to suspend claims pending in American courts. Such claims have, of course, an existence apart from the attachments which accompanied them. In terminating these claims through Executive Order No. 12294 the President purported to act under authority of both the IEEPA and 22 U.S.C. § 1732, the so-called "Hostage Act."

---

6. Although petitioner concedes that the President could have forbidden attachments, it nevertheless argues that once he allowed them the President permitted claimants to acquire property interests in their attachments. Petitioner further argues that only the licenses to obtain the attachments were made revocable, not the attachments themselves. It is urged that the January 19, 1981, order revoking all licenses only affected petitioner's right to obtain future attachments. We disagree. As noted above, the regulations specifically provided that any attachment is null and void "unless licensed," and all licenses may be revoked at any time. Moreover, common sense defies petitioner's reading of the regulations. The President could hardly have intended petitioner and other similarly situated claimants to have the power to take control of the frozen assets out of his hands.

Our construction of petitioner's attachments as being "revocable," "contingent," and "in every sense subordinate to the President's power under the IEEPA," in effect answers petitioner's claim that even if the President had the authority to nullify the attachments and transfer the assets, the exercise of such would constitute an unconstitutional taking of property in violation of the Fifth Amendment absent just compensation. We conclude that because of the President's authority to prevent or condition attachments, and because of the orders he issued to this effect, petitioner did not acquire any "property" interest in its attachments of the sort that would support a constitutional claim for compensation.

We conclude that although the IEEPA authorized the nullification of the attachments, it cannot be read to authorize the suspension of the claims. The claims of American citizens against Iran are not in themselves transactions involving Iranian property or efforts to exercise any rights with respect to such property. An *in personam* lawsuit, although it might eventually be reduced to judgment and that judgment might be executed upon, is an effort to establish liability and fix damages and does not focus on any particular property within the jurisdiction. The terms of the IEEPA therefore do not authorize the President to suspend claims in American courts. This is the view of all the courts which have considered the question.

The Hostage Act, passed in 1868, provides:

> "Whenever it is made known to the President that any citizen of the United States has been unjustly deprived of his liberty by or under the authority of any foreign government, it shall be the duty of the President forthwith to demand of that government the reasons of such imprisonment; and if it appears to be wrongful and in violation of the rights of American citizenship, the President shall forthwith demand the release of such citizen, and if the release so demanded is unreasonably delayed or refused, the President shall use such means, not amounting to acts of war, as he may think necessary and proper to obtain or effectuate the release; and all the facts and proceedings relative thereto shall as soon as practicable be communicated by the President to Congress."

We are reluctant to conclude that this provision constitutes specific authorization to the President to suspend claims in American courts. Although the broad language of the Hostage Act suggests it may cover this case, there are several difficulties with such a view. The legislative history indicates that the Act was passed in response to a situation unlike the recent Iranian crisis. Congress in 1868 was concerned with the activity of certain countries refusing to recognize the citizenship of naturalized Americans travelling abroad, and repatriating such citizens against their will. These countries were not interested in returning the citizens in exchange for any sort of ransom. This also explains the reference in the Act to imprisonment "in violation of the rights of American citizenship." Although the Iranian hostage-taking violated international law and common decency, the hostages were not seized out of any refusal to recognize their American citizenship—they were seized precisely *because of* their American citizenship. The legislative history is also somewhat ambiguous on the question whether Congress contemplated Presidential action such as that involved here or rather simply reprisals directed against the offending foreign country and *its* citizens.

Concluding that neither the IEEPA nor the Hostage Act constitutes specific authorization of the President's action suspending claims, however, is not to say that these statutory provisions are entirely irrelevant to the question of the validity of the President's action. We think both statutes highly relevant in the looser sense of indicating congressional acceptance of a broad scope for executive action in circumstances such as those presented in this case. . . . [T]he IEEPA delegates broad authority to the President to act in times of national emergency with respect to property of a foreign country. The Hostage Act similarly indicates congressional willingness that the President have broad discretion when responding to the hostile acts of foreign sovereigns. . . . An original version of the Act, which authorized the President to suspend trade with a foreign country and even arrest citizens of that country in the United States in retaliation, was rejected because "there may be a great variety of cases arising where other and different means would be equally effective, and where the end desired could be accomplished without resorting to such dangerous and violent measures."

Although we have declined to conclude that the IEEPA or the Hostage Act directly authorizes the President's suspension of claims for the reasons noted, we cannot ignore the general tenor of Congress' legislation in this area in trying to determine whether the President is acting alone or at least with the acceptance of Congress. As we have noted, Congress cannot anticipate and legislate with regard to every possible action the President may find it necessary to take or every possible situation in which he might act. Such failure of Congress specifically to delegate authority does not, "especially . . . in the areas of foreign policy and national security," imply "congressional disapproval" of action taken by the Executive. *Haig v. Agee*, 453 U.S. 280, 291. On the contrary, the enactment of legislation closely related to the question of the President's authority in a particular case which evinces legislative intent to accord the President broad discretion may be considered to "invite" "measures on independent presidential responsibility," *Youngstown*, 343 U.S., at 637 (Jackson, J., concurring). At least this is so where there is no contrary indication of legislative intent and when, as here, there is a history of congressional acquiescence in conduct of the sort engaged in by the President. It is to that history which we now turn.

Not infrequently in affairs between nations, outstanding claims by nationals of one country against the government of another country are "sources of friction" between the two sovereigns. *United States v. Pink*, 315 U.S. 203, 225 (1942). To resolve these difficulties, nations have often entered into agreements settling the claims of their respective nationals. As one treatise writer puts it, international agreements settling claims by nationals of one state against the government of another "are established international practice reflecting traditional international theory." L. Henkin, Foreign Affairs and the Constitution 262 (1972). Consistent with that principle, the United States has repeatedly exercised its sovereign authority to settle the claims of its nationals against foreign countries. Though those settlements have sometimes been made by treaty, there has also been a longstanding practice of settling such claims by executive agreement without the advice and consent of the Senate.[8] Under such agreements, the President has agreed to renounce or extinguish claims of United States nationals against foreign governments in return for lump-sum payments or the establishment of arbitration procedures. To be sure, many of these settlements were encouraged by the United States claimants themselves, since a claimant's only hope of obtaining any payment at all might lie in having his Government negotiate a diplomatic settlement on his behalf. But it is also undisputed that the "United States has sometimes disposed of the claims of its citizens without their consent, or even without consultation with them, usually without exclusive regard for their interests, as distinguished from those of the nation as a whole." Henkin, *supra*, at 262-263. It is clear that the practice of settling claims continues today. Since 1952, the President has entered into at least 10 binding settlements with foreign nations, including an $80 million settlement with the People's Republic of China.[9]

---

8. At least since the case of the "Wilmington Packet" in 1799, Presidents have exercised the power to settle claims of United States nationals by executive agreement. . . .

9. Those agreements are [1979] 30 U.S.T. 1957 (People's Republic of China); [1976] 27 U.S.T. 3933 (Peru); [1976] 27 U.S.T. 4214 (Egypt); [1974] 25 U.S.T. 227 (Peru); [1973] 24 U.S.T. 522 (Hungary); [1969] 20 U.S.T. 2654 (Japan); [1965] 16 U.S.T. 1 (Yugoslavia); [1963] 14 U.S.T. 969 (Bulgaria); [1960] 11 U.S.T. 1953 (Poland); [1960] 11 U.S.T. 317 (Rumania).

Crucial to our decision today is the conclusion that Congress has implicitly approved the practice of claim settlement by executive agreement. This is best demonstrated by Congress' enactment of the International Claims Settlement Act of 1949, 22 U.S.C. § 1621. The Act had two purposes: (1) to allocate to United States nationals funds received in the course of an executive claims settlement with Yugoslavia, and (2) to provide a procedure whereby funds resulting from future settlements could be distributed. To achieve these ends Congress created the International Claims Commission, now the Foreign Claims Settlement Commission, and gave it jurisdiction to make final and binding decisions with respect to claims by United States nationals against settlement funds. 22 U.S.C. § 1623(a). By creating a procedure to implement future settlement agreements, Congress placed its stamp of approval on such agreements. . . .

Over the years Congress has frequently amended the International Claims Settlement Act to provide for particular problems arising out of settlement agreements, thus demonstrating Congress' continuing acceptance of the President's claim settlement authority. With respect to the Executive Agreement with the People's Republic of China, for example, Congress established an allocation formula for distribution of the funds received pursuant to the Agreement. 22 U.S.C. § 1627(f). As with legislation involving other executive agreements, Congress did not question the fact of the settlement or the power of the President to have concluded it. In 1976, Congress authorized the Foreign Claims Settlement Commission to adjudicate the merits of claims by United States nationals against East Germany, so that the Executive would "be in a better position to negotiate an adequate settlement . . . of these claims." S.Rep. No. 94-1188, p. 2 (1976); 22 U.S.C. § 1644b. Similarly, Congress recently amended the International Claims Settlement Act to facilitate the settlement of claims against Vietnam. 22 U.S.C. §§ 1645, 1645a(5) (1976 ed., Supp. IV). The House Report stated that the purpose of the legislation was to establish an official inventory of losses of private United States property in Vietnam so that recovery could be achieved "through future direct Government-to-Government negotiation of private property claims." H.R.Rep. No. 96-915, pp. 2-3, U. S. Code Cong. & Admin. News, 1980, pp. 7328, 7329-7330. Finally, the legislative history of the IEEPA further reveals that Congress has accepted the authority of the Executive to enter into settlement agreements. Though the IEEPA was enacted to provide for some limitation on the President's emergency powers, Congress stressed that "[n]othing in this act is intended . . . to interfere with the authority of the President to [block assets], or to impede the settlement of claims of U.S. citizens against foreign countries." S.Rep. No. 95-466, p. 6 (1977); 50 U.S.C. § 1706(a)(1).[10]

---

10. Indeed, Congress has consistently failed to object to this longstanding practice of claim settlement by executive agreement, even when it has had an opportunity to do so. In 1972, Congress entertained legislation relating to congressional oversight of such agreements. But Congress took only limited action, requiring that the text of significant executive agreements be transmitted to Congress. 1 U.S.C. § 112b. . . . Congress, though legislating in the area has left "untouched" the authority of the President to enter into settlement agreements.

The legislative history of 1 U.S.C. § 112b further reveals that Congress has accepted the President's authority to settle claims. During the hearings on the bill, Senator Case, the sponsor of the Act, stated with respect to executive claim settlements:

"I think it is a most interesting [area] in which we have accepted the right of the President, one individual, acting through his diplomatic force, to adjudicate and settle claims of American nationals against foreign countries. But that is a fact."

Transmittal of Executive Agreements to Congress: Hearings on S. 596 before the Senate Committee on Foreign Relations, 92d Cong., 1st Sess., 74 (1971).

In addition to congressional acquiescence in the President's power to settle claims, prior cases of this Court have also recognized that the President does have some measure of power to enter into executive agreements without obtaining the advice and consent of the Senate. In *United States v. Pink*, 315 U.S. 203 (1942), for example, the Court upheld the validity of the Litvinov Assignment, which was part of an Executive Agreement whereby the Soviet Union assigned to the United States amounts owed to it by American nationals so that outstanding claims of other American nationals could be paid. The Court explained that the resolution of such claims was integrally connected with normalizing United States' relations with a foreign state....

Petitioner raises two arguments in opposition to the proposition that Congress has acquiesced in this longstanding practice of claims settlement by executive agreement. First, it suggests that all pre-1952 settlement claims, and corresponding court cases such as *Pink*, should be discounted because of the evolution of the doctrine of sovereign immunity. Petitioner observes that prior to 1952 the United States adhered to the doctrine of absolute sovereign immunity, so that absent action by the Executive there simply would be no remedy for a United States national against a foreign government. When the United States in 1952 adopted a more restrictive notion of sovereign immunity, by means of the so-called "Tate" letter, it is petitioner's view that United States nationals no longer needed executive aid to settle claims and that, as a result, the President's authority to settle such claims in some sense "disappeared." Though petitioner's argument is not wholly without merit, it is refuted by the fact that since 1952 there have been at least 10 claims settlements by executive agreement. Thus, even if the pre-1952 cases should be disregarded, congressional acquiescence in settlement agreements since that time supports the President's power to act here.

Petitioner next asserts that Congress divested the President of the authority to settle claims when it enacted the Foreign Sovereign Immunities Act of 1976 (hereinafter FSIA), 28 U.S.C. §§ 1330, 1602 *et seq.* The FSIA granted personal and subject-matter jurisdiction in the federal district courts over commercial suits brought by claimants against those foreign states which have waived immunity. 28 U.S.C. § 1330. Prior to the enactment of the FSIA, a foreign government's immunity to suit was determined by the Executive Branch on a case-by-case basis. According to petitioner, the principal purpose of the FSIA was to depoliticize these commercial lawsuits by taking them out of the arena of foreign affairs—where the Executive Branch is subject to the pressures of foreign states seeking to avoid liability through a grant of immunity—and by placing them within the exclusive jurisdiction of the courts. Petitioner thus insists that the President, by suspending its claims, has circumscribed the jurisdiction of the United States courts in violation of Art. III of the Constitution.

We disagree. In the first place, we do not believe that the President has attempted to divest the federal courts of jurisdiction. Executive Order No. 12294 purports only to "suspend" the claims, not divest the federal court of "jurisdiction." As we read the Executive Order, those claims not within the jurisdiction of the Claims Tribunal will "revive" and become judicially enforceable in United States courts. This case, in short, illustrates the difference between modifying federal-court jurisdiction and directing the courts to apply a different rule of law. The President has exercised the power, acquiesced in by Congress, to settle claims and, as such, has simply effected a change in the substantive law governing the lawsuit. Indeed, the very example of sovereign immunity belies petitioner's argument. No one would suggest that a determination of sovereign immunity divests the federal courts of "jurisdiction." Yet, petitioner's argument, if accepted, would have required courts prior to the enactment of the FSIA to reject as an encroachment on their jurisdiction the President's determination of a foreign state's sovereign immunity.

Petitioner also reads the FSIA much too broadly. The principal purpose of the FSIA was to codify contemporary concepts concerning the scope of sovereign immunity and withdraw from the President the authority to make binding determinations of the sovereign immunity to be accorded foreign states. The FSIA was thus designed to remove one particular barrier to suit, namely sovereign immunity, and cannot be fairly read as *prohibiting* the President from settling claims of United States nationals against foreign governments. It is telling that the Congress which enacted the FSIA considered but rejected several proposals designed to limit the power of the President to enter into executive agreements, including claims settlement agreements. It is quite unlikely that the same Congress that rejected proposals to limit the President's authority to conclude executive agreements sought to accomplish that very purpose *sub silentio* through the FSIA. And, as noted above, just one year after enacting the FSIA, Congress enacted the IEEPA, where the legislative history stressed that nothing in the IEEPA was to impede the settlement of claims of United States citizens. It would be surprising for Congress to express this support for settlement agreements had it intended the FSIA to eliminate the President's authority to make such agreements.

In light of all of the foregoing—the inferences to be drawn from the character of the legislation Congress has enacted in the area, such as the IEEPA and the Hostage Act, and from the history of acquiescence in executive claims settlement—we conclude that the President was authorized to suspend pending claims pursuant to Executive Order No. 12294. As Justice Frankfurter pointed out in *Youngstown*, "a systematic, unbroken, executive practice, long pursued to the knowledge of the Congress and never before questioned . . . may be treated as a gloss on 'Executive Power' vested in the President by § 1 of Art. II." Past practice does not, by itself, create power, but "long-continued practice, known to and acquiesced in by Congress, would raise a presumption that the [action] had been [taken] in pursuance of its consent. . . ." *United States v. Midwest Oil Co.*, 236 U.S. 459, 474 (1915). See *Haig v. Agee*, 453 U.S., at 291, 292. Such practice is present here and such a presumption is also appropriate. In light of the fact that Congress may be considered to have consented to the President's action in suspending claims, we cannot say that action exceeded the President's powers.

Our conclusion is buttressed by the fact that the means chosen by the President to settle the claims of American nationals provided an alternative forum, the Claims Tribunal, which is capable of providing meaningful relief. The Solicitor General also suggests that the provision of the Claims Tribunal will actually *enhance* the opportunities for claimants to recover their claims, in that the Agreement removes a number of jurisdictional and procedural impediments faced by claimants in United States courts. Although being overly sanguine about the chances of United States claimants before the Claims Tribunal would require a degree of naiveté which should not be demanded even of judges, the Solicitor General's point cannot be discounted. Moreover, it is important to remember that we have already held that the President has the *statutory* authority to nullify attachments and to transfer the assets out of the country. The President's power to do so does not depend on his provision of a forum whereby claimants can recover on those claims. The fact that the President has provided such a forum here means that the claimants are receiving something in return for the suspension of their claims, namely, access to an international tribunal before which they may well recover something on their claims. Because there does appear to be a real "settlement" here, this case is more easily analogized to the more traditional claim settlement cases of the past.

Just as importantly, Congress has not disapproved of the action taken here. Though Congress has held hearings on the Iranian Agreement itself, Congress has not enacted legislation, or even passed a resolution, indicating its displeasure with the Agreement. Quite the contrary, the relevant Senate Committee has stated that the establishment of the Tribunal is "of vital importance to the United States." S.Rep.No. 97-71, p. 5 (1981).[13] We are thus clearly not confronted with a situation in which Congress has in some way resisted the exercise of Presidential authority.

Finally, we re-emphasize the narrowness of our decision. We do not decide that the President possesses plenary power to settle claims, even as against foreign governmental entities. As the Court of Appeals for the First Circuit stressed, "[t]he sheer magnitude of such a power, considered against the background of the diversity and complexity of modern international trade, cautions against any broader construction of authority than is necessary." *Chas. T. Main Int'l, Inc. v. Khuzestan Water & Power Authority*, 651 F.2d, at 814. But where, as here, the settlement of claims has been determined to be a necessary incident to the resolution of a major foreign policy dispute between our country and another, and where, as here, we can conclude that Congress acquiesced in the President's action, we are not prepared to say that the President lacks the power to settle such claims.

V

We do not think it appropriate at the present time to address petitioner's contention that the suspension of claims, if authorized, would constitute a taking of property in violation of the Fifth Amendment to the United States Constitution in the absence of just compensation.[14] Both petitioner and the Government concede that the question whether the suspension of the claims constitutes a taking is not ripe for review. However, this contention, and the possibility that the President's actions may effect a taking of petitioner's property, make ripe for adjudication the question whether petitioner will have a remedy at law in the Court of Claims under the Tucker Act, 28 U.S.C. § 1491, in such an event. That the fact and extent of the taking in this case is yet speculative is inconsequential because "there must be at the time of taking 'reasonable, certain and adequate provision for obtaining compensation.' " *Regional Rail Reorganization Act Cases*, 419 U.S. 102, 124-125 (1974), quoting *Cherokee Nation v. Southern Kansas R. Co.*, 135 U.S. 641, 659 (1890).

It has been contended that the "treaty exception" to the jurisdiction of the Court of Claims, 28 U.S.C. § 1502, might preclude the Court of Claims from exercising

---

13. Contrast congressional reaction to the Iranian Agreements with congressional reaction to a 1973 Executive Agreement with Czechoslovakia. There the President sought to settle over $105 million in claims against Czechoslovakia for $20.5 million. Congress quickly demonstrated its displeasure by enacting legislation requiring that the Agreement be renegotiated. *See* Lillich, *The Gravel Amendment to the Trade Reform Act of 1974*, 69 Am. J. Int'l Law 837, 839-840 (1975). Though Congress has shown itself capable of objecting to executive agreements, it has rarely done so and has not done so in this case.

14. Though we conclude that the President has settled petitioner's claims against Iran, we do not suggest that the settlement has terminated petitioner's possible taking claim against the United States. We express no views on petitioner's claims that it has suffered a taking.

jurisdiction over any takings claims the petitioner might bring. At oral argument, however, the Government conceded that § 1502 would not act as a bar to petitioner's action in the Court of Claims. We agree. Accordingly, to the extent petitioner believes it has suffered an unconstitutional taking by the suspension of the claims, we see no jurisdictional obstacle to an appropriate action in the United States Court of Claims under the Tucker Act.

The judgment of the District Court is accordingly affirmed, and the mandate shall issue forthwith.

It is so ordered.

Justice STEVENS, concurring in part.

In my judgment the possibility that requiring this petitioner to prosecute its claim in another forum will constitute an unconstitutional "taking" is so remote that I would not address the jurisdictional question considered in Part V of the Court's opinion. However, I join the remainder of the opinion.

Justice POWELL, concurring and dissenting in part.

I join the Court's opinion except its decision that the nullification of the attachments did not effect a taking of property interests giving rise to claims for just compensation. The nullification of attachments presents a separate question from whether the suspension and proposed settlement of claims against Iran may constitute a taking. I would leave both "taking" claims open for resolution on a case-by-case basis in actions before the Court of Claims. The facts of the hundreds of claims pending against Iran are not known to this Court and may differ from the facts in this case. I therefore dissent from the Court's decision with respect to attachments. The decision may well be erroneous,[1] and it certainly is premature with respect to many claims.

. . . The Court holds that parties whose valid claims are not adjudicated or not fully paid may bring a "taking" claim against the United States in the Court of Claims, the jurisdiction of which this Court acknowledges. The Government must pay just compensation when it furthers the Nation's foreign policy goals by using as "bargaining chips" claims lawfully held by a relatively few persons and subject to the jurisdiction of our courts. The extraordinary powers of the President and Congress upon which our decision rests cannot, in the circumstances of this case, displace the Just Compensation Clause of the Constitution.

---

1. To what extent could Congress have legislatively proscribed claims settlements by executive agreement, or at least claims settlements that are not part of a process of recognition? Note the Court's apparently greater tentativeness in *Dames & Moore* in endorsing presidential authority, as compared to *Pink*. (Could that tentativeness be the consequence of the time pressure the federal courts faced for decision—time pressure we have observed in other important separation of powers cases?) Did the President have any constitutional power to nullify claims against Iranian assets apart

---

1. Even though the Executive Orders purported to make attachments conditional, there is a substantial question whether the Orders themselves may have effected a taking by making conditional the attachments that claimants against Iran otherwise could have obtained without condition. Moreover, because it is settled that an attachment entitling a creditor to resort to specific property for the satisfaction of a claim is a property right compensable under the Fifth Amendment, there is a question whether the revocation of the license under which petitioner obtained its attachments suffices to render revocable the attachments themselves.

from IEEPA? Is that power tied to national emergencies? On what constitutional authority is it based?

2. On what basis, if any, could it be argued that, to the extent claimants against Iran do not recover 100 per cent of their claims through the international tribunal, those claimants still do *not* have any "takings" claim against the United States? What if the U.S. had provided, instead of the possibility of arbitration, a fixed settlement of all outstanding private claims against Iran for 75 cents on the dollar? 50 cents? 10 cents? *See Shanghai Power Co. v. United States*, 4 Cl. Ct. 237 (Ct. Cl. 1983), *aff'd*, 765 F.2d 159 (Fed. Cir. 1985), *cert. denied*, 474 U.S. 909 (1985) (Presidential act in recognition of People's Republic of China settling corporation's claim against PRC for one-sixth its value held not a taking).

Consider, in this connection, the Supreme Court's holding that the Constitution creates no "property" protected by the due process clauses of the fifth and fourteenth amendments; rather, property interests "are created and their dimensions are defined by existing rules or understandings that stem from an independent [legal] source . . . [and] that secure certain benefits and that support claims of entitlement to those benefits." *Board of Regents of State Colleges v. Roth*, 408 U.S. 564, 577 (1972). Did Dames & Moore face a situation in which the "existing understanding" was (and is) that U.S. nationals who do business abroad take their chances with the political branches in securing their claims against other nations? (Intriguingly, the Dames & Moore subsidiary whose claim was at issue in the above case had contractually agreed to litigate its contract claims in Iran. Should that affect the takings analysis?)

3. If, under the *mistaken* impression that the President has the authority to nullify attachments of foreign assets, U.S. banks holding attached assets release them to the foreign government, would the domestic claimants have a successful claim against the banks? If so, would the banks have a good claim against the United States? Should the Supreme Court have written a stronger endorsement of executive power in international emergencies, to avoid future doubts from interfering with the resolution of similar crises?

4. Considering note 14 of the majority opinion and the views of Justice Powell, do you think it was a mistake for President Carter to have granted a general license authorizing limited judicial proceedings against Iran?

5. Prior to 1976, the President had judicially recognized authority to grant immunity to foreign governments involved in U.S. litigation. In 1976, Congress enacted the Foreign Sovereign Immunities Act, 28 U.S.C. §§ 1602-1611, proscribing immunities in certain classes of cases, including any case in which the action is based on a foreign state's commercial activities in the U.S. Is the Act conclusive as to the President's authority? Consider, in reading the next chapter, if it would make a difference if the President's purpose in conferring immunity were to permit a friendly foreign power to marshal its assets in wartime.

6. The Supreme Court's decision in *Dames & Moore* hardly halted the tide of litigation prompted by the Iranian hostage crisis. At least two courts reached the takings question reserved in *Dames & Moore*, and found that, as a matter of law, no taking occurred. *E-Systems Inc. v. United States*, 2 Cl. Ct. 271 (1983); *American Int'l Group v. Islamic Republic of Iran*, 657 F.2d 430 (D.C. Cir. 1981). *See also Itek Corporation v. First National Bank of Boston*, 730 F.2d 19 (1st Cir. 1984).

Complex litigation likewise followed concerning a host of substantive and procedural issues that defy brief summary. For example, standby letters of credit were originally exempted from coverage by the blocking regulations, but were covered in subsequent amendments. Litigation concerning these multi-party international arrangements generally involved an American corporation attempting to enjoin an American bank from making payment on letters of credit in favor of an Iranian party to which the American corporation would ultimately be liable. *See* Getz, *Enjoining the International Standby Letter of Credit: The Iranian Letter of Credit Cases*, 21 Harv. Int'l L. J. 189, 198-200 (1980). Similarly, on the status of possessory liens against Iranian property, *see E-Systems Inc., supra.*

As of November, 1985, about 130 American companies had won a total of about $370 million from Iran through the Iran-United States Claims Tribunal. The nine-member panel, consisting of three American, three Iranian, and three neutral judges, are responsible for resolving over 3,800 claims filed with the tribunal. Approximately 86 per cent of the claims are private claims by individuals or companies against the government of the other country—overwhelmingly suits by American parties against Iran. Other claims involve disputes between the two governments or between banks of the two countries. Ironically, the time taken by the tribunal to begin processing the claims had at least one beneficial effect; the $1 billion security fund initially created for the settlement of claims grew substantially beyond $1 billion because interest on the fund exceeded the amount of the awards paid out. See Henderson, *Bringing It All Back Home*, Wash. Post Nat'l Weekly Edition, Nov. 4, 1985, at 22.

7. For overviews of the legal issues, international and domestic, raised by the Iranian Hostage Agreement, *see* Note, *The Iranian Hostage Agreement Under International and United States Law*, 81 Colum. L. Rev. 822 (1981); Sympoisum, Dames & Moore v. Regan, 29 U.C.L.A. L. Rev. 977 (1982). For a critical view of the Supreme Court's acquiescence, based on legislative silence, in the President's removal of U.S. citizens' commercial claims from the jurisdiction of U.S. courts, *see* Marks and Grabow, *The President's Foreign Economic Powers After* Dames & Moore v. Regan: *Legislation by Acquiescence*, 68 Cornell L. Rev. 68 (1982). On the takings issues not reached by the Court, *see also* Trimble, *Foreign Policy Frustrated*—Dames & Moore, *Claims Court Jurisdiction and a New Raid on the Treasury*, 84 Colum. L. Rev. 317 (1984).

D. Other Aspects of Congress' Role in Foreign Policy

1. Foreign Policy and Foreign Commerce

a. Foreign Trade and the International Emergency Economic Powers Act

Despite the Court's expansive reading of in *Dames & Moore* of the International Emergency Economic Powers Act (IEEPA), IEEPA was enacted in 1977 to limit the broad emergency powers previously delegated to the President under the Trading with the Enemy Act (TWEA), § 301(1), 55 Stat. 838, 839-40 (1941). Prior to the amendment of the TWEA, that act conferred extensive powers on the President both in wartime and in "any other period of national emergency" that the President might declare. Congress repealed the peacetime powers delegated by the TWEA, Trading

With the Enemy Act Amendments, Pub. L. No. 95-223, 91 Stat. 1625 (1977), and adopted the IEEPA in its place. The basic change enacted in the IEEPA was not in the range of powers delegated to the President, which was nearly identical in both acts, but rather a seeming change in the scope of the power delegated to declare national emergencies.[*] Congress authorized the declaration of a national emergency based only on "any unusual and extraordinary threat, which has its source in whole or substantial part outside the United States, to the national security, foreign policy, or the economy of the United States...." 50 U.S.C. § 1701 (1982).

How much, however, did this statutory change really change the scope of presidential power? Consider in this connection a pre-IEEPA case concerning the President's peacetime TWEA powers, *United States v. Yoshida International, Inc.*, 526 F.2d 560 (C.C.P.A. 1975). Yoshida sought to invalidate an import duty surcharge imposed by President Nixon because of "an exceptionally severe and worsening balance of payments deficit" experienced by the U.S. in the summer of 1971. As described by the court:

> The gold reserve backing of the U.S. dollar had dropped from $17.8 billion in 1960 to less than $10.4 billion in June of 1971, reflecting a growing lack of confidence in the U.S. dollar abroad. Foreign exchange rates were being controlled by some of our major trading partners in such a way as to overvalue the U.S. dollar. That action, by stimulating U.S. imports and restraining U.S. exports, contributed substantially to the balance of payments deficit. As one step in a program designed to meet the economic crisis,[4] the President issued Proclamation 4074, which in relevant part stated:
>
> WHEREAS, there has been a prolonged decline in the international monetary reserves of the United States, and our trade and international competitive position is seriously threatened and, as a result, our continued ability to assure our security could be impaired;
>
> WHEREAS, the balance of payments position of the United States requires the imposition of a surcharge on dutiable imports;
>
> A. I hereby declare a national emergency during which I call upon the public and private sector to make the efforts necessary to strengthen the international economic position of the United States.
>
> B. (1) I hereby terminate in part for such period as may be necessary and modify prior Presidential Proclamations which carry out trade agreements in-

---

[*] A related effort to circumscribe the President's powers regarding national emergencies was the National Emergencies Act, Pub.L. No. 94-412, 90 Stat. 1255 (1976). That act prescribed procedures for the declaration of national emergencies, for their termination, and for presidential reporting to Congress in connection with national emergencies. To end the practice of declaring national emergencies of unjustifiably indefinite duration, Congress provided that any emergency not otherwise terminated would terminate one year after its declaration unless the President should "publish in the Federal Register and transmit to the Congress a notice stating that such emergency is to continue in effect" beyond its anniversary. 50 U.S.C. § 1622(d) (1982).

4. The Proclamation in suit was part of a "New Economic Policy," which involved suspension of the convertibility of foreign held dollars into gold, reductions in taxes, Federal spending and foreign aid, a 90-day wage-price freeze, and imposition of the surcharge "(a)s a temporary measure." "Address to the Nation Outlining a New Economic Policy: 'The Challenge of Peace'," Public Papers of the Presidents of the United States Richard Nixon 1971 886 (1972)....

sofar as such proclamations are inconsistent with . . . the terms of this Proclamation.

(2) Such proclamations are suspended only insofar as is required to assess a surcharge in the form of a supplemental duty amounting to 10 percent ad valorem. Such supplemental duty shall be imposed on all dutiable articles [with certain exceptions,] . . . .

526 F.2d at 567.

The court commenced its legal analysis with the following premise:

The people of the new United States, in adopting the Constitution, granted the power to "lay and collect duties" and to "regulate commerce" to the Congress, not to the Executive. U.S. Constitution, Art. I, Sec. 8, clauses 1 and 3. Nonetheless, . . . Congress, beginning as early as 1794 and continuing into 1974, has delegated the exercise of much of the power to regulate foreign commerce to the Executive. . . . It is nonetheless clear that no undelegated power to regulate commerce, or to set tariffs, inheres in the Presidency.

526 F.2d at 571-72. The court then concluded that no delegated power sufficient to sustain the Nixon proclamation could be found in either the Tariff Act of 1930, 19 U.S.C. § 1351(a)(6), or the Trade Expansion Act of 1962, 19 U.S.C. § 1885(b) (1982).

The court nonetheless upheld the proclamation as an exercise of "national emergency" power under the TWEA. Because the TWEA did not expressly limit the President's power to declare an emergency, the propriety of that declaration did not present a hard question. Would it present any harder a question under the IEEPA, which permits a declaration of emergency in the face of an "unusual and extraordinary threat, which has its source in whole or substantial part outside the United States, to the . . . the economy of the United States . . . ?"

The more difficult question, the court believed was:

whether Congress, having itself regulated imports by employing duties as a regulatory tool, and having delegated to the President, for use in national emergencies, the power to regulate imports, intended to permit the President to employ the same regulatory tool, and what, if any, limitations lay upon his use thereof.

526 F.2d at 574. The court concluded, however, that the language of the TWEA—which in this respect is identical to the language of the IEEPA—did not categorically prohibit the use of tariffs as a form of import "regulation," so long as the measure was facially a reasonable response to the emergency presented. Because the proclamation was so tailored, the court upheld it.

Again, does the IEEPA change the analysis? It seems unlikely that courts will relish an intense role in reviewing the President's determinations whether a national emergency exists or whether particular measures represent an appropriate response. Would the Nixon tariff surcharge fare any less well under the IEEPA than it did under the TWEA? If the IEEPA were not construed to permit a tariff surcharge as a response to a national economic emergency caused by foreign sources, would the President have any inherent article II authority to sustain his initiative under *Youngstown*?

b. Trade Expansion Act

Independent Gasoline Marketers Council v. Duncan
492 F.Supp. 614 (D.D.C. 1980)

AUBREY E. ROBINSON, Jr., District Judge.

In these consolidated actions Plaintiffs Independent Gasoline Marketers Council, Inc. . . . and Marathon Oil Corporation, seek to enjoin . . . [implementation of] the Petroleum Import Adjustment Program ("PIAP" or "the Program") proclaimed by the President of the United States in Proclamation 4744 (45 Fed.Reg. 22864; April 3, 1980), as amended. . . . This Program was created as a result of the report to the President on March 14, 1979, by the Treasury Secretary, acting pursuant to Section 232(b) of the Trade Expansion Act of 1962 as amended (TEA), that oil was being imported into the United States "in such quantities and under such circumstances as to threaten to impair the national security." 44 Fed.Reg. 18818 (March 29, 1979). The investigation upon which this determination was founded had been initiated on March 15, 1978, by W. Michael Blumenthal, former Secretary of the Treasury, in the exercise of his authority under Section 232. Information and advice were solicited from the Secretary of Defense, the Secretary of Energy, the Secretary of State, the Secretary of Commerce, the Federal Reserve Board, the Central Intelligence Agency and other appropriate officers of the United States regarding the effects on national security of the imports of petroleum and petroleum products. Those matters specified in Section 232(c) of the TEA and other relevant factors were considered.

The Treasury Secretary found that the level of imported oil threatened our national security. He recommended that President Carter take action. The President's response was the enactment of the PIAP, which was implemented primarily to lower domestic gasoline consumption by raising the retail price of all gasoline by $.10 per gallon. Its mechanism may be summarized as follows: Under the PIAP, a license fee would be imposed on imported crude oil and gasoline. The amount of the fee (presently estimated at $4.62 per barrel of crude oil and $4.35 per barrel of gasoline) would float, and would be determined by the effect of the fee on the retail price of gasoline. The PIAP would be terminated if and when Congress increases the present $.04 per gallon excise tax to $.14 per gallon. . . .

In economic terms, the PIAP may best be viewed as a demand-side disincentive.[3] . . . The PIAP mechanism completely undermines this demand-side disincentive, however, by contemplating that the cost of the fee would eventually be paid by consumers of both domestic and imported gasoline. Thus, the imposition of the fee would not put imported oil at a competitive disadvantage with domestic oil, and the demand for imported oil would not decrease proportionately to domestic oil. Rather, the specific demand-side disincentive initially placed on imported oil is, under the PIAP, transformed into a generalized demand-side disincentive on the purchase of all gasoline.[4]

---

3. A demand-side disincentive lowers demand for a given good by artificially raising its price. A supply-side disincentive (such as a quota) decreases the availability of a given good. The Supreme Court has referred to demand-side disincentives as "monetary measures," and supply-side disincentives as "quantitative measures." See FEA v. Algonquin, 426 U.S. 548, 561 (1976).

4. Defendants estimate that the PIAP would reduce overall gasoline consumption by 56,000 to 100,000 barrels per day.

Because of the displacement of the initial import fee onto both domestic and imported oil, and the nature of the fee itself, the PIAP could not act as a disincentive to reduce imports. . . . Rather than attempt to directly decrease the amount of oil imported into the United States, the PIAP attempts to decrease the total amount of oil consumed, and therefore could have only a collateral effect on the retailing of foreign oil.

Under Section 232 of the Trade Expansion Act, 19 U.S.C. § 1862(b), if the Secretary of Commerce[5] has found after an appropriate investigation that imports of an article "threaten to impair the national security," the President is authorized to "take such action, and for such time, as he deems necessary to adjust the imports of such article" so as to lessen the threat to national security. Defendants argue that the TEA standing alone authorizes the Petroleum Import Adjustment Program. They contend first that Section 232 empowers the President to impose license fees as he has done in the PIAP. They argue further that the TEA gives the President authority to channel the impact of that fee to gasoline sales because doing so will (a) enable the program to have the desired effect on imports and (b) equitably distribute the burden of the program throughout the nation.

In *FEA v. Algonquin, SNG, Inc.*, 426 U.S. 548 (1976), the Supreme Court held that Section 232 authorizes the President to impose a system of license fees as a means of controlling imports. In that case, respondents had argued that the section empowers the President to control imports only by imposing "direct" controls such as quotas and not through the use of license fees. In holding to the contrary, the Court found that the statute authorizes not only quantitative restraints that affect the supply of imported goods, but also monetary measures, such as license fees, that control imports by affecting demand. The Court noted that a license fee itself "as much as a quota has its initial and direct impact on imports, albeit on their price as opposed to their quantity." Although concluding that the statute authorizes a license fee, the Court cautioned that its conclusion does not mean that "*any* action the President might take, as long as it has even a remote impact on imports, is also so authorized."

Algonquin is not dispositive of the instant action. The import fee approved by the Supreme Court in that case directly affected the price of imported oil relative to domestic oil. Standing alone, the import fee component of the PIAP would have a similar effect. In the context of the PIAP mechanism as a whole, however, the import fee has no "initial and direct impact on imports" similar to that of the fee approved in *Algonquin*. Nor is it intended to have such a result. . . . No monetary burden is imposed on imported oil that is not imposed on domestic oil. . . . Any impact on imports will be indirect and will result from the general gasoline conservation fee, not from the initial import fee.

To determine whether the Trade Expansion Act authorizes the PIAP, the Court must look to the design of the program as a whole. Analysis of the manner in which PIAP would function belies Defendants' contention that it is structured to lower demand for imported oil in particular rather than demand for oil generally. Two aspects of the program undercut Defendants' argument. First, . . . the initial import fee is com-

---

5. Prior to January 2, 1980, investigatory responsibility under the TEA vested in the Secretary of the Treasury. *See* Exec. Order No. 12175, 44 Fed.Reg. 70703 (Dec. 10, 1979); Reorganization Plan No. 3 of 1979, 44 Fed.Reg. 69273 (Dec. 3, 1979).

pletely offset by [PIAP's pricing] mechanism. Second, assuming a stable level of domestic oil production, the per barrel import fee would decrease if the level of imports rose. The rationale underlying PIAP thus reduces to the contention that TEA empowers the President to impose a $.10 per gallon "conservation fee" on all gasoline so as to lower demand for the product. The TEA provides no such authority.

TEA does not authorize the President to impose general controls on domestically produced goods either through a monetary mechanism or through a quantitative device. The statute provides for regulation of imports. A regulation on imports may incidentally regulate domestic goods. The regulation of domestic oil contemplated by PIAP, however, is not incidental to regulation of imported oil. Rather, it is a primary purpose of the program, and is essential to the goal of reducing demand for all gasoline regardless of its source. Moreover, the impact of the oil conservation fee is greater on domestically produced oil than on imported oil since the former comprises roughly sixty (60) per cent of all crude oil utilized today, and Defendants acknowledge that the PIAP's effect on import levels will be slight.

In *Algonquin*, the Supreme Court indicated that TEA does not authorize "any action the President might take, as long as it has even a remote impact on imports." Any possible benefits of the PIAP on levels of oil imports are far too remote and indirect for the TEA alone to support the program. The remoteness of the program's effect on imports is apparent from three factors. First, the quantitative impact of the program on import levels will admittedly be slight. Second, the program imposes broad controls on domestic goods to achieve that slight impact. Third, Congress has thus far denied the President authority to reduce gasoline consumption through a gasoline conservation levy. PIAP is an attempt to circumvent that stumbling block in the guise of an import control measure. TEA alone does not sanction this attempt to exercise authority that has been deliberately withheld from the President by the Congress.

[The court next rejected government arguments that any portions of the PIAP not authorized by the TEA were sustainable under the Emergency Petroleum Allocation Act (EPAA), 15 U.S.C. § 751, et seq. Whether or not the EPAA could authorize such a program, the President had not complied with the prescribed procedures for invoking EPAA authority.]

Defendants finally contend that, because of the national security aspects presented by this nation's consumption of imported oil, the President has authority, independent of Congress, to impose a gasoline conservation fee. The extent of the "inherent" nature of Presidential power was delineated by the Supreme Court in Youngstown Sheet & Tube Co. v. Sawyer, 343 U.S. 579 (1952). [The court quoted Justice Black's passage emphasizing the vesting of lawmaking powers in Congress.] It is clear that Congress, not the President, must decide whether the imposition of a gasoline conservation fee is good policy.

On this issue, Congress has already spoken. The Energy Policy and Conservation Act, (EPCA) 42 U.S.C. § 6201, et seq., gives the President the authority to prescribe a "plan which imposes reasonable restrictions on the public or private use of energy which are necessary to reduce energy consumption." 42 U.S.C. § 6262(a)(1). Section 202 of that Act provides that

(2) An energy conservation contingency plan under this section may not

(A) impose rationing or any tax, tariff, or user fee;

(B) contain any provision respecting the price of petroleum products....

42 U.S.C. § 6262(a)(2). Congress has thus precluded the use of demand-side disincentives to lower overall gasoline consumption.[10] It is imperative to note that the EPCA is not effective until the President has found the existence of a severe energy supply interruption. 42 U.S.C. § 6261(b). Thus, even in times of severe energy supply interruptions, the President may not use monetary measures to decrease demand. The imposition of the gasoline conservation fee is contrary to manifest Congressional intent....

The gasoline conservation fee at issue in the instant litigation does not fall within the inherent powers of the President, is not sanctioned by the statutes cited by Defendants, and is contrary to manifest Congressional intent. The Court has no choice but to grant Plaintiffs the relief they seek.

Did the *Independent Gasoline Marketers Council* improperly confuse questions as to the scope of power delegated by the TEA and questions whether the President properly implemented those powers that were delegated? Consider this critique:

> The court's opinion... did not articulate the standard of review it was applying to factual judgments about the likely effect of the program on imports, which the court correctly regarded as vital to the legality of the program under the TEA. Because the year-old Treasury report had recommended no particular action, it did not provide support for the intended effects of the President's program. To fill the gap in the record, the Government filed an affidavit by Secretary of Energy Duncan, which argued that the program would "maximize the conservation effect and the reduction of imports" resulting from the initial fee on imported oil. Secretary Duncan appended a copy of a brief memorandum he and Treasury Secretary Miller had sent the President formally recommending adoption of the program on grounds that it would reduce gasoline consumption, "thereby reducing the level of oil imports." The court cited neither document and, in the end, apparently simply disagreed with the President's judgment.
>
> Finally, the court found that the President's action contravened a statute forbidding the imposition of fees on gasoline as part of contingency plans for conservation in case of supply disruptions.[243] The court viewed the President's program as "an attempt to circumvent" this restriction on his authority "in the guise of an import control measure."[244]
>
> The court's analysis was flawed. It should first have decided whether the President's action would have been legal if it had produced the effects claimed for it, or whether it exceeded his statutory authority on its face. If the court were prepared to conclude that the President's program was in conflict with

---

10. In commenting on an original executive proposal rejected in the version passed by the Congress, the House Report to the EPCA stated that "the Committee finds the President's strategy to use price as the principal means of achieving conservation unacceptable because it so harshly impacts on the poor and low income members of our society." H.R.Rep. No. 94-340, 94th Cong., 1st Sess. 6 (1975), U.S.Code Cong. & Admin.News 1975, pp. 1762, 1768.

243. Energy Policy and Conservation Act, 42 U.S.C. §§ 6201-6422 (Supp. III 1979).

244. 492 F. Supp. at 618. The Government subsequently appealed; Congress responded with legislation, passed over the President's veto, specifically repealing the program. 126 Cong. Rec. S6376-87 (daily ed. June 6, 1980); 126 Cong. Rec. H4600-02 (daily ed. June 5, 1980).

the statutory limitation on his authority to include fees on gasoline in contingency plans, it should have rested its holding squarely on that provision. The resulting precedent would have had minimal effect on the President's import authority under the TEA. Instead, the court confused its determination of the extent of the President's statutory authority with its review of the factual basis for his action in a fashion that led to creation of an unnecessarily narrow statutory precedent. The court should have relied on the Government's affidavits for the purpose of elaborating the President's rationale that a fee applied to retail sales of all gasoline would reduce imports, and it should have deferred to that judgment if the Government could have supported the order's rationality on the administrative record.

Bruff, *Judicial Review and the President's Statutory Powers*, 68 Va. L. Rev. 1, 54-55 (1982).

c. Sales of Military Equipment to Iran

In November, 1986, President Reagan confirmed reports that the United States had in 1985 and 1986 facilitated six sales of TOW anti-tank missiles, Hawk anti-aircraft missiles, and spare parts for missile systems to Iran. Certain of the missiles had been previously sold to Israel; Israel agreed to sell their missiles to Iran if the U.S. approved and agreed to replenish the Israeli arsenal. Other missiles and parts were sold directly by the U.S. government to Iran. The Administration originally defended all of the transactions as part of an attempt to improve relations generally with Iran. Critics charged that the sales were, in fact, an attempt to buy the release of Americans held hostage in Lebanon by Islamic revolutionary groups believed to be under Iranian influence. It was further alleged that the operation was conducted by the staff of the National Security Council, rather than by the Central Intelligence Agency, for the central purpose of avoiding legally required congressional oversight of the operations involved. (Further discussion of these events appears in subsection 3 of this section of Chapter Six.)

Among the issues raised by these sales was their legality under various statutes regulating the international sale of arms, statutes clearly within Congress's power to regulate foreign trade. *See* Celada, Laws Implicated By Shipments of Military Materials to Iran (Congressional Research Service Memorandum, Nov. 24, 1986). A hint of the complexities involved appears in the following passage from the report of a Special Review Board ("Tower Commission") established by President Reagan on December 1, 1986 to review the controversial activities of the National Security Council staff:

> The Arms Export Control Act, the principal U.S. statute governing arms sales abroad, makes it unlawful to export arms without a license. Exports of arms by U.S. government agencies, however, do not require a license if they are otherwise authorized by law. Criminal penalties—fines and imprisonment—are provided for willful violations.
>
> The initial arms transfers in the Iran initiative involved the sale and shipment by Israel of U.S.-origin missiles. The usual way for such international retransfer of arms to be authorized under U.S. law is pursuant to the Arms Export Control Act. This Act requires that the President consent to any transfers by another

country of arms exported under the Act and imposes three conditions before such Presidential consent may be given:

(a) the United States would itself transfer the arms in question to the recipient country;

(b) a commitment in writing has been obtained from the recipient country against unauthorized retransfer of significant arms, such as missiles; and

(c) a prior written certification regarding the retransfer is submitted to the Congress if the defense equipment, such as missiles, has an acquisition cost of 14 million dollars or more. 22 U.S.C. 2753 (a), (d).

In addition, the Act generally imposes restrictions on which countries are eligible to receive U.S. arms and on the purposes for which arms may be sold.[2]

The other possible avenue whereby government arms transfers to Iran may be authorized by law would be in connection with intelligence operations conducted under the National Security Act. This Act requires that the Director of Central Intelligence and the heads of other intelligence agencies keep the two Congressional intelligence committees "fully and currently informed" of all intelligence activities under their responsibility. 50 U.S.C. 413. Where prior notice of significant intelligence activities is not given, the intelligence committees are to be informed "in a timely fashion." In addition, the so called Hughes-Ryan Amendment to the Foreign Assistance Act requires that "significant anticipated intelligence activities" may not be conducted by the CIA unless and until the President finds that "each such operation is important to the national security of the United States." 22 U.S.C. 2422.

When the Israelis began transferring arms to Iran in August, 1985, they were not acting on their own. U.S. officials had knowledge about the essential elements of the proposed shipments. The United States shared some common purpose in the transfers and received a benefit from them—the release of a hostage. Most importantly, Mr. McFarlane [the National Security Adviser] communicated prior U.S. approval to the Israelis for the shipments, including an undertaking for replenishment. But for this U.S. approval, the transactions may not have gone forward. In short, the United States was an essential participant in the arms transfers to Iran that occurred in 1985.

Whether this U.S. involvement in the arms transfers by the Israelis was lawful depends fundamentally upon whether the President approved the transactions before they occurred. In the absence of Presidential approval, there does not appear to be any authority in this case for the United States to engage in the transfer of arms or consent to the transfer by another country. The arms transfers to Iran in 1985 and hence the Iran initiative itself would have proceeded contrary to U.S. law.

The Attorney General reached a similar judgment with respect to the activities of the CIA in facilitating the November, 1985 shipment by the Israelis of HAWK missiles.

---

2. It may be possible to authorize transfers by another country under the Arms Export Control Act without obtaining the President's consent. As a practical matter, however, the legal requirements may not differ significantly. For example, section 614(2) permits the President to waive the requirements of the Act. But this waiver authority may not be exercised unless it is determined that the international arms sales are "vital to the national security interests of the United States." Moreover, before granting a waiver, the President must consult with and provide written justification to the foreign affairs and appropriations committees of the Congress. 22 U.S.C. 2374(3).

In a letter to the Board, the Attorney General concluded that with respect to the CIA assistance, "a finding under the Hughes-Ryan Amendment would be required."[4]

The Board was unable to reach a conclusive judgment about whether the 1985 shipments of arms to Iran were approved in advance by the President. On balance the Board believes that it is plausible to conclude that he did approve them in advance.

Yet even if the President in some sense consented to or approved the transactions, a serious question of law remains. It is not clear that the form of the approval was sufficient for purposes of either the Arms Export Control Act or the Hughes-Ryan Amendment. The consent did not meet the conditions of the Arms Export Control Act, especially in the absence of a prior written commitment from the Iranians regarding unauthorized retransfer.

Under the National Security Act, it is not clear that mere oral approval by the President would qualify as a Presidential finding that the initiative was vital to the national security interests of the United States. The approval was never reduced to writing. It appears to have been conveyed to only one person. The President himself has no memory of it. And there is contradictory evidence from the President's advisors about how the President responded when he learned of the arms shipments which the approval was to support. In addition, the requirement for Congressional notification was ignored. In these circumstances, even if the President approved of the transactions, it is difficult to conclude that his actions constituted adequate legal authority.

... [T]he legal underpinning of the Iran initiative during 1985 was at best highly questionable. The Presidential Finding of January 17, 1986, formally approved the Iran initiative as a covert intelligence operation under the National Security Act. This ended the uncertainty about the legal status of the initiative and provided legal authority for the United States to transfer arms directly to Iran.

> The National Security Act also requires notification of Congress of covert intelligence activities. If not done in advance, notification must be "in a timely fashion." The Presidential finding of January 17 directed that Congressional notification be withheld, and this decision appears to have never been reconsidered. While there was surely justification to suspend Congressional notification in advance of a particular transaction relating to a hostage release, the law would seem to require disclosure where, as in the Iran case, a pattern of relative inactivity occurs over an extended period. To do otherwise prevents the Congress from fulfilling its proper oversight responsibilities.

J. Tower, et al., Report of the President's Special Review Board IV 8-9 (1987).

Assuming that at least some of the arms transfers to Iran occurred under procedures that did not comply with all relevant provisions of law, could the President argue (a) persuasively or even (b) plausibly that he had inherent authority to effect the arms transfers in pursuit of his foreign policy without respect to the statutes involved? What would be the constitutional basis for such authority? Review the cases earlier

---

4. Apparently no determination was made at the time as to the legality of these activities even though serious concerns about legality were expressed by the Deputy Director of CIA, a Presidential finding was sought by CIA officials before any further CIA activities in support of the Iran initiative were undertaken, and the CIA counsel, Mr. Stanley Sporkin, advised that as a matter of prudence any new finding should seek to ratify the prior CIA activities.

in this chapter. Could you have written a memorandum responsibly supporting the President's authority to make the transfers based solely on his constitutional powers? How does *Youngstown* shape your analysis? The Tower Commission had this to say about the apparent involvement of Administration lawyers in decisionmaking relevant to the Iran initiative:

> Throughout the Iran initiative, significant questions of law do not appear to have been adequately addressed. In the face of a sweeping statutory prohibition and explicit requirements relating to Presidential consent to arms transfers by third countries, there appears to have been at the outset in 1985 little attention, let alone systematic analysis, devoted to how Presidential actions would comply with U.S. law. The Board has found no evidence that an evaluation was ever done during the life of the operation to determine whether it continued to comply with the terms of the January 17 Presidential Finding. Similarly, when a new prohibition was added to the Arms Export Control Act in August of 1986 to prohibit exports to countries on the terrorism list (a list which contained Iran), no evaluation was made to determine whether this law affected authority to transfer arms to Iran in connection with intelligence operations under the National Security Act. This lack of legal vigilance markedly increased the chances that the initiative would proceed contrary to law.

Id. at IV 9. What is your assessment? Is the Comission "pussyfooting" in the last quoted sentence? Over a vigorous dissent, the majority joint report for the congressional committees investigating the Iran-Contra affair went further than the Tower Commisssion in condemning what it perceived as a "disdain" for law shared by key Reagan Administration officials. *See generally* S. Rep. No. 216, 100th Cong., 1st Sess. (1987); H.R. Rep. No. 433, 100th Cong., 1st Sess. (1987).

While the committees in both Houses conducted their investigations, President Reagan announced a comprehensive review of executive branch procedures concerning covert operations in order to implement the recommendations of the Tower Commisssion. On August 7, 1987, the President promised specific reform measures, including the reduction of all future "Findings" pertaining to national security operations to writing, except in cases of "extreme emergency"; forbearance from issuing any retroactive "Findings"; and a requirement that agencies designated by the President for the discharge of covert operations comply with all procedures applicable to the President in notifying Congress concerning such operations. *See* Letter to the Chairman and Vice Chairman of the Senate Select Committee on Intelligence Regarding Procedures for Presidential Approval and Notification of Congress, 23 Weekly Comp. Pres. Doc. 910 (Aug. 7, 1987). The joint congressional report, however, suggested stronger reform, recommending that Congress enact a requirement of advance notification, except in emergencies, of all covert operations. As you review the discussion of the War Powers Resolution in Chapter Seven, consider the degree to which notification requirements effectively foster legal and political accountability. How might you draft such requirements for covert operations both to facilitate effective oversight and to respect the constitutional authority of the President?

2. *Foreign Policy and the Independent Regulatory Agencies*

Westinghouse Electric Corp. v. U.S. Nuclear Regulatory Commission
598 F.2d 759 (3d Cir. 1979).

ADAMS, Circuit Judge.

On December 23, 1977, the United States Nuclear Regulatory Commission (NRC) suspended for approximately two years its decisionmaking process regarding proposals for the recycling of spent nuclear fuel and the use in nuclear reactors of plutonium recovered from that fuel. This suspension was announced in an order terminating informal rulemaking and related licensing proceedings concerning this subject. In part, the decision to place a moratorium upon these deliberations was taken in deference to President Carter's stated objective of deferring domestic plutonium recycling while the United States initiated a multinational evaluation of alternative fuel cycles that would pose a lesser risk of international proliferation of nuclear weapons. Petitions for review were filed requesting us to set aside and enjoin the NRC's order on the grounds that, in terminating these proceedings, the NRC violated the Atomic Energy Act (AEA)[1] and the National Environmental Policy Act (NEPA).[2] Because we conclude that the NRC acted within the scope of its authority and that there is no requirement to have a NEPA statement at this time, the petitions for review will be denied.

I.

For over two decades, the federal government, initially through the Atomic Energy Commission (AEC) and later through the NRC, a successor agency to the AEC, has been exploring, together with the private sector, the feasibility of reprocessing spent nuclear fuel and employing the plutonium recovered from such fuel in nuclear reactors utilized to generate electricity. Commercial implementation of the plutonium recycling process would have the advantages of conserving uranium resources and of alleviating the problem of disposing of radioactive wastes, but might also pose the dangers of a proliferation of nuclear weapons and the possible sabotage of reprocessing facilities. This is so because, unlike the slightly "enriched" uranium currently used in nuclear reactors, plutonium can be employed in the production of nuclear explosives and might be diverted to that end by foreign governments or by terrorists.

Recognizing that a decision to implement a wide-scale program for the commercial recycling of plutonium constitutes a major federal action significantly affecting the environment, and thereby necessitating an environmental impact statement (EIS) in order to comply with § 102(2)(C) of NEPA, the AEC in 1974 commenced work on a Generic Environmental Statement on the Use of Recycled Plutonium in Mixed Oxide Fuel in Light Water Cooled Reactors (GESMO). Concomitant with the GESMO informal rulemaking proceeding, the Commission . . . conducted adjudicatory licensing proceedings on applications by private companies dealing with the construction and operation of nuclear fuel reprocessing plants, some of which were already pending

---

1. 42 U.S.C. §§ 2011-2296 (1976).

2. 42 U.S.C. §§ 4321-4347 (1976).

when GESMO was undertaken. Among the applications before the Commission were those of Allied-General Nuclear Services ... for a license to operate the nearly-completed fuel reprocessing plant that it had permission to construct at Barnwell, South Carolina, and of Westinghouse Electric Corp.... for a license to construct a similar plant at Anderson, South Carolina.

One of the concerns expressed while the rulemaking and adjudicatory proceedings were progressing was that dangers to world security might ensue from the commercial reprocessing of nuclear fuel. For example, the AEC staff's first draft of GESMO, which was published on August 21, 1974, prompted a number of critical comments by the public. These included a letter from the President's Council on Environmental Quality that was directed at GESMO's failure (a) to address the proliferation dangers, (b) to explore what safeguards were available, and (c) to weigh the possibility of developing alternative sources of energy. In response to this criticism, the staff undertook to reassess its study and to supplement the draft GESMO with an analysis of proliferation risks and safeguards.[10] And, on October 28, 1976, President Ford discussed the risks entailed in plutonium recycling in a statement on nuclear policy. He declared that the nation "should pursue reprocessing and recycling in the future only if they are found to be consistent with our international (non-proliferation) objectives."

President Carter disclosed his administration's policy concerning plutonium recycling on April 7, 1977. Noting with alarm the serious proliferation risks of plutonium recycling, the President stated that part of the government's response would be to "defer indefinitely the commercial reprocessing and recycling of plutonium produced in the U.S. nuclear power programs," and to sponsor an international nuclear fuel cycle evaluation (INFCE) program aimed at developing alternative processes with lower proliferation risks.

Almost immediately thereafter, a motion was filed to terminate the GESMO proceeding, and ... the NRC announced its intention to reassess "the future course and scope of GESMO, the review of recycle-related applications, and the matter of interim licensing," and invited GESMO participants, the Executive Branch, and other interested persons to submit their views on the subject. President Carter's position was explained on October 4, 1977, in a letter by Stuart Eizenstat, Assistant to the President for Domestic Affairs and Policy.[15] The NRC then solicited further public comment on the President's position and on several alternative courses of action.[16]

---

10. In November, 1975, after an earlier announcement and the receipt of comments, the NRC published a policy statement declaring that a study of safeguard alternatives would be included in GESMO and weighed in NRC's final decision on the subject of wide-scale commercial recycling of plutonium. That statement also specified the procedures and schedule to be followed for GESMO hearings and set forth criteria under which interim licensing of non-experimental, recycle-related activities would be considered. See 40 Fed.Reg. 53056 (1975), corrected, 40 Fed.Reg. 59497 (1975). Various environmental groups sought review of this policy statement in the Court of Appeals for the Second Circuit. That court affirmed the NRC's hearing procedures but held that the interim licensing of recycle-related activities on a commercial basis violated NEPA. The Supreme Court vacated and remanded that judgment for consideration of mootness after the NRC's order of December 23, 1977.

15. Mr. Eizenstat's letter stated in pertinent part:

The President believes that our goal of stopping the spread of nuclear weapons capability among non-weapons states can be significantly improved by a halt in purex reprocessing. Last April 7, he stated that the U.S. should "defer indefinitely the commercial reprocessing

Thereafter, on December 23, 1977, the NRC issued an order terminating the GESMO proceeding as well as most proceedings relating to pending or future plutonium-recycle license applications. Among other things, the order also committed the NRC "to re-examine the above matter after the completion of the ongoing alternative fuel cycle studies, now expected to take about two years," and to publish shortly after the decision a statement of the reasons underlying the decision....

... Westinghouse filed petitions in this Court ... challenging the termination of both GESMO and the licensing proceedings with respect to its Anderson, South Carolina facility. Four days later, Allied-General ... filed a similar petition....

As explained by the NRC in considerable detail in its May 8 Memorandum of Decision, the December 23 Order terminating GESMO and related licensing proceedings was prompted by the President's policy initiatives as well as by the pendency of studies into alternative fuel cycles. With respect to the first reason for termination, the NRC noted in its Memorandum that although the proceedings in question concern domestic activities, it is appropriate for the NRC to weigh the foreign policy implications as well, because the AEA requires that the common defense and security be considered in making any domestic licensing decision. "[I]n the absence of a clear statutory mandate to the contrary" and in view of Congress' reception of the Administration's nuclear policy,[38] the NRC deemed it proper to accord "substantial defer-

---

and recycling of the plutonium produced in U.S. nuclear power programs". The Administration has proposed an accelerated research and development program to examine alternative fuel cycles not involving direct access to plutonium. The President has also asked other countries to join us in an International Nuclear Fuel Cycle Evaluation to examine alternative approaches to advanced nuclear technologies. The GESMO proceedings and related licensing requests may impact these non- proliferation initiatives. While the studies and analyses done by the Commission staff, if available in published form, may be of value to the International Nuclear Fuel Cycle Evaluation, the President believes that his non-proliferation initiatives would be assisted both domestically and internationally if the Commission were to terminate the GESMO proceedings. Specifically, the President believes that the following actions would be helpful in achieving the Administration's goals:

* Publication of the Commission's assessment of safeguards issues.

* Termination of staff reviews and hearings relating to recycle activities. (Continuation of these activities could lead other nations to question the United States commitment to deter commercial reprocessing and plutonium recycle.)

* Denial of interim licensing of fuel cycle facilities.

* Denial of interim licensing for use of mixed oxide fuel in reactors, except in small quantities for experimental purposes.

The letter is reprinted at 42 Fed.Reg. 57186 (1977).

16. *See* 42 Fed.Reg. 57185 (1977). The notice described four possible courses of action: (1) terminating GESMO and denying the related license applications; (2) continuing as before; (3) taking an intermediate course of action, such as deferring further consideration of GESMO and the related proceedings pending completion of ongoing national and international studies; or (4) continuing GESMO to some convenient stopping point, such as completion of the health, safety, and environmental hearings.

38. Congress explicitly supported the alternative fuel cycle studies proposed by the President in § 105 of the Nuclear Non-Proliferation Act of 1978, Pub.L.No.95-242, 92 Stat. 120, which was pending in the Senate at the time of the December 23 decision (having already passed the House of Representatives) and was enacted before the May 8 Memorandum was released. Section 105 states:

The President shall take immediate initiatives to invite all nuclear supplier and recipient

ence" to the President's request that it terminate the proceedings, since "the President is the national spokesman in the area of foreign policy." In addition, the NRC examined the President's request and reasoned that indeed the country's international prerogatives would be compromised were the proceedings to continue.[40] ...

The NRC carefully examined policy-based arguments tendered by various commentors that the proceedings ought to be continued, but was not persuaded by them. It emphasized that its decision to terminate the GESMO and related licensing proceedings "does not involve their final disposition on the merits," and is taken because "the present state of studies and national fuel cycle policy evaluations precludes an informed decision on the merits of plutonium recycle at this time." Finally, the NRC noted that the President and Congress have indicated that they may reassess their positions after the studies are completed, and that the NRC is committed to reexamine its December 23 decision "in light of the completed studies, expected to take about two years, and any revisions of the Administration's policies." ...

In passing the Atomic Energy Act of 1954, Congress enacted "a regulatory scheme which is virtually unique in the degree to which broad responsibility is reposed in the administering agency, free of close prescription in its charter as to how it shall proceed in achieving the statutory objectives." ... Given this broad delegation of authority to the NRC to choose the necessary means by which to implement the general policy objectives of the AEA, we cannot say that the NRC must inexorably proceed with the processing of license applications and the development of a final GESMO when in its judgment to do so would endanger the attainment of its statutory objectives. ...

Inasmuch as we conclude that the NRC may, in its discretion, delay processing applications and refuse to accept new ones when there are sound reasons for doing so, we must now examine whether in the present case this discretion was abused or was exercised in a manner not in conformity with statutory dictates. ... [W]e are satisfied, at least for now, that the NRC has not abused its discretion in refusing to continue the pending proceedings on the ground that it cannot yet formulate a generic standard or make a determination on the question of inimicality [to national security and public safety]. When and if it ever becomes apparent that the NRC has *de facto* denied the license applications despite the applicants' compliance with the pertinent regulations and without making a finding of inimicality, or that the moratorium is of unreasonable duration, judicial recourse will be available to the aggrieved parties.

Petitioners also maintain that the NRC impermissibly terminated the GESMO and related licensing proceedings at the request of the President and in deference to his foreign policy pronouncement. They charge that in failing to act independently of the

---

nations to reevaluate all aspects of the nuclear fuel cycle, with emphasis on alternatives to an economy based on the separation of pure plutonium or the presence of high enriched uranium, methods to deal with spent fuel storage, and methods to improve the safeguards for existing nuclear technology. ...

22 U.S.C. § 3224 (Supp.1979). In addition, Congress endorsed the non-proliferation goals of the Administration, as well as its efforts to encourage international cooperation, in §§ 2 and 3 of that Act, 22 U.S.C. §§ 3201-02. ...

40. The NRC recognized that the United States' initiatives to discourage other nations from reprocessing spent fuel would be undermined if at the same time it continued to pursue domestic commercial reprocessing, since American arguments that the marginal economic benefits are outweighed by the grave security dangers would lose their credibility.

Executive Branch, the NRC contravened Congress' express intent that the Commission be completely free from presidential influence and control.[65] According to petitioners, the fact that the President has primary responsibility over foreign affairs does not justify the NRC's derogation from Congress' plan, since foreign affairs powers are vested in Congress as well. And, petitioners assert, Congress exercised its share of those powers by legislating that with respect to nuclear energy, which inevitably touches upon the sensitive area of foreign affairs, a strict separation is to prevail between the President and the Commission. This is particularly so, petitioners declare, in the context of domestic licensing. In contrast, in the area of international arrangements, such as export licensing, Congress has legislated a divergence from this scheme by making Commission decisions subject to approval by the President.

Although petitioners' argument is resonant with constitutional subtleties concerning the "twilight zone" in which congressional and presidential powers overlap, neither the authority reposed in the NRC nor the agency's exercise of that authority in this case require us to venture into that largely unchartered area. The legislative history produced by petitioners makes clear that Congress intended that the Commission be independent not only from pressures brought to bear by the President, but from all external pressures. Representative is the view expressed by Senator Magnuson:

> Actually, the AEC was established by Congress with the hope and aim of making it the most sensitive agency of Government, more independent than any other, and to be protected from Congress itself, and from all other interference, including Executive interference.

Independence, however, does not mean that the Commission must ignore or reject positions espoused by the President, by Congress or by other parties. The Commission was "charged with a most sensitive and most vital responsibility," a responsibility that cannot possibly be performed properly if the Commission is oblivious or nonresponsive to actions being taken by others, whether within or outside the government. When it created independent administrative agencies, Congress undoubtedly desired that they interact with the three branches of the government much as the legislative body interacts with the executive branch, with "separateness but interdependence, autonomy but reciprocity," so that "practice will integrate the dispersed powers into a workable government."

As previously set forth, the NRC is directed in many provisions of the AEA to consider "the common defense and security." Any contemplation of these sensitive matters necessarily touches upon areas that are also within the domain of the President and of Congress. It was therefore appropriate for the NRC to take note of the relevant developments in the executive and legislative branches and to ascertain, with the help of interested parties, what bearing these developments may have on its own agenda. As we understand the NRC's actions here, that is all it did, and it maintained its independence from both those branches while making an informed decision to suspend its proceedings.

---

65. Expressions of congressional intent that the Commission be independent of the Executive Branch may be found throughout the debates surrounding the passage of the AEA, which took place against the backdrop of the Dixon-Yates controversy. That controversy arose when the President attempted to instruct the Commission to enter into a contract with particular utilities for the provision of electricity to certain Commission facilities. . . .

There is no evidence that the President improperly interfered with the NRC's decisionmaking process, or that the NRC capitulated to the President. Instead, the agency appears to have examined the President's position, and agreed with the President's contention that continuation of the proceedings would adversely affect the President's nonproliferation efforts. Then, after determining that Congress had not exercised its constitutional powers in this area in a contrary manner, neither through the AEA nor through subsequent legislation, the NRC decided that it would be prudent to terminate the proceedings for a time so that the President might pursue his objectives. Given this record, we cannot say that the NRC abused its discretion or acted arbitrarily, capriciously, or not in accordance with the law when it rested its decision in part on a desire not to obstruct the goal of securing international nonproliferation....

[T]he petitions for review will be denied.

---

1. As the preceding case illustrates, the "independence" of "independent agencies" does not preclude presidential communication with such agencies (indeed, the President, like any "interested person," may submit comments with respect to informal rulemaking under 5 U.S.C. § 553), and does not preclude such agencies from basing administrative decisions on factors brought to their attention through executive communications. Recall, from Chapter Four, *Sierra Club v. Costle*, in which Judge Wald stated that presidential jawboning did not invalidate a statutorily authorized administrative decision, even if the decision was different from another statutorily authorized decision the agency might have made without such pressure.

But was this the only issue involved in this case? Although Stuart Eizenstat reported on October 4, 1977 that it was President Carter's position that the commercial reprocessing and recycling of plutonium "should" be deferred (see note 15), the court more accurately reports that the President, on April 4, 1977, said that such processes "would" be deferred. As a Department of Justice lawyer, how would you have responded on April 3, 1977 if asked whether the President had the authority to make his intended statement on April 4? Could the President lawfully have directed a 20-year moratorium on U.S. commercial reprocessing and recycling of plutonium? Could the President lawfully have directed the action that the Nuclear Regulatory Commission took in this case? Assuming that Congress did not provide by statute for presidential review of the foreign policy aspects of NRC licensing decisions, how should a Presidential attempt to prevent licensing on foreign policy grounds be analyzed under *Youngstown* and *Curtiss-Wright*? To use the APA's judicial review standard, 5 U.S.C § 706(2)(A), would it be "arbitrary and capricious" for the NRC to decline licenses on the ground that, in considering the "common defense and security" under statute, it will treat as conclusive any presidential determination that a license would not serve the interests of the "common defense and security?"

2. The court states in *Westinghouse* that "Congress intended the Commission be independent not only from pressures brought to bear by the President, but from all external pressures." This characterization is reminiscent of Justice White's description of the General Accounting Office in *Bowsher v. Synar*, discussed in Chapter Four. Which, if any, functions of the Nuclear Regulatory Commission could Congress vest in an office structured like the position of Comptroller General, in the interest of "total" independence? Did the NRC's actions regarding the recycling issue exhibit

such independence? Would the agency have conformed as readily to the policy views of President Carter had Congress not endorsed them?

3. The *Westinghouse* case implicates the question we asked after *Curtiss-Wright* and *Waterman Steamship* whether Congress may vest regulatory authority with the potential to affect our foreign relations in an official subordinate to the President, but proscribe presidential supervision of that authority. If such legislation would be constitutionally problematic—an open question—then it might also follow that statutes conferring regulatory authority with the potential to affect our foreign relations should be interpreted, in the absence of contrary language, to imply a power *pro tanto* of presidential review. Conversely, if a regulatory statute expressly precludes presidential review, perhaps the agency's implied powers should be construed narrowly whenever a broader construction would give the agency power to affect our foreign relations. You may find the following note useful to assess the wisdom of these hypotheses.

Note: CAB Review of Air Carrier Acquisitions

U.S. and foreign air carriers seeking to engage in air transportation between the U.S. and foreign countries were required until recently to obtain certificates authorizing such transportation from the Civil Aeronautics Board, an independent agency created in 1938 and disbanded at the end of 1984. Because our international aviation is conducted under the provisions of sensitive and complex multilateral and bilateral air transport agreements, CAB decisions to issue, deny, or permit changes in such certificates affected the terms of our international air service and therefore could affect our relations with other countries. For example, the CAB might propose to include in a newly awarded certificate a condition requiring the recipient airline to provide low-cost budget fares to a particular foreign country. If such fares would in fact be lower than fares offered by the national airline of that foreign country on the same route, the displeasure of the other government would be obvious. Indeed, depending on the terms of the applicable bilateral aviation agreement, the other government might well be expected to disapprove the new low fares required by the CAB's condition. The U.S. Government would probably retaliate by disapproving selected fares of the other government's national airline, and a serious government-to-government dispute regarding airline pricing would result.

In some circumstances, the U.S. Government may wish to engage a foreign country in such a controversy in the hope of establishing more attractive fares in a particular market. At other times, depending on the totality of our bilateral relationship with the foreign government in question, the U.S. Government might prefer a less confrontational approach. To ensure that CAB decisions regarding international air certificates are consistent with the foreign policy principles adopted by the Executive Branch, § 801(a) of the Federal Aviation Act, 49 U.S.C. App. § 1461(a) (1982), provided in part:

> The issuance, denial, transfer, amendment, cancellation, suspension, or revocation of, and the terms, conditions, and limitations contained in, any certificate authorizing an air carrier to engage in foreign air transportation, or any permit issuable to any foreign air carrier under section 402 of this Act [49 U.S.C. App. 1372], shall be presented to the President for review. The President shall have the right to disapprove any such Board action concerning such cer-

tificates or permits solely upon the basis of foreign relations or national defense considerations which are within the President's jurisdiction, but not upon the basis of economic or carrier selection considerations.... Any such Board action so disapproved shall be null and void....

Between 1980 and 1984, the question arose in three CAB proceedings whether § 801(a) applied to CAB decisions approving one airline's acquisition of control of another airline when the transaction, while likely to lead to an eventual transfer of one or the other airline's certificates to engage in foreign air transportation, does not require any *immediate* transfer of certificates, and thus may not fall within the language of §801, read literally. The issue in each case was whether the *de facto* transfer of control over the certificates in question—by virtue of the acquisition—constituted a "transfer" within the meaning of § 801(a).

For example, Texas International Airlines applied to the CAB in 1980 to acquire Continental Airlines as a wholly-owned subsidiary. Continental was to continue operating under its own name, and thus no certificate transfers were contemplated. But Continental had long provided the main airline services to and within the Trust Territory of the Pacific Islands, thereby contributing importantly to the effective discharge of certain U.S. treaty obligations. Executive branch agencies, learning of the proposed acquisition, worried that Texas International, badly in need of cash at the time, planned to liquidate Continental, thereby terminating its Pacific services. The agencies argued that the CAB should therefore transmit its decision to the President for review under § 801(a), whether or not any certificates were transferred or modified. The Board decided, for reasons relating to the promotion of U.S. carrier competition, to delete certain Mexican routes from the airlines' certificates, and to send the decision to the President because of those amendments. Thus, the Board found it unnecessary to rule on the applicability of § 801(a) to acquisitions involving no certificate transfers whatsoever.

The Board did address the issue in another case one year later. The Department of Transportation, in Air Florida System-Western Show Cause Proceeding, Order No. 82-1-148 (C.A.B. Jan. 29, 1982) had urged that the CAB submit for presidential review its decision on a petition by Air Florida System, Inc. (AFSI) for approval of a voting trust agreement allowing it to acquire a controlling share of Western Air Lines. Again, no certificate changes were contemplated in the short term. The Department of Transportation had written:

> 3. It has been the consistent view of the Department of Transportation that Section 801 cannot be so narrowly construed as not to apply to a proceeding of this nature. Congress has recognized that foreign relations and national defense considerations, which are within the President's exclusive jurisdiction, may be affected by the transfer of a U.S. air carrier's certificate to engage in foreign air transportation. The potential foreign policy or national defense implications of an air carrier acquisition do not change merely because what is being transferred is control over the holder of the certificate as opposed to the certificate itself. Such a conclusion would be a triumph of form over substance and avoid effective and timely Presidential review of the foreign relations and national defense implications of the acquisition. If, for example, at a subsequent date Air Florida were to seek to amend the permits (which it would control in the name of Western) pursuant to a consolidation, liquidation, or another form

of inter-company transaction, Presidential review occurring only at that time could hardly be found to preserve those Presidential prerogatives intended by Congress to be exercised pursuant to Section 801. The issues reserved to the President ripen at the time of the transfer of control, and are no longer open by the time subsequent inter-company transactions take place.

Statement of the Department of Transportation, at 3-4 (Dec. 7, 1981).

As you read the CAB's decision on this point, which follows, consider whether you regard the Board's or the executive branch's position better-founded. Should § 801 be interpreted to include only those decisions precisely within its language, or should the CAB have been required to determine if its § 408 approval would have the same effect as a § 801 decision with respect to the same parties? What if the airlines structured their arrangement precisely to avoid presidential interference? Note that the CAB decision finds support in two Court of Appeals decisions rendered in 1958 and 1966. Should a later climate of deregulation and relative instability in the airline industry affect a court's attitude towards the Federal Aviation Act?

PRESIDENTIAL REVIEW

Western argued that any order approving the proposed acquisition should be subject to review by the President under § 801 of the Act. This position received support from the Departments of State and Transportation and encountered opposition from AFSI. All proponents of Presidential review concede that the language of the statute does not require such a result. They argue instead that Congress intended that § 801 be read expansively and assert that Presidential review is appropriate here because the acquisition of stock control by AFSI will be similar in practical effect to a transfer of Western's foreign certificates.

The proponents do not address themselves to the fact that we have never sent to the President under § 801 any § 408 decision that involved transfer of control but did not take action with respect to a foreign certificate. Such a consistent Board interpretation requires at least that this acquisition of control be legally distinguished from others. The proponents of review have offered no reason why years of settled practice should be disturbed in this instance.

The proponents have stated the proposition that Congress intended an expansive reading of the section that would subject to Presidential review Board orders that had effects similar to the transfer of a certificate. In fact, this position is not supported by the evidence of Congressional intent that accompanied passage of the Airline Deregulation Act of 1978. Although the Deregulation Act did not alter the language dealing with the sorts of Board actions that should be sent to the President, it did substantially limit the President's previously unfettered discretion as to the exercise of his right to review.[94] The only direct Congressional commentary on the changes

---

94. The changes in § 801 accomplished by the Airline Deregulation Act are as follows:

Pre-ADA	Post-ADA
1. Board actions "subject to the approval of the President"	1. Board actions "presented to the President for review"
2. "overseas or foreign" certificates covered	2. only "foreign" certificates covered

is contained in the House Report accompanying H.R. 12611, which proposed the amendments to § 801 that were later adopted in the final Act:

Presidential Review of International Route Cases

Section 801 of the Federal Aviation Act does not impose any specific standards for the President to follow in reviewing decisions of the CAB on international air routes. From time to time questions have arisen as to whether this section permits the President to substitute his judgment for that of the CAB as to which routes will best serve the interests of the traveling public. The committee believes that this type of judgment should be made by the CAB which is an arm of Congress and that the President should only disapprove CAB decisions when the decision would create difficulties in our foreign relations or national security.[95]

In addition to changes to § 801, Congress also amended § 408 to deemphasize public interest concerns and accentuate the antitrust policies that guide court review of combinations in unregulated sectors of the economy, and limited the types of combinations subject to Board approval. These changes also suggest a more limited role for Presidential action in the cases of mergers and acquisitions. Given this background, we are not persuaded that the expansive view of § 801 urged upon us is supported by the actions of Congress.

Leaving aside Congressional intent, the proposition that § 801 should be read expansively is inconsistent with the court decisions. In *ALPA v. CAB*[96] it was argued that a § 408 transaction approved by the Board had in fact transferred control of Saturn, a foreign certificate holder, even though Saturn was the surviving corporation, and therefore § 801 review was necessary. The court observed that Saturn held the certificate before and after the transaction and therefore the Board's decision should not have been sent to the President.[97] The argument that Board actions that have the

---

3.	copies of applications for certificates to be sent to President prior to hearing	3. requirement eliminated
4.	all decisions to be submitted to President before publication	4. requirement eliminated
5.	no limitation on President's power to disapprove	5. President's right to disapprove limited to "foreign relations or national defense considerations . . . but not economic or carrier selection considerations."
6.	no requirement that President give reasons for disapproval	6. requirement that President issue public document, giving reasons for disapproval, within 60 days
7.	no similar language	*7. disapproved Board action is null and void; action not disapproved is action of Board and subject to judicial review.

* This language is apparently in response to the *Waterman* case which held, in general, that *Board actions submitted to the President were completely unreviewable by courts, whatever action the President took.*

95. H.R. Rep. No. 95-1211, 95th Cong., 2d Sess. 19 (1978).

96. *Airline Pilots Ass'n Int'l v. Civil Aeronautics Board.*, 360 F.2d 837 (D.C. Cir. 1966).

97. The court suggested that the result might be different if the parties deliberately and

same practical effects as those enumerated in § 801 should be sent to the President was laid to rest in *Pan Am v. CAB* in 1958.[98] The Board had granted an exemption from the § 401 certificate requirement for the carriage of international mail. That exemption had the same effect as the grant of a certificate, but the court held that the decision should not have been sent to the President.

> Section 801 contains no reference to exemptions although it recites explicitly a whole series of Board actions relative to certificates affected by the statute. True, the exemption has operative effects not unlike an amendment of a certificate, but the extraordinary power vested in the Executive should not be expanded beyond the needs of the foreign relations considerations which have been relied on to justify the grant.[99]

Thus, in the context of both a certificate exemption and a transfer of control, courts have not read § 801 expansively and have specifically rejected the "same practical effects" argument.

Consequently, in this case, as we have done consistently in the past, we must follow the express dictates of § 801: since we are taking no action with respect to the certificates of either Air Florida or Western, this order will not be sent to the President for review.

---

1. What action would you have advised the President to take if he objected to the CAB decision?

2. The CAB's functions with respect to authorizing foreign air transportation were transferred on the CAB's demise to the U.S. Department of Transportation (DOT), an executive agency. 49 U.S.C. § 1551. DOT subsequently established a system for formal adjudications within the department on matters relating to air carrier certificates. Its decisions continue to be reviewable by the President under § 801 of the Federal Aviation Act. Is the transfer of functions likely to eliminate the conflict described in the above note? Assuming an adjudicative system in DOT structurally identical to the CAB structure (except that DOT is not a multi-headed agency), what impact is the transfer of CAB functions to a "non-independent" executive agency likely to have in terms of policy control by the President?

3. Foreign Policy and the Appropriations Power

Note: The Iran-Contra Initiative

As noted above, it was disclosed in November, 1986 that the United States had, since August, 1985, engaged in a series of secret arms deals involving Iran. Less than two weeks after initial U.S. confirmation of the deals, it was further revealed that National Security Council (NSC) staff had facilitated the diversion of profits from the arms sales to the support of military forces (the "Contras") seeking to overthrow

---

"irrationally" structured the transactions in a "patently artificial attempt to bypass the White House." 360 F.2d at 841. There is no evidence of any such attempt in this case.

98. *Pan American World Airways, Inc. v. Civil Aeronautics Board.*, 261 F.2d 754 (D.C. Cir. 1958), *cert. denied*, 359 U.S. 912 (1959).

99. 261 F.2d at 756.

the government of Nicaragua. This funding occurred during a period for which Congress had imposed a series of restrictions on military and intelligence appropriations (the so-called "Boland Amendments") proscribing the use of those appropriations for the military or paramilitary assistance of the Contra forces. These limitations were imposed despite the vigorous opposition of the Administration, for which support of the Contras was considered a foreign policy priority. (These amendments may be viewed as part of a trend over the last 15 years toward congressional resort to appropriations riders to impose substantive limitations on the statutory authority of the executive branch. Recall *Brown v. Califano*, reprinted in Chapter Four, concerning the use of appropriations statutes to regulate the implementation of Title VI of the Civil Rights Act of 1964.)

Whether the use of National Security Council staff to facilitate Contra support violated the then-current Boland Amendment is a complex question, in no small part because the various Contra aid restrictions enacted by Congress differed in their precise terms, and those differences make for rich argument over legislative intent. In order to further debate on the issue, Rep. William V. Alexander, Jr. of Arkansas took the unusual step on June 15, 1987 of inserting into the Congressional record the legislative history of each of these provisions. 133 Cong. Rec. H4585-4987 (daily ed. June 15, 1987). This compilation includes a chart of the twelve Contra aid restrictions enacted between December, 1982 and October, 1986. During fiscal year 1985—the period chiefly relevant to the initiation of the Contra funding initiative—Congress provided:

> [N]o funds available to the Central Intelligence Agency, the Department of Defense, or any other agency or entity of the United States involved in intelligence activities may be obligated or expended for the purpose or which would have the effect of supporting, directly or indirectly, military or paramilitary operations in Nicaragua by any nation, group, organization, movement, or individual.

Department of Defense Appropriations Act 1985, § 8066, enacted in Further Continuing Appropriations Act, Pub. L. No. 98-473, 98 Stat. 1935 (1984). Whether this proscription applied to the NSC's 1985 activities involving the Contras depends, statutorily, on whether the NSC is to be viewed as "agency or entity of the United States," and, if so, whether it is "involved in intelligence activities," within the intent of the statute. *See* the discussion of the National Security Council in Chapter Three, above.

Note that the appropriations act was a so-called "continuing resolution," funding all those government agencies that had not been funded by the beginning of the fiscal year, October 1, 1984. Recall that, without this appropriation, most administrative operations of the executive branch would have had to shut down. It is in this context that President Reagan signed the statute containing the fiscal year 1985 Boland Amendment. Does this example help explain the temptation to use appropriations acts to impose substantive limits on government authority? Would the context in which the President signed the act excuse any failure scrupulously to obey it?

Whatever the proper resolution of these questions, it is clear that the Contra support initiative raises important constitutional questions concerning both presidential and congressional authorities.

For example, on the congressional side, are there limits to Congress' power to regulate presidential attempts to raise money from private citizens or from other countries in support of his foreign affairs objectives? Presumably, the Boland Amendment is unproblematic if it is simply a limitation on the government accounts on which the President may properly draw for such a fund-raising effort. Congress could surely tell the President to use the State Department, but not the Treasury Department for such an effort. Some members of Congress have argued, however, that the Boland Amendment was essentially a comprehensive ban on attempts by anyone involved in government intelligence work to undertake any initiative in support of the Contras. Could Congress have provided: "No officer of the Government of the United States may raise funds from any source in support of military or paramilitary activity in Nicaragua"? What would be the source of Congress's authority for such a statute? If Congress lacks authority for such a statute, could it permissibly enact the same proscription in the form of an appropriations rider? That is, does its spending power for the general welfare give it greater leeway in this context than when it legislates pursuant to its substantive regulatory powers? Would such a view undermine any notion of inherent presidential authority to accomplish anything that he cannot accomplish on his own salary?

On the executive side, does the President have inherent authority to undertake covert fund-raising initiatives in support of his foreign affairs objectives? (For example, would the Contra initiative have been lawful even if the executive found itself, because of the Boland Amendment, in its weakest legal position under Justice Jackson's *Youngstown* analysis?) If so, what are the implications for the article I vesting of the appropriations power in Congress as a source of "checks and balances?" Even if the Boland Amendment did not expressly proscribe the NSC activities that took place, is the argument for inherent presidential authority strong enough to withstand the suggestion that the NSC initiative undermined the "faithful execution of the laws" given the policy of non-aid to the Contras implicit in that amendment? Would it be relevant to the legal analysis whether the fund-raising was covert, and hence, resistant to ordinary mechanisms of governmental accountability, or public, and thus subject to a full and educated congressional response?

On November 18, 1987, the House and Senate committees investigating the Iran-Contra affair issued their final report. S. Rep. No. 216, 100th Cong., 1st Sess. (1987); H.R. Rep. No. 433, 100th Cong., 1st Sess. (1987). The Democratic majorities of both committees, together with three Republican Senators, concluded that the Administration had engaged in "an evasion of the letter and the spirit" of the law, and laid blame partially with President Reagan, whose solicitation of foreign donations for the Contras assertedly "set the stage" for his subordinates' "disdain" for legal restrictions. Two Senate and the six House Republicans contended that the Boland amendments were unconstitutional. A helpful summary of the lengthy report appears at 45 Cong. Q. 2847-59 (1987). *See also* J. Tower, et al., Report of the President's Special Review Board (1987); Preliminary Inquiry into the Sale of Arms to Iran and Possible Diversion of Funds to the Nicaraguan Resistance, S. Rept. No. 100-7, 100th Cong., 1st Sess. (1987). Note that the preceding discussion has focused entirely on the constitutional issues lurking behind this episode; testimony before Congress also established that executive branch officials had intentionally lied to congressional committees to prevent their discovery of the Contra funding operation. (Do this and the Watergate episode suggest that perjury and obstruction of justice charges are likely the inevitable outgrowths of secret policy gone wrong?) Presumably, prosecutions for perjury before Congress would not raise any separation of powers problem.

4. Immigration and Foreign Policy

Yet another area of congressional authority with obvious ramifications for our foreign policy concerns the regulation of immigration. The full import of immigration law for foreign affairs could only be assessed in a work as long as this entire book. For the sake of completeness, however, at least some mention of the foreign affairs aspects of immigration law is warranted. For a comprehensive review of American immigration law, see T.A. Aleinikoff and D. Martin, Immigration Process and Policy (1985).

For over 40 years, our foreign policy was affected by Congress' enactment of a national origin quota formula, basing the proportion of admissible aliens on the nationality breakdown of the 1920 U.S. census. The resulting scheme, first implemented in 1924, was heavily weighted in favor of the United Kingdom and Northern European countries. The quota system was not repealed until 1965. Act of October 3, 1965, P.L. 89-236, 79 Stat. 911. For an historical overview, see Select Commission on Immigration and Refugee Policy, Staff Report on U.S. Immigration Policy and the National Interest (1981).

Currently, critical foreign affairs issues are raised by the executive branch's implementation of authority delegated by Congress to handle the influx of refugees. *See,* for example, *Jean v. Nelson*, 472 U.S. 846 (1985), holding that officials of the Immigration and Naturalization Service are barred from considering race and national origin in making decisions whether to "parole" Haitian refugees into the United States under 8 U.S.C. § 1182(d)(5)(A); *Hotel and Restaurant Employees Union v. Smith*, 594 F. Supp. 502 (D.D.C. 1984), *aff'd in part, rev'd in part*, 804 F.2d 1256 (D.C. Cir. 1986), holding unreviewable a decision by the Attorney General not to grant El Salvadoran refugees "extended voluntary departure" status, which would have had the effect of insulating them from deportation procedures until an end to the political turmoil in El Salvador. *See also United States v. Frade*, 709 F.2d 1387 (11th Cir. 1983), reversing the conviction of two clerics under the Trading with the Enemy Act for helping to transport and land illegal aliens during the 1980 Cuban boat lift. The current legal framework for the admission of refugees is set by the Refugee Act of 1980, Pub. L. No. 96-212, 94 Stat. 102. *See generally* Martin, *The Refugee Act of 1980: Its Past and Future*, 1982 Mich. Y.B. Int'l L. Stud. 91; G. Loescher & J. Scanlan, Calculated Kindness: Refugees and America's Half-Open Door, 1945-Present (1986).

The executive branch also may exercise its discretion to deny visas to aliens on foreign affairs grounds, including an alien's intent to engage in activities that the executive branch believes to be "prejudicial to the public interest... of the United States." 8 U.S.C. § 1182(a)(27). Notwithstanding the first and fifth amendments, such activities may include speech making and even the alien's mere presence in the United States. *See Kleindienst v. Mandel*, 408 U.S. 753 (1972); *but see Abourezk v. Reagan*, 592 F. Supp. 880 (D.D.C. 1984), *rev'd*, 785 F.2d 1043 (D.C. Cir. 1986), *aff'd by equally divided court*, 108 S. Ct. 252 (1987).

E. Individual Rights and the Government's "Monopoly" in Foreign Policy

Note: The Logan Act

Materials in this chapter have referred often to the overriding interest of the federal government in the conduct of foreign policy, and to the presumptive authority of the

President in managing our foreign affairs. Of obvious concern in this connection is the prospect for the disruption of our foreign relations—or the frustration of the current President's policy objectives—by actions of private citizens that may affect our relationship with other nations.

A statute that tries to preserve the federal government's monopoly in foreign affairs is the Logan Act, 18 U.S.C. § 953, adopted in 1799, which provides as follows:

> Any citizen of the United States, wherever he may be, who, without authority of the United States, directly or indirectly commences or carries on any correspondence or intercourse with any foreign government or any officer or agent thereof, with intent to influence the measures or conduct of any foreign government or of any officer or agent thereof, in relation to any disputes or controversies with the United States, or to defeat the measures of the United States, shall be fined not more than $5,000 or imprisoned not more than three years, or both.
>
> This section shall not abridge the right of a citizen to apply, himself or his agent, to any foreign government or the agents thereof for redress of any injury which he may have sustained from such government or any of its agents or subjects.

(A related statute aimed at protecting the government's monopoly over military policy is the Neutrality Act, 18 U.S.C. §960, explored in Chapter Seven.)

The statute is named after Dr. George Logan, a Philadelphia Quaker, a doctor and a Republican, who sailed to France in the 1790's to speak with French officials in order to help relax tensions with America. Although the French greeted his efforts with enthusiasm, President Adams successfully recommended that Congress take action to curb the "temerity and impudence of individuals affecting to interfere in public affairs between France and the United States." Although Logan's name was immortalized through this bill, most historians have noted that he accomplished little or nothing by his efforts and may even have done positive harm by his interference. *See generally* Vagts, *The Logan Act: Paper Tiger or Sleeping Giant?* 60 Am. J. Int'l. L. 268 (1966).

There is no reported decision of any conviction under this statute. A review, however, of some reported instances of its invocation in prosecutions either contemplated or actually commenced and abandoned, suggests the kinds of contexts in which the Government is likely to be especially sensitive about its foreign affairs monopoly. Because the Act poses first amendment problems, its threatened use—and the consequent chilling effect on speech—may be as important as the prospect of a conviction.

The Logan Act has been invoked mostly during tense periods in United States history. During the early 1800's, the United States was negotiating with Spain over territory and, on two occasions, accused persons informally of violating the Logan Act. In both of these instances, the Administration was irritated with what it felt was interference in its negotiation through individual correspondence with Spain. Neither instance led to an indictment.

Other occasions during which the Logan Act has been involved occurred during the Civil War and World War I. There were no indictments during the Civil War, although one Mr. Bunch, the British Consul in Charleston, South Carolina lost his position after the Secretary of War accused Bunch of violating the Logan Act, based on his having invited the Confederacy to declare its adherence to the Convention of Paris on naval warfare. World War I presented an international scene somewhat similar to that in which the Logan Act arose and resulted in American citizens privately urging warring nations to settle their disputes. Although threats of indictments were made, none of them were followed through.

More recent historical examples have shown a similar pattern. Following the Korean War, Army Private John O. Martin was charged with having violated the Logan Act. During his two years as a prisoner of war, he was alleged to have collaborated with the enemy. (Charges were dropped as the court held that the Army did not have proper jurisdiction to try the case.)

The Logan Act was mentioned in *U.S. v. Peace Information Center*, 97 F. Supp. 255, 261 (D.D.C. 1951), a case in which the defendant, the Peace Information Center, was charged with violating the Foreign Agents Registration Act of 1938. The court discussed the Federal Government's broad power to deal with the external relations of the United States, naming the Logan Act as an example of the implementation of that power. Rather than invoking the Logan Act against a defendant like the Peace Information Center, however, the Government had chosen to create the Foreign Agents Registration Act of 1938 as a way to deal with the citizens of the United States who attempt to conduct correspondence *on behalf of* a foreign government. *See also Copeland v. Secretary of State*, 226 F. Supp. 20 (S.D.N.Y 1964), *vacated*, 378 U.S. 588 (1974).

Several controversial invocations of the Logan Act have occurred in recent years. Jesse Jackson was threatened with prosecution under the Act in 1980 when it was reported that a Libyan diplomat had given $10,000 to his Operation PUSH. In 1983, the Justice Department dropped its investigation because it found no evidence that Jackson had acted on behalf of Libya. Former Attorney General Ramsey Clark was similarly threatened with prosecution by President Carter, for having defied the President's ban on travel to Iran and having attended a conference in Teheran during the Iranian hostage crisis. Criminal charges were not filed.

In 1980, a case involving former CIA agent Philip Agee arose because the Department of State revoked his passport on national security grounds. One Court of Appeals judge argued that the revocation was partly justified by Agee's violation of the Logan Act through correspondence with Iranian terrorists, encouraging them to prevail in their unlawful demands on the United States to deliver all records of CIA intelligence operations in Iran. *Agee v. Muskie*, 629 F.2d 80, 112-113 (D.C. Cir. 1980) (McKinnon, J., dissenting). The Court of Appeals' holding that the Department of State needed clearer congressional authorization in order to revoke Agee's passport was reversed by the Supreme Court. *Haig v. Agee*, 453 U.S. 280 (1981) (reprinted below).

Jesse Jackson again raised a Logan Act problem in 1981, when he negotiated with the Syrian foreign ministry to release Lt. Robert O. Goodman, Jr., a U.S. flier held captive in Syria. When Jackson returned home a hero, having secured Goodman's release, no charges were filed.

After 186 years without prosecuting any Logan Act offense to conclusion, may the government still constitutionally rely on it consistently with due process? Until 1960, the State Department had a regulation under which Americans who proposed to advise foreign governments with respect to disputes with the United States could obtain clearance. At present, however, there is no established procedure through which any party can obtain approval of such activities. How then, is a citizen to learn what the Act technically permits or proscribes? Does the Act's facial breadth in proscribing speech make it void for vagueness under the First Amendment? What does it mean to "defeat a measure" of the United States? Is it always possible, for example, to distinguish correspondence relevant to a legitimate business deal from the conduct of foreign policy?

A substantially litigated area in which the government's foreign policy concerns pose tensions with individual rights is the area of international travel. The scope of the executive's powers in constraining such travel is clouded by the silence of the relevant statutes concerning standards for withholding or revoking passports. In *Kent v. Dulles*, 357 U.S. 116 (1958), the Court reviewed a challenge to a State Department regulation denying passports to applicants because of their alleged Communist beliefs and associations and their refusals to file affidavits concerning present or past membership in the Communist Party. Rather than confront difficult issues concerning the permissible grounds for passport denial, the Court held that, absent a clear statement from Congress, it would not conclude that Congress had granted the executive branch administrative authority with such serious individual rights implications. Seven years later, however, in *Zemel v. Rusk*, 381 U.S. 1 (1965), the Court held that the Secretary of State could restrict travel for all citizens to Cuba, but only after finding implicit authority for area travel restrictions in light of congressional acquiescence in a long-standing executive branch practice of implementing them. Such acquiescence was deemed a clear statement of legislative intent. (*See also Regan v. Wald*, 468 U.S. 222 (1984), upholding Treasury Department regulations restricting travel-related economic transactions—and hence travel—in an effort to prevent Cuba from earning hard currency through U.S. tourism.) *Kent* and *Zemel* are the focus of the following decision, which poses the question whether the Court still perceives international travel restrictions as posing difficult constitutional issues and whether it still follows a restrictive approach to statutory interpretation in divining authority to limit that travel.

Haig v. Agee
453 U.S. 280 (1981)

Chief Justice BURGER delivered the opinion of the Court.

The question presented is whether the President, acting through the Secretary of State, has authority to revoke a passport on the ground that the holder's activities in foreign countries are causing or are likely to cause serious damage to the national security or foreign policy of the United States.

I

A

Philip Agee, an American citizen, currently resides in West Germany.[1] From 1957 to 1968, he was employed by the Central Intelligence Agency. He held key positions

---

1. Agee has been deported from Great Britain, France, and the Netherlands. Dirty Work: The CIA in Western Europe 286-300 (P. Agee & L. Wolf eds. 1978).

in the division of the Agency that is responsible for covert intelligence gathering in foreign countries. In the course of his duties at the Agency, Agee received training in clandestine operations, including the methods used to protect the identities of intelligence employees and sources of the United States overseas. He served in undercover assignments abroad and came to know many Government employees and other persons supplying information to the United States. The relationships of many of these people to our Government are highly confidential; many are still engaged in intelligence gathering.

In 1974, Agee called a press conference in London to announce his "campaign to fight the United States CIA wherever it is operating." He declared his intent "to expose CIA officers and agents and to take the measures necessary to drive them out of the countries where they are operating." Since 1974, Agee has, by his own assertion, devoted consistent effort to that program, and he has traveled extensively in other countries in order to carry it out. To identify CIA personnel in a particular country, Agee goes to the target country and consults sources in local diplomatic circles whom he knows from his prior service in the United States Government. He recruits collaborators and trains them in clandestine techniques designed to expose the "cover" of CIA employees and sources. Agee and his collaborators have repeatedly and publicly identified individuals and organizations located in foreign countries as undercover CIA agents, employees, or sources. The record reveals that the identifications divulge classified information, violate Agee's express contract not to make any public statements about Agency matters without prior clearance by the Agency,[5] have prejudiced the ability of the United States to obtain intelligence, and have been followed by episodes of violence against the persons and organizations identified.[7]

In December 1979, the Secretary of State revoked Agee's passport and delivered an explanatory notice to Agee in West Germany. The notice states in part:

---

5. As a condition for his employment by the Agency, Agee contracted that "[i]n consideration of my employment by CIA I undertake not to publish or to participate in the publication of any information or material relating to the Agency, its activities or intelligence activities generally, either during or after the term of my employment by the Agency without specific prior approval by the Agency." This language is identical to the clause which we construed in *Snepp v. United States*, 444 U.S. 507, 508 (1980).

7. In December 1975, Richard Welch was murdered in Greece after the publication of an article in an Englisha-alanguage newspaper in Athens naming Welch as CIA Chief of Station. In July 1980, two days after a Jamaica press conference at which Agee's principal collaborator identified Richard Kinsman as CIA Chief of Station in Jamaica, Kinsman's house was strafed with automatic gunfire. Four days after the same press conference, three men approached the Jamaica home of another man similarly identified as an Agency officer. Police challenged the men and gunfire was exchanged. In January 1981, two American officials of the American Institute for Free Labor Development, previously identified as a CIA front by Agee and discussed extensively in Agee's book Inside the Company: CIA Diary, were assassinated in El Salvador.

The Secretary does not assert that Agee has specifically incited anyone to commit murder. However, affidavits of the CIA's Deputy Director for Operations set out and support his judgment that Agee's purported identifications are "thinly-veiled invitations to violence," that "Agee's actions could, in today's circumstances, result in someone's death," and that Agee's conduct has "markedly increased the likelihood of individuals so identified being the victims of violence." One of those affidavits also shows that the ultimate effectiveness of Agee's program depends on activities of hostile foreign groups, and that such groups can be expected to engage in physical surveillance, harassment, kidnaping, and, in extreme cases, murder of United States officials abroad.

"The Department's action is predicated upon a determination made by the Secretary under the provisions of [22 CFR] Section 51.70(b)(4) that your activities abroad are causing or are likely to cause serious damage to the national security or the foreign policy of the United States. The reasons for the Secretary's determination are, in summary, as follows: Since the early 1970's it has been your stated intention to conduct a continuous campaign to disrupt the intelligence operations of the United States. In carrying out that campaign you have travelled in various countries (including, among others, Mexico, the United Kingdom, Denmark, Jamaica, Cuba, and Germany), and your activities in those countries have caused serious damage to the national security and foreign policy of the United States. Your stated intention to continue such activities threatens additional damage of the same kind."

The notice also advised Agee of his right to an administrative hearing and offered to hold such a hearing in West Germany on 5 days' notice.

Agee at once filed suit against the Secretary. He alleged that the regulation invoked by the Secretary, 22 CFR § 51.70(b)(4) (1980), has not been authorized by Congress and is invalid; that the regulation is impermissibly overbroad; that the revocation prior to a hearing violated his Fifth Amendment right to procedural due process; and that the revocation violated a Fifth Amendment liberty interest in a right to travel and a First Amendment right to criticize Government policies. He sought declaratory and injunctive relief, and he moved for summary judgment on the question of the authority to promulgate the regulation and on the constitutional claims. For purposes of that motion, Agee conceded the Secretary's factual averments and his claim that Agee's activities were causing or were likely to cause serious damage to the national security or foreign policy of the United States. The District Court held that the regulation exceeded the statutory powers of the Secretary under the Passport Act of 1926, 22 U.S.C. § 211a, granted summary judgment for Agee, and ordered the Secretary to restore his passport.

B

A divided panel of the Court of Appeals affirmed. *Agee v. Muskie*, 629 F.2d 80 (D.C. Cir. 1980). It held that the Secretary was required to show that Congress had authorized the regulation either by an express delegation or by implied approval of a "substantial and consistent" administrative practice, *Zemel v. Rusk*, 381 U.S. 1, 12 (1965). The court found no express statutory authority for the revocation. It perceived only one other case of actual passport revocation under the regulation since it was promulgated and only five other instances prior to that in which passports were actually denied "even arguably for national security or foreign policy reasons." The Court of Appeals took note of the Secretary's reliance on "a series of statutes, regulations, proclamations, orders and advisory opinions dating back to 1856," but declined to consider those authorities, reasoning that "the criterion for establishing congressional assent by inaction is the actual imposition of sanctions and not the mere assertion of power." ... The court also regarded it as material that most of the Secretary's authorities dealt with powers of the Executive Branch "during time of war or national emergency" or with respect to persons "engaged in criminal conduct." ...

II

The principal question before us is whether the statute authorizes the action of the Secretary pursuant to the policy announced by the challenged regulation.[17]

A

1

... [W]e begin with the language of the statute. The Passport Act of 1926 provides in pertinent part:

> "The Secretary of State may grant and issue passports, and cause passports to be granted, issued, and verified in foreign countries by diplomatic representatives of the United States... under such rules as the President shall designate and prescribe for and on behalf of the United States, and no other person shall grant, issue, or verify such passports." 22 U.S.C. § 211a.

This language is unchanged since its original enactment in 1926.

The Passport Act does not in so many words confer upon the Secretary a power to revoke a passport. Nor, for that matter, does it expressly authorize denials of passport applications. Neither, however, does any statute expressly limit those powers. It is beyond dispute that the Secretary has the power to deny a passport for reasons not specified in the statutes. For example, in *Kent v. Dulles*, 357 U.S. 116 (1958), the Court recognized congressional acquiescence in Executive policies of refusing passports to applicants "participating in illegal conduct, trying to escape the toils of the law, promoting passport frauds, or otherwise engaging in conduct which would violate the laws of the United States." In *Zemel*, the Court held that "the weightiest considerations of national security" authorized the Secretary to restrict travel to Cuba at the time of the Cuban missile crisis. Agee concedes that if the Secretary may deny a passport application for a certain reason, he may revoke a passport on the same ground.

2

Particularly in light of the "broad rule making authority granted in the [1926] Act," a consistent administrative construction of that statute must be followed by the courts " 'unless there are compelling indications that it is wrong.' " *E. I. du Pont de Nemours & Co. v. Collins*, 432 U.S. 46, 55 (1977). This is especially so in the areas of foreign policy and national security, where congressional silence is not to be equated with congressional disapproval....

Applying these considerations to statutory construction, the *Zemel* Court observed:

> "[B]ecause of the changeable and explosive nature of contemporary international relations, and the fact that the Executive is immediately privy to information which cannot be swiftly presented to, evaluated by, and acted upon by the legislature, *Congress—in giving the Executive authority over matters of*

---

17. In light of our decision on this issue, we have no occasion in this case to determine the scope of "the very delicate, plenary and exclusive power of the President as the sole organ of the federal government in the field of international relations—a power which does not require as a basis for its exercise an act of Congress, but which, of course, like every other governmental power, must be exercised in subordination to the applicable provisions of the Constitution." See *United States v. Curtiss-Wright Export Corp.*, 299 U.S. 304 (1936).

foreign affairs—must of necessity paint with a brush broader than that it customarily wields in domestic areas."

381 U.S., at 17 (emphasis supplied). Matters intimately related to foreign policy and national security are rarely proper subjects for judicial intervention. . . .

B

1

A passport is, in a sense, a letter of introduction in which the issuing sovereign vouches for the bearer and requests other sovereigns to aid the bearer. Very early, the Court observed:

> "[A passport] is a document, which, from its nature and object, is addressed to foreign powers; purporting only to be a request, that the bearer of it may pass safely and freely; and is to be considered rather in the character of a political document, by which the bearer is recognised, in foreign countries, as an American citizen; and which, by usage and the law of nations, is received as evidence of the fact." *Urtetiqui v. D'Arcy*, 9 Pet. 692, 698 (1835).

With the enactment of travel control legislation making a passport generally a requirement for travel abroad,[22] a passport took on certain added characteristics. Most important for present purposes, the only means by which an American can lawfully leave the country or return to it—absent a Presidentially granted exception—is with a passport. See 8 U.S.C. § 1185(b) (1976 ed., Supp. IV). As a travel control document, a passport is both proof of identity and proof of allegiance to the United States. Even under a travel control statute, however, a passport remains in a sense a document by which the Government vouches for the bearer and for his conduct.

The history of passport controls since the earliest days of the Republic shows congressional recognition of Executive authority to withhold passports on the basis of substantial reasons of national security and foreign policy. Prior to 1856, when there was no statute on the subject, the common perception was that the issuance of a passport was committed to the sole discretion of the Executive and that the Executive would exercise this power in the interests of the national security and foreign policy of the United States. This derived from the generally accepted view that foreign policy was the province and responsibility of the Executive. From the outset, Congress endorsed not only the underlying premise of Executive authority in the areas of foreign policy and national security, but also its specific application to the subject of passports. Early Congresses enacted statutes expressly recognizing the Executive authority with respect to passports.

The first Passport Act, adopted in 1856, provided that the Secretary of State "shall be authorized to grant and issue passports . . . under such rules as the President shall designate and prescribe for and on behalf of the United States. . . ." § 23, 11 Stat. 60. This broad and permissive language worked no change in the power of the Executive to issue passports; nor was it intended to do so. The Act was passed to centralize passport authority in the Federal Government and specifically in the Secretary of State. In all other respects, the 1856 Act "merely confirmed an authority

---

22. With exceptions during the War of 1812 and the Civil War, passports were not mandatory until 1918. It was not until 1978 that passports were required by statute in non-emergency peacetime.

already possessed and exercised by the Secretary of State. This authority was ancillary to his broader authority to protect American citizens in foreign countries and was necessarily incident to his general authority to conduct the foreign affairs of the United States under the Chief Executive." Senate Committee on Government Operations, Reorganization of the Passport Functions of the Department of State, 86th Cong., 2d Sess., 13 (Comm. Print 1960).

The President and the Secretary of State consistently construed the 1856 Act to preserve their authority to withhold passports on national security and foreign policy grounds. Thus, as an emergency measure in 1861, the Secretary issued orders prohibiting persons from going abroad or entering the country without passports; denying passports to citizens who were subject to military service unless they were bonded; and absolutely denying passports to persons "on errands hostile and injurious to the peace of the country and dangerous to the Union." 3 J. Moore, A Digest of International Law 920 (1906); U. S. Dept. of State, The American Passport 49-54 (1898). An 1869 opinion of Attorney General Hoar held that the granting of a passport was not "obligatory in any case." 13 Op. Atty.Gen. 89, 92....

In 1903, President Theodore Roosevelt promulgated a rule providing that "[t]he Secretary of State has the right in his discretion to refuse to issue a passport, and will exercise this right towards anyone who, he has reason to believe, desires a passport to further an unlawful or improper purpose." Subsequent Executive Orders issued between 1907 and 1917 cast no doubt on this position. This policy was enforced in peacetime years to deny passports to citizens whose conduct abroad was "likely to embarrass the United States" or who were "disturbing, or endeavoring to disturb, the relations of this country with the representatives of foreign countries."

By enactment of the first travel control statute in 1918, Congress made clear its expectation that the Executive would curtail or prevent international travel by American citizens if it was contrary to the national security. The legislative history reveals that the principal reason for the 1918 statute was fear that "renegade Americans" would travel abroad and engage in "transference of important military information" to persons not entitled to it. The 1918 statute left the power to make exceptions exclusively in the hands of the Executive, without articulating specific standards. Unless the Secretary had power to apply national security criteria in passport decisions, the purpose of the Travel Control Act would plainly have been frustrated.

Against this background, and while the 1918 provisions were still in effect, Congress enacted the Passport Act of 1926. The legislative history of the statute is sparse. However, Congress used language which is identical in pertinent part to that in the 1856 statute, as amended, and the legislative history clearly shows congressional awareness of the Executive policy. There is no evidence of any intent to repudiate the longstanding administrative construction. Absent such evidence, we conclude that Congress, in 1926, adopted the longstanding administrative construction of the 1856 statute.

The Executive construed the 1926 Act to work no change in prior practice and specifically interpreted it to authorize denial of a passport on grounds of national security or foreign policy. Indeed, by an unbroken line of Executive Orders, regulations, instructions to consular officials, and notices to passport holders, the President and the Department of State left no doubt that likelihood of damage to national security or foreign policy of the United States was the single most important criterion in passport decisions.... This history of administrative construction was repeatedly communicated to Congress, not only by routine promulgation of Executive Orders and regulations, but also by specific presentations. . . .

In 1966, the Secretary of State promulgated the regulations at issue in this case. 22 CFR §§ 51.70(b)(4), 51.71(a) (1980). Closely paralleling the 1956 regulation, these provisions authorize revocation of a passport where "[t]he Secretary determines that the national's activities abroad are causing or are likely to cause serious damage to the national security or the foreign policy of the United States."

Zemel recognized that congressional acquiescence may sometimes be found from nothing more than silence in the face of an administrative policy. Here, however, the inference of congressional approval "is supported by more than mere congressional inaction." Twelve years after the promulgation of the regulations at issue and 22 years after promulgation of the similar 1956 regulation, Congress enacted the statute making it unlawful to travel abroad without a passport even in peacetime. 8 U.S.C. § 1185(b) (1976 ed., Supp. IV). Simultaneously, Congress amended the Passport Act of 1926 to provide that "[u]nless authorized by law," in the absence of war, armed hostilities, or imminent danger to travelers, a passport may not be geographically restricted.[48] Title 8 U.S.C. § 1185(b) must be read *in pari materia* with the Passport Act.

The 1978 amendments are weighty evidence of congressional approval of the Secretary's interpretation, particularly that in the 1966 regulations. Despite the long-standing and officially promulgated view that the Executive had the power to withhold passports for reasons of national security and foreign policy, Congress in 1978, "though it once again enacted legislation relating to passports, left completely untouched the broad rule-making authority granted in the earlier Act." *Zemel*, *supra*, at 12.

3

Agee argues that the only way the Executive can establish implicit congressional approval is by proof of longstanding and consistent *enforcement* of the claimed power: that is, by showing that many passports were revoked on national security and foreign policy grounds. For this proposition, he relies on *Kent*. A necessary premise for Agee's contention is that there were frequent occasions for revocation and that the claimed Executive power was exercised in only a few of those cases. However, if there were no occasions—or few—to call the Secretary's authority into play, the absence of frequent instances of enforcement is wholly irrelevant. The exercise of a power emerges only in relation to a factual situation, and the continued validity of the power is not diluted simply because there is no need to use it.

The history is clear that there have been few situations involving substantial likelihood of serious damage to the national security or foreign policy of the United

---

48. Act of Oct. 7, 1978, § 124, 92 Stat. 971, 22 U.S.C. § 211a (1976 ed., Supp. IV). This amendment added the following language to the Passport Act:

"Unless authorized by law, a passport may not be designated as restricted for travel to or for use in any country other than a country with which the United States is at war, where armed hostilities are in progress, or where there is imminent danger to the public health or the physical safety of United States travellers."

The statute provides that the purpose of this amendment is "achieving greater United States compliance with the provisions of the Final Act of the Conference on Security and Cooperation in Europe (signed at Helsinki on August 1, 1975)." 92 Stat. 971.

States as a result of a passport holder's activities abroad, and that in the cases which have arisen, the Secretary has consistently exercised his power to withhold passports. Perhaps the most notable example of enforcement of the administrative policy, which surely could not have escaped the attention of Congress, was the 1948 denial of a passport to a Member of Congress who sought to go abroad to support a movement in Greece to overthrow the existing government. Another example was the 1954 revocation of a passport held by a man who was supplying arms to groups abroad whose interests were contrary to positions taken by the United States. In 1970, the Secretary revoked passports of two persons who sought to travel to the site of an international airplane hijacking.

The Secretary has construed and applied his regulations consistently, and it would be anomalous to fault the Government because there were so few occasions to exercise the announced policy and practice. Although a pattern of actual enforcement is one indicator of Executive policy, it suffices that the Executive has "openly asserted" the power at issue. *Kent* is not to the contrary. There, it was shown that the claimed governmental policy had not been enforced consistently. The Court stressed that "as respects Communists these are scattered rulings and not consistently of one pattern." In other words, the Executive had allowed passports to some Communists, but sought to deny one to Kent. The Court had serious doubts as to whether there was in reality any definite policy in which Congress could have acquiesced. Here, by contrast, there is no basis for a claim that the Executive has failed to enforce the policy against others engaged in conduct likely to cause serious damage to our national security or foreign policy. . . .

Agee also contends that the statements of Executive policy are entitled to diminished weight because many of them concern the powers of the Executive in wartime. However, the statute provides no support for this argument. History eloquently attests that grave problems of national security and foreign policy are by no means limited to times of formally declared war.

4

Relying on the statement of the Court in *Kent* that "illegal conduct" and problems of allegiance were, "so far as relevant here, . . . the only [grounds] which it could fairly be argued were adopted by Congress in light of prior administrative practice," Agee argues that this enumeration was exclusive and is controlling here. This is not correct.

The *Kent* Court had no occasion to consider whether the Executive had the power to revoke the passport of an individual whose *conduct* is damaging the national security and foreign policy of the United States. *Kent* involved denials of passports solely on the basis of political beliefs entitled to First Amendment protection. Although finding it unnecessary to reach the merits of that constitutional problem, the *Kent* Court emphasized the fact that "[w]e deal with *beliefs*, with *associations*, with *ideological* matters." 357 U.S., at 130 (emphasis supplied). . . .

The protection accorded beliefs standing alone is very different from the protection accorded conduct. Thus, in *Aptheker v. Secretary of State*, [378 U.S. 500 (1964)], the Court held that a statute which, like the policy at issue in *Kent*, denied passports to Communists solely on the basis of political beliefs unconstitutionally "establishes an irrebuttable presumption that individuals who are members of the specified organizations will, if given passports, engage in activities inimical to the security of the United States." The Court recognized that the legitimacy of the objective of safeguarding our national security is "obvious and unarguable." The Court explained that the statute at issue was not the least restrictive alternative available: "The prohibition against travel is supported only by a tenuous relationship between the bare fact of organizational membership and the activity Congress sought to proscribe."

Beliefs and speech are only part of Agee's "campaign to fight the United States CIA." In that sense, this case contrasts markedly with the facts in *Kent* and *Aptheker*. No presumptions, rebuttable or otherwise, are involved, for Agee's conduct in foreign countries presents a serious danger to American officials abroad and serious danger to the national security.

We hold that the policy announced in the challenged regulations is "sufficiently substantial and consistent" to compel the conclusion that Congress has approved it.

III

Agee also attacks the Secretary's action on three constitutional grounds: first, that the revocation of his passport impermissibly burdens his freedom to travel; second, that the action was intended to penalize his exercise of free speech and deter his criticism of Government policies and practices; and third, that failure to accord him a prerevocation hearing violated his Fifth Amendment right to procedural due process.

In light of the express language of the passport regulations, which permits their application only in cases involving likelihood of "serious damage" to national security or foreign policy, these claims are without merit.

Revocation of a passport undeniably curtails travel, but the freedom to travel abroad with a "letter of introduction" in the form of a passport issued by the sovereign is subordinate to national security and foreign policy considerations; as such, it is subject to reasonable governmental regulation. The Court has made it plain that the *freedom* to travel outside the United States must be distinguished from the *right* to travel within the United States. . . .

It is "obvious and unarguable" that no governmental interest is more compelling than the security of the Nation. Protection of the foreign policy of the United States is a governmental interest of great importance, since foreign policy and national security considerations cannot neatly be compartmentalized. Measures to protect the secrecy of our Government's foreign intelligence operations plainly serve these interests. . . .

Not only has Agee jeopardized the security of the United States, but he has also endangered the interests of countries other than the United States—thereby creating serious problems for American foreign relations and foreign policy. Restricting Agee's foreign travel, although perhaps not certain to prevent all of Agee's harmful activities, is the only avenue open to the Government to limit these activities.

Assuming, *arguendo*, that First Amendment protections reach beyond our national boundaries, Agee's First Amendment claim has no foundation. The revocation of Agee's passport rests in part on the content of his speech: specifically, his repeated disclosures of intelligence operations and names of intelligence personnel. Long ago, however, this Court recognized that "[n]o one would question but that a government might prevent actual obstruction to its recruiting service or the publication of the sailing dates of transports or the number and location of troops." *Near v. Minnesota ex rel. Olson*, 283 U.S. 697, 716 (1931). Agee's disclosures, among other things, have the declared purpose of obstructing intelligence operations and the recruiting of intelligence personnel. They are clearly not protected by the Constitution. The mere fact that Agee is also engaged in criticism of the Government does not render his conduct beyond the reach of the law.

To the extent the revocation of his passport operates to inhibit Agee, "it is an inhibition of *action*," rather than of speech. *Zemel*, 381 U.S., at 16-17 (emphasis supplied). Agee is as free to criticize the United States Government as he was when he held a passport—always subject, of course, to express limits on certain rights by virtue of his contract with the Government.

On this record, the Government is not required to hold a prerevocation hearing. In *Cole v. Young*, 351 U.S. 536 (1956), we held that federal employees who hold "sensitive" positions "where they could bring about any discernible adverse effects on the Nation's security" may be suspended without a presuspension hearing. For the same reasons, when there is a substantial likelihood of "serious damage" to national security or foreign policy as a result of a passport holder's activities in foreign countries, the Government may take action to ensure that the holder may not exploit the sponsorship of his travels by the United States.... The Constitution's due process guarantees call for no more than what has been accorded here: a statement of reasons and an opportunity for a prompt postrevocation hearing.[62]

We reverse the judgment of the Court of Appeals and remand for further proceedings consistent with this opinion.

Reversed and remanded.

Justice BLACKMUN, concurring.

There is some force, I feel, in Justice Brennan's observations, that today's decision cannot be reconciled fully with all the reasoning of *Zemel v. Rusk* and, particularly, of *Kent v. Dulles*, and that the Court is cutting back somewhat upon the opinions in those cases *sub silentio*. I would have preferred to have the Court disavow forthrightly the aspects of *Zemel* and *Kent* that may suggest that evidence of a longstanding Executive policy or construction in this area is not probative of the issue of congressional authorization. Nonetheless, believing this is what the Court in effect has done, I join its opinion.

Justice BRENNAN, with whom Justice MARSHALL joins, dissenting.

... This is not a complicated case. The Court has twice articulated the proper mode of analysis for determining whether Congress has delegated to the Executive Branch the authority to deny a passport under the Passport Act of 1926. The analysis is hardly confusing, and I expect that had the Court faithfully applied it, today's judgment would affirm the decision below.

In *Kent v. Dulles*, ... [b]ecause the Passport Act of 1926—the same statute at issue here—did not expressly authorize the denial of passports to alleged Communists, the Court examined cases of actual passport refusals by the Secretary to determine whether "it could be fairly argued" that this category of passport refusals was "adopted by Congress in light of prior administrative practice." The Court was unable to find such prior administrative practice, and therefore held that the regulation was unauthorized.

In *Zemel v. Rusk*, the issue was whether the Secretary could restrict travel for all citizens to Cuba. In holding that he could, the Court expressly approved the holding

---

62. We do not decide that these procedures are constitutionally required.

in *Kent*.... In reaching its decision, the Court in *Zemel* relied upon numerous occasions when the State Department had restricted travel to certain international areas. ... As in *Kent* and *Zemel*, there is no dispute here that the Passport Act of 1926 does not *expressly* authorize the Secretary to revoke Agee's passport. Therefore, the sole remaining inquiry is whether there exists "with regard to the sort of passport [revocation] involved [here], an administrative *practice* sufficiently substantial and consistent to warrant the conclusion that Congress had implicitly approved it." *Zemel v. Rusk*, 381 U.S., at 12 (emphasis added). The Court today, citing to this same page in *Zemel* applies a test markedly different from that of *Zemel* and *Kent* and in fact expressly disavowed by the latter.... [N]either *Zemel* nor *Kent* holds that a longstanding Executive *policy* or *construction* is sufficient proof that Congress has implicitly authorized the Secretary's action. The cases hold that an administrative *practice* must be demonstrated; in fact *Kent* unequivocally states that mere *construction* by the Executive—no matter how longstanding and consistent—is *not* sufficient....

The Court's requirement in *Kent* of evidence of the Executive's *exercise* of discretion as opposed to its possession of discretion may best be understood as a preference for the strongest proof that Congress knew of and acquiesced in that authority. The presence of sensitive constitutional questions in the passport revocation context cautions against applying the normal rule that administrative constructions in cases of statutory construction are to be given great weight. Only when Congress had maintained its silence in the face of a consistent and substantial pattern of actual passport denials or revocations—where the parties will presumably object loudly, perhaps through legal action, to the Secretary's exercise of discretion—can this Court be sure that Congress is aware of the Secretary's actions and has implicitly approved that exercise of discretion. Moreover, broad statements by the Executive Branch relating to its discretion in the passport area lack the precision of definition that would follow from concrete applications of that discretion in specific cases. Although Congress might register general approval of the Executive's overall policy, it still might disapprove of the Executive's pattern of applying that broad rule in specific categories of cases.

Not only does the Court ignore the *Kent-Zemel* requirement that Executive discretion be supported by a consistent administrative practice, but it also relies on the very Executive construction and policy deemed irrelevant in *Kent*. Thus, noting that "[t]he President and the Secretary of State consistently construed the 1856 (Passport) Act to preserve their authority to withhold passports on national security and foreign policy grounds," the Court reaches out to hold that "Congress, in 1926, adopted the longstanding administrative construction of the 1856 statute." The Court quotes from 1869 and 1901 opinions of the Attorneys General. But *Kent* expressly cited both of these opinions as examples of Executive constructions *not* relevant to the determination whether Congress had implicitly approved the Secretary's exercise of authority. The Court similarly relies on four Executive Orders issued between 1907 and 1917 to buttress its position, even though *Kent* expressly cited the same four Orders as examples of Executive constructions inapposite to the proper inquiry. Where the Court in *Kent* discounted the constructions of the Act made by "[t]he scholars, the courts, the Chief Executive, and the Attorneys General," today's Court decides this case on the basis of constructions evident from "an unbroken line of Executive Orders, regulations, instructions to consular officials,and notices to passport holders."[7] The

---

7. Even if the Court were correct to use administrative constructions of passport leg-

Court's reliance on material expressly abjured in *Kent* becomes understandable only when one appreciates the paucity of recorded administrative practice—the only evidence upon which *Kent* and *Zemel* permit reliance—with respect to passport denials or revocations based on foreign policy or national security considerations relating to an individual. The Court itself identifies only three occasions over the past 33 years when the Secretary has revoked passports for such reasons. And only one of these cases involved a revocation pursuant to the regulations challenged in this case. Yet, in 1979 alone, there were 7,835,000 Americans traveling abroad.

... [N]o one is "faulting" the Government because there are only few occasions when it has seen fit to deny or revoke passports for foreign policy or national security reasons. The point that *Kent* and *Zemel* make, and that today's opinion should make, is that the Executive's authority to revoke passports touches an area fraught with important constitutional rights, and that the Court should therefore "construe narrowly all delegated powers that curtail or dilute them." The presumption is that Congress must expressly delegate authority to the Secretary to deny or revoke passports for foreign policy or national security reasons before he may exercise such authority....

III

I suspect that this case is a prime example of the adage that "bad facts make bad law." Philip Agee is hardly a model representative of our Nation. And the Executive Branch has attempted to use one of the only means at its disposal, revocation of a passport, to stop respondent's damaging statements. But ... it is important to remember that this decision applies not only to Philip Agee, whose activities could be perceived as harming the national security, but also to other citizens who may merely disagree with Government foreign policy and express their views.[9]

... [T]he Court professes to rely on, but in fact departs from, the two precedents in the passport regulation area, *Zemel* and *Kent*. Of course it is always easier to fit oneself within the safe haven of *stare decisis* than boldly to overrule precedents of several decades' standing. Because I find myself unable to reconcile those cases with

---

islation, it is by no means certain that the Executive *did* construe the Acts to give it the discretion alleged here, since it sometimes referred to the unqualified rights of citizens to passports. See, *e.g.*, 15 Op.Atty.Gen. 114, 117 (1876); 13 Op.Atty.Gen. 397, 398 (1871). Indeed the State Department has sought legislation from Congress to provide the sort of authority exercised in this case. See S. 4110, § 103(6), 85th Cong., 2d Sess. (1958); Hearings on S. 2770, S. 3998, S. 4110, and S. 4137 before the Senate Committee on Foreign Relations, 85th Cong., 2d Sess., 1, 4 (1958); see also H.R. 14895, § 205(e), 89th Cong., 2d Sess. (1966). This hardly suggests that the Executive thought it had such authority.

9. An excerpt from the petitioner's portion of the oral argument is particularly revealing:

"QUESTION: General McCree, supposing a person right now were to apply for a passport to go to Salvador, and when asked the purpose of his journey, to say, to denounce the United States policy in Salvador in supporting the junta. And the Secretary of State says, I just will not issue a passport for that purpose. Do you think that he can consistently do that in the light of our previous cases?

"MR. McCREE: I would say, yes, he can. Because we have to vest these—The President of the United States and the Secretary of State working under him are charged with conducting the foreign policy of the Nation, and the freedom of speech that we enjoy domestically may be different from that that we can exercise in this context."

The reach of the Secretary's discretion is potentially staggering.

the decision in this case, however, and because I disagree with the Court's *sub silentio* overruling of those cases, I dissent.[10]

1. This case does not involve an executive claim of inherent constitutional power to revoke passports on national security grounds; the issue presented was one of the scope of a statutory delegation. Why was it not dispositive that the Passport Act not only did not specify criteria for the revocation of passports, but it did not expressly confer any passport revocation authority at all? Why, if the statute tacitly confers standardless revocation authority, is the resulting delegation of legislative power nevertheless constitutional? (Does the absence of express statutory support for the majority view suggest that the majority perceives, but does not wish to rely on an article II basis for the Secretary of State's regulation?) Is there any constitutional obligation of the executive branch to promulgate criteria for passport revocation before purporting to exercise such authority?

2. The Justices disagree on what needs to be shown in this case to demonstrate congressional knowledge of and acquiescence in an administrative interpretation. Perhaps the burden each side would place on the executive reflects its appraisal of the seriousness of the constitutional issues posed by the revocation of Agee's passport or of passports in general. In your view, which side is right?

3. The majority attributes the scant administrative history of national security-based passport controls to the relative lack of instances in which a passport holder's activities abroad involved "substantial likelihood of serious damage to the national security or foreign policy of the United States." Does the Logan Act history support this view?

4. Do you agree with footnote 7 to the dissent that executive branch efforts to secure *express* statutory authority for particular activities belie arguments on behalf of the executive that *implicit* statutory authority already exists for those activities?

---

10. Because I conclude that the regulation is invalid as an unlawful exercise of authority by the Secretary under the Passport Act of 1926, I need not decide the important constitutional issues presented in this case. However, several parts of the Court's whirlwind treatment of Agee's constitutional claims merit comment, either because they are extreme oversimplifications of constitutional doctrine or mistaken views of the law and facts of this case.

First, the Court states [that the revocation of Agee's passport inhibits *action*, not *speech*]. Under the Court's rationale, ... a 40 year prison sentence imposed upon a person who criticized the Government's food stamp policy would represent only an "inhibition of action." After all, the individual would remain free to criticize the United States Government, albeit from a jail cell.

... [Moreover, t]he Court seems to misunderstand the prior precedents of this Court, for Agee's speech is undoubtedly protected by the Constitution.... [I]t may be that respondent's First Amendment right to speak is outweighed by the Government's interest in national security, [but] ... revocation of his passport obviously does implicate First Amendment rights by chilling his right to speak, and therefore the Court's responsibility must be to balance that infringement against the asserted governmental interests to determine whether the revocation contravenes the First Amendment....

Second, ... [t]he District Court nowhere held that respondent lacked standing to contend vagueness and overbreadth.... [I]t is strange indeed to suggest that an individual whose activities admittedly fall within the core of the challenged regulation does not have standing to argue overbreadth. After all, the purpose of the overbreadth doctrine in First Amendment cases is precisely to permit a person who falls within the legislation nevertheless to challenge the wide sweep of the legislation as it affects another's protected activity....

Would the Court's adoption of this position as a rule of statutory construction deter salutary executive branch efforts to prompt Congress to clarify executive authority?

5. On what ground does the majority deny that Agee had a right to a hearing before the termination of his passport? Is a post-revocation hearing constitutionally required?

6. Note from footnote 9 to the dissent the Solicitor General's answer on the scope of the Secretary of State's power. Did he give the correct answer? Would there have been a preferable answer?

7. Passport revocation has proven an almost wholly ineffectual response to the sort of problem posed by Philip Agee. What else could or should the government do? In 1982, Congress enacted the Intelligence Identities Protection Act, 50 U.S.C. §421 *et seq.* That Act provides, in part:

> Whoever, having or having had authorized access to classified information that identifies a covert agent, intentionally discloses any information identifying such covert agent to any individual not authorized to receive classified information, knowing that the information disclosed so identifies such covert agent and that the United States is taking affirmative measures to conceal such covert agent's intelligence relationship to the United States, shall be fined not more than $50,000 or imprisoned not more than ten years or both.

50 U.S.C. § 421(a) (1982). The Act also creates lesser included offenses for persons who commit disclosures of the kind outlawed in § 421(a), if (1) such persons have authorized access to classified information, whether or not that information identified the covert agent in question, § 421(b), or (2) such persons are engaged "in the course of a pattern of activities intended to identify and expose covert agents and with reason to believe that such activities would impair or impede the foreign intelligence activities of the United States," § 421 (c). Opponents of the legislation insisted it was unconstitutional to criminalize the publication of agents' names if such information is derived from public documents, on which Agee and others have claimed to rely. Schwartz, *A Constitutional Disaster*, The Nation, Jul. 3, 1982, at 11-13. The argument has yet to be tested in court. What do you think?

8. For fuller assessments of *Haig v. Agee*, see Farber, *National Security, The Right to Travel, and the Court*, 1981 Sup. Ct. Rev. 263; Koffler & Gershman, *The New Seditious Libel*, 69 Cornell L. Rev. 816 (1984).

Chapter 7
The President as Commander in Chief

A number of problems posed thus far have dealt with the President's power to respond to what he perceives as emergency circumstances. *See*, e.g., *Youngstown*; *New York Times v. United States*; *In re Debs*; and *United States v. United States District Court*. The analyses of the President's legal powers in these, and most, emergency situations involve some assessment of the reach of the "faithful execution" clause of article II, viewed against the backdrop of relevant legislative action or inaction. Indeed, Congress has devoted considerable attention to problems of emergency responses by the executive, and has enacted statutes granting the President a broad range of powers in various national emergencies. For an excellent historical discussion, *see* Special Senate Committee on National Emergencies and Delegated Emergency Powers, A Brief History of Emergency Powers in the United States: A Working Paper, 93d Cong., 2d Sess. (Comm. Print 1974). On the declaration and congressional reporting procedures required in national emergencies, *see* National Emergencies Act, Pub. L. No. 94-412, 90 Stat. 1255 (1976).

Additional considerations present themselves, however, with respect to the President's use of troops in emergency actions, and his invocation of other emergency powers during wartime. The President, by express constitutional text, serves as "Commander in Chief of the Army and Navy of the United States, and of the Militia of the several States, when called into the actual Service of the United States." Art. II., § 2, cl. 1. Furthermore, because those emergencies in which a military response would appear useful often, although certainly not always, involve other nations, it may be that the President derives additional authority from his constitutional role in foreign affairs, discussed in Chapter Six.

Section A of this chapter considers the President's powers to commit troops to military action prior to Congressional authorization. Although Congress' military powers under the Constitution, art. I, § 8, cls. 1, 10-16, clearly permit it to vest in the President a wide range of military functions, history has repeatedly demonstrated the appeal of executive action more immediate than legislative deliberation might permit. Consider, in this regard, Hamilton's brief and modest characterization of the President's military powers in the Federalist No. 69, and the Supreme Court's approval of Lincoln's more expansive interpretation of his war powers, construed in conjunction with his duty to take care that the laws be faithfully executed. Section A then offers executive, legislative, and judicial views on the legality of U.S. involvement in Vietnam, and materials on the War Powers Resolution, Congress' major attempt thus far to circumscribe the President's military powers.

Section B considers the scope of the President's domestic powers in wartime, especially as they affect civil liberties and the organization of the economy. Finally, Section C discusses the President's peacetime use of troops in law enforcement.

A. Power to Commit Troops

1. *Scope of the Commander in Chief Clause*

THE FEDERALIST, NO. 69 (HAMILTON)

The President is to be the "commander-in-chief of the army and navy of the United States, and of the militia of the several States, when called into the actual service of the United States...." In most ... particulars the power of the President will resemble equally that of the king of Great Britain and of the governor of New York. The most material points of difference are these: *First*. The President will have only the occasional command of such part of the militia of the nation as by legislative provision may be called into the actual service of the Union. The king of Great Britain and the governor of New York have at all times the entire command of all the militia within their several jurisdictions. In this article, therefore, the power of the President would be inferior to that of either the monarch or the governor. *Secondly*. The President is to be commander-in-chief of the army and navy of the United States. In this respect his authority would be nominally the same with that of the king of Great Britain, but in substance much inferior to it. It would amount to nothing more than the supreme command and direction of the military and naval forces, as first General and admiral of the Confederacy; while that of the British king extends to the *declaring* of war and to the *raising* and *regulating* of fleets and armies; all of which, by the Constitution under consideration, would appertain to the legislature. The governor of New York, on the other hand, is by the constitution of the State vested only with the command of its militia and navy. But the constitutions of several of the States expressly declare their governors to be commanders-in-chief as well of the army as navy; and it may well be a question, whether those of New Hampshire and Massachusetts, in particular, do not, in this instance, confer larger powers upon their respective governors than could be claimed by a President of the United States.

The Prize Cases

67 U.S. (2 Black) 635 (1863)

[Abraham Lincoln's victory in the 1860 election was a culmination of a series of events leading to the secession of the Southern states, and on December 20, 1860, South Carolina became the first state to withdraw from the Union. Other states of the deep South followed. Efforts on the part of the Buchanan administration to check secession failed, and one by one most of the federal forts in the South were taken over by secessionists.

On February 4, 1861—a month before Lincoln's inauguration—six Southern states sent representatives to Montgomery, Alabama, to set up a new, independent government. With Jefferson Davis at its head, the Confederate States of America came into being.

Lincoln was prepared to conciliate the South, but would not recognize that the Union could be divided. The test of his position came early in his Administration when he learned that the federal troops at Fort Sumter, South Carolina, one of the few military installations in the South still in federal control, had to be promptly supplied or withdrawn. Lincoln determined that supplies must be sent even if doing so provoked the Confederates into firing on the fort. (In fact, some historians contend this decision was made *because* it would provoke just such a response.) On April 12, 1861, just before Federal supply ships arrived, Confederate guns opened fire upon Fort Sumter, precipitating a war which is still the most costly in American lives of any in the nation's history.

By proclamations of April 19 and 27, 1861, President Lincoln established a blockade of Southern ports and provided that any vessel attempting to violate the blockade could be taken as prize. 12 Stat. 1258, 1259. Although subsequently ratified, the blockade was declared before Congress had a chance to assemble and take action on the matter. The immediate purpose of the blockade was to cripple the Confederacy because it needed foreign markets for its crops and manufactured goods, and required food supplies that it could not produce.

Because the United States never admitted that the southern ports were not ports of the United States, it would have been legally possible to proclaim them closed and thereby avoid the international law implications of a blockade. This was, in fact, the course of action recommended to President Lincoln by Secretary of the Navy Welles.

But serious difficulties stood in the way of relying exclusively on such a measure. Most notably, such a closing would have been impossible to enforce because the United States did not control the land on which the ports were located or by which they were surrounded. The only means by which the United States Navy could act against neutral shipping was to resort to international law and the law of the blockade.

The four vessels involved in the Prize Cases had been captured by public vessels of the United States for attempting to violate the blockade. They were taken on behalf of the United States and in each case condemned by the district court exercising its jurisdiction as provided in the proclamations.]

Justice GRIER.

There are certain propositions of law which must necessarily affect the ultimate decision of these cases.... They are, 1st. Had the President a right to institute a blockade of ports in possession of persons in armed rebellion against the Government, on the principles of international law, as known and acknowledged among civilized States?

2d. Was the property of persons domiciled or residing within those States a proper subject of capture on the sea as "enemies' property?"

I. Neutrals have a right to challenge the existence of a blockade *de facto*, and also the authority of the party exercising the right to institute it. They have a right to enter the ports of a friendly nation for the purposes of trade and commerce, but are bound to recognize the rights of a belligerent engaged in actual war, to use this mode of coercion, for the purpose of subduing the enemy.

That a blockade *de facto* actually existed, and was formally declared and notified by the President on the 27th and 30th of April, 1861, is an admitted fact in these cases.

That the President, as the Executive Chief of the Government and Commander-in-chief of the Army and Navy, was the proper person to make such notification, has not been, and cannot be disputed.

The right of prize and capture has its origin in the "*jus belli*," and is governed and adjudged under the law of nations. To legitimate the capture of a neutral vessel or property on the high seas, a war must exist *de facto*, and the neutral must have a knowledge or notice of the intention of one of the parties belligerent to use this mode of coercion against a port, city, or territory, in possession of the other.

Let us enquire whether, at the time this blockade was instituted, a state of war existed which would justify a resort to these means of subduing the hostile force.... [I]t is not necessary to constitute war, that both parties should be acknowledged as independent nations or sovereign States. A war may exist where one of the belligerents claims sovereign rights as against the other.

... A civil war is never solemnly declared; it becomes such by its accidents—the number, power, and organization of the persons who originate and carry it on. When the party in rebellion occupy and hold in a hostile manner a certain portion of territory; have declared their independence; have cast off their allegiance; have organized armies; have commenced hostilities against their former sovereign, the world acknowledges them as belligerents, and the contest a *war*. *They* claim to be in arms to establish their liberty and independence, in order to become a sovereign State, while the sovereign party treats them as insurgents and rebels who owe allegiance, and who should be punished with death for their treason.... [T]he parties to a civil war usually concede to each other belligerent rights. They exchange prisoners, and adopt the other courtesies and rules common to public or national wars.... As a civil war is never publicly proclaimed, *eo nomine* against insurgents, its actual existence is a fact in our domestic history which the Court is bound to notice and to know....

By the Constitution, Congress alone has the power to declare a national or foreign war. It cannot declare war against a State, or any number of States, by virtue of any clause in the Constitution. The Constitution confers on the President the whole Executive power. He is bound to take care that the laws be faithfully executed. He is Commander-in-chief of the Army and Navy of the United States, and of the militia of the several States when called into the actual service of the United States. He has no power to initiate or declare a war either against a foreign nation or a domestic State. But by the Acts of Congress of February 28th, 1795, and 3d of March, 1807, he is authorized to call out the militia and use the military and naval forces of the United States in case of invasion by foreign nations, and to suppress insurrection against the government of a State or of the United States.

If a war be made by invasion of a foreign nation, the President is not only authorized but bound to resist force by force ... without waiting for any special legislative authority. And whether the hostile party be a foreign invader, or States organized in rebellion, it is none the less a war, although the declaration of it be *"unilateral."* ...

The battles of Palo Alto and Resaca de la Palma had been fought before the passage of the Act of Congress of May 13th, 1846, which recognized *"a state of war as existing by the act of the Republic of Mexico."* This act not only provided for the future prosecution of the war, but was itself a vindication and ratification of the Act of the President in accepting the challenge without a previous formal declaration of war by Congress.

This greatest of civil wars was not gradually developed by popular commotion, tumultuous assemblies, or local unorganized insurrections. However long may have been its previous conception, it nevertheless sprung forth suddenly from the parent brain, a Minerva in the full panoply of *war*. The President was bound to meet it in the shape it presented itself, without waiting for Congress to baptize it with a name; and no name given to it by him or them could change the fact.

... Foreign nations acknowledge it as war by a declaration of neutrality. The condition of neutrality cannot exist unless there be two belligerent parties.... As soon as the news of the attack on Fort Sumter, and the organization of a government by the seceding States, assuming to act as belligerents, could become known in Europe, to wit, on the 13th of May, 1861, the Queen of England issued her proclamation of neutrality, "recognizing hostilities as existing between the Government of the United States of American and *certain States* styling themselves the Confederate States of America." This was immediately followed by similar declarations or silent acquiescence by other nations. After such an official recognition by the sovereign, a citizen of a foreign State is estopped to deny the existence of a war with all its consequences as regards neutrals....

Whether the President in fulfilling his duties, as Commander-in-chief, in suppressing an insurrection, has met with such armed hostile resistance, and a civil war of such alarming proportions as will compel him to accord to them the character of belligerents, is a question to be decided *by him*, and this Court must be governed by the decisions and acts of the political department of the Government to which this power was entrusted. "He must determine what degree of force the crisis demands." The proclamation of blockade is itself official and conclusive evidence to the Court that a state of war existed which demanded and authorized a recourse to such a measure, under the circumstances peculiar to the case.

If it were necessary to the technical existence of a war, that it should have a legislative sanction, we find it in almost every act passed at the extraordinary session of the Legislature of 1861, which was wholly employed in enacting laws to enable the Government to prosecute the war with vigor and efficiency. And finally, in 1861, we find Congress...passing an act "approving, legalizing, and making valid all the acts, proclamations, and orders of the President, &c., as if they had been *issued and done under the previous express authority* and direction of the Congress of the United States."

Without admitting that such an act was necessary under the circumstances, it is plain that if the President had in any manner assumed powers which it was necessary should have the authority or sanction of Congress,...this ratification has operated to perfectly cure the defect....

The objection made to this act of ratification, that it is *ex post facto*, and therefore unconstitutional and void, might possibly have some weight on the trial of an indictment in a criminal Court. But precedents from that source cannot be received as authoritative in a tribunal administering public and international law.

On this first question therefore we are of the opinion that the President had a right, *jure belli*, to institute a blockade of ports in possession of the States in rebellion, which neutrals are bound to regard.

> [In the remainder of the majority opinion, Justice Grier concluded that the property of all persons residing within the territory of the States in rebellion that is captured on the high seas may lawfully be treated as enemy property.]

Justice NELSON, dissenting.

[An] objection taken to the seizure of this vessel and cargo is, that there was no existing war between the United States and the States in insurrection within the meaning of the law of nations, which drew after it the consequences of a public or civil war[, which,] . . . when duly commenced by proclamation or otherwise, . . . entitles both of the belligerent parties to all the rights of war against each other, and as respects neutral nations. . . . Chancellor Kent . . . observes, "as war cannot lawfully be commenced on the part of the United States without an act of Congress, such act is, of course, a formal notice to all the world, and equivalent to the most solemn declaration."

The legal consequences resulting from a state of war between two countries at this day are well understood, and will be found described in every approved work on the subject of international law. The people of the two countries become immediately the enemies of each other—all intercourse commercial or otherwise between them unlawful—all contracts existing at the commencement of the war suspended, and all made during its existence utterly void. . . . [I]nterdiction of trade and intercourse direct or indirect is absolute and complete by the mere force and effect of war itself. All the property of the people of the two countries on land or sea are subject to capture and confiscation by the adverse party as enemies' property. . . . The ports of the respective countries may be blockaded, and letters of marque and reprisal granted as rights of war, and the law of prizes as defined by the law of nations comes into full and complete operation, resulting from maritime captures, *jure belli*. . . . [T]he same code which has annexed to the existence of a war all these disturbing consequences has declared that the right of making war belongs exclusively to the supreme or sovereign power of the State.

This power in all civilized nations is regulated by the fundamental laws or municipal constitution of the country. By our Constitution this power is lodged in Congress. Congress shall have power "to declare war, grant letters of marque and reprisal, and make rules concerning captures on land and water." . . .

In the case of a rebellion or resistance of a portion of the people of a country against the established government, there is no doubt, if in its progress and enlargement the government thus sought to be overthrown sees fit, it may by the competent power recognize or declare the existence of a state of civil war, which will draw after it all the consequences and rights of war between the contending parties as in the case of a public war. . . . It is not to be denied, therefore, that if a civil war existed between that portion of the people in organized insurrection to overthrow this Government at the time this vessel and cargo were seized, and if she was guilty of a violation of the blockade, she would be lawful prize of war. But before this insurrection against the established Government can be dealt with on the footing of a civil war, within the meaning of the law of nations and the Constitution of the United States, and which will draw after it belligerent rights, it must be recognized or declared by the war-making power of the Government. No power short of this can change the legal status of the Government or the relations of its citizens from that of peace to a state of war, or bring into existence all those duties and obligations of neutral third parties growing out of a state of war. . . . There is no difference in this respect between a civil or a public war.

. . . [S]ome confusion existed on the argument [in these cases] as to the definition of a war that drew after it all the rights of prize of war. . . . An idea seemed to be entertained that all that was necessary to constitute a war was organized hostility in the district of country in a state of rebellion. . . . With a view to enforce this idea, we had, during the argument, an imposing historical detail of the several measures adopted by the Confederate States to enable them to resist the authority of the general

Government, and of many bold and daring acts of resistance and of conflict. It was said that war was to be ascertained by looking at the armies and navies or public force of the contending parties, and the battles lost and won. . . .

Now, in one sense, no doubt this is war, and may be a war of the most extensive and threatening dimensions and effects, but it is a statement simply of its existence in a material sense, and has no relevancy or weight when the question is what constitutes war in a legal sense, in the sense of the law of nations, and of the Constitution of the United States? For it must be a war in this sense to attach to it all the consequences that belong to belligerent rights. Instead, therefore, of inquiring after armies and navies, and victories lost and won, or organized rebellion against the general Government, the inquiry should be into the law of nations and into the municipal fundamental laws of the Government. . . . [C]ivil war, . . . under our system of government, can exist only by an act of Congress, which requires the assent of two of the great departments of the Government, the Executive and Legislative.

We have thus far been speaking of the war power under the Constitution of the United States, and as known and recognized by the law of nations. But we are asked, what would become of the peace and integrity of the Union in case of an insurrection at home or invasion from abroad if this power could not be exercised by the President in the recess of Congress, and until that body could be assembled?

The framers of the Constitution fully comprehended this question, and provided for the contingency. Indeed, it would have been surprising if they had not, as a rebellion had occurred in the State of Massachusetts while the Convention was in session, and which had become so general that it was quelled only by calling upon the military power of the State. The Constitution declares that Congress shall have power "to provide for calling forth the militia to execute the laws of the Union, suppress insurrections, and repel invasions." Another clause, "that the President shall be Commander-in-chief of the Army and Navy of the United States, and of the militia of the several States when called into the actual service of the United States;" and, again, "He shall take care that the laws shall be faithfully executed." Congress passed laws on this subject in 1792 and 1795. 1 United States Laws, pp. 264, 424.

The last Act provided that whenever the United States shall be invaded or be in imminent danger of invasion from a foreign nation, it shall be lawful for the President to call forth such number of the militia most convenient to the place of danger, and in case of insurrection in any State against the Government thereof, it shall be lawful for the President, on the application of the Legislature of such State, if in session, or if not, of the Executive of the State, to call forth such number of militia of any other State or States as he may judge sufficient to suppress such insurrection.

The 2d section provides, that when the laws of the United States shall be opposed, or the execution obstructed in any State by combinations too powerful to be suppressed by the course of judicial proceedings, it shall be lawful for the President to call forth the militia of such State, or of any other State or States as may be necessary to suppress such combinations; and by the Act 3 March, 1807, (2 U. S. Laws, 443,) it is provided that in case of insurrection or obstruction of the laws, either in the United States or of any State or Territory, where it is lawful for the President to call forth the militia for the purpose of suppressing such insurrection, and causing the laws to be executed, it shall be lawful to employ for the same purpose such part of the land and naval forces of the United States as shall be judged necessary. It will be seen, therefore, that ample provision has been made under the Constitution and laws against any sudden and unexpected disturbance of the public peace from insurrection at home or invasion from abroad. The whole military and naval power of the country is put under the control of the President to meet the emergency. He may call out a force in proportion to its necessities, one regiment or fifty, one ship-of-war or any number at his discretion. If, like the insurrection in the State of Pennsylvania in 1793, the disturbance is confined to a small district of country, a few regiments of the militia may be sufficient to suppress it. If of the dimension of the present, when it first broke out, a much larger force would be required. But whatever its numbers, whether great or small, that may be required, ample provision is here made; and whether great or small, the nature of the power is the same. It is the exercise of a power under the municipal laws of the country and not under the law of nations; and, as we see, furnishes the most ample means of repelling attacks from abroad or suppressing disturbances at home until the assembling of Congress, who can, if it be deemed necessary, bring into operation the war power, and thus change the nature and character of the contest. Then, instead of being carried on under the municipal law of 1795, it would be under the law of nations, and the Acts of Congress as war measures with all the rights of war.

. . . It has also been argued that [the] power of the President from necessity should be construed as vesting him with the war power, or the Republic might greatly suffer or be in danger from the attacks of the hostile party before the assembling of Congress. But we have seen that the whole military and naval force are in his hands under the municipal laws of the country. He can meet the adversary upon land and water with all the forces of the Government. The truth is, this idea of the existence of any necessity for clothing the President with the war power, under the Act of 1795, is simply a monstrous exaggeration; for, besides having the command of the whole of the army and navy, Congress can be assembled within any thirty days, if the safety of the country requires that the war power shall be brought into operation.

. . . Certainly it cannot rightfully be said that the President has the power to convert a loyal citizen into a belligerent enemy or confiscate his property as enemy's property. Congress assembled on the call for an extra session the 4th of July, 1861, and among the first acts passed was one in which the President was authorized by proclamation to interdict all trade and intercourse between all the inhabitants of States in insurrection and the rest of the United States, subjecting vessel and cargo to capture and condemnation as prize, and also to direct the capture of any ship or vessel belonging in whole or in part to any inhabitant of a State whose inhabitants are declared by the proclamation to be in a state of insurrection, found at sea or in any part of the rest of the United States. Act of Congress of 13th of July, 1861, secs. 5, 6. . . . The President's Proclamation was issued on the 16th of August following, and embraced Georgia, North and South Carolina, part of Virginia, Tennessee, Alabama, Louisiana, Texas, Arkansas, Mississippi and Florida. This Act of Congress, we think, recognized a state of civil war between the Government and the Confederate States, and made it territorial. . . .

[W]hen the Government of the United States recognizes a state of civil war to exist between a foreign nation and her colonies, but remaining itself neutral, the Courts are bound to consider as lawful all those acts which the new Government may direct against the enemy, and we admit the President who conducts the foreign relations of the Government may fitly recognize or refuse to do so, the existence of civil war in the foreign nation under the circumstances stated. But this is a very different question from the one before us, which is whether the President can recognize or declare a civil war, under the Constitution, with all its belligerent rights, between his own Government and a portion of its citizens in a state of insurrection. That power, as we have seen, belongs to Congress. We agree when such a war is recognized or declared to exist by the war-making power, but not otherwise, it is the duty of the Courts to follow the decision of the political power of the Government. . . .

Congress on the 6th of August, 1862, passed an Act confirming all acts, proclamations, and orders of the President, after the 4th of March, 1861, respecting the army and navy, and legalizing them, so far as was competent for that body, and it has been suggested, but scarcely argued, that this legislation on the subject had the effect to bring into existence an *ex post facto* civil war with all the rights of capture and confiscation, *jure belli*, from the date referred to. An *ex post facto* law is defined, when, after an action, indifferent in itself, or lawful, is committed, the Legislature then, for the first time, declares it to have been a crime and inflicts punishment upon the person who committed it. The principle is sought to be applied in this case. Property of the citizen or foreign subject engaged in lawful trade at the time, and illegally captured, which must be taken as true if a confirmatory act be necessary, may be held and confiscated by subsequent legislation. . . . Here the captures were without any Constitutional authority, and void; and, on principle, no subsequent ratification could make them valid. . . .

Chief Justice TANEY, Justice CATRON and Justice CLIFFORD, concurred in the dissenting opinion of Justice Nelson.

––––––––

1. Note that the issue dividing the majority and dissent in *The Prize Cases* was not whether the President acted lawfully in mustering a defense to the Confederate insurrection. What was the issue? Does it follow from the majority opinion that the President needed no statutory authority lawfully to resist the insurrection with armed force?

2. Presumably, in prescribing a constitutional separation of powers for the prosecution of war, the Constitution is concerned with serious dangers that would attend allowing the President unilaterally to raise an army, declare war, and command the troops. What are those dangers? Are they absent in cases of civil insurrection? What justifies the result in *The Prize Cases*?

3. Note that *The Prize Cases* were decided by the slimmest of margins. Given that the dissenters agreed that the President's acts in resisting the Confederacy were lawful, why do they think it important to maintain the distinction between hostilities aimed personally at insurgents and a public or territorial war, which only Congress could declare?

4. Should *The Prize Cases* be read as holding that any legal challenge to a presidential determination of military emergency should be regarded as presenting a nonjusticiable political question? What about a legal challenge to the degree of presidential response to a military emergency?

5. Should the Court have resolved *The Prize Cases* differently if Congress had not yet statutorily ratified Lincoln's actions?

6. Do the statutes on insurrection to which the dissent refers pertain to cases of insurrection by the states? If not, where would the dissent leave executive power in such a case?

2. *Case Study: Vietnam*

Meeker,*the Legality of United States Participation in the Defense of Viet-Nam

54 Dept. State Bull. 474 (1966)

IV. THE PRESIDENT HAS FULL AUTHORITY TO COMMIT UNITED STATES FORCES IN THE COLLECTIVE DEFENSE OF SOUTH VIET-NAM

There can be no question in present circumstances of the President's authority to commit United States forces to the defense of South Viet-Nam. The grant of authority to the President in article II of the Constitution extends to the actions of the United States currently undertaken in Viet-Nam. In fact, however, it is unnecessary to determine whether this grant standing alone is sufficient to authorize the actions taken in Viet-Nam. These actions rest not only on the exercise of Presidential powers under article II but on the SEATO treaty—a treaty advised and consented to by the Senate—and on actions of the Congress, particularly the joint resolution of August 10, 1964. When these sources of authority are taken together...there can be no question of the legality under domestic law of United States actions in Viet-Nam.

A. THE PRESIDENT'S POWER UNDER ARTICLE II OF THE CONSTITUTION EXTENDS TO THE ACTIONS CURRENTLY UNDERTAKEN IN VIET-NAM

Under the Constitution, the President, in addition to being Chief Executive, is Commander in Chief of the Army and Navy. He holds the prime responsibility for the conduct of United States foreign relations. These duties carry very broad powers, including the power to deploy American forces abroad and commit them to military operations when the President deems such action necessary to maintain the security and defense of the United States.

At the Federal Constitutional Convention in 1787, it was originally proposed that Congress have the power "to make war." There were objections that legislative proceedings were too slow for this power to be vested in Congress; it was suggested that the Senate might be a better repository. Madison and Gerry then moved to substitute "to declare war" for "to make war," "leaving to the Executive the power to repel sudden attacks." It was objected that this might make it too easy for the Executive to involve the nation in war, but the motion carried with but one dissenting vote.

In 1787 the world was a far larger place, and the framers probably had in mind attacks upon the United States. In the 20th century, the world has grown much smaller. An attack on a country far from our shores can impinge directly on the nation's security. In the SEATO treaty, for example, it is formally declared that an armed attack against Viet-Nam would endanger the peace and safety of the United States.

Since the Constitution was adopted there have been at least 125 instances in which the President has ordered the armed forces to take action or maintain positions abroad without obtaining prior congressional authorization, starting with the "undeclared war" with France (1798-1800). For example, President Truman ordered 250,000

---

*The author of this article, Leonard Meeker, was then Legal Adviser to the U.S. Department of State.

troops to Korea during the Korean war of the early 1950's. President Eisenhower dispatched 14,000 troops to Lebanon in 1958.

The Constitution leaves to the President the judgment to determine whether the circumstances of a particular armed attack are so urgent and the potential consequences so threatening to the security of the United States that he should act without formally consulting the Congress.

B. THE SOUTHEAST ASIA COLLECTIVE DEFENSE TREATY AUTHORIZES THE PRESIDENT'S ACTIONS

Under article VI of the United States Constitution, "all treaties made, or which shall be made, under the Authority of the United States, shall be the supreme Law of the Land." Article IV, paragraph 1, of the SEATO treaty establishes as a matter of law that a Communist armed attack against South Viet-Nam endangers the peace and safety of the United States. In this same provision the United States has undertaken a commitment in the SEATO treaty to "act to meet the common danger in accordance with its constitutional processes" in the event of such an attack.

Under our Constitution it is the President who must decide when an armed attack has occurred. He has also the constitutional responsibility for determining what measures of defense are required when the peace and safety of the United States are endangered. If he considers that deployment of U. S. forces to South Viet-Nam is required, and that military measures against the source of Communist aggression in North Viet-Nam are necessary, he is constitutionally empowered to take those measures.

The SEATO treaty specifies that each party will act "in accordance with its constitutional processes."

It has recently been argued that the use of land forces in Asia is not authorized under the treaty because their use to deter armed attack was not contemplated at the time the treaty was considered by the Senate. Secretary Dulles testified at that time that we did not intend to establish (1) a land army in Southeast Asia capable of deterring Communist aggression, or (2) an integrated headquarters and military organization like that of NATO; instead, the United States would reply on "mobile striking power" against the sources of aggression. However, the treaty obligation in article IV, paragraph 1, to meet the common danger in the event of armed aggression, is not limited to particular modes of military action. What constitutes an adequate deterrent or an appropriate response, in terms of military strategy, may change; but the essence of our commitment to act to meet the common danger, as necessary at the time of an armed aggression, remains. In 1954 the forecast of military judgment might have been against the use of substantial United States ground forces in Viet-Nam. But that does not preclude the President from reaching a different military judgment in different circumstances, 12 years later.

C. THE JOINT RESOLUTION OF CONGRESS OF AUGUST 10, 1964, AUTHORIZES UNITED STATES PARTICIPATION IN THE COLLECTIVE DEFENSE OF SOUTH VIET-NAM

. . . Following the North Vietnamese attacks in the Gulf of Tonkin against United States destroyers, Congress adopted, by a Senate vote of 88-2 and a House vote of 416-0, a joint resolution containing a series of important declarations and provisions of law.

Section 1 resolved that "the Congress approves and supports the determination of the President, as Commander in Chief, to take all necessary measures to repel any armed attack against the forces of the United States and to prevent further aggression." Thus, the Congress gave its sanction to specific actions by the President to repel attacks against United States naval vessels in the Gulf of Tonkin and elsewhere in the western Pacific. Congress further approved the taking of "all necessary measures . . . to prevent further aggression." . . .

The joint resolution then went on to provide in section 2:

> The United States regards as vital to its national interest and to world peace the maintenance of international peace and security in southeast Asia. Consonant with the Constitution of the United States and the Charter of the United Nations and in accordance with its obligations under the Southeast Asia Collective Defense Treaty, the United States is, therefore, prepared, as the President determines, to take all necessary steps, including the use of armed force, to assist any member or protocol state of the Southeast Asia Collective Defense Treaty requesting assistance in defense of its freedom.

Section 2 thus constitutes an authorization to the President, in his discretion, to act—using armed force if he determines that is required—to assist South Viet-Nam at its request in defense of its freedom. . . .

It has been suggested that the legislative history of the joint resolution shows an intention to limit United States assistance to South Viet-Nam to aid, advice, and training. This suggestion is based on an amendment offered from the floor by Senator [Gaylord] Nelson which would have added the following to the text:

> The Congress also approves and supports the efforts of the President to bring the problem of peace in Southeast Asia to the Security Council of the United Nations, and the President's declaration that the United States, seeking no extension of the present military conflict, will respond to provocation in a manner that is "limited and fitting." Our continuing policy is to limit our role to the provision of aid, training assistance, and military advice, and it is the sense of Congress that, except when provoked to a greater response, we should continue to attempt to avoid a direct military involvement in the Southeast Asian conflict.[25]

Senator [J. W.] Fulbright, who had reported the joint resolution from the Foreign Relations Committee, spoke on the amendment as follows:

> It states fairly accurately what the President has said would be our policy, and what I stated my understanding was as to our policy; also what other Senators have stated. In other words, it states that our response should be appropriate and limited to the provocation, which the Senator states as "respond to provocation in a manner that is limited and fitting," and so forth. . . .

> The Senator has put into his amendment a statement of policy that is unobjectionable. However, I cannot accept the amendment under the circumstances. I do not believe it is contrary to the joint resolution, but it is an enlargement. I am informed that the House is now voting on this resolution. The House joint

---

25. 110 *Cong. Rec.* 18459 (Aug. 7, 1964).

resolution is about to be presented to us. I cannot accept the amendment and go to conference with it, and thus take responsibility for delaying matters.

I do not object to it as a statement of policy. I believe it is an accurate reflection of what I believe is the President's policy, judging from his own statements....

Senator Nelson's amendment related the degree and kind of U. S. response in Viet-Nam to "provocation" on the other side; the response should be "limited and fitting." The greater the provocation, the stronger are the measures that may be characterized as "limited and fitting." Bombing of North Vietnamese naval bases was a "limited and fitting" response to the attacks on U. S. destroyers in August 1964, and the subsequent actions taken by the United States and South Viet-Nam have been an appropriate response to the increased war of aggression carried on by North Viet-Nam since that date. Moreover, Senator Nelson's proposed amendment did not purport to be a restriction on authority available to the President but merely a statement concerning what should be the continuing policy of the United States.

Congressional realization of the scope of authority being conferred by the joint resolution is shown by the legislative history of the measure as a whole. The following exchange between Senators Cooper and Fulbright is illuminating:

> Mr. COOPER [John Sherman Cooper].... The Senator will remember that the SEATO Treaty, in article IV, provides that in the event an armed attack is made ... upon one of the protocol states such as South Vietnam, the ... United States, would then take such action as might be appropriate, after resorting to their constitutional processes. I assume that would mean, in the case of the United States, that Congress would be asked to grant the authority to act.
>
> Does the Senator consider that in enacting this resolution we are satisfying that requirement of article IV of the Southeast Asia Collective Defense Treaty? In other words, are we now giving the President advance authority to take whatever action he may deem necessary respecting South Vietnam and its defense, or with respect to the defense of any other country included in the treaty?
>
> Mr. FULBRIGHT. I think that is correct.
>
> Mr. COOPER. Then, looking ahead, if the President decided that it was necessary to use such force as could lead into war, we will give that authority by this resolution?
>
> Mr. FULBRIGHT. That is the way I would interpret it. If a situation later developed in which we thought the approval should be withdrawn it could be withdrawn by concurrent resolution.

The August 1964 joint resolution continues in force today. Section 2 of the resolution provides that it shall expire "when the President shall determine that the peace and security of the area is reasonably assured by international conditions created by action of the United Nations or otherwise, except that it may be terminated earlier by concurrent resolution of the Congress." The President has made no such determination, nor has Congress terminated the joint resolution.[28]

Instead, Congress in May 1965 approved an appropriation of $700 million to meet the expense of mounting military requirements in Viet-Nam. (Public Law 89-18, 79

---

28. On March 1, 1966, the Senate voted, 92-5, to table an amendment that would have repealed the joint resolution.

Stat. 109.) The President's message asking for this appropriation states that this was "not a routine appropriation. For each Member of Congress who supports this request is also voting to persist in our efforts to halt Communist aggression in South Vietnam." The appropriation act constitutes a clear congressional endorsement and approval of the actions taken by the President.

On March 1, 1966, the Congress continued to express its support of the President's policy by approving a $4.8 billion supplemental military authorization by votes of 392-4 and 93-2. An amendment that would have limited the President's authority to commit forces to Viet-Nam was rejected in the Senate by a vote of 94-2.

D. NO DECLATATION OF WAR BY THE CONGRESS IS REQUIRED TO AUTHORIZE UNITED STATES PARTICIPATION IN THE COLLECTIVE DEFENSE OF SOUTH VIET-NAM

No declaration of war is needed to authorize American actions in Viet-Nam. As shown in the preceding sections, the President has ample authority to order the participation of United States armed forces in the defense of South Viet-Nam.

Over a very long period in our history, practice and precedent have confirmed the constitutional authority to engage United States forces in hostilities without a declaration of war. This history extends from the undeclared war with France and the war against the Barbary pirates at the end of the 18th century to the Korean war of 1950-53.

James Madison, one of the leading framers of the Constitution, and Presidents John Adams and Jefferson all construed the Constitution, in their official actions during the early years of the Republic, as authorizing the United States to employ its armed forces abroad in hostilities in the absence of any congressional declaration of war. Their views and actions constitute highly persuasive evidence as to the meaning and effect of the Constitution. History has accepted the interpretation that was placed on the Constitution by the early Presidents and Congresses in regard to the lawfulness of hostilities without a declaration of war. The instances of such action in our history are numerous.

In the Korean conflict, where large-scale hostilities were conducted with an American troop participation of a quarter of a million men, no declaration of war was made by the Congress. The President acted on the basis of his constitutional responsibilities. While the Security Council, under a treaty of this country—the United Nations Charter—recommended assistance to the Republic of Korea against the Communist armed attack, the United States had no treaty commitment at that time obligating us to join in the defense of South Korea. In the case of South Viet-Nam we have the obligation of the SEATO treaty and clear expressions of congressional support. If the President could act in Korea without a declaration of war, *a fortiori* he is empowered to do so now in Viet-Nam. It may be suggested that a declaration of war is the only available constitutional process by which congressional support can be made effective for the use of United States armed forces in combat abroad. But the Constitution does not insist on any rigid formalism. It gives Congress a choice of ways in which to exercise its powers. In the case of Viet-Nam the Congress has supported the determination of the President by the Senate's approval of the SEATO treaty, the adoption of the joint resolution of August 10, 1964, and the enactment of the necessary authorizations and appropriations.

V. CONCLUSION

... The United States has commitments to assist South Viet-Nam in defending itself against Communist aggression from the North. The United States gave undertakings to this effect at the conclusion of the Geneva conference in 1954. Later that year the United States undertook an international obligation in the SEATO treaty to defend South Viet-Nam against Communist armed aggression. And during the past decade the United States has given additional assurance to the South Vietnamese Government.

The Geneva accords of 1954 provided for a cease-fire and regroupment of contending forces, a division of Viet-Nam into two zones, and a prohibition on the use of either zone for the resumption of hostilities or to "further an aggressive policy." From the beginning, North Viet-Nam violated the Geneva accords through a systematic effort to gain control of South Viet-Nam by force. In the light of these progressive North Vietnamese violations, the introduction into South Viet-Nam beginning in late 1961 of substantial United States military equipment and personnel, to assist in the defense of the South, was fully justified; substantial breach of an international agreement by one side permits the other side to suspend performance of corresponding obligations under the agreement.... United States actions in Viet-Nam, taken by the President and approved by the Congress, do not require any declaration of war, as shown by a long line of precedents for the use of United States armed forces abroad in the absence of any congressional declaration of war.

National Commitments

S. Rept. No. 129 (Comm. on Foreign Relations),
91st Cong., 1st Sess. (1969)

· · ·

1. THE INTENT OF THE FRAMERS

There is no uncertainty or ambiguity about the intent of the framers of the Constitution with respect to the war power. Greatly dismayed by the power of the British Crown to commit Great Britain—and with it the American colonies—to war, fearful of the possible development of monarchical tendencies in their new republic, and fearful as well of the dangers of large standing armies and military defiance of civilian authority, they vested the power to commit the United States to war exclusively in Congress. This power was not, like certain others, divided between the executive and the legislature; it was conferred upon Congress and Congress alone.

It was understood by the framers—and subsequent usage confirmed their understanding—that the President in his capacity as Commander in Chief of the Armed Forces would have the right, indeed the duty, to use the Armed Forces to repel sudden attacks on the United States, even in advance of Congressional authorization to do so. It was further understood that he would direct and lead the Armed Forces and put them to any use specified by Congress but that this did not extend to the initiation of hostilities. As Senator Ervin said in his statement to the committee, "... a distinction must be drawn between defensive warfare and offensive warfare."

The Constitutional Convention had at first proposed to give Congress the power to "*make war*" but changed this to "*declare war*." The purpose of the change was not to enlarge Presidential power in any significant degree (it was supported by delegates who subsequently refused to sign the Constitution on the ground that it gave too much power to the President) but to permit him to take action to repel sudden attacks. Madison's notes on the proceedings of the convention report the change of wording as follows:

> Mr. Madison and Mr. Gerry *moved* to insert *"declare,"* striking out *"make"* war; leaving to the Executive the power to repel sudden attacks.[15]

It should be remembered as well that the Congress was not expected to be in session for more than 1 month a year and that it was thought that it would be dangerous to leave the country defenseless during the long adjournment. Were the matter being considered now, in our age of long congressional sessions, rapid transportation, and instantaneous communication, one may wonder whether it would be thought necessary to concede the Executive any authority at all in this field. In any case it was authority to repel sudden attacks—that and nothing more—that the framers conceded to the President....

Relatively little attention was given by the Constitutional Convention to the comparative roles of President and Congress in making war. The probable reason, a recent scholar suggests, is that the full power to initiate the use of the armed forces was assumed by everyone to rest with Congress; seeing no issue of separation of powers, they gave the matter scant attention.[17]

The evidence is abundant that the framers did not intend the executive to have the power to initiate war....

2. THE WAR POWER FROM 1789 TO 1900

The early Presidents carefully respected Congress's authority to initiate war. President Adams took action to protect American ships from French attacks on the Atlantic only to the extent that Congress authorized him to do so; even in the case of this "limited war" between the United States and revolutionary France the President did not regard himself as free to use the Armed Forces without authorization by Congress.

Early in his term of office President Jefferson sent a naval squadron to the Mediterranean to protect American commerce against piracy, but it was not at first permitted to engage in offensive action against the Barbary pirates. On December 8, 1801, President Jefferson, having judged that offensive action was necessary, sent the following message to Congress:

> Tripoli, the least considerable of the Barbary States, had come forward with demands unfounded either in right or in compact, and had permitted itself to denounce war on our failure to comply before a given day. The style of the demand admitted but one answer. I sent a small squadron of frigates into the Mediterranean...with orders to protect our commerce against the threatened attack....Our commerce in the Mediterranean was blockaded and that of the Atlantic in peril....

Then, referring to the capture of one of the Tripolitan ships by the American ship *Enterprise*, Jefferson continued:

---

15. *The Records of the Federal Convention of 1787*, 4 volumes. (Max Farrand, editor, New Haven and London: Yale University Press, 1966), vol. 2, p. 318.

17. Robert William Russell, *The United States Congress and the Power To Use Military Force Abroad*, Ph. D. thesis, Fletcher School of Law and Diplomacy, 1967, pp. 58-59.

...Unauthorized by the Constitution, without the sanction of Congress, to go beyond the line of defense, the vessel, being disabled from committing further hostilities, was liberated with its crew. The Legislature will doubtless consider whether, by authorizing measures of offense also, they will place our force on an equal footing with that of its adversaries. I communicate all material information on this subject, that in the exercise of this important function confided by the Constitution to the Legislature exclusively their judgment may form itself on a knowledge and consideration of every circumstance of weight.[19]

The Monroe Doctrine is often cited as an instance and precedent for the making of foreign commitments by executive action. In fact a distinction was made at the time between a statement of policy and its implementation, the latter being regarded as falling within the province of Congress. In reply to an inquiry by the Government of Colombia in 1824 as to what action the United States might take in response to possible European intervention against the New Latin American republics, Secretary of State John Quincy Adams replied:

With respect to the question, "in what manner the Government of the United States intends to resist on its part any interference of the Holy Alliance for the purpose of subjugating the new republics or interfering in their political forms" you understand that by the Constitution of the United States, the ultimate decision of this question belongs to the Legislative Department of the Government....[20]

In 1846 President Polk sent American forces into the disputed territory between Corpus Christi and the Rio Grande River, precipitating the clash which began the Mexican War. The constitutionality of this act is uncertain but Abraham Lincoln, then a Congressman from Illinois, was certain that it was unconstitutional. He wrote:

... Allow the President to invade a neighboring nation, whenever *he* shall deem it necessary to repel an invasion, and you allow him to do so, *whenever he may choose to say* he deems it necessary for such purpose—and you allow him to make war at pleasure. Study to see if you can fix *any limit* to his power in this respect, after you have given him so much as you propose....

The provision of the Constitution giving the warmaking power to Congress, was dictated, as I understand it, by the following reasons. Kings had always been involving and impoverishing their people in wars, pretending generally, if not always, that the good of the people was the object. This, our Convention undertook to be the most oppressive of all Kingly oppressions; and they resolved to so frame the Constitution that *no one man* should hold the power of bringing this oppression upon us.[21]

---

19. U. S. Congress, Joint Committee on Printing, *Compilation of Messages and Papers of the Presidents*, 20 volumes (James D. Richardson, editor, New York: Bureau of National Literature, Inc., 1897), vol. 1, p. 314.

20. John Quincy Adams to Don Jose Maria Salazar, Aug. 6, 1824, quoted in *The Record of American Diplomacy* (Ruhl J. Bartlett, editor, third edition, New York: Alfred A. Knopf, 1954), p. 185.

21. Letter to William H. Herndon, Feb 15, 1848, in *The Collected Works of Abraham Lincoln*, 9 volumes (New Brunswick: Rutgers University Press, 1953), vol. 1, pp. 451-452.

During the 19th century American Armed Forces were used by the President on his own authority for such purposes as suppressing piracy, suppressing the slave trade by American ships, "hot pursuit" of criminals across frontiers, and protecting American lives and property in backward areas or areas where government had broken down. Such limited uses of force without authorization by Congress, not involving the initiation of hostilities against foreign governments, came to be accepted practice, sanctioned by usage though not explicitly by the Constitution.

Some Presidents, notably Polk, Grant, and McKinley, interpreted their powers as Commander in Chief broadly, while others, such as the early Presidents and Buchanan and Cleveland, were scrupulously deferential to the war power of Congress. Summarizing the war power in the 19th century, Robert William Russell writes:

> It is not a simple matter to arrive at conclusions concerning this period in which the constitutional interpretation was far from consistent, where Grant's extreme view is sandwiched between the conservative views of Buchanan and Cleveland. But there was one opinion that enjoyed wide acceptance: the President could constitutionally employ American military force outside the nation as long as he did not use it to commit "acts of war." While the term was never precisely defined, an "act of war" in this context usually meant *the use of military force against a sovereign nation* without that nation's *consent* and without that nation's having declared war upon or used force against the United States. To perform acts of war the President needed the authorization of Congress. Even when a foreign state initiated military acts of war, the President always sought *post hoc* congressional approval for his response.
>
> This dividing line between the proper spheres of legislative and executive authority was sufficiently flexible to permit the President to use military force in the unimportant cases, while preserving the role of Congress in important decisions. The acts of war doctrine was probably a step beyond what the framers intended when they changed the congressional power from "make" war to "declare" war, and was certainly a move in the direction of Presidential power compared to the cautious stance of Washington, Adams, Jefferson, and Madison. The central objective which the Constitution sought—congressional authority to approve the initiation of major conflicts—was undamaged, but a certain fraying of the edges had occurred. This slight deterioration was greatly accelerated during the following 50 years.[22]

3. THE EXPANSION OF EXECUTIVE POWER IN THE 20TH CENTURY, 1900-41

The use of the Armed Forces against sovereign nations without authorization by Congress became common practice in the 20th century. President Theodore Roosevelt used the Navy to prevent Colombian forces from suppressing insurrection in the province of Panama and intervened militarily in Cuba and the Dominican Republic. Presidents Taft and Wilson also sent armed forces to the Caribbean and Central America without Congressional authorization. In Haiti, the Dominican Republic, and Nicaragua these interventions resulted in the establishment of American military governments.

---

22. Russell, *The United States Congress and the Power To Use Military Force Abroad,* pp. 242-243.

President Wilson seized the Mexican port of Vera Cruz in 1914 as an act of reprisal, in order, he said, to "enforce respect" for the government of the United States. The two Houses of Congress adopted separate resolutions in support of President Wilson's action but the Senate did not complete action on its resolution until after the seizure of Vera Cruz. After the Mexican bandit Pancho Villa raided the town of Columbus, N. Mex., in 1916, President Wilson sent a force under General Pershing into Mexico in "hot pursuit" of the bandits; the expedition turned into a prolonged intervention of nearly 2 years and almost brought about war with Mexico. The Senate adopted a resolution supporting the President after General Pershing's force had entered Mexico; this resolution was never reported out of the Foreign Affairs Committee of the House of Representatives.

The military powers which had been acquired by Presidents in the 19th century— for purposes of "hot pursuit" and the protection of American lives and property, and under treaties which conferred rights and obligations on the United States—were not serious infringements on Congress' war power because they had been used for the most part against individuals or bands of pirates or bandits and not against sovereign states. Roosevelt, Taft, and Wilson used these powers to engage in military action against sovereign states, thereby greatly expanding the scope of executive power over the use of the armed forces and setting precedents for the greater expansions of executive power which were to follow. The Congresses of that era did not see fit to resist or oppose these incursions of their constitutional authority; indeed, as we have noted, one or both Houses of Congress gave retroactive approval to President Wilson's unauthorized interventions in Mexico.

Roosevelt, Taft, and Wilson asserted no general or "inherent" Presidential power to make war. Indeed, when it came to full-scale conflict with Germany, President Wilson explicitly acknowledged the war power of the Congress. *Advising* Congress to declare war on Germany in his war message of April 2, 1917, the President said:

> I have called the Congress into extraordinary session because there are serious, very serious, choices of policy to be made, and made immediately, which it is neither right nor constitutionally permissible that I should assume the responsibility of making.[23]

President Franklin Roosevelt expanded executive power over the use of the Armed Forces to an unprecedented degree. The exchange of overaged American destroyers for British bases in the Western Hemisphere was accomplished by executive agreement, in violation of the Senate's treaty power, and was also a violation of the international law of neutrality, giving Germany legal cause, had she chosen to take it, to declare war on the United States. The transaction was an *emergency* use of Presidential power, taken in the belief that it might be essential to save Great Britain from invasion.

In 1941 President Roosevelt, on his own authority, committed American forces to the defense of Greenland and Iceland and authorized American naval vessels to escort convoys to Iceland provided that at least one ship in each convoy flew the American or Icelandic flag. When the American destroyer *Greer* was fired on by a German submarine, . . . President Roosevelt utilized the occasion to announce that thereafter American naval vessels would shoot on sight against German and Italian ships west

---

23. *The Public Papers of Woodrow Wilson: War and Peace*, 2 volumes (Ray Stannard Baker and William E. Dodd, editors, New York and London: Harper Bros.), vol. 1, p. 6.

of the 26th meridian. By the time Germany and Italy declared war on the United States, in the wake of the Japanese attack on Pearl Harbor, the United States had already been committed by its President, acting on his own authority, to an undeclared naval war in the Atlantic. Roosevelt, however, achieved his objective without asserting a general or "inherent" Presidential power to commit the Armed Forces abroad.

4. THE PASSING OF THE WAR POWER FROM CONGRESS TO THE EXECUTIVE AFTER WORLD WAR II

The trend initiated by Theodore Roosevelt, Taft, and Wilson, and accelerated by Franklin Roosevelt, continued at a rapid rate under Presidents Truman, Eisenhower, Kennedy, and Johnson, bringing the country to the point at which the real power to commit the country to war is now in the hands of the President. The trend which began in the early 20th century has been consummated and the intent of the framers of the Constitution as to the war power substantially negated.

By the late 1940's there had developed a kind of ambivalence as to the war power in the minds of officials in the executive branch, Members of Congress and, presumably, the country at large. On the one hand, it was and still is said that Congress alone has the power to declare war; on the other hand it was widely believed, or at least conceded, that the President in his capacity as Commander in Chief had the authority to use the Armed Forces in any way he saw fit. Noting that the President has in fact exercised power over the Armed Forces we have come to assume that he is entitled to do so. The actual possession of a power has given rise to a belief in its constitutional legitimacy.

The fact that Congress has acquiesced in, or at the very least has failed to challenge, the transfer of the war power from itself to the executive, is probably the most important single fact accounting for the speed and virtual completeness of the transfer. Why has Congress agreed to this rearrangement of powers which is without constitutional justification, and at its own expense?

To some degree, it seems to be the result of the unfamiliarity of the United States with its new role as a world power. Lacking guidelines of experience for the accommodation of our constitutional system to the new demands that have been made upon it, Congress has acquiesced in the resort to expedients in foreign policy making which we have already noted. In addition, the fact that so many of the great policy decisions of the postwar era have been made in an atmosphere of real or contrived urgency has put tremendous pressure on Members of Congress to set aside apprehensions as to the exercise of power by the executive lest they cause some fatal delay or omission in the nation's foreign policy.

Another possible factor in congressional passivity is that Congress may have permitted itself to be overawed by the cult of executive expertise. Like the newly rich who go beyond the bounds of good taste in material display, the newly powerful may go beyond the bounds of good judgment in their intellectual display. A veritable army of foreign policy experts has sprung up in government and in the universities in recent years, contributing greatly to our knowledge and skill in foreign relations but also purveying the belief that foreign policy is an occult science which ordinary citizens, including Members of Congress, are simply too stupid to grasp. Many Members of Congress seem to have accepted this viewpoint, forgetting the point made by Professor Bartlett that "... there are no experts in wisdom concerning human affairs or in determining the national interest, and there is nothing in the realm of foreign policy that cannot be understood by the average American citizen."[24]

There may also be a historical memory at work in Congress' acceptance of executive predominance in foreign relations. The Senate, it has long been widely agreed, acted with disastrous irresponsibility in its rejection of the Covenant of the League of Nations in 1919. Since at least 1945, when the Senate ratified the United Nations Charter with virtually no debate, Congress has been doing a kind of penance for its prewar isolationism, and that penance has sometimes taken the form of overly hasty acquiescence in proposals for the acceptance of one form or another of international responsibility. Congress, it seems clear, was deficient in vision during the 1920's and 1930's, but so were Presidents Harding, Coolidge, Hoover, and—prior to 1938— Roosevelt.... In its deference to the executive in foreign affairs, Congress has conceded him, and the experts around him, a kind of infallibility which the wisest among them would readily acknowledge they do not have. Versailles, like Munich, has conveyed more lessons than were in it; its only lesson, as far as the workings of the American government are concerned, is the need not of congressional diffidence but of congressional responsibility—and the same counsel could profitably be heeded by the executive as well.

Returning to our chronology, we can detect the ambivalence about the executive's control of the armed forces in events of the post-World War II period....

There seems to have been general agreement that the United Nation's Charter, the NATO Treaty, and the other postwar security treaties did not change the relative powers of Congress and the President with respect to the use of the Armed Forces. There was little agreement, however, on what exactly those relative powers were— not, in the committee's opinion, because there could be any real doubt on constitutional grounds but because, as the trend toward executive control accelerated, constitutional considerations were neglected and the *de facto* power of the President came to be accepted as a constitutional power. As E. S. Corwin wrote in 1949, in many American minds—

> ... the President's power to repel sudden attacks had developed into an undefined power ... to employ without congressional authorization the Armed Forces in the protection of American rights and interests abroad whenever necessary.[27]

Dr. Russell comments:

> ... The intriguing aspect of this new interpretation of the constitutional division of powers is that it occurred at a point in American history when the older, specific categories under which force had been used by Presidents had disappeared. The right to intervene in Latin America was no longer maintained and the right to protect lives and property by armed force had been renounced. The areas where Presidents wished to use armed force were no longer primitive nations, but major powers against whom the use of armed force could not be easily disguised as anything but acts of war. If Presidents wished to exercise the power to use armed force abroad for general purposes without the consent of Congress they needed to assert a broader explanation of the President's con-

---

24. "U.S. Commitments to Foreign Powers," p. 20.

27. Edward S. Corwin, "Who Has the Power To Make War?" *New York Times Magazine*, July 31, 1949, p. 14.

stitutional authority than the right to use armed force in all cases except acts of war. What they needed to establish complete independence from congressional control was to assert that the President had a general constitutional power to use armed force to protect U.S. "interests" or "security." With no established limits on when Presidents might use force or on the quantity used, there would be no need to go to Congress.[28]

President Truman committed American Armed Forces to Korea in 1950 without Congressional authorization. Congressional leaders and the press were simultaneously informed of the decision but the decision had already been made.

President Truman himself made no public explanation of his use of the war power but an article in the Department of State Bulletin asserted that "the President, as Commander in Chief of the Armed Forces of the United States, has full control over the use thereof." The article pointed to past instances in which the President had used the Armed Forces in what was said to be "the broad interests of American foreign policy" and also asserted that there was a "traditional power of the President to use the Armed Forces of the United States without consulting Congress."[29] Here, clearly expostulated, is a doctrine of general or "inherent" Presidential power—something which had not been claimed by previous Presidents. [Yet, s]carcely a voice of dissent was raised in Congress at the time of Truman's action....

In 1951 the Senate Committees on Foreign Relations and Armed Services held joint hearings to discuss President Truman's plan for sending six divisions of American soldiers to Europe. Secretary of State Acheson gave the committees the following interpretation of the President's powers:

> Not only has the President the authority to use the Armed Forces in carrying out the broad foreign policy of the United States and implementing treaties, but it is equally clear that this authority may not be interfered with by the Congress in the exercise of powers which it has under the Constitution.

Acheson thought it inappropriate even to discuss constitutional matters:

> We are in a position in the world today where the argument as to who has the power to do this, that, or the other thing, is not exactly what is called for from America in this very critical hour.[32]

President Eisenhower exhibited some ambivalence as to his authority to use the Armed Forces. He conceded the authority of Congress, for example in the following statement at a press conference on March 10, 1954:

> There is going to be no involvement of America in war unless it is a result of the constitutional process that is placed upon Congress to declare it. Now let us have that clear....[33]

---

28. *The United States Congress and the Power to Use Military Force Abroad*, p. 389.

29. *Department of State Bulletin*, vol. 23, No. 578, July 31, 1950, pp. 173-177.

32. "Assignment of Ground Forces of the United States to Duty in the European Area," *Hearing by Committees on Foreign Relations and Armed Services*. U. S. Senate, 82nd Cong., first sess., on S. Con. Res. 8, Feb. 1-28, 1951 (Washington: U.S. Government Printing Office, 1951), pp. 92-93.

33. *Public Papers of the Presidents of the United States: Eisenhower, 1954* (Washington: U.S. Government Printing Office, 1960), p. 306.

But, in asking Congress for "presidential authority to use American Armed Forces to protect Formosa and the Pescadores," he said:

> Authority for some of the action which might be required would be inherent in the authority of the Commander in Chief. Until congress can act I would not hesitate, so far as my constitutional powers extend, to take whatever emergency action might be forced upon us in order to protect the rights and security of the United States.
>
> However, a suitable congressional resolution would clearly and publicly establish the authority of the President as Commander in Chief to employ the Armed Forces of this Nation promptly and effectively for the purposes indicated if in his judgment it became necessary.[34]

The burden of President Eisenhower's message seems to have been that, although he regarded himself as having some authority to dispose of the Armed Forces, he did not regard it as entirely certain that he did have it or in what amount. It was presumably in order to put this authority on an unquestionable basis that he asked for a congressional resolution.

It is significant that in the case of the Formosa resolution President Eisenhower asked for *authority* rather than mere approval or support and that under the resolution adopted by Congress the President was "*authorized* to employ the Armed Forces," upon his own finding of necessity, for the defense of Formosa and the Pescadores. The use of the word *authorize* by both President and Congress strongly implied recognition by both that the authority to commit the armed forces lay with the Congress, to grant or withhold. The committee emphasizes this point as one which may have significance in possible future congressional action on resolutions pertaining to the use of the Armed Forces.

Although the word *authorize* was used in the Formosa resolution, the authorization was an extremely broad one, empowering the President to employ the Armed Forces to defend Formosa and the Pescadores "as he determines necessary." It can be argued that an authorization so general and imprecise amounts to an unconstitutional alienation of its war power on the part of the Congress. Indeed, Senate opposition to the Formosa resolution centered on the contention that the language of the resolution sought to enable the President to wage war without a declaration of war by Congress. During the debate on the resolution Senator Morse said that, "under the Constitution of the United States, no President has the right to commit an act of war against a sovereign power."[35]

Subsequent resolutions involving the possible use of armed force abandoned the principle of *authorization*, demonstrating not only ambivalence as to the extent of the President's authority but a lack of attention to the underlying constitutional question. The Middle East resolution of 1957, the Cuba resolution of 1962, and the Gulf of Tonkin resolution of 1964 dropped the vital concept of congressional authorization and instead used terminology which, by failing to express a grant of power by Congress, implied acceptance of the view that the President already had the power

---

34. *Congressional Record*, 84th Cong., first sess., vol. 101, pt. 1, Senate, Jan. 24, 1955, p. 601.

35. *Congressional Record*, 84th Cong., first sess., vol. 101, pt. 1, Senate, Jan. 24, 1955, p. 766.

to use the Armed Forces in the ways proposed and that, the resolutions were no more than expressions of congressional support and national unity. The prevailing attitude in each instance seems to have been one of concern not with constitutional questions but with the problem at hand and with the need for a method of dealing with it, heightened in all three cases by a sense of urgency. Nonetheless, precedents were set.

The debate on the Middle East resolution of 1957 revealed two dominant attitudes on the war power; first, a reluctance to define it with precision, and, second, growing senatorial acceptance of the view that the President, in his capacity as Commander in Chief, could commit the Armed Forces to defend what he might regard as the "vital interest" of the nation. In testimony before the Committees on Foreign Relations and Armed Services, Secretary of State Dulles refused to express an opinion as to whether or not the President could commit the Armed Forces in the absence of the resolution. Senator Fulbright, whose view has changed with time and experience, thought at the time that the President had power as Commander in Chief to use the Armed Forces to defend the "vital interests" of the country and that the resolution would have the effect of limiting that power.[36] This viewpoint was widely shared at the time. In their report the two committees struck out the word "authorize" and expressed satisfaction at having avoided the necessity of defining the relative powers of Congress and the President.[37] The debate on the floor of the Senate showed preponderant, but far from unanimous, support for this expansive view of Presidential authority.[38] The final resolution said that, "if the President determines the necessity thereof, the United States is prepared to use armed force" to defend Middle Eastern nations against Communist aggression, "provided that such employment shall be consonant with the treaty obligations of the United States and with the Constitution of the United States." What exactly was thought to be required for the use of force to be "consonant with the Constitution" was by this time more obscure than ever. When President Eisenhower sent 14,000 American troops to Lebanon in 1958, he said that they were being sent "to protect American lives and by their presence there to encourage the Lebanese Government in defense of Lebanese sovereignty and integrity." No reference was made to the resolution of the previous year.

In September 1962 Congress adopted a joint resolution pertaining to Cuba. The Kennedy administration favored a concurrent resolution expressing the sense of Congress that the President "possesses all necessary authority" to prevent Cuba, "by whatever means may be necessary, including the use of arms," from "exporting its aggressive purposes" in the hemisphere, to prevent the establishment of a foreign, i.e., Soviet, military base in Cuba, and to support Cuban aspirations for self-determination. Senator Russell opposed the concurrent resolution favored by the administration. "I do not believe," he said, "that the Armed Services Committee is going to make a constitutional assertion that the President of the United States has the right

---

36. "The President's Proposal on the Middle East," Hearings before the Committees on Foreign Relations and Armed Services, U.S. Senate, 85th Cong., first sess., Jan. 14 to Feb. 11, 1957 (Washington: U.S. Government Printing Office, 1957), pp. 111-119.

37. "To Promote Peace and Stability in the Middle East," S. Rept. No. 70, 85th Cong., first sess. (Washington: U.S. Government Printing Office, 1957), p. 9.

38. Russell, *The United States Congress and the Power To Use Military Force Abroad*, pp. 416-420.

to declare war, and that is what this does."[39] The resolution as finally adopted was a joint resolution, stating that "the United States is determined" to do those things spelled out in the abandoned concurrent resolution.

The Cuban missile crisis occurred 1 month later. Two hours before he went on television on October 22, 1962, to announce the "quarantine" on shipments of offensive missiles to Cuba, President Kennedy met with the congressional leadership and briefed them on the decisions which had, of course, already been made. In the belief that they had a *duty* to give the President their best judgment, certain Senators expressed opinions as to possible wise courses of action. This was the extent of congressional participation in the greatest crisis of the postwar era, the one crisis which brought the world to the brink of nuclear war. Finding the congressional advice in some cases "captious and inconsistent," Theodore Sorensen later wrote that the President's meeting with the congressional leadership was the "only sour note of the day."[40] ...

The Gulf of Tonkin resolution represents the extreme point in the process of constitutional erosion that began in the first years of this century. Couched in broad terms, the resolution constitutes an acknowledgment of virtually unlimited Presidential control of the Armed Forces. It is of more than historical importance that the Congress now ask itself why it was prepared to acquiesce in the transfer to the executive of a power which, beyond any doubt, was intended by the Constitution to be exercised by Congress.

Several answers suggest themselves:

First, in the case of each of the resolutions discussed, Congress was confronted with a situation that seemed to be urgent and, lacking firm historical guidelines for the discharge of its foreign policy responsibilities in a real or seeming emergency, it acquiesced in an expedient which seemed to meet the needs of the moment, the foremost of which at the time of each of the resolutions seemed to be an expression of national unity. In the case of the Gulf of Tonkin resolution, the Senate responded to the administration's contention that the effect of the resolution would be lost if it were not enacted quickly. The desired effect was a resounding expression of national unity and support for the President at a moment when it was felt that the country had been attacked. In order, therefore, to avoid the delay that would arise from a careful analysis of the language of the resolution and the further delay that would arise if the resolution had to go to a Senate-House conference to reconcile differing versions, the Foreign Relations Committee and the entire Senate speedily approved the resolution in the language in which it had already been adopted by the House of Representatives. The prevailing attitude was not so much that Congress was granting or acknowledging the executive's authority to take certain actions but that it was expressing unity and support for the President in a moment of national crisis and, therefore, that the exact words in which it expressed those sentiments were not of primary importance.

---

39. "Situation in Cuba," *Hearings before the Senate Foreign Relations and Armed Services Committees*, U.S. Senate, 87th Cong., second sess., September 1962 (Washington: U.S. Government Printing Office, 1962), p. 72.

40. *Kennedy* (New York: Harper & Row, 1965), p. 702

Second, in the course of two decades of cold war the country and its leaders became so preoccupied with questions of national security as to have relatively little time or thought for constitutional matters....

Third, in the case of the Gulf of Tonkin resolution, there was a discrepancy between the language of the resolution and the intent of Congress. Although the language of the resolution lends itself to the interpretation that Congress was consenting in advance to a full-scale war in Asia should the President think it necessary, that was not the expectation of Congress at the time. In adopting the resolution Congress was closer to believing that it was helping to *prevent* a large-scale war by taking a firm stand than it was laying the legal basis for the conduct of such a war.... Its expectations were shaped by events outside of the formal legislative record, notably the national election campaign then in progress, in which President Johnson's basic position as to Vietnam was expressed in his assertion that "... we are not about to send American boys 9,000 or 10,000 miles away from home to do what Asian boys ought to be doing for themselves."[44] It is difficult, therefore, to credit Under Secretary of State Katzenbach's contention that the Gulf of Tonkin resolution, combined with the SEATO Treaty, was the "functional equivalent" of a declaration of war.[45] In adopting a resolution with such sweeping language, however, Congress committed the error of making a *personal* judgment as to how President Johnson would implement the resolution when it had a responsibility to make an *institutional* judgment, first, as to what *any* President would do with so great an acknowledgment of power, and, second, as to whether, under the Constitution, Congress had the right to grant or concede the authority in question.

From the executive's point of view these questions are academic, because every President since World War II has asserted at one time or another that he had the authority to commit the Armed Forces to conflict without the consent of Congress. The Johnson administration was not entirely consistent in its interpretations of the Gulf of Tonkin resolution, but on a number of occasions it was asserted that the President would have full authority to conduct the war in Vietnam on its full scale even in the absence of the resolution....

The exact view of the executive as to the meaning of Congress constitutional power to "declare war" remains somewhat obscure. In his testimony before the Foreign Relations Committee on August 17, 1967, Under Secretary Katzenbach referred to a declaration of war as something which is "outmoded in the international arena" and also as something that would not "correctly reflect the limited objectives of the United States with respect to Vietnam."[48] The Under Secretary ... asked: "What could a declaration of war have done that would have given the President more authority and a clearer voice of the Congress of the United States than that did?"[49]...

The burden of the Under Secretary's remarks seems to have been, first, that the Gulf of Tonkin resolution was not a declaration of war but its "functional equivalent," and, second, that declarations of war are inappropriate when the nation's purposes are "limited" and in any case are "outmoded in the international arena."... The committee is reluctant to believe that the executive feels itself free to alter on its own

---

44. Remarks in Memorial Hall, Akron University, Akron, Ohio, Oct. 21, 1964.

45. "U.S. Commitments to Foreign Powers," p. 82.

48. "U.S. Commitments to Foreign Powers," p. 81.

49. *Ibid.* pp. 81, 83.

authority a provision of the Constitution which it believes to be "outmoded in the international arena." Nor can the committee accept the view that "limited" wars can be undertaken by the executive without the consent of Congress; neither the Constitution nor the conduct of American Presidents prior to 1950—with one or two possible exceptions—justify that interpretation of the Constitution. It is obvious that the question of authority to commit the United States to war is in need of clarification.

One final occurrence must be mentioned to complete our chronology. On April 28, 1965, after consulting his advisers and briefing the leaders of Congress, President Johnson sent American Armed Forces to the Dominican Republic. As in the instances of Korea in 1950 and Lebanon in 1958, American forces were sent to a foreign country without reference to any resolution or other act or expression of Congress. The congressional leadership were informed but that cannot be equated with obtaining the consent of Congress.

Great emphasis has been placed by the Executive on its diligence in "informing" and "consulting" the Congress on foreign policy decisions. "Consistently," says the Department of State . . . , "Congress is informed and consulted concerning both the implementation of existing commitments and policy and the planning of new initiatives." Unfortunately, the terms "consult" and "inform" are used interchangeably, although the distinction between solicitation of advice in advance of a decision and the provision of information in the wake of a decision would seem to be a significant one. In fact, recent administrations have been fairly conscientious about "informing" the congressional leadership—although not the Congress itself—of their foreign policy decisions. . . . [I]n matters involving the commitment of the Armed Forces to hostilities abroad, the Constitution requires that the consent of Congress be obtained in advance of action by the executive. . . .

President Nixon's four immediate predecessors—Eisenhower a shade less than the others—all asserted unrestricted executive authority to commit the Armed Forces without the consent of Congress, and Congress, for the most part, has acquiesced in the transfer of its war power to the executive. The evolution traced in these pages is the basis of the committee's contention that the intent of the framers of the Constitution with respect to the exercise of the war power has been virtually nullified. . . .

6. CONCLUSION: THE RESTORATION OF CONSTITUTIONAL BALANCE

. . . The committee is strongly of the view that a restoration of the division of war powers specified by the Constitution and generally adhered to during more than a century of national experience is both compatible with modern conditions and essential to constitutional government. . . .

Claims to unlimited executive authority over the use of armed force are made on grounds of both legitimacy and necessity. . . . Failing of constitutional and historical legitimacy, the case for unlimited executive power over the Armed Forces has final resort to the spurious and dangerous doctrine of "inherent powers of the Presidency." . . . [Besides the arguments for executive power based on executive branch expertise in foreign affairs, t]he other principal argument made in support of emergency powers over foreign policy is the necessity of speed in response to a grave threat to the nation's security or survival. To this the committee has two responses:

First, a useful distinction can be made between speed and haste. In a number of situations in recent years which were characterized as emergencies, American policy would have profited from brief delays to permit deliberation and consultation with the Congress. In the case of the joint resolutions adopted by Congress pertaining to Formosa, the Middle East, Cuba and the Gulf of Tonkin, not one was a matter of the greatest urgency although that did not in each case seem clear at the time. In the case of the Gulf of Tonkin resolution, a delay of a week or two would have permitted Congress both to ascertain the facts regarding the occurrence in the Gulf of Tonkin and to record its intentions in a legislative record; the retaliatory attacks on the North Vietnamese ports had already been made when the resolution was put before Congress, so that a delay would have had no military consequences.

Second, the committee is well aware that there have been, and may in the future again be, instances of great national emergency such as the Cuban missile crisis when prompt action is essential. In such instances consultation with the Congress is by no means out of the question; Congress has demonstrated on many occasions that it is capable of acting as speedily as the executive. Should the urgency or the need of secrecy be judged so great, however, as to preclude any form of consultation with Congress, the President, as we have noted, has unchallenged authority to respond to a sudden attack upon the United States. This authority is recognized as nothing less than a duty and it is inconceivable that the Congress would fail to support the President in response to a direct attack on the United States.

Finally, should the President find himself confronted with a situation of such complexity and ambiguity as to leave him without guidelines for constitutional action, it would be far better for him to take the action he saw fit without attempting to justify it in advance and leave it to Congress or the courts to evaluate his action in retrospect. A single unconstitutional act, later explained or pronounced unconstitutional, is preferable to an act dressed up in some spurious, precedent-setting claim of legitimacy. As a member of the Nation's first Congress, Alexander White, of Virginia, said:

> It would be better for the President to extend his powers on some extraordinary occasions, even where he is not strictly justified by the Constitution, than the legislature should grant an improper power to be exercised at all times.... [58]

For all of the foregoing reasons the committee rejects the contention that the war powers as spelled out in the Constitution are obsolete and strongly recommends that the Congress reassert its constitutional authority over the use of the Armed Forces. No constitutional amendment or legislative enactment is required for this purpose; all that is required is the restoration of constitutional procedures which have been permitted to atrophy.

... If Congress makes clear that it intends to exercise these powers, it is most unlikely that the executive will fail to respect that intention. Napoleon is credited with the maxim that "the tools belong to the man that can use them." Only Congress, by exercising its constitutional powers, can prevent them from passing into other hands.

The committee does not believe that formal declarations of war are the only available means by which Congress can authorize the President to initiate limited or general hostilities. Joint resolutions such as those pertaining to Formosa, the Middle East, and the Gulf of Tonkin are a proper method of granting authority, provided that they are precise as to what is to be done and for what period of time, and provided that

---

58. *The Annals of Congress*, June 18, 1789, vol. 1, p. 537.

they do in fact *grant authority* and not merely express approval of undefined action to be taken by the President. That distinction is of the greatest importance. As used in the recent past, joint resolutions have been instruments of political control over the Congress in the hand of the President, enabling him to claim support for any action he may choose to take and so phrased as to express Congressional acquiescence in the constitutionally unsound contention that the President in his capacity as Commander in Chief has the authority to commit the country to war.

The committee therefore recommends that, in considering future resolutions involving the use or possible use of the Armed Forces, Congress—

(1) debate the proposed resolution at sufficient length to establish a legislative record showing the intent of Congress;

(2) use the words *authorize* or *empower* or such other language as will leave no doubt that Congress alone has the right to authorize the initiation of war and that, in granting the President authority to use the Armed Forces, Congress is granting him power that he would not otherwise have;

(3) state in the resolution as explicitly as possible under the circumstances the kind of military action that is being authorized and the place and purpose of its use; and

(4) put a time limit on the resolution, thereby assuring Congress the opportunity to review its decision and extend or terminate the President's authority to use military force....

The Supreme Court never ruled whether the Vietnam War was legal, or even whether its legality was a political question. As you read the following dissent from a denial of certiorari in a case that would have presented these issues, consider whether the Court behaved responsibly in failing to exercise its discretionary review powers. *Compare* Henkin, *On Drawing Lines*, 82 Harv. L. Rev. 63, 90-91 (1968) (defending denials of certiorari), *with* Hughes, *Civil Disobedience and the Political Question Doctrine*, 43 N.Y.U. L. Rev. 1, 15 (1968) (criticizing Court's failure to give reasoned response to civil disobedients protesting legality of war). *See also* Note, *Congress, the President, and the Power to Commit Forces to Combat*, 81 Harv. L. Rev. 1771 (1968); Van Alstyne, *Congress, the President, and the Power to Declare War*, 121 U. Pa. L. Rev. 1088 (1966).

Mora v. McNamara
389 U.S. 934 (1967)

Petition for writ of certiorari to the United States Court of Appeals for the District of Columbia Circuit. Denied.

Justice MARSHALL took no part in the consideration or decision of this petition.

Justice STEWART, with whom Justice DOUGLAS joins, dissenting.

The petitioners were drafted into the United States Army in late 1965, and six months later were ordered to a West Coast replacement station for shipment to Vietnam. They brought this suit to prevent the Secretary of Defense and the Secretary of the Army from carrying out those orders, and requested a declaratory judgment that the present United States military activity in Vietnam is "illegal." The District Court dismissed the suit, and the Court of Appeals affirmed.

There exist in this case questions of great magnitude. Some are akin to those referred to by Justice Douglas in *Mitchell v. United States*, 386 U.S. 972.* But there are others:

I. Is the present United States military activity in Vietnam a "war" within the meaning of Article I, Section 8, Clause 11 of the Constitution?

II. If so, may the Executive constitutionally order the petitioners to participate in that military activity, when no war has been declared by the Congress?

III. Of what relevance to Question II are the present treaty obligations of the United States?

IV. Of what relevance to Question II is the joint Congressional ("Tonkin Gulf") Resolution of August 10, 1964?

   (a) Do present United States military operations fall within the terms of the Joint Resolution?

   (b) If the Joint Resolution purports to give the Chief Executive authority to commit United States forces to armed conflict limited in scope only by his own absolute discretion, is the Resolution a constitutionally impermissible delegation of all or part of Congress' power to declare war?

These are large and deeply troubling questions. Whether the Court would ultimately reach them depends, of course, upon the resolution of serious preliminary issues of justiciability. We cannot make these problems go away simply by refusing to hear the case of three obscure Army privates. I intimate not even tentative views upon any of these matters, but I think the Court should squarely face them by granting certiorari and setting this case for oral argument.

Justice DOUGLAS, with whom Justice STEWART concurs, dissenting.

The questions posed by Mr. Justice Stewart cover the wide range of problems which the Senate Committee on Foreign Relations recently explored,[1] in connection with the SEATO Treaty of February 19, 1955, and the Tonkin Gulf Resolution. Mr. Katzenbach, representing the Administration, testified that he did not regard the Tonkin Gulf Resolution to be "a declaration of war" and that while the Resolution was not "constitutionally necessary" it was "politically, from an international viewpoint and from a domestic viewpoint, extremely important." He added:

> The use of the phrase "to declare war" as it was used in the Constitution of the United States had a particular meaning in terms of the events and the practices which existed at the time it was adopted. . . .

> [I]t was recognized by the Founding Fathers that the President might have to take emergency action to protect the security of the United States, but that if there was going to be another use of the armed forces of the United States, that was a decision which Congress should check the Executive on, which Congress

---

*In *Mitchell*, the convicted defendant in a prosecution for failure to report for induction contended that the war in Vietnam was being conducted in violation of various treaties. Justice Douglas dissented from the denial of certiorari.

1. Hearings on S.Res. No. 151, 90th Cong., 1st Sess. (1967).

should support. It was for that reason that the phrase was inserted in the Constitution.

Now, over a long period of time, . . . there have been many uses of the military forces of the United States for a variety of purposes without a congressional declaration of war. But it would be fair to say that most of these were relatively minor uses of force. . . .

A declaration of war would not, I think, correctly reflect the very limited objectives of the United States with respect to Vietnam. It would not correctly reflect our efforts there, what we are trying to do, the reasons why we are there, to use an outmoded phraseology, to declare war.

The view that Congress was intended to play a more active role in the initiation and conduct of war than the above statements might suggest has been espoused by Senator Fulbright (Cong. Rec., Oct. 11, 1967, p. 14683-14690), quoting Thomas Jefferson who said:

We have already given . . . one effectual check to the Dog of War by transferring the power of letting him loose from the Executive to the Legislative body, from those who are to spend to those who are to pay.

These opposed views are reflected in the *Prize Cases*, 2 Black 635, a five-to-four decision rendered in 1863. Justice Grier, writing for the majority, emphasized the arguments for strong presidential powers. Justice Nelson, writing for the minority of four, read the Constitution more strictly, emphasizing that what is war in actuality may not constitute war in the constitutional sense. During all subsequent periods in our history—through the Spanish-American War, the Boxer Rebellion, two World Wars, Korea, and now Vietnam—the two points of view urged in the *Prize Cases* have continued to be voiced.

A host of problems is raised. Does the President's authority to repel invasions and quiet insurrections, do his powers in foreign relations and his duty to execute faithfully the laws of the United States, including its treaties, justify what has been threatened of petitioners? What is the relevancy of the Gulf of Tonkin Resolution and the yearly appropriations in support of the Vietnam effort?

The London Treaty (59 Stat. 1546), the SEATO Treaty (6 U.S.T. 81, 1955), the Kellogg-Briand Pact (46 Stat. 2343), and Article 39 of Chapter VII of the UN Charter [59 Stat. 1043 (1945)] deal with various aspects of wars of "aggression." Do any of them embrace hostilities in Vietnam, or give rights to individuals affected to complain, or in other respects give rise to justiciable controversies?

There are other treaties or declarations that could be cited. Perhaps all of them are wide of the mark. There are sentences in our opinions which, detached from their context, indicate that what is happening is none of our business:

Certainly it is not the function of the Judiciary to entertain private litigation— even by a citizen—which challenges the legality, the wisdom, or the propriety of the Commander-in-Chief in sending our armed forces abroad or to any particular region.

Johnson v. Eisentrager, 339 U.S. 763, 789.

We do not, of course, sit as a committee of oversight or supervision. What resolutions the President asks and what the Congress provides are not our concern. With respect to the Federal Government, we sit only to decide actual cases or controversies within judicial cognizance that arise as a result of what the Congress or the President or a judge does or attempts to do to a person or his property.

In *Ex parte Milligan*, 4 Wall. 2, the Court relieved a person of the death penalty imposed by a military tribunal, holding that only a civilian court had power to try him for the offense charged. Speaking of the purpose of the Founders in providing constitutional guarantees, the Court said:

> They knew . . . the nation they were founding, be its existence short or long, would be involved in war; how often or how long continued, human foresight could not tell; and that unlimited power, wherever lodged at such a time, was especially hazardous to freemen. For this, and other equally weighty reasons, they secured the inheritance they had fought to maintain, by incorporating in a written constitution the safeguards which *time* had proved were essential to its preservation. Not one of these safeguards can the President, or Congress, or the Judiciary disturb, except the one concerning the writ of *habeas corpus*.

. . . These petitioners should be told whether their case is beyond judicial cognizance. If it is not, we should then reach the merits of their claims, on which I intimate no views whatsoever.

Notes and Questions on Vietnam

1. On what bases does Leonard Meeker assert that the President was empowered to conduct the war in Southeast Asia? Does it follow, even if the war was lawful, that it was a "war" within the meaning of article I? For example, would the lawfulness of the war justify legislatively unauthorized domestic emergency measures to assure the prosecution of the war? (Recall *Youngstown*.) If not, does it follow that the Vietnam experience has left a purpose for declaring war more important than gratuitous formality?

2. Would it be plausible or useful for Congress and the President today to try to settle on the constitutional understanding that Dr. Russell finds in nineteenth century practice, that "the President could constitutionally employ American military force outside the nation as long as he did not use it to commit 'acts of war?' "

3. To what extent is the linchpin of Meeker's argument his observation that the world has "grown much smaller" since 1787? How much military and foreign affairs power should this circumstance be deemed to have vested in the President? Does it strengthen or weaken the case for unilateral presidential power to terminate treaties? (In connection with Meeker's description of the SEATO Treaty and the obligations undertaken by the United States, recall Judge McKinnon's arguments in *Goldwater v. Carter* based on the fact that the nation, not the President, is party to the treaty.) Does the advent of the nuclear age help explain the growth of executive power since World War II? Does it justify those developments?

4. Note that the Tonkin Gulf resolution provided that it could be terminated by concurrent resolution of Congress. Would such a termination be constitutional under *Chadha*? If not, how could Congress rescind any grant of warmaking power to the President? In the Vietnam period, Congress ultimately found the most effective check on executive power to be limitations on the use of appropriations. Are such limitations on the use of funds for conducting hostilities constitutional? Are they appropriate?

5. Why, given the history of legislative acquiescence in the Vietnam War, did Congress never declare war on Vietnam? Note that it has always been understood that Congress may authorize limited hostile engagements short of a declared war. *Cf. Bas v. Tingy*, 4 U.S. (4 Dall.) 37 (1800) (awarding shipowner compensation under federal statute dealing with recapture of ships from "the enemy"; France deemed "the enemy" although Congress never declared war in naval hostilities with France between 1798 and 1800). Is popular consensus behind a war effort what makes the collateral consequences of a declaration of war constitutional, for all practical purposes, on the domestic front? Should it be a legitimate objection to the imposition of extraordinary wartime burdens on particular individuals, for example, the draft, that such burdens are legitimate only if there is sufficient popular backing to produce a declaration of war? *See Orlando v. Laird*, 443 F.2d 1039 (2d Cir.), *cert. denied*, 404 U.S. 869 (1971) (Congressional action ratifying Vietnam military operations sufficient to justify compelling soldiers to participate in hostilities); *but cf. Mitchell v. Laird*, 488 F.2d 611 (D.C. Cir. 1973) (dismissing suit to enjoin Vietnam War as presenting political question, but opining in dictum that Congress had not authorized Vietnam War in a "Constitutionally satisfactory form"). Should this issue be regarded as justiciable? In addition to *Mora*, compare *Atlee v. Laird*, 347 F. Supp. 689 (E.D. Pa. 1972) (three-judge court), *aff'd sub nom Atlee v. Richardson*, 411 U.S. 911 (1973), *with Massachusetts v. Laird*, 400 U.S. 886 (1970) (Douglas, J., dissenting from denial of motion for leave to file a bill of complaint).

6. Does history confirm Meeker's argument that the Constitution supported the President's authority to commit troops to Vietnam? Do he and the Senate read history consistently? As you read the War Powers Resolution, which follows, consider whether Congress, through explicit legislation, can overcome the historical gloss on constitutional text. Alternatively, should the President ever be able to argue that he has accrued war powers originally vested in Congress through a kind of adverse possession?

7. So long as the President's war-making powers, in the absence of a declaration of war, are limited by appropriations and substantive legislation, should we be worried that the United States can become engaged in *de facto* war without a declaration of war? Is the current practice more salutary than requiring a declaration of war in each instance of international belligerency?

8. The Senate report cites with approval Jefferson's constitutionally punctilious handling of the Barbary Pirates. Do modern circumstances in any way limit the attractiveness or practicability of his approach?

9. How useful do you believe are the various suggestions in the Senate report for a more responsible congressional exercise of its war powers? Is it a meaningful check on the President to require congressional authorization for the use of military force if Congress is likely to grant such authority in extremely broad terms? Is it realistic to expect Congress, in a crisis situation, to draft such authorizations more closely or with any greater precision than it has in the past? Should Congress ever put time limits on its grants of authority? (Consider, in this connection, the impact of the War Powers Resolution in the case study of Lebanon, below.)

10. Do courts have any proper role to play in keeping military operations within statutorily authorized bounds? Consider in this regard, *Holtzman v. Schlesinger*, 414 U.S. 1304 (Marshall, Circuit Justice, 1973) (declining to vacate court of appeals stay of district court order enjoining Cambodia bombing). Courts are now revisiting that

issue with respect to military operations in Central America. *Ramirez de Arellano v. Weinberger*, 745 F.2d 1500 (D.C. Cir. 1984) (en banc), *vacated*, 471 U.S. 1113 (1985), *on remand*, 788 F.2d 762 (D.C. Cir. 1986) (holding justiciable the claim of a U.S. citizen that his private ranch in Honduras was being unlawfully used for U.S. military operations); *Sanchez-Espinoza v. Reagan*, 568 F. Supp. 596 (D.D.C. 1983), *aff'd*, 770 F.2d 202 (D.C. Cir. 1985) (holding challenges to military operations in Nicaragua nonjusticiable); *Crockett v. Reagan*, 558 F. Supp. 893 (D.D.C. 1982) *aff'd*, 720 F.2d 1355 (D.C. Cir. 1983), *cert. denied*, 467 U.S. 1251 (1984) (holding challenge to military aid to El Salvador nonjusticiable).

3. Congress' Efforts to Limit the President's Authority to Commit Troops: The War Powers Resolution

The key separation of powers development emanating from the Vietnam experience was Congress' enactment of the War Powers Resolution. The following materials are intended to provoke analysis of that Resolution, its rationale, and the prospects for its successful implementation.

a. The Resolution and Its History

War Powers Resolution

Pub. L. 93-148, 87 Stat. 555, codified at 50 U.S.C. 1541 *et seq.*

Section 1. This joint resolution may be cited as the "War Powers Resolution".

PURPOSE AND POLICY

Sec. 2. (a) It is the purpose of this joint resolution to fulfill the intent of the framers of the Constitution of the United States and insure that the collective judgment of both the Congress and the President will apply to the introduction of United States Armed Forces into hostilities, or into situations where imminent involvement in hostilities is clearly indicated by the circumstances, and to the continued use of such forces in hostilities or in such situations.

(b) Under article I, section 8, of the Constitution, it is specifically provided that the Congress shall have the power to make all laws necessary and proper for carrying into execution, not only its own powers but also all other powers vested by the Constitution in the Government of the United States, or in any department or officer thereof.

(c) The constitutional powers of the President as Commander-in-Chief to introduce United States Armed Forces into hostilities, or into situations where imminent involvement in hostilities is clearly indicated by the circumstances, are exercised only pursuant to (1) a declaration of war, (2) specific statutory authorization, or (3) a national emergency created by attack upon the United States, its territories or possessions, or its armed forces.

CONSULTATION

Sec. 3. The President in every possible instance shall consult with Congress before introducing United States Armed Forces into hostilities or into situations where imminent involvement in hostilities is clearly indicated by the circumstances, and after every such introduction shall consult regularly with the Congress until United States

Armed Forces are no longer engaged in hostilities or have been removed from such situations.

REPORTING

Sec. 4. (a) In the absence of a declaration of war, in any case in which United States Armed Forces are introduced—

(1) into hostilities or into situations where imminent involvement in hostilities is clearly indicated by the circumstances;

(2) into the territory, airspace or waters of a foreign nation, while equipped for combat, except for deployments which relate solely to supply, replacement, repair, or training of such forces; or

(3) in numbers which substantially enlarge United States Armed Forces equipped for combat already located in a foreign nation;

the President shall submit within 48 hours to the Speaker of the House of Representatives and to the President pro tempore of the Senate a report, in writing, setting forth—

(A) the circumstances necessitating the introduction of United States Armed Forces;

(B) the constitutional and legislative authority under which such introduction took place; and

(C) the estimated scope and duration of the hostilities or involvement.

(b) The President shall provide such other information as the Congress may request in the fulfillment of its constitutional responsibilities with respect to committing the Nation to war and to the use of United States Armed Forces abroad.

(c) Whenever United States Armed Forces are introduced into hostilities or into any situation described in subsection (a) of this section, the President shall, so long as such armed forces continue to be engaged in such hostilities or situation, report to the Congress periodically on the status of such hostilities or situation as well as on the scope and duration of such hostilities or situation, but in no event shall he report to the Congress less often than once every six months.

CONGRESSIONAL ACTION

Sec. 5. (a) Each report submitted pursuant to section 4(a)(1) shall be transmitted to the Speaker of the House of Representatives and to the President pro tempore of the Senate on the same calendar day. . . . If, when the report is transmitted, the Congress has adjourned sine die or has adjourned for any period in excess of three calendar days, the Speaker of the House of Representatives and the President pro tempore of the Senate, if they deem it advisable (or if petitioned by at least 30 percent of the membership of their respective Houses) shall jointly request the President to convene Congress in order that it may consider the report and take appropriate action pursuant to this section.

(b) Within sixty calendar days after a report is submitted or is required to be submitted pursuant to section 4(a)(1), whichever is earlier, the President shall terminate any use of United States Armed Forces with respect to which such report was submitted (or required to be submitted), unless the Congress (1) has declared war or has enacted a specific authorization for such use of United States Armed Forces,

(2) has extended by law such sixty-day period, or (3) is physically unable to meet as a result of an armed attack upon the United States. Such sixty-day period shall be extended for not more than an additional thirty days if the President determines and certifies to the Congress in writing that unavoidable military necessity respecting the safety of United States Armed Forces requires the continued use of such armed forces in the course of bringing about a prompt removal of such forces.

(c) Notwithstanding subsection (b), at any time that United States Armed Forces are engaged in hostilities outside the territory of the United States, its possessions and territories without a declaration of war or specific statutory authorization, such forces shall be removed by the President if the Congress so directs by concurrent resolution.

> [Sections 6 and 7 of the Resolution provide for expedited consideration of legislative action to be taken pursuant to the Resolution in the event of U.S. military engagements.]

INTERPRETATION OF JOINT RESOLUTION

Sec. 8. (a) Authority to introduce United States Armed Forces into hostilities or into situations wherein involvement in hostilities is clearly indicated by the circumstances shall not be inferred—

> (1) from any provision of law (whether or not in effect before the date of the enactment of this joint resolution) including any provision contained in any appropriation Act, unless such provision specifically authorizes the introduction of United States Armed Forces into hostilities or into such situations and states that it is intended to constitute specific statutory authorization within the meaning of this joint resolution; or

> (2) from any treaty heretofore or hereafter ratified unless such treaty is implemented by legislation specifically authorizing the introduction of United States Armed Forces into hostilities or into such situations and stating that it is intended to constitute specific statutory authorization within the meaning of this joint resolution.

. . .

(c) For purposes of this joint resolution, the term "introduction of United States Armed Forces" includes the assignment of members of such armed forces to command, coordinate, participate in the movement of, or accompany the regular or irregular military forces of any foreign country or government when such military forces are engaged, or there exists an imminent threat that such forces will become engaged, in hostilities.

(d) Nothing in this joint resolution—

> (1) is intended to alter the constitutional authority of the Congress or of the President, or the provisions of existing treaties; or

> (2) shall be construed as granting any authority to the President with respect to the introduction of United States Armed Forces into hostilities or into situations wherein involvement in hostilities is clearly indicated by the circumstances which authority he would not have had in the absence of this joint resolution.

SEPARABILITY CLAUSE

Sec. 9. If any provision of this joint resolution or the application thereof to any person or circumstance is held invalid, the remainder of the joint resolution and the application of such provision to any other person or circumstance shall not be affected thereby.

. . .

President Nixon's Veto of the War Powers Resolution
H. Doc. No. 171, 93d Cong., 1st Sess. (1973)

To the House of Representatives:

I hereby return without my approval House Joint Resolution 542—the War Powers Resolution. While I am in accord with the desire of the Congress to assert its proper role in the conduct of our foreign affairs, the restrictions which this resolution would impose upon the authority of the President are both unconstitutional and dangerous to the best interests of our Nation.

The proper roles of the Congress and the Executive in the conduct of foreign affairs have been debated since the founding of our country. Only recently, however, has there been a serious challenge to the wisdom of the Founding Fathers in choosing not to draw a precise and detailed line of demarcation between the foreign policy powers of the two branches.

The Founding Fathers understood the impossibility of foreseeing every contingency that might arise in this complex area. They acknowledged the need for flexibility in responding to changing circumstances. They recognized that foreign policy decisions must be made through close cooperation between the two branches and not through rigidly codified procedures.

These principles remain as valid today as they were when our Constitution was written. Yet House Joint Resolution 542 would violate those principles by defining the President's powers in ways which would strictly limit his constitutional authority.

CLEARLY UNCONSTITUTIONAL

House Joint Resolution 542 would attempt to take away, by a mere legislative act, authorities which the President has properly exercised under the Constitution for almost 200 years. One of its provisions would automatically cut off certain authorities after sixty days unless the Congress extended them. Another would allow the Congress to eliminate certain authorities merely by the passage of a concurrent resolution— an action which does not normally have the force of law, since it denies the President his constitutional role in approving legislation.

I believe that both these provisions are unconstitutional....

UNDERMINING OUR FOREIGN POLICY

While I firmly believe that a veto of House Joint Resolution 542 is warranted solely on constitutional grounds, I am also deeply disturbed by the practical consequences of this resolution. For it would seriously undermine this Nation's ability to act decisively and convincingly in time of international crisis. As a result, the confidence of our allies in our ability to assist them could be diminished and the respect of our adversaries for our deterrent posture could decline. A permanent and substantial element of unpredictability would be injected into the world's assessment of American behavior, further increasing the likelihood of miscalculation and war.

If this resolution had been in operation, America's effective response to a variety of challenges in recent years would have been vastly complicated or even made impossible. We may well have been unable to respond in the way we did during the Berlin crisis of 1961, the Cuban missile crisis of 1962, the Congo rescue operation in 1964, and the Jordanian crisis of 1970—to mention just a few examples....

While all the specific consequences of House Joint Resolution 542 cannot yet be predicted, it is clear that it would undercut the ability of the United States to act as an effective influence for peace. For example, the provision automatically cutting off certain authorities after 60 days unless they are extended by the Congress could work to prolong or intensify a crisis. Until the Congress suspended the deadline, there would be at least a chance of United States withdrawal and an adversary would be tempted therefore to postpone serious negotiations until the 60 days were up. Only after the Congress acted would there be a strong incentive for an adversary to negotiate. In addition, the very existence of a deadline could lead to an escalation of hostilities in order to achieve certain objectives before the 60 days expired.

The measure would jeopardize our role as a force for peace in other ways as well. It would, for example, strike from the President's hand a wide range of important peacekeeping tools by eliminating his ability to exercise quiet diplomacy backed by subtle shifts in our military deployments. It would also cast into doubt authorities which Presidents have used to undertake certain humanitarian relief missions in conflict areas, to protect fishing boats from seizure, to deal with ship or aircraft hijackings, and to respond to threats of attack. Not the least of the adverse consequences of this resolution would be the prohibition contained in section 8 against fulfilling our obligations under the NATO treaty as ratified by the Senate. Finally, since the bill is somewhat vague as to when the 60 day rule would apply, it could lead to extreme confusion and dangerous disagreements concerning the prerogatives of the two branches, seriously damaging our ability to respond to international crises.

FAILURE TO REQUIRE POSITIVE CONGRESSIONAL ACTION

I am particularly disturbed by the fact that certain of the President's constitutional powers as Commander in Chief of the Armed Forces would terminate automatically under this resolution 60 days after they were invoked. No overt Congressional action would be required to cut off these powers—they would disappear automatically unless the Congress extended them. In effect, the Congress is here attempting to increase its policy-making role through a provision which requires it to take absolutely no action at all.

In my view, the proper way for the Congress to make known its will on such foreign policy questions is through a positive action, with full debate on the merits of the issue and with each member taking the responsibility of casting a yes or no vote after considering those merits. The authorization and appropriations process represents one of the ways in which such influence can be exercised. I do not, however, believe that the Congress can responsibly contribute its considered, collective judgment on such grave questions without full debate and without a yes or no vote. Yet this is precisely what the joint resolution would allow. It would give every future Congress the ability to handcuff every future President merely by doing nothing and sitting still. In my view, one cannot become a responsible partner unless one is prepared to take responsible action.

STRENGTHENING COOPERATION BETWEEN THE CONGRESS AND THE EXECUTIVE BRANCHES

The responsible and effective exercise of the war powers requires the fullest co-operation between the Congress and the Executive and the prudent fulfillment by each branch of its constitutional responsibilities. House Joint Resolution 542 includes certain constructive measures which would foster this process by enhancing the flow of information from the executive branch to the Congress. Section 3, for example, calls for consultations with the Congress before and during the involvement of the United States forces in hostilities abroad. This provision is consistent with the desire of this Administration for regularized consultations with the Congress in an even wider range of circumstances....

RICHARD NIXON.

THE WHITE HOUSE, *October 24, 1973*

War Powers: A Test of Compliance—Relative to the Danang Sealift, the Evacuation of Phnom Penh, the Evacuation of Saigon, and the Mayaguez Incident

Hearings Before the House Comm. on Int'l Rel.,
94th Cong., 1st Sess. 46-48 (1975)

Legislative History of the Consultation Provision of the War Powers Resolution

. . .

Explanation of Consultation Provision in H.J. Res. 542 from House Report 93-287

Section 2. Consultation

This section directs that the President *"in every possible instance shall consult with the leadership and appropriate committees of the Congress before committing United States Armed Forces to hostilities or to situations where hostilities may be imminent....*

The use of the word "every" reflects the committee's belief that such consultation *prior* to the commitment of armed forces should be inclusive. In other words, it should apply in extraordinary and emergency circumstances—even when it is not possible to get formal congressional approval in the form of a declaration of war or other specific authorization. At the same time, through use of the word "possible" it recognizes that a situation may be so dire, e.g. hostile missile attack underway, and require such instantaneous action that no prior consultation will be possible....

The second element of section 2 relates to situations *after* a commitment of forces has been made (with or without prior consultation). In that instance, it imposes upon the President, through use of the word "shall," the obligation to *"consult regularly...."*

A considerable amount of attention was given to the definition of *consultation.* Rejected was the notion that consultation should be synonymous with merely being informed. Rather, consultation in this provision means that a decision is pending on a problem and that Members of Congress are being asked by the President for their advice and opinions and, in appropriate circumstances, their approval of action contemplated. Furthermore, for consultation to be meaningful, the President himself must participate and all information relevant to the situation must be made available.

In the context of this and following sections of the resolution, a *commitment* of armed forces commences when the President makes the final decision to act and issues orders putting that decision into effect.

The word *hostilities* was substituted for the phrase *armed conflict* during the subcommittee drafting process because it was considered to be somewhat broader in scope. In addition to a situation in which fighting actually has begun, *hostilities* also encompasses a state of confrontation in which no shots have been fired but where there is a clear and present danger of armed conflict. *"Imminent hostilities"* denotes a situation in which there is a clear potential either for such a state of confrontation or for actual armed conflict.

· · ·

Explanation by Senator Jacob Javits of the Conference Report

Congressional Record, October 10, 1973, p. 33549

Consultation

Section 3, the provisions establishing a statutory requirement of advance consultation as well as continuing consultation with the Congress, [is] to be read as maximal rather than minimal. The consultation requirement is not discretionary for the President; he is obliged by law to consult before the introduction of forces into hostilities and to continue consultations so long as the troops are engaged. This section does take account of the contingency that there may be instances of such great suddenness in which it is not possible to consult in advance....

It is important to note that, while consultation is a statutorily established requirement in this legislation, the President does not acquire or derive any authority respecting the use of the Armed Forces through the consultation process per se— although "consultation" may lead to a declaration of war or the enactment of specific statutory authorization. In other words, consultation is not a substitute for specific statutory authorization.

Section 3 is rather intended to reestablish the historic, consultative tradition between the executive and the Congress respecting foreign affairs and international security matters, which has generally prevailed throughout our Nation's history. The breakdown in recent years of this consultative tradition has contributed heavily to strains between the executive and the Congress, and in my judgment is an important contributory element in the constitutional crisis now confronting our Nation with respect to the war powers.

Questions on the War Powers Resolution

1. As a general matter, is Congress constitutionally empowered to define its own and the President's war powers? *See* Carter, *The Constitutionality of the War Powers Resolution*, 70 Va. L. Rev. 101 (1984). If so, are any of the provisions of the War

Powers Resolution constitutionally objectionable on their face: the cataloguing of the President's powers; the consultation requirements; the reporting requirements; the 60-day cut-off provisions; the legislative veto provision? How does section 8(d)(1), added in conference, affect the constitutionality of section (2)(c)? How does it affect the impact of (2)(c)?

2. Is the legislative veto provision constitutional after *Chadha*? If not, how would you rule on the severability question? *See* Comment, *Congressional Control of Presidential War-Making Under the War Powers Act: The Status of a Legislative Veto after* Chadha, 132 U. Pa. L. Rev. 1217 (1984).

3. Do you view the 60-day cutoff provisions as wise on foreign policy grounds?

4. Note that the circumstances Congress describes in section 2(c) of the resolution as permitting the President to introduce U.S. armed forces into hostilities do not concede any general authority to use military force for the protection of U.S. persons and property abroad. Presidents, however, have asserted such power, relying on 19th century precedent. Consider the following excerpt from a massive treatise on the Constitution produced by the Congressional Research Service in the Library of Congress, The Constitution of the United States of America: Analysis and Interpretation, S. Doc. No. 82, 92d Cong., 2d Sess. 562-63 (1973):

> In 1854, one Lieutenant Hollins, in command of a United States warship, bombarded the town of Greytown, Nicaragua because of the refusal of local authorities to pay reparations for an attack by a mob on the United States consul. Upon his return to the United States, Hollins was sued in a federal court by Durand for the value of certain property which was alleged to have been destroyed in the bombardment. His defense was based upon the orders of the President and Secretary of the Navy and was sustained by Justice Nelson, on circuit.[2] "As the Executive head of the nation, the President is made the only legitimate organ of the General Government, to open and carry on correspondence or negotiations with foreign nations, in matters concerning the interests of the country or of its citizens. It is to him, also, the citizens abroad must look for protection of person and of property, and for the faithful execution of the laws existing and intended for their protection. . . .
>
> "Now, as it respects the interposition of the Executive abroad, for the protection of the lives or property of the citizen, the duty must, of necessity, rest in the discretion of the President. Acts of lawless violence, or of threatened violence to the citizen or his property, cannot be anticipated and provided for; and the protection, to be effectual or of any avail, may, not unfrequently, require the most prompt and decided action. Under our system of Government, the citizen abroad is as much entitled to protection as the citizen at home. The great object and duty of Government is the protection of the lives, liberty, and property of the people composing it, whether abroad or at home; and any Government failing in the accomplishment of the object, or the performance of the duty, is not worth preserving."

This incident and this case were but two items in the 19th century advance of the concept that the President had the duty and the responsibility to protect American lives and property abroad through the use of armed forces if deemed

---

2. *Durand v. Hollins*, 8 Fed. Cas. 111 (No. 4186) (C.C.S.D.N.Y. 1860).

necessary.[4] The duty could be said to grow out of the inherent powers of the Chief Executive or perhaps out of his obligation to "take Care that the Laws be faithfully executed." Although there were efforts made at times to limit this presidential power narrowly to the protection of persons and property rather than to the promotion of broader national interests,[7] no such distinction was observed in practice and so grew the concepts which have become the source of serious national controversy in the 1960's and 1970's, the power of the President to use troops abroad to observe national commitments and protect the national interest without seeking prior approval from Congress.[8]

See also In re Neagle, 135 U.S. 1 (1890), excerpted in Chapter Five. Should Congress have included the general protection of U.S. persons and property abroad as a constitutionally sufficient ground for presidential use of military force? If the President has any such power, does its omission from section 2 render the resolution unconstitutional? Why not? (Note that Presidents have taken the position that War Powers Resolution is simply inapplicable to military actions for the protection of U.S. persons and property abroad.)

5. For an intriguing set of essays analyzing the implications of the separation of powers for nuclear warfare, partly against the backdrop of Congress' experience with the War Powers Resolution, *see* First Use of Nuclear Weapons: Under the Constitution, Who Decides? (P. Raven-Hansen, ed. 1987). A helpful bibliography of war powers literature generally appears *id*. at 233-242.

b. Implementation

At least as controversial as the enactment itself of the War Powers Resolution is the debate whether its implementation has had any salutary effect on the distribution of war powers between Congress and the President. The thoughtful published perspectives on this issue include Glennon, *The War Powers Resolution Ten Years Later: More Politics Than Law*, 78 Am. J. Int'l L. 71 (1984); Note, *A Defense of the War Powers Resolution*, 93 Yale L. J. 1330 (1984); Note, *The Future of the War Powers Resolution*, 36 Stan. L. Rev. 1407 (1984); Note, *The War Powers Resolution: A Tool for Balancing Power Through Negotiation*, 70 Va. L. Rev. 1037 (1974); Symposium, *The War Powers Resolution*, 17 Loyola L.A. L. Rev. 579 (1984); and Vance, *Striking the Balance: Congress and the President Under the War Powers Resolution*, 133 U. Pa. L. Rev. 79 (1984).

The first formal invocation of the Resolution came in 1975, when President Ford had three occasions to file brief reports with Congress concerning the evacuation of U.S. citizens from Cambodia and from Saigon, and the seizure of the *S.S. Mayaguez*,

---

4. *See* United States Solicitor of the Department of State, *Right to Protect Citizens in Foreign Countries by Landing Forces* (Washington: 3d. rev. ed. 1934); M. Offutt, *The Protection of Citizens Abroad by the Armed Forces of the United States* (Baltimore: 1928).

7. E. Corwin, *The President: Office and Powers 1787-1957* (New York: 4th ed. 1957), 198-201.

8. In 1965, President Johnson landed troops in the Dominican Republic during a revolution, assertedly to protect the lives of United States citizens threatened by the rebels, 52 Dept. State Bull. 738 (1965), but no doubt also to serve other interests, i.e., "to help prevent another Communist state in this hemisphere." Id., 743. It should be noted that after evacuation of United States citizens had been completed, the United States military presence was increased from 400 Marines to over 20,000 troops. *New York Times*, September 5, 1965, p. 1, col. 4.

a U.S. merchant vessel. Each of these reports was facially consistent with obligations imposed on the President by Section 4 of the War Powers Resolution, although none of the reports conceded the authority of Congress to impose such requirements. Furthermore, some members of Congress complained that the reports and the limited Congressional consultation that preceded them did not represent a serious effort by the executive branch to involve Congress in military decision making. Former New York Senator Jacob Javits, a primary author of the War Powers Resolution, testified before a congressional committee:

> To a disturbing extent, consultations with the Congress prior to the Mayaguez incident resembled the old, discredited practice of informing selected members of Congress a few hours in advance at the implementation of decisions already taken within the Executive Branch. It is unclear whether this relapse was from force of habit or was calculated to test the mettle and resoluteness of the Congress.

War Powers: A Test of Compliance—Relative to the Danang Sealift, the Evacuation of Phnom Penh, the Evacuation of Saigon, and the Mayaguez Incident, Hearings Before the House Comm. on Int'l Rel., 94th Cong., 1st Sess. 61 (1975). The seriousness of the executive branch's commitment to the War Powers Resolution process was further called into question regarding President Carter's decision to attempt a military rescue in 1980 of American hostages held in Iran. The President's report to Congress and his counsel's legal opinion on the requirement for consultation with Congress follow.

1.) Iranian Hostage Rescue Attempt

President Carter's Report to Speaker O'Neill Concerning the Abortive Rescue Attempt in Iran (Apr. 26, 1980)

Public Papers of the Presidents: Jimmy Carter, 1980-81, at 777

Dear Mr. Speaker: Because of my desire that Congress be informed on this matter and consistent with the reporting provisions of the War Powers Resolution of 1973 (Public Law 93-148), I submit this report.

On April 24, 1980, elements of the United States Armed Forces under my direction commenced the positioning stage of a rescue operation which was designed, if the subsequent stages had been executed, to effect the rescue of the American hostages who have been held captive in Iran since November 4, 1979, in clear violation of international law and the norms of civilized conduct among nations. The subsequent phases of the operation were not executed. Instead, for the reasons described below, all these elements were withdrawn from Iran and no hostilities occurred.

The sole objective of the operation that actually occurred was to position the rescue team for the subsequent effort to withdraw the American hostages. The rescue team was under my overall command and control and required my approval before executing the subsequent phases of the operation designed to effect the rescue itself. . . .

Beginning approximately 10:30 AM EST on April 24, six U.S. C-130 transport aircraft and eight RH-53 helicopters entered Iran airspace. Their crews were not equipped for combat. Some of the C-130 aircraft carried a force of approximately 90 members of the rescue team equipped for combat, plus various support personnel.

From approximately 2 to 4 PM EST the six transports and six of the eight helicopters landed at a remote desert site in Iran approximately 200 miles from Teheran where they disembarked the rescue, commenced refueling operations and began to prepare for the subsequent phases.

During the flight to the remote desert site, two of the eight helicopters developed operating difficulties. . . . Of the six helicopters which landed at the remote desert site, one developed a serious hydraulic problem and was unable to continue with the mission. The operational plans called for a minimum of six helicopters in good operational condition able to proceed from the desert site. . . . When the number of helicopters available to continue dropped to five, . . . I decided to cancel the mission and ordered the United States Armed Forces involved to return from Iran.

During the process of withdrawal, one of the helicopters accidentally collided with one of the C-130 aircraft, which was preparing to take off, resulting in the death of eight personnel and the injury of several others. At this point, the decision was made to load all surviving personnel aboard the remaining C-130 aircraft and to abandon the remaining helicopters at the landing site. . . . No United States Armed Forces remain in Iran.

The remote desert area was selected to conceal this phase of the mission from discovery. At no time during the temporary presence of United States Armed Forces in Iran did they encounter Iranian forces of any type. . . .

At one point during the period in which United States Armed Forces elements were on the ground at the desert landing site a bus containing forty-four Iranian civilians happened to pass along a nearby road. The bus was stopped and then disabled. Its occupants were detained by United States Armed Forces elements until their departure, and then released unharmed. One truck closely followed by a second vehicle also passed by while United States Armed Forces elements were on the ground. These elements stopped the truck by a shot into its headlights. The driver ran to the second vehicle which then escaped across the desert. Neither of these incidents affected the subsequent decision to terminate the mission.

Our rescue team knew, and I knew, that the operation was certain to be dangerous. We were all convinced that if and when the rescue phase of the operation had been commenced, it had an excellent chance of success. . . . The mission on which they were embarked was a humanitarian mission. It was not directed against Iran. It was not directed against the people of Iran. It caused no Iranian casualties.

This operation was ordered and conducted pursuant to the President's powers under the Constitution as Chief Executive and as Commander-in-Chief of the United States Armed Forces, expressly recognized in Section 8(d)(1) of the War Powers Resolution. In carrying out this operation, the United States was acting wholly within its right, in accordance with Article 51 of the United Nations Charter, to protect and rescue its citizens where the government of the territory in which they are located is unable or unwilling to protect them.

Sincerely, Jimmy Carter.

Legal Opinion by Lloyd Cutler, President's Counsel, on War Powers Consultation Relative to the Iran Rescue Mission (May 9, 1980)

Subcomm. on Int'l Security and Scientific Affairs of the House Comm. on Foreign Affairs, War Powers Resolution: Relevant Documents, Correspondence, Reports, 98th Cong., 1st Sess. 50 (1983)

1. In my opinion, the President's decision to use the armed forces in an attempt to rescue the American hostages in Iran, without consulting Congress before taking this action, was a lawful exercise of his constitutional powers as President and Commander-in-Chief, and did not violate the War Powers Resolution of 1973.

2. The President's constitutional power to use the armed forces to rescue Americans illegally detained abroad is clearly established. *In re Neagle*, 135 U.S. 1, *Durand v. Hollins*, 8 Fed. Cases 111. This power was expressly recognized in the Senate version of the War Powers Resolution, and is not negated by the final version of the Resolution, especially where, as here, those to be rescued include United States Marines.

3. His inherent constitutional power to conduct this kind of rescue operation, which depends on total surprise, includes the power to act before consulting Congress, if the President concludes, as he did in this case, that to do so would unreasonably endanger the success of the operation and the safety of those to be rescued.

4. Section 3 of the War Powers Resolution does require consulting with Congress "in every possible instance" before introducing United States Armed Forces into "hostilities or into situations where imminent involvement in hostilities is clearly indicated by the circumstances." In this case, the first stage of the operation—introducing the rescue team into Iran during the night of April 24—did not involve any hostilities. The rescue effort itself was not to be initiated before the following night, and could have been aborted before any involvement in hostilities was "clearly indicated," and this is in fact what occurred.

5. In any event, Section 8(d)(1) of the War Powers Resolution provides that nothing in it "is intended to alter the constitutional authority of the Congress or of the President." If Section 3 were read to require prior consultation in these precise circumstances—where the President has inherent constitutional authority to conduct a rescue operation dependent on surprise and reasonable ground to believe that prior consultation would unreasonably endanger the success of the operation and the safety of those to be rescued—this would raise grave issues as to the constitutionality of Section 3. Since statutes and joint resolutions are to be read where possible in a manner that does not raise such grave constitutional issues, Section 3 and Section 8(d)(1), read together, should not be construed to require prior consultation under the precise circumstances of this case.

————————

Do you agree with the Cutler opinion? In particular, is there force to his argument in paragraph 5? If so, how far does the argument extend?

2.) Case Study: Lebanon

The most serious controversy during the Reagan Administration concerning the War Powers Resolution concerned the President's authority to deploy Marines in Lebanon to help stabilize the Lebanese Government:

The Administration decided in August 1982, to send a contingent of U.S. Marines to Beirut as part of a multinational force to help facilitate the PLO's evacuation from the Lebanese capital. On August 20, 1982, following consultations with President Reagan on the use of U.S. forces in such a role, Senators Percy and Pell wrote to the President, recommending that he report this deployment under Section 4(a)(1) of the War Powers Resolution. On August 21, 800 French troops arrived, the first contingent of the Multinational Forces (MNF), and on August 25, 800 U.S. Marines landed in Beirut. President Reagan reported to the Congress "consistent with the War Powers Resolution" but stated the Marines would not be in a hostile situation and would be withdrawn within 30 days. . . . On September 11, the Marines were withdrawn.

On September 16, President Bashir Gemayal of Lebanon was assassinated, and on September 16-18, a massacre took place at the Sabra and Shatila Palestinian refugee camps. President Reagan announced on September 21 that U.S. Marines would return to Lebanon as part of an international force. On September 24, Senators Percy and Pell again wrote to the President recommending that the reintroduction of U.S. troops be reported under Section 4(a)(1). On September 29, U.S. Marines took over the Beirut airport area and President Reagan submitted a report "consistent with the War Powers Resolution" but insisting that the Marines were "not expected to become engaged in hostilities." On December 15, 1982, 14 Committee Members wrote to the President to say they "would expect Congress to be involved at the earliest possible stage . . . and that formal Congressional authorization would be sought before undertaking long-term or expanded commitments or extending indefinitely the present level of operations."

S. Rept. No. 98-242, 98th Cong., 1st Sess. 1-2 (1983).

Over a year after the Marines' initial deployment (and after appropriating $151 million in economic and military assistance for Lebanon), Congress enacted the Multinational Force in Lebanon Resolution, Pub. L. 98-119, 97 Stat. 805 (1983), which both authorized the continued use of U.S. armed forces, expressly under the War Powers Resolution, and provided that such authority would expire in 18 months. As you read the Resolution, the President's signing statement, and the excerpts from the Senate Foreign Relations Committee report, which follow, how do you evaluate the utility of the War Powers Resolution? Do political momentum and the capacity for initiative so favor the President that the Resolution is doomed to be ineffective in controlling Presidential use of military force? Could it be argued that the 1983 resolution on Lebanon represents a significant victory for congressional government, in that it represents a formal assertion of congressional control, which the President signed into law? Is yet a third hypothesis possible—that the War Powers Resolution is effective chiefly because its existence necessarily prompts Congress to engage with the President in vigorous negotiations over the use of military force—negotiations which may or may not ultimately constrain Presidential authority, but which heighten the degree of accountability and consensus underlying the President's policies?

Readers should recall that, within two weeks after the President signed the Resolution, 241 U.S. Marines were killed in an attack on Marine barracks at the Beirut airport. Further casualties and mounting public and congressional criticism of U.S. policy resulted in an offshore evacuation of the Marines in February, 1984, and their withdrawal less than two months later from the Multinational Force.

Multinational Force in Lebanon Resolution*
Pub. L. No. 98-119, 97 Stat. 805 (1983)

. . .

FINDINGS AND PURPOSE
SEC. 2.(a) The Congress finds that—

. . .

(5) United States Armed Forces participating in the Multinational Force in Lebanon are now in hostilities requiring authorization of their continued presence under the War Powers Resolution.

(b) The Congress determines that the requirements of section 4(a)(1) of the War Powers Resolution became operative on August 29, 1983. Consistent with section 5(b) of the War Powers Resolution, the purpose of this joint resolution is to authorize the continued participation of United States Armed Forces in the Multinational Force in Lebanon.

(c) The Congress intends this joint resolution to constitute the necessary specific statutory authorization under the War Powers Resolution for continued participation by United States Armed Forces in the Multinational Force in Lebanon.

AUTHORIZATION FOR CONTINUED PARTICIPATION OF UNITED STATES ARMED FORCES IN THE MULTINATIONAL FORCE IN LEBANON

SEC. 3. The President is authorized, for purposes of section 5(b) of the War Powers Resolution, to continue participation by United States Armed Forces in the Multinational Force in Lebanon, subject to the provisions of section 6 of this joint resolution. Such participation shall be limited to performance of the functions, and shall be subject to the limitations, specified in the agreement establishing the Multinational Force in Lebanon as set forth in the exchange of letters between the Governments of the United States and Lebanon dated September 25, 1982, except that this shall not preclude such protective measures as may be necessary to ensure the safety of the Multinational Force in Lebanon.

. . .

STATEMENTS OF POLICY

SEC. 5. (a) The Congress declares that the participation of the armed forces of other countries in the Multinational Force in Lebanon is essential to maintain the international character of the peacekeeping function in Lebanon.

(b) The Congress believes that it should continue to be the policy of the United States to promote continuing discussions with Israel, Syria, and Lebanon with the objective of bringing about the withdrawal of all foreign troops from Lebanon and establishing an environment which will permit the Lebanese Armed Forces to carry out their responsibilities in the Beirut area.

---

*Additional text to this resolution appears in the Appendix, *infra*.

(c) It is the sense of the Congress that, not later than one year after the date of enactment of this joint resolution and at least once a year thereafter, the United States should discuss with the other members of the Security Council of the United Nations the establishment of a United Nations peacekeeping force to assume the responsibilities of the Multinational Force in Lebanon. An analysis of the implications of the response to such discussions for the continuation of the Multinational Force in Lebanon shall be included in the reports required under paragraph (3) of section 4 of this resolution.

DURATION OF AUTHORIZATION FOR UNITED STATES PARTICIPATION IN THE MULTINATIONAL FORCE IN LEBANON

SEC. 6. The participation of United States Armed Forces in the Multinational Force in Lebanon shall be authorized for purposes of the War Powers Resolution until the end of the eighteen-month period beginning on the date of enactment of this resolution unless the Congress extends such authorization, except that such authorization shall terminate sooner upon the occurrence of any one of the following:

(1) the withdrawal of all foreign forces from Lebanon, unless the President determines and certifies to the Congress that continued United States Armed Forces participation in the Multinational Force in Lebanon is required after such withdrawal in order to accomplish the purposes specified in the September 25, 1982, exchange of letters providing for the establishment of the Multinational Force in Lebanon; or

(2) the assumption by the United Nations or the Government of Lebanon of the responsibilities of the Multinational Force in Lebanon; or

(3) the implementation of other effective security arrangements in the area; or

(4) the withdrawal of all other countries from participation in the Multinational Force in Lebanon.

· · ·

President Reagan's Signing Statement on Multinational Force in Lebanon Resolution (Oct. 12, 1983)

Papers of the Presidents: Ronald Reagan, 1983, at 1444

I am pleased to sign into law today S.J. Res. 159, the Multinational Force in Lebanon Resolution. This resolution provides important support for the United States presence and policies in Lebanon and facilitates the pursuit of United States interests in that region on the bipartisan basis that has been the traditional hallmark of American foreign policy. In my view, the participation and support of the Congress are exceedingly important on matters of such fundamental importance to our national security interests, particularly where United States Armed Forces have been deployed in support of our policy objectives abroad....

The text of this resolution states a number of congressional findings, determinations, and assertions on certain matters. It is, of course, entirely appropriate for Congress to express its views on these subjects in this manner. However, I do not necessarily join in or agree with some of these expressions. For example, with regard to the congressional determination that the requirements of section 4(a)(1) of the War Powers

Resolution became operative on August 29, 1983, I would note that the initiation of isolated or infrequent acts of violence against United States Armed Forces does not necessarily constitute actual or imminent involvement in hostilities, even if casualties to those forces result. I think it reasonable to recognize the inherent risk and imprudence of setting any precise formula for making such determinations....

There have been historic differences between the legislative and executive branches of government with respect to the wisdom and constitutionality of section 5(b) of the War Powers Resolution. That section purports to require termination of the use of United States Armed Forces...unless Congress, within 60 days, enacts a specific authorization for that use or otherwise extends the 60-day period. In light of these historic differences, I would like to emphasize my view that the imposition of such arbitrary and inflexible deadlines creates unwise limitations on Presidential authority to deploy United States Forces in the interests of United States national security. For example, such deadlines can undermine foreign policy judgments, adversely affect our ability to deploy United States Armed Forces in support of these judgments, and encourage hostile elements to maximize United States casualties in connection with such deployments.

I believe it is, therefore, important for me to state, in signing this resolution, that I do not and cannot cede any of the authority vested in me under the Constitution as President and as Commander in Chief of United States Armed Forces. Nor should my signing be viewed as any acknowledgment that the President's constitutional authority can be impermissibly infringed by statute, that congressional authorization would be required if and when the period specified in section 5(b) of the War Powers Resolution might be deemed to have been triggered and the period had expired, or that section 6 of the Multinational Force in Lebanon Resolution may be interpreted to revise the President's constitutional authority to deploy United States Armed Forces....

Multinational Force in Lebanon Resolution
S. Rept. No. 98-242, 98th Cong., 1st Sess. 1-18 (1983)

The Committee on Foreign Relations, to which was referred the joint resolution (S.J. Res. 159) having considered the same, reports favorably thereon....

BACKGROUND
... On March 1, 1983, Senator Percy introduced the Lebanon Emergency Assistance Act to provide $100 million in military aid loans and $150 million in economic aid to Lebanon. The Committee reported that bill on May 5 with a requirement that Congress authorize "any substantial change in the number or role of United States Armed Forces in Lebanon...." President Reagan signed it into law on June 27.

In mid-August of this year, fighting broke out between Lebanese Army units and Moslem militia men in South and West Beirut and on August 28, U.S. Marines at the Beirut airport came under fire for the first time. They returned fire, but there were no Marine casualties. However, on August 29, 2 U.S. Marines died and 14 were wounded by hostile shelling. The Marines returned fire, including the use of a helicopter gunship. On August 31, the Senate received a report from President Reagan "consistent with Section 4 of the War Powers Resolution," explaining the circumstances of the Marine casualties but expressing the view that the danger to U.S. forces would be temporary.

On September 3, Israel began its re-deployment to the Awali River. On September 4, heavy fighting broke out between Druze and Christian militia for control of the Chouf. President Reagan told Congressional leaders that the United States had no plans to commit additional troops. On September 6, two more U.S. Marines were killed and two wounded during shelling of the Beirut airport. On September 8, U.S. Navy ships were used to fire back at guns shelling Marine positions.

On September 12, Senator Mathias introduced S.J. Resolution 159, triggering the expedited procedures of Section 6 of the War Powers Resolution. On September 13, following heavy attacks by Druze, Syrian and Palestinian forces on strategic heights overlooking Beirut, the White House said the Marines are now authorized to call on naval and air power not only to defend themselves directly but also to aid other MNF forces and the Lebanese Army in certain circumstances. On September 14, Senator Byrd introduced S.J. Resolution 163, making a congressional determination that Section 4(a)(1) of the War Powers Resolution applied to the situation in Lebanon. On September 19, U.S. navy ships fired several hundred shells to help the Lebanese Army beat back attacks on Suq al Gharb, a mountain village on a strategic ridge near Beirut. On September 20, following negotiations with the White House and House Leaders, Senators Baker and Percy introduced S.J. Resolution 166. A companion measure was introduced in the House....

COMMITTEE COMMENTS

United States Policy in Lebanon

American objectives The Committee believes that Lebanon cannot be isolated from the wider issues of peace and security in the Middle East.... In a letter to the Congress on August 24, President Reagan stated that the deployment of the Marines would not in itself resolve the problems of Lebanon. Nevertheless, the Marines would improve the prospects for realizing our objectives in Lebanon: a permanent cessation of hostilities; establishment of a strong, representative central government; withdrawal of all foreign forces; restoration of control by the Lebanese Government throughout the country; and establishment of conditions under which Lebanon no longer can be used as a launching point for attacks against Israel.

These objectives remain the basis of our policy in Lebanon as outlined by Secretary Shultz before the Foreign Relations Committee on September 21, 1983. Similar objectives are cited in the resolution reported out by the Committee.

The Committee notes that a number of steps are being taken to attain these broad policy objectives. American participation in the multinational force is only one of these. Diplomacy remains the principal component, and the diplomatic efforts are supported by the peacekeeping efforts of the Multinational Force. While progress has not been as rapid as hoped for during the past year, important steps have been taken. In May, the Government of Israel and Lebanon with the assistance of the United States reached agreement on the withdrawal of Israeli forces from Lebanon. Unfortunately, Syria has not been willing to discuss the withdrawal of its forces despite a formal request from the Government of Lebanon.... [W]ith American encouragement, the Government of President Gemayal has begun the process of reconciliation with dissident segments of the population....

The Committee supports these attempts and believes the Government of Lebanon must represent fairly all communal and ethnic groups. Injustice and privilege must be eliminated, and security concerns alleviated, if the Lebanese will ever reassert national sovereignty.

The Committee also supports efforts to rebuild national institutions which were fractured by 8 years of civil conflict and foreign occupation. Foremost of these institutions is a truly national army. Much progress has been made in a relatively short period of time. Significant American aid has helped finance equipment for a mechanized brigade and American personnel have helped train several brigades. . . . The committee recognizes the difficulty of rebuilding a national Army in such a fragmented society and has no illusion that the task will be easily accomplished. The MNF provides important symbolic and other support for this task.

The role of the marines The Multinational Force, which includes a contingent of U.S. Marines, is another vehicle for implementing our broader policy objectives in Lebanon. The Committee agrees with Secretary Shultz's assurance that "it is not the mission of our Marines, or of the MNF as a whole, to maintain the military balance in Lebanon by themselves. . . . They are an important deterrent, a symbol of the international backing behind the legitimate Government of Lebanon. . . ."

The Committee understands that the role of the Marines is limited. The authorization of the presence of the Marines does not remove previous limitations on their deployment. Marine activities are restricted to the "Beirut area" and the number of Marine combat troops based onshore will remain approximately 1,200. The Resolution specifically states that it does not modify Section 4 of the Lebanese Emergency Assistance Act of 1983 which require congressional authorization for any substantial expansion in the number or role of the U.S. peacekeeping forces.

18-Month authorization The Committee voted to authorize the continued presence of U.S. forces for an additional 18 months rather than for a shorter period of 6 months. The debate centered on three issues: (1) would the shorter period place the Marines in a more dangerous position; (2) how would American policy objectives be affected by the shorter period; and (3) how would the congressional prerogatives be affected by a longer period.

The Executive Branch opposed any reference to a specific time period. The 18-month period was part of a compromise reached by the Majority Leadership of the Senate and House with the Executive Branch.

A strong concern was expressed that the compromise might fall apart if Congress imposed a shorter period. This concern prevailed in the Committee's deliberations. Senator Mathias observed that "we are dealing with a very delicate process here." The Senator expressed concern that the broad principles of the War Powers compromise might be abandoned and not reach the floor if the shorter 6-month period was adopted by the Committee. . . .

During the Committee's hearings and debate, witnesses and Members expressed fears that a shorter time period could result in increased hostile fire on the Marines and complicate the efforts to negotiate a ceasefire and political settlement.

Marine Corps Commandant Paul X. Kelley testified to the Committee on September 13 that a short time limit might stimulate more attacks on the Marines in an effort to encourage a public outcry for their withdrawal. He commented that "I am concerned that we could impose what could prove to be a dangerous time constraint that would be misread by our potential adversaries.... It would encourage hostile forces or forces inimical to the best interests, the life and limb of Marines. It would encourage them to be more provocative in an attempt to arouse public sentiment.... There still is a possibility that hostile forces would use this as an opportunity to up the ante against our Marines."

A great deal of concern was also expressed about how a short time period would be interpreted in the Middle East, especially in Damascus. The Syrians are aiding the Druze, who have been shelling Marine positions. Senator Percy said a 6-month time limit "might send a false signal which might encourage and place great incentive on the part of the Syrians to make attacks." Members warned that attacks might be increased in an effort to alter American opinions in advance of another debate over the extension of the forces 6 months from now.

A short time period also might encourage the anti-government forces to drag their feet in negotiations. The United States has been prodding the government of Amin Gemayal to take part in talks aimed at forming a broader government of conciliation. President Gemayal recently issued a call for such a conference. But the Syrians have been blocking these efforts, even vetoing the proposed participation of the Lebanese Prime Minister and Speaker of the House, both Muslims. Many believe the Syrians are stalling for time, hoping that continued military pressure on the Lebanese Army and on the Multinational Force will result in the military collapse of the former and the withdrawal of the latter.

Assistant Secretary of State Nicholas Veliotes described the diplomatic problem in the September 13 hearing, saying, "There would be no incentive on the part of those who oppose our policy in Lebanon to seek anything other than a series of violent confrontations, thinking to wait for the time limit and then influence American opinion in the Congress. We think that a six-month authorization would be a grave error."

By contrast, approval of an 18-month time period shows that the United States is willing to exercise patience as well as diplomacy, to give the peacekeeping efforts and negotiations a chance. Secretary of State Shultz testified on September 21 that "the 18-month period seemed like a long enough period so that you had some room for maneuver, and it had the effect of allowing people who were concerned both on the Congressional side of this constitutional issue and the Presidential side both to keep their principles intact." ...

In acting on the Resolution, the Committee also approved two amendments by Senator Mathias which provide Congress with additional check reins. Congress will receive reports from the Administration every 3 months on the current situation. More important, from the procedural view, the Resolution was amended to ensure that in the event a resolution to repeal the authorization is reported by this committee or the House Foreign Affairs Committee, it will be considered in each House under expedited procedures....

WAR POWERS

Applicability of the War Powers Resolution

(1) *Actual or imminent hostilities* Section 2(b) of this Resolution includes a Congressional determination that actual or imminent hostilities involving U.S. Armed Forces clearly came into being on August 29, 1983.

The President's report to the Congress describes the circumstances surrounding the heavy exchanges of fire on that date:

> On August 29, sporadic fighting between Lebanese Armed Forces and various armed factions took place in South Beirut; from time to time during the course of this fighting, positions in the vicinity of the Beirut airport manned by U.S. Marines of the MNF came under small-arms fire (without injury to U.S. personnel), and this fire was returned. On August 29, fighting erupted again. Marine positions came under mortar, rocket, and small-arms fire, with the result that two Marines were killed and fourteen wounded. In addition, several artillery rounds fell near the USS Iwo Jima (an amphibious support vessel lying offshore), with no resulting damage or injuries. As contemplated by their rules of engagement; U.S. Marines returned fire with artillery, small arms, and, in one instance, rocket fire from a helicopter gunship....

Such exchanges have continued, with additional casualties and fatalities, until the present. Naval gunfire support on specific locations has been carried out in an effort to protect our forces on the ground. In addition, tactical air support and reconnaissance has been authorized. Although there have been continuing efforts to arrange a ceasefire and to achieve a broader, more permanent arrangement which would reduce the occurrence or imminence of hostilities, there is no immediate indication that this situation will soon change significantly. Therefore, the hostile situation has been a continuing one.

In enacting the War Powers Resolution in 1973, Congress made little effort to go beyond the "plain meaning" of key terms "hostilities" and "situations where imminent involvement in hostilities is clearly indicated by the circumstances." These terms originated in the early Senate version of the Resolution and prompted little subsequent discussion. The House Foreign Affairs Committee later substituted them for its original phrase, "armed conflict," because the term "hostilities" was considered "somewhat broader in scope." "In addition to a situation in which fighting actually has begun," the Committee wrote, "hostilities also encompasses a state of confrontation in which no shots have been fired but where there is a clear and present danger of armed conflict."

In short, the exchange of fire with hostile forces would indicate an outbreak of hostilities, and a high probability of such exchanges would suggest "imminent involvement." Brief, non-recurring situations such as occasional sniper fire would not suggest the continuing dangers associated with an ongoing set of hostile circumstances.

Arguments have been made that a hostile situation was not indicated by the present circumstances because the Marines:

(a) Only returned rather than initiated fire;

(b) Acted only in self-defense;

(c) Remained essentially in one location, rather than taking offensive actions;

(d) Performed a mission of "peacekeeping," "presence," or "interposition".

However, there is nothing in the legislative history of the War Powers Act to indicate that any of these considerations would alter the fact that "hostilities" are indicated. ...Nor is it necessary or sufficient that fatalities occur in order to conclude that hostilities are involved.

(2) *Need for authorization or extension* The requirements of Section 5(b) of the War Powers Resolution speak for themselves. . . . Two points about this [section] should be emphasized, however. First, the actual submission of a report by the President is not a prerequisite to the operation of the requirement for an authorization. The language "submitted or is required to be submitted" was obviously intended to cover situations in which the required report is either not submitted at all or is submitted late. In other words, the President does not need to certify that a hostile situation is involved under Section 4 in order to be bound by the requirement for an authorization in Section 5.

Second, the available 30-day extension of the deadline is not simply a matter of Presidential discretion. The President must certify that he is in the course of withdrawing U.S. forces and needs the extra time in order to do so safely because of "unavoidable military necessity."

(3) *Congressional procedures* Assuming that hostilities involving U.S. forces can be said to have begun on August 29, the 60-day period began on August 31, since that is when the report would have been due. (It also happens to be the date on which the President's report of August 30 was actually submitted, which is the alternative starting point.) . . .

Under Section 6 of the War Powers Resolution, the Committee Resolution becomes the pending business in the Senate as soon as it is reported, after which the Senate has up to three calendar days to vote on it. Further procedures are prescribed to assure Committee and floor consideration by the House and a House-Senate Conference prior to the 60-day deadline. The House Foreign Affairs Committee approved a nearly identical resolution on September 22 by a vote of 30 to 6. . . .

Constitutional considerations

This is the first time since the enactment of the War Powers Resolution on November 7, 1973, that Congress has faced the task of considering a specific authorization for the involvement of U.S. Armed Forces in hostilities. The text and history of the War Powers Resolution provide little guidance as to how such an authorization should be drafted. . . .

(1) *Declaration of war analogy* One approach is to regard the task of Congress in enacting a specific authorization as similar to its function in declaring war. . . . By this analogy, the role of Congress is to decide the general question of whether a particular commitment of forces to hostilities in a given part of the world is worth the costs and risks expected from it. Once having exercised this broad judgment—and acting as a check upon Presidential excesses—Congress arguably should not seek to limit or direct the activities of the Armed Forces. Such decisions (so the argument might run) were meant to be exercised only by the President as Commander in Chief, under Article II, Section 2. Frustration with the efforts of the Continental Congress to prosecute the Revolutionary War and subsequent conflicts led the drafters of the Constitution to limit Congressional involvement to the power to "declare" rather than to "make" war as originally proposed. Thus, declarations of war have typically been brief, general statements, without time limits or other specific restrictions.

(2) *Legislative limitations* A different approach to the drafting of a specific authorization is to enact particular limitations or criteria which circumscribe the scope of the commitment. Such specifications might include the duration, location, size, cost and mission of U.S. deployments, as well as requirements based upon future

THE PRESIDENT AS COMMANDER IN CHIEF

developments. Presidents have traditionally resisted such constraints as infringements on the Commander in Chief power, but no definitive resolution of such questions has ever been achieved.

Members of Congress are therefore confronted with the need to decide a novel issue regarding the role appropriate of the legislative branch: how far should the Congress go in defining the authority being granted to the President in a situation of hostilities? Is it appropriate for Congress to try to predict, and to protect legislatively against, every foreseeable risk which our forces might encounter in their mission, or to anticipate and define each angle of Presidential flexibility to respond to events? Or is it part of the responsibility which Congress is insisting upon for itself under the Constitution to recognize the inevitable risks and costs of any foreign military involvement—and to accept such risks as part of the decision to approve its initiation or continuation?

Scope of Senate Joint Resolution 159

The authorization recommended by the Committee takes a middle ground on the question of general approval and specific limitations. While confining its terms to the mandate of the Multinational Force and preserving existing statutory provisions relating to "any substantial expansion in the number or role," the resolution recognizes the possible need for "protective measures to ensure the safety of the Multinational Force."

As Chairman of the Committee, Senator Percy, has argued, any suggestion that the terms of this authorization resemble the Tonkin Gulf Resolution of 1964 or amount to a "blank check" for Presidential actions is simply unfounded. The resolution is limited and specific in a number of respects.

(1) *Duration* Attention has focused on the 18-month duration of this proposed authorization, as if time limitations are the only effective measure of statutory restraints. Six months has become the benchmark of those who regard this proposal as a "blank check." In fact, however, any time limit is an arbitrary choice, having little to do with the events in Lebanon or the policy choices involved in maintaining a Multinational Force....

(2) *Active oversight* Whatever the time limits, the test of Congressional responsibility will be the degree to which Congress actively follows the situation in Lebanon and, if necessary, takes steps to adjust this authorization once it is enacted.... Congress must follow through in the exercise of its responsibilities through oversight and amendment. Such an approach is far preferable to restrictions which avoid the difficult choices and prevent the possibility of decision through inaction.

(3) *Limited mandate* The authorization contained in this resolution is limited to the functions of the Multinational Force in Lebanon. Section 6 of the resolution provides that U.S. participation "shall be subject to the limitations, specified in the agreement establishing the Multinational Force in Lebanon" of September 25, 1982....

Three principal limitations on the U.S. role are contained in that agreement: the number of U.S. troops will be approximately 1,200, they will operate in the Beirut area in support of the Lebanese Government, and they are not expected to perform a combat mission....

(4) *Protective measures* The Committee recognizes that performing the role of peacekeeping forces is a new and unfamiliar role, not only for the troops themselves,

but for the U.S. Government and the American public as well. Having to stand between
hostile forces in the same, sometimes vulnerable locations without taking and maintaining the offensive can be a difficult posture to maintain, particularly for United
States Marines. From time to time, U.S. forces must respond to direct attacks or take
protective actions for their own defense. The Committee does not believe that such
actions necessarily change the role of the U.S. forces, so long as the task of the U.S.
forces is not to duplicate or supplant the functions of the Lebanese Armed Forces or
to redeploy from the Beirut area, or in other respects to exceed the limited mandate
of the Multinational Force or the limitations of the Lebanon Emergency Assistance
Act of 1983.

From the outset of the Multinational Force, it has been assumed that the various
national contingents are part of a common effort. Therefore, not only do they have
the usual right to defend themselves, as recognized in the September 25 agreement,
but also a general responsibility to come to each other's assistance when called upon
to do so. The resolution therefore acknowledges the possible necessity of actions "to
ensure the safety" of other contingents of the Force.

(5) *Limitations on expansion* "Any substantial expansion in the number or role
in Lebanon of United States Armed Forces" would call into play the provision of
Section 4(a) of the Lebanon Emergency Assistance Act, requiring the President to
seek authorization for such expansion....

However, during the Committee's hearing on September 21 with Secretary of State
Shultz, some question arose as to whether the Reagan Administration felt constrained
by this provision.

> Senator SARBANES.... Is it the Administration's position that what they
> need to do is consult with the Congress, or that they need to obtain an au-
> thorization from the Congress, that they could not expand the number or role
> without a specific Congressional authorization?
>
> Secretary SHULTZ. I think the President, or perhaps any of you if you were
> President, thinking about your role, your Constitutional role as Commander in
> Chief, would be very reluctant to tie your hands and say that you could only
> order U.S. forces to do something or other after the Congress had authorized
> it.
>
> Senator SARBANES. So it is your position, then, that you could substantially
> expand them without a Congressional authorization?
>
> Secretary SHULTZ. The constitutional reservation goes to the President's role
> as Commander in Chief, and therefore to his capacity to be in charge of the
> deployment of the armed forces of the United States. I have no doubt that he
> will continue to assert that role.

The Committee is concerned that Secretary of State Shultz seemed reluctant to
accept the need for an authorization to expand substantially the number or role of
U.S. forces in Lebanon as required by law. That provision was adopted after very
careful deliberation by this Committee and on the basis of very clear assurances by
the Reagan Administration that it would seek an authorization for that purpose.
However, it is true, as the legislative history of this provision clearly reveals, that
Congress did not insist upon specific prior authorization for any such expansion in
numbers or role.... The Administration strongly opposed any such requirement and,

in the end, the Congress did not insist upon it. The following statement by Congressman Hamilton during the final debate on June 1 on a House-Senate compromise version of the bill, described the congressional interpretation of this provision:

> The requirement for congressional authorization is not meant to impede the performance of the limited functions currently being performed by the U.S. Marines in Beirut or to interfere with their ability to defend themselves if attacked. However, any decision to expand significantly the role in Lebanon of United States Armed Forces would require statutory authorization.

> If possible, the President should obtain authorization from the Congress before any significant change is made in the size or role of the U.S. forces in Lebanon. The Congress is aware, however, that in order to promote peace within Lebanon and fulfill international commitments, the deployment of a new or expanded peacekeeping force involving U.S. forces might be necessary prior to final passage of congressional authorization. However, congressional action should be obtained at the earliest possible time. In any case, the Congress expects full consultations by the executive branch with the Congress in a timely fashion should any change be contemplated in the size or role of U.S. forces in Lebanon, including any change in conjunction with the creation of a new peacekeeping force.

In its own final deliberations on this provision, the Committee acted on the basis of assurances contained in an April 20 letter from Deputy Secretary of State Kenneth Dam:

THE DEPUTY SECRETARY OF STATE,
Washington, April 20, 1983.

Hon. CHARLES H. PERCY,
Chairman, Committee on Foreign Relations,
U.S. Senate

DEAR MR. CHAIRMAN: I understand that the House Foreign Affairs Committee has adopted an amendment to the Lebanon supplemental which provides that the President shall obtain statutory authorization from the Congress with respect to the introduction of U.S. Armed Forces into Lebanon in conjunction with agreements for the withdrawal of foreign forces and the creation of a new multinational force. *I understand that this language was deliberately drafted so as not to interfere with the President's ability to begin such an introduction, if circumstances urgently require it, while Congress is considering his request for statutory authorization.*

Under these circumstances, the HFAC amendment correctly described what this administration intends to do, is consistent with what we have done in comparable situations in the past (such as the Sinai Multinational Force), and is therefore acceptable to us. *It is our intention to seek authorization from Congress as soon as possible following the completion of the ongoing negotiations, and we trust that Congress and the executive branch would then work expeditiously together with the objective of obtaining such authorization, if at all possible, prior to such new deployments.*

I strongly hope that your committee will not find it necessary to deal with this question in the context of section 4(a)(1) of the war powers resolution. It would be

highly premature and unwise, and potentially damaging to the integrity of the resolution, for Congress to prejudge the possible applicability of that section to future
arrangements which have not yet been negotiated and future circumstances which
cannot yet be predicted. Such an action, which would amount to a public finding that
U.S. forces will be exposed to an imminent risk of involvement in hostilities, is in no
way a foregone conclusion, and could give entirely the wrong public impression as
to what results these negotiations are intended to produce. Surely it would be far
preferable for Congress to reserve judgment on this matter (as we will) until it can
evaluate the circumstances as they develop, knowing that the provisions of the war
powers resolution will, of course, remain available.

I appreciate this opportunity to comment on your committee's work, and hope
that we can arrive at a result which accommodates our mutual interests in this matter.

Sincerely,

KENNETH W. DAM.

[Emphasis added.]

The Committee expects that the commitments made by the Administration on this
point will be kept.

Institutional accommodations

This resolution is the reflection of a delicate compromise, carefully constructed in
recognition of the firmly-held positions of both the legislative and executive branches
However, the Committee believes that the resolution is fully consistent with, and
supportive of, the constitutional role of Congress recognized in the War Powers
Resolution. As our former colleague Jacob Javits—the principal Senate author of the
War Powers Resolution—expressed it in a statement provided to all Members prior
to the markup:

> The Administration and the Congress have each gained a major point in the
> proposed compromise on the War Powers Resolution. Congress has established
> the proposition that it may set the clock running under the resolution even if
> the President does not trigger it by giving the appropriate notice under the
> proper section of the resolution when U.S. troops are deployed abroad into
> hostilities or the imminent threat of them. The President has gained the point
> that for the situation in Lebanon the authority Congress gives him to continue
> their involvement must be by joint not concurrent resolution, thereby, requiring
> the President's signature. This compromise avoids a constitutional crisis at this
> juncture. Though it may not settle the issue, it is an important step along the
> way.

MINORITY VIEWS

We strongly oppose the joint resolution on Lebanon sponsored by Senators Baker
and Percy and approved in the Foreign Relations Committee by a vote of 9-7. In our
judgment, its enactment would constitute (1) a dereliction of Congressional responsibility to uphold the principles and procedures of the War Powers Resolution of 1973;
(2) a failure to require of the Administration a clearly articulated and persuasive
statement of the mission which U.S. Marines have been deployed in Lebanon to
implement; and (3) an 18-month "blank check" under which the Administration
could pursue hitherto unspecified military objectives in Lebanon while asserting that

it is operating with full Congressional sanction. These gravely serious flaws warrant elaboration:

(1) *Dereliction of congressional responsibility relating to the War Powers Resolution* The Baker-Percy language has been presented as a "bipartisan compromise" which, in the interest of avoiding a dispute over "legalisms," would allow Congress and the executive to affirm principles which are in conflict. This would present, it is argued, a united front regarding U.S. policy in Lebanon.

We do not believe that the issues surrounding proper implementation of the War Powers Resolution are mere "legalisms." At issue are constitutional questions of immense gravity. The War Powers Resolution is law, a law passed over President Nixon's veto by overwhelming majorities in both houses. The reservations expressed by the executive branch about the resolution's constitutionality do not diminish or compromise its legal standing. In the absence of a Supreme Court ruling, only Congress can change or nullify that law. But by failing to demand adherence to obligations prescribed in the Resolution, Congress would abdicate its responsibility to uphold the law. In any event, Congress must not concede to the executive branch the contention that the War Powers Resolution is not binding in all of its particulars.

One approach, first proposed by Minority Leader Byrd and advocated in Committee by Senator Cranston, would have limited any joint resolution to a simple declaration that key provisions of section 4(a) of the War Powers Resolution were triggered by hostilities in Lebanon on August 29, 1983, which resulted in the deaths of 2 Marines. Enactment of such a resolution would not entail a withdrawal of U.S. forces from Lebanon. It would, however, achieve the essential result of affirming unmistakably the applicability of War Powers Resolution procedures, including the requirement for Congressional authorization for the maintenance of U.S. forces in Lebanon beyond 60-90 days. Unfortunately, this proposal was defeated in Committee by a vote of 9-7.

The determined unwillingness of the administration to recognize that the procedures stipulated by the War Powers Resolution are now in fact required became starkly evident during the Secretary of State's testimony before the Committee. Under questioning on September 21 about the relationship between the Baker-Percy resolution and future U.S. actions in Lebanon, Secretary Shultz was assiduously careful to reserve for the Commander in Chief a full range of options—regarding the scope of operations, the number of U.S. forces, and the duration of the involvement—even in disregard if necessary of the War Powers Resolution framework the Baker-Percy resolution would purportedly impose on the U.S. presence there. Congress cannot ignore what this means. The Administration is prepared to participate in a procedure which would give some appearance of creating a War Powers Resolution framework without really conceding that any such framework exists.

Not only is the War Powers Resolution the law; its applicability to the situation in Lebanon is manifest. Accordingly, we believe strongly that any resolution passed should allow no ambiguity as to whether the procedures set forth in the War Powers Resolution are required. By intentionally side-stepping the issue, the Baker-Percy resolution fails to meet that test.

(2) *The absence of a clearly defined policy* The constitutional ambiguity of the Baker-Percy resolution is paralleled by an alarming vagueness concerning the mission of the U.S. forces whose presence in Lebanon the resolution would purport to authorize. One year ago, on August 25, 1982, when U.S. Marines were first introduced

into Lebanon, their mission was limited and precise: to provide a temporary buffer that would allow the evacuation from Lebanon of elements of the Palestine Liberation Organization within a specified period of time. Shortly thereafter, when the Marines were reintroduced into Lebanon, they were deployed to perform, as part of a Multinational Force, the less precisely-worded mission set forth in the September 25, 1982, exchange of letters between the United States and Lebanese Governments. That agreement did, however, make clear that the U.S. military role would be confined to "the Beirut area" and would preclude involvement in combat.

While citing the September 25 agreement, the Baker-Perry resolution is drafted so as to be susceptible to an extremely broad—almost infinitely elastic—interpretation of the mission associated with the presence of the U.S. forces in Lebanon. The "purposes" cited in Section 2 include "the removal of all foreign forces from Lebanon" and the restoration of "full control by the Government of Lebanon over its own territory." Thus, over the period of 1 year, the stated mission of U.S. forces in Lebanon has expanded from a limited role, the feasibility of which Congress could evaluate, to a role too nebulous for Congress to evaluate and too far-reaching for U.S. military forces alone possibly to accomplish. Consequently, the effect of the resolution is to provide Congressional acquiescence in a policy involving American soldiers in a commitment the scope of which has yet to be defined even by its proponents.

A major advantage of the Byrd-Cranston proposal to invoke section 4(a)(1) of the War Powers Resolution is that it would require the Administration to submit for Congressional evaluation a clear statement of military mission. This the Baker-Percy resolution would not do. It is not an example of any "Vietnam syndrome" to find in that resolution a disturbing similarity to the "Gulf of Tonkin" resolution of 1964 which, being comparably vague and invoking the necessity of protecting American forces, was used by a different Administration to assert that it possessed Congressional support for an Indochina policy which proved to be one of ever-widening involvement.

(3) *An 18-month blank check* Since we take as serious the Administration's patent unwillingness to be bound by the stipulations of the War Powers Resolution, the duration of the Baker-Percy "authorization" is technically a moot point. Practically, however, a shorter "authorization" would at least require that Congress face again the issues—constitutional and policy—which Congress faces now but which the Baker-Percy formulation would allow it negligently to defer. Accordingly, we supported—but failed in a 9-8 vote to achieve—the substitution of a 6-month "authorization" period, after which these issues would again necessarily be joined if U.S. forces remain in Lebanon. We reject the argument that a time period shorter than 18 months will endanger the lives of American soldiers by inviting hostile action against them intended to sway U.S. public opinion against a continued U.S. presence. If the Administration had offered a clearly-defined mission in Lebanon for the U.S. Armed Forces and had also acknowledged its legal obligations under the War Powers Resolution, such a limited "authorization" might be unnecessary. But if the Baker-Percy formulation is to be adopted, it should certainly stipulate a duration short enough to require Congress to review soon the crucial questions surrounding the United States involvement in Lebanon. We believe in any case that to pass this resolution would represent a grave abdication of congressional responsibility.

CLAIBORNE PELL.

JOSEPH R. BIDEN, JR.

JOHN GLENN.

PAUL S. SARBANES, JR.

EDWARD ZORINSKY.

PAUL TSONGAS.

ALAN CRANSTON.

CHRISTOPHER J. DODD.

1. Why do the proponents of the Multinational Force in Lebanon Resolution view it as a significant assertion of congressional authority? Why do the opponents disagree? What is your assessment?

2. On what grounds, if any, could the executive argue that the resolution is unconstitutional? What is Congress' rebuttal?

3. Does it seem to you that the War Powers Resolution had any impact on the course of interbranch negotiation regarding Lebanon? Which event(s) in the history of Marine involvement in Lebanon should have been regarded as triggering the Resolution's procedural requirements? Was the President's report to Congress on September 29, 1982 already tardy? Did the Resolution play any different role from the role it played (if any) in the Iran rescue attempt? If you think so, why?

4. How does the committee report affect your assessment of President Nixon's opposition to the imposition of deadlines governing the availability of military force?

3.) *Note: Grenada, Libya, and the Persian Gulf*

Besides the Marine deployment in Lebanon, the most controversial uses of overt military force by the Reagan Administration occurred (1) on October 25, 1983, with the United States invasion of Grenada, (2) on April 14, 1986, with the bombing of targets in Libya; and (3) in connection with efforts through 1987 to protect Kuwaiti oil tankers from Iranian attack in the Persian Gulf.

Grenada. The Grenada invasion was a response to an unstable political situation prompted by the assassination a week earlier of Prime Minister Maurice Bishop. A new government was established under a "Revolutionary Military Council" under the leadership of the Army Commander General. The purported purposes of the invasion were to assist in restoring law and order to Grenada, and to protect approximately 1,000 Americans living on the island. The entire armed conflict lasted only a week, and all combat troops were removed by December 15, 1983.

Because of the brevity of the invasion, there was insufficient time for a Lebanon-like controversy with Congress to develop. For a largely negative answer, however, to the question whether the Administration respected the consultation and reporting requirements of the War Powers Resolution, *see* Rubner, *President Reagan, the War Powers Resolution, and Grenada*, 100 Pol. Sci. Q. 627 (1985-86). *See also* Committee on Grenada, *International Law and the United States Action in Grenada: A Report*, 18 Int'l Lawyer 331 (1984). A lawsuit brought by members of the House of Representatives challenging the invasion as unconstitutional was dismissed as moot. *Conyers v. Reagan*, 765 F.2d 1124 (D.C. Cir. 1985).

Of equal controversy was a decision by the Department of Defense to exclude the U.S. press from Grenada during the invasion. For two days, the press was kept away, assertedly to insure the success of the initial surprise attack and to protect the correspondents' safety. The White House subsequently admitted that the press ban was inappropriate and probably unnecessary for protecting the secrecy of the military operation. Although a subsequent law suit challenging the press ban was dismissed as moot, *Flynt v. Weinberger*, 588 F. Supp. 57 (D.D.C. 1984), *vacated in part, aff'd in part*, 762 F.2d 134 (D.C. Cir. 1985), the Defense Department responded to the Grenada experience by establishing a commission to recommend better means of handling press coverage during military emergencies. Following that panel's recommendations, the Defense Department designated a rotating pool of reporters who could be called at a moment's notice to cover military invasions or other unanticipated military operations.

Libya. The Libya bombing in April, 1986, followed a heightening of tension between Libya and the United States resulting from U.S. charges of Libyan-sponsored international terrorism and a naval confrontation in the Libyan-claimed Gulf of Sidra. President Reagan stated that he finally ordered the air strike against five military targets on April 16 after "irrefutable" proof linked Libya to sponsorship of an April 5 bombing of a Berlin discotheque, which killed an American soldier and wounded 50 others. The asserted rationale for the bombing was the national right of self-defense.

The Administration briefed about a dozen members of Congress concerning the attack several hours before the strike. At the time of the briefing, the U.S. Air Force planes involved in the strike had already left their bases in England; the Administration later said the planes would have been recalled in the face of any strong congressional objections to the plan. President Reagan sent a report to Congress on April 16, "consistent with the War Powers Resolution," formally noting the strike and its rationale. While the report satisfied some members of Congress that the War Powers Resolution had been respected, others charged that it amounted to mere notification and not the consultation that the Resolution requires.

In general, congressional reaction to the attack itself mixed support for retaliation against Libya with concern about the decisionmaking process that led to the attack. The latter concern, however, was not entirely in one direction. While some asserted the need for tightening the War Powers Resolution's consultation requirements, others called for new legislation expressly authorizing greater presidential flexibility in responding to asserted acts of international terrorism. One House member has argued that Congress' failure to invoke the resolution in connection with the Libya bombing— an initiative with consensus support—does not belie the resolution's potential force in the face of more controversial initiatives. Torricelli, *The War Powers Resolution After the Libya Crisis*, 7 Pace L. Rev. 661 (1987).

Persian Gulf. In December, 1986, Kuwait asked the United States for protection against attacks on its oil tankers in the Persian Gulf as a result of the Iran-Iraq war. In particular, Kuwait asked that the tankers be reflagged as the property of "shell" U.S. companies. Controversy over increased U.S. naval involvement in the Gulf mounted sharply, however, when an Iraqi warplane on May 21, 1987 accidentally attacked a frigate, the *USS Stark*, killing 37 on board. The Reagan Administration announced it would postpone reflagging, which did not occur until late July. *See* Overview of the Situation in the Persian Gulf, Hearings and Markup Before the House Comm. on Foreign Affairs, 100th Cong., 1st Sess. (1987).

Despite mine damage to a reflagged tanker and a U.S. helicopter attack on an Iranian minelaying ship, the Administration refused to concede the applicability of the War Powers Resolution. By October, 1987, legislative measures to invoke the War Powers Resolution or otherwise to control the U.S. reflagging program had failed to pass more than one House. After an October 16 Iranian missile attack on a reflagged tanker and the retaliatory destruction by the U.S. of an Iranian oil platform three days later, however, the Senate voted on October 21, 1987 to require the President to report within 30 days on the status of the reflagging program, which would trigger Congress's consideration, within another 30 days, of an expedited joint resolution on U.S. policy in the Gulf. S.J. Res. 194, 100th Cong., 1st Sess. (1987), *reprinted in* 133 Cong. Rec. S14657-58 (daily ed. Oct. 21, 1987). For a helpful chronology, *see* Towell, *Senate Shows Its Ambivalence in Votes on Gulf*, 46 Cong. Q. Weekly Rep. 2595 (1987). By November, Congress's unwillingness or inability to use the War Powers Resolution effectively to assert Congress's voice in Persian Gulf policymaking had raised obvious questions as to its utility. Cohen, *Making War*, 19 Nat'l J. 2516 (1987). On December 18, 1987, a D.C. district Court judge dismissed as nonjusticiable a suit by 111 Democratic members of Congress to enjoin presidential compliance with the Act.

What lessons, if any, do you draw from these episodes as to the importance of the War Powers Resolution? Does it serve any function? Could it? How, if at all, could the process be improved, if you think it needs improvement? What are the prospects for congressional enforcement of the Resolution through litigation? Recall the earlier discussions of the political question doctrine and of congressional standing.

4.) *Note: Covert Warmaking and the Neutrality Act*

The legislative history of the War Powers Resolution makes clear that it addresses only conventional military operations—the introduction by the President of "United States Armed Forces" into hostilities or situations where hostilities are imminent. Increasingly, however, the twentieth century has witnessed the growth of covert paramilitary action as a tool of U.S. foreign policy. This phenomenon poses equally profound questions as to the proper allocation of constitutional responsibility for national policymaking.

As in foreign policy (see the discussion of the Logan Act in Chapter Six), Congress early attempted by statute to secure a government monopoly over military policy. In 1794, Congress adopted the Neutrality Act, which provides in its current form:

> Whoever, within the United States, knowingly begins or sets on foot or provides or prepares a means for or furnishes the money for, or takes part in, any military or naval expedition or enterprise to be carried on from thence against the territory or dominion of any foreign prince or state, or of any colony, district, or people with whom the United States is at peace, shall be fined not more than $3,000 or imprisoned not more than three years, or both.

18 U.S.C. § 960 (1982).

The Neutrality Act, unlike the Logan Act, has been the basis of criminal prosecutions, as recently as 1985. *United States v. Ramirez*, 765 F.2d 438 (5th Cir. 1985), *cert. denied*, 474 U.S. 1063 (1986) (dismissing selective prosecution challenge to conviction for Neutrality Act violations directed at Cuba and Nicaragua). Undoubtedly, the most famous of these was the prosecution of Aaron Burr for allegedly preparing a military expedition against Mexico. *United States v. Burr*, 25 F. Cas. 201 (C.C.D. Va. 1807) (No. 14,694a) (upholding indictment as charging acts violative of Neutrality Act).

Besides their differing histories, there is arguably an important difference between the constitutional underpinnings of the two acts. The Logan Act, in proscribing the private conduct of foreign diplomacy, protects *executive* management of foreign policy. Private persons who secure from the State Department the "authority of the United States" to communicate with foreign governments do not run afoul of the Act. 18 U.S.C. § 963. The President is thus protected against interference with his initiatives by unauthorized private persons, but has flexibility under the Act regarding the deployment of private persons to assist in those initiatives.

The Neutrality Act, however, is a blanket prohibition against the conduct of military operations against countries with which the United States is at peace. The difference in wording likely reflects an early understanding (persisting through the Act's several reenactments) that the Act's function was to protect Congress' control of military policy. This inference is buttressed by the date of the statutory enactment—a time roughly contemporaneous with the original decision to vest in Congress the power to declare war, and a time during which Congress (and the Continental Congress before it) exercised its power to issue "Letters of Marque and Reprisal," U.S. Const., art. I, § 8, cl. 11. These letters were instruments authorizing private persons to conduct military hostilities for the United States. For a comprehensive review of the "letters of marque and reprisal" power and its current implications for covert warmaking, *see* Lobel, *Covert War and Congressional Authority: Hidden War and Forgotten Power*, 134 U. Pa. L. Rev. 1035 (1986). For an equally global treatment of the history and interpretation of the Neutrality Act, *see* Lobel, *The Rise and Decline of the Neutrality Act: Sovereignty and Congressional War Powers in United States Foreign Policy*, 24 Harv. Int'l L. J. 1 (1983).

If this analysis of the Neutrality Act and its underlying theory is correct, an important issue arises whether the Act circumscribes covert warmaking by government officials, even with presidential backing. A corollary issue is whether such a prohibition could be enforced effectively. The Ninth Circuit has held that a member of Congress and private citizens lack standing to secure review of an Attorney General decision under the Ethics in Government Act not to seek the appointment of independent counsel to investigate alleged Neutrality Act violations by government officials making war against Nicaragua. *Dellums v. Smith*, 797 F.2d 817 (9th Cir. 1986), *rev'g*, 573 F. Supp. 1489 (N.D. Cal. 1983). Likewise, the District of Columbia Circuit has barred private suits under the Neutrality Act for damages or injunctive relief. *Sanchez-Espinoza v. Reagan*, 770 F.2d 202 (D.C. Cir. 1985).

In your view, is the Neutrality Act relevant to an assessment whether the President may lawfully authorize covert paramilitary operations? Whether he may engage in fund-raising from private parties and third countries to support such operations? Are your answers any different with respect to actions by the Director of Central Intelligence, the National Security Adviser, or one of their ambitious subordinates, should they conduct a paramilitary operation that is not revealed to the President?

B. DOMESTIC PRESIDENTIAL POWERS IN WARTIME

1. Civil Liberties

No crisis in U.S. history has more forcefully threatened the Constitution than our civil war, and no war has gone further in testing the limits of presidential emergency powers. *See generally* J.G. Randall, Constitutional Problems Under Lincoln (1963). The most celebrated of Lincoln's invocations of emergency power is the Emancipation Proclamation of January 1, 1863, by which the President purported to free all persons held as slaves in the Confederate states. That proclamation, reprinted in the Appendix, *infra*, rested on Lincoln's power "as commander-in-chief of the army and navy ... [to employ] a fit and necessary war measure for suppressing ... rebellion...." 12 Stat. 1268 (1861). Against arguments that the proclamation was an unauthorized taking of private property without just compensation, supporters urged that the rights of belligerents, which belonged to the government under *The Prize Cases*, *supra*, included the right to free an enemy's slaves. *See generally* Randall, *supra*, at 371-404.

Another source of profound controversy was Lincoln's decision in 1861 to suspend "the privilege of the writ of *habeas corpus*." U.S. Const., art. I, § 9, par. 2. The legal issue was not whether the privilege could be suspended; the Constitution expressly authorizes suspension "when in cases of rebellion or invasion the public safety may require it." *Id*. The Constitution is silent, however, as to who is empowered to make the determination of necessity and to suspend the privilege. Lincoln's determination to suspend the privilege without prior congressional authorization was an attempt to preclude judicial challenges to military arrests, the trial of civilians before military commissions, and other acts which, if unconstitutional, might have subjected the government or its officers to suits for injunctive or monetary relief. Although Lincoln asked Congress in 1861 to approve the legality of his actions, it was not until 1863 that Congress acted on the subject, passing legislation worded ambiguously as to whether Congress was approving the President's actions or exercising its own suspension powers.[1]

The seriousness of the *habeas corpus* controversy is well illustrated by the case of *Ex Parte Merryman*, 17 F.Cas. 144 (C.C.D. Md. 1861) (No. 9487). Merryman, lieutenant of a secessionist drill company, was among hundreds of persons arrested and placed under Union military custody in the first year of the war. Chief Justice Taney issued a writ of *habeas corpus* to the arresting general, which the general, acting on Lincoln's suspension order, refused to honor. When a marshal sought to serve a writ of attachment for contempt against the general, Union soldiers refused him entrance to Fort McHenry. Taney responded: "I have exercised all the power which the constitution and laws confer upon me, but that power has been resisted by a force too strong for me to overcome." 17 F. Cas. at 153. As for the President's outright defiance of his order, Taney indicated he would order the proceedings in the case to be transmitted to Lincoln personally, in the hope that the President might determine that his general misconstrued the President's order: "It will then remain for that high officer, in fulfillment of his obligation to 'take care that the laws be faithfully executed,' to determine what measures he will take to cause the civil process of the United States to be respected and enforced." *Id*.

Intriguingly, the Supreme Court did not address the legal issues surrounding the suspension of *habeas corpus* until after the war's end. One Milligan had been arrested in 1864 and convicted by a military commission in Indiana of conspiring to release Confederate prisoners and to make war against the United States. The Supreme Court issued the following opinion, notwithstanding uncertainty whether Milligan had been executed as scheduled on May 19, 1865.

---

1. Act of March 3, 1863, 12 Stat. 755.

Ex Parte Milligan

71 U.S. (4 Wall.) 2 (1867)

Justice DAVIS delivered the opinion of the court.

On the 10th day of May, 1865, Lambdin P. Milligan presented a petition to the Circuit Court of the United States for the District of Indiana, to be discharged from an alleged unlawful imprisonment. The case made by the petition is this: Milligan is a citizen of the United States; has lived for twenty years in Indiana; and, at the time of the grievances complained of, was not, and never had been in the military or naval service of the United States. On the 5th day of October, 1864, while at home, he was arrested by order of General Alvin P. Hovey, commanding the military district of Indiana; and has ever since been kept in close confinement.

On the 21st day of October, 1864, he was brought before a military commission, convened at Indianapolis, by order of General Hovey, tried on certain charges and specifications; found guilty, and sentenced to be hanged; and the sentence ordered to be executed on Friday, the 19th day of May, 1865.

On the 2d day of January, 1865, after the proceedings of the military commission were at an end, the Circuit Court of the United States for Indiana met at Indianapolis and empanelled a grand jury, who were charged to inquire whether the laws of the United States had been violated; and, if so, to make presentments. The court adjourned on the 27th day of January, having, prior thereto, discharged from further service the grand jury, who did not find any bill of indictment or make any presentment against Milligan for any offence whatever; and, in fact, since his imprisonment, no bill of indictment has been found or presentment made against him by any grand jury of the United States. Milligan insists that said military commission had no jurisdiction to try him upon the charges preferred, or upon any charges whatever; because he was a citizen of the United States and the State of Indiana, and had not been, since the commencement of the late Rebellion, a resident of any of the States whose citizens were arrayed against the government, and that the right of trial by jury was guaranteed to him by the Constitution of the United States. The prayer of the petition was, that under the act of Congress, approved March 3d, 1863, entitled, "An act relating to *habeas corpus* and regulating judicial proceedings in certain cases," he may be brought before the court, and either turned over to the proper civil tribunal to be proceeded against according to the law of the land or discharged from custody altogether.

With the petition were filed the order for the commission, the charges and specifications, the findings of the court, with the order of the War Department reciting that the sentence was approved by the President of the United States, and directing that it be carried into execution without delay. The petition was presented and filed in open court by the counsel for Milligan; at the same time the District Attorney of the United States for Indiana appeared, and, by the agreement of counsel, the application was submitted to the court. The opinions of the judges of the Circuit Court were opposed on three questions, which are certified to the Supreme Court:

1st. "On the facts stated in said petition and exhibits, ought a writ of *habeas corpus* to be issued?"

2d. "On the facts stated in said petition and exhibits, ought the said Lambdin P. Milligan to be discharged from custody as in said petition prayed?"

3d. "Whether, upon the facts stated in said petition and exhibits, the military commission mentioned therein had jurisdiction legally to try and sentence said Milligan in manner and form as in said petition and exhibits is stated?"

The importance of the main question presented by this record cannot be overstated; for it involves the very framework of the government and the fundamental principles of American liberty. During the late wicked Rebellion, the temper of the times did not allow that calmness in deliberation and discussion so necessary to a correct conclusion of a purely judicial question. *Then*, considerations of safety were mingled with the exercise of power; and feelings and interests prevailed which are happily terminated. *Now* that the public safety is assured, this question, as well as all others, can be discussed and decided without passion or the admixture of any element not required to form a legal judgment....

Milligan claimed his discharge from custody by virtue of the act of Congress "relating to *habeas corpus*, and regulating judicial proceedings in certain cases," approved March 3d, 1863. Did that act confer jurisdiction on the Circuit Court of Indiana to hear this case?...This law was passed in a time of great national peril, when our heritage of free government was in danger. An armed rebellion against the national authority, of greater proportions than history affords an example of, was raging; and the public safety required that the privilege of the writ of *habeas corpus* should be suspended. The President had practically suspended it, and detained suspected persons in custody without trial; but his authority to do this was questioned. It was claimed that Congress alone could exercise this power; and that the legislature, and not the President, should judge of the political considerations on which the right to suspend it rested. The privilege of this great writ had never before been withheld from the citizen; and as the exigence of the times demanded immediate action, it was of the highest importance that the lawfulness of the suspension should be fully established.... The President was authorized ... to suspend the privilege of the writ of *habeas corpus*, whenever, in his judgment, the public safety required; and he did, by proclamation, bearing date the 15th of September, 1863, reciting, among other things, the authority of this statute, suspend it. The suspension of the writ does not authorize the arrest of any one, but simply denies to one arrested the privilege of this writ in order to obtain his liberty.

It is proper, therefore, to inquire under what circumstances the courts could rightfully refuse to grant this writ, and when the citizen was at liberty to invoke its aid.

The second and third sections of the law are explicit on these points.... The public safety demanded, if the President thought proper to arrest a suspected person, that he should not be required to give the cause of his detention on return to a writ of *habeas corpus*. But it was not contemplated that such person should be detained in custody beyond a certain fixed period, unless certain judicial proceedings, known to the common law, were commenced against him. The Secretaries of State and War were directed to furnish to the judges of the courts of the United States, a list of the names of all parties, not prisoners of war, resident in their respective jurisdictions, who then were or afterwards should be held in custody by the authority of the President, and who were citizens of states in which the administration of the laws in the Federal tribunals was unimpaired. After the list was furnished, if a grand jury of the district convened and adjourned, and did not indict or present one of the persons thus named, he was entitled to his discharge; and it was the duty of the judge of the court to order him brought before him to be discharged, if he desired it.…

Milligan, in his application to be released from imprisonment, averred the existence of every fact necessary under the terms of this law to give the Circuit Court of Indiana jurisdiction.…

[I]t is said that this case is ended, as the presumption is, that Milligan was hanged in pursuance of the order of the President. Although we have no judicial information on the subject, yet the inference is that he is alive; for otherwise learned counsel would not appear for him and urge this court to decide his case. It can never be in this country of written constitution and laws, with a judicial department to interpret them, that any chief magistrate would be so far forgetful of his duty, as to order the execution of a man who denied the jurisdiction that tried and convicted him; *after* his case was before Federal judges with power to decide it, who, being unable to agree on the grave questions involved, had, according to known law, sent it to the Supreme Court of the United States for decision. But even the suggestion is injurious to the Executive, and we dismiss it from further consideration.…

The controlling question in the case is this: Upon the *facts* stated in Milligan's petition, and the exhibits filed, had the military commission mentioned in it *jurisdiction*, legally, to try and sentence him?…

Every trial involves the exercise of judicial power; and from what source did the military commission that tried him derive their authority? Certainly no part of judicial power of the country was conferred on them; because the Constitution expressly vests it "in one supreme court and such inferior courts as the Congress may from time to time ordain and establish," and it is not pretended that the commission was a court ordained and established by Congress. They cannot justify on the mandate of the President; because he is controlled by law, and has his appropriate sphere of duty, which is to execute, not to make, the laws; and there is "no unwritten criminal code to which resort can be had as a source of jurisdiction."

But it is said that the jurisdiction is complete under the "laws and usages of war."

It can serve no useful purpose to inquire what those laws and usages are, whence they originated, where found, and on whom they operate; they can never be applied to citizens in states which have upheld the authority of the government, and where the courts are open and their process unobstructed. This court has judicial knowledge that in Indiana the Federal authority was always unopposed, and its courts always open to hear criminal accusations and redress grievances; and no usage of war could sanction a military trial there for any offence whatever of a citizen in civil life, in nowise connected with the military service. Congress could grant no such power; and to the honor of our national legislature be it said, it has never been provoked by the state of the country even to attempt its exercise. One of the plainest constitutional provisions was, therefore, infringed when Milligan was tried by a court not ordained and established by Congress, and not composed of judges appointed during good behavior.

Why was he not delivered to the Circuit Court of Indiana to be proceeded against according to law? No reason of necessity could be urged against it; because Congress had declared penalties against the offences charged, provided for their punishment, and directed that court to hear and determine them. And soon after this military tribunal was ended, the Circuit Court met, peacefully transacted its business, and adjourned. It needed no bayonets to protect it, and required no military aid to execute its judgments. It was held in a state, eminently distinguished for patriotism, by judges commissioned during the Rebellion, who were provided with juries, upright, intelligent, and selected by a marshal appointed by the President. The government had no right to conclude that Milligan, if guilty, would not receive in that court merited punishment; for its records disclose that it was constantly engaged in the trial of similar offences, and was never interrupted in its administration of criminal justice. If it was dangerous, in the distracted condition of affairs, to leave Milligan unrestrained of his liberty, because he "conspired against the government, afforded aid and comfort to rebels, and incited the people to insurrection," the *law* said arrest him, confine him closely, render him powerless to do further mischief; and then present his case to the grand jury of the district, with proofs of his guilt, and, if indicted, try him according to the course of the common law. If this had been done, the Constitution would have been vindicated, the law of 1863 enforced, and the securities for personal liberty preserved and defended.

Another guarantee of freedom was broken when Milligan was denied a trial by jury. The great minds of the country have differed on the correct interpretation to be given to various provisions of the Federal Constitution; and judicial decision has been often invoked to settle their true meaning; but until recently no one ever doubted that the right of trial by jury was fortified in the organic law against the power of attack. ... [T]his right—one of the most valuable in a free country—is preserved to every one accused of crime who is not attached to the army, or navy, or militia in actual service....

The discipline necessary to the efficiency of the army and navy, required other and swifter modes of trial than are furnished by the common law courts; and, in pursuance of the power conferred by the Constitution, Congress has declared the kinds of trial, and the manner in which they shall be conducted, for offences committed while the party is in the military or naval service. Every one connected with these branches of the public service is amenable to the jurisdiction which Congress has created for their government, and, while thus serving, surrenders his right to be tried by the civil courts. *All other persons*, citizens of states where the courts are open, if charged with crime, are guaranteed the inestimable privilege of trial by jury....

It is claimed that martial law covers with its broad mantle the proceedings of this military commission. The proposition is this: that in a time of war the commander of an armed force (if in his opinion the exigencies of the country demand it, and of which he is to judge), has the power, within the lines of his military district, to suspend all civil rights and their remedies, and subject citizens as well as soldiers to the rule of *his will*; and in the exercise of his lawful authority cannot be restrained, except by his superior officer or the President of the United States.

If this position is sound to the extent claimed, then when war exists, foreign or domestic, and the country is subdivided into military departments for mere convenience, the commander of one of them can, if he chooses, within his limits, on the plea of necessity, with the approval of the Executive, substitute military force for and to the exclusion of the laws, and punish all persons, as he thinks right and proper, without fixed or certain rules. The statement of this proposition shows its importance; for, if true, republican government is a failure, and there is an end of liberty regulated by law. Martial law, established on such a basis, destroys every guarantee of the

Constitution, and effectually renders the "military independent of and superior to the civil power"—the attempt to do which by the King of Great Britain was deemed by our fathers such an offence, that they assigned it to the world as one of the causes which impelled them to declare their independence. Civil liberty and this kind of martial law cannot endure together; the antagonism is irreconcilable; and, in the conflict, one or the other must perish.

This nation, as experience has proved, cannot always remain at peace, and has no right to expect that it will always have wise and humane rulers, sincerely attached to the principles of the Constitution. Wicked men, ambitious of power, with hatred of liberty and contempt of law, may fill the place once occupied by Washington and Lincoln; and if this right is conceded, and the calamities of war again befall us, the dangers to human liberty are frightful to contemplate. If our fathers had failed to provide for just such a contingency, they would have been false to the trust reposed in them. They knew—the history of the world told them—the nation they were founding, be its existence short or long, would be involved in war; how often or how long continued, human foresight could not tell; and that unlimited power, wherever lodged at such a time, was especially hazardous to freemen. For this, and other equally weighty reasons, they secured the inheritance they had fought to maintain, by incorporating in a written constitution the safeguards which *time* had proved were essential to its preservation. Not one of these safeguards can the President, or Congress, or the Judiciary disturb, except the one concerning the writ of *habeas corpus*.

It is essential to the safety of every government that, in a great crisis, like the one we have just passed through, there should be a power somewhere of suspending the writ of *habeas corpus*. In every war, there are men of previously good character, wicked enough to counsel their fellow-citizens to resist the measures deemed necessary by a good government to sustain its just authority and overthrow its enemies; and their influence may lead to dangerous combinations. In the emergency of the times, an immediate public investigation according to law may not be possible; and yet, the peril to the country may be too imminent to suffer such persons to go at large.... The Constitution goes no further. It does not say after a writ of *habeas corpus* is denied a citizen, that he shall be tried otherwise than by the course of the common law; if it had intended this result, it was easy by the use of direct words to have accomplished it....

It will be borne in mind that this is not a question of the power to proclaim martial law, when war exists in a community and the courts and civil authorities are overthrown. Nor is it a question what rule a military commander, at the head of his army, can impose on states in rebellion to cripple their resources and quell the insurrection. The jurisdiction claimed is much more extensive. The necessities of the service, during the late Rebellion, required that the loyal states should be placed within the limits of certain military districts and commanders appointed in them; and, it is urged, that this, in a military sense, constituted them the theater of military operations; and, as in this case, Indiana had been and was again threatened with invasion by the enemy, the occasion was furnished to establish martial law. The conclusion does not follow from the premises. If armies were collected in Indiana, they were to be employed in another locality, where the laws were obstructed and the national authority disputed. On *her* soil there was no hostile foot; if once invaded, that invasion was at an end, and with it all pretext for martial law. Martial law cannot arise from a *threatened* invasion. The necessity must be actual and present; the invasion real, such as effectually closes the courts and deposes the civil administration. It is difficult to see how the *safety* of the country required martial law in Indiana. If any of her citizens were plotting treason, the power of arrest could secure them, until the government was prepared for their trial, when the courts were open and ready to try them. It was as easy to protect witnesses before a civil as a military tribunal; and as there could be no wish to convict, except on sufficient legal evidence, surely an ordained and established court was better able to judge of this than a military tribunal composed of gentlemen not trained to the profession of the law.

It follows, from what has been said on this subject, that there are occasions when martial rule can be properly applied. If, in foreign invasion or civil war, the courts are actually closed, and it is impossible to administer criminal justice according to law, *then*, on the theatre of active military operations, where war really prevails, there is a necessity to furnish a substitute for the civil authority, thus overthrown, to preserve the safety of the army and society; and as no power is left but the military, it is allowed to govern by martial rule until the laws can have their free course. As necessity creates the rule, so it limits its duration; for, if this government is continued *after* the courts are reinstated, it is a gross usurpation of power. Martial rule can never exist where the courts are open, and in the proper and unobstructed exercise of their jurisdiction. It is also confined to the locality of actual war. Because, during the late Rebellion it could have been enforced in Virginia, where the national authority was overturned and the courts driven out, it does not follow that it should obtain in Indiana, where that authority was never disputed, and justice was always administered. And so in the case of a foreign invasion, martial rule may become a necessity in one state, when, in another, it would be "mere lawless violence." . . .

To the third question, then, on which the judges below were opposed in opinion, an answer in the negative must be returned. . . .

The two remaining questions in this case must be answered in the affirmative. The suspension of the privilege of the writ of *habeas corpus* does not suspend the writ itself. The writ issues as a matter of course; and on the return made to it the court decides whether the party applying is denied the right of proceeding any further with it.

If the military trial of Milligan was contrary to law, then he was entitled, on the facts stated in his petition, to be discharged from custody by the terms of the act of Congress of March 3d, 1863. . . .

But it is insisted that Milligan was a prisoner of war, and, therefore, excluded from the privileges of the statute. It is not easy to see how he can be treated as a prisoner of war, when he lived in Indiana for the past twenty years, was arrested there, and had not been, during the late troubles, a resident of any of the states in rebellion. If in Indiana he conspired with bad men to assist the enemy, he is punishable for it in the courts of Indiana; but, when tried for the offence, he cannot plead the rights of war; for he was not engaged in legal acts of hostility against the government, and only such persons, when captured, are prisoners of war. If he cannot enjoy the immunities attaching to the character of a prisoner of war, how can he be subject to their pains and penalties? . . .

(The CHIEF JUSTICE, with Justices WAYNE, SWAYNE, MILLER concurred separately in the judgment.)

1. As the preceding case indicates, military law—the ordinary law that applies to military affairs—is a discrete species of executive power, which this text does not pursue. *See generally* D. Zillman, et al., Cases and Materials on the Military in American Society (1978). It should not be confused with "martial law," which is the extraordinary rule of civilians by military authorities because of military emergency. "It is an unbending rule of law, that the exercise of military power, where the rights of the citizen are concerned, shall never be pushed beyond that which the exigency requires." *Raymond v. Thomas*, 91 U.S. 712, 716 (1876).

2. What does the Court mean by stating that suspension of the "privilege of the Writ" does not suspend the writ itself?

3. Justice Black relied on *Milligan* in deciding *Duncan v. Kahanamoku*, 327 U.S. 304 (1946), in which the Court held invalid a declaration of martial law by the governor of the Territory of Hawaii on December 7, 1941, suspending, with the President's subsequent approval, the writ of habeas corpus in that territory. The animating event, of course, was the bombing of Pearl Harbor, which set off considerable panic as to the vulnerability of Hawaii and the west coast to Japanese attack. Can the two cases be reconciled with *Ex parte Quirin*, 317 U.S. 1 (1942), in which the Court upheld the trial and condemnation of a group of Nazi saboteurs by a presidentially convened tribunal of military officers, although the United States was not in the war zone and civilian courts were operating? (The *Quirin* court summarily held *Milligan* inapplicable to "enemy belligerents," including belligerents who are citizens of the United States.) A common feature of *Milligan* and *Quirin* was the apparent judicial uncertainty, at the time the Court acted in each case, whether the petitioners were still alive. A common feature of *Milligan* and *Duncan* was the fact that each case was decided during peacetime.

4. Does *Milligan* stand for the proposition that federal courts have inherent jurisdiction to determine the limits of their own jurisdiction?

Korematsu v. United States
323 U.S. 214 (1944)

Justice BLACK delivered the opinion of the Court.

The petitioner, an American citizen of Japanese descent, was convicted in a federal district court for remaining in San Leandro, California, a "Military Area," contrary to Civilian Exclusion Order No. 34 of the Commanding General of the Western Command, U.S. Army, which directed that after May 9, 1942, all persons of Japanese ancestry should be excluded from that area. No question was raised as to petitioner's loyalty to the United States. . . .

It should be noted, to begin with, that all legal restrictions which curtail the civil rights of a single racial group are immediately suspect. That is not to say that all such restrictions are unconstitutional. It is to say that courts must subject them to the most rigid scrutiny. Pressing public necessity may sometimes justify the existence of such restrictions; racial antagonism never can.

In the instant case prosecution of the petitioner was begun by information charging violation of an Act of Congress, of March 21, 1942, 56 Stat. 173, which provides that

> ... whoever shall enter, remain in, leave, or commit any act in any military area or military zone prescribed, under the authority of an Executive order of the President, by the Secretary of War, or by any military commander designated by the Secretary of War, contrary to the restrictions applicable to any such area or zone or contrary to the order of the Secretary of War or any such military commander, shall, if it appears that he knew or should have known of the existence and extent of the restrictions or order and that his act was in violation thereof, be guilty of a misdemeanor and upon conviction shall be liable to a fine of not to exceed $5,000 or to imprisonment for not more than one year, or both, for each offense.

Exclusion Order No. 34, which the petitioner knowingly and admittedly violated was one of a number of military orders and proclamations, all of which were substantially based upon Executive Order No. 9066, 7 Fed.Reg. 1407. That order, issued after we were at war with Japan, declared that "the successful prosecution of the war requires every possible protection against espionage and against sabotage to national-defense material, national-defense premises, and national-defense utilities. . . . "

One of the series of orders and proclamations, a curfew order, which like the exclusion order here was promulgated pursuant to Executive Order 9066, subjected all persons of Japanese ancestry in prescribed West Coast military areas to remain in their residences from 8 p.m. to 6 a.m. As is the case with the exclusion order here, that prior curfew order was designed as a "protection against espionage and against sabotage." In Hirabayashi v. United States, 320 U.S. 81, we sustained a conviction obtained for violation of the curfew order. The Hirabayashi conviction and this one thus rest on the same 1942 Congressional Act and the same basic executive and military orders, all of which orders were aimed at the twin dangers of espionage and sabotage.

The 1942 Act was attacked in the *Hirabayashi* case as an unconstitutional delegation of power; it was contended that the curfew order and other orders on which it rested were beyond the war powers of the Congress, the military authorities and of the President, as Commander in Chief of the Army; and finally that to apply the curfew order against none but citizens of Japanese ancestry amounted to a constitutionally prohibited discrimination solely on account of race. . . . We upheld the curfew order as an exercise of the power of the government to take steps necessary to prevent espionage and sabotage in an area threatened by Japanese attack.

In the light of the principles we announced in the *Hirabayashi* case, we are unable to conclude that it was beyond the war power of Congress and the Executive to exclude those of Japanese ancestry from the West Coast war area at the time they did. True, exclusion from the area in which one's home is located is a far greater deprivation than constant confinement to the home from 8 p.m. to 6 a.m. Nothing short of apprehension by the proper military authorities of the gravest imminent danger to the public safety can constitutionally justify either. But exclusion from a threatened area, no less than curfew, has a definite and close relationship to the prevention of espionage and sabotage. The military authorities, charged with the primary responsibility of defending our shores, concluded that curfew provided inadequate protection and ordered exclusion. They did so, as pointed out in our *Hirabayashi* opinion, in accordance with Congressional authority to the military to say who should, and who should not, remain in the threatened areas. In this case the petitioner challenges the assumptions upon which we rested our conclusions in the *Hirabayashi* case. He also urges that by May 1942, when Order No. 34 was promulgated, all danger of Japanese invasion of the West Coast had disappeared. After careful consideration of these contentions we are compelled to reject them.

Here, as in the *Hirabayashi* case, " ... we cannot reject as unfounded the judgment of the military authorities and of Congress that there were disloyal members of that population, whose number and strength could not be precisely and quickly ascertained. We cannot say that the war-making branches of the Government did not have ground for believing that in a critical hour such persons could not readily be isolated and separately dealt with, and constituted a menace to the national defense and safety, which demanded that prompt and adequate measures be taken to guard against it."

Like curfew, exclusion of those of Japanese origin was deemed necessary because of the presence of an unascertained number of disloyal members of the group, most of whom we have no doubt were loyal to this country. It was because we could not reject the finding of the military authorities that it was impossible to bring about an immediate segregation of the disloyal from the loyal that we sustained the validity of the curfew order as applying to the whole group. In the instant case, temporary exclusion of the entire group was rested by the military on the same ground. The judgment that exclusion of the whole group was for the same reason a military imperative answers the contention that the exclusion was in the nature of group punishment based on antagonism to those of Japanese origin. That there were members of the group who retained loyalties to Japan has been confirmed by investigations made subsequent to the exclusion. Approximately five thousand American citizens of Japanese ancestry refused to swear unqualified allegiance to the United States and to renounce allegiance to the Japanese Emperor, and several thousand evacuees requested repatriation to Japan.[2]

We uphold the exclusion order as of the time it was made and when the petitioner violated it. In doing so, we are not unmindful of the hardships imposed by it upon a large group of American citizens. But hardships are part of war, and war is an aggregation of hardships. All citizens alike, both in and out of uniform, feel the impact of war in greater or lesser measure. Citizenship has its responsibilities as well as its privileges, and in time of war the burden is always heavier. Compulsory exclusion of large groups of citizens from their homes, except under circumstances of direst emergency and peril, is inconsistent with our basic governmental institutions. But when under conditions of modern warfare our shores are threatened by hostile forces, the power to protect must be commensurate with the threatened danger.

It is argued that on May 30, 1942, the date the petitioner was charged with remaining in the prohibited area, there were conflicting orders outstanding, forbidding him both to leave the area and to remain there. Of course, a person cannot be convicted

---

2. Hearings before the Subcommittee on the National War Agencies Appropriation Bill for 1945, Part II, 608-726; Final Report, Japanese Evacuation from the West Coast, 1942, 309-327; Hearings before the Committee on Immigration and Naturalization, House of Representatives, 78th Cong., 2d Sess., on H.R. 2701 and other bills to expatriate certain nationals of the United States, pp. 37-42, 49-58.

for doing the very thing which it is a crime to fail to do. But the outstanding orders here contained no such contradictory commands.

There was an order issued March 27, 1942, which prohibited petitioner and others of Japanese ancestry from leaving the area, but its effect was specifically limited in time "until and to the extent that a future proclamation or order should so permit or direct." 7 Fed. Reg. 2601. That "future order," the one for violation of which petitioner was convicted, was issued May 3, 1942, and it did "direct" exclusion from the area of all persons of Japanese ancestry, before 12 o'clock noon, May 9; furthermore it contained a warning that all such persons found in the prohibited area would be liable to punishment under the March 21, 1942 Act of Congress. Consequently, the only order in effect touching the petitioner's being in the area on May 30, 1942, the date specified in the information against him, was the May 3 order which prohibited his remaining there, and it was that same order, which he stipulated in his trial that he had violated, knowing of its existence. There is therefore no basis for the argument that on May 30, 1942, he was subject to punishment, under the March 27 and May 3rd orders, whether he remained in or left the area.

It does appear, however, that on May 9, the effective date of the exclusion order, the military authorities had already determined that the evacuation should be effected by assembling together and placing under guard all those of Japanese ancestry, at central points, designated as "assembly centers," in order "to insure the orderly evacuation and resettlement of Japanese voluntarily migrating from military area No. 1 to restrict and regulate such migration." Public Proclamation No. 4, 7 Fed. Reg. 2601. And on May 19, 1942, eleven days before the time petitioner was charged with unlawfully remaining in the area, Civilian Restrictive Order No. 1, 8 Fed. Reg. 982, provided for detention of those of Japanese ancestry in assembly or relocation centers. It is now argued that the validity of the exclusion order cannot be considered apart from the orders requiring him, after departure from the area, to report and to remain in an assembly or relocation center. The contention is that we must treat these separate orders as one and inseparable; that, for this reason, if detention in the assembly or relocation center would have illegally deprived the petitioner of his liberty, the exclusion order and his conviction under it cannot stand.

We are thus being asked to pass at this time upon the whole subsequent detention program in both assembly and relocation centers, although the only issues framed at the trial related to petitioner's remaining in the prohibited area in violation of the exclusion order. Had petitioner here left the prohibited area and gone to an assembly center we cannot say either as a matter of fact or law that his presence in that center would have resulted in his detention in a relocation center. Some who did report to the assembly center were not sent to relocation centers, but were released upon condition that they remain outside the prohibited zone until the military orders were modified or lifted. This illustrates that they pose different problems and may be governed by different principles. The lawfulness of one does not necessarily determine the lawfulness of the others. This is made clear when we analyze the requirements of the separate provisions of the separate orders. These separate requirements were that those of Japanese ancestry (1) depart from the area; (2) report to and temporarily remain in an assembly center; (3) go under military control to a relocation center there to remain for an indeterminate period until released conditionally or unconditionally by the military authorities.... There is no reason why violations of these orders, insofar as they were promulgated pursuant to congressional enactment, should not be treated as separate offenses. The *Endo* case (*Ex parte Mitsuye Endo*) 323 U.S. 283,* graphically illustrates the difference between the validity of an order to exclude and the validity of a detention order after exclusion has been effected. Since the petitioner has not been convicted of failing to report or to remain in an assembly or relocation center, we cannot in this case determine the validity of those separate provisions of the order. It is sufficient here for us to pass upon the order which petitioner violated. To do more would be to go beyond the issues raised, and to decide momentous questions not contained within the framework of the pleadings or the evidence in this case. It will be time enough to decide the serious constitutional issues which petitioner seeks to raise when an assembly or relocation order is applied or is certain to be applied to him, and we have its terms before us.

Some of the members of the Court are of the view that evacuation and detention in an Assembly Center were inseparable. After May 3, 1942, the date of Exclusion Order No. 34, Korematsu was under compulsion to leave the area not as he would choose but via an Assembly Center. The Assembly Center was conceived as a part of the machinery for group evacuation. The power to exclude includes the power to do it by force if necessary. And any forcible measure must necessarily entail some degree of detention or restraint whatever method of removal is selected. But whichever view is taken, it results in holding that the order under which petitioner was convicted was valid. It is said that we are dealing here with the case of imprisonment of a citizen in a concentration camp solely because of his ancestry, without evidence or inquiry concerning his loyalty and good disposition towards the United States. Our task would be simple, our duty clear, were this a case involving the imprisonment of a loyal citizen in a concentration camp because of racial prejudice. Regardless of the true nature of the assembly and relocation centers—and we deem it unjustifiable to call them concentration camps with all the ugly connotations that term implies—we are dealing specifically with nothing but an exclusion order.... Korematsu was not excluded from the Military Area because of hostility to him or his race. He *was* excluded because we are at war with the Japanese Empire, because the properly constituted military authorities feared an invasion of our West Coast and felt constrained to take proper security measures, because they decided that the military urgency of the situation demanded that all citizens of Japanese ancestry be segregated from the West Coast temporarily, and finally, because Congress, reposing its confidence in this time of war in our military leaders—as inevitably it must—determined that they should have the power to do just this. There was evidence of disloyalty on the part of some, the military authorities considered that the need for action was great, and time was short. We cannot—by availing ourselves of the calm perspective of hindsight—now say that at that time these actions were unjustified.

Affirmed.

Justice FRANKFURTER, concurring.

... I am unable to see how the legal considerations that led to the decision in *Hirabayashi*, fail to sustain the military order which made the conduct now in controversy a crime. And so I join in the opinion of the Court....

**Endo held that neither the relevant statutes or executive orders permitted a U.S. citizen of Japanese ancestry, whose loyalty was conceded, to be detained at a relocation camp by civilian authorities.

The provisions of the Constitution which confer on the Congress and the President powers to enable this country to wage war are as much part of the Constitution as provisions looking to a nation at peace.... [T]he validity of action under the war power must be judged wholly in the context of war. That action is not to be stigmatized as lawless because like action in times of peace would be lawless.... The respective spheres of action of military authorities and of judges are of course very different. But within their sphere, military authorities are no more outside the bounds of obedience to the Constitution than are judges within theirs.... To recognize that military orders are "reasonably expedient military precautions" in time of war and yet to deny them constitutional legitimacy makes of the Constitution an instrument for dialectic subtleties not reasonably to be attributed to the hard-headed Framers, of whom a majority had had actual participation in war. If a military order such as that under review does not transcend the means appropriate for conducting war, such action by the military is as constitutional as would be any authorized action by the Interstate Commerce Commission within the limits of the constitutional power to regulate commerce. And being an exercise of the war power explicitly granted by the Constitution for safeguarding the national life by prosecuting war effectively, I find nothing in the Constitution which denies to Congress the power to enforce such a valid military order by making its violation an offense triable in the civil courts. To find that the Constitution does not forbid the military measures now complained of does not carry with it approval of that which Congress and the Executive did. That is their business, not ours.

Justice ROBERTS.

I dissent, because I think the indisputable facts exhibit a clear violation of Constitutional rights.

This is not a case of keeping people off the streets at night as was *Hirabayashi*, 320 U.S. 81, nor a case of temporary exclusion of a citizen from an area for his own safety or that of the community, nor a case of offering him an opportunity to go temporarily out of an area where his presence might cause danger to himself or to his fellows. On the contrary, it is the case of convicting a citizen as a punishment for not submitting to imprisonment in a concentration camp, based on his ancestry, and solely because of his ancestry, without evidence or inquiry concerning his loyalty and good disposition towards the United States....

A chronological recitation of events will make it plain that the petitioner's supposed offense did not, in truth, consist in his refusal voluntarily to leave the area which included his home in obedience to the order excluding him therefrom. Critical attention must be given to the dates and sequence of events.

December 8, 1941, the United States declared war on Japan.

February 19, 1942, the President issued Executive Order No. 9066....

February 20, 1942, Lieutenant General DeWitt was designated Military Commander of the Western Defense Command embracing the westernmost states of the Union,—about one-fourth of the total area of the nation.

March 2, 1942, General DeWitt promulgated Public Proclamation No. 1, which recites that the entire Pacific Coast is "particularly subject to attack, to attempted invasion ... and, in connection therewith, is subject to espionage and acts of sabotage." It states that "as a matter of military necessity" certain military areas and zones are established known as Military Areas Nos. 1 and 2. It adds that "Such persons or classes of persons as the situation may require" will, by subsequent orders, "be excluded from all of Military Area No. 1" and from certain zones in Military Area No. 2. Subsequent proclamations were made which, together with Proclamation No. 1, included in such areas and zones all of California, Washington, Oregon, Idaho, Montana, Nevada and Utah, and the southern portion of Arizona. The orders required that if any person of Japanese, German or Italian ancestry residing in Area No. 1 desired to change his habitual residence he must execute and deliver to the authorities a Change of Residence Notice.

San Leandro, the city of petitioner's residence, lies in Military Area No. 1. On March 2, 1942, the petitioner, therefore, had notice that, by Executive Order, the President, to prevent espionage and sabotage, had authorized the Military to exclude him from certain areas and to prevent his entering or leaving certain areas without permission. He was on notice that his home city had been included, by Military Order, in Area No. 1, and he was on notice further that, at sometime in the future, the Military Commander would make an order for the exclusion of certain persons, not described or classified, from various zones including that in which he lived. March 21, 1942, Congress enacted [18 U.S.C. § 97a]. . . . This is the Act under which the petitioner was charged.

March 24, 1942, General DeWitt instituted the curfew for certain areas within his command, by an order the validity of which was sustained in *Hirabayashi v. United States, supra.*

March 24, 1942, General DeWitt began to issue a series of exclusion orders relating to specified areas.

March 27, 1942, by Proclamation No. 4, the General recited that "it is necessary, in order to provide for the welfare and to insure the orderly evacuation and resettlement of Japanese *voluntarily migrating* from Military Area No. 1 to restrict and regulate such migration"; and ordered that, as of March 29, 1942, "all alien Japanese and persons of Japanese ancestry who are within the limits of Military Area No. 1, be and they are hereby prohibited from leaving that area for any purpose until and to the extent that a future proclamation or order of this headquarters shall so permit or direct."[5] . . .

May 3, 1942, General DeWitt issued Civilian Exclusion Order No. 34 providing that, after 12 o'clock May 8, 1942, all persons of Japanese ancestry, both alien and non-alien, were to be excluded from a described portion of Military Area No. 1, which included the County of Alameda, California. The order required a responsible member of each family and each individual living alone to report, at a time set, at a Civil Control Station for instructions to go to an Assembly Center, and added that any person failing to comply with the provisions of the order who was found in the described area after the date set would be liable to prosecution under the Act of March 21, 1942. It is important to note that the order, by its express terms, had no application to persons within the bounds "of an established Assembly Center pursuant to instructions from this Headquarters. . . . " The obvious purpose of the orders made, taken together, was to drive all citizens of Japanese ancestry into Assembly Centers within the zones of their residence, under pain of criminal prosecution.

---

5. The italics in the quotation are mine. The use of the word 'voluntarily' exhibits a grim irony probably not lost on petitioner and others in like case. Either so, or its use was a disingenuous attempt to camouflage the compulsion which was to be applied.

The predicament in which the petitioner thus found himself was this: He was forbidden, by Military Order, to leave the zone in which he lived; he was forbidden, by Military Order, after a date fixed, to be found within that zone unless he were in an Assembly Center located in that zone. General DeWitt's report to the Secretary of War concerning the programme of evacuation and relocation of Japanese makes it entirely clear, if it were necessary to refer to that document,—and, in the light of the above recitation, I think it is not,—that an Assembly Center was a euphemism for a prison. No person within such a center was permitted to leave except by Military Order. In the dilemma that he dare not remain in his home, or voluntarily leave the area, without incurring criminal penalties, and that the only way he could avoid punishment was to go to an Assembly Center and submit himself to military imprisonment, the petitioner did nothing.

. . . [Following his conviction, Korematsu] was at once taken into military custody and lodged in an Assembly Center. We further know that, on March 18, 1942, the President had promulgated Executive Order No. 9102 establishing the War Relocation Authority under which so-called Relocation Centers, a euphemism for concentration camps, were established pursuant to cooperation between the military authorities of the Western Defense Command and the Relocation Authority, and that the petitioner has been confined either in an Assembly Center, within the zone in which he had lived or has been removed to a Relocation Center where, as the facts disclosed in Ex parte Endo, 323 U.S. 283, demonstrate, he was illegally held in custody.

The Government has argued this case as if the only order outstanding at the time the petitioner was arrested and informed against was Exclusion Order No. 34 ordering him to leave the area in which he resided, which was the basis of the information against him. . . . This, I think, is a substitution of an hypothetical case for the case actually before the court. . . . This case cannot . . . be decided on any such narrow ground as the possible validity of a Temporary Exclusion Order under which the residents of an area are given an opportunity to leave and go elsewhere in their native land outside the boundaries of a military area. To make the case turn on any such assumption is to shut our eyes to reality. . . .

[The] stark realities are met by the suggestion that it is lawful to compel an American citizen to submit to illegal imprisonment on the assumption that he might, after going to the Assembly Center, apply for his discharge by suing out a writ of habeas corpus, as was done in the *Endo* case. . . . [I]t is a new doctrine of constitutional law that one indicted for disobedience to an unconstitutional statute may not defend on the ground of the invalidity of the statute but must obey it though he knows it is no law and, after he has suffered the disgrace of conviction and lost his liberty by sentence, then, and not before, seek, from within prison walls, to test the validity of the law. . . . I would reverse the judgment of conviction.

Justice MURPHY, dissenting.

This exclusion of "all persons of Japanese ancestry, both alien and non-alien," from the Pacific Coast area on a plea of military necessity in the absence of martial law ought not to be approved. Such exclusion goes over "the very brink of constitutional power" and falls into the ugly abyss of racism. In dealing with matters relating to the prosecution and progress of a war, we must accord great respect and consideration to the judgments of the military authorities who are on the scene and who have full knowledge of the military facts. The scope of their discretion must, as a matter of necessity and common sense, be wide. And their judgments ought not to be overruled lightly by those whose training and duties ill-equip them to deal intelligently with matters so vital to the physical security of the nation.

At the same time, however, it is essential that there be definite limits to military discretion, especially where martial law has not been declared. Individuals must not be left impoverished of their constitutional rights on a plea of military necessity that has neither substance nor support. Thus, like other claims conflicting with the asserted constitutional rights of the individual, the military claim must subject itself to the judicial process of having its reasonableness determined and its conflicts with other interests reconciled. "What are the allowable limits of military discretion, and whether or not they have been overstepped in a particular case, are judicial questions." *Sterling v. Constantin*, 287 U.S. 378, 401.

The judicial test of whether the Government, on a plea of military necessity, can validly deprive an individual of any of his constitutional rights is whether the deprivation is reasonably related to a public danger that is so "immediate, imminent, and impending" as not to admit of delay and not to permit the intervention of ordinary constitutional processes to alleviate the danger. *United States v. Russell*, 13 Wall. 623, 627-28. Civilian Exclusion Order No. 34, banishing from a prescribed area of the Pacific Coast "all persons of Japanese ancestry, both alien and non-alien," clearly does not meet that test. Being an obvious racial discrimination, the order deprives all those within its scope of the equal protection of the laws as guaranteed by the Fifth Amendment. It further deprives these individuals of their constitutional rights to live and work where they will, to establish a home where they choose and to move about freely. In excommunicating them without benefit of hearings, this order also deprives them of all their constitutional rights to procedural due process. Yet no reasonable relation to an "immediate, imminent, and impending" public danger is evident to support this racial restriction which is one of the most sweeping and complete deprivations of constitutional rights in the history of this nation in the absence of martial law.

It must be conceded that the military and naval situation in the spring of 1942 was such as to generate a very real fear of invasion of the Pacific Coast, accompanied by fears of sabotage and espionage in that area. The military command was therefore justified in adopting all reasonable means necessary to combat these dangers. In adjudging the military action taken in light of the then apparent dangers, we must not erect too high or too meticulous standards; it is necessary only that the action have some reasonable relation to the removal of the dangers of invasion, sabotage and espionage. But the exclusion, either temporarily or permanently, of all persons with Japanese blood in their veins has no such reasonable relation. And that relation is lacking because the exclusion order necessarily must rely for its reasonableness upon the assumption that all persons of Japanese ancestry may have a dangerous tendency to commit sabotage and espionage and to aid our Japanese enemy in other ways. It is difficult to believe that reason, logic or experience could be marshalled in support of such an assumption.

That this forced exclusion was the result in good measure of this erroneous assumption of racial guilt rather than bona fide military necessity is evidenced by the Commanding General's Final Report on the evacuation from the Pacific Coast area.[1]

---

1. Final Report, Japanese Evacuation from the West Coast, 1942, by Lt. Gen. J. L. DeWitt. This report is dated June 5, 1943, but was not made public until January, 1944.

In it he refers to all individuals of Japanese descent as "subversive," as belonging to "an enemy race" whose "racial strains are undiluted," and as constituting "over 112,000 potential enemies . . . at large today" along the Pacific Coast.[2] In support of this blanket condemnation of all persons of Japanese descent, however, no reliable evidence is cited to show that such individuals were generally disloyal,[3] or had generally so conducted themselves in this area as to constitute a special menace to defense installations or war industries, or had otherwise by their behavior furnished reasonable ground for their exclusion as a group.

Justification for the exclusion is sought, instead, mainly upon questionable racial and sociological grounds not ordinarily within the realm of expert military judgment, supplemented by certain semi-military conclusions drawn from an unwarranted use of circumstantial evidence. Individuals of Japanese ancestry are condemned because they are said to be "a large, unassimilated, tightly knit racial group, bound to an enemy nation by strong ties of race, culture, custom and religion."[4] They are claimed to be given to "emperor worshipping ceremonies[5] and to "dual citizenship."[6] Japanese language schools and allegedly pro-Japanese organizations are cited as evidence of possible group disloyalty, together with facts as to certain persons being educated and residing at length in Japan. It is intimated that many of these individuals deliberately resided "adjacent to strategic points," thus enabling them "to carry into

---

2. Further evidence of the Commanding General's attitude toward individuals of Japanese ancestry is revealed in his voluntary testimony on April 13, 1943, in San Francisco before the House Naval Affairs Subcommittee to Investigate Congested Areas, Part 3, pp. 739-40 (78th Cong., 1st Sess.):

I don't want any of them [persons of Japanese ancestry] here. They are a dangerous element. There is no way to determine their loyalty. The west coast contains too many vital installations essential to the defense of the country to allow any Japanese on this coast. . . . The danger of the Japanese was, and is now—if they are permitted to come back—espionage and sabotage. It makes no difference whether he is an American citizen, he is still a Japanese. American citizenship does not necessarily determine loyalty. . . . But we must worry about the Japanese all the time until he is wiped off the map. Sabotage and espionage will make problems as long as he is allowed in this area. . . .

3. The Final Report, p. 9, casts a cloud of suspicion over the entire group by saying that "while it was *believed* that *some* were loyal, it was known that many were not." (Italics added.)

4. Final Report, p. vii; see also pp. 9, 17. To the extent that assimilation is a problem, it is largely the result of certain social customs and laws of the American general public. Studies demonstrate that persons of Japanese descent are readily susceptible to integration in our society if given the opportunity. Strong, The Second-Generation Japanese Problem (1934); Smith, Americans in Process (1937); Mears, Resident Orientals on the American Pacific Coast (1928); Millis, The Japanese Problem in the United States (1942). The failure to accomplish an ideal status of assimilation, therefore, cannot be charged to the refusal of these persons to become Americanized or to their loyalty to Japan. And the retention by some persons of certain customs and religious practices of their ancestors is no criterion of their loyalty to the United States.

5. Final Report, pp. 10-11. No sinister correlation between the emperor worshipping activities and disloyalty to America was shown.

6. Final Report, p. 22. The charge of "dual citizenship" springs from a misunderstanding of the simple fact that Japan in the past used the doctrine of *jus sanguinis*, as she had a right to do under international law, and claimed as her citizens all persons born of Japanese nationals wherever located. Japan has greatly modified this doctrine, however, by allowing all Japanese born in the United States to renounce any claim of dual citizenship and by releasing her claim as to all born in the United States after 1925. . . .

execution a tremendous program of sabotage on a mass scale should any considerable number of them have been inclined to do so."[9] The need for protective custody is also asserted. The report refers without identity to "numerous incidents of violence" as well as to other admittedly unverified or cumulative incidents. From this, plus certain other events not shown to have been connected with the Japanese Americans, it is concluded that the "situation was fraught with danger to the Japanese population itself" and that the general public "was ready to take matters into its own hands."[10] Finally, it is intimated, though not directly charged or proved, that persons of Japanese ancestry were responsible for three minor isolated shellings and bombings of the Pacific Coast area,[11] as well as for unidentified radio transmissions and night signalling.

The main reasons relied upon by those responsible for the forced evacuation, therefore, do not prove a reasonable relation between the group characteristics of Japanese Americans and the dangers of invasion, sabotage and espionage. The reasons appear, instead, to be largely an accumulation of much of the misinformation, half-truths and insinuations that for years have been directed against Japanese Americans by people with racial and economic prejudices—the same people who have been among the foremost advocates of the evacuation.[12] A military judgment based upon such racial and sociological considerations is not entitled to the great weight ordinarily given the judgments based upon strictly military considerations. Especially is this so when every charge relative to race, religion, culture, geographical location, and legal and economic status has been substantially discredited by independent studies made by experts in these matters.

The military necessity which is essential to the validity of the evacuation order thus resolves itself into a few intimations that certain individuals actively aided the enemy, from which it is inferred that the entire group of Japanese Americans could not be trusted to be or remain loyal to the United States. No one denies, of course, that there were some disloyal persons of Japanese descent on the Pacific Coast who did all in their power to aid their ancestral land. Similar disloyal activities have been

---

9. Final Report, p. 10; see also pp. vii, 9, 15-17. This insinuation, based purely upon speculation and circumstantial evidence, completely overlooks the fact that the main geographic pattern of Japanese population was fixed many years ago with reference to economic, social and soil conditions....

10. Final Report, pp. 8-9. This dangerous doctrine of protective custody, as proved by recent European history, should have absolutely no standing as an excuse for the deprivation of the rights of minority groups. In this instance, moreover, there are only two minor instances of violence on record involving persons of Japanese ancestry.

11. Final Report, p. 18. One of these incidents (the reputed dropping of incendiary bombs on an Oregon forest) occurred on Sept. 9, 1942—a considerable time after the Japanese Americans had been evacuated from their homes and placed in Assembly Centers.

12. Special interest groups were extremely active in applying pressure for mass evacuation. Mr. Austin E. Anson, managing secretary of the Salinas Vegetable Grower-Shipper Association, has frankly admitted that "We're charged with wanting to get rid of the Japs for selfish reasons.... We do. It's a question of whether the white man lives on the Pacific Coast or the brown men. They came into this valley to work, and they stayed to take over.... They undersell the white man in the markets.... They work their women and children while the white farmer has to pay wages for his help. If all the Japs were removed tomorrow, we'd never miss them in two weeks, because the white farmers can take over and produce everything the Jap grows. And we don't want them back when the war ends, either." Quoted by Taylor in his article "The People Nobody Wants," 214 Sat. Eve. Post 24, 66 (May 9, 1942).

engaged in by many persons of German, Italian and even more pioneer stock in our country. But to infer that examples of individual disloyalty prove group disloyalty and justify discriminatory action against the entire group is to deny that under our system of law individual guilt is the sole basis for deprivation of rights. Moreover, this inference, which is at the very heart of the evacuation orders, has been used in support of the abhorrent and despicable treatment of minority groups by the dictatorial tyrannies which this nation is now pledged to destroy. To give constitutional sanction to that inference in this case, however well-intentioned may have been the military command on the Pacific Coast, is to adopt one of the cruelest of the rationales used by our enemies to destroy the dignity of the individual and to encourage and open the door to discriminatory actions against other minority groups in the passions of tomorrow.

No adequate reason is given for the failure to treat these Japanese Americans on an individual basis by holding investigations and hearings to separate the loyal from the disloyal, as was done in the case of persons of German and Italian ancestry. See House Report No. 2124 (77th Cong., 2d Sess.) 247-52. It is asserted merely that the loyalties of this group "were unknown and time was of the essence." Yet nearly four months elapsed after Pearl Harbor before the first exclusion order was issued; nearly eight months went by until the last order was issued; and the last of these "subversive" persons was not actually removed until almost eleven months had elapsed. Leisure and deliberation seem to have been more of the essence than speed. And the fact that conditions were not such as to warrant a declaration of martial law adds strength to the belief that the factors of time and military necessity were not as urgent as they have been represented to be.

Moreover, there was no adequate proof that the Federal Bureau of Investigation and the military and naval intelligence services did not have the espionage and sabotage situation well in hand during this long period. Nor is there any denial of the fact that not one person of Japanese ancestry was accused or convicted of espionage or sabotage after Pearl Harbor while they were still free,[15] a fact which is some evidence of the loyalty of the vast majority of these individuals and of the effectiveness of the established methods of combatting these evils. It seems incredible that under these circumstances it would have been impossible to hold loyalty hearings for the mere 112,000 persons involved—or at least for the 70,000 American citizens—especially when a large part of this number represented children and elderly men and women.[16] Any inconvenience that may have accompanied an attempt to conform to procedural due process cannot be said to justify violations of constitutional rights of individuals.

I dissent, therefore, from this legalization of racism....

---

15. The Final Report, p. 34, makes the amazing statement that as of February 14, 1942, "The very fact that no sabotage has taken place to date is a disturbing and confirming indication that such action will be taken." Apparently, in the minds of the military leaders, there was no way that the Japanese Americans could escape the suspicion of sabotage.

16. During a period of six months, the 112 alien tribunals or hearing boards set up by the British Government shortly after the outbreak of the present war summoned and examined approximately 74,000 German and Austrian aliens. These tribunals determined whether each individual enemy alien was a real enemy of the Allies or only a "friendly enemy." About 64,000 were freed from internment and from any special restrictions, and only 2,000 were interned. Kempner, "The Enemy Alien Problem in the Present War," 34 Amer. Journ. of Int. Law 443, 444-46; House Report No. 2124 (77th Cong., 2d Sess.), 280-1.

Justice JACKSON, dissenting.

 Korematsu was born on our soil, of parents born in Japan. The Constitution makes him a citizen of the United States by nativity and a citizen of California by residence. No claim is made that he is not loyal to this country. There is no suggestion that apart from the matter involved here he is not law-abiding and well disposed. Korematsu, however, has been convicted of an act not commonly a crime. It consists merely of being present in the state whereof he is a citizen, near the place where he was born, and where all his life he has lived.

 Even more unusual is the series of military orders which made this conduct a crime. They forbid such a one to remain, and they also forbid him to leave. They were so drawn that the only way Korematsu could avoid violation was to give himself up to the military authority. This meant submission to custody, examination, and transportation out of the territory, to be followed by indeterminate confinement in detention camps.

 A citizen's presence in the locality, however, was made a crime only if his parents were of Japanese birth. Had Korematsu been one of four—the others being, say, a German alien enemy, an Italian alien enemy, and a citizen of American-born ancestors, convicted of treason but out on parole—only Korematsu's presence would have violated the order. The difference between their innocence and his crime would result, not from anything he did, said, or thought, different than they, but only in that he was born of different racial stock.

 Now, if any fundamental assumption underlies our system, it is that guilt is personal and not inheritable. Even if all of one's antecedents had been convicted of treason, the Constitution forbids its penalties to be visited upon him, for it provides that "no attainder of treason shall work corruption of blood, or forfeiture except during the life of the person attainted." [Article 3, § 3, cl. 2.] But here is an attempt to make an otherwise innocent act a crime merely because this prisoner is the son of parents as to whom he had no choice, and belongs to a race from which there is no way to resign. If Congress in peace-time legislation should enact such a criminal law, I should suppose this Court would refuse to enforce it.

 But the "law" which this prisoner is convicted of disregarding is not found in an act of Congress, but in a military order. Neither the Act of Congress nor the Executive Order of the President, nor both together, would afford a basis for this conviction. It rests on the orders of General DeWitt. And it is said that if the military commander had reasonable military grounds for promulgating the orders, they are constitutional and become law, and the Court is required to enforce them. There are several reasons why I cannot subscribe to this doctrine.

 It would be impracticable and dangerous idealism to expect or insist that each specific military command in an area of probable operations will conform to conventional tests of constitutionality. When an area is so beset that it must be put under military control at all, the paramount consideration is that its measures be successful, rather than legal. The armed services must protect a society, not merely its Constitution.... Defense measures will not, and often should not, be held within the limits that bind civil authority in peace. No court can require such a commander in such circumstances to act as a reasonable man; he may be unreasonably cautious and exacting. Perhaps he should be. But a commander in temporarily focusing the life of a community on defense is carrying out a military program; he is not making law in the sense the courts know the term. He issues orders, and they may have a certain authority as military commands, although they may be very bad as constitutional law. But if we cannot confine military expedients by the Constitution, neither would I distort the Constitution to approve all that the military may deem expedient. That is what the Court appears to be doing, whether consciously or not. I cannot say, from any evidence before me, that the orders of General DeWitt were not reasonably expedient military precautions, nor could I say that they were. But even if they were permissible military procedures, I deny that it follows that they are constitutional. If, as the Court holds, it does follow, then we may as well say that any military order will be constitutional and have done with it.

The limitation under which courts always will labor in examining the necessity for a military order are illustrated by this case. How does the Court know that these orders have a reasonable basis in necessity? No evidence whatever on that subject has been taken by this or any other court. There is sharp controversy as to the credibility of the DeWitt report. So the Court, having no real evidence before it, has no choice but to accept General DeWitt's own unsworn, self-serving statement, untested by any cross-examination, that what he did was reasonable. And thus it will always be when courts try to look into the reasonableness of a military order.

In the very nature of things military decisions are not susceptible of intelligent judicial appraisal. They do not pretend to rest on evidence, but are made on information that often would not be admissible and on assumptions that could not be proved. Information in support of an order could not be disclosed to courts without danger that it would reach the enemy. Neither can courts act on communications made in confidence. Hence courts can never have any real alternative to accepting the mere declaration of the authority that issued the order that it was reasonably necessary from a military viewpoint. Much is said of the danger to liberty from the Army program for deporting and detaining these citizens of Japanese extraction. But a judicial construction of the due process clause that will sustain this order is a far more subtle blow to liberty than the promulgation of the order itself. A military order, however unconstitutional, is not apt to last longer than the military emergency. Even during that period a succeeding commander may revoke it all. But once a judicial opinion rationalizes such an order to show that it conforms to the Constitution, or rather rationalizes the Constitution to show that the Constitution sanctions such an order, the Court for all time has validated the principle of racial discrimination in criminal procedure and of transplanting American citizens. The principle then lies about like a loaded weapon ready for the hand of any authority that can bring forward a plausible claim of an urgent need. Every repetition imbeds that principle more deeply in our law and thinking and expands it to new purposes.... Nothing better illustrates this danger than does the Court's opinion in this case. It argues that we are bound to uphold the conviction of Korematsu because we upheld one in *Hirabayashi*, when we sustained these orders in so far as they applied a curfew requirement to a citizen of Japanese ancestry. I think we should learn something from that experience.

In that case we were urged to consider only the curfew feature, that being all that technically was involved, because it was the only count necessary to sustain Hirabayashi's conviction and sentence. We yielded, and the Chief Justice guarded the opinion as carefully as language will do.... However, in spite of our limiting words we did validate a discrimination of the basis of ancestry for mild and temporary deprivation of liberty. Now the principle of racial discrimination is pushed from support of mild measures to very harsh ones, and from temporary deprivations to indeterminate ones. And the precedent which it is said requires us to do so is *Hirabayashi*. . . . How far the principle of this case would be extended before plausible reasons would play out, I do not know.

I should hold that a civil court cannot be made to enforce an order which violates constitutional limitations even if it is a reasonable exercise of military authority. The courts can exercise only the judicial power, can apply only law, and must abide by the Constitution, or they cease to be civil courts and become instruments of military policy.

Of course the existence of a military power resting on force, so vagrant, so centralized, so necessarily heedless of the individual, is an inherent threat to liberty. But I would not lead people to rely on this Court for a review that seems to me wholly delusive. The military reasonableness of these orders can only be determined by military superiors. If the people ever let command of the war power fall into irresponsible and unscrupulous hands, the courts wield no power equal to its restraint. The chief restraint upon those who command the physical forces of the country, in the future as in the past, must be their responsibility to the political judgments of their contemporaries and to the moral judgments of history.

My duties as a justice as I see them do not require me to make a military judgment as to whether General DeWitt's evacuation and detention program was a reasonable military necessity. I do not suggest that the courts should have attempted to interfere with the Army in carrying out its task. But I do not think they may be asked to execute a military expedient that has no place in law under the Constitution. I would reverse the judgment and discharge the prisoner.

Notes and Questions on Japanese Internment and its Aftermath

1. What standard of review did the Court apply in assessing the facts alleged in justification of the military orders that Korematsu disobeyed? How *should* the Court have determined whether the facts of *Korematsu* demonstrated the taking of "proper security measures" based on a reasonable assessment of "military urgency" or "the imprisonment of a citizen in a concentration camp solely because of his ancestry?" Even if, contrary to Justice Jackson, the military legitimacy of security measures taken in wartime will be deemed by courts to afford those measures a presumption of legal validity, did not Korematsu demonstrate enough to overcome that presumption? Did the military meet even a burden of going forward with evidence?

2. How much good would Jackson's "lend no aid" position have done actually to protect Japanese-Americans against unlawful detention? Insofar as his argument rests on the fact that Korematsu's conviction rested wholly on disobedience of a military order, would that conviction, under Jackson's analysis, stand on better ground if the President and Congress had more clearly authorized that order? (Recall *Kent v. Dulles* and *Hampton v. Mow Sun Wong*, reviewed in the materials on delegation in Chapter Two, in which the Court invalidated administrative decisions with foreign policy and national security implications on the ground that they had not been authorized with sufficient clarity by those political actors most competent to assess foreign policy and national security.)

3. Imagine that, before any of the *Korematsu* events had occurred, you had been asked to advise the Department of the Army in 1942 on the following question: If military authorities determine the existence of a situation of grave imminent danger to public safety, may the Army constitutionally impose restrictions on the movements of a local U.S. population if, in the view of the Army, such restrictions are closely and definitely related to avoiding sabotage and espionage? How would you proceed to address the question at hand?

4. Quite recently, Korematsu succeeded in having his conviction overturned. *Korematsu v. U.S.*, 584 F. Supp. 1406 (N.D. Cal. 1984). A federal district court in California granted a writ of *coram nobis* based on findings that the government deliberately omitted relevant information and provided misleading information in papers submitted to the Supreme Court concerning whether the military orders at issue were reasonably related to the security and defense of the nation and to the prosecution of the war. The government's assertions as to mootness and the statute of limitations failed; the court found that Korematsu continued to suffer the consequences of his conviction and that the statute of limitations was not a bar because much of the evidence needed for his post-conviction challenge had only recently been discovered by a Commission on Wartime Relocation and Internment of Civilians, established by Congress in 1980. Wartime Relocation and Internment Act, Pub. L. No. 96-317, 52, 95 Stat. 964 (1980). *See also* Irons, "Return of the Yellow Peril," *The Nation*, Oct. 19, 1985, at 361, discussing the 1985 reversal of the conviction of Gordon Hirabayashi for violation of a curfew order, upheld by the Supreme Court in *Hirabayashi v. U.S.*, 320 U.S. 81 (1943).

In *Hohri v. U.S.*, 782 F.2d 227 (D.C. Cir. 1986), a group of Japanese-American victims of the evacuation sued the U.S. to recover damages for injuries arising out of the wartime internment. They persuaded the D.C. Circuit that the government's fraudulent concealment of facts undermining its claims of military necessity tolled the applicable statute of limitations on at least certain of their claims until 1980. (The Supreme Court, however, vacated the judgment on the ground that the district court's decision adverse to the plaintiffs should have been appealed to the U.S. Court of Appeals for the Federal Circuit. *United States v. Hohri*, 107 S.Ct. 2246 (1987).) The Court of Appeals rejected the government's argument that, unlike Korematsu's post-conviction petition, the plaintiffs' damage actions could have been filed timely based on information available prior to the work of the 1980 commission. The Court was not moved by the fact that the plaintiffs had had other options for relief available to them earlier. In 1948, Congress created a mechanism for the reimbursement of Japanese-American victims through the American Japanese Evacuation Claims Act. Claims were permitted against the government for property loss, resulting in the filing of 26,000 claims and the distribution of $37 million in damages. The deadline for relief under the Act was 1950. Legislation is now pending in Congress to settle the *Hohri* litigation.

In overturning Korematsu's conviction and holding the statute of limitations tolled on takings claims, the federal courts found, through the report by the Commission on Wartime Relocation and Internment of Civilians, Personal Justice Denied (1983), that the U.S. Department of Justice had information at its disposal directly contradictory to the report by General DeWitt that military necessity justified exclusion and internment of persons of Japanese ancestry without regard to individual identity.

Executive Order 9066, upon which the military relied as authority for the evacuation and internment of Japanese Americans, was adopted at the behest of General DeWitt. DeWitt's so-called Final Report of June 5, 1943 based the War Department's anti-espionage program on a number of alleged facts: supposed signaling from shore to enemy submarines; the FBI's discovery of arms and contraband during raids on Japanese-American homes and businesses on the West Coast; the danger posed to evacuees by vigilantes; the concentration of a number of Japanese ethnic organizations which might allegedly shelter pro-Japanese attitudes or activities such as emperor-worship.

Reading the Final Report while preparing to defend the exclusion before the Supreme Court, Justice Department attorneys were, of course, drawn to the signaling contention as directly relevant to military operations. The claim was investigated by the FCC and found to be so utterly unsubstantiated that, in its brief to the Supreme Court, the Justice Department was careful not to rely on DeWitt's Final Report as a factual basis for the military decision it had to defend. There had not been any identifiable shore-to-ship signaling. Similarly, the arms and contraband argument had earlier been dismissed. The Department of Justice concluded that, although the FBI did confiscate arms and contraband from some ethnic Japanese, most items were those frequently in the possession of law-abiding citizens. Thus, neither of these "facts" justified military exclusion.

DeWitt's third argument, protecting the Japanese Americans against vigilantism, had some factual credibility. There were serious episodes of violent crimes against ethnic Japanese on the West Coast. The obvious issue raised by these incidents, however, is whether the government could properly discharge its duty to the victims of crime by imprisoning the victims. Would such police protection, in any event, be relevant to the operations of military authorities?

Finally, an argument that the Japanese were dangerously located near sensitive military installations failed to take account of similar circumstances concerning other ethnic groups. The 1980 Commission concluded that Italian-Americans were located in more strategic coastal locations than the Japanese.

Although the Government's brief in *Korematsu* thus contained few hard facts, Justice Black asserts in his opinion that the military orders were not based on "racial prejudice." The data relied on by the Court, however, derived in part from allegations of disloyalty based on cultural characteristics of the Japanese, such as their alleged community solidarity and commitment to separate language schools. These allegations are scorned in Justice Murphy's dissent, which notes that "not one person of Japanese ancestry was accused or convicted of espionage or sabotage after Pearl Harbor while they were still free."

A. Imagine that you, as a Justice Department lawyer in 1942, were aware that key facts asserted by the military in justification for the Japanese evacuation orders were unsubstantiated. Does your ethical obligation to the courts require you (1) to refrain from relying on those facts in making your argument? (2) to divulge your factual understanding to the courts? (3) to confess error?

B. Imagine that you, as a Justice Department lawyer in 1942, believe that the military's actions—even if justified in fact—were *motivated* by racial prejudice, would your conclusion affect your participation in a conduct of the Government's defense?

5. Two excellent books providing additional background information on the Japanese internment cases are J. tenBroek, E. Barnhart, and F. Matson, Prejudice, War and the Constitution (1954), and P. Irons, Justice at War (1983).

2. *Mobilization and Regulation of the Economy*
Note: Presidential Economic Controls During World War II

The power normally associated with the President's constitutional role as Commander in Chief of the Armed Forces is the power to command military troops in wartime. Presidents have also, however, asserted wartime domestic power to regulate the economy in support of the war effort.

The most innovative uses of economic controls occurred during World War II, under President Roosevelt. Some of these and their judicial reception are summarized in the following excerpt from Constitution of the United States of America: Analysis and Interpretation, S. Doc. No. 82, 92d Cong., 2d Sess. 453-59 (1973).

> [I]n exercising both the powers which he claimed as Commander-in-Chief and those which Congress conferred upon him to meet the emergency, Mr. [Franklin] Roosevelt employed new emergency agencies, created by himself and responsible directly to him, rather than the established departments or existing independent regulatory agencies.[3] . . .
>
> *Presidential Government of Labor Relations.* The most important segment of the home front regulated by what were in effect presidential edicts was the field of labor relations. Exactly six months before Pearl Harbor, on June 7, 1941, Mr. Roosevelt, citing his proclamation thirteen days earlier of an unlimited national emergency, issued an Executive Order seizing the North American Aviation Plant at Inglewood, California, where, on account of a strike, production was at a standstill.[11] Attorney General Jackson justified the seizure as growing out of the "duty constitutionally and inherently rested upon the President to exert his civil and military as well as his moral authority to keep the defense efforts of the United States a going concern," as well as "to obtain supplies for which Congress has appropriated the money, and which it has directed the President to obtain."[12] Other seizures followed, and on January 12, 1942, Mr. Roosevelt, by Executive Order 9017, created the National War Labor Board. "Whereas," the order read in part, "by reason of the state of war declared to exist by joint resolution of Congress, . . . , the national interest demands that there shall be no interruption of any work which contributes to the effective prosecution of the war; and Whereas as a result of a conference of representatives of labor and industry which met at the call of the President on December 17, 1941, it has been agreed that for the duration of the war there shall be no strikes or lockouts, and that all labor disputes shall be settled by peaceful means, and that a National War Labor Board be established for a peaceful adjustment of such disputes. Now, therefore, by virtue of the authority vested in me by the Constitution and the

---

3. For a listing of the agencies and an account of their creation to the close of 1942, *see* Vanderbilt, "War Powers and Their Administration," in *1942 Annual Survey of American Law* (New York Univ.), 106.

11. E.O. 8773, 6 *Fed. Reg.* 2777 (1941).

12. E. Corwin, *Total War and the Constitution* (New York: 1946), 47-48.

statutes of the United States, it is hereby ordered: 1. There is hereby created in the Office for Emergency Management a National War Labor Board...."[13] In this field, too, Congress intervened by means of the War Labor Disputes Act of June 25, 1943,[14] which, however, still left ample basis for presidential activity of a legislative character.[15]

Sanctions Implementing Presidential Directives. To implement his directives as Commander-in-Chief in wartime, and especially those which he issued in governing labor disputes, President Roosevelt often resorted to "sanctions," which may be described as penalties lacking statutory authorization. Ultimately, the President sought to put sanctions in this field on a systematic basis. The order empowered the Director of Economic Stabilization, on receiving a report from the National War Labor Board that someone was not complying with its orders, to issue "directives" to the appropriate department or agency requiring that privileges, benefits, rights, or preferences enjoyed by the noncomplying party be withdrawn.[16]

Sanctions were also occasionally employed by statutory agencies, such as OPA, to supplement the penal provisions of the Emergency Price Control Act of January 30, 1942.[17] In the case of *Steuart & Bro. v. Bowles*,[18] the Supreme Court had the opportunity to regularize this type of executive emergency legislation. Here a retail dealer in fuel oil was charged with having violated a rationing order of OPA by obtaining large quantities of oil from its supplier without surrendering ration coupons, by delivering many thousands of gallons of fuel oil without requiring ration coupons, and so on, and was prohibited by the agency from receiving oil for resale or transfer for the ensuing year. The offender conceded the validity of the rationing order in support of which the suspension order was issued but challenged the validity of the latter as imposing a penalty that Congress had not enacted and asked the district court to enjoin it.

The court refused to do so and was sustained by the Supreme Court in its position. Said Justice Douglas, speaking for the Court: "Without rationing, the fuel tanks of a few would be full; the fuel tanks of many would be empty. Some localities would have plenty; communities less favorably situated would suffer.

---

13. 7 *Fed. Reg.* 237 (1942).

14. 57 Stat. 163 (1943).

15. "During the course of the year [1945] the President directed the seizure of many of the nation's industries in the course of labor disputes. The total number of facilities taken over is significant: two railroad systems, one public utility, nine industrial companies, the transportation systems of two cities, the motor carriers in one city, a towing company and a butadiene plant. In addition thereto the President on April 10 seized 218 bituminous coal mines belonging to 162 companies and on May 7, 33 more bituminous mines of 24 additional companies. The anthracite coal industry fared no better; on May 3 and May 7 all the mines of 365 companies and operators were taken away from the owners, and on October 6 the President ordered the seizure of 54 plants and pipe lines of 29 petroleum producing companies in addition to four taken over prior thereto...." Vanderbilt, "War Powers and their Administration," *1945 Annual Survey of American Law* (N.Y. Univ.), 254, 271-273.

16. E.O. 9370, 8 *Fed. Reg.* 11463 (1943).

17. 56 Stat. 23 (1942).

18. 322 U.S. 398 (1944).

Allocation or rationing is designed to eliminate such inequalities and to treat all alike who are similarly situated.... But middlemen—wholesalers and retailers—bent on defying the rationing system could raise havoc with it.... From the viewpoint of a rationing system a middleman who distributes the product in violation and disregard of the prescribed quotas is an inefficient and wasteful conduit.... Certainly we would not say that the President would lack the power under this Act to take away from a wasteful factory and route to an efficient one a previous supply of material needed for the manufacture of articles of war. ... Yet if the President has the power to channel raw materials into the most efficient industrial units and thus save scarce materials from wastage it is difficult to see why the same principle is not applicable to the distribution of fuel oil."[19] Sanctions were, therefore, constitutional when the deprivations they wrought were a reasonably implied amplification of the substantive power which they supported and were directly conservative of the interests which this power was created to protect and advance. It is certain, however, that sanctions not uncommonly exceeded this pattern.[20]

Constitutional Status of Presidential Agencies. The question of the legal status of the presidential agencies was dealt with judicially but once. This was in the decision of the United States Court of Appeals of the District of Columbia in *Employers Group v. National War Labor Board*, [143 F.2d 145 (D.C. Cir. 1944)] which was a suit to annul and enjoin a "directive order" of the War Labor Board. The Court refused the injunction on the ground that at the time when the directive was issued any action of the Board was "informatory," "at most advisory." In support of this view the Court quoted approvingly a statement by the chairman of the Board itself: "These orders are in reality mere declarations of the equities of each industrial dispute, as determined by a tripartite body in which industry, labor, and the public share equal responsibility; and the appeal of the Board is to the moral obligation of employers and workers to abide by the nonstrike, no-lock-out agreement and ... to carry out the directives of the tribunal created under that agreement by the Commander in Chief." Nor, the Court continued, had the later War Labor Disputes Act vested War Labor Boards orders with any greater authority, with the result that they were still judicially unenforceable and unreviewable. Following this theory, the War Labor Board was not an office wielding power, but a purely advisory body, such as Presidents have frequently created in the past without the aid or consent of Congress. Congress itself, nevertheless, both in its appropriation acts and in other legislation, treated the presidential agencies as in all respects offices....

The Postwar Period. The end of active hostilities did not terminate either the emergency or the federal-governmental response to it. President Truman proclaimed the termination of hostilities on December 31, 1946,[21] and Congress enacted a joint resolution which repealed a great variety of wartime statutes and set termination dates for others in July, 1947.[22] Signing the resolution, the

---

19. *Id.*, 404-405.

20. E. Corwin, *The President: Office and Powers 1787-1957* (New York: 4th ed. 1957), 249-250.

21. Proc. 2714, 12 *Fed. Reg.* 1 (1947).

22. S.J. Res. 123, 61 Stat. 449 (1947).

President said that the emergencies declared in 1939 and 1940 continued to exist and that it was "not possible at this time to provide for terminating all war and emergency powers."[23] The hot war was giving way to the Cold War.

Congress thereafter enacted a new Housing and Rent Act to continue the controls begun in 1942[24] and continued the draft.[25] With the outbreak of the Korean War, legislation was enacted establishing general presidential control over the economy again[1] and by executive order the President created agencies to exercise the power.[2] The Court continued to assume the existence of a state of wartime emergency prior to Korea but with misgivings. In *Woods v. Cloyd W. Miller Co.*,[3] the Court held constitutional the new rent control law on the ground that cessation of hostilities did not conclude the Government's powers but that the power continued to remedy the evil arising out of the emergency. Yet for the Court, Justice Douglas noted: "We recognize the force of the argument that the effects of war under modern conditions may be felt in the economy for years and years, and that if the war power can be used in days of peace to treat all the wounds which war inflicts on our society, it may not only swallow up all other powers of Congress but largely obliterate the Ninth and Tenth Amendments as well. There are no such implications in today's decision." Justice Jackson, while concurring, noted that he found the war power "the most dangerous one to free government in the whole catalogue of powers" and cautioned that its exercise should "be scrutinized with care." And in *Ludecke v. Watkins*,[6] four Justices were prepared to hold that the presumption in the statute under review of continued war with Germany was fiction and not be utilized.

But the postwar was a time of reaction against the wartime exercise of power by President Roosevelt and President Truman was not permitted the same liberties. The Twenty-second Amendment writing into permanent law the two term custom, the "Great Debate" about our participation in NATO, the attempt to limit the treaty-making power, and other actions, bespoke the reaction. The Supreme Court signalized this reaction when it struck down the President's action in seizing the steel industry while it was struck during the Korean War.

Powers of the President Under the War Labor Disputes Act to Seize Properties Affected by Strikes
40 Op. A.G. 312 (1944)

MY DEAR MR. PRESIDENT: My opinion has been requested on the legality of a proposed Executive order directing the Secretary of Commerce to take possession of and to operate certain plants and facilities of Montgomery Ward and Company in

---

23. *Woods v. Cloyd W. Miller Co.*, 333 U.S. 138, 140 n. 3 (1948).

24. 61 Stat. 193 (1947).

25. 62 Stat. 604 (1948), as amended, 50 U.S.C. App. § 451 et. seq.

1. Defense Production Act of 1950, 64 Stat. 798.

2. E.O. 10161, 15 *Fed. Reg.* 6105 (1950).

3. 333 U.S. 138 (1948).

6. 335 U.S. 160 (1948).

Chicago, Illinois, in which a strike is now in progress.... In my opinion, the facts ... justify the following conclusions:

(1) Montgomery Ward and Company is engaged in activities of a kind essential to the maintenance of our war economy. An interruption or stoppage of the Company's activities would have an adverse effect upon the war effort.

(2) There is a real and present danger that the labor dispute that is now interrupting the operations of the plants and facilities of the Company in Chicago may extend throughout the nation and interrupt the operations of other plants and facilities of the Company. There is an equally real and present danger that the dispute will breed other labor controversies that will interrupt the operations of plants and facilities of other companies, both in the Chicago area and elsewhere, that are engaged in making or distributing goods or performing services that are essential to the war effort.

(3) There is now no reason to expect that the disputes between the Company and its employees in Chicago and elsewhere in the United States will be settled promptly and peacefully either by agreement or by the machinery that Congress has set up in the War Labor Disputes Act.

The basic legal question is whether you have the authority to take possession of and to operate the plants and facilities of Montgomery Ward and Company in Chicago in order to prevent a serious interference with the war effort. Section 3 of the War Labor Disputes Act provides in part as follows: "The power of the President under the foregoing provisions of this section to take immediate possession of any plant upon a failure to comply with any such provisions, and the authority granted by this section for the use and operation by the United States or in its interests of any plant of which possession is so taken, shall also apply as hereinafter provided to any plant, mine, or facility equipped for the manufacture, production, or mining of any articles or materials which may be required for the war effort or which may be useful in connection therewith. Such power and authority may be exercised by the President through such department or agency of the Government as he may designate, and may be exercised with respect to any such plant, mine, or facility whenever the President finds, after investigation, and proclaims that there is an interruption of the operation of such plant, mine, or facility as a result of a strike or other labor disturbance, that the war effort will be unduly impeded or delayed by such interruption, and that the exercise of such power and authority is necessary to insure the operation of such plant, mine, or facility in the interest of the war effort...."

On the basis of the facts that have been summarized, and the conclusions that those facts justify, it is my opinion, first, that the plants and facilities of Montgomery Ward are the kind of plants and facilities whose seizure is authorized by section 3 and, second, that you may properly make the findings required by section 3 as a condition precedent to the exercise of the power that it confers. I believe, therefore, that section 3 of the War Labor Disputes Act authorizes you to take possession of and to operate the plants and facilities of Montgomery Ward and Company.

It is not necessary, however, to rely solely upon the provisions of section 3 of the War Labor Disputes Act. As Chief Executive and as Commander-in-Chief of the Army and Navy, the President possesses an aggregate of powers that are derived from the Constitution and from various statutes enacted by the Congress for the purpose of carrying on the war. The Constitution lays upon the President the duty "to take care that the laws be faithfully executed." The Constitution also places on the President the responsibility and invests in him the powers of Commander-in-Chief of the Army and Navy. In time of war when the existence of the nation is at stake, this aggregate of powers includes authority to take reasonable steps to prevent nation-wide labor disturbances that threaten to interfere seriously with the conduct of the war. The fact that the initial impact of these disturbances is on the production or distribution of essential civilian goods is not a reason for denying the Chief Executive and the Commander-in-Chief of the Army and Navy the power to take steps to protect the nation's war effort. In modern war the maintenance of a healthy, orderly, and stable civilian economy is essential to successful military effort. The Congress has recognized this fact by enacting such statutes as the Emergency Price Control Act of 1942; the act of October 2, 1942, entitled "An Act to Amend the Emergency Price Control Act of 1942, to aid in preventing inflation, and for other purposes"; the Small Business Mobilization Law of June 11, 1942; and the War Labor Disputes Act. Even in the absence of section 3 of the War Labor Disputes Act, therefore, I believe that by the exercise of the aggregate of your powers as Chief Executive and Commander-in-Chief, you could lawfully take possession of and operate the plants and facilities of Montgomery Ward and Company if you found it necessary to do so to prevent injury to the country's war effort.

I conclude that in the circumstances of this case section 3 of the War Labor Disputes Act and your constitutional and statutory powers as Chief Executive and Commander-in-Chief of the Army and of the Navy, considered either separately or together, authorize you to direct the Secretary of Commerce to take possession of and to operate the plants and facilities of Montgomery Ward and Company in Chicago, Illinois.

The proposed Executive order, presented by the Chairman of the National War Labor Board and forwarded for my consideration by the Director of the Bureau of the Budget, has my approval as to form and legality.

Respectfully yours, FRANCIS BIDDLE.

———————

The strike that precipitated the preceding opinion is perhaps best known for the newspaper photograph it produced of U.S. army troops carrying the head of Montgomery Ward out of his office. Do you agree with Attorney General Biddle's interpretation of the Constitution? Should this opinion provoke any reassessment of *Youngstown*?

C. Peace Time Authority to Use Troops for Law Enforcement ("Posse Comitatus")

In addition to the President's powers to use military force abroad, it has been urged that the President has both constitutional and statutory power to use armed force for domestic law enforcement. Sections 331, 332 and 333 of Title 10, United States Code, expressly authorize the President to use militia to suppress insurrections against states, suppress rebellions against federal law enforcement, and suppress domestic insurrections generally. The President's discretion under these sections is limited by certain procedural requirements, including the requirement under section 334 of Title 10 that the President order insurgents to disperse prior to the deployment of military force.

The most general statutory limitation on the President's ability to use military force for law enforcement purposes is, however, the so-called Posse Comitatus Act, 18 U.S.C. 1385. It provides:

> Whoever, except in cases and under circumstances expressly authorized by the Constitution or Act of Congress, willfully uses any part of the Army or Air Force as a posse comitatus or otherwise to execute the laws shall be fined not more than $10,000 or imprisoned not more than two years or both.

The Act was specifically adopted to prevent the use of troops in U.S. marshals' posses, which had been widespread prior to the Civil War. Note, however, that the Act expressly omits reference to the Coast Guard, which has statutory authority to assist in the enforcement of all federal laws applicable on the high seas. 10 U.S.C. § 2.

The President's authority to use federal troops to suppress resistance to the enforcement of federal law is reviewed in the following Attorney General opinion, which comments on the most famous modern use of military force for law enforcement purposes—the desegregation of the Little Rock, Arkansas public schools. Would you regard it as desirable for Congress to expand the President's authority to use military force for law enforcement purposes? For example, should a branch of the military conducting routine air exercises be allowed to engage in aerial surveillance photography on behalf of the Drug Enforcement Administration or the Environmental Protection Agency? Should military intelligence agencies be authorized to use their intelligence gathering capacity on behalf of the Federal Bureau of Investigation? What dangers, if any, do you foresee should Congress expand the military role in law enforcement?

President's Power to Use Federal Troops to Suppress Resistance to Enforcement of Federal Court Orders— Little Rock, Arkansas

41 Op. A.G. 313 (1957)

[The Little Rock School Board, in 1955, formulated a plan for the gradual desegregation of Little Rock public schools, to begin with the high school in 1957. In a suit by black students and their parents challenging the plan as too slow, a U.S. district court held the plan adequate under *Brown v. Board of Education (II)*, 349 U.S. 294 (1955). *Aaron v. Cooper*, 143 F. Supp. 855 (E.D. Ark. 1956). While the school board was pursuing steps to implement its plan, a state court issued an order enjoining the desegregation effort, based on testimony by Governor Orval E. Faubus that implementation of the plan might lead to violence. *Thomason v. Cooper*, 2 Race Rel. L. Rep. 931 (Pulaski County Ch. Ct. Aug. 29, 1957). The next day, the U.S. district court issued an order forbidding implementation of the state decree and interference with desegregation.

Notwithstanding the federal order, Governor Faubus, on September 2, 1957, stationed national guard troops at Little Rock Central High School with the ostensible purpose of preserving the peace. Faubus' order made clear, however, that, in the name of "peace and good order," integration would not be permitted to proceed. The school board responded by asking black students to stay away from the school until further legal proceedings resolved the impasse.

In response to a school board petition for further guidance, the U.S. district court, on September 3 again ordered integration. Notwithstanding this order, Governor

Faubus again ordered the national guard to maintain segregation. The federal court responded, in part, by asking the United States to enter the case as *amicus curiae* and to petition for an injunction against the governor of Arkansas on the ground that his use of the state military force was unconstitutional.]

MY DEAR MR. PRESIDENT: I am formally submitting to you in this opinion the legal advice which I have given you on separate recent occasions on certain questions arising in the school desegregation case in Little Rock, Arkansas, between September 3, 1957, and October 1, 1957. Because of the grave constitutional issues involved, and the direct bearing of those issues upon the action taken by you as President of the United States, I believe it advisable that this advice should be made into a permanent record.

·   ·   ·

While we were preparing for the hearing [in which the federal district court requested the participation of the Justice Department], it became increasingly evident that the normal judicial procedure might be inadequate to prevent obstruction of the orders of the court. The activities of agitators which had commenced after the Governor had placed the National Guard at the school presented a threat of concerted obstruction.

You accordingly asked for advice as to your power and duty as President to aid in the execution of the court's orders if obstruction should continue after the September 20th hearing and further action by the court. Between the dates of September 10th and September 24th I gave you the advice which I am now setting forth.

Whenever interference and obstruction to enforcement of law exists, and domestic violence is interposed to frustrate the judicial process, it is the primary and mandatory duty of the authorities of the State to suppress the violence and to remove any obstruction to the orderly enforcement of law. This same duty fully exists where the domestic violence is interposed in opposition to the enforcement of Federal law rather than to the local law of the State....

The supremacy of Federal law is ensured by clause 3 of Article VI providing that: "the Members of the several State Legislatures, and all executive and judicial Officers, both of the United States and of the several States, shall be bound by Oath or Affirmation, to support this Constitution;...."... The obligation which the Federal Constitution imposes upon State officers to uphold Federal law is in accord with their primary responsibility to maintain order within the State. Acts of violent or forcible resistance to Federal law disrupt peace and order in the State and violate State law. It is the duty of State officers in such circumstances to suppress the disorders in a manner which will not nullify and will permit the effectuation of State and Federal law.

When State officers refuse or fail to discharge their duty in this respect, it becomes the responsibility of the national Government, through the Chief Executive, to dispel any such forcible resistance to Federal law. Otherwise, lawlessness would be permitted to exist for lack of any counteracting force. Shortly before the hearings on September 20, the attorneys for Governor Faubus and his codefendants filed an affidavit of bias and prejudice seeking to disqualify Judge Davies. They also filed motions to dismiss the pleadings filed by the United States as *amicus curiae* on the grounds of lack of jurisdiction and failure to convene a three-judge court, as well as a motion to quash the service of the subpoenas which had been served on the commanding officers of the Arkansas National Guard. At the hearing on September 20, the court heard argument on these motions and denied them. At that point, the attorneys for Governor Faubus and his codefendants announced their position that the Governor could not be questioned in a United States court "or anywhere" as to the exercise of his judgment in the performance of a duty under the Constitution and laws of a State. They then requested permission to leave the hearing. They were excused by the court with the explanation that the hearing would proceed notwithstanding their withdrawal.

The Department of Justice then placed witnesses on the stand, including the Mayor of Little Rock, the Chief of Police, and local school authorities. These witnesses gave unchallenged testimony of local peaceful relations among the races in Little Rock for a quarter of a century, including the removal of seating restrictions based upon race in local buses in January 1957, and the absence of any indication that violence or disorder would be present upon the opening of the school term. The attorneys for the Governor and his codefendants remained absent during the taking of the testimony by the court and chose not to take advantage of their right to cross-examine the witnesses, to present evidence on their behalf, and to assist the court in its functions. After hearing the witnesses, the court announced:

> It is very clear to this Court from the evidence and the testimony adduced upon the hearing today that the plan of integration adopted by the Little Rock School Board and approved by this Court and the Court of Appeals for the Eighth Circuit has been thwarted by the Governor of Arkansas by the use of National Guard troops.
>
> It is equally demonstrable from the testimony here today that there would have been no violence in carrying out the plan of integration and that there has been no violence.

Late on September 20, the court handed down its decree enjoining the Governor of Arkansas and his National Guard commanders from further interference with the orders of that court. The Governor thereupon announced that he was withdrawing the National Guard from the school. No stay of enforcement of the court's order was sought by the Governor or others.

The local authorities of Little Rock announced their intention of maintaining order in support of the decrees of the court. The test of the ability of those authorities to control the situation came on September 23d. At the opening of the school, a mob of about 1,000 persons assembled. When the Negro children who were entitled to admission to the school arrived violence broke out. After three hours of riot and tumult, the Negro children were removed from the school by orders of the Mayor and local officials. Mob force had successfully frustrated the carrying out of the orders of the court and had demonstrably overpowered such police forces as could be mustered by the local officials. The Governor did not use his powers to support the local authorities. I thereupon advised you that you then had the undoubted power, under the Constitution and laws of the United States, to call the National Guard into service and to use those forces, together with such of the Armed Forces as you considered necessary, to suppress the domestic violence, obstruction and resistance of law then and there existing.

I further advised you, and do again advise you, that your power so to act rested upon both your powers as President under the Constitution and the powers vested in you by the Congress under Federal law, particularly as reflected by sections 332 and 333 of title 10 of the United States Code.

The Supreme Court has recognized the constitutional power and responsibility which reposes in the National Government to compel obedience to law and order. (*Ex parte Siebold*, 100 U.S. 371, 395 (1879)): "We hold it to be an incontrovertible principle, that the government of the United States may, by means of physical force, exercised through its official agents, execute on every foot of American soil the powers and functions that belong to it. This necessarily involves the power to command obedience to its laws, and hence the power to keep the peace to that extent." To similar effect was the declaration by the Court in a later case (*In Re Debs*, 158 U.S. 564, 582 (1894)): "The entire strength of the nation may be used to enforce in any part of the land the full and free exercise of all national powers and the security of all rights entrusted by the Constitution to its care.... If the emergency arises, the army of the Nation, and all its militia, are at the service of the Nation to compel obedience to its laws."

In addition to the constitutional power in the President in such matters, a series of statutes of broad sweep enable the President to deal effectively with civil disturbances within a State when compelling circumstances are present. By section 331 of title 10 of the United States Code, the President may use the State militia and the Armed Forces of the United States, upon call of the State legislature or of its Governor if the legislature cannot be convened, to put down any insurrection against a State Government. This authority was not appropriate for use and was not used in Little Rock.

Under section 332 of title 10, the President is vested with similar authority as to the militia and Armed Forces when, in his judgment, unlawful obstructions, combinations, or assemblages, or rebellion against the authority of the United States make it impracticable to enforce the laws of the United States in any State by the ordinary course of judicial proceedings. A third statute, section 333 of title 10, gives the President like powers to suppress in a State any insurrection, domestic violence, unlawful combination, or conspiracy which so hinders the execution of the laws of the State and of the United States that any class of its people is deprived of a right, privilege, immunity, or protection named in the Constitution and secured by law, and the constituted authorities of the State are unable, fail, or refuse to protect the right, privilege, or immunity, or to give that protection, or which opposes or obstructs the execution of the laws of the United States or impedes the course of justice under those laws. Congress declared in this statute that when the execution of the laws is so hindered, without State protection, the State shall be considered to have denied the equal protection of the laws secured by the Constitution.

In order that the authority of either of these two sections of the Code may be invoked, it is required that the President first issue a proclamation, as set forth in section 334 of title 10. You issued an appropriate proclamation (No. 3204, September 23, 1957) prior to the issuance of Executive Order No. 10730 of September 24, 1957. This Executive order cited, as a basis for the authorized use of Federal forces, the Constitution and statutes of the United States, including particularly the above-noted sections 332 and 333 of title 10. As applied to the Little Rock events, I advised you that unlawful obstructions, combinations, or assemblages made it impracticable to enforce the laws of the United States in Little Rock by the ordinary course of judicial proceedings (10 U.S.C. 332). The facts upon which these conclusions were based were reported to you as they occurred, and included an account of the determined group of hundreds of men and women bent upon overpowering the local peace officers, the several incidents of violence with their very real and discernible trend toward a larger-scale inflammatory assault, the action of the Mayor and local authorities in ordering the withdrawal of the Negro students so as to appease the unruly mob, the admission of local authorities that such peace officers as they could command were unable to cope with the disorderly assemblage, and the indifference or refusal of the Governor of the State to supply a sufficient force to quell the lawless movement. I also advised you that the local strength of the United States Marshal was insufficient to achieve enforcement of the order of the United States District Court, and that, because of the local situation and the need for timely action, it would not have been reasonable, or effective in the circumstances, to attempt to have the Marshal enlist the support of the citizenry to carry out the court order. In accordance with the salutary policy that the agents of the Federal Bureau of Investigation shall not be used as a national police, you rejected suggestions originating outside the Federal Government that such agents be called upon to enforce the court's orders.

These facts were still present on the day after issuance of the proclamation. The street mobs reassembled. The Mayor of Little Rock wired you on September 24, as follows:

THE IMMEDIATE NEED FOR FEDERAL TROOPS IS URGENT. THE MOB IS MUCH LARGER IN NUMBERS AT 8 AM THAN AT ANY TIME YESTERDAY PEOPLE ARE CONVERGING ON THE SCENE FROM ALL DIRECTIONS MOB IS ARMED AND ENGAGING IN FISTICUFFS AND OTHER ACTS OF VIOLENCE. SITUATION IS OUT OF CONTROL AND POLICE CANNOT DISPERSE THE MOB I AM PLEADING TO YOU AS PRESIDENT OF THE UNITED STATES IN THE INTEREST OF HUMANITY LAW AND ORDER AND THE CAUSE OF DEMOCRACY WORLD WIDE TO PROVIDE THE NECESSARY FEDERAL TROOPS WITHIN SEVERAL HOURS. ACTION BY YOU WILL RESTORE PEACE AND ORDER AND COMPLIANCE WITH YOUR PROCLAMATION.

Thereupon you ordered the use of United States troops and the federalization of the Arkansas National Guard.

This, in sum, was in my view—and I so advised you—a situation which compelled action by the Chief Executive under provisions of law designed to uphold the strength of law enforcement and the standing and authority of the courts.

I also advised you that the execution of the laws of Arkansas and of the United States within the State of Arkansas was being hindered by unlawful combinations so as to deprive people in that State of a right, privilege, immunity, or protection named in the Constitution and secured by law, and that the appropriate State authorities were unable, unwilling, or failed to protect that right, privilege, immunity, or to give that protection. The requisites of law were met. (10 U.S.C. 333.)

During the course of consideration relative to the use of Federal troops, attention also was given to the "Posse Comitatus Act" (18 U.S.C. 1385). . . . I pointed out to you that the act, by its specific terms, excepts from its prohibition the use of the Army or Air Force as a posse comitatus or otherwise to execute the law "in cases and under circumstances expressly authorized by the Constitution or Act of Congress." I advised you that your authority to dispatch Federal troops to Little Rock would be predicated upon express statutory right (10 U.S.C. 332, 333), and, therefore, would be within the exception contained in the Posse Comitatus Act. Although there has been no judicial decision on this question, the advice given you has support in a long line of opinions of past Attorneys General and in Executive action.[6] The legislative history surrounding this act fully supports this view. In brief, it discloses that, at the time the Posse Comitatus Act was enacted, the predecessors to 10 U.S.C. 332, 333 were in force and the Congress did not intend or interpret the act as impairing whatever powers the President had under those statutes. The sponsors of the Posse Comitatus Act expressly so stated during the course of the debates.[7] This was also the view of President Hayes who approved the Posse Comitatus Act. In his diary entry for July 30, 1878, President Hayes wrote:

> The whiskey cases in the South call for wise and firm conduct. No doubt the Government is a good deal crippled in its means of enforcing the laws by the proviso attached to the Army Appropriation Bill which prohibits the use of the Army as a *posse comitatus* to aid United States officers in the execution of process. The states may and do employ state military force to support as a *posse comitatus* the state civil authorities. If a conflict of jurisdiction occurs between the State and the United States on any question, the United States is thus placed at a great disadvantage. But in the last resort, I am confident that the laws give the Executive ample power to enforce obedience to United States process. The machinery is cumbersome and its exercise will tend to give undue importance to petty attempts to resist or evade the laws. But I must use such machinery as the laws give. Senator Beck, a supporter of the provision, stated with respect to the use of troops to enforce the laws: "Wherever the law authorizes it, it is admitted to be right; ..." (*ibid.*, 4240). "Without passion or haste, the enforcement of the laws must go on. If the sheriffs or other state officers resist the laws, and by the aid of state militia do it successfully, that is a case of rebellion to be dealt with under the laws framed to enable the Executive to subdue combinations or conspiracies too powerful to be suppressed by the

---

6. 16 Op. A.G. 162, 164 (1878); 17 Op. 242 (1881); 17 Op. 333, 335 (1882); 19 Op. 293, 296 (1889); 19 Op. 570, 571 (1890). An account of the action of President Cleveland in reference to the Pullman strike in 1894 and that of President Wilson in connection with unlawful assemblages in Arkansas in 1914 is set forth in *Federal Aid in Domestic Disturbances*, Sen. Doc. No. 263, 67th Cong., 2d sess., pp. 197, 321; Sen. Ex. Doc. No. 7, vol. 2, 53d Cong., 3d sess., p. XX (1894-95).

7. The predecessors of 10 U.S.C. 332, 333 were part of title 69 of the Revised Statutes of 1873 when the Posse Comitatus Act was enacted. The sponsors of the legislation were aware of title 69 and stated that the new legislation would not affect the powers contained in that title. 7 Cong. Rec. 3846, 4243. Congressman Knott, who introduced the provision, said:

> [T]his amendment expressly excepts those cases and those circumstances in which troops are now authorized by any act of Congress to be employed in the enforcement of said law (ibid., 3847).

. . .

> There are, as I have already remarked, particular cases in which Congress has provided that the Army may be used, which this bill does not militate against, such as the case of the enforcement of the neutrality laws, the enforcement of the collection of customs duties and of the civil-rights bill, and one or two other instances. But this amendment is designed to put a stop to the practice, which has become fearfully common, of military officers of every grade answering the call of every marshal and deputy marshal to aid in the enforcement of the laws (*ibid.*, 3849).

ordinary civil officers of the United States. This involves proclamations, the movement of United States land and naval forces, and possibly the calling out of volunteers, and this looks like war. It is like the Whiskey Rebellion in the time of Washington. That precedent, if the case demands it, will be followed. Good citizens who wish to avoid such a result must see to it that neither their State Governments nor mobs undertake to prevent United States officers from enforcing the laws. My duty is plain. The laws must be enforced.[8]

There are in any event grave doubts as to the authority of the Congress to limit the constitutional powers of the President to enforce the laws and preserve the peace under circumstances which he deems appropriate. However, that consideration was not reached because of the express congressional authority for the action taken.

Finally, much of what the Supreme Court said in the Debs case has special and peculiar relevance to the Little Rock situation. There, a Federal district court issued a sweeping order enjoining strikers in the Pullman company riots at Chicago in 1894. When the mobs continued their lawless course, Federal troops, both regular and National Guardsmen, were dispatched to the city and actively intervened to restore order. In reviewing this situation, the Supreme Court pointed out that what had happened at Chicago transcended municipal boundaries (*In Re Debs*, 158 U.S. 592):

> That the bill filed in this case alleged special facts calling for the exercise of all the powers of the court is not open to question. The picture drawn in it of the vast interests involved, not merely of the city of Chicago and the State of Illinois, but of all the States, and the general confusion into which the interstate commerce of the country was thrown; the forcible intervention with that commerce; the attempted exercise by individuals of powers belonging only to government, and the threatened continuance of such invasions of public right, presented a condition of affairs which called for the fullest exercise of all the powers of the courts. If ever there was a special exigency, one which demanded that the court should do all that courts can do, it was disclosed by this bill, and we need not turn to the public history of the day, which only reaffirms with clearest emphasis all its allegations.

In Little Rock, the "vast interests involved" also reached beyond the confines of that one city and, as publicly stated by you and the Secretary of State, vitally affected our country's international relations. When an unruly mob arrogates to itself the power to nullify a constitutionally-secured right, a statutory prescription, and a court order, it may reasonably be assumed that the danger of a fast-moving, destructive volcanic force is immediately present. Success of the unlawful assemblage in Little Rock inevitably would have led to mob rule, and a probable breakdown of law and order in an ever-increasing area. When a local and State Government is unable or unwilling to meet such a threat, the Federal Government is not impotent....

Respectfully, HERBERT BROWNELL, Jr.

---

1. The Little Rock struggle provoked a major Supreme Court reassertion of the Court's role as ultimate arbiter of the Constitution. *Cooper v. Aaron*, 358 U.S. 1 (1958). Indeed, all nine justices underscored their commitment to that view by signing the *Cooper* opinion individually. A fuller account of the events leading up to *Cooper*

---

8. Diary and Letters of Rutherford Brichard Hayes (1929), vol. 3, pp. 492-493.

appears in T. Freyer, The Little Rock Crisis: A Constitutional Interpretation (1984). For an exploration by a Little Rock native of both the immediate post-*Brown* politics in Little Rock and the aftermath of *Cooper*, see I. Spitzberg, Jr., Racial Politics in Little Rock 1954-1964 (1987). The implications of *Cooper* for the Supreme Court are discussed in Farber, *The Supreme Court and the Rule of Law:* Cooper v. Aaron *Revisited*, 1982 U. Ill. L. Rev. 387.

2. The Kennedy and Johnson Administrations were widely criticized for failing to use federal law enforcement powers more aggressively to protect civil rights—for example, during the Birmingham, Alabama demonstrations of April, 1963, and during Mississippi's "Freedom Summer" of 1964. In an important set of lectures, Professor Burke Marshall, formerly President Kennedy's assistant attorney general in charge of the Civil Rights Division of the Justice Department, defended the Kennedy Administration's efforts as an attempt to preserve constitutional principles of federalism while trying to secure the constitutional rights of blacks and of civil rights protesters. Marshall warned that the durability of federalism would give way unless states accepted new federal antidiscrimination legislation, and abandoned their pattern of defiance to federal law. B. Marshall, Federalism and Civil Rights (1964). To understand fully the urgency of the demands on the Kennedy Administration, one should read M. L. King, Jr., Letter from Birmingham City Jail (1963), an essay that ranks among the classic defenses of civil disobedience and was perhaps the most influential explanation of black unwillingness to accept further gradualism as a strategy for securing civil rights. *See also* M. L. King, Jr., Why We Can't Wait (1964).

3. The Supreme Court is expected to decide during its October, 1987 term a case in which the plaintiffs, residents of the Pine Ridge Indian Reservation in South Dakota, persuaded the Eighth Circuit that, if their "seizure" by military personnel and removal to the Village of Wounded Knee, South Dakota violated the Posse Comitatus Act, it would be "unreasonable" and hence in violation of the fourth amendment as a matter of law. *Bissonette v. Haig*, 800 F.2d 812 (8th Cir. 1986) (en banc), *cert. granted*, 107 S. Ct. 1283 (1987). The Court of Appeals held that, although not all seizures in violation of statute would be unconstitutional, the Posse Comitatus Act is "a criminal law of long standing, itself expressive of an authentically American tradition of even longer standing," 800 F.2d at 816, which provides "at least *prima facie* evidence of what society as a whole regards as reasonable." *Id*. at 814. The dissenters in the 5-4 ruling argued that using the Posse Comitatus Act as the measure of liability in a personal damages action under the Constitution would undermine Congress' decision not to create a private right of action to enforce a criminal statute. *Id*. at 817.

Chapter 8

The Transfer of Power

The Constitution determines, and various statutes relate to, how the President is to be elected, how he may be removed by Congress, and how the government is to proceed in cases of presidential disability or removal from office. Yet the operation of the relevant law, perhaps more conspicuously than in other contexts, is conditioned by deeply entrenched political phenomena, for example, the political party system, that are beyond the express contemplation of the Constitution.

We consider here at least the basic contours of this body of law for three reasons. First, although the constitutional provisions affecting election and removal do not *per se* vest power in the President, the political possibilities that the law creates for election and removal affect the exercise of the powers we have already considered. Conversely, one's analysis of the proper exercise of those powers will have implications for designing appropriate processes for choosing, removing, and replacing Presidents. Finally, some consideration of these issues is necessary to round out the institutional portrait of the presidential office.

Section A of this chapter considers the nomination of presidential and vice-presidential candidates. Section B deals with presidential elections and campaign regulation. Section C considers issues relevant to presidential impeachment. Section D concerns problems of presidential disability and succession.

A. Nomination of Presidential and Vice Presidential Candidates

1. Political Parties and Law Generally

a. Development of Parties and Nominating Systems

Two features of our presidential election process are most critical to any comprehension of it. First, what transpires on Election Day every four years is not a nationwide election of the President, but fifty state-run contests for presidential electors who conduct the actual presidential choice through an obscure constitutional process the following month. Second, a very great deal of the political process that determines the Presidency is controlled by political parties, which are, for most legal purposes, private associations. This section provides a capsule summary of this history of U.S. political parties, the processes by which they choose presidential candidates, and several recurring proposals for reform.

History of Parties. Those who drafted the 1787 Constitution did not anticipate— indeed, they hoped to forestall—political party organization. *See* The Federalist No. 10 (J. Madison); G. Wills, Explaining America (1981). Parties developed, however, within several years of nationhood, crystalizing first as factions in Congress. Historian

Arthur Schlesinger has proffered an essentially functionalist explanation for their development—party organization was simply too attractive to be passed up as a device for the accomplishment of critically important goals. These included broadening representation for the wide range of salient interests having a stake in the new country, providing channels for the recruitment and mobilization of both political leaders and their supporters, helping to define areas of agreement and disagreement among competing political groups, and developing mechanisms for the containment of political differences. *See generally* A. M. Schlesinger, Jr., *Introduction*, in 1 History of U.S. Political Parties (A. M. Schlesinger, Jr. ed. 1973).

Arguably, the United States is in its fourth or fifth party system. Between 1794 and 1814, the party competitors were the Federalists and the Democratic-Republicans, led by Jefferson. Although the Jeffersonian ideology was more egalitarian, the parties exhibited few major differences over domestic policy. Unsuccessful Federalist opposition to the War of 1812 underscored its sectional orientation, however, and threats of party leaders to sponsor a New England secession discredited the party and hastened its demise.

Subsequent factionalism among the Jeffersonians created a split between Jacksonian Democrats and the Whigs, the predominant parties between 1828 and 1854. The formation of a party around a strong presidential personality gave the President, for the first time, a new freedom of action based on his independent constituency. The Whig faction dissolved after the Kansas-Nebraska Act of 1854, the so-called "Conscience Whigs" joining Free Soil Democrats to launch a Republican ticket in 1856.

The Republican party achieved dominance between 1860 and 1932 as the party of industrialization. After the Civil War, the Democratic party espoused a more egalitarian economic philosophy, but the parties did not achieve thoroughgoing distinctiveness in this respect until the infusion of protest groups into the Democratic party generated the William Jennings Bryan nomination in 1896. That nomination prompted a further shift of elite opinion towards the Republicans and realigned the parties sectionally. What eventually ended Republican dominance was the party's seeming inability to respond to economic chaos following the 1929 stock market crash.

The fourth party system, traced to Franklin Roosevelt's 1932 election, is rooted in Roosevelt's success at forging a new alliance behind a government agenda of economic regulation and social reform. Roosevelt's program supplied the dominant rhetoric of political discourse through at least the 1960's, when racial conflict and dissension over the Vietnam War again polarized the electorate. Because Democrats will have held the White House for only 4 years in the 1968-1988 period, political scientists have hypothesized the possible reemergence of a nationally dominant Republican party. It seems premature, however, to sound the deathknell of the FDR coalition, given the Democrats' continuing predominance in state elections and their resounding comeback in the 1986 U.S. senate elections.

Evolution of Nominating Systems. The literature on the development and operation of various nominating systems for national candidates is immense. Helpful introductions include S. J. Wayne, The Road to the White House: The Politics of Presidential Elections (2d ed. 1984), and N. Polsby and A. Wildavsky, Presidential Elections: Strategies of American Electoral Politics (6th ed. 1984).

The presidential elections of 1788 and 1792 fit the framers' anticipated vision of nonpartisan electors disinterestedly choosing an esteemed national leader; their unanimous selection was George Washington. By 1796, however, the Federalist and Anti-federalist factions had organized sufficiently in Congress to conduct separate meetings for the purpose of recommending candidates to electors faithful to one or the other faction. The Federalists chose John Adams; the Anti-federalists selected New York Governor George Clinton.

During the 1790's, state legislatures chose presidential electors for their respective states. The embryonic organization of political parties thus brought with it a partisan selection of electors with the expectation, even today not embodied in any enforceable law, that the electors would support their respective parties' presidential candidates. *See* Ray v. Blair, 343 U.S. 214 (1952) (rejecting facial challenge to constitutionality of required party pledge that candidates for elector would support nominees of the national party, but not reaching issue of pledge's enforceability).

These developments played havoc with the electoral college system, which provided for only a single presidential ballot without the designation of a vice-president. Because the President would be the top electoral vote-getter, the more numerous party in the electoral college could secure the election of its presidential candidate only by withholding some votes from its preferred vice-presidential candidate. As a result, the second-best vote-getter, who would become vice-president under the Constitution, could be a candidate from a different party. That was precisely the result in 1796, when Thomas Jefferson became John Adams' vice-president. The twelfth amendment, ratified in 1804, cured the defect by providing for separate presidential and vice-presidential ballots.

By 1800, the congressional meetings for nominating national candidates had become full-fledged partisan caucuses. This electoral mechanism, however, was never entirely regularized, and dissension within the caucuses posed the possibility that a party's electors would fail to unite behind the party's nominee. Additionally, as noted by Professor Wayne, *supra*, the caucuses went beyond the original spirit of the Constitution not just by importing partisanship into the election, but by establishing congressional control of the presidential selection.

In 1820, there was only one effective caucus; the Federalists had all but disappeared as a party. Still, the Democratic-Republican caucus was beset by factionalism and uneven participation by party members. The 1824 caucus failed to nominate any national candidate who would win a majority of the electoral college; thus, for the second time,[1] a presidential election was decided by the throwback mechanism of resolution by the House of Representatives.

During the 1820's, the nomination process decentralized. State and local party organizations, state legislatures, or local conventions all nominated candidates. Despite Jackson's 1828 reelection, however, party organizers understood that such decentralization was dysfunctional in a national election. As a result, political parties—starting with the Anti-Masons and the anti-Jackson National Republicans (who became the Whigs) in 1831, and the Democratic-Republicans (who became the Democrats) in 1832—began to hold national conventions. The delegates, party leaders, were chosen by state conventions or meetings of local party elites. At the outset, the process involved little rank-and-file participation.

---

1. The House of Representatives had to choose in 1800 between Jefferson and Burr, the Republican candidates for president and vice-president, who garnered equal numbers of votes in the electoral college.

The utility of broad-based competition between two mass parties was reinforced by the adoption by most state legislatures by the 1830's of the unit-rule for electoral college selection. Under the unit-rule, the party prevailing in any state contest for choosing presidential electors would win all the electoral college votes allocated to that state. It thus made little sense to promote marginal or narrowly based minor party efforts (although many such parties did arise), because winning even a substantial minority of a state's popular vote in a presidential election would not have any influence on the electoral college.

Near the turn of the twentieth century, the Progressive movement attacked the presidential nomination process as the domain of party bosses, and targeted that process for reform. The Progressive demand for a popular selection of delegates to the national nominating conventions bore fruit first in Florida in 1904. By 1912, thirteen states held primaries, Oregon had adopted the first presidential preference primary, and former President Theodore Roosevelt launched the first campaign for a party's nomination based on primaries.

The surge of interest in primaries declined after World War I, with a reassertion of control by party leaders. According to Professor Wayne, primaries were not critical for winning the nomination until the 1970's. After the disastrous 1968 Democratic national convention, however, rank-and-file demands for greater participation, plus a legal and media climate more conducive to effective primary campaigning, led to a new spurt of primaries. George McGovern and Jimmy Carter proved the utility of primary campaigning for building a movement towards the nomination, and primaries have clearly become of central importance to the 1988 candidate selection process. (For an essay bemoaning the trend towards primaries and the demise of the truly deliberative nominating convention, *see* Walzer, *Democracy v. Elections*, The New Republic, Jan. 3 & 10, 1981, at 17-19.)

Proposals for Reform. The democratization of the process by which state parties choose delegates to national nominating conventions hardly limits the debatable issues relevant to structuring state processes. First, it should be stressed that not all states have been persuaded of the benefits of primaries. Iowa, for example, which currently holds the first delegate selection process of the presidential season, still adheres to a caucus/convention system. Its supporters insist it is less expensive and less draining on the candidates than a primary, because it depends more on grass-roots organization and less on media hype, and helps build local party strength. Party activists have a larger role to play, which may result in candidates who are more ideologically oriented, but which may also result in candidates with a firmer early base of strong organizational support. Critics of caucuses insist primaries are more open, induce a larger turnout, and are simpler. Other recurring issues for dispute include (a) whether to impose representativeness requirements for state delegations to a national convention—whether to assure party leaders, racial minorities, women, younger or older party members, labor, or any other group a guaranteed voice at the convention; (b) whether independent voters should be permitted to participate in the nomination of party candidates (the "open" vs. "closed" primary debate); (c) what the relationship should be between primary or caucus outcomes and the actual distribution of seats in the state delegation—purely proportional vs. weighted formulas;[2] (d) the scheduling

---

2. Perhaps the most heatedly debated issue is the justifiability of threshold rules—rules that bar representation for any candidate's delegates in the state delegation to the national convention unless that candidate receives at least a minimum threshold of support in the state primary or convention.

of primaries and caucuses close to or much earlier than the convention; and (e) proposals for a national primary or regional primaries to replace state contests. The materials in the following sections consider the first three issues. *Democratic Party of the United States v. Wisconsin ex rel. La Follette* provides a brief discussion of the various Democratic Party attempts since 1968 at rule reform in these respects. In addition to the Wayne and the Polsby and Wildavsky books cited above, *see* Presidential Politics: Readings on Nominations and Elections (J. Lengle and B. Shafer 2d ed. 1983) for further discussion of all the above issues.

b. Legal Control of Political Parties

Advocates of electoral reform face a difficult issue: should changes be imposed on the parties by state legislatures or by Congress, or should the parties themselves decide whether to change. The issue arises because, despite their critical importance to the obviously governmental function of conducting elections, the parties are deemed by courts to be private associations embodying their members' first amendment rights. The following case considers the degree to which political parties are subject to legislative control.

Democratic Party of the United States v. Wisconsin ex rel. La Follette
450 U.S. 107 (1981)

Justice STEWART delivered the opinion of the Court.

The charter of the appellant Democratic Party of the United States (National Party) provides that delegates to its National Convention shall be chosen through procedures in which only Democrats can participate. Consistently with the charter, the National Party's Delegate Selection Rules provide that only those who are willing to affiliate publicly with the Democratic Party may participate in the process of selecting delegates to the Party's National Convention. The question on this appeal is whether Wisconsin may successfully insist that its delegates to the Convention be seated, even though those delegates are chosen through a process that includes a binding state preference primary election in which voters do not declare their party affiliation. The Wisconsin Supreme Court held that the National Convention is bound by the Wisconsin primary election results, and cannot refuse to seat the delegates chosen in accord with Wisconsin law.

I

Rule 2A of the Democratic Selection Rules for the 1980 National Convention states: "Participation in the delegate selection process in primaries or caucuses shall be restricted to Democratic voters only who publicly declare their party preference and have that preference publicly recorded." . . .

The election laws of Wisconsin allow non-Democrats—including members of other parties and independents—to vote in the Democratic primary without regard to party affiliation and without requiring a public declaration of party preference. The voters in Wisconsin's "open" primary express their choice among Presidential candidates for the Democratic Party's nomination; they do not vote for delegates to the National

Convention. Delegates to the National Convention are chosen separately, after the primary, at caucuses of persons who have stated their affiliation with the Party. But these delegates, under Wisconsin law, are bound to vote at the National Convention in accord with the results of the open primary election.[6] Accordingly, while Wisconsin's open Presidential preference primary does not itself violate National Party rules, the State's mandate that the results of the primary shall determine the allocation of votes cast by the State's delegates at the National Convention does.

In May 1979, the Democratic Party of Wisconsin (State Party) submitted to the Compliance Review Commission of the National Party its plan for selecting delegates to the 1980 National Convention. The plan incorporated the provisions of the State's open primary laws, and, as a result the Commission disapproved it as violating Rule 2A. Since compliance with Rule 2A was a condition of participation at the Convention, for which no exception could be made, the National Party indicated that Wisconsin delegates who were bound to vote according to the results of the open primary would not be seated.

The State Attorney General then brought an original action in the Wisconsin Supreme Court on behalf of the State. Named as respondents in the suit were the National Party and the Democratic National Committee ... and the State Party.... The State sought a declaration that the Wisconsin delegate selection system was constitutional as applied to the [national party and committee] and that the [national party and committee] could not lawfully refuse to seat the Wisconsin delegation at the Convention. The State Party responded by agreeing that state law may validly be applied against it and the National Party, and cross-claimed against the National Party, asking the court to order the National Party to recognize the delegates selected in accord with Wisconsin law. The National Party argued that under the First and Fourteenth Amendments it could not be compelled to seat the Wisconsin delegation in violation of Party rules.

The Wisconsin Supreme Court entered a judgment declaring that the State's system of selecting delegates to the Democratic National Convention is constitutional and binding on the appellants. 93 Wis.2d 473, 287 N.W.2d 519....

II

Rule 2A can be traced to efforts of the National Party to study and reform its nominating procedures and internal structure after the 1968 Democratic National Convention. The Convention, the Party's highest governing authority, directed the Democratic National Committee (DNC) to establish a Commission on Party Structure and Delegate Selection (McGovern/Fraser Commission). This Commission concluded that a major problem faced by the Party was that rank-and-file Party members had been underrepresented at its Convention, and that the Party should "find methods which would guarantee every American *who claims a stake in the Democratic Party* the opportunity to make his judgment felt in the presidential nominating process."

---

6. The Convention delegates are bound for a limited period by the outcome of the Presidential preference vote in their respective districts or by the outcome of the total Presidential vote in the State at large. Wis. Stat. § 8.12(3)(b) (1977). Each delegate must pledge to support the candidate to whom the delegate is bound and to vote for that candidate on the first ballot and on any additional ballot, unless the candidate dies or releases the delegate or until the candidate fails to receive at least one-third of the votes authorized to be cast. Thereafter the delegate's vote at the Convention is based on personal preference. § 8.12(3)(c) 5.

Commission on Party Structure and Delegate Selection, Mandate for Reform: A Report of the Commission on Party Structure and Delegate Selection to the Democratic National Committee 8 (Apr. 1970) (emphasis added) (hereafter Mandate for Reform). The Commission stressed that Party nominating procedures should be as open and accessible as possible to all persons who wished to join the Party,[15] but expressed the concern that "a full opportunity for all Democrats to participate is diluted if members of other political parties are allowed to participate in the selection of delegates to the Democratic National Convention." Id., at 47.

The 1972 Democratic National Convention also established a Commission on Delegate Selection and Party Structure (Mikulski Commission). This Commission reiterated many of the principles announced by the McGovern/Fraser Commission, but went further to propose binding rules directing state parties to restrict participation in the delegate selection process to Democratic voters. Commission on Delegate Selection and Party Structure, Democrats All: A Report of the Commission on Delegate Selection and Party Structure 2, 15 (Dec. 6, 1973) (hereafter Democrats All). The DNC incorporated these recommendations into the Delegate Selection Rules for the 1976 Convention. . . .

Rule 2A took its present form in 1976. . . . [I]t restricted participation in the delegate selection process in primaries or caucuses to "Democratic voters only who publicly declare their party preference and have that preference publicly recorded." But the 1976 Delegate Selection Rules allowed for an exemption from any rule, including Rule 2A, that was inconsistent with state law if the state party was unable to secure changes in the law.

In 1975, the Party established yet another commission to review its nominating procedures, the Commission on Presidential Nomination and Party Structure (Winograd Commission). This Commission was particularly concerned with what it believed to be the dilution of the voting strength of Party members in States sponsoring open or "crossover" primaries. Indeed, the Commission based its concern in part on a study of voting behavior in Wisconsin's open primary. See Adamany, Cross-Over Voting and the Democratic Party's Reform Rules, 70 Am. Pol. Sci. Rev. 536, 538-539 (1976).

The Adamany study, assessing the Wisconsin Democratic primaries from 1964 to 1972, found that crossover voters comprised 26% to 34% of the primary voters; that the voting patterns of crossover voters differed significantly from those of participants who identified themselves as Democrats; and that crossover voters altered the composition of the delegate slate chosen from Wisconsin.[19] The Winograd Commission thus

---

15. The McGovern/Fraser Commission adopted guidelines to eliminate state party practices that limited the access of rank-and-file Democrats to the candidate selection procedures, as well as those that tended to dilute the influence of each Democrat who took advantage of expanded opportunities to participate. Mandate for Reform, at 12. . . . See also Segal, Delegate Selection Standards: The Democratic Party's Experience, 38 Geo. Wash. L. Rev. 873, 880-881 (1970).

19. In 1964, crossovers made up 26% of the participants in the Wisconsin Democratic primary. Seven percent of those identifying themselves as Democrats voted for Governor George Wallace, but 62% of the crossovers voted for him. Three-quarters of Governor Wallace's support in the Democratic primary came from crossover voters. Adamany, Cross-Over Voting and the Democratic Party's Reform Rules, 70 Am. Pol. Sci. Rev. 536, 541 (1976).

In 1968, crossovers constituted 28% of the participants in the Wisconsin Democratic primary.

recommended that the Party strengthen its rules against crossover voting, Openness, Participation and Party Building: Reforms for a Stronger Democratic Party 68 (Feb. 17, 1978) (hereafter Openness, Participation), predicting that continued crossover voting "could result in a convention delegation which did not fairly reflect the division of preferences among Democratic identifiers in the electorate." And it specifically recommended that "participation in the delegate selection process in primaries or caucuses . . . be restricted to Democratic voters only who publicly declare their party preference and have that preference publicly recorded." Accordingly, the text of Rule 2A was retained, but a new Rule, 2B, was added, prohibiting any exemptions from Rule 2A.

III

The question in this case is not whether Wisconsin may conduct an open primary election if it chooses to do so, or whether the National Party may require Wisconsin to limit its primary election to publicly declared Democrats. Rather, the question is whether, once Wisconsin has opened its Democratic Presidential preference primary to voters who do not publicly declare their party affiliation, it may then bind the National Party to honor the binding primary results, even though those results were reached in a manner contrary to National Party rules. . . . [T]his issue was resolved, we believe, in *Cousins v. Wigoda*, 419 U.S. 477 (1975).

In *Cousins* the Court reviewed the decision of an Illinois court holding that state law exclusively governed the seating of a state delegation at the 1972 Democratic National Convention, and enjoining the National Party from refusing to seat delegates selected in a manner in accord with state law although contrary to National Party rules. . . . The Court reversed the state judgment, holding that "Illinois' interest in protecting the integrity of its electoral process cannot be deemed compelling in the context of the selection of delegates to the National Party Convention." That disposition controls here.

The *Cousins* Court relied upon the principle that "[t]he National Democratic Party and its adherents enjoy a constitutionally protected right of political association." This First Amendment freedom to gather in association for the purpose of advancing shared beliefs is protected by the Fourteenth Amendment from infringement by any State. And the freedom to associate for the "common advancement of political beliefs," necessarily presupposes the freedom to identify the people who constitute the association, and to limit the association to those people only. "Any interference with the freedom of a party is simultaneously an interference with the freedom of its adherents." *Sweezy v. New Hampshire*, 354 U.S. 234, 250.

Here, the members of the National Party, speaking through their rules, chose to define their associational rights by limiting those who could participate in the processes

---

Forty-eight percent of those who said they were Democrats voted for Senator Eugene McCarthy, while 39% voted for President Johnson. Of the crossovers, however, 70% voted for Senator McCarthy, while only 14% voted for President Johnson. Participation of crossovers increased Senator McCarthy's margin of victory over President Johnson in Wisconsin by 2½ times.

In 1972, crossovers amounted to 34% of the participants. Fifty-one percent of the self-identified Democrats voted for Senator George McGovern, while only 7% voted for Governor Wallace. Of the crossovers, however, only 33% voted for Senator McGovern, while 29% voted for Governor Wallace. The study figures indicate that two-thirds of Governor Wallace's support in the Democratic primary came from crossover voters. The study found that "the participation of crossover voters will . . . alter the composition of national convention delegations." . . .

leading to the selection of delegates to their National Convention. On several occasions this Court has recognized that the inclusion of persons unaffiliated with a political party may seriously distort its collective decisions—thus impairing the party's essential functions—and that political parties may accordingly protect themselves "from intrusion by those with adverse political principles." *Ray v. Blair*, 343 U.S. 214, 221-222. In *Rosario v. Rockefeller*, 410 U.S. 752, for example, the Court sustained the constitutionality of a requirement—there imposed by a state statute—that a voter enroll in the party of his choice at least 30 days before the general election in order to vote in the next party primary. The purpose of that statute was "to inhibit party 'raiding,' whereby voters in sympathy with one party designate themselves as voters of another party so as to influence or determine the results of the other party's primary."[23] ...

The State argues that its law places only a minor burden on the National Party. The National Party argues that the burden is substantial, because it prevents the Party from "screen[ing] out those whose affiliation is ... slight, tenuous, or fleeting," and that such screening is essential to build a more effective and responsible Party. But it is not for the courts to mediate the merits of this dispute. For even if the State were correct, a State, or a court, may not constitutionally substitute its own judgment for that of the Party. A political party's choice among the various ways of determining the makeup of a State's delegation to the party's national convention is protected by the Constitution. And as is true of all expressions of First Amendment freedoms, the courts may not interfere on the ground that they view a particular expression as unwise or irrational.

IV

We must consider, finally, whether the State has compelling interests that justify the imposition of its will upon the appellants.... The State asserts a compelling interest in preserving the overall integrity of the electoral process, providing secrecy of the ballot, increasing voter participation in primaries, and preventing harassment of voters. But all those interests go to the conduct of the Presidential preference primary—not to the imposition of voting requirements upon those who, in a separate process, are eventually selected as delegates. Therefore, the interests advanced by the State do not justify its substantial intrusion into the associational freedom of members of the National Party.

V

... [The] judgment [of the Wisconsin Supreme Court] is reversed....

Justice POWELL, with whom Justice BLACKMUN and Justice REHNQUIST join, dissenting.

... Because I believe that this law does not impose a substantial burden on the associational freedom of the National Party, and actually promotes the free political activity of the citizens of Wisconsin, I dissent.

---

23. The extent to which "raiding" is a motivation of Wisconsin voters matters not. As the Winograd Commission acknowledged, "the existence of 'raiding' has never been conclusively proven by survey research." Openness, Participation 68. The concern of the National Party is, rather, with crossover voters in general, regardless of their motivation.

I

The Wisconsin open primary law was enacted in 1903. . . . As the Wisconsin Supreme Court described in its opinion below:

> The primary was aimed at stimulating popular participation in politics thereby ending boss rule, corruption, and fraudulent practices which were perceived to be part of the party caucus or convention system. Robert M. La Follette, Sr., supported the primary because he believed that citizens should nominate the party candidates; that the citizens, not the party bosses, could control the party by controlling the candidate selection process; and that the candidates and public officials would be more directly responsible to the citizens.

As noted in the opinion of the Court, the open primary law only recently has come into conflict with the rules of the National Democratic Party. The new Rule 2A was enacted as part of a reform effort aimed at opening up the party to greater popular participation. This particular rule, however, has the ironic effect of calling into question a state law that was intended itself to open up participation in the nominating process and minimize the influence of "party bosses."

II

The analysis in this kind of First Amendment case has two stages. If the law can be said to impose a burden on the freedom of association, then the question becomes whether this burden is justified by a compelling state interest. . . . In my view, . . . any burden here is not constitutionally significant, and the State has presented at least a formidable argument linking the law to compelling state interests.

A

In analyzing the burden imposed on associational freedoms in this case, the Court treats the Wisconsin law as the equivalent of one regulating delegate selection, and, relying on *Cousins v. Wigoda*, 419 U.S. 477 (1975), concludes that any interference with the National Party's accepted delegate-selection procedures impinges on constitutionally protected rights. It is important to recognize, however, that the facts of this case present issues that differ considerably from those we dealt with in *Cousins*. In *Cousins*, we reversed a determination that a state court could interfere with the Democratic Convention's freedom to select one delegation from the State of Illinois over another. At issue in the case was the power of the National Party to reject a delegation chosen in accordance with state law because the State's delegate-selection procedures violated party rules regarding participation of minorities, women, and young people, as well as other matters. The state court had ordered the Convention to seat the delegation chosen under state law, rather than the delegation preferred by the Convention itself. In contrast with the direct state regulation of the delegate-selection process at issue in *Cousins*, this case involves a state statutory scheme that regulates delegate *selection* only indirectly. . . .

. . . Wisconsin merely requires that the delegates "vote in accordance with the results of the Wisconsin open primary." While this regulation affecting participation in the primary is hardly insignificant, it differs substantially from the direct state interference in delegate selection at issue in *Cousins*. . . . All that Wisconsin has done is to require the major parties to allow voters to affiliate with them—for the limited purpose of participation in a primary—*secretly*, in the privacy of the voting booth.

The Democrats remain free to require public affiliation from anyone wishing any greater degree of participation in party affairs....

In evaluating the constitutional significance of this relatively minimal state regulation of party membership requirements, I am unwilling—at least in the context of a claim by one of the two major political parties—to conclude that every conflict between state law and party rules concerning participation in the nomination process creates a burden on associational rights....

It goes without saying that nomination of a candidate for President is a principal function performed by a national political party, and Wisconsin has, to an extent, regulated the terms on which a citizen may become a "member" of the group of people permitted to influence that decision. If appellant National Party were an organization with a particular ideological orientation or political mission, perhaps this regulation would present a different question. In such a case, the state law might well open the organization to participation by persons with incompatible beliefs and interfere with the associational rights of its founders.

The Democratic Party, however, is not organized around the achievement of defined ideological goals. Instead, the major parties in this country "have been characterized by a fluidity and overlap of philosophy and membership." *Rosario v. Rockefeller*, 410 U.S. 752, 769 (1973) (POWELL, J., dissenting). It can hardly be denied that this party generally has been composed of various elements reflecting most of the American political spectrum.[4] The Party does take positions on public issues, but these positions vary from time to time, and there never has been a serious effort to establish for the Party a monolithic ideological identity by excluding all those with differing views. As a result, it is hard to see what the Democratic Party has to fear from an open primary plan. Wisconsin's law may influence to some extent the outcome of a primary contest by allowing participation by voters who are unwilling to affiliate with the Party publicly. It is unlikely, however, that this influence will produce a delegation with preferences that differ from those represented by a substantial number of delegates from other parts of the country. Moreover, it seems reasonable to conclude that, insofar as the major parties do have ideological identities, an open primary merely allows relatively independent voters to cast their lot with the party that speaks to their present concerns. By attracting participation by relatively independent-minded

---

4. This perception need not be taken as a criticism of the American party structure. The major parties have played a key role in forming coalitions and creating consensus on national issues. "Broad-based political parties supply an essential coherence and flexibility to the American political scene. They serve as coalitions of different interests that combine to seek national goals." *Branti v. Finkel*, 445 U.S. 507, 532 (1980) (Powell, J., dissenting). As Professor Ranney has written:

> (E)ach party has sought winning coalitions by attempting accommodations among competing interests it hopes will appeal to more contributors and voters than will the rival accommodations offered by the opposition party. This strategy, it is conceded, has resulted in vague, ambiguous, and overlapping party programs and in elections that offer the voters choices between personalities and, at most, general programmatic tendencies, certainly not unequivocal choices between sharply different programs. But this...is not a vice but a virtue, for it has enabled Americans through all but one era of their history to manage their differences with relatively little violence and to preserve the world's oldest constitutional democratic regime.

A. Ranney, Curing the Mischiefs of Faction 201 (1975).

voters, the Wisconsin plan arguably may enlarge the support for a party at the general election.

It is significant that the Democratic Party of Wisconsin, which represents those citizens of Wisconsin willing to take part publicly in Party affairs, is here *defending* the state law. Moreover, the National Party's apparent concern that the outcome of the Wisconsin Presidential primary will be skewed cannot be taken seriously when one considers the alternative delegate-selection methods that are acceptable to the Party under its rules. Delegates pledged to various candidates may be selected by a caucus procedure involving a small minority of Party members, as long as all participants in the process are publicly affiliated. While such a process would eliminate "crossovers," it would be at least as likely as an open primary to reflect inaccurately the views of a State's Democrats. In addition, the National Party apparently is quite willing to accept public affiliation immediately before primary voting, which some States permit. As Party affiliation becomes this easy for a voter to change in order to participate in a particular primary election, the difference between open and closed primaries loses its practical significance.

In sum, I would hold that the National Party has failed to make a sufficient showing of a burden on its associational rights.[9]

B

The Court does not dispute that the State serves important interests by its open primary plan. Instead the Court argues that these interests are irrelevant because they do not support a requirement that the outcome of the primary be binding on delegates chosen for the convention. This argument, however, is premised on the unstated assumption that a nonbinding primary would be an adequate mechanism for pursuing the state interests involved. This assumption is unsupportable because the very purpose of a Presidential primary, as enunciated as early as 1903 when Wisconsin passed its first primary law, was to give control over the nomination process to individual voters. Wisconsin cannot do this, and still pursue the interests underlying an open primary, without making the open primary binding.

If one turns to the interests asserted, it becomes clear that they are substantial. As explained by the Wisconsin Supreme Court:

> The state's interest in maintaining a primary and in not restricting voting in the presidential preference primary to those who publicly declare and record their party preference is to preserve the overall integrity of the electoral process by encouraging increased voter participation in the political process and providing secrecy of the ballot, thereby ensuring that the primary itself and the political party's participation in the primary are conducted in a fair and orderly manner.

---

9. Of course, the National Party could decide that it no longer wishes to be a relatively nonideological party, but it has not done so. Such a change might call into question the institutionalized status achieved by the two major parties in state and federal law. It cannot be denied that these parties play a central role in the electoral process in this country, to a degree that has led this Court on occasion to impose constitutional limitations on party activities. See *Smith v. Allwright*, 321 U.S. 649 (1944); *Terry v. Adams*, 345 U.S. 461 (1953). Arguably, the special status of the major parties is an additional factor favoring state regulation of the electoral process even in the face of a claim by such a party that this regulation has interfered with its First Amendment rights.

. . .

> In guaranteeing a private primary ballot, the open primary serves the state interest of encouraging voters to participate in selecting the candidates of their party which, in turn, fosters democratic government. Historically the primary was initiated in Wisconsin in an effort to enlarge citizen participation in the political process and to remove from the political bosses the process of selecting candidates. 93 Wis.2d, at 512-513, 287 N.W.2d, at 536-537 (footnote omitted).

The State's interest in promoting the freedom of voters to affiliate with parties and participate in party primaries has been recognized in the decisions of this Court. In several cases, we have dealt with challenges to state laws restricting voters who wish to change party affiliation in order to participate in a primary. We have recognized that voters have a right of free association that can be impaired unconstitutionally if such state laws become too burdensome....

Here, Wisconsin has attempted to ensure that the prospect of public party affiliation will not inhibit voters from participating in a Democratic primary.... [T]he National Party's rule requiring public affiliation for primary voters is not itself an unconstitutional interference with voters' freedom of association.... The State of Wisconsin[, however,] has determined that some voters are deterred from participation by a public affiliation requirement,[13] and the validity of that concern is not something that we should second-guess.[14]

III

The history of state regulation of the major political parties suggests a continuing accommodation of the interests of the parties with those of the States and their citizens. In the process, "the States have evolved comprehensive, and in many respects complex, election codes regulating in most substantial ways, with respect to both federal and state elections, the time, place, and manner of holding primary and general elections, the registration and qualifications of voters, and the selection and qualification of

---

13. A related concern is the prevention of undue influence by a particular political organization or "machine." The Progressives who promoted the idea of a primary election perceived a need to combat political professionals who controlled access to governmental power. ... The *open* primary carries this process one step further by eliminating some potential pressures from political organizations on voters to affiliate with a particular party. Although one well may question the wisdom of a state law that undermines the influence of party professionals and may tend to weaken parties themselves, the state interests involved are neither illegitimate nor insubstantial.... [T]he Democratic Party of Wisconsin has filed a brief in *support* of the validity of the Wisconsin plan.

14. A more difficult question in this case is whether Wisconsin can satisfy the second component of the "compelling interest test"—whether it can show that it has no "less drastic way of satisfying its legitimate interests." The answer to this question depends in many cases on how the state interest is conceived. Here, a state interest in protecting voters from the possible coercive effects of public party affiliation cannot be satisfied by any law except one that allows private party affiliation. On the other hand, if the state interest is described more generally, in terms of increasing voter freedom or participation, there may well be less "drastic" alternatives available to Wisconsin. Because of my conclusion that there is no significant burden on the associational freedoms of appellant National Party in this case, and because the Court's analysis does not reach this question, I express no view on whether the State has shown a sufficient interest in this particular method of regulating the electoral process to satisfy a less-drastic-means inquiry.

candidates." *Storer v. Brown*, 415 U.S. 724, 730 (1974). Today, the Court departs from this process of accommodation. It does so, it seems to me, by upholding a First Amendment claim by one of the two major parties without any serious inquiry into the extent of the burden on associational freedoms and without due consideration of the countervailing state interests.

---

1. Do you agree with the majority's assessment of the relative weights of the competing interests involved in this case? Could the result in *La Follette* be defended more persuasively in terms of the state's diminished interest in regulating the political process when the selection of national officials is at stake? Cf. *Anderson v. Celebrezze*, 460 U.S. 780 (1983) (invalidating state ballot access requirements for third-party presidential candidates). A recent decision, *Tashjian v. Republican Party of Connecticut*, 107 S. Ct. 544 (1986), suggests a negative answer. In *Tashjian*, the court invalidated, 5-4, a state statute prohibiting political parties from permitting independent voters to vote in party primaries for congressional and gubernatorial elections. The majority balanced the competing interests the same way as *La Follette*. It regarded the law as an attempt by the Democratic state legislature to impede efforts by the vastly outnumbered Republican state party to broaden its appeal in elections by choosing candidates attractive to independent voters. Is it true, however, that a political party has the same associational interest in combining with voters who refuse to register as members, as it does in excluding independents from party processes? Could a political party insist, contrary to state law, that out-of-staters or minors be allowed to vote in state primaries? Would the party's associational claim be any different or less weighty?

2. Given their importance in the selection of the President, should the parties be viewed legally as autonomous private organizations expressing their members' will? Or should at least the dominant political parties be viewed as arms of government subject to constitutional norms? On the state level, that question vexed the Supreme Court in a series of "state action" cases, overturning party-imposed racial exclusions from Texas state and local primaries as unconstitutional. *Nixon v. Herndon*, 273 U.S. 536 (1927); *Nixon v. Condon*, 286 U.S. 73 (1932); *Smith v. Allwright*, 321 U.S. 649 (1944); *Terry v. Adams*, 345 U.S. 461 (1953).

The Supreme Court has never squarely addressed the issue as to presidential elections. In *Ripon Society v. National Republican Party*, 525 F.2d 567 (D.C. Cir. 1975) (en banc), *cert. den.*, 424 U.S. 933 (1976), excerpted below, the court of appeals held that the requirements of "one-person, one-vote" do not apply to a national political party's allocation of seats to state delegations to a national nominating convention. The court reserved the question whether the allocation function was "government action" subject to constitutional control because the "one-person, one-vote" requirement would be inapplicable in any event. Four members of the court, however, stated their view in separate concurrences that no government action was present in the conduct of national conventions, repudiating the holdings of two earlier cases. *Georgia v. National Democratic Party*, 447 F.2d 1271 (D.C. Cir. 1971), *cert. den.*, 404 U.S. 858 (1971); *Bode v. National Democratic Party*, 452 F.2d 1302 (D.C. Cir.), *cert. den.*, 404 U.S. 1019 (1972).

The arguments for and against regarding political parties as government actors in connection with presidential elections may be briefly catalogued. The appearance of government action is strong because candidate selection is a process integral to the general election, which is paradigmatic government action; the states typically provide automatic ballot placement to the nominees of the major parties; and the processes of national candidate selection are both regulated and substantially funded by the federal and state governments. *Georgia v. National Democratic Party, supra; cf. Ripon Society v. National Republican Party,* 525 F.2d at 616 (BAZELON, C. J., dissenting). On the other hand, candidate selection is not traditionally viewed as a government function. *La Follette* and *Tashjian* suggest political parties are constitutionally immune to a significant range of government regulation regarding their candidate selection processes. No government regulation requires or controls the conduct of national conventions. Finally, the Supreme Court has rejected the argument that extensive government funding of private activity alone subjects that activity to constitutional norms. *Cf. Rendell-Baker v. Kohn,* 457 U.S. 830 (1982) (private school almost entirely financed through state payments held not a state actor for purposes of personnel discharge decisions).

What do you think? Consider, as you read the next section on representational issues within parties, what the implications might be of regularly regarding the major parties as state actors subject to constitutional norms. Can the racial exclusion cases be persuasively distinguished? Could a state ever grant ballot access to the candidate selected by an all-white primary? An all-male primary? A religiously exclusive primary? Could the courts manageably or sensibly pursue the distinction Justice Powell urges between major, heterogeneous parties and ideological parties?

2. Representation Within Political Parties

Because of the considerable independent power that political parties wield in the Presidential selection process, there is extraordinary interest within each party in determining the rules for the selection of national convention delegates. Traditionally, the Democratic party has fought these fights more intensely at the national level, while the Republican party has adopted a more hands-off attitude with respect to its individual state organizations. As the following case indicates, however, Republican Party rule-makers have faced one policy dispute of national significance, namely, by what criteria the party should set the size of the respective states' national convention delegations.

Ripon Society v. National Republican Party
525 F.2d 567 (D.C. Cir. 1975) (en banc),
cert. den., 424 U.S. 933 (1976)

McGOWAN, Circuit Judge:

. . .

I

The subject of the appeal is the delegate allocation formula adopted by the National Republican Party for its 1976 convention. The Ripon Society and nine individual plaintiffs have secured the judgment of the District Court that parts of that formula are unconstitutional. 369 F.Supp. 368 (D.D.C.1974)....

[The 1976] formula was adopted, on a vote of 910 to 434, by the delegates to the 1972 convention. It provides as follows: 1,605 delegates, or 72 percent of the total, are allocated according to the states' electoral college votes, each state to receive three delegates per presidential elector; 312 delegates, or 14 percent, are awarded as "victory bonuses" to states voting for the Republican candidate in the last presidential election, each such state to receive a number of additional delegates equal to 60 percent of its electoral college vote, or 20 percent of its electoral college-based delegation (the "proportional victory bonus"); 245 delegates, or 11 percent, are divided equally among the states that voted for the last Republican presidential candidate, each such state to receive five delegates on this basis (the "uniform victory bonus"); 50 delegates, or 2 percent, are awarded to the states for Republican election successes at the state level, one such delegate for each Republican governor, senator, or majority of United States Representatives which the state elects in 1972 or a succeeding year prior to the 1976 convention (this bonus will be considered part of the "uniform victory bonus"); and 30 delegates, or 1 percent, are divided among the District of Columbia (14), Puerto Rico (8), Guam and the Virgin Islands (4 each).

Declaratory and injunctive relief was sought on the ground that the formula as a whole, and in particular its various victory bonus features, denied plaintiffs equal protection of the laws. Plaintiffs proposed that the Republican National Committee be permitted to fashion a new formula subject to the constraints that (1) a "substantial" number of delegates be allocated according to the Republican vote in one or more recent elections, (2) the remaining delegates be apportioned on the basis of population or electoral college vote, (3) the District of Columbia be treated for allocation purposes as a state, and (4) the territories receive a number of delegates no greater than what they would be entitled to on a population basis.

The district judge granted relief only in part. Ruling on cross-motions for summary judgment, he forbade the use of uniform victory bonuses, but upheld the formula in other respects. 369 F.Supp. at 376. Plaintiffs have appealed the denial of additional relief; defendants have appealed the granting of any relief at all.

II

[The court decided that this suit involved plaintiffs with standing to seek relief on each of the claims presented, but declined to rule whether the party's choice of a delegate allocation formula amounted to "state action," finding it unnecessary to reach what the court took to be a difficult constitutional issue.]

III

Having assumed *arguendo* that defendants are subject to justiciable constitutional limitations, we confront the question of whether those limitations have been exceeded in this case. Our discussion falls into two parts, the first dealing with what in general the Constitution requires in the allocation of delegates to a national political convention, and the second inquiring as to whether this particular formula satisfies those requirements.

A. Applicability of One Person, One Vote.

. . . [P]laintiffs rely primarily on the constitutional guarantee of equal protection. They analogize the Republican National Convention to the state legislatures in which that guarantee has been held to require representation on a "one man, one vote" basis. Plaintiffs propose that the constituency whose members are each to have "one vote" be either the entire population of a state, or that part of it that voted Republican in one or more past elections. Their entire argument is couched in terms of the challenged formula's deviations from proportionality to those constituencies. Although they would apparently accept some such deviations, they would set as an outer limit the deviations present in the electoral college. The disproportionality introduced by the victory bonus system they do not consider justifiable....

The fact that the conduct of a national political convention may be subject to the Equal Protection Clause does not in itself establish the applicability of the one person, one vote rule. Manifestly, a given constitutional command may not require of one part of the state what it requires of another. The army and the park commissioner are not equally constrained by the First Amendment; the President is not subject to the same restraints in making appointments as Congress is in passing legislation. And indeed it is clear that the Equal Protection Clause does not impose the same one person, one vote rule upon all elected and decision-making bodies, even if they are formally and indisputably organs of the state.... [The court cited cases permitted exceptions to the "one-person, one-vote" rule for elections to choose the boards of directors for water management districts.]

... The constitutional command is not one person, one vote but equal protection of the laws, and what it requires by way of representation in a given assembly must depend on the purposes for which the assembly is convened and the nature of the decisions it makes. The Supreme Court's inquiry into these matters has led it to the conclusion that where the assembly exercises formal governmental powers one person, one vote is ordinarily required. A similar inquiry in other contexts may well reveal that the public and private interests in making decisions through some other scheme of representation outweigh the interests served by numerically equal apportionment....

From the [beginnings of the party convention system in the 1840's], delegate votes at the convention were apportioned according to each State's electoral college vote. Indeed it is somewhat ironic that the convention, the first major reform of the nominating process, brought with it an apportionment scheme that bore no relation at all to the relative strength of the parties in the various states, whereas the [predecessor] congressional caucus reflected that strength quite accurately.

There was recurrent criticism of electoral college-based apportionment, particularly in the Republican Party, where it gave inordinate control to delegates from southern States in which the Party had no hope of electoral success. Reform finally came in 1913, and in a way which presents a second irony for this case: the electoral college basis was in effect retained, but an extra vote was awarded to congressional districts which had voted Republican in past elections. Party strength was thus reinstated as a basis for delegate apportionment through a bonus vote system such as the one to which plaintiffs so strenuously object. The Party has employed some such mixture of electoral college-based and bonus votes ever since.... In requesting that we impose a one person, one vote rule on the Republican Party, plaintiffs are ... inviting us to take into judicial hands a process of change and adaptation that still continues within the Party.

We have twice declined that invitation in [*Georgia v. National Democratic Party*, 447 F.2d 1271 (D.C. Cir.), *cert. den.*, 404 U.S. 858 (1971), and *Bode v. National Democratic Party*, 452 F.2d 1302 (D.C. Cir. 1971), *cert. den.*, 404 U.S. 1019 (1972)]. It is particularly significant that in the latter case we expressly upheld the parties' long-standing practice of apportioning delegates according to electoral college strength. The Democratic Party formula challenged in *Bode* allocated 54 percent of the delegates on that basis. Although it allocated the remaining 46 percent according to Democratic voting strength as measured in past elections, it was not for that reason, or even because of the analogy to the electoral college itself, that we sustained the formula. Electoral college apportionment was perceived to have an "independent rationality for its use," which was that it reflected "a judgment exercised toward maintaining and enlarging party appeal on a national scale." 452 F.2d at 1309.

In thus upholding electoral college apportionment we have in effect already discarded the notion that national convention delegates must represent some constituency on a one person, one vote basis. Electoral college apportionment obviously is not related to any set of Republican Party members or adherents. It bears some relation to total population, but only a very rough one.[46]

. . . [A] party might well wish to impose conditions on delegate selection which are inconsistent with an unconstrained, mathematically equal system of representation. The Democratic Party recently did so by establishing quotas for the membership in state delegations of minorities, women, and young people.[53] Could a national convention take the more drastic step of refusing for some reason perceived to be in the Party's best interests to seat a State's delegation *at all?* Apparently so. The Supreme Court stated in *Cousins v. Wigoda* that "[t]he Convention was under no obligation to seat the respondents (whom the Illinois court ordered seated) but was free . . . to leave the Chicago seats vacant and thus defeat the objective." 419 U.S. at 488.

"Equal" apportionment of delegates among the states is presumably sought in order to insure "equal" representation of the people in those states. Yet the actual selection of delegates at the state level varies from the highly democratic to the opposite extreme. In a number of states the selection is made not in a primary election but through a series of local, county, and state caucuses and conventions. Often these are malapportioned,[54] and often voter participation is so slight as to make the selection process one virtually (or even officially) of appointment by party officials. A practice that is more defensible perhaps, though scarcely more "democratic," is the granting of *ex officio* delegate status to party officials or public office holders, presumably because of their special wisdom and expertise.

There are a number of respects, then, in which the parties conduct their affairs other than by giving equal attention to the preferences of all voters, or even all party

---

46. Electors from large States represent up to 4.4 times as many people as do electors from small States. One of Alaska's three electors represents 100,724 people according to the 1970 census. One of New York's forty-one electors represents 443,677 people.

53. The quotas were not mandatory, but, as one member of the Commission which conceived the quota system reports, "most state delegations chose to play it safe by making sure they had close to the required percentages of each favored group." Ranney, *Changing the Rules of the Nominating Game*, Choosing the President 78 n. 1 (Barber ed., 1974). A comparable committee of Republicans was appointed to recommend changes in the rules for selection of delegates to that Party's 1972 convention. One of its recommendations, not accepted, was that "each State (shall) include in its delegation to the Republican national convention delegates under 25 years of age in numerical equity to their voting strength within the State." II *Report of the Delegates and Organization Committee* 5-9 (Republican National Committee publication, 1971).

54. . . . The delegate selection procedures of the states are surveyed in *Developments in the Law-Elections*, 88 Harv. L. Rev. 1111, 1153-54 (1975). . . .

adherents.[57] Perhaps this is not surprising. A party is after all more than a forum for all its adherents' views. It is an organized attempt to see the most important of those views put into practice through control of the levers of government.[58] One party may think that the best way to do this is through a "strictly democratic" majoritarianism. But another may think it can only be done (let us say) by giving the proven party professional a greater voice than the newcomer. Which of these approaches is the more efficacious we cannot say, but the latter certainly seems a more accurate description of how political parties operate in reality.

What is important for our purposes is that a party's choice, as among various ways of governing itself, of the one which seems best calculated to strengthen the party and advance its interests, deserves the *protection* of the Constitution as much if not more than its condemnation. The express constitutional rights of speech and assembly are of slight value indeed if they do not carry with them a concomitant right of political association. Speeches and assemblies are after all not ends in themselves but means to effect change through the political process. If that is so, there must be a right not only to form political associations but to organize and direct them in the way that will make them most effective....

Last term the Court in *Cousins v. Wigoda* placed the internal workings of a political party squarely within the protection of the First Amendment.... If First Amendment rights are exercised when a Party determines the make-up, or perhaps even the existence, of state delegations, we think the same is true when it determines their size.

The First Amendment is of course not our only concern. We are keenly aware that "[a]s a practical matter, the ultimate choice of the mass of voters is predetermined when the nominations have been made." If the right to vote is a right to true participation in the elective process, then it is heavily implicated in the nomination process.

---

57. It will perhaps add to our perspective to note that the United States is virtually unique among western democracies in the degree to which the selection of party candidates is entrusted even to the party rank and file. Elsewhere this is regarded as a function of the party leadership. See L. Epstein, Political Parties in Western Democracies 201-32 (1967). The British system for selecting candidates for Parliament is judged in the cited study to be far more typical, and is described in the following terms:

The types of local leaders dominating the process vary from party to party and from locality to locality. They may, for instance (in the Labour party), be trade-union leaders rather than just political activists. But in any case they are relatively few in number. Candidate selection is not the business of the party rank and file.... There is no need—in fact, it is usually regarded as undesirable—for aspirants to campaign before the membership. Candidate selection is meant to be oligarchical.

Id. at 220....

58. This point is driven home by the difficulty of determining what exactly is the "constituency" of a national convention. Is it the entire population, much of which may have not the slightest interest in what the convention decides? Is it the registered party membership, a class which does not even exist in some states? Plaintiffs contend that it is the set of voters who voted for the party's candidates in past elections. That is a different set for each election, of course, a fact that only serves to demonstrate that the circumstances of those elections may have been such as to attract to the party's candidates large numbers of voters who retain no continuing interest in its fortunes. If we cannot identify with any confidence the set of people whose preferences are to be given equal and accurate expression at a party convention, then perhaps we must admit that that is not the primary purpose of such a convention at all. The primary purpose is to chart a course for the advancement of the party's ideals, and it is in that light that the requirements of equal protection are to be discerned.

We do not deny this, but rest our judgment on the view that, as between that right and the right of free political association, the latter is more in need of protection in this case. . . . [T]he right to organize a party in the way that will make it the most effective political organization seems clearly at stake here. The right of one person to one vote is of course preserved in the general election. . . . Persons not heard in one [major] party may be welcomed in the other, and if there are enough such defections, the offending party may lose the general election, as both parties must be well aware.

We conclude, therefore, that the Equal Protection Clause, assuming it is applicable, does not require the representation in presidential nominating conventions of some defined constituency on a one person, one vote basis. It is satisfied if the representational scheme and each of its elements rationally advance some legitimate interest of the party in winning elections or otherwise achieving its political goals. We turn, then, to the question of whether the challenged formula meets this test.

B. Justifications of the Challenged Formula.

By far the greatest number of delegates (72 percent) are allocated according to the electoral college vote of the States. We upheld this as a basis of representation in *Bode*. . . . A State's share of the electoral college vote . . . precisely reflects the relative importance of the state to the party in terms of winning the presidential election. As we stated in *Bode*, "the primary function of a national party convention . . . is to select among a field of available persons Presidential and Vice-Presidential candidates most competent to perform the duties of office, *yet capable of attracting a sufficient number of popular votes to carry the requisite number of States in the election*." 452 F.2d at 1309 (emphasis added).

The "requisite number of States" is the number with a majority of electoral college votes. The delegates from those states will presumably know best what kind of candidate is likely to carry them. It may be helpful, or even necessary, to have running mates who actually come from those states. If so, it may be wise, especially if it is thought that delegates from other states may ignore this fact in favor of their "favorite sons," to "build in" for candidates from large states the advantage of large home-state delegations. Assuming, as we have, the constitutional validity of delegate allocation measures taken to improve the Party's chances for victory, this one is hardly irrational.

It could stand some improvement, of course. As between two states of equal electoral importance, a party could more profitably focus its attention on the one in which it has a chance of victory. This purpose we think is rationally served by the victory bonus system. A state which has gone Republican in the past may do so again. If electoral college apportionment weights the vote of the states according to the value of the prize, the victory bonus system does the same according to the likelihood of winning it.

The victory bonus system may help to keep a state in the Republican camp not only by orienting party policies to that state's interests, but also by providing a reward and incentive for the efforts of that state's party organization. Whether or not it is an effective incentive, it may be the only one that a national party has to offer. In any case, having accepted the legitimacy of such party-strengthening measures, we can hardly say that it is irrational. . . .

It is urged that this formula represents nothing more than an effort by party members from strongly Republican states to perpetuate their control. But it seems to us that the First Amendment protects their power to do precisely that. The Party could have chosen a delegate allocation scheme calculated to broaden its base, by giving special influence to delegates from States where the party is weak. Instead it appears to have chosen to consolidate its gains in states where it has been strong. We are not about to hold that this is an irrational way to seek political success. As for those aspects of the formula which treat the states on a uniform basis and thus give disproportionate influence to the smaller states, how could we say that they do not rationally serve the important cause of cohesiveness among the various state parties, when it took precisely such a scheme to bring about the union of the states themselves?

We therefore hold that the formula does not violate the Equal Protection Clause. To the extent that voting rights are involved, warranting close judicial scrutiny, these rights are offset by the First Amendment rights exercised by the Party in choosing the formula it did. We must emphasize that this is only true because the formula rationally advances legitimate party interests in political effectiveness. The same might not always hold true. There are no racial or other invidious classifications here. If there were, the Party's entitlement to constitutional protection would be as slight as those of the victims would be strong. Similarly, we have said that voting rights are not as heavily implicated in a nomination as in an election. It might be otherwise in a case where there is only one party with a realistic chance to win the election, and where a vote in the nominating process is the only effective vote that can be cast.[65]

These *caveats* have no significance in the present context other than to suggest that, although courts should be slow to interfere with the internal processes of political parties, circumstances can be conceived of wherein they may grant relief. Where such circumstances do not exist, *Georgia*, *Bode*, and this case should serve to discourage resort to this court for the resolution of intra-party differences.

The judgment of the District Court is reversed, and the case is remanded with directions to dismiss the complaint.

[The separate concurring opinions of Judges MACKINNON, DANAHER, TAMM, and WILKEY are omitted.]

BAZELON, Chief Judge (dissenting):

III

... [T]he minority [of this court] is simply wrong in asserting that a national political convention is a "nongovernmental" body to which the one-person-one-vote rule is not applicable.... [I]t would boggle the mind to hold that the Kansas City Junior College District performed "governmental" functions while the national convention of a major political party does not.[10] Prevailing doctrine does not require such an absurdity.

---

65. We may distinguish *Gray v. Sanders*, 372 U.S. 368 (1963), on this basis. It is clearly the Supreme Court case most closely in point. Having first announced the one person, one vote rule, it applied that rule to a primary election held to select candidates for state-wide offices. Georgia's practice of giving unequal weight to votes cast in different districts was invalidated.... It was, however, a case dominated by the fact of one party rule in Georgia. The District Court had noted that it was "known to all that the Democratic candidate has, without exception, at least during the present century, been the choice of the voters at the General election." *Sanders v. Gray*, 203 F.Supp. 158, 167 (N.D.Ga.1962)....

10. *See Hadley v. Junior College Dist.*, 397 U.S. 50 (1970).

... [T]he proper definition of a party's constituency is nonjusticiable. What is justiciable is the following: once a party defines a constituency for itself, courts will require that the party not malapportion the members of that constituency so as to deprive some constituents of their right to vote....

IV

The majority's central argument is that the national parties are so undemocratic already that enforcement of the right to an equal vote for all party constituents makes little sense. Why is not an opposite conclusion equally plausible and indeed convincing? The structure of state legislatures and for that matter the Congress may well be undemocratic in particulars, for example the committee structure, the caucus, the system of patronage distribution. But surely it does not follow that malapportionment of legislative districts is thereby sanctioned. The whole purpose of reapportionment is to give all voters an equal place at the democratic starting line. What thereafter occurs is but the natural workings of the democratic process in which temporary majorities make necessary political decisions. The whole drift of reapportionment—the one-person-one-vote principle—is to prevent these temporary majorities from entrenching themselves in a manner that prevents the natural working of the democratic process *in the future*. Reapportionment derives its immense constitutional legitimacy from its prevention of this entrenchment.

This is the main error of the court's way: it assumes that decisions of a temporary majority in the organization of the party and the use of the party's political power are no different from entrenchment of the temporary majority in the very process of political choice. The court then leaps to the improbable conclusion that malapportionment of political parties either does not violate the one-person-one-vote principle or is outside the one-person-one-vote principle.... [However,] equality at the starting line is just as important, if not more important, in the convention context than in the general election context, since for the great mass of voters their choice has already been determined by the convention's decision.

... [T]he party itself seems to admit quite openly that the purpose of the victory bonus and its consequent malapportionment is not, as the majority on rehearing would have it, as some sort of "reward" or as a measure of "probable success" in capturing a state's electoral college votes. Rather, the purpose is an ideological compromise designed to apportion power within the party by means of a territorial discrimination....

Generally the court seems to assume that if a malapportionment might be helpful in winning elections or aid in the organization or solidarity of the party, it is permissible. But this reasoning destroys the one-person-one-vote principle. All malapportionment may have some legitimate objective—in winning elections or in ensuring party national solidarity.... The court ... is simply holding that the one-person-one-vote principle is not applicable to political parties, without directly arguing the point, under the guise of "balancing." This is true, since there is no malapportionment conceivable, including overt racial discrimination, which could not be justified on similar grounds.

Of course, the court intimates it would not tolerate overt racial discrimination (although it approves here a territorial discrimination which has largely the same effect). But why? Surely in some areas it would be rational indeed, unfortunately so, to exclude blacks or other minorities to ensure party victory or solidarity. If the court were to reach a different result in such a case, then it will be pure *ipse dixit*. And, after all, *Reynolds v. Sims* expressly extended the proscription of denial of the right to vote on the basis of racial discrimination to proscription of denial based on territorial discrimination.

Stripped of its rational exterior, I read the majority opinion . . . as telling us something of this sort:

> The reapportionment decisions were intensely controversial and involved a radical extension of judicial power. We will not extend those decisions nor the philosophy of judicial power they embody even if logically compelled, absent either more public demand than we can perceive or clear guidance from the Supreme Court. We simply do not believe the principle of one-person-one-vote is sufficiently important to overcome these concerns of institutional competence and popular approval, which have always lain on the horizon of the reapportionment decisions and which counsel studied conservation of the power of judicial review.

This sort of judicial statesmanship is not so much wrong as insensitive to the principles of legitimacy that underlie a democratic state. . . . The principle of legitimacy is this, repeated again and again in support of controversial but necessary public decisions: if you disagree with present public policy, run for office or vote to throw the rascals out. Go through the legitimate processes of democratic government—the "system"— and popular change will follow. But the court tells us this is naive ideology, fit for high school textbooks perhaps, but surely not as a constitutional command in the "real world." . . .

---

1. As a matter of policy, should political parties, in the governance of their own internal processes, respect constitutional norms that apply to state elections? Intriguingly, the disputes over group interest representation in the Republican and Democratic parties mirror constitutional disputes that have been waged with respect to state legislatures. As the preceding opinion demonstrates, the key issue in the Republican party has been the propriety of departing from "one person-one vote" principles in the allocation of delegate strength by state. The Democrats, by contrast, have had less trouble with this issue than the issue of "voting dilution" with respect to minority groups and other possibly "discrete and insular" interests within the party.

In 1984, presidential candidate Jesse Jackson argued that party rules create unfair barriers to the representation of minorities in the national candidate selection process. Despite affirmative action requirements in the selection of delegates to the national convention, minority candidates are disadvantaged, in his view, by rules that deny candidates a share of convention delegates proportional to their electoral success. These include so-called threshold requirements—requirements that a candidate achieve some minimum support in a state primary or convention before being awarded any seats in the state delegation to the national convention—and so-called "winner-take-all" or "winner-take-more" bonus delegate schemes. He argued further that the early scheduling of primaries and caucuses gives an advantage to better financed candidates over candidates not yet familiar to voters. (This protest may appear ironic given Jackson's early lead in the 1988 presidential preference polls, based largely on his name recognition in the Democratic Party.) His recommendations were that the party abandon the "front-loading" of primaries, eliminate awards of bonus delegates, eliminate thresholds, and require states to comply faithfully with affirmative action requirements. R. Walters, Unfair Reflection of Minority Participation in the Presidential Nomination Process of the Democratic Party (Unpublished Paper Prepared for the "Jesse Jackson for President in 1984" Campaign); *see also* Kirschten, Democrats Weigh Party Rules Changes to Meet Jesse Jackson's Demands, National Journal, May 12, 1984, at 921.

How do you assess the merits of the policy positions advocated by the Ripon Society and by the 1984 Jackson campaign?

2. Is national discipline through party rulemaking more or less helpful to national electoral success than state-by-state decisionmaking on delegate selection? For the 1988 election, it is clear that the Democratic Party is trying to contain its enthusiasm for massive rule changes. Is this stance appropriate in light of its most recent experiences in presidential elections? Do you think that party rules for the nomination process had a genuine impact on that electoral record?

3. Should disputes over the composition of national nominating conventions be treated as justiciable? If you think not, is there any legislative authority after *La Follette* competent to impose rules on the parties in order to reform the nomination process significantly?

B. Presidential Elections

1. Campaign Finance

There is no election-related issue of greater legal or political complexity than the subject of money. Presidential elections are subject to the Federal Election Campaign Act, 2 U.S.C. § 431 *et seq.* (1982), which imposes a variety of conditions on campaign finance. These include extensive registration and reporting requirements, limits on contributions, limits on expenditures by candidates or by national or state committees of parties that receive federal funds. The Act also establishes the Federal Election Commission to police federal campaign finance generally. For helpful introductions to the myriad policy issues connected with this subject, *see* H. Alexander, Financing Politics (3d ed. 1984), and M. J. Malbin, ed., Money and Politics in the U.S.: Financing Elections in the 1980's (1984). For an excellent study of the political action committee (PAC) phenomenon, *see* J. Cantor, *Political Action Committees: Their Evolution and Growth and Their Implications for the Political System, in Campaign Finance Reform, Hearings Before the Task Force on Elections of the H. Comm. on Administration*, 97th Cong., 2d Sess. 287-386 (1982). For a highly critical appraisal of PAC's by an experienced political observer, *see* E. Drew, Politics and Money (1983). For a review of the constitutional limitations on legislative power to regulate campaign finance, *see* 3 R. Rotunda, J. Nowak, & J. Young, Treatise on Constitutional Law: Substance and Procedure §§ 20.50-.52 (1986).

Of major concern in the Presidential context are the Presidential Election Campaign Fund Act, 26 U.S.C. § 9001 *et seq.*, which provides for the funding of both national conventions and general election campaigns, and the Presidential Primary Matching Payment Account Act, 26 U.S.C. § 9031 *et seq.*, which provides limited public funding for presidential primary campaigns. Here we consider first the constitutionality of the current statutory scheme for public funding of presidential elections, and then, the legality, under current statutes, of the incumbent President's use of the resources of his office to gain electoral advantages.

Buckley v. Valeo
424 U.S. 1 (1976)

[In *Buckley*, the Supreme Court decided a series of challenges to various provisions of the Federal Election Campaign Act of 1971, and related provisions of the Internal Revenue Code. In Chapter Four, we considered that portion of *Buckley* invalidating the method of appointments enacted for the Federal Election Commission. With respect to those portions of the Act that regulated campaign finance, the Court upheld the Act's reporting and disclosure requirements, ruled that the provisions limiting contributions to candidates for federal political office are constitutional, and invalidated certain provisions limiting expenditures by contributors or groups relative to an identified candidate. In the portion of the *per curiam* decision that follows, the Court upheld the scheme for public financing of presidential campaigns. Six Justices joined this opinion; the Chief Justice and Justice Rehnquist dissented. Justice Stevens did not participate.]

III. PUBLIC FINANCING OF PRESIDENTIAL ELECTION CAMPAIGNS

A series of statutes for the public financing of Presidential election campaigns produced the scheme now found in § 6096 and Subtitle H of the Internal Revenue Code of 1954, 26 U.S.C. §§ 6096, 9001-9012, 9031-9042.... Appellants ... [contend] that the legislation violates the First and Fifth Amendments. We find no merit in their claims and affirm.

A. Summary of Subtitle H

Section 9006 establishes a Presidential Election Campaign Fund (Fund), financed from general revenues in the aggregate amount designated by individual taxpayers, under § 6096, who on their income tax returns may authorize payment to the Fund of one dollar of their tax liability in the case of an individual return or two dollars in the case of a joint return. The Fund consists of three separate accounts to finance (1) party nominating conventions, (2) general election campaigns, and (3) primary campaigns.

Chapter 95 of Title 26, which concerns financing of party nominating conventions and general election campaigns, distinguishes among "major," "minor," and "new" parties. A major party is defined as a party whose candidate for President in the most recent election received 25% or more of the popular vote, § 9002(6). A minor party is defined as a party whose candidate received at least 5% but less than 25% of the vote at the most recent election, § 9002(7). All other parties are new parties, § 9002(8), including both newly created parties and those receiving less than 5% of the vote in the last election.

Major parties are entitled to $2,000,000 to defray their national committee Presidential nominating convention expenses, must limit total expenditures to that amount, and may not use any of this money to benefit a particular candidate or delegate. A minor party receives a portion of the major-party entitlement determined by the ratio of the votes received by the party's candidate in the last election to the average of the votes received by the major parties' candidates. The amounts given to the parties and the expenditure limit are adjusted for inflation, using 1974 as the base year. No financing is provided for new parties, nor is there any express provision for financing independent candidates or parties not holding a convention.

For expenses in the general election campaign, § 9004(a)(1) entitles each major-party candidate to $20,000,000. This amount is also adjusted for inflation. See § 9004(a)(1). To be eligible for funds the candidate must pledge not to incur expenses in excess of the entitlement under § 9004(a)(1) and not to accept private contributions except to the extent that the fund is insufficient to provide the full entitlement. Minor-party candidates are also entitled to funding, again based on the ratio of the vote received by the party's candidate in the preceding election to the average of the major-party candidates. Minor-party candidates must certify that they will not incur campaign expenses in excess of the major-party entitlement and that they will accept private contributions only to the extent needed to make up the difference between that amount and the public funding grant. New-party candidates receive no money prior to the general election, but any candidate receiving 5% or more of the popular vote in the election is entitled to post-election payments according to the formula applicable to minor-party candidates. Similarly, minor-party candidates are entitled to post-election funds if they receive a greater percentage of the average major-party vote than their party's candidate did in the preceding election; the amount of such payments is the difference between the entitlement based on the preceding election and that based on the actual vote in the current election. A further eligibility requirement for minor- and new-party candidates is that the candidate's name must appear on the ballot, or electors pledged to the candidate must be on the ballot, in at least 10 States.

Chapter 96 establishes a third account in the Fund, the Presidential Primary Matching Payment Account. § 9037(a). This funding is intended to aid campaigns by candidates seeking Presidential nomination "by a political party," § 9033(b)(2), in "primary elections," § 9032(7). The threshold eligibility requirement is that the candidate raise at least $5,000 in each of 20 States, counting only the first $250 from each person contributing to the candidate. In addition, the candidate must agree to abide by the spending limits in § 9035. Funding is provided according to a matching formula: each qualified candidate is entitled to a sum equal to the total private contributions received, disregarding contributions from any person to the extent that total contributions to the candidate by that person exceed $250. Payments to any candidate under Chapter 96 may not exceed 50% of the overall expenditure ceiling accepted by the candidate.

B. Constitutionality of Subtitle H

Appellants argue that Subtitle H is invalid (1) as "contrary to the 'general welfare,'" Art. I, § 8, (2) because any scheme of public financing of election campaigns is inconsistent with the First Amendment, and (3) because Subtitle H invidiously discriminates against certain interests in violation of the Due Process Clause of the Fifth Amendment. We find no merit in these contentions. Appellants' "general welfare" contention erroneously treats the General Welfare Clause as a limitation upon congressional power. It is rather a grant of power, the scope of which is quite expansive, particularly in view of the enlargement of power by the Necessary and Proper Clause. *McCulloch v. Maryland*, 4 Wheat. 316, 420 (1819). Congress has power to regulate

Presidential elections and primaries; and public financing of Presidential elections as a means to reform the electoral process was clearly a choice within the granted power. It is for Congress to decide which expenditures will promote the general welfare: "[T]he power of Congress to authorize expenditure of public moneys for public purposes is not limited by the direct grants of legislative power found in the Constitution." *United States v. Butler*, 297 U.S. 1, 66 (1936). Any limitations upon the exercise of that granted power must be found elsewhere in the Constitution. In this case, Congress was legislating for the "general welfare"—to reduce the deleterious influence of large contributions on our political process, to facilitate communication by candidates with the electorate, and to free candidates from the rigors of fundraising. Whether the chosen means appear "bad," "unwise," or "unworkable" to us is irrelevant; Congress has concluded that the means are "necessary and proper" to promote the general welfare, and we thus decline to find this legislation without the grant of power in Art. I, § 8.

Appellants' challenge to the dollar check-off provision (§ 6096) fails for the same reason. They maintain that Congress is required to permit taxpayers to designate particular candidates or parties as recipients of their money. But the appropriation to the Fund in § 9006 is like any other appropriation from the general revenue except that its amount is determined by reference to the aggregate of the one- and two-dollar authorization on taxpayers' income tax returns. This detail does not constitute the appropriation any less an appropriation by Congress.[124] The fallacy of appellants' argument is therefore apparent; every appropriation made by Congress uses public money in a manner to which some taxpayers object.

Appellants next argue that "by analogy" to the Religion Clauses of the First Amendment public financing of election campaigns, however meritorious, violates the First Amendment. We have, of course, held that the Religion Clauses . . . require Congress, and the States through the Fourteenth Amendment, to remain neutral in matters of religion. The government may not aid one religion to the detriment of others or impose a burden on one religion that is not imposed on others, and may not even aid all religions. But the analogy is patently inapplicable to our issue here.

Although "Congress shall make no law . . . abridging the freedom of speech, or of the press," Subtitle H is a congressional effort, not to abridge, restrict, or censor speech, but rather to use public money to facilitate and enlarge public discussion and participation in the electoral process, goals vital to a self-governing people. Thus, Subtitle H furthers, not abridges, pertinent First Amendment values.[127] Appellants

---

124. The scheme involves no compulsion upon individuals to finance the dissemination of ideas with which they disagree. The § 6096 check-off is simply the means by which Congress determines the amount of its appropriation.

127. The historical bases of the Religion and Speech Clauses are markedly different. Intolerable persecutions throughout history led to the Framers' firm determination that religious worship—both in method and belief—must be strictly protected from government intervention. "Another purpose of the Establishment Clause rested upon an awareness of the historical fact that governmentally established religions and religious persecutions go hand in hand." Engel v. Vitale, 370 U.S. 421, 432 (1962). But the central purpose of the Speech and Press Clauses was to assure a society in which "uninhibited, robust, and wide-open" public debate concerning matters of public interest would thrive, for only in such a society can a healthy representative democracy flourish. Legislation to enhance these First Amendment values is the rule, not the exception. Our statute books are replete with laws providing financial assistance to the exercise of free speech, such as aid to public broadcasting and other forms of educational media, 47

argue, however, that as constructed public financing invidiously discriminates in vi-olation of the Fifth Amendment. We turn therefore to that argument.

Equal protection analysis in the Fifth Amendment area is the same as that under the Fourteenth Amendment. In several situations concerning the electoral process, the principle has been developed that restrictions on access to the electoral process must survive exacting scrutiny. The restriction can be sustained only if it furthers a "vital" governmental interest, *American Party of Texas v. White*, 415 U.S. 767, 780-781 (1974), that is "achieved by a means that does not unfairly or unnecessarily burden either a minority party's or an individual candidate's equally important interest in the con-tinued availability of political opportunity." *Lubin v. Panish*, 415 U.S. 709, 716 (1974). These cases, however, dealt primarily with state laws requiring a candidate to satisfy certain requirements in order to have his name appear on the ballot. These were, of course, direct burdens not only on the candidate's ability to run for office but also on the voter's ability to voice preferences regarding representative government and contemporary issues. In contrast, the denial of public financing to some Presidential candidates is not restrictive of voters' rights and less restrictive of candidates'.[128] Subtitle H does not prevent any candidate from getting on the ballot or any voter from casting a vote for the candidate of his choice; the inability, if any, of minor-party candidates to wage effective campaigns will derive not from lack of public funding but from their inability to raise private contributions. Any disadvantage suffered by operation of the eligibility formulae under Subtitle H is thus limited to the claimed denial of the enhancement of opportunity to communicate with the electorate that the formulae afford eligible candidates. But eligible candidates suffer a countervailing denial. As we more fully develop later, acceptance of public financing entails voluntary acceptance of an expenditure ceiling. Noneligible candidates are not subject to that limitation. Accordingly, we conclude that public financing is generally less restrictive of access to the electoral process than the ballot-access regulations dealt with in prior cases. In any event, Congress enacted Subtitle H in furtherance of sufficiently important governmental interests and has not unfairly or unnecessarily burdened the political opportunity of any party or candidate.

It cannot be gainsaid that public financing as a means of eliminating the improper influence of large private contributions furthers a significant governmental interest. In addition, the limits on contributions necessarily increase the burden of fundraising, and Congress properly regarded public financing as an appropriate means of relieving major-party Presidential candidates from the rigors of soliciting private contributions. The States have also been held to have important interests in limiting places on the ballot to those candidates who demonstrate substantial popular support. Congress' interest in not funding hopeless candidacies with large sums of public money, nec-essarily justifies the withholding of public assistance from candidates without signif-icant public support. Thus, Congress may legitimately require "some preliminary

---

U.S.C. §§ 390-399, and preferential postal rates and antitrust exemptions for newspapers, 39 CFR § 132.2 (1975); 15 U.S.C. §§ 1801-1804.

128. Appellants maintain that denial of funding is a more severe restriction than denial of access to the ballot, because write-in candidates can win elections, but candidates without funds cannot. New parties will be unfinanced, however, only if they are unable to get private financial support, which presumably reflects a general lack of public support for the party. Public financing of some candidates does not make private fundraising for others any more difficult; indeed, the elimination of private contributions to major-party Presidential candidates might make more private money available to minority candidates.

showing of a significant modicum of support," *Jenness v. Fortson*, 403 U.S., at 442, as an eligibility requirement for public funds. This requirement also serves the important public interest against providing artificial incentives to "splintered parties and unrestrained factionalism." *Storer v. Brown*, 415 U.S., at 736. At the same time Congress recognized the constitutional restraints against inhibition of the present opportunity of minor parties to become major political entities if they obtain widespread support....

1. General Election Campaign Financing

Appellants insist that Chapter 95 falls short of the constitutional requirement in that its provisions supply larger, and equal, sums to candidates of major parties, use prior vote levels as the sole criterion for pre-election funding, limit new-party candidates to post-election funds, and deny any funds to candidates of parties receiving less than 5% of the vote. These provisions, it is argued, ... work invidious discrimination against minor and new parties in violation of the Fifth Amendment. We disagree.

As conceded by appellants, the Constitution does not require Congress to treat all declared candidates the same for public financing purposes. As we said in *Jenness v. Fortson*, "there are obvious differences in kind between the needs and potentials of a political party with historically established broad support, on the one hand, and a new or small political organization on the other.... Sometimes the grossest discrimination can lie in treating things that are different as though they were exactly alike...." 403 U.S., at 441-442. Since the Presidential elections of 1856 and 1860, when the Whigs were replaced as a major party by the Republicans, no third party has posed a credible threat to the two major parties in Presidential elections. Third parties have been completely incapable of matching the major parties' ability to raise money and win elections. Congress was, of course, aware of this fact of American life, and thus was justified in providing both major parties full funding and all other parties only a percentage of the major-party entitlement. Identical treatment of all parties, on the other hand, "would not only make it easy to raid the United States Treasury, it would also artificially foster the proliferation of splinter parties." The Constitution does not require the Government to "finance the efforts of every nascent political group," merely because Congress chose to finance the efforts of the major parties.

Furthermore, appellants have made no showing that the election funding plan disadvantages nonmajor parties by operating to reduce their strength below that attained without any public financing. First, such parties are free to raise money from private sources, and by our holding today new parties are freed from any expenditure limits, although admittedly those limits may be a largely academic matter to them. But since any major-party candidate accepting public financing of a campaign voluntarily assents to a spending ceiling, other candidates will be able to spend more in relation to the major-party candidates. The relative position of minor parties that do qualify to receive some public funds because they received 5% of the vote in the previous Presidential election is also enhanced. Public funding for candidates of major parties is intended as a substitute for private contributions; but for minor-party candidates such assistance may be viewed as a supplement to private contributions since these candidates may continue to solicit private funds up to the applicable spending limit. Thus, we conclude that the general election funding system does not work an invidious discrimination against candidates of nonmajor parties.

Appellants challenge reliance on the vote in past elections as the basis for determining eligibility. That challenge is foreclosed, however, by our holding in *Jenness v. Fortson*, that popular vote totals in the last election are a proper measure of public support. And Congress was not obliged to select instead from among appellants' suggested alternatives. Congress could properly regard the means chosen as preferable, since the alternative of petition drives presents cost and administrative problems in validating signatures, and the alternative of opinion polls might be thought inappropriate since it would involve a Government agency in the business of certifying polls or conducting its own investigation of support for various candidates, in addition to serious problems with reliability.

Appellants next argue, relying on the ballot-access decisions of this Court, that the absence of any alternative means of obtaining pre-election funding renders the scheme unjustifiably restrictive of minority political interests.... Our decisions finding a need for an alternative means turn on the nature and extent of the burden imposed in the absence of available alternatives. We have earlier stated our view that Chapter 95 is far less burdensome upon and restrictive of constitutional rights than the regulations involved in the ballot-access cases. Moreover, expenditure limits for major parties and candidates may well improve the chances of nonmajor parties and their candidates to receive funds and increase their spending....

Appellants' reliance on the alternative-means analyses of the ballot-access cases generally fails to recognize a significant distinction from the instant case. The primary goal of all candidates is to carry on a successful campaign by communicating to the voters persuasive reasons for electing them. In some of the ballot-access cases the States afforded candidates alternative means for qualifying for the ballot, a step in any campaign that, with rare exceptions, is essential to successful effort. Chapter 95 concededly provides only one method of obtaining pre-election financing; such funding is, however, not as necessary as being on the ballot. Plainly, campaigns can be successfully carried out by means other than public financing; they have been up to this date, and this avenue is still open to all candidates. And, after all, the important achievements of minority political groups in furthering the development of American democracy were accomplished without the help of public funds. Thus, the limited participation or nonparticipation of nonmajor parties or candidates in public funding does not unconstitutionally disadvantage them.

Of course, nonmajor parties and their candidates may qualify for post-election participation in public funding and in that sense the claimed discrimination is not total. Appellants contend, however, that the benefit of any such participation is illusory due to § 9004(c), which bars the use of the money for any purpose other than paying campaign expenses or repaying loans that had been used to defray such expenses. The only meaningful use for post-election funds is thus to repay loans; but loans, except from national banks, are "contributions" subject to the general limitations on contributions, 18 U.S.C. § 591(e) (1970 ed., Supp. IV). Further, they argue, loans are not readily available to nonmajor parties or candidates before elections to finance their campaigns. Availability of post-election funds therefore assertedly gives them nothing. But in the nature of things the willingness of lenders to make loans will depend upon the pre-election probability that the candidate and his party will attract 5% or more of the voters. When a reasonable prospect of such support appears, the party and candidate may be an acceptable loan risk since the prospect of post-election participation in public funding will be good.

Finally, appellants challenge the validity of the 5% threshold requirement for general election funding. They argue that, since most state regulations governing ballot access have threshold requirements well below 5%, and because in their view the 5% requirement here is actually stricter than that upheld in *Jenness v. Fortson*, the requirement is unreasonable. We have already concluded that the restriction under Chapter 95 is generally less burdensome than ballot-access regulations.... [U]nder Chapter 95 a Presidential candidate needs only 5% or more of the actual vote, not the larger universe of eligible voters.... In any event, the choice of the percentage requirement that best accommodates the competing interests involved was for Congress to make. Without any doubt a range of formulations would sufficiently protect the public fisc and not foster factionalism, and would also recognize the public interest in the fluidity of our political affairs. We cannot say that Congress' choice falls without the permissible range.

2. Nominating Convention Financing

The foregoing analysis and reasoning sustaining general election funding apply in large part to convention funding under Chapter 95 and suffice to support our rejection of appellants' challenge to these provisions. Funding of party conventions has increasingly been derived from large private contributions, and the governmental interest in eliminating this reliance is as vital as in the case of private contributions to individual candidates. The expenditure limitations on major parties participating in public financing enhance the ability of nonmajor parties to increase their spending relative to the major parties; further, in soliciting private contributions to finance conventions, parties are not subject to the $1,000 contribution limit pertaining to candidates. We therefore conclude that appellants' constitutional challenge to the provisions for funding nominating conventions must also be rejected.

3. Primary Election Campaign Financing

Appellants' final challenge is to the constitutionality of Chapter 96, which provides funding of primary campaigns. They contend that these provisions are constitutionally invalid (1) because they do not provide funds for candidates not running in party primaries and (2) because the eligibility formula actually increases the influence of money on the electoral process. In not providing assistance to candidates who do not enter party primaries, Congress has merely chosen to limit at this time the reach of the reforms encompassed in Chapter 96. This Congress could do without constituting the reforms a constitutionally invidious discrimination. The governing principle was stated in *Katzenbach v. Morgan*, 384 U.S. 641, 657 (1966):

> "[I]n deciding the constitutional propriety of the limitations in such a reform measure we are guided by the familiar principles that a 'statute is not invalid under the Constitution because it might have gone farther than it did,' that a legislature need not 'strike at all evils at the same time,' and that 'reform may take one step at a time, addressing itself to the phase of the problem which seems most acute to the legislative mind.' "

The choice to limit matching funds to candidates running in primaries may reflect that concern about large private contributions to candidates centered on primary races and that there is no historical evidence of similar abuses involving contributions to candidates who engage in petition drives to qualify for state ballots. Moreover, assistance to candidates and nonmajor parties forced to resort to petition drives to gain ballot access implicates the policies against fostering frivolous candidacies, creating a system of splintered parties, and encouraging unrestrained factionalism.

The eligibility requirements in Chapter 96 are surely not an unreasonable way to measure popular support for a candidate, accomplishing the objective of limiting subsidization to those candidates with a substantial chance of being nominated. Counting only the first $250 of each contribution for eligibility purposes requires candidates to solicit smaller contributions from numerous people. Requiring the money to come from citizens of a minimum number of States eliminates candidates whose appeal is limited geographically; a President is elected not by popular vote, but by winning the popular vote in enough States to have a majority in the Electoral College.

We also reject as without merit appellants' argument that the matching formula favors wealthy voters and candidates. The thrust of the legislation is to reduce financial barriers and to enhance the importance of smaller contributions. Some candidates undoubtedly could raise large sums of money and thus have little need for public funds, but candidates with lesser fundraising capabilities will gain substantial benefits from matching funds. In addition, one eligibility requirement for matching funds is acceptance of an expenditure ceiling, and candidates with little fundraising ability will be able to increase their spending relative to candidates capable of raising large amounts in private funds.

For the reasons stated, we reject appellants' claims that Subtitle H is facially unconstitutional. . . .

Chief Justice BURGER, concurring in part and dissenting in part.

. . . I dissent from Part III sustaining the constitutionality of the public financing provisions of Subtitle H.

Since the turn of this century when the idea of Government subsidies for political campaigns first was broached, there has been no lack of realization that the use of funds from the public treasury to subsidize political activity of private individuals would produce substantial and profound questions about the nature of our democratic society. . . .

The Court chooses to treat this novel public financing of political activity as simply another congressional appropriation whose validity is "necessary and proper" to Congress' power to regulate and reform elections and primaries. . . . No holding of this Court is directly in point, because no federal scheme allocating public funds in a comparable manner has ever been before us. . . . The public monies at issue here are not being employed simply to police the integrity of the electoral process or to provide a forum for the use of all participants in the political dialogue, as would, for example, be the case if free broadcast time were granted. Rather, we are confronted with the Government's actual financing, out of general revenues, a segment of the political debate itself. As Senator Howard Baker remarked during the debate on this legislation:

> "I think there is something politically incestuous about the Government financing and, I believe, inevitably then regulating, the day-to-day procedures by which the Government is selected. . . .

> "I think it is extraordinarily important that the Government not control the machinery by which the public expresses the range of its desires, demands, and dissent." 120 Cong. Rec. 8202 (1974).

... [T]he Court points to no basis for predicting that the historical pattern of "varying measures of control and surveillance," which usually accompany grants from Government will not also follow in this case. Up to now, the Court has always been extraordinarily sensitive, when dealing with First Amendment rights, to the risk that the "flag tends to follow the dollars." Yet, here, where Subtitle H specifically requires the auditing of records of political parties and candidates by Government inspectors, the Court shows little sensitivity to the danger it has so strongly condemned in other contexts. Up to now, this Court has scrupulously refrained, absent claims of invidious discrimination, from entering the arena of intraparty disputes concerning the seating of convention delegates. An obvious underlying basis for this reluctance is that delegate selection and the management of political conventions have been considered a strictly private political matter, not the business of Government inspectors. But once the Government finances these national conventions by the expenditure of millions of dollars from the public treasury, we may be providing a springboard for later attempts to impose a whole range of requirements on delegate selection and convention activities. . . .

Assuming, *arguendo*, that Congress could validly appropriate public money to subsidize private political activity, it has gone about the task in Subtitle H in a manner which is not, in my view, free of constitutional infirmity. . . . Congress has not itself appropriated a specific sum to attain the ends of the Act but has delegated to a limited group of citizens—those who file tax returns—the power to allocate general revenue for the Act's purposes—and of course only a small percentage of that limited group has exercised the power. There is nothing to assure that the "fund" will actually be adequate for the Act's objectives. Thus, I find it difficult to see a rational basis for concluding that this scheme would, in fact, attain the stated purposes of the Act when its own funding scheme affords no real idea of the amount of the available funding.

I agree with Justice REHNQUIST that the scheme approved by the Court today invidiously discriminates against minor parties. . . . [T]he present system could preclude or severely hamper access to funds before a given election by a group or an individual who might, at the time of the election, reflect the views of a major segment or even a majority of the electorate. The fact that there have been few drastic realignments in our basic two-party structure in 200 years is no constitutional justification for freezing the status quo of the present major parties at the expense of such future political movements. When and if some minority party achieves majority status, Congress can readily deal with any problems that arise. In short, I see grave risks in legislation, enacted by incumbents of the major political parties, which distinctly disadvantages minor parties or independent candidates. This Court has, until today, been particularly cautious when dealing with enactments that tend to perpetuate those who control legislative power.

I would also find unconstitutional the system of matching grants which makes a candidate's ability to amass private funds the sole criterion for eligibility for public funds. Such an arrangement can put at serious disadvantage a candidate with a potentially large, widely diffused—but poor—constituency. The ability of a candidate's supporters to help pay for his campaign cannot be equated with their willingness to cast a ballot for him. . . .

Justice REHNQUIST, concurring in part and dissenting in part.

. . . I concur in so much of Part III of the Court's opinion as holds that the public funding of the cost of a Presidential election campaign is a permissible exercise of congressional authority under the power to tax and spend granted by Art. I, but dissent from Part III-B-1 of the Court's opinion, which holds that certain aspects of the statutory treatment of minor parties and independent candidates are constitutionally valid. . . .

The limits imposed by the First and Fourteenth Amendments on governmental action may vary in their stringency depending on the capacity in which the government is acting. The government as proprietor, is, I believe, permitted to affect putatively protected interests in a manner in which it might not do if simply proscribing conduct across the board. . . .

The statute before us was enacted by Congress, not with the aim of managing the Government's property nor of regulating the conditions of Government employment, but rather with a view to the regulation of the citizenry as a whole. The case for me, then, presents the First Amendment interests of the appellants at their strongest, and the legislative authority of Congress in the position where it is most vulnerable to First Amendment attacks. . . .

While I am not sure that I agree with the Court's comment, that "public financing is generally less restrictive of access to the electoral process than the ballot-access regulations dealt with in prior cases," in any case that is not, under my view, an adequate answer to appellants' claim. The electoral laws relating to ballot access which were examined in [this Court's earlier decisions] all arose out of state efforts to regulate minor party candidacies and the actual physical size of the ballot. If the States are to afford a republican form of government, they must by definition provide for general elections and for some standards as to the contents of the official ballots which will be used at those elections. The decision of the state legislature to enact legislation embodying such regulations is therefore not in any sense an optional one; there must be some standards, however few, which prescribe the contents of the official ballot if the popular will is to be translated into a choice among candidates. . . .

Congress, on the other hand, while undoubtedly possessing the legislative authority to undertake the task if it wished, is not obliged to address the question of public financing of Presidential elections at all. When it chooses to legislate in this area, so much of its action as may arguably impair First Amendment rights lacks the same sort of mandate of necessity as does a State's regulation of ballot access.

Congress, of course, does have an interest in not "funding hopeless candidacies with large sums of public money," and may for that purpose legitimately require " 'some preliminary showing of a significant modicum of support,' *Jenness v. Fortson*, as an eligibility requirement for public funds." But Congress in this legislation has done a good deal more than that. It has enshrined the Republican and Democratic Parties in a permanently preferred position, and has established requirements for funding minor-party and independent candidates to which the two major parties are not subject. Congress would undoubtedly be justified in treating the Presidential candidates of the two major parties differently from minor-party or independent Presidential candidates, in view of the long demonstrated public support of the former. But because of the First Amendment overtones of the appellants' Fifth Amendment equal protection claim something more than a merely rational basis for the difference in treatment must be shown, as the Court apparently recognizes. I find it impossible to subscribe to the Court's reasoning that because no third party has posed a credible threat to the two major parties in Presidential elections since 1860, Congress may by law attempt to assure that this pattern will endure forever.

I would hold that, as to general election financing, Congress has not merely treated the two major parties differently from minor parties and independents, but has discriminated in favor of the former in such a way as to run afoul of the Fifth and First Amendments to the United States Constitution.

---

1. Which of the opinions above most appropriately balances the first amendment concerns relevant to the public funding of electoral campaigns, taking into account the proper roles of court and legislature in doing the balancing?

2. Under the majority's reasoning, could Congress provide for differential postal subsidies for political parties based on their past political support? For one judge's negative answer, *see Greenberg v. Bolger,* 497 F.Supp. 756 (E.D.N.Y. 1980). What is the impact on this analysis of *Harris v. McRae,* 448 U.S. 297 (1980), holding that Congress is not required to provide public funding for medically necessary abortions even though a woman's right to choose an abortion is constitutionally protected, and Congress funds other medically necessary procedures related to pregnancy and childbirth? (Recall also that no state currently provides full funding generally for parents to send their children to private schools, although (a) the states fund public schools, and (b) the right of parents to choose private schools for their children is constitutionally protected, *Pierce v. Society of Sisters,* 268 U.S. 510 (1925).) Could Congress fund public transportation to the polls for voters pledged to candidates of the major parties? How are the cases distinguishable?

3. *Buckley* follows *United States v. Butler,* 297 U.S. 1 (1936), in giving Congress broad leeway to determine what constitutes the "general welfare" for public funding purposes. Is the Court too generous? Could it successfully evolve a requirement, as some states have tried, that the purposes for which public monies are spent be "public purposes," as distinguished from "private purposes?" Are political controls sufficient (or the only practicable avenue) for policing the use of public funds? How would the purposes of the public funding scheme challenged in *Buckley* fare under a "public purpose" test?

4. The Court upholds the federal tax check-off scheme although it does not permit the taxpayer to designate the recipient, either candidate or party, of the taxpayer's dollar. Is the appellant's suggested alternative, permitting such a designation, more or less objectionable on constitutional or policy grounds? This practice, too, varies among the states that employ tax write-offs for the public funding of state elections.

5. The Court in *Buckley* treats the advantages enjoyed by major parties under the public funding scheme as justified by Congress' putatively neutral interest in avoiding undue factionalism by ensuring that public funds be used to support political parties that enjoy substantial support. Is this a fair characterization of the policy underlying public funding, or is the scheme actually one of self-dealing by Democrats and Republicans, entrenching their dominant political position? The Court's characterization presumably turns on a perception that the electoral success of major versus minor parties will not, in fact, be much affected one way or the other by public funding. Is this perception justified? Is it an appropriate premise for adjudicating the minor parties' rights?

6. Supreme Court decisions determining the constitutionality of facially neutral election regulations that disparately burden third parties generally conform to a two-stage analysis characteristic of many of the Court's recent substantive due process cases: first, the Court determines whether the challenged regulation "substantially"

burdens a constitutionally protected interest; then, if it does, the Court subjects the regulation to a heightened form of scrutiny, *see, e.g., Anderson v. Celebrezze,* 460 U.S. 780 (1983). Did the *Buckley* majority persuasively determine that the burden of the public funding scheme on third parties was relatively insubstantial? Should the "weighing" process have taken greater account of the nature of the burden, that is, incumbents helping incumbents? For an illustration of the unpredictability of the "substantiality" determination, *see Munro v. Socialist Workers Party,* 107 S.Ct. 533 (1986), finding that the challenged change in Washington's ballot access rules was not sufficiently burdensome to warrant strict scrutiny, although the change had the impact of all but eliminating third parties from the general election ballot in all statewide elections.

Winpisinger v. Watson
628 F.2d 133 (D.C. Cir.) *cert. denied,* 446 U.S. 929 (1980)

Opinion PER CURIAM.

Appellants, supporters of Senator Edward M. Kennedy in his quest for the Presidential nomination of the Democratic Party, appeal from the dismissal by the district court of their action alleging that the defendants, members of President Carter's administration and the Carter-Mondale Committee, have illegally employed their public authority and expended federal funds to promote the President's renomination. Appellants contend that this results in constitutional violations by diminishing the effect of their efforts for Senator Kennedy. They accordingly seek declaratory and injunctive relief against the practices detailed in their complaint.

The district court . . . dismissed the complaint for lack of standing by appellants to bring the action.

We affirm, both on the basis of lack of standing and on the ground that prudential considerations would preclude the court from exercising jurisdiction in any event.

I. THE COMPLAINT

. . . The gravamen of appellants' allegations is . . . :

This is an action for declaratory judgment and injunction against defendants' misuse of federal power and federal funds to purchase the Presidential renomination of Jimmy Carter, impairing the operation of the Nation's elective process embodied in the Constitution and injuring plaintiffs' constitutional rights under the First and Fifth Amendments, as voters, contributors and participants in the process of Presidential nomination. Defendants are Presidential subordinates engaged in a concerted course of conduct designed to use the public treasury for salaries, travel expenses, costs of meetings and other political outlays; to grant and withhold public employment based upon political support by the employee; and to promise and award federal programs and funds to communities as political inducements and rewards, all in order to obtain support for President Carter's renomination. . . .

. . . Appellants contend, for example, that defendant [presidential chief of staff, Hamilton] Jordan said that federal employees who were not barred from political activity by federal law are expected to perform political activities only for President

Carter and that anyone in that category supporting Senator Kennedy would be dismissed.[6] Similarly, President Carter is alleged to have instructed the defendant members of his Administration to require their subordinates who were outside of the protection of the Civil Service Merit System to support his candidacy or suffer the threat of dismissal for refusing to do so.

Several types of charges dealing with the alleged misuse of federal funds are also made. The defendant federal officials are alleged to have used their time during normal working hours, for which time they are paid out of the federal treasury for their work as federal officials, on trips made and activities conducted for the principal purpose of promoting President Carter's renomination campaign. Allegations are also made that on trips taken for campaign purposes only partial reimbursement to the federal treasury was made, if at all, and only after the trip was actually taken. This delay in making reimbursement acts, according to the complaint, as an interest free loan by the treasury to the Carter-Mondale Committee.

Similarly, the allegation is made that federal funds are being used to publish materials favorable to the President. For example, defendant [presidential aide Anne] Wexler is alleged to have had thousands of copies of a 49-page pamphlet entitled "The Record of President Carter's Administration" printed and mailed at federal expense. The purpose for this pamphlet is alleged to be the generation of support for the Carter campaign. Defendant [presidential aide Sarah] Weddington is alleged to have mailed 6,200 copies of a letter and glossy poster displaying 100 photographs of women appointees in the Carter Administration two days after Senator Kennedy criticized "the Carter position concerning women" in a speech. Other allegations in the complaint contend that Kennedy supporters were not invited to attend Presidential functions, or to travel on the President's aircraft "Air Force One" because of their preference for Senator Kennedy.

Political patronage in hiring is also contained in the allegations of the complaint; the defendant federal officials are alleged to have hired federal employees on the basis of political affiliation. For example, appellants contend that the 275,000 people to be hired to take the 1980 census are to be chosen on the basis of "patronage conferred upon those political figures who had or would support the Carter candidacy." . . .

Finally, appellants contend that the granting of federal funds to states and cities has been conditioned upon officials of those entities supporting the Carter candidacy, and that the timing of the announcement of federal grants has been coordinated to provide the maximum benefit to President Carter's renomination campaign. As a corollary to this allegation, appellants charge that in areas where official support has been for Senator Kennedy, assistance has been denied.

Collectively, appellants contend that the use by the defendant federal officials of the resources of the federal government provide the Carter-Mondale Committee with federal support. This, in turn, is alleged to harm appellants in four distinct ways. As supporters of Senator Kennedy, they charge that the challenged actions violate their First Amendment right to "free expression and free association in the electoral process in support of their preferred candidates." As voters, they argue that these practices

---

6. Such dismissals would be unconstitutional under the recent decision in *Branti v. Finkel* [excerpted in Chapter Four]. [Ed.: Is this statement accurate? As to which government employees would it likely be inaccurate?]

are alleged to "diminish, dilute and nullify plaintiffs' votes, plaintiffs' lawful contributions of money, and their other efforts to nominate the candidates of their choice."

As contributors to Senator Kennedy's campaign they claim infringement of a right to effectiveness of their contributions equal to those of President Carter's supporters. And two appellants, candidates for delegate seats at the Democratic National Convention, assert that the conduct complained of has lessened their chances of selection.

In addition, appellants assume several more general positions. Violation of appellants' rights to equal protection of the laws, secured by the Fifth Amendment, is alleged to occur by defendants "depriving plaintiffs of an equal voice in the Democratic Presidential nomination process by their use of the federal treasury and federal power in support of the Carter nomination." And violations of laws relating to the election process, appropriations and the legislative authority of Congress are also alleged. . . .

II. STANDING

The district court dismissed this action for lack of standing. The court did not reach, for that reason, the issue of whether prudential considerations would also bar plaintiffs' claims. Although we affirm the dismissal, we do so on the basis of both lack of standing and prudential concerns. . . . [W]e do not consider these two concepts to be clearly severable in this case; consequently, we rely upon both grounds for our affirmance.

A

. . . The district court held that the plaintiffs failed to demonstrate standing because they failed to allege a "distinct and palpable injury" to themselves, quoting *Warth v. Seldin*, 422 U.S. 490, 501 (1975) which is direct and concrete, and not abstract, remote or speculative, citing *O'Shea v. Littleton*, 414 U.S. 488 (1974). The court further held that plaintiffs must establish an injury "that fairly can be traced to the challenged action of the defendant, and not injury that results from the independent action of some third party not before the Court," citing *Simon v. Eastern Kentucky Welfare Rights Org.*, 426 U.S. 26, 41-42 (1976) and *Duke Power Co. v. Carolina Env. Study Group*, 438 U.S. 59, 98 (1978). In conclusion the court found that the plaintiffs' inability to influence the election process or to induce support for Senator Kennedy may turn on "a number of factors that are unrelated to defendants' alleged abuses." This variety of factors operating on the electorate at any given time would require extreme speculation to establish a relationship between the defendants' alleged conduct, and the plaintiffs' injury. . . .

In sum, the district court concluded that the appellants had failed to show either injury in fact to themselves or a causal connection between the injury and the defendants' conduct. . . . [W]e agree with the conclusions of the district court.

B

. . . The endless number of diverse factors potentially contributing to the outcome of state presidential primary elections, caucuses and conventions forecloses any reliable conclusion that voter support of a candidate is "fairly traceable" to any particular event. In the case before us, whether an appellant is viewed in the character of a voter, contributor, a noncontributing supporter or a candidate for a delegate post, a court would have to accept a number of very speculative inferences and assumptions in any endeavor to connect his alleged injury with activities attributed to appellees. Courts are powerless to confer standing when the causal link is too tenuous. . . .

III. PRUDENTIAL BARRIERS

Although the district court declined to address the question of whether prudential considerations would also preclude maintenance of this action, we feel that they are inextricably linked to the question of standing in this case.... A fair characterization of the [appellants'] accusations would necessarily include the observation that they relate, quite literally, to virtually every discretionary decision made by the Administration acting through these high government officials. Consequently, any relief, to be effective, would have to be as broad as the authority of the high offices held by the federal defendants. Whether shaped as declaratory relief, or injunctive relief, or both, the court's judgment would have to interject itself into practically every facet of the Executive Branch of the federal government, on a continuing basis, for the purpose of appraising whether considerations other than pure public service motivated a particular defendant in the performance of his or her official duties.

Prudential barriers upon courts clearly preclude judicial interference in the daily responsibilities of these defendants and the resultant shift of such decisionmaking from the Executive to the Judicial Branch.... The judiciary is not to act as a management overseer of the Executive Branch....

Providing the requested relief would unquestionably bring the court and the Executive Branch into conflict because the court would be placed in the position of evaluating every discretionary consideration, including those which result in a decision not to take a particular action, for traces of political expediency. This would necessarily require the court to determine how the particular matter would be resolved if detached from the political consequences to President Carter's renomination efforts.... [T]he sweeping breadth of complaint would require correspondingly broad relief. The courts are not suited to undertake a neutral consideration of every Executive action, ranging from White House invitations and space reservations on the Presidential aircraft to the decision to award funds to a particular state or other political subdivision for general or specific projects.

... [W]hile we accord due respect to the Seventh Circuit's opinion in *Shakman* [*v. Democratic Organization of Cook County*, 435 F.2d 267 (7th Cir. 1970), *cert. denied*, 402 U.S. 909 (1971)], we find it distinguishable from the case at bar.[32] *Shakman* accorded standing to an independent candidate, and a supporter, to challenge alleged abuses which utilized the incumbent party's position to use a system of coercing political activity through the threat of arbitrary dismissal for failure to participate. *Shakman* dealt with an identifiable system of abuses, involving a single County, not a coordinate branch of the federal government. Additionally, the district court, on remand, was aided by a consent judgment entered into by a number of the defendants. The district court left open, for further developments, the remedy to be applied in *Shakman*.

It is axiomatic that the request for declaratory relief is discretionary with the court, and that the request should be denied where "it will not terminate the controversy

---

32. We note that *Shakman* was a 2-1 decision, Judge Swygert dissenting on the ground of inappropriateness of judicial intervention, the thesis we maintain here. We also note that *Shakman* was decided in 1970, prior to many of the Supreme Court opinions reassessing the standing requirement.... It should also be noted that unlike the government employees in *Shakman*, the defendants here have no fixed hours, are not paid on an hourly basis and their working day is largely within their own discretion.

or serve a useful purpose." ... In keeping with the Constitution's separation of powers of the three branches we elect to exercise such discretion by refusing to hear this case which would set a precedent by placing the judiciary in the middle of myriads of fundamental decisions that the framers of the Constitution considered they were vesting in the executive branch of government. Similarly, an injunction must be drawn with sufficient specificity to remedy the harm shown. The relief which appellants request would be so broad as to cause judicial intrusion into virtually every facet of the Executive Branch; narrower relief would be ineffective.

... We affirm the order of the district court dismissing the action....

---

1. Could the resource advantages of incumbency ever practically be controlled by statute or consent decree? If so, should they be? How would a court differentiate between "campaign" activities of the President's special assistants and their "ordinary" tasks of promoting the President and his programs?

2. Political scientists generally agree that, at least at the outset of a campaign, the marginal utility of a dollar of campaign spending is greater for challengers than for incumbents. Hence, critics of legislative attempts to impose contribution or expenditure limitations on election campaigns label such measures as "incumbent protection acts." Are there practicable ways of limiting the overall rate of increase in campaign spending without insulating incumbents from a fair challenge? Could a system of differential spending limits for challengers and incumbents be structured constitutionally? Would an incumbent legislature ever enact it?

2. Electoral College

The most arcane feature of U.S. presidential elections is, of course, the electoral college. Under the electoral college system, the choice of President is not determined by the popular vote, but by the impact of state elections on the choice of electors, whose votes, in turn, control the outcome. Perhaps its greatest role in popular political culture is providing election night newscasters with scenarios for unlikely—but constitutionally plausible—electoral nightmares, which are typically spun out while the East Coast audience waits for returns from the late-closing western states.[1] For a brief, but thorough review of the electoral college process, see W. Berns, After the People Vote: Steps in Choosing the President (1983).

The materials that follow summarize the key arguments that have been brought on behalf of continuing the electoral college system or abandoning it in favor of a direct election process.

Direct Popular Election of the President and Vice President of the United States

S. Rept. No. 609, 95th Cong., 1st Sess. (1977)

The Committee on the Judiciary, to which was referred the resolution (S.J. Res. 1) proposing an amendment to the Constitution of the United States relating to the

---

1. For example, if Democratic President-Elect A dies the night before Inauguration Day, who becomes President, Democratic Vice-President-elect B or Republican loser C? Answer: C. B received no electoral votes for President. (Don't worry: Once inaugurated, C, in a fit of statesmanship, could resign. B would become President, and could appoint a new Vice-President. See the discussion below of the 25th amendment.)

direct popular election of the President and the Vice President of the United States, having considered the same, . . . recommends that the joint resolution do pass. . . .

DEFECTS AND DEFICIENCIES IN THE PRESENT SYSTEM

The appearance of political party candidates as early as 1800 meant, in effect, that Hamilton's concept of a "select assembly" of independent electors already had lost its purpose only a decade after its embodiment in the Constitution. A Senate report published in 1806 caustically noted that the free and independent electors had "degenerated into mere agents in a case which requires no agency and where the agent must be useless if he is faithful and dangerous if he is not." More than 145 years later, however, the elector still retains this constitutionally guaranteed independence. In January 1969, Congress confirmed this 18th century prerogative by accepting the vote of a popularly chosen Republican elector from North Carolina who had cast his vote in the Electoral College for George Wallace, the American Independent Party candidate. Again in 1973, a Republican elector from Virginia was allowed to cast his vote for one Dr. John Hospers of the Liberation Party. An elector from Washington, Mike Padden, cast his vote for his personal choice, Ronald Reagan in 1976.

How dangerous is the anachronistic elector? Historically, as the late Justice Jackson paraphrased Gilbert and Sullivan, "they always voted at their party's beck and call and never thought of thinking for themselves at all." The prospect of unknown electors auctioning off the Presidency to the highest bidder, nevertheless, is all too real. That is the lesson of 1968, when the present electoral system brought us to the brink of a constitutional crisis. A shift from Nixon to Humphrey of only 42,000 popular votes in three States would have denied Nixon an electoral majority and given Wallace, with his 46 electoral votes, the balance of power. As the former Alabama Governor explained in an exclusive interview with *U.S. News & World Report* (September 30, 1968):

> *Question.* If none of the three candidates get a majority, is the election going to be decided in the Electoral College or in the House of Representatives?
>
> WALLACE. I think it would be settled in the Electoral College.
>
> *Question.* Two of the candidates get together or their electors get together and determine who is to be President?
>
> WALLACE. That is right.

. . . [E]liminating the elector . . . is not a cure-all for what ails our present electoral machinery. The elector, in fact, is merely a symptom of what the American Bar Association's Special Commission on Electoral Reform aptly described as our "archaic, undemocratic, complex, ambiguous, indirect, and dangerous" method of electing a President.

After a 10 month study, the Commission concluded that the entire electoral system should be replaced, and popular choice substituted for political chance.

Among other things, the present system can elect a President who has fewer popular votes than the opponent and thus is not the first choice of the voters; awards all of a State's electoral votes to the winner of the State popular vote, whether the candidate's margin is 1 vote or 1 million votes; cancels out all of the popular votes cast for the losing candidate in a State and casts these votes for the winner; assigns to each State a minimum of three electoral votes regardless of population and voter turnout; and provides for a patently undemocratic method for choosing a President in the event no candidate receives an electoral majority.

The major defect of the present electoral system—the unit rule—is not even a constitutional provision. The unit rule or "winner-take-all" formula is the State practice of awarding all of its electoral votes to the statewide popular vote winner. In effect, millions of voters are disfranchised if they vote for the losing candidate in their State because the full voting power of the State—its electoral vote—is awarded to the candidate they opposed....

A practical consequence of this disfranchisement is that it discourages the minority party in traditionally one-party States. Simply stated, where there is no hope of carrying the statewide popular vote the size of the voter turnout for the likely loser is meaningless. This necessarily leads to the atrophy of the party structure in many States. By the same token, the prospective winner has little incentive to turn out the vote because the margin of victory likewise is meaningless. In sum, the unit rule has the unhealthy political effect of both discouraging second parties in areas of one-party dominance and discouraging voting. This is reflected most clearly in the poor voter turnout in U.S. Presidential elections in comparison to most other democratic nations.

A byproduct of the unit rule is the distortions it produces in the value of individual votes. Winner-take-all means that a single voter has the power to cast the "swing" vote in his State, throwing the entire bloc of electoral votes to one candidate or the other. The voter's power is thus enhanced or diminished according to how many electoral votes the voter is able to affect, that is, whether the voter comes from a large or small electoral vote State. It is therefore possible for 11 "swing" votes in the largest States and one from the District of Columbia to decide the election, even though the candidate did not get a single popular vote in all of the other States. Ultimately, the swing voter derives influence from the inherent possibility of the electoral college system that the majority of the electoral votes will not produce the same winner as the plurality of popular votes. There is, of course, no swing vote with direct election. With direct election all votes count the same.

The most dangerous result of the unit rule of our present electoral system is the lack of guarantee that the candidate with the most popular votes will win.

This dangerous prospect, more than anything else, condemns the present system as an imperfect device for recording the sentiment of American voters. In 1824, 1876, and again in 1888 this system produced Presidents who were not the popular choice of the voters. On numerous other occasions in this century, a shift of less than 1 percent of the popular vote would have produced an electoral majority for the candidate who received fewer popular votes. In 1948, for example, a shift of less than 30,000 popular votes in three States would have given Governor Dewey an electoral vote majority—despite President Truman's 2 million-plus popular vote margin.

In a runaway election—like that of 1972—any system will produce an electoral victory for the popular vote winner. It is the accuracy of the results produced in closely contested elections, however, that determines the true soundness of an electoral system. Based on this criterion, the committee concluded that the present system is clearly defective. A computer study of Presidential elections over the last 50 years revealed, for example, that in elections as close as that of 1960 the present system offered only a 50-50 chance that the electoral result would agree with the popular vote. For an election as close as 1968, where some 500,000 popular votes separated the candidates, there was one chance in three that the electoral vote winner would not be the popular vote winner as well. According to the evidence, the danger of an electoral backfire is clear and present.

THE OPPONENTS' ARGUMENTS AND SOME COUNTERPOINTS

In the 10 years the proposal for the direct popular election of the President has been before the Congress, through many weeks of hearings and many days of floor debate, the arguments on this question have been sharpened and refined. . . .

THE EFFECT OF DIRECT ELECTION ON THE
TWO-PARTY SYSTEM

Opponents of direct election have alleged that abolition of the electoral college would tend to proliferate the party structure and weaken the two major parties. They believe that the winner-take-all or unit rule feature of the present system is the most important institutional guarantee for the two-party system. A well known political scientist has summarized their argument as follows: "Under the present system, the votes cast for a minor party candidate in any state are lost except in the unlikely event he runs ahead of the major party candidate. On the other hand all of the votes cast for a minor party under a popular vote would count toward the total vote of its candidate. Therefore, the carryover of votes from state to state, which would be possible under direct election, would cause the proliferation of third parties."

However, a careful study of the dynamics of the electoral college reveals that it does not discourage third parties, and . . . actually encourages them . . . in two respects. First, it provides incentives for the regional third party candidate such as George Wallace in 1968. Wallace perceived that by carrying a large bloc of States with a thin margin, he might be able to throw the two major candidates into a deadlock and thereby see the contest settled in the House of Representatives.

The winner-take-all rule also enhances the chances of national third-party candidates when they can gather votes in large, closely balanced states. For example, as Lawrence Longley testified before the subcommittee, Eugene McCarthy in 1976,

> with less than 1 percent of the popular vote, came close to tilting the election through his strength in close pivotal States. In four States, (Iowa, Maine, Alabama and Oregon) totaling 26 electoral votes, McCarthy's vote exceeded the margin by which Ford defeated Carter. In those States, McCarthy's candidacy may have swung those States to Carter. Even more significantly, had McCarthy been on the New York ballot, it is likely Ford would have carried that State with its 41 electoral votes, and with it the election—despite Carter's national vote majority.

Most authorities agree that the deterrence of third parties is related to factors other than the electoral college. An excellent case in point is the abortive attempt of the "peace" forces to organize a fourth party after the 1968 Democratic Convention. In 1968, "Peace Party" probably could not have garnered a plurality in enough states to have a significant impact on the electoral college, and the unit rule undoubtedly played some role in their ultimate decision not to proceed. . . .

It is much more likely that the Peace Party failed in 1968 for two reasons totally unrelated to the structure of the electoral college—two reasons why nationwide third parties will also be deterred under direct election. First, . . . the organizers realized that their efforts would take votes from the major party candidate closest to them in conviction and insure the victory of the major party candidate most undesirable to them. The Peace Party would have been more apt to garner a Humphrey vote than a Nixon vote, and thus by entering the field they would have enhanced the prospects of Nixon. Second, nationwide third party movements are discouraged by the fact that they must compete with the major parties for a single office—the Presidency. Planners of a Peace Party in 1968 were discouraged by the realization that they would have little to show for their efforts, for unlike the European coalition governments, the Presidency is held by one person and would be the exclusive prize of one of the major parties. On the other hand, if all the Peace Party wanted was to "spoil" the Democratic Party's chances, then the electoral college system was best suited to its purposes. All they needed to do was to run in New York and California to insure a Democratic defeat.

Scholars who have studied the two-party system in this country and compared it to similar systems throughout the world have a variety of theories as to its cause; but none suggest the electoral college. Most political scientists believe that the major institutional influence on the two-party system is the election of almost all officials in the U.S. in single-member districts. This theory stems originally from the writings of Maurice Duverger, who has found that almost every government in the world which elects its officials from single-member districts and by plurality vote has only two major parties, while countries that use multi-member districts and proportional representation have a multitude of parties. Duverger and other scholars have found that the electoral mechanics of the single member district, in terms of its effect on the party system, are such that they tend to force factions to combine in order to be certain of capturing a popular vote plurality and victory.

It was the conclusion of the committee's majority that direct popular election would work affirmatively to strengthen the two-party system. First, by counting every popular vote regardless of where it is cast, direct election would spread and foster two-party competition on a nationwide scale. The goal of both major parties would be to "get out the vote" in every State. Simply carrying a State, the objective under the present system, would no longer be the ultimate objective. The net result, therefore, would be increased party activity—particularly in what are now one-party States....

FEDERALISM AND DIRECT ELECTION

Perhaps the most frequent argument made by opponents of direct election is that the electoral college is an important component in preserving the power of the States in our Federal system. Even at the Constitutional Convention, however, the electoral college was not intended to serve that purpose.

The electoral college was effected primarily as a compromise between advocates of popular election such as James Madison, James Wilson and Gouverneur Morris and those who wanted the executive chosen by the legislative branch. The manner of choosing the President was debated sporadically over the summer of 1787, and resolved finally by the contrivance of an appointed Committee of Eleven in the early days of September as a matter of practical politics. It worked well as an arbitration device in 1787 but quickly diminished in utility thereafter.

It is clear that the well-known Great Compromise between large and small states was not a major factor in shaping the electoral college. As Neal Peirce has explained in his book, "The People's President,"

The Great Compromise was devised to settle the dispute over representation in Congress, not the electoral college.... At no point in the minutes of the Convention can one find any reference to the application of the Great Compromise to the electoral college's apportionment as important to the Federal system or to the overall structure of the Constitution which was adopted. Indeed, it was never mentioned directly at all. Only in "The Federalist Papers," where James Madison argued at one point that the electoral base for the Presidency would be a "compound" of national and state factors because of the mixed apportionment base, does the argument appear. But no more than indirect reference was made to the apportionment of the electoral college in the State ratifying conventions, or in fact by any of the Nation's leaders until some years after ratification of the Constitution. The argument that the founding fathers viewed the special Federal nature of electoral college apportionment as central to the institution of the Presidency, or to the entire Constitution, is simply false. The small States thought they would gain special advantage, but by another provision—their equal votes in the House in contingent elections.

In the latest hearings on the proposed direct election amendment before the Subcommittee on the Constitution, Professor Emeritus Paul Freund of Harvard addressed the question of whether changing to direct election as a means of electing the President would affect a change on the concept of federalism as conceived by the framers of the Constitution. His reply was that such a change would be much less radical than that of the 17th Amendment in 1913 when we abandoned the indirect election of Senators and thereby abandoned the design of the framers. The original vision of the writers of the Constitution about the selection of the Executive soon proved unworkable. A whole new set of circumstances such as the growth of political parties arose and quickly required the revision of the 12th amendment....

The fundamental tenets of federalism remain today as they did in 1787; the balance between State governments and the Federal Government, and the varying representation in the two Houses of Congress. Perhaps no better response has been given to the questions about direct election which arise under the name of federalism than that of Senator Mike Mansfield in 1961:

> The Federal system is not strengthened through an antiquated device which has not worked as it was intended to work when it was included in the Constitution and which, if anything, has become a divisive force in the Federal system by pitting groups of States against groups of States. As I see the Federal system in contemporary practice, the House of Representatives is the key to the protection of district interests as to district interests, just as the Senate is the key to the protection of State interests as State interests. These instrumentalities, and particularly the Senate, are the principal constitutional safeguards of the Federal system, but the Presidency has evolved, out of necessity, into the principal political office, as the courts have become the principal legal bulwark beyond districts, beyond States, for safeguarding the interests of all the people in all the States. And since such is the case, in my opinion, the Presidency should be subject to the direct and equal control of all the people.

As Senator Robert Dole remarked in testifying before the Subcommittee for the second time in 1977, direct election serves to enhance real "commonsense" federalism. ... Dole explains that with direct election, Presidential candidates would no longer be able to ignore areas in small as well as large States, simply because their supporters are in a clear majority or clear minority....

IMPACT OF DIRECT ELECTION ON THE SMALLER STATES

... Under the unit rule, all of the State's electoral votes are awarded to the candidate who wins a popular vote plurality—regardless of whether the plurality is 1 vote or 1 million votes. The consequence of this "winner-take-all" system is that Presidential campaigns and political power are concentrated in the large, closely contested urban States, where entire State blocs of electoral votes can be won by the narrowest of margins....

There is little doubt that with direct election, candidates will continue to travel more often to heavily populated areas than sparsely populated ones. But with direct election, at least communities of the same size will hold the same attraction whether they are in a large or a small State....

DIRECT ELECTION WOULD REDUCE THE DANGER OF VOTER FRAUD

According to the minority report from the Committee on the Judiciary in 1970, "One of the most calamitous and probable consequences of direct popular election will be the increased incidence of election fraud." The argument is that if fraud occurs under the present system, the impact is limited to determining the outcome on one State alone. "The incentive to steal votes is now restricted to close contests in States which have a sufficiently large electoral vote to alter the final result. Thus, fraud can be profitable only in a few States, and is seldom capable of affecting the national outcome."

In reality, the incentive to steal votes "now" as described above is a fair argument for why the electoral college system itself encourages fraud. A relatively few irregular votes can reap a healthy reward in the form of a bloc of electoral votes, because of the unit rule. In short, under the present system, fraudulent popular votes are likely to have a greater impact than a like number of fraudulent popular votes under direct election.

We may cite New York in 1976 as an example. Cries of voting irregularities arose on election night. At stake were 41 electoral votes—more than enough to elect Ford over Carter in the electoral college. Carter's popular margin was 290,000. The calls for recount were eventually dropped, but if fraud had been present in New York, Carter's plurality of 290,000 would have been enough to determine the outcome of the election. Under direct election, at least 1.7 million votes, Carter's national margin, would have had to have been irregular to determine the outcome.

Opponents of direct election charge that a popular vote would increase the incentive for fraud because in a close election every vote would count. It is precisely for this reason that we would have better policing of the polling places by the parties themselves, and possibly even better counting methods and procedural safeguards. The kinds of fraud and voting irregularities which have occurred under the electoral college are frequently in places controlled by one party. And under the electoral college system, there is no incentive for the other party to watch the polls when there is no possibility of carrying the electoral votes.

DIRECT ELECTION AND VOTE RECOUNTS

... It is common sense that a candidate will desire a recount only when the candidate perceives that it may change the results in the candidate's favor. And that change of fortune is more likely with the electoral college system than it is with direct election. For example, in 1976, if Ford had carried Ohio and Hawaii he would have gained the electoral majority and would have won the election. A shift of only 9,245 votes in these two States would have accomplished that result. The number of votes nation-wide needed to change the result with a direct election was Carter's plurality of 1.7 million....

Further, recounts will remain unlikely under direct election as they have been with the electoral college system in that experience has shown that overall election recounts generally reveal an almost minuscule shift in number and percent of votes and almost never change the result....

RUNOFF

The proposed amendment requires the winning candidate to obtain at least 40 percent of the total vote in order to win. Failing that plurality a runoff of the top two candidates is required. The 40 percent figure was arrived at because it was felt necessary to establish a reasonable plurality requirement indicating a legitimate mandate to govern. On the other hand, it was decided that a requirement that was set too high might disrupt the stability of our political system by too easily triggering a runoff.

... To turn once again to some indirect method of choice such as the Congress to resolve the selection of the President would mean that the choice would be useless if it reflects the will of the people and mischievous if it does not. All the dangers of deals made with third party candidates which now exist with the electoral college would be retained, with no improvement in the means of expressing the wishes of the voters themselves.

A review of Presidential elections shows that the likelihood of a runoff is dim. Only one President, Lincoln, has received less than 40 percent of the popular vote. In 1860 Lincoln received only 39.79 percent of the vote but his name did not appear on the ballot in 10 States.

Further, it appears very unlikely that neither major party candidate would receive a 40 percent plurality—even with a third party candidate in the race. Under the terms of Senate Joint Resolution 1, a splinter party would have to poll at least 20 percent of the total popular vote—and in most instances more—before triggering the runoff. That is considered unlikely in view of the strong two-party system in the United States. In 1968, for example, the most significant third party bid since 1924 could only produce 13.5 percent of the popular vote for George Wallace.

Even more to the point, the committee reviewed the four-way race in 1912, noting that in the face of challenges by an incumbent President and a popular former President, Woodrow Wilson still received more than 40 percent of the popular vote. The four-way race in 1948, involving Truman, Dewey, Thurmond, and Wallace, likewise produced a candidate with well over 40 percent of the popular vote. The likelihood of a major party candidate receiving the required plurality, therefore, is not confined merely to third party races but to multiparty contests as well.

The question has been raised as to whether the runoff might not unnecessarily encourage third parties to enter Presidential elections. As analyzed by Prof. Paul Freund of Harvard University before the subcommittee on July 28, 1977, third parties have four motivations to place a candidate in the field. They may hope to win or at least be placed in the runoff; to register the strengths of their movement or cause; to deadlock the election or play a spoiler role; or finally to cause the defeat of a particular major party candidate.

If the motive is to win, the third party obviously must register 40 percent. If it is to place in the runoff, the party must keep both major parties from achieving 40 percent, while at the same time defeating one of the major parties, an extremely difficult task.

If the minor party's aim is to effect a deadlock and exert maximum power in a contingency election, then the electoral college is probably more attractive a system than direct election. To prevent a majority in the electoral vote is far easier for a strong regional candidate than it would be to achieve at least 20 percent of the popular vote while neither major party achieved 40 percent.

Assuming, however, that a minor party candidate or group of candidates is able to garner 20 percent of the popular vote and simultaneously preclude either major party candidate from receiving at least 40 percent of the remaining votes, the bargaining position obtained may be less than would at first appear. The ability of the candidate to control the votes of all those individuals who once claimed to support him is not tantamount to the influence held by a candidate over electors pledged to that candidate....

RACIAL AND MINORITY GROUP VOTING POWER UNDER ELECTORAL COLLEGE AND DIRECT ELECTION SYSTEMS

Some have defended the present electoral college approach on the theory that the system as it operates gives disproportionate voting influence to racial or ethnic minorities, thereby offsetting some of the economic or social deprivations historically suffered by these groups. The late Prof. Alexander M. Bickel of Yale Law School was a major proponent of this view.... This conclusion in respect to racial groups has been undermined in recent years, however, by empirical analyses which have been done of voting power under the electoral college....

Perhaps the one aspect of the electoral college system which carries with it the greatest burden for ethnic or racial minorities is the unit rule provision. This system, which awards all of a State's electoral votes to the candidate who wins a majority of the popular vote, can have an impact on minority voting strength that is little short of devastating.... [T]he direct election approach is the only method of insuring that minority and ethnic group voters across the country exercise the voting power which their numbers command....

A final question is answered by direct election, and that is the question of fundamental fairness. With direct election every vote would count. Every vote would count the same, urban or rural, black or white, rich or poor; north, south, east or west. And the person with the most votes would win. Only direct election accomplishes this result....

J. A. Best, Prepared Statement on "The Case for the Electoral College"*

The Electoral College and Direct Election, Hearings Before the
Subcomm. on the Constitution of the U.S. Comm. on the Judiciary,
95th Cong., 1st Sess. (1977)

. . . The distinctive element of the electoral college system is the federal unit rule principle not the office of presidential elector. This system emerged in 1832 at the same time as the national party nominating convention system.

. . . The organizing principle of the American system of government is the principle of the concurrent majority under which coalition-building and compromise create broad cross-sectional majorities that provide moderate government and are resistant to tyranny. . . .

The following case for the electoral college system is not a case for the system established by the Founders in the Constitution. Contrary to the usual understanding, the date of the emergence of our current presidential election system is approximately 1832 not 1789. The original system devised by the Founders not only did not work as they had intended but was a mere embryo of the system as we know it today. . . .

The Constitution left it to the states to decide how their presidential electors would be selected. As a result, a diversity of methods were employed during the first eleven presidential elections. As late as 1828, one fourth of the states did not use the unit rule. In 1828, Maine, Maryland, New York and Tennessee used the district method of aggregating popular votes and in Delaware and South Carolina the electors were chosen by the state legislature. By 1832, all but two states had adopted the unit rule; Maryland used the district system and in South Carolina the electors were chosen by the legislature. 1832 was the year when the system assumed its peculiar, characteristic form.

. . . Faithless electors make headlines and arouse our moral indignation, but they have had no practical effect on any election. More than 17,000 electoral votes have been cast since the founding, and less than 10 of them can be called faithless or miscast. If the office of elector alone were abolished, the system as we know it would not be altered. . . . The actual, the paramount question about the electoral college system is whether the popular vote for President should be aggregated under the federal unit rule principle.

No electoral system is neutral. Every electoral system, as a practical matter, favors certain groups and interests and discriminates against others. Therefore, the issue is not whether the electoral college has biases, but rather whether the biases of the electoral college are compatible with and supportive of the American idea of democracy, whether the electoral college is an integral part of our system of government. As Senator John Kennedy put it, when he and Senator Paul Douglas led the fight against a proposal to change the system, "It is not only the unit vote for the Presidency we are talking about, but a whole solar system of governmental power. If it is proposed to change the balance of power of one of the elements of the solar system, it is necessary to consider the others."

*Copyright 1977. American Political Science Association. Reprinted by permission. The author's footnotes are omitted.

What, then, is this "solar system," what is the American idea of democracy? It is, has been, and was intended to be a system of concurrent majorities designed to balance two very high but frequently incompatible things—liberty and equality. We are not, have never been and were not intended to be a simple majoritarian democracy, the regime whose dedication to equality is so singleminded that it will readily sacrifice liberty to achieve its goal. No attentive reader of the constitution or of the *Federalist Papers* can fail to recognize the Founder's overwhelming fear of majority faction, of majority tyranny....

Our "solar system of governmental power" is filled with devices or intermediary institutions to protect minorities, to prevent the formation of all-national majorities and to limit the power of ordinary majorities. To mention just five of the most obvious and important ones, there are the Constitution itself, the amendment procedure, the Supreme Court of the United States, the United States Senate and, of course, the electoral college system.... None of these institutions and procedures operates simply under the principle of one citizen, one equally weighted direct vote....

As it actually operates, the electoral college system has a significant number of biases. It has a bias in favor of: (1) the winner of a cross-sectional popular plurality, (2) a single election, (3) the two-party system, (4) large, competitive two-party states and well organized or self-conscious minorities in urban-suburban areas in such states, (5) ideologically moderate candidates and parties, and (6) electoral certainty. It has a bias against: (1) sectional candidacies, (2) contingency elections, (3) third parties, (4) homogeneous regions and one-party states, (5) ideologically extremist candidates and parties, and (6) the premium on fraud. These biases must be closely examined to determine how they operate and interact....

The system is essentially a plurality system that magnifies the national plurality winner's margin of victory in the electoral vote. Because the unit rule awards 100 percent of a state's electoral vote to the candidate who achieves a statewide plurality, the President-Elect will receive a higher percentage of the electoral vote than he has won in the popular vote. In the thirty-six elections held since 1832, the average increase in the national plurality winner's margin in the electoral votes is 19.3 percent. In every election but one, the multiplier effect of the unit rule worked to the advantage of the undisputed winner of the popular plurality.

This does not mean that the multiplier effect gives the plurality candidate a greater mandate. The electorate largely misses the fact of the electoral college; and election analysts know full well that the multiplier effect is artificial, that the real mandate is derived from the popular vote. What this multiplier effect does mean is that the system is biased in favor of the winner of the national popular plurality, and that it makes a contingency election highly improbable.

There is but one addendum to this bias of the electoral college system, but one exception to the advantage given to the plurality winner: the bias against a purely or predominantly sectional candidacy. A candidate whose appeal is sectional and not cross-sectional, a candidate whose popular vote support is geographically narrow and deep loses the advantage of the multiplier effect. There are no electoral vote bonuses for candidates who win a state by a landslide. The top prize is 100 percent of a state's electoral votes whether a candidate polls a simple plurality or 85 percent of the statewide popular vote.

This bias against sectional candidacies is clearly illustrated by the election of 1888, when Grover Cleveland, who had a narrow popular plurality, lost to Benjamin Harrison, after running a sectional campaign. Cleveland emphasized the sectional tariff issue and increased the Democratic party's margins in the already solid South by 5 to 17 percent over the election of 1884. The average increase in the Southern states was 9 percent. To put it mildly, this strategy was dysfunctional since the unit rule gives greater rewards to candidates who muster a statewide plurality than to candidates who win a state by a landslide, such as Cleveland's 83 percent in South Carolina. Any votes a candidate gathers in excess of a statewide plurality are "wasted" because they do not yield electoral votes. In a closely contested election, geographic concentration of the popular votes is as strategically undesirable as it is politically undesirable.

Furthermore, the multiplier effect works well, produces a plurality President, even in the closest elections, and it will continue to work well as long as our power oriented parties give as much concern to the distribution of their popular votes as to the number of their popular votes. In the closest election in our history, the election of 1880, when Garfield led Hancock by a minuscule 0.1 percent of the popular votes, Garfield won 57.9 percent of the electoral vote for a magnification of 9.6 percent over his popular vote. In 1960, the second closest election, when Kennedy apparently led Nixon by less than 0.2 percent of the popular vote, it increased Kennedy's electoral vote percentage by 6.7 percent.... Under the unit rule the distribution of the popular votes may be as important as the number. Not every sectional dispute can be moderated by an election system, but the antisectional bias of an electoral system ... should be prized.

A word must be said about the shift-in-votes argument used by several analysts to suggest that the system is not a reliable plurality system. In large part this argument is a parlor game of speculation in which numbers are moved from one column to another in a political vacuum and often without regard to the election laws. Several analysts have argued that a switch of less than 1 percent of the votes in New York in the 1844 election would have made Henry Clay a runner-up President. As a simple mathematical proposition, it is true. But it abstracts from the political world where such shifts would have to occur. What would produce such a shift? Is it likely that whatever produced such a shift would have no effects in any other state? If the cause of such a shift is some political act (and if it is not, does this mean that votes are cast randomly and arbitrarily?), then the effect would not be isolated to one state but could change or reverse the results in other closely contested states.... Unless the proposed shifts occurs in *and are limited to* the states selected in our game of speculation, the predicted result will not obtain.... What experience has demonstrated is that the electoral college system is a system strongly biased in favor of the winner of a cross-sectional popular plurality.

Is this bias functional given the American idea of democracy? Plurality systems are an aberration of majoritarian theory which requires that elected officials have the support of a majority of *all* citizens.... In practice the majority requirement is too stringent. It would necessitate compulsory voting. Run-off elections with all their attendant cost, confusion, intrigue and delay would become the rule if the majority requirement were strictly enforced....

[O]ur plurality Presidencies compare quite favorably with our majority Presidencies. For fifteen presidential terms we have been governed by a minority President, one who received a plurality rather than a majority of the popular vote. Among these terms are seven that have been rated among the best in our history: those of Polk, Lincoln, Cleveland twice, Wilson twice and Truman....

We have good reason to know that sectional candidacies breed civil strife and civil war. We are a continental nation; we are a heterogeneous people with a wide variety of religious, racial, ethnic, economic and ideological interests that must be consulted and considered. The electoral college bias in favor of broad cross-sectional candidacies is highly functional in such a nation.

The federal-geographic rider works in the electoral college the same way that it does for the Congress. It incorporates the Presidency into the system of concurrent majorities. It forces candidates to create broad coalitions. It provides the incentive to our national parties, as James MacGregor Burns pointed out, "to widen and 'flatten out' their vote." In fact, Burns has concluded that this is "the historic achievement of the presidential party," the party whose strategy is shaped by the electoral college....

The multiplier effect of the unit rule not only favors the plurality candidate, it produces a single election. Once the electoral college system had fully evolved, the likelihood of contingency elections became remote. We have not had one since the unit rule was adopted by almost all of the states. And, in light of recent history, it seems more probable that the Twenty-fifth Amendment, dealing with vice presidential vacancies and presidential disabilities, will be far more important to the institution of the Presidency than the contingency election procedures established by the Founders.

The contingency procedure is utilized only if no candidate receives a majority of the electoral votes. This could occur in an election with more than two serious candidates. The electoral college, however, discriminates against both sectional and national third parties, and the multiplier effect continues to magnify the plurality winner's margin of victory in the electoral vote. In years when more than two candidates won electoral votes, the average increase in the plurality candidate's electoral vote over his popular vote was 17.1 percent, only 2.2 percent less than the average for all elections....

The college's bias against national third parties is widely recognized, but its bias against sectional third parties is not as clearly understood. A sectional candidate is under a severe handicap because the unit rule favors a cross-sectional vote distribution pattern. Many of the popular votes for a sectional candidate are "wasted" because of their narrow and deep distribution.

Despite the sectional third party candidate's apparent advantage over a national third party candidate, he cannot win the election. It is feared, however, that he could deadlock the college and provoke a contingency election.... To deadlock the college, a candidate would have to win some electoral votes. Then he would have to ... take votes away from both of the major parties, and these votes must be strategically placed in specific states. Too much here or too little there not only will mean failure to deadlock but also could produce an electoral vote landslide for one of the two major party candidates. While such a candidate is raiding the major parties, they are not complacent and indulgent. They rush out to secure their followers and to recapture those who have strayed. The efforts of the major parties and the prospect of casting a wasted vote in a close election create strong counter-pressures on the voters to whom the third party candidate must appeal.

The third party candidacy of George Wallace in 1968 is a classic example of the single election bias of the college. Wallace was a sectional candidate who ran a national campaign and amassed 4,100,000 votes outside the South for which he received no electoral votes. Although he won 13.5 percent of the popular vote, he won only 8 percent of the electoral vote, less than half of the average distortion of the multiplier effect in three-way electoral vote contests. His attempt to deadlock the college was a dismal failure. . . .

The result of the 1968 Wallace deadlock strategy is merely a part of a larger pattern, a pattern of defeat for third party strategies. There have been eleven presidential elections in which a third party candidate won electoral votes. In none of these elections were we close to a deadlock, and in five of them the victor's percentage of the electoral vote surpassed sixty percent. Several of these third party candidates polled high percentages of the popular vote: Millard Fillmore received 21 percent in 1856. Robert La Follette received 17 percent in 1924. None of these prodigious efforts were any match for the multiplier effect of the unit rule. In 1856, Buchanan won with an electoral vote of 58.7 percent for an increase of 13 percent over his popular vote. In 1860, Lincoln jumped from a popular vote of merely 38.7 percent to an electoral vote of 59.4 percent, an increase of 19.7 percent. In 1924, Coolidge won an electoral vote landslide with 71.7 percent for an increase of 17.7 percent over his popular vote.

As it actually operates, the college has a bias in favor of a single election. . . . [I]t makes for stability, reduces uncertainty, prevents intrigue, shortens the period of interregnum, and allows time for the smooth transition of power. Over and above these things, the single election bias of the college supports the two-party system, the system that, in the words of Austin Ranney and Willmore Kendall, "more than any other American Institution, consciously, actively and directly nurtures consensus."

The college's bias in favor of the two-party system is sustained not only by its bias against sectional and national third parties, but also by its bias in favor of a single election. Frequent contingency elections of any kind would weaken or destroy the two-party system whose vitality may depend, as Schattschneider argued, upon its control over nominations. If, as is the case under the current system, a contingency election is highly unlikely, disenchanted partisan factions have little to gain and a great deal to lose by bucking the party nomination procedure. But if the electoral system has no bias toward a single election, if a contingency election is probable, then the second-chance psychology will spread. The parties could fragment as factional leaders scramble to enter the contest. . . .

In this continental, heterogeneous nation, the two-party system has developed as an extra-constitutional institution to perform a critically necessary function, a coalition-building, unifying function. Madison's idea was to divide and diversify, to encourage the development of numerous contending minority factions rather than a monolithic majority faction. That could be a sound plan if and only if something would serve to create coalitions, concurrent majorities, that could govern. . . . Thus, a major problem posed by the Madisonian system of a large heterogeneous federal republic, with its cultural pluralism and its separation of powers, was to provide some unity and coherence, to provide political majorities.

The two-party system arose in response to this necessity for coalition-building. Not surprisingly, our national party nominating convention system arose at the same time that the unit rule reached full development, 1832-1836. The two-party system is an integral part of the American idea of democracy, and the electoral college's bias in its favor is highly desirable. It is especially desirable at this moment in our history when the two-party system is somewhat indisposed, when the other non-institutional supports for two-partyism have decayed, when politics is individualized and the number of Independents is rising.

The college's partiality is not simply for two-partyism; it prefers moderate candidates and parties. The federal-geographic dispersion requirement quells tendencies to organize parties on class, racial, religious, ethnic, economic or ideological lines. Such factions cannot readily combine their votes across state lines. Even if the two-party system were to survive the abandonment of the unit rule, the parties could be drastically changed becoming highly ideological and dysfunctionally immoderate. Absent the unit rule, factionalism could run wild as candidates would be relieved of the necessity to create broad coalitions. Now, a victorious strategy cannot be based on narrow appeals and extravagant promises to popular majorities in one section of the country such as the populous Eastern megalopolis, or to a dominant racial group, the whites, or to a dominant religious group, the Christians, or to a single-interest constituency such as the anti-forced-busing faction....

The system also has a bias in favor of large competitive, two-party states and of urban and suburban voters in such states. Again it is the unit rule that accounts for this partiality. The most populous states have large blocs of electoral votes at their disposal, and if they are competitive, if each of the two major parties has a real chance of victory in such states, they will become the major battlegrounds. Since these states are much more representative of the diversity of the nation as a whole than the homogeneous one-party states, these are the most appropriate and functional battlegrounds. The kinds of coalitions that can win in such states are the kinds of coalitions that can win a cross-sectional victory and therefore can govern. Within such states urban-suburban voters have an apparent advantage.... [I]t balances the rural-small-town bias of the Congress.

Although no election system can completely prevent fraud, the current system does have a bias against fraud because of the unit rule. Under any system, the closer the election the greater the inducement to cheat. But when, as now, each state is a separate electoral arena, the state boundaries quarantine the disease.... Furthermore, because of the multiplier effect, close popular vote contests are not always close electoral vote contests, and the point of the fraudulent activity is to affect the electoral votes through the popular votes....

As a result of this bias, few elections are likely to be contested by the loser even when he has good reason to suspect fraud in some states because the fraudulent activity does not always determine the victory. The candidate who demands a recount in the hope of reversing the results must not only pick up votes and/or invalidate some of the votes for his opponent, but he must do so in particular states....

If federalism is an anachronism, if cross-sectional, concurrent majorities are no longer necessary to maintain liberty, then perhaps we should abandon federalism for the national legislature as well as for the executive. To do one without the other, particularly to make the President the recipient of the only all-national mandate could change our governmental solar system, could change the balance in executive-legislative relationships to the advantage of the President. The authenticity of the voice of the Congress, speaking for a concurrent majority, could be seriously undermined by a truly plebiscitary President claiming to speak most directly and clearly for the general will. The sobering experience of the Watergate era should make us reluctant to further aggrandize the Presidency.

Is the electoral college system compatible with and supportive of the American idea of democracy? The answer, I believe, is yes.... The system looks to the formation of concurrent rather than simple arithmetical majorities, but the organizing principle of the whole governmental system is the concurrent majority. But above all else, the system balances the principles of liberty and equality because it at once utilizes the numerical votes of factions while restraining their destructive potential.

---

1. By which arguments are you more persuaded—Professor Best's or those of the committee report? How much weight do you attach to arguments stressing imagined "horribles," for example, that a single vote's difference in each of just a few states could alter the electoral outcome?

2. Note that the virtues Professor Best attributes to the electoral college flow not from its constitutionally prescribed structure, but from the universal state adoption of the unit rule, which is a matter of discretion with each state. Is it plausible to argue that 150 years of practice have effectively amended the Constitution? Could a state legislature abandon the unit rule? Could it constitutionally determine that it will choose the state's electors without any popular vote at all in the state? (The constitutional text permits such an outcome; should that be the end of the interpretive inquiry?)

C. Impeachment

Besides elections, the one constitutionally prescribed means for presidential removal is impeachment. The following study surveys the law and history of impeachment practice. As you read the materials that follow, consider what guidance, if any, the existence of an impeachment option provides for constitutional interpretation on other questions. For example, does the Constitution's express provision for a single means of congressional participation in the removal of officers of the United States buttress the Supreme Court's refusal to sanction any further role for Congress in the removal of officers? Recall *Myers v. United States* and *Bowsher v. Synar*, both excerpted in Chapter Four. Does the existence of an impeachment option suggest that other congressional efforts to police executive wrongdoing—special prosecutor legislation, for example—are beyond Congress' powers? Or, conversely, does the impracticability of impeachment buttress Congress' case that additional mechanisms are legitimate, at least as long as they do not aggrandize Congress' direct powers regarding removal?

Note also that the following materials were produced in connection with proceedings to consider the impeachment of Richard Nixon in the wake of the Watergate scandal. Despite the dispassionate tone of the House Judiciary Committee staff report, the House was under Democratic control, and it is worth considering to what degree the study should be read as an advocacy document. [The executive branch likewise proffered scholarly studies on impeachment, with the prefatory disclaimers that they were not to be regarded as taking an official position, and, indeed, were not intended to reach "ultimate conclusions." Office of Legal Counsel, U.S. Department of Justice, Legal Aspects of Impeachment: An Overview (with 4 appendices) (1974).] President Nixon argued, for example, that impeachment, by clear implication of the constitutional text, could be based on only criminal offenses. Is this argument wholly without foundation? Would such a doctrine usefully prevent Congress from impeaching merely unpopular Presidents? *See* St. Clair, *et al., Analysis of the Constitutional Standard for Presidential Impeachment*, in Presidential Impeachment: A Documentary Overview 40-73 (M. B. Schnapper ed. 1974). Or would it unjustifiably constrain Congress from protecting the government against gross, but not criminal, abuses of power? *See generally* R. Berger, Impeachment: The Constitutional Problems (1973); C. Black, Impeachment (1974). For another view generally concurring with the House study that follows, *see* Committee on Legislation, Association of the Bar of the City of New York, The Law of Presidential Impeachment (1974).

Constitutional Grounds for Presidential Impeachment
Report by the Staff of the Impeachment Inquiry of the House Committee on the Judiciary (Comm. Print), 93d Cong., 2d Sess. (1974)

I. Introduction

The Constitution deals with the subject of impeachment and conviction at six places. The scope of the power is set out in Article II, Section 4:

> The President, Vice President and all civil Officers of the United States, shall be removed from Office on Impeachment for, and Conviction of, Treason, Bribery, or other high Crimes and Misdemeanors.

Other provisions deal with procedures and consequences. Article I, Section 2 states:

> The House of Representatives . . . shall have the sole Power of Impeachment.

Similarly, Article I, Section 3, describes the Senate's role:

> The Senate shall have the sole Power to try all Impeachments. When sitting for that Purpose, they shall be on Oath or Affirmation. When the President of the United States is tried, the Chief Justice shall preside: And no Person shall be convicted without the Concurrence of two thirds of the Members present.

The same section limits the consequences of judgment in cases of impeachment:

> Judgment in Cases of Impeachment shall not extend further than to removal from Office, and disqualification to hold and enjoy any Office of honor, Trust or Profit under the United States: but the Party convicted shall nevertheless be liable and subject to Indictment, Trial, Judgment and Punishment, according to Law.

Of lesser significance, although mentioning the subject, are: Article II, Section 2:

> The President . . . shall have Power to grant Reprieves and Pardons for Offences against the United States, except in Cases of Impeachment.

Article III, Section 2:

> The Trial of all Crimes, except in Cases of Impeachment, shall be by Jury. . . .

. . . This memorandum offers no fixed standards for determining whether grounds for [the] impeachment [of Richard Nixon] exist. The framers did not write a fixed standard. Instead they adopted from English history a standard sufficiently general and flexible to meet future circumstances and events, the nature and character of which they could not foresee.

II. The Historical Origins of Impeachment

The Constitution provides that the President " ... shall be removed from Office on Impeachment for, and Conviction of, Treason, Bribery, or other high Crimes and Misdemeanors." The framers could have written simply "or other crimes"—as indeed they did in the provision for extradition of criminal offenders from one state to another. They did not do that. If they had meant simply to denote seriousness, they could have done so directly. They did not do that either. They adopted instead a unique phrase used for centuries in English parliamentary impeachments, for the meaning of which one must look to history. ...

A. THE ENGLISH PARLIAMENTARY PRACTICE

Alexander Hamilton wrote, in No. 65 of *The Federalist*, that Great Britain had served as "the model from which [impeachment] has been borrowed." ...

Parliament developed the impeachment process as a means to exercise some measure of control over the power of the King. An impeachment proceeding in England was a direct method of bringing to account the King's ministers and favorites—men who might otherwise have been beyond reach. Impeachment, at least in its early history, has been called "the most powerful weapon in the political armoury, short of civil war." It played a continuing role in the struggles between King and Parliament that resulted in the formation of the unwritten English constitution. In this respect impeachment was one of the tools used by the English Parliament to create more responsive and responsible government and to redress imbalances when they occurred.

The long struggle by Parliament to assert legal restraints over the unbridled will of the King ultimately reached a climax with the execution of Charles I in 1649 and the establishment of the Commonwealth under Oliver Cromwell. In the course of that struggle, Parliament sought to exert restraints over the King by removing those of his ministers who most effectively advanced the King's absolutist purposes. Chief among them was Thomas Wentworth, Earl of Strafford. The House of Commons impeached him in 1640. As with earlier impeachments, the thrust of the charge was damage to the state. The first article of impeachment alleged

> That he ... hath traitorously endeavored to subvert the Fundamental Laws and Government of the Realms ... and in stead thereof, to introduce Arbitrary and Tyrannical Government against Law. ...

The other articles against Strafford included charges ranging from the allegation that he had assumed regal power and exercised it tyrannically to the charge that he had subverted the rights of Parliament.

Characteristically, impeachment was used in individual cases to reach offenses, as perceived by Parliament, against the system of government. The charges, variously denominated "treason," "high treason," "misdemeanors," "malversations," and "high Crimes and Misdemeanors," thus included allegations of misconduct as various as the kings (or their ministers) were ingenious in devising means of expanding royal power.

At the time of the Constitutional Convention the phrase "high Crimes and Misdemeanors" had been in use for over 400 years in impeachment proceedings in Parliament.[6] It first appears in 1386 in the impeachment of the King's Chancellor,

---

6. ... The basis for what became the impeachment procedure apparently originated in

Michael de la Pole, Earl of Suffolk. Some of the charges may have involved common law offenses. Others plainly did not. . . .

The phrase does not reappear in impeachment proceedings until 1450. In that year articles of impeachment against William de la Pole, Duke of Suffolk (a descendant of Michael), charged him with several acts of high treason, but also with "high Crimes and Misdemeanors," including such various offenses as "advising the King to grant liberties and privileges to certain persons to the hindrance of the due execution of the laws," "procuring offices for persons who were unfit, and unworthy of them" and "squandering away the public treasure."

Impeachment was used frequently during the reigns of James I (1603-1625) and Charles I (1628-1649). During the period from 1620 to 1649 over 100 impeachments were voted by the House of Commons. Some of these impeachments charged high treasons, as in the case of Strafford; others charged high crimes and misdemeanors. The latter included both statutory offenses, particularly with respect to the Crown monopolies, and non-statutory offenses. For example, Sir Henry Yelverton, the King's Attorney General, was impeached in 1621 of high crimes and misdemeanors in that he failed to prosecute after commencing suits, and exercised authority before it was properly vested in him.

There were no impeachments during the Commonwealth (1649-1660). Following the end of the Commonwealth and the Restoration of Charles II (1660-1685) a more powerful Parliament expanded somewhat the scope of "high Crimes and Misdemeanors" by impeaching officers of the Crown for such things as negligent discharge of duties[14] and improprieties in office.[15]

The phrase "high Crimes and Misdemeanors" appears in nearly all of the comparatively few impeachments that occurred in the eighteenth century. Many of the charges involved abuse of official power or trust. . . .

The impeachment of Warren Hastings, first attempted in 1786 and concluded in 1795, is particularly important because contemporaneous with the American Convention debates. Hastings was the first Governor-General of India. The articles indicate that Hastings was being charged with high crimes and misdemeanors in the form of gross maladministration, corruption in office, and cruelty toward the people of India.

Two points emerge from the 400 years of English parliamentary experience with the phrase "high Crimes and Misdemeanors." First, the particular allegations of misconduct alleged damage to the state in such forms as misapplication of funds, abuse of official power, neglect of duty, encroachment on Parliament's prerogatives, corruption, and betrayal of trust. Second, the phrase "high Crimes and Misdemeanors" was confined to parliamentary impeachments; it had no roots in the ordinary

---

1341, when the King and Parliament alike accepted the principle that the King's ministers were to answer in Parliament for their misdeeds. Offenses against Magna Charta, for example, were failing for technicalities in the ordinary courts, and therefore Parliament provided that offenders against Magna Charta be declared in Parliament and judged by their peers.

14. Peter Pett, Commissioner of the Navy, was charged in 1668 with negligent preparation for an invasion by the Dutch, and negligent loss of a ship. The latter charge was predicated on alleged willful neglect in failing to insure that the ship was brought to a mooring.

15. Chief Justice Scroggs was charged in 1680, among other things, with browbeating witnesses and commenting on their credibility, and with cursing and drinking to excess, thereby bringing "the highest scandal on the public justice of the kingdom."

criminal law, and the particular allegations of misconduct under that heading were not necessarily limited to common law or statutory derelictions or crimes.

B. THE INTENTION OF THE FRAMERS

The debates on impeachment at the Constitutional Convention in Philadelphia focus principally on its applicability to the President. The framers sought to create a responsible though strong executive; they hoped, in the words of Elbridge Gerry of Massachusetts, that "the maxim would never be adopted here that the chief Magistrate could do [no] wrong." Impeachment was to be one of the central elements of executive responsibility in the framework of the new government as they conceived it.

The constitutional grounds for impeachment of the President received little direct attention in the Convention; the phrase "other high Crimes and Misdemeanors" was ultimately added to "Treason" and "Bribery" with virtually no debate. There is evidence, however, that the framers were aware of the technical meaning the phrase had acquired in English impeachments....

1. THE PURPOSE OF THE IMPEACHMENT REMEDY

Among the weaknesses of the Articles of Confederation apparent to the delegates to the Constitutional Convention was that they provided for a purely legislative form of government whose ministers were subservient to Congress. One of the first decisions of the delegates was that their new plan should include a separate executive, judiciary, and legislature. However, the framers sought to avoid the creation of a too-powerful executive. The Revolution had been fought against the tyranny of a king and his council, and the framers sought to build in safeguards against executive abuse and usurpation of power. They explicitly rejected a plural executive, despite arguments that they were creating "the foetus of monarchy," because a single person would give the most responsibility to the office....

James Wilson, in the Pennsylvania convention, described the security furnished by a single executive as one of its "very important advantages":

> The executive power is better to be trusted when it has no screen. Sir, we have a responsibility in the person of our President; he cannot act improperly, and hide either his negligence or inattention; he cannot roll upon any other person the weight of his criminality; no appointment can take place without his nomination; and he is responsible for every nomination he makes.... Add to all this, that officer is placed high, and is possessed of power far from being contemptible, yet not a *single privilege* is annexed to his character; far from being above the laws, he is amenable to them in his private character as a citizen, and in his public character by *impeachment*."

As Wilson's statement suggests, the impeachability of the President was considered to be an important element of his responsibility. Impeachment had been included in the proposals before the Constitutional Convention from its beginning. A specific provision, making the executive removable from office on impeachment and conviction for "mal-practice or neglect of duty," was unanimously adopted even before it was decided that the executive would be a single person.[33]

---

33. Just before the adoption of this provision, a proposal to make the executive removable from office by the legislature upon request of a majority of the state legislatures had been overwhelmingly rejected. In the course of debate on this proposal, it was suggested that the

The only major debate on the desirability of impeachment occurred when it was moved that the provision for impeachment be dropped, a motion that was defeated by a vote of eight states to two. . . . The one argument made by the opponents of impeachment to which no direct response was made during the debate was that the executive would be too dependent on the legislature—that, as Charles Pinckney put it, the legislature would hold impeachment "as a rod over the Executive and by that means effectually destroy his independence." That issue, which involved the forum for trying impeachments and the mode of electing the executive, troubled the Convention until its closing days. Throughout its deliberations on ways to avoid executive subservience to the legislature, however, the Convention never reconsidered its early decision to make the executive removable through the process of impeachment.

2. ADOPTION OF "HIGH CRIMES AND MISDEMEANORS"

Briefly, and late in the Convention, the framers addressed the question how to describe the grounds for impeachment consistent with its intended function. They did so only after the mode of the President's election was settled in a way that did not make him (in the words of James Wilson) "the Minion of the Senate."

The draft of the Constitution then before the Convention provided for his removal upon impeachment and conviction for "treason or bribery." George Mason objected that these grounds were too limited:

> Why is the provision restrained to Treason & bribery only? Treason as defined in the Constitution will not reach many great and dangerous offenses. Hastings is not guilty of Treason. Attempts to subvert the Constitution may not be Treason as above defined—As bills of attainder which have saved the British Constitution are forbidden, it is the more necessary to extend; the power of impeachments.

Mason then moved to add the word "maladministration" to the other two grounds. Maladministration was a term in use in six of the thirteen state constitutions as a ground for impeachment, including Mason's home state of Virginia.

When James Madison objected that "so vague a term will be equivalent to a tenure during pleasure of the Senate," Mason withdrew "maladministration" and substituted "high crimes and misdemeanors agst. the State," which was adopted eight states to three, apparently with no further debate.

That the framers were familiar with English parliamentary impeachment proceedings is clear. . . . The Convention had earlier demonstrated its familiarity with the term "high misdemeanor."[51] A draft constitution had used "high misdemeanor" in its provision for the extradition of offenders from one state to another. The Convention, apparently unanimously struck "high misdemeanor" and inserted "other crime," "in

---

legislature "should have power to remove the Executive at pleasure"—a suggestion that was promptly criticized as making him "the mere creature of the Legislature" in violation of "the fundamental principle of good Government," and was never formally proposed to the Convention.

51. As a technical term, a "high" crime signified a crime against the system of government, not merely a serious crime. "This element of injury to the commonwealth—that is, to the state itself and to its constitution—was historically the criterion for distinguishing a 'high' crime or misdemeanor from an ordinary one. The distinction goes back to the ancient law of treason, which differentiated 'high' from 'petit' treason." Bestor, Book Review, 49 Wash. L. Rev. 255, 263-64 (1973). See 4 W. Blackstone, Commentaries 75.

order to comprehend all proper cases: it being doubtful whether 'high misdemeanor' had not a technical meaning too limited."

The "technical meaning" referred to is the parliamentary use of the term "high misdemeanor." Blackstone's *Commentaries on the Laws of England*—a work cited by delegates in other portions of the Convention's deliberations and which Madison later described (in the Virginia ratifying convention) as "a book which is in every man's hand"—included "high misdemeanors" as one term for positive offenses "against the king and government." The "first and principal" high misdemeanor, according to Blackstone, was "mal-administration of such high officers, as are in public trust and employment," usually punished by the method of parliamentary impeachment.

"High Crimes and Misdemeanors" has traditionally been considered a "term of art," like such other constitutional phrases as "levying war" and "due process." The Supreme Court has held that such phrases must be construed, not according to modern usage, but according to what the framers meant when they adopted them. . . .

3. GROUNDS FOR IMPEACHMENT

Mason's suggestion to add "maladministration," Madison's objection to it as "vague," and Mason's substitution of "high crimes and misdemeanors agst. the State" are the only comments in the Philadelphia convention specifically directed to the constitutional language describing the grounds for impeachment of the President. Mason's objection to limiting the grounds to treason and bribery was that treason would "not reach many great and dangerous offences" including "[a]ttempts to subvert the Constitution." His willingness to substitute "high Crimes and Misdemeanors," especially given his apparent familiarity with the English use of the term as evidenced by his reference to the Warren Hastings impeachment, suggests that he believed "high Crimes and Misdemeanors" would cover the offenses about which he was concerned.

Contemporaneous comments on the scope of impeachment are persuasive as to the intention of the framers. In *Federalist* No. 65, Alexander Hamilton described the subject of impeachment as

> those offences which proceed from the misconduct of public men, or, in other words, from the abuse or violation of some public trust. They are of a nature which may with peculiar propriety be denominated POLITICAL, as they relate chiefly to injuries done immediately to the society itself.

Comments in the state ratifying conventions also suggest that those who adopted the Constitution viewed impeachment as a remedy for usurpation or abuse of power or serious breach of trust. . . . [T]he framers who discussed impeachment in the state ratifying conventions, as well as other delegates who favored the Constitution, implied that it reached offenses against the government, and especially abuses of constitutional duties. The opponents did not argue that the grounds for impeachment had been limited to criminal offenses.

An extensive discussion of the scope of the impeachment power . . . in the House of Representatives in the First Session of the First Congress. . . . lends support to the view that the framers intended the impeachment power to reach failure of the President to discharge the responsibilities of his office. . . . One further piece of contemporary evidence is provided by the *Lectures on Law* delivered by James Wilson of Pennsylvania in 1790 and 1791. Wilson described impeachments in the United States as "confined to political characters, to political crimes and misdemeanors, and to political punishment."...

Impeachment, as Justice Joseph Story wrote in his *Commentaries on the Constitution* in 1833, applies to offenses of "a political character"....

C. THE AMERICAN IMPEACHMENT CASES

Thirteen officers have been impeached by the House since 1787; one President, one cabinet officer, one United States Senator, and ten Federal judges.[84] In addition there have been numerous resolutions and investigations in the House not resulting in impeachment. However, the action of the House in declining to impeach an officer is not particularly illuminating. The reasons for failing to impeach are generally not stated, and may have rested upon a failure of proof, legal insufficiency of the grounds, political judgment, the press of legislative business, or the closeness of the expiration of the session of Congress. On the other hand, when the House has voted to impeach an officer, a majority of the Members necessarily have concluded that the conduct alleged constituted grounds for impeachment.[85]

Does Article III, Section 1 of the Constitution, which states that judges "shall hold their Offices during good Behaviour," limit the relevance of the ten impeachments of judges with respect to presidential impeachment standards as has been argued by some? It does not. The argument is that "good behavior" implies an additional ground for impeachment of judges not applicable to other civil officers. However, the only impeachment provision discussed in the Convention and included in the Constitution is Article II, Section 4, which by its express terms, applies to all civil officers, including judges, and defines impeachment offenses as "Treason, Bribery, and other high Crimes and Misdemeanors."

In any event, the interpretation of the "good behavior" clause adopted by the House has not been made clear in any of the judicial impeachment cases. Whichever view is taken, the judicial impeachments have involved an assessment of the conduct of the officer in terms of the constitutional duties of his office. In this respect, the impeachments of judges are consistent with the three impeachments of non-judicial officers.

Each of the thirteen American impeachments involved charges of misconduct incompatible with the official position of the officeholder. This conduct falls into three broad categories: (1) exceeding the constitutional bounds of the powers of the office in derogation of the powers of another branch of government; (2) behaving in a manner grossly incompatible with the proper function and purpose of the office; and (3) employing the power of the office for an improper purpose or for personal gain.

---

84. Eleven of these officers were tried in the Senate. Articles of impeachment were presented to the Senate against a twelfth (Judge English), but he resigned shortly before the trial. The thirteenth (Judge Delahay) resigned before articles could be drawn. [Ed. note: Since this report was written, an additional federal judge was impeached and convicted. President Nixon's resignation obviated a vote on his impeachment.]

85. Only four of the thirteen impeachments—all involving judges—have resulted in conviction in the Senate and removal from office. While conviction and removal show that the Senate agreed with the House that the charges on which conviction occurred stated legally sufficient grounds for impeachment, acquittals offer no guidance on this question, as they may have resulted from a failure of proof, other factors, or a determination by more than one third of the Senators (as in the Blount and Belknap impeachments) that trial or conviction was inappropriate for want of jurisdiction.

1. EXCEEDING THE POWERS OF THE OFFICE IN DEROGATION OF THOSE OF ANOTHER BRANCH OF GOVERNMENT

The first American impeachment, of Senator William Blount in 1797, was based on allegations that Blount attempted to incite the Creek and Cherokee Indians to attack the Spanish settlers of Florida and Louisiana, in order to capture the territory for the British. . . .

The impeachment of President Andrew Johnson in 1868 also rested on allegations that he had exceeded the power of his office and had failed to respect the prerogatives of Congress. The Johnson impeachment grew out of a bitter partisan struggle over the implementation of Reconstruction in the South following the Civil War. Johnson was charged with violation of the Tenure of Office Act, which purported to take away the President's authority to remove members of his own cabinet and specifically provided that violation would be a "high misdemeanor," as well as a crime. Believing the Act unconstitutional, Johnson removed Secretary of War Edwin M. Stanton and was impeached three days later. . . . The removal of Stanton[, however,] was more a catalyst for the impeachment than a fundamental cause. The issue between the President and Congress was which of them should have the constitutional—and ultimately even the military—power to make and enforce Reconstruction policy in the South. The Johnson impeachment, like the British impeachments of great ministers, involved issues of state going to the heart of the constitutional division of executive and legislative power.

2. BEHAVING IN A MANNER GROSSLY INCOMPATIBLE WITH THE PROPER FUNCTION AND PURPOSE OF THE OFFICE

Judge John Pickering was impeached in 1803, largely for intoxication on the bench. . . . Seventy-three years later another judge, Mark Delahay, was impeached for intoxication both on and off the bench but resigned before articles of impeachment were adopted.

A similar concern with conduct incompatible with the proper exercise of judicial office appears in the decision of the House to impeach Associate Supreme Court Justice Samuel Chase in 1804. The [Democratic-Republican-controlled] House alleged that [federalist] Justice Chase had permitted his partisan views to influence his conduct of two trials held while he was conducting circuit court several years earlier. . . .

Judge West H. Humphreys was impeached in 1862 on charges that he joined the Confederacy without resigning his federal judgeship. . . .

Judicial favoritism and failure to give impartial consideration to cases before him were also among the allegations in the impeachment of Judge George W. English in 1926.

3. EMPLOYING THE POWER OF THE OFFICE FOR AN IMPROPER PURPOSE OR PERSONAL GAIN

Two types of official conduct for improper purposes have been alleged in past impeachments. The first type involves vindictive use of their office by federal judges; the second, the use of office for personal gain.

Judge James H. Peck was impeached in 1826 for charging with contempt a lawyer who had publicly criticized one of his decisions, imprisoning him, and ordering his disbarment for 18 months. . . .

Some of the articles in the impeachment of Judge Charles Swayne (1903) alleged that he maliciously and unlawfully imprisoned two lawyers and a litigant for contempt.

Six impeachments have alleged the use of office for personal gain or the appearance of financial impropriety while in office. Secretary of War William W. Belknap was impeached in 1876 of high crimes and misdemeanors for conduct that probably constituted bribery and certainly involved the use of his office for highly improper purposes—receiving substantial annual payments through an intermediary in return for his appointing a particular post trader at a frontier military post in Indian territory.

The impeachments of Judges Charles Swayne (1903), Robert W. Archibald (1912), George W. English (1926) each involved charges of the use of office for direct or indirect personal monetary gain....

III. The Criminality Issue

The phrase "high Crimes and Misdemeanors" may connote "criminality" to some. This likely is the predicate for some of the contentions that only an indictable crime can constitute impeachable conduct. Other advocates of an indictable-offense requirement would establish a criminal standard of impeachable conduct because that standard is definite, can be known in advance and reflects a contemporary legal view of what conduct should be punished. A requirement of criminality would require resort to familiar criminal laws and concepts to serve as standards in the impeachment process. Furthermore, this would pose problems concerning the applicability of standards of proof and the like pertaining to the trial of crimes.

The central issue raised by these concerns is whether requiring an indictable offense as an essential element of impeachable conduct is consistent with the purposes and intent of the framers in establishing the impeachment power and in setting a constitutional standard for the exercise of that power.... The impeachment of a President must occur only for reasons at least as pressing as those needs of government that give rise to the creation of criminal offenses. But this does not mean that the various elements of proof, defenses, and other substantive concepts surrounding an indictable offense control the impeachment process. Nor does it mean that state or federal criminal codes are necessarily the place to turn to provide a standard under the United States Constitution. Impeachment is a constitutional remedy. The framers intended that the impeachment language they employed should reflect the grave misconduct that so injures or abuses our constitutional institutions and form of government as to justify impeachment.

This view is supported by the historical evidence of the constitutional meaning of the words "high Crimes and Misdemeanors." That evidence is set out above....

The published records of the state ratifying conventions do not reveal an intention to limit the grounds of impeachment to criminal offenses....

The post-convention statements and writings of Alexander Hamilton, James Wilson, and James Madison—each a participant in the Constitutional Convention—show that they regarded impeachment as an appropriate device to deal with offenses against constitutional government by those who hold civil office, and not a device limited to criminal offenses.

The American experience with impeachment, which is summarized above, reflects the principle that impeachable conduct need not be criminal. Of the thirteen impeachments voted by the House since 1789, at least ten involved one or more allegations that did not charge a violation of criminal law.

Impeachment and the criminal law serve fundamentally different purposes. Impeachment is the first step in a remedial process—removal from office and possible disqualification from holding future office. The purpose of impeachment is not personal punishment; its function is primarily to maintain constitutional government. Furthermore, the Constitution itself provides that impeachment is no substitute for the ordinary process of criminal law since it specifies that impeachment does not immunize the officer from criminal liability for his wrongdoing.

The general applicability of the criminal law also makes it inappropriate as the standard for a process applicable to a highly specific situation such as removal of a President. The criminal law sets a general standard of conduct that all must follow. It does not address itself to the abuses of presidential power. In an impeachment proceeding a President is called to account for abusing powers that only a President possesses.

Other characteristics of the criminal law make criminality inappropriate as an essential element of impeachable conduct. While the failure to act may be a crime, the traditional focus of criminal law is prohibitory. Impeachable conduct, on the other hand, may include the serious failure to discharge the affirmative duties imposed on the President by the Constitution. Unlike a criminal case, the cause for the removal of a President may be based on his entire course of conduct in office. In particular situations, it may be a course of conduct more than individual acts that has a tendency to subvert constitutional government.

To confine impeachable conduct to indictable offenses may well be to set a standard so restrictive as not to reach conduct that might adversely affect the system of government. Some of the most grievous offenses against our constitutional form of government may not entail violations of the criminal law....

A requirement of criminality would be incompatible with the intent of the framers to provide a mechanism broad enough to maintain the integrity of constitutional government. Impeachment is a constitutional safety valve; to fulfill this function, it must be flexible enough to cope with exigencies not now foreseeable. Congress has never undertaken to define impeachable offenses in the criminal code. Even respecting bribery, which is specifically identified in the Constitution as grounds for impeachment, the federal statute establishing the criminal offense for civil officers generally was enacted over seventy-five years after the Constitutional Convention....

Impeachment of Richard M. Nixon, President of the United States

H. Rept. No. 1305, 93d Cong., 2d Sess. (1974)

The committee on the Judiciary ... recommends that the House exercise its constitutional power to impeach Richard M. Nixon, President of the United States, and that articles of impeachment be exhibited to the Senate as follows:

RESOLUTION

Impeaching Richard M. Nixon, President of the United States, of high crimes and misdemeanors.

Resolved. That Richard M. Nixon, President of the United States, is impeached for high crimes and misdemeanors, and that the following articles of impeachment be exhibited to the Senate:

. . .

ARTICLE I

In his conduct of the office of President of the United States, Richard M. Nixon, in violation of his constitutional oath faithfully to execute the office of President of the United States and to the best of his ability, preserve, protect and defend the Constitution of the United States, and in violation of his constitutional duty to take care that the laws be faithfully executed, has prevented, obstructed, and impeded the administration of justice in that:

On June 17, 1972, and prior thereto, agents of the Committee for the Re-election of the President committed unlawful entry of the headquarters of the Democratic National Committee in Washington, District of Columbia, for the purpose of securing political intelligence. Subsequent thereto, Richard M. Nixon, using the powers of his high office, engaged personally and through his subordinates and agents, in a course of conduct or plan designed to delay, impede, and obstruct the investigation of such unlawful entry; to cover up, conceal and protect those responsible; and to conceal the existence and scope of other unlawful covert activities.

The means used to implement this course of conduct or plan included one or more of the following:

(1) making or causing to be made false or misleading statements to lawfully authorized investigative officers and employees of the United States;

(2) withholding relevant and material evidence or information from lawfully authorized investigative officers and employees of the United States;

(3) approving, condoning, acquiescing in, and counseling witnesses with respect to the giving of false or misleading statements to lawfully authorized investigative officers and employees of the United States and false or misleading testimony in duly instituted judicial and congressional proceedings;

(4) interfering or endeavoring to interfere with the conduct of investigations by the Department of Justice of the United States, the Federal Bureau of Investigation, the Office of Watergate Special Prosecution Force, and Congressional Committees;

(5) approving, condoning, and acquiescing in, the surreptitious payment of substantial sums of money for the purpose of obtaining the silence or influencing the testimony of witnesses, potential witnesses or individuals who participated in such unlawful entry and other illegal activities;

(6) endeavoring to misuse the Central Intelligence Agency, an agency of the United States;

(7) disseminating information received from officers of the Department of Justice of the United States to subjects of investigations conducted by lawfully authorized investigative officers and employees of the United States, for the purpose of aiding and assisting such subjects in their attempts to avoid criminal liability;

(8) making false or misleading public statements for the purpose of deceiving the people of the United States into believing that a thorough and complete

investigation had been conducted with respect to allegations of misconduct on the part of personnel of the executive branch of the United States and personnel of the Committee for the Re-election of the President, and that there was no involvement of such personnel in such misconduct; or

(9) endeavoring to cause prospective defendants, and individuals duly tried and convicted, to expect favored treatment and consideration in return for their silence or false testimony or rewarding individuals for their silence or false testimony.

In all of this, Richard M. Nixon has acted in a manner contrary to his trust as President and subversive of constitutional government to the great prejudice of the cause of law and justice and to the manifest injury of the people of the United States.

Wherefore Richard M. Nixon, by such conduct, warrants impeachment and trial, and removal from office.

ARTICLE II

Using the powers of the office of President of the United States, Richard M. Nixon, in violation of his constitutional oath faithfully to execute the office of President of the United States and, to the best of his ability, preserve, protect and defend the Constitution of the United States, and in disregard of his constitutional duty to take care that the laws be faithfully executed, has repeatedly engaged in conduct violating the constitutional rights of citizens, impairing the due and proper administration of justice and the conduct of lawful inquiries, or contravening the laws governing agencies of the executive branch and the purposes of these agencies.

This conduct has included one or more of the following:

(1) He has, acting personally and through his subordinates and agents, endeavored to obtain from the Internal Revenue Service, in violation of the constitutional rights of citizens, confidential information contained in income tax returns for purposes not authorized by law, and to cause, in violation of the constitutional rights of citizens, income tax audits or other income tax investigations to be initiated or conducted in a discriminatory manner.

(2) He misused the Federal Bureau of Investigation, the Secret Service, and other executive personnel, in violation or disregard of the constitutional rights of citizens, by directing or authorizing such agencies or personnel to conduct or continue electronic surveillance or other investigations for purposes unrelated to national security, the enforcement of laws, or any other lawful function of his office; he did direct, authorize, or permit the use of information obtained thereby for purposes unrelated to national security, the enforcement of laws, or any other lawful function of his office; and he did direct the concealment of certain records made by the Federal Bureau of Investigation of electronic surveillance.

(3) He has, acting personally and through his subordinates and agents, in violation or disregard of the constitutional rights of citizens, authorized and permitted to be maintained a secret investigative unit within the office of the President, financed in part with money derived from campaign contributions, which unlawfully utilized the resources of the Central Intelligence Agency, engaged in covert and unlawful activities, and attempted to prejudice the constitutional right of an accused to a fair trial.

(4) He has failed to take care that the laws were faithfully executed by failing to act when he knew or had reason to know that his close subordinates endeavored to impede and frustrate lawful inquiries by duly constituted executive, judicial, and legislative entities concerning the unlawful entry into the headquarters of the Democratic National Committee, and the cover-up thereof, and concerning other unlawful activities, including those relating to the confirmation of Richard Kleindienst as Attorney General of the United States, the electronic surveillance of private citizens, the break-in into the offices of Dr. Lewis Fielding, and the campaign financing practices of the Committee to Re-elect the President.

(5) In disregard of the rule of law, he knowingly misused the executive power by interfering with agencies of the executive branch, including the Federal Bureau of Investigation, the Criminal Division, and the Office of Watergate Special Prosecution Force, of the Department of Justice, and the Central Intelligence Agency, in violation of his duty to take care that the laws be faithfully executed.

In all of this, Richard M. Nixon has acted in a manner contrary to his trust as President and subversive of constitutional government, to the great prejudice of the cause of law and justice and to the manifest injury of the people of the United States.

Wherefore Richard M. Nixon, by such conduct, warrants impeachment and trial, and removal from office.

ARTICLE III

In his conduct of the office of President of the United States, Richard M. Nixon, contrary to his oath faithfully to execute the office of President of the United States and, to the best of his ability, preserve, protect, and defend the Constitution of the United States, and in violation of his constitutional duty to take care that the laws be faithfully executed, has failed without lawful cause or excuse to produce papers and things as directed by duly authorized subpoenas issued by the Committee on the Judiciary of the House of Representatives on April 11, 1974, May 15, 1974, May 30, 1974, and June 24, 1974, and willfully disobeyed such subpoenas. The subpoenaed papers and things were deemed necessary by the Committee in order to resolve by direct evidence fundamental, factual questions relating to Presidential direction, knowledge, or approval of actions demonstrated by other evidence to be substantial grounds for impeachment of the President. In refusing to produce these papers and things, Richard M. Nixon, substituting his judgment as to what materials were necessary for the inquiry, interposed the powers of the Presidency against the lawful subpoenas of the House of Representatives, thereby assuming to himself functions and judgments necessary to the exercise of the sole power of impeachment vested by the Constitution in the House of Representatives.

In all of this, Richard M. Nixon has acted in a manner contrary to his trust as President and subversive of constitutional government, to the great prejudice of the cause of law and justice, and to the manifest injury of the people of the United States.

Wherefore Richard M. Nixon, by such conduct, warrants impeachment and trial, and removal from office.

. . .

PROPOSED ARTICLE OF CONCEALMENT OF INFORMATION
ABOUT BOMBING OPERATIONS IN CAMBODIA

On July 30, 1974, the Committee considered a proposed Article of Impeachment dealing with the unauthorized bombing of Cambodia and the concealment from the Congress of that bombing:

> In his conduct of the office of President of the United States, Richard M. Nixon, in violation of his constitutional oath faithfully to execute the office of President of the United States and, to the best of his ability, preserve, protect, and defend the Constitution of the United States, and in disregard of his constitutional duty to take care that the laws be faithfully executed, on and subsequent to March 17, 1969, authorized, ordered, and ratified the concealment from the Congress of the facts and the submission to the Congress of false and misleading statements concerning the existence, scope and nature of American bombing operations in Cambodia in derogation of the power of the Congress to declare war, to make appropriations and to raise and support armies, and by such conduct warrants impeachment and trial and removal from office.

The Committee, by a vote of 26-12, decided not to report the proposed Article to the House.

The article charged that the President had concealed the bombing in Cambodia from the Congress and that he had submitted, personally and through his aides, false and misleading statements to the Congress concerning that bombing. The investigation of those allegations centered upon the initial decision to bomb Cambodia; the type, scope, extent and nature of the bombing missions; the reporting and recording system used internally within the military and the Administration; and the statements made by Administration officials to Congress and to the public both during the military operation and after it had ceased.

On February 11, 1969, the President received the initial request to institute the bombing from his military advisors. On March 17, 1969, after a series of National Security Council meetings, the President approved the request and directed that the operation be undertaken under tight security.

On March 18, 1969, the bombing of Cambodia commenced with B-52 strikes under the code name MENU OPERATION. These strikes continued until May 26, 1970, almost one month after the American incursion into Cambodia. The operational reports prepared after each mission stated that these strikes had taken place in South Vietnam rather than in Cambodia.

Between April 24 and May 24, 1970, American planes conducted tactical air strikes in Cambodia under the code name "regular" PATIO. No operational reports were made with respect to these strikes. Similarly, prior to June 30, 1970, an unspecified number of tactical air strikes occurred in various parts of Cambodia. Again no regular reports were prepared.

On May 14, 1970, a one day series of "special" PATIO sorties were conducted, operational reports stated that the strikes had occurred in Laos rather than Cambodia. The tactical air sorties with the code name "regular" FREEDOM DEAL were accurately reported as having occurred in Cambodia. A series of tactical air bombing missions in Cambodia called "special" FREEDOM DEAL occurred outside the boundaries designated for FREEDOM DEAL bombing, although the operational reports indicated otherwise.

On July 1, 1973, Congress enacted P.L. 93-50 and P.L. 93-52 providing for the cessation of all bombing in Cambodia by August 15, 1973. At that time the bombing had not been formally acknowledged by the President or his representatives.

Later, during the Senate Armed Services Committee hearings on the Cambodian bombing, military and Administration officials explained that the bombing was not publicized because of the delicate diplomatic and military situation in Southeast Asia prior to the American incursion into Cambodia. They stated that it was their understanding that Cambodia's ruler, Prince Sihanouk, had privately agreed to the bombing of Cambodia prior to his overthrow. It was further stated that certain Members of Congress had been informed of the military action and that this constituted sufficient notice to Congress of the President's military decision. Finally, the submission of false data to Congress was said to have resulted from the highly classified nature of the accurate bombing statistics.

The Committee considered the views of the supporters of this proposed Article of Impeachment that the President's conduct constituted ground for impeachment because the Constitution vests the power to make war in Congress and implicitly prohibits the Executive from waging an undeclared war. Stating that impeachment is a process for redefining the powers of the President, the supporters argued that the President, by issuing false and misleading statements, failed to provide Congress with complete and accurate information and thereby prevented Congress from responsibly exercising its powers to declare war, to raise and support armies, and to make appropriations. They stated that informing a few selected members of the Congress about the Cambodian bombing did not constitute the constitutionally required notice, particularly inasmuch as the President's contemporaneous public statements were contrary to the facts and the selected Members were committed to a course of action involving war that did not represent the views of a substantial portion of American citizens. The supporters also stated that Congress had not ratified the President's conduct through inaction or by its 1973 limitation on bombing because Congress did not know of the bombing until after it voted the authorization. Finally, they asserted that the technicalities or merits of the war in Southeast Asia, the acquiescence or protests of Prince Sihanouk, and the arguably similar conduct of past Presidents were irrelevant to the question of President Nixon's constitutional accountability in usurping Congress' war-making and appropriations powers.

The Committee did not agree to the article for a variety of reasons. The two principal arguments in opposition to it were that President Nixon was performing his constitutional duty in ordering the bombing and that Congress had been given sufficient notice of the bombing. Several Members stated that the president as Commander-in-Chief was acting to protect American troops and that other Presidents had engaged in similar military activities without prior Congressional consent. Examining the bombing of Cambodia from the perspective of Congressional responsibility, the opponents of the Article concluded that, even if President Nixon usurped Congressional power, Congress shared the blame through acquiescence or ratification of his actions. They stated that the President had provided sufficient notice of the military actions to Congress by informing key Members. Finally, they said that the passage of the War Powers Resolution in 1973 mooted the question raised by the Article.

PROPOSED ARTICLE OF EMOLUMENTS AND TAX EVASION

On July 30, 1974, the Committee considered the following proposed Article:

In his conduct of the office of President of the United States, Richard M. Nixon, in violation of his constitutional oath faithfully to execute the office of the President of the United States, and, to the best of his ability, preserve, protect and defend the Constitution of the United States, and in violation of his constitutional duty to take care that the laws be faithfully executed, did receive emoluments from the United States in excess of the compensation provided by law pursuant to Article II, Section 1, of the Constitution, and did willfully attempt to evade the payment of a portion of Federal income taxes due and owing by him for the years 1969, 1970, 1971, and 1972, in that:

(1) He, during the period for which he has been elected President, unlawfully received compensation in the form of government expenditures at and on his privately-owned properties located on or near San Clemente, California, and Key Biscayne, Florida.

(2) He knowingly and fraudulently failed to report certain income and claimed deductions in the years 1969, 1970, 1971, and 1972 on his Federal income tax returns which were not authorized by law, including deductions for a gift of papers to the United States valued at approximately $576,000.

In all of this, Richard M. Nixon has acted in a manner contrary to his trust as President and subversive of constitutional government, to the great prejudice of the cause of law and justice and to the manifest injury of the people of the United States.

After debate, by a vote of 26 to 12, the Committee decided not to report the Article to the House.

This Article was based upon allegations in two areas. The expenditure of federal funds on the President's privately-owned properties at San Clemente, California, and Key Biscayne, Florida, was alleged to constitute a violation of Article II, Section 1, Clause 7, of the Constitution. That clause reads, "The President shall, at stated Times, receive for his Services, a Compensation, which shall neither be increased nor diminished during the Period for which he shall have been elected, and he shall not receive within that Period any other Emolument from the United States, or any of them." The second allegation is that the President knowingly and fraudulently failed to report certain income and claimed certain improper deductions on his federal income tax returns.

A. EXPENDITURE OF FEDERAL FUNDS ON THE PRESIDENT'S PROPERTIES

Several investigations have been undertaken with regard to the amount and propriety of Federal expenditures at or near the President's properties in San Clemente, California and Key Biscayne, Florida. The House Committee on Government Operations found that a total of $17 million had been spent by the Federal Government in connection with the President's properties, including personnel costs, communication costs, and amounts expended on adjacent Federal facilities. The staff of the Joint Committee on Internal Revenue Taxation found that the President realized more than $92,000 in personal income from government expenditures on his properties in the years 1969 through 1972. The Internal Revenue Service concluded that the President realized more than $67,000 in personal income from government expenditures on his properties in those years.

The federal expenditures at San Clemente which were found to be primarily for the President's personal benefit included payments for such items as a sewer system, a heating system, a fireplace exhaust fan, enlargement of den windows, refurbishing or construction of outbuildings, paving, and boundary and structural surveys. Expenditures brought into question at Key Biscayne included expenditures for such items as the reconstruction of a shuffleboard court and the building of a fence and hedge system. The Government also made significant expenditures for landscape construction and maintenance on both properties.

The proponents of this section of the Article argued that the President, personally and through his agents, supervised the planning and execution of non-protective government expenditures at his private homes for his personal enrichment. The opponents maintained that a majority of the questionable expenditures were made pursuant to a Secret Service request, that there was no direct evidence of the President's awareness at the time of the expenditures that payment for these items were made out of public rather than personal funds, and that this section of the Article did not rise to the level of an impeachable offense.

B. INTERNAL REVENUE CODE VIOLATIONS

In examining the President's income tax returns for the years 1969 through 1972, the Internal Revenue Service found that his reported income should have been increased by more than $230,000 and that deductions claimed in excess of $565,000 should be disallowed, for a total error in reported taxable income of more than $796,000. The staff of the Joint Committee on Internal Revenue Taxation determined that the President's improper deductions and unreported income for that period totaled more than $960,000. Central to the tax section of the proposed Article was the charitable deduction claimed by the President for the years 1969-1972 for a gift of his private papers claimed to have been made to the Government in 1969 which was allegedly worth $576,000.

Both the IRS and the Joint Committee staff disallowed this deduction as not having been made on or before July 25, 1969, the last day on which a gift of such papers could entitle the donor to a tax deduction. While the papers allegedly donated were physically delivered to the National Archives on March 27, 1969, they were part of a larger mass of papers, and the selection of the papers given was not completed until March 27, 1970. The President's attorneys argued that in February 1969, the President told an aide that he wanted to make a gift, but no contemporary record of this instruction was produced. A deed of gift, signed not by President Nixon but by a White House attorney who had no written authority to sign on behalf of the President was not delivered to the Archives until April 1970, although on its face it appears to have been executed on April 21, 1969. The IRS and Joint Committee staff investigations established that the deed was actually executed on April 10, 1970, and backdated to the 1969 date (before the deduction cut-off date of July 25, 1969). It was found that through the end of 1969, the National Archives, the donee, thought that no gift had been made. Finally, even though the deed contained restrictions limiting access to the papers, the President's 1969 tax return stated that the gift was made without restrictions.

The IRS assessed a five percent negligence penalty against the President. An internal IRS memorandum recommending against the assertion of a fraud penalty stated that as of late March 1974 there was not sufficient evidence available to assert such a penalty. On April 2, 1974 IRS Commissioner Alexander wrote to Special Prosecutor Jaworski recommending a grand jury investigation into possible violations of law arising out of the preparation of the President's 1969 income tax return. Commissioner Alexander stated that the IRS was unable to complete its processing of the matter because of the lack of cooperation of some of the witnesses and because of many inconsistencies in the testimony of individuals to the IRS. The Joint Committee staff report did not address the question of fraud.

The Joint Committee staff did submit questions to the President concerning the gift-of-papers deduction and other tax matters. The President did not answer the questions.

The proponents of this Article argued that the President knew that no gift of papers had been made by July 25, 1969, and that the deduction was improper. They noted that it was contrary to rational tax planning for such a large gift to be made so early in the year. They pointed to the President's personal involvement in a similar gift in 1968, and memoranda and incidents in 1969 which showed his interest in his personal financial affairs in general and the gift-of-papers deduction in particular. They referred to the opinion of an expert on criminal tax fraud matters that if this were the case of an ordinary taxpayer, the case would be referred to a grand jury for prosecution. It was argued that the President took advantage of his office in claiming this unlawful deduction, knowing that the tax return of a President would receive only cursory examination by the IRS.

The opponents of the tax fraud section stated that the President had not knowingly underpaid his taxes, but relied on attorneys and agents; that the IRS failure to assess a fraud penalty was dispositive; and that even if fraud were shown, the offense of tax evasion did not rise to the level of an impeachable offense. Some who voted against the Article were of the opinion that the evidence before the Committee did not satisfy the standard of "clear and convincing proof" which some Members thought applicable.

Some of the Members who opposed the proposed Article argued that there was no clear and convincing evidence that the President had committed tax fraud and stated that the President had not knowingly underpaid his taxes, but rather relied on attorneys and agents. Opponents of the proposed Article also asserted that an impeachment inquiry in the House and trial in the Senate are inappropriate forums to determine the President's culpability for tax fraud, and that this kind of offense can be properly redressed through the ordinary processes of the criminal law. Finally they argued that even if tax fraud were proved, it was not the type of abuse of power at which the remedy of impeachment is directed.

---

1. Do you believe that all of the counts contained in the articles of impeachment voted against Richard Nixon amounted to impeachable offenses? In light of the materials you read in Chapter Three concerning executive privilege and Congress, is the proposed article III, focusing on Nixon's resistance to congressional subpoenas, appropriate? If you think it is, would a President's refusal to obey Congress' subpoenas always amount to an impeachable offense, or would your conclusion depend on the nature of the congressional inquiry at issue?

2. Do any of the recommended articles of impeachment charge abuses of power as serious as the allegations in the proposed—but rejected—article on the concealment of information about bombing operations in Cambodia? Are you persuaded by the majority's arguments for rejecting that article? (For a highly critical assessment of U.S. military and foreign policy in Southeast Asia and its impact on Cambodia, see W. Shawcross, Sideshow (1979).) Would you regard presidential complicity in the events discussed in Chapter Six with respect to the diversion of funds from Iranian arms sales to the Contras as an impeachable offense? Would the majority's arguments on the proposed Cambodia article apply to a proposed impeachment article based on the Contra episode?

3. Given Nixon's position that the "offenses" alleged were not "high crimes and misdemeanors" under the Constitution, should he have been able to seek judicial review of that question? Before his Senate trial? After conviction? Recall the "political question" doctrine discussed earlier, in the Note on that topic in Chapter Four and in Chapter Six with respect to treaty termination.

4. The impeachments of President Andrew Johnson and of Justice Samuel Chase, referred to above in the House staff report, were highly politicized disputes. For fuller accounts, see, respectively, M. Benedict, The Impeachment and Trial of Andrew Johnson (1973), and J. Elsmere, Justice Samuel Chase (1980). The story of the journalistic investigations that gave impetus to the Nixon impeachment efforts is told in B. Woodward and C. Bernstein, All the President's Men (1974). For a popular account of the work of the House Judiciary Committee in connection with Watergate, see H. Fields, High Crimes and Misdemeanors (1978). An account of the scandal and Congress' response told by the Senate's most conspicuous leader during the Watergate period is S. J. Ervin, Jr., The Whole Truth: The Watergate Conspiracy (1980).

D. Presidential and Vice-Presidential Succession

Besides elections and removals from office through impeachment, death and disability provide the other occasions for transfers of presidential power. Succession problems are now governed by the twenty-fifth amendment and by 3 U.S.C. 1982, in which Congress, pursuant to art. II, § 1, par. 6, provided "for the Case of Removal, Death, Resignation, or Inability, both of the President and the Vice President." For general histories of presidential successions as well as instances of presidential illness, see J.D. Feerick, From Failing Hands: The Story of Presidential Succession (1965); J.D. Feerick, The Twenty-Fifth Amendment: Its Complete History and Earliest Applications (1976); and A. Sindler, Unchosen Presidents (1976). The fascinating story of Woodrow Wilson, whose wife, together with his chief aide, Colonel House, virtually ran the White House after Wilson suffered a paralytic stroke 18 months prior to the end of his second term, is told in A.L. and J.L. George, Woodrow Wilson and Colonel House (1964).

The following memorandum prepared shortly after ratification of the twenty-fifth amendment reviews the circumstances that prompted adoption of that amendment and the amendment's proffered reforms. The history of art. II, § 1, par. 6, and the law of succession prior to the twenty-fifth amendment is further reviewed at 42 Op. Att'y Gen. 69 (1961).

R. Celada, Presidential Continuity and Vice Presidential Vacancy Amendment

Congressional Research Service Memorandum (Mar. 13, 1967),
reprinted in Application of the 25th Amendment to Vacancies in the
Office of the Vice-President: Legislative History, House Committee on
the Judiciary (Comm. Print), 93d Cong., 1st Sess. 451-67 (1973)

At least three times in our history, during the administrations of Garfield, who lay in the twilight zone between life and death for eighty days before succumbing to an assassin's bullet, Wilson who, after suffering a stroke, spent the last eighteen months of his term in a state of at least semi-invalidism, and Eisenhower who had three separate and serious illnesses, the President of the United States, for varying periods, has been unable to carry out the duties of his office. Although the Constitution provides that when a President is disabled the Vice President shall take over, it does this in language so ambiguous that there is disagreement about whether the Vice President becomes President for the balance of the term or simply acts as President until the disability is ended. Moreover, no specific method is set forth for determining when presidential inability begins or ends. Nor is the responsibility for making such determination clearly spelled out.

Despite the virtual unanimity of informed contemporary opinion that existing law empowers the Vice President to make the determination that a President is disabled and thereafter to assume the powers and duties of the presidential office until the inability is ended, no Vice President has ever done so. Historical precedents as well as the weight of informed opinion are inclined toward the conclusion that no Vice President will act until the constitutional ambiguities have been removed. The cries for a solution to the problem have intensified as Americans have apprehended the dread possibility of a nation immobilized in a moment of maximum peril because there might be neither a fit President nor someone unquestionably authorized to act in his stead.

Following his third illness, President Eisenhower attempted to fill in some of the constitutional gaps by entering into a working agreement with Vice President Nixon. The terms of the agreement provided that whenever the President informed the Vice President that he was unable to act the Vice President would assume the powers and duties of the presidential office until the inability had ended. If, however, the President were unable to communicate the existence of his inability, the Vice President would assume the duties of the office after such consultation as seemed to him appropriate under the circumstances. In either case the President, himself, would determine when the inability had ended and at that time resume the powers and duties of his office. Similar agreements were made between President Kennedy and Vice President Johnson and between President Johnson and Speaker McCormack who was next in line of succession until the inauguration of Vice President-elect Humphrey. A similar agreement also exists between President Johnson and Vice President Humphrey.

There has been general agreement that however valuable these working agreements might be nothing short of an amendment to the Constitution will give the person who assumes the duties of the presidential office the air of legitimacy so indispensable to their successful execution.

Furthermore, although three Attorneys General have expressed the view that these agreements are "consistent with the correct interpretation of . . . the Constitution" their legal standing continues to present a nagging question. Since the Supreme Court does not render advisory opinions it is extremely doubtful that the matter could ever be resolved in advance of the crisis. Not until the assassination of President Kennedy, however, had there been anything approaching a consensus on precisely what the amendment to the Constitution should provide. That consensus was embodied in the resolution proposed by the 89th Congress. . . .

Article II, section 1, clause 6 of the Constitution now provides that—

> In Case of the Removal of the President from Office, or of his Death, Res-
> ignation, or Inability to discharge the Powers and Duties of the said Office, the
> Same shall devolve on the Vice President, and the Congress may by Law provide
> for the Case of Removal, Death, Resignation, or Inability, both of the President
> and Vice President, declaring what Officer shall then act as President, and such
> Officer shall act accordingly, until the Disability be removed, or a President shall
> be elected.

Constitutional scholars have debated for many years the meaning of Article II, section 1, clause 6. The crux of the disability problem arises from the first clause. . . . The second clause relating to the congressional power has been implemented from time to time through the enactment of statutes setting forth the succession to the office of President in the event of the removal, death, and resignation, or inability of *both* the President and Vice President. Although the latter clause also raises several problems of constitutional interpretation, these more properly relate to presidential succession and are outside the scope of this paper.[2]

Turning to the first clause, it will be noted that it outlines four situations in which the Vice President may be called upon to act as President. Three of these, namely, removal, death, and resignation, obviously contemplate the permanent exclusion of the President for the balance of his term. The source of the uncertainty arises in connection with the fourth contingency, specifically, the "Inability to discharge the Powers and Duties of the said Office." Did the Framers intend such "inability" to permanently exclude the President, even in the event of recovery, from resuming the discharge of his powers and duties? Another question arises from the remaining language of the first clause which provides "the Same shall devolve on the Vice President." To what do the words "the Same" refer? In other words, what is it that "devolves" on the Vice President? Is it the "Office" of the President or the presidential "Powers and Duties"? If the former interpretation prevails, the contingency of inability like the other three would operate to effect a permanent exclusion. However, if the latter interpretation prevails, the powers and duties would once again attach to the office upon the President's recovery.

---

2. The principal issue arising from the second clause concerns the legal propriety of placing legislative officers in the order of presidential succession. Despite the inclusion of such persons in two of the three succession laws passed by Congress—including that currently in effect—debate on the matter continues unabated. The specific points at issue are (1) whether the Speaker and the President pro tempore are "officers" in the sense of Article II, section 1, clause 6; (2) whether a legislative officer (named to act as President) who resigns his office thereafter is eligible to act as President; and (3) whether it violates the constitutional principle of separation of powers for a Member of Congress to act as President.

Historical investigation and the weight of constitutional authority tend to support the conclusion that under Article II, section 1, clause 6 of the Constitution the Vice President merely discharges the powers and duties of the Presidency during the President's inability. The sole dissenting voice in this otherwise harmonious picture springs from actual practice whereby Vice Presidents have *become* Presidents upon the latter's death. The precedent was established by John Tyler's succession upon the death of William Henry Harrison on April 4, 1841. In her authoritative volume, *Presidential Succession* [14 (1951)], Ruth C. Silva describes these events, in part as follows:

> . . . The presidential office was vacant for the first time. It was then decided that in conformity with the Constitution, Vice President Tyler was to be the President for the remaining three years and eleven months of Harrison's term. Exactly who made this decision is uncertain. Legend tells us that the precedent was established merely because Tyler claimed presidential status. The Cabinet had decided, so the story goes, that Mr. Tyler should be officially styled "Vice President of the United States, acting President." But Tyler is supposed to have promptly determined that he would enjoy all the dignities and honors which he assumed he had inherited.

Although objections were raised in Congress and in the press, Tyler's assumption established the precedent that when the presidential office is vacant, the Vice President becomes the President for the remainder of the term. As a consequence, on each of the eight occasions that the Vice President has assumed office because of the death of the President, he has taken the presidential oath. Notwithstanding that succession in these instances arose from one of the contingencies that contemplates a permanent exclusion, namely, death, they threw a cloud on a disabled President's claim to office upon full recovery.

These precedents combined with the ambiguities of Article II, section 1, clause 6 served to throttle any action in the event of a presidential crisis. Arthur, Garfield's Vice President, emphatically declined to take any steps whatsoever to assume the powers of the President. Vice President Marshall flatly refused to assume any of the powers of the presidency because of the constitutional uncertainty as to whether Wilson could resume his office when he recovered.

Adding to this already highly uncertain situation was the recurrent and troubling problem of vice presidential vacancy. Between the years 1787 and 1965, eight Presidents died in office.[6] Seven Vice Presidents also died in office and one resigned.[7] As a result of these occurrences, the nation has been without a Vice President more than twenty percent of the time during its history.

It became apparent that in order to adequately correct the flaws in our constitutional system it was necessary to accomplish the following objectives:

(1) To establish once and for all that the Vice President *assumes* the presidential *office* upon removal from office, death, or resignation of the President;

---

6. The eight Vice Presidents who succeeded to the Presidency were John Tyler (Harrison), Millard Fillmore (Taylor), Andrew Johnson (Lincoln), Chester A. Arthur (Garfield), Theodore Roosevelt (McKinley), Calvin Coolidge (Harding), Harry S. Truman (Roosevelt), and Lyndon B. Johnson (Kennedy).

7. The seven Vice Presidents who died in office were George Clinton, Elbridge Gerry, William R. King, Henry Wilson, Thomas A. Hendricks, Garrett A. Hobart, and James Sherman. The only Vice President to have ever resigned was John C. Calhoun.

(2) To provide that in the event of the fourth contingency, namely, inability, the Vice President shall exercise the powers and duties of the office of President;

(3) To establish the procedure for determining the existence of an inability and its termination; and

(4) To provide for filling a vacancy occurring in the Vice Presidency....

After more than eighty years of study by congressional committees, attorneys general, constitutional experts and bar association committees, the Congress, in the dying moments of 1963, began to act on a presidential continuity amendment. Sparked by the assassination of President Kennedy which alerted the American people as never before to the dangerous constitutional void, hearings were scheduled for early 1964.[8] Even as the nation mourned the loss of the President many thoughts were troubled by the prospect of the political crisis which might have followed had the fallen leader lingered on in hopeless and permanent incapacity.... Also, the record of Vice President Johnson's prior heart attack and advanced ages of the two immediate successors doubtless contributed to the general desire for a prompt solution....

The amendment proposed to the States by the 89th Congress meets the four basic objectives noted earlier. It affirms the historical practice by which a Vice President has become President upon the death of the President, further extending the practice to the contingencies of resignation or removal from office. In order to assure that the second highest office will always be occupied, it requires the President to nominate a person to be Vice President whenever there is a vacancy in that office. The nominee is to take office as Vice President upon confirmation by a majority in both Houses of Congress.

The proposal permits the President to declare himself disabled and to declare the end of his disability. The declarations are to be reduced to writing and transmitted to the Speaker of the House of Representatives and the President pro tempore of the Senate. In the interim, the Vice President becomes Acting President. If a President does not declare the existence of his inability, the Vice President and a majority of the "principal officers of the executive departments" may declare the President disabled by transmitting their written declaration to this effect to the presiding legislative officers of the House and Senate. In such an event the Vice President is to undertake the discharge of the presidential powers and duties as Acting President. If for any reason the Cabinet proves not to be a workable instrument in this matter, Congress is empowered to set up another body to work with the Vice President.

"Thereafter" the President may announce his own recovery and "resume the powers and duties of his office." However, if the Vice President and a majority of the Cabinet disagree with the President, they have four days to send a written declaration of the fact to the Speaker and the President pro tempore. At this point the Congress is responsible for a final decision. If Congress is not in session, it would have to assemble within forty-eight hours of receipt of the declaration. From the time of receipt Congress has twenty-one days in which to decide the issue. Pending the decision, the Vice President is to continue as Acting President. If Congress fails to arrive at a decision, or if more than one-third of the membership of either House sides with the President, the President is to resume his powers and duties. If two-thirds of the membership of

8. Presidential Inability and Vacancies in the Office of Five Presidents. Hearings before the subcommittee on Constitutional Amendments of the Committee on the Judiciary. United States Senate, 88th Cong., 2d Sess. (1964).

each House support the Vice President and the Cabinet, the Vice President is to continue as Acting President.

Note: Reagan-Bush Temporary Power Transfer

The first occasion for using the procedure outlined in section 3 of the 25th Amendment for a temporary transfer of power to the Vice President occurred on July 13, 1985. Just before receiving anesthesia for abdominal surgery to remove a cancerous polyp, President Reagan transferred presidential authority to Vice President George Bush by letter. Reagan's letter was carefully drafted to avoid invoking the 25th Amendment unambiguously, out of an apparent anxiety over binding future Presidents to what Reagan thought might be an unfortunate precedent. Thus, Bush was not formally designated "acting President," a phrase used in the 25th Amendment, although White House officials acknowledged that Bush played that role while Reagan was on the operating table. The texts of President Reagan's July 13th letters transferring power to Vice President Bush and then withdrawing it follow:

Dear Mr. President (Mr. Speaker):

I am about to undergo surgery during which time I will be briefly and temporarily incapable of discharging the Constitutional powers and duties of the Office of the President of the United States.

After consultations with my Counsel and the Attorney General, I am mindful of the provisions of Section 3 of the 25th Amendment to the Constitution and of the uncertainties of its application to such brief and temporary periods of incapacity. I do not believe that the drafters of this Amendment intended its application to situations such as the instant one.

Nevertheless, consistent with my longstanding arrangement with Vice President George Bush, and not intending to set a precedent binding anyone privileged to hold this Office in the future, I have determined and it is my intention and direction that Vice President George Bush shall discharge those powers and duties in my stead commencing with the administration of anesthesia to me in this instance.

I shall advise you and the Vice President when I determine that I am able to resume the discharge of the Constitutional powers and duties of this Office.

May God bless this Nation and us all.

Sincerely,

Ronald Reagan

Dear Mr. President (Mr. Speaker):

Following up on my letter to you of this date, please be advised I am able to resume the discharge of the Constitutional powers and duties of the Office of the President of the United States. I have informed the Vice President of my determination and my resumption of those powers and duties.

Sincerely,

Ronald Reagan

Weekly Comp. Pres. Doc. (July 13, 1985).

For a legal analysis of the delegability of presidential functions during periods of disability, prepared in the wake of the 1981 attempted assassination of President Reagan, *see* 5 Op. Off. of Legal Coun. 91 (1981).

Chapter 9
Epilogue: The Future Presidency

Changes in the needs of the country and of government occasionally surface proposals for major institutional reform of the Presidency. Although none has been undertaken since the Twenty-second Amendment, which limited the President to two terms of office, far-reaching proposals—such as creating line-item veto power, discussed in Chapter Four—continue to be made. *See, e.g.,* C. Hardin, Presidential Power and Accountability: Towards a New Constitution (1974) (proposing reorganization of Congress and the executive to achieve stronger checks and balances); D. L. Robinson, "To the Best of My Ability": The Presidency and the Constitution (1987) (proposing electoral reforms including establishment of council of former Presidents empowered to call elections within four-year cycle). Two especially good representatives of the burgeoning bicentennial literature debating structural reforms to the Constitution are J. Sundquist, Constitutional Reform and Effective Government (1986), and Separation of Powers—Does it Still Work? (R.A. Goldwin and A. Kaufman, eds. 1986).

In 1982, C. Douglas Dillon, Treasury Secretary in the Kennedy Administration, and President Carter's legal counsel, Lloyd Cutler, established a Committee on the Constitutional System, a nonpartisan corporation devoted to the study of the Constitution and the analysis of potential reforms in the structure of government. *See* Reforming American Government: The Bicentennial Papers of the Committee on the Constitutional System (D. L. Robinson ed. 1985). Cutler had argued in a 1980 article that the separation of powers, particularly in its impact on the President, was anachronistic. Although he did not advocate particular reforms, Cutler recommended consideration of a variety of measures that might afford our system of government more of the virtues of government coordination he perceives in parliamentary regimes. In his view, some such reforms are necessary for three major reasons. First, the federal government now makes an unprecedented number of significant allocative choices for which it is difficult to achieve a broad political consensus. Second, the increasing interdependence of the world makes the stability and predictability of our foreign policy especially important. Third, Congress itself has undergone a decentralization of power, which makes cooperation between Congress and the executive branch increasingly difficult. The flavor of Cutler's analysis is captured in the following passage:

L. Cutler, to Form a Government*
Foreign Affairs, Fall, 1980, at 126-129

A particular shortcoming in need of a remedy is the structural inability of our government to propose, legislate and administer a balanced program for governing.

In parliamentary terms, one might say that under the U.S. Constitution it is not now feasible to "form a Government." The separation of powers between the legislative and executive branches, whatever its merits in 1793, has become a structure that almost guarantees stalemate today. As we wonder why we are having such a difficult time making decisions we all know must be made, and projecting our power and leadership, we should reflect on whether this is one big reason.

We elect one presidential candidate over another on the basis of our judgment of the overall program he presents, his ability to carry it out, and his capacity to adapt his program to new developments as they arise. We elected President Carter, whose program included, as one of its most important elements, the successful completion of the SALT II negotiations that his two predecessors had been conducting since 1972. President Carter did complete and sign a SALT II Treaty, in June 1979, which he and his Cabinet regarded as very much in the national security interests of the United States. . . . But because we do not "form a Government," it has not been possible for President Carter to carry out this major part of his program.

Of course the constitutional requirement of Senate advice and consent to treaties presents a special situation. The case for the two-thirds rule was much stronger in 1793, when events abroad rarely affected this isolated continent, and when "entangling foreign alliances" were viewed with a skeptical eye. Whether it should be maintained in an age when most treaties deal with such subjects as taxation and trade is open to question. No parliamentary regime anywhere in the world has a similar provision. But in the American case—at least for major issues like SALT—there is merit to the view that treaties should indeed require the careful bipartisan consultation essential to win a two-thirds majority. This is the principle that Woodrow Wilson fatally neglected in 1919. But it has been carefully observed by recent Presidents, including President Carter for the Panama Canal Treaties and the SALT II Treaty. In each of these cases there was a clear prior record of support by previous Republican Administrations, and there would surely have been enough votes for fairly rapid ratification if the President could have counted on the total or near-total support of his own party—if, in short, he had truly formed a Government, with a legislative majority which takes the responsibility for governing.

Treaties may indeed present special cases, and I do not argue here for any change in the historic two-thirds requirement. But our inability to "form a Government" able to ratify SALT II is replicated regularly over the whole range of legislation required to carry out any President's overall program, foreign and domestic. Although the enactment of legislation takes only a simple majority of both Houses, that majority is very difficult to achieve. Any part of the President's legislative program may be defeated, or amended into an entirely different measure, so that the legislative record of any presidency may bear little resemblance to the overall program the President wanted to carry out. Energy and the budget provide two current and critical examples. Indeed, SALT II itself could have been presented for approval by a simple majority of each House under existing arms control legislation, but the Administration deemed this task even more difficult than achieving a two-thirds vote in the Senate. And this difficulty is of course compounded when the President's party does not even hold the majority of the seats in both Houses, as was the case from 1946 to 1948, from 1954 to 1960 and from 1968 to 1976—or almost half the duration of the last seven Administrations.

The Constitution does not require or even permit in such a case the holding of a new election, in which those who oppose the President can seek office to carry out their own overall program. Indeed, the opponents of each element of the President's overall program usually have a different makeup from one element to another. They would probably be unable to get together on any overall program of their own, or to obtain the congressional votes to carry it out. As a result the stalemate continues, and because we do not form a Government, we have no overall program at all. We cannot fairly hold the President accountable for the success or failure of his overall program, because he lacks the constitutional power to put that program into effect.

Compare this with the structure of parliamentary governments. A parliamentary government may have no written constitution, as in the United Kingdom. Or it may have a written constitution, as in West Germany, Japan and Ireland, that in other respects—such as an independent judiciary and an entrenched Bill of Rights—closely resembles our own. But while there may be a ceremonial President or, as in Japan, an Emperor, the executive consists of those members of the legislature chosen by the elected legislative majority. The majority elects a Premier or Prime Minister from among its number, and he selects other leading members of the majority as the members of his Cabinet. The majority as a whole is responsible for forming and conducting the "government." If any key part of its overall program is rejected by the legislature, or if a vote of "no confidence" is carried, the "Government" must resign and either a new "Government" must be formed out of the existing legislature or a new legislative election must be held. If the program *is* legislated, the public can judge the results, and can decide at the next regular election whether to reelect the majority or turn it out. At all times the voting public knows who is in charge, and whom to hold accountable for success or failure.

Do you agree with Cutler's point of view? Does the record of western parliamentary democracies since World War II sustain his confidence in parliamentary structure?

To help assess the profound impact that changes in the presidential office can have, consider the following materials on the recurring proposal to afford the President a single six-year term. Note that this debate involves essentially the same issues as do debates whether to repeal the twenty-second amendment and permit the President indefinite eligibility for reelection.

One Six-year Presidential Term

Hearing Before the Subcommittee on Crime of the House Committee
on the Judiciary, 93d Cong., 1st Sess. 4-16, 19-28, 42-46 (1973)

*Testimony of Theodore C. Sorensen, Former Special Counsel to
President Kennedy*

MR. SORENSEN.... From the earliest beginnings of our Nation this and similar proposals have been put forward under very distinguished sponsorship and for very thoughtful reasons. Presidents, ex-Presidents, Senators, Congressmen and commentators in great number from every political point of view have from time to time favored the concept of a single-term Presidency, as did in fact a substantial number of members of the original Constitutional Convention; and this recommendation has generally included a lengthening of the present 4-year term.... Those members of both parties who have over the years advocated this amendment in order to diminish the role of reelection politics in the White House, and in order to curb the abuse of

Presidential might for political ends, can now—and I am sorry to say—find in the revelations of recent months ample confirmation of their worst fears.

For this Nation now knows that, solely to further the reelection of the President, the laws of this land were violated, the rights and privacy of opposition leaders were infringed, law enforcement agencies and courts as well as the Congress and public were deceived and denied essential facts, large corporations were intimidated or encouraged to purchase influence, and the political processes and ethical standards of this country were warped and distorted as never before by acts of political sabotage and espionage financed by unprecedented amounts of secret cash.... Because these events have rightly been deplored by members of both parties, it is understandable that renewed consideration is now being given to proposals such as this as a way of limiting the Presidency, making it less necessary for any future incumbent to mix politics with public duty, and banning any future "Committee To Re-elect the President."

But in that context the proposed amendment is, in my opinion, a mistaken solution based upon a mistaken premise. For, frankly speaking, the collection of sorry and scandalous episodes now lumped under the all-embracing label of Watergate reveals serious flaws not in the Presidency but in the President; and whenever the Congress concludes in this or any other instance that Executive misconduct is so grievous as to strike at the very heart of our system, then the remedy is to change not the Presidency but the President. No constitutional amendment is required to prevent or correct malfeasance on the part of any President from any party.

Moreover, with or without Watergate, I would be strongly opposed to the proposed constitutional amendment for the following reasons:

First, this proposal, contrary to the intentions of some of its backers, does not curb the power of the President—it curbs the power of the people.

Support for the notion that this measure would curb Presidential powers comes not only from its proponents but also its opponents, who often express the fear that it would render every President impotent by giving him a "lameduck" status from his first day in office. But this alleged weakness of lameducks—at least until their final months in office, after the selection of a successor—is, in my opinion, greatly exaggerated. A one-term President will still have all the powers given him by the Constitution and Congress in conducting foreign affairs, in originating budget and legislative items, in controlling appointments and patronage, in appealing directly to the people, in lending or withholding his political support from other candidates and in influencing his own party's choice of a successor.

Indeed there is reason to believe that the opposite danger is more real: that a President not subject to the healthy democratic discipline of facing the electorate again, who takes office free from any review of his stewardship by the people, will be too powerful and independent, too unresponsive to the public needs and interests and too irresponsible in his exercise of power.

For example, suppose President Nixon had known after winning reelection last November that the possibility of another race for the Presidency was still open to him; suppose he had thought he might face the voting public again. Would he then have so readily engaged without public explanation in the intensive Christmas bombing of North Vietnam; would he then have continued the bombing of Cambodia without congressional authorization long after our forces were withdrawn from Vietnam; would he have stretched the doctrine of Executive privilege to unprecedented limits in the defiance of congressional and grand jury requests; would he have sought to dismantle programs mandated by the Congress for the public good; would he have avoided the press for so extraordinarily long a period this spring and summer?

I do not know. No one knows.... But the point I am making is that no future President, Democrat or Republican, should be tempted from his very first day in office onward with the knowledge that he too will be in a similar position of public unaccountability, that he too can exploit the ambiguities of the Constitution free from electoral review, because he will not be allowed another term.

Even placing a President in that position under our present system by virtue of the 22d amendment, once he is reelected for a second term, is dangerous enough; but at least that President is more likely to be restrained by the patterns and precedents he sets in his first reviewable term, and at least the public is given 4 years to observe him in office and to decide as best it can whether he can be entrusted with that second unreviewable term.

That is why a one-term Presidency, far from curing the abuses of Presidential power, may only increase them. The power of the people, on the other hand, would be clearly and significantly curbed by this amendment. It would deny them the right they have now to return a good President to office for a second term; and it would deny them the right they have now to get rid of a bad President after 4 years of office. The two-term limitation imposed by the 22d amendment already places one curb of doubtful necessity upon the power of the electorate; and further restriction in that direction would be not only unnecessary but undemocratic. Moreover, the passage of time has not altered the wisdom of the Constitutional Convention's decision, which was the result of intensive deliberation by its members, that less than 4 years is too short for a good President and more than 4 years is too long for a bad one.

Second, this proposal, contrary to the intentions of some of its backers, does not reduce the role of politics in the White House—nor should that role be reduced.

It is said by some backers of this amendment that a President eligible for reelection is required to consider the public's view of certain difficult decisions he must make; that he is required to take time out from his office to travel among the people soliciting their opinions and support; and that he is required to undergo hostile attacks and harassment from the Members of the Congress, the opposition and the press who are seeking his defeat at the polls. All that is perfectly true; and all that is healthy.

For this country decided long ago that an appointed President, no matter how statesmanlike and brilliant he might be, would not be as successful in that office as an elected President—one who knows how to deal with politicians, how to mobilize support, how to stay abreast of public opinion, how to debate his adversaries, and how to organize his energies and resources for an exhausting campaign. For that same reason it is highly desirable that our President be a politician, that he worry about his reelection and that he be subject to all the same vicissitudes of politics to which the Congress and other elected officials are subject.

He should be the head of his party, not above party. The two-party system in this country needs to be strengthened, not weakened (as this proposed amendment would do). It is sad that Watergate has caused some people to turn away from party politics. For it was not the Republican Party or the Republican National Committee that broke the locks and the law at Watergate but a separate Presidential committee that kept its efforts and funds largely aloof from other campaigning Republicans. That is not surprising, nor is it irrelevant to this proposed amendment. For a national party that knows it must go back to the public time and time again for support is more likely to maintain a lawful and responsible posture than a candidate who knows he will never face the voters again. Party responsibility helps build stability and continuity in our political system; and I would hope that every future President, without neglecting his obligations to the national interest, will recognize his role as the head of the party which put him forward and not be encouraged to disregard it.

But in truth this amendment would not diminish politics either in the White House or in congressional-Executive relations anyway. It might only increase them. Today, during the first few years of a President's first term, the amount of political maneuvering in the legislative branch and elsewhere with an eye to succeeding him is ordinarily nonexistent within his own party and relatively subdued in the opposition. But were he forbidden to seek a second term, the maneuvering in both parties would begin immediately upon his inauguration, continue until his successor was chosen, and still continue without respite in both parties upon that new President's inauguration for his one term. Meanwhile, the President himself, even without the need to worry about his own reelection, would still be engaged in politics on a wide scale in order to influence the passage of his legislative programs, the success of his party in the midterm elections and the choice of his successor.

In short, . . . I regard the proposed amendment as the worst of ideas offered with the best of intentions. I do believe that our political system is in serious need of reform, particularly our election and campaign finance laws. I also believe that the imbalance between Presidential and congressional powers must be righted, primarily by the Congress more fully asserting its own powers. . . . But the pending amendment cannot solve any of our problems and could instead make them worse. . . .

MR. CONYERS. Mr. Sorensen, would you agree with the observation that there is really nothing inherently sacred about two 4-year terms, that it is first of all a matter of political judgment as to what length of time a President should be allowed to perpetuate himself in office?

Mr. SORENSEN. That is exactly correct, Mr. Chairman. The fact of the matter is, most Presidents in this century did not serve two full terms. . . . President Taft sought a second term and was defeated. President Coolidge decided not to seek a second term. President Hoover sought a second term and was defeated. Also, President [Theodore] Roosevelt decided not to seek a second full term.

So that President Wilson, President [Franklin] Roosevelt, President Eisenhower, and President Nixon were the only ones who did seek a second term and were successful. . . .

MR. CONYERS. . . . There may be times when . . . questions of national and international significance don't need anybody to indulge in political activities. We need to bring nonpolitical judgments to many of the important questions that the most powerful office in the world is confronted with. . . .

MR. SORENSEN. I know that even opponents of this amendment have in the past testified that we can rely upon Presidents to avoid political considerations and make statesmanlike decisions on these great issues. Frankly, I don't believe that for a minute. We can rely upon them to make nonpartisan judgments, but to say they are going to exclude politics from their minds, exclude where public opinion stands on a particular issue, where the Congress stands on a particular issue, the long range interest of the country, how it is going to be affected by an issue—I think that is very unrealistic. . . .

MR. THORNTON. . . . [C]ertain bureaucratic institutions on the national scene are rather removed from being responsive to the people. The Office of Management and Budget is one that we are concerned about. It is difficult to affect their decisions. Is it your thought that the people of this country really want their Government to be responsive to their will rather than removed from political control?

MR. SORENSEN. Obviously, lines have to be drawn. I am told that the technology of communications has now developed to the point where the President could go on television and say, "All those who favor the bombing of North Vietnam, press this button twice, and all those who oppose it, press it once." I would be very much against the introduction of such a system. I don't believe the American public really wants that kind of rule by public opinion. But they do want government that is responsive. . . .

MR. THORNTON. In that light, I wonder if any information can be gained from history as to whether Presidents during their second 4-year terms were less political in their decisions than they were in their first 4-year terms.

As you know, our country is now bound to that rule. However, until the time of Franklin Roosevelt, it was bound by the Washington decision not to seek a third term by tradition, which was almost as strong, and it was assumed that the second 4-year term was the last. . . .

MR. SORENSEN. I see no evidence of the fact that any President in his second term, knowing that he would not face the voters again, eschewed politics as a result. Woodrow Wilson in his second term was as political as he was in his first term. The same is true of Franklin Roosevelt in each of his terms. President Eisenhower showed no diminution of political interest; indeed, I always had the feeling he was becoming more interested in politics the longer he stayed in the White House. And there is some indication that President Nixon thus far in his second term has been political. . . .

MR. FISH. Do you have any thoughts on the length of the congressional term, either leaving the Presidency as it is, a 4-year term with option to renew, or in the event that a 6-year term is adopted?

MR. SORENSEN. Yes. Frankly, I think 4 years would be a more appropriate term for Members of the House of Representatives.

MR. FISH. Would you have that coincide with the term of office of the President or the congressional reelection fall halfway between? . . . In other words, perhaps one of the solutions to this—and you talked in terms of responsiveness, et cetera—is something closer to a parliamentary system, in which the House would come up for elections with the President on a routine basis.

MR. SORENSEN. Yes, I would favor that. . . .

MR. FISH. I take it from your testimony that you don't agree with the argument that a President is a lameduck, either in his second term or if he has just one term.

MR. SORENSEN. Not in terms of weakening his powers. The primary effect of lameduck status is to increase the amount of political maneuvering going on in his party and in the opposition party in the Congress.

MR. FISH. One final area, Mr. Sorensen. . . . An article by [Kennedy aide] Kenneth O'Donnell from Life magazine, August 7, 1970 [reported] a meeting in 1963 between

President Kennedy and Senator Mansfield..., during which the President had had second thoughts about Mansfield's argument for complete military withdrawal from Vietnam and agreed with the Senator's thinking. And this is a quote. " 'But I can't do that until 1965, after I'm reelected,' Kennedy told Mansfield." ...

I was wondering if you had any comment on the accuracy of the statement, or were you privy to it—

MR. SORENSEN. . . . I was not privy to it, I had no idea as to its accuracy. Senator Mansfield, I believe, has said he knows of no explicit statement to that effect made to him.

I think we should bear in mind, without getting into a long debate over Vietnam war history, that President Kennedy refused, rejected the advice of those who said he should put combat troop divisions in Vietnam and bomb North Vietnam.

It is very possible that he felt certain decisions should be taken in his second term, not because they would affect his reelection, but because he hoped at that time to have a broader and stronger mandate from the public and larger margin in the Congress. . . .

[H]e felt, as Jefferson said, great decisions cannot be forced on slender majorities. He was elected with less than 50 percent of the vote, and by plurality of two- or three-tenths of 1 percent. . . . He therefore felt that he needed an opportunity in his first term to prove himself to the public, to win a larger mandate from the public, to win a larger margin of support in the House, and then he could move ahead more effectively.

MR. CONYERS. I see. Well, of course, the issue of Vietnam wasn't before the American people in 1960, as I recall, nor was it before the Congress. We never declared war as we should have, or that, at least is my understanding. So that whether he had a majority in the Congress or not, could it not be argued, would have no bearing on an Executive decision in the first place. It wasn't up to Congress to determine whether the President should authorize a few thousand troops for the Vietnam war as it began, or a few advisers which led to a few thousand troops, which in turn led to one of the most questionable wars in our history. So whether he had a majority or a minority in the Congress politically, could not one argue that this would have had no bearing at all on his own decisions as the Chief Executive Officer?

MR. SORENSEN. That might be true of a Chief Executive Officer who intended to bypass the Congress and not to involve it in the great decisions. But President Kennedy discovered, for example, in the area of civil rights, that his Executive proclamations, even though they were not matters on which the Congress was required to vote, nevertheless had a considerable impact upon his support within the Congress. And I think he may very well have felt that a decision on Vietnam that the Congress was unwilling to support would hamper his legislative program in that body. . . .

MR. COHEN. . . . Much has been made about Kenneth O'Donnell's statement that President Kennedy would have pulled the troops out of Vietnam if he had not had to face reelection, and therefore would have saved thousands of American lives and Vietnamese lives.

It seems to me President Johnson retired from the office because of the tremendous public outcry against the war, at least that is the major speculation, and had he not had to face reelection, could we plausibly argue he would have continued the war. Would you agree with that?

MR. SORENSEN. No. I think that by 1968, President Johnson was fed up with the recommendations for continuing and escalating the war. He realized that it was an impossible track that he was on. He also was looking for ways of turning it around, regardless of whether he sought reelection or not....

MR. COHEN. An issue which you have touched upon in your statement deals with Congress' reassertion of its constitutional powers and prerogatives. Perhaps you are familiar with [President Johnson's adviser] Jack Valenti's statement concerning the 6-year term. Let me just quote the last sentence, where he suggests, "In short, a President needs to be freed from any major pressures that might divert him from his primary function as our leader."

It seems to me inherent in this particular argument, is the presumption that there is an overwhelmingly strong Executive in that situation, who can ignore or be free from public pressures. If you have a strong President free from political pressures as such, Congress has a choice of either adopting his proposals, in which instance they could just be labeled a rubber stamp; or No. 2, continue to oppose those which it feels are inconsistent with the needs of the public and thereby be labeled irresponsible partisans.

Do you agree that imbalance could be created by a 6-year term of the Presidency?

MR. SORENSEN. Yes, I do. I am very much for a strong President and a strong Congress. And I think the two working together can best provide the leadership that this country requires. There is no reason why the President should not be subject to the same kind of public pressures as the Congress is subject to.

MR. COHEN. One of the arguments I understand will be offered by subsequent witnesses is that many programs over the years become ingrown or deeply ingrained in our system, and they have become so deeply rooted that special interests would perpetuate them well beyond their usefulness. With a 6-year term the President has the flexibility and freedom to make vast changes without fear of retaliation at the polls.

The question I would ask you is, could a President even with a 6-year term accomplish this objective while Congress is elected, or the House of Representatives is elected, every 2 years? In your opinion, could that be possible?

MR. SORENSEN. I doubt it. I agree there are many ingrained programs protected by special interests. The fault there lies largely in our electoral system and our campaign finance laws, and no President, whether his term is 6 years or otherwise, is going to be able on his own to get rid of those ingrained programs....

MR. COHEN. What is your opinion about the other portion of this bill, which would put a 70-year age limitation on office?

MR. SORENSEN. Is that on Presidents only?

MR. COHEN. There is legislation, also, which would apply to Senators and Representatives. Would you support that as well?...

MR. SORENSEN. My general posture is one of against limitations on the public's right to choose whomever they wish for public office. I think there have been occasions in the past where individuals have held on to office well past the age of their effectiveness, but I would doubt very much I would set that at age 70.

MR. COHEN.... The chairman suggested in his line of questioning that perhaps we should have nonpolitical judgments being exercised by this powerful office....

The same argument, it seems to me, is being made along that line that we should have a nonpolitical caretaker as Vice President.

I take it from your statement that you disagree with that?

MR. SORENSEN. I want to again draw the distinction between the words nonpolitical and nonpartisan. I doubt very much that it would be either possible or appropriate to have a nonpolitical Vice President, one who did not know about and did not care about politics and political machinery in this country. It is possible, I suppose, to have a nonpartisan Vice President.

MR. COHEN. But the notion of a nonpolitical or nonpartisan caretaker is somewhat inconsistent with your notion of the office itself.

MR. SORENSEN. Bear in mind that the duties of the Vice President are considerably different from the duties of the President.

MR. COHEN. For the time being, but it may be transformed rather immediately.

MR. SORENSEN. Yes.

Testimony of Hon. Charles E. Chamberlain, a Representative in Congress from the State of Michigan

MR. CHAMBERLAIN. . . . I first introduced this proposal [for a single 6-year presidential term] in July 1971, feeling that because of the tremendous responsibilities of the Presidential office, the time had come to reexamine the fundamental question of whether any President can fulfill his duties as head of state if he is preoccupied with the demands of reelection. Clearly, the events of the past year point up the prudence of that concern and the dangers of White House preoccupation with election politics. We can no longer postpone serious bipartisan debate of the one-term proposal.

You will recall that in 1947 Congress passed the 22d amendment, subsequently ratified in 1951, to limit our Presidents to two terms in office. I believe passage of that amendment was wise, both for the sake of representative democracy and for the benefit of the man who must shoulder the burdens of that office. Yet our experience over the past 20 years suggests to me, and others as well, that we need to go further.

One of the popular ways of viewing the President is to think of him as a leader who wears many hats: that of leader of all the people, that of administrative head of the Government, that of legislative leader, that of chief foreign policymaker, that of Commander-in-Chief of all our military forces, and that of party leader. In considering these manifold areas of responsibility which directly affect world peace and domestic well-being of every American citizen, the legitimate question has been raised as to whether a President can devote the fullest measure of his time and talents to the pressing duties of state if he must be preoccupied with the concerns of reelection. The problem has been well stated by former Presidential assistant, Jack Valenti, who has written—and I believe this may be a quote that was alluded to earlier:

> The man who holds that office has to deal with problems so monstrous, so disruptive, so resistant to permanent solution that the reelection process is no longer suitable. The President cannot be allowed to be diverted from his hard duties and even harder decisions by the so-called normalcies of politics and reelections.

While the demands on the modern Presidency make the need for a change in election procedure that much more pressing, interest in a 6-year term for the Chief Executive actually dates back to the early days of our Republic. Considerable discussion of a 6-year term took place at the Constitutional Convention in 1787, and well over a hundred amendments have been offered to achieve that purpose since the Constitution became operative. During his Presidency, Thomas Jefferson declared himself in favor of a single 8-year term, while Presidents Jackson, Polk, William Henry Harrison, Andrew Johnson, Cleveland, and Taft, at one time or another, advocated the 6-year, nonrenewable term.

In 1912, the House Committee on the Judiciary reported a resolution to amend the Constitution to provide a single, 6-year term. In its report to the House, the committee stated in part:

> The President should be ineligible to a second term, because being ineligible there will be no temptation improperly to use the powers and patronage of that exalted office.

And further:

> It will make the President the Chief Executive of the whole people and not the leader of a mere faction or the chief of a political party.

Considering 4 years an inadequate period of time in which a President may act to realize the goals of the platform on which he was elected, the committee felt that "6 years, coupled with the freedom from anxiety for reelection, would give sufficient opportunity to the President to properly organize his administration and to bring about real accomplishments within the bounds of his duties and powers under the Constitution." In conclusion the committee wrote:

> This amendment, if submitted and ratified, will increase the efficiency of the administration of the President; will remove the temptation to build up a political machine by the abuse of patronage and power; and will save the President from the humiliating necessity of going to the stump to repel assaults made upon him.

It is equally interesting to note that in 1913 the Senate actually approved a proposed constitutional amendment for a 6-year term, but since President Woodrow Wilson objected, the measure died in the House Judiciary Committee.

With the passage of time, the powers and responsibilities of the Presidency have, of course, increased dramatically. We all know that. If there were reason and justification for considering such a course of action 60 years ago, how much more justified we are in proposing a 6-year term today when the burdens of that high office have multiplied to previously unimagined complexity. As Washington columnist, Marquis Childs, has written:

> The difficulties facing a President today are so enormous, so complex, so riddled with partisanship that no Chief Executive can emerge at the end of four years with the prospect of a majority of the electorate.

I find that judgment to be sound. In the light of Watergate, we know that the President would be better able to direct his energies both toward the administration of the Government and the implementation of his programs were he accorded a longer term and relieved of the partisan political concerns involving reelection to office. We know that the pressures on a President are tremendous. While I do not suggest that the office of the Presidency be made immune to the legitimate problems of state, I do think that removal of the concern over reelection would permit a President to act more efficiently in what is best for the country.

... [W]e have already accepted a time limitation with the passage of the 22d amendment and arguments against creating a "lameduck" Presidency lose much of their validity when we realize that a President is already a "lameduck" for his entire second term of 4 years. While I have no illusions that a 6-year term will be a panacea, I am satisfied that this is a matter that should be carefully reviewed and studied and that we should seriously ask ourselves if such a change would not further improve our system of government....

MR. CONYERS.... Do you give any credence to the notion that Presidents are in politics to begin with, so that any attempt to diminish the political aspects of the office of the Presidency cannot be accomplished by a one-term of office [limit]?

MR. CHAMBERLAIN. No, I don't think we are ever going to remove the President of the United States from legitimate political concerns. It is a political office, and the President should very well be occupied with political matters. But what I am saying is that I feel we should be trying to minimize his participation in partisan political affairs after he becomes the President of the United States....

I feel that we have arrived at that point in the history of our country with all of our technological advances, with our atomic bombs and instant communication and satellites and everything else, when we should minimize the political activities of our President after he has taken his oath of office, and have him motivated by just two basic concerns: (1) to do the best job he can as President and find his place in history, and (2) to make his peace with his maker and not have to be concerned about "how will I get reelected."

MR. CONYERS.... Do you feel that the late President Johnson would have reacted differently and perhaps caused a different historical result with respect to Vietnam? Do you feel that the present officeholder of the Presidency of the United States would have a different outlook had he not been forced to seek reelection?...

MR. CHAMBERLAIN.... I feel that when President Johnson was elected—when he first took office in 1963, at the death of the late President Kennedy, the whole problem of Vietnam was put in neutral for about a year, if you recall. From November 1963 until November 1964 we weren't going to become involved. And then after the election in 1964, we did become more involved.

I think that the President's conduct in that 1 year was guided very materially by his desire to be reelected. I also feel from 1964 and 1968 he pursued a course of conduct that he felt would cause him to be reelected, this did not materialize and he did not run for reelection.

In fairness, I must also say that I feel that President Nixon in his first term conducted himself, so far as the war was concerned, with the intentions of being a candidate for a second term himself.

Now, I can't tell you what either of these Presidents might have done differently, I really don't know. But I think that we all must recognize the fact that they did have their eyes on the calendar, that the decisions that they made did have this one element in them, each of them. And I say that when we have gone through the ordeal that we have gone through for these many years, the longest war our Nation has ever been engaged in, and its many complex aspects, and the greatly increased duties of the President, I feel that it is well that we try to minimize his political concerns....

MR. THORNTON.... It seems to me the thrust of your presentation is that with the complexities of government which now exist, the tremendous bureaucracy, the difficulty in finding effective means to affect the governmental process, that a 6-year term is needed to enable the President to cope with these complex problems. Is that a fair description?

MR. CHAMBERLAIN. Yes, indeed, I will subscribe to that.

MR. THORNTON. And following that, the thought is that this would strengthen the President in his ability to cope with these governmental processes.

MR. CHAMBERLAIN. I think so. To the extent that he will not be concerned with these political considerations.

MR. THORNTON. The next thought which occurs to me is whether indeed in maintaining the balance of power between the executive and legislative branch, whether a stronger Executive is what is needed today in the democratic system?

MR. CHAMBERLAIN.... I think we have abdicated our responsibility in many areas and given it to the President. I don't see how the reassertion of the powers that belong to the Congress are going to alter attitudes, certainly my attitude toward a 6-year term. I would still think it would be consistent.

We want a strong President for our country. We have always looked to him for leadership but that doesn't mean we should abdicate our own prerogatives.

MR. THORNTON. Certainly I agree the course for the Congress is to reassert its responsibility in various areas. The point I am really getting at is whether there has not been in modern years a tendency to glorify the office of the Presidency and to identify that office as being the office that can do no wrong, that stands above the other branches of Government, and whether that is desirable.

MR. CHAMBERLAIN. Well, we do have three coequal branches, but there is no doubt about it, the Presidency is the focal point of our Government and always has been. And the reason Presidents get all of the publicity is because this is where the ultimate decisions are made on so many great issues, and the press and everybody else, concentrates on the office of the President, no matter who is there. This has always been so and I presume it will continue. So I don't know how we can change that, even with any length of the term....

MR. FISH.... I wonder if you could address yourself to the principal argument of the prior witness, Mr. Sorensen, because I think this is a rather challenging expression by him. He maintains the proposal for a single 6-year term, contrary to the intentions of some of its backers, does not curb the power of the President, but rather curbs the power of the people....

MR. CHAMBERLAIN. Well, this is not a new argument, and I believe that I alluded to it in my own statement, when I said that the first I must concede, Mr. Fish, is that a President that is reelected for his second 4-year term is a lameduck for 4 years, and so every argument that has been made against the single 6-year term is applicable to the second 4-year term. Every one of them.

Now, for me to try to say that the extension of the Presidential term for two additional years does not in fact remove the President to that extent from the people, I readily concede that a valid argument just can't be made against it. Should we extend the term of the President we remove him from the people to that extent. But there comes a time when you must balance the pros and cons. This is the decision your committee is going to make.

Now, as to accountability and conceding that a 6-year term would free the President from many political pressures, I suppose in pure theory that the argument you suggest could be made. But more realistically, I think any President, no matter who he is, or of what party, is going to want to leave that office with a favorable impression on the people of the country. He is going to want to be loved and have history treat him well and he can't do this if he is going to ignore public opinion and his own commitments that he has made, his own responsibilities to his party, and all up and down the line. . . .

MR. FISH. Could I ask you, sir, why in your legislation—and this is true of most of the bills before us—the single term is set at 6 years and not 5 or 7 or 8?

MR. CHAMBERLAIN. Well, I certainly wouldn't want to say there is any magic in 6 years. If your committee, in its wisdom and the House wanted to work its will and say 5 or 7, that would be agreeable with me.

I question, however, that we would want to accept a 4-year limit and just say a President shall only have one 4-year term. I don't think that that would be in the interest of the country at the present time.

So if you want to make it 5, 5-1/2, all right. But the 6 kind of fits in with the calendar and the senatorial, and the House terms. I think it could probably be woven into our election fabric a little more easily.

MR. FISH. If we did have a single 6-year term, would you recommend any changes in the terms of either U.S. Senators or Members of the House?

MR. CHAMBERLAIN. I think not. . . . [W]hen you say 4-year term, it is going to take the pressure off the Members for an added 2 years before they have to face the electorate. We hear our colleagues in the other body speak of having 5 years off and 1 year to campaign, and maybe that is good, they can be statesmen during the 5-year period, that was the theory. But it is said that you people in the House are running for election all the while. You don't have time to do your work, to consider the legislation that is coming before the Congress.

And there is a measure of validity and merit to that argument, but this is precisely, in my judgment, what our Founding Fathers wanted. They wanted to have one House of this Congress here that was immediately responsible to the will of the people. And how is that going to be unless you are going to keep the pressure on and have them running for reelection all the while. . . .

Now, one thought came to mind as I was listening to the prior witness, and that is the 4-year term that coincided with the President's term. This would be very helpful in terms of partisan policy, Republican or Democrat. Hopefully, for all partisans, the Congress would be of the party of the President. But I recall the election of 1964 when President Johnson won by a very heavy majority. I believe, Mr. Chairman, you were serving in that Congress with me, too, and we had 140 Republicans in the minority, we had 295 Democrats in the majority.

Now, if we had had a single 4-year term, there would have been a better than 2 to 1 majority in the House for a 4-year period. If you recall, we had the Great Society programs before the Congress at that time. And for 2 years we were very prolific in our legislative activity. In 1966, the House of Representatives went back to the people and the people blew the whistle on the Great Society, and 47 additional Republicans were elected. That changed the lineup considerably in the House. . . .

Now, getting back to what Mr. Fish had to say, the President being removed from the people for this 6-year term. Certainly the people are going to have this opportunity to express themselves with the Congress every 2 years, and if things get too far out of line during this 6-year term, the Congress is going to have its say. The people are going to be electing their House of Representatives, unless we change it, of course. But in answering the question that was put to me, I think the 2-year term, as hard as it is on the Members is best for the country. I would not urge its change.

MR. FISH. . . . I would like to talk a little about the Vice President in this context, because if my memory is right, we have had several Presidents who were first Vice Presidents.

In your testimony, you tell us that you favor the 22d amendment which limits the term of office to two terms, and from the testimony of the previous witness we heard testimony that actually only one President in this century has served more than two terms, and not many have served even two terms, but have been defeated or decided not to run.

It would seem to me inherent in your proposal is a possibility of an 11-year term for the President, in that a Vice President who becomes President in the first year of his administration has a right to seek reelection. And he would be seeking reelection for the full 6-year term after serving a 5-year term.

If the process is to squeeze it down from 8 to 6 years, aren't we opening up the possibility that one man would have a term considerably longer than 6 years?

MR. CHAMBERLAIN. I would have to concede that that is so, that we are doing that. Unless, of course, your committee or the Congress in its wisdom altered or made some changes in the Vice Presidency, or would possibly provide that he might not be able to succeed himself. That [could] be done, too.

But in any event, Mr. Fish, that man is going to have to go to the people again at some time for reelection if he is to have his term beyond 6 years. Should he seek the Presidency again he must give an accounting of his stewardship and the people will have to make the judgment as to whether or not they want to renew his contract. And if they say "yes," it would be because they did in fact trust him.

The other aspect of this, too, I would think, is that the pressures of this office are tremendous. We all know that. They are really beyond our comprehension. Perhaps only the President himself may have a full realization of the weight and the loneliness of that office. But I think there would perhaps be an awful lot of self-discipline on the part of that individual if he had in fact assumed the Presidency after a short period as Vice President, say within the first year of a new term of the President. And having had it for 5 years, I think he might say—do I want to go another 6 at this time. . . .

MR. COHEN. . . . Edmund Burke pointed out the role of an elected official was not simply to give you his energy but also his judgment.

One of the things which you talked about during your testimony was the traditional dilemma that faces all of us, and that is voting your conscience rather than for your constituents; you find the two are not necessarily compatible on every issue.

It seems to me that is a dilemma we all face and one that is healthy in our system. I don't see any substantial benefit to remove that dilemma from a President any more than from a Senator or Representative.

I also note in your statement that you quote from Jefferson, supporting the longer term. But he also retracted that later on, and in a letter back in 1805, he said:

> I originally supported the position of electing a President for seven years and who was forever ineligible thereafter. I have since become sensible . . . seven years is too long to be irremovable and there should be a peaceable way of withdrawing a man in midway who has been doing wrong. Service for eight years with power to remove after the first four comes close to my principle . . .

MR. CHAMBERLAIN. I certainly stand corrected.

MR. COHEN. He did take that position initially, he then changed his mind, but it leads to another facet of my question. You quoted from Jack Valenti, who supports the 6-year term. . . . Mr. Valenti . . . says:

> Watergate cries out as the important reason in favor of a six-year term. Watergate became a cancer not in its breaking-and-entering but in its cover-up attempts. There would have been no reason to cover up had there been no need (as campaign aides saw it) to re-elect the President. Presidential aides in their zeal to guarantee reelection pursued an activity that would never have been imagined if that damnable re-election campaign wasn't in full bloom. Thus, Watergate presents itself as Exhibit A in the case for the six-year term.

Would you subscribe to that line of reasoning?

MR. CHAMBERLAIN. I don't think that during the current deliberations of this committee you can fully disassociate your considerations from the Watergate issue. It is here, it isn't going to go away, it is in the back of people's minds, and we have to accept it. But at the same time, I don't feel that it is paramount or controlling. . . .

MR. COHEN. It just comes back to the point I tried to make about Jefferson's comment, there must be some more immediate way or peaceable way to remove a President, and he suggested it come at the end of the 4-year term. If you take the alternative of a 6-year term with no reelection, then you do bring up the specter, and it is not exactly a desirable one for many of the Congressmen, of impeachment proceedings as the only other alternative.

MR. CHAMBERLAIN. Very traumatic and I can't take issue with what you say. You have indeed pointed up the other side of the coin. . . .

Prepared Statement of Prof. Thomas E. Cronin, The Case Against the Single Six-Year Presidential Term

One of the more persistent remedies in discussion of the presidency, in light of the Watergate scandals, is that presidents should be removed from "politics." The assumption is that once elected, presidents should provide leadership for all people and cast aside partisan calculations. He should do what is "right" even if this means that his party might lose votes, his friend suffer financial losses, or his own political future be damaged.

Those who want to take the politics out of the presidency usually want to deemphasize the divisive aspects of both electoral politics and partisanship and somehow elevate the presidency above selfish ambitions. Implicit is the hope that the dignity of the office can be enhanced by encouraging presidents to act so as never to favor one party over another, one region over another, or one class over another. The verdict is rendered that the roles of politician and statesman are incompatible. Critics voice disapproval when presidents appoint well known party workers or campaign contributors to key administration or ambassadorial posts. Appointments, critics say, should be made on merit alone, above politics! Then, too, presidents look unstatesmanlike to some when they appear at fund raising dinners or intervene in state and congressional political elections.

The proposed Constitutional amendment championed by Senator Mike Mansfield (D-Mont.) and George Aiken (R-Vt.) in the 92d and 93d Congresses and suggested by President Nixon in the wake of the Watergate scandals, would extend the term of a president to six years but make presidents ineligible to run a second time. Such a change, it is hoped, might give a president greater courage and freedom in the exercise of his responsibilities. Arguing that we must liberate the presidency from "unnecessary political burdens," Mansfield says that it is intolerable that a president "is compelled to devote his time, energy and talents to what can be termed only as purely political tasks.... a president facing reelection faces... a host of demands that range from attending the needs of political office holders, office seekers, financial backers and all the rest, to riding herd on the day-to-day developments within the pedestrian partisan arena."

The six-year term proposal is supported by those who feel the country's chief executive should be more businesslike and that reducing his political activities would assure more time and energy for planning and systematic program implementation. Some hope, moreover, that it would enable a president to overcome his deference to special interests and the timidity that results from having to keep his eye on the forthcoming election. Several former White House aides have given support to the concept of a six-year term and offer this type of rationale: From a former administrative aide to Lyndon Johnson:

"I would favor one six-year term for the presidency. I don't think the president should be concerned and involved with politics and the considerations of becoming elected for another term. The president's obligations should be devoted to a whole nation and not to any one section of it."

A Nixon foreign policy aide offered this view:

"I am in favor of a six-year term because we frankly don't have enough time to get going as it is. We are working on several things now that are just developing and will have to be dropped this year or next because of the political restraints involved in the election... there can be some excellent results if we keep pushing. But we are being held back—some of the president's political aides are already sending us memos to that effect."

And a former national security counselor to President Johnson writes;

"The four-year presidential term with its tremendous pressures on the incumbent to lay the groundwork for his reelection inhibits... long-range nonpartisan political thinking... We have seen all too much of White House pressures for dramatic quick fixes on the grounds that "the president needs something fast before he comes up for reelection." The single six-year term would seem to provide an atmosphere in which ... long term planning and less partisan solutions might have a chance to flourish."

Support for a six-year term without reelection also came from President Johnson, himself, who felt that four years is not long enough for a president to develop and carry out major reform programs. From the day a new president assumes office, he is racing against an almost impossible time schedule. National budgets are made a year and a half, or two years, in advance and even then uncontrollable fiscal and political factors prohibit a new president from significantly reordering national priorities. Johnson and several former aides argued that the most needed reforms take more than four years to formulate, pass, fund, and implement. The case for this reform, said Johnson in 1971, is stronger now than ever before: "The growing burdens of the office exact an enormous physical toll on the man himself and place incredible demands on his time. Under these circumstances the old belief that a president can carry out the responsibilities of the office and at the same time undergo the rigors of campaigning is, in my opinion, no longer valid."

While the proposal's adoption at this time is unlikely, it does have beguiling aspects. Its likely consequences are, however, far less attractive than they may seem at first. Woodrow Wilson offered this trenchant perspective: "The argument is not that it is clearly known now just how long each president should remain in office. Four years is too long a term for a president who is not the true spokesman of the people, who is imposed upon and does not lead. It is too short a term for a president who is doing, or attempting a great work of reform, and who has not had time to finish it.

To change the term to six years would be to increase the likelihood of its being too long, without any assurance that it would in happy cases, be long enough. A fixed constitutional limitation to a single term of office is highly arbitrary and unsatisfactory from any point of view."

The proposed divorce (between the presidency and politics) presupposes a significantly different type of political system than ours, which is glued together in large measure by ambiguity, compromise, and the extensive sharing of powers. In light of the requisites of democracy, the presidency must be a highly political office, and the president an expert practitioner of the art of politics. Quite simply, there is no other way for presidents to negotiate favorable coalitions within the country, Congress and the executive branch, and to gather the authority needed to translate ideas into accomplishments. A president who remains aloof from politics, campaigns, and partisan alliances does so at the risk of becoming the prisoner of events, special interests, or his own whims.

Most of the men who have been effective presidents have also been highly political: they knew how to stretch the limited resources of the office, they loved politics and enjoyed the responsibilities of party leadership. The nation has been well served by sensitive politicians, disciplined by the general thrust of partisan and public thinking. Many of the least political presidents were also the least successful and seemingly the least suited temperamentally to the rigors of the office. The best have been those who listened to people, who responded to majority as well as to intense minority sentiment, who saw that political parties are often the most important vehicle for communicating voter preferences to those in public office, and who were attentive to the diversity and intensity of public attitudes, even as they attempted to educate and to influence the direction of opinion.

President Nixon told the nation during his Watergate crisis that the presidency had to come first and politics second. This, he said, is why he did not involve himself in the 1972 election campaign. This is a pleasing posture, of course, but its implications are misleading and in large measure wrong. Everything a president does has political consequences, and every political act by a president has implications for the state of the presidency. As a nation we might just as well grow up to the full recognition that presidents will and must be political and they ought to be vigorous partisan leaders as well. Bipartisanship rarely has served us well. James MacGregor Burns aptly notes that, "Almost as many crimes have been committed in the name of mindless bipartisanship as in the name of mindless patriotism." Recognition of the reality of presidents as partisan political leaders might also serve to underscore the seriousness of the lack of an opposition party that can challenge a president's program, challenge the presidential establishment, and that is eager and able to proclaim alternative national priorities.

If our national leaders do become isolated or insulated from the mood of the public, then electing our presidents for longer terms would only encourage this tendency. Frequent elections necessarily remain a chief means of motivating responsive and responsible behavior. An apolitical president, disinterested in reelection, motivated by personal principle or moralistic abstractions, and aloof from the concerns of our political parties, could be a highly irresponsible president. Elections customarily force an assessment of presidential performance. Elections are welcomed when promises have been kept and feared when performance has been unsatisfactory. Is it a mere coincidence, or were President Nixon's troop withdrawal rates aimed toward the election of 1972, or the Johnson-Humphrey bombing halt of 1968 aimed toward that election? President Nixon's significant economic "game plan" reversal in 1971 and President Johnson's vain efforts at peace negotiations in 1967 and 1968 unmistakably were related to the action-forcing character of American elections.

Though important national policy change is a slow process, it does not necessarily follow that a six-year term is an appropriate remedy. Frequently policy changes which have frustrated the White House have come slowly because they have been highly controversial and support was not adequately assembled. Mobilization of support is just as much a presidential responsibility as proclaiming the need, and support would be no less crucial with a seven-year or even eleven-year term. Only a shrewdly political president who is also his party's leader, sensitive to political moods, and allied with dozens of political and party elites, can build the coalitions that can bridge the separation of powers in Washington, and offset strong forces bent on thwarting progress.

Often, when the White House is frustrated in attempting reform, the proposed changes have not been adequately planned or tested. In the case of the Johnson administration it is now well known that too many policies were pronounced prematurely; sometimes policy was "made" by press release and the administration acted as though bill-signing ceremonies were the culmination of the policy-making process. The Johnson administration also was frustrated in its attempt to implement sweeping domestic policy changes precisely because too much emphasis was placed on "getting the laws on the books" to the neglect of developing the managerial and bureaucratic organizations necessary for imaginative administration of these laws. A White House that becomes overly transfixed with a legislative box score or that succumbs to the unquenchable thirst for quick political credit may, at least for a while, appear to be accomplishing great innovations. But translating paper victories into genuine policy accomplishments requires far more than monopolization of the legislative process.

In the early history of the presidency, presidents who were unable to mobilize support within Congress were also unable to maintain reasonable support within their own executive branch. Keeping in the good graces of a president, who had partisans of his own in Congress, became politically prudent for cabinet members who had program or political ambitions of their own. According to political scientist James S. Young, presidential effectiveness depended in large measure on political-partisan leadership skills.

What was true in the past remains true today: effective national leadership requires what the Constitution tried to discourage, that a party or faction disperse its members or its influence across the branches of government. A president under normal circumstances who ignores this or retreats from these partisan and political responsibilities is unlikely to achieve much substantive policy innovation.

Moreover, as Clark Clifford, a former counselor to three presidents put it: "A president who can never again be a candidate is a president whose coattails are permanently in mothballs." A president elected to a six-year term with reelection forbidden would be a president inescapably confronted with a bureaucracy of the permanent government, as well as his senior political appointees even less responsive to him than now. Even when presidents are both popular and eligible for reelection their dependence on the senior and mid-career services of the permanent government can never be overestimated. This is well summed up in a wonderfully wry, albeit overstated, Washington observation that the "bureaucracy eats presidents for lunch." When it is known that a chief executive is to leave by a certain date, bureaucratic entrepreneurs suddenly enjoy wider degrees of discretion and independence. Used or not, reeligibility is a potentially significant political resource in the hands of a president, and denying that resource will diminish the leadership discretion of future presidents who desire to be activist policy initiators. It could have the same effect as the Twenty-Second Amendment; though, to be sure, this is not a propitious time to expend much energy on repealing the Twenty-Second Amendment; it was, in enactment, a massive vote of no-confidence in the political judgment of future generations. As Henry Steele Commager once put it, "We substitute *our* judgment for theirs on the crucial matter of electing a President."

One may sympathize with President Johnson's predicament in 1968, when he was losing popularity, when the American public was disillusioned with his war policies, and his domestic programs were running into a myriad of implementation difficulties. Many of his domestic efforts had become controversial, many were underfunded or not funded at all, and those that received funding often foundered on the shoals of Johnson's Vietnam-generated inflation or from intergovernmental obstacles not anticipated by White House domestic program architects. It is doubtful, however, that much would have been different under a Constitutional six-year term.

A six-year term might induce some otherwise timid president to propose more courageous and far-reaching policies. But that was hardly a Johnson deficiency. A six-year term might make those who are overly concerned with party patronage and party machinery less so. But this was clearly not a Johnson preoccupation. A six-year term might permit a greater degree of program follow-through, monitoring, and evaluation. But this apparently was never a personal Johnson interest. Nor would a six-year presidential term have been any guarantee that much of the Watergate scandals would not have occurred anyway.

The idea of a set single six-year presidential term is the last gasp of those who cling to the hope that we can separate national leadership from the crucible of politics, or of those who contend that our presidency is overly beholden to the workings of a patronage or spoils system. Neither is the case: the former remains an impossibility while the latter is a problem whose time largely has passed. So, too, the notion that intense conflicts over policy choices can be somehow removed from the presidency is undesirable. The conflicts that surround the presidency and require a president to act as public mediator mirror existing and potential conflicts over values in the society at large. If our presidents were not asked to resolve political conflicts they would not be fulfilling those responsibilities which rightly are associated with democratic leadership.

———————

1. What effects do you think the single six-year term proposal might have on the President's ability to discharge the constitutional responsibilities you have studied? Note that the Mexican presidency is a strong one despite a single-term requirement and substantial intrigue over succession within the ruling party throughout the incumbent's term. Are there features particular to our party system or our structures or traditions of governance that sustain Sorenson's negative view of the proposal?

2. What would be the impact of the proposal on the President's political accountability? Is there any predictable relationship between decreased accountability and increased efficiency? Could we wind up with a decrease in both?

3. In general, do you perceive the national changes experienced since 1789 as profound enough to require constitutional change in the Presidency, or have you been persuaded that the current constitutional structure is sufficiently flexible to permit any sound adjustment of government performance to changing national needs?

APPENDIX: SELECTED STATUTES AND PRESIDENTIAL DOCUMENTS*

2 U.S.C. §§ 621-23, 631-42, 651-56—Congressional Budget and Fiscal
Operations 813

2 U.S.C. §§ 681-88—Impoundment Control 831

2 U.S.C. §§ 901-09, 921-22—Emergency Power to Eliminate Budget Deficits .. 836

3 U.S.C. §§ 301-03—Delegation of Presidential Functions 864

5 U.S.C. § 5503—Recess Appointments 865

5 U.S.C. § 7211—Employees' Right to Petition Congress.......................865

18 U.S.C. § 793—Espionage..866

18 U.S.C. § 1505—Interference with Government Proceedings..................868

22 U.S.C. § 2370(e)(2)—Hickenlooper Amendment.............................868

28 U.S.C. §§ 511-19—Functions of the Attorney General 869

28 U.S.C. §§ 591-598—Independent Counsel....................................870

28 U.S.C. §§ 2671-80—Federal Tort Claims Act 883

31 U.S.C. §§ 703, 711-12, 717, 719—Comptroller General Functions 887

40 U.S.C. §§ 471, 486(a)—Federal Procurement 891

44 U.S.C. §§ 2201-07—Presidential Records 892

50 U.S.C. note following § 1541—Multinational Force in Lebanon
Resolution 897

50 U.S.C. §§ 1701-05—International Emergency Economic Powers............ 900

50 U.S.C. App. §§ 2-3, 5—Trading With the Enemy Act 903

Proclamation of January 1, 1863 (Emancipation Proclamation)............... 907

Exec. Order No. 10340 908

Exec. Order No. 11615 910

Exec. Order No. 12092 912

Exec. Order No. 12291 913

Exec. Order No. 12498 918

UNITED STATES CODE—SELECTED PROVISIONS
TITLE 2—THE CONGRESS

Congressional Budget and Fiscal Operations

§ 621. Congressional declaration of purpose

The Congress declares that it is essential—

---

* The statutes appear as they were amended through December 16, 1987.

(1) to assure effective congressional control over the budgetary process;

(2) to provide for the congressional determination each year of the appropriate level of Federal revenues and expenditures;

(3) to provide a system of impoundment control;

(4) to establish national budget priorities; and

(5) to provide for the furnishing of information by the executive branch in a manner that will assist the Congress in discharging its duties.

§ 622. Definitions

For purposes of this Act—

(1) The terms "budget outlays" and "outlays" mean, with respect to any fiscal year, expenditures and net lending of funds under budget authority during such year.

(2) The term "budget authority" means authority provided by law to enter into obligations which will result in immediate or future outlays involving Government funds or to collect offsetting receipts[.], except that such term does not include authority to insure or guarantee the repayment of indebtedness incurred by another person or government.

(3) The term "tax expenditures" means those revenue losses attributable to provisions of the Federal tax laws which allow a special exclusion, exemption, or deduction from gross income or which provide a special credit, a preferential rate of tax, or a deferral of tax liability; and the term "tax expenditures budget" means an enumeration of such tax expenditures.

(4) The term "concurrent resolution on the budget" means—

(A) a concurrent resolution setting forth the congressional budget for the United States Government for a fiscal year as provided in section 301 [2 U.S.C. § 632]; and

(B) any other concurrent resolution revising the congressional budget for the United States Government for a fiscal year as described in section 304 [2 U.S.C. § 635].

(C) [Redesignated]

(5) The term "appropriation Act" means an Act referred to in section 105 of title 1, United States Code [1 U.S.C. § 105].

(6) The term "deficit" means, with respect to any fiscal year, the amount by which total budget outlays for such fiscal year exceed total revenues for such fiscal year. In calculating the deficit for purposes of comparison with the maximum deficit amount under the Balanced Budget and Emergency Deficit Control Act of 1985 and in calculating the excess deficit for purposes of sections 251 and 252 of such Act [2 U.S.C. §§ 901, 902] (notwithstanding section 710(a) of the Social Security Act [42 U.S.C. § 911(a)]), for any fiscal year, the receipts of the Federal Old-Age and Survivors Insurance Trust Fund and the Federal Disability Insurance Trust Fund for such fiscal year and the taxes payable under sections 1401(a), 3101(a), and 3111(a) of the Internal Revenue Code of 1954 [26 U.S.C. §§ 1401(a), 3101(a), 3111(a)] during such fiscal year shall be included in total revenues for such fiscal year, and the disbursements of each such Trust Fund for such fiscal year shall be

included in total budget outlays for such fiscal year. Notwithstanding any other provision of law except to the extent provided by section 710(a) of the Social Security Act [42 U.S.C. § 911(a)], the receipts, revenues, disbursements, budget authority, and outlays of each off-budget Federal entity for a fiscal year shall be included in total budget authority, total budget outlays, and total revenues and the amounts of budget authority and outlays set forth for each major functional category, for such fiscal year. Amounts paid by the Federal Financing Bank for the purchase of loans made or guaranteed by a department, agency, or instrumentality of the Government of the United States shall be treated as outlays of such department, agency, or instrumentality.

(7) The term "maximum deficit amount" means—

   (A) with respect to the fiscal year beginning October 1, 1985, $171,900,000,000;

   (B) with respect to the fiscal year beginning October 1, 1986, $144,000,000,000;

   (C) with respect to the fiscal year beginning October 1, 1987, $108,000,000,000;*

   (D) with respect to the fiscal year beginning October 1, 1987, $144,000,000,000;

   (E) with respect to the fiscal year beginning October 1, 1988, $136,000,000,000;

   (F) with respect to the fiscal year beginning October 1, 1989, $100,000,000,000;

   (G) with respect to the fiscal year beginning October 1, 1990, $64,000,000,000;

   (H) with respect to the fiscal year beginning October 1, 1991, $28,000,000,000; and

   (I) with respect to the fiscal year beginning October 1, 1992, zero.

(8) The term "off-budget Federal entity" means any entity (other than a privately-owned Government-sponsored entity)—

   (A) which is established by Federal law, and

   (B) the receipts and disbursements of which are required by law to be excluded from the totals of—

      (i) the budget of the United States Government submitted by the President pursuant to section 1105 of title 31, United States Code [31 U.S.C. § 1105], or

      (ii) the budget adopted by the Congress pursuant to title III of this Act [2 U.S.C. §§ 631 et seq.].

(9) The term "entitlement authority" means spending authority described by section 401(c)(2)(C) [31 U.S.C. § 1351(c)(2)(C)].

(10) The term "credit authority" means authority to incur direct loan obligations or to incur primary loan guarantee commitments.

---

* Clauses (A) through (C) of this paragraph were added by the Balanced Budget and Emergency Deficit Control Act of 1985, Pub. L. No. 99-177, § 201(a)(1), 99 Stat. 1039. The Balanced Budget and Emergency Deficit Control Reaffirmation Act of 1987, Pub. L. No. 100-119, § 106(a), 101 Stat. 780, substituted new clauses (D) through (F) for like-lettered clauses also enacted in 1985, and added new clauses (G) through (I). Because the 1985 version of clause (C) and the 1987 version of clause (D) both prescribe maximum deficit amounts for fiscal 1988, Congress presumably intended the 1987 act to repeal the earlier provision for fiscal 1988, but mislabeled the clauses. Errors of this sort are commonly corrected by "housekeeping" provisions of later legislation.

§ 623. Continuing study of additional budget reform proposals [Omitted.]

§ 631. Timetable

The timetable with respect to the congressional budget process for any fiscal year is as follows:

On or before:	Action to be completed:
First Monday after January 3	President submits his budget.
February 15	Congressional Budget Office submits report to Budget Committees.
February 25...........................	Committees submit views and estimates to Budget Committees.
April 1	Senate Budget Committee reports concurrent resolution on the budget.
April 15	Congress completes action on concurrent resolution on the budget.
May 15................................	Annual appropriation bills may be considered in the House.
June 10...............................	House Appropriations Committee reports last annual appropriation bill.
June 15...............................	Congress completes action on reconciliation legislation.
June 30...............................	House completes action on annual appropriation bills.
October 1	Fiscal year begins.

§ 632. Annual adoption of concurrent resolution on the budget.

(a) **Content of concurrent resolution on the budget.** On or before April 15 of each year, the Congress shall complete action on a concurrent resolution on the budget for the fiscal year beginning on October 1 of such year. The concurrent resolution shall set forth appropriate levels for the fiscal year beginning on October 1 of such year, and planning levels for each of the two ensuing fiscal years, for the following—

(1) totals of new budget authority, budget outlays, direct loan obligations, and primary loan guarantee commitments;

(2) total Federal revenues and the amount, if any, by which the aggregate level of Federal revenues should be increased or decreased by bills and resolutions to be reported by the appropriate committees;

(3) the surplus or deficit in the budget;

(4) new budget authority, budget outlays, direct loan obligations, and primary loan guarantee commitments for each major functional category, based on allocations of the total levels set forth pursuant to paragraph (1); and

(5) the public debt.

(b) Additional matters in concurrent resolution. The concurrent resolution on the budget may—

(1) set forth, if required by subsection (f), the calendar year in which, in the opinion of the Congress, the goals for reducing unemployment set forth in section 4(b) of the Employment Act of 1946 [15 U.S.C. § 1022a(b)] should be achieved;

(2) include reconciliation directives described in section 310 [2 U.S.C. § 641];

(3) require a procedure under which all or certain bills or resolutions providing new budget authority or new entitlement authority for such fiscal year shall not be enrolled until the Congress has completed action on any reconciliation bill or reconciliation resolution or both required by such concurrent resolution to be reported in accordance with section 310(b) [2 U.S.C. § 641(b)]; and

(4) set forth such other matters, and require such other procedures, relating to the budget, as may be appropriate to carry out the purposes of this Act.

(c) Consideration of procedures or matters which have the effect of changing any rule of the House of Representatives. If the Committee on the Budget of the House of Representatives reports any concurrent resolution on the budget which includes any procedure or matter which has the effect of changing any rule of the House of Representatives, such concurrent resolution shall then be referred to the Committee on Rules with instructions to report it within five calendar days (not counting any day on which the House is not in session). The Committee on Rules shall have jurisdiction to report any concurrent resolution referred to it under this paragraph with an amendment or amendments changing or striking out any such procedure or matter.

(d) Views and estimates of other committees. On or before February 25 of each year, each committee of the House of Representatives having legislative jurisdiction shall submit to the Committee on the Budget of the House and each committee of the Senate having legislative jurisdiction shall submit to the Committee on the Budget of the Senate its views and estimates (as determined by the committee making such submission) with respect to all matters set forth in subsections (a) and (b) which relate to matters within the jurisdiction or functions of such committee. The Joint Economic Committee shall submit to the Committees on the Budget of both Houses its recommendations as to the fiscal policy appropriate to the goals of the Employment Act of 1946. Any other committee of the House of Representatives or the Senate may submit to the Committee on the Budget of its House, and any joint committee of the Congress may submit to the Committees on the Budget of both Houses, its views and estimates with respect to all matters set forth in subsections (a) and (b) which relate to matters within its jurisdiction or functions.

(e) Hearings and report. In developing the concurrent resolution on the budget referred to in subsection (a) for each fiscal year, the Committee on the Budget of each House shall hold hearings and shall receive testimony from Members of Congress and such appropriate representatives of Federal departments and agencies, the general public, and national organizations as the committee deems desirable. Each of the recommendations as to short-term and medium-term goals set forth in the report submitted by the members of the Joint Economic Committee under subsection (d) may be considered by the Committee on the Budget of each House as part of its consideration of such concurrent resolution, and its report may reflect its views thereon, including its views on how the estimates of revenues and levels of budget authority and outlays set forth in such concurrent resolution are designed to achieve any goals it is recommending. The report accompanying such concurrent resolution shall include, but not be limited to—

(1) a comparison of revenues estimated by the committee with those estimated in the budget submitted by the President;

(2) a comparison of the appropriate levels of total budget outlays and total new budget authority, total direct loan obligations, total primary loan guarantee commitments, as set forth in such concurrent resolution, with those estimated or requested in the budget submitted by the President;

(3) with respect to each major functional category, an estimate of budget outlays and an appropriate level of new budget authority for all proposed programs and for all existing programs (including renewals thereof), with the estimate and level for existing programs being divided between permanent authority and funds provided in appropriation Acts, and with each such division being subdivided between controllable amounts and all other amounts;

(4) an allocation of the level of Federal revenues recommended in the concurrent resolution among the major sources of such revenues;

(5) the economic assumptions and objectives which underlie each of the matters set forth in such concurrent resolution and any alternative economic assumptions and objectives which the committee considered;

(6) projections (not limited to the following), for the period of five fiscal years beginning with such fiscal year, of the estimated levels of total budget outlays and total new budget authority, the estimated revenues to be received, and the estimated surplus or deficit, if any, for each fiscal year in such period, and the estimated levels of tax expenditures (the tax expenditures budget) by major functional categories;

(7) a statement of any significant changes in the proposed levels of Federal assistance to State and local governments;

(8) information, data, and comparisons indicating the matter in which, and the basis on which, the committee determined each of the matters set forth in the concurrent resolution; and

(9) allocations described in section 302(a) [2 U.S.C. § 633(a)].

(f) Achievement of goals for reducing unemployment.

(1) If, pursuant to section 4(c) of the Employment Act of 1946 [15 U.S.C. § 1022a(c)], the President recommends in the Economic Report that the goals for reducing unemployment set forth in section 4(b) of such Act [15 U.S.C. § 1022a(b)] be achieved in a year after the close of the five-year period prescribed by such subsection, the concurrent resolution on the budget for the fiscal year beginning after the date on which such Economic Report is received by the Congress may set forth the year in which, in the opinion of the Congress, such goals can be achieved.

(2) After the Congress has expressed its opinion pursuant to paragraph (1) as to the year in which the goals for reducing unemployment set forth in section 4(b) of the Employment Act of 1946 [15 U.S.C. § 1022a(b)] can be achieved, if, pursuant to section 4(e) of such Act [15 U.S.C. § 1022a(e)], the President recommends in the Economic Report that such goals be achieved in a year which is different from the year in which the Congress has expressed its opinion that such goals should be achieved, either in its action pursuant to paragraph (1) or in its most recent

action pursuant to this paragraph, the concurrent resolution on the budget for the fiscal year beginning after the date on which such Economic Report is received by the Congress may set forth the year in which, in the opinion of the Congress, such goals can be achieved.

(3) It shall be in order to amend the provision of such resolution setting forth such year only if the amendment thereto also proposes to alter the estimates, amounts, and levels (as described in subsection (a)) set forth in such resolution in germane fashion in order to be consistent with the economic goals (as described in sections 3(a)(2) and 4(b) of the Employment Act of 1946 [15 U.S.C. §§ 1022(a)(2), 1022a(b)]) which such amendment proposes can be achieved by the year specified in such amendment.

(g) Economic assumptions.

(1) It shall not be in order in the Senate to consider any concurrent resolution on the budget for a fiscal year, or any amendment thereto, or any conference report thereon, that sets forth amounts and levels that are determined on the basis of more than one set of economic and technical assumptions.

(2) The joint explanatory statement accompanying a conference report on a concurrent resolution on the budget shall set forth the common economic assumptions upon which such joint statement and conference report are based, or upon which any amendment contained in the joint explanatory statement to be proposed by the conferees in the case of technical disagreement, is based.

(3) Subject to periodic reestimation based on changed economic conditions or technical estimates, determinations under titles III and IV of the Congressional Budget Act of 1974 shall be based upon such common economic and technical assumptions.

(h) Budget committees consultation with committees. The Committee on the Budget of the House of Representatives shall consult with the committees of its House having legislative jurisdiction during the preparation, consideration, and enforcement of the concurrent resolution on the budget with respect to all matters which relate to the jurisdiction or functions of such committees.

(i) Maximum deficit amount may not be exceeded.

(1) (A) Except as provided in paragraph (2), it shall not be in order in either the House of Representatives or the Senate to consider any concurrent resolution on the budget for a fiscal year under this section, or to consider any amendment to such a concurrent resolution, or to consider a conference report on such a concurrent resolution, if the level of total budget outlays for such fiscal year that is set forth in such concurrent resolution or conference report exceeds the recommended level of Federal revenues set forth for that year by an amount that is greater than the maximum deficit amount for such fiscal year as determined under section 3(7) [2 U.S.C. § 622(7)], or if the adoption of such amendment would result in a level of total budget outlays for that fiscal year which exceeds the recommended level of Federal revenues for that fiscal year, by an amount that is greater than the maximum deficit amount for such fiscal year as determined under section 3(7) [2 U.S.C. § 622(7)].

(B) In the House of Representatives the point of order established under subparagraph (A) with respect to the consideration of a conference report or with respect to the consideration of a motion to concur, with or without an amendment or amendments, in a Senate amendment, the stage of disagreement having been reached, may be waived only by a vote of three-fifths of the Members present and voting, a quorum being present.

(2) (A) Paragraph (1) of this subsection shall not apply if a declaration of war by the Congress is in effect.

(B) Paragraph (1) shall not apply to the consideration of any concurrent resolution on the budget for fiscal year 1988 or fiscal year 1989, or amendment thereto or conference report thereon, if such concurrent resolution or conference report provides, or in the case of an amendment if the concurrent resolution as changed by the adoption of such amendment would provide for deficit reduction from a budget baseline estimate as specified in section 251(a)(6) of the Balanced Budget and Emergency Deficit Control Act of 1985 for such fiscal year (based on laws in effect on January 1 of the calendar year during which the fiscal year begins) equal to or greater than the maximum amount of unachieved deficit reduction for such fiscal year as specified in section 251(a)(3)(A) of such Act.

(C) For purposes of the application of subparagraph (B), the amount of deficit reduction for a fiscal year provided for in a concurrent resolution, or amendment thereto or conference report thereon, shall be determined on the basis of estimates made by the Committee on the Budget of the House of Representatives or of the Senate as the case may be.

§ 633. Committee allocations [Omitted.]

§ 634. Adoption of first concurrent resolution on the budget prior to consideration of legislation providing new budget authority, new spending authority, or changes in revenues or public debt limit

(a) In general. It shall not be in order in either the House of Representatives or the Senate to consider any bill or resolution (or amendment thereto) as reported to the House or Senate which provides—

(1) new budget authority for a fiscal year;

(2) an increase or decrease in revenues to become effective during a fiscal year;

(3) an increase or decrease in the public debt limit to become effective during a fiscal year;

(4) new entitlement authority to become effective during a fiscal year; or

(5) new credit authority for a fiscal year,

until the concurrent resolution on the budget for such fiscal year has been agreed to pursuant to section 301 [2 U.S.C. § 632].

(b) Exceptions. Subsection (a) does not apply to any bill or resolution—

(1) providing new budget authority which first becomes available in a fiscal year following the fiscal year to which the concurrent resolution applies; or

(2) increasing or decreasing revenues which first become effective in a fiscal year following the fiscal year to which the concurrent resolution applies.

After May 15 of any calendar year, subsection (a) does not apply in the House of Representatives to any general appropriation bill, or amendment thereto, which provides new budget authority for the fiscal year beginning in such calendar year.

(c) Waiver in the Senate.

(1) The committee of the Senate which reports any bill or resolution (or amendment thereto) to which subsection (a) applies may at or after the time it reports such bill or resolution (or amendment), report a resolution to the Senate (A) providing for the waiver of subsection (a) with respect to such bill or resolution (or amendment), and (B) stating the reasons why the waiver is necessary. The resolution shall then be referred to the Committee on the Budget of the Senate. That committee shall report the resolution to the Senate within 10 days after the resolution is referred to it (not counting any day on which the Senate is not in session) beginning with the day following the day on which it is so referred, accompanied by that committee's recommendations and reasons for such recommendations with respect to the resolution. If the committee does not report the resolution within such 10-day period, it shall automatically be discharged from further consideration of the resolution and the resolution shall be placed on the calendar.

(2) During the consideration of any such resolution, debate shall be limited to one hour, to be equally divided between, and controlled by, the majority leader and minority leader or their designees, and the time on any debatable motion or appeal shall be limited to twenty minutes, to be equally divided between, and controlled by, the mover and the manager of the resolution. In the event the manager of the resolution is in favor of any such motion or appeal, the time in opposition thereto shall be controlled by the minority leader or his designee. Such leaders, or either of them, may, from the time under their control on the passage of such resolution, allot additional time to any Senator during the consideration of any debatable motion or appeal. No amendment to the resolution is in order.

(3) If, after the Committee on the Budget has reported (or been discharged from further consideration of) the resolution, the Senate agrees to the resolution, then subsection (a) shall not apply with respect to the bill or resolution (or amendment thereto) to which the resolution so agreed to applies.

§ 635. Revisions of concurrent resolutions on the budget

(a) **In general.** At any time after the concurrent resolution on the budget for a fiscal year has been agreed to pursuant to section 301 [2 U.S.C. § 632], and before the end of such fiscal year, the two Houses may adopt a concurrent resolution on the budget which revises or reaffirms the concurrent resolution on the budget for such fiscal year most recently agreed to.

(b) **Maximum deficit amount may not be exceeded.** The provisions of section 301(i) [2 U.S.C. § 632(i)] shall apply with respect to concurrent resolutions on the budget under this section (and amendments thereto and conference reports thereon) in the same way they apply to concurrent resolutions on the budget under such section 301(i) [2 U.S.C. § 632(i)] (and amendments thereto and conference reports thereon).

(c) **Economic assumptions.** The provisions of section 301(g) shall apply with respect to concurrent resolutions on the budget under this section (and amendments thereto and conference reports thereon) in the same way they apply to concurrent resolutions on the budget under such section 301(g) (and amendments thereto and conference reports thereon).

§ 636. Consideration of concurrent resolutions on the budget [omitted.]

§ 637. Budget Committee handling of legislation dealing with Congressional budget

No bill or resolution, and no amendment to any bill or resolution, dealing with any matter which is within the jurisdiction of the Committee on the Budget of either House shall be considered in that House unless it is a bill or resolution which has been reported by the Committee on the Budget of that House (or from the consideration of which such committee has been discharged) or unless it is an amendment to such a bill or resolution.

§ 638. House committee action on all appropriation bills to be completed by June 10

On or before June 10 of each year, the Committee on Appropriations of the House of Representatives shall report annual appropriation bills providing new budget authority under the jurisdiction of all of its subcommittees for the fiscal year which begins on October 1 of that year.

§ 639. Reports, summaries, and projections of Congressional budget actions

(a) Reports on legislation providing new budget authority, new spending authority, or new credit authority, or providing an increase or decrease in revenues or tax expenditures.

(1) Whenever a committee of either House reports to its House a bill or resolution, or committee amendment thereto, providing new budget authority (other than continuing appropriations), new spending authority described in section 401(c)(2) [2 U.S.C. § 651(c)(2)], or new credit authority, or providing an increase or decrease in revenues or tax expenditures for a fiscal year, the report accompanying that bill or resolution shall contain a statement, or the committee shall make available such a statement in the case of an approved committee amendment which is not reported to its House, prepared after consultation with the Director of the Congressional Budget Office—

(A) comparing the levels in such measure to the appropriate allocations in the reports submitted under section 302(b) [2 U.S.C. § 633(b)] for the most recently agreed to concurrent resolution on the budget for such fiscal year;

(B) including an identification of any new spending authority described in section 401(c)(2) [2 U.S.C. § 651(c)(2)] which is contained in such measure and a justification for the use of such financing method instead of annual appropriations;

(C) containing a projection by the Congressional Budget Office of how such measure will affect the levels of such budget authority, budget outlays, spending authority, revenues, tax expenditures, direct loan obligations, or primary loan guarantee commitments under existing law for such fiscal year and each of the four ensuing fiscal years, if timely submitted before such report is filed; and

(D) containing an estimate by the Congressional Budget Office of the level of new budget authority for assistance to State and local governments provided by such measure, if timely submitted before such report is filed.

(2) Whenever a conference report is filed in either House and such conference report or any amendment reported in disagreement or any amendment contained in the joint statement of managers to be proposed by the conferees in the case of technical disagreement on such bill or resolution provides new budget authority (other than continuing appropriations), new spending authority described in section 401(c)(2) [2 U.S.C. § 651(c)(2)], or new credit authority, or provides an increase or decrease in revenues for a fiscal year, the statement of managers accompanying such conference report shall contain the information described in paragraph (1), if available on a timely basis. If such information is not available when the conference report is filed, the committee shall make such information available to Members as soon as practicable prior to the consideration of such conference report.

(b) Up-to-date tabulations of Congressional budget action.

(1) The Director of the Congressional Budget Office shall issue to the committees of the House of Representatives and the Senate reports on at least a monthly basis detailing and tabulating the progress of congressional action on bills and resolutions providing new budget authority, new spending authority described in section 401(c)(2) [2 U.S.C. § 451(c)(2)], or new credit authority, or providing an increase or decrease in revenues or tax expenditures for a fiscal year. Such reports shall include but are not limited to an up-to-date tabulation comparing the appropriate aggregate and functional levels (including outlays) included in the most recently adopted concurrent resolution on the budget with the levels provided in bills and resolutions reported by committees or adopted by either House or by the Congress, and with the levels provided by law for the fiscal year preceding such fiscal year.

(2) The Committee on the Budget of each House shall make available to Members of its House summary budget scorekeeping reports. Such reports—

(A) shall be made available on at least a monthly basis, but in any case frequently enough to provide Members of each House an accurate representation of the current status of congressional consideration of the budget;

(B) shall include, but are not limited to, summaries of tabulations provided under subsection (b)(1); and

(C) shall be based on information provided under subsection (b)(1) without substantive revision.

The chairman of the Committee on the Budget of the House of Representatives shall submit such reports to the Speaker.

(c) Five-year projection of Congressional budget action. As soon as practicable after the beginning of each fiscal year, the Director of the Congressional Budget Office shall issue a report projecting for the period of 5 fiscal years beginning with such fiscal year—

(1) total new budget authority and total budget outlays each fiscal year in such period;

(2) revenues to be received and the major sources thereof, and the surplus or deficit, if any, for each fiscal year in such period;

(3) tax expenditures for each fiscal year in such period;

(4) entitlement authority for each fiscal year in such period; and

(5) credit authority for each fiscal year in such period.

§ 640. House approval of regular appropriation bills

It shall not be in order in the House of Representatives to consider any resolution providing for an adjournment period of more than three calendar days during the month of July until the House of Representatives has approved annual appropriation bills providing new budget authority under the jurisdiction of all the subcommittees of the Committee on Appropriations for the fiscal year beginning on October 1 of such year. For purposes of this section, the chairman of the Committee on Appropriations of the House of Representatives shall periodically advise the Speaker as to changes in jurisdiction among its various subcommittees.

§ 641. Reconciliation

(a) Inclusion of reconciliation directives in concurrent resolutions on the budget. A concurrent resolution on the budget for any fiscal year, to the extent necessary to effectuate the provisions and requirements of such resolution, shall—

(1) specify the total amount by which—

(A) new budget authority for such fiscal year;

(B) budget authority initially provided for prior fiscal years;

(C) new entitlement authority which is to become effective during such fiscal year; and

(D) credit authority for such fiscal year,

contained in laws, bills, and resolutions within the jurisdiction of a committee, is to be changed and direct that committee to determine and recommend changes to accomplish a change of such total amount;

(2) specify the total amount by which revenues are to be changed and direct that the committees having jurisdiction to determine and recommend changes in the revenue laws, bills, and resolutions to accomplish a change of such total amount;

(3) specify the amounts by which the statutory limit on the public debt is to be changed and direct the committee having jurisdiction to recommend such change; or

(4) specify and direct any combination of the matters described in paragraphs (1), (2), and (3).

(b) Legislative procedure. If a concurrent resolution containing directives to one or more committees to determine and recommend changes in laws, bills, or resolutions is agreed to in accordance with subsection (a), and—

(1) only one committee of the House or the Senate is directed to determine and recommend changes, that committee shall promptly make such determination and recommendations and report to its House reconciliation legislation containing such recommendations; or

(2) more than one committee of the House or the Senate is directed to determine and recommend changes, each such committee so directed shall promptly make such determination and recommendations and submit such recommendations to

the Committee on the Budget of its House, which, upon receiving all such recommendations, shall report to its House reconciliation legislation carrying out all such recommendations without any substantive revision.

For purposes of this subsection, a reconciliation resolution is a concurrent resolution directing the Clerk of the House of Representatives or the Secretary of the Senate, as the case may be, to make specified changes in bills and resolutions which have not been enrolled.

(c) **Compliance with reconciliation directions.** Any committee of the House of Representatives or the Senate that is directed, pursuant to a concurrent resolution on the budget, to determine and recommend changes of the type described in paragraphs (1) and (2) of subsection (a) with respect to laws within its jurisdiction, shall be deemed to have complied with such directions—

(1) if—

(A) the amount of the changes of the type described in paragraph (1) of such subsection recommended by such committee do not exceed or fall below the amount of the changes such committee was directed by such concurrent resolution to recommend under such paragraph by more than 20 percent of the total of the amounts of the changes such committee was directed to make under paragraphs (1) and (2) of such subsection, and

(B) the amount of the changes of the type described in paragraph (2) of such subsection recommended by such committee do not exceed or fall below the amount of the changes such committee was directed by such concurrent resolution to recommend under that paragraph by more than 20 percent of the total of the amounts of the changes such committee was directed to make under paragraphs (1) and (2) of such subsection; and

(2) if the total amount of the changes recommended by such committee is not less than the total of the amounts of the changes such committee was directed to make under paragraphs (1) and (2) of such subsection.

(d) **Limitation on amendments to reconciliation bills and resolutions.**

(1) It shall not be in order in the House of Representatives to consider any amendment to a reconciliation bill or reconciliation resolution if such amendment would have the effect of increasing any specific budget outlays above the level of such outlays provided in the bill or resolution (for the fiscal years covered by the reconciliation instructions set forth in the most recently agreed to concurrent resolution on the budget), or would have the effect of reducing any specific Federal revenues below the level of such revenues provided in the bill or resolution (for such fiscal years), unless such amendment makes at least an equivalent reduction in other specific budget outlays, an equivalent increase in other specific Federal revenues, or an equivalent combination thereof (for such fiscal years), except that a motion to strike a provision providing new budget authority or new entitlement authority may be in order.

(2) It shall not be in order in the Senate to consider any amendment to a reconciliation bill or reconciliation resolution if such amendment would have the effect of decreasing any specific budget outlay reductions below the level of such outlay reductions provided (for the fiscal years covered) in the reconciliation instructions which relate to such bill or resolution set forth in a resolution providing for reconciliation, or would have the effect of reducing Federal revenue increases below

the level of such revenue increases provided (for such fiscal years) in such instructions relating to such bill or resolution, unless such amendment makes a reduction in other specific budget outlays, an increase in other specific Federal revenues, or a combination thereof (for such fiscal years) at least equivalent to any increase in outlays or decrease in revenues provided by such amendment, except that a motion to strike a provision shall always be in order.

(3) Paragraphs (1) and (2) shall not apply if a declaration of war by the Congress is in effect.

(4) For purposes of this section, the levels of budget outlays and Federal revenues for a fiscal year shall be determined on the basis of estimates made by the Committee on the Budget of the House of Representatives or of the Senate, as the case may be.

(5) The Committee on Rules of the House of Representatives may make in order amendments to achieve changes specified by reconciliation directives contained in a concurrent resolution on the budget if a committee or committees of the House fail to submit recommended changes to its Committee on the Budget pursuant to its instruction.

(e) Procedure in the Senate.

(1) Except as provided in paragraph (2), the provisions of section 305 [2 U.S.C. § 636] for the consideration in the Senate of concurrent resolutions on the budget and conference reports thereon shall also apply to the consideration in the Senate of reconciliation bills reported under subsection (b) and conference reports thereon.

(2) Debate in the Senate on any reconciliation bill reported under subsection (b), and all amendments thereto and debatable motions and appeals in connection therewith, shall be limited to not more than 20 hours.

(f) Completion of reconciliation process.

(1) In general. Congress shall complete action on any reconciliation bill or reconciliation resolution reported under subsection (b) not later than June 15 of each year.

(2) Point of order in the House of Representatives. It shall not be in order in the House of Representatives to consider any resolution providing for an adjournment period of more than three calendar days during the month of July until the House of Representatives has completed action on the reconciliation legislation for the fiscal year beginning on October 1 of the calendar year to which the adjournment resolution pertains, if reconciliation legislation is required to be reported by the concurrent resolution on the budget for such fiscal year.

(g) Limitation on changes to the Social Security Act. Notwithstanding any other provision of law, it shall not be in order in the Senate or the House of Representatives to consider any reconciliation bill or reconciliation resolution reported pursuant to a concurrent resolution on the budget agreed to under section 301 or 304 [2 U.S.C. § 632 or 635], or a resolution pursuant to section 254(b) of the Balanced Budget and Emergency Deficit Control Act of 1985 [2 U.S.C. § 904(b)], or any amendment thereto or conference report thereon, that contains recommendations with respect to the old-age, survivors, and disability insurance program established under title II of the Social Security Act [42 U.S.C. §§ 401 et seq.].

§ 642. New budget authority, new spending authority, and revenue legislation to be within appropriate levels

(a) Legislation subject to point of order. Except as provided by subsection (b), after the Congress has completed action on a concurrent resolution on the budget for a fiscal year, it shall not be in order in either the House of Representatives or the Senate to consider any bill, resolution, or amendment providing new budget authority for such fiscal year, providing new entitlement authority effective during such fiscal year, or reducing revenues for such fiscal year, or any conference report on any such bill or resolution, if—

(1) the enactment of such bill or resolution as reported;

(2) the adoption and enactment of such amendment; or

(3) the enactment of such bill or resolution in the form recommended in such conference report;

would cause the appropriate level of total new budget authority or total budget outlays set forth in the most recently agreed to concurrent resolution on the budget for such fiscal year to be exceeded, or would cause revenues to be less than the appropriate level of total revenues set forth in such concurrent resolution or, in the Senate, would otherwise result in a deficit for such fiscal year that—

(A) for fiscal year 1989 or any subsequent fiscal year, exceeds the maximum deficit amount specified for such fiscal year in section 3(7); and

(B) for fiscal year 1988 or 1989, exceeds the amount of the estimated deficit for such fiscal year based on laws and regulations in effect on January 1 of the calendar year in which such fiscal year begins as measured using the budget baseline specified in section 251(a)(6) of the Balanced Budget and Emergency Deficit Control Act of 1985 minus $23,000,000,000 for fiscal year 1988 or $36,000,000,000 for fiscal year 1989;

except to the extent that paragraph (1) of section 301(i) or section 304(b), as the case may be, does not apply by reason of paragraph (2) of such subsection.

(b) Exception in the House of Representatives. Subsection (a) shall not apply in the House of Representatives to any bill, resolution , or amendment which provides new budget authority or new entitlement authority effective during such fiscal year, or to any conference report on any such bill or resolution, if—

(1) the enactment of such bill or resolution as reported;

(2) the adoption and enactment of such amendment; or

(3) the enactment of such bill or resolution in the form recommended in such conference report,

would not cause the appropriate allocation of new discretionary budget authority or new entitlement authority made pursuant to section 302(a) [2 U.S.C. § 633(a)] for such fiscal year, for the committee within whose jurisdiction such bill, resolution, or amendment falls, to be exceeded.

(c) Determination of budget levels. For purposes of this section, the levels of new budget authority, budget outlays, new entitlement authority, and revenues for a fiscal year shall be determined on the basis of estimates made by the Committee on the Budget of the House of Representatives or of the Senate, as the case may be.

§ 651. Bills providing new spending authority

(a) **Controls on legislation providing spending authority.** It shall not be in order in either the House of Representatives or the Senate to consider any bill, resolution, or conference report, as reported to its House which provides new spending authority described in subsection (c)(2)(A) or (B) (or any amendment which provides such new spending authority), unless that bill, resolution, conference report, or amendment also provides that such new spending authority as described in subsection (c)(2)(A) or (B) is to be effective for any fiscal year only to such extent or in such amounts as are provided in appropriation Acts.

(b) **Legislation providing entitlement authority.**

(1) It shall not be in order in either the House of Representatives or the Senate to consider any bill or resolution which provides new spending authority described in subsection (c)(2)(C) (or any amendment which provides such new spending authority) which is to become effective before the first day of the fiscal year which begins during the calendar year in which such bill or resolution is reported.

(2) If any committee of the House of Representatives or the Senate reports any bill or resolution which provides new spending authority described in subsection (c)(2)(C) which is to become effective during a fiscal year and the amount of new budget authority which will be required for such fiscal year if such bill or resolution is enacted as so reported exceeds the appropriate allocation of new budget authority reported under section 302(b) [2 U.S.C. § 633(b)] in connection with the most recently agreed to concurrent resolution on the budget for such fiscal year, such bill or resolution shall then be referred to the Committee on Appropriations of that House with instructions to report it, with the committee's recommendations, within 15 calendar days (not counting any day on which that House is not in session) beginning with the day following the day on which it is so referred. If the Committee on Appropriations of either House fails to report a bill or resolution referred to it under this paragraph within such 15-day period, the committee shall automatically be discharged from further consideration of such bill or resolution and such bill or resolution shall be placed on the appropriate calendar.

(3) The Committee on Appropriations of each House shall have jurisdiction to report any bill or resolution referred to it under paragraph (2) with an amendment which limits the total amount of new spending authority provided in such bill or resolution.

(c) **Definitions.**

(1) For purposes of this section, the term "new spending authority" means spending authority not provided by law on the effective date of this Act, including any increase in or addition to spending authority provided by law on such date.

(2) For purposes of paragraph (1), the term "spending authority" means authority (whether temporary or permanent)—

(A) to enter into contracts under which the United States is obligated to make outlays, the budget authority for which is not provided in advance by appropriation Acts;

(B) to incur indebtedness (other than indebtedness incurred under chapter 31 of title 31 of the United States Code [31 U.S.C. §§ 3101 et seq.]) for the repayment of which the United States is liable, the budget authority for which is not provided in advance by appropriation Acts;

(C) to make payments (including loans and grants), the budget authority for which is not provided for in advance by appropriation Acts, to any person or government if, under the provisions of the law containing such authority, the United States is obligated to make such payments to persons or governments who meet the requirements established by such law;

(D) to forego the collection by the United States of proprietary offsetting receipts, the budget authority for which is not provided in advance by appropriation Acts to offset such foregone receipts; and

(E) to make payments by the United States (including loans, grants, and payments from revolving funds) other than those covered by subparagraph (A), (B), (C), or (D), the budget authority for which is not provided in advance by appropriation Acts.

Such term does not include authority to insure or guarantee the repayment of indebtedness incurred by another person or government.

(d) Exceptions.

(1) Subsections (a) and (b) shall not apply to new spending authority if the budget authority for outlays which will result from such new spending authority is derived—

(A) from a trust fund established by the Social Security Act [42 U.S.C. §§ 301 et seq.] (as in effect on the date of the enactment of this Act); or

(B) from any other trust fund, 90 percent or more of the receipts of which consist or will consist of amounts (transferred from the general fund of the Treasury) equivalent to amounts of taxes (related to the purposes for which such outlays are or will be made) received in the Treasury under specified provisions of the Internal Revenue Code of 1954 [26 U.S.C. §§ 1 et seq.].

(2) Subsections (a) and (b) shall not apply to new spending authority which is an amendment to or extension of the State and Local Fiscal Assistance Act of 1972, or a continuation of the program of fiscal assistance to State and local governments provided by that Act, to the extent so provided in the bill or resolution providing such authority.

(3) Subsections (a) and (b) shall not apply to new spending authority to the extent that—

(A) the outlays resulting therefrom are made by an organization which is (i) a mixed-ownership Government corporation (as defined in section 201 of the Government Corporation Control Act), or (ii) a wholly owned Government corporation (as defined in section 101 of such Act) which is specifically exempted by law from compliance with any or all of the provisions of that Act, as of the date of enactment of the Balanced Budget and Emergency Deficit Control Act of 1985 [enacted Dec. 12, 1985]; or

(B) the outlays resulting therefrom consist exclusively of the proceeds of gifts or bequests made to the United States for a specific purpose.

§ 652. Legislation providing new credit authority

(a) Controls on legislation providing new credit authority. It shall not be in order in either the House of Representatives or the Senate to consider any bill, resolution, or conference report, as reported to its House, or any amendment which provides new credit authority described in subsection (b)(1), unless that bill, resolution, conference report, or amendment also provides that such new credit authority is to be effective for any fiscal year only to such extent or in such amounts as are provided in appropriation Acts.

(b) **Definition.** For purposes of this Act, the term "new credit authority" means credit authority (as defined in section 3(10) of this Act [2 U.S.C. 622(10)]) not provided by law on the effective date of this section, including any increase in or addition to credit authority provided by law on such date.

§ 653. Analysis by Congressional Budget Office

(a) The Director of the Congressional Budget Office shall, to the extent practicable, prepare for each bill or resolution of a public character reported by any committee of the House of Representatives or the Senate (except the Committee on Appropriations of each House), and submit to such committee—

> (1) an estimate of the costs which would be incurred in carrying out such bill or resolution in the fiscal year in which it is to become effective and in each of the 4 fiscal years following such fiscal year, together with the basis for each such estimate;

> (2) an estimate of the cost which would be incurred by State and local governments in carrying out or complying with any significant bill or resolution in the fiscal year in which it is to become effective and in each of the four fiscal years following such fiscal year, together with the basis for each such estimate;

> (3) a comparison of the estimates of costs described in paragraph [paragraphs] (1) and (2) with any available estimates of costs made by such committee or by any Federal agency; and

> (4) a description of each method for establishing a Federal financial commitment contained in such bill or resolution.

The estimates, comparison, and description so submitted shall be included in the report accompanying such bill or resolution if timely submitted to such committee before such report is filed.

(b) For purposes of subsection (a)(2), the term "local government" has the same meaning as in section 103 of the Intergovernmental Cooperation Act of 1968 [42 U.S.C. § 4201].

(c) For purposes of subsection (a)(2), the term "significant bill or resolution" is defined as any bill or resolution which in the judgment of the Director of the Congressional Budget Office is likely to result in an annual cost to State and local governments of $200,000,000 or more, or is likely to have exceptional fiscal consequences for a geographic region or a particular level of government.

§ 654. Study by the General Accounting Office of forms of federal financial commitment that are not reviewed annually by Congress [Omitted.]

§ 655. Off-budget agencies, programs, and activities

(a) Notwithstanding any other provision of law, budget authority, credit authority, and estimates of outlays and receipts for activities of the Federal budget which are off-budget immediately prior to the date of enactment of this section [Dec 12, 1986], not including activities of the Federal Old-Age and Survivors Insurance and Federal Disability Insurance Trust Funds, shall be included in a budget submitted pursuant to section 1105 of title 31, United States Code [31 U.S.C. § 1105], and in a concurrent resolution on the budget reported pursuant to section 301 or section 304 of this Act [2 U.S.C. § 632 or 635] and shall be considered, for purposes of this Act, budget authority, outlays, and spending authority in accordance with definitions set forth in this Act.

(b) All receipts and disbursements of the Federal Financing Bank with respect to any obligations which are issued, sold, or guaranteed by a Federal agency shall be treated as a means of financing such agency for purposes of section 1105 of title 31, United States Code [31 U.S.C. § 1105], and for purposes of this Act.

§ 656. Member User Group

The Speaker of the House of Representatives, after consulting with the Minority Leader of the House, may appoint a Member User Group for the purpose of reviewing budgetary scorekeeping rules and practices of the House and advising the Speaker from time to time on the effect and impact of such rules and practices.

Impoundment Control

§ 681. Disclaimer

Nothing contained in this Act, or in any amendments made by this Act, shall be construed as—

(1) asserting or conceding the constitutional powers or limitations of either the Congress or the President;

(2) ratifying or approving any impoundment heretofore or hereafter executed or approved by the President or any other Federal officer or employee, except insofar as pursuant to statutory authorization then in effect;

(3) affecting in any way the claims or defenses of any party to litigation concerning any impoundment; or

(4) superseding any provision of law which requires the obligation of budget authority or the making of outlays thereunder.

§ 682. Definitions

For purposes of this part [2 U.S.C. §§ 682 et seq.]—

(1) "deferral of budget authority" includes—

(A) withholding or delaying the obligation or expenditure of budget authority (whether by establishing reserves or otherwise) provided for projects or activities; or

(B) any other type of executive action or inaction which effectively precludes the obligation or expenditures of budget authority, including authority to obligate by contract in advance of appropriations as specifically authorized by law;

(2) "Comptroller General" means the Comptroller General of the United States;

(3) "rescission bill" means a bill or joint resolution which only rescinds, in whole or in part, budget authority proposed to be rescinded in a special message transmitted by the President under section 1012 [2 U.S.C. § 683], and upon which the Congress completes action before the end of the first period of 45 calendar days of continuous session of the Congress after the date on which the President's message is received by the Congress;

(4) "impoundment resolution" means a resolution of the House of Representatives or the Senate which only expresses its disapproval of a proposed deferral of budget authority set forth in a special message transmitted by the President under section 1013 [2 U.S.C. §684]; and

(5) continuity of a session of the Congress shall be considered as broken only by an adjournment of the Congress sine die, and the days on which either House is not in session because of an adjournment of more than 3 days to a day certain shall be excluded in the computation of the 45-day period referred to in paragraph (3) of this section and in section 1012 [2 U.S.C. § 683], and the 25-day periods referred to in sections 1016 [2 U.S.C. § 687] and 1017(b)(1) [2 U.S.C. § 1408(b)(1)]. If a special message is transmitted under section 1012 [2 U.S.C. § 683] during any Congress and the last session of such Congress adjourns sine die before the expiration of 45 calendar days of continuous session (or a special message is so transmitted after the last session of the Congress adjourns sine die), the message shall be deemed to have been retransmitted on the first day of the succeeding Congress and the 45-day period referred to in paragraph (3) of this section and in section 1012 [2 U.S.C. § 683] (with respect to such message) shall commence on the day after such first day.

§ 683. Rescission of budget authority

(a) **Transmittal of special message.** Whenever the President determines that all or part of any budget authority will not be required to carry out the full objectives or scope of programs for which it is provided or that such budget authority should be rescinded for fiscal policy or other reasons (including the termination of authorized projects or activities for which budget authority has been provided), or whenever all or part of budget authority provided for only one fiscal year is to be reserved from obligation for such fiscal year, the President shall transmit to both Houses of Congress a special message specifying—

(1) the amount of budget authority which he proposes to be rescinded or which is to be so reserved;

(2) any account, department, or establishment of the Government to which such budget authority is available for obligation, and the specific project or governmental functions involved;

(3) the reasons why the budget authority should be rescinded or is to be so reserved;

(4) to the maximum extent practicable, the estimated fiscal, economic, and budgetary effect of the proposed rescission or of the reservation; and

(5) all facts, circumstances, and considerations relating to or bearing upon the proposed rescission or the reservation and the decision to effect the proposed rescission or the reservation, and to the maximum extent practicable, the estimated

effect of the proposed rescission or the reservation upon the objects, purposes, and programs for which the budget authority is provided.

(b) Requirement to make available for obligation. Any amount of budget authority proposed to be rescinded or that is to be reserved as set forth in such special message shall be made available for obligation unless, within the prescribed 45-day period, the Congress has completed action on a rescission bill rescinding all or part of the amount proposed to be rescinded or that is to be reserved. Funds made available for obligation under this procedure may not be proposed for rescission again.

§ 684. Proposed deferrals of budget authority

(a) Transmittal of special message. Whenever the President, the Director of the Office of Management and Budget, the head of any department or agency of the United States, or any officer or employee of the United States proposes to defer any budget authority provided for a specific purpose or project, the President shall transmit to the House of Representatives and the Senate a special message specifying—

(1) the amount of the budget authority proposed to be deferred;

(2) any account, department, or establishment of the Government to which such budget authority is available for obligation, and the specific projects or governmental functions involved;

(3) the period of time during which the budget authority is proposed to be deferred;

(4) the reasons for the proposed deferral, including any legal authority invoked to justify the proposed deferral;

(5) to the maximum extent practicable, the estimated fiscal, economic, and budgetary effect of the proposed deferral; and

(6) all facts, circumstances, and considerations relating to or bearing upon the proposed deferral and the decision to effect the proposed deferral, including an analysis of such facts, circumstances, and considerations in terms of their application to any legal authority, including specific elements of legal authority, invoked to justify such proposed deferral, and to the maximum extent practicable, the estimated effect of the proposed deferral upon the objects, purposes, and programs for which the budget authority is provided.

A special message may include one or more proposed deferrals of budget authority. A deferral may not be proposed for any period of time extending beyond the end of the fiscal year in which the special message proposing the deferral is transmitted to the House and the Senate.

(b) Consistency with legislative policy. Deferrals shall be permissible only—

(1) to provide for contingencies;

(2) to achieve savings made possible by or through changes in requirements or greater efficiency of operations; or

(3) as specifically provided by law.

No officer or employee of the United States may defer any budget authority for any other purpose.

(c) Exception. The provisions of this section do not apply to any budget authority proposed to be rescinded or that is to be reserved as set forth in a special message required to be transmitted under section 1012 [2 U.S.C. § 683].

§ 685. Transmission of messages; publication

(a) **Delivery to House and Senate.** Each special message transmitted under section 1012 or 1013 [2 U.S.C. §§ 683, 684], shall be transmitted to the House of Representatives and the Senate on the same day, and shall be delivered to the Clerk of the House of Representatives if the House is not in session, and to the Secretary of the Senate if the Senate is not in session. Each special message so transmitted shall be referred to the appropriate committee of the House of Representatives and the Senate. Each such message shall be printed as a document of each House.

(b) **Delivery to Comptroller General.** A copy of each special message transmitted under section 1012 or 1013 [2 U.S.C. §§ 683, 684] shall be transmitted to the Comptroller General on the same day it is transmitted to the House of Representatives and the Senate. In order to assist the Congress in the exercise of its functions under sections 1012 and 1013 [2 U.S.C. §§ 683, 684], the Comptroller General shall review each such message and inform the House of Representatives and the Senate as promptly as practicable with respect to—

(1) in the case of a special message transmitted under section 1012 [2 U.S.C. § 683], the facts surrounding the proposed rescission or the reservation of budget authority (including the probable effects thereof); and

(2) in the case of a special message transmitted under section 1013 [2 U.S.C. § 684], (A) the facts surrounding each proposed deferral of budget authority (including the probable effects thereof) and (B) whether or not (or to what extent), in his judgment, such proposed deferral is in accordance with existing statutory authority.

(c) **Transmission of supplementary messages.** If any information contained in a special message transmitted under section 1012 or 1013 [2 U.S.C. §§ 683, 684] is subsequently revised, the President shall transmit to both Houses of Congress and the Comptroller General a supplementary message stating and explaining such revision. Any such supplementary message shall be delivered, referred, and printed as provided in subsection (a). The Comptroller General shall promptly notify the House of Representatives and the Senate of any changes in the information submitted by him under subsection (b) which may be necessitated by such revision.

(d) **Printing in Federal Register.** Any special message transmitted under section 1012 or 1013 [2 U.S.C. §§ 683, 684], and any supplementary message transmitted under subsection (c), shall be printed in the first issue of the Federal Register published after such transmittal.

(e) **Cumulative reports of proposed rescissions, reservations, and deferrals of budget authority.**

(1) The President shall submit a report to the House of Representatives and the Senate, not later than the 10th day of each month during a fiscal year, listing all budget authority for that fiscal year with respect to which, as of the first day of such month—

(A) he has transmitted a special message under section 1012 [2 U.S.C. § 683] with respect to a proposed rescission or a reservation; and

(B) he has transmitted a special message under section 1013 [2 U.S.C. § 684] proposing a deferral.

Such report shall also contain, with respect to each such proposed rescission or deferral, or each such reservation, the information required to be submitted in the special message with respect thereto under section 1012 or 1013 [2 U.S.C. §§ 683, 684].

(2) Each report submitted under paragraph (1) shall be printed in the first issue of the Federal Register published after its submission.

§ 686. Reports by Comptroller General

(a) **Failure to transmit special message.** If the Comptroller General finds that the President, the Director of the Office of Management and Budget, the head of any department or agency of the United States, or any other officer or employee of the United States—

(1) is to establish a reserve or proposes to defer budget authority with respect to which the President is required to transmit a special message under section 1012 or 1013 [2 U.S.C. §§ 683, 684]; or

(2) he ordered, permitted, or approved the establishment of such a reserve or a deferral of budget authority;

and that the President has failed to transmit a special message with respect to such a reserve or deferral, the Comptroller General shall make a report on such reserve or deferral and any available information concerning it to both Houses of Congress. The provisions of this part [2 U.S.C. §§ 682 et seq.] shall apply with respect to such reserve or deferral in the same manner and with the same effect as if such report of the Comptroller General were a special message transmitted by the President under section 1012 or 1013 [2 U.S.C. §§ 683, 684], and, for purposes of this part [2 U.S.C. §§ 682 et seq.], such report shall be considered a special message transmitted under section 1012 or 1013 [2 U.S.C. §§ 683, 684].

(b) **Incorrect classification of special message.** If the President has transmitted a special message to both Houses of Congress in accordance with section 1012 or 1013 [2 U.S.C. §§ 683, 684], and the Comptroller General believes that the President so transmitted the special message in accordance with one of those sections when the special message should have been transmitted in accordance with the other of those sections, the Comptroller General shall make a report to both Houses of the Congress setting forth his reasons.

§ 687. Suits by Comptroller General

If, under this title, budget authority is required to be made available for obligation and such budget authority is not made available for obligation, the Comptroller General is hereby expressly empowered, through attorneys of his own selection, to bring a civil action in the United States District Court for the District of Columbia to require such budget authority to be made available for obligation, and such court is hereby expressly empowered to enter in such civil action, against any department, agency, officer, or employee of the United States, any decree, judgment, or order which may be necessary or appropriate to make such budget authority available for obligation. No civil action shall be brought by the Comptroller General under this section until the expiration of 25 calendar days of continuous session of the Congress following the date on which an explanatory statement by the Comptroller General of the circumstances giving rise to the action contemplated has been filed with the Speaker of the House of Representatives and the President of the Senate.

§ 688. Procedure in House of Representatives and Senate [Omitted.]

Emergency Power to Eliminate Budget Deficits

§ 901. Reporting of Excess Deficits

(a) **Initial estimates, determinations, and reports by OMB and CBO.**

(1) **Estimates and determinations.**—The Director of the Office of Management and Budget and the Director of the Congressional Budget Office (in this part referred to as the "Directors") shall with respect to each fiscal year and in accordance with the requirements, specifications, definitions, and calculations required by this part—

(A) estimate the budget levels of total revenues and outlays that may be anticipated for such fiscal year as of August 15 of the calendar year in which such fiscal year begins (or as of October 10, 1987, in the case of fiscal year 1988),

(B) determine whether the projected deficit for such fiscal year will exceed the maximum deficit amount for such fiscal year and whether such deficit excess will be greater than $10,000,000,000 (zero in the case of fiscal year 1993),

(C) estimate the amount of net deficit reduction in the budget baseline that has occurred since January 1 of the calendar year in which such fiscal year begins, and

(D) estimate the rate of real economic growth that will occur during such fiscal year, the rate of real economic growth that will occur during each quarter of such fiscal year, and the rate of real economic growth that will have occurred during each of the last two quarters of the preceding fiscal year.

(2) **Reports.**—

(A) Based on the estimates and determinations required in paragraph (1) and in accordance with the requirements, specifications, definitions, and calculations required by this part, the Director of Congressional Budget Office (in this part referred to as the "Director of CBO") shall issue a report to the Director of the Office of Management and Budget (in this part referred to as the "Director of OMB") and to the Congress on August 20 of the calendar year in which the fiscal year begins (or on October 15, 1987, in the case of fiscal year 1988) estimating the budget baseline levels of total revenues and total outlays for such fiscal year, identifying the amount of any deficit excess for such fiscal year, stating whether such excess is greater than $10,000,000,000 (zero in the case of fiscal year 1993), estimating the amount of net deficit reduction in the budget baseline that has occurred since January 1 of the calendar year in which such fiscal year begins, specifying the estimated rate of real economic growth for such fiscal year, for each quarter of such fiscal year, and for each of the last two quarters of the preceding fiscal year, indicating whether the estimate includes two or more consecutive quarters of negative real economic growth, estimating the aggregate amount of required outlay reductions, and specifying, by account for non-defense programs and by account for defense programs the budget baseline from which reductions are taken and the amounts and percentages by which such accounts must be reduced during such fiscal year in order to make the reductions required by this part.

(B) The Director of OMB shall issue a report to the President and the Congress on August 25 of the calendar year in which the fiscal year begins (or on October 20, 1987, in the case of the fiscal year 1988) containing the same information required in subparagraph (A) and the information required in clauses (i) and (ii) for such fiscal year as follows:

(i) The Director of OMB shall identify and explain any differences between the amount set forth in such report and the corresponding amount set forth in the report of the Director of CBO under subparagraph (A) with respect to—

(I) the aggregate amount of required outlay reductions;

(II) the aggregate of resources to be sequestered from defense accounts (by type of sequesterable resource) and from non-defense accounts (by type of sequesterable resource); and

(III) the amount of sequesterable resources for any budget account that is to be reduced if such difference is greater than $5,000,000.

(ii) The Director of OMB shall calculate and set forth for defense programs (by type of sequesterable resource) and for non-defense programs (by type of sequesterable resource), the amount of reductions in budgetary resources that would be required by this part using his estimate of the aggregate amount of required outlay reductions and applying the technical assumptions (including outlay rates) and methodologies used in the report of the Director of CBO under subparagraph (A). The Director of OMB shall identify and explain any differences between these estimates and such corresponding amounts set forth under clause (i).

(iii) In the report for a fiscal year (except fiscal year 1988) issued under this subparagraph, the Director of OMB shall assume that the aggregate outlay rate for defense programs covered by paragraph (6)(C), calculated using data on sequesterable resources and account outlay rates applicable to such fiscal year, shall not differ by more than one-half of 1 percent from such aggregate outlay rate calculated using the same data on sequesterable resources but using account outlay rates calculated arithmetically using the applicable sequesterable resources and outlays contained in the report submitted under this Act for the preceding fiscal year as proposed by the Director of OMB. For purposes of this subparagraph, an aggregate outlay rate shall be the average of account outlay rates (expressed as a percentage) with each account outlay rate (as defined in section 257(13)) given a weight that is proportional to the account's share of total sequesterable resources. The calculation of the non-defense aggregate outlay rate for programs covered by paragraph (6)(C), shall be determined using the procedures and restrictions used for determining the aggregate defense outlay rate.

(iv) The report issued under this subparagraph for any fiscal year (except fiscal year 1988) may not assume aggregate outlays for the health insurance programs under title XVIII of the Social Security Act (before taking into account legislation enacted or regulations prescribed after the current services budget is submitted) which deviate by more than 1 percent from the amount of outlays estimated for such programs in the current services budget submitted by the President pursuant to section 1109(a) of title 31, United States Code, for such fiscal year. For fiscal year 1988 the report issued under this subparagraph shall assume aggregate outlays for such programs (before taking into account legislation enacted or regulations promulgated as final after August 20, 1987) equal to the amount assumed for such programs by the Director of OMB in the report submitted to the Temporary Joint Committee on Deficit Reduction on August 20, 1987, except that, unless necessary to comply with requirements provided in law, any change in administrative procedures that increases or decreases the average number of days for the payment of claims under title XVIII of the Social Security Act, compared to such average in the preceding fiscal year, shall not be taken into account for purposes of this Act.

(C)(i) The technical and economic assumptions used by the Director of CBO to calculate the excess deficit shall also be used by the Director of CBO to calculate the unachieved deficit reduction, required outlay reductions and the amounts and percentages by which budgetary resources must be reduced.

(ii) The technical and economic assumptions used by the Director of OMB to calculate the excess deficit shall also be used by the Director of OMB to calculate the required outlay reductions, the unachieved deficit reduction and the amounts and percentages by which budgetary resources must be reduced.

(iii) For fiscal year 1988, except as specified in subparagraph (B)(iv), the Director of OMB shall use the same economic and technical assumptions (including outlay rates) that the Director of OMB used in the report submitted to the Temporary Joint Committee on Deficit Reduction on August 20, 1987.

(iv) For fiscal year 1989 and subsequent fiscal years, to the extent that the report submitted by the President for such fiscal year under section 1106(a) of title 31, United States Code, uses economic and technical assumptions (including outlay rates) that differ from those that will be used by the Director of OMB in the report to be submitted under subparagraph (B) for such fiscal year, the report submitted by the President shall explain and identify such differences. Such report shall provide an estimate of the deficit excess and net deficit reduction in the budget baseline consistent with the estimates that will be used by the Director of OMB in the report to be submitted under subparagraph (B) for such fiscal year. The report submitted by the Director of OMB under subparagraph (B) for such fiscal year shall use the economic and technical assumptions that the report submitted by the President indicated would be used by such Director.

(3) **Determination of Reductions.**—

(A) The aggregate amount of required outlay reductions for a fiscal year shall be determined as follows:

(i) The aggregate required outlay reductions shall be—

(I) for fiscal year 1988, the amount of unachieved deficit reduction;

(II) for fiscal year 1989, zero if the deficit excess is equal to or less than $10,000,000,000, or if not, the lesser of the deficit excess or the amount of unachieved deficit reduction; or

(III) for fiscal year 1990, 1991, 1992, or 1993, zero if the deficit excess for such fiscal year is equal to or less than the amount of the margin for such fiscal year specified in paragraph (10) of section 257, or if not, the amount of the deficit excess for such fiscal year.

The unachieved deficit reduction shall be $23,000,000,000 in the case of fiscal year 1988 and $36,000,000,000 in the case of fiscal year 1989, minus the net deficit reduction in the budget baseline for such fiscal year, but such unachieved deficit reduction shall not exceed $23,000,000,000 in the case of fiscal year 1988 or $36,000,000,000 in the case of fiscal year 1989. Net deficit reduction in the budget baseline for a fiscal year shall be the amount of the estimated deficit for such fiscal year based on laws enacted by, and regulations promulgated as final by, the snapshot date, as measured using the budget baseline specified in paragraph (6), subtracted from the amount of the estimated deficit for such fiscal year based on laws enacted by, and regulations promulgated as final by, January 1 of the calendar year in which such fiscal year begins as measured by using the budget baseline specified in paragraph (6). Both such deficit estimates for a fiscal year shall be made using the same economic and technical assumptions.

(ii) As used in this paragraph, the term "snapshot date" means—

(I) for fiscal year 1988, in the case of an initial report submitted under subsection (a), October 10, 1987, and in the case of a final report submitted under subsection (c), the latest possible date before its submission;

(II) for fiscal year 1989 and subsequent fiscal years, in the case of an initial report submitted under subsection (a), August 15, and in the case of a final report submitted under subsection (c), the latest possible date before its submission.

(B) Subject to the exemptions, exceptions, limitations, special rules, and definitions set forth in this section and in sections 255, 256, and 257, one-half of the aggregate required outlay reductions shall be made under accounts within major functional category 050 (in this part referred to as outlays under "defense programs"), and shall be made in accordance with the rules prescribed in subsection (d), and the other half of the aggregate required outlay reductions shall be made under other accounts of the Federal Government (in this part referred to as "non-defense programs").

(C) The amount by which outlays for automatic spending increases scheduled to take effect during the fiscal year are to be reduced shall be credited as reductions in outlays under non-defense programs, and the total amount of reductions in outlays under non-defense programs required under subparagraph (B) shall be reduced accordingly.

(D) The maximum reduction permissible for each program to which an exception, limitation, or special rule set forth in subsection (c) or (f) of section 256 applies shall be credited as reductions in outlays under non-defense programs, and the amount of reductions in outlays under non-defense programs shall be further reduced by the amount of the reduction determined with respect to each such program.

(E)(i) Sequestrations and reductions under the remaining non-defense programs shall be applied on a uniform percentage basis so as to reduce new budget authority; new loan guarantee commitments or limitations; new direct loan obligations, commitments, or limitations; obligation limitations; and spending authority as defined in section 401(c)(2) of the Congressional Budget Act of 1974 to the extent necessary to achieve any remaining required outlay reductions; except that each of the programs to which the special rules set forth in subsections (d) and (k) of section 256 apply shall not be reduced by more than the percentages specified in such subsections and the uniform percentage reduction applicable to all other programs under this clause shall be increased (if necessary) to a level sufficient to achieve any remaining required outlay reductions.

(ii) For purposes of determining reductions under clause (i), any reduction in outlays of the Commodity Credit Corporation under an order issued by the President under section 252 for a fiscal year, with respect to contracts entered into during that fiscal year, that will occur during the succeeding fiscal year, shall be credited as reductions in outlays for the fiscal year in which the order is issued.

The determination of which accounts are within major functional category 050 and which are not, for purposes of subparagraph (B), shall be made by the Directors in a manner consistent with the budget submitted by the President for the fiscal year 1986; except that for such purposes no part of the accounts entitled "Federal Emergency Management Agency, Salaries and Expenses (58-0100-0-1-999)" and "Federal Emergency Management Agency, Emergency management planning and assistance (58-0101-0-1-999)" shall be treated as being within functional category 050.

(4) **Additional Specifications.**—The reports submitted under paragraph (2) must also specify (with respect to the fiscal year involved)—

(A) the amount and percentage increase of the automatic spending increase (if any) which is scheduled to take effect in the case of each program providing for such increases, and the amount and percentage increase (if any) of each such increase which will take effect after reduction under this part;

(B) the amount of the savings (if any) to be achieved in the application of each of the special rules set forth in subsections (c) through (l) of section 256, along with a statement of (i) the new Federal matching rate resulting from the application of subsection (e) of that section, and (ii) the amount of the percentage reduction in payments to the States under section 204 of the Federal-State Extended Unemployment Compensation Act of 1970; and

(C)(i) for defense programs, by account, the reduction (stated in terms of both percentage and amount) in new budget authority and unobligated balances, together with the estimated outlay reductions resulting therefrom; and

(ii) for non-defense programs, by account, the reduction, stated in terms of both percentage and amount, in new budget authority; new loan guarantee commitments or limitations; new direct loan obligations, commitments, or limitations; obligation limitations; and spending authority as defined in section 401(c)(2) of the Congressional Budget Act of 1974; together with the estimated outlay reductions resulting therefrom.

(5) **Basis for Directors' Estimates, Determinations, and Specifications.**—The estimates, determinations, and specifications of the Directors under the preceding provisions of this subsection and under subsection (c) shall utilize the budget baseline, criteria, and guidelines set forth in paragraph (6) and in sections 255, 256, and 257. In estimating the deficit, the excess deficit and unachieved deficit reduction for an initial report under paragraph (2) or a final report under subsection (c), the Directors shall use the budget baseline set forth in paragraph (6) based on laws enacted by, and regulations promulgated as final by, the snapshot date applicable to such report.

(6) **Budget Baseline.**—In estimating the deficit excess and net deficit reduction in the budget baseline and in computing the amounts and percentages by which accounts must be reduced during a fiscal year as set forth in any report required under this subsection for such fiscal year, the budget baseline shall be determined by—

(A) assuming (subject to subparagraph (B)) the continuation of current revenue law and, in the case of spending authority as defined in section 401(c)(2) of the Congressional Budget Act of 1974, funding for current law at levels sufficient to fully make all payments required under such law;

(B) assuming that expiring provisions of law providing revenues and spending authority as defined in section 401(c)(2) of the Congressional Budget Act of 1974 do expire, except that excise taxes dedicated to a trust fund, and agricultural price support programs administered through the Commodity Credit Corporation are extended at current rates, and contract authority for transportation trust funds is extended at current levels;

(C) in the case of all accounts to which subparagraph (A) does not apply—

(i) assuming for an account (except as provided by clause (ii)), appropriations at the level specified in enacted annual appropriations or continuing appropriations enacted for the entire fiscal year, and in addition, estimates of appropriations to cover the costs of Federal pay adjustments as set forth in subparagraph (D)(ii) (unless funding for such pay adjustments are provided for in such measure as explained in the joint explanatory statement of managers accompanying such appropriations);

(ii) assuming, if no annual appropriations or continuing appropriations for the entire fiscal year have been enacted for an account, subject to subparagraph (D)(iii), appropriations at the level provided for the previous fiscal year, (I) adjusted to reflect the full 12-month costs (without absorption) of the pay adjustment that occurred in such fiscal year, (II) inflated as specified in subparagraph (D)(i), and (III) increased to cover the increased costs to agencies of personnel benefits (other than pay) required by law;

(D)(i)as required by subparagraph (C)(ii)(II), assuming that the inflator shall equal—

(I) in the case of fiscal year 1988—

(aa) for personnel costs, the rate of Federal pay adjustments for statutory pay systems and elements of military pay if such adjustments have been enacted into law or (on or after October 1 of the fiscal year) have been established pursuant to law for such fiscal year or, if not, 4.2 percent, multiplied by the proportion of the fiscal year for which the pay adjustments will be effective, multiplied by 78 percent; and

(bb) for all other costs, 4.2 percent;

(II) in the case of fiscal year 1989 and subsequent fiscal years—

(aa) for 70 percent of personnel costs, the rate of Federal pay adjustments for statutory pay systems and elements of military pay if such adjustments have been enacted into law or (on or after October 1 of the fiscal year) have been established pursuant to law for such fiscal year or, if not, at the inflation rate specified in subclause (II)(bb), multiplied by the proportion of the fiscal year for which the pay adjustments will be effective, multiplied by 78 percent; and

(bb) for all other costs, the percentage by which the average of the estimated gross national product implicit price deflator for such fiscal year exceeds the average of such estimated deflator for the prior fiscal year (and the Director of OMB shall use such percentage as estimated in the budget submitted by the President under section 1105(a) for such fiscal year, but such use shall not constrain the economic assumptions the Director may use under paragraph (2)(C));

(ii) if required by subparagraph (C)(i), assuming appropriations for a fiscal year in an amount sufficient to—

(I) cover any Federal pay adjustment for statutory pay systems (including associated adjustments in benefit costs) if such adjustments have been enacted into law or, on or after October 1 of the fiscal year, have been established pursuant to law for such fiscal year;

(II) cover any pay adjustments for elements of military pay (including associated adjustments in benefit costs) if such adjustments are specifically enacted into law or occur pursuant to adjustments for statutory pay systems if such adjustments have been enacted into law or, on or after October 1 of the fiscal year, have been established pursuant to law;

reduced by 22 percent;

(iii) assuming for the purposes of subparagraph (C)(ii) that the amount provided for an account for the previous fiscal year is the amount provided in any enacted annual appropriations or continuing appropriations enacted for the entire fiscal year, as modified by any enacted supplemental appropriations or rescission bills, and if a temporary continuing appropriation is in effect for the previous fiscal year, then the amount provided for such account for the previous fiscal year shall be assumed to be the amount that would have been enacted if such continuing appropriations were in effect for the entire fiscal year;

(E) assuming that medicare spending levels for inpatient hospital services will be based upon the regulations most recently issued in final form or proposed by the Health Care Financing Administration pursuant to sections 1886(b)(3)(B), 1886(d)(3)(A), and 1886(e)(4) of the Social Security Act;

(F) assuming that, unless otherwise required by law, advance deficiency payments and paid land diversion payments under the Agricultural Act of 1949 will be made in accordance with applicable regulations and payment rates for 1987;

(G) assuming that the increase in revenues attributable to any increase in appropriations available for administration and enforcement of the Internal Revenue Code of 1986 (over the amount actually appropriated for the previous fiscal year) is consistent on a proportional basis with the increase in revenues projected to result from the increased appropriations for such purposes in the budget submitted under section 1105(a) of title 31, United States Code, for such fiscal year;

(H) assuming, unless otherwise provided by law, that the increase for Veterans' compensation (36-0153-0-1-701) for a fiscal year will be the same as that required by law for Veterans' pensions;

(I) assuming, for purposes of this paragraph and subparagraph (A)(i) of paragraph (3), that the sale of an asset or prepayment of a loan shall not alter the deficit or produce any net deficit reduction in the budget baseline, except that the budget baseline estimate shall include asset sales mandated by law before September 18, 1987, and routine, ongoing asset sales and loan prepayments at levels consistent with agency operations in fiscal year 1986;

(J) assuming that deferrals proposed during the period beginning October 1 of such fiscal year and ending with the snapshot date for such fiscal year shall not be taken into account in determining such budget baseline; and

(K) assuming that the transfer of Government actions from one fiscal year to another fiscal year, as described in section 202 of the Balanced Budget and Emergency Deficit Control Reaffirmation Act of 1987, shall not be taken into account except to the extent provided in such section.

Terms used in this paragraph shall have the meanings defined in sections 256 and 257.

(b) Dates for submission and printing of reports. Each report submitted under this section shall be submitted to the Federal Register on the day that it is issued and printed on the following day. If the date specified for the submission of a report by the Directors or its printing in the Federal Register under this section falls on a Sunday or legal holiday, such report shall be submitted or printed on the following day.

(c) Revised estimates, determinations, and reports.

(1) **Reports by CBO.**—On November 15 of fiscal year 1988 and on October 10 of subsequent fiscal years, the Director of CBO shall issue a revised report to Congress and the Director of OMB—

(A) indicating whether and to what extent, as a result of laws enacted and regulations promulgated as final after August 15 of the calendar year in which the fiscal year begins (or after October 10, 1987, in the case of the fiscal year 1988) the aggregate amount of required outlay reductions identified in the report submitted under subsection (a)(2)(A) has been eliminated, reduced, or increased,

(B) adjusting the determinations made under subsection (a)(2)(A) to the extent necessary, and

(C) specifying by programs, projects, and activities for defense accounts, the budget baseline from which reductions are taken and the amounts and percentages by which such programs, projects, and activities must be reduced.

(2) **Reports by OMB.**—On November 20 of fiscal year 1988 and on October 15 of subsequent fiscal years, the Director of OMB shall submit to the President and

the Congress a report revising the report issued under subsection (a)(2)(B), adjusting the estimates, determinations, and specifications contained in the report and taking into account for the purposes of required determinations and comparisons the revised report issued by the Director of CBO under paragraph (1). This report shall contain all of the determinations and comparisons required in, and shall be based on the same economic and technical assumptions, employ the same methodologies, and utilize the same definition of the budget baseline and the same criteria and guidelines as, the report issued under subsection (a)(2)(B), and shall provide for the determination of reductions in the manner specified in subsection (a)(3). In addition, this report shall specify by programs, projects, and activities for defense accounts, the budget baseline from which reductions are taken and the amounts by which such programs, projects, and activities must be reduced.

(d) Sequestration of defense programs.

(1) **Determination of Uniform Percentage.**—The total amount of reductions in outlays under defense programs required for a fiscal year under subsection (a)(3)(B) shall be calculated as a percentage of the total amount of outlays for the fiscal year estimated to result from new budget authority and unobligated balances for defense programs.

(2) **Sequestration of New Budget Authority and Unobligated Balances.**—

(A) Sequestration to achieve the required reduction in outlays under defense programs shall be made by reducing new budget authority and unobligated balances (if any) in each program, project, or activity under accounts within defense programs by the percentage determined under paragraph (1), computed on the basis of the combined outlay rate for new budget authority and unobligated balances for such program, project, or activity determined under subparagraph (B).

(B) If the outlay rate for unobligated balances is not available for any program, project, or activity, the outlay rate used shall be the outlay rate for new budget authority.

(3) **Flexibility with Respect to Military Personnel Accounts.**—

(A) Notwithstanding paragraphs (1) and (2), with respect to a fiscal year the President may, with respect to any military personnel account—

(i) exempt any program, project, or activity within such account from the order;

(ii) provide for a lower uniform percentage to be applied to reduce any program, project, or activity within such account than would otherwise apply; or

(iii) take actions described in both clauses (i) and (ii).

(B) If the President uses the authority under subparagraph (A), the total amount by which outlays are not reduced for such fiscal year in military personnel accounts by reason of the use of such authority shall be determined. Additional reductions in outlays under defense programs in such total amount shall be achieved by a uniform percentage sequestration of new budget authority and unobligated balances in each program, project, and activity within each account within major functional category 050 other than those military personnel accounts for which the authority provided under subparagraph (A) has been exercised, computed on the basis of the outlay rate for each such program, project, and activity determined under paragraphs (1) and (2).

(C) The President may not use the authority provided by subparagraph (A) unless he notifies the Congress on or before October 10, 1987, in the case of fiscal year 1988, or August 15 of the calendar year in which the fiscal year begins in the case of any subsequent fiscal year, of the manner in which such authority will be exercised. The Directors shall reflect the results of authority exercised under this paragraph in the reports required under section 251(a)(2).

(e) **Exception.** The preceding provisions of this section shall not apply if a declaration of war by the Congress is in effect.

§ 902. Presidential Order

(a) **Issuance of initial order.**

(1) **In General.**—On August 25 (or October 20, 1987, in the case of fiscal year 1988), following the submission of a report by the Director of OMB under section 251(a)(2)(B), the President, in strict accordance with the requirements of paragraph (2) and section 251(a)(3) and (4) and subject to the exemptions, exceptions, limitations, special rules, and definitions set forth in sections 255, 256, and 257, shall make all the reductions specified in such report by issuing an order that (notwithstanding the Impoundment Control Act of 1974)—

(A) in accordance with such report, suspends the operation of each provision of Federal law that would (but for such order) require an automatic spending increase to take effect during such fiscal year in such a manner as to prevent such increase from taking effect, or reduce such increase, in accordance with such report; and

(B) in accordance with such report, sequesters new budget authority; unobligated balances; new loan guarantee commitments or limitations; new direct loan obligations, commitments, or limitations; spending authority as defined in section 401(c)(2) of the Congressional Budget Act of 1974; and obligation limitations—

(i) for funds provided in annual appropriation Acts, from each affected program, project, and activity (as set forth in the most recently enacted applicable appropriation Acts and accompanying committee reports for the program, project, or activity involved, including joint resolutions providing continuing appropriations and committee reports accompanying Acts referred to in such resolutions), applying the same reduction percentage as the percentage by which the account involved is reduced in the report submitted under section 251(a)(2)(B) or from each affected budget account if the program, project, or activity is not so set forth, and

(ii) for funds not provided in annual appropriation Acts, from each budget account activity as identified in the program and financing schedules contained in the appendix to the Budget of the United States Government for that fiscal year, applying the same reduction percentage as the percentage by which the account is reduced in such report.

(2) **Order to be Based on Director of OMB's Report.**—The order must provide for reductions in the manner specified in section 251(a)(3), must incorporate the provisions of the report submitted under section 251(a)(2)(B), and must be consistent

with such report in all respects. The President may not modify or recalculate any of the estimates, determinations, specifications, bases, amounts, or percentages set forth in such report in determining the reductions to be specified in the order with respect to programs, projects, and activities, or with respect to budget activities, within an account.

(3) **Order Required if No Reductions Are Needed.**—If the report submitted under section 251(a)(2)(B) states that no aggregate outlay reductions are required for a fiscal year, the order issued by the President shall so state.

(4) **Effect of Sequestration Under Initial Order.**—

(A) **In General.**—Notwithstanding section 257(7), amounts sequestered under an order issued by the President under paragraph (1) shall be withheld from obligation or expenditure pending the issuance of a final order under subsection (b) and shall be permanently sequestered or reduced in accordance with such final order upon the issuance of such order.

(B) **Special Rule Concerning Reduction of Payments Under The Medicare Program.**—

(i) **In General.**—With respect to services furnished during the interim period (as defined in clause (iii)) for any fiscal year, and notwithstanding any other provision of this Act, payments under the health insurance programs under title XVIII of the Social Security Act shall not be reduced by an initial order under this subsection for that fiscal year.

(ii) **Director of OMB to Determine Annualized Percentage Reduction.**—The Director of OMB, in consultation with the Secretary of Health and Human Services, shall determine a percentage reduction which shall apply to payments under the health insurance programs under title XVIII of the Social Security Act for services furnished in any fiscal year after the interim period for that year, such that the reduction made in such payments under the final order under subsection (b) for that year shall achieve a total reduction of 2 percent (or, if lower, the uniform percentage reduction provided under section 251(a)(3)(E)(i)) in such payments for such fiscal year as determined on a 12-month basis.

(iii) **Interim Period.**—In this subparagraph, the term "interim period" means, with respect to a fiscal year, the period beginning on October 1 of the fiscal year and ending on the date of the issuance of the final order under subsection (b) with respect to that fiscal year.

(5) **Accompanying Message.**—Not later than the 15th day beginning after the President issues an initial order under paragraph (1) for any fiscal year, the President shall transmit to both Houses of Congress a single message containing all the information required by section 251(a)(4) and further specifying in strict accordance with paragraph (2)—

(A) within each account, for each program, project, and activity, or budget account activity, the base from which each sequestration or reduction is taken and the amounts which are to be sequestered or reduced for each such program, project, and activity or budget account activity; and

(B) such other supporting details as the President may determine to be appropriate.

Upon receipt in the Senate and the House of Representatives, the message (and any accompanying proposals made under subsection (c)(1)) shall be referred to all committees with jurisdiction over programs, projects, and activities affected by the order.

(6) **Effective Date of Initial Order.**—

(A) **Fiscal Year 1988.**—The order issued by the President under paragraph (1) with respect to fiscal year 1988 shall be effective as of the day it is issued (and the President shall withhold from obligation or expenditure as provided in paragraph (4), pending the issuance of the final order under subsection (b), any amounts that are sequestered under such order).

(B) **Fiscal Years 1989–1993.**—The order issued by the President under paragraph (1) with respect to the fiscal year 1989 or any subsequent fiscal year shall be effective as of October 1 of such fiscal year (and the President shall withhold from obligation or expenditure as provided in paragraph (4), pending the issuance of the final order under subsection (b), any amounts that are sequestered under such order).

(7) **Treatment of Automatic Spending Increases.**—

(A) **Fiscal Years 1987–1993.**—Notwithstanding any other provision of law, any automatic spending increase that would (but for this clause) be first paid during the period beginning with the first day of such fiscal year and ending with the date on which a final order is issued pursuant to subsection (b) shall be suspended until such final order becomes effective, and the amounts that would otherwise be expended during such period with respect to such increases shall be withheld. If such final order provides that automatic spending increases shall be reduced to zero during such fiscal year, the increases suspended pursuant to the preceding sentence and any legal rights thereto shall be permanently cancelled. If such final order provides for the payment of the full amount of such increases, the increases suspended pursuant to such sentence shall be restored to the extent necessary to pay such reduced or full increases, and lump-sum payments in the amounts necessary to pay such reduced or full increases shall be made, for the period for which such increases were suspended pursuant to this clause.

(B) **Prohibition Against Recoupment.**—Notwithstanding subparagraph (A), if an amount required to be withheld is paid, no recoupment shall be made against an individual to whom payment was made.

(C) **Effect of Lump-Sum Payments on Needs-Related Programs.**—Lump-sum payments made under the last sentence of subparagraph (A) shall not be considered as income or resources or otherwise taken into account in determining the eligibility of any individual for aid, assistance, or benefits under any Federal or federally assisted program which conditions such eligibility to any extent upon the income or resources of such individual or his or her family or household, or in determining the amount or duration of such aid, assistance, or benefits.

(b) **Issuance of final order.**

(1) **In General.**—October 15 of the fiscal year (or on November 20, 1987, in the case of fiscal year 1988), after the submission of the revised report by the Director of OMB under section 251(c)(2), the President shall issue a final order under this section to make all of the reductions and sequestrations specified in such report,

but only to the extent and in the manner provided in such report. The order issued under this subsection—

(A) shall include the same reductions and sequestrations as the initial order issued under subsection (a), adjusted to the extent necessary to take account of any changes in relevant amounts or percentages determined by the Director of OMB in the revised report submitted under section 251(c)(2), and shall include a reduction in payments under the health care programs under title XVIII of the Social Security Act determined in accordance with subsection (a)(4)(B)(ii),

(B) shall make such reductions and sequestrations in strict accordance with the requirements of sections 251(a)(3) and (4), and

(C) shall utilize the same criteria and guidelines as those which were used in the issuance of such initial order under subsection (a).

The provisions of section 251(a)(3) shall apply to the revised report submitted under section 251(c)(2) and to the order issued under this subsection in the same manner as such provisions apply to the initial report issued under section 251(a)(2)(B) and to the order issued under subsection (a).

(2) **Order Required If Deficit Reduction Is Achieved.**—If the Director of OMB issues a revised report under section 251(c)(2) stating that as a result of laws enacted and regulations promulgated as final after August 15 of the calendar year in which such fiscal year begins (or October 10, 1987, in the case of fiscal year 1988) no deficit reduction is necessary to fully satisfy the requirements of section 251(a)(3)(A), the order issued under this subsection shall so state and shall make available for obligation and expenditure any amounts withheld pursuant to subsection (a)(4) or (a)(7).

(3) **Effective Date of Final Order.**—

(A) The final order issued by the President under paragraph (1) shall become effective on the date of its issuance, and shall supersede the initial order issued under subsection (a)(1).

(B) Any modification or suspension by such order of the operation of a provision of law that would (but for such order) require an automatic spending increase to take effect during the fiscal year shall apply for the one-year period beginning with the date on which such automatic increase would have taken effect during such fiscal year (but for such order).

(4) **Accompanying Message.**—Not later than the 15th day beginning after the President issues a final order under paragraph (1) for any fiscal year, the President shall transmit to both Houses of Congress a single message in the same manner as, and containing all the information required by, subsection (a)(5).

(c) **Proposal of alternatives by the President.**

(1) **In General.**—A message transmitted pursuant to subsection (a)(5) with respect to a fiscal year may be accompanied by a proposal setting forth in full detail alternative ways to reduce the deficit for such fiscal year in an amount not less than the deficit reduction required under section 251(a)(3) for such fiscal year.

(2) **Flexibility Among Defense Programs, Projects, and Activities.**—

(A) Subject to subparagraphs (B), (C), and (D), and subsection (d), new budget authority and unobligated balances for any programs, projects, or activities within major functional category 050 (other than a military personnel account) may be further reduced beyond the amount specified in an order issued by the President under subsection (b)(1) for such fiscal year. To the extent such additional reductions are made and result in additional outlay reductions, the President may provide for lesser reductions in new budget authority and unobligated balances for other programs, projects, or activities within major functional category 050 for such fiscal year, but only to the extent that the resulting outlay increases do not exceed the additional outlay reductions, and no such program, project, or activity may be increased above the level actually made available by law in appropriation Acts (before taking sequestration into account). In making calculations under this subparagraph, the President shall use account outlay rates that are identical to those used in the report by the Director of OMB under section 251(c)(2).

(B) No actions taken by the President under subparagraph (A) for a fiscal year may result in a domestic base closure or realignment that would otherwise be subject to section 2687 of title 10, United States Code.

(C) The President may not exercise the authority provided by this paragraph for a fiscal year unless—

> (i) the President submits a single report to Congress specifying changes proposed to be made for such fiscal year pursuant to this paragraph; and

> (ii) a joint resolution affirming or modifying the changes proposed by the President pursuant to this paragraph becomes law.

(D) Within 5 calendar days of session after the President submits a report to Congress under subparagraph (C)(i) for a fiscal year, but before November 25, 1987, for fiscal year 1988 or, in the case of any subsequent fiscal year, before October 20 of such fiscal year, the majority leader of each House of Congress shall (by request) introduce a joint resolution which contains provisions affirming the changes proposed by the President pursuant to this paragraph.

(E)(i) The matter after the resolving clause in any joint resolution introduced pursuant to subparagraph (D) shall be as follows: "That the report of the President as submitted on [Insert Date] under section 252(c)(2)(C)(i) is hereby approved."

> (ii) The title of the joint resolution shall be "Joint resolution approving the report of the President submitted under section 252(c)(2)(C)(i) of the Balanced Budget and Emergency Deficit Control Act of 1985."

> (iii) Such joint resolution shall not contain any preamble.

(F)(i) A joint resolution introduced in the House of Representatives under subparagraph (D) shall be referred to the Committee on Appropriations, and if not reported within 5 calendar days (excluding Saturdays, Sundays, and legal holidays) from the date of introduction shall be considered as having been discharged therefrom and shall be placed on the appropriate calendar pending disposition of such joint resolution in accordance with this subsection.

> (ii) A joint resolution introduced in the Senate under subparagraph (D) shall be referred to the Committee on Appropriations, and if not reported within 5 calendar days (excluding Saturdays, Sundays, and legal holidays) from the date of introduction shall be considered as having been discharged therefrom and shall be placed on the appropriate calendar pending disposition of such

joint resolution in accordance with this subsection. In the Senate, no amendment made in the Committee on Appropriations shall be in order other than an amendment (in the nature of a substitute) that is germane or relevant to the provisions of the joint resolution or to the order issued under section 252(b)(1) insofar as they relate to major function 050 (national defense).

(iii) On or after the third calendar day (excluding Saturdays, Sundays, and legal holidays) beginning after a joint resolution is placed on the appropriate calendar, notwithstanding any rule or precedent of the Senate, including Rule 22 of the Standing Rules of the Senate, it is in order (even though a previous motion to the same effect has been disagreed to) for any Member of the respective House to move to proceed to the consideration of the joint resolution, and all points of order against the joint resolution (and against consideration of the joint resolution) are waived, except for points of order under titles III and IV of the Congressional Budget Act of 1974. The motion is not in order after the eighth calendar day (excluding Saturdays, Sundays, and legal holidays) beginning after such joint resolution is placed on the appropriate calendar. The motion is highly privileged in the House of Representatives and is privileged in the Senate and is not debatable. The motion is not subject to amendment, or to a motion to postpone, or to a motion to proceed to the consideration of other business. A motion to reconsider the vote by which the motion is agreed to or disagreed to shall not be in order. If a motion to proceed to the consideration of the joint resolution is agreed to, the respective House shall immediately proceed to consideration of the joint resolution without intervening motion, order, or other business, and the joint resolution shall remain the unfinished business of the respective House until disposed of.

(G)(i) In the Senate, debate on a joint resolution introduced under subparagraph (D), amendments thereto, and all debatable motions and appeals in connection therewith shall be limited to not more than 10 hours, which shall be divided equally between the majority leader and the minority leader (or their designees). In the House, general debate on a joint resolution introduced under subparagraph (D) shall be limited to not more than 4 hours which shall be equally divided between the chairman of the Committee on Appropriations and the ranking minority member of such committee.

(ii) A motion to postpone, or a motion to proceed to the consideration of other business is not in order. A motion to reconsider the vote by which the joint resolution is agreed to or disagreed to is not in order. In the Senate, a motion to recommit the joint resolution is not in order. In the House, a motion further to limit debate is in order and not debatable. In the House, a motion to recommit, with or without instructions, is in order.

(H)(i) In the House of Representatives, an amendment and any amendment to an amendment is debatable for not to exceed 30 minutes to be equally divided between the proponent of the amendment and a Member opposed thereto.

(ii) No amendment that is not germane or relevant to the provisions of the joint resolution or to the order issued under section 252(b)(1) insofar as they relate to major function 050 (national defense) shall be in order in the Senate. In the Senate, an amendment, any amendment to an amendment, or any debatable motion or appeal is debatable for not to exceed 30 minutes to be equally divided between the majority leader and the minority leader (or their designees).

(iii) In the Senate, an amendment that is otherwise in order shall be in order notwithstanding the fact that it amends the joint resolution in more than one place or amends language previously amended. It shall not be in order in the Senate to vote on the question of agreeing to such a joint resolution or any amendment thereto unless the figures then contained in such joint resolution or amendment are mathematically consistent.

(iv) It shall not be in order in the Senate to consider any amendment to any joint resolution introduced under subparagraph (D) or any conference report thereon if such amendment or conference report would have the effect of decreasing any specific budget outlay reductions below the level of such outlay reductions provided in such joint resolutions unless such amendment or conference report makes a reduction in other specific budget outlays at least equivalent to any increase in outlays provided by such amendment or conference report.

(v) For purposes of the application of clause (iv), the level of outlays and specific budget outlay reductions provided in an amendment shall be determined on the basis of estimates made by the Committee on the Budget of the Senate.

(I) Immediately following the conclusion of the debate on a joint resolution introduced under subparagraph (D), a single quorum call at the conclusion of the debate if requested in accordance with the rules of the appropriate House, and the disposition of any amendments under subparagraph (H) (except in the House of Representatives for the motion to recommit and the disposition of any amendment proposed in a motion to recommit which has been adopted), the vote on final passage of the joint resolution shall occur.

(J) Appeals from the decisions of the Chair relating to the application of the rules of the Senate or the House of Representatives, as the case may be, to the procedure relating to a joint resolution described in subparagraph (D) shall be decided without debate.

(K) In the Senate, points of order under titles III and IV of the Congressional Budget Act of 1974 (including points of order under sections 302(c), 303(a), 306, and 401(b)(1)) are applicable to a conference report on the joint resolution or any amendments in disagreement thereto.

(L) If, before the passage by the Senate of a joint resolution of the Senate introduced under subparagraph (D), the Senate receives from the House of Representatives a joint resolution introduced under subparagraph (D), then the following procedures shall apply:

(i) The joint resolution of the House of Representatives shall not be referred to a committee.

(ii) With respect to a joint resolution introduced under subparagraph (D) in the Senate—

(I) the procedure in the Senate shall be the same as if no joint resolution had been received from the House; but

(II) (aa) the vote on final passage shall be on the joint resolution of the House if it is identical to the joint resolution then pending for passage in the Senate; or

(bb) if the joint resolution from the House is not identical to the joint resolution then pending for passage in the Senate and the Senate then passes it, the Senate shall be considered to have passed the joint resolution as amended by the text of the Senate joint resolution.

(iii) Upon disposition of the joint resolution received from the House, it shall no longer be in order to consider the joint resolution originated in the Senate.

(M) If the Senate receives from the House of Representatives a joint resolution introduced under subparagraph (D) after the Senate has disposed of a Senate originated joint resolution which is identical to the House passed joint resolution, the action of the Senate with regard to the disposition of the Senate originated joint resolution shall be deemed to be the action of the Senate with regard to the House originated joint resolution. If it is not identical to the House passed joint resolution, then the Senate shall be considered to have passed the joint resolution of the House as amended by the text of the Senate joint resolution.

(d) Existing programs, projects, and activities not to be eliminated. No action taken by the President under subsection (a) or (b) of this section shall have the effect of eliminating any program, project, or activity of the Federal Government.

(e) Relative budget priorities not to be altered. Nothing in the preceding provisions of this section shall be construed to give the President new authority to alter the relative priorities in the Federal budget that are established by law, and no person who is or becomes eligible for benefits under any provision of law shall be denied eligibility by reason of any order issued under this part.

(f) Part-year appropriations.

(1) **Effect of Final Order on Part-Year Appropriation.**—If, at the time the President issues a final order for any fiscal year, there is in effect an Act making or continuing appropriations for part of the fiscal year for any budget account which is subject to reduction under the order, then the amount sequestered upon issuance of the order for that account shall be equal to the reduction amount for such account required by the final order multiplied by a fraction the numerator of which is the number of days during the fiscal year with respect to which the Act applies and the denominator of which is 365.

(2) **Effect of Subsequent Appropriation on Final Order.**—

(A) If, after the issuance of a final order for a fiscal year under subsection (b), an Act referred to in paragraph (1) is extended or an Act making or continuing appropriations for part of the fiscal year for the account is enacted, then additional amounts determined in the same manner shall be sequestered.

(B) Upon enactment of a full-year appropriation (including a continuing appropriation for the full year) for the account, the full amount of the sequestration specified by the final order, reduced by the sum of amounts previously sequestered and savings achieved by such appropriation measure when the amount enacted is less than the budget baseline for such account, shall be sequestered, except that the sum shall not exceed the amount specified in the final order for the account.

(3) **Effective Date of Sequestrations.**—Amounts required to be sequestered by the President under paragraph (1) or (2) shall be sequestered not later than the close of the fifth calendar day beginning after the date of enactment into law of the relevant Act referred to in paragraph (1) or (2).

(g) Printing of orders. Each initial order and final order issued under this section shall be submitted to the Federal Register on the date it is issued and printed on the following day. If the date specified for the issuance of an order or its printing in the Federal Register under this section falls on a Sunday or legal holiday, such order shall be issued or printed on the following day.

§ 903. Compliance report by Comptroller General

On or before November 15 of each fiscal year (or December 15, 1987, in the case of the fiscal year 1988), the Comptroller General shall submit to the Congress and the President a report on—

(1) the extent to which each order issued by the President under section 252 for such fiscal year complies with all of the requirements contained in section 252, either certifying that the order fully and accurately complies with such requirements or indicating the respects in which it does not;

(2) the extent to which each report of the Director of OMB under section 251 for such fiscal year complies with all of the requirements contained in this part, either certifying that the report fully and accurately complies with such requirements or indicating the respects in which it does not; and

(3) any recommendations of the Comptroller General for improving the procedures set forth in this part.

§ 904. Congressional action

(a) Special procedures in the event of a recession.

(1) **In General.**—The Director of the Congressional Budget Office shall notify the Congress at any time if—

(A) during the period consisting of the quarter during which such notification is given, the quarter preceding such notification, and the four quarters following such notification, such Office or the Office of Management and Budget has determined that real economic growth is projected or estimated to be less than zero with respect to each of any two consecutive quarters within such period, or

(B) the Department of Commerce preliminary reports of actual real economic growth (or any subsequent revision thereof) indicate that the rate of real economic growth for each of the most recent reported quarter and the immediately preceding quarter is less than one percent.

Upon such notification the Majority Leader of each House shall introduce a joint resolution (in the form set forth in paragraph (2)) declaring that the conditions specified in this paragraph are met and suspending the relevant provisions of this title for the remainder of the current fiscal year or for the following fiscal year or both.

(2) **Form of Joint Resolution.—**

(A) The matter after the resolving clause in any joint resolution introduced pursuant to paragraph (1) shall be as follows: "That the Congress declares that the conditions specified in section 254(a)(1) of the Balanced Budget and Emergency Deficit Control Act of 1985 [2 U.S.C. § 904(a)(1)] are met; and—

(i) the provisions of sections 3(7), 301(i), 302(f), 304(b), and 311(a) of the Congressional Budget and Impoundment Control Act of 1974 [2 U.S.C. §§ 622(7), 632(i), 633(f), 635(b), 642(a)], section 1106(c) of title 31, United States Code [31 U.S.C. § 1106(c)], and part C of the Balanced Budget and Emergency Deficit Control Act of 1985 [2 U.S.C. §§ 901 et seq.] are suspended for the remainder of the current fiscal year, and

(ii) the provisions of sections 3(7), 301(i), 304(b), and 311(a) [2 U.S.C. §§ 622(7), 632(i), 633(f), 642(a)] (insofar as it relates to section 3(7)) 622(7)] of the Congressional Budget and Impoundment Control Act of 1974, sections 302(f) and 311(a) [2 U.S.C. §§ 633(f), 642(a)] (except insofar as it relates to section 3(7)) of that Act [2 U.S.C. § 622(7)] (but only if a concurrent resolution on the budget under section 301 of that Act [2 U.S.C. § 632], for the fiscal year following the current fiscal year, has been agreed to prior to the introduction of this joint resolution), sections 1105(f) and 1106(c) of title 31, United States Code [31 U.S.C. §§ 1105(f), 1106(c)], and part C of the Balanced Budget and Emergency Deficit Control Act of 1985 [2 U.S.C. §§ 901 et seq.] are suspended for the fiscal year following the current fiscal year.

This joint resolution shall not have the effect of suspending any final order which was issued for the current fiscal year under section 252(b) of the Balanced Budget and Emergency Deficit Control Act of 1985 [2 U.S.C. § 902(b)] if such order was issued before the date of the enactment of this joint resolution."

(B) The title of the joint resolution shall be "Joint resolution suspending certain provisions of law pursuant to section 254(a)(2) of the Balanced Budget and Emergency Deficit Control Act of 1985 [2 U.S.C. § 904(a)(2)]."; and the joint resolution shall not contain any preamble.

(3) **Committee Action.**—Each joint resolution introduced pursuant to paragraph (1) shall be referred to the Committee on the Budget of the House involved; and such Committee shall report the joint resolution to its House without amendment on or before the fifth day on which such House is in session after the date on which the joint resolution is introduced. If the Committee fails to report the joint resolution within the five-day period referred to in the preceding sentence, it shall be automatically discharged from further consideration of the joint resolution, and the joint resolution shall be placed on the appropriate calendar.

(4) **Consideration of Joint Resolution.**—

(A) A vote on final passage of a joint resolution reported to a House of the Congress or discharged pursuant to paragraph (3) shall be taken on or before the close of the fifth calendar day of session of such House after the date on which the joint resolution is reported to such House or after the Committee has been discharged from further consideration of the joint resolution. If prior to the passage by one House of a joint resolution of that House, that House receives the same joint resolution from the other House, then—

(i) the procedure in that House shall be the same as if no such joint resolution had been received from the other House, but

(ii) the vote on final passage shall be on the joint resolution of the other House.

When the joint resolution is agreed to, the Clerk of the House of Representatives (in the case of a House joint resolution agreed to in the House of Representatives) or the Secretary of the Senate (in the case of a Senate joint resolution agreed to in the Senate) shall cause the joint resolution to be engrossed, certified, and transmitted to the other House of the Congress as soon as practicable.

(B)(i) A motion in the House of Representatives to proceed to the consideration of a joint resolution under this paragraph shall be highly privileged and not debatable. An amendment to the motion shall not be in order, nor shall it be in order to move to reconsider the vote by which the motion is agreed to or disagreed to.

(ii) Debate in the House of Representatives on a joint resolution under this paragraph shall be limited to not more than five hours, which shall be divided equally between those favoring and those opposing the joint resolution. A motion to postpone, made in the House of Representatives with respect to the consideration of a joint resolution under this paragraph, and a motion to proceed to the consideration of other business, shall not be in order. A motion further to limit debate shall not be debatable. It shall not be in order to move to table or to recommit a joint resolution under this paragraph or to move to reconsider the vote by which the joint resolution is agreed to or disagreed to.

(iii) All appeals from the decisions of the Chair relating to the application of the Rules of the House of Representatives to the procedure relating to a joint resolution under this paragraph shall be decided without debate.

(iv) Except to the extent specifically provided in the preceding provisions of this subsection or in subparagraph (D), consideration of a joint resolution under this subparagraph shall be governed by the Rules of the House of Representatives.

(C)(i) A motion in the Senate to proceed to the consideration of a joint resolution under this paragraph shall be privileged and not debatable. An amendment to the motion shall not be in order, nor shall it be in order to move to reconsider the vote by which the motion is agreed to or disagreed to.

(ii) Debate in the Senate on a joint resolution under this paragraph, and all debatable motions and appeals in connection therewith, shall be limited to not more than five hours. The time shall be equally divided between, and controlled by, the majority leader and the minority leader or their designees.

(iii) Debate in the Senate on any debatable motion or appeal in connection with a joint resolution under this paragraph shall be limited to not more than one hour, to be equally divided between, and controlled by, the mover and the manager of the joint resolution, except that in the event the manager of the joint resolution is in favor of any such motion or appeal, the time in opposition thereto shall be controlled by the minority leader or his designee.

(iv) A motion in the Senate to further limit debate on a joint resolution under this paragraph is not debatable. A motion to table or to recommit a joint resolution under this paragraph is not in order.

(D) No amendment to a joint resolution considered under this paragraph shall be in order in either the House of Representatives or the Senate.

(b) **Congressional response to Presidential order.**

(1) **Reporting of resolutions, and reconciliation bills and resolutions, in the Senate.—**

(A) Committee Alternatives to Presidential Order. Within two days after the submission of a report by the Director of OMB under section 251(c)(2), each standing committee of the Senate may submit to the Committee on the Budget of the Senate information of the type described in section 301(d) of the Congressional Budget Act of 1974 [2 U.S.C. § 632(d)] with respect to alternatives to the order envisioned by such report insofar as such order affects laws within the jurisdiction of the committee.

(B) **Initial Budget Committee Action.**—Not later than two days after issuance of a final order by the President under section 252(b) [2 U.S.C. § 902(b)] with respect to a fiscal year, the Committee on the Budget of the Senate may report to the Senate a resolution. The resolution may affirm the impact of the order issued under such section, in whole or in part. To the extent that any part of the order is not affirmed, the resolution shall state which parts are not affirmed and shall contain instructions to committees of the Senate of the type referred to in section 310(a) of the Congressional Budget Act of 1974 [2 U.S.C. § 641(a)], sufficient to achieve at least the total level of deficit reduction contained in those sections which are not affirmed.

(C) **Response of Committees.**—Committees instructed pursuant to subparagraph (B), or affected thereby, shall submit their responses to the Budget Committee no later than 10 days after the resolution referred to in subparagraph (B) is agreed to, except that if only one such Committee is so instructed such Committee shall, by the same date, report to the Senate a reconciliation bill or reconciliation resolution containing its recommendations in response to such instructions. A committee shall be considered to have complied with all instructions to it pursuant to a resolution adopted under subparagraph (B) if it has made recommendations with respect to matters within its jurisdiction which would result in a reduction in the deficit at least equal to the total reduction directed by such instructions.

(D) **Budget Committee Action.**—Upon receipt of the recommendations received in response to a resolution referred to in subparagraph (B), the Budget Committee shall report to the Senate a reconciliation bill or reconciliation resolution, or both, carrying out all such recommendations without any substantive revisions. In the event that a committee instructed in a resolution referred to in subparagraph (B) fails to submit any recommendation (or, when only one committee is instructed, fails to report a reconciliation bill or resolution) in response to such instructions, the Budget Committee shall include in the reconciliation bill or reconciliation resolution reported pursuant to this subparagraph legislative language within the jurisdiction of the noncomplying committee to achieve the amount of deficit reduction directed in such instructions.

(E) **Point of Order.**—It shall not be in order in the Senate to consider any reconciliation bill or reconciliation resolution reported under subparagraph (D) with respect to a fiscal year, any amendment thereto, or any conference report thereon if—

(i) the enactment of such bill or resolution as reported;

(ii) the adoption and enactment of such amendment; or

(iii) the enactment of such bill or resolution in the form recommended in such conference report, would cause the amount of the deficit for such fiscal year to exceed the maximum deficit amount for such fiscal year, and for fiscal year 1988 or 1989, exceed the amount of the estimated deficit for such fiscal year based on laws and regulations in effect on January 1 of the calendar year in which such fiscal year begins as measured using the budget baseline specified in section 251(a)(6) of the Balanced Budget and Emergency Deficit Control Act of 1985 minus $23,000,000,000 for fiscal year 1988 or $36,000,000,000 for fiscal year 1989;

unless the report submitted under section 251(c)(1) [2 U.S.C. § 901(c)(1)] projects negative real economic growth for such fiscal year, or for each of any two consecutive quarters during such fiscal year.

(F) **Treatment of Certain Amendments.**—In the Senate, an amendment which adds to a resolution reported under subparagraph (B) an instruction of the type referred to in such subparagraph shall be in order during the consideration of such resolution if such amendment would be in order but for the fact that it would be held to be nongermane on the basis that the instruction constitutes new matter.

(G) **Definition.**—For purposes of subparagraphs (A), (B), and (C), the term "day" shall mean any calendar day on which the Senate is in session.

(2) **Procedures.**

(A) **In General.**—Except as provided in subparagraph (B), in the Senate the provisions of sections 305 and 310 of the Congressional Budget Act of 1974 [2 U.S.C. §§ 636, 641] for the consideration of concurrent resolutions on the budget and conference reports thereon shall also apply to the consideration of resolutions, and reconciliation bills and reconciliation resolutions reported under this paragraph and conference reports thereon.

(B) **Limit on Debate.**—Debate in the Senate on any resolution reported pursuant to paragraph (1)(B), and all amendments thereto and debatable motions and appeals in connection therewith, shall be limited to 10 hours.

(C) **Limitation on Amendments.**—Section 310(d)(2) of the Congressional Budget Act [2 U.S.C. § 641(d)(2)] shall apply to reconciliation bills and reconciliation resolutions reported under this subsection.

(D) **Bills and resolutions received from the House.**—Any bill or resolution received in the Senate from the House, which is a companion to a reconciliation bill or reconciliation resolution of the Senate for the purposes of this subsection, shall be considered in the Senate pursuant to the provisions of this subsection.

(E) **Definition.**—For purposes of this subsection, the term "resolution" means a simple, joint, or concurrent resolution.

(c) **Certain resolutions treated as reconciliation bills.** Resolutions described in subsection (b) of this section and bills reported as a result thereof shall be considered in the Senate to be reconciliation bills or resolutions for purposes of the Congressional Budget Act of 1974.

§ 905. **Exempt programs and activities** [Omitted.]

§ 906. **Exceptions, limitations, and special rules** [Omitted.]

§ 907. **Definitions**

For purposes of this title:

(1) The term "automatic spending increase" (except as otherwise provided in sections 255 and 256 [2 U.S.C. §§ 905, 906]) means increases in budget outlays due to changes in indexes in the following Federal programs: National Wool Act (12-4336-0-3-351); Special milk program (12-3502-0-1-605); and Vocational rehabilitation (91-0301-0-1-506). For purposes of the preceding provisions of this paragraph, programs are identified by the designated budget account identification code numbers set forth in the Budget of the United States Government, 1986—Appendix.

(2) The terms "budget outlays" and "budget authority" have the meaning given to such terms in sections 3(1) and 3(2), respectively, of the Congressional Budget and Impoundment Control Act of 1974 [2 U.S.C. § 622(1), (2)].

(3) The term "concurrent resolution on the budget" has the meaning given to such term in section 3(4) of the Congressional Budget and Impoundment Control Act of 1974 [2 U.S.C. § 622(4)].

(4) The term "deficit" has the meaning given to such term in section 3(6) of the Congressional Budget and Impoundment Control Act of 1974 [2 U.S.C. § 622(6)].

(5) The term "maximum deficit amount," with respect to any fiscal year, means the maximum deficit amount for such fiscal year determined under section 3(7) of the Congressional Budget and Impoundment Control Act of 1974 [2 U.S.C. § 622(7)].

(6) The term "real economic growth," with respect to any fiscal year, means the growth in the gross national product during such fiscal year, adjusted for inflation, consistent with Department of Commerce definitions.

(7) The terms "sequester" and "sequestration" (subject to section 252(a)(4)) refer to or mean the reduction or cancellation of new budget authority; unobligated balances, new loan guarantee commitments or limitations; new direct loan obligations, commitments, or limitations; spending authority as defined in section 401(c)(2) of the Congressional Budget Act of 1974; and obligation limitations.

(8) The term "account" means an item for which appropriations are made in any appropriation Act used to determine the budget base, and, for items not provided for in appropriation Acts, such term means an item for which there is a designated budget account identification code number in the Appendix to the President's budget.

(9) The term "sequesterable resource" means new budget authority; unobligated balances; new loan guarantee commitments or limitations; new direct loan obligations, commitments, or limitations; spending authority as defined in section 401(c)(2) of the Congressional Budget Act of 1974; and obligation limitations for budget accounts, programs, projects, and activities that are not exempt from reduction or sequestration under this part.

(10) The term "margin" means $10,000,000,000 with respect to each of fiscal years 1988 through 1992 and zero with respect to fiscal year 1993.

. . .

(12) The sale of an asset means the sale to the public of any asset, whether physical or financial, owned in whole or in part by the United States. The term "prepayment of a loan" means payments to the United States made in advance of the schedules set by law or contract when the financial asset is first acquired, such as the pre-

payment to the Federal Financing Bank of loans guaranteed by the Rural Electrification Administration. If a law or contract allows a flexible payment schedule, the term "in advance" shall mean in advance of the slowest payment schedule allowed under such law or contract.

(13) The term "outlay rate," with respect to any budget account, program, project, or activity, means—

   (A) the ratio of outlays resulting in the fiscal year involved from new budgetary resources for such budget account, program, project, or activity to such new budgetary resources; or

   (B) the ratio of outlays resulting in the fiscal year involved from unobligated balances for such budget account, program, project, or activity to such unobligated balances.

(14) The term "combined outlay rate," with respect to any budget account, program, project, or activity, means the weighted average (by budgetary resources) of the ratios determined under subparagraphs (A) and (B) of paragraph (13) for such budget account, program, project, or activity.

§ 908. Modification of Presidential order

(a) **Introduction of joint resolution.** At any time after the Director of OMB issues a report under section 251(c)(2) for a fiscal year, but before the close of the tenth calendar day of session in that session of Congress beginning after the date of issuance of such report, the majority leader of either House of Congress may introduce a joint resolution which contains provisions directing the President to modify the most recent order issued under section 252 for such fiscal year. After the introduction of the first such joint resolution in either House of Congress in any calendar year, then no other joint resolution introduced in such House in such calendar year shall be subject to the procedures set forth in this section.

(b) **Procedures for consideration of joint resolutions.**

   (1) **No Referral to Committee.**—A joint resolution introduced in the Senate or the House of Representatives under subsection (a) shall not be referred to a committee of the Senate or the House of Representatives, as the case may be, and shall be placed on the appropriate calendar pending disposition of such joint resolution in accordance with this subsection.

   (2) **Immediate Consideration.**—On or after the third calendar day (excluding Saturdays, Sundays, and legal holidays) beginning after a joint resolution is introduced under subsection (a), notwithstanding any rule or precedent of the Senate, including Rule 22 of the Standing Rules of the Senate, it is in order (even though a previous motion to the same effect has been disagreed to) for any Member of the respective House to move to proceed to the consideration of the joint resolution, and all points of order against the joint resolution (and against consideration of the joint resolution) are waived, except for points of order under titles III or IV of the Congressional Budget Act of 1974. The motion is not in order after the eighth calendar day (excluding Saturdays, Sundays, and legal holidays) beginning after a joint resolution (to which the motion applies) is introduced. The motion is highly privileged in the House of Representatives and is privileged in the Senate and is not debatable. The motion is not subject to amendment, or to a motion to postpone,

or to a motion to proceed to the consideration of other business. A motion to reconsider the vote by which the motion is agreed to or disagreed to shall not be in order. If a motion to proceed to the consideration of the joint resolution is agreed to, the respective House shall immediately proceed to consideration of the joint resolution without intervening motion, order, or other business, and the joint resolution shall remain the unfinished business of the respective House until disposed of.

(3) **Debate.**—

(A) In the Senate, debate on a joint resolution introduced under subsection (a), amendments thereto, and all debatable motions and appeals in connection therewith shall be limited to not more than 10 hours, which shall be divided equally between the majority leader and the minority leader (or their designees). In the House, general debate on a joint resolution introduced under subsection (a) shall be limited to not more than 4 hours which shall be equally divided between the majority and minority leaders.

(B) A motion to postpone, or a motion to proceed to the consideration of other business is not in order. A motion to reconsider the vote by which the joint resolution is agreed to or disagreed to is not in order. In the Senate, a motion to recommit the joint resolution is not in order. In the House, a motion further to limit debate is in order and not debatable. In the House, a motion to recommit is in order.

(C) (i) In the House of Representatives, an amendment and any amendment thereto is debatable for not to exceed 30 minutes to be equally divided between the proponent of the amendment and a Member opposed thereto.

(ii) No amendment that is not germane or relevant to the provisions of the joint resolution or to the order issued under section 252(b)(1) shall be in order in the Senate. In the Senate, an amendment, any amendment to an amendment, or any debatable motion or appeal is debatable for not to exceed 30 minutes to be equally divided between the majority leader and the minority leader (or their designees).

(iii) In the Senate, an amendment that is otherwise in order shall be in order notwithstanding the fact that it amends the joint resolution in more than one place or amends language previously amended. It shall not be in order in the Senate to vote on the question of agreeing to such a joint resolution or any amendment thereto unless the figures then contained in such joint resolution or amendment are mathematically consistent.

(4) **Vote on Final Passage.**—Immediately following the conclusion of the debate on a joint resolution introduced under subsection (a), a single quorum call at the conclusion of the debate if requested in accordance with the rules of the appropriate House, and the disposition of any amendments under paragraph (3) (except for the motion to recommit in the House of Representatives), the vote on final passage of the joint resolution shall occur.

(5) **Appeals.**—Appeals from the decisions of the Chair relating to the application of the rules of the Senate or the House of Representatives, as the case may be, to the procedure relating to a joint resolution described in subsection (a) shall be decided without debate.

(6) **Conference Reports.**—In the Senate, points of order under titles III and IV of the Congressional Budget Act of 1974 (including points of order under sections 302(c), 303(a), 306, and 401(b)(1)) are applicable to a conference report on the joint resolution or any amendments in disagreement thereto.

(7) **Resolution from Other House.**—If, before the passage by the Senate of a joint resolution of the Senate introduced under subsection (a), the Senate receives from the House of Representatives a joint resolution introduced under subsection (a), then the following procedures shall apply:

(A) The joint resolution of the House of Representatives shall not be referred to a committee.

(B) With respect to a joint resolution introduced under subsection (a) in the Senate—

(i) the procedure in the Senate shall be the same as if no joint resolution had been received from the House; but

(ii)(I) the vote on final passage shall be on the joint resolution of the House if it is identical to the joint resolution then pending for passage in the Senate; or

(II) if the joint resolution from the House is not identical to the joint resolution then pending for passage in the Senate and the Senate then passes it, the Senate shall be considered to have passed the joint resolution as amended by the text of the Senate joint resolution.

(C) Upon disposition of the joint resolution received from the House, it shall no longer be in order to consider the resolution originated in the Senate.

(8) **Senate Action on House Resolution.**—If the Senate receives from the House of Representatives a joint resolution introduced under subsection (a) after the Senate has disposed of a Senate originated resolution which is identical to the House passed joint resolution, the action of the Senate with regard to the disposition of the Senate originated joint resolution shall be deemed to be the action of the Senate with regard to the House originated joint resolution. If it is not identical to the House passed joint resolution, then the Senate shall be considered to have passed the joint resolution of the House as amended by the text of the Senate joint resolution.

§ 909. Prohibition of counting as savings the transfer of government actions from one year to another

(a) **In general.** Except as otherwise provided in this section, any law or regulation that has the effect of transferring an outlay, receipt, or revenue of the United States from one fiscal year to an adjacent fiscal year shall not be treated as altering the deficit or producing net deficit reduction in any fiscal year for purposes of the Congressional Budget Act of 1974 and the Balanced Budget and Emergency Deficit Control Act of 1985.

(b) **Exceptions.** Subsection (a) shall not apply if the law making the transfer stipulates that such transfer—

(1) is a necessary (but secondary) result of a significant policy change;

(2) provides for contingencies; or

(3) achieves savings made possible by changes in program requirements or by greater efficiency of operations.

§ 921. Revenue estimates [Omitted.]

§ 922. Judicial review

(a) **Expedited review.**

(1) Any Member of Congress may bring an action, in the United States District Court for the District of Columbia, for declaratory judgment and injunctive relief on the ground that any order that might be issued pursuant to section 252 [2 U.S.C. § 902] violates the Constitution.

(2) Any Member of Congress, or any other person adversely affected by any action taken under this title, may bring an action, in the United States District Court for the District of Columbia, for declaratory judgment and injunctive relief concerning the constitutionality of this title.

(3) Any Member of Congress may bring an action, in the United States District Court for the District of Columbia, for declaratory and injunctive relief on the ground that the terms of an order issued under section 252 [2 U.S.C. § 902] do not comply with the requirements of this title.

(4) A copy of any complaint in an action brought under paragraph (1), (2), or (3) shall be promptly delivered to the Secretary of the Senate and the Clerk of the House of Representatives, and each House of Congress shall have the right to intervene in such action.

(5) Any action brought under paragraph (1), (2), or (3) shall be heard and determined by a three-judge court in accordance with section 2284 of title 28, United States Code [28 U.S.C. § 2284].

Nothing in this section or in any other law shall infringe upon the right of the House of Representatives to intervene in an action brought under paragraph (1), (2), or (3) without the necessity of adopting a resolution to authorize such intervention.

(b) **Appeal to Supreme Court.** Notwithstanding any other provision of law, any order of the United States District Court for the District of Columbia which is issued pursuant to an action brought under paragraph (1), (2), or (3) of subsection (a) shall be reviewable by appeal directly to the Supreme Court of the United States. Any such appeal shall be taken by a notice of appeal filed within 10 days after such order is entered; and the jurisdictional statement shall be filed within 30 days after such order is entered. No stay of an order issued pursuant to an action brought under paragraph (1), (2), or (3) of subsection (a) shall be issued by a single Justice of the Supreme Court.

(c) **Expedited consideration.** It shall be the duty of the District Court for the District of Columbia and the Supreme Court of the United States to advance on the docket and to expedite to the greatest possible extent the disposition of any matter brought under subsection (a).

(d) **Noncompliance with sequestration procedures.**

(1) If it is finally determined by a court of competent jurisdiction that an order issued by the President under section 252(b) [2 U.S.C. § 902(b)] for any fiscal year—

(A) does not reduce automatic spending increases under any program specified in section 257(1) [2 U.S.C. § 907(1)] to the extent that such increases are required to be reduced by part C of this title [2 U.S.C. §§ 901 et seq.] (or reduces such increases by a greater extent than is so required),

(B) does not sequester the amount of new budget authority, new loan guarantee commitments, new direct loan obligations, or spending authority which is required to be sequestered by such part (or sequesters more than that amount) with respect to any program, project, activity, or account, or

(C) does not reduce obligation limitations by the amount by which such limitations are required to be reduced under such part (or reduces such limitations by more than that amount) with respect to any program, project, activity, or account,

the President shall, within 20 days after such determination is made, revise the order in accordance with such determination.

(2) If the order issued by the President under section 252(b) [2 U.S.C. § 902(b)] for any fiscal year—

(A) does not reduce any automatic spending increase to the extent that such increase is required to be reduced by part C of this title [2 U.S.C. §§ 901 et seq.],

(B) does not sequester any amount of new budget authority, new loan guarantee commitments, new direct loan obligations, or spending authority which is required to be sequestered by such part [2 U.S.C. §§ 901 et seq.], or

(C) does not reduce any obligation limitation by the amount by which such limitation is required to be reduced under such part [2 U.S.C. §§ 901 et seq.],

on the claim or defense that the constitutional powers of the President prevent such sequestration or reduction or permit the avoidance of such sequestration or reduction, and such claim or defense is finally determined by the Supreme Court of the United States to be valid, then the entire order issued pursuant to section 252(b) [2 U.S.C. § 902(b)] for such fiscal year shall be null and void.

(e) **Timing of relief.** No order of any court granting declaratory or injunctive relief from the order of the President issued under section 252 [2 U.S.C. § 902], including but not limited to relief permitting or requiring the expenditure of funds sequestered by such order, shall take effect during the pendency of the action before such court, during the time appeal may be taken, or, if appeal is taken, during the period before the court to which such appeal is taken has entered its final order disposing of such action.

(f) **Alternative procedures for the joint reports of the directors.**

(1) In the event that any of the reporting procedures described in section 251 are invalidated, then any report of the Director of CBO under section 251(a)(2)(A) or 251(c)(1) shall be transmitted to the joint committee established under this subsection.

(2) Upon the invalidation of any such procedure there is established a Temporary Joint Committee on Deficit Reduction, composed of the entire membership of the Budget Committees of the House of Representatives and the Senate. The Chairman of these two committees shall act as Co-Chairmen of the Joint Committee. Actions taken by the Joint Committee shall be determined by the majority vote of the

members representing each House. The purposes of the Joint Committee are to receive the reports of the Director of CBO as described in paragraph (1), and to report (with respect to each such report of the Director of CBO) a joint resolution as described in paragraph (3).

(3) No later than 5 days after the receipt of a report of the Director of CBO in accordance with paragraph (1), the Joint Committee shall report to the House of Representatives and the Senate a joint resolution setting forth the contents of the report of the Director of CBO.

(4) The provisions relating to the consideration of a joint resolution under section 254(a)(4) [2 U.S.C. § 904(a)(4)] shall apply to the consideration of a joint resolution reported pursuant to this subsection in the House of Representatives and the Senate, except that debate in each House shall be limited to two hours.

(5) Upon its enactment, the joint resolution shall be deemed to be the report received by the President under section 251(a)(2)(B) or (c)(2) (whichever is applicable).

(g) Preservation of other rights. The rights created by this section are in addition to the rights of any person under law, subject to subsection (e).

(h) Economic data, assumptions, and methodologies. The economic data and economic assumptions, used by the Director of OMB in computing the base levels of total revenues and total budget outlays, as specified in any report issued by the Director of OMB under section 251(a)(2)(B) or (c)(2) shall not be subject to review in any judicial or administrative proceeding.

TITLE 3—THE PRESIDENT
Delegation of Functions

§ 301. General authorization to delegate functions; publication of delegations

The President of the United States is authorized to designate and empower the head of any department or agency in the executive branch, or any official thereof who is required to be appointed by and with the advice and consent of the Senate, to perform without approval, ratification, or other action by the President (1) any function which is vested in the President by law, or (2) any function which such officer is required or authorized by law to perform only with or subject to the approval, ratification, or other action of the President: Provided, That nothing contained herein shall relieve the President of his responsibility in office for the acts of any such head or other official designated by him to perform such functions. Such designation and authorization shall be in writing, shall be published in the Federal Register, shall be subject to such terms, conditions, and limitations as the President may deem advisable, and shall be revocable at any time by the President in whole or in part.

§ 302. Scope of delegation of functions

The authority conferred by this chapter [3 U.S.C. §§ 301 et seq.] shall apply to any function vested in the President by law if such law does not affirmatively prohibit delegation of the performance of such function as herein provided for, or specifically designate the officer or officers to whom it may be delegated. This chapter [3 U.S.C. §§ 301 et seq.] shall not be deemed to limit or derogate from any existing or inherent right of the President to delegate the performance of functions vested in him by law, and nothing herein shall be deemed to require express authorization in any case in which such an official would be presumed in law to have acted by authority or direction of the President.

§ 303. Definitions

As used in this chapter [3 U.S.C. §§ 301 et seq.], the term "function" embraces any duty, power, responsibility, authority, or discretion vested in the President or other officer concerned, and the terms "perform" and "performance" may be construed to mean "exercise."

TITLE 5—GOVERNMENT OPERATIONS AND EMPLOYEES
Pay Administration

§ 5503. Recess appointments

(a) Payment for services may not be made from the Treasury of the United States to an individual appointed during a recess of the Senate to fill a vacancy in an existing office, if the vacancy existed while the Senate was in session and was by law required to be filled by and with the advice and consent of the Senate, until the appointee has been confirmed by the Senate. This subsection does not apply—

(1) if the vacancy arose within 30 days before the end of the session of the Senate;

(2) if, at the end of the session, a nomination for the office, other than the nomination of an individual appointed during the preceding recess of the Senate, was pending before the Senate for its advice and consent; or

(3) if a nomination for the office was rejected by the Senate within 30 days before the end of the session and an individual other than the one whose nomination was rejected thereafter receives a recess appointment.

(b) A nomination to fill a vacancy referred to by paragraph (1), (2), or (3) of subsection (a) of this section shall be submitted to the Senate not later than 40 days after the beginning of the next session of the Senate.

Antidiscrimination; Right to Petition Congress

§ 7211. Employees' right to petition Congress

The right of employees, individually or collectively, to petition Congress or a Member of Congress, or to furnish information to either House of Congress, or to a committee or Member thereof, may not be interfered with or denied.

TITLE 18—CRIMES AND CRIMINAL PROCEDURE
Espionage and Censorship

§ 793. Gathering, transmitting, or losing defense information

(a) Whoever, for the purpose of obtaining information respecting the national defense with intent or reason to believe that the information is to be used to the injury of the United States, or to the advantage of any foreign nation, goes upon, enters, flies over, or otherwise obtains information concerning any vessel, aircraft, work of defense, navy yard, naval station, submarine base, fueling station, fort, battery, torpedo station, dockyard, canal, railroad, arsenal, camp, factory, mine, telegraph, telephone, wireless, or signal station, building, office, research laboratory or station or other place connected with the national defense owned or constructed, or in progress of construction by the United States or under the control of the United States, or of any of its officers, departments, or agencies, or within the exclusive jurisdiction of the United States, or any place in which any vessel, aircraft, arms, munitions, or other materials or instruments for use in time of war are being made, prepared, repaired, stored, or are the subject of research or development, under any contract or agreement with the United States, or any department or agency thereof, or with any person on behalf of the United States, or otherwise on behalf of the United States, or any prohibited place so designated by the President by proclamation in time of war or in case of national emergency in which anything for the use of the Army, Navy, or Air Force is being prepared or constructed or stored, information as to which prohibited place the President has determined would be prejudicial to the national defense; or

(b) Whoever, for the purpose aforesaid, and with like intent or reason to believe, copies, takes, makes, or obtains, or attempts, to copy, take, make, or obtain any sketch, photograph, photographic negative, blueprint, plan, map, model, instrument, appliance, document, writing, or note of anything connected with the national defense; or

(c) Whoever, for the purpose aforesaid, receives or obtains or agrees or attempts to receive or obtain from any person, or from any source whatever, any document, writing, code book, signal book, sketch, photograph, photographic negative, blueprint, plan, map, model, instrument, appliance, or note, of anything connected with the national defense, knowing or having reason to believe, at the time he receives or obtains, or agrees or attempts to receive or obtain it, that it has been or will be obtained, taken, made, or disposed of by any person contrary to the provisions of this chapter [18 U.S.C. §§ 792 et seq.]; or

(d) Whoever, lawfully having possession of, access to, control over, or being entrusted with any document, writing, code book, signal book, sketch, photograph, photographic negative, blueprint, plan, map, model, instrument, appliance, or note relating to the national defense, or information relating to the national defense which information the possessor has reason to believe could be used to the injury of the United States or to the advantage of any foreign nation, willfully communicates, delivers, transmits or causes to be communicated, delivered, or transmitted or attempts to communicate, deliver, transmit or cause to be communicated, delivered or transmitted the same to any person not entitled to receive it, or willfully retains the same and fails to deliver it on demand to the officer or employee of the United States entitled to receive it; or

(e) Whoever having unauthorized possession of, access to, or control over any document, writing, code book, signal book, sketch, photograph, photographic negative, blueprint, plan, map, model, instrument, appliance, or note relating to the national defense, or information relating to the national defense which information the possessor has reason to believe could be used to the injury of the United States or to the advantage of any foreign nation, willfully communicates, delivers, transmits or causes to be communicated, delivered, or transmitted, or attempts to communicate, deliver, transmit or cause to be communicated, delivered, or transmitted the same to any person not entitled to receive it, or willfully retains the same and fails to deliver it to the officer or employee of the United States entitled to receive it; or

(f) Whoever, being entrusted with or having lawful possession or control of any document, writing, code book, signal book, sketch, photograph, photographic negative, blueprint, plan, map, model, instrument, appliance, note, or information, relating to the national defense, (1) through gross negligence permits the same to be removed from its proper place of custody or delivered to anyone in violation of his trust, or to be lost, stolen, abstracted, or destroyed, or (2) having knowledge that the same has been illegally removed from its proper place of custody or delivered to anyone in violation of his trust, or lost, or stolen, abstracted, or destroyed, and fails to make prompt report of such loss, theft, abstraction, or destruction to his superior officer—

Shall be fined not more than $10,000 or imprisoned not more than ten years, or both.

(g) If two or more persons conspire to violate any of the foregoing provisions of this section, and one or more of such persons do any act to effect the object of the conspiracy, each of the parties to such conspiracy shall be subject to the punishment provided for the offense which is the object of such conspiracy.

(h)(1) Any person convicted of a violation of this section shall forfeit to the United States, irrespective of any provision of State law, any property constituting, or derived from, any proceeds the person obtained, directly or indirectly, from any foreign government, or any faction or party or military or naval force within a foreign country, whether recognized or unrecognized by the United States, as the result of such violation.

(2) The court, in imposing sentence on a defendant for a conviction of a violation of this section, shall order that the defendant forfeit to the United States all property described in paragraph (1) of this subsection.

(3) The provisions of subsections (b), (c), and (e) through (o) of section 413 of the Comprehensive Drug Abuse Prevention and Control Act of 1970 (21 U.S.C. 853(b), (c) and (e)-(o) [21 U.S.C. § 853(b), (c), (e)-(o)] shall apply to—

(A) property subject to forfeiture under this subsection;

(B) any seizure or disposition of such property; and

(C) any administrative or judicial proceeding in relation to such property, if not inconsistent with this subsection.

(4) Notwithstanding section 524(c) of title 28 [28 U.S.C. § 524(c)], there shall be deposited in the Crime Victims Fund in the Treasury all amounts from the forfeiture

of property under this subsection remaining after the payment of expenses for forfeiture and sale authorized by law.

Obstruction of Justice

§ 1505. Obstruction of proceedings before departments, agencies, and committees

Whoever, with intent to avoid, evade, prevent, or obstruct compliance, in whole or in part, with any civil investigative demand duly and properly made under the Antitrust Civil Process Act [15 U.S.C. §§ 1311 et seq.], willfully withholds, misrepresents, removes from any place, conceals, covers up, destroys, mutilates, alters, or by other means falsifies any documentary material, answers to written interrogatories, or oral testimony, which is the subject of such demand; or attempts to do so or solicits another to do so; or whoever corruptly, or by threats or force, or by any threatening letter or communication influences, obstructs, or impedes or endeavors to influence, obstruct, or impede the due and proper administration of the law under which any pending proceeding is being had before any department or agency of the United States, or the due and proper exercise of the power of inquiry under which any inquiry or investigation is being had by either House, or any committee of either House or any joint committee of the Congress—

Shall be fined not more than $5,000 or imprisoned not more than five years, or both.

TITLE 22 —FOREIGN RELATIONS AND INTERCOURSE
Foreign Assistance

§ 2370. Prohibitions against furnishing assistance

Nationalization, expropriation or seizure of property of United States citizens, or taxation or other exaction having same effect; failure to compensate or to provide relief from taxes, exactions, or conditions; report on full value of property by Foreign Claims Settlement Commission; act of state doctrine

(e)(2) Notwithstanding any other provision of law, no court in the United States shall decline on the ground of the federal act of state doctrine to make a determination on the merits giving effect to the principles of international law in a case in which a claim of title or other right to property is asserted by any party including a foreign state (or a party claiming through such state) based upon (or traced through) a confiscation or other taking after January 1, 1959, by an act of that state in violation of the principles of international law, including the principles of compensation and the other standards set out in this subsection: *Provided*, That this subparagraph shall not be applicable (1) in any case in which an act of a foreign state is not contrary to international law or with respect to a claim of title or other right to property acquired pursuant to an irrevocable letter of credit of not more than 180 days duration issued in good faith prior to the time of the confiscation or other taking, or (2) in any case with respect to which the President determines that application of the act of state doctrine is required in that particular case by the foreign policy interests of the United States and a suggestion to this effect is filed on his behalf in that case with the court.

TITLE 28—JUDICIARY AND JUDICIAL PROCEDURE
The Attorney General

§ 511. Attorney General to advise the President

The Attorney General shall give his advice and opinion on questions of law when required by the President.

§ 512. Attorney General to advise heads of executive departments

The head of an executive department may require the opinion of the Attorney General on questions of law arising in the administration of his department.

§ 513. Attorney General to advise Secretaries of military departments

When a question of law arises in the administration of the Department of the Army, the Department of the Navy, or the Department of the Air Force, the cognizance of which is not given by statute to some other officer from whom the Secretary of the military department concerned may require advice, the Secretary of the military department shall send it to the Attorney General for disposition.

§ 514. Legal services on pending claims in departments and agencies

When the head of an executive department or agency is of the opinion that the interests of the United States require the service of counsel on the examination of any witness concerning any claim, or on the legal investigation of any claim, pending in the department or agency, he shall notify the Attorney General, giving all facts necessary to enable him to furnish proper professional service in attending the examination or making the investigation, and the Attorney General shall provide for the service.

§ 515. Authority for legal proceedings; commission, oath, and salary for special attorneys

(a) The Attorney General or any other officer of the Department of Justice, or any attorney specially appointed by the Attorney General under law, may, when specifically directed by the Attorney General, conduct any kind of legal proceeding, civil or criminal, including grand jury proceedings and proceedings before committing magistrates, which United States attorneys are authorized by law to conduct, whether or not he is a resident of the district in which the proceeding is brought.

(b) Each attorney specially retained under authority of the Department of Justice shall be commissioned as special assistant to the Attorney General or special attorney, and shall take the oath required by law. Foreign counsel employed in special cases are not required to take the oath. The Attorney General shall fix the annual salary of a special assistant or special attorney at not more than $12,000.

§ 516. Conduct of litigation reserved to Department of Justice

Except as otherwise authorized by law, the conduct of litigation in which the United States, an agency, or officer thereof is a party, or is interested, and securing evidence therefor, is reserved to officers of the Department of Justice, under the direction of the Attorney General.

§ 517. Interests of United States in pending suits

The Solicitor General, or any officer of the Department of Justice, may be sent by the Attorney General to any State or district in the United States to attend to the interests of the United States in a suit pending in a court of the United States, or in a court of a State, or to attend to any other interest of the United States.

§ 518. Conduct and argument of cases

(a) Except when the Attorney General in a particular case directs otherwise, the Attorney General and the Solicitor General shall conduct and argue suits and appeals in the Supreme Court and suits in the United States Claims Court or in the United States Court of Appeals for the Federal Circuit and in the Court of International Trade in which the United States is interested.

(b) When the Attorney General considers it in the interests of the United States, he may personally conduct and argue any case in a court of the United States in which the United States is interested, or he may direct the Solicitor General or any officer of the Department of Justice to do so.

§ 519. Supervision of litigation

Except as otherwise authorized by law, the Attorney General shall supervise all litigation to which the United States, an agency, or officer thereof is a party, and shall direct all United States attorneys, assistant United States attorneys, and special attorneys appointed under section 543 of this title in the discharge of their respective duties.

Independent Counsel

§ 591. Applicability of provisions of this chapter

(a) **Preliminary investigation with respect to certain covered persons.**—The Attorney General shall conduct a preliminary investigation in accordance with section 592 whenever the Attorney General receives information sufficient to constitute grounds to investigate whether any person described in subsection (b) of this section may have violated any Federal criminal law other than a violation classified as a Class B or C misdemeanor or an infraction.

(b) Persons to whom subsection (a) applies.—The persons referred to in subsection (a) of this section are—

(1) The President and Vice President;

(2) any individual serving in a position listed in section 5312 of title 5;

(3) any individual working in the Executive Office of the President who is compensated at a rate of pay at or above level II of the Executive Schedule under section 5313 of title 5;

(4) any Assistant Attorney General and any individual working in the Department of Justice who is compensated at a rate of pay at or above level III of the Executive Schedule under section 5314 of title 5;

(5) The Director of Central Intelligence, the Deputy Director of Central Intelligence, and the Commissioner of Internal Revenue;

(6) any individual who leaves any office or position described in any of paragraphs (1) through (5) of this subsection, during the incumbency of the President under whom such individual served in the office or position plus one year after such incumbency, but in no event longer than a period of three years after the individual leaves the office or position;

(7) any individual who held an office or position described in any of paragraphs (1) through (5) of this subsection during the incumbency of one President and who continued to hold the office or position for not more than 90 days into the term of the next President, during the 1-year period after the individual leaves the office or position; and

(8) the chairman and treasurer of the principal national campaign committee seeking the election or reelection of the President, and any officer of that committee exercising authority at the national level, during the incumbency of the President.

(c) Preliminary Investigation With Respect to Persons Not Listed in Subsection (b).—The Attorney General may conduct a preliminary investigation in accordance with section 592 if—

(1) the Attorney General receives information sufficient to constitute grounds to investigate whether any person other than a person described in subsection (b) may have violated any Federal criminal law other than a violation classified as a Class B or C misdemeanor or an infraction; and

(2) the Attorney General determines that an investigation or prosecution of the person, with respect to the information received, by the Attorney General or other officer of the Department of Justice may result in a personal, financial, or political conflict of interest.

(d) Examination of Information to Determine Need for Preliminary Investigation.—

(1) **Factors to be considered.**—In determining under subsection (a) or (c) for section 592(c)(2)) whether grounds to investigate exist, the Attorney General shall consider only—

(A) the specificity of the information received; and

(B) the credibility of the course of the information.

(2) **Time period for making determination.**—The Attorney General shall determine whether grounds to investigate exist not later than 15 days after the information is first received. If within that 15-day period the Attorney General determines that the information is not specific or is not from a credible source, then the Attorney General shall close the matter. If within that 15-day period the Attorney General determines that the information is specific and from a credible source, the Attorney General shall, upon making that determination, commence a preliminary investigation with respect to that information. If the Attorney General is unable to determine, within that 15-day period, whether the information is specific and from a credible source, the Attorney General shall, at the end of that 15-day period, commence a preliminary investigation with respect to that information.

(c) **Recusal of Attorney General.**—

(1) **When recusal is required.**—If information received under this chapter involves the Attorney General or a person with whom the Attorney General has a current or recent personal or financial relationship, the Attorney General shall recuse himself or herself by designating the next most senior officer in the Department of Justice whom that information does not involve and who does not have a current or recent personal or financial relationship with such person to perform the duties assigned under this chapter to the Attorney General with respect to that information.

(2) **Requirements for recusal determination.**—The Attorney General shall, before personally making any other determination under this chapter with respect to information received under this chapter, determine under paragraph (1) whether to recuse himself or herself with respect to that information. A determination to recuse shall be in writing, shall identify the facts considered by the Attorney General, and shall set forth the reasons for the recusal. The Attorney General shall file this determination with any notification or application submitted to the division of the court under this chapter with respect to the information involved.

§592. Preliminary investigation and application for appointment of an independent counsel

(a) **Conduct of Preliminary Investigation.**—

(1) **In General.**—A preliminary investigation conducted under this chapter shall be of such matters as the Attorney General considers appropriate in order to make a determination, under subsection (b) or (c), on whether further investigation is warranted, with respect to each potential violation, or allegation of a violation, of criminal law. The Attorney General shall make such determination not later than 90 days after the preliminary investigation is commenced, except that, in the case of a preliminary investigation commenced after a congressional request under subsection (g), the Attorney General shall make such determination not later than 90 days after the request is received. The Attorney General shall promptly notify the division of the court specified in section 593(a) of the commencement of such preliminary investigation and the date of such commencement.

(2) **Limited Authority of Attorney General.**—(A) In conducting preliminary investigations under this chapter, the Attorney General shall have no authority to convene grand juries, plea bargain, grant immunity, or issue subpoenas.

(B)(i) The Attorney General shall not base a determination under this chapter that information with respect to a violation of criminal law by a person is not specific and from a credible source upon a determination that such person lacked the state of mind required for the violation of criminal law.

(ii) The Attorney General shall not base a determination under this chapter that there are no reasonable grounds to believe that further investigation is warranted, upon a determination that such person lacked the state of mind required for the violation of criminal law involved, unless there is clear and convincing evidence that the person lacked such state of mind.

(3) **Extension of time for preliminary investigation.**—The Attorney General may apply to the division of the court for a single extension, for a period of not more than 60 days, of the 90-day period referred to in paragraph (1). The division of the court may, upon a showing of good cause, grant such extension.

(b) **Determination That Further Investigation Not Warranted.**—

(1) **Notification of division of the court.**—If the Attorney General, upon completion of a preliminary investigation under this chapter, determines that there are no reasonable grounds to believe that further investigation is warranted, the Attorney General shall promptly so notify the division of the court, and the division of the court shall have no power to appoint an independent counsel with respect to the matters involved.

(2) **Form of notification.**—Such notification shall contain a summary of the information received and a summary of the results of the preliminary investigation.

(c) **Determination That Further Investigation is Warranted.**—

(1) **Application for appointment of independent counsel.**—The Attorney General shall apply to the division of the court for the appointment of an independent counsel if—

(A) the Attorney General, upon completion of a preliminary investigation under this chapter, determines that there are reasonable grounds to believe that further investigation is warranted; or

(B) the 90-day period referred to in subsection (a)(1), and any extension granted under subsection (a)(3), have elapsed and the Attorney General has not filed a notification with the division of the court under subsection (b)(1).

In determining under this chapter whether reasonable grounds exist to warrant further investigation, the Attorney General shall comply with the written or other established policies of the Department of Justice with respect to the conduct of criminal investigations.

(2) **Receipt of additional information.**—If, after submitting a notification under subsection (b)(1), the Attorney General receives additional information sufficient to constitute grounds to investigate the matters to which such notification related, the Attorney General shall—

(A) conduct such additional preliminary investigation as the Attorney General considers appropriate for a period of not more than 90 days after the date on which such additional information is received; and

(B) otherwise comply with the provisions of this section with respect to such additional preliminary investigation to the same extent as any other preliminary investigation under this section.

(d) **Contents of Application.**—Any application for the appointment of an independent counsel under this chapter shall contain sufficient information to assist the division of the court in selecting an independent counsel and in defining that independent counsel's prosecutorial jurisdiction so that the independent counsel has adequate authority to fully investigate and prosecute the subject matter and all matters related to that subject matter.

(c) **Disclosure of Information.**—Except as otherwise provided in this chapter, no officer or employee of the Department of Justice or an office of independent counsel may, without leave of the division of the court, disclose to any individual outside the Department of Justice or such office any notification, application, or any other document, materials, or memorandum supplied to the division of the court under this chapter. Nothing in this chapter shall be construed as authorizing the withholding of information from the Congress.

(f) **Limitation of Judicial Review.**—The Attorney General's determination under this chapter to apply to the division of the court for the appointment of an independent counsel shall not be reviewable in any court.

(g) **Congressional Request.**—

(1) **By judiciary committee or members thereof.**—The Committee on the Judiciary of either House of the Congress, or a majority of majority party members or a majority of all nonmajority party members of either such committee, may request in writing that the Attorney General apply for the appointment of an independent counsel.

(2) **Report by attorney general pursuant to request.**—Not later than 30 days after the receipt of a request under paragraph (1), the Attorney General shall submit, to the committee making the request, or to the committee on which the persons making the request serve, a report on whether the Attorney General has begun or will begin a preliminary investigation under this chapter of the matters with respect to which the request is made, in accordance with subsection (a) or (c) of section 591, as the case may be. The report shall set forth the reasons for the Attorney General's decision regarding such preliminary investigation as it relates to each of the matters with respect to which the congressional request is made. If there is such a preliminary investigation, the report shall include the date on which the preliminary investigation began or will begin.

(3) **Submission of information in response to congressional request.**—At the same time as any notification, application, or any other document, material, or memorandum is supplied to the division of the court pursuant to this section with respect to a preliminary investigation of any matter with respect to which a request is made under paragraph (1), such notification, application, or other document, material, or memorandum shall be supplied to the committee making the request, or to the committee on which the persons making the request serve. If no application for the appointment of an independent counsel is made to the division of the court under this section pursuant to such a preliminary investigation, the Attorney General shall submit a report to that committee stating the reasons why such application was not made, addressing each matter with respect to which the congressional request was made.

(4) **Disclosure of information.**—Any report, notification, application, or other document, material, or memorandum supplied to a committee under this subsection shall not be revealed to any third party, except that the committee may, either on its own initiative or upon the request of the Attorney General, make public such

portion or portions of such report, notification, application, document, material, or memorandum as will not in the committee's judgment prejudice the rights of any individual.

§ 593. Duties of the division of the court

(a) **Reference to division of the court.**—The division of the court to which this chapter refers is the division established under section 49 of this title.

(b) **Appointment and Jurisdiction of Independent Counsel.**—

(1) **Authority.**—Upon receipt of an application under section 592(c), the division of the court shall appoint an appropriate independent counsel and shall define that independent counsel's prosecutorial jurisdiction.

(2) **Qualifications of independent counsel.**—The division of the court shall appoint as independent counsel an individual who has appropriate experience and who will conduct the investigation and any prosecution in a prompt, responsible, and cost-effective manner. The division of the court shall seek to appoint as independent counsel an individual who will serve to the extent necessary to complete the investigation and any prosecution without undue delay. The division of the court may not appoint as an independent counsel any person who holds any office of profit or trust under the United States.

(3) **Scope of prosecutorial jurisdiction.**—In defining the independent counsel's prosecutorial jurisdiction, the division of the court shall assure that the independent counsel has adequate authority to fully investigate and prosecute the subject matter with respect to which the Attorney General has requested the appointment of the independent counsel, and all matters related to that subject matter. Such jurisdiction shall also include the authority to investigate and prosecute Federal crimes, other than those classified as Class B or C misdemeanors or infractions, that may arise out of the investigation or prosecution of the matter with respect to which the Attorney General's request was made, including perjury, obstruction of justice, destruction of evidence, and intimidation of witnesses.

(4) **Disclosure of identity and prosecutorial jurisdiction.**—An independent counsel's identity and prosecutorial jurisdiction (including any expansion under subsection (c)) may not be made public except upon the request of the Attorney General or upon a determination of the division of the court that disclosure of the identity and prosecutorial jurisdiction of such independent counsel would be in the best interests of justice. In any event, the identity and prosecutorial jurisdiction of such independent counsel shall be made public when any indictment is returned, or any criminal information is filed, pursuant to the independent counsel's investigation.

(c) **Expansion of Jurisdiction.**—

(1) **In General.**—The division of the court, upon the request of the Attorney General, may expand the prosecutorial jurisdiction of an independent counsel, and such expansion may be in lieu of the appointment of another independent counsel.

(2) **Procedure for request by independent counsel.**—(A) If the independent counsel discovers or receives information about possible violations of criminal laws by persons as provided in section 591, which are not covered by the prosecutorial jurisdiction of the independent counsel, the independent counsel may submit such information to the Attorney General. The Attorney General shall then conduct a

preliminary investigation of the information in accordance with the provisions of section 592, except that such preliminary investigation shall not exceed 30 days from the date such information is received. In making the determinations required by section 592, the Attorney General shall give great weight to any recommendations of the independent counsel.

(B) If the Attorney General determines, after according great weight to the recommendations of the independent counsel, that there are no reasonable grounds to believe that further investigation is warranted, the Attorneys General shall promptly so notify the division of the court and the division of the court shall have no power to expand the jurisdiction of the independent counsel or to appoint another independent counsel with respect to the matters involved.

(C) If—

(i) the Attorney General determines that there are reasonable grounds to believe that further investigation is warranted; or

(ii) the 30-day period referred to in subparagraph (A) elapses without a notification to the division of the court that no further investigation is warranted, the division of the court shall expand the jurisdiction of the appropriate independent counsel to include the matters involved or shall appoint another independent counsel to investigate such matters.

(d) Return for Further Explanation.—Upon receipt of a notification under section 592 or subsection (c)(2)(B) of this section from the Attorney General that there are no reasonable grounds to believe that further investigation is warranted with respect to information received under this chapter, the division of the court shall have no authority to overrule this determination but may return the matter to the Attorney General for further explanation of the reasons for such determination.

(e) Vacancies.—If a vacancy in office arises by reason of the resignation, death or removal of an independent counsel, the division of the court may appoint an independent counsel to complete the work of the independent counsel whose resignation, death or removal caused the vacancy, except that, in the case of a vacancy arising by reason of the removal of an independent counsel, the division of the court may appoint an acting independent counsel to serve until any judicial review of such removal is completed.

(f) Attorneys' Fees.—

(1) **Award of fees.**—Upon the request of an individual who is the subject of an investigation conducted by an independent counsel pursuant to this chapter, the division of the court may, if no indictment is brought against such individual pursuant to that investigation, award reimbursement for those reasonable attorneys' fees incurred by that individual during that investigation which would not have been incurred but for the requirements of this chapter. The division of the court shall notify the Attorney General of any request for attorneys' fees under this subsection.

(2) **Evaluation of fees.**—The division of the court may direct the Attorney General to file a written evaluation of any request for attorneys' fees under this subsection, analyzing for each expense—

(A) the sufficiency of the documentation;

(B) the need or justification for the underlying item; and

(C) the reasonableness of the amount of money requested.

(g) Disclosure of Information.—The division of the court may, subject to section 594(h)(2), allow the disclosure of any notification, application, or any other document, material, or memorandum supplied to the division of the court under this chapter.

(h) Amicus Curiae Briefs.—When presented with significant legal issues, the division of the court may disclose sufficient information about the issues to permit the filing of timely amicus curiae briefs.

§ 594. Authority and duties of an independent counsel

(a) Authorities.—Notwithstanding any other provision of law, an independent counsel appointed under this chapter shall have, with respect to all matters in such independent counsel's prosecutorial jurisdiction established under this chapter, full power and independent authority to exercise all investigative and prosecutorial functions and powers of the Department of Justice, the Attorney General, and any other officer or employee of the Department of Justice, except that the Attorney General shall exercise direction or control as to those matters that specifically require the Attorney General's personal action under section 2516 of title 18. Such investigative and prosecutorial functions and powers shall include—

(1) conducting proceedings before grand juries and other investigations;

(2) participating in court proceedings and engaging in any litigation, including civil and criminal matters, that such independent counsel deems necessary;

(3) appealing any decision of a court in any case or proceeding in which such independent counsel participates in an official capacity;

(4) reviewing all documentary evidence available from any source;

(5) determining whether to contest the assertion of any testimonial privilege;

(6) receiving appropriate national security clearances and, if necessary, contesting in court (including, where appropriate, participating in camera proceedings) any claim of privilege or attempt to withhold evidence on grounds of national security;

(7) making applications to any Federal court for a grant of immunity to any witness, consistent with applicable statutory requirements, or for warrants, subpoenas, or other court orders, and, for purposes of sections 6003, 6004, and 6005 of title 18, exercising the authority vested in a United States attorney or the Attorney General;

(8) inspecting, obtaining, or using the original or a copy of any tax return, in accordance with the applicable statutes and regulations, and, for purposes of section 6103 of the Internal Revenue Code of 1986, and the regulations issued thereunder, exercising the powers vested in a United States attorney or the Attorney General.

(9) initiating and conducting prosecutions in any court of competent jurisdiction, framing and signing indictments, filing information, and handling all aspects of any case in the name of the United States; and

(10) consulting with the United States Attorney for the district in which any violation of law with respect to which the independent counsel is appointed was alleged to have occurred.

(b) Compensation.—An independent counsel appointed under this chapter shall receive compensation at the per diem rate equal to the annual rate of basic pay for level IV of the Executive Schedule under section 5315 of title 5.

(c) **Additional personnel.**—For the purposes of carrying out the duties of an office of independent counsel, such independent counsel may appoint, fix the compensation, and assign the duties of such employees as such independent counsel deems necessary (including investigators, attorneys, and part-time consultants). The positions of all such employees are exempted from the competitive service. No such employee may be compensated at a rate exceeding the maximum rate of pay payable for GS-18 of the General Schedule under section 5332 of title 5.

(d) **Assistance of Department of Justice.**—

(1) **In carrying out functions.**—An independent counsel may request assistance from the Department of Justice in carrying out the functions of the independent counsel, and the Department of Justice shall provide that assistance, which may include access to any records, files, or other materials relevant to matters within such independent counsel's prosecutorial jurisdiction, and the use of the resources and personnel necessary to perform such independent counsel's duties.

(2) **Payment of and reports on expenditures of independent counsel.**—The Department of Justice shall pay all costs relating to the establishment and operation of any office of independent counsel. The Attorney General shall submit to the Congress, not later than 30 days after the end of each fiscal year, a report on amounts paid during that fiscal year for expenses of investigations and prosecutions by independent counsel. Each such report shall include a statement of all payments made for activities of independent counsel but may not reveal the identity or prosecutorial jurisdiction of any independent counsel which has not been disclosed under section 593(b)(4).

(e) **Referral of Other matters to an independent counsel.**—An independent counsel may ask the Attorney General or the division of the court to refer to the independent counsel matters related to the independent counsel's prosecutorial jurisdiction, and the Attorney General or the division of the court, as the case may be, may refer such matters. If the Attorney General refers a matter to an independent counsel on the Attorney General's own initiative, the independent counsel may accept such referral if the matter relates to the independent counsel's prosecutorial jurisdiction. If the Attorney General refers any matter to the independent counsel pursuant to the independent counsel's request, or if the independent counsel accepts a referral made by the Attorney General on the Attorney General's own initiative, the independent counsel shall so notify the division of the court.

(f) **Compliance with policies of the Department of Justice.**—An independent counsel shall, except where not possible, comply with the written or other established policies of the Department of Justice respecting enforcement of the criminal laws.

(g) **Dismissal of matters.**—The independent counsel shall have full authority to dismiss matters within the independent counsel's prosecutorial jurisdiction without conducting an investigation or at any subsequent time before prosecution, if to do so would be consistent with the written or other established policies of the Department of Justice with respect to the enforcement of criminal laws.

(h) **Reports by Independent Counsel.**—

(1) **Required reports.**—An independent counsel shall—

(A) file with the division of the court, with respect to the 6-month period beginning on the date of his or her appointment, and with respect to each 6-month period thereafter until the office of that independent counsel terminates, a report which identifies and explains major expenses, and summarizes all other expenses, incurred by that office during the 6-month period with respect to which the report is filed, and estimates future expenses of that office; and

(B) before the termination of the independent counsel's office under section 596(b), file a final report with the division of the court, setting forth fully and completely a description of the work of the independent counsel, including the disposition of all cases brought, and the reasons for not prosecuting any matter within the prosecutorial jurisdiction of such independent counsel.

(2) **Disclosure of information in reports.**—The division of the court may release to the Congress, the public, or any appropriate person, such portions of a report made under this subsection as the division of the court considers appropriate. The division of the court shall make such orders as are appropriate to protect the rights of any individual named in such report and to prevent undue interference with any pending prosecution. The division of the court may make any portion of a final report filed under paragraph (1)(B) available to any individual named in such report for the purposes of receiving within a time limit set by the division of the court any comments or factual information that such individual may submit. Such comments and factual information, in whole or in part, may, in the discretion of the division of the court, be included as an appendix to such final report.

(i) **Independence from Department of Justice.**—Each independent counsel appointed under this chapter, and the persons appointed by that independent counsel under subsection (c), are separate from and independent of the Department of Justice for purposes of sections 202 through 209 of title 18.

(j) **Standards of conduct applicable to independent counsel, persons serving in the office of an independent counsel, and their law firms.**—

(1) **Restriction on employment while independent counsel and appointees are serving.**—(a) During the period in which an independent counsel is serving under this chapter.—

(i) such independent counsel, and

(ii) any person associated with a firm with which such independent counsel is associated, may not represent in any matter any person involved in any investigation or prosecution under this chapter.

(B) During the period in which any person appointed by an independent counsel under subsection (c) is serving in the office of independent counsel, such persons may not represent in any matter any person involved in any investigation or prosecution under this chapter.

(2) **Post employment restrictions on independent counsel and appointees.**—(A) Each independent counsel and each person appointed by that independent counsel under subsection (c) may not, for 3 years following the termination of the service under this chapter of that independent counsel or appointed persons, as the case may be, represent any person in any matter if that individual was the subject of an investigation or prosecution under this chapter that was conducted by that independent counsel.

(B) Each independent counsel and each person appointed by that independent counsel under subsection (c) may not, for 1 year following this chapter of that independent counsel or appointed person, as the case may be, represent any person in any matter involving any investigation or prosecution under this chapter.

(3) One-year ban on representation by members of firms of independent counsel.— Any person who is associated with a firm with which an independent counsel is associated or becomes associated after termination of the service of that independent counsel under this chapter may not, for 1 year following such termination, represent any person in any matter involving any investigation or prosecution under this chapter.

(4) Definitions.—For purposes of this subsection—

(A) the term "firm" means a law firm whether organized as a partnership or corporation; and

(B) a person is 'associated' with a firm if that person is an officer, director, partner, or other member or employee of that firm.

(k) Custody of records of an independent counsel.—

(1) Transfer of records.—Upon termination of the office of an independent counsel, that independent counsel shall transfer to the Archivist of the United States all records which have been created or received by that office. Before this transfer, the independent counsel shall clearly indentify which of these records are subject to rule 6(e) of the Federal Rules of Criminal Procedure as grand jury materials and which of these records have been classified as national security information. Any records which were compiled by an independent counsel and, upon termination of the independent counsel's office, were stored with the division of the court or elsewhere before the enactment of the Independent Counsel Reauthorization Act of 1987, shall also be transferred to the Archivist of the United States by the division of the court or the person in possession of such records.

(2) Maintenance, use, and disposal of records.—Records transferred to the Archivist under this chapter shall be maintained, used, and disposed of in accordance with chapters 21, 29, and 33 of title 44.

(3) Access to records.—

(A) **In general.—**Subject to paragraph (4), access to the records transferred to the Archivist under this chapter shall be governed by section 552 of title 5.

(B) **Access by Department of Justice.—**The Archivist shall, upon written application by the Attorney General, disclose any such records to the Department of Justice for purposes of an ongoing law enforcement investigation or court proceeding, except that, in the case of grand jury materials, such records shall be so disclosed only by order of the court of jurisdiction under rule 6(e) of the Federal Rules of Criminal Procedure.

(C) **Exception.—**Notwithstanding any restriction on access imposed by law, the Archivist and persons employed by the National Archives and Records Administration who are engaged in the performance of normal archival work shall be permitted access to the records transferred to the Archivist under this chapter.

(4) Records provided by Congress.—Records of an investigation conducted by a committee of the House of Representatives or the Senate which are provided to an independent counsel to assist in an investigation or prosecution conducted by that independent counsel.—

(A) shall be maintained as a separate body of records within the records of the independent counsel; and

(B) shall, after the records have been transferred to the Archivist under this chapter, be made available, except as provided in paragraph (3)(B) and (C), in accordance with the rules governing release of the records of the House of Congress that provided the records to the independent counsel.

Subparagraph (B) shall not apply to those records which have been surrendered pursuant to grand jury or court proceedings.

§ 595. Congressional oversight

(a) Oversight of conduct of independent counsel.—

(1) **Congressional oversight.—**The appropriate committees of the Congress shall have oversight jurisdiction with respect to the official conduct of any independent counsel appointed under this chapter, and such independent counsel shall have the duty to cooperate with the exercise of such oversight jurisdiction.

(2) **Reports to Congress.—**An independent counsel appointed under this chapter shall submit to the Congress such statements or reports on the activities of such independent counsel as the independent counsel considers appropriate.

(b) Oversight of conduct of Attorney General.—Within 15 days after receiving an inquiry about a particular case under this chapter, which is a matter of public knowledge, from a committee of the Congress with jurisdiction over this chapter, the Attorney General shall provide the following information to that committee with respect to that case:

(1) When the information about the case was received.

(2) Whether a preliminary investigation is being conducted, and if so, the date it began.

(3) Whether an application for the appointment of an independent counsel or a notification that further investigation is not warranted has been filed with the division of the court, and if so, the date of such filing.

(c) Information relating to impeachment.—As independent counsel shall advise the House of Representatives of any substantial and credible information which such independent counsel receives, in carrying out the independent counsel's responsibilities under this chapter, that may constitute grounds for an impeachment. Nothing in this chapter or section 49 of this title shall prevent the Congress or either House thereof from obtaining information in the course of an impeachment proceeding.

§ 596. Removal of an independent counsel; termination of office

(a) Removal; report on removal.—

(1) **Grounds for removal.—**An independent counsel appointed under this chapter may be removed from office, other than by impeachment and conviction, only by the personal action of the Attorney General and only for good cause, physical disability, mental incapacity, or any other condition that substantially impairs the performance of such independent counsel's duties.

(2) **Report to division of the Court and Congress.—**If an independent counsel is removed from office, the Attorney General shall promptly submit to the division of

the court and the Committees on the Judiciary of the Senate and the House of Representatives a report specifying the facts found and the ultimate grounds for such removal. The committees shall make available to the public such report, except that each committee may, if necessary to protect the rights of any individual named in the report or to prevent undue interference with any pending prosecution, postpone or refrain from publishing any or all of the report. The division of the court may release any or all of such report in accordance with section 594(h)(2).

(3) **Judicial review of removal.**—An independent counsel removed from office may obtain judicial review of the removal in a civil action commenced in the United States District Court for the District of Columbia. A member of the division of the court may not hear or determine any such civil action or any appeal of a decision in any such civil action. The independent counsel may be reinstated or granted other appropriate relief by order of the court.

(b) **Termination of office.**—

(1) **Termination by action of independent counsel.**—An office of independent counsel shall terminate when—

(A) the independent counsel notifies the Attorney General that the investigation of all matters within the prosecutorial jurisdiction of such independent counsel or accepted by such independent counsel under section 594(e), and any resulting prosecutions, have been completed or so substantially completed that it would be appropriate for the Department of Justice to complete such investigations and prosecutions; and

(B) the independent counsel files a report in full compliance with section 594(h)(1)(B).

(2) The division of the court, either on its own motion or upon the request of the Attorney General, may terminate an office of independent counsel at any time, on the ground that the investigation of all matters within the prosecutorial jurisdiction of such independent counsel or accepted by such independent counsel under section 594(e), and any resulting prosecutions, have been completed or so substantially completed that it would be appropriate for the Department of Justice to complete such investigations and prosecutions. At the time of such termination, the independent counsel shall file the final report required by section 594(h)(1)(B).

(c) **Audits.**—After the termination of the office of an independent counsel, the Comptroller-General shall conduct an audit of the expenditures of that office, and shall submit to the appropriate committees of the Congress a report on the audit.

§ 597. Relationship with Department of Justice

(a) **Suspension of other investigations or proceedings.**—Whenever a matter is in the prosecutorial jurisdiction of an independent counsel or has been accepted by an independent counsel under section 594(e), the Department of Justice, the Attorney General, and all other officers and employees of the Department of Justice shall suspend all investigations and proceedings regarding such matter, except to the extent required by section 594(d)(1), and except insofar as such independent counsel agrees in writing that such investigation or proceedings may be continued by the Department of Justice.

(b) **Presitation of amicus curiae permitted.**—Nothing in this chapter shall prevent the Attorney General or the Solicitor General from making a presentation as amicus curiae to any court as to issues of law raised by any case or proceeding in which an independent counsel participates in an official capacity or any appeal of such a case or proceeding.

§ 598. Severability

If any provision of this chapter or the application thereof to any person or circumstance is held invalid, the remainder of this chapter and the application of such provision to other persons not similarly situated or to other circumstances shall not be affected by such invalidation.

§ 599. Termination of effect of chapter

This chapter shall cease to be effective five years after the date of enactment of the Independent Counsel Reauthorization Act of 1987, except that this chapter shall continue in effect with respect to then pending matters before an independent counsel that in the judgment of such counsel require such continuation until that independent counsel determines such matters have been completed.

Tort Claims Procedure

§ 2671. Definitions

As used in this chapter [28 U.S.C. §§ 2671 et seq.] and sections 1346(b) and 2401(b) of this title [28 U.S.C. §§ 1346(b) and 2401(b)] the term "Federal agency" includes the executive departments, the military departments, independent establishments of the United States, and corporations primarily acting as, instrumentalities or agencies of the United States but does not include any contractor with the United States.

"Employee of the government" includes officers or employees of any federal agency, members of the military or naval forces of the United States, members of the National Guard while engaged in training or duty under section 316, 502, 503, 504, or 505 of title 32 [32 U.S.C. §§ 316, 502, 503, 504, or 505], and persons acting on behalf of a federal agency in an official capacity, temporarily or permanently in the service of the United States, whether with or without compensation.

"Acting within the scope of his office or employment," in the case of a member of the military or naval forces of the United States or a member of the National Guard as defined in section 101(3) of title 32 [32 U.S.C. § 101(3)], means acting in line of duty.

§ 2672. Administrative adjustment of claims

The head of each Federal agency or his designee, in accordance with regulations prescribed by the Attorney General, may consider, ascertain, adjust, determine, compromise, and settle any claim for money damages against the United States for injury or loss of property or personal injury or death caused by the negligent or wrongful act or omission of any employee of the agency while acting within the scope of his office or employment, under circumstances where the United States, if a private person, would be liable to the claimant in accordance with the law of the place where the act or omission occurred: Provided, That any award, compromise, or settlement in excess of $25,000 shall be effected only with the prior written approval of the Attorney General or his designee.

Subject to the provisions of this title relating to civil actions on tort claims against the United States, any such award, compromise, settlement, or determination shall be final and conclusive on all officers of the Government, except when procured by means of fraud.

Any award, compromise, or settlement in an amount of $2,500 or less made pursuant to this section shall be paid by the head of the Federal agency concerned out of appropriations available to that agency. Payment of any award, compromise, or settlement in an amount in excess of $2,500 made pursuant to this section or made by the Attorney General in any amount pursuant to section 2677 of this title [28 U.S.C. § 2677] shall be paid in a manner similar to judgments and compromises in like causes and appropriations or funds available for the payment of such judgments and compromises are hereby made available for the payment of awards, compromises, or settlements under this chapter [28 U.S.C. §§ 2671, 2672, 2674-2680].

The acceptance by the claimant of any such award, compromise, or settlement shall be final and conclusive on the claimant, and shall constitute a complete release of any claim against the United States and against the employee of the government whose act or omission gave rise to the claim, by reason of the same subject matter.

§ 2673. [Repealed]

§ 2674. Liability of United States

The United States shall be liable, respecting the provisions of this title relating to tort claims, in the same manner and to the same extent as a private individual under like circumstances, but shall not be liable for interest prior to judgment or for punitive damages.

If, however, in any case wherein death was caused, the law of the place where the act or omission complained of occurred provides, or has been construed to provide, for damages only punitive in nature, the United States shall be liable for actual or compensatory damages, measured by the pecuniary injuries resulting from such death to the persons respectively, for whose benefit the action was brought, in lieu thereof.

§ 2675. Disposition by federal agency as prerequisite; evidence

(a) An action shall not be instituted upon a claim against the United States for money damages for injury or loss of property or personal injury or death caused by the negligent or wrongful act or omission of any employee of the Government while acting within the scope of his office or employment, unless the claimant shall have first presented the claim to the appropriate Federal agency and his claim shall have been finally denied by the agency in writing and sent by certified or registered mail. The failure of an agency to make final disposition of a claim within six months after it is filed shall, at the option of the claimant any time thereafter, be deemed a final denial of the claim for purposes of this section. The provisions of this subsection shall not apply to such claims as may be asserted under the Federal Rules of Civil Procedure by third party complaint, cross-claim, or counterclaim.

(b) Action under this section shall not be instituted for any sum in excess of the amount of the claim presented to the federal agency, except where the increased amount is based upon newly discovered evidence not reasonably discoverable at the time of presenting the claim to the federal agency, or upon allegation and proof of intervening facts, relating to the amount of the claim.

(c) Disposition of any claim by the Attorney General or other head of a federal agency shall not be competent evidence of liability or amount of damages.

§ 2676. Judgment as bar

The judgment in an action under section 1346(b) of this title [28 U.S.C. § 1346(b)] shall constitute a complete bar to any action by the claimant, by reason of the same subject matter, against the employee of the government whose act or omission gave rise to the claim.

§ 2677. Compromise

The Attorney General or his designee may arbitrate, compromise, or settle any claim cognizable under section 1346(b) of this title [28 U.S.C. § 1346(b)], after the commencement of an action thereon.

§ 2678. Attorney fees; penalty

No attorney shall charge, demand, receive, or collect for services rendered, fees in excess of 25 per centum of any judgment rendered pursuant to section 1346(b) of this title or any settlement made pursuant to section 2677 of this title [28 U.S.C. § 2677], or in excess of 20 per centum of any award, compromise, or settlement made pursuant to section 2672 of this title [28 U.S.C. § 2672].

Any attorney who charges, demands, receives, or collects for services rendered in connection with such claim any amount in excess of that allowed under this section, if recovery be had, shall be fined not more than $2,000 or imprisoned not more than one year, or both.

§ 2679. Exclusiveness of remedy

(a) The authority of any federal agency to sue and be sued in its own name shall not be construed to authorize suits against such federal agency on claims which are cognizable under section 1346(b) of this title [28 U.S.C. § 1346(b)], and the remedies provided by this title in such cases shall be exclusive.

(b) The remedy against the United States provided by sections 1346(b) and 2672 of this title [28 U.S.C. §§ 1346(b) and 2672] for injury or loss of property or personal injury or death, resulting from the operation by any employee of the Government of any motor vehicle while acting within the scope of his office or employment, shall hereafter be exclusive of any other civil action or proceeding by reason of the same subject matter against the employee or his estate whose act or omission gave rise to the claim.

(c) The Attorney General shall defend any civil action or proceeding brought in any court against any employee of the Government or his estate for any such damage or injury. The employee against whom such civil action or proceeding is brought shall deliver within such time after date of service or knowledge of service as determined by the Attorney General, all process served upon him or an attested true copy thereof to his immediate superior or to whomever was designated by the head of his department to receive such papers and such person shall promptly furnish copies of the pleadings and process therein to the United States attorney for the district embracing the place wherein the proceeding is brought, to the Attorney General, and to the head of his employing Federal agency.

(d) Upon a certification by the Attorney General that the defendant employee was acting within the scope of his employment at the time of the incident out of which the suit arose, any such civil action or proceeding commenced in a State court shall be removed without bond at any time before trial by the Attorney General to the district court of the United States for the district and division embracing the place wherein it is pending and the proceedings deemed a tort action brought against the United States under the provisions of this title and all references thereto. Should a United States district court determine on a hearing on a motion to remand held before a trial on the merits that the case so removed is one in which a remedy by suit within the meaning of subsection (b) of this section is not available against the United States, the case shall be remanded to the State court.

(e) The Attorney General may compromise or settle any claim asserted in such civil action or proceeding in the manner provided in section 2677, and with the same effect.

§ 2680. Exceptions

The provisions of this chapter and section 1346(b) of this title [28 U.S.C. § 1346(b)] shall not apply to—

(a) Any claim based upon an act or omission of an employee of the Government, exercising due care, in the execution of a statute or regulation, whether or not such statute or regulation be valid, or based upon the exercise or performance or the failure to exercise or perform a discretionary function or duty on the part of a federal agency or an employee of the Government, whether or not the discretion involved be abused.

(b) Any claim arising out of the loss, miscarriage, or negligent transmission of letters or postal matter.

(c) Any claim arising in respect of the assessment or collection of any tax or customs duty, or the detention of any goods or merchandise by any officer of customs or excise or any other law-enforcement officer.

(d) Any claim for which a remedy is provided by sections 741-752, 781-790 of Title 46 [46 U.S.C. §§ 741 et seq.], relating to claims or suits in admiralty against the United States.

(e) Any claim arising out of an act or omission of any employee of the Government in administering the provisions of sections 1-31 of Title 50, Appendix [50 Appx U.S.C. §§ et seq.].

(f) Any claim for damages caused by the imposition or establishment of a quarantine by the United States.

(g) [Repealed]

(h) Any claim arising out of assault, battery, false imprisonment, false arrest, malicious prosecution, abuse of process, libel, slander, misrepresentation, deceit, or interference with contract rights: *Provided*, That, with regard to acts or omissions of investigative or law enforcement officers of the United States Government, the provisions of this chapter and section 1346(b) of this title [28 U.S.C. § 1346(b)] shall apply to any claim arising, on or after the date of the enactment of this proviso, out of assault, battery, false imprisonment, false arrest, abuse of process, or malicious prosecution. For the purpose of this subsection, "investigative or law enforcement officer" means any officer of the United States who is empowered by law to execute searches, to seize evidence, or to make arrests for violations of Federal law.

(i) Any claim for damages caused by the fiscal operations of the Treasury or by the regulation of the monetary system.

(j) Any claim arising out of the combatant activities of the military or naval forces, or the Coast Guard, during time of war.

(k) Any claim arising in a foreign country.

(l) Any claim arising from the activities of the Tennessee Valley Authority.

(m) Any claim arising from the activities of the Panama Canal Company.

(n) Any claim arising from the activities of a Federal land bank, a Federal intermediate credit bank, or a bank for co-operatives.

TITLE 31—MONEY AND FINANCE

General Accounting Office

§ 703. Comptroller General and Deputy Comptroller General

(a)(1) The Comptroller General and Deputy Comptroller General are appointed by the President, by and with the advice and consent of the Senate.

(2) When a vacancy occurs in the office of Comptroller General or Deputy Comptroller General, a commission is established to recommend individuals to the President for appointment to the vacant office. The commission shall be composed of—

(A) the Speaker of the House of Representatives;

(B) the President pro tempore of the Senate;

(C) the majority and minority leaders of the House of Representatives and the Senate;

(D) the chairmen and ranking minority members of the Committee on Governmental Affairs of the Senate and the Committee on Government Operations of the House; and

(E) when the office of Deputy Comptroller General is vacant, the Comptroller General.

(3) A commission established because of a vacancy in the office of the Comptroller General shall recommend at least 3 individuals. The President may ask the commission to recommend additional individuals.

(b) Except as provided in subsection (e) of this section, the term of the Comptroller General is 15 years. The Comptroller General may not be reappointed. The term of the Deputy Comptroller General expires on the date an individual is appointed Comptroller General. The Deputy Comptroller General may continue to serve until a successor is appointed.

(c) The Deputy Comptroller General—

(1) carries out duties and powers prescribed by the Comptroller General; and

(2) acts for the Comptroller General when the Comptroller General is absent or unable to serve or when the office of Comptroller General is vacant.

(d) The Comptroller General shall designate an officer or employee of the General Accounting Office to act as Comptroller General when the Comptroller General and Deputy Comptroller General are absent or unable to serve or when the offices of Comptroller General and Deputy Comptroller General are vacant.

(e)(1) A Comptroller General or Deputy Comptroller General retires on becoming 70 years of age. Either may be removed at any time by—

(A) impeachment; or

(B) joint resolution of Congress, after notice and an opportunity for a hearing, only for—

(i) permanent disability;

(ii) inefficiency;

(iii) neglect of duty;

(iv) malfeasance; or

(v) a felony or conduct involving moral turpitude.

(2) A Comptroller General or Deputy Comptroller General removed from office under paragraph (1) of this subsection may not be reappointed to the office.

(f) The annual rate of basic pay of the—

(1) Comptroller General is equal to the rate for level II of the Executive Schedule [5 U.S.C. § 5313]; and

(2) Deputy Comptroller General is equal to the rate for level III of the Executive Schedule [5 U.S.C. § 5314].

§ 711. General authority

The Comptroller General may—

(1) prescribe regulations to carry out the duties and powers of the Comptroller General;

(2) delegate the duties and powers of the Comptroller General to officers and employees of the General Accounting Office as the Comptroller General decides is necessary to carry out those duties and powers;

(3) regulate the practice of representatives of persons before the Office; and

(4) administer oaths to witnesses when auditing and settling accounts.

§ 712. Investigating the use of public money

The Comptroller General shall—

(1) investigate all matters related to the receipt, disbursement, and use of public money;

(2) estimate the cost to the United States Government of complying with each restriction on expenditures of a specific appropriation in a general appropriation law and report each estimate to Congress with recommendations the Comptroller General considers desirable;

(3) analyze expenditures of each executive agency the Comptroller General believes will help Congress decide whether public money has been used and expended economically and efficiently;

(4) make an investigation and report ordered by either House of Congress or a committee of Congress having jurisdiction over revenue, appropriations, or expenditures; and

(5) give a committee of Congress having jurisdiction over revenue, appropriations, or expenditures the help and information the committee requests.

§ 717. Evaluating programs and activities of the United States Government

(a) In this section, "agency" means a department, agency, or instrumentality of the United States Government (except a mixed-ownership Government corporation) or the District of Columbia government.

(b) The Comptroller General shall evaluate the results of a program or activity the Government carries out under existing law—

(1) on the initiative of the Comptroller General;

(2) when either House of Congress orders an evaluation; or

(3) when a committee of Congress with jurisdiction over the program or activity requests the evaluation.

(c) The Comptroller General shall develop and recommend to Congress ways to evaluate a program or activity the Government carries out under existing law.

(d)(1) On request of a committee of Congress, the Comptroller General shall help the committee to—

(A) develop a statement of legislative goals and ways to assess and report program performance related to the goals, including recommended ways to assess performance, information to be reported, responsibility for reporting, frequency of reports, and feasibility of pilot testing; and

(B) assess program evaluations prepared by and for an agency.

(2) On request of a member of Congress, the Comptroller General shall give the member a copy of the material the Comptroller General compiles in carrying out this subsection that has been released by the committee for which the material was compiled.

§ 719. Comptroller General reports

(a) At the beginning of each regular session of Congress, the Comptroller General shall report to Congress (and to the President when requested by the President) on the work of the Comptroller General. A report shall include recommendations on—

(1) legislation the Comptroller General considers necessary to make easier the prompt and accurate making and settlement of accounts; and

(2) other matters related to the receipt, disbursement, and use of public money the Comptroller General considers advisable.

(b)(1) The Comptroller General shall include in the report to Congress under subsection (a) of this section—

(A) a review of activities under sections 717(b)-(d) and 731(e)(2) of this title [31 U.S.C. §§ 717(b)-(d), 731(e)(2)], including recommendations under section 717(c) of this title [31 U.S.C. § 717(c)];

(B) information on carrying out duties and powers of the Comptroller General under clauses (A) and (C) of this paragraph, subsections (g) and (h) of this section, and sections 717, 731(e)(2), 734, 1112, and 1113 of this title [31 U.S.C. §§ 717, 731(e)(2), 734, 1112, and 1113]; and

(C) the name of each officer and employee of the General Accounting Office assigned or detailed to a committee of Congress, the committee to which the officer or employee is assigned or detailed, the length of the period of assignment or detail, a statement on whether the assignment or detail is finished or continuing, and compensation paid out of appropriations available to the Comptroller General for the period of the assignment or detail that has been completed.

(2) In a report under subsection (a) of this section or in a special report to Congress when Congress is in session, the Comptroller General shall include recommendations on greater economy and efficiency in public expenditures.

(c) The Comptroller General shall report to Congress—

(1) specially on expenditures and contracts an agency makes in violation of law;

(2) on the adequacy and effectiveness of—

(A) administrative audits of accounts and claims in an agency; and

(B) inspections by an agency of offices and accounts of fiscal officials; and

(3) as frequently as practicable on audits carried out under sections 713 and 714 of this title [31 U.S.C. §§ 713, 714].

(d) The Comptroller General shall report each year to the Committees on Finance and Governmental Affairs of the Senate, the Committees on Ways and Means and Government Operations of the House of Representatives, and the Joint Committee on Taxation. Each report shall include—

(1) procedures and requirements the Comptroller General, the Commissioner of Internal Revenue, and the Director of the Bureau of Alcohol, Tobacco, and Firearms, prescribe to protect the confidentiality of returns and return information made available to the Comptroller General under section 713(b)(1) of this title [31 U.S.C. § 713(b)(1)];

(2) the scope and subject matter of audits under section 713 of this title [31 U.S.C. § 713]; and

(3) findings, conclusions, or recommendations the Comptroller General develops as a result of an audit under section 713 of this title [31 U.S.C. § 713], including significant evidence of inefficiency or mismanagement.

(e) The Comptroller General shall report on analyses carried out under section 712(3) of this title [31 U.S.C. § 712(3)] to the Committees on Governmental Affairs and

Appropriations of the Senate, the Committees on Government Operations and Appropriations of the House, and the committees with jurisdiction over legislation related to the operation of each executive agency.

(f) The Comptroller General shall give the President information on expenditures and accounting the President requests.

(g) When the Comptroller General submits a report to Congress, the Comptroller General shall deliver copies of the report to—

(1) the Committees on Governmental Affairs and Appropriations of the Senate;

(2) the Committees on Government Operations and Appropriations of the House;

(3) a committee of Congress that requested information on any part of a program or activity of a department, agency, or instrumentality of the United States Government (except a mixed-ownership Government corporation) or the District of Columbia government that is the subject of any part of a report; and

(4) any other committee of Congress requesting a copy.

(h)(1) The Comptroller General shall prepare—

(A) each month a list of reports issued during the prior month; and

(B) at least once each year a list of reports issued during the prior 12 months.

(2) A copy of each list shall be sent to each committee of Congress and each member of Congress. On request, the Comptroller General promptly shall provide a copy of a report to a committee or member.

(i) On request of a committee of Congress, the Comptroller General shall explain to and discuss with the committee or committee staff a report the Comptroller General makes that would help the committee—

(1) evaluate a program or activity of an agency within the jurisdiction of the committee; or

(2) in its consideration of proposed legislation.

TITLE 40—PUBLIC BUILDINGS, PROPERTY, AND WORKS

Management and Disposal of Government Property

§ 471. Congressional declaration of policy

It is the intent of the Congress in enacting this legislation to provide for the Government an economical and efficient system for (a) the procurement and supply of personal property and nonpersonal services, including related functions such as contracting, inspection, storage, issue, specifications, property identification and classification, transportation and traffic management, establishment of pools or systems for transportation of Government personnel and property by motor vehicle within specific areas, management of public utility services, repairing and converting, establishment of inventory levels, establishment of forms and procedures, and representation before Federal and State regulatory bodies; (b) the utilization of available property; (c) the disposal of surplus property; and (d) records management.

§ 486. Policies, regulations, and delegations

(a) **Promulgation by President.** The President may prescribe such policies and directives, not inconsistent with the provisions of this Act, as he shall deem necessary to effectuate the provisions of said Act, which policies and directives shall govern the Administrator and executive agencies in carrying out their respective functions hereunder.

TITLE 44—PUBLIC PRINTING AND DOCUMENTS

Presidential Records

§ 2201. Definitions

As used in this chapter—

(1) The term "documentary material" means all books, correspondence, memorandums, documents, papers, pamphlets, works of art, models, pictures, photographs, plates, maps, films, and motion pictures, including, but not limited to, audio, audiovisual, or other electronic or mechanical recordations.

(2) The term "Presidential records" means documentary materials, or any reasonably segregable portion thereof, created or received by the President, his immediate staff, or a unit or individual of the Executive Office of the President whose function is to advise and assist the President, in the course of conducting activities which relate to or have an effect upon the carrying out of the constitutional, statutory, or other official or ceremonial duties of the President. Such term—

(A) includes any documentary materials relating to the political activities of the President or members of his staff, but only if such activities relate to or have a direct effect upon the carrying out of constitutional, statutory, or other official or ceremonial duties of the President; but

(B) does not include any documentary materials that are (i) official records of an agency (as defined in section 552(e) of title 5, United States Code); (ii) personal records; (iii) stocks of publications and stationery; or (iv) extra copies of documents produced only for convenience of reference, when such copies are clearly so identified.

(3) The term "personal records" means all documentary materials, or any reasonably segregable portion therof,[2] of a purely private or nonpublic character which do not relate to or have an effect upon the carrying out of the constitutional,

---

2 So in original. Probably should be "thereof."

statutory, or other official or ceremonial duties of the President. Such term includes—

(A) diaries, journals, or other personal notes serving as the functional equivalent of a diary or journal which are not prepared or utilized for, or circulated or communicated in the course of, transacting Government business;

(B) materials relating to private political associations, and having no relation to or direct effect upon the carrying out of constitutional, statutory, or other official or ceremonial duties of the President; and

(C) materials relating exclusively to the President's own election to the office of the Presidency; and materials directly relating to the election of a particular individual or individuals to Federal, State, or local office, which have no relation to or direct effect upon the carrying out of constitutional, statutory, or other official or ceremonial duties of the President.

(4) The term "Archivist" means the Archivist of the United States.

(5) The term "former President," when used with respect to Presidential records, means the former President during whose term or terms of office such Presidential records were created.

§ 2202. Ownership of Presidential records

The United States shall reserve and retain complete ownership, possession, and control of Presidential records; and such records shall be administered in accordance with the provisions of this chapter.

§ 2203. Management and custody of Presidential records

(a) Through the implementation of records management controls and other necessary actions, the President shall take all such steps as may be necessary to assure that the activities, deliberations, decisions, and policies that reflect the performance of his constitutional, statutory, or other official or ceremonial duties are adequately documented and that such records are maintained as Presidential records pursuant to the requirements of this section and other provisions of law.

(b) Documentary materials produced or received by the President, his staff, or units or individuals in the Executive Office of the President the function of which is to advise and assist the President, shall, to the extent practicable, be categorized as Presidential records or personal records upon their creation or receipt and be filed separately.

(c) During his term of office, the President may dispose of those of his Presidential records that no longer have administrative, historical, informational, or evidentiary value if—

(1) the President obtains the views, in writing, of the Archivist concerning the proposed disposal of such Presidential records; and

(2) the Archivist states that he does not intend to take any action under subsection (e) of this section.

(d) In the event the Archivist notifies the President under subsection (c) that he does intend to take action under subsection (e), the President may dispose of such Presidential records if copies of the disposal schedule are submitted to the appropriate Congressional Committees at least 60 calendar days of continuous session of Congress in advance of the proposed disposal date. For the purpose of this section, continuity of session is broken only by an adjournment of Congress sine die, and the days on which either House is not in session because of an adjournment of more than three days to a day certain are excluded in the computation of the days in which Congress is in continuous session.

(e) The Archivist shall request the advice of the Committee on Rules and Administration and the Committee on Governmental Affairs of the Senate and the Committee on House Administration and the Committee on Government Operations of the House of Representatives with respect to any proposed disposal of Presidential records whenever he considers that—

(1) these particular records may be of special interest to the Congress; or

(2) consultation with the Congress regarding the disposal of these particular records is in the public interest.

(f)(1) Upon the conclusion of a President's term of office, or if a President serves consecutive terms upon the conclusion of the last term, the Archivist of the United States shall assume responsibility for the custody, control, and preservation of, and access to, the Presidential records of that President. The Archivist shall have an affirmative duty to make such records available to the public as rapidly and completely as possible consistent with the provisions of this Act.

(2) The Archivist shall deposit all such Presidential records in a Presidential archival depository or another archival facility operated by the United States. The Archivist is authorized to designate, after consultation with the former President, a director at each depository or facility, who shall be responsible for the care and preservation of such records.

(3) The Archivist is authorized to dispose of such Presidential records which he has appraised and determined to have insufficient administrative, historical, informational, or evidentiary value to warrant their continued preservation. Notice of such disposal shall be published in the Federal Register at least 60 days in advance of the proposed disposal date. Publication of such notice shall constitute a final agency action for purposes of review under chapter 7 of title 5, United States Code.

§ 2204. Restrictions on access to Presidential records

(a) Prior to the conclusion of his term of office or last consecutive term of office, as the case may be, the President shall specify durations, not to exceed 12 years, for which access shall be restricted with respect to information, in a Presidential record, within one or more of the following categories:

(1)(A) specifically authorized under criteria established by an Executive order to be kept secret in the interest of national defense or foreign policy and (B) in fact properly classified pursuant to such Executive order;

(2) relating to appointments to Federal office;

(3) specifically exempted from disclosure by statute (other than sections 552 and 552b of title 5, United States Code), provided that such statute (A) requires that the material be withheld from the public in such a manner as to leave no discretion

on the issue, or (B) establishes particular criteria for withholding or refers to particular types of material to be withheld;

(4) trade secrets and commercial or financial information obtained from a person and privileged or confidential;

(5) confidential communications requesting or submitting advice, between the President and his advisers, or between such advisers; or

(6) personnel and medical files and similar files the disclosure of which would constitute a clearly unwarranted invasion of personal privacy.

(b)(1) Any President record or reasonably segregable portion thereof containing information within a category restricted by the President under subsection (a) shall be so designated by the Archivist and access thereto shall be restricted until the earlier of—

(A)(i) the date on which the former President waives the restriction on disclosure of such record, or

(ii) the expiration of the duration specified under subsection (a) for the category of information on the basis of which access to such record has been restricted; or

(B) upon a determination by the Archivist that such record or reasonably segregable portion thereof, or of any significant element or aspect of the information contained in such record or reasonably segregable portion thereof, has been placed in the public domain through publication by the former President, or his agents.

(2) Any such record which does not contain information within a category restricted by the President under subsection (a), or contains information within such a category for which the duration of restricted access has expired, shall be exempt from the provisions of subsection (c) until the earlier of—

(A) the date which is 5 years after the date on which the Archivist obtains custody of such record pursuant to section 2203(d)(1); or

(B) the date on which the Archivist completes the processing and organization of such records or integral file segment thereof.

(3) During the period of restricted access specified pursuant to subsection (b)(1), the determination whether access to a Presidential record or reasonably segregable portion thereof shall be restricted shall be made by the Archivist, in his discretion, after consultation with the former President, and, during such period, such determinations shall not be subject to judicial review, except as provided in subsection (e) of this section. The Archivist shall establish procedures whereby any person denied access to a Presidential record because such record is restricted pursuant to a determination made under this paragraph, may file an administrative appeal of such determination. Such procedures shall provide for a written determination by the Archivist or his designee, within 30 working days after receipt of such an appeal, setting forth the basis for such determination.

(c)(1) Subject to the limitations on access imposed pursuant to subsections (a) and (b), Presidential records shall be administered in accordance with section 552 of title 5, United States Code, except that paragraph (b)(5) of that section shall not be available for purposes of withholding any Presidential record, and for the purposes of such section such records shall be deemed to be records of the National Archives and

Records Administration. Access to such records shall be granted on nondiscriminatory terms.

(2) Nothing in this Act shall be construed to confirm, limit, or expand any constitutionally-based privilege which may be available to an incumbent or former President.

(d) Upon the death or disability of a President or former President, any discretion or authority the President or former President may have had under this chapter shall be exercised by the Archivist unless otherwise previously provided by the President or former President in a written notice to the Archivist.

(e) The United States District Court for the District of Columbia shall have jurisdiction over any action initiated by the former President asserting that a determination made by the Archivist violates the former President's rights or privileges.

§ 2205. Exceptions to restricted access

Notwithstanding any restrictions on access imposed pursuant to section 2204—

(1) the Archivist and persons employed by the National Archives and Records Administration who are engaged in the performance of normal archival work shall be permitted access to Presidential records in the custody of the Archivist;

(2) subject to any rights, defenses, or privileges which the United States or any agency or person may invoke, Presidential records shall be made available—

(A) pursuant to subpoena or other judicial process issued by a court of competent jurisdiction for the purposes of any civil or criminal investigation or proceeding;

(B) to an incumbent President if such records contain information that is needed for the conduct of current business of his office and that is not otherwise available; and

(C) to either House of Congress, or, to the extent of matter within its jurisdiction, to any committee or subcommittee thereof if such records contain information that is needed for the conduct of its business and that is not otherwise available; and

(3) the Presidential records of a former President shall be available to such former President or his designated representative.

§ 2206. Regulations

The Archivist shall promulgate in accordance with section 553 of title 5, United States Code, regulations necessary to carry out the provisions of this chapter. Such regulations shall include—

(1) provisions for advance public notice and description of any Presidential records scheduled for disposal pursuant to section 2203(f)(3);

(2) provisions for providing notice to the former President when materials to which access would otherwise be restricted pursuant to section 2204(a) are to be made available in accordance with section 2205(2);

(3) provisions for notice by the Archivist to the former President when the disclosure of particular documents may adversely affect any rights and privileges which the former President may have; and

(4) provisions for establishing procedures for consultation between the Archivist and appropriate Federal agencies regarding materials which may be subject to section 552(b)(7) of title 5, United States Code.

§ 2207. Vice-Presidential records

Vice-Presidential records shall be subject to the provisions of this chapter in the same manner as Presidential records. The duties and responsibilities of the Vice President, with respect to Vice-Presidential records, shall be the same as the duties and responsibilities of the President under this chapter with respect to Presidential records. The authority of the Archivist with respect to Vice-Presidential records shall be the same as the authority of the Archivist under this chapter with respect to Presidential records, except that the Archivist may, when the Archivist determines that it is in the public interest, enter into an agreement for the deposit of Vice-Presidential records in a non-Federal archival depository. Nothing in this chapter shall be construed to authorize the establishment of separate archival depositories for such Vice-Presidential records.

TITLE 50—WAR AND NATIONAL DEFENSE
Note following § 1541—MULTINATIONAL FORCE IN LEBANON RESOLUTION

SHORT TITLE

Section 1. This joint resolution may be cited as the "Multinational Force in Lebanon Resolution."

FINDINGS AND PURPOSE

Section 2. (a) The Congress finds that—

(1) the removal of all foreign forces from Lebanon is an essential United States foreign policy objective in the Middle East;

(2) in order to restore full control by the Government of Lebanon over its own territory, the United States is currently participating in the multinational peacekeeping force (hereafter in this resolution referred to as the "Multinational Force in Lebanon") which was established in accordance with the exchange of letters between the Governments of the United States and Lebanon dated September 25, 1982;

(3) the Multinational Force in Lebanon better enables the Government of Lebanon to establish its unity, independence, and territorial integrity;

(4) progress toward national political reconciliation in Lebanon is necessary; and

(5) United States Armed Forces participating in the Multinational Force in Lebanon are now in hostilities requiring authorization of their continued presence under the War Powers Resolution.

(b) The Congress determines that the requirements of section 4(a)(1) of the War Powers Resolution became operative on August 29, 1983. Consistent with section

5(b) of the War Powers Resolution, the purpose of this joint resolution is to authorize the continued participation of United States Armed Forces in the Multinational Force in Lebanon.

(c) The Congress intends this joint resolution to constitute the necessary specific statutory authorization under the War Powers Resolution for continued participation by United States Armed Forces in the Multinational Force in Lebanon.

AUTHORIZATION FOR CONTINUED PARTICIPATION OF UNITED STATES ARMED FORCES IN THE MULTINATIONAL FORCE IN LEBANON

Section 3. The President is authorized, for purposes of section 5(b) of the War Powers Resolution, to continue participation by United States Armed Forces in the Multinational Force in Lebanon, subject to the provisions of section 6 of this joint resolution. Such participation shall be limited to performance of the functions, and shall be subject to the limitations, specified in the agreement establishing the Multinational Force in Lebanon as set forth in the exchange of letters between the Governments of the United States and Lebanon dated September 25, 1981, except that this shall not preclude such protective measures as may be necessary to ensure the safety of the Multinational Force in Lebanon.

REPORTS TO THE CONGRESS

Section 4. As required by section 4(c) of the War Powers Resolution, the President shall report periodically to the Congress with respect to the situation in Lebanon, but in no event shall he report less often than once every three months. In addition to providing the information required by that section on the status, scope, and duration of hostilities involving United States Armed Forces, such reports shall describe in detail—

(1) the activities being performed by the Multinational Force in Lebanon;

(2) the present composition of the Multinational Force in Lebanon, including a description of the responsibilities and deployment of the armed forces of each participating country;

(3) the results of efforts to reduce and eventually eliminate the Multinational Force in Lebanon;

(4) how continued United States participation in the Multinational Force in Lebanon is advancing United States foreign policy interests in the Middle East; and

(5) what progress has occurred toward national political reconciliation among all Lebanese groups.

STATEMENTS OF POLICY

Section 5. (a) The Congress declares that the participation of the armed forces of other countries in the Multinational Force in Lebanon is essential to maintain the international character of the peacekeeping function in Lebanon.

(b) The Congress believes that it should continue to be the policy of the United States to promote continuing discussions with Israel, Syria, and Lebanon with the objective of bringing about the withdrawal of all foreign troops from Lebanon and establishing an environment which will permit the Lebanese Armed Forces to carry out their responsibilities in the Beirut area.

(c) It is the sense of the Congress that, not later than one year after the date of enactment of this joint resolution and at least once a year thereafter, the United States should discuss with the other members of the Security Council of the United Nations the establishment of a United Nations peacekeeping force to assume the responsibilities of the Multinational Force in Lebanon. An analysis of the implications of the response to such discussions for the continuation of the Multinational Force in Lebanon shall be included in the reports required under paragraph (3) of section 4 of this resolution.

DURATION OF AUTHORIZATION FOR UNITED STATES PARTICIPATION IN THE MULTINATIONAL FORCE IN LEBANON

Section 6. The participation of United States Armed Forces in the Multinational Force in Lebanon shall be authorized for purposes of the War Powers Resolution until the end of the eighteen-month period beginning on the date of enactment of this resolution unless the Congress extends such authorization, except that such authorization shall terminate sooner upon the occurrence of any one of the following:

(1) the withdrawal of all foreign forces from Lebanon, unless the President determines and certifies to the Congress that continued United States Armed Forces participation in the Multinational Force in Lebanon is required after such withdrawal in order to accomplish the purposes specified in the September 25, 1982, exchange of letters providing for the establishment of the Multinational Force in Lebanon; or

(2) the assumption by the United Nations or the Government of Lebanon of the responsibilities of the Multinational Force in Lebanon; or

(3) the implementation of other effective security arrangements in the area; or

(4) the withdrawal of all other countries from participation in the Multinational Force in Lebanon.

INTERPRETATION OF THIS RESOLUTION

Section 7. (a) Nothing in this joint resolution shall preclude the President from withdrawing United States Armed Forces participation in the Multinational Force in Lebanon if circumstances warrant, and nothing in this joint resolution shall preclude the Congress by joint resolution from directing such a withdrawal.

(b) Nothing in this joint resolution modifies, limits, or supersedes any provision of the War Powers Resolution or the requirements of section 4(a) of the Lebanon Emergency Assistance Act of 1983, relating to congressional authorization for any substantial expansion in the number or role of United States Armed Forces in Lebanon.

CONGRESSIONAL PRIORITY PROCEDURES FOR AMENDMENTS

Section 8. (a) Any joint resolution or bill introduced to amend or repeal this Act shall be referred to the Committee on Foreign Affairs of the House of Representatives or the Committee on Foreign Relations of the Senate, as the case may be. Such joint resolution or bill shall be considered by such committee within fifteen calendar days and may be reported out, together with its recommendation, unless such House shall otherwise determine pursuant to its rules.

(b) Any joint resolution or bill so reported shall become the pending business of the House in question (in the case of the Senate the time for debate shall be equally divided between the proponents and the opponents) and shall be voted on within three calendar days thereafter, unless such House shall otherwise determine by the yeas and nays.

(c) Such a joint resolution or bill passed by one House shall be referred to the committee of the other House named in subsection (a) and shall be reported out by such committee together with its recommendations within fifteen calendar days and shall thereupon become the pending business of such House and shall be voted upon within three calendar days, unless such House shall otherwise determine by the yeas and nays.

(d) In the case of any disagreement between the two Houses of Congress with respect to a joint resolution or bill passed by both Houses, conferees shall be promptly appointed and the committee of conference shall make and file a report with respect to such joint resolution within six calendar days after the legislation is referred to the committee of conference. Notwithstanding any rule in either House concerning the printing of conference reports or concerning any delay in the consideration of such reports, such report shall be acted on by both Houses not later than six calendar days after the conference report is filed. In the event the conferees are unable to agree within forty-eight hours, they shall report back to their respective Houses in disagreement.

International Emergency Economic Powers

§ 1701. Unusual and extraordinary threat; declaration of national emergency; exercise of Presidential authorities

(a) Any authority granted to the President by section 203 [50 U.S.C. § 1702] may be exercised to deal with any unusual and extraordinary threat, which has its source in whole or substantial part outside the United States, to the national security, foreign policy, or economy of the United States, if the President declares a national emergency with respect to such threat.

(b) The authorities granted to the President by section 203 [50 U.S.C. § 1702] may only be exercised to deal with an unusual and extraordinary threat with respect to which a national emergency has been declared for purposes of this title [50 U.S.C. §§ 1701 et seq.] and may not be exercised for any other purpose. Any exercise of such authorities to deal with any new threat shall be based on a new declaration of national emergency which must be with respect to such threat.

§ 1702. Presidential authorities

(a)(1) At the times and to the extent specified in section 202 [50 U.S.C. § 1701], the President may, under such regulations as he may prescribe, by means of instructions, licenses, or otherwise—

(A) investigate, regulate, or prohibit—

(i) any transactions in foreign exchange,

(ii) transfers of credit or payments between, by, through, or to any banking institution, to the extent that such transfers or payments involve any interest of any foreign country or a national thereof,

(iii) the importing or exporting of currency or securities; and

(B) investigate, regulate, direct and compel, nullify, void, prevent or prohibit, any acquisition, holding, withholding, use, transfer, withdrawal, transportation, importation or exportation of, or dealing in, or exercising any right, power, or privilege with respect to, or transactions involving, any property in which any foreign country or a national thereof has any interest;

by any person, or with respect to any property, subject to the jurisdiction of the United States.

(2) In exercising the authorities granted by paragraph (1), the President may require any person to keep a full record of, and to furnish under oath, in the form of reports or otherwise, complete information relative to any act or transaction referred to in paragraph (1) either before, during, or after the completion thereof, or relative to any interest in foreign property, or relative to any property in which any foreign country or any national thereof has or has had any interest, or as may be otherwise necessary to enforce the provisions of such paragraph. In any case in which a report by a person could be required under this paragraph, the President may require the production of any books of account, records, contracts, letters, memoranda, or other papers, in the custody or control of such person.

(3) Compliance with any regulation, instruction, or direction issued under this title [50 U.S.C. §§ 1701 et seq.] shall to the extent thereof be a full acquittance and discharge for all purposes of the obligation of the person making the same. No person shall be held liable in any court for or with respect to anything done or omitted in good faith in connection with the administration of, or pursuant to and in reliance on, this title, or any regulation, instruction, or direction issued under this title.

(b) The authority granted to the President by this section does not include the authority to regulate or prohibit, directly or indirectly—

(1) any postal, telegraphic, telephonic, or other personal communication, which does not involve a transfer of anything of value; or

(2) donations, by persons subject to the jurisdiction of the United States, of articles, such as food, clothing, and medicine, intended to be used to relieve human suffering, except to the extent that the President determines that such donations (A) would seriously impair his ability to deal with any national emergency declared under section 202 of this title [50 U.S.C. § 1701], (B) are in response to coercion against the proposed recipient or donor, or (C) would endanger Armed Forces of the United States which are engaged in hostilities or are in a situation where imminent involvement in hostilities is clearly indicated by the circumstances.

§ 1703. Consultation and reports

(a) **Consultation with Congress.** The President, in every possible instance, shall consult with the Congress before exercising any of the authorities granted by this title [50

U.S.C. §§ 1701 et seq.] and shall consult regularly with the Congress so long as such authorities are exercised.

(b) Report to Congress upon exercise of Presidential authorities. Whenever the President exercises any of the authorities granted by this title [50 U.S.C. §§ 1701 et seq.], he shall immediately transmit to the Congress a report specifying—

(1) the circumstances which necessitate such exercise of authority;

(2) why the President believes those circumstances constitute an unusual and extraordinary threat, which has its source in whole or substantial part outside the United States, to the national security, foreign policy, or economy of the United States;

(3) the authorities to be exercised and the actions to be taken in the exercise of those authorities to deal with those circumstances;

(4) why the President believes such actions are necessary to deal with those circumstances; and

(5) any foreign countries with respect to which such actions are to be taken and why such actions are to be taken with respect to those countries.

(c) Periodic follow-up reports. At least once during each succeeding six-month period after transmitting a report pursuant to subsection (b) with respect to an exercise of authorities under this title [50 U.S.C. §§ 1701 et seq.], the President shall report to the Congress with respect to the actions taken, since the last such report, in the exercise of such authorities, and with respect to any changes which have occurred concerning any information previously furnished pursuant to paragraphs (1) through (5) of subsection (b).

(d) Supplemental requirements. The requirements of this section are supplemental to those contained in title IV of the National Emergencies Act [50 U.S.C. § 1641].

§ 1704. Authority to issue regulations

The President may issue such regulations, including regulations prescribing definitions, as may be necessary for the exercise of the authorities granted by this title [50 U.S.C. §§ 1701 et seq.].

§ 1705. Penalties

(a) A civil penalty of not to exceed $10,000 may be imposed on any person who violates any license, order, or regulation issued under this title [50 U.S.C. §§ 1701 et seq.].

(b) Whoever willfully violates any license, order, or regulation issued under this title [50 U.S.C. §§ 1701 et seq.] shall, upon conviction, be fined not more than $50,000, or, if a natural person, may be imprisoned for not more than ten years, or both; and any officer, director, or agent of any corporation who knowingly participates in such violation may be punished by a like fine, imprisonment, or both.

TITLE 50, APPENDIX—WAR AND NATIONAL DEFENSE

Trading With the Enemy Act

§ 2. Definitions

The word "enemy," as used herein, shall be deemed to mean, for the purposes of such trading and of this Act—

(a) Any individual, partnership, or other body of individuals, of any nationality, resident within the territory (including that occupied by the military and naval forces) of any nation with which the United States is at war, or resident outside the United States and doing business within such territory, and any corporation incorporated within such territory of any nation with which the United States is at war or incorporated within any country other than the United States and doing business within such territory.

(b) The government of any nation with which the United States is at war, or any political or municipal subdivision thereof, or any officer, official, agent, or agency thereof.

(c) Such other individuals, or body or class of individuals, as may be natives, citizens, or subjects of any nation with which the United States is at war, other than citizens of the United States, wherever resident or wherever doing business, as the President, if he shall find the safety of the United States or the successful prosecution of the war shall so require, may, by proclamation, include with the term "enemy."

The words "ally of enemy," as used herein, shall be deemed to mean—

(a) Any individual, partnership, or other body of individuals, of any nationality, resident within the territory (including that occupied by the military and naval forces) of any nation which is an ally of a nation with which the United States is at war, or resident outside the United States and doing business within such territory, and any corporation incorporated within such territory of such ally nation, or incorporated within any country other than the United States and doing business within such territory.

(b) The government of any nation which is an ally of a nation with which the United States is at war, or any political or municipal subdivision of such ally nation, or any officer, official, agent, or agency thereof.

(c) Such other individuals, or body or class of individuals, as may be natives, citizens, or subjects of any nation which is an ally of a nation with which the United States is at war, other than citizens of the United States, wherever resident or wherever doing business, as the President, if he shall find the safety of the United States or the successful prosecution of the war shall so require, may, be proclamation, include within the term "ally of enemy."

The word "person,"as used herein, shall be deemed to mean an individual, partnership, association, company, or other unincorporated body of individuals, or corporation or body politic.

The words "United States," as used herein, shall be deemed to mean all land and water, continental or insular, in any way within the jurisdiction of the United States or occupied by the military or naval forces thereof.

The words "the beginning of the war," as used herein, shall be deemed to mean midnight ending the day on which Congress has declared, or shall declare war or the existence of a state of war.

The words "end of the war," as used herein, shall be deemed to mean the date of proclamation of exchange of ratifications of the treaty of peace, unless the President shall, by proclamation, declare a prior date, in which case the date so proclaimed shall be deemed to be the "end of the war" within the meaning of this Act.

The words "bank or banks," as used herein, shall be deemed to mean and include national banks, State banks, trust companies, or other banks or banking associations doing business under the laws of the United States, or of any State of the United States.

The words "to trade," as used herein, shall be deemed to mean—

(a) Pay, satisfy, compromise, or give security for the payment or satisfaction of any debt or obligation.

(b) Draw, accept, pay, present for acceptance or payment, or indorse any negotiable instrument or chose in action.

(c) Enter into, carry on, complete, or perform any contract, agreement, or obligation.

(d) Buy or sell, loan or extend credit, trade in, deal with, exchange, transmit, transfer, assign, or otherwise dispose of, or receive any form of property.

(e) To have any form of business or commercial communication or intercourse with.

§ 3. Acts prohibited

It shall be unlawful—

(a) For any person in the United States, except with the license of the President, granted to such person, or to the enemy, or ally of enemy, as provided in this Act, to trade, or attempt to trade, either directly or indirectly, with, to, or from, or for, or on account of, or on behalf of, or for the benefit of, any other person, with knowledge or reasonable cause to believe that such other person is an enemy or ally of enemy, or is conducting or taking part in such trade, directly or indirectly, for, or on account of, or on behalf of, or for the benefit of, an enemy or ally of enemy.

(b) For any person, except with the license of the President, to transport or attempt to transport into or from the United States, or for any owner, master, or other person in charge of a vessel of American registry to transport or attempt to transport from any place to any other place, any subject or citizen of an enemy or ally of enemy nation, with knowledge or reasonable cause to believe that the person transported or attempted to be transported is such subject or citizen.

(c) For any person (other than a person in the service of the United States Government or of the Government of any nation, except that of an enemy or ally of enemy nation, and other than such persons or classes of persons as may be exempted hereunder by the President or by such person as he may direct), to send, or take out of, or bring into, or attempt to send, or take out of, or bring into the United States, any letter or other writing or tangible form of communication, except in the regular course of the mail; and it shall be unlawful for any person to send, take, or transmit, or attempt to send, take, or transmit out of the United States, any letter or other writing, book, map, plan, or other paper, picture, or any telegram, cablegram, or wireless message, or other form of communication intended for or to be delivered, directly or indirectly, to an enemy or ally of enemy: *Provided, however*, That any person may send, take, or transmit out of the United States anything herein forbidden if he shall first submit the same to the President, or to such officer as the President may direct, and shall obtain the license or consent of the President, under such rules and regulations, and with such exemptions, as shall be prescribed by the President.

(**d**) Whenever, during the present war, the President shall deem that the public safety demands it, he may cause to be censored under such rules and regulations as he may from time to time establish, communications by mail, cable, radio, or other means of transmission passing between the United States and any foreign country he may from time to time specify, or which may be carried by any vessel or other means of transportation touching at any port, place, or territory of the United States and bound to or from any foreign country. Any person who wilfully evades or attempts to evade the submission of any such communication to such censorship or wilfully uses or attempts to use any code or other device for the purpose of concealing from such censorship the intended meaning of such communication shall be punished as provided in section sixteen of this Act [50 U.S.C. Appx. § 16].

§ 5. Suspension of provisions relating to ally of enemy; regulation of transactions in foreign exchange of gold or silver, property transfers, vested interests, enforcement and penalties

(**a**) The President, if he shall find it compatible with the safety of the United States, and with the successful prosecution of the war, may, by proclamation, suspend the provisions of this Act so far as they apply to an ally of enemy, and he may revoke or renew such suspension from time to time; and the President may grant licenses, special or general, temporary or otherwise, and for such period of time and containing such provisions and conditions as he shall prescribe, to any person or class of persons to do business as provided in subsection (a) of section four hereof [50 U.S.C. Appx. § 4(a)] and perform any act made unlawful without such license in section three hereof [50 U.S.C. Appx. § 3], and to file and prosecute applications under subsection (b) of section ten hereof [50 U.S.C. Appx. § 10(b)]; and he may revoke or renew such licenses from time to time, if he shall be of opinion that such grant or revocation or renewal shall be compatible with the safety of the United States and with the successful prosecution of the war; and he may make such rules and regulations, not inconsistent with law, as may be necessary and proper to carry out the provisions of this Act; and the President may exercise any power or authority conferred by this Act through such officer or officers as he shall direct.

If the President shall have reasonable cause to believe that any act is about to be performed in violation of section three hereof [50 U.S.C. Appx. § 3] he shall have authority to order the postponement of the performance of such act for a period not exceeding ninety days, pending investigation of the facts by him.

(**b**)(1) During the time of war, the President may, through any agency that he may designate, and under such rules and regulations as he may prescribe, by means of instructions, licenses, or otherwise—

(A) investigate, regulate, or prohibit, any transactions in foreign exchange, transfers of credit or payments between, by, through, or to any banking institution, and the importing, exporting, hoarding, melting, or earmarking of gold or silver coin or bullion, currency or securities, and

(B) investigate, regulate, direct and compel, nullify, void, prevent or prohibit, any acquisition holding, withholding, use, transfer, withdrawal, transportation, importation or exportation of, or dealing in, or exercising any right, power, or privilege with respect to, or transactions involving, any property in which any foreign country or a national thereof has any interest,

by any person, or with respect to any property, subject to the jurisdiction of the United States; and any property or interest of any foreign country or national thereof shall vest, when, as, and upon the terms, directed by the President, in such agency or person as may be designated from time to time by the President, and upon such terms and conditions as the President may prescribe such interest or property shall be held, used, administered, liquidated, sold, or otherwise dealt with in the interest of and for the benefit of the United States, and such designated agency or person may perform any and all acts incident to the accomplishment or furtherance of these purposes; and the President shall, in the manner hereinabove provided, require any person to keep a full record of, and to furnish under oath, in the form of reports or otherwise, complete information relative to any act or transaction referred to in this subdivision either before, during, or after the completion thereof, or relative to any interest in foreign property, or relative to any property in which any foreign country or any national thereof has or has had any interest, or as may be otherwise necessary to enforce the provisions of this subdivision, and in any case in which a report could be required, the President may, in the manner hereinabove provided, require the production, or if necessary to the national security or defense, the seizure, of any books of account, records, contracts, letters, memoranda, or other papers, in the custody or control of such person.

(2) Any payment, conveyance, transfer, assignment, or delivery of property or interest therein, made to or for the account of the United States, or as otherwise directed, pursuant to this subdivision or any rule, regulation, instruction, or direction issued hereunder shall to the extent thereof be a full acquittance and discharge for all purposes of the obligation of the person making the same; and no person shall be held liable in any court for or in respect to anything done or omitted in good faith in connection with the administration of, or in pursuance of and in reliance on, this subdivision, or any rule, regulation, instruction, or direction issued hereunder.

(3) As used in this subdivision the term "United States" means the United States and any place subject to the jurisdiction thereof, [including the Philippine Islands, and the several courts of first instance of the Commonwealth of the Philippine Islands shall have jurisdiction in all cases, civil or criminal, arising under this subdivision in the Philippine Islands and concurrent jurisdiction with the district courts of the United States of all cases, civil or criminal, arising upon the high seas]: *Provided, however,* That the foregoing shall not be construed as a limitation upon the power of the President, which is hereby conferred, to prescribe from time to time, definitions, not inconsistent with the purposes of this subdivision, for any or all of the terms used in this subdivision. As used in this section the term "person" means an individual, partnership, association, or corporation.

January 1, 1863.

BY THE PRESIDENT OF THE UNITED STATES OF AMERICA:

A PROCLAMATION

WHEREAS, on the twenty-second day of September, in the year of our Lord one thousand eight hundred and sixty-two, a proclamation was issued by the President of the United States, containing, among other things, the following, to wit:

"That on the first day of January, in the year of our Lord one thousand eight hundred and sixty-three, all persons held as slaves within any state or designated part of a state, the people whereof shall then be in rebellion against the United States, shall be then, thenceforward, and forever, free; and the Executive Government of the United States, including the military and naval authority thereof, will recognize and maintain the freedom of such persons, and will do no act or acts to repress such persons, or any of them, in any efforts they may make for their actual freedom.

"That the Executive will on the first day of January aforesaid, by proclamation, designate the states and parts of states, if any, in which the people thereof, respectively, shall then be in rebellion against the United States; and the fact that any state, or the people thereof, shall on that day be in good faith represented in the Congress of the United States, by members chosen thereto at elections wherein a majority of the qualified voters of such states shall have participated, shall, in the absence of strong countervailing testimony, be deemed conclusive evidence that such state, and the people thereof, are not then in rebellion against the United States."

Now, therefore, I, ABRAHAM LINCOLN, President of the United States, by virtue of the power in me vested as commander-in-chief of the army and navy of the United States, in time of actual armed rebellion against the authority and Government of the United States, and as a fit and necessary war measure for suppressing said rebellion, do, on this first day of January, in the year of our Lord one thousand eight hundred and sixty-three, and in accordance with my purpose so to do, publicly proclaimed for the full period of one hundred days from the day first above mentioned, order and designate as the states and parts of states wherein the people thereof, respectively, are this day in rebellion against the United States, the following, to wit:

Arkansas, Texas, Louisiana, (except the parishes of St. Bernard, Plaquemines, Jefferson, St. John, St. Charles, St. James, Ascension, Assumption, Terre Bonne, Lafourche, St. Mary, St. Martin, and Orleans, including the city of New Orleans,) Mississippi, Alabama, Florida, Georgia, South Carolina, North Carolina, and Virginia, (except the forty-eight counties designated as West Virginia, and also the counties of Berkeley, Accomac, Northampton, Elizabeth City, York, Princess Ann, and Norfolk, including the cities of Norfolk and Portsmouth,) and which excepted parts are for the present left precisely as if this proclamation were not issued.

And by virtue of the power and for the purpose aforesaid, I do order and declare that all persons held as slaves within said designated states and parts of states are, and henceforward shall be, free; and that the Executive Government of the United States, including the military and naval authorities thereof, will recognize and maintain the freedom of said persons.

And I hereby enjoin upon the people so declared to be free to abstain from all violence, unless in necessary self-defence; and I recommend to them that, in all cases when allowed, they labor faithfully for reasonable wages.

And I further declare and make known that such persons, of suitable condition, will be received into the armed service of the United States to garrison forts, positions, stations, and other places, and to man vessels of all sorts in said service.

And upon this act, sincerely believed to be an act of justice, warranted by the Constitution upon military necessity, I invoke the considerate judgment of mankind and the gracious favor of Almighty God.

In witness whereof, I have hereunto set my hand and caused the seal of the United States to be affixed.

Done at the city of Washington this first day of January, in the year of our Lord one thousand eight hundred and sixty-three, and of the Independence of [L. S.]   the United States of America the eighty-seventh.

ABRAHAM LINCOLN.

By the President:

WILLIAM H. SEWARD, *Secretary of State.*

Exec. Order No. 10340

April 10, 1952, 17 F. R. 3139

Directing the Secretary of Commerce to Take Possession of and Operate the Plants and Facilities of Certain Steel Companies

WHEREAS on December 16, 1950, I proclaimed the existence of a national emergency which requires that the military, naval, air, and civilian defenses of this country be strengthened as speedily as possible to the end that we may be able to repel any and all threats against our national security and to fulfill our responsibilities in the efforts being made throughout the United Nations and otherwise to bring about a lasting peace; and

WHEREAS American fighting men and fighting men of other nations of the United Nations are now engaged in deadly combat with the forces of aggression in Korea, and forces of the United States are stationed elsewhere overseas for the purpose of participating in the defense of the Atlantic Community against aggression; and

WHEREAS the weapons and other materials needed by our armed forces and by those joined with us in the defense of the free world are produced to a great extent in this country, and steel is an indispensable component of substantially all of such weapons and materials; and

WHEREAS steel is likewise indispensable to the carrying out of programs of the Atomic Energy Commission of vital importance to our defense efforts; and

WHEREAS a continuing and uninterrupted supply of steel is also indispensable to the maintenance of the economy of the United States, upon which our military strength depends; and

WHEREAS a controversy has arisen between certain companies in the United States producing and fabricating steel and the elements thereof and certain of their workers represented by the United Steel Workers of America, CIO, regarding terms and conditions of employment; and

WHEREAS the controversy has not been settled through the processes of collective bargaining or through the efforts of the Government, including those of the Wage Stabilization Board, to which the controversy was referred on December 22, 1951, pursuant to Executive Order No. 10233,[20] and a strike has been called for 12:01 A.M., April 9, 1952; and

WHEREAS a work stoppage would immediately jeopardize and imperil our national defense and the defense of those joined with us in resisting aggression, and would add to the continuing danger of our soldiers, sailors, and airmen engaged in combat in the field; and

WHEREAS in order to assure the continued availability of steel and steel products during the existing emergency, it is necessary that the United States take possession of and operate the plants, facilities, and other property of the said companies as hereinafter provided:

NOW, THEREFORE, by virtue of the authority vested in me by the Constitution and laws of the United States, and as President of the United States and Commander in Chief of the armed forces of the United States, it is hereby ordered as follows:

1. The Secretary of Commerce is hereby authorized and directed to take possession of all or such of the plants, facilities, and other property of the companies named in the list attached hereto [List of specific Steel Companies and Plants omitted], or any part thereof, as he may deem necessary in the interests of national defense; and to operate or to arrange for the operation thereof and to do all things necessary for, or incidental to, such operation.

2. In carrying out this order the Secretary of Commerce may act through or with the aid of such public or private instrumentalities or persons as he may designate; and all Federal agencies shall cooperate with the Secretary of Commerce to the fullest extent possible in carrying out the purposes of this order.

3. The Secretary of Commerce shall determine and prescribe terms and conditions of employment under which the plants, facilities, and other properties possession of which is taken pursuant to this order shall be operated. The Secretary of Commerce shall recognize the rights of workers to bargain collectively through representatives of their own choosing and to engage in concerted activities for the purpose of collective bargaining, adjustment of grievances, or other mutual aid or protection, provided that such activities do not interfere with the operation of such plants, facilities, and other properties.

4. Except so far as the Secretary of Commerce shall otherwise provide from time to time, the managements of the plants, facilities, and other properties possession of which is taken pursuant to this order shall continue their functions, including the collection and disbursement of funds in the usual and ordinary course of business in the names of their respective companies and by means of any instrumentalities used by such companies.

5. Except so far as the Secretary of Commerce may otherwise direct, existing rights and obligations of such companies shall remain in full force and effect, and there may be made, in due course, payments of dividends on stock, and of principal, interest, sinking funds, and all other distributions upon bonds, debentures, and other obligations, and expenditures may be made for other ordinary corporate or business purposes.

6. Whenever in the judgment of the Secretary of Commerce further possession and operation by him of any plant, facility, or other property is no longer necessary or expedient in the interest of national defense, and the Secretary has reason to believe that effective future operation is assured, he shall return the possession and operation and such plant, facility, or other property to the company in possession and control thereof at the time possession was taken under this order.

7. The Secretary of Commerce is authorized to prescribe and issue such regulations and orders not inconsistent herewith as he may deem necessary or desirable for carrying out the purposes of this order; and he may delegate and authorize subdelegation of such of his functions under this order as he may deem desirable.

HARRY S. TRUMAN

THE WHITE HOUSE
April 8th, 1952; 9:50 p.m. e.s.t.

Exec. Order No. 11615

August 17, 1971, 36 F.R. 15727

Providing for Stabilization of Prices, Rents, Wages, and Salaries

WHEREAS, in order to stabilize the economy, reduce inflation, and minimize unemployment, it is necessary to stabilize prices, rents, wages, and salaries; and

WHEREAS, the present balance of payments situation makes it especially urgent to stabilize prices, rents, wages, and salaries in order to improve our competitive position in world trade and to protect the purchasing power of the dollar:

NOW, THEREFORE, by virtue of the authority vested in me by the Constitution and statutes of the United States, including the Economic Stabilization Act of 1970 (P.L. 91-379, 84 Stat. 799), as amended,[92] it is hereby ordered as follows:

Section 1. (a) Prices, rents, wages, and salaries shall be stabilized for a period of 90 days from the date hereof at levels not greater than the highest of those pertaining to a substantial volume of actual transactions by each individual, business, firm or other entity of any kind during the 30-day period ending August 14, 1971, for like or similar commodities or services. If no transactions occurred in that period, the ceiling will be the highest price, rent, salary or wage in the nearest preceding 30-day period in which transactions did occur. No person shall charge, assess, or receive, directly or indirectly in any transaction prices or rents in any form higher than those permitted hereunder, and no person shall, directly or indirectly, pay or agree to pay in any transaction wages or salaries in any form, or to use any means to obtain payment of wages and salaries in any form, higher than those permitted hereunder, whether by retroactive increase or otherwise.

(b) Each person engaged in the business of selling or providing commodities or services shall maintain available for public inspection a record of the highest prices or rents charged for such or similar commodities or services during the 30-day period ending August 14, 1971.

(c) The provisions of sections 1 and 2 hereof shall not apply to the prices charged for raw agricultural products.

Sec. 2. (a) There is hereby established the Cost of Living Council which shall act as an agency of the United States and which is hereinafter referred to as the Council.

(b) The Council shall be composed of the following members: The Secretary of the Treasury, the Secretary of Agriculture, the Secretary of Commerce, the Secretary of Labor, the Director of the Office of Management and Budget, the Chairman of the Council of Economic Advisers, the Director of the Office of Emergency Preparedness, and the Special Assistant to the President for Consumer Affairs. The Secretary of the Treasury shall serve as Chairman of the Council and the Chairman of the Council of Economic Advisers shall serve as Vice Chairman. The Chairman of the Board of Governors of the Federal Reserve System shall serve as adviser to the Council.

(c) Under the direction of the Chairman of the Council a Special Assistant to the President shall serve as Executive Director of the Council, and the Executive Director is authorized to appoint such personnel as may be necessary to assist the Council in the performance of its functions.

Section 3. (a) Except as otherwise provided herein, there are hereby delegated to the Council all of the powers conferred on the President by the Economic Stabilization Act of 1970.

(b) The Council shall develop and recommend to the President additional policies, mechanisms, and procedures to maintain economic growth without inflationary increases in prices, rents, wages, and salaries after the expiration of the 90-day period specified in Section 1 of this Order.

(c) The Council shall consult with representatives of agriculture, industry, labor and the public concerning the development of policies, mechanisms and procedures to maintain economic growth without inflationary increases in prices, rents, wages, and salaries.

(d) In all of its actions the Council will be guided by the need to maintain consistency of price and wage policies with fiscal, monetary, international and other economic policies of the United States.

(e) The Council shall inform the public, agriculture, industry, and labor concerning the need for controlling inflation and shall encourage and promote voluntary action to that end.

Sec. 4. (a) The Council, in carrying out the provisions of this Order, may (i) prescribe definitions for any terms used herein, (ii) make exceptions or grant exemptions, (iii) issue regulations and orders, and (iv) take such other actions as it determines to be necessary and appropriate to carry out the purposes of this Order.

(b) The Council may redelegate to any agency, instrumentality or official of the United States any authority under this Order, and may, in administering this Order, utilize the services of any other agencies, Federal or State, as may be available and appropriate.

(c) On request of the Chairman of the Council, each Executive department or agency is authorized and directed, consistent with law, to furnish the Council with available information which the Council may require in the performance of its functions.

(d) All Executive departments and agencies shall furnish such necessary assistance as may be authorized by section 214 of the Act of May 3, 1945 (59 Stat. 134; 31 U.S.C. 691).

Sec. 5. The Council may require the maintenance of appropriate records or other evidence which are necessary in carrying out the provisions of this Order, and may require any person to maintain and produce for examination such records or other evidence, in such form as it shall require, concerning prices, rents, wages, and salaries and all related matters. The Council may make such exemptions from any requirement otherwise imposed as are consistent with the purposes of this Order. Any type of record or evidence required under regulations issued under this Order shall be retained for such period as the Council may prescribe.

Sec. 6. The expenses of the Council shall be paid from such funds of the Treasury Department as may be available therefor.

Sec. 7. (a) Whoever willfully violates this Order or any order or regulation issued under authority of this Order shall be fined not more than $5,000 for each such violation.

(b) The Council shall in its discretion request the Department of Justice to bring actions for injunctions authorized under Section 205 of the Economic Stabilization Act of 1970 whenever it appears to the Council that any person has engaged, is engaged, or is about to engage in any acts or practices constituting a violation of any regulation or order issued pursuant to this Order.

RICHARD NIXON

THE WHITE HOUSE,
August 15, 1971.

Exec. Order No. 12092
Nov. 1, 1978, 43 F.R. 51375
Prohibition Against Inflationary Procurement Practices

By the authority vested in me as President and as Commander in Chief of the Armed Forces by the Constitution and statutes of the United States of America, including Section 2(c) and 3(a) of the Council on Wage and Price Stability Act, as amended (12 U.S.C. 1904 note) and Section 205(a) of the Federal Property and Administrative Services Act of 1949, as amended (40 U.S.C. 486(a)), and in order to encourage noninflationary pay and price behavior by private industry and labor, and to provide for the procurement by Executive agencies and Military Departments of personal property and services at prices and wage rates which are noninflationary, it is hereby ordered as follows:

1–101. The Chairman of the Council on Wage and Price Stability shall:

(a) Monitor company pay and price practices in order to determine compliance with the standards set forth in Section 1–102 of this Order;

(b) Promulgate regulations and guidance to further define these standards, and provide for appropriate exemptions and exceptions;

(c) Publish, or cause to be published, in accordance with procedures designed to ensure fairness and due process, the names of individuals or companies which are not in compliance with the standards;

(d) Promulgate procedures to be used in proceedings before the Council on matters pertaining to the standards, and take such other action as may be necessary and consistent with the purposes of this Section.

1–102. Noninflationary wage and price behavior shall be measured by the following standards:

(a) For prices, noninflationary price behavior is the deceleration by companies of their current rate of average price increase by at least 0.5 percentage points from their historical rate of annual price increase during 1976–1977 except where profits have not increased.

(b) For pay, noninflationary pay behavior is the holding of pay increases to not more than 7 percent annually above their recent historical levels.

(c) These standards, which shall be further defined by the Chairman of the Council on Wage and Price Stability, shall be subject to certain limitations and exemptions as determined by the Chairman.

1–103. In order to ensure economy and efficiency in government procurement, the head of each Executive agency and Military Department shall ensure that their contracts incorporate, on and after January 1, 1979, a clause which requires compliance by the contractor, and by his subcontractors and suppliers, with the standards set forth in Section 1–102 of this Order.

1–104. Each Executive agency and each Military Department shall comply with the directions of the Administrator for Federal Procurement Policy, who, in accord with Section 6 of the Office of Federal Procurement Policy Act (41 U.S.C. 405), shall be responsible for the overall direction of the implementation of Section 1–103 including the issuance of regulations and procedures for determining exceptions and granting exemptions.

JIMMY CARTER

THE WHITE HOUSE,
November 1, 1978.

Exec. Order No. 12291
Feb. 17, 1981, 46 F.R. 13193
Federal Regulation

By the authority vested in me as President by the Constitution and laws of the United States of America, and in order to reduce the burdens of existing and future regulations, increase agency accountability for regulatory actions, provide for presidential oversight of the regulatory process, minimize duplication and conflict of regulations, and insure well-reasoned regulations, it is hereby ordered as follows:

Section 1. Definitions. For the purposes of this Order:

(a) "Regulation" or "rule" means an agency statement of general applicability and future effect designed to implement, interpret, or prescribe law or policy or describing the procedure or practice requirements of an agency, but does not include:

(1) Administrative actions governed by the provisions of Sections 556 and 557 of Title 5 of the United States Code;

(2) Regulations issued with respect to a military or foreign affairs function of the United States; or

(3) Regulations related to agency organization, management, or personnel.

(b) "Major rule" means any regulation that is likely to result in:

(1) An annual effect on the economy of $100 million or more;

(2) A major increase in costs or prices for consumers, individual industries, Federal, State, or local government agencies, or geographic regions; or

(3) Significant adverse effects on competition, employment, investment, productivity, innovation, or on the ability of United States-based enterprises to compete with foreign-based enterprises in domestic or export markets.

(c) "Director" means the Director of the Office of Management and Budget.

(d) "Agency" means any authority of the United States that is an "agency" under 444 U.S.C. 3502(1), excluding those agencies specified in 44 U.S.C. 3502(10).

(e) "Task Force" means the Presidential Task Force on Regulatory Relief.

Section 2. General Requirements. In promulgating new regulations, reviewing existing regulations, and developing legislative proposals concerning regulation, all agencies, to the extent permitted by law, shall adhere to the following requirements:

(a) Administrative decisions shall be based on adequate information concerning the need for and consequences of proposed government action;

(b) Regulatory action shall not be undertaken unless the potential benefits to society for the regulation outweigh the potential costs to society;

(c) Regulatory objectives shall be chosen to maximize the net benefits to society;

(d) Among alternative approaches to any given regulatory objective, the alternative involving the least net cost to society shall be chosen; and

(e) Agencies shall set regulatory priorities with the aim of maximizing the aggregate net benefits to society, taking into account the condition of the particular industries affected by regulations, the condition of the national economy, and other regulatory actions contemplated for the future.

Section 3. Regulatory Impact Analysis and Review.

(a) In order to implement Section 2 of this Order, each agency shall, in connection with every major rule, prepare, and to the extent permitted by law consider, a Regulatory Impact Analysis. Such Analyses may be combined with any Regulatory Flexibility Analyses performed under 5 U.S.C. 603 and 604.

(b) Each agency shall initially determine whether a rule it intends to propose or to issue is a major rule, *provided that*, the Director, subject to the direction of the Task Force, shall have authority, in accordance with Sections 1(b) and 2 of this Order, to prescribe criteria for making such determinations, to order a rule to be treated as a major rule, and to require any set of related rules to be considered together as a major rule.

(c) Except as provided in Section 8 of this Order, agencies shall prepare Regulatory Impact Analyses of major rules and transmit them, along with all notices of proposed rulemaking and all final rules, to the Director as follows:

(1) If no notice of proposed rulemaking is to be published for a proposed major rule that is not an emergency rule, the agency shall prepare only a final Regulatory

Impact Analysis, which shall be transmitted, along with the proposed rule, to the Director at least 60 days prior to the publication of the major rule as a final rule;

(2) With respect to all other major rules, the agency shall prepare a preliminary Regulatory Impact Analysis, which shall be transmitted, along with a notice of proposed rulemaking, to the Director at least 60 days prior to the publication of a notice of proposed rulemaking, and a final Regulatory Impact Analysis, which shall be transmitted along with the final rule at least 30 days prior to the publication of the major rule as a final rule;

(3) For all rules other than major rules, agencies shall submit to the Director, at least 10 days prior to publication, every notice of proposed rulemaking and final rule.

(d) To permit each proposed major rule to be analyzed in light of the requirements stated in Section 2 of this Order, each preliminary and final Regulatory Impact Analysis shall contain the following information:

(1) A description of the potential benefits of the rule, including any beneficial effects that cannot be quantified in monetary terms, and the identification of those likely to receive the benefits;

(2) A description of the potential costs of the rule, including any adverse effects that cannot be quantified in monetary terms, and the identification of those likely to bear the costs;

(3) A determination of the potential net benefits of the rule, including an evaluation of effects that cannot be quantified in monetary terms;

(4) A description of alternative approaches that could substantially achieve the same regulatory goal at lower cost, together with an analysis of this potential benefit and costs and a brief explanation of the legal reasons why such alternatives, if proposed, could not be adopted; and

(5) Unless covered by the description required under paragraph (4) of this subsection, an explanation of any legal reasons why the rule cannot be based on the requirements set forth in Section 2 of this Order.

(e)(1) The Director, subject to the direction of the Task Force, which shall resolve any issues raised under this Order or ensure that they are presented to the President, is authorized to review any preliminary or final Regulatory Impact Analysis, notice of proposed rulemaking, or final rule based on the requirements of this Order.

(2) The Director shall be deemed to have concluded review unless the Director advises an agency to the contrary under subsection (f) of this Section;

(A) Within 60 days of a submission under subsection (c)(1) or a submission of a preliminary Regulatory Impact Analysis or notice of proposed rulemaking under subsection (c)(2);

(B) Within 30 days of the submission of a final Regulatory Impact Analysis and a final rule under subsection (c)(2); and

(C) Within 10 days of the submission of a notice of proposed rulemaking or final rule under subsection (c)(3).

(f)(1) Upon the request of the Director, an agency shall consult with the Director concerning the review of a preliminary Regulatory Impact Analysis or notice of proposed rulemaking under this Order, and shall, subject to Section 8(a)(2) of this Order, refrain from publishing its preliminary Regulatory Impact Analysis or notice of proposed rulemaking until such review is concluded.

(2) Upon receiving notice that the Director intends to submit views with respect to any final Regulatory Impact Analysis or final rule, the agency shall, subject to Section 8(a)(2) of this Order, refrain from publishing its final Regulatory Impact Analysis or final rule until the agency has responded to the Director's views, and incorporated those views and the agency's response in the rulemaking file.

(3) Nothing in this subsection shall be construed as displacing the agencies' responsibilities delegated by law.

(g) For every rule for which an agency publishes a notice of proposed rulemaking, the agency shall include in its notice:

(1) A brief statement setting forth the agency's initial determination whether the proposed rule is a major rule, together with the reasons underlying that determination; and

(2) For each proposed major rule, a brief summary of the agency's preliminary Regulatory Impact Analysis.

(h) Agencies shall make their preliminary and final Regulatory Impact Analyses available to the public.

(i) Agencies shall initiate reviews of currently effective rules in accordance with the purposes of this Order, and perform Regulatory Impact Analyses of currently effective major rules. The Director, subject to the direction of the Task Force, may designate currently effective rules for review in accordance with this Order, and establish schedules for reviews and Analyses under this Order.

Section 4. Regulatory Review. Before approving any final major rule, each agency shall:

(a) Make a determination that the regulation is clearly within the authority delegated by law and consistent with congressional intent, and include in the Federal Register at the time of promulgation a memorandum of law supporting that determination.

(b) Make a determination that the factual conclusions upon which the rule is based have substantial support in the agency record, viewed as a whole, with full attention to public comments in general and the comments of persons directly affected by the rule in particular.

Section 5. Regulatory Agendas.

(a) Each agency shall publish, in October and April of each year, an agenda of proposed regulations that the agency has issued or expects to issue, and currently effective rules that are under agency review pursuant to this Order. These agendas may be incorporated with the agendas published under 5 U.S.C. 602, and must contain at the minimum:

(1) A summary of the nature of each major rule being considered, the objectives and legal basis for the issuance of the rule, and an approximate schedule for completing action on any major rule for which the agency has issued a notice of proposed rulemaking;

(2) The name and telephone number of a knowledgeable agency official for each item on the agenda; and

(3) A list of existing regulations to be reviewed under the terms of this Order, and a brief discussion of each such regulation.

(b) The Director, subject to the direction of the Task Force, may, to the extent permitted by law:

(1) Require agencies to provide additional information in an agenda; and

(2) Require publication of the agenda in any form.

Section 6. The Task Force and Office of Management and Budget.

(a) To the extent permitted by law, the Director shall have authority, subject to the direction of the Task Force, to:

(1) Designate any proposed or existing rule as a major rule in accordance with Section 1(b) of this Order;

(2) Prepare and promulgate uniform standards for the identification of major rules and the development of Regulatory Impact Analyses;

(3) Require an agency to obtain and evaluate, in connection with a regulation, any additional relevant data from any appropriate source;

(4) Waive the requirements of Sections 3, 4, or 7 of this Order with respect to any proposed or existing major rule;

(5) Identify duplicative, overlapping and conflicting rules, existing or proposed, and existing or proposed rules that are inconsistent with the policies underlying statutes governing agencies other than the issuing agency or with the purposes of this Order, and, in each such case, require appropriate interagency consultation to minimize or eliminate such duplication, overlap, or conflict;

(6) Develop procedures for estimating the annual benefits and costs of agency regulations, on both an aggregate and economic or industrial sector basis, for purposes of compiling a regulatory budget;

(7) In consultation with interested agencies, prepare for consideration by the President recommendations for changes in the agencies' statutes; and

(8) Monitor agency compliance with the requirements of this Order and advise the President with respect to such compliance.

(b) The Director, subject to the direction of the Task Force, is authorized to establish procedures for the performance of all functions vested in the Director by this Order. The Director shall take appropriate steps to coordinate the implementation of the analysis, transmittal, review, and clearance provisions of this Order with the authorities and requirements provided for or imposed upon the Director and agencies under the Regulatory Flexibility Act, 5 U.S.C. 601 *et seq.*, and the Paperwork Reduction Plan Act of 1980, 44 U.S.C. 3501 *et seq.*

. . .

Section 8. Exemptions.

(a) The procedures prescribed by this Order shall not apply to:

(1) Any regulation that responds to an emergency situation, *provided that*, any such regulation shall be reported to the Director as soon as is practicable, the agency shall publish in the Federal Register a statement of the reasons why it is impracticable for the agency to follow the procedures of this Order with respect to such a rule, and the agency shall prepare and transmit as soon as is practicable a Regulatory Impact Analysis of any such major rule; and

(2) Any regulation for which consideration or reconsideration under the terms of this Order would conflict with deadlines imposed by statute or by judicial order,

provided that, any such regulation shall be reported to the Director together with a brief explanation of the conflict, the agency shall publish in the Federal Register a statement of the reasons why it is impracticable for the agency to follow the procedures of this Order with respect to such a rule, and the agency, in consultation with the Director, shall adhere to the requirements of this Order to the extent permitted by statutory or judicial deadlines.

(b) The Director, subject to the direction of the Task Force, may, in accordance with the purposes of this Order, exempt any class or category of regulations from any or all requirements of this Order.

Section 9. Judicial Review. This Order is intended only to improve the internal management of the Federal government, and is not intended to create any right or benefit, substantive or procedural, enforceable at law by a party against the United States, its agencies, its officers or any person. The determinations made by agencies under Section 4 of this Order, and any Regulatory Impact Analyses for any rule, shall be made part of the whole record of agency action in connection with the rule.

Section 10. Revocations. Executive Orders No. 12044, as amended, and No. 12174 are revoked.

RONALD REAGAN

THE WHITE HOUSE
February 17, 1981.

Exec. Order No. 12498

Jan. 4, 1985, 50 F.R. 1036

Regulatory Planning Process

By the authority vested in me as President by the Constitution and laws of the United States of America, and in order to create a coordinated process for developing on an annual basis the Administration's Regulatory Program, establish Administration regulatory priorities, increase the accountability of agency heads for the regulatory actions of their agencies, provide for Presidential oversight of the regulatory process, reduce the burdens of existing and future regulations, minimize duplication and conflict of regulations, and enhance public and Congressional understanding of the Administration's regulatory objectives, it is hereby ordered as follows:

Section 1. General Requirements. (a) There is hereby established a regulatory planning process by which the Administration will develop and publish a Regulatory Program for each year. To implement this process, each Executive agency subject to executive Order No. 12291 shall submit to the Director of the Office of Management and Budget (OMB) each year, starting in 1985, a statement of its regulatory policies, goals, and objectives for the coming year and information concerning all significant regulatory actions underway or planned; however, the Director may exempt from this Order such agencies or activities as the Director may deem appropriate in order to achieve the effective implementation of this Order.

(b) The head of each Executive agency subject to this Order shall ensure that all regulatory actions are consistent with the goals of the agency and of the Administration, and will be appropriately implemented.

(c) This program is intended to complement the existing regulatory planning and review procedures of agencies and the Executive branch, including the procedures established by Executive Order No. 12291.

(d) To assure consistency with the goals of the Administration, the head of each agency subject to this Order shall adhere to the regulatory principles stated in Section 2 of Executive Order No. 12291, including those elaborated by the regulatory policy guidelines set forth in the August 11, 1983, Report of the Presidential Task Force on Regulatory Relief, "Reagan Administration Regulatory Achievements."

Section 2. Agency Submission of Draft Regulatory Program. (a) The head of each agency shall submit to the Director an overview of the agency's regulatory policies, goals, and objectives for the program year and such information concerning all significant regulatory actions of the agency, planned or underway, including actions taken to consider whether to initiate rulemaking; requests for public comment; and the development of documents that may influence, anticipate, or could lead to the commencement of rulemaking proceedings at a later date, as the Director deems necessary to develop the Administration's Regulatory Program. This submission shall constitute the agency's draft regulatory program. The draft regulatory program shall be submitted to the Director each year, on a date to be specified by the Director, and shall cover the period from April 1 through March 31 of the following year.

(b) The overview portion of the agency's submission should discuss the agency's broad regulatory purposes, explain how they are consistent with the Administration's regulatory principles, and include a discussion of the significant regulatory actions, as defined by the Director, that it will take. The overview should specifically discuss the significant regulatory actions of the agency to revise or rescind existing rules.

(c) Each agency head shall categorize and describe the regulatory actions described in subsection (a) in such format as the Director shall specify and provide such additional information as the Director may request; however, the Director shall, by Bulletin or Circular, exempt from the requirements of this Order any class or category of regulatory action that the Director determines is not necessary to review in order to achieve the effective implementation of the program.

Section 3. Review, Compilation, and Publication of the Administration's Regulatory Program. (a) In reviewing each agency's draft regulatory program, the Director shall (i) consider the consistency of the draft regulatory program with the Administration's policies and priorities and the draft regulatory programs submitted by other agencies; and (ii) identify such further regulatory or deregulatory actions as may, in his view, be necessary in order to achieve such consistency. In the event of disagreement over the content of the agency's draft regulatory program, the agency head or the Director may raise issues for further review by the President or by such appropriate Cabinet Council or other forum as the President may designate.

(b) Following the conclusion of the review process established by subsection (a), each agency head shall submit to the Director, by a date to be specified by the Director, the agency's final regulatory plan for compilation and publication as the Administration's Regulatory Program for that year. The Director shall circulate a draft of the Administration's Regulatory Program for agency comment, review, and interagency consideration, if necessary, before publication.

(c) After development of the Administration's Regulatory Program for the year, if the agency head proposes to take a regulatory action subject to the provisions of

Section 2 and not previously submitted for review under this process, or if the agency head proposes to take a regulatory action that is materially different from the action described in the agency's final Regulatory Program, the agency head shall immediately advise the Director and submit the action to the Director for review in such format as the Director may specify. Except in the case of emergency situations, as defined by the Director, or statutory or judicial deadlines, the agency head shall refrain from taking the proposed regulatory action until the review of this submission by the Director is completed. As to those regulatory actions not also subject to Executive Order No. 12291, the Director shall be deemed to have concluded that the proposal is consistent with the purposes of this Order, unless he notifies the agency head to the contrary within 10 days of its submission. As to those regulatory actions subject to Executive Order No. 12291, the Director's review shall be governed by the provisions of Section 3(e) of that Order.

(d) Absent unusual circumstances, such as new statutory or judicial requirements or unanticipated emergency situations, the Director may, to the extent permitted by law, return for reconsideration any rule submitted for review under Executive Order No. 12291 that would be subject to Section 2 but was not included in the agency's final Regulatory Program for that year; or any other significant regulatory action that is materially different from those described in the Administration's Regulatory Program for that year.

Section 4. Office of Management and Budget. The Director of the Office of Management and Budget is authorized, to the extent permitted by law, to take such actions as may be necessary to carry out the provisions of this Order.

Section 5. Judicial Review. This Order is intended only to improve the internal management of the Federal government, and is not intended to create any right or benefit, substantive or procedural, enforceable at law by a party against the United States, its agencies, its officers or any person.

RONALD REAGAN

THE WHITE HOUSE,
January 4, 1985.

CONSTITUTION OF THE UNITED STATES

We the People of the United States, in Order to form a more perfect Union, establish Justice, insure domestic Tranquility, provide for the common defence, promote the general Welfare, and secure the Blessings of Liberty to ourselves and our Posterity, do ordain and establish this Constitution for the United States of America.

Article I.

SECTION 1. All legislative Powers herein granted shall be vested in a Congress of the United States, which shall consist of a Senate and House of Representatives.

SECTION 2. The House of Representatives shall be composed of Members chosen every second Year by the People of the several States, and the Electors in each State shall have the Qualifications requisite for Electors of the most numerous Branch of the State Legislature.

No Person shall be a Representative who shall not have attained to the Age of twenty-five Years, and been seven Years a Citizen of the United States, and who shall not, when elected, be an Inhabitant of that State in which he shall be chosen.

Representatives and direct Taxes shall be apportioned among the several States which may be included within this Union, according to their respective Numbers, which shall be determined by adding to the whole Number of free Persons, including those bound to Service for a Term of Years, and excluding Indians not taxed, three-fifths of all other Persons. The actual Enumeration shall be made within three Years after the first Meeting of the Congress of the United States, and within every subsequent Term of ten Years in such Manner as they shall by Law direct. The Number of Representatives shall not exceed one for every thirty Thousand, but each State shall have at Least one Representative; and until such enumeration shall be made, the State of New Hampshire shall be entitled to chuse three, Massachusetts eight, Rhode Island and Providence Plantations one, Connecticut five, New York six, New Jersey four, Pennsylvania eight, Delaware one, Maryland six, Virginia ten, North Carolina five, South Carolina five, and Georgia three.

When vacancies happen in the Representation from any State, the Executive Authority thereof shall issue Writs of Election to fill such Vacancies.

The House of Representatives shall chuse their Speaker and other Officers; and shall have the sole Power of Impeachment.

SECTION 3. The Senate of the United States shall be composed of two Senators from each State chosen by the Legislature thereof, for six Years and each Senator shall have one Vote.

Immediately after they shall be assembled in Consequence of the first Election, they shall be divided as equally as may be into three Classes. The Seats of the Senators of the first Class shall be vacated at the Expiration of the second Year, of the second Class at the Expiration of the fourth Year, and of the third Class at the Expiration of the sixth Year, so that one-third may be chosen every second Year; and if Vacancies happen by Resignation, or otherwise, during the Recess of the Legislature of any State, the Executive thereof may make temporary Appointments until the next Meeting of the Legislature, which shall then fill such Vacancies.

No person shall be a Senator who shall not have attained to the Age of thirty Years, and been nine Years a Citizen of the United States, who shall not, when elected, be an Inhabitant of that State for which he shall be chosen.

The Vice President of the United States shall be President of the Senate, but shall have no Vote, unless they be equally divided.

The Senate shall chuse their other Officers, and also a President pro tempore, in the absence of the Vice President, or when he shall exercise the Office of President of the United States.

The Senate shall have the sole Power to try all Impeachments. When sitting for that Purpose, they shall be on Oath or Affirmation. When the President of the United States is tried, the Chief Justice shall preside: And no Person shall be convicted without the Concurrence of two-thirds of the Members present.

Judgment in Cases of Impeachment shall not extend further than to removal from Office and disqualification to hold and enjoy any Office of honor, Trust or Profit under the United States; but the Party convicted shall nevertheless be liable and subject to Indictment, Trial, Judgment and Punishment, according to Law.

SECTION 4. The Times, Places and Manner of holding Elections for Senators and Representatives, shall be prescribed in each State by the Legislature thereof; but the Congress may at any time by Law make or alter such Regulations, except as to the Place of Chusing Senators.

The Congress shall assemble at least once in every Year, and such Meeting shall be on the first Monday in December, unless they shall by Law appoint a different Day.

SECTION 5. Each House shall be the Judge of the Elections, Returns and Qualifications of its own Members, and a Majority of each shall constitute a Quorum to do Business; but a smaller number may adjourn from day to day, and may be authorized to compel the Attendance of absent Members, in such Manner, and under such Penalties as each House may provide.

Each House may determine the Rules of its Proceedings, punish its Members for disorderly Behavior, and, with the Concurrence of two-thirds, expel a Member.

Each House shall keep a Journal of its Proceedings, and from time to time publish the same, excepting such Parts as may in their Judgment require Secrecy; and the Yeas and Nays of the Members of either House on any question shall, at the Desire of one-fifth of those Present, be entered on the Journal.

Neither House, during the Session of Congress, shall, without the Consent of the other, adjourn for more than three days, nor to any other Place than that in which the two Houses shall be sitting.

SECTION 6. The Senators and Representatives shall receive a Compensation for their Services, to be ascertained by Law, and paid out of the Treasury of the United States. They shall in all Cases, except Treason, Felony and Breach of the Peace, be privileged from Arrest during their Attendance at the Session of their respective Houses, and in going to and returning from the same; and for any Speech or Debate in either House, they shall not be questioned in any other Place.

No Senator or Representative shall, during the Time for which he was elected, be appointed to any civil Office under the Authority of the United States, which shall have been created, or the Emoluments whereof shall have been increased during such time; and no Person holding any Office under the United States, shall be a Member of either House during his Continuance in Office.

SECTION 7. All Bills for raising Revenue shall originate in the House of Representatives; but the Senate may propose or concur with Amendments as on other Bills.

Every Bill which shall have passed the House of Representatives and the Senate, shall, before it become a Law, be presented to the President of the United States; If he approve he shall sign it, but if not he shall return it, with his Objections to that House in which it shall have originated, who shall enter the Objections at large on their Journal, and proceed to reconsider it. If after such Reconsideration two thirds of that House shall agree to pass the Bill, it shall be sent, together with the Objections, to the other House, by which it shall likewise be reconsidered, and if approved by two thirds of that House, it shall become a Law. But in all such Cases the Votes of both Houses shall be determined by Yeas and Nays, and the Names of the Persons voting for and against the Bill shall be entered on the Journal of each House respectively. If any Bill shall not be returned by the President within ten Days (Sundays excepted) after it shall have been presented to him, the Same shall be a Law, in like Manner as if he had signed it, unless the Congress by their Adjournment prevent its Return, in which Case it shall not be a Law.

Every Order, Resolution, or Vote to which the Concurrence of the Senate and House of Representatives may be necessary (except on a question of Adjournment) shall be presented to the President of the United States; and before the Same shall take Effect, shall be approved by him, or being disapproved by him, shall be repassed by two-thirds of the Senate and House of Representatives, according to the Rules and Limitations prescribed in the Case of a Bill.

SECTION 8. The Congress shall have Power

To lay and collect Taxes, Duties, Imposts and Excises, to pay the Debts and provide for the common Defence and general Welfare of the United States; but all Duties, Imposts and Excises shall be uniform throughout the United States;

To borrow money on the credit of the United States;

To regulate Commerce with foreign Nations, and among the several States, and with the Indian Tribes;

To establish an uniform Rule of Naturalization, and uniform Laws on the subject of Bankruptcies throughout the United States;

To coin Money, regulate the Value thereof, and of foreign Coin, and fix the Standard of Weights and Measures;

To provide for the Punishment of counterfeiting the Securities and current Coin of the United States;

To establish Post Offices and post Roads;

To promote the Progress of Science and useful Arts, by securing for limited Times to Authors and Inventors the exclusive Right to their respective Writings and Discoveries;

To constitute Tribunals inferior to the supreme Court;

To define and punish Piracies and Felonies committed on the high Seas, and Offences against the Law of Nations;

To declare War, grant Letters of Marque and Reprisal, and make Rules concerning Captures on Land and Water;

To raise and support Armies, but no Appropriation of Money to that Use shall be for a longer Term than two Years;

To provide and maintain a Navy;

To make Rules for the Government and Regulation of the land and naval Forces;

To provide for calling forth the Militia to execute the Laws of the Union, suppress Insurrections and repel Invasions;

To provide for organizing, arming, and disciplining the Militia, and for governing such Part of them as may be employed in the Service of the United States, reserving to the States respectively, the Appointment of the Officers, and the Authority of training the Militia according to the discipline prescribed by Congress;

To exercise exclusive Legislation in all Cases whatsoever, over such District (not exceeding ten Miles square) as may, by Cession of particular States, and the acceptance of Congress, become the Seat of the Government of the United States, and to exercise like Authority over all Places purchased by the Consent of the Legislature of the State in which the Same shall be, for the Erection of Forts, Magazines, Arsenals, dock-Yards, and other needful buildings;—And

To make all Laws which shall be necessary and proper for carrying into Execution the foregoing Powers, and all other Powers vested by this Constitution in the Government of the United States, or in any Department or Officer thereof.

SECTION 9. The Migration or Importation of such Persons as any of the States now existing shall think proper to admit, shall not be prohibited by the Congress prior to the Year one thousand eight hundred and eight, but a tax or duty may be imposed on such Importation, not exceeding ten dollars for each Person.

The privilege of the Writ of Habeas Corpus shall not be suspended, unless when in Cases of Rebellion or Invasion the public Safety may require it.

No Bill of Attainder or ex post facto Law shall be passed.

No capitation, or other direct, Tax shall be laid, unless in Proportion to the Census or Enumeration herein before directed to be taken.

No Tax or Duty shall be laid on Articles exported from any State.

No Preference shall be given by any Regulation of Commerce or Revenue to the Ports of one State over those of another: nor shall Vessels bound to, or from, one State, be obliged to enter, clear, or pay Duties in another.

No Money shall be drawn from the Treasury, but in Consequence of Appropriations made by Law; and a regular Statement and Account of the Receipts and Expenditures of all public Money shall be published from time to time.

No Title of Nobility shall be granted by the United States: And no Person holding any Office of Profit or Trust under them, shall, without the Consent of the Congress, accept of any present, Emolument, Office, or Title, of any kind whatever, from any King, Prince, or foreign State.

SECTION 10. No State shall enter into any Treaty, Alliance, or Confederation; grant Letters of Marque and Reprisal; coin Money; emit Bills of Credit; make any Thing but gold and silver Coin a Tender in Payment of Debts; pass any Bill of Attainder, ex post facto Law, or Law impairing the Obligation of Contracts, or grant any Title of Nobility.

No State shall, without the Consent of the Congress, lay any Imposts or Duties on Imports or Exports, except what may be absolutely necessary for executing its inspection Laws: and the net Produce of all Duties and Imposts, laid by any State on Imports or Exports, shall be for the Use of the Treasury of the United States; and all such Laws shall be subject to the Revision and Controul of the Congress.

No State shall, without the Consent of Congress, lay any duty of Tonnage, keep Troops, or Ships of War in time of Peace, enter into any Agreement or Compact with another State, or with a foreign Power, or engage in War, unless actually invaded, or in such imminent Danger as will not admit of delay.

Article II.

SECTION 1. The executive Power shall be vested in a President of the United States of America. He shall hold his Office during the Term of four Years, and, together with the Vice President, chosen for the same Term, be elected as follows.

Each State shall appoint, in such Manner as the Legislature thereof may direct, a Number of Electors, equal to the whole Number of Senators and Representatives to which the State may be entitled in the Congress: but no Senator or Representative, or Person holding an Office of Trust or Profit under the United States, shall be appointed an Elector.

The Electors shall meet in their respective States, and vote by Ballot for two persons, of whom one at least shall not be an Inhabitant of the same State with themselves. And they shall make a List of all the Persons voted for, and of the Number of Votes for each; which List they shall sign and certify, and transmit sealed to the Seat of the Government of the United States, directed to the President of the Senate. The President of the Senate shall, in the Presence of the Senate and House of Representatives, open all the Certificates, and the Votes shall then be counted. The Person having the greatest Number of Votes shall be the President, if such Number be a Majority of the whole Number of Electors appointed; and if there be more than one who have such Majority, and have an equal Number of Votes, then the House of Representatives shall immediately chuse by Ballot one of them for President; and if no Person have a Majority, then from the five highest on the List the said House shall in like Manner chuse the President. But in chusing the President, the Votes shall be taken by States, the Representation from each State having one Vote; a quorum for this Purpose shall consist of a Member or Members from two thirds of the States, and a Majority of all the States shall be necessary to a Choice. In every Case, after the Choice of the President, the Person having the greatest Number of Votes of the Electors shall be the Vice President. But if there should remain two or more who have equal Votes, the Senate shall chuse from them by Ballot the Vice-President.

The Congress may determine the Time of the chusing the Electors, and the Day on which they shall give their Votes; which Day shall be the same throughout the United States.

No person except a natural born Citizen, or a Citizen of the United States, at the time of the Adoption of this Constitution, shall be eligible to the Office of President; neither shall any Person be eligible to that Office who shall not have attained to the age of thirty-five Years, and been fourteen Years a Resident within the United States.

In Case of the Removal of the President from Office, or his Death, Resignation, or Inability to Discharge the Powers and Duties of the said Office, the same shall devolve on the Vice President, and the Congress may by Law provide for the Case of Removal, Death, Resignation or Inability, both of the President and Vice President, declaring what Officer shall then act as President, and such Officer shall act accordingly, until the Disability be removed, or a President be elected.

The President shall, at stated Times, receive for his Services, a Compensation, which shall neither be encreased nor diminished during the Period for which he shall have been elected, and he shall not receive within that Period any other Emolument from the United States, or any of them.

Before he enter on the Execution of his Office, he shall take the following Oath or Affirmation:

"I do solemnly swear (or affirm) that I will faithfully execute the Office of President of the United States, and will to the best of my Ability, preserve, protect and defend the Constitution of the United States."

SECTION 2. The President shall be Commander in Chief of the Army and Navy of the United States, and of the Militia of the several States, when called into the actual Service of the United States; he may require the Opinion, in writing, of the principal Officer in each of the executive Departments, upon any subject relating to the Duties of their respective Offices, and he shall have Power to Grant Reprieves and Pardons for Offenses against the United States, except in Cases of Impeachment.

He shall have Power, by and with the Advice and Consent of the Senate, to make Treaties, provided two-thirds of the Senators present concur; and he shall nominate, and by and with the Advice and Consent of the Senate, shall appoint Ambassadors, other public Ministers and Consuls, Judges of the supreme Court, and all other Officers of the United States, whose Appointments are not herein otherwise provided for, and which shall be established by Law: but the Congress may by Law vest the Appointment of such inferior Officers, as they think proper, in the President alone, in the Courts of Law, or in the Heads of Departments.

The President shall have Power to fill up all Vacancies that may happen during the Recess of the Senate, by granting Commissions which shall expire at the End of their next Session.

SECTION 3. He shall from time to time give to the Congress Information of the State of the Union, and recommend to their Consideration such Measures as he shall judge necessary and expedient; he may, on extraordinary Occasions, convene both Houses, or either of them, and in Case of Disagreement between them, with Respect to the Time of Adjournment, he may adjourn them to such Time as he shall think proper; he shall receive Ambassadors and other public Ministers; he shall take Care that the Laws be faithfully executed, and shall Commission all the Officers of the United States.

SECTION 4. The President, Vice-President and all civil Officers of the United States, shall be removed from Office on Impeachment for, and Conviction of, Treason, Bribery, or other high Crimes and Misdemeanors.

Article III.

SECTION 1. The judicial Power of the United States shall be vested in one supreme Court, and in such inferior Courts as the Congress may from time to time ordain and establish. The Judges, both of the supreme and inferior Courts, shall hold their Offices during good Behaviour, and shall, at stated Times, receive for their Services, a Compensation, which shall not be diminished during their Continuance in Office.

SECTION 2. The judicial Power shall extend to all Cases, in Law and Equity, arising under this Constitution, the Laws of the United States, and Treaties made, or which shall be made, under their Authority;—to all Cases affecting Ambassadors, other public Ministers and Consuls;—to all Cases of admiralty and maritime Jurisdiction;—to Controversies to which the United States shall be a party;—to Controversies between two or more States;—between a State and Citizens of another State;—between Citizens of different States; between Citizens of the same State claiming Lands under Grants of different States, and between a State, or the Citizens thereof, and foreign States, Citizens, or Subjects.

In all Cases affecting Ambassadors, other public Ministers and Consuls, and those in which a State shall be a Party, the supreme Court shall have original Jurisdiction. In all the other Cases before mentioned, the supreme Court shall have appellate Jurisdiction, both as to Law and Fact, with such Exceptions, and under such Regulations as the Congress shall make.

The trial of all Crimes, except in Cases of Impeachment, shall be by Jury; and such Trial shall be held in the State where the said Crimes shall have been committed; but when not committed within any State, the Trial shall be at such Place or Places as the Congress may by Law have directed.

SECTION 3. Treason against the United States, shall consist only in levying War against them, or in adhering to their Enemies, giving them Aid and Comfort. No Person shall be convicted of Treason unless on the Testimony of two Witnesses to the same overt Act, or on Confession in open Court.

The Congress shall have Power to declare the Punishment of Treason, but no Attainder of Treason shall work Corruption of Blood, or Forfeiture except during the Life of the Person attainted.

Article IV.

SECTION 1. Full Faith and Credit shall be given in each State to the public Acts, Records, and judicial Proceedings of every other State. And the Congress may by general Laws prescribe the Manner in which such Acts, Records, and Proceedings shall be proved, and the Effect thereof.

SECTION 2. The Citizens of each State shall be entitled to all Privileges and Immunities of Citizens in the several States.

A Person charged in any State with Treason, Felony, or other Crime, who shall flee from Justice, and be found in another State, shall on demand of the executive Authority of the State from which he fled, be delivered up, to be removed to the State having Jurisdiction of the Crime.

No Person held to Service or Labour in one State, under the Laws thereof, escaping into another, shall, in Consequence of any Law or Regulation therein, be discharged from such Service or Labour, but shall be delivered up on Claim of the Party to whom such Service or Labour may be due.

SECTION 3. New States may be admitted by the Congress into this Union; but no new State shall be formed or erected within the Jurisdiction of any other State; nor any State be formed by the Junction of two or more States, or parts of States, without the Consent of the Legislatures of the States concerned as well as of the Congress.

The Congress shall have Power to dispose of and make all needful Rules and Regulations respecting the Territory or other Property belonging to the United States; and nothing in this Constitution shall be so construed as to Prejudice any Claims of the United States, or of any particular State.

SECTION 4. The United States shall guarantee to every State in this Union a Republican Form of Government, and shall protect each of them against Invasion; and on Application of the Legislature, or of the Executive (when the Legislature cannot be convened) against domestic Violence.

Article V.

The Congress, whenever two-thirds of both Houses shall deem it necessary, shall propose Amendments to this Constitution, or, on the Application of the Legislatures of two-thirds of the several States, shall call a Convention for proposing Amendments, which, in either Case, shall be valid, to all Intents and Purposes, as part of this Constitution, when ratified by the Legislatures of three-fourths of the several States, or by Conventions in three-fourths thereof, as the one or the other Mode of Ratification may be proposed by the Congress: Provided that no Amendment which may be made prior to the Year One thousand eight hundred and eight shall in any Manner affect the first and fourth Clauses in the Ninth Section of the first Article; and that no State, without its Consent, shall be deprived of its equal Suffrage in the Senate.

Article VI.

All Debts contracted and Engagements entered into, before the Adoption of this Constitution, shall be as valid against the United States under this Constitution, as under the Confederation.

This Constitution, and the Laws of the United States which shall be made in Pursuance thereof; and all Treaties made, or which shall be made, under the Authority of the United States, shall be the supreme Law of the Land; and the Judges in every State shall be bound thereby, any Thing in the Constitution or laws of any State to the Contrary notwithstanding.

The Senators and Representatives before mentioned, and the Members of the several State Legislatures, and all executive and judicial Officers, both of the United States and of the several States, shall be bound, by Oath or Affirmation, to support this Constitution; but no religious Test shall ever be required as a Qualification to any Office or public Trust under the United States.

Article VII.

The Ratification of the Conventions of nine States shall be sufficient for the Establishment of this Constitution between the States so ratifying the Same.

Done in Convention, by the Unanimous Consent of the States present, the Seventeenth Day of September, in the Year of our Lord one thousand seven hundred and Eighty-seven and of the Independence of the United States of America the Twelfth. In Witness whereof We have hereunto subscribed our Names.

Attest: *William Jackson,* Secretary

   George Washington PRESIDENT AND DEPUTY FROM VIRGINIA

NEW HAMPSHIRE
John Langdon
Nicholas Gilman
MASSACHUSETTS
Nathaniel Gorham
Rufus King
NEW YORK
Alexander Hamilton
NEW JERSEY
William Livingston
David Brearley
William Paterson
Jonathan Dayton

PENNSYLVANIA
Benjamin Franklin
Thomas Mifflin
Robert Morris
George Clymer
Thomas FitzSimons
Jared Ingersoll
James Wilson
Gouverneur Morris
DELAWARE
George Read
Gunning Bedford, Jr.
John Dickinson
Richard Bassett
Jacob Broom
CONNECTICUT
William Samuel Johnson
Roger Sherman

MARYLAND
James McHenry
Dan of St. Thomas Jenifer
Daniel Carroll
VIRGINIA
John Blair
James Madison, Jr.
NORTH CAROLINA
William Blount
Richard Dobbs Spaight
Hugh Williamson
SOUTH CAROLINA
John Rutledge
Charles Cotesworth Pinckney
Charles Pinckney
Pierce Butler
GEORGIA
William Few
Abraham Baldwin

AMENDMENTS

Amendment I

Congress shall make no law respecting an establishment of religion, or prohibiting the free exercise thereof; or abridging the freedom of speech, or of the press; or the right of the people peaceably to assemble, and to petition the Government for a redress of grievances.

Amendment II

A well regulated Militia, being necessary to the security of a free State, the right of the people to keep and bear Arms, shall not be infringed.

Amendment III

No Soldier shall, in time of peace be quartered in any house, without the consent of the Owner, nor in time of war, but in a manner to be prescribed by law.

Amendment IV

The right of the people to be secure in their persons, houses, papers, and effects, against unreasonable searches and seizures, shall not be violated; and no Warrants shall issue, but upon probable cause, supported by Oath or affirmation, and particularly describing the place to be searched, and the persons or things to be seized.

Amendment V

No person shall be held to answer for a capital, or otherwise infamous crime, unless on a presentment or indictment of a Grand Jury, except in cases arising in the land or naval forces, or in the Militia, when in actual service in time of War or public danger; nor shall any person be subject for the same offence to be twice put in jeopardy of life or limb; nor shall be compelled in any criminal case to be a witness against himself; nor be deprived of life, liberty, or property, without due process of law; nor shall private property be taken for public use, without just compensation.

Amendment VI

In all criminal prosecutions, the accused shall enjoy the right to a speedy and public trial, by an impartial jury of the State and district wherein the crime shall have been committed, which district shall have been previously ascertained by law, and to be informed of the nature and cause of the accusation; to be confronted with the witnesses against him; to have compulsory process for obtaining witnesses in his favor, and to have the Assistance of Counsel for his defence.

Amendment VII

In suits at common law, where the value in controversy shall exceed twenty dollars, the right of trial by jury shall be preserved, and no fact tried by a jury, shall be otherwise reexamined in any Court of the United States, than according to the rules of the common law.

Amendment VIII

Excessive bail shall not be required, nor excessive fines imposed, nor cruel and unusual punishments inflicted.

Amendment IX

The enumeration in the Constitution, of certain rights, shall not be construed to deny or disparage others retained by the people.

Amendment X

The powers not delegated to the United States by the Constitution, nor prohibited by it to the States, are reserved to the States respectively, or to the people.

Amendment XI

The Judicial power of the United States shall not be construed to extend to any suit in law or equity, commenced or prosecuted against one of the United States by Citizens of another State, or by Citizens or Subjects of any Foreign State.

Amendment XII

The Electors shall meet in their respective states and vote by ballot for President and Vice-President, one of whom, at least, shall not be an inhabitant of the same state with themselves; they shall name in their ballots the person voted for as President, and in distinct ballots the person voted for as Vice-President, and they shall make distinct lists of all persons voted for as President, and of all persons voted for as Vice-President, and of the number of votes for each, which lists they shall sign and certify, and transmit sealed to the seat of the government of the United States, directed to the President of the Senate;—the President of the Senate shall, in presence of the Senate and House of Representatives, open all the certificates and the votes shall then be counted;—The person having the greatest number of votes for President shall be the President, if such number be a majority of the whole number of Electors appointed; and if no person have such a majority, then from the persons having the highest numbers not exceeding three on the list of those voted for as President, the House of Representatives shall chuse immediately, by ballot, the President. But in chusing the President, the votes shall be taken by states, the representation from each state having one vote; a quorum for this purpose shall consist of a member or members from two-thirds of the states, and a majority of all the states shall be necessary to a choice. And if the House of Representatives shall not chuse a President whenever the right of choice shall devolve upon them, before the fourth day of March next following, then the Vice-President shall act as President, as in the case of the death or other constitutional disability of the President. The person having the greatest number of votes as Vice-President, shall be the Vice-President, if such number be a majority of the whole number of Electors appointed, and if no person have a majority, then from the two highest numbers on the list, the Senate shall chuse the Vice-President; a quorum for the purpose shall consist of two-thirds of the whole number of Senators, and a majority of the whole number shall be necessary to a choice. But no person constitutionally ineligible to the office of President shall be eligible to that of Vice-President of the United States.

Amendment XIII

SECTION 1. Neither slavery nor involuntary servitude, except as a punishment for crime whereof the party shall have been duly convicted, shall exist within the United States, or any place subject to their jurisdiction.

SECTION 2. Congress shall have power to enforce this article by appropriate legislation.

Amendment XIV

SECTION 1. All persons born or naturalized in the United States, and subject to the jurisdiction thereof, are citizens of the United States and of the State wherein they reside. No State shall make or enforce any law which shall abridge the privileges or immunities of citizens of the United States; nor shall any State deprive any person of life, liberty, or property, without due process of law; nor deny to any person within its jurisdiction the equal protection of the laws.

SECTION 2. Representatives shall be apportioned among the several States according to their respective numbers, counting the whole number of persons in each State, excluding Indians not taxed. But when the right to vote at any election for the choice of electors for President and Vice President of the United States, Representatives in Congress, the Executive and Judicial officers of a State, or the members of the Legislature thereof, is denied to any of the male inhabitants of such State, being twenty-one years of age, and citizens of the United States, or in any way abridged, except for participation in rebellion, or other crime, the basis of representation therein shall be reduced in the proportion which the number of such male citizens shall bear to the whole number of male citizens twenty-one years of age in such State.

SECTION 3. No person shall be a Senator or Representative in Congress, or elector of President and Vice-President, or hold any office, civil or military, under the United

States, or under any State, who, having previously taken an oath, as a member of Congress, or as an officer of the United States, or as a member of any State legislature, or as an executive or judicial officer of any State, to support the Constitution of the United States, shall have engaged in insurrection or rebellion against the same, or given aid or comfort to the enemies thereof. But Congress may by a vote of two-thirds of each House, remove such disability.

SECTION 4. The validity of the public debt of the United States, authorized by law, including debts incurred for payment of pensions and bounties for services in suppressing insurrection or rebellion, shall not be questioned. But neither the United States nor any State shall assume or pay any debt or obligation incurred in aid of insurrection or rebellion against the United States, or any claim for the loss or emancipation of any slave; but all such debts, obligations and claims shall be held illegal and void.

SECTION 5. The Congress shall have power to enforce, by appropriate legislation, the provisions of this article.

Amendment XV

SECTION 1. The right of citizens of the United States to vote shall not be denied or abridged by the United States or by any State on account of race, color, or previous condition of servitude.

SECTION 2. The Congress shall have power to enforce this article by appropriate legislation.

Amendment XVI

The Congress shall have power to lay and collect taxes on incomes, from whatever source derived, without apportionment among the several States, and without regard to any census or enumeration.

Amendment XVII

The Senate of the United States shall be composed of two Senators from each State, elected by the people thereof, for six years; and each Senator shall have one vote. The electors in each State shall have the qualifications requisite for electors of the most numerous branch of the State legislatures.

When vacancies happen in the representation of any State in the Senate, the executive authority of such State shall issue writs of election to fill such vacancies: Provided, That the legislature of any State may empower the executive thereof to make temporary appointments until the people fill the vacancies by election as the legislature may direct.

This amendment shall not be so construed as to affect the election or term of any Senator chosen before it becomes valid as part of the Constitution.

Amendment XVIII

SECTION 1. After one year from the ratification of this article the manufacture, sale, or transportation of intoxicating liquors within, the importation thereof into, or the exportation thereof from the United States and all territory subject to the jurisdiction thereof for beverage purposes is hereby prohibited.

SECTION 2. The Congress and the several States shall have concurrent power to enforce this article by appropriate legislation.

SECTION 3. This article shall be inoperative unless it shall have been ratified as an amendment to the Constitution by the legislatures of the several States as provided in the Constitution, within seven years of the date of the submission hereof to the States by Congress.

Amendment XIX

The right of citizens of the United States to vote shall not be denied or abridged by the United States or by any State on account of sex.

Congress shall have power to enforce this article by appropriate legislation.

Amendment XX

SECTION 1. The terms of the President and Vice President shall end at noon on the 20th day of January, and the terms of Senators and Representatives at noon on the 3d day of January, of the years in which such terms would have ended if this article had not been ratified; and the terms of their successors shall then begin.

SECTION 2. The Congress shall assemble at least once in every year, and such meeting shall begin at noon on the 3d day of January, unless they shall by law appoint a different day.

SECTION 3. If, at the time fixed for the beginning of the term of the President, the President elect shall have died, the Vice President elect shall become President. If a President shall not have been chosen before the time fixed for the beginning of his term, or if the President elect shall have failed to qualify, then the Vice President elect shall act as President until a President shall have qualified; and the Congress may by law provide for the case wherein neither a President elect nor a Vice President elect shall have qualified, declaring who shall then act as President, or the manner in which one who is to act shall be selected, and such person shall act accordingly until a President or Vice President shall have qualified.

SECTION 4. The Congress may by law provide for the case of the death of any of the persons from whom the House of Representatives may chuse a President whenever the right of choice shall have devolved upon them, and for the case of the death of any of the persons from whom the Senate may chuse a Vice President whenever the right of choice shall have devolved upon them.

SECTION 5. Sections 1 and 2 shall take effect on the 15th day of October following the ratification of this article.

SECTION 6. This article shall be inoperative unless it shall have been ratified as an amendment to the Constitution by the legislatures of three-fourths of the several States within seven years from the date of its submission.

Amendment XXI

SECTION 1. The eighteenth article of amendment to the Constitution of the United States is hereby repealed.

SECTION 2. The transportation or importation into any State, Territory, or possession of the United States for delivery or use therein of intoxicating liquors, in violation of the laws thereof, is hereby prohibited.

SECTION 3. This article shall be inoperative unless it shall have been ratified as an amendment to the Constitution by conventions in the several States, as provided in the Constitution, within seven years from the date of the submission hereof to the States by the Congress.

Amendment XXII

SECTION 1. No person shall be elected to the office of the President more than twice, and no person who has held the office of President, or acted as President, for more than two years of a term to which some other person was elected President shall be elected to the office of the President more than once. But this Article shall not apply to any person holding the office of President when this Article was proposed by the Congress, and shall not prevent any person who may be holding the office of President, or acting as President, during the term within which this Article becomes operative from holding the office of President or acting as President during the remainder of such term.

SECTION 2. This article shall be inoperative unless it shall have been ratified as an amendment to the Constitution by the legislatures of three-fourths of the several states within seven years from the date of its submission to the States by the Congress.

Amendment XXIII

SECTION 1. The District constituting the seat of Government of the United States shall appoint in such manner as the Congress may direct:

A number of electors of President and Vice President equal to the whole number of Senators and Representatives in Congress to which the District would be entitled if it were a State, but in no event more than the least populous State; they shall be in addition to those appointed by the states, but they shall be considered, for the purposes of the election of President and Vice President, to be electors appointed by a State; and they shall meet in the District and perform such duties as provided by the twelfth article of amendment.

SECTION 2. The Congress shall have power to enforce this article by appropriate legislation.

Amendment XXIV

SECTION 1. The right of citizens of the United States to vote in any primary or other election for President or Vice President, for electors for President or Vice President, or for Senator or Representative in Congress, shall not be denied or abridged by the United States or any State by reason of failure to pay any poll tax or other tax.

SECTION 2. The Congress shall have power to enforce this article by appropriate legislation.

Amendment XXV

SECTION 1. In case of the removal of the President from office or of his death or resignation, the Vice President shall become President.

SECTION 2. Whenever there is a vacancy in the office of the Vice President, the President shall nominate a Vice President who shall take office upon confirmation by a majority vote of both Houses of Congress.

SECTION 3. Whenever the President transmits to the President pro tempore of the Senate and the Speaker of the House of Representatives his written declaration that he is unable to discharge the powers and duties of his office, and until he transmits to them a written declaration to the contrary, such powers and duties shall be discharged by the Vice President as Acting President.

SECTION 4. Whenever the Vice President and a majority of either the principal officers of the executive departments or of such other body as Congress may by law provide, transmit to the President pro tempore of the Senate and the Speaker of the House of Representatives their written declaration that the President is unable to discharge the powers and duties of his office, the Vice President shall immediately assume the powers and duties of the office as Acting President.

Thereafter, when the President transmits to the President pro tempore of the Senate and the Speaker of the House of Representatives his written declaration that no inability exists, he shall resume the powers and duties of his office unless the Vice President and a majority of either the principal officers of the executive department or of such other body as Congress may by law provide, transmit within four days to the President pro tempore of the Senate and the Speaker of the House of Representatives their written declaration that the President is unable to discharge the powers and duties of his office. Thereupon Congress shall decide the issue, assembling within forty-eight hours for that purpose if not in session. If the Congress, within twenty-one days after receipt of the latter written declaration, or, if Congress is not in session, within twenty-one days after Congress is required to assemble, determines by two-thirds vote of both Houses that the President is unable to discharge the powers and duties of his office, the Vice President shall continue to discharge the same as Acting President; otherwise, the President shall resume the powers and duties of his office.

Amendment XXVI

SECTION 1. The right of citizens of the United States, who are eighteen years of age or older, to vote shall not be denied or abridged by the United States or by any State on account of age.

SECTION 2. The Congress shall have the power to enforce this article by appropriate legislation.

Index

Appointment powers of President:
  executive officers, 259-269; judges,
  271-290
Appropriations: lapses in, 368-375; riders,
  375-379, 589-591
Articles of confederation, 4-5
Attorney General: litigation powers of,
  426-429

Buchanan, James: on the presidency, 15-16
Budget and spending processes, generally,
  366-368

Campaign finance, 734-750
Civil service, President's power over, 269-
  271
Claims settlements, 551-568
Commander in Chief powers (see "War
  Powers")
Confirmation, Senate power of, 228-233
Congressional standing, 409-419
Constitutional interpretation, theories of,
  27-29, 418-419

Delegation doctrine, 64-88

Electoral college, 750-765
Electronic surveillance, 483-502
Execution of laws: criminal laws, 429-438,
  unconstitutional laws, 396-409;
  unjustified laws, 419-426
Executive agreements, 541-568
Executive branch: general statutory
  regulation of, 217-228; presidential
  management and supervision of, 332-
  366
Executive-congressional relationship,
  generally, 47-64
Executive-judicial relationship, generally,
  31-46
Executive orders: generally, 88-101; private
  enforcement of, 101-102
Executive privilege: presidential privacy
  privilege, 162-171; state secrets
  privilege, 171-180; vis-a-vis Congress
  generally, 180-208; vis-a-vis courts
  generally, 162-171

Foreign affairs powers of President,
  generally, 507-520

Foreign policy and foreign commerce, 568-
  578

Gorsuch, Anne, 187-200
Government lawyers, ethics of, 32-34, 37-
  38, 696

Immigration, foreign policy and, 592
Immunities of executive officers from
  damages liability, 233-257
Impeachment, 765-784
Impoundment, 379-390
Independent agencies: constitutional status
  of, 305-306, 319-327; foreign policy
  and, 579-589
Independent counsel, 444-458
Inherent powers of President: generally,
  458-466; over public lands, 466-472;
  to enforce constitutional rights, 472-
  482; to protect national security, 483-
  506
International Emergency Economic Powers
  Act (IEEPA), 552-570
Iran-Contra affair, 575-578, 589-591

Jackson, Andrew: on the presidency, 14-15
Japanese internment, 680-697
Jefferson, Thomas: on the presidency, 14

Law enforcement, use of troops for, 702-
  710 (See also "Execution of laws")
Lincoln, Abraham: and Civil War
  constitutional crises, 672-673; on the
  presidency, 16
Logan Act, 592-595

Multinational Force in Lebanon
  Resolution, 655-657; history of, 657-
  669

National security agencies, oversight of,
  492-497
National security information:
  classification of, 154-156;
  nondisclosure of generally, 137-149
Neutrality Act, 671-672
Nixon, Richard M., proposed
  impeachment of, 775-784

Pardon power, 439-443
Political parties: development of, 711-715;
    legal control of, 715-725;
    representation within, 725-734
Political question doctrine, 208-210
Posse Comitatus Act, 702-710
Preclearance agreements, 149-154, 156-162
Presidency: creation of, 4-12; organization
    and management of, 20-26; proposed
    reforms of, 390-393, 791-811
Presidential documents, regulation of
    access to, 210-217
Presidential succession, 784-790
Prosecutorial discretion, 438-439

Recess appointments: of judges, 283-290
Recognition power, 544-551
Regulatory process, presidential
    participation in, 337-366
Removal powers: first amendment limits,
    327-331; generally, 290-326
Roosevelt, Franklin: on the presidency, 19-
    20; on the Supreme Court, 274-279
Roosevelt, Theodore: on the presidency, 17

Special prosecutors (see "Independent
    counsel")

Taft, William Howard: on the presidency,
    18-19

Trade Expansion Act, 571-575
Travel restrictions, foreign policy and, 595-
    608
Treaties: legal impact of, 523-525;
    permissible scope of, 523
Treaty powers, generally, 520-525
Treaty termination, 525-541

Veto power: generally, 102-105; line-item,
    390-393
Vetoes, legislative, 112-135
Vetoes, pocket, 106-112
Vietnam, war powers and, 618-623, 637-
    642

War powers: and civil liberties, 672-697;
    and economic mobilization, 47-61,
    697-702; and covert warmaking, 671-
    672; generally, 610-617, 623-637
War Powers Resolution, 642-645, 647-651;
    and Grenada, 669-670; and Iran, 651-
    653; and Lebanon, 653-669; and
    Libya, 670; and Persian Gulf, 670-
    671; veto of, 645-647
Washington, George: on the presidency,
    12-14
Watt, James, 200-208
Wilson, Woodrow: on the presidency, 17